The Almanac of American Education

2018

The Almanac of American Education

2018

10th Edition
Edited by Hannah Anderson Krog

Bernan Press

Lanham, MD

Published by Bernan Press
An imprint of The Rowman & Littlefield Publishing Group, Inc.
4501 Forbes Boulevard, Suite 200, Lanham, Maryland 20706
www.rowman.com
800-462-6420

Unit A, Whitacre Mews, 26-34 Stannary Street, London SE11 4AB

ISBN: 978-1-64143-258-0
E-ISBN: 978-1-64143-259-7

♾™ The paper used in this publication meets the minimum requirements of American National Standard for Information Sciences—Permanence of Paper for Printed Library Materials, ANSI/NISO Z39.48-1992.

Manufactured in the United States of America.

Contents

Tables

PART A—NATIONAL EDUCATION STATISTICS

ENROLLMENT TABLES

HISTORICAL ENROLLMENT TABLES

ATTAINMENT TABLES

PART C—COUNTY EDUCATION STATISTICS

Figures

PART C—COUNTY EDUCATION STATISTICS

Preface

The *Almanac of American Education* serves as a guide to understanding and comparing the quality of education at the national, state, and county levels. Compiled from sources such as the U.S. Census Bureau and the National Center for Education Statistics (NCES), the *Almanac* contains historical and current data, insightful analysis, and useful graphics that paint a compelling picture of the state of education in the United States.

The 10th edition of the *Almanac* includes tables updated from the 9th edition alongside several new tables and figures.

The *Almanac* is organized into three sections: Part A—National Education Statistics; Part B—Region and State Education Statistics; and Part C—County Education Statistics. Most of the data presented in Part A are no longer available in print form from the Census Bureau. Additional tables in Part A are excerpted from the *Digest of Education Statistics* from the NCES, providing an overview of higher education in the United States. The data in Parts B and C have been specially tabulated for this publication from data obtained from the NCES, the Census Bureau, and other sources.

The *Almanac*'s contents and coverage allow users to answer—and ask—important questions about education, including:

- What are the nationwide trends in earnings by educational attainment level?

- Is the earnings gap between high school graduates and college graduates growing or shrinking?
- Which states have the highest and lowest high school dropout rates?
- Was there a relationship between childhood poverty rates and state-level expenditures per student?
- Which states have the largest county-to-county variation in high-school graduation rates?

The data in this volume meet the publication standards of the federal statistical agencies from which they were obtained. Every effort has been made to select accurate, meaningful, and useful data. All statistical data are subject to error arising from sampling variability, reporting errors, incomplete coverage, imputation, and other causes. The responsibility of the editors and publisher of this volume is limited to reasonable care in the reproduction and presentation of data obtained from established sources.

Hannah Anderson Krog has edited several previous titles for Bernan Press including *State Profiles: The Population and Economy of Each U.S. State* and *Patterns of Economic Change*. She earned her bachelor of arts in journalism from the University of Maryland.

Much appreciation is due to the federal agency personnel who prepared the original data and generously responded to our requests for assistance.

PART A
NATIONAL EDUCATION STATISTICS

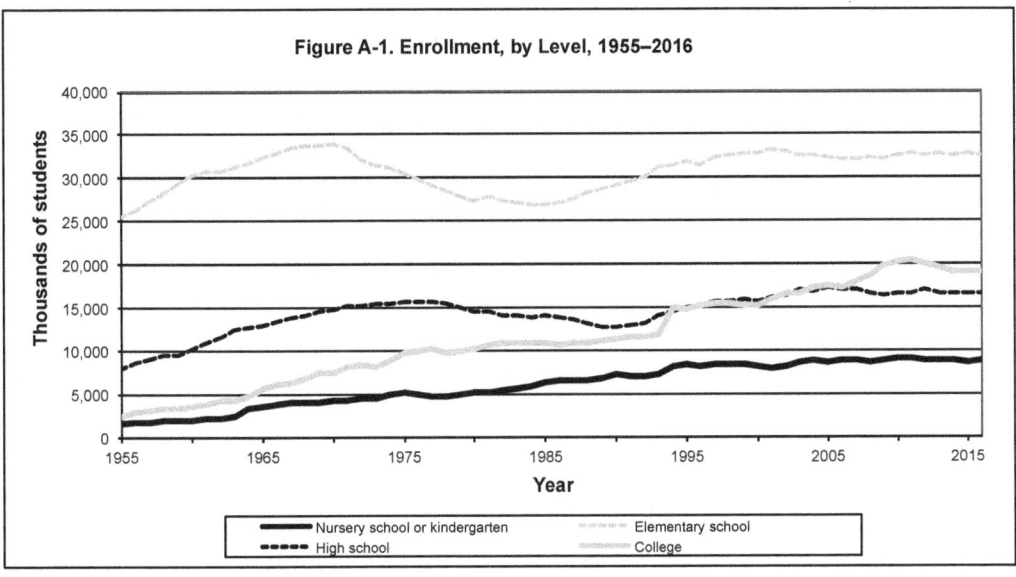

Figure A-1. Enrollment, by Level, 1955–2016

More than 77 million people were enrolled in school in 2016. Total enrollment had decreased in the late 1970s and early 1980s, but began to rise again by the late in 1980s, continuing to increase through 2011. College enrollment increased in 2016, after decreasing each year from 2011 through 2015. Elementary school enrollment has remained between 32 and 33 million since 1997, similar to the baby boom levels of the 1960s but never quite reaching the nearly 34 million elementary school enrollees of 1970. High-school enrollment in 2016 increased slightly from the 2015 level, with 133,000 more students enrolled nationwide. College enrollment also saw a slight increase of 95,000 students from 2015 to 2016, but 2016 college enrollment was still 1.2 million below the peak enrollment level of 2011. (Table A-9)

In 2016, 25.1 percent of people age 3 years and over were enrolled in school. For the population 3 to 4 years old, 53.8 percent were enrolled in nursery school or kindergarten, and 46.2 percent were not enrolled in school. Among the population 18 to 24 years old, 47.4 percent were enrolled in school (41.2 percent enrolled in college), as were 13.2 percent of 25 to 29 year olds. The proportion of 30 to 44 year olds enrolled in school was 4.7 percent. (Table A-1)

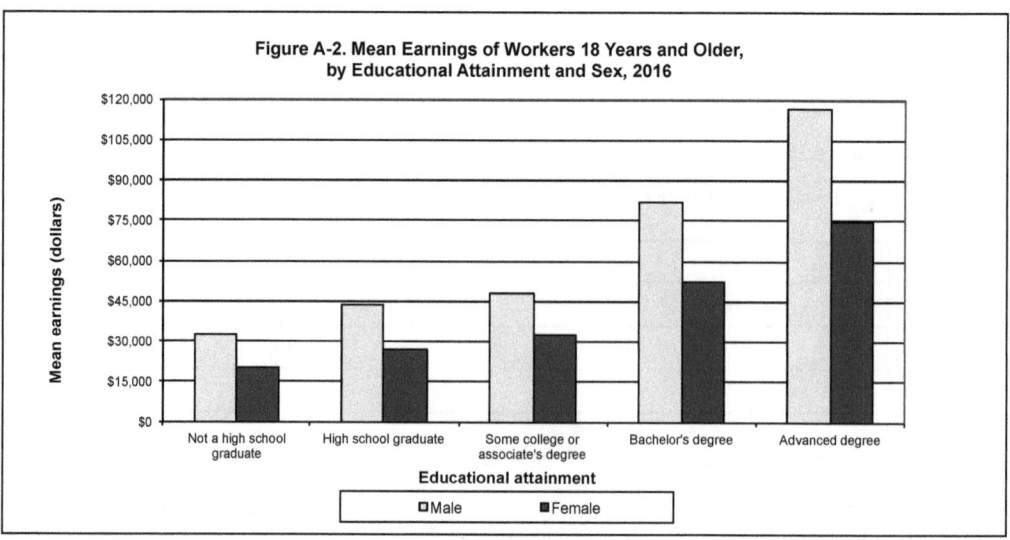

Figure A-2. Mean Earnings of Workers 18 Years and Older, by Educational Attainment and Sex, 2016

In 2016, the wage gap between males and females age 18 years and older was seen for all levels of educational attainment. The largest gap was between males and females without a high-school diploma: the mean earnings of females without a high-school diploma were 38.5 percent less than the mean earnings of males without a high-school diploma ($19,974 versus $32,463). (Table A-27)

In 2015, the median annual earnings for men 25 years old and over was $52,310; for women it was $41,680, with half of the men or women earning more than this amount and half earning less. For those who attended but did not finish high school, the median annual earnings were $32,140 for men, $22,670 for women. For high school graduates, including GED, median earnings were $41,570 for men and $31,250 for women. Men with bachelor's degrees had median earnings of $71,390 while women with bachelor's degrees had median earnings of $51,680. Workers with a professional degree had the highest median earnings, $131,190 for men and $82,310 for women. Men continued to earn more than women at all levels of educational attainment by 30 percent or more. (Table A-28)

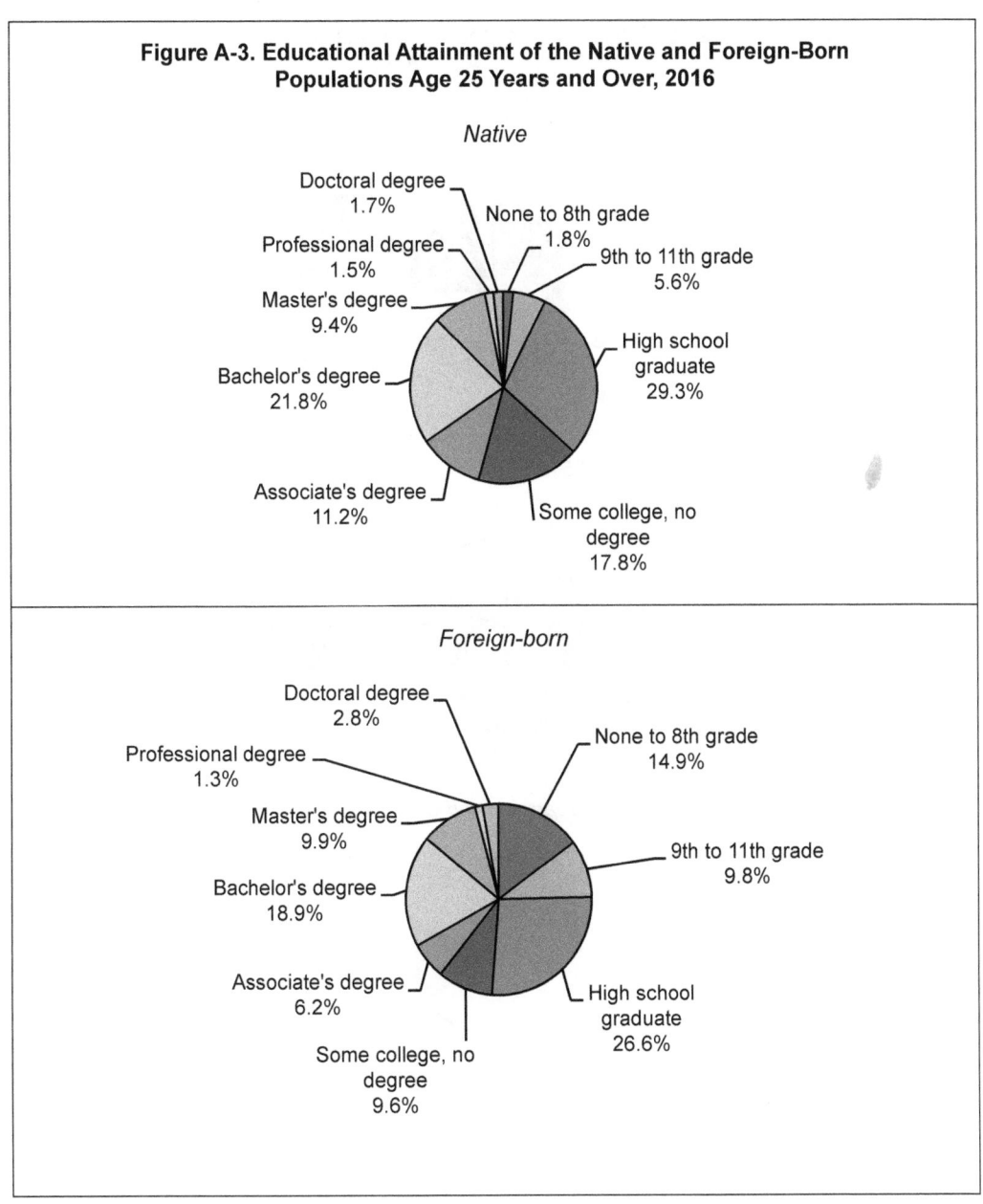

Figure A-3. Educational Attainment of the Native and Foreign-Born Populations Age 25 Years and Over, 2016

Native

- Doctoral degree 1.7%
- Professional degree 1.5%
- Master's degree 9.4%
- Bachelor's degree 21.8%
- Associate's degree 11.2%
- None to 8th grade 1.8%
- 9th to 11th grade 5.6%
- High school graduate 29.3%
- Some college, no degree 17.8%

Foreign-born

- Doctoral degree 2.8%
- Professional degree 1.3%
- Master's degree 9.9%
- Bachelor's degree 18.9%
- Associate's degree 6.2%
- Some college, no degree 9.6%
- None to 8th grade 14.9%
- 9th to 11th grade 9.8%
- High school graduate 26.6%

In 2017, 82.5 percent of the population age 25 years and older in the United States was native-born, and 17.5 percent of the population was foreign-born. The foreign-born population had a much larger proportion of people with less than a 9th-grade education. Nearly 15 percent of the foreign-born population was in this category, compared to 1.8 percent of the native population. However, the foreign-born population also had a higher proportion of people with doctoral degrees than the native population (2.8 percent, compared to 1.7 percent of natives). (Table A-24)

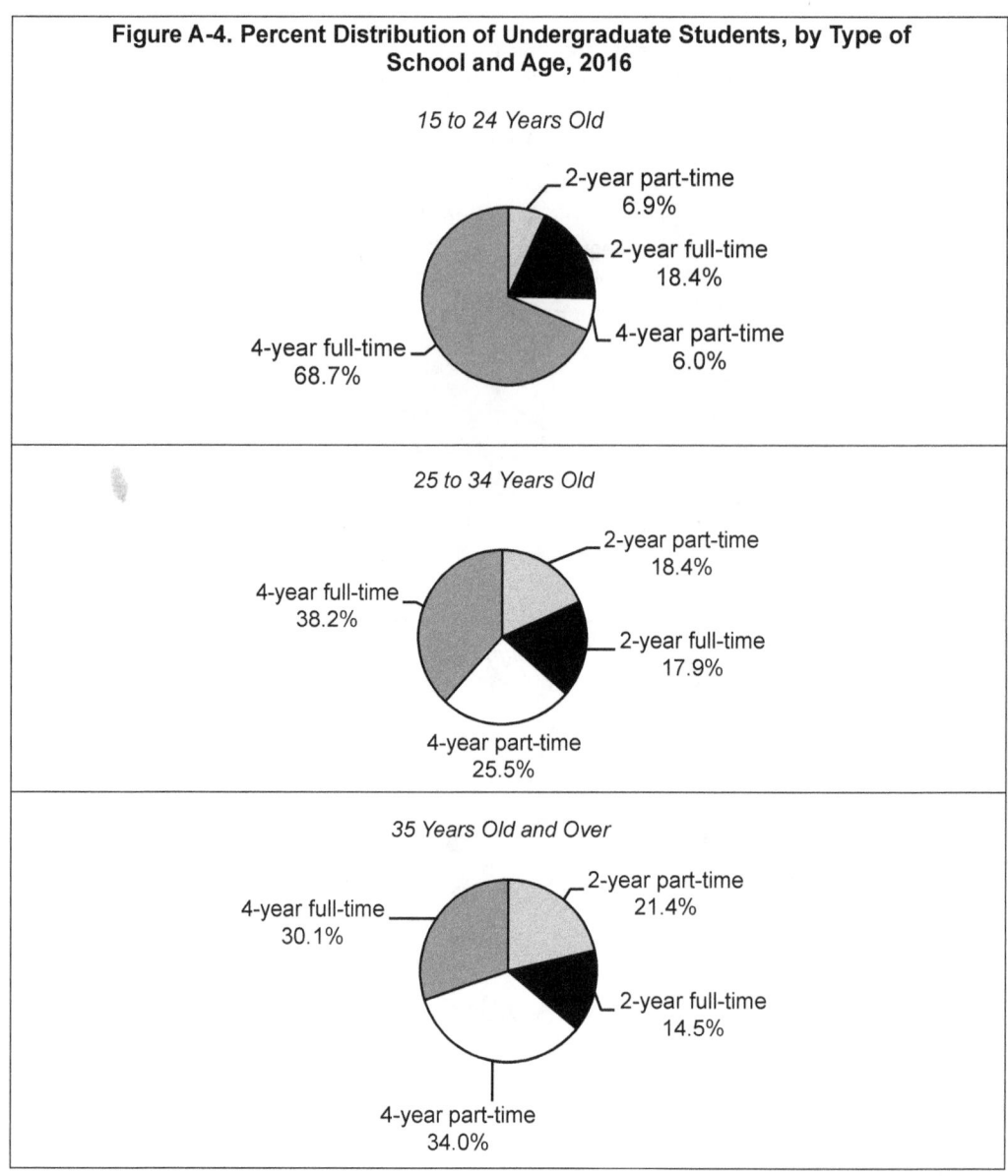

Figure A-4. Percent Distribution of Undergraduate Students, by Type of School and Age, 2016

15 to 24 Years Old

- 2-year part-time 6.9%
- 2-year full-time 18.4%
- 4-year part-time 6.0%
- 4-year full-time 68.7%

25 to 34 Years Old

- 2-year part-time 18.4%
- 2-year full-time 17.9%
- 4-year part-time 25.5%
- 4-year full-time 38.2%

35 Years Old and Over

- 2-year part-time 21.4%
- 2-year full-time 14.5%
- 4-year part-time 34.0%
- 4-year full-time 30.1%

In 2016, more than 19 million students 15 years old and over were enrolled in colleges and universities. More than 15 million of them were undergraduates. A higher percent of under-graduates attending four-year colleges were full-time students (83.7 percent) compared to those attending two-year colleges (64.0 percent full-time). The proportion of full-time to part-time college students decreased as age increased. Among students 14 to 19 years old, 91.8 percent were full-time students, followed by 87.5 percent of 20- to 21-year-olds, 79.4 percent of 22- to 24-year-olds, 56.2 percent of 25- to 34-year-olds, and 44.6 percent of students 35 years and over. Among graduate students, 62.3 percent were full-time students in 2016. Until 2008, the reverse was true: part-time students outnumbered full-time in graduate programs most years. (Tables A-5, A-9 and A-16)

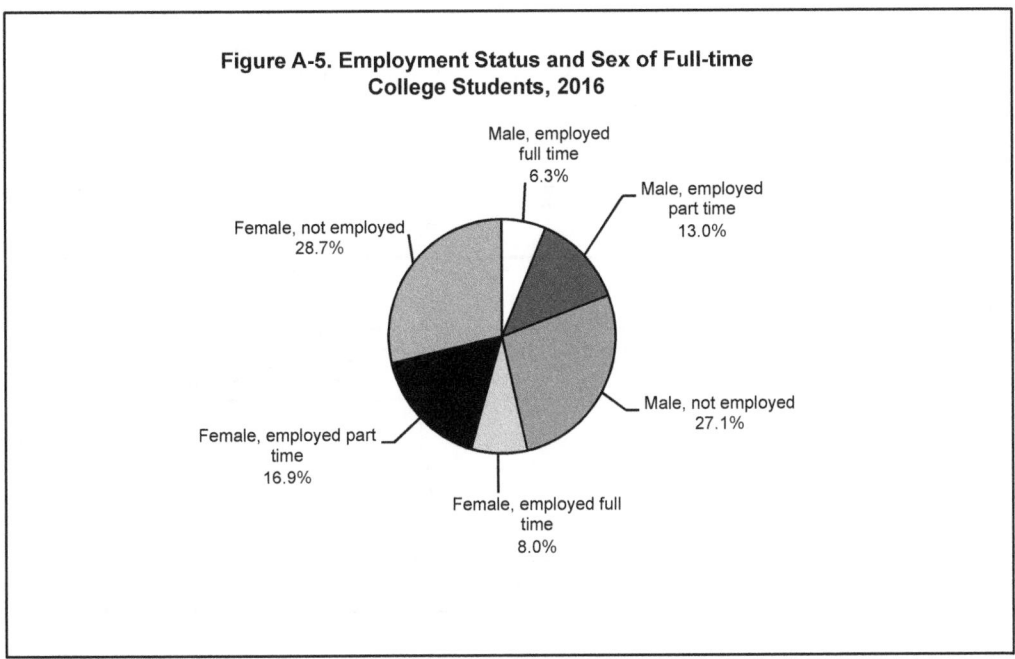

Figure A-5. Employment Status and Sex of Full-time College Students, 2016

Male, employed full time 6.3%

Male, employed part time 13.0%

Female, not employed 28.7%

Male, not employed 27.1%

Female, employed part time 16.9%

Female, employed full time 8.0%

In 2016, women made up 54.3 percent of all undergraduate students. In contrast, only 42.2 percent of all undergraduate students in 1970 were women. By the end of the 1970s, the proportions of men and women were more equal; since then, women's share has steadily increased, staying above 55 percent in most years since the early 1990s and reaching its highest levels of 56.9 percent in 2005 and 56.8 percent in 2012. Among Black students, 57.9 percent were female. Among Hispanic college students, 56.8 percent were female. The proportion of female to male Asian students fell to 47.3 percent female in 2016 from 53.5 percent in 2015. Among graduate students, women accounted for 57.6 percent of enrollment in 2016. (Tables A-15 and A-16)

In 2016, 64.7 percent of male college students were employed—either full- or part-time—and 53.9 percent of female college students were employed. Among those who were enrolled in vocational courses, 69.1 percent were employed, either full-time or part-time. (Tables A–5 and A-6)

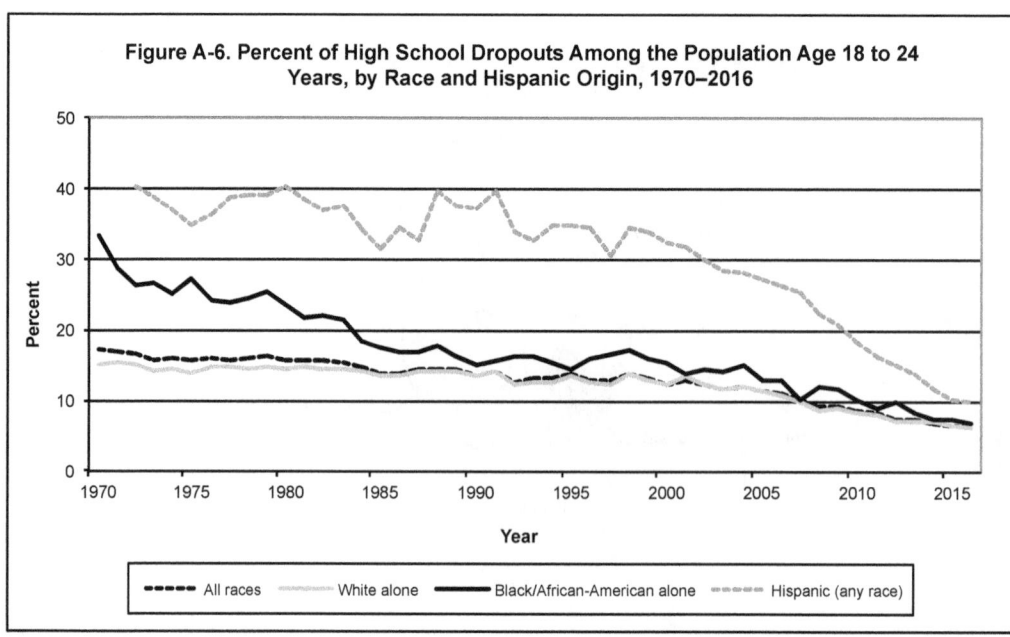

Figure A-6. Percent of High School Dropouts Among the Population Age 18 to 24 Years, by Race and Hispanic Origin, 1970–2016

The high school dropout rate has continually declined since 1970. In 1967, almost 20 percent of the population between the ages of 18 and 24 years had dropped out of high school. By 2012, that rate had dropped below 8 percent, and by 2015 it fell to 6.4 percent, where it stayed in 2016. Although the proportion of dropouts has declined for all races, it declined most dramatically for the population identifying as Black. In 1967, 34.5 percent of Blacks between the ages of 18 and 24 years had dropped out of high school. By 2011, that rate had dropped to 8.9 percent, and in 2016, it was 6.9 percent. During that same period, the dropout rate for whites was 17.9 percent in 1967, dropping to 8.2 percent in 2011 and 6.3 percent in 2016. The population who identified as Hispanic continues to have the highest dropout rate for the 18- to 24-year-old population, at 9.9 percent in 2016. The dropout rate is lowest among Asians, at 3.0 percent. In addition, in 2016, the dropout rate for females (3.9 percent) was lower than the rate for males (5.1 percent). (Tables A-12 and A-13)

In 1940, only one in four Americans had completed high school. By 1966, the ratio had only increased to 1 in 2—just less than half of the U.S. population 25 years old and over. As of 2017, 89.6 percent of Americans age 25 years and over were high school graduates. (Table A-18)

The percentage of college graduates, which constituted just 4.6 percent of the population in 1940, had risen to 9.8 percent by 1966. By 2017, college graduates constituted 34.2 percent of the population 25 years old and over. Women have now surpassed men with their percentage of college graduates. In 2017, 33.7 percent of males and 34.6 percent of females age 25 and over were college graduates. (Table A-18)

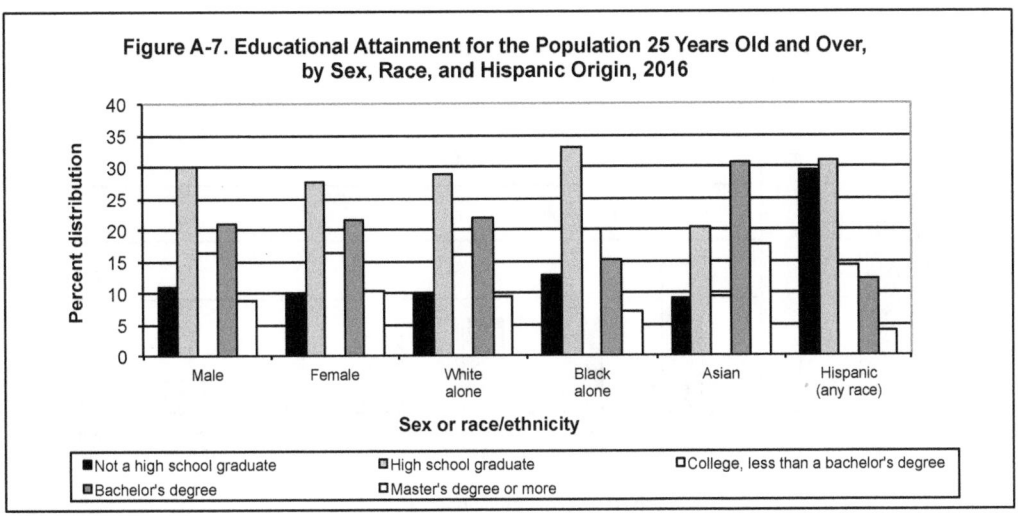

Figure A-7. Educational Attainment for the Population 25 Years Old and Over, by Sex, Race, and Hispanic Origin, 2016

In 2016, 89.6 percent of Americans 25 years old and over were high school graduates, and 34.2 percent held a bachelor's degree or higher. For people age 25 to 29 years, 92.5 percent had a high school diploma or higher and 35.7 percent held a bachelor's degree or higher. Women 25 years of age and over had slightly higher rates of high school attainment and college attainment, at 90.0 percent and 34.6 percent, respectively. Among race and ethnic groups (age 25 and older) in 2016, Asians had the highest high school graduation rate (90.9 percent), followed by Whites (90.1 percent), Blacks (87.3 percent), and Hispanics (70.5 percent). More than half (54.8 percent) of Asians had graduated from college, followed by Whites (34.6 percent), Blacks (23.9 percent), and Hispanics (17.2 percent). (Tables A-17, A-18, and A-26)

In 2017, 39.4 percent of civilians over 25 years of age in the labor force held a bachelor's degree or more. About 7.3 percent of the labor force had not graduated from high school, compared to 10.4 percent of all civilians (in or out of the labor force) over 25 years of age. (Table A-21)

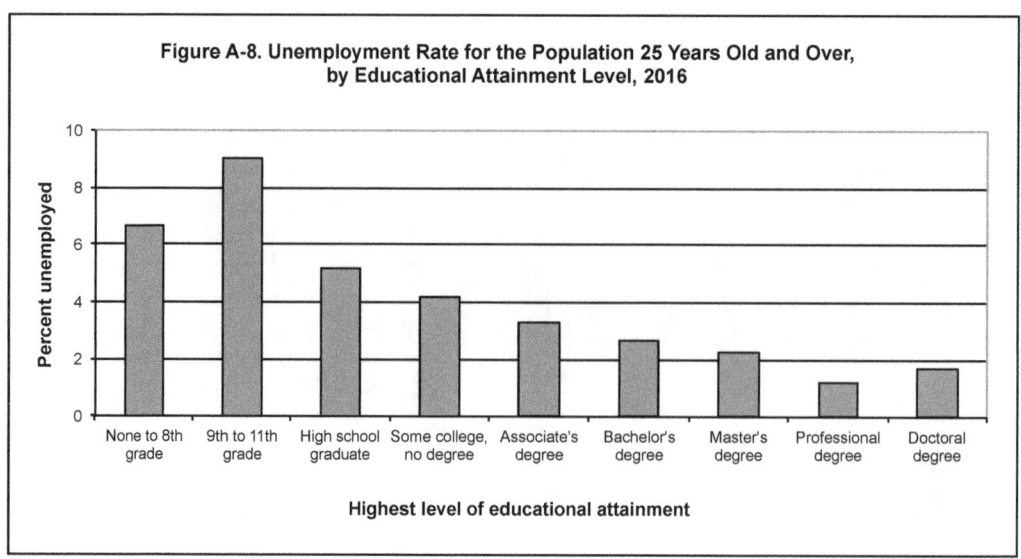

Figure A-8. Unemployment Rate for the Population 25 Years Old and Over, by Educational Attainment Level, 2016

Unemployment data for 2017 show once again that the more education a person has obtained, the less likely he or she will be unemployed. The unemployment rate for the population age 25 and over with a 9th to 11th grade education was 9.0 percent in 2017. For high-school graduates, the rate of unemployment was 5.2 percent; for civilians with a bachelor's degree, it was 2.7 percent. With a doctoral degree, this percentage dropped to 1.7; and the lowest unemployment rate was for those with a professional degree (1.2 percent). The overall unemployment rate in 2017 was 3.9 percent. The unemployment rate for men (4.1 percent) was higher than that for women (3.8 percent). In 2017, the labor force participation rate was 70.8 percent for men, and 58.0 percent for women. (Table A-21)

For persons 25 years old and over, professional and related occupations provided the most jobs in 2017. This category includes teachers, lawyers, scientists, artists, doctors, nurses, and other healthcare professionals. Nearly 73.4 percent of those employed in professional and related occupations held a bachelor's degree or more. In contrast, less than 9 percent of those employed in farming, forestry and fishing, construction, maintenance, production, and transportation occupations had reached this level of educational attainment. Farming, forestry, and fishing employed the greatest percent of people without a high-school diploma (35.8 percent), and service occupations employed the highest number of people without a high-school diploma (3.1 million). (Table A-22)

The educational and health services industry was the largest employer in the United States and employed more than 32 million people in 2017. More than half (56 percent) of the population in the education and health services industry held a bachelor's degree or higher, and 29.2 percent of workers in this field had a master's degree or higher. Mining was the smallest industry in terms of employment, with 693,000 workers, of whom 208,000 (30 percent) held a bachelor's degree or higher. (Table A-23)

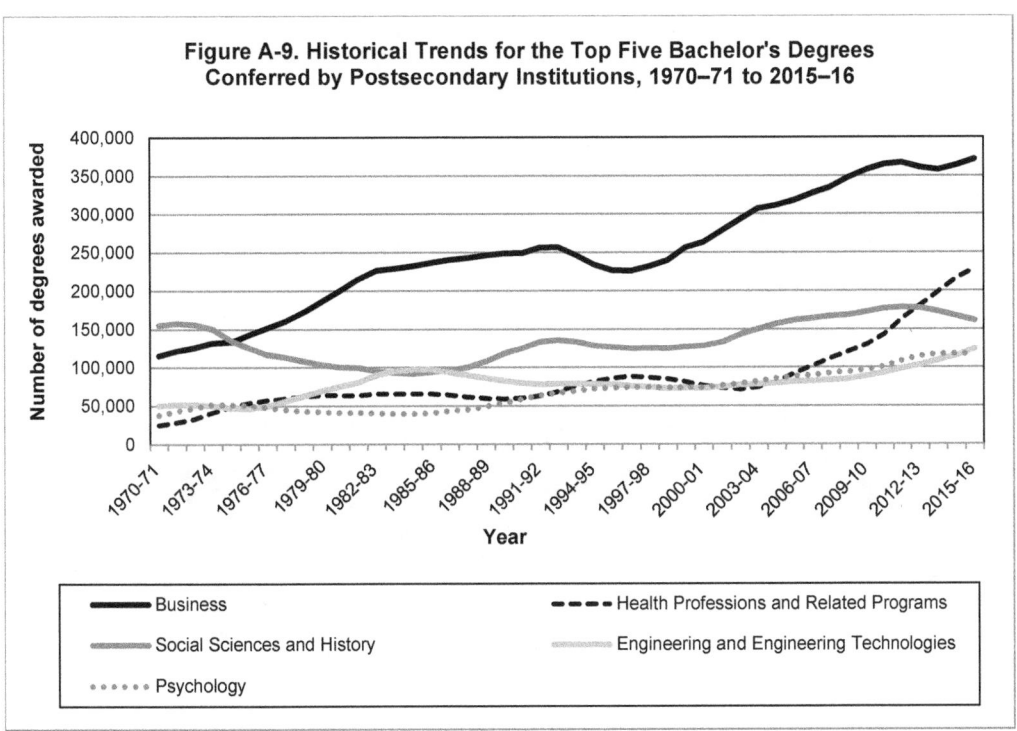

Figure A-9. Historical Trends for the Top Five Bachelor's Degrees Conferred by Postsecondary Institutions, 1970–71 to 2015–16

The top five bachelor's degrees conferred by postsecondary institutions in the United States during the 2015–2016 school year were: business (371,694 bachelor's degrees conferred), health professions and related programs (228,896 bachelor's degrees), social sciences and history (161,230 bachelor's degrees), engineering and engineering technologies (124,009 bachelor's degrees), and psychology (117,440 bachelor's degrees). The top three master's programs in 2015–2016 with the most graduates were: business (186,834 master's degrees conferred), education (145,781 master's degrees conferred), and health professions and related programs (110,348 master's degrees conferred). (Table A-37)

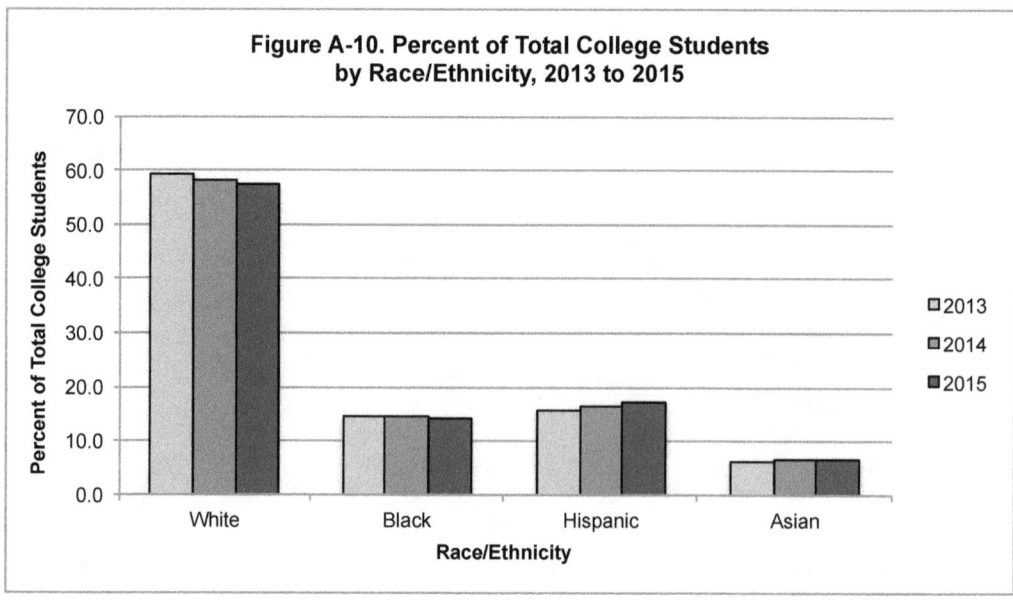

The past three years has saw an increase in the percent of Hispanic and Asian college students, with a correlating decrease in the percent of college students who identified as White or Black. In 2013, college students were 59.3 percent White, 14.7 percent Black, 15.8 percent Hispanic, and 6.1 Asian. In 2015, 57.6 percent of college students were White, 14.1 percent were black, 17.3 percent were Hispanic, and 6.5 percent were Asian. (Table A-35) Private for-profit institution attendance costs in 2015 were between public and private non-profit costs, with on-campus living at $30,406 and off-campus (living with family) at $22,407. (Table A-37)

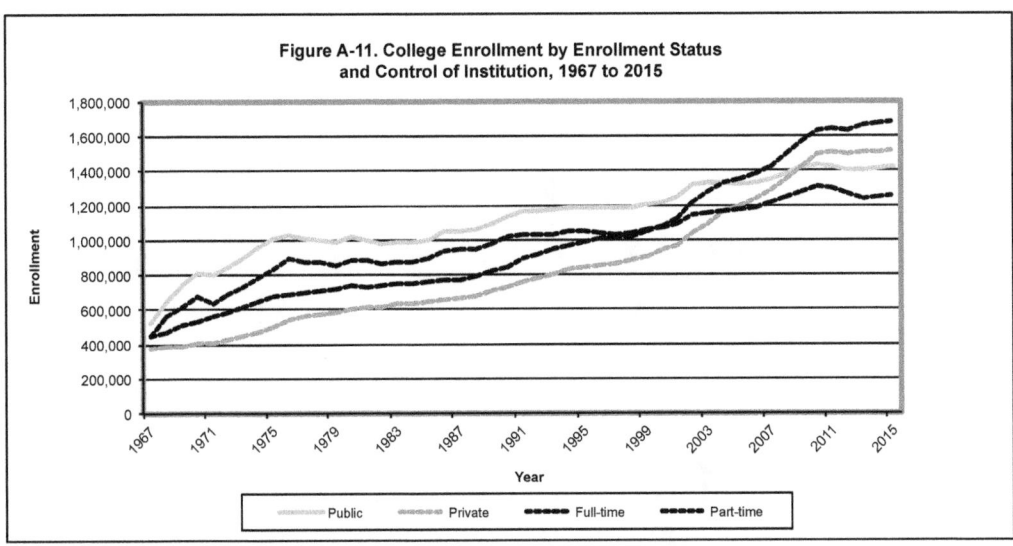

Figure A-11. College Enrollment by Enrollment Status and Control of Institution, 1967 to 2015

College enrollment increased 37.3 percent between 2000 and 2010, but it has decreased each year since 2010. In 2016, nearly 20 million students were enrolled in college, with almost 14.6 million in public institutions. Enrollment in private colleges increased from about 3.6 million students in 2000 to nearly 5.3 million students in 2016. Public 4-year colleges continued to enroll the most students, increasing 44.4 percent since 2000 to 8.7 million students. Public 2-year colleges saw a smaller increase of 2.5 percent, from 5.7 million students in 2000 to 5.8 million students in 2016. There have been more females than males enrolled in college since 1979, and the percentage of females remained at its highest point of 57 percent in 2014 and 2015. (Tables A-29 and A-30)

PART A

NATIONAL EDUCATION STATISTICS

■ Enrollment Tables

Table A-1. Enrollment Status of the Population 3 Years Old and Over, by Sex, Age, Race, Hispanic Origin, Foreign Born, and Foreign-Born Parentage, October 2016

(Numbers in thousands; percent; civilian noninstitutionalized population.)

| Age, sex, race, Hispanic origin, and nativity | Population | Enrolled in school | | | | | | | | |
| | | Total | | Nursery or kindergarten | | Elementary | | High school | |
	Number	Number	Percent	Number	Percent	Number	Percent	Number	Percent
ALL RACES									
Both Sexes									
Total	307,516	77,232	25.1	8,764	2.8	32,604	10.6	16,668	5.4
3 and 4 years old	7,971	4,289	53.8	4,289	53.8	*	*	*	*
5 and 6 years old	8,050	7,507	93.3	4,415	54.8	3,092	38.4	*	*
7 to 9 years old	12,369	12,093	97.8	60	0.5	12,033	97.3	*	*
10 to 13 years old	16,535	16,288	98.5	*	*	16,008	96.8	280	1.7
14 and 15 years old	8,271	8,107	98.0	*	*	1,343	16.2	6,739	81.5
16 and 17 years old	8,475	7,879	93.0	*	*	55	0.6	7,608	89.8
18 and 19 years old	8,266	5,741	69.5	*	*	29	0.4	1,541	18.6
20 and 21 years old	8,286	4,597	55.5	*	*	9	0.1	171	2.1
22 to 24 years old	13,340	3,841	28.8	*	*	9	0.1	99	0.7
25 to 29 years old	22,410	2,966	13.2	*	*	11	*	73	0.3
30 to 34 years old	21,335	1,364	6.4	*	*	6	*	23	0.1
35 to 44 years old	39,887	1,495	3.7	*	*	4	*	66	0.2
45 to 54 years old	42,291	717	1.7	*	*	4	*	40	0.1
55 years old and over	90,030	349	0.4	*	*	3	*	27	*
Male									
Total	150,027	38,351	25.6	4,487	3.0	16,682	11.1	8,538	5.7
3 and 4 years old	4,067	2,201	54.1	2,201	54.1	*	*	*	*
5 and 6 years old	4,125	3,824	92.7	2,259	54.8	1,566	38.0	*	*
7 to 9 years old	6,300	6,141	97.5	27	0.4	6,114	97.0	*	*
10 to 13 years old	8,435	8,294	98.3	*	*	8,190	97.1	104	1.2
14 and 15 years old	4,212	4,159	98.7	*	*	738	17.5	3,417	81.1
16 and 17 years old	4,296	3,981	92.7	*	*	39	0.9	3,866	90.0
18 and 19 years old	4,192	2,860	68.2	*	*	14	0.3	903	21.5
20 and 21 years old	4,214	2,165	51.4	*	*	*	*	80	1.9
22 to 24 years old	6,636	1,832	27.6	*	*	4	0.1	56	0.8
25 to 29 years old	11,142	1,311	11.8	*	*	11	0.1	36	0.3
30 to 34 years old	10,535	582	5.5	*	*	3	*	6	0.1
35 to 44 years old	19,550	580	3.0	*	*	1	*	30	0.2
45 to 54 years old	20,676	277	1.3	*	*	*	*	20	0.1
55 years old and over	41,649	144	0.3	*	*	3	*	20	*
Female									
Total	157,489	38,881	24.7	4,277	2.7	15,923	10.1	8,130	5.2
3 and 4 years old	3,904	2,088	53.5	2,088	53.5	*	*	*	*
5 and 6 years old	3,925	3,682	93.8	2,156	54.9	1,526	38.9	*	*
7 to 9 years old	6,069	5,951	98.1	33	0.5	5,919	97.5	*	*
10 to 13 years old	8,100	7,994	98.7	*	*	7,819	96.5	176	2.2
14 and 15 years old	4,059	3,948	97.3	*	*	605	14.9	3,322	81.8
16 and 17 years old	4,178	3,899	93.3	*	*	17	0.4	3,742	89.6
18 and 19 years old	4,075	2,881	70.7	*	*	15	0.4	638	15.7
20 and 21 years old	4,072	2,431	59.7	*	*	8	0.2	91	2.2
22 to 24 years old	6,705	2,009	30.0	*	*	4	0.1	43	0.6
25 to 29 years old	11,268	1,655	14.7	*	*	*	*	37	0.3
30 to 34 years old	10,800	782	7.2	*	*	3	*	17	0.2
35 to 44 years old	20,337	914	4.5	*	*	3	*	36	0.2
45 to 54 years old	21,615	440	2.0	*	*	4	*	19	0.1
55 years old and over	48,381	205	0.4	*	*	*	*	7	*
WHITE ALONE OR IN COMBINATION									
Both Sexes									
Total	243,453	58,973	24.2	6,742	2.8	25,148	10.3	12,728	5.2
3 and 4 years old	6,101	3,283	53.8	3,283	53.8	*	*	*	*
5 and 6 years old	6,192	5,801	93.7	3,426	55.3	2,375	38.4	*	*
7 to 9 years old	9,447	9,260	98.0	33	0.4	9,227	97.7	*	*
10 to 13 years old	12,794	12,602	98.5	*	*	12,396	96.9	206	1.6
14 and 15 years old	6,392	6,286	98.4	*	*	1,033	16.2	5,237	81.9
16 and 17 years old	6,556	6,071	92.6	*	*	50	0.8	5,857	89.3
18 and 19 years old	6,392	4,455	69.7	*	*	29	0.5	1,110	17.4
20 and 21 years old	6,303	3,530	56.0	*	*	8	0.1	104	1.6

* = Quantity equals zero or rounds to zero.

Table A-1. Enrollment Status of the Population 3 Years Old and Over, by Sex, Age, Race, Hispanic Origin, Foreign Born, and Foreign-Born Parentage, October 2016—*Continued*

(Numbers in thousands; percent; civilian noninstitutionalized population.)

Age, sex, race, Hispanic origin, and nativity	Population Number	Enrolled in school College undergraduate or graduate Number	Enrolled in school College undergraduate or graduate Percent	Not enrolled in school Total Number	Not enrolled in school Total Percent	Not enrolled in school High school graduate Number	Not enrolled in school High school graduate Percent	Not enrolled in school Not high school graduate Number	Not enrolled in school Not high school graduate Percent
ALL RACES									
Both Sexes									
Total	307,516	19,196	6.2	230,284	74.9	199,749	65	30,535	9.9
3 and 4 years old	7,971	*	*	3,682	46.2	*	*	3,682	46.2
5 and 6 years old	8,050	*	*	543	6.7	*	*	543	6.7
7 to 9 years old	12,369	*	*	276	2.2	*	*	276	2.2
10 to 13 years old	16,535	*	*	246	1.5	*	*	246	1.5
14 and 15 years old	8,271	25	0.3	164	2.0	34	0.4	129	1.6
16 and 17 years old	8,475	216	2.5	595	7.0	172	2	423	5.0
18 and 19 years old	8,266	4,171	50.5	2,525	30.5	1,993	24.1	532	6.4
20 and 21 years old	8,286	4,417	53.3	3,690	44.5	3,163	38.2	527	6.4
22 to 24 years old	13,340	3,733	28	9,499	71.2	8,647	64.8	852	6.4
25 to 29 years old	22,410	2,882	12.9	19,444	86.8	17,774	79.3	1,670	7.5
30 to 34 years old	21,335	1,336	6.3	19,971	93.6	18,139	85	1,832	8.6
35 to 44 years old	39,887	1,425	3.6	38,392	96.3	34,382	86.2	4,010	10.1
45 to 54 years old	42,291	673	1.6	41,575	98.3	37,065	87.6	4,510	10.7
55 years old and over............	90,030	319	0.4	89,681	99.6	78,380	87.1	11,301	12.6
Male									
Total	150,027	8,644	5.8	111,676	74.4	96,156	64.1	15,520	10.3
3 and 4 years old	4,067	*	*	1,866	45.9	*	*	1,866	45.9
5 and 6 years old	4,125	*	*	300	7.3	*	*	300	7.3
7 to 9 years old	6,300	*	*	159	2.5	*	*	159	2.5
10 to 13 years old	8,435	*	*	141	1.7	*	*	141	1.7
14 and 15 years old	4,212	3	0.1	53	1.3	5	0.1	48	1.1
16 and 17 years old	4,296	76	1.8	315	7.3	78	1.8	237	5.5
18 and 19 years old	4,192	1,944	46.4	1,332	31.8	1,028	24.5	303	7.2
20 and 21 years old	4,214	2,085	49.5	2,049	48.6	1,725	40.9	324	7.7
22 to 24 years old	6,636	1,771	26.7	4,804	72.4	4,298	64.8	506	7.6
25 to 29 years old	11,142	1,264	11.3	9,831	88.2	8,906	79.9	925	8.3
30 to 34 years old	10,535	574	5.4	9,952	94.5	8,958	85	994	9.4
35 to 44 years old	19,550	550	2.8	18,970	97.0	16,771	85.8	2,199	11.2
45 to 54 years old	20,676	256	1.2	20,399	98.7	18,030	87.2	2,369	11.5
55 years old and over............	41,649	121	0.3	41,505	99.7	36,357	87.3	5,148	12.4
Female									
Total	157,489	10,551	6.7	118,608	75.3	103,593	65.8	15,015	9.5
3 and 4 years old	3,904	*	*	1,816	46.5	*	*	1,816	46.5
5 and 6 years old	3,925	*	*	243	6.2	*	*	243	6.2
7 to 9 years old	6,069	*	*	117	1.9	*	*	117	1.9
10 to 13 years old	8,100	*	*	105	1.3	*	*	105	1.3
14 and 15 years old	4,059	21	0.5	111	2.7	29	0.7	82	2.0
16 and 17 years old	4,178	140	3.3	280	6.7	94	2.3	186	4.4
18 and 19 years old	4,075	2,227	54.7	1,193	29.3	965	23.7	229	5.6
20 and 21 years old	4,072	2,331	57.3	1,641	40.3	1,438	35.3	203	5.0
22 to 24 years old	6,705	1,962	29.3	4,695	70.0	4,349	64.9	346	5.2
25 to 29 years old	11,268	1,618	14.4	9,613	85.3	8,869	78.7	745	6.6
30 to 34 years old	10,800	762	7.1	10,018	92.8	9,180	85	838	7.8
35 to 44 years old	20,337	876	4.3	19,423	95.5	17,611	86.6	1,811	8.9
45 to 54 years old	21,615	417	1.9	21,175	98.0	19,034	88.1	2,141	9.9
55 years old and over............	48,381	198	0.4	48,176	99.6	42,023	86.9	6,153	12.7
WHITE ALONE OR IN COMBINATION									
Both Sexes									
Total	243,453	14,355	5.9	184,480	75.8	160,848	66.1	23,631	9.7
3 and 4 years old	6,101	*	*	2,818	46.2	*	*	2,818	46.2
5 and 6 years old	6,192	*	*	391	6.3	*	*	391	6.3
7 to 9 years old	9,447	*	*	186	2.0	*	*	186	2.0
10 to 13 years old	12,794	*	*	192	1.5	*	*	192	1.5
14 and 15 years old	6,392	16	0.3	105	1.6	*	*	105	1.6
16 and 17 years old	6,556	164	2.5	486	7.4	136	2.1	350	5.3
18 and 19 years old	6,392	3,316	51.9	1,937	30.3	1,554	24.3	383	6.0
20 and 21 years old	6,303	3,418	54.2	2,773	44.0	2,394	38.0	379	6.0

* = Quantity equals zero or rounds to zero.

Table A-1. Enrollment Status of the Population 3 Years Old and Over, by Sex, Age, Race, Hispanic Origin, Foreign Born, and Foreign-Born Parentage, October 2016—*Continued*

(Numbers in thousands; percent; civilian noninstitutionalized population.)

Age, sex, race, Hispanic origin, and nativity	Population Number	Enrolled in school							
		Total		Nursery or kindergarten		Elementary		High school	
		Number	Percent	Number	Percent	Number	Percent	Number	Percent
22 to 24 years old	10,135	2,772	27.4	*	*	4	*	56	0.6
25 to 29 years old	16,929	2,153	12.7	*	*	11.0	0.1	43	0.3
30 to 34 years old	16,332	969	5.9	*	*	6	*	21	0.1
35 to 44 years old	30,813	1,026	3.3	*	*	2	*	46	0.1
45 to 54 years old	33,608	500	1.5	*	*	4	*	29	0.1
55 years old and over	75,461	266	0.4	*	*	3	*	21	*
Male									
Total	119,855	29,350	24.5	3,500	2.9	12,927	10.8	6,508	5.4
3 and 4 years old	3,103	1,715	55.3	1,715	55.3	*	*	*	*
5 and 6 years old	3,181	2,980	93.7	1,772	55.7	1,208	38.0	*	*
7 to 9 years old	4,817	4,715	97.9	13	0.3	4,702	97.6	*	*
10 to 13 years old	6,555	6,440	98.2	*	*	6,375	97.3	65	1.0
14 and 15 years old	3,278	3,236	98.7	*	*	573	17.5	2,659	81.1
16 and 17 years old	3,356	3,095	92.2	*	*	34	1.0	3,005	89.5
18 and 19 years old	3,233	2,211	68.4	*	*	14	0.4	650	20.1
20 and 21 years old	3,208	1,635	51.0	*	*	*	*	34	1.1
22 to 24 years old	5,094	1,309	25.7	*	*	4	0.1	20	0.4
25 to 29 years old	8,481	905	10.7	*	*	11	0.1	19	0.2
30 to 34 years old	8,207	404	4.9	*	*	3	*	6	0.1
35 to 44 years old	15,363	414	2.7	*	*	1	*	19	0.1
45 to 54 years old	16,674	188	1.1	*	*	*	*	17	0.1
55 years old and over	35,305	103	0.3	*	*	3	*	14	*
Female									
Total	123,597	29,624	24.0	3,242	2.6	12,221	9.9	6,220	5.0
3 and 4 years old	2,998	1,568	52.3	1,568	52.3	*	*	*	*
5 and 6 years old	3,011	2,821	93.7	1,654	54.9	1,168	38.8	*	*
7 to 9 years old	4,630	4,545	98.2	20	0.4	4,525	97.7	*	*
10 to 13 years old	6,239	6,162	98.8	*	*	6,021	96.5	141	2.3
14 and 15 years old	3,113	3,051	98.0	*	*	460	14.8	2,578	82.8
16 and 17 years old	3,200	2,975	93.0	*	*	15	0.5	2,852	89.1
18 and 19 years old	3,159	2,245	71.0	*	*	15	0.5	460	14.6
20 and 21 years old	3,095	1,894	61.2	*	*	8	0.3	70	2.2
22 to 24 years old	5,042	1,464	29.0	*	*	*	*	36	0.7
25 to 29 years old	8,448	1,248	14.8	*	*	*	*	24	0.3
30 to 34 years old	8,125	564	6.9	*	*	3	*	15	0.2
35 to 44 years old	15,450	613	4.0	*	*	1	*	27	0.2
45 to 54 years old	16,934	312	1.8	*	*	4	*	12	0.1
55 years old and over	40,155	163	0.4	*	*	*	*	7	*
BLACK ALONE OR IN COMBINATION									
Both Sexes									
Total	43,482	13,507	31.1	1,589	3.7	5,749	13.2	3,090	7.1
3 and 4 years old	1,487	779	52.4	779	52.4	*	*	*	*
5 and 6 years old	1,449	1,350	93.2	789	54.5	561	38.7	*	*
7 to 9 years old	2,259	2,208	97.7	20	0.9	2,188	96.8	*	*
10 to 13 years old	2,885	2,850	98.8	*	*	2,785	96.6	64	2.2
14 and 15 years old	1,428	1,375	96.3	*	*	208	14.6	1,164	81.5
16 and 17 years old	1,509	1,434	95.0	*	*	6	0.4	1,395	92.4
18 and 19 years old	1,399	941	67.2	*	*	*	*	338	24.2
20 and 21 years old	1,403	668	47.6	*	*	*	*	60	4.3
22 to 24 years old	2,176	592	27.2	*	*	*	*	21	1.0
25 to 29 years old	3,577	450	12.6	*	*	*	*	20	0.6
30 to 34 years old	3,038	263	8.7	*	*	*	*	2	0.1
35 to 44 years old	5,626	378	6.7	*	*	1	*	19	0.3
45 to 54 years old	5,580	164	2.9	*	*	*	*	6	0.1
55 years old and over	9,665	57	0.6	*	*	*	*	*	*
Male									
Total	20,320	6,574	32.4	765	3.8	2,890	14.2	1,637	8.1
3 and 4 years old	738	355	48.1	355	48.1	*	*	*	*
5 and 6 years old	745	676	90.8	399	53.5	278	37.3	*	*
7 to 9 years old	1,130	1,091	96.6	11	1.0	1,080	95.6	*	*

* = Quantity equals zero or rounds to zero.

Table A-1. Enrollment Status of the Population 3 Years Old and Over, by Sex, Age, Race, Hispanic Origin, Foreign Born, and Foreign-Born Parentage, October 2016—*Continued*

(Numbers in thousands; percent; civilian noninstitutionalized population.)

Age, sex, race, Hispanic origin, and nativity	Population	Enrolled in school: College undergraduate or graduate		Not enrolled in school: Total		Not enrolled in school: High school graduate		Not enrolled in school: Not high school graduate	
	Number	Number	Percent	Number	Percent	Number	Percent	Number	Percent
22 to 24 years old	10,135	2,712	26.8	7,363	72.6	6,706	66.2	657	6.5
25 to 29 years old	16,929	2,099	12.4	14,776	87.3	13,490	79.7	1,286	7.6
30 to 34 years old	16,332	942	5.8	15,363	94.1	13,821	84.6	1,542	9.4
35 to 44 years old	30,813	979	3.2	29,786	96.7	26,498	86.0	3,289	10.7
45 to 54 years old	33,608	467	1.4	33,108	98.5	29,686	88.3	3,423	10.2
55 years old and over	75,461	242	0.3	75,195	99.6	66,564	88.2	8,630	11.4
Male									
Total	119,855	6,415	5.4	90,506	75.5	78,249	65.3	12,257	10.2
3 and 4 years old	3,103	*	*	1,389	44.7	*	*	1,389	44.7
5 and 6 years old	3,181	*	*	201	6.3	*	*	201	6.3
7 to 9 years old	4,817	*	*	102	2.1	*	*	102	2.1
10 to 13 years old	6,555	*	*	115	1.8	*	*	115	1.8
14 and 15 years old	3,278	3	0.1	43	1.3	*	*	43	1.3
16 and 17 years old	3,356	56	1.7	261	7.8	67	2.0	194	5.8
18 and 19 years old	3,233	1,547	47.8	1,022	31.6	813	25.1	209	6.5
20 and 21 years old	3,208	1,602	49.9	1,572	49.0	1,334	41.6	238	7.4
22 to 24 years old	5,094	1,284	25.2	3,785	74.3	3,388	66.5	397	7.8
25 to 29 years old	8,481	876	10.3	7,576	89.3	6,822	80.4	754	8.9
30 to 34 years old	8,207	396	4.8	7,802	95.1	6,941	84.6	862	10.5
35 to 44 years old	15,363	394	2.6	14,949	97.3	13,132	85.5	1,817	11.8
45 to 54 years old	16,674	171	1.0	16,486	98.9	14,612	87.6	1,874	11.2
55 years old and over	35,305	87	0.2	35,202	99.7	31,141	88.2	4,061	11.5
Female									
Total	123,597	7,940	6.4	93,974	76.0	82,599	66.8	11,374	9.2
3 and 4 years old	2,998	*	*	1,430	47.7	*	*	1,430	47.7
5 and 6 years old	3,011	*	*	189	6.3	*	*	189	6.3
7 to 9 years old	4,630	*	*	85	1.8	*	*	85	1.8
10 to 13 years old	6,239	*	*	77	1.2	*	*	77	1.2
14 and 15 years old	3,113	13	0.4	62	2.0	*	*	62	2.0
16 and 17 years old	3,200	108	3.4	225	7.0	69	2.2	156	4.9
18 and 19 years old	3,159	1,770	56.0	915	29.0	741	23.5	174	5.5
20 and 21 years old	3,095	1,816	58.7	1,201	38.8	1,060	34.2	141	4.6
22 to 24 years old	5,042	1,428	28.3	3,578	71.0	3,318	65.8	260	5.1
25 to 29 years old	8,448	1,224	14.5	7,200	85.2	6,668	78.9	532	6.3
30 to 34 years old	8,125	546	6.7	7,560	93.1	6,880	84.7	680	8.4
35 to 44 years old	15,450	585	3.8	14,837	96.0	13,366	86.5	1,472	9.5
45 to 54 years old	16,934	296	1.7	16,622	98.2	15,073	89.0	1,548	9.1
55 years old and over	40,155	155	0.4	39,993	99.6	35,424	88.2	4,569	11.4
BLACK ALONE OR IN COMBINATION									
Both Sexes									
Total	43,482	3,079	7.1	29,975	68.9	25,245	58.1	4,729	10.9
3 and 4 years old	1,487	*	*	709	47.6	*	*	709	47.6
5 and 6 years old	1,449	*	*	99	6.8	*	*	99	6.8
7 to 9 years old	2,259	*	*	51	2.3	*	*	51	2.3
10 to 13 years old	2,885	*	*	35	1.2	*	*	35	1.2
14 and 15 years old	1,428	3	0.2	53	3.7	34	2.4	18	1.3
16 and 17 years old	1,509	32	2.1	76	5.0	19	1.3	57	3.8
18 and 19 years old	1,399	602	43.1	458	32.8	360	25.7	99	7.1
20 and 21 years old	1,403	607	43.3	735	52.4	619	44.1	117	8.3
22 to 24 years old	2,176	572	26.3	1,583	72.8	1,457	66.9	127	5.8
25 to 29 years old	3,577	430	12.0	3,128	87.4	2,854	79.8	274	7.6
30 to 34 years old	3,038	261	8.6	2,775	91.3	2,583	85.0	192	6.3
35 to 44 years old	5,626	357	6.4	5,249	93.3	4,754	84.5	495	8.8
45 to 54 years old	5,580	157	2.8	5,416	97.1	4,742	85.0	674	12.1
55 years old and over	9,665	57	0.6	9,608	99.4	7,824	80.9	1,784	18.5
Male									
Total	20,320	1,283	6.3	13,746	67.6	11,434	56.3	2,312	11.4
3 and 4 years old	738	*	*	383	51.9	*	*	383	51.9
5 and 6 years old	745	*	*	69	9.2	*	*	69	9.2
7 to 9 years old	1,130	*	*	39	3.4	*	*	39	3.4

* = Quantity equals zero or rounds to zero.

Table A-1. Enrollment Status of the Population 3 Years Old and Over, by Sex, Age, Race, Hispanic Origin, Foreign Born, and Foreign-Born Parentage, October 2016—*Continued*

(Numbers in thousands; percent; civilian noninstitutionalized population.)

Age, sex, race, Hispanic origin, and nativity	Population	Enrolled in school								
		Total		Nursery or kindergarten		Elementary		High school	
	Number	Number	Percent	Number	Percent	Number	Percent	Number	Percent
10 to 13 years old	1,467	1,449	98.8	*	*	1,418	96.6	32	2.2
14 and 15 years old	743	732	98.5	*	*	110	14.8	622	83.7
16 and 17 years old	755	720	95.4	*	*	5	0.6	701	92.8
18 and 19 years old	686	459	66.9	*	*	*	*	208	30.4
20 and 21 years old	713	315	44.2	*	*	*	*	35	4.9
22 to 24 years old	1,009	260	25.8	*	*	*	*	13	1.3
25 to 29 years old	1,694	208	12.3	*	*	*	*	13	0.7
30 to 34 years old	1,407	102	7.3	*	*	*	*	*	*
35 to 44 years old	2,540	121	4.8	*	*	*	*	10	0.4
45 to 54 years old	2,531	67	2.6	*	*	*	*	3	0.1
55 years old and over	4,164	19	0.4	*	*	*	*	*	*
Female									
Total	23,162	6,933	29.9	823	3.6	2,859	12.3	1,454	6.3
3 and 4 years old	749	424	56.6	424	56.6	*	*	*	*
5 and 6 years old	705	674	95.6	391	55.5	283	40.2	*	*
7 to 9 years old	1,129	1,117	98.9	9	0.8	1,108	98.1	*	*
10 to 13 years old	1,418	1,400	98.8	*	*	1,368	96.5	33	2.3
14 and 15 years old	685	643	93.9	*	*	98	14.4	542	79.1
16 and 17 years old	754	713	94.6	*	*	1	0.1	695	92.1
18 and 19 years old	713	482	67.6	*	*	*	*	130	18.2
20 and 21 years old	691	353	51.1	*	*	*	*	26	3.7
22 to 24 years old	1,167	332	28.5	*	*	*	*	8	0.6
25 to 29 years old	1,884	242	12.8	*	*	*	*	7	0.4
30 to 34 years old	1,631	161	9.9	*	*	*	*	2	0.1
35 to 44 years old	3,087	256	8.3	*	*	1	*	9	0.3
45 to 54 years old	3,048	97	3.2	*	*	*	*	3	0.1
55 years old and over	5,501	39	0.7	*	*	*	*	*	*
ASIAN ALONE OR IN COMBINATION									
Both Sexes									
Total	19,811	5,669	28.6	669	3.4	2,207	11.1	1014	5.1
3 and 4 years old	574	363	63.2	363	63.2	*	*	*	*
5 and 6 years old	541	490	90.7	299	55.4	191	35.3	*	*
7 to 9 years old	853	837	98.1	6	0.7	831	97.4	*	*
10 to 13 years old	1,122	1108	98.8	*	*	1086	96.8	22	2.0
14 and 15 years old	499	490	98.2	*	*	90	18.0	396	79.3
16 and 17 years old	542	509	94.0	*	*	4	0.7	488	90.1
18 and 19 years old	487	382	78.4	*	*	*	*	69	14.2
20 and 21 years old	587	433	73.7	*	*	*	0.1	12	2.0
22 to 24 years old	951	444	46.7	*	*	4	0.5	13	1.3
25 to 29 years old	1,706	351	20.6	*	*	*	*	4	0.2
30 to 34 years old	1,834	118	6.4	*	*	*	*	*	*
35 to 44 years old	3,146	78	2.5	*	*	*	*	*	*
45 to 54 years old	2,687	39	1.5	*	*	*	*	4	0.1
55 years old and over	4,282	26	0.6	*	*	*	*	7	0.2
Male									
Total	9,450	2,894	30.6	315	3.3	1,151	12.2	491	5.2
3 and 4 years old	290	174	60.1	174	60.1	*	*	*	*
5 and 6 years old	280	245	87.5	139	49.5	107	38.1	*	*
7 to 9 years old	446	438	98.2	3	0.6	435	97.5	*	*
10 to 13 years old	578	572	98.9	*	*	562	97.3	9	1.6
14 and 15 years old	233	231	99.0	*	*	42	18.1	189	81.0
16 and 17 years old	266	242	91.1	*	*	4	1.5	231	87.0
18 and 19 years old	244	186	76.3	*	*	*	*	27	11.2
20 and 21 years old	290	223	76.9	*	*	*	0.1	11	3.9
22 to 24 years old	511	266	52.1	*	*	*	*	13	2.5
25 to 29 years old	848	182	21.4	*	*	*	*	4	0.5
30 to 34 years old	813	59	7.2	*	*	*	*	*	*
35 to 44 years old	1,480	40	2.7	*	*	*	*	*	*
45 to 54 years old	1,275	14	1.1	*	*	*	*	*	*
55 years old and over	1,897	22	1.2	*	*	*	*	7	0.4

* = Quantity equals zero or rounds to zero.

Table A-1. Enrollment Status of the Population 3 Years Old and Over, by Sex, Age, Race, Hispanic Origin, Foreign Born, and Foreign-Born Parentage, October 2016—*Continued*

(Numbers in thousands; percent; civilian noninstitutionalized population.)

Age, sex, race, Hispanic origin, and nativity	Population	Enrolled in school — College undergraduate or graduate		Not enrolled in school — Total		Not enrolled in school — High school graduate		Not enrolled in school — Not high school graduate	
	Number	Number	Percent	Number	Percent	Number	Percent	Number	Percent
10 to 13 years old	1,467	*	*	17	1.2	*	*	17	1.2
14 and 15 years old	743	*	*	11	1.5	5	0.7	6	0.8
16 and 17 years old	755	14	1.9	35	4.6	4	0.5	31	4.1
18 and 19 years old	686	250	36.5	227	33.1	163	23.8	64	9.3
20 and 21 years old	713	280	39.3	398	55.8	321	45.0	77	10.8
22 to 24 years old	1,009	247	24.5	749	74.2	664	65.8	85	8.4
25 to 29 years old	1,694	195	11.5	1,486	87.7	1,369	80.8	117	6.9
30 to 34 years old	1,407	102	7.3	1,305	92.7	1,221	86.8	83	5.9
35 to 44 years old	2,540	112	4.4	2,418	95.2	2,166	85.3	252	9.9
45 to 54 years old	2,531	63	2.5	2,464	97.4	2,150	84.9	315	12.4
55 years old and over	4,164	19	0.4	4,146	99.6	3,372	81.0	773	18.6
Female									
Total	23,162	1,797	7.8	16,229	70.1	13,811	59.6	2,418	10.4
3 and 4 years old	749	*	*	325	43.4	*	*	325	43.4
5 and 6 years old	705	*	*	31	4.4	*	*	31	4.4
7 to 9 years old	1,129	*	*	12	1.1	*	*	12	1.1
10 to 13 years old	1,418	*	*	17	1.2	*	*	17	1.2
14 and 15 years old	685	3	0.5	41	6.1	29	4.3	12	1.8
16 and 17 years old	754	18	2.3	41	5.4	15	2.0	26	3.5
18 and 19 years old	713	352	49.3	231	32.4	197	27.6	35	4.9
20 and 21 years old	691	328	47.4	337	48.9	298	43.2	39	5.7
22 to 24 years old	1,167	325	27.8	835	71.5	793	68.0	42	3.6
25 to 29 years old	1,884	234	12.4	1,642	87.2	1,486	78.9	157	8.3
30 to 34 years old	1,631	159	9.7	1,470	90.1	1,362	83.5	108	6.6
35 to 44 years old	3,087	246	8.0	2,831	91.7	2,588	83.8	242	7.9
45 to 54 years old	3,048	94	3.1	2,952	96.8	2,592	85.0	359	11.8
55 years old and over	5,501	39	0.7	5,462	99.3	4,451	80.9	1,011	18.4
ASIAN ALONE OR IN COMBINATION									
Both Sexes									
Total	19,811	1,780	9.0	14,142	71.4	12,386	62.5	1,756	8.9
3 and 4 years old	574	*	*	211	36.8	*	*	211	36.8
5 and 6 years old	541	*	*	50	9.3	*	*	50	9.3
7 to 9 years old	853	*	*	16	1.9	*	*	16	1.9
10 to 13 years old	1,122	*	*	14	1.2	*	*	14	1.2
14 and 15 years old	499	5	0.9	9	1.8	*	*	9	1.8
16 and 17 years old	542	17	3.2	33	6.0	15	2.7	18	3.3
18 and 19 years old	487	313	64.2	105	21.6	88	18.1	17	3.6
20 and 21 years old	587	421	71.7	154	26.3	138	23.5	17	2.8
22 to 24 years old	951	427	44.9	507	53.3	481	50.5	27	2.8
25 to 29 years old	1,706	346	20.3	1,355	79.4	1,281	75.1	74	4.4
30 to 34 years old	1,834	118	6.4	1,716	93.6	1,639	89.4	77	4.2
35 to 44 years old	3,146	78	2.5	3,067	97.5	2,881	91.6	186	5.9
45 to 54 years old	2,687	35	1.3	2,648	98.5	2,360	87.8	288	10.7
55 years old and over	4,282	20	0.5	4,255	99.4	3,504	81.8	752	17.6
Male									
Total	9,450	937	9.9	6,556	69.4	5,816	61.5	739	7.8
3 and 4 years old	290	*	*	116	39.9	*	*	116	39.9
5 and 6 years old	280	*	*	35	12.5	*	*	35	12.5
7 to 9 years old	446	*	*	8	1.8	*	*	8	1.8
10 to 13 years old	578	*	*	6	1.1	*	*	6	1.1
14 and 15 years old	233	*	*	2	1.0	*	*	2	1.0
16 and 17 years old	266	7	2.5	24	8.9	9	3.3	15	5.6
18 and 19 years old	244	159	65.2	58	23.7	48	19.8	10	3.9
20 and 21 years old	290	211	72.9	67	23.1	62	21.4	5	1.7
22 to 24 years old	511	254	49.7	244	47.9	235	45.9	10	2.0
25 to 29 years old	848	178	20.9	666	78.6	642	75.7	24	2.8
30 to 34 years old	813	59	7.2	755	92.8	723	88.8	32	3.9
35 to 44 years old	1,480	40	2.7	1,440	97.3	1,350	91.2	89	6.0
45 to 54 years old	1,275	14	1.1	1,261	98.9	1,147	89.9	114	9.0
55 years old and over	1,897	16	0.8	1,874	98.8	1,601	84.4	273	14.4

* = Quantity equals zero or rounds to zero.

Table A-1. Enrollment Status of the Population 3 Years Old and Over, by Sex, Age, Race, Hispanic Origin, Foreign Born, and Foreign-Born Parentage, October 2016—*Continued*

(Numbers in thousands; percent; civilian noninstitutionalized population.)

Age, sex, race, Hispanic origin, and nativity	Population	Enrolled in school							
		Total		Nursery or kindergarten		Elementary		High school	
	Number	Number	Percent	Number	Percent	Number	Percent	Number	Percent
Female									
Total	10,361	2,775	26.8	353	3.4	1,056	10.2	523	5.0
3 and 4 years old	284	189	66.4	189	66.4	*	*	*	*
5 and 6 years old	261	245	94.0	161	61.7	84	32.3	*	*
7 to 9 years old	407	399	98.0	3	0.8	396	97.2	*	*
10 to 13 years old	545	537	98.6	*	*	524	96.2	13	2.3
14 and 15 years old	266	260	97.6	*	*	48	18.0	207	77.9
16 and 17 years old	276	267	96.7	*	*	*	*	257	93.0
18 and 19 years old	243	195	80.4	*	*	*	*	42	17.2
20 and 21 years old	297	210	70.6	*	*	*	*	*	0.1
22 to 24 years old	441	178	40.4	*	*	4	1.0	*	*
25 to 29 years old	858	169	19.7	*	*	*	*	*	*
30 to 34 years old	1021	60	5.8	*	*	*	*	*	*
35 to 44 years old	1,666	38	2.3	*	*	*	*	*	*
45 to 54 years old	1,411	25	1.7	*	*	*	*	4	0.3
55 years old and over	2,385	4	0.2	*	*	*	*	*	*
HISPANIC (OF ANY RACE)									
Both Sexes									
Total	54,325	17,865	32.9	2,113	3.9	8,148	15.0	3,943	7.3
3 and 4 years old	2,026	1003	49.5	1003	49.5	*	*	*	*
5 and 6 years old	2,100	1,953	93.0	1,089	51.9	864	41.1	*	*
7 to 9 years old	3,171	3,074	97.0	21	0.7	3,053	96.3	*	*
10 to 13 years old	4,073	4,009	98.4	*	*	3,897	95.7	112	2.8
14 and 15 years old	1,951	1,904	97.6	*	*	300	15.4	1,597	81.9
16 and 17 years old	1,973	1,847	93.6	*	*	17	0.8	1,748	88.6
18 and 19 years old	1,825	1,248	68.4	*	*	1	*	363	19.9
20 and 21 years old	1,894	978	51.7	*	*	3	0.1	27	1.5
22 to 24 years old	2,821	753	26.7	*	*	*	*	21	0.7
25 to 29 years old	4,560	513	11.3	*	*	4	0.1	18	0.4
30 to 34 years old	4,401	208	4.7	*	*	3	0.1	14	0.3
35 to 44 years old	8,240	257	3.1	*	*	*	*	29	0.4
45 to 54 years old	6,739	85	1.3	*	*	4	0.1	5	0.1
55 years old and over	8,554	33	0.4	*	*	3	*	7	0.1
Male									
Total	27,198	8,853	32.6	1,100	4.0	4,171	15.3	2,000	7.4
3 and 4 years old	1,039	527	50.7	527	50.7	*	*	*	*
5 and 6 years old	1,074	987	91.8	562	52.3	425	39.5	*	*
7 to 9 years old	1,610	1,551	96.3	11	0.7	1,540	95.7	*	*
10 to 13 years old	2,071	2,031	98.1	*	*	1,989	96.0	42	2.0
14 and 15 years old	991	975	98.4	*	*	193	19.5	779	78.6
16 and 17 years old	1,030	962	93.4	*	*	13	1.3	923	89.6
18 and 19 years old	894	593	66.3	*	*	1	0.1	209	23.3
20 and 21 years old	960	441	46.0	*	*	*	*	4	0.4
22 to 24 years old	1,436	335	23.4	*	*	*	*	8	0.6
25 to 29 years old	2,343	219	9.3	*	*	4	0.2	4	0.2
30 to 34 years old	2,268	82	3.6	*	*	3	0.1	3	0.1
35 to 44 years old	4,167	106	2.5	*	*	*	*	15	0.4
45 to 54 years old	3,376	26	0.8	*	*	*	*	5	0.2
55 years old and over	3,939	18	0.5	*	*	3	0.1	7	0.2
Female									
Total	27,127	9,012	33.2	1,013	3.7	3,977	14.7	1,943	7.2
3 and 4 years old	986	475	48.2	475	48.2	*	*	*	*
5 and 6 years old	1,025	966	94.2	527	51.4	439	42.8	*	*
7 to 9 years old	1,560	1,523	97.6	10	0.6	1,513	97.0	*	*
10 to 13 years old	2,002	1,978	98.8	*	*	1,908	95.3	70	3.5
14 and 15 years old	960	929	96.8	*	*	107	11.1	818	85.3
16 and 17 years old	943	885	93.9	*	*	3	0.4	825	87.5
18 and 19 years old	930	655	70.5	*	*	*	*	154	16.6
20 and 21 years old	934	537	57.5	*	*	3	0.3	24	2.5
22 to 24 years old	1,385	418	30.2	*	*	*	*	12	0.9
25 to 29 years old	2,218	294	13.3	*	*	*	*	14	0.6
30 to 34 years old	2,132	126	5.9	*	*	*	*	11	0.5

* = Quantity equals zero or rounds to zero.

Table A-1. Enrollment Status of the Population 3 Years Old and Over, by Sex, Age, Race, Hispanic Origin, Foreign Born, and Foreign-Born Parentage, October 2016—*Continued*

(Numbers in thousands; percent; civilian noninstitutionalized population.)

Age, sex, race, Hispanic origin, and nativity	Population	Enrolled in school		Not enrolled in school					
		College undergraduate or graduate		Total		High school graduate		Not high school graduate	
	Number	Number	Percent	Number	Percent	Number	Percent	Number	Percent
Female									
Total..............................	10,361	843	8.1	7,586	73.2	6,569	63.4	1017	9.8
3 and 4 years old	284	*	*	96	33.6	*	*	96	33.6
5 and 6 years old	261	*	*	16	6.0	*	*	16	6.0
7 to 9 years old	407	*	*	8	2.0	*	*	8	2.0
10 to 13 years old	545	*	*	8	1.4	*	*	8	1.4
14 and 15 years old	266	5	1.7	6	2.4	*	*	6	2.4
16 and 17 years old	276	10	3.8	9	3.3	6	2.2	3	1.1
18 and 19 years old	243	153	63.3	47	19.6	40	16.3	8	3.2
20 and 21 years old	297	209	70.5	87	29.4	76	25.5	12	3.9
22 to 24 years old	441	174	39.4	263	59.6	246	55.8	17	3.8
25 to 29 years old	858	169	19.7	689	80.3	639	74.5	50	5.9
30 to 34 years old	1021	60	5.8	961	94.2	916	89.8	45	4.4
35 to 44 years old	1,666	38	2.3	1,628	97.7	1,531	91.9	97	5.8
45 to 54 years old	1,411	21	1.5	1,387	98.3	1,213	85.9	174	12.3
55 years old and over............	2,385	4	0.2	2,381	99.8	1,902	79.8	479	20.1
HISPANIC (OF ANY RACE)									
Both Sexes									
Total..............................	54,325	3,661	6.7	36,460	67.1	24,501	45.1	11,959	22.0
3 and 4 years old	2,026	*	*	1,023	50.5	*	*	1,023	50.5
5 and 6 years old	2,100	*	*	147	7.0	*	*	147	7.0
7 to 9 years old	3,171	*	*	96	3.0	*	*	96	3.0
10 to 13 years old	4,073	*	*	64	1.6	*	*	64	1.6
14 and 15 years old	1,951	6	0.3	47	2.4	*	*	47	2.4
16 and 17 years old	1,973	82	4.2	126	6.4	43	2.2	83	4.2
18 and 19 years old	1,825	884	48.5	576	31.6	430	23.6	146	8.0
20 and 21 years old	1,894	948	50.1	915	48.3	742	39.2	174	9.2
22 to 24 years old	2,821	732	26.0	2,068	73.3	1,740	61.7	328	11.6
25 to 29 years old	4,560	491	10.8	4,047	88.7	3,166	69.4	881	19.3
30 to 34 years old	4,401	191	4.3	4,193	95.3	3,120	70.9	1,073	24.4
35 to 44 years old	8,240	228	2.8	7,983	96.9	5,613	68.1	2,369	28.8
45 to 54 years old	6,739	75	1.1	6,654	98.7	4,514	67.0	2,140	31.8
55 years old and over............	8,554	23	0.3	8,521	99.6	5,134	60.0	3,387	39.6
Male									
Total..............................	27,198	1,582	5.8	18,345	67.4	12,086	44.4	6,259	23.0
3 and 4 years old	1,039	*	*	512	49.3	*	*	512	49.3
5 and 6 years old	1,074	*	*	88	8.2	*	*	88	8.2
7 to 9 years old	1,610	*	*	59	3.7	*	*	59	3.7
10 to 13 years old	2,071	*	*	40	1.9	*	*	40	1.9
14 and 15 years old	991	3	0.3	16	1.6	*	*	16	1.6
16 and 17 years old	1,030	26	2.5	68	6.6	27	2.6	41	4.0
18 and 19 years old	894	383	42.8	302	33.7	212	23.7	90	10.0
20 and 21 years old	960	437	45.6	519	54.0	421	43.9	98	10.2
22 to 24 years old	1,436	327	22.8	1,101	76.6	893	62.2	208	14.4
25 to 29 years old	2,343	210	9.0	2,124	90.7	1,582	67.5	542	23.1
30 to 34 years old	2,268	76	3.4	2,186	96.4	1,569	69.2	617	27.2
35 to 44 years old	4,167	91	2.2	4,061	97.5	2,785	66.8	1,275	30.6
45 to 54 years old	3,376	21	0.6	3,350	99.2	2,214	65.6	1,136	33.6
55 years old and over............	3,939	8	0.2	3,921	99.5	2,382	60.5	1,539	39.1
Female									
Total..............................	27,127	2,079	7.7	18,115	66.8	12,416	45.8	5,700	21.0
3 and 4 years old	986	*	*	511	51.8	*	*	511	51.8
5 and 6 years old	1,025	*	*	59	5.8	*	*	59	5.8
7 to 9 years old	1,560	*	*	37	2.4	*	*	37	2.4
10 to 13 years old	2,002	*	*	24	1.2	*	*	24	1.2
14 and 15 years old	960	4	0.4	31	3.2	*	*	31	3.2
16 and 17 years old	943	56	6.0	58	6.1	16	1.7	42	4.4
18 and 19 years old	930	501	53.9	275	29.5	218	23.5	56	6.1
20 and 21 years old	934	511	54.7	397	42.5	321	34.3	76	8.1
22 to 24 years old	1,385	405	29.3	967	69.8	846	61.1	121	8.7
25 to 29 years old	2,218	281	12.7	1,923	86.7	1,584	71.4	340	15.3
30 to 34 years old	2,132	115	5.4	2,007	94.1	1,550	72.7	456	21.4

* = Quantity equals zero or rounds to zero.

Table A-1. Enrollment Status of the Population 3 Years Old and Over, by Sex, Age, Race, Hispanic Origin, Foreign Born, and Foreign-Born Parentage, October 2016—*Continued*

(Numbers in thousands; percent; civilian noninstitutionalized population.)

| Age, sex, race, Hispanic origin, and nativity | Population | Enrolled in school | | | | | | | |
| | | Total | | Nursery or kindergarten | | Elementary | | High school | |
	Number	Number	Percent	Number	Percent	Number	Percent	Number	Percent
35 to 44 years old	4,073	151	3.7	*	*	*	*	15	0.4
45 to 54 years old	3,363	59	1.7	*	*	4	0.1	*	*
55 years old and over	4,615	15	0.3	*	*	*	*	*	*
FOREIGN–BORN									
Both Sexes									
Total	43,578	5,097	11.7	138	0.3	1,207	2.8	1,179	2.7
3 and 4 years old	135	55	40.7	55	40.7	*	*	*	*
5 and 6 years old	187	166	88.6	83	44.1	83	44.4	*	*
7 to 9 years old	393	375	95.4	*	*	375	95.4	*	*
10 to 13 years old	680	661	97.1	*	*	644	94.6	17	2.5
14 and 15 years old	457	441	96.5	*	*	93	20.3	344	75.2
16 and 17 years old	595	553	92.9	*	*	3	0.5	524	88.2
18 and 19 years old	726	491	67.6	*	*	5	0.6	146	20.2
20 and 21 years old	924	500	54.1	*	*	*	*	38	4.1
22 to 24 years old	1,626	581	35.8	*	*	*	*	30	1.9
25 to 29 years old	3,470	539	15.5	*	*	*	*	25	0.7
30 to 34 years old	4,332	241	5.6	*	*	3	0.1	7	0.2
35 to 44 years old	9,234	308	3.3	*	*	1	*	28	0.3
45 to 54 years old	8,485	134	1.6	*	*	1	*	9	0.1
55 years old and over	12,334	54	0.4	*	*	*	*	11	0.1
Male									
Total	21,013	2,550	12.1	58	0.3	611	2.9	561	2.7
3 and 4 years old	73	21	29.6	21	29.6	*	*	*	*
5 and 6 years old	93	78	84.7	36	39.2	42	45.4	*	*
7 to 9 years old	210	195	92.5	*	*	195	92.5	*	*
10 to 13 years old	335	325	96.8	*	*	318	94.8	7	2.1
14 and 15 years old	172	172	100.0	*	*	51	29.7	121	70.3
16 and 17 years old	311	279	89.8	*	*	3	1.0	269	86.5
18 and 19 years old	382	256	66.9	*	*	*	*	82	21.6
20 and 21 years old	497	271	54.6	*	*	*	0.1	22	4.5
22 to 24 years old	880	336	38.1	*	*	*	*	19	2.2
25 to 29 years old	1,845	310	16.8	*	*	*	*	12	0.6
30 to 34 years old	2,106	100	4.8	*	*	3	0.1	3	0.1
35 to 44 years old	4,406	126	2.9	*	*	*	*	13	0.3
45 to 54 years old	4,165	50	1.2	*	*	*	*	2	*
55 years old and over	5,538	31	0.6	*	*	*	*	11	0.2
Female									
Total	22,565	2,547	11.3	80	0.4	596	2.6	618	2.7
3 and 4 years old	63	34	53.6	34	53.6	*	*	*	*
5 and 6 years old	94	87	92.4	46	49.0	41	43.5	*	*
7 to 9 years old	183	180	98.8	*	*	180	98.8	*	*
10 to 13 years old	345	336	97.4	*	*	326	94.4	10	3.0
14 and 15 years old	284	268	94.4	*	*	41	14.6	222	78.2
16 and 17 years old	284	274	96.4	*	*	*	*	256	90.0
18 and 19 years old	344	235	68.4	*	*	5	1.3	64	18.7
20 and 21 years old	426	228	53.5	*	*	*	*	15	3.6
22 to 24 years old	746	246	33.0	*	*	*	*	11	1.4
25 to 29 years old	1,626	229	14.1	*	*	*	*	13	0.8
30 to 34 years old	2,226	141	6.3	*	*	*	*	4	0.2
35 to 44 years old	4,828	182	3.8	*	*	1	*	15	0.3
45 to 54 years old	4,320	84	1.9	*	*	1	*	7	0.2
55 years old and over	6,796	22	0.3	*	*	*	*	*	*

* = Quantity equals zero or rounds to zero.

Table A-1. Enrollment Status of the Population 3 Years Old and Over, by Sex, Age, Race, Hispanic Origin, Foreign Born, and Foreign-Born Parentage, October 2016—*Continued*

(Numbers in thousands; percent; civilian noninstitutionalized population.)

Age, sex, race, Hispanic origin, and nativity	Population	Enrolled in school		Not enrolled in school					
		College undergraduate or graduate		Total		High school graduate		Not high school graduate	
	Number	Number	Percent	Number	Percent	Number	Percent	Number	Percent
35 to 44 years old	4,073	137	3.4	3,922	96.3	2,828	69.4	1,094	26.8
45 to 54 years old	3,363	54	1.6	3,305	98.3	2,300	68.4	1,004	29.9
55 years old and over	4,615	15	0.3	4,600	99.7	2,752	59.6	1,848	40.1
FOREIGN–BORN									
Both Sexes									
Total	43,578	2,574	5.9	38,480	88.3	28,354	65.1	10,126	23.2
3 and 4 years old	135	*	*	80	59.3	*	*	80	59.3
5 and 6 years old	187	*	*	21	11.4	*	*	21	11.4
7 to 9 years old	393	*	*	18	4.6	*	*	18	4.6
10 to 13 years old	680	*	*	20	2.9	*	*	20	2.9
14 and 15 years old	457	5	1.0	16	3.5	*	*	16	3.5
16 and 17 years old	595	25	4.2	42	7.1	19	3.1	23	3.9
18 and 19 years old	726	340	46.8	235	32.4	179	24.7	56	7.7
20 and 21 years old	924	462	50.0	424	45.9	340	36.8	84	9.1
22 to 24 years old	1,626	551	33.9	1,045	64.2	816	50.2	228	14.0
25 to 29 years old	3,470	514	14.8	2,931	84.5	2,268	65.4	664	19.1
30 to 34 years old	4,332	232	5.4	4,090	94.4	3,135	72.4	955	22.0
35 to 44 years old	9,234	279	3.0	8,927	96.7	6,747	73.1	2,180	23.6
45 to 54 years old	8,485	124	1.5	8,351	98.4	6,176	72.8	2,176	25.6
55 years old and over	12,334	43	0.3	12,280	99.6	8,674	70.3	3,606	29.2
Male									
Total	21,013	1,320	6.3	18,462	87.9	13,403	63.8	5,060	24.1
3 and 4 years old	73	*	*	51	70.4	*	*	51	70.4
5 and 6 years old	93	*	*	14	15.3	*	*	14	15.3
7 to 9 years old	210	*	*	16	7.5	*	*	16	7.5
10 to 13 years old	335	*	*	11	3.2	*	*	11	3.2
14 and 15 years old	172	*	*	*	*	*	*	*	*
16 and 17 years old	311	7	2.2	32	10.2	14	4.6	17	5.6
18 and 19 years old	382	173	45.3	126	33.1	92	24.2	34	8.9
20 and 21 years old	497	249	50.0	226	45.4	183	36.8	43	8.6
22 to 24 years old	880	316	35.9	545	61.9	393	44.6	152	17.3
25 to 29 years old	1,845	298	16.1	1,535	83.2	1,119	60.7	416	22.5
30 to 34 years old	2,106	95	4.5	2,005	95.2	1,483	70.4	522	24.8
35 to 44 years old	4,406	113	2.6	4,281	97.1	3,136	71.2	1,145	26.0
45 to 54 years old	4,165	48	1.2	4,115	98.8	2,989	71.8	1,125	27.0
55 years old and over	5,538	21	0.4	5,506	99.4	3,992	72.1	1,514	27.3
Female									
Total	22,565	1,254	5.6	20,018	88.7	14,952	66.3	5,066	22.5
3 and 4 years old	63	*	*	29	46.4	*	*	29	46.4
5 and 6 years old	94	*	*	7	7.6	*	*	7	7.6
7 to 9 years old	183	*	*	2	1.2	*	*	2	1.2
10 to 13 years old	345	*	*	9	2.6	*	*	9	2.6
14 and 15 years old	284	5	1.6	16	5.6	*	*	16	5.6
16 and 17 years old	284	18	6.4	10	3.6	4	1.5	6	2.1
18 and 19 years old	344	166	48.4	109	31.6	87	25.2	22	6.3
20 and 21 years old	426	213	49.9	198	46.5	157	36.8	41	9.7
22 to 24 years old	746	235	31.5	500	67.0	424	56.8	76	10.2
25 to 29 years old	1,626	216	13.3	1,396	85.9	1,149	70.6	248	15.3
30 to 34 years old	2,226	137	6.1	2,085	93.7	1,652	74.2	433	19.4
35 to 44 years old	4,828	166	3.4	4,646	96.2	3,611	74.8	1,035	21.4
45 to 54 years old	4,320	76	1.8	4,237	98.1	3,186	73.7	1,051	24.3
55 years old and over	6,796	22	0.3	6,774	99.7	4,682	68.9	2,092	30.8

* = Quantity equals zero or rounds to zero.

Table A-1. Enrollment Status of the Population 3 Years Old and Over, by Sex, Age, Race, Hispanic Origin, Foreign Born, and Foreign-Born Parentage, October 2016—*Continued*

(Numbers in thousands; percent; civilian noninstitutionalized population.)

| Age, sex, race, Hispanic origin, and nativity | Population | Enrolled in school | | | | | | | |
| | | Total | | Nursery or kindergarten | | Elementary | | High school | |
	Number	Number	Percent	Number	Percent	Number	Percent	Number	Percent
CHILDREN OF FOREIGN– BORN PARENTS									
Both Sexes									
Total	78,569	20,864	26.6	2,237	2.8	8,541	10.9	4,404	5.6
3 and 4 years old	2,058	1,105	53.7	1,105	53.7	*	*	*	*
5 and 6 years old	2,074	1,919	92.5	1,122	54.1	797	38.4	*	*
7 to 9 years old	3,250	3,157	97.2	10	0.3	3,148	96.9	*	*
10 to 13 years old	4,388	4,312	98.3	*	*	4,202	95.8	110	2.5
14 and 15 years old	2,154	2,116	98.2	*	*	347	16.1	1,759	81.6
16 and 17 years old	2,145	2,010	93.7	*	*	10	0.5	1,921	89.6
18 and 19 years old	2,088	1,525	73.0	*	*	13	0.6	404	19.3
20 and 21 years old	2,254	1,389	61.6	*	*	3	0.1	65	2.9
22 to 24 years old	3,628	1,285	35.4	*	*	8	0.2	54	1.5
25 to 29 years old	6,468	1032	16.0	*	*	4	0.1	31	0.5
30 to 34 years old	6,493	369	5.7	*	*	3	*	10	0.2
35 to 44 years old	12,357	405	3.3	*	*	1	*	30	0.2
45 to 54 years old	11,001	176	1.6	*	*	4	*	9	0.1
55 years old and over	18,212	64	0.4	*	*	*	*	11	0.1
Male									
Total	38,479	10,365	26.9	1,161	3.0	4,324	11.2	2,224	5.8
3 and 4 years old	1,085	595	54.8	595	54.8	*	*	*	*
5 and 6 years old	1033	951	92.1	564	54.6	387	37.5	*	*
7 to 9 years old	1,637	1,584	96.8	3	0.2	1,581	96.6	*	*
10 to 13 years old	2,221	2,176	98.0	*	*	2,129	95.9	47	2.1
14 and 15 years old	1056	1037	98.3	*	*	196	18.6	838	79.4
16 and 17 years old	1,088	1014	93.2	*	*	10	0.9	976	89.7
18 and 19 years old	1,085	776	71.5	*	*	9	0.8	247	22.8
20 and 21 years old	1,106	660	59.7	*	*	*	*	36	3.2
22 to 24 years old	1,923	669	34.8	*	*	4	0.2	35	1.8
25 to 29 years old	3,355	485	14.5	*	*	4	0.1	12	0.4
30 to 34 years old	3,133	134	4.3	*	*	3	0.1	6	0.2
35 to 44 years old	6,037	184	3.0	*	*	*	*	14	0.2
45 to 54 years old	5,482	62	1.1	*	*	*	*	2	*
55 years old and over	8,239	37	0.4	*	*	*	*	11	0.1
Female									
Total	40,090	10,499	26.2	1,076	2.7	4,216	10.5	2,179	5.4
3 and 4 years old	973	511	52.5	511	52.5	*	*	*	*
5 and 6 years old	1041	968	93.0	558	53.6	410	39.3	*	*
7 to 9 years old	1,613	1,573	97.5	7	0.4	1,566	97.1	*	*
10 to 13 years old	2,168	2,136	98.5	*	*	2,073	95.6	63	2.9
14 and 15 years old	1,099	1,079	98.2	*	*	150	13.7	920	83.8
16 and 17 years old	1,057	996	94.2	*	*	*	*	945	89.4
18 and 19 years old	1,003	749	74.6	*	*	5	0.5	156	15.6
20 and 21 years old	1,148	729	63.5	*	*	3	0.2	30	2.6
22 to 24 years old	1,705	616	36.1	*	*	4	0.3	19	1.1
25 to 29 years old	3,113	547	17.6	*	*	*	*	19	0.6
30 to 34 years old	3,359	235	7.0	*	*	*	*	4	0.1
35 to 44 years old	6,320	221	3.5	*	*	1	*	16	0.3
45 to 54 years old	5,519	114	2.1	*	*	4	0.1	7	0.1
55 years old and over	9,973	27	0.3	*	*	*	*	*	*

* = Quantity equals zero or rounds to zero.

Table A-1. Enrollment Status of the Population 3 Years Old and Over, by Sex, Age, Race, Hispanic Origin, Foreign Born, and Foreign-Born Parentage, October 2016—*Continued*

(Numbers in thousands; percent; civilian noninstitutionalized population.)

| Age, sex, race, Hispanic origin, and nativity | Population | Enrolled in school | | Not enrolled in school | | | | | |
| | | College undergraduate or graduate | | Total | | High school graduate | | Not high school graduate | |
	Number	Number	Percent	Number	Percent	Number	Percent	Number	Percent
CHILDREN OF FOREIGN– BORN PARENTS									
Both Sexes									
Total	78,569	5,683	7.2	57,705	73.4	44,695	56.9	13,010	16.6
3 and 4 years old	2,058	*	*	952	46.3	*	*	952	46.3
5 and 6 years old	2,074	*	*	155	7.5	*	*	155	7.5
7 to 9 years old	3,250	*	*	92	2.8	*	*	92	2.8
10 to 13 years old	4,388	*	*	76	1.7	*	*	76	1.7
14 and 15 years old	2,154	11	0.5	38	1.8	*	*	38	1.8
16 and 17 years old	2,145	79	3.7	135	6.3	43	2.0	92	4.3
18 and 19 years old	2,088	1,108	53.1	563	27.0	431	20.6	132	6.3
20 and 21 years old	2,254	1,321	58.6	864	38.4	728	32.3	136	6.0
22 to 24 years old	3,628	1,223	33.7	2,343	64.6	1,999	55.1	344	9.5
25 to 29 years old	6,468	997	15.4	5,436	84.0	4,594	71.0	842	13.0
30 to 34 years old	6,493	356	5.5	6,124	94.3	5,023	77.4	1,101	17.0
35 to 44 years old	12,357	373	3.0	11,953	96.7	9,565	77.4	2,387	19.3
45 to 54 years old	11,001	163	1.5	10,825	98.4	8,466	77.0	2,359	21.4
55 years old and over............	18,212	53	0.3	18,148	99.6	13,846	76.0	4,302	23.6
Male									
Total	38,479	2,655	6.9	28,114	73.1	21,550	56.0	6,564	17.1
3 and 4 years old	1,085	*	*	490	45.2	*	*	490	45.2
5 and 6 years old	1033	*	*	82	7.9	*	*	82	7.9
7 to 9 years old	1,637	*	*	53	3.2	*	*	53	3.2
10 to 13 years old	2,221	*	*	44	2.0	*	*	44	2.0
14 and 15 years old	1056	3	0.2	18	1.7	*	*	18	1.7
16 and 17 years old	1,088	27	2.5	74	6.8	27	2.5	48	4.4
18 and 19 years old	1,085	520	47.9	309	28.5	223	20.6	85	7.9
20 and 21 years old	1,106	624	56.5	446	40.3	381	34.4	65	5.8
22 to 24 years old	1,923	630	32.8	1,254	65.2	1,031	53.6	223	11.6
25 to 29 years old	3,355	469	14.0	2,870	85.5	2,353	70.1	517	15.4
30 to 34 years old	3,133	125	4.0	2,999	95.7	2,395	76.4	605	19.3
35 to 44 years old	6,037	170	2.8	5,854	97.0	4,577	75.8	1,276	21.1
45 to 54 years old	5,482	61	1.1	5,420	98.9	4,187	76.4	1,233	22.5
55 years old and over............	8,239	26	0.3	8,202	99.6	6,376	77.4	1,826	22.2
Female									
Total	40,090	3,028	7.6	29,590	73.8	23,145	57.7	6,446	16.1
3 and 4 years old	973	*	*	462	47.5	*	*	462	47.5
5 and 6 years old	1041	*	*	73	7.0	*	*	73	7.0
7 to 9 years old	1,613	*	*	40	2.5	*	*	40	2.5
10 to 13 years old	2,168	*	*	32	1.5	*	*	32	1.5
14 and 15 years old	1,099	8	0.7	20	1.8	*	*	20	1.8
16 and 17 years old	1,057	51	4.8	61	5.8	16	1.5	45	4.2
18 and 19 years old	1,003	588	58.6	254	25.4	208	20.7	47	4.7
20 and 21 years old	1,148	696	60.7	419	36.5	347	30.2	72	6.3
22 to 24 years old	1,705	593	34.8	1,089	63.9	968	56.7	121	7.1
25 to 29 years old	3,113	527	16.9	2,566	82.4	2,241	72.0	325	10.4
30 to 34 years old	3,359	231	6.9	3,124	93.0	2,628	78.2	496	14.8
35 to 44 years old	6,320	203	3.2	6,099	96.5	4,988	78.9	1,111	17.6
45 to 54 years old	5,519	103	1.9	5,405	97.9	4,279	77.5	1,126	20.4
55 years old and over............	9,973	27	0.3	9,946	99.7	7,469	74.9	2,476	24.8

* = Quantity equals zero or rounds to zero.

Table A-2. Single Grade of Enrollment and High School Graduation Status for Population 3 Years Old and Over, by Sex, Age (Single Years for 3 to 24 Years), Race, and Hispanic Origin, October 2016

(Numbers in thousands; percent; civilian noninstitutionalized population.)

| Age, sex, race, and Hispanic origin | Population | Enrolled | | Nursery | Kinder-garten | Enrolled | | | | | | | | |
| | | Number | Percent | | | Elementary grades | | | | | | | | |
						1	2	3	4	5	6	7	8
ALL RACES													
Both Sexes													
Total	307,516	77,232	25.1	4,746	4,017	3,922	3,942	4,241	4,191	4,194	4,051	4,003	4,060
3 years old	3,978	1,656	41.6	1,622	34	*	*	*	*	*	*	*	*
4 years old	3,993	2,633	65.9	2,413	220	*	*	*	*	*	*	*	*
5 years old	4,061	3,660	90.1	667	2,821	147	26	*	*	*	*	*	*
6 years old	3,989	3,847	96.4	45	882	2,750	135	34	*	*	*	*	*
7 years old	4,046	3,929	97.1	*	60	924	2,717	192	36	*	*	*	*
8 years old	4,117	4,024	97.7	*	*	86	909	2,792	211	26	*	*	*
9 years old	4,206	4,140	98.4	*	*	15	133	1,112	2,666	191	23	*	*
10 years old	4,257	4,177	98.1	*	*	*	22	88	1,133	2,778	135	20	*
11 years old	4,034	3,985	98.8	*	*	*	*	23	123	1,047	2,588	172	32
12 years old	4,050	4,001	98.8	*	*	*	*	*	22	129	1,115	2,553	174
13 years old	4,193	4,126	98.4	*	*	*	*	*	*	23	131	1,033	2,667
14 years old	4,082	4,010	98.2	*	*	*	*	*	*	*	25	142	1,030
15 years old	4,188	4,097	97.8	*	*	*	*	*	*	*	5	30	111
16 years old	4,246	3,994	94.1	*	*	*	*	*	*	*	19	4	32
17 years old	4,229	3,885	91.9	*	*	*	*	*	*	*	1	*	*
18 years old	4,203	3,133	74.5	*	*	*	*	*	*	*	*	14	3
19 years old	4,063	2,608	64.2	*	*	*	*	*	*	*	*	11	*
20 years old	4,029	2,425	60.2	*	*	*	*	*	*	*	*	9	*
21 years old	4,257	2,172	51.0	*	*	*	*	*	*	*	*	*	*
22 years old	4,335	1,646	38.0	*	*	*	*	*	*	*	*	*	*
23 years old	4,469	1,180	26.4	*	*	*	*	*	*	*	*	4	*
24 years old	4,536	1015	22.4	*	*	*	*	*	*	*	*	4	*
25 to 29 years old	22,410	2,966	13.2	*	*	*	*	*	*	*	1	*	10
30 to 34 years old	21,335	1,364	6.4	*	*	*	*	*	*	*	3	3	*
35 to 39 years old	20,545	823	4.0	*	*	*	*	*	*	*	*	1	1
40 to 44 years old	19,342	672	3.5	*	*	*	*	*	*	*	1	*	*
45 to 49 years old	20,728	427	2.1	*	*	*	*	*	*	*	*	*	*
50 to 54 years old	21,563	289	1.3	*	*	*	*	*	*	*	3	1	*
55 to 59 years old	21,883	171	0.8	*	*	*	*	*	*	*	*	*	*
60 to 64 years old	19,605	44	0.2	*	*	*	*	*	*	*	*	*	*
65 years and over	48,542	134	0.3	*	*	*	*	*	*	*	3	*	*
Male													
Total	150,027	38,351	25.6	2,438	2,049	1,989	2,079	2,087	2,173	2,138	2,111	2,050	2,056
3 years old	2,013	855	42.5	835	19	*	*	*	*	*	*	*	*
4 years old	2,053	1,346	65.6	1,230	116	*	*	*	*	*	*	*	*
5 years old	2,104	1,887	89.7	349	1,459	62	18	*	*	*	*	*	*
6 years old	2,021	1,937	95.9	24	427	1,380	84	23	*	*	*	*	*
7 years old	2,052	1,984	96.7	*	27	497	1,347	94	18	*	*	*	*
8 years old	2,124	2,073	97.6	*	*	41	542	1,363	115	14	*	*	*
9 years old	2,124	2,084	98.1	*	*	9	78	551	1,346	87	14	*	*
10 years old	2,216	2,170	97.9	*	*	*	12	39	633	1,401	70	15	*
11 years old	2,017	1,997	99.0	*	*	*	*	17	54	566	1,261	84	16
12 years old	2,070	2,038	98.5	*	*	*	*	8	50	663	1,245	67
13 years old	2,132	2,088	98.0	*	*	*	*	*	*	20	67	603	1,299
14 years old	2,095	2,070	98.8	*	*	*	*	*	*	*	13	71	581
15 years old	2,117	2,088	98.6	*	*	*	*	*	*	*	3	10	61
16 years old	2,156	2,012	93.3	*	*	*	*	*	*	*	15	2	21
17 years old	2,140	1,969	92.0	*	*	*	*	*	*	*	1	*	*
18 years old	2,154	1,567	72.7	*	*	*	*	*	*	*	*	10	*
19 years old	2,038	1,293	63.5	*	*	*	*	*	*	*	*	4	*
20 years old	2,026	1,128	55.6	*	*	*	*	*	*	*	*	*	*
21 years old	2,188	1,038	47.4	*	*	*	*	*	*	*	*	*	*
22 years old	2,105	774	36.8	*	*	*	*	*	*	*	*	*	*
23 years old	2,240	590	26.3	*	*	*	*	*	*	*	*	*	*
24 years old	2,290	468	20.4	*	*	*	*	*	*	*	*	4	*
25 to 29 years old	11,142	1,311	11.8	*	*	*	*	*	*	*	1	*	10
30 to 34 years old	10,535	582	5.5	*	*	*	*	*	*	*	*	3	*
35 to 39 years old	10,093	305	3.0	*	*	*	*	*	*	*	*	*	*
40 to 44 years old	9,457	275	2.9	*	*	*	*	*	*	*	1	*	*
45 to 49 years old	10,154	162	1.6	*	*	*	*	*	*	*	*	*	*

* = Quantity zero or rounds to zero.

Table A-2. Single Grade of Enrollment and High School Graduation Status for Population 3 Years Old and Over, by Sex, Age (Single Years for 3 to 24 Years), Race, and Hispanic Origin, October 2016—*Continued*

(Numbers in thousands; percent; civilian noninstitutionalized population.)

Age, sex, race, and Hispanic origin	Enrolled — High school 9	10	11	12	Enrolled — Undergraduate college 1	2	3	4	Enrolled — Graduate school 1	2+	Not enrolled H.S. grad	Not enrolled Not grad	Not enrolled Number	Not enrolled Percent
ALL RACES														
Both Sexes														
Total	4,134	4,254	4,018	4,261	4,494	4,444	3,617	2,942	1,352	2,347	199,749	30,535	230,284	74.9
3 years old	*	*	*	*	*	*	*	*	*	*	*	2,322	2,322	58.4
4 years old	*	*	*	*	*	*	*	*	*	*	*	1,360	1,360	34.1
5 years old	*	*	*	*	*	*	*	*	*	*	*	401	401	9.9
6 years old	*	*	*	*	*	*	*	*	*	*	*	142	142	3.6
7 years old	*	*	*	*	*	*	*	*	*	*	*	117	117	2.9
8 years old	*	*	*	*	*	*	*	*	*	*	*	93	93	2.3
9 years old	*	*	*	*	*	*	*	*	*	*	*	66	66	1.6
10 years old	*	*	*	*	*	*	*	*	*	*	*	80	80	1.9
11 years old	*	*	*	*	*	*	*	*	*	*	*	49	49	1.2
12 years old	8	*	*	*	*	*	*	*	*	*	*	49	49	1.2
13 years old	258	14	*	*	*	*	*	*	*	*	*	68	68	1.6
14 years old	2,607	194	12	*	*	*	*	*	*	*	*	73	73	1.8
15 years old	1,032	2,593	249	52	15	*	3	*	5	2	34	57	91	2.2
16 years old	155	1,115	2,320	283	30	*	14	*	21	2	44	207	251	5.9
17 years old	38	198	1,081	2,419	134	11	3	*	*	*	129	215	344	8.1
18 years old	16	50	188	1,058	1,678	103	11	*	11	*	790	281	1,071	25.5
19 years old	3	18	49	159	950	1,172	236	11	*	*	1,203	251	1,454	35.8
20 years old	*	4	24	80	393	876	938	83	14	3	1,343	261	1,604	39.8
21 years old	*	*	12	51	151	448	617	789	44	60	1,820	266	2,086	49.0
22 years old	*	3	24	9	155	328	309	564	161	93	2,456	233	2,689	62.0
23 years old	*	8	4	7	92	224	257	317	112	153	2,939	350	3,289	73.6
24 years old	*	3	12	30	85	138	195	252	113	184	3,252	269	3,521	77.6
25 to 29 years old	5	12	13	42	349	495	453	425	417	744	17,774	1,670	19,444	86.8
30 to 34 years old	*	7	1	15	159	226	214	168	162	406	18,139	1,832	19,971	93.6
35 to 39 years old	2	6	10	17	95	153	142	111	79	205	17,662	2,060	19,722	96.0
40 to 44 years old	*	6	7	18	85	99	92	83	96	185	16,721	1,950	18,670	96.5
45 to 49 years old	2	9	10	6	39	71	69	66	55	101	18,025	2,276	20,301	97.9
50 to 54 years old	3	3	3	3	40	49	38	41	21	83	19,039	2,234	21,274	98.7
55 to 59 years old	*	*	*	1	25	30	14	17	29	55	19,456	2,255	21,711	99.2
60 to 64 years old	1	*	*	*	3	12	2	2	7	17	17,605	1,956	19,561	99.8
65 years and over	3	10	*	12	18	9	9	13	4	52	41,318	7,090	48,408	99.7
Male														
Total	2,153	2,179	2,039	2,166	2,078	1,974	1,676	1,347	548	1021	96,156	15,520	111,676	74.4
3 years old	*	*	*	*	*	*	*	*	*	*	*	1,159	1,159	57.5
4 years old	*	*	*	*	*	*	*	*	*	*	*	707	707	34.4
5 years old	*	*	*	*	*	*	*	*	*	*	*	217	217	10.3
6 years old	*	*	*	*	*	*	*	*	*	*	*	83	83	4.1
7 years old	*	*	*	*	*	*	*	*	*	*	*	69	69	3.3
8 years old	*	*	*	*	*	*	*	*	*	*	*	50	50	2.4
9 years old	*	*	*	*	*	*	*	*	*	*	*	40	40	1.9
10 years old	*	*	*	*	*	*	*	*	*	*	*	46	46	2.1
11 years old	*	*	*	*	*	*	*	*	*	*	*	20	20	1.0
12 years old	5	*	*	*	*	*	*	*	*	*	*	32	32	1.5
13 years old	93	6	*	*	*	*	*	*	*	*	*	43	43	2.0
14 years old	1,320	77	9	*	*	*	*	*	*	*	*	24	24	1.2
15 years old	592	1,289	113	18	3	*	*	*	*	*	5	24	29	1.4
16 years old	93	615	1,101	141	9	*	5	*	8	2	26	118	144	6.7
17 years old	28	113	598	1,177	39	11	3	*	*	*	52	119	171	8.0
18 years old	7	25	109	618	756	26	5	*	11	*	420	167	587	27.3
19 years old	*	14	26	102	504	533	105	5	*	*	609	136	745	36.5
20 years old	*	4	21	37	196	393	429	39	8	*	745	153	899	44.4
21 years old	*	*	9	9	81	245	316	325	26	27	979	171	1,150	52.6
22 years old	*	3	14	9	92	154	139	268	52	43	1,205	126	1,331	63.2
23 years old	*	4	4	4	41	107	132	183	41	74	1,440	210	1,650	73.7
24 years old	*	3	8	7	30	54	102	143	44	73	1,654	169	1,823	79.6
25 to 29 years old	3	12	13	8	143	232	215	185	161	328	8,906	925	9,831	88.2
30 to 34 years old	*	*	*	6	29	92	92	76	70	181	8,958	994	9,952	94.5
35 to 39 years old	2	3	3	4	29	52	51	37	27	96	8,651	1,137	9,788	97.0
40 to 44 years old	*	3	4	10	35	28	40	27	47	80	8,120	1,062	9,182	97.1
45 to 49 years old	2	*	3	2	22	22	28	26	19	38	8,788	1,204	9,991	98.4

* = Quantity zero or rounds to zero.

Table A-2. Single Grade of Enrollment and High School Graduation Status for Population 3 Years Old and Over, by Sex, Age (Single Years for 3 to 24 Years), Race, and Hispanic Origin, October 2016—*Continued*

(Numbers in thousands; percent; civilian noninstitutionalized population.)

| Age, sex, race, and Hispanic origin | Population | Enrolled | | Enrolled | | | | | | | | | | |
		Number	Percent	Nursery	Kinder-garten	1	2	3	4	5	6	7	8
50 to 54 years old	10,522	114	1.1	*	*	*	*	*	*	*	*	*	*
55 to 59 years old	10,619	59	0.6	*	*	*	*	*	*	*	*	*	*
60 to 64 years old	9,337	24	0.3	*	*	*	*	*	*	*	*	*	*
65 years and over	21,693	60	0.3	*	*	*	*	*	*	*	3	*	*
Female													
Total	157,489	38,881	24.7	2,308	1,969	1,933	1,862	2,154	2,019	2,056	1,941	1,953	2,004
3 years old	1,964	801	40.8	786	15	*	*	*	*	*	*	*	*
4 years old	1,940	1,287	66.3	1,183	104	*	*	*	*	*	*	*	*
5 years old	1,957	1,773	90.6	318	1,362	85	8	*	*	*	*	*	*
6 years old	1,968	1,910	97.0	21	455	1,371	51	11	*	*	*	*	*
7 years old	1,993	1,945	97.6	*	33	427	1,370	97	18	*	*	*	*
8 years old	1,994	1,950	97.8	*	*	45	367	1,429	96	13	*	*	*
9 years old	2,082	2,056	98.8	*	*	6	55	561	1,321	104	9	*	*
10 years old	2,041	2,007	98.3	*	*	*	10	49	500	1,378	65	5	*
11 years old	2,017	1,987	98.5	*	*	*	*	7	69	481	1,327	89	16
12 years old	1,980	1,963	99.1	*	*	*	*	*	15	79	452	1,308	107
13 years old	2,062	2,037	98.8	*	*	*	*	*	*	3	64	429	1,368
14 years old	1,988	1,940	97.6	*	*	*	*	*	*	*	12	72	449
15 years old	2,071	2,009	97.0	*	*	*	*	*	*	*	2	21	50
16 years old	2,090	1,983	94.9	*	*	*	*	*	*	*	4	2	10
17 years old	2,089	1,916	91.7	*	*	*	*	*	*	*	*	*	*
18 years old	2,050	1,566	76.4	*	*	*	*	*	*	*	*	5	3
19 years old	2,025	1,315	64.9	*	*	*	*	*	*	*	*	7	*
20 years old	2,003	1,297	64.8	*	*	*	*	*	*	*	*	8	*
21 years old	2,069	1,134	54.8	*	*	*	*	*	*	*	*	*	*
22 years old	2,230	872	39.1	*	*	*	*	*	*	*	*	*	*
23 years old	2,229	590	26.5	*	*	*	*	*	*	*	*	4	*
24 years old	2,246	547	24.4	*	*	*	*	*	*	*	*	*	*
25 to 29 years old	11,268	1,655	14.7	*	*	*	*	*	*	*	*	*	*
30 to 34 years old	10,800	782	7.2	*	*	*	*	*	*	*	3	*	*
35 to 39 years old	10,452	518	5.0	*	*	*	*	*	*	*	*	1	1
40 to 44 years old	9,885	397	4.0	*	*	*	*	*	*	*	*	1	*
45 to 49 years old	10,575	265	2.5	*	*	*	*	*	*	*	*	*	*
50 to 54 years old	11,041	175	1.6	*	*	*	*	*	*	*	3	1	*
55 to 59 years old	11,264	112	1.0	*	*	*	*	*	*	*	*	*	*
60 to 64 years old	10,268	20	0.2	*	*	*	*	*	*	*	*	*	*
65 years and over	26,849	74	0.3	*	*	*	*	*	*	*	*	*	*
WHITE ALONE NON-HISPANIC													
Both Sexes													
Total	189,195	40,606	21.5	2,499	1,956	1,912	1,987	2,099	2,061	2,174	2,149	2,136	2,122
3 years old	1,966	846	43.0	842	4	*	*	*	*	*	*	*	*
4 years old	1,978	1,342	67.8	1,273	69	*	*	*	*	*	*	*	*
5 years old	1,987	1,805	90.8	361	1,373	64	8	*	*	*	*	*	*
6 years old	2,004	1,941	96.9	23	496	1,357	54	11	*	*	*	*	*
7 years old	1,977	1,918	97.0	*	16	455	1,361	67	19	*	*	*	*
8 years old	2,057	2,014	97.9	*	*	21	494	1,398	89	12	*	*	*
9 years old	2,085	2,061	98.9	*	*	15	66	570	1,322	76	11	*	*
10 years old	2,204	2,164	98.2	*	*	*	3	48	585	1,463	58	8	*
11 years old	2,051	2,020	98.5	*	*	*	*	5	38	529	1,375	60	13
12 years old	2,198	2,177	99.0	*	*	*	*	*	8	84	631	1,409	39
13 years old	2,144	2,110	98.4	*	*	*	*	*	*	10	42	540	1,409
14 years old	2,191	2,172	99.1	*	*	*	*	*	*	*	21	61	591
15 years old	2,233	2,195	98.3	*	*	*	*	*	*	*	2	19	39
16 years old	2,273	2,129	93.7	*	*	*	*	*	*	*	4	4	21
17 years old	2,251	2,040	90.6	*	*	*	*	*	*	*	*	*	*
18 years old	2,268	1,698	74.9	*	*	*	*	*	*	*	*	13	3
19 years old	2,295	1,516	66.1	*	*	*	*	*	*	*	*	11	*
20 years old	2,124	1,323	62.3	*	*	*	*	*	*	*	*	6	*
21 years old	2,313	1,220	52.7	*	*	*	*	*	*	*	*	*	*
22 years old	2,346	894	38.1	*	*	*	*	*	*	*	*	*	*
23 years old	2,475	619	25.0	*	*	*	*	*	*	*	*	*	*
24 years old	2,543	525	20.6	*	*	*	*	*	*	*	*	4	*

* = Quantity zero or rounds to zero.

Table A-2. Single Grade of Enrollment and High School Graduation Status for Population 3 Years Old and Over, by Sex, Age (Single Years for 3 to 24 Years), Race, and Hispanic Origin, October 2016—*Continued*

(Numbers in thousands; percent; civilian noninstitutionalized population.)

Age, sex, race, and Hispanic origin	Enrolled										Not enrolled		Not enrolled	
	High school				Undergraduate college				Graduate school		H.S. grad	Not grad	Number	Percent
	9	10	11	12	1	2	3	4	1	2+				
50 to 54 years old	3	3	3	3	11	18	9	19	10	35	9,243	1,165	10,408	98.9
55 to 59 years old	*	*	*	*	12	7	4	4	20	12	9,372	1,188	10,559	99.4
60 to 64 years old	1	*	*	*	2	7	2	2	4	5	8,314	999	9,313	99.7
65 years and over	3	4	*	12	2	4	*	7	*	26	18,672	2,961	21,632	99.7
Female														
Total	1,980	2,075	1,979	2,095	2,416	2,470	1,941	1,596	804	1,326	103,593	15,015	118,608	75.3
3 years old	*	*	*	*	*	*	*	*	*	*	*	1,163	1,163	59.2
4 years old	*	*	*	*	*	*	*	*	*	*	*	653	653	33.7
5 years old	*	*	*	*	*	*	*	*	*	*	*	184	184	9.4
6 years old	*	*	*	*	*	*	*	*	*	*	*	58	58	3.0
7 years old	*	*	*	*	*	*	*	*	*	*	*	48	48	2.4
8 years old	*	*	*	*	*	*	*	*	*	*	*	43	43	2.2
9 years old	*	*	*	*	*	*	*	*	*	*	*	26	26	1.2
10 years old	*	*	*	*	*	*	*	*	*	*	*	34	34	1.7
11 years old	*	*	*	*	*	*	*	*	*	*	*	29	29	1.5
12 years old	3	*	*	*	*	*	*	*	*	*	*	18	18	0.9
13 years old	164	9	*	*	*	*	*	*	*	*	*	24	24	1.2
14 years old	1,287	117	2	*	*	*	*	*	*	*	*	48	48	2.4
15 years old	441	1,304	136	34	11	*	3	*	5	2	29	33	63	3.0
16 years old	62	500	1,218	142	21	*	9	*	14	*	18	89	107	5.1
17 years old	10	85	483	1,243	95	*	*	*	*	*	76	97	173	8.3
18 years old	9	26	78	441	922	77	7	*	*	*	370	113	484	23.6
19 years old	3	3	23	56	446	639	131	6	*	*	594	115	710	35.1
20 years old	*	*	4	43	197	483	509	44	6	3	598	108	705	35.2
21 years old	*	*	3	42	70	203	301	464	17	33	840	95	936	45.2
22 years old	*	*	10	*	63	174	170	296	109	49	1,251	107	1,358	60.9
23 years old	*	4	*	3	51	118	125	134	72	80	1,499	140	1,639	73.5
24 years old	*	*	4	22	55	83	93	109	69	111	1,599	99	1,698	75.6
25 to 29 years old	2	*	*	35	206	262	238	240	256	415	8,869	745	9,613	85.3
30 to 34 years old	*	7	1	9	87	143	122	92	92	225	9,180	838	10,018	92.8
35 to 39 years old	*	3	7	13	66	101	90	74	52	109	9,011	924	9,934	95.0
40 to 44 years old	*	3	2	9	50	71	52	56	49	105	8,601	888	9,488	96.0
45 to 49 years old	*	9	7	4	17	50	41	39	36	63	9,238	1,072	10,310	97.5
50 to 54 years old	*	*	*	*	29	32	29	22	11	48	9,797	1,069	10,866	98.4
55 to 59 years old	*	*	*	1	14	23	10	13	9	43	10,085	1,067	11,152	99.0
60 to 64 years old	*	*	*	*	1	5	*	*	2	12	9,292	957	10,248	99.8
65 years and over	*	6	*	*	16	6	9	6	4	27	22,646	4,129	26,776	99.7
WHITE ALONE NON-HISPANIC														
Both Sexes														
Total	2,207	2,204	2,130	2,220	2,309	2,462	1,962	1,822	777	1,417	136,423	12,166	148,589	78.5
3 years old	*	*	*	*	*	*	*	*	*	*	*	1,120	1,120	57.0
4 years old	*	*	*	*	*	*	*	*	*	*	*	636	636	32.2
5 years old	*	*	*	*	*	*	*	*	*	*	*	182	182	9.2
6 years old	*	*	*	*	*	*	*	*	*	*	*	63	63	3.1
7 years old	*	*	*	*	*	*	*	*	*	*	*	59	59	3.0
8 years old	*	*	*	*	*	*	*	*	*	*	*	42	42	2.1
9 years old	*	*	*	*	*	*	*	*	*	*	*	23	23	1.1
10 years old	*	*	*	*	*	*	*	*	*	*	*	40	40	1.8
11 years old	*	*	*	*	*	*	*	*	*	*	*	31	31	1.5
12 years old	5	*	*	*	*	*	*	*	*	*	*	21	21	1.0
13 years old	99	9	*	*	*	*	*	*	*	*	*	34	34	1.6
14 years old	1,414	80	5	*	*	*	*	*	*	*	*	19	19	0.9
15 years old	571	1,420	119	18	1	*	3	*	3	*	*	38	38	1.7
16 years old	81	584	1,291	123	6	*	6	*	11	*	17	127	144	6.3
17 years old	20	66	588	1,314	46	7	*	*	*	*	76	135	211	9.4
18 years old	4	13	76	570	957	52	7	*	3	*	445	126	570	25.1
19 years old	*	3	7	74	540	762	113	6	*	*	662	116	778	33.9
20 years old	*	*	16	39	171	482	556	50	3	*	676	125	802	37.7
21 years old	*	*	3	13	49	203	347	545	23	37	997	96	1,093	47.3
22 years old	*	3	2	1	61	170	165	351	101	41	1,352	100	1,452	61.9
23 years old	*	8	*	5	27	111	148	155	74	91	1,698	157	1,855	75.0
24 years old	*	*	8	18	40	71	78	151	44	112	1,916	102	2,018	79.4

* = Quantity zero or rounds to zero.

Table A-2. Single Grade of Enrollment and High School Graduation Status for Population 3 Years Old and Over, by Sex, Age (Single Years for 3 to 24 Years), Race, and Hispanic Origin, October 2016—*Continued*

(Numbers in thousands; percent; civilian noninstitutionalized population.)

Age, sex, race, and Hispanic origin	Population	Enrolled Number	Enrolled Percent	Nursery	Kinder-garten	1	2	3	4	5	6	7	8
25 to 29 years old	12,441	1,652	13.3	*	*	*	*	*	*	*	1	*	6
30 to 34 years old	12,041	799	6.6	*	*	*	*	*	*	*	3	*	*
35 to 39 years old	11,730	422	3.6	*	*	*	*	*	*	*	*	*	1
40 to 44 years old	11,122	352	3.2	*	*	*	*	*	*	*	1	*	*
45 to 49 years old	12,850	250	1.9	*	*	*	*	*	*	*	*	*	*
50 to 54 years old	14,181	167	1.2	*	*	*	*	*	*	*	*	*	*
55 to 59 years old	15,355	108	0.7	*	*	*	*	*	*	*	*	*	*
60 to 64 years old	14,132	21	0.2	*	*	*	*	*	*	*	*	*	*
65 years and over	37,381	103	0.3	*	*	*	*	*	*	*	*	*	*
Male													
Total	92,728	20,265	21.9	1,308	1,003	990	1,045	1052	1,027	1098	1,147	1,126	1,071
3 years old	1010	448	44.4	444	4	*	*	*	*	*	*	*	*
4 years old	1,010	696	68.9	661	35	*	*	*	*	*	*	*	*
5 years old	1,013	924	91.3	192	702	28	3	*	*	*	*	*	*
6 years old	1,025	995	97.1	11	260	687	25	11	*	*	*	*	*
7 years old	1,007	972	96.5	*	2	254	671	35	9	*	*	*	*
8 years old	1,053	1,035	98.2	*	*	12	307	659	51	6	*	*	*
9 years old	1,063	1,055	99.2	*	*	9	38	317	642	38	10	*	*
10 years old	1,110	1,089	98.1	*	*	*	*	26	304	713	38	8	*
11 years old	1,078	1,064	98.7	*	*	*	*	4	20	298	700	29	12
12 years old	1,134	1,121	98.8	*	*	*	*	*	1	35	354	714	14
13 years old	1,100	1,074	97.6	*	*	*	*	*	*	7	33	313	692
14 years old	1,126	1,121	99.6	*	*	*	*	*	*	*	11	37	312
15 years old	1,145	1,123	98.1	*	*	*	*	*	*	*	*	6	20
16 years old	1,171	1,087	92.8	*	*	*	*	*	*	*	*	2	15
17 years old	1,152	1,047	90.9	*	*	*	*	*	*	*	*	*	*
18 years old	1,161	844	72.7	*	*	*	*	*	*	*	*	9	*
19 years old	1,190	787	66.2	*	*	*	*	*	*	*	*	4	*
20 years old	1,132	649	57.3	*	*	*	*	*	*	*	*	*	*
21 years old	1,139	550	48.3	*	*	*	*	*	*	*	*	*	*
22 years old	1,130	439	38.9	*	*	*	*	*	*	*	*	*	*
23 years old	1,261	300	23.8	*	*	*	*	*	*	*	*	*	*
24 years old	1,247	237	19.0	*	*	*	*	*	*	*	*	4	*
25 to 29 years old	6,203	724	11.7	*	*	*	*	*	*	*	1	*	6
30 to 34 years old	5,989	330	5.5	*	*	*	*	*	*	*	*	*	*
35 to 39 years old	5,833	162	2.8	*	*	*	*	*	*	*	*	*	*
40 to 44 years old	5,499	143	2.6	*	*	*	*	*	*	*	1	*	*
45 to 49 years old	6,367	98	1.5	*	*	*	*	*	*	*	*	*	*
50 to 54 years old	7,024	66	0.9	*	*	*	*	*	*	*	*	*	*
55 to 59 years old	7,527	35	0.5	*	*	*	*	*	*	*	*	*	*
60 to 64 years old	6,863	12	0.2	*	*	*	*	*	*	*	*	*	*
65 years and over	16,966	38	0.2	*	*	*	*	*	*	*	*	*	*
Female													
Total	96,467	20,341	21.1	1,191	953	922	942	1,047	1034	1,076	1,002	1,010	1,052
3 years old	956	398	41.6	398	*	*	*	*	*	*	*	*	*
4 years old	968	646	66.8	612	34	*	*	*	*	*	*	*	*
5 years old	975	881	90.4	169	671	36	5	*	*	*	*	*	*
6 years old	979	946	96.7	12	235	670	28	*	*	*	*	*	*
7 years old	970	947	97.6	*	14	201	690	32	10	*	*	*	*
8 years old	1,003	980	97.6	*	*	9	187	740	38	6	*	*	*
9 years old	1,021	1,007	98.6	*	*	5	29	253	680	38	2	*	*
10 years old	1,094	1,075	98.3	*	*	*	3	21	281	750	20	*	*
11 years old	973	956	98.2	*	*	*	*	*	19	231	675	31	1
12 years old	1,064	1,056	99.2	*	*	*	*	*	7	48	278	695	25
13 years old	1,043	1,035	99.2	*	*	*	*	*	*	3	9	228	717
14 years old	1,066	1,051	98.6	*	*	*	*	*	*	*	10	24	279
15 years old	1,088	1,072	98.5	*	*	*	*	*	*	*	2	13	19
16 years old	1,102	1,042	94.6	*	*	*	*	*	*	*	4	2	6
17 years old	1,100	993	90.3	*	*	*	*	*	*	*	*	*	*
18 years old	1,107	854	77.1	*	*	*	*	*	*	*	*	5	3
19 years old	1,105	729	66.0	*	*	*	*	*	*	*	*	7	*
20 years old	992	674	67.9	*	*	*	*	*	*	*	*	6	*
21 years old	1,175	670	57.0	*	*	*	*	*	*	*	*	*	*
22 years old	1,216	455	37.4	*	*	*	*	*	*	*	*	*	*

* = Quantity zero or rounds to zero.

Table A-2. Single Grade of Enrollment and High School Graduation Status for Population 3 Years Old and Over, by Sex, Age (Single Years for 3 to 24 Years), Race, and Hispanic Origin, October 2016—*Continued*

(Numbers in thousands; percent; civilian noninstitutionalized population.)

Age, sex, race, and Hispanic origin	Enrolled										Not enrolled		Not enrolled	
	High school				Undergraduate college				Graduate school		H.S. grad	Not grad	Number	Percent
	9	10	11	12	1	2	3	4	1	2+				
25 to 29 years old	3	3	4	19	181	276	220	261	246	432	10,334	455	10,789	86.7
30 to 34 years old	*	*	*	7	84	110	142	99	115	239	10,736	506	11,242	93.4
35 to 39 years old	2	*	3	5	57	63	60	58	44	129	10,780	528	11,308	96.4
40 to 44 years old	*	3	*	5	28	40	55	48	47	126	10,259	510	10,769	96.8
45 to 49 years old	2	6	3	3	22	49	34	45	24	63	11,943	656	12,599	98.1
50 to 54 years old	3	*	3	3	20	32	8	26	10	61	13,251	764	14,015	98.8
55 to 59 years old	*	*	*	1	8	21	12	13	22	31	14,284	962	15,246	99.3
60 to 64 years old	1	*	*	*	3	5	*	2	2	8	13,348	764	14,111	99.8
65 years and over	*	6	*	5	9	9	9	13	4	47	33,651	3,627	37,278	99.7
Male														
Total	1,158	1,103	1,133	1,125	1,097	1,105	973	798	323	583	66,212	6,251	72,463	78.1
3 years old	*	*	*	*	*	*	*	*	*	*	*	562	562	55.6
4 years old	*	*	*	*	*	*	*	*	*	*	*	315	315	31.1
5 years old	*	*	*	*	*	*	*	*	*	*	*	88	88	8.7
6 years old	*	*	*	*	*	*	*	*	*	*	*	30	30	2.9
7 years old	*	*	*	*	*	*	*	*	*	*	*	36	36	3.5
8 years old	*	*	*	*	*	*	*	*	*	*	*	19	19	1.8
9 years old	*	*	*	*	*	*	*	*	*	*	*	9	9	0.8
10 years old	*	*	*	*	*	*	*	*	*	*	*	21	21	1.9
11 years old	*	*	*	*	*	*	*	*	*	*	*	14	14	1.3
12 years old	3	*	*	*	*	*	*	*	*	*	*	13	13	1.2
13 years old	24	6	*	*	*	*	*	*	*	*	*	26	26	2.4
14 years old	727	32	3	*	*	*	*	*	*	*	*	5	5	0.4
15 years old	336	684	70	6	1	*	*	*	*	*	*	22	22	1.9
16 years old	43	321	635	64	*	*	2	*	4	*	9	75	84	7.2
17 years old	13	43	341	626	16	7	*	*	*	*	30	74	105	9.1
18 years old	*	4	47	346	418	17	*	*	3	*	244	73	317	27.3
19 years old	*	3	7	42	307	373	50	*	*	*	352	50	403	33.8
20 years old	*	*	12	13	86	218	293	26	*	*	401	82	483	42.7
21 years old	*	*	1	5	32	98	173	210	17	15	525	63	588	51.7
22 years old	*	3	*	1	45	83	91	168	35	15	643	48	690	61.1
23 years old	*	4	*	2	7	56	75	90	32	35	879	82	961	76.2
24 years old	*	*	8	3	12	30	38	79	17	46	946	65	1,010	81.0
25 to 29 years old	3	3	4	3	73	125	104	111	96	194	5,236	243	5,479	88.3
30 to 34 years old	*	*	*	3	46	31	67	41	50	91	5,389	270	5,659	94.5
35 to 39 years old	2	*	*	*	16	23	35	16	18	52	5,358	313	5,671	97.2
40 to 44 years old	*	*	*	3	9	8	29	18	23	52	5,057	299	5,356	97.4
45 to 49 years old	2	*	*	*	18	16	12	19	8	25	5,887	382	6,269	98.5
50 to 54 years old	3	*	3	3	5	12	*	12	3	25	6,536	421	6,958	99.1
55 to 59 years old	*	*	*	*	4	3	2	*	16	9	6,952	541	7,493	99.5
60 to 64 years old	1	*	*	*	2	2	*	2	*	4	6,412	439	6,851	99.8
65 years and over	*	*	*	5	*	4	*	7	*	23	15,356	1,572	16,927	99.8
Female														
Total	1,049	1,101	997	1,095	1,212	1,357	990	1023	454	833	70,211	5,915	76,126	78.9
3 years old	*	*	*	*	*	*	*	*	*	*	*	558	558	58.4
4 years old	*	*	*	*	*	*	*	*	*	*	*	321	321	33.2
5 years old	*	*	*	*	*	*	*	*	*	*	*	94	94	9.6
6 years old	*	*	*	*	*	*	*	*	*	*	*	33	33	3.3
7 years old	*	*	*	*	*	*	*	*	*	*	*	24	24	2.4
8 years old	*	*	*	*	*	*	*	*	*	*	*	24	24	2.4
9 years old	*	*	*	*	*	*	*	*	*	*	*	15	15	1.4
10 years old	*	*	*	*	*	*	*	*	*	*	*	19	19	1.7
11 years old	*	*	*	*	*	*	*	*	*	*	*	17	17	1.8
12 years old	3	*	*	*	*	*	*	*	*	*	*	8	8	0.8
13 years old	75	3	*	*	*	*	*	*	*	*	*	8	8	0.8
14 years old	687	49	2	*	*	*	*	*	*	*	*	15	15	1.4
15 years old	236	736	49	12	*	*	3	*	3	*	*	16	16	1.5
16 years old	37	263	656	59	5	*	4	*	7	*	8	51	60	5.4
17 years old	7	23	246	687	30	*	*	*	*	*	45	61	106	9.7
18 years old	4	8	29	224	539	35	7	*	*	*	200	53	253	22.9
19 years old	*	*	*	32	233	389	62	6	*	*	310	66	376	34.0
20 years old	*	*	4	26	85	264	262	24	3	*	275	43	318	32.1
21 years old	*	*	3	8	17	105	175	334	6	22	472	33	505	43.0
22 years old	*	*	2	*	16	87	74	184	66	26	709	52	761	62.6

* = Quantity zero or rounds to zero.

Table A-2. Single Grade of Enrollment and High School Graduation Status for Population 3 Years Old and Over, by Sex, Age (Single Years for 3 to 24 Years), Race, and Hispanic Origin, October 2016—*Continued*

(Numbers in thousands; percent; civilian noninstitutionalized population.)

Age, sex, race, and Hispanic origin	Population	Enrolled Number	Enrolled Percent	Nursery	Kinder-garten	Elementary grades 1	2	3	4	5	6	7	8
23 years old	1,214	319	26.3	*	*	*	*	*	*	*	*	*	*
24 years old	1,296	288	22.2	*	*	*	*	*	*	*	*	*	*
25 to 29 years old	6,238	929	14.9	*	*	*	*	*	*	*	*	*	*
30 to 34 years old	6,053	470	7.8	*	*	*	*	*	*	*	3	*	*
35 to 39 years old	5,897	260	4.4	*	*	*	*	*	*	*	*	*	1
40 to 44 years old	5,623	209	3.7	*	*	*	*	*	*	*	*	*	*
45 to 49 years old	6,482	152	2.3	*	*	*	*	*	*	*	*	*	*
50 to 54 years old	7,157	100	1.4	*	*	*	*	*	*	*	*	*	*
55 to 59 years old	7,827	74	0.9	*	*	*	*	*	*	*	*	*	*
60 to 64 years old	7,269	9	0.1	*	*	*	*	*	*	*	*	*	*
65 years and over	20,415	64	0.3	*	*	*	*	*	*	*	*	*	*
BLACK ALONE													
Both Sexes													
Total	40,039	11,684	29.2	620	668	599	592	702	645	577	570	595	576
3 years old	641	274	42.7	254	20	*	*	*	*	*	*	*	*
4 years old	594	354	59.5	306	48	*	*	*	*	*	*	*	*
5 years old	580	531	91.5	60	445	23	2	*	*	*	*	*	*
6 years old	598	571	95.5	*	134	405	23	8	*	*	*	*	*
7 years old	654	640	97.8	*	20	152	429	37	1	*	*	*	*
8 years old	625	609	97.6	*	*	19	116	450	25	*	*	*	*
9 years old	642	621	96.8	*	*	*	11	201	369	36	4	*	*
10 years old	649	631	97.2	*	*	*	11	4	209	368	38	*	*
11 years old	587	580	98.8	*	*	*	*	1	27	156	357	27	13
12 years old	528	527	99.8	*	*	*	*	13	17	127	349	20
13 years old	679	670	98.7	*	*	*	*	*	*	39	194	385
14 years old	611	601	98.5	*	*	*	*	*	*	*	4	22	139
15 years old	623	584	93.7	*	*	*	*	*	*	*	*	2	18
16 years old	641	611	95.2	*	*	*	*	*	*	*	*	*	1
17 years old	631	597	94.5	*	*	*	*	*	*	*	*	*	*
18 years old	603	443	73.5	*	*	*	*	*	*	*	*	*	*
19 years old	641	393	61.2	*	*	*	*	*	*	*	*	*	*
20 years old	631	334	52.9	*	*	*	*	*	*	*	*	*	*
21 years old	666	292	43.8	*	*	*	*	*	*	*	*	*	*
22 years old	658	231	35.2	*	*	*	*	*	*	*	*	*	*
23 years old	665	151	22.8	*	*	*	*	*	*	*	*	*	*
24 years old	687	180	26.2	*	*	*	*	*	*	*	*	*	*
25 to 29 years old	3,342	425	12.7	*	*	*	*	*	*	*	*	*	*
30 to 34 years old	2,856	249	8.7	*	*	*	*	*	*	*	*	*	*
35 to 39 years old	2,753	223	8.1	*	*	*	*	*	*	*	*	1	*
40 to 44 years old	2,533	150	5.9	*	*	*	*	*	*	*	*	*	*
45 to 49 years old	2,642	82	3.1	*	*	*	*	*	*	*	*	*	*
50 to 54 years old	2,734	74	2.7	*	*	*	*	*	*	*	*	*	*
55 to 59 years old	2,625	24	0.9	*	*	*	*	*	*	*	*	*	*
60 to 64 years old	2,247	23	1.0	*	*	*	*	*	*	*	*	*	*
65 years and over	4,471	10	0.2	*	*	*	*	*	*	*	*	*	*
Male													
Total	18,651	5,689	30.5	284	343	290	296	339	363	293	275	294	281
3 years old	318	124	38.9	113	11	*	*	*	*	*	*	*	*
4 years old	310	169	54.5	143	25	*	*	*	*	*	*	*	*
5 years old	303	276	91.0	28	243	2	2	*	*	*	*	*	*
6 years old	294	269	91.5	*	52	199	15	4	*	*	*	*	*
7 years old	332	322	97.0	*	11	81	213	16	1	*	*	*	*
8 years old	336	322	95.9	*	*	8	51	246	16	*	*	*	*
9 years old	305	291	95.2	*	*	*	8	70	192	16	4	*	*
10 years old	352	339	96.5	*	*	*	7	2	134	180	16	*	*
11 years old	274	274	99.7	*	*	*	*	*	14	92	146	20	1
12 years old	248	247	99.7	*	*	*	*	*	6	5	85	143	9
13 years old	362	358	99.0	*	*	*	*	*	*	*	21	123	187
14 years old	308	307	99.5	*	*	*	*	*	*	*	2	8	84
15 years old	314	309	98.3	*	*	*	*	*	*	*	*	*	*
16 years old	304	294	96.6	*	*	*	*	*	*	*	*	*	*
17 years old	334	317	94.9	*	*	*	*	*	*	*	*	*	*
18 years old	319	237	74.2	*	*	*	*	*	*	*	*	*	*

* = Quantity zero or rounds to zero.

Table A-2. Single Grade of Enrollment and High School Graduation Status for Population 3 Years Old and Over, by Sex, Age (Single Years for 3 to 24 Years), Race, and Hispanic Origin, October 2016—*Continued*

(Numbers in thousands; percent; civilian noninstitutionalized population.)

Age, sex, race, and Hispanic origin	Enrolled — High school				Enrolled — Undergraduate college				Enrolled — Graduate school		Not enrolled H.S. grad	Not enrolled Not grad	Not enrolled Number	Not enrolled Percent
	9	10	11	12	1	2	3	4	1	2+				
23 years old	*	4	*	3	21	55	73	65	43	56	819	75	894	73.7
24 years old	*	*	*	15	28	41	40	72	27	66	970	37	1,008	77.8
25 to 29 years old	*	*	*	16	107	151	116	151	150	239	5,098	212	5,310	85.1
30 to 34 years old	*	*	*	4	38	80	76	57	64	148	5,347	236	5,583	92.2
35 to 39 years old	*	*	3	5	40	40	25	42	27	78	5,422	215	5,637	95.6
40 to 44 years old	*	3	*	2	19	32	26	30	24	74	5,202	211	5,413	96.3
45 to 49 years old	*	6	3	3	4	34	22	27	16	38	6,056	275	6,330	97.7
50 to 54 years old	*	*	*	*	15	20	8	14	7	37	6,714	343	7,057	98.6
55 to 59 years old	*	*	*	1	5	17	10	13	6	22	7,332	422	7,753	99.1
60 to 64 years old	*	*	*	*	1	2	*	*	2	4	6,936	324	7,260	99.9
65 years and over	*	6	*	*	9	6	9	6	4	24	18,295	2,055	20,350	99.7
BLACK ALONE														
Both Sexes														
Total	630	711	581	733	657	757	489	435	205	342	23,965	4,390	28,355	70.8
3 years old	*	*	*	*	*	*	*	*	*	*	*	367	367	57.3
4 years old	*	*	*	*	*	*	*	*	*	*	*	241	241	40.5
5 years old	*	*	*	*	*	*	*	*	*	*	*	49	49	8.5
6 years old	*	*	*	*	*	*	*	*	*	*	*	27	27	4.5
7 years old	*	*	*	*	*	*	*	*	*	*	*	14	14	2.2
8 years old	*	*	*	*	*	*	*	*	*	*	*	15	15	2.4
9 years old	*	*	*	*	*	*	*	*	*	*	*	21	21	3.2
10 years old	*	*	*	*	*	*	*	*	*	*	*	18	18	2.8
11 years old	*	*	*	*	*	*	*	*	*	*	*	7	7	1.2
12 years old	*	*	*	*	*	*	*	*	*	*	*	1	1	0.2
13 years old	51	*	*	*	*	*	*	*	*	*	*	9	9	1.3
14 years old	396	36	4	*	*	*	*	*	*	*	*	9	9	1.5
15 years old	145	357	52	10	*	*	*	*	*	*	34	5	39	6.3
16 years old	23	192	323	60	5	*	*	*	7	*	10	21	31	4.8
17 years old	8	71	137	363	18	*	*	*	*	*	6	29	34	5.5
18 years old	7	19	25	179	189	15	*	*	8	*	107	52	160	26.5
19 years old	*	15	16	44	120	141	53	5	*	*	213	35	248	38.8
20 years old	*	4	*	24	59	146	97	4	*	*	252	46	298	47.1
21 years old	*	*	5	21	36	76	71	77	2	4	312	63	374	56.2
22 years old	*	*	*	5	28	61	15	98	13	12	404	22	427	64.8
23 years old	*	*	4	*	20	33	24	50	5	16	468	46	514	77.2
24 years old	*	*	*	12	12	21	38	55	22	21	456	51	507	73.8
25 to 29 years old	*	4	9	7	73	68	50	62	60	91	2,668	249	2,917	87.3
30 to 34 years old	*	*	*	2	36	68	26	19	26	72	2,438	170	2,607	91.3
35 to 39 years old	*	6	5	7	19	60	54	19	6	44	2,293	237	2,530	91.9
40 to 44 years old	*	*	*	*	25	41	20	21	25	18	2,172	211	2,383	94.1
45 to 49 years old	*	3	*	*	4	3	14	14	21	22	2,283	277	2,560	96.9
50 to 54 years old	*	3	*	*	6	10	23	10	8	14	2,293	367	2,660	97.3
55 to 59 years old	*	*	*	*	4	6	1	*	*	13	2,280	321	2,601	99.1
60 to 64 years old	*	*	*	*	*	7	2	*	4	9	1,894	331	2,224	99.0
65 years and over	*	*	*	*	5	*	*	*	*	5	3,380	1,081	4,461	99.8
Male														
Total	319	392	281	422	281	327	176	197	89	147	10,843	2,119	12,962	69.5
3 years old	*	*	*	*	*	*	*	*	*	*	*	195	195	61.1
4 years old	*	*	*	*	*	*	*	*	*	*	*	141	141	45.5
5 years old	*	*	*	*	*	*	*	*	*	*	*	27	27	9.0
6 years old	*	*	*	*	*	*	*	*	*	*	*	25	25	8.5
7 years old	*	*	*	*	*	*	*	*	*	*	*	10	10	3.0
8 years old	*	*	*	*	*	*	*	*	*	*	*	14	14	4.1
9 years old	*	*	*	*	*	*	*	*	*	*	*	15	15	4.8
10 years old	*	*	*	*	*	*	*	*	*	*	*	12	12	3.5
11 years old	*	*	*	*	*	*	*	*	*	*	*	1	1	0.3
12 years old	*	*	*	*	*	*	*	*	*	*	*	1	1	0.3
13 years old	27	*	*	*	*	*	*	*	*	*	*	4	4	1.0
14 years old	192	15	4	*	*	*	*	*	*	*	*	2	2	0.5
15 years old	71	219	13	6	*	*	*	*	*	*	5	*	5	1.7
16 years old	17	92	149	30	2	*	*	*	4	*	4	7	10	3.4
17 years old	8	34	63	205	7	*	*	*	*	*	*	17	17	5.1
18 years old	3	6	23	112	85	1	*	*	8	*	56	26	82	25.8

* = Quantity zero or rounds to zero.

Table A-2. Single Grade of Enrollment and High School Graduation Status for Population 3 Years Old and Over, by Sex, Age (Single Years for 3 to 24 Years), Race, and Hispanic Origin, October 2016—*Continued*

(Numbers in thousands; percent; civilian noninstitutionalized population.)

Age, sex, race, and Hispanic origin	Population	Enrolled Number	Enrolled Percent	Nursery	Kinder-garten	1	2	3	4	5	6	7	8
19 years old	293	171	58.3	*	*	*	*	*	*	*	*	*	*
20 years old	304	143	46.9	*	*	*	*	*	*	*	*	*	*
21 years old	368	168	45.7	*	*	*	*	*	*	*	*	*	*
22 years old	298	85	28.3	*	*	*	*	*	*	*	*	*	*
23 years old	315	90	28.4	*	*	*	*	*	*	*	*	*	*
24 years old	321	77	23.9	*	*	*	*	*	*	*	*	*	*
25 to 29 years old	1,587	205	12.9	*	*	*	*	*	*	*	*	*	*
30 to 34 years old	1,308	97	7.4	*	*	*	*	*	*	*	*	*	*
35 to 39 years old	1,247	57	4.6	*	*	*	*	*	*	*	*	*	*
40 to 44 years old	1,138	61	5.4	*	*	*	*	*	*	*	*	*	*
45 to 49 years old	1,196	28	2.3	*	*	*	*	*	*	*	*	*	*
50 to 54 years old	1,251	36	2.9	*	*	*	*	*	*	*	*	*	*
55 to 59 years old	1,227	1	0.1	*	*	*	*	*	*	*	*	*	*
60 to 64 years old	977	12	1.3	*	*	*	*	*	*	*	*	*	*
65 years and over	1,807	5	0.3	*	*	*	*	*	*	*	*	*	*
Female													
Total	21,388	5,995	28.0	336	325	309	296	363	283	284	295	300	295
3 years old	323	150	46.5	141	9	*	*	*	*	*	*	*	*
4 years old	285	185	65.0	162	23	*	*	*	*	*	*	*	*
5 years old	277	255	92.1	32	202	21	*	*	*	*	*	*	*
6 years old	304	302	99.3	*	83	207	9	4	*	*	*	*	*
7 years old	322	317	98.6	*	9	71	217	21	*	*	*	*	*
8 years old	289	287	99.5	*	*	10	65	203	9	*	*	*	*
9 years old	337	331	98.2	*	*	*	2	131	177	20	*	*	*
10 years old	297	291	98.0	*	*	*	4	2	76	188	22	*	*
11 years old	313	307	98.0	*	*	*	*	1	14	63	211	6	11
12 years old	280	280	100.0	*	*	*	*	*	8	12	42	206	12
13 years old	317	312	98.4	*	*	*	*	*	*	*	18	71	198
14 years old	302	295	97.5	*	*	*	*	*	*	*	2	14	55
15 years old	309	275	89.0	*	*	*	*	*	*	*	*	2	18
16 years old	337	317	94.0	*	*	*	*	*	*	*	*	*	1
17 years old	297	280	94.1	*	*	*	*	*	*	*	*	*	*
18 years old	283	206	72.8	*	*	*	*	*	*	*	*	*	*
19 years old	348	222	63.7	*	*	*	*	*	*	*	*	*	*
20 years old	327	191	58.4	*	*	*	*	*	*	*	*	*	*
21 years old	298	124	41.5	*	*	*	*	*	*	*	*	*	*
22 years old	360	147	40.8	*	*	*	*	*	*	*	*	*	*
23 years old	350	62	17.7	*	*	*	*	*	*	*	*	*	*
24 years old	366	104	28.3	*	*	*	*	*	*	*	*	*	*
25 to 29 years old	1,755	220	12.5	*	*	*	*	*	*	*	*	*	*
30 to 34 years old	1,548	152	9.8	*	*	*	*	*	*	*	*	*	*
35 to 39 years old	1,506	166	11.0	*	*	*	*	*	*	*	*	1	*
40 to 44 years old	1,395	89	6.4	*	*	*	*	*	*	*	*	*	*
45 to 49 years old	1,446	54	3.7	*	*	*	*	*	*	*	*	*	*
50 to 54 years old	1,484	38	2.6	*	*	*	*	*	*	*	*	*	*
55 to 59 years old	1,398	23	1.6	*	*	*	*	*	*	*	*	*	*
60 to 64 years old	1,270	11	0.8	*	*	*	*	*	*	*	*	*	*
65 years and over	2,664	5	0.2	*	*	*	*	*	*	*	*	*	*
ASIAN ALONE													
Both Sexes													
Total	18,198	4,720	25.9	304	214	179	208	226	247	205	232	227	257
3 years old	207	103	49.7	103	1	*	*	*	*	*	*	*	*
4 years old	230	172	74.6	153	18	*	*	*	*	*	*	*	*
5 years old	238	201	84.3	44	140	15	2	*	*	*	*	*	*
6 years old	199	191	95.7	5	48	131	*	7	*	*	*	*	*
7 years old	217	215	98.9	*	6	29	163	14	3	*	*	*	*
8 years old	226	213	94.4	*	*	4	43	151	14	2	*	*	*
9 years old	226	226	100.0	*	*	*	*	49	166	11	*	*	*
10 years old	241	238	98.7	*	*	*	*	7	63	151	18	*	*
11 years old	232	225	97.0	*	*	*	*	*	1	36	161	27	*
12 years old	227	223	98.4	*	*	*	*	*	*	*	40	150	30
13 years old	213	213	100.0	*	*	*	*	*	*	5	6	29	162
14 years old	189	187	98.8	*	*	*	*	*	*	*	*	12	51

* = Quantity zero or rounds to zero.

Table A-2. Single Grade of Enrollment and High School Graduation Status for Population 3 Years Old and Over, by Sex, Age (Single Years for 3 to 24 Years), Race, and Hispanic Origin, October 2016—*Continued*

(Numbers in thousands; percent; civilian noninstitutionalized population.)

| Age, sex, race, and Hispanic origin | Enrolled | | | | | | | | | | Not enrolled | | Not enrolled | |
| | High school | | | | Undergraduate college | | | | Graduate school | | H.S. grad | Not grad | Number | Percent |
	9	10	11	12	1	2	3	4	1	2+				
19 years old	*	11	8	30	46	56	15	5	*	*	92	30	122	41.7
20 years old	*	4	*	22	31	61	25	*	*	*	137	24	161	53.1
21 years old	*	*	5	4	19	56	32	47	2	4	154	46	200	54.3
22 years old	*	*	*	5	9	23	7	35	1	4	202	11	214	71.7
23 years old	*	*	4	*	15	17	12	25	*	16	195	30	225	71.6
24 years old	*	*	*	4	*	8	24	34	6	*	209	36	245	76.1
25 to 29 years old	*	4	8	*	36	38	24	27	19	49	1,270	111	1,382	87.1
30 to 34 years old	*	*	*	*	10	28	8	12	13	26	1,142	70	1,212	92.6
35 to 39 years old	*	3	3	4	7	13	5	3	3	16	1,068	122	1,190	95.4
40 to 44 years old	*	*	*	*	12	15	4	2	17	12	968	109	1,077	94.6
45 to 49 years old	*	*	*	*	*	*	10	2	8	8	1,027	141	1,169	97.7
50 to 54 years old	*	3	*	*	*	5	9	7	4	8	1,054	161	1,215	97.1
55 to 59 years old	*	*	*	*	*	*	1	*	*	*	1058	167	1,225	99.9
60 to 64 years old	*	*	*	*	*	5	2	*	4	1	811	154	965	98.7
65 years and over	*	*	*	*	2	*	*	*	*	3	1,390	411	1,802	99.7
Female														
Total	311	319	301	311	375	431	312	238	117	195	13,122	2,270	15,392	72.0
3 years old	*	*	*	*	*	*	*	*	*	*	*	173	173	53.5
4 years old	*	*	*	*	*	*	*	*	*	*	*	100	100	35.0
5 years old	*	*	*	*	*	*	*	*	*	*	*	22	22	7.9
6 years old	*	*	*	*	*	*	*	*	*	*	*	2	2	0.7
7 years old	*	*	*	*	*	*	*	*	*	*	*	4	4	1.4
8 years old	*	*	*	*	*	*	*	*	*	*	*	2	2	0.5
9 years old	*	*	*	*	*	*	*	*	*	*	*	6	6	1.8
10 years old	*	*	*	*	*	*	*	*	*	*	*	6	6	2.0
11 years old	*	*	*	*	*	*	*	*	*	*	*	6	6	2.0
12 years old	*	*	*	*	*	*	*	*	*	*	*	*	*	*
13 years old	24	*	*	*	*	*	*	*	*	*	*	5	5	1.6
14 years old	203	21	*	*	*	*	*	*	*	*	*	8	8	2.5
15 years old	74	139	40	4	*	*	*	*	*	*	29	5	34	11.0
16 years old	6	99	174	30	3	*	*	*	4	*	6	14	20	6.0
17 years old	*	37	74	158	11	*	*	*	*	*	6	12	18	5.9
18 years old	5	13	2	67	104	15	*	*	*	*	51	26	77	27.2
19 years old	*	3	8	14	74	84	39	*	*	*	122	5	126	36.3
20 years old	*	*	*	3	27	85	72	4	*	*	115	22	136	41.6
21 years old	*	*	*	16	18	20	39	30	*	*	158	17	174	58.5
22 years old	*	*	*	*	19	38	8	63	11	8	202	11	213	59.2
23 years old	*	*	*	8	5	16	12	25	5	*	273	16	288	82.3
24 years old	*	*	*	8	12	12	14	21	16	21	247	15	262	71.7
25 to 29 years old	*	*	*	7	37	31	26	36	41	42	1,398	137	1,536	87.5
30 to 34 years old	*	*	*	2	26	40	18	8	13	46	1,296	100	1,396	90.2
35 to 39 years old	*	3	3	3	11	47	50	16	3	28	1,225	115	1,340	89.0
40 to 44 years old	*	*	*	*	12	27	16	19	8	6	1,205	102	1,306	93.6
45 to 49 years old	*	3	*	*	4	3	3	13	12	15	1,256	136	1,392	96.3
50 to 54 years old	*	*	*	*	6	5	15	3	4	6	1,240	206	1,446	97.4
55 to 59 years old	*	*	*	*	4	6	*	*	*	13	1,222	153	1,375	98.4
60 to 64 years old	*	*	*	*	*	3	*	*	*	8	1,083	177	1,260	99.2
65 years and over	*	*	*	*	3	*	*	*	*	2	1,990	670	2,659	99.8
ASIAN ALONE														
Both Sexes														
Total	153	247	231	207	300	258	313	230	169	315	11,812	1,665	13,478	74.1
3 years old	*	*	*	*	*	*	*	*	*	*	*	104	104	50.3
4 years old	*	*	*	*	*	*	*	*	*	*	*	58	58	25.4
5 years old	*	*	*	*	*	*	*	*	*	*	*	37	37	15.7
6 years old	*	*	*	*	*	*	*	*	*	*	*	8	8	4.3
7 years old	*	*	*	*	*	*	*	*	*	*	*	2	2	1.1
8 years old	*	*	*	*	*	*	*	*	*	*	*	13	13	5.6
9 years old	*	*	*	*	*	*	*	*	*	*	*	*	*	*
10 years old	*	*	*	*	*	*	*	*	*	*	*	3	3	1.3
11 years old	*	*	*	*	*	*	*	*	*	*	*	7	7	3.0
12 years old	3	*	*	*	*	*	*	*	*	*	*	4	4	1.6
13 years old	6	6	*	*	*	*	*	*	*	*	*	*	*	*
14 years old	110	14	*	*	*	*	*	*	*	*	*	2	2	1.2

* = Quantity zero or rounds to zero.

Table A-2. Single Grade of Enrollment and High School Graduation Status for Population 3 Years Old and Over, by Sex, Age (Single Years for 3 to 24 Years), Race, and Hispanic Origin, October 2016—*Continued*

(Numbers in thousands; percent; civilian noninstitutionalized population.)

| Age, sex, race, and Hispanic origin | Population | Enrolled | | Enrolled | | | | | | | | | |
| | | Number | Percent | Nursery | Kinder-garten | Elementary grades | | | | | | | |
						1	2	3	4	5	6	7	8
15 years old	221	215	97.1	*	*	*	*	*	*	*	3	4	14
16 years old	229	220	96.0	*	*	*	*	*	*	*	4	*	*
17 years old	231	213	92.3	*	*	*	*	*	*	*	*	*	*
18 years old	220	183	82.9	*	*	*	*	*	*	*	*	*	*
19 years old	184	129	70.1	*	*	*	*	*	*	*	*	*	*
20 years old	249	194	78.0	*	*	*	*	*	*	*	*	*	*
21 years old	240	175	73.1	*	*	*	*	*	*	*	*	*	*
22 years old	296	171	57.9	*	*	*	*	*	*	*	*	*	*
23 years old	277	136	49.1	*	*	*	*	*	*	*	*	4	*
24 years old	302	100	33.1	*	*	*	*	*	*	*	*	*	*
25 to 29 years old	1,582	332	21.0	*	*	*	*	*	*	*	*	*	*
30 to 34 years old	1,700	108	6.4	*	*	*	*	*	*	*	*	*	*
35 to 39 years old	1,478	38	2.6	*	*	*	*	*	*	*	*	*	*
40 to 44 years old	1,524	34	2.3	*	*	*	*	*	*	*	*	*	*
45 to 49 years old	1,389	31	2.2	*	*	*	*	*	*	*	*	*	*
50 to 54 years old	1,226	8	0.6	*	*	*	*	*	*	*	*	*	*
55 to 59 years old	1,060	20	1.9	*	*	*	*	*	*	*	*	*	*
60 to 64 years old	962	*	*	*	*	*	*	*	*	*	*	*	*
65 years and over	2,184	7	0.3	*	*	*	*	*	*	*	*	*	*
Male													
Total	8,643	2,407	27.8	152	97	97	122	127	112	110	130	102	122
3 years old	98	46	47.4	46	1	*	*	*	*	*	*	*	*
4 years old	132	93	70.3	84	9	*	*	*	*	*	*	*	*
5 years old	120	94	78.0	22	61	8	2	*	*	*	*	*	*
6 years old	102	98	96.3	*	23	75	*	*	*	*	*	*	*
7 years old	101	99	98.3	*	3	10	82	5	*	*	*	*	*
8 years old	134	129	96.2	*	*	4	38	79	7	*	*	*	*
9 years old	110	110	100.0	*	*	*	*	39	70	1	*	*	*
10 years old	127	127	100.0	*	*	*	*	4	34	82	7	*	*
11 years old	123	120	98.2	*	*	*	*	*	1	22	86	11	*
12 years old	115	111	96.9	*	*	*	*	*	*	*	25	73	10
13 years old	105	105	100.0	*	*	*	*	*	*	5	6	13	77
14 years old	93	91	97.5	*	*	*	*	*	*	*	*	4	26
15 years old	94	94	100.0	*	*	*	*	*	*	*	3	*	8
16 years old	120	114	94.8	*	*	*	*	*	*	*	4	*	*
17 years old	93	81	87.5	*	*	*	*	*	*	*	*	*	*
18 years old	105	88	83.8	*	*	*	*	*	*	*	*	*	*
19 years old	110	74	66.8	*	*	*	*	*	*	*	*	*	*
20 years old	122	97	79.2	*	*	*	*	*	*	*	*	*	*
21 years old	120	91	76.0	*	*	*	*	*	*	*	*	*	*
22 years old	148	92	62.0	*	*	*	*	*	*	*	*	*	*
23 years old	142	89	62.6	*	*	*	*	*	*	*	*	*	*
24 years old	166	54	32.5	*	*	*	*	*	*	*	*	*	*
25 to 29 years old	810	181	22.3	*	*	*	*	*	*	*	*	*	*
30 to 34 years old	761	53	7.0	*	*	*	*	*	*	*	*	*	*
35 to 39 years old	698	17	2.4	*	*	*	*	*	*	*	*	*	*
40 to 44 years old	715	21	2.9	*	*	*	*	*	*	*	*	*	*
45 to 49 years old	651	14	2.1	*	*	*	*	*	*	*	*	*	*
50 to 54 years old	574	1	0.1	*	*	*	*	*	*	*	*	*	*
55 to 59 years old	492	16	3.2	*	*	*	*	*	*	*	*	*	*
60 to 64 years old	411	*	*	*	*	*	*	*	*	*	*	*	*
65 years and over	951	7	0.7	*	*	*	*	*	*	*	*	*	*
Female													
Total	9,555	2,313	24.2	152	117	81	86	99	135	95	102	125	135
3 years old	110	57	51.8	57	*	*	*	*	*	*	*	*	*
4 years old	98	79	80.5	69	9	*	*	*	*	*	*	*	*
5 years old	118	107	90.7	21	79	7	*	*	*	*	*	*	*
6 years old	97	92	95.2	5	25	56	*	7	*	*	*	*	*
7 years old	116	115	99.5	*	3	19	81	9	3	*	*	*	*
8 years old	92	85	91.8	*	*	*	5	72	6	2	*	*	*
9 years old	116	116	100.0	*	*	*	*	9	96	11	*	*	*
10 years old	114	111	97.3	*	*	*	*	2	29	68	11	*	*
11 years old	110	105	95.7	*	*	*	*	*	*	14	75	16	*
12 years old	112	112	100.0	*	*	*	*	*	*	*	15	77	20

* = Quantity zero or rounds to zero.

Table A-2. Single Grade of Enrollment and High School Graduation Status for Population 3 Years Old and Over, by Sex, Age (Single Years for 3 to 24 Years), Race, and Hispanic Origin, October 2016—*Continued*

(Numbers in thousands; percent; civilian noninstitutionalized population.)

Age, sex, race, and Hispanic origin	Enrolled										Not enrolled		Not enrolled	
	High school				Undergraduate college				Graduate school		H.S. grad	Not grad	Number	Percent
	9	10	11	12	1	2	3	4	1	2+				
15 years old	24	150	12	3	*	*	*	*	2	2	*	6	6	2.9
16 years old	11	57	128	19	*	*	*	*	*	*	4	6	9	4.0
17 years old	*	6	55	139	14	*	*	*	*	*	10	7	18	7.7
18 years old	*	8	6	30	130	9	*	*	*	*	30	8	38	17.1
19 years old	*	*	10	3	37	46	33	*	*	*	47	8	55	29.9
20 years old	*	*	8	*	30	57	93	6	*	*	47	8	55	22.0
21 years old	*	*	3	*	23	26	51	61	7	3	59	6	64	26.9
22 years old	*	*	4	3	14	30	29	48	27	17	118	6	124	42.1
23 years old	*	*	*	2	4	20	21	37	15	32	128	13	141	50.9
24 years old	*	3	*	*	*	5	11	16	34	31	198	4	202	66.9
25 to 29 years old	*	4	*	*	14	34	52	35	54	139	1,178	72	1,250	79.0
30 to 34 years old	*	*	*	*	10	11	16	14	15	43	1,521	71	1,592	93.6
35 to 39 years old	*	*	*	*	*	7	*	11	4	16	1,342	98	1,440	97.4
40 to 44 years old	*	*	*	*	7	4	3	*	7	13	1,407	82	1,489	97.7
45 to 49 years old	*	*	4	*	5	4	5	*	3	10	1,186	172	1,358	97.8
50 to 54 years old	*	*	*	*	4	*	*	3	1	*	1,105	113	1,218	99.4
55 to 59 years old	*	*	*	*	8	4	*	*	*	8	932	109	1,041	98.1
60 to 64 years old	*	*	*	*	*	*	*	*	*	*	839	123	962	100.0
65 years and over	*	*	*	7	*	*	*	*	*	*	1,664	513	2,177	99.7
Male														
Total	76	120	109	95	162	134	143	128	76	193	5,548	689	6,236	72.2
3 years old	*	*	*	*	*	*	*	*	*	*	*	51	51	52.6
4 years old	*	*	*	*	*	*	*	*	*	*	*	39	39	29.7
5 years old	*	*	*	*	*	*	*	*	*	*	*	26	26	22.0
6 years old	*	*	*	*	*	*	*	*	*	*	*	4	4	3.7
7 years old	*	*	*	*	*	*	*	*	*	*	*	2	2	1.7
8 years old	*	*	*	*	*	*	*	*	*	*	*	5	5	3.8
9 years old	*	*	*	*	*	*	*	*	*	*	*	*	*	*
10 years old	*	*	*	*	*	*	*	*	*	*	*	*	*	*
11 years old	*	*	*	*	*	*	*	*	*	*	*	2	2	1.8
12 years old	3	*	*	*	*	*	*	*	*	*	*	4	4	3.1
13 years old	4	*	*	*	*	*	*	*	*	*	*	*	*	*
14 years old	56	6	*	*	*	*	*	*	*	*	*	2	2	2.5
15 years old	7	68	8	*	*	*	*	*	*	*	*	*	*	*
16 years old	7	35	52	16	*	*	*	*	*	*	4	3	6	5.2
17 years old	*	*	21	57	4	*	*	*	*	*	4	7	12	12.5
18 years old	*	4	6	11	68	*	*	*	*	*	9	8	17	16.2
19 years old	*	*	7	*	27	20	21	*	*	*	35	2	37	33.2
20 years old	*	*	8	*	23	33	32	1	*	*	24	2	25	20.8
21 years old	*	*	3	*	9	16	29	30	3	*	25	3	29	24.0
22 years old	*	*	4	3	8	16	7	26	12	16	54	2	56	38.0
23 years old	*	*	*	2	3	13	15	27	5	24	49	4	53	37.4
24 years old	*	3	*	*	*	*	6	8	14	23	112	*	112	67.5
25 to 29 years old	*	4	*	*	8	17	21	27	28	75	605	24	629	77.7
30 to 34 years old	*	*	*	*	4	8	7	8	3	23	676	31	707	93.0
35 to 39 years old	*	*	*	*	*	3	*	*	*	13	639	43	681	97.6
40 to 44 years old	*	*	*	*	*	*	3	*	7	10	647	47	694	97.1
45 to 49 years old	*	*	*	*	*	4	2	*	3	4	576	61	637	97.9
50 to 54 years old	*	*	*	*	*	*	*	*	1	*	523	51	574	99.9
55 to 59 years old	*	*	*	*	8	4	*	*	*	4	421	56	476	96.8
60 to 64 years old	*	*	*	*	*	*	*	*	*	*	384	27	411	100.0
65 years and over	*	*	*	7	*	*	*	*	*	*	761	183	944	99.3
Female														
Total	77	127	122	112	138	124	170	103	93	122	6,265	977	7,241	75.8
3 years old	*	*	*	*	*	*	*	*	*	*	*	53	53	48.2
4 years old	*	*	*	*	*	*	*	*	*	*	*	19	19	19.5
5 years old	*	*	*	*	*	*	*	*	*	*	*	11	11	9.3
6 years old	*	*	*	*	*	*	*	*	*	*	*	5	5	4.8
7 years old	*	*	*	*	*	*	*	*	*	*	*	1	1	0.5
8 years old	*	*	*	*	*	*	*	*	*	*	*	8	8	8.2
9 years old	*	*	*	*	*	*	*	*	*	*	*	*	*	*
10 years old	*	*	*	*	*	*	*	*	*	*	*	3	3	2.7
11 years old	*	*	*	*	*	*	*	*	*	*	*	5	5	4.3
12 years old	*	*	*	*	*	*	*	*	*	*	*	*	*	*

* = Quantity zero or rounds to zero.

Table A-2. Single Grade of Enrollment and High School Graduation Status for Population 3 Years Old and Over, by Sex, Age (Single Years for 3 to 24 Years), Race, and Hispanic Origin, October 2016—*Continued*

(Numbers in thousands; percent; civilian noninstitutionalized population.)

Age, sex, race, and Hispanic origin	Population	Enrolled Number	Enrolled Percent	Nursery	Kinder-garten	1	2	3	4	5	6	7	8
13 years old	108	108	100.0	*	*	*	*	*	*	*	*	15	84
14 years old	96	96	100.0	*	*	*	*	*	*	*	*	8	25
15 years old	127	120	94.9	*	*	*	*	*	*	*	*	4	6
16 years old	109	106	97.3	*	*	*	*	*	*	*	*	*	*
17 years old	138	132	95.6	*	*	*	*	*	*	*	*	*	*
18 years old	115	95	82.1	*	*	*	*	*	*	*	*	*	*
19 years old	74	56	75.0	*	*	*	*	*	*	*	*	*	*
20 years old	127	97	76.9	*	*	*	*	*	*	*	*	*	*
21 years old	120	84	70.3	*	*	*	*	*	*	*	*	*	*
22 years old	148	79	53.7	*	*	*	*	*	*	*	*	*	*
23 years old	135	47	34.9	*	*	*	*	*	*	*	*	4	*
24 years old	135	46	33.9	*	*	*	*	*	*	*	*	*	*
25 to 29 years old	771	151	19.5	*	*	*	*	*	*	*	*	*	*
30 to 34 years old	940	55	5.9	*	*	*	*	*	*	*	*	*	*
35 to 39 years old	780	21	2.7	*	*	*	*	*	*	*	*	*	*
40 to 44 years old	809	13	1.7	*	*	*	*	*	*	*	*	*	*
45 to 49 years old	738	17	2.3	*	*	*	*	*	*	*	*	*	*
50 to 54 years old	651	7	1.1	*	*	*	*	*	*	*	*	*	*
55 to 59 years old	568	4	0.7	*	*	*	*	*	*	*	*	*	*
60 to 64 years old	551	*	*	*	*	*	*	*	*	*	*	*	*
65 years and over	1,233	*	*	*	*	*	*	*	*	*	*	*	*
HISPANIC (OF ANY RACE)													
Both Sexes													
Total	54,325	17,865	32.9	1079	1,034	1076	1,000	1,031	1,049	1,075	991	990	936
3 years old	1,013	370	36.5	352	17	*	*	*	*	*	*	*	*
4 years old	1,013	633	62.5	545	88	*	*	*	*	*	*	*	*
5 years old	1,057	959	90.7	165	740	40	14	*	*	*	*	*	*
6 years old	1,043	994	95.3	16	168	741	56	12	*	*	*	*	*
7 years old	1,027	988	96.2	*	21	252	651	56	8	*	*	*	*
8 years old	1,034	1,004	97.1	*	*	43	219	653	77	13	*	*	*
9 years old	1,110	1,083	97.6	*	*	*	53	266	695	61	8	*	*
10 years old	987	969	98.1	*	*	*	8	27	211	677	33	12	*
11 years old	1,076	1075	99.9	*	*	*	*	17	57	288	631	79	3
12 years old	1022	1000	97.8	*	*	*	*	*	1	29	276	617	77
13 years old	987	965	97.8	*	*	*	*	*	*	6	31	231	586
14 years old	946	905	95.7	*	*	*	*	*	*	*	*	38	225
15 years old	1004	999	99.4	*	*	*	*	*	*	*	*	5	32
16 years old	986	936	95.0	*	*	*	*	*	*	*	6	*	10
17 years old	988	911	92.2	*	*	*	*	*	*	*	1	*	*
18 years old	945	696	73.6	*	*	*	*	*	*	*	*	1	*
19 years old	879	552	62.8	*	*	*	*	*	*	*	*	*	*
20 years old	904	502	55.5	*	*	*	*	*	*	*	*	3	*
21 years old	989	476	48.1	*	*	*	*	*	*	*	*	*	*
22 years old	948	305	32.2	*	*	*	*	*	*	*	*	*	*
23 years old	972	250	25.7	*	*	*	*	*	*	*	*	*	*
24 years old	901	199	22.0	*	*	*	*	*	*	*	*	*	*
25 to 29 years old	4,560	513	11.3	*	*	*	*	*	*	*	*	*	4
30 to 34 years old	4,401	208	4.7	*	*	*	*	*	*	*	*	3	*
35 to 39 years old	4,281	133	3.1	*	*	*	*	*	*	*	*	*	*
40 to 44 years old	3,959	124	3.1	*	*	*	*	*	*	*	*	*	*
45 to 49 years old	3,597	46	1.3	*	*	*	*	*	*	*	*	*	*
50 to 54 years old	3,142	39	1.2	*	*	*	*	*	*	*	3	1	*
55 to 59 years old	2,521	19	0.8	*	*	*	*	*	*	*	*	*	*
60 to 64 years old	2,027	*	*	*	*	*	*	*	*	*	*	*	*
65 years and over	4,006	14	0.4	*	*	*	*	*	*	*	3	*	*
Male													
Total	27,198	8,853	32.6	572	528	510	537	498	555	564	492	512	504
3 years old	520	203	39.0	199	4	*	*	*	*	*	*	*	*
4 years old	519	324	62.5	278	46	*	*	*	*	*	*	*	*
5 years old	550	493	89.6	83	383	16	11	*	*	*	*	*	*
6 years old	524	494	94.2	13	83	342	44	12	*	*	*	*	*
7 years old	525	506	96.3	*	11	135	326	30	3	*	*	*	*
8 years old	520	503	96.6	*	*	16	121	319	39	7	*	*	*

* = Quantity zero or rounds to zero.

Table A-2. Single Grade of Enrollment and High School Graduation Status for Population 3 Years Old and Over, by Sex, Age (Single Years for 3 to 24 Years), Race, and Hispanic Origin, October 2016—*Continued*

(Numbers in thousands; percent; civilian noninstitutionalized population.)

Age, sex, race, and Hispanic origin	Enrolled										Not enrolled		Not enrolled	
	High school				Undergraduate college				Graduate school		H.S. grad	Not grad	Number	Percent
	9	10	11	12	1	2	3	4	1	2+				
13 years old	2	6	*	*	*	*	*	*	*	*	*	*	*	*
14 years old	54	9	*	*	*	*	*	*	*	*	*	*	*	*
15 years old	17	82	4	3	*	*	*	*	2	2	*	6	6	5.1
16 years old	4	22	77	3	*	*	*	*	*	*	*	3	3	2.7
17 years old	*	6	34	82	10	*	*	*	*	*	6	*	6	4.4
18 years old	*	4	*	19	62	9	*	*	*	*	20	*	21	17.9
19 years old	*	*	3	3	10	27	12	*	*	*	12	6	18	25.0
20 years old	*	*	*	*	7	25	61	5	*	*	23	7	29	23.1
21 years old	*	*	*	*	13	10	22	31	4	3	33	2	36	29.7
22 years old	*	*	*	*	6	14	22	21	15	*	65	4	68	46.3
23 years old	*	*	*	*	*	7	7	10	10	8	79	9	88	65.1
24 years old	*	*	*	*	*	5	5	9	20	7	85	4	89	66.1
25 to 29 years old	*	*	*	*	7	17	30	8	25	64	572	48	621	80.5
30 to 34 years old	*	*	*	*	6	3	8	6	11	20	844	40	884	94.1
35 to 39 years old	*	*	*	*	*	4	*	11	4	3	704	55	759	97.3
40 to 44 years old	*	*	*	*	7	3	*	*	*	3	760	36	796	98.3
45 to 49 years old	*	*	4	*	5	*	2	*	*	6	609	112	721	97.7
50 to 54 years old	*	*	*	*	4	*	*	3	*	*	582	62	644	98.9
55 to 59 years old	*	*	*	*	*	*	*	*	*	4	511	53	564	99.3
60 to 64 years old	*	*	*	*	*	*	*	*	*	*	456	96	551	100.0
65 years and over	*	*	*	*	*	*	*	*	*	*	903	330	1,233	100.0
HISPANIC (OF ANY RACE)														
Both Sexes														
Total	1037	1007	915	984	1106	946	768	433	166	243	24,501	11,959	36,460	67.1
3 years old	*	*	*	*	*	*	*	*	*	*	*	643	643	63.5
4 years old	*	*	*	*	*	*	*	*	*	*	*	380	380	37.5
5 years old	*	*	*	*	*	*	*	*	*	*	*	98	98	9.3
6 years old	*	*	*	*	*	*	*	*	*	*	*	49	49	4.7
7 years old	*	*	*	*	*	*	*	*	*	*	*	39	39	3.8
8 years old	*	*	*	*	*	*	*	*	*	*	*	30	30	2.9
9 years old	*	*	*	*	*	*	*	*	*	*	*	27	27	2.4
10 years old	*	*	*	*	*	*	*	*	*	*	*	18	18	1.9
11 years old	*	*	*	*	*	*	*	*	*	*	*	1	1	0.1
12 years old	*	*	*	*	*	*	*	*	*	*	*	22	22	2.2
13 years old	107	6	*	*	*	*	*	*	*	*	*	22	22	2.2
14 years old	588	52	2	*	*	*	*	*	*	*	*	41	41	4.3
15 years old	275	600	61	19	6	*	*	*	*	*	*	6	6	0.6
16 years old	46	275	478	90	19	*	9	*	3	*	9	40	49	5.0
17 years old	10	49	267	532	45	3	3	*	*	*	34	43	77	7.8
18 years old	4	5	63	230	363	26	5	*	*	*	180	69	249	26.4
19 years old	3	6	16	38	238	208	45	*	*	*	250	77	327	37.2
20 years old	*	*	*	17	115	170	167	17	11	3	319	84	402	44.5
21 years old	*	*	*	10	52	149	132	110	8	16	423	90	513	51.9
22 years old	*	*	8	*	40	67	90	62	14	24	539	104	643	67.8
23 years old	*	*	4	*	34	56	59	72	15	11	597	126	722	74.3
24 years old	*	*	4	4	23	43	60	29	16	20	604	98	702	78.0
25 to 29 years old	2	*	*	16	64	115	122	57	50	82	3,166	881	4,047	88.7
30 to 34 years old	*	7	1	7	30	63	28	29	5	36	3,120	1,073	4,193	95.3
35 to 39 years old	*	*	2	5	20	15	22	30	21	19	2,963	1,185	4,148	96.9
40 to 44 years old	*	3	6	14	25	14	14	13	11	24	2,650	1,184	3,834	96.9
45 to 49 years old	*	*	3	2	8	11	11	6	3	2	2,360	1,191	3,551	98.7
50 to 54 years old	*	*	*	*	16	7	3	2	2	4	2,154	949	3,103	98.8
55 to 59 years old	*	*	*	*	5	*	*	4	7	3	1,667	836	2,502	99.2
60 to 64 years old	*	*	*	*	*	*	*	*	*	*	1,294	733	2,027	100.0
65 years and over	3	4	*	*	4	*	*	*	*	*	2,173	1,819	3,992	99.6
Male														
Total	528	528	435	509	498	389	339	196	70	90	12,086	6,259	18,345	67.4
3 years old	*	*	*	*	*	*	*	*	*	*	*	317	317	61.0
4 years old	*	*	*	*	*	*	*	*	*	*	*	195	195	37.5
5 years old	*	*	*	*	*	*	*	*	*	*	*	57	57	10.4
6 years old	*	*	*	*	*	*	*	*	*	*	*	30	30	5.8
7 years old	*	*	*	*	*	*	*	*	*	*	*	20	20	3.7
8 years old	*	*	*	*	*	*	*	*	*	*	*	17	17	3.4

* = Quantity zero or rounds to zero.

Table A-2. Single Grade of Enrollment and High School Graduation Status for Population 3 Years Old and Over, by Sex, Age (Single Years for 3 to 24 Years), Race, and Hispanic Origin, October 2016—*Continued*

(Numbers in thousands; percent; civilian noninstitutionalized population.)

Age, sex, race, and Hispanic origin	Population	Enrolled Number	Enrolled Percent	Nursery	Kinder-garten	1	2	3	4	5	6	7	8
9 years old	565	543	96.1	*	*	*	31	116	365	31	*	*	*
10 years old	545	532	97.7	*	*	*	4	7	127	378	8	7	*
11 years old	510	510	99.9	*	*	*	*	12	20	133	303	42	*
12 years old	536	522	97.3	*	*	*	*	*	1	8	167	316	30
13 years old	479	467	97.4	*	*	*	*	*	*	6	5	123	291
14 years old	491	475	96.8	*	*	*	*	*	*	*	*	18	147
15 years old	499	499	100.0	*	*	*	*	*	*	*	*	4	24
16 years old	516	487	94.5	*	*	*	*	*	*	*	6	*	7
17 years old	515	475	92.3	*	*	*	*	*	*	*	1	*	*
18 years old	480	347	72.2	*	*	*	*	*	*	*	*	1	*
19 years old	414	246	59.4	*	*	*	*	*	*	*	*	*	*
20 years old	404	199	49.4	*	*	*	*	*	*	*	*	*	*
21 years old	556	242	43.5	*	*	*	*	*	*	*	*	*	*
22 years old	475	122	25.7	*	*	*	*	*	*	*	*	*	*
23 years old	471	106	22.5	*	*	*	*	*	*	*	*	*	*
24 years old	489	107	21.9	*	*	*	*	*	*	*	*	*	*
25 to 29 years old	2,343	219	9.3	*	*	*	*	*	*	*	*	*	4
30 to 34 years old	2,268	82	3.6	*	*	*	*	*	*	*	*	3	*
35 to 39 years old	2,181	57	2.6	*	*	*	*	*	*	*	*	*	*
40 to 44 years old	1,986	49	2.5	*	*	*	*	*	*	*	*	*	*
45 to 49 years old	1,807	18	1.0	*	*	*	*	*	*	*	*	*	*
50 to 54 years old	1,569	8	0.5	*	*	*	*	*	*	*	*	*	*
55 to 59 years old	1,233	8	0.6	*	*	*	*	*	*	*	*	*	*
60 to 64 years old	966	*	*	*	*	*	*	*	*	*	*	*	*
65 years and over	1,740	10	0.6	*	*	*	*	*	*	*	3	*	*
Female													
Total	27,127	9,012	33.2	506	506	567	463	534	494	511	499	477	433
3 years old	493	167	33.9	154	13	*	*	*	*	*	*	*	*
4 years old	494	309	62.5	267	42	*	*	*	*	*	*	*	*
5 years old	507	466	92.0	82	357	24	3	*	*	*	*	*	*
6 years old	518	500	96.5	3	85	399	13	*	*	*	*	*	*
7 years old	502	482	96.1	*	10	116	325	26	5	*	*	*	*
8 years old	514	501	97.5	*	*	27	97	334	38	5	*	*	*
9 years old	544	539	99.1	*	*	*	21	149	331	31	8	*	*
10 years old	443	437	98.7	*	*	*	3	20	84	299	25	5	*
11 years old	566	565	99.9	*	*	*	*	5	37	155	328	38	3
12 years old	486	478	98.3	*	*	*	*	*	21	108	301	47	
13 years old	508	499	98.1	*	*	*	*	*	*	26	108	294	
14 years old	455	430	94.5	*	*	*	*	*	*	*	20	78	
15 years old	505	499	98.8	*	*	*	*	*	*	*	2	7	
16 years old	470	449	95.6	*	*	*	*	*	*	*	*	3	
17 years old	473	435	92.1	*	*	*	*	*	*	*	*	*	
18 years old	465	349	75.1	*	*	*	*	*	*	*	*	*	
19 years old	465	306	65.8	*	*	*	*	*	*	*	*	*	
20 years old	501	303	60.5	*	*	*	*	*	*	*	3	*	
21 years old	433	234	54.1	*	*	*	*	*	*	*	*	*	
22 years old	472	183	38.7	*	*	*	*	*	*	*	*	*	
23 years old	501	144	28.7	*	*	*	*	*	*	*	*	*	
24 years old	412	91	22.2	*	*	*	*	*	*	*	*	*	
25 to 29 years old	2,218	294	13.3	*	*	*	*	*	*	*	*	*	
30 to 34 years old	2,132	126	5.9	*	*	*	*	*	*	*	*	*	
35 to 39 years old	2,100	76	3.6	*	*	*	*	*	*	*	*	*	
40 to 44 years old	1,973	75	3.8	*	*	*	*	*	*	*	*	*	
45 to 49 years old	1,790	28	1.6	*	*	*	*	*	*	*	*	*	
50 to 54 years old	1,573	31	1.9	*	*	*	*	*	*	*	3	1	
55 to 59 years old	1,289	11	0.9	*	*	*	*	*	*	*	*	*	
60 to 64 years old	1061	*	*	*	*	*	*	*	*	*	*	*	
65 years and over	2,266	4	0.2	*	*	*	*	*	*	*	*	*	

* = Quantity zero or rounds to zero.

Table A-2. Single Grade of Enrollment and High School Graduation Status for Population 3 Years Old and Over, by Sex, Age (Single Years for 3 to 24 Years), Race, and Hispanic Origin, October 2016—*Continued*

(Numbers in thousands; percent; civilian noninstitutionalized population.)

Age, sex, race, and Hispanic origin	Enrolled High school 9	10	11	12	Enrolled Undergraduate college 1	2	3	4	Enrolled Graduate school 1	2+	Not enrolled H.S. grad	Not enrolled Not grad	Not enrolled Number	Not enrolled Percent
9 years old	*	*	*	*	*	*	*	*	*	*	*	22	22	3.9
10 years old	*	*	*	*	*	*	*	*	*	*	*	12	12	2.3
11 years old	*	*	*	*	*	*	*	*	*	*	*	*	*	0.1
12 years old	*	*	*	*	*	*	*	*	*	*	*	14	14	2.7
13 years old	42	*	*	*	*	*	*	*	*	*	*	13	13	2.6
14 years old	283	25	2	*	*	*	*	*	*	*	*	16	16	3.2
15 years old	163	278	19	9	3	*	*	*	*	*	*	*	*	*
16 years old	26	174	217	49	6	*	3	*	*	*	9	19	28	5.5
17 years old	7	34	155	262	10	3	3	*	*	*	17	22	40	7.7
18 years old	4	5	25	134	164	8	5	*	*	*	90	43	133	27.8
19 years old	*	6	4	30	117	69	20	*	*	*	122	46	168	40.6
20 years old	*	*	*	3	52	70	60	6	8	*	153	52	204	50.6
21 years old	*	*	*	1	26	88	79	37	4	8	269	46	314	56.5
22 years old	*	*	*	*	24	32	23	30	4	8	291	62	353	74.3
23 years old	*	*	4	*	15	19	25	38	4	*	277	89	365	77.5
24 years old	*	*	*	4	17	16	34	22	11	4	325	57	382	78.1
25 to 29 years old	*	*	*	4	25	49	63	25	23	25	1,582	542	2,124	90.7
30 to 34 years old	*	*	*	3	10	21	13	3	3	26	1,569	617	2,186	96.4
35 to 39 years old	*	*	*	*	5	8	7	19	7	11	1,476	648	2,124	97.4
40 to 44 years old	*	3	4	7	14	4	4	7	*	6	1,309	627	1,937	97.5
45 to 49 years old	*	*	3	2	4	*	*	6	*	2	1,153	635	1,789	99.0
50 to 54 years old	*	*	*	*	6	*	*	*	2	*	1061	500	1,561	99.5
55 to 59 years old	*	*	*	*	*	*	*	4	4	*	807	418	1,225	99.4
60 to 64 years old	*	*	*	*	*	*	*	*	*	*	591	375	966	100.0
65 years and over	3	4	*	*	*	*	*	*	*	*	984	745	1,729	99.4
Female														
Total	509	479	480	475	608	556	429	236	96	154	12,416	5,700	18,115	66.8
3 years old	*	*	*	*	*	*	*	*	*	*	*	326	326	66.1
4 years old	*	*	*	*	*	*	*	*	*	*	*	185	185	37.5
5 years old	*	*	*	*	*	*	*	*	*	*	*	41	41	8.0
6 years old	*	*	*	*	*	*	*	*	*	*	*	18	18	3.5
7 years old	*	*	*	*	*	*	*	*	*	*	*	20	20	3.9
8 years old	*	*	*	*	*	*	*	*	*	*	*	13	13	2.5
9 years old	*	*	*	*	*	*	*	*	*	*	*	5	5	0.9
10 years old	*	*	*	*	*	*	*	*	*	*	*	6	6	1.3
11 years old	*	*	*	*	*	*	*	*	*	*	*	1	1	0.1
12 years old	*	*	*	*	*	*	*	*	*	*	*	8	8	1.7
13 years old	65	6	*	*	*	*	*	*	*	*	*	9	9	1.9
14 years old	305	27	*	*	*	*	*	*	*	*	*	25	25	5.5
15 years old	112	322	42	10	4	*	*	*	*	*	*	6	6	1.2
16 years old	19	102	261	42	13	*	6	*	3	*	*	21	21	4.4
17 years old	4	15	112	270	35	*	*	*	*	*	16	21	37	7.9
18 years old	*	*	37	95	199	18	*	*	*	*	90	26	116	24.9
19 years old	3	*	11	7	121	138	25	*	*	*	128	30	159	34.2
20 years old	*	*	*	14	63	100	106	11	3	3	166	32	198	39.5
21 years old	*	*	*	10	25	61	53	73	4	8	155	44	199	45.9
22 years old	*	*	8	*	16	35	66	32	10	15	248	42	290	61.3
23 years old	*	*	*	*	19	36	33	34	11	11	320	37	357	71.3
24 years old	*	*	4	*	6	26	26	8	5	16	278	42	320	77.8
25 to 29 years old	2	*	*	12	39	66	59	32	27	58	1,584	340	1,923	86.7
30 to 34 years old	*	7	1	3	20	42	15	27	2	10	1,550	456	2,007	94.1
35 to 39 years old	*	*	2	5	15	7	15	11	14	7	1,488	537	2,024	96.4
40 to 44 years old	*	*	1	7	11	10	10	7	11	18	1,341	557	1,898	96.2
45 to 49 years old	*	*	*	*	3	11	11	*	3	*	1,207	555	1,762	98.4
50 to 54 years old	*	*	*	*	10	7	3	2	*	4	1,093	449	1,542	98.1
55 to 59 years old	*	*	*	*	5	*	*	*	3	3	860	417	1,277	99.1
60 to 64 years old	*	*	*	*	*	*	*	*	*	*	703	357	1061	100.0
65 years and over	*	*	*	*	4	*	*	*	*	*	1,188	1,074	2,262	99.8

* = Quantity zero or rounds to zero.

Table A-3. Nursery and Primary School Enrollment of Population 3 to 6 Years Old, by Control of School, Attendance Status, Age, Race, Hispanic Origin, Mother's Labor Force Status and Education, and Family Income, October 2016

(Numbers in thousands; civilian noninstitutionalized population)

| Characteristic | Total | Not enrolled | Enrolled in nursery school | | | | | | | | |
| | | | Total | | | Public | | | Private | | |
			Total	Part-day	Full-day	Total	Part-day	Full-day	Total	Part-day	Full-day
3 TO 6 YEARS OLD											
Total............	16,021	4,225	4,746	2,185	2,562	2,806	1,302	1,504	1,941	883	1,058
Race and Hispanic origin											
White alone...........	11,496	2,995	3,445	1,758	1,687	1,984	1027	957	1,461	731	730
White alone non-Hispanic........	7,934	2,001	2,499	1,316	1,183	1,275	695	580	1,224	621	603
Black alone............	2,414	684	620	145	475	457	125	332	163	19	144
Asian alone............	875	208	304	115	189	138	63	75	166	53	114
Hispanic (of any race)...........	4,125	1,170	1079	491	588	791	350	441	287	140	147
Labor force status of mother:											
Children not living with mother........	1,701	493	502	231	271	376	182	193	126	49	77
Mother employed part-time........	2,339	508	746	374	372	400	177	224	345	197	148
Mother employed full-time........	6,516	1,466	2,064	775	1,289	1,111	458	653	953	317	636
Mother unemployed........	521	157	99	51	48	73	37	36	26	14	12
Mother not in the labor force........	4,944	1,601	1,336	753	583	845	447	398	491	306	185
Education of mother:											
Children not living with mother........	1,701	493	502	231	271	376	182	193	126	49	77
Elementary: 0 to 8 years...........	605	205	111	54	57	97	50	47	15	4	11
High school: 9 to 11 years........	931	279	215	78	137	195	73	122	20	5	16
High school graduate........	3,408	1,089	838	375	463	661	296	364	178	79	99
Some college or associate's degree...........	4,167	1,080	1,218	538	680	764	326	437	455	212	243
Bachelor's degree or more...........	5,209	1,080	1,862	908	953	714	373	341	1,147	535	613
Family income:											
Less than $20,000...........	2,136	691	514	173	341	443	150	293	71	23	48
$20,000 to $29,999...........	1,316	371	293	120	173	243	110	133	50	9	40
$30,000 to $39,999...........	1,474	428	399	173	226	309	149	160	90	24	66
$40,000 to $49,999...........	1,142	342	303	139	164	225	113	112	77	26	51
$50,000 to $74,999...........	2,290	634	670	304	366	394	171	223	275	133	142
$75,000 and over...........	4,779	975	1,751	859	893	677	359	318	1,075	500	575
Not reported...........	2,885	784	817	418	400	514	250	264	303	168	135
3 AND 4 YEARS OLD											
Total............	7,971	3,682	4,034	1,856	2,178	2,310	1,078	1,233	1,724	778	946
Race and Hispanic origin											
White alone...........	5,683	2,632	2,892	1,486	1,405	1,615	844	772	1,276	643	634
White alone non-Hispanic........	3,944	1,756	2,115	1,123	992	1049	577	471	1,067	546	521
Black alone............	1,236	608	560	125	434	398	107	291	162	18	144
Asian alone............	438	163	256	91	165	107	48	60	148	43	106
Hispanic (of any race)...........	2,026	1,023	898	411	486	639	285	353	259	126	133
Labor force status of mother:											
Children not living with mother........	889	440	427	202	226	311	157	154	117	45	72
Mother employed part-time........	1,146	435	656	333	323	341	151	189	315	181	134
Mother employed full-time........	3,190	1,322	1,765	654	1111	940	398	542	825	256	569
Mother unemployed........	227	141	77	38	39	51	24	27	26	14	12
Mother not in the labor force........	2,518	1,345	1,109	630	479	668	348	320	441	282	159
Education of mother:											
Children not living with mother........	889	440	427	202	226	311	157	154	117	45	72
Elementary: 0 to 8 years...........	290	178	105	50	55	91	46	45	15	4	11
High school: 9 to 11 years........	404	228	156	58	98	141	53	88	15	5	11
High school graduate........	1,730	973	688	303	385	525	231	294	163	71	91
Some college or associate's degree...........	2,061	945	1039	457	582	644	275	369	395	182	213
Bachelor's degree or more...........	2,596	919	1,619	787	832	599	315	284	1,020	472	548
Family income:											
Less than $20,000...........	1,115	617	442	129	313	374	109	265	68	20	48
$20,000 to $29,999...........	604	334	237	97	140	191	88	104	46	9	37
$30,000 to $39,999...........	718	346	345	165	180	265	144	121	80	21	59
$40,000 to $49,999...........	572	312	242	107	136	181	93	88	62	14	48
$50,000 to $74,999...........	1,153	547	577	264	312	334	148	186	242	116	126
$75,000 and over...........	2,419	846	1,533	750	782	566	292	274	967	458	508
Not reported...........	1,390	679	658	344	315	399	204	195	259	140	120
5 YEARS OLD											
Total............	4,061	401	667	301	366	454	197	257	213	104	109
Race and Hispanic origin											
White alone...........	2,902	258	514	245	269	333	157	176	181	88	92

* = Quantity zero or rounds to zero.

Table A-3. Nursery and Primary School Enrollment of Population 3 to 6 Years Old, by Control of School, Attendance Status, Age, Race, Hispanic Origin, Mother's Labor Force Status and Education, and Family Income, October 2016—Continued

(Numbers in thousands; civilian noninstitutionalized population.)

| Characteristic | Enrolled in kindergarten | | | | | | | | | Enrolled in elementary school | | |
| | Total | | | Public | | | Private | | | | | |
	Total	Part-day	Full-day	Total	Part-day	Full-day	Total	Part-day	Full-day	Total	Public	Private
3 TO 6 YEARS OLD												
Total..............	3,958	777	3,180	3,597	718	2,879	361	59	301	3,092	2,813	278
Race and Hispanic origin												
White alone.............	2,826	570	2,256	2,548	515	2,033	278	55	223	2,230	2,040	191
White alone non-Hispanic	1,941	369	1,572	1,685	315	1,370	256	53	202	1,494	1,343	151
Black alone.................	648	94	553	611	94	517	37	*	37	462	423	40
Asian alone	207	64	144	182	60	122	26	4	22	155	141	13
Hispanic (of any race)	1,013	239	774	987	237	750	26	2	24	864	819	45
Labor force status of mother...............												
Children not living with mother....................	414	65	349	406	65	341	7	*	7	293	278	15
Mother employed part-time	627	168	459	556	152	404	71	16	55	457	414	43
Mother employed full-time..................	1,625	255	1,370	1,486	240	1,245	140	15	125	1,361	1,237	123
Mother unemployed	164	28	136	153	26	127	11	2	9	101	100	1
Mother not in the labor force	1,127	261	866	995	235	761	132	27	105	880	784	96
Education of mother...................												
Children not living with mother....................	414	65	349	406	65	341	7	*	7	293	278	15
Elementary: 0 to 8 years	140	30	109	139	30	109	*	*	*	150	136	14
High school: 9 to 11 years	250	33	217	246	33	212	4	*	4	187	187	*
High school graduate	829	153	676	787	151	636	42	3	40	651	605	46
Some college or associate's degree	1,068	214	854	970	198	772	98	16	82	800	738	62
Bachelor's degree or more	1,256	281	975	1,048	240	808	208	40	168	1,011	870	141
Family income...................												
Less than $20,000	571	100	471	551	98	453	20	2	18	359	336	23
$20,000 to $29,999	370	75	295	355	74	281	16	1	14	283	270	13
$30,000 to $39,999	335	61	275	319	57	263	16	4	12	312	300	12
$40,000 to $49,999	271	60	211	247	53	195	23	7	17	226	213	13
$50,000 to $74,999	557	92	465	492	89	403	66	4	62	428	376	52
$75,000 and over........................	1,154	236	918	980	212	767	175	24	151	898	771	127
Not reported	698	154	544	654	137	517	45	18	27	585	548	38
3 AND 4 YEARS OLD												
Total..............	254	52	202	221	39	182	33	13	21	*	*	*
Race and Hispanic origin												
White alone.............	160	32	128	143	22	121	17	9	7	*	*	*
White alone non-Hispanic	72	13	59	57	4	53	16	9	6	*	*	*
Black alone.................	68	7	61	58	7	51	10	*	10	*	*	*
Asian alone	19	9	11	13	5	7	6	3	3	*	*	*
Hispanic (of any race)	105	26	79	104	26	78	1	*	1	*	*	*
Labor force status of mother...............												
Children not living with mother....................	22	4	19	22	4	19	*	*	*	*	*	*
Mother employed part-time	56	23	33	46	16	30	9	7	2	*	*	*
Mother employed full-time..................	103	13	90	97	12	85	6	*	5	*	*	*
Mother unemployed	9	*	9	9	*	9	*	*	*	*	*	*
Mother not in the labor force	64	12	51	46	7	38	18	5	13	*	*	*
Education of mother...................												
Children not living with mother....................	22	4	19	22	4	19	*	*	*	*	*	*
Elementary: 0 to 8 years	7	*	7	7	*	7	*	*	*	*	*	*
High school: 9 to 11 years	20	*	20	20	*	20	*	*	*	*	*	*
High school graduate	70	14	56	64	12	52	5	1	4	*	*	*
Some college or associate's degree	77	21	56	61	17	44	16	4	12	*	*	*
Bachelor's degree or more	58	14	44	46	7	40	12	7	5	*	*	*
Family income...................												
Less than $20,000	56	9	47	50	9	41	6	*	6	*	*	*
$20,000 to $29,999	33	2	30	32	2	30	*	*	*	*	*	*
$30,000 to $39,999	27	4	23	27	4	23	*	*	*	*	*	*
$40,000 to $49,999	17	3	14	14	3	12	3	*	2	*	*	*
$50,000 to $74,999	29	11	18	24	10	14	5	1	4	*	*	*
$75,000 and over........................	41	2	39	33	*	33	8	1	6	*	*	*
Not reported	52	21	31	41	11	30	11	10	1	*	*	*
5 YEARS OLD												
Total..............	2,821	529	2,292	2,601	502	2,099	220	27	193	172	142	30
Race and Hispanic origin												
White alone.............	2,013	392	1,621	1,840	365	1,475	173	27	146	118	105	13

* = Quantity zero or rounds to zero.

Table A-3. Nursery and Primary School Enrollment of Population 3 to 6 Years Old, by Control of School, Attendance Status, Age, Race, Hispanic Origin, Mother's Labor Force Status and Education, and Family Income, October 2016—*Continued*

(Numbers in thousands; civilian noninstitutionalized population)

Characteristic	Total	Not enrolled	Enrolled in nursery school								
			Total			Public			Private		
			Total	Part-day	Full-day	Total	Part-day	Full-day	Total	Part-day	Full-day
White alone non-Hispanic	1,987	182	361	178	183	207	103	105	153	75	78
Black alone	580	49	60	19	41	59	18	41	1	1	*
Asian alone	238	37	44	25	19	25	15	11	18	10	8
Hispanic (of any race)	1,057	98	165	68	97	136	54	83	29	15	14
Labor force status of mother											
Children not living with mother	421	42	70	26	43	60	23	38	9	4	6
Mother employed part-time	622	60	86	40	46	58	24	34	28	16	12
Mother employed full-time	1,671	101	278	111	167	153	51	102	126	61	65
Mother unemployed	148	10	22	13	9	22	13	9	*	*	*
Mother not in the labor force	1,199	189	211	110	100	161	87	74	50	24	26
Education of mother											
Children not living with mother	421	42	70	26	43	60	23	38	9	4	6
Elementary: 0 to 8 years	127	22	6	4	2	6	4	2	*	*	*
High school: 9 to 11 years	305	44	55	16	39	50	16	34	5	*	5
High school graduate	832	82	127	60	67	112	53	59	15	7	8
Some college or associate's degree	1,068	96	179	81	98	119	51	68	60	30	30
Bachelor's degree or more	1,309	115	230	114	116	106	51	55	123	63	61
Family income											
Less than $20,000	524	58	63	35	28	61	33	28	3	3	*
$20,000 to $29,999	346	28	53	22	30	49	22	27	4	*	4
$30,000 to $39,999	368	54	54	8	46	44	5	39	10	3	7
$40,000 to $49,999	274	15	54	26	28	38	14	25	15	12	3
$50,000 to $74,999	597	64	93	39	53	59	22	37	33	17	17
$75,000 and over	1,185	96	211	103	108	103	61	42	108	42	66
Not reported	767	86	139	67	72	99	39	60	40	28	12
6 YEARS OLD											
Total	3,989	142	45	27	18	41	27	14	4	*	4
Race and Hispanic origin											
White alone	2,911	105	40	27	13	36	26	9	4	*	4
White alone non-Hispanic	2,004	63	23	15	8	19	15	4	4	*	4
Black alone	598	27	*	*	*	*	*	*	*	*	*
Asian alone	199	8	5	*	5	5	*	5	*	*	*
Hispanic (of any race)	1,043	49	16	11	5	16	11	5	*	*	*
Labor force status of mother											
Children not living with mother	391	11	5	3	1	5	3	1	*	*	*
Mother employed part-time	570	14	4	2	2	2	2	*	2	*	2
Mother employed full-time	1,655	44	20	10	10	19	10	9	2	*	1
Mother unemployed	146	7	*	*	*	*	*	*	*	*	*
Mother not in the labor force	1,227	67	16	12	4	16	12	4	*	*	*
Education of mother											
Children not living with mother	391	11	5	3	1	5	3	1	*	*	*
Elementary: 0 to 8 years	188	5	*	*	*	*	*	*	*	*	*
High school: 9 to 11 years	222	7	4	4	*	4	4	*	*	*	*
High school graduate	846	34	23	13	11	23	13	11	*	*	*
Some college or associate's degree	1,038	39	*	*	*	*	*	*	*	*	*
Bachelor's degree or more	1,304	46	13	7	5	9	7	2	4	*	4
Family income											
Less than $20,000	497	16	8	8	*	8	8	*	*	*	*
$20,000 to $29,999	366	8	3	*	3	3	*	3	*	*	*
$30,000 to $39,999	387	28	*	*	*	*	*	*	*	*	*
$40,000 to $49,999	296	15	6	6	*	6	6	*	*	*	*
$50,000 to $74,999	540	23	1	1	*	1	1	*	*	*	*
$75,000 and over	1,175	33	8	5	3	7	5	3	*	*	*
Not reported	727	18	20	7	13	16	7	9	4	*	4

* = Quantity zero or rounds to zero.

Table A-3. Nursery and Primary School Enrollment of Population 3 to 6 Years Old, by Control of School, Attendance Status, Age, Race, Hispanic Origin, Mother's Labor Force Status and Education, and Family Income, October 2016—*Continued*

(Numbers in thousands; civilian noninstitutionalized population.)

Characteristic	Enrolled in kindergarten									Enrolled in elementary school		
	Total			Public			Private					
	Total	Part-day	Full-day	Total	Part-day	Full-day	Total	Part-day	Full-day	Total	Public	Private
White alone non-Hispanic	1,373	250	1,123	1,220	224	996	153	25	127	72	59	13
Black alone	445	67	378	425	67	358	20	*	20	26	17	8
Asian alone	140	37	104	134	37	97	7	*	7	17	15	2
Hispanic (of any race)	740	167	573	716	165	551	24	2	22	54	54	*
Labor force status of mother												
Children not living with mother	306	40	266	301	40	262	5	*	5	3	3	*
Mother employed part-time	448	109	339	394	100	294	54	9	45	29	25	4
Mother employed full-time	1,199	191	1008	1,102	178	923	97	12	84	93	73	21
Mother unemployed	112	17	95	101	15	86	11	2	9	4	4	*
Mother not in the labor force	757	173	584	703	169	534	54	4	50	43	37	5
Education of mother												
Children not living with mother	306	40	266	301	40	262	5	*	5	3	3	*
Elementary: 0 to 8 years	94	26	68	94	26	68	*	*	*	5	5	*
High school: 9 to 11 years	193	25	168	188	25	164	4	*	4	13	13	*
High school graduate	595	107	489	572	107	465	23	*	23	27	23	4
Some college or associate's degree	739	141	598	684	132	553	54	9	45	53	53	*
Bachelor's degree or more	894	191	703	760	173	588	133	18	115	71	45	26
Family income												
Less than $20,000	388	65	323	373	63	311	14	2	12	15	15	*
$20,000 to $29,999	251	50	201	244	50	194	7	*	7	14	14	*
$30,000 to $39,999	235	45	190	223	45	179	11	*	11	26	22	4
$40,000 to $49,999	193	44	149	180	40	140	13	3	9	12	12	*
$50,000 to $74,999	424	69	355	387	66	321	37	3	34	17	7	10
$75,000 and over	833	152	681	714	137	576	119	14	104	45	29	16
Not reported	498	106	393	480	101	379	18	5	13	44	44	*
6 YEARS OLD												
Total	882	196	686	775	177	598	108	19	88	2,919	2,671	248
Race and Hispanic origin												
White alone	654	146	507	566	128	438	88	18	70	2,113	1,935	177
White alone non-Hispanic	496	105	390	408	87	321	88	18	69	1,422	1,285	137
Black alone	134	20	114	128	20	108	7	*	7	437	405	31
Asian alone	48	19	29	36	18	18	12	1	12	138	126	11
Hispanic (of any race)	168	46	121	167	46	121	*	*	*	810	765	45
Labor force status of mother												
Children not living with mother	85	22	63	83	22	61	3	*	3	290	275	15
Mother employed part-time	124	36	88	116	36	81	8	*	8	428	389	39
Mother employed full-time	323	52	272	286	50	237	37	2	35	1,267	1,165	103
Mother unemployed	43	11	32	43	11	32	*	*	*	97	96	1
Mother not in the labor force	306	76	231	246	59	188	60	17	43	837	747	90
Education of mother												
Children not living with mother	85	22	63	83	22	61	3	*	3	290	275	15
Elementary: 0 to 8 years	38	4	34	38	4	34	*	*	*	145	131	14
High school: 9 to 11 years	37	9	28	37	9	28	*	*	*	174	174	*
High school graduate	164	33	132	150	31	119	14	1	13	624	582	42
Some college or associate's degree	253	53	200	225	50	176	28	3	25	746	685	62
Bachelor's degree or more	305	76	229	242	61	181	63	15	48	940	825	115
Family income												
Less than $20,000	128	26	102	128	26	102	*	*	*	344	321	23
$20,000 to $29,999	86	23	64	79	21	57	8	1	7	269	256	13
$30,000 to $39,999	73	12	61	69	8	61	4	4	*	286	278	8
$40,000 to $49,999	61	13	48	53	10	43	8	3	5	214	201	13
$50,000 to $74,999	104	13	92	81	13	68	23	*	23	412	370	42
$75,000 and over	281	82	199	233	75	158	49	8	41	853	742	111
Not reported	148	27	121	132	24	108	16	3	13	541	504	38

* = Quantity zero or rounds to zero.

Table A-4. Current Grade for People 15 to 24 Years Old Enrolled in School, and Highest Grade Completed for People with Selected Enrollment and Completion Status, by Sex, Age, Race, and Hispanic Origin, October 2016

(Numbers in thousands; civilian noninstitutionalized population.)

Age, sex, race, and Hispanic origin	Total	Enrolled — Current grade							Not enrolled — Enrolled last year — Highest grade completed						Not enrolled last year
		Less than 9th grade	9th grade	10th grade	11th grade	12th grade	College (graduated this year)	Other college	Less than 9th grade	9th grade	10th grade	11th or 12th, no diploma	New HS graduate	Other[1]	
ALL RACES															
Both Sexes															
Total	42,556	247	1,244	3,992	3,962	4,148	2,199	10,362	9	69	126	337	954	2,423	12,483
15 years old	4,188	146	1,032	2,593	249	52	10	14	1	9	8	10	5	5	52
16 years old	4,246	54	155	1,115	2,320	283	19	49	4	41	60	33	15	4	95
17 years old	4,229	1	38	198	1,081	2,419	100	48	*	5	38	97	50	41	112
18 years old	4,203	18	16	50	188	1,058	1,361	442	*	8	20	129	475	111	327
19 years old	4,063	11	3	18	49	159	570	1,798	1	5	*	38	259	277	875
20 to 24 years old	21,626	17	*	18	76	176	138	8,011	4	*	*	30	148	1,985	11,022
Male															
Total	21,455	130	720	2,071	2,003	2,122	1027	4,853	2	36	78	191	493	1,107	6,621
15 years old	2,117	73	592	1,289	113	18	3	*	1	8	*	*	*	*	20
16 years old	2,156	38	93	615	1,101	141	6	18	1	16	38	22	4	3	61
17 years old	2,140	1	28	113	598	1,177	34	18	*	4	27	45	24	19	52
18 years old	2,154	10	7	25	109	618	606	192	*	5	12	87	271	57	154
19 years old	2,038	4	*	14	26	102	302	844	1	4	*	19	120	138	464
20 to 24 years old	10,850	5	*	14	56	67	76	3,780	*	*	*	19	74	890	5,870
Female															
Total	21,101	117	524	1,921	1,959	2,026	1,172	5,510	7	33	48	146	461	1,316	5,862
15 years old	2,071	73	441	1,304	136	34	7	14	*	2	8	10	5	5	32
16 years old	2,090	17	62	500	1,218	142	13	31	3	25	21	11	12	*	34
17 years old	2,089	*	10	85	483	1,243	66	30	*	1	11	52	26	22	60
18 years old	2,050	8	9	26	78	441	756	250	*	3	7	43	204	54	173
19 years old	2,025	7	3	3	23	56	268	954	*	1	*	19	139	140	411
20 to 24 years old	10,777	13	*	4	20	110	62	4,231	4	*	*	12	75	1,095	5,152
WHITE ALONE															
Total	31,285	182	955	2,868	2,869	2,978	1,629	7,643	7	47	99	224	704	1,835	9,244
15 years old	3,062	95	792	1,909	175	33	7	6	1	8	4	3	*	*	28
16 years old	3,114	44	121	815	1,704	189	17	37	3	26	54	26	6	4	69
17 years old	3,091	1	30	112	808	1,758	61	40	*	4	31	81	40	33	93
18 years old	3,087	18	9	17	122	784	1,013	329	*	5	12	77	367	91	243
19 years old	3,057	11	3	3	18	111	439	1,390	*	4	*	26	181	193	678
20 to 24 years old	15,875	13	*	11	42	102	93	5,843	4	*	*	10	111	1,515	8,133
WHITE ALONE NON-HISPANIC															
Total	23,120	126	676	2,096	2,110	2,173	1,195	5,782	7	43	85	145	520	1,414	6,748
15 years old	2,233	60	571	1,420	119	18	1	6	1	8	1	*	*	*	28
16 years old	2,273	29	81	584	1,291	123	4	19	3	23	43	13	6	*	55
17 years old	2,251	*	20	66	588	1,314	37	16	*	4	29	57	23	25	73
18 years old	2,268	17	4	13	76	570	780	238	*	3	12	47	287	62	160
19 years old	2,295	11	*	3	7	74	325	1,096	*	4	*	22	121	156	476
20 to 24 years old	11,801	10	*	11	29	75	48	4,407	4	*	*	6	83	1,171	5,956
BLACK ALONE															
Total	6,446	20	183	658	563	718	238	1,436	1	11	22	64	177	345	2,011
15 years old	623	19	145	357	52	10	*	*	*	*	5	*	5	5	23
16 years old	641	1	23	192	323	60	2	10	1	8	5	2	6	*	10
17 years old	631	*	8	71	137	363	10	8	*	*	6	12	6	*	11
18 years old	603	*	7	19	25	179	145	67	*	4	7	26	67	6	50
19 years old	641	*	*	15	16	44	65	253	*	*	*	9	67	59	114
20 to 24 years old	3,308	*	*	4	9	62	16	1,098	*	*	*	16	25	274	1,804

[1]Other includes people whose response to questions on educational attainment did not fall into one of the listed categories (e.g., completed high school (not last year), but enrolled in college or some other type of school last year).
* = Quantity zero or rounds to zero.

Table A-4. Current Grade for People 15 to 24 Years Old Enrolled in School, and Highest Grade Completed for People with Selected Enrollment and Completion Status, by Sex, Age, Race, and Hispanic Origin, October 2016—*Continued*

(Numbers in thousands; civilian noninstitutionalized population.)

Age, sex, race, and Hispanic origin	Total	Enrolled — Current grade							Not enrolled — Enrolled last year — Highest grade completed						Not enrolled last year
		Less than 9th grade	9th grade	10th grade	11th grade	12th grade	College (graduated this year)	Other college	Less than 9th grade	9th grade	10th grade	11th or 12th, no diploma	New HS graduate	Other[1]	
ASIAN ALONE															
Total	2,449	30	35	223	227	200	146	876	*	*	*	20	12	157	524
15 years old	221	21	24	150	12	3	*	5	*	*	*	6	*	*	*
16 years old	229	4	11	57	128	19	*	*	*	*	*	*	*	*	9
17 years old	231	*	*	6	55	139	14	*	*	*	*	4	1	7	6
18 years old	220	*	*	8	6	30	100	39	*	*	*	4	5	7	22
19 years old	184	*	*	*	10	3	19	97	*	*	*	2	6	14	33
20 to 24 years old	1,363	5	*	3	15	6	12	736	*	*	*	3	*	129	453
HISPANIC (OF ANY RACE)															
Total	9,517	57	338	934	902	941	541	2,113	1	4	18	96	208	480	2,885
15 years old	1004	37	275	600	61	19	6	*	*	*	3	3	*	*	*
16 years old	986	16	46	275	478	90	13	18	1	3	10	18	*	3	14
17 years old	988	1	10	49	267	532	28	24	*	*	5	24	19	8	20
18 years old	945	1	4	5	63	230	296	98	*	2	*	36	94	35	83
19 years old	879	*	3	6	16	38	145	346	*	*	*	4	60	44	219
20 to 24 years old	4,715	3	*	*	17	31	53	1,627	*	*	*	10	35	390	2,548

[1]Other includes people whose response to questions on educational attainment did not fall into one of the listed categories (e.g., completed high school (not last year), but enrolled in college or some other type of school last year).
* = Quantity zero or rounds to zero.

Table A-5. Type of College and Year Enrolled for College Students 15 Years Old and Over, by Age, Sex, Race, Attendance Status, Control of School, Disability Status, and Enrollment Status, October 2016

(Numbers in thousands; civilian noninstitutionalized population.)

Characteristic	Total enrolled	Undergraduate college								Graduate school	
		All colleges				Two-year college		Four-year college			
		1st year	2nd year	3rd year	4th year	1st year	2nd or higher	1st year	2nd or higher	1st year	2nd or higher
BOTH SEXES	19,196	4,494	4,444	3,617	2,942	1,879	2,467	2,615	8,535	1,352	2,347
Full-Time Students											
Total	14,421	3,497	3,378	2,885	2,355	1,250	1,531	2,247	7,088	820	1,484
Age.											
15–19 years old	4,053	2,545	1,189	267	9	813	312	1,732	1,154	38	5
20–24 years old	6,859	610	1,576	2,077	1,807	246	757	364	4,703	355	433
25–34 years old	2,500	247	432	354	365	149	297	98	854	323	779
35 years old and over	1,009	95	181	187	174	42	165	53	377	104	267
Race.											
White alone	10,373	2,493	2,509	2,104	1,754	858	1,107	1,635	5,261	532	981
White alone non-Hispanic	8,135	1,818	1,930	1,595	1,474	595	786	1,223	4,213	445	873
Black alone	2,064	479	530	385	355	207	264	272	1,005	120	196
Asian alone	1,349	268	221	263	197	72	98	196	583	137	263
Hispanic (of any race)	2,571	804	666	571	311	335	369	469	1,179	93	126
Employment Status.											
Full time	2,065	278	385	347	344	103	245	175	831	216	494
Part time	4,309	920	1,173	879	780	393	533	526	2,299	190	368
Not employed	8,047	2,299	1,820	1,659	1,231	754	753	1,545	3,958	414	622
Control of School.											
Public	11,068	2,950	2,722	2,232	1,712	1,185	1,407	1,765	5,260	529	924
Private	3,352	548	656	653	643	66	124	482	1,828	292	561
Disability Status.											
No disability	14,022	3,402	3,286	2,786	2,313	1,201	1,451	2,201	6,933	794	1,441
Any disability	399	95	93	99	42	50	80	46	154	27	43
Part-Time Students											
Total	4,775	997	1,065	732	587	628	936	368	1,448	531	863
Age.											
15–19 years old	359	261	96	*	2	162	76	99	22	*	*
20–24 years old	1,291	266	437	240	198	180	386	86	489	89	60
25–34 years old	1,717	261	289	313	228	168	289	94	540	256	371
35 years old and over	1,408	209	243	179	159	120	185	89	396	186	432
Race.											
White alone	3,528	745	767	520	451	478	686	267	1,052	393	652
White alone non-Hispanic	2,614	491	532	368	348	294	467	197	781	332	544
Black alone	821	178	228	104	81	108	147	69	265	86	146
Asian alone	235	31	37	50	33	12	54	19	66	32	52
Hispanic (of any race)	1,090	302	280	197	122	211	273	91	325	73	117
Employment Status.											
Full time	2,855	432	570	423	394	256	491	176	896	402	634
Part time	1,070	290	316	190	113	188	279	102	340	57	104
Not employed	850	274	179	119	80	184	166	90	212	72	125
Control of School.											
Public	3,903	890	903	619	495	601	861	289	1,157	374	622
Private	872	107	162	113	92	27	76	80	291	157	241
Disability Status.											
No disability	4,621	971	1,037	691	582	603	899	368	1,410	515	826
Any disability	154	26	29	41	5	25	38	*	37	16	37
MALE	8,644	2,078	1,974	1,676	1,347	932	1,108	1,146	3,889	548	1,021
Full-Time Students											
Total	6,701	1,653	1,497	1,380	1,099	655	696	998	3,282	361	710
Age.											
15–19 years old	1,863	1,206	513	117	5	450	139	756	497	18	2
20–24 years old	3,238	299	729	1,013	860	125	371	173	2,231	139	198
25–34 years old	1,189	116	192	169	164	61	117	55	407	162	387
35 years old and over	411	32	63	81	71	18	69	14	146	41	123
Race.											
White alone	4,774	1,164	1,086	1034	793	441	481	723	2,433	254	441
White alone non-Hispanic	3,844	889	865	808	663	335	338	554	1,999	215	404
Black alone	904	213	244	155	169	114	135	99	432	46	77
Asian alone	720	141	113	129	110	39	54	102	299	59	168
Hispanic (of any race)	1,115	361	261	256	140	166	153	195	504	44	54
Employment Status.											

* = Quantity zero or rounds to zero.

Table A-5. Type of College and Year Enrolled for College Students 15 Years Old and Over, by Age, Sex, Race, Attendance Status, Control of School, Disability Status, and Enrollment Status, October 2016—*Continued*

(Numbers in thousands; civilian noninstitutionalized population.)

Characteristic	Total enrolled	Undergraduate college								Graduate school	
		All colleges				Two-year college		Four-year college			
		1st year	2nd year	3rd year	4th year	1st year	2nd or higher	1st year	2nd or higher	1st year	2nd or higher
Full time	913	113	161	175	133	39	110	73	359	94	237
Part time	1,876	445	498	365	342	209	184	237	1020	64	162
Not employed	3,912	1,095	838	840	625	406	401	688	1,902	203	311
Control of School											
Public	5,091	1,387	1,188	1,084	784	618	643	769	2,414	234	413
Private	1,611	266	309	296	315	36	52	230	868	126	298
Disability Status											
No disability	6,501	1,589	1,464	1,327	1,085	619	662	970	3,215	351	685
Any disability	200	64	34	53	14	35	34	28	67	10	26
Part-Time Students											
Total	1,943	425	476	296	247	278	412	147	608	188	311
Age											
15–19 years old	161	105	56	*	*	61	43	44	13	*	*
20–24 years old	618	140	224	105	98	103	197	37	230	32	19
25–34 years old	649	100	123	138	97	60	108	40	250	69	122
35 years old and over	516	80	74	53	52	53	64	26	115	88	170
Race											
White alone	1,449	328	361	230	187	213	318	116	460	128	215
White alone non-Hispanic	1,036	208	240	165	135	120	212	88	328	108	180
Black alone	313	68	83	22	28	53	52	15	81	42	70
Asian alone	115	21	21	14	17	6	18	15	34	17	25
Hispanic (of any race)	467	137	128	84	56	109	122	28	146	26	36
Employment Status											
Full time	1,180	199	247	191	154	123	211	75	382	144	245
Part time	462	127	161	75	47	79	139	47	144	19	33
Not employed	301	99	68	30	46	75	62	25	82	25	33
Control of School											
Public	1,625	381	412	262	205	264	382	117	497	133	232
Private	319	44	65	34	42	14	30	30	111	55	78
Disability Status											
No disability	1,884	419	457	280	245	272	387	147	596	180	302
Any disability	59	6	19	16	2	6	25	*	12	8	9
FEMALE	10,551	2,416	2,470	1,941	1,596	947	1,360	1,469	4,646	804	1,326
Full-Time Students											
Total	7,720	1,844	1,881	1,505	1,256	596	836	1,248	3,806	460	774
Age											
15–19 years old	2,191	1,339	675	150	4	363	173	976	656	19	2
20–24 years old	3,621	311	847	1,064	947	121	386	191	2,472	216	235
25–34 years old	1,311	131	240	185	201	89	179	43	447	161	392
35 years old and over	598	63	118	106	103	24	97	39	231	63	144
Race											
White alone	5,599	1,329	1,423	1,070	961	417	626	912	2,827	277	540
White alone non-Hispanic	4,292	930	1,065	787	810	261	448	669	2,214	230	469
Black alone	1,160	266	286	230	185	93	129	173	573	73	119
Asian alone	629	127	108	134	87	34	45	94	284	78	95
Hispanic (of any race)	1,456	443	404	316	171	169	216	274	675	49	72
Employment Status											
Full time	1,151	165	224	172	211	63	135	102	472	121	257
Part time	2,434	474	675	514	438	184	348	290	1,278	127	206
Not employed	4,135	1,205	982	818	607	348	352	857	2,056	212	311
Control of School											
Public	5,978	1,563	1,533	1,148	928	567	764	996	2,846	294	511
Private	1,742	281	347	357	328	29	72	252	960	166	263
Disability Status											
No disability	7,521	1,813	1,822	1,459	1,227	581	790	1,231	3,718	443	757
Any disability	199	32	59	46	28	15	46	17	88	17	17

* = Quantity zero or rounds to zero.

Table A-5. Type of College and Year Enrolled for College Students 15 Years Old and Over, by Age, Sex, Race, Attendance Status, Control of School, Disability Status, and Enrollment Status, October 2016—*Continued*

(Numbers in thousands; civilian noninstitutionalized population.)

Characteristic	Total enrolled	Undergraduate college								Graduate school	
		All colleges				Two-year college		Four-year college			
		1st year	2nd year	3rd year	4th year	1st year	2nd or higher	1st year	2nd or higher	1st year	2nd or higher
Part-Time Students											
Total	2,832	571	589	436	340	351	524	221	840	344	552
Age											
15–19 years old	198	156	40	*	2	100	33	55	9	*	*
20–24 years old	673	125	214	135	100	76	189	49	259	58	41
25–34 years old	1,069	162	166	175	131	108	181	54	290	187	248
35 years old and over	893	129	169	126	107	66	121	63	281	98	263
Race											
White alone	2,079	416	407	290	263	265	368	151	592	265	438
White alone non-Hispanic	1,578	283	291	203	213	173	254	109	453	224	364
Black alone	509	109	145	82	53	55	95	55	184	44	76
Asian alone	121	11	16	36	16	7	36	4	32	15	27
Hispanic (of any race)	624	165	152	113	65	102	151	63	180	47	81
Employment Status											
Full time	1,674	233	322	232	240	133	280	101	515	258	389
Part time	609	163	155	115	66	109	140	54	196	39	71
Not employed	548	175	111	89	34	109	104	66	129	47	92
Control of School											
Public	2,278	509	492	357	289	338	479	171	660	241	390
Private	554	62	97	78	50	13	46	49	180	103	163
Disability Status											
No disability	2,737	551	579	410	336	331	511	220	815	335	524
Any disability	95	20	10	25	4	20	13	*	25	8	28

* = Quantity zero or rounds to zero.

Table A-6. Employment Status and Enrollment in Vocational Courses for the Population 15 Years Old and Over, by Sex, Age, Educational Attainment, and College Enrollment, October 2016[1]

(Numbers in thousands; percent; civilian noninstitutionalized population.)

Characteristic	Total	Enrolled in vocational courses		Employed full-time	Enrolled in vocational courses		Employed part-time	Enrolled in vocational courses		Not employed	Enrolled in vocational courses	
	Total	Number	Percent	Total	Number	Percent	Total	Number	Percent	Total	Number	Percent
BOTH SEXES												
Total...........................	258,509	3,585	1.4	124,822	1,798	1.4	28,048	681	2.4	105,640	1,106	1.0
Age.................................												
15 to 19 years old..............	20,929	268	1.3	1,432	38	2.7	3,702	79	2.1	15,795	152	1.0
20 to 24 years old..............	21,626	640	3.0	8,983	169	1.9	4,902	176	3.6	7,742	295	3.8
25 to 34 years old..............	43,745	962	2.2	29,462	526	1.8	4,397	165	3.8	9,886	271	2.7
35 to 44 years old..............	39,887	607	1.5	28,128	388	1.4	3,689	82	2.2	8,070	137	1.7
45 to 64 years old..............	83,780	892	1.1	51,307	623	1.2	7,813	106	1.4	24,660	162	0.7
65 years and over...............	48,542	216	0.4	5,509	54	1.0	3,545	73	2.1	39,488	88	0.2
Educational attainment..................	258,509	3,585	1.4	124,822	1,798	1.4	28,048	681	2.4	105,640	1,106	1.0
Not a high school graduate.......	39,297	135	0.3	8,812	36	0.4	3,839	17	0.4	26,646	82	0.3
High school graduate only........	72,099	693	1.0	32,954	276	0.8	7,372	100	1.4	31,773	317	1.0
Some college or associate's degree..................	70,474	1,447	2.1	34,479	608	1.8	9,736	355	3.6	26,259	484	1.8
Bachelor's degree or more........	76,640	1,310	1.7	48,578	877	1.8	7,101	209	2.9	20,962	223	1.1
College enrollment........................	258,509	3,585	1.4	124,822	1,798	1.4	28,048	681	2.4	105,640	1,106	1.0
Enrolled in college....................	19,196	1,140	5.9	4,920	377	7.7	5,380	328	6.1	8,896	436	4.9
Not enrolled in college.............	239,314	2,445	1.0	119,902	1,421	1.2	22,668	354	1.6	96,744	670	0.7
MALE												
Total...........................	125,006	1,675	1.3	70,674	902	1.3	10,221	267	2.6	44,111	506	1.1
Age.................................												
15 to 19 years old..............	10,605	132	1.2	799	23	2.9	1,726	31	1.8	8,080	78	1.0
20 to 24 years old..............	10,850	299	2.8	4,882	66	1.3	2,184	83	3.8	3,784	150	4.0
25 to 34 years old..............	21,677	427	2.0	16,664	258	1.6	1,492	61	4.1	3,521	107	3.0
35 to 44 years old..............	19,550	257	1.3	16,201	211	1.3	863	15	1.7	2,486	31	1.2
45 to 64 years old..............	40,632	431	1.1	28,783	309	1.1	2,273	33	1.5	9,576	89	0.9
65 years and over...............	21,693	129	0.6	3,346	34	1.0	1,684	43	2.6	16,664	51	0.3
Educational attainment..................	125,006	1,675	1.3	70,674	902	1.3	10,221	267	2.6	44,111	506	1.1
Not a high school graduate.......	20,065	79	0.4	6,213	16	0.3	1,677	11	0.6	12,176	52	0.4
High school graduate only........	36,500	350	1.0	20,565	168	0.8	2,937	37	1.3	12,999	145	1.1
Some college or associate's degree..................	32,293	643	2.0	18,509	290	1.6	3,428	139	4.1	10,356	214	2.1
Bachelor's degree or more........	36,148	603	1.7	25,387	428	1.7	2,179	80	3.7	8,582	95	1.1
College enrollment........................	125,006	1,675	1.3	70,674	902	1.3	10,221	267	2.6	44,111	506	1.1
Enrolled in college....................	8,644	473	5.5	2,094	141	6.7	2,337	134	5.7	4,213	198	4.7
Not enrolled in college.............	116,362	1,201	1.0	68,580	761	1.1	7,883	133	1.7	39,898	307	0.8
FEMALE												
Total...........................	133,503	1,910	1.4	54,147	896	1.7	17,827	414	2.3	61,529	600	1.0
Age.................................												
15 to 19 years old..............	10,324	137	1.3	634	15	2.3	1,976	48	2.4	7,715	74	1.0
20 to 24 years old..............	10,777	341	3.2	4,101	104	2.5	2,718	92	3.4	3,958	144	3.6
25 to 34 years old..............	22,068	535	2.4	12,798	267	2.1	2,905	104	3.6	6,365	164	2.6
35 to 44 years old..............	20,337	351	1.7	11,927	177	1.5	2,826	67	2.4	5,584	107	1.9
45 to 64 years old..............	43,148	461	1.1	22,524	314	1.4	5,540	73	1.3	15,083	73	0.5
65 years and over...............	26,849	87	0.3	2,164	20	0.9	1,861	29	1.6	22,824	37	0.2
Educational attainment..................	133,503	1,910	1.4	54,147	896	1.7	17,827	414	2.3	61,529	600	1.0
Not a high school graduate.......	19,232	56	0.3	2,599	21	0.8	2,162	6	0.3	14,471	29	0.2
High school graduate only........	35,599	343	1.0	12,389	108	0.9	4,436	63	1.4	18,775	172	0.9
Some college or associate's degree..................	38,181	804	2.1	15,969	319	2.0	6,308	216	3.4	15,903	270	1.7
Bachelor's degree or more........	40,492	707	1.7	23,190	449	1.9	4,922	129	2.6	12,380	128	1.0
College enrollment........................	133,503	1,910	1.4	54,147	896	1.7	17,827	414	2.3	61,529	600	1.0
Enrolled in college....................	10,551	667	6.3	2,826	236	8.3	3,042	194	6.4	4,683	237	5.1
Not enrolled in college.............	122,952	1,243	1.0	51,322	661	1.3	14,785	220	1.5	56,846	362	0.6

[1]People enrolled in vocational courses are not considered to be enrolled in school for all tables. People enrolled in regular school below the college level are not asked about vocational enrollment in the CPS. They are counted in this table as not enrolled in vocational courses.

Table A-7. Enrollment Status of High School Graduates 15 to 24 Years Old, by Type of School, Attendance Status, and Sex, October 2016

(Numbers in thousands; civilian noninstitutionalized population.)

Characteristic	Total	Enrolled in college or vocational school						Not enrolled	
		2-year college		4-year college		Graduate school	Vocational school	Employed	Not employed
		Full-time	Part-time	Full-time	Part-time				
ALL RACES									
Both sexes	26,475	2,111	784	7,897	693	980	267	10,307	3,436
Graduated this year	3,152	621	125	1,381	67	4	33	540	381
Graduated earlier	23,322	1,490	659	6,516	626	976	234	9,767	3,055
Male	12,965	1,068	392	3,639	324	408	134	5,419	1,582
Graduated this year	1,520	344	38	608	33	4	19	297	177
Graduated earlier	11,445	724	353	3,031	291	404	115	5,122	1,405
Female	13,510	1,043	392	4,259	369	572	133	4,888	1,854
Graduated this year	1,632	277	87	773	34	*	14	243	203
Graduated earlier	11,878	766	305	3,485	335	572	119	4,645	1,650
WHITE ALONE									
Both sexes	19,602	1,549	570	5,905	506	672	195	7,833	2,372
Graduated this year	2,333	451	96	1022	55	4	24	420	259
Graduated earlier	17,268	1,098	474	4,882	451	668	171	7,413	2,113
Male	9,699	750	292	2,718	263	263	98	4,189	1,126
Graduated this year	1,125	239	31	435	26	4	18	239	132
Graduated earlier	8,574	510	261	2,283	237	259	80	3,950	994
Female	9,902	799	278	3,187	242	409	97	3,645	1,246
Graduated this year	1,208	212	65	587	29	*	7	182	127
Graduated earlier	8,694	587	213	2,599	214	409	90	3,463	1,119
WHITE ALONE, NON-HISPANIC									
Both sexes	14,773	1,064	346	4,655	327	542	149	6,010	1,680
Graduated this year	1,715	312	58	789	36	*	16	328	176
Graduated earlier	13,059	752	288	3,867	291	542	133	5,683	1,503
Male	7,326	548	173	2,191	168	218	80	3,123	826
Graduated this year	867	183	20	350	15	*	9	195	94
Graduated earlier	6,460	365	153	1,841	152	218	70	2,928	732
Female	7,447	516	173	2,464	160	324	69	2,887	853
Graduated this year	848	129	38	439	21	*	7	133	82
Graduated earlier	6,599	387	135	2,025	139	324	62	2,754	772
BLACK ALONE									
Both sexes	3,914	320	118	992	112	109	39	1,516	708
Graduated this year	415	74	23	136	5	*	7	83	86
Graduated earlier	3,499	246	95	856	107	109	31	1,433	621
Male	1,780	181	59	420	21	44	18	715	321
Graduated this year	169	45	7	44	*	*	*	38	34
Graduated earlier	1,611	135	52	375	21	44	18	678	287
Female	2,134	140	59	572	91	64	21	801	386
Graduated this year	246	28	17	91	5	*	7	45	52
Graduated earlier	1,888	111	42	481	86	64	14	756	334
ASIAN ALONE									
Both sexes	1,659	119	29	670	31	170	13	454	173
Graduated this year	158	30	*	109	7	*	*	6	5
Graduated earlier	1,501	90	29	561	23	170	13	447	167
Male	854	69	17	332	23	97	7	255	55
Graduated this year	85	15	*	59	6	*	*	4	*
Graduated earlier	769	54	17	273	17	97	7	251	55
Female	805	50	13	338	7	73	7	199	118
Graduated this year	73	15	*	50	1	*	*	2	5
Graduated earlier	732	36	13	288	7	73	7	197	113
HISPANIC (OF ANY RACE)									
Both sexes	5,579	580	280	1,404	221	139	54	2,119	782
Graduated this year	749	199	43	277	18	4	8	114	86
Graduated earlier	4,831	381	237	1,127	203	136	45	2,005	697
Male	2,716	263	149	603	98	51	18	1,191	344
Graduated this year	335	102	16	112	11	4	8	44	38
Graduated earlier	2,381	160	133	491	87	47	10	1,147	306
Female	2,863	317	131	802	123	88	35	928	438
Graduated this year	413	96	27	165	7	*	*	70	48
Graduated earlier	2,450	221	104	637	116	88	35	858	391

* = Quantity zero or rounds to zero.

Table A-8. Enrollment Status for Families with Children 5 to 24 Years Old, by Control of School, Race, Type of Family, and Family Income, October 2016

(Numbers in thousands; civilian noninstitutionalized population.)

Characteristic	Total	Families with no dependents 5 to 24 years old[1]	None enrolled in elementary or high school	Public only	Public and private	Private only	None enrolled in college	One enrolled in college	Two or more enrolled in college
			Kindergarten, elementary, and high school enrollment status				College enrollment status		
ALL RACES									
All Families	83,555	44,445	8,128	28,177	671	2,134	32,635	5,506	970
Less than $20,000	7,385	3,312	592	3,328	63	91	3,772	275	26
$20,000 to $74,999	30,140	15,970	2,796	10,566	151	657	12,187	1,747	236
$75,000 and over	26,950	13,941	2,853	8,856	285	1,014	10,206	2,333	469
Not reported	19,081	11,222	1,887	5,427	173	372	6,470	1,151	238
Married-couple families	60,687	35,897	4,831	17,809	481	1,669	20,331	3,690	769
Less than $20,000	2,854	1,801	170	849	12	22	979	68	7
$20,000 to $74,999	20,420	12,445	1,388	6,062	90	435	6,866	937	172
$75,000 and over	23,813	12,710	2,264	7,651	257	931	8,727	1,953	423
Not reported	13,600	8,942	1,009	3,247	123	281	3,760	732	167
Unmarried householder[3]	22,869	8,548	3,298	10,368	191	465	12,304	1,816	201
Less than $20,000	4,531	1,511	421	2,479	51	69	2,794	207	20
$20,000 to $74,999	9,720	3,525	1,408	4,504	61	222	5,321	810	64
$75,000 and over	3,137	1,231	589	1,205	29	83	1,479	380	46
Not reported	5,480	2,280	879	2,180	50	91	2,710	419	71
WHITE ALONE									
All Families	66,120	36,693	6,221	20,996	479	1,731	24,433	4,206	787
Less than $20,000	4,844	2,300	375	2,075	30	64	2,358	170	16
$20,000 to $74,999	23,764	13,246	2,075	7,804	118	522	9,062	1,273	184
$75,000 and over	22,631	11,971	2,394	7,203	213	850	8,355	1,909	396
Not reported	14,881	9,176	1,377	3,914	119	294	4,658	855	191
Married-couple families	50,843	30,760	3,984	14,316	361	1,422	16,459	2,961	663
Less than $20,000	2,185	1,402	122	631	8	22	731	45	7
$20,000 to $74,999	17,048	10,668	1,111	4,818	75	376	5,516	718	147
$75,000 and over	20,264	11,045	1,941	6,309	192	778	7,240	1,615	364
Not reported	11,346	7,645	810	2,558	86	246	2,973	583	146
Unmarried householder[3]	15,277	5,933	2,236	6,681	118	309	7,974	1,246	125
Less than $20,000	2,660	898	253	1,444	22	42	1,627	125	9
$20,000 to $74,999	6,716	2,577	964	2,986	42	146	3,546	555	38
$75,000 and over	2,367	926	453	894	21	73	1,115	294	32
Not reported	3,535	1,531	567	1,356	33	48	1,685	273	46
WHITE ALONE NON-HISPANIC									
All Families	53,942	32,169	4,851	15,009	406	1,508	18,105	3,086	583
Less than $20,000	2,975	1,625	231	1,057	14	48	1,261	81	9
$20,000 to $74,999	18,242	11,339	1,473	4,910	91	430	6,050	763	90
$75,000 and over	20,573	11,190	2,117	6,290	204	772	7,392	1,646	345
Not reported	12,152	8,015	1,030	2,752	97	258	3,402	596	138
Married-couple families	43,050	27,671	3,211	10,582	324	1,262	12,625	2,259	495
Less than $20,000	1,351	996	62	271	5	17	338	17	*
$20,000 to $74,999	13,421	9,379	782	2,882	60	317	3,553	414	74
$75,000 and over	18,621	10,434	1,738	5,558	183	708	6,483	1,390	313
Not reported	9,658	6,862	629	1,870	76	220	2,252	437	107
Unmarried householder[3]	10,892	4,498	1,640	4,427	82	246	5,480	827	88
Less than $20,000	1,624	629	169	786	9	31	923	63	9
$20,000 to $74,999	4,821	1,960	691	2,027	31	113	2,497	349	15
$75,000 and over	1,952	756	379	732	21	64	909	255	32
Not reported	2,494	1,153	401	882	21	38	1,150	160	31
BLACK ALONE									
All Families	10,205	4,379	1,146	4,341	115	224	5,082	675	69
Less than $20,000	1,915	719	164	984	28	19	1,115	75	6
$20,000 to $74,999	3,969	1,649	453	1,750	28	89	2,029	269	21
$75,000 and over	1,750	777	213	663	37	60	770	174	28
Not reported	2,572	1,235	316	943	22	56	1,167	156	14

[1]Unmarried (or married with spouse absent) child, grandchild, brother/sister or other relative.
[2]No spouse present.
[3]May be of any race.
* = Quantity zero or rounds to zero.

Table A-8. Enrollment Status for Families with Children 5 to 24 Years Old, by Control of School, Race, Type of Family, and Family Income, October 2016—*Continued*

(Numbers in thousands; civilian noninstitutionalized population.)

Characteristic	Total	Families with no dependents 5 to 24 years old[1]	Families with dependents 5 to 24 years old[2]						
			Kindergarten, elementary, and high school enrollment status				College enrollment status		
			None enrolled in elementary or high school	Public only	Public and private	Private only	None enrolled in college	One enrolled in college	Two or more enrolled in college
Married-couple families	4,621	2,544	414	1,487	59	118	1,732	315	30
Less than $20,000	388	228	30	125	4	*	145	14	*
$20,000 to $74,999	1,790	999	150	593	10	39	676	106	9
$75,000 and over	1,326	630	125	477	37	57	559	122	14
Not reported	1,117	687	108	292	9	21	352	72	7
Unmarried householder[3]	5,585	1,836	732	2,854	56	107	3,350	360	39
Less than $20,000	1,528	490	134	860	25	19	970	61	6
$20,000 to $74,999	2,179	651	303	1,157	18	49	1,353	163	12
$75,000 and over	424	147	88	186	*	3	211	52	14
Not reported	1,454	548	207	651	13	35	815	84	7
ASIAN ALONE									
All Families	4,741	2,329	505	1,739	48	120	1,879	448	85
Less than $20,000	289	168	27	90	*	3	93	23	4
$20,000 to $74,999	1,406	681	162	545	1	16	550	147	28
$75,000 and over	1,922	921	185	701	25	90	783	182	36
Not reported	1,125	559	130	402	23	11	453	97	16
Married-couple families	3,759	1,866	325	1,420	44	103	1,535	297	61
Less than $20,000	173	116	12	45	*	*	49	8	*
$20,000 to $74,999	1,037	529	90	407	1	9	413	79	16
$75,000 and over	1,685	782	155	638	25	84	713	153	36
Not reported	864	439	67	329	18	10	360	57	8
Unmarried householder[3]	983	463	180	319	4	17	344	151	24
Less than $20,000	115	53	15	45	*	3	44	14	4
$20,000 to $74,999	369	152	72	138	*	7	137	68	12
$75,000 and over	237	139	30	62	*	6	69	29	*
Not reported	261	119	63	74	4	1	93	40	8
HISPANIC[3]									
All Families	13,592	5,022	1,554	6,694	80	242	7,106	1,236	228
Less than $20,000	2,103	765	171	1,135	16	16	1,223	104	12
$20,000 to $74,999	6,145	2,067	685	3,264	27	102	3,417	558	103
$75,000 and over	2,341	898	314	1037	14	78	1,097	295	50
Not reported	3,002	1,292	384	1,259	23	45	1,369	279	62
Married-couple families	8,500	3,382	850	4,064	38	165	4,171	766	180
Less than $20,000	897	430	70	389	3	5	428	33	7
$20,000 to $74,999	3,926	1,388	356	2,103	15	63	2,135	324	80
$75,000 and over	1,865	707	228	852	9	70	859	249	50
Not reported	1,812	858	196	720	11	27	750	161	44
Unmarried householder[3]	5,092	1,640	704	2,631	42	76	2,935	470	48
Less than $20,000	1,206	335	102	746	13	11	795	71	5
$20,000 to $74,999	2,219	679	329	1,161	12	39	1,283	234	24
$75,000 and over	476	191	86	185	5	9	239	46	*
Not reported	1,191	434	187	540	12	18	619	118	19

[1]Unmarried (or married with spouse absent) child, grandchild, brother/sister or other relative.
[2]No spouse present.
[3]May be of any race.
* = Quantity zero or rounds to zero.

PART A

NATIONAL EDUCATION STATISTICS

■ **Historical Enrollment Tables**

Table A-9. School Enrollment of the Population 3 Years Old and Over, by Level and Control of School, Selected Race, and Hispanic Origin, October 1955–2016

(Numbers in thousands; civilian noninstitutionalized population.)

Year, race, and Hispanic origin	Total enrolled	Nursery school			Kindergarten			Elementary school		
		Total	Public	Private	Total	Public	Private	Total	Public	Private
ALL RACES										
2016	77,232	4,746	2,806	1,941	4,017	3,654	364	32,604	29,978	2,627
2015	77,066	4,532	2,610	1,922	4,073	3,644	428	32,826	30,173	2,653
2014	77,214	4,694	2,693	2,001	4,069	3,617	453	32,622	29,805	2,817
2013	77,772	4,682	2,558	2,124	4,150	3,725	425	32,873	30,171	2,702
2012	78,426	4,628	2,732	1,896	4,138	3,684	454	32,683	29,865	2,818
2011	79,043	4,946	2,904	2,042	4,214	3,732	482	32,872	29,965	2,907
2010	78,519	4,835	2,776	2,059	4,172	3,764	408	32,663	29,841	2,822
2009	77,288	4,708	2,744	1,964	4,132	3,767	365	32,238	29,365	2,874
2008	76,353	4,614	2,632	1,982	4,047	3,578	469	32,344	29,162	3,182
2007	75,967	4,628	2,570	2,058	4,132	3,656	476	32,169	29,052	3,117
2006	75,197	4,688	2,519	2,169	4,039	3,552	487	32,089	28,975	3,113
2005	75,780	4,603	2,480	2,123	3,912	3,349	563	32,438	29,072	3,366
2004	75,461	4,739	2,487	2,252	3,992	3,417	575	32,556	29,166	3,389
2003	74,911	4,928	2,567	2,361	3,719	3,098	622	32,565	29,204	3,361
2002	74,046	4,471	2,246	2,225	3,571	2,976	594	33,132	29,658	3,474
2001	73,124	4,289	2,161	2,128	3,737	3,145	591	33,166	29,800	3,366
2000	72,214	4,401	2,217	2,184	3,832	3,173	659	32,898	29,378	3,520
1999	72,395	4,578	2,269	2,309	3,825	3,167	658	32,873	29,264	3,609
1998	72,109	4,577	2,265	2,313	3,828	3,128	700	32,573	29,124	3,449
1997	72,031	4,500	2,254	2,246	3,933	3,271	663	32,369	29,308	3,061
1996	70,297	4,212	1,868	2,344	4,034	3,353	681	31,515	28,153	3,362
1995	69,769	4,399	2,012	2,387	3,877	3,174	704	31,815	28,384	3,431
1994[1]	69,272	4,259	1,940	2,319	3,863	3,278	585	31,512	28,131	3,381
1993[r]	64,414	3,032	1,258	1,774	4,275	3,589	686	31,219	28,278	2,941
1993	62,730	3,018	1,230	1,788	4,180	3,499	681	30,604	27,688	2,914
1992	62,082	2,899	1,098	1,801	4,130	3,507	623	30,165	27,066	3,102
1991	61,276	2,933	1,094	1,839	4,152	3,531	621	29,591	26,632	2,958
1990	60,588	3,401	1,212	2,188	3,899	3,332	567	29,265	26,591	2,674
1989	59,236	2,877	971	1,906	3,868	3,293	575	28,637	25,897	2,740
1988	58,847	2,639	838	1,770	3,958	3,420	538	28,223	25,443	2,778
1987	58,691	2,587	848	1,739	4,018	3,423	595	27,524	24,760	2,765
1986	58,153	2,554	835	1,719	3,961	3,328	633	27,121	24,163	2,958
1985	58,014	2,491	854	1,637	3,815	3,221	594	26,866	23,803	3,063
1984	57,313	2,354	761	1,593	3,484	2,953	531	26,838	24,120	2,718
1983	57,745	2,350	809	1,541	3,361	2,706	656	27,198	24,203	2,994
1982	57,905	2,153	729	1,423	3,299	2,746	553	27,412	24,381	3,031
1981	58,390	2,058	663	1,396	3,161	2,616	545	27,795	24,758	3,037
1980	57,348	1,987	633	1,354	3,176	2,690	486	27,449	24,398	3,051
1979	57,854	1,869	636	1,233	3,025	2,593	432	27,865	24,756	3,109
1978	58,616	1,824	587	1,237	2,989	2,493	496	28,490	25,252	3,238
1977	60,013	1,618	562	1,056	3,191	2,665	526	29,234	25,983	3,251
1976	60,482	1,526	476	1,050	3,490	2,962	528	29,774	26,698	3,075
1975	60,969	1,748	574	1,174	3,393	2,851	542	30,446	27,166	3,279
1974	60,259	1,607	423	1,184	3,252	2,726	526	31,126	27,956	3,169
1973	59,392	1,324	400	924	3,074	2,582	493	31,469	28,201	3,268
1972	60,142	1,283	402	881	3,135	2,636	499	32,242	28,693	3,549
1971	61,106	1,066	317	749	3,263	2,689	574	33,507	29,829	3,678
1970	60,357	1,096	333	763	3,183	2,647	536	33,950	30,001	3,949
1969	59,913	860	245	615	3,276	2,682	594	33,788	29,825	3,964
1968	58,791	816	262	554	3,268	2,709	559	33,761	29,527	4,234
1967	57,656	713	230	484	3,312	2,678	635	33,440	28,877	4,562
1966	56,167	688	215	473	3,115	2,527	588	32,916	28,208	4,706
1965	54,701	520	127	393	3,057	2,439	618	32,474	27,596	4,878
1964	52,490	471	91	380	2,830	2,349	481	31,734	26,811	4,923
1963	50,356	NA	NA	NA	2,340	1,936	404	31,245	26,502	4,742
1962	48,704	NA	NA	NA	2,319	1,914	405	30,661	26,148	4,513
1961	47,708	NA	NA	NA	2,299	1,926	373	30,718	26,221	4,497
1960	46,260	NA	NA	NA	2,092	1,691	401	30,349	25,814	4,535
1959	44,370	NA	NA	NA	2,032	1,678	354	29,382	24,680	4,702
1958	42,900	NA	NA	NA	1,991	1,569	422	28,184	23,800	4,385
1957	41,166	NA	NA	NA	1,824	1,471	353	27,248	23,076	4,172
1956	39,353	NA	NA	NA	1,758	1,566	192	26,169	22,474	3,695
1955	37,426	NA	NA	NA	1,628	1,365	263	25,458	22,078	3,379
WHITE ALONE										
2016	56,007	3,445	1,984	1,461	2,859	2,578	281	23,732	21,786	1,946
2015	56,056	3,230	1,778	1,452	2,970	2,630	340	23,863	21,776	2,088
2014	56,343	3,354	1,814	1,540	2,866	2,557	309	23,886	21,677	2,209
2013	56,914	3,346	1,740	1,606	2,933	2,588	345	24,238	22,090	2,148

Note: Data shown for 1955 to 1966 for the Black population are for Black and Other races.
NA = Not available.
[1]Prior to 1994, total enrolled does not include the 35 and over population.
r = Revised, controlled to 1990 census based population estimates; previous 1993 data controlled to 1980 census based population estimates.

Table A-9. School Enrollment of the Population 3 Years Old and Over, by Level and Control of School, Selected Race, and Hispanic Origin, October 1955–2016—*Continued*

(Numbers in thousands; civilian noninstitutionalized population.)

Year, race, and Hispanic origin	High school			College			
	Total	Public	Private	Total	Public	Private	Full-time
ALL RACES							
2016	16,668	15,330	1,338	19,196	14,971	4,225	14,421
2015	16,535	15,358	1,177	19,101	15,175	3,926	14,236
2014	16,654	15,379	1,275	19,175	15,325	3,850	14,400
2013	16,601	15,468	1,133	19,467	15,514	3,953	14,228
2012	17,047	15,704	1,343	19,930	15,778	4,152	14,602
2011	16,613	15,426	1,187	20,397	16,134	4,263	14,903
2010	16,574	15,338	1,236	20,275	16,153	4,122	14,600
2009	16,445	15,269	1,177	19,764	15,722	4,042	14,364
2008	16,715	15,397	1,319	18,632	14,739	3,893	13,245
2007	17,082	15,804	1,278	17,956	14,072	3,884	12,656
2006	17,149	15,617	1,532	17,232	13,466	3,766	12,070
2005	17,354	15,934	1,420	17,472	13,435	4,037	12,237
2004	16,791	15,498	1,293	17,383	13,652	3,731	11,990
2003	17,062	15,785	1,276	16,638	13,109	3,529	11,490
2002	16,374	15,064	1,310	16,497	12,834	3,664	11,141
2001	16,059	14,830	1,230	15,873	12,421	3,452	10,404
2000	15,770	14,431	1,339	15,314	12,008	3,305	10,159
1999	15,916	14,638	1,278	15,203	11,659	3,544	10,112
1998	15,584	14,299	1,285	15,547	11,984	3,563	10,184
1997	15,793	14,634	1,159	15,436	12,091	3,345	10,236
1996	15,309	14,113	1,197	15,226	12,014	3,212	9,839
1995	14,963	13,750	1,213	14,715	11,372	3,343	9,544
1994[1]	14,616	13,539	1,077	15,022	11,694	3,329	9,573
1993[r]	13,989	12,985	1,004	11,901	9,440	2,461	8,706
1993	13,522	12,542	977	11,409	9,031	2,374	8,308
1992	13,219	12,268	952	11,671	9,282	2,386	8,503
1991	13,010	12,069	945	11,589	9,078	2,511	8,461
1990	12,719	11,818	903	11,306	8,889	2,417	8,154
1989	12,786	11,980	806	11,066	8,576	2,490	7,905
1988	13,093	12,095	998	10,937	8,663	2,278	7,771
1987	13,647	12,577	1,070	10,915	8,556	2,361	7,560
1986	13,912	12,746	1,166	10,605	8,153	2,452	7,507
1985	13,979	12,764	1,215	10,863	8,379	2,483	7,720
1984	13,777	12,721	1,057	10,859	8,467	2,392	7,822
1983	14,010	12,792	1,218	10,825	8,185	2,640	7,711
1982	14,123	13,004	1,118	10,919	8,354	2,565	7,736
1981	14,642	13,523	1,119	10,734	8,159	2,576	7,569
1980	14,556	NA	NA	10,180	NA	NA	7,147
1979	15,116	13,994	1,122	9,978	7,699	2,280	7,010
1978	15,475	14,231	1,244	9,838	7,427	2,410	6,979
1977	15,753	14,505	1,248	10,217	7,925	2,292	7,196
1976	15,742	14,541	1,201	9,950	7,739	2,211	7,176
1975	15,683	14,503	1,180	9,697	7,704	1,994	7,105
1974	15,447	14,275	1,172	8,827	6,905	1,922	6,351
1973	15,347	14,162	1,184	8,179	6,224	1,955	6,089
1972	15,169	14,015	1,155	8,313	6,337	1,976	6,314
1971	15,183	14,057	1,126	8,087	6,271	1,816	6,204
1970	14,715	13,545	1,170	7,413	5,699	1,714	5,763
1969	14,553	13,400	1,153	7,435	5,439	1,995	5,810
1968	14,145	12,793	1,352	6,801	4,948	1,854	5,357
1967	13,790	12,498	1,292	6,401	4,540	1,861	4,976
1966	13,364	11,985	1,377	6,085	4,178	1,908	4,847
1965	12,975	11,517	1,457	5,675	3,840	1,835	4,414
1964	12,812	11,403	1,410	4,643	3,025	1,618	3,556
1963	12,438	11,186	1,251	4,336	2,897	1,439	3,260
1962	11,516	10,431	1,085	4,208	2,820	1,388	3,237
1961	10,959	9,817	1,141	3,731	2,376	1,354	2,902
1960	10,249	9,215	1,033	3,570	2,307	1,262	2,681
1959	9,616	8,571	1,045	3,340	2,120	1,220	2,464
1958	9,482	8,485	998	3,242	2,088	1,155	NA
1957	8,956	8,059	897	3,138	2,054	1,084	NA
1956	8,543	7,668	875	2,883	1,824	1,059	NA
1955	7,961	7,181	780	2,379	1,515	864	NA
WHITE ALONE							
2016	12,071	11,017	1,053	13,901	10,846	3,054	10,373
2015	12,133	11,199	934	13,859	11,039	2,821	10,254
2014	12,283	11,315	969	13,953	11,227	2,727	10,506
2013	12,157	11,270	887	14,240	11,378	2,862	10,281

Note: Data shown for 1955 to 1966 for the Black population are for Black and Other races.

NA = Not available.

[1]Prior to 1994, total enrolled does not include the 35 and over population.

r = Revised, controlled to 1990 census based population estimates; previous 1993 data controlled to 1980 census based population estimates.

Table A-9. School Enrollment of the Population 3 Years Old and Over, by Level and Control of School, Selected Race, and Hispanic Origin, October 1955–2016—*Continued*

(Numbers in thousands; civilian noninstitutionalized population.)

Year, race, and Hispanic origin	Total enrolled	Nursery school			Kindergarten			Elementary school		
		Total	Public	Private	Total	Public	Private	Total	Public	Private
2012	57,702	3,393	1,925	1,468	2,940	2,584	355	24,187	21,928	2,260
2011	59,647	3,624	1,997	1,627	3,198	2,806	393	24,864	22,419	2,445
2010	59,236	3,659	1,992	1,668	3,069	2,745	324	24,680	22,395	2,284
2009	58,586	3,404	1,832	1,572	3,154	2,860	293	24,575	22,257	2,319
2008	58,244	3,479	1,830	1,649	3,121	2,748	373	24,552	21,986	2,565
2007	58,021	3,545	1,880	1,665	3,223	2,836	387	24,431	21,869	2,562
2006	57,419	3,624	1,815	1,809	3,084	2,701	382	24,472	21,923	2,549
2005	58,013	3,542	1,767	1,775	3,056	2,611	445	24,652	21,858	2,795
2004	57,585	3,566	1,703	1,863	3,043	2,571	472	24,773	21,889	2,883
2003[2]	57,391	3,909	1,918	1,990	2,866	2,367	499	24,711	21,893	2,818
2002	57,501	3,473	1,613	1,860	2,760	2,240	520	25,625	22,703	2,922
2001	56,649	3,278	1,484	1,794	2,893	2,394	499	25,729	22,848	2,881
2000	56,344	3,392	1,539	1,853	2,998	2,453	545	25,562	22,538	3,024
1999	56,713	3,590	1,571	2,019	2,956	2,422	534	25,628	22,552	3,076
1998	56,515	3,549	1,598	1,951	2,933	2,356	577	25,489	22,547	2,942
1997	56,587	3,489	1,572	1,917	3,078	2,532	546	25,289	22,679	2,610
1996	55,378	3,284	1,314	1,970	3,163	2,596	567	24,692	21,785	2,907
1995	55,186	3,553	1,435	2,118	3,032	2,440	592	24,963	22,010	2,954
1994[1]	54,823	3,376	1,330	2,046	3,010	2,505	505	24,786	21,903	2,883
1993[r]	51,034	2,434	851	1,583	3,323	2,730	593	24,637	22,078	2,559
1993	49,985	2,447	843	1,604	3,273	2,681	592	24,249	21,714	2,535
1992	49,713	2,387	785	1,602	3,256	2,727	529	23,932	21,213	2,718
1991	49,156	2,447	810	1,637	3,274	2,766	508	23,547	20,948	2,599
1990	48,897	2,830	869	1,961	3,081	2,609	472	23,343	20,984	2,359
1989	47,923	2,393	712	1,681	3,118	2,611	506	22,867	20,468	2,399
1988	47,672	2,234	651	1,583	3,192	2,722	471	22,541	20,086	2,455
1987	47,471	2,204	630	1,574	3,120	2,591	529	22,037	19,538	2,498
1986	47,267	2,144	601	1,543	3,161	2,589	572	21,761	19,090	2,671
1985	47,452	2,087	617	1,470	3,060	2,545	515	21,593	18,817	2,776
1984	46,941	1,915	543	1,372	2,788	2,319	469	21,730	19,282	2,449
1983	47,423	1,932	563	1,369	2,769	2,181	588	22,054	19,340	2,714
1982	47,662	1,783	504	1,279	2,677	2,189	489	22,297	19,583	2,713
1981	48,169	1,685	447	1,238	2,597	2,130	467	22,663	19,924	2,739
1980	47,673	1,637	432	1,205	2,595	2,172	423	22,510	19,743	2,768
1979	48,225	1,537	428	1,110	2,437	2,069	368	22,959	20,174	2,785
1978	48,843	1,456	351	1,105	2,452	2,009	444	23,524	20,551	2,973
1977	50,151	1,314	372	942	2,611	2,153	458	24,262	21,312	2,950
1976	50,761	1,246	318	929	2,881	2,423	457	24,776	21,947	2,829
1975	51,430	1,432	392	1,040	2,845	2,363	483	25,412	22,351	3,059
1974	50,992	1,340	293	1,048	2,745	2,268	477	26,051	23,063	2,990
1973	50,617	1,087	242	845	2,584	2,139	445	26,531	23,506	3,025
1972	51,314	1,079	285	794	2,633	2,185	448	27,185	23,869	3,316
1971	52,081	888	225	664	2,735	2,207	527	28,187	24,720	3,466
1970	51,719	893	198	695	2,706	2,233	473	28,638	24,923	3,715
1969	51,465	676	136	539	2,803	2,289	515	28,572	24,803	3,768
1968	50,608	664	163	501	2,775	2,272	504	28,634	24,580	4,054
1967	49,721	564	134	429	2,840	2,254	587	28,415	24,044	4,371
1966	48,620	564	127	437	2,693	2,163	530	28,012	23,469	4,542
1965	47,451	451	93	358	2,648	2,086	562	27,679	22,976	4,703
1964	44,850	NA	NA	NA	2,157	1,795	362	27,099	22,381	4,718
1963	43,815	NA	NA	NA	2,064	1,699	365	26,709	22,181	4,527
1962	42,501	NA	NA	NA	2,025	1,667	358	26,272	21,922	4,350
1961	42,498	NA	NA	NA	1,968	1,618	350	26,294	22,014	4,281
1960	40,348	NA	NA	NA	1,849	1,485	364	26,035	21,696	4,339
1959	38,857	NA	NA	NA	1,758	1,434	324	25,395	20,854	4,541
1958	37,662	NA	NA	NA	1,769	1,383	386	24,380	20,178	4,203
1957	36,132	NA	NA	NA	1,595	1,258	337	23,610	19,595	4,015
1956	34,641	NA	NA	NA	1,544	1,364	180	22,740	19,186	3,554
1955	32,929	NA	NA	NA	1,484	1,244	240	22,185	18,947	3,238
WHITE ALONE NON-HISPANIC										
2016	40,606	2,499	1,275	1,224	1,956	1,697	259	16,640	14,939	1,701
2015	41,145	2,410	1,143	1,268	2,022	1,748	273	16,879	15,095	1,783
2014	41,456	2,477	1,159	1,317	1,990	1,726	264	16,904	15,008	1,897
2013	42,025	2,531	1,089	1,442	1,968	1,691	277	17,309	15,379	1,930
2012	42,776	2,509	1,227	1,283	2,011	1,691	320	17,413	15,401	2,012
2011	44,951	2,743	1,332	1,411	2,238	1,903	335	17,830	15,670	2,160

Note: Data shown for 1955 to 1966 for the Black population are for Black and Other races.

NA = Not available.

[1]Prior to 1994, total enrolled does not include the 35 and over population.

[2]Starting in 2003 respondents could identify more than one race. Except as noted, the race data in this table from 2003 onward represent those respondents who indicated only one race category.

[r] = Revised, controlled to 1990 census based population estimates; previous 1993 data controlled to 1980 census based population estimates.

Table A-9. School Enrollment of the Population 3 Years Old and Over, by Level and Control of School, Selected Race, and Hispanic Origin, October 1955–2016—*Continued*

(Numbers in thousands; civilian noninstitutionalized population.)

Year, race, and Hispanic origin	High school			College			
	Total	Public	Private	Total	Public	Private	Full-time
2012	12,554	11,494	1,060	14,628	11,530	3,098	10,694
2011	12,548	11,542	1,007	15,412	12,161	3,251	11,205
2010	12,570	11,525	1,045	15,258	12,179	3,079	10,818
2009	12,425	11,419	1,006	15,027	11,948	3,079	10,847
2008	12,687	11,585	1,103	14,405	11,432	2,973	10,256
2007	12,986	11,886	1,100	13,835	10,855	2,979	9,696
2006	12,966	11,694	1,273	13,273	10,338	2,936	9,236
2005	13,296	12,109	1,187	13,466	10,303	3,163	9,392
2004	12,823	11,684	1,138	13,381	10,478	2,904	9,257
2003[2]	13,036	11,939	1,097	12,870	10,101	2,769	8,855
2002	12,862	11,730	1,132	12,781	9,774	3,007	8,613
2001	12,540	11,473	1,067	12,208	9,503	2,705	7,909
2000	12,392	11,259	1,133	11,999	9,364	2,636	7,945
1999	12,487	11,374	1,113	12,053	9,185	2,868	7,886
1998	12,142	11,013	1,130	12,401	9,518	2,883	8,012
1997	12,290	11,287	1,003	12,442	9,713	2,729	8,127
1996	12,052	10,999	1,053	12,188	9,567	2,622	7,849
1995	11,617	10,574	1,042	12,021	9,311	2,711	7,773
1994[1]	11,430	10,514	916	12,222	9,472	2,751	7,722
1993[r]	10,960	10,124	836	9,685	7,695	1,990	6,996
1993	10,651	9,834	819	9,366	7,428	1,940	6,739
1992	10,480	9,648	833	9,658	7,653	2,001	6,985
1991	10,309	9,467	841	9,579	7,464	2,118	6,919
1990	10,177	9,370	807	9,466	7,411	2,056	6,776
1989	10,172	9,443	730	9,374	7,219	2,158	6,658
1988	10,462	9,571	890	9,245	7,302	1,940	6,488
1987	10,967	10,019	947	9,143	7,113	2,034	6,275
1986	11,259	10,229	1,030	8,943	6,821	2,122	6,253
1985	11,378	10,258	1,120	9,334	7,131	2,203	6,597
1984	11,240	10,266	974	9,269	7,163	2,105	6,672
1983	11,425	10,339	1,086	9,242	6,949	2,293	6,532
1982	11,577	10,541	1,036	9,328	7,102	2,227	6,579
1981	12,062	11,035	1,027	9,162	6,906	2,256	6,452
1980	12,056	NA	NA	8,875	NA	NA	6,212
1979	12,583	11,549	1,033	8,709	6,672	2,037	6,058
1978	12,897	11,741	1,156	8,514	6,368	2,145	5,974
1977	13,152	11,980	1,172	8,812	6,743	2,069	6,165
1976	13,214	12,093	1,121	8,644	6,657	1,987	6,170
1975	13,224	12,112	1,112	8,516	6,724	1,792	6,183
1974	13,073	11,966	1,107	7,781	6,049	1,732	5,575
1973	13,091	11,967	1,124	7,324	5,550	1,773	5,408
1972	12,959	11,876	1,083	7,458	5,644	1,814	5,678
1971	12,998	11,937	1,061	7,273	5,624	1,650	5,560
1970	12,723	11,599	1,124	6,759	5,168	1,591	5,221
1969	12,588	11,502	1,085	6,827	4,967	1,860	5,307
1968	12,280	11,007	1,272	6,255	4,501	1,753	4,919
1967	11,997	10,769	1,228	5,905	4,155	1,750	4,604
1966	11,643	10,312	1,329	5,708	3,914	1,795	4,556
1965	11,356	9,961	1,395	5,317	3,568	1,749	4,111
1964	11,257	9,898	1,359	4,338	2,798	1,540	NA
1963	10,994	9,782	1,212	4,050	2,680	1,370	NA
1962	10,270	9,217	1,053	3,934	2,620	1,314	NA
1961	9,737	8,635	1,102	3,498	2,205	1,293	NA
1960	9,122	8,124	999	3,342	2,126	1,215	NA
1959	8,586	7,572	1,014	3,118	1,960	1,158	NA
1958	8,484	7,501	982	3,030	1,928	1,101	NA
1957	7,995	7,121	874	2,932	1,924	1,006	NA
1956	7,670	6,825	845	2,687	1,704	983	NA
1955	7,036	6,303	733	2,224	1,429	795	NA
WHITE ALONE NON-HISPANIC							
2016	8,760	7,839	921	10,749	8,219	2,530	8,135
2015	8,931	8,087	843	10,904	8,526	2,377	8,226
2014	9,018	8,155	862	11,068	8,775	2,292	8,456
2013	8,869	8,109	760	11,348	8,889	2,459	8,362
2012	9,193	8,252	941	11,650	8,977	2,672	8,604
2011	9,437	8,535	902	12,703	9,842	2,861	9,333

Note: Data shown for 1955 to 1966 for the Black population are for Black and Other races.
NA = Not available.
[1]Prior to 1994, total enrolled does not include the 35 and over population.
[2]Starting in 2003 respondents could identify more than one race. Except as noted, the race data in this table from 2003 onward represent those respondents who indicated only one race category.
[r] = Revised, controlled to 1990 census based population estimates; previous 1993 data controlled to 1980 census based population estimates.

Table A-9. School Enrollment of the Population 3 Years Old and Over, by Level and Control of School, Selected Race, and Hispanic Origin, October 1955–2016—*Continued*

(Numbers in thousands; civilian noninstitutionalized population.)

Year, race, and Hispanic origin	Total enrolled	Nursery school			Kindergarten			Elementary school		
		Total	Public	Private	Total	Public	Private	Total	Public	Private
2010....................	44,968	2,766	1,274	1,492	2,120	1,842	278	17,942	15,960	1,981
2009....................	45,470	2,575	1,188	1,387	2,252	1,990	262	18,244	16,198	2,046
2008....................	45,373	2,710	1,213	1,497	2,206	1,884	323	18,349	16,029	2,320
2007....................	45,334	2,711	1,225	1,486	2,279	1,929	351	18,306	15,998	2,307
2006....................	45,386	2,769	1,152	1,616	2,288	1,940	348	18,622	16,322	2,301
2005....................	46,338	2,810	1,211	1,599	2,308	1,936	372	18,858	16,335	2,523
2004....................	46,095	2,840	1,153	1,687	2,325	1,917	408	19,093	16,447	2,646
2003[2]....................	46,440	3,184	1,382	1,802	2,245	1,804	440	19,252	16,735	2,517
2002....................	46,725	2,881	1,172	1,709	2,065	1,585	480	20,124	17,495	2,628
2001....................	46,110	2,725	1,054	1,671	2,203	1,781	422	20,298	17,693	2,605
2000....................	46,660	2,854	1,149	1,705	2,346	1,846	500	20,574	17,747	2,827
1999....................	47,292	3,044	1,146	1,898	2,307	1,839	468	20,779	17,960	2,819
1998....................	47,386	2,964	1,136	1,828	2,336	1,790	547	20,806	18,107	2,699
1997....................	47,776	2,956	1,143	1,813	2,456	1,970	486	20,839	18,426	2,413
1996....................	46,947	2,767	922	1,845	2,590	2,081	509	20,447	17,808	2,639
1995....................	48,019	3,104	1,129	1,975	2,551	2,047	504	21,256	18,518	2,738
1994[1]....................	47,679	3,024	1,090	1,934	2,522	2,059	462	21,170	18,555	2,615
1993....................	43,827	2,277	720	1,557	2,779	2,239	540	20,961	18,617	2,344
BLACK ALONE										
2016....................	11,684	620	457	163	668	631	37	4,855	4,522	333
2015....................	11,544	703	501	202	618	596	23	4,883	4,647	236
2014....................	11,796	746	557	189	690	605	86	4,844	4,587	257
2013....................	11,824	683	465	218	736	691	46	4,848	4,625	224
2012....................	11,918	708	516	193	646	598	48	4,856	4,583	273
2011....................	12,037	794	562	232	559	503	56	4,902	4,658	245
2010....................	11,969	698	522	175	736	682	54	4,795	4,498	298
2009....................	11,748	811	640	171	619	578	41	4,749	4,424	325
2008....................	11,421	706	548	158	601	545	56	4,993	4,665	329
2007....................	11,475	700	485	215	605	548	56	4,926	4,572	353
2006....................	11,400	715	513	202	608	536	71	4,952	4,608	344
2005....................	11,384	719	542	177	538	486	52	5,106	4,747	359
2004....................	11,540	825	600	224	596	535	61	5,159	4,905	254
2003[2]....................	11,408	697	484	212	558	495	63	5,245	4,942	302
2002....................	11,703	725	503	221	598	543	55	5,545	5,210	335
2001....................	11,630	787	537	250	605	536	69	5,478	5,160	318
2000....................	11,503	726	531	195	629	547	82	5,481	5,133	347
1999....................	11,282	729	569	160	632	558	74	5,388	5,002	386
1998....................	11,411	761	528	233	689	592	97	5,332	5,031	301
1997....................	11,270	796	582	214	632	571	61	5,332	5,049	284
1996....................	10,851	702	459	243	634	545	89	5,171	4,846	325
1995....................	10,753	663	478	185	653	564	89	5,185	4,845	340
1994[1]....................	10,702	721	513	208	662	603	59	5,086	4,709	378
1993[r]....................	9,786	433	320	113	721	649	72	5,009	4,733	276
1993....................	9,470	414	307	107	687	618	69	4,865	4,599	266
1992....................	9,150	374	250	124	688	625	63	4,730	4,494	234
1991....................	9,031	360	244	117	676	598	79	4,672	4,445	229
1990....................	8,854	431	283	148	636	574	62	4,627	4,428	199
1989....................	8,707	366	216	150	601	557	44	4,528	4,296	232
1988....................	8,609	286	168	118	591	547	44	4,538	4,289	250
1987....................	8,712	277	164	113	699	658	41	4,402	4,206	194
1986....................	8,556	315	200	115	647	600	47	4,326	4,134	193
1985....................	8,444	332	212	120	625	562	63	4,307	4,131	175
1984....................	8,226	340	179	161	563	513	51	4,123	3,947	177
1983....................	8,199	326	215	111	476	427	48	4,153	3,964	189
1982....................	8,262	305	192	113	508	463	45	4,194	3,974	220
1981....................	8,350	284	182	102	474	412	62	4,291	4,087	204
1980....................	8,251	294	180	115	490	440	50	4,259	4,058	202
1979....................	8,317	278	185	95	497	443	54	4,296	4,053	243
1978....................	8,416	312	210	102	451	414	38	4,356	4,154	202
1977....................	8,564	250	171	78	496	447	50	4,387	4,166	221
1976....................	8,518	226	146	80	542	482	60	4,430	4,256	175
1975....................	8,400	276	171	105	468	426	42	4,509	4,344	165
1974....................	8,215	227	121	106	463	416	47	4,585	4,455	131
1973....................	7,834	210	146	64	423	391	32	4,473	4,277	196
1972....................	7,959	185	113	72	448	402	46	4,573	4,382	191
1971....................	8,179	151	90	61	464	422	42	4,877	4,712	165
1970....................	7,829	178	129	49	426	374	53	4,868	4,668	200
1969....................	7,680	170	102	68	425	361	64	4,785	4,633	151

Note: Data shown for 1955 to 1966 for the Black population are for Black and Other races.
NA = Not available.
[1]Prior to 1994, total enrolled does not include the 35 and over population.
[2]Starting in 2003 respondents could identify more than one race. Except as noted, the race data in this table from 2003 onward represent those respondents who indicated only one race category.
[r] = Revised, controlled to 1990 census based population estimates; previous 1993 data controlled to 1980 census based population estimates.

Table A-9. School Enrollment of the Population 3 Years Old and Over, by Level and Control of School, Selected Race, and Hispanic Origin, October 1955–2016—*Continued*

(Numbers in thousands; civilian noninstitutionalized population.)

Year, race, and Hispanic origin	High school			College			
	Total	Public	Private	Total	Public	Private	Full-time
2010.............................	9,528	8,598	930	12,613	9,900	2,713	9,122
2009.............................	9,573	8,655	919	12,826	10,022	2,803	9,368
2008.............................	9,783	8,798	986	12,324	9,630	2,694	8,925
2007.............................	10,171	9,204	966	11,867	9,141	2,726	8,379
2006.............................	10,222	9,072	1,150	11,485	8,821	2,664	8,105
2005.............................	10,647	9,566	1,081	11,715	8,852	2,863	8,246
2004.............................	10,266	9,221	1,044	11,571	8,928	2,643	8,082
2003[2].............................	10,463	9,473	990	11,295	8,742	2,553	7,810
2002.............................	10,419	9,388	1,031	11,236	8,488	2,749	7,673
2001.............................	10,281	9,331	950	10,602	8,133	2,469	6,980
2000.............................	10,250	9,222	1,029	10,636	8,202	2,434	7,105
1999.............................	10,344	9,314	1,030	10,818	8,158	2,660	7,162
1998.............................	10,170	9,131	1,039	11,109	8,435	2,674	7,251
1997.............................	10,280	9,358	922	11,245	8,688	2,558	7,378
1996.............................	10,107	9,148	959	11,034	8,584	2,450	7,178
1995.............................	10,084	9,094	991	11,024	8,439	2,585	7,194
1994[1].............................	9,786	8,951	835	11,178	8,568	2,610	7,152
1993.............................	9,216	8,449	767	8,594	6,772	1,822	6,247
BLACK ALONE							
2016.............................	2,656	2,556	100	2,885	2,271	614	2,064
2015.............................	2,515	2,420	95	2,826	2,260	566	2,045
2014.............................	2,581	2,451	130	2,934	2,284	650	2,055
2013.............................	2,699	2,588	111	2,857	2,340	517	2,092
2012.............................	2,669	2,528	141	3,038	2,507	531	2,168
2011.............................	2,635	2,545	91	3,146	2,541	605	2,279
2010.............................	2,657	2,552	105	3,083	2,495	587	2,223
2009.............................	2,680	2,592	89	2,889	2,322	567	2,061
2008.............................	2,639	2,524	115	2,481	1,975	506	1,690
2007.............................	2,743	2,627	116	2,501	1,968	533	1,683
2006.............................	2,792	2,628	165	2,334	1,816	518	1,628
2005.............................	2,723	2,592	131	2,298	1,800	498	1,526
2004.............................	2,660	2,584	76	2,301	1,831	470	1,504
2003[2].............................	2,765	2,691	74	2,144	1,773	371	1,416
2002.............................	2,558	2,451	107	2,278	1,868	410	1,468
2001.............................	2,531	2,412	119	2,230	1,766	463	1,475
2000.............................	2,502	2,350	152	2,164	1,721	443	1,351
1999.............................	2,536	2,427	109	1,998	1,587	411	1,372
1998.............................	2,614	2,515	99	2,016	1,595	421	1,284
1997.............................	2,605	2,516	89	1,903	1,546	357	1,280
1996.............................	2,443	2,338	105	1,901	1,519	381	1,179
1995.............................	2,481	2,370	111	1,772	1,353	419	1,117
1994[1].............................	2,434	2,313	121	1,800	1,439	361	1,147
1993[r].............................	2,317	2,197	120	1,305	1,006	299	951
1993.............................	2,244	2,128	115	1,261	973	288	914
1992.............................	2,152	2,072	72	1,217	980	237	904
1991.............................	2,100	2,044	56	1,220	1,004	217	900
1990.............................	1,975	1,909	65	1,188	963	227	869
1989.............................	2,069	2,027	42	1,139	932	208	833
1988.............................	2,079	2,016	62	1,114	894	220	801
1987.............................	2,140	2,056	84	1,193	977	218	852
1986.............................	2,130	2,040	91	1,138	896	242	859
1985.............................	2,131	2,068	63	1,049	860	190	767
1984.............................	2,061	2,002	59	1,138	918	220	810
1983.............................	2,143	2,057	86	1,102	858	245	806
1982.............................	2,128	2,073	55	1,127	865	263	800
1981.............................	2,168	2,102	65	1,133	898	235	815
1980.............................	2,200	NA	NA	1,007	NA	NA	723
1979.............................	2,245	2,171	74	1,002	814	188	748
1978.............................	2,276	2,211	65	1,020	822	199	753
1977.............................	2,327	2,269	59	1,103	916	187	803
1976.............................	2,258	2,187	71	1,062	887	175	817
1975.............................	2,199	2,140	59	948	782	166	742
1974.............................	2,125	2,072	54	814	659	155	589
1973.............................	2,044	1,988	56	685	537	147	536
1972.............................	2,025	1,971	54	727	582	145	525
1971.............................	2,006	1,951	55	680	532	148	534
1970.............................	1,834	1,794	41	522	422	100	427
1969.............................	1,808	1,751	57	492	372	120	401

Note: Data shown for 1955 to 1966 for the Black population are for Black and Other races.
NA = Not available.
[1]Prior to 1994, total enrolled does not include the 35 and over population.
[2]Starting in 2003 respondents could identify more than one race. Except as noted, the race data in this table from 2003 onward represent those respondents who indicated only one race category.
[r] = Revised, controlled to 1990 census based population estimates; previous 1993 data controlled to 1980 census based population estimates.

Table A-9. School Enrollment of the Population 3 Years Old and Over, by Level and Control of School, Selected Race, and Hispanic Origin, October 1955–2016—*Continued*

(Numbers in thousands; civilian noninstitutionalized population.)

Year, race, and Hispanic origin	Total enrolled	Nursery school			Kindergarten			Elementary school		
		Total	Public	Private	Total	Public	Private	Total	Public	Private
1968	7,448	132	89	43	448	397	51	4,716	4,569	146
1967	7,196	140	92	47	418	375	44	4,618	4,444	173
1966	7,547	125	88	37	420	364	56	4,904	4,739	165
1965	7,252	72	37	35	407	353	54	4,796	4,620	176
1964	6,807	NA	NA	NA	312	275	37	4,634	4,430	205
1963	6,541	NA	NA	NA	276	237	39	4,536	4,321	215
1962	6,203	NA	NA	NA	294	247	47	4,389	4,226	163
1961	6,210	NA	NA	NA	331	308	23	4,424	4,207	216
1960	5,910	NA	NA	NA	243	206	37	4,313	4,118	195
1959	5,513	NA	NA	NA	274	244	30	3,987	3,826	161
1958	5,238	NA	NA	NA	222	186	36	3,804	3,621	182
1957	5,034	NA	NA	NA	229	213	16	3,638	3,483	155
1956	4,712	NA	NA	NA	214	202	12	3,429	3,287	142
1955	4,498	NA	NA	NA	144	121	23	3,273	3,131	142
ASIAN ALONE[3]										
2016	4,720	304	138	166	214	188	26	1,781	1,658	123
2015	4,567	244	102	142	215	188	27	1,704	1,552	152
2014	4,449	257	105	152	179	147	32	1,643	1,476	167
2013	4,375	242	113	129	165	149	16	1,576	1,402	174
2012	4,275	208	90	118	224	196	28	1,540	1,388	152
2011	3,779	212	120	92	209	189	21	1,469	1,336	133
2010	3,815	223	97	127	196	181	15	1,488	1,358	130
2009	3,515	239	107	132	167	146	21	1,296	1,170	125
2008	3,545	205	110	95	144	119	24	1,356	1,168	188
2007	3,470	171	77	94	137	112	25	1,421	1,305	115
2006	3,287	143	65	78	162	149	13	1,235	1,105	130
2005	3,377	185	80	105	138	99	39	1,228	1,137	91
2004	3,409	165	72	93	164	152	12	1,239	1,153	86
2003[2]	3,312	138	56	82	122	93	29	1,258	1,122	136
2002	3,787	217	85	132	157	137	20	1,431	1,237	195
2001	3,803	161	91	70	181	161	20	1,409	1,263	146
2000	3,442	222	91	132	152	124	28	1,350	1,257	93
1999	3,621	205	96	109	195	148	47	1,461	1,343	118
1998	3,386	196	77	118	145	120	25	1,380	1,190	189
1997	3,261	168	59	108	161	110	51	1,329	1,186	144
1996	3,258	183	63	120	177	158	19	1,255	1,144	111
1995	1,863	76	28	47	75	62	13	697	622	74
1994[1]	2,057	76	27	50	74	60	14	785	707	78
1993	2,321	100	38	62	139	125	14	1,012	930	82
HISPANIC (OF ANY RACE)										
2016	17,865	1,079	791	287	1,034	1,008	26	8,148	7,835	313
2015	17,362	933	735	198	1,090	1,020	70	8,187	7,824	364
2014	17,122	1,016	769	248	1,044	991	54	8,085	7,699	386
2013	16,971	991	781	210	1,090	1,018	73	7,942	7,680	262
2012	17,043	988	781	206	1,050	1,009	41	7,841	7,566	275
2011	16,131	1,010	766	244	1,042	984	58	7,716	7,401	315
2010	15,670	994	794	200	1,050	1,002	49	7,403	7,052	351
2009	14,528	930	717	213	965	933	32	7,058	6,716	342
2008	13,967	844	668	177	961	910	51	6,742	6,450	292
2007	13,708	905	711	194	990	954	37	6,582	6,299	284
2006	13,111	911	707	205	846	798	48	6,394	6,109	285
2005	12,809	797	601	196	804	725	79	6,330	5,991	339
2004	12,509	787	591	196	769	699	70	6,184	5,895	290
2003	11,929	768	561	206	694	633	61	5,974	5,651	322
2002	11,544	637	476	161	727	688	39	5,909	5,585	324
2001	11,163	593	452	141	728	641	87	5,779	5,478	301
2000	10,163	574	419	154	687	639	48	5,224	5,012	213
1999	9,936	585	458	127	666	594	73	5,088	4,829	259
1998	9,528	618	492	126	639	608	31	4,831	4,568	262
1997	9,220	548	436	112	648	589	59	4,644	4,427	217
1996	8,818	533	403	130	602	539	63	4,443	4,162	281
1995	8,563	510	350	160	558	465	93	4,434	4,165	269
1994[1]	8,183	400	278	122	559	516	43	4,162	3,848	314
1993[r]	7,651	231	169	62	639	576	63	4,027	3,779	248
1993	6,689	194	142	52	538	484	53	3,534	3,317	217

Note: Data shown for 1955 to 1966 for the Black population are for Black and Other races.
NA = Not available.
[1]Prior to 1994, total enrolled does not include the 35 and over population.
[2]Starting in 2003 respondents could identify more than one race. Except as noted, the race data in this table from 2003 onward represent those respondents who indicated only one race category.
[3]The data shown prior to 2003 consists of those identifying themselves as "Asian or Pacific Islanders."

Table A-9. School Enrollment of the Population 3 Years Old and Over, by Level and Control of School, Selected Race, and Hispanic Origin, October 1955–2016—*Continued*

(Numbers in thousands; civilian noninstitutionalized population.)

Year, race, and Hispanic origin	High school			College			
	Total	Public	Private	Total	Public	Private	Full-time
1968	1,718	1,656	62	434	359	75	338
1967	1,651	1,605	46	370	280	90	271
1966	1,721	1,673	48	282	NA	NA	210
1965	1,619	1,556	62	358	272	86	218
1964	1,556	1,505	51	306	227	78	NA
1963	1,444	1,404	39	286	217	69	NA
1962	1,246	1,214	32	274	200	74	NA
1961	1,222	1,182	39	233	171	61	NA
1960	1,127	1,092	34	227	180	46	NA
1959	1,030	999	31	222	160	62	NA
1958	998	981	17	212	160	53	NA
1957	961	939	22	206	132	74	NA
1956	873	843	30	196	120	76	NA
1955	926	878	48	155	86	69	NA
ASIAN ALONE[3]							
2016	837	776	62	1,585	1,163	421	1,349
2015	787	727	60	1,616	1,232	384	1,340
2014	827	766	61	1,543	1,202	341	1,247
2013	817	741	76	1,576	1,144	432	1,260
2012	857	778	79	1,447	1,078	369	1,175
2011	685	635	50	1,204	936	268	963
2010	586	542	43	1,322	969	353	1,090
2009	582	530	53	1,231	950	282	972
2008	620	564	56	1,220	918	301	917
2007	638	616	23	1,103	841	261	896
2006	663	611	51	1,084	862	223	866
2005	642	596	46	1,184	904	279	948
2004	650	619	31	1,191	928	263	881
2003[2]	632	585	47	1,162	833	328	901
2002	723	664	59	1,258	1,040	218	951
2001	771	736	35	1,280	1,026	254	921
2000	668	622	46	1,049	831	218	792
1999	719	666	53	1,041	779	261	787
1998	650	599	51	1,016	783	233	821
1997	656	600	57	947	712	235	721
1996	644	606	38	999	816	183	710
1995	399	375	24	617	470	147	456
1994[1]	399	365	34	723	548	174	530
1993	428	390	37	641	519	122	542
HISPANIC (OF ANY RACE)							
2016	3,943	3,787	156	3,661	3,050	612	2,571
2015	3,777	3,658	120	3,374	2,861	514	2,343
2014	3,681	3,545	136	3,295	2,799	496	2,352
2013	3,729	3,596	133	3,219	2,768	452	2,179
2012	3,765	3,633	131	3,400	2,948	451	2,397
2011	3,410	3,294	116	2,953	2,515	438	2,041
2010	3,344	3,219	125	2,879	2,478	401	1,868
2009	3,142	3,052	90	2,434	2,122	312	1,651
2008	3,192	3,066	126	2,227	1,919	308	1,434
2007	3,058	2,902	156	2,172	1,888	284	1,459
2006	2,990	2,856	134	1,968	1,664	304	1,246
2005	2,937	2,824	113	1,942	1,625	316	1,255
2004	2,793	2,685	108	1,975	1,676	299	1,276
2003	2,779	2,667	112	1,714	1,480	235	1,139
2002	2,614	2,513	101	1,656	1,374	283	1,004
2001	2,363	2,246	117	1,700	1,445	255	1,005
2000	2,253	2,144	108	1,426	1,219	207	873
1999	2,290	2,200	91	1,307	1,093	214	765
1998	2,077	1,978	98	1,363	1,137	226	801
1997	2,119	2,035	84	1,260	1,079	181	797
1996	2,018	1,922	96	1,223	1,031	192	708
1995	1,854	1,772	83	1,207	1,037	170	709
1994[1]	1,874	1,781	92	1,187	1,019	169	640
1993[1]	1,722	1,653	69	1,029	872	157	686
1993	1,556	1,496	60	867	731	134	573

Note: Data shown for 1955 to 1966 for the Black population are for Black and Other races.

NA = Not available.

[1]Prior to 1994, total enrolled does not include the 35 and over population.

[2]Starting in 2003 respondents could identify more than one race. Except as noted, the race data in this table from 2003 onward represent those respondents who indicated only one race category.

[3]The data shown prior to 2003 consists of those identifying themselves as "Asian or Pacific Islanders."

Table A-9. School Enrollment of the Population 3 Years Old and Over, by Level and Control of School, Selected Race, and Hispanic Origin, October 1955–2016—*Continued*

(Numbers in thousands; civilian noninstitutionalized population.)

Year, race, and Hispanic origin	Total enrolled	Nursery school			Kindergarten			Elementary school		
		Total	Public	Private	Total	Public	Private	Total	Public	Private
1992	6,598	209	139	70	554	493	60	3,525	3,271	252
1991	6,306	215	146	69	552	525	27	3,461	3,240	221
1990	6,072	242	153	88	475	446	29	3,301	3,107	197
1989	5,722	181	95	86	404	382	21	3,219	3,031	188
1988	5,588	151	111	40	461	445	16	3,160	2,954	207
1987	5,619	226	138	88	439	399	39	3,048	2,861	187
1986	5,513	179	114	65	465	421	44	2,995	2,787	208
1985	5,070	168	105	63	364	315	49	2,803	2,607	196
1984	4,284	117	78	39	293	267	26	2,384	2,218	166
1983	4,618	108	60	48	335	285	50	2,548	2,323	225
1982	4,478	83	46	37	329	291	37	2,501	2,276	225
1981	4,551	131	68	63	306	282	24	2,474	2,239	235
1980	4,263	146	70	75	263	234	30	2,363	2,134	228
1979	3,608	89	50	39	226	210	16	1,934	1,745	189
1978	3,455	87	47	39	231	198	33	1,893	1,704	188
1977	3,516	75	30	46	220	206	14	1,874	1,654	220
1976	3,623	68	38	30	262	242	20	1,934	1,768	165
1975	3,741	85	47	39	235	218	17	2,062	1,858	204
1974	3,620	85	37	48	225	207	18	2,040	1,780	260
1973	3,171	68	41	27	171	165	6	1,884	1,712	172
1972	3,257	61	43	18	241	227	14	1,879	1,705	173
WHITE ALONE OR IN COMBINATION										
2016	58,973	3,695	2,119	1,576	3,046	2,746	300	25,148	23,034	2,114
2015	59,162	3436	1890	1546	3133	2762	371	25,493	23,271	2223
2014	59,281	3,575	1,942	1,634	3,125	2,791	334	25,391	23,054	2,337
2013	60,066	3,650	1,896	1,754	3,166	2,813	353	25,776	23,510	2,266
2012	60,618	3601	2058	1543	3177	2799	378	25,613	23,244	2369
2011	61,979	3,833	2,132	1,702	3,393	2,988	405	25,989	23,474	2,516
2010	61,498	3,880	2,130	1,749	3,188	2,848	339	25,844	23,469	2,375
2009	60,778	3,582	1,931	1,651	3,271	2,974	298	25,629	23,238	2,391
2008	60,309	3,642	1,927	1,715	3,247	2,863	385	25,498	22,849	2,649
2007	59,896	3,689	1,959	1,730	3,339	2,946	393	25,321	22,689	2,632
2006	59,391	3,765	1,895	1,871	3,213	2,820	393	25,424	22,809	2,615
2005	60,035	3,642	1,819	1,823	3,179	2,715	463	25,682	22,794	2,888
2004	59,427	3,682	1,762	1,920	3,169	2,670	498	25,691	22,682	3,009
2003	59,184	4,039	1,989	2,050	3,002	2,477	525	25,581	22,686	2,895
BLACK ALONE OR IN COMBINATION										
2016	13,507	792	561	231	797	749	48	5,749	5,332	417
2015	13,248	820	594	226	710	680	29	5,883	5,598	285
2014	13,387	840	624	216	830	739	91	5,720	5,409	312
2013	13,517	852	560	291	855	804	51	5,637	5,378	259
2012	13,534	834	613	221	799	744	55	5,603	5,299	305
2011	13,288	904	649	255	696	628	68	5,524	5,253	271
2010	13,105	798	589	210	809	743	66	5,402	5,069	333
2009	12,825	894	687	206	674	632	42	5,295	4,942	353
2008	12,542	776	589	187	668	609	59	5,593	5,225	368
2007	12,401	788	546	242	673	617	57	5,395	5,030	365
2006	12,261	801	568	234	678	607	71	5,365	5,002	363
2005	12,118	763	563	200	593	531	62	5,504	5,122	382
2004	12,303	864	622	242	676	606	70	5,540	5,251	289
2003	12,144	787	526	262	637	559	78	5,604	5,276	327
ASIAN ALONE OR IN COMBINATION										
2016	5,669	402	170	232	266	233	34	2,207	1,990	217
2015	5,417	334	125	209	256	211	44	2,047	1,830	217
2014	5,353	320	122	198	255	214	41	2,078	1,857	221
2013	5,399	367	157	210	240	214	26	2,026	1,780	246
2012	5,154	268	118	150	270	232	38	1,939	1,733	206
2011	4,571	273	139	134	257	235	22	1,860	1,686	173
2010	4,591	297	132	165	230	212	18	1,876	1,696	180
2009	4,117	316	140	175	195	170	25	1,571	1,410	160
2008	4,122	267	143	123	188	156	32	1,570	1,351	219
2007	4,025	219	94	125	179	151	28	1,664	1,513	151
2006	3,849	189	78	111	203	181	22	1,497	1,331	166
2005	3,964	220	94	126	159	118	41	1,495	1,362	133
2004	3,943	208	82	127	191	169	21	1,497	1,350	148
2003	3,817	164	73	90	148	111	38	1,507	1,346	161

Note: Data shown for 1955 to 1966 for the Black population are for Black and Other races.
NA = Not available.
[1]Prior to 1994, total enrolled does not include the 35 and over population.
[r] = Revised, controlled to 1990 census based population estimates; previous 1993 data controlled to 1980 census based population estimates.

Table A-9. School Enrollment of the Population 3 Years Old and Over, by Level and Control of School, Selected Race, and Hispanic Origin, October 1955–2016—*Continued*

(Numbers in thousands; civilian noninstitutionalized population.)

Year, race, and Hispanic origin	High school			College			
	Total	Public	Private	Total	Public	Private	Full-time
1992	1,494	1,435	59	813	710	104	487
1991	1,357	1,299	61	721	607	115	481
1990	1,437	1,374	64	617	515	100	380
1989	1,278	1,231	48	642	557	82	416
1988	1,163	1,113	49	654	592	60	414
1987	1,239	1,160	80	668	551	115	414
1986	1,197	1,116	81	677	540	137	418
1985	1,156	1,090	167	579	464	116	381
1984	966	909	57	524	433	91	356
1983	1,104	1,027	77	523	441	82	335
1982	1,072	995	77	493	398	96	312
1981	1,130	1,056	74	510	398	112	343
1980	1,048	NA	NA	443	NA	NA	294
1979	920	875	45	440	365	75	314
1978	868	825	43	377	315	62	231
1977	928	836	92	418	357	60	287
1976	932	867	65	427	354	73	297
1975	948	886	61	411	358	53	287
1974	916	858	59	354	297	57	247
1973	758	707	51	290	247	43	201
1972	834	784	50	242	213	29	178
WHITE ALONE OR IN COMBINATION							
2016	12,728	11,627	1,102	14,355	11,223	3,132	10,731
2015	12,805	11,813	992	14,295	11,365	2930	10,581
2014	12,879	11,824	1,055	14,310	11,503	2,807	10,778
2013	12,732	11,803	929	14,743	11,768	2,975	10,647
2012	13,110	12,010	1101	15,117	11,919	3198	11,038
2011	12,979	11,952	1,027	15,785	12,449	3,336	11,476
2010	13,001	11,924	1,077	15,586	12,460	3,127	11,062
2009	12,905	11,877	1,029	15,391	12,236	3,155	11,150
2008	13,184	12,050	1,133	14,738	11,692	3,046	10,511
2007	13,433	12,302	1,131	14,114	11,058	3,056	9,912
2006	13,425	12,115	1,309	13,564	10,569	2,995	9,433
2005	13,741	12,516	1,225	13,791	10,561	3,230	9,618
2004	13,218	12,047	1,170	13,668	10,711	2,957	9,468
2003	13,398	12,267	1,131	13,164	10,366	2,798	9,048
BLACK ALONE OR IN COMBINATION							
2016	3,090	2,959	131	3,079	2,435	644	2,219
2015	2,850	2,730	120	2,985	2,364	621	2,163
2014	2,898	2,730	168	3,099	2,405	694	2,185
2013	3,055	2,921	134	3,118	2,542	577	2,297
2012	2,962	2,816	146	3,335	2,752	583	2,373
2011	2,847	2,752	95	3,317	2,676	641	2,401
2010	2,846	2,724	122	3,250	2,641	610	2,354
2009	2,932	2,836	97	3,030	2,434	596	2,178
2008	2,886	2,769	118	2,619	2,065	554	1,779
2007	2,915	2,792	122	2,630	2,059	571	1,774
2006	2,971	2,798	174	2,444	1,907	537	1,702
2005	2,870	2,729	141	2,387	1,866	521	1,585
2004	2,811	2,726	85	2,412	1,922	490	1,591
2003	2,889	2,800	89	2,227	1,846	381	1,482
ASIAN ALONE OR IN COMBINATION							
2016	1,014	922	92	1,780	1,324	455	1,512
2015	960	879	81	1,821	1,385	436	1,501
2014	988	893	96	1,712	1,337	375	1,392
2013	1,000	909	91	1,766	1,295	471	1,412
2012	1,060	949	111	1,617	1,201	415	1,300
2011	825	757	68	1,356	1,053	302	1,063
2010	722	668	54	1,467	1,089	378	1,205
2009	701	636	65	1,334	1,033	301	1,061
2008	758	690	68	1,340	1,009	331	1,009
2007	760	718	42	1,204	917	287	988
2006	806	743	63	1,154	918	235	900
2005	792	726	67	1,297	993	305	1,036
2004	786	743	43	1,260	980	281	936
2003	736	674	62	1,262	925	337	965

Note: Data shown for 1955 to 1966 for the Black population are for Black and Other races.
NA = Not available.
[1]Prior to 1994, total enrolled does not include the 35 and over population.
r = Revised, controlled to 1990 census based population estimates; previous 1993 data controlled to 1980 census based population estimates.

Table A-10. Percentage of the Population 3 Years Old and Over Enrolled in School, by Age, Sex, Race, and Hispanic Origin, October 1947–2016

(Percent; civilian noninstitutionalized population.)

Year, sex, race, and Hispanic origin	Total enrolled 3 to 34 years old	Total enrolled 3 years old and over	Age											
			3 and 4	5 and 6	7 to 9	10 to 13	14 and 15	16 and 17	18 and 19	20 and 21	22 to 24	25 to 29	30 to 34	35 and over
ALL RACES														
Both Sexes														
2016..............	55.2	25.1	53.8	93.3	97.8	98.5	98.0	93.0	69.5	55.5	28.8	13.2	6.4	1.5
2015..............	55.2	25.3	52.7	94.2	97.3	98.0	98.0	93.7	68.5	53.3	28.8	13.2	6.6	1.6
2014..............	55.2	25.6	54.5	93.4	97.7	97.5	97.8	92.9	68.4	51.4	29.6	13.1	6.4	1.8
2013..............	55.8	25.9	54.9	93.8	97.9	98.2	98.4	93.7	67.1	52.8	29.7	13.3	6.7	1.8
2012..............	56.6	26.4	53.5	93.2	98.0	98.0	98.2	95.8	69.0	54.0	30.7	14.0	7.5	1.9
2011..............	56.8	26.9	52.4	95.1	98.0	98.5	98.6	95.7	71.1	52.7	31.1	14.8	7.7	2.0
2010..............	56.5	26.9	53.2	94.5	97.7	98.2	98.1	96.1	69.2	52.4	28.9	14.6	8.3	2.1
2009..............	56.5	26.7	52.4	94.1	97.7	98.5	98.0	94.6	68.9	51.7	30.4	13.5	8.1	2.1
2008..............	56.2	26.6	52.8	93.8	98.3	98.9	98.6	95.2	66.0	50.1	28.2	13.2	7.3	2.0
2007..............	56.1	26.6	54.5	94.7	98.1	98.6	98.7	94.3	66.8	48.4	27.3	12.4	7.2	1.9
2006..............	56.2	26.7	55.7	94.6	98.2	98.3	98.3	94.5	65.5	47.5	26.7	11.7	7.2	1.9
2005..............	56.5	27.1	53.6	95.4	98.6	98.6	98.0	95.1	67.6	48.7	27.3	11.9	6.9	2.0
2004..............	56.2	27.2	54.0	95.4	98.1	98.6	98.5	94.5	64.4	48.9	26.3	13.0	6.6	2.0
2003..............	56.2	27.2	55.1	94.5	98.1	98.4	97.5	94.9	64.5	48.3	27.8	11.8	6.8	1.9
2002..............	56.1	27.3	54.5	95.2	98.0	98.5	98.4	94.3	63.3	47.8	25.6	12.1	6.6	2.1
2001..............	55.7	27.2	52.2	95.3	98.2	98.4	98.1	93.4	61.0	45.5	25.1	11.7	6.8	2.0
2000..............	55.9	27.5	52.1	95.6	98.1	98.3	98.7	92.8	61.2	44.1	24.6	11.4	6.7	1.9
1999..............	56.0	27.7	54.2	96.0	98.5	98.8	98.2	93.6	60.6	45.3	24.5	11.1	6.2	2.1
1998..............	55.8	27.9	52.1	95.6	98.8	99.0	98.4	93.9	62.2	44.8	24.9	11.9	6.6	2.1
1997..............	55.6	28.3	52.6	96.6	98.8	99.3	98.9	94.3	61.5	45.9	26.4	11.8	5.7	2.3
1996..............	54.1	27.8	48.3	94.0	97.2	98.1	98.0	92.8	61.5	44.4	24.8	11.9	6.1	2.3
1995..............	53.7	27.8	48.7	96.0	98.7	99.1	98.9	93.6	59.4	44.9	23.2	11.6	6.0	2.2
1994..............	53.3	27.9	47.3	96.7	99.3	99.4	98.8	94.4	60.2	44.9	24.1	10.8	6.7	2.3
1993ʳ..............	51.9	NA	40.1	95.3	99.5	99.5	98.9	93.9	61.4	42.6	23.5	10.2	5.9	NA
1993..............	51.8	26.9	40.4	95.4	99.5	99.5	98.9	94.0	61.6	42.7	23.6	10.2	5.9	2.2
1992..............	51.4	26.9	39.7	95.5	99.4	99.4	99.1	94.1	61.4	44.0	23.7	9.8	6.1	2.1
1991..............	50.7	26.9	40.5	95.4	99.6	99.7	98.8	93.3	59.6	42.0	22.2	10.2	6.2	2.2
1990..............	50.2	26.8	44.4	96.5	99.7	99.6	99.0	92.5	57.3	39.7	21.0	9.7	5.8	2.1
1989..............	49.1	26.4	39.1	95.2	99.2	99.4	98.8	92.7	56.0	38.5	19.9	9.3	5.7	2.0
1988..............	48.7	26.5	38.2	96.0	99.6	99.7	98.9	91.6	55.7	39.1	18.3	8.3	5.9	2.1
1987..............	48.6	26.6	38.3	95.1	99.6	99.5	98.6	91.7	55.6	38.7	17.5	9.0	5.9	1.8
1986..............	48.2	26.6	39.0	95.3	99.3	99.1	97.6	92.3	54.6	33.0	17.9	8.8	6.0	1.8
1985..............	48.3	26.8	38.9	96.1	99.1	99.3	98.1	91.7	51.6	35.3	16.9	9.2	6.1	1.7
1984..............	47.9	26.6	36.3	94.5	99.0	99.4	97.8	91.5	50.1	33.9	17.3	9.1	6.3	1.5
1983..............	48.4	27.1	37.6	95.4	98.9	99.4	98.3	91.7	50.4	32.5	16.6	9.6	6.4	1.7
1982..............	48.6	27.4	36.4	95.0	99.2	99.1	98.5	90.6	47.8	34.0	16.8	9.6	6.3	1.6
1981..............	48.9	27.9	36.0	94.0	99.2	99.3	98.0	90.6	49.0	31.6	16.5	9.0	6.9	1.7
1980..............	49.7	28.2	36.7	95.7	99.1	99.4	98.2	89.0	46.4	31.0	16.3	9.3	6.5	1.6
1979..............	50.3	28.7	35.1	95.8	99.2	99.1	98.1	89.2	45.0	30.2	15.8	9.6	6.4	1.7
1978..............	51.2	29.3	34.2	95.3	99.3	99.0	98.4	89.1	45.4	29.5	16.3	9.4	6.4	1.6
1977..............	52.5	NA	32.0	95.8	99.5	99.4	98.5	88.9	46.2	31.8	16.5	10.8	6.9	NA
1976..............	53.1	31.7	31.3	95.5	99.2	99.2	98.2	89.1	46.2	32.0	17.1	10.0	6.3	3.9
1975..............	53.7	NA	31.5	94.7	99.3	99.3	98.2	89.0	46.9	31.2	16.2	10.1	6.6	NA
1974..............	53.6	NA	28.8	94.2	99.1	99.5	97.9	87.9	43.1	30.2	15.1	9.6	5.7	NA
1973..............	53.5	NA	24.2	92.5	99.1	99.2	97.5	88.3	42.9	30.1	14.5	8.5	4.5	NA
1972..............	54.9	NA	24.4	91.9	99.0	99.3	97.6	88.9	46.3	31.4	14.8	8.6	4.6	NA
1971..............	56.2	NA	21.2	91.6	99.1	99.2	98.6	90.2	49.2	32.2	15.4	8.0	4.9	NA
1970..............	56.4	NA	20.5	89.5	99.2	99.2	98.1	90.0	47.7	31.9	14.9	7.5	4.2	NA
1969..............	57.0	NA	16.1	88.4	99.3	99.1	98.1	89.7	50.2	34.1	15.4	7.9	4.8	NA
1968..............	56.7	NA	15.7	87.6	99.1	99.1	98.0	90.2	50.4	31.2	13.8	7.0	3.9	NA
1967..............	56.6	NA	14.2	87.4	99.4	99.1	98.2	88.8	47.6	33.3	13.6	6.6	4.0	NA
1966..............	56.1	NA	12.5	85.1	99.3	99.3	98.6	88.5	47.2	29.9	13.2	6.5	2.7	NA
1965..............	55.5	NA	10.6	84.4	99.3	99.4	98.9	87.4	46.3	27.6	13.2	6.1	3.2	NA
1964..............	54.5	NA	9.5	83.3	99.0	99.0	98.6	87.7	41.6	26.3	9.9	5.2	2.6	NA
1963..............	58.5	NA	NA	82.7	99.4	99.3	98.4	87.1	40.9	25.0	11.4	4.9	2.5	NA
1962..............	57.8	NA	NA	82.2	99.2	99.3	98.0	84.3	41.8	23.0	10.3	5.0	2.6	NA
1961..............	56.8	NA	NA	81.7	99.4	99.3	97.6	83.6	38.0	21.5	8.4	4.4	2.0	NA
1960..............	56.4	NA	NA	80.7	99.6	99.5	97.8	82.6	38.4	19.4	8.7	4.9	2.4	NA
1959..............	55.5	NA	NA	80.0	99.4	99.4	97.5	82.9	36.8	18.8	8.6	5.1	2.2	NA
1958..............	54.8	NA	NA	80.4	99.5	99.5	96.9	80.6	37.6	------13.4------		5.7	2.2	NA
1957..............	53.6	NA	NA	78.6	99.5	99.5	97.1	80.5	34.9	------14.0------		5.5	1.8	NA
1956..............	52.3	NA	NA	77.6	99.4	99.2	96.9	78.4	35.4	------12.8------		5.1	1.9	NA
1955..............	50.8	NA	NA	78.1	99.2	99.2	95.9	77.4	31.5	------11.1------		4.2	1.6	NA

Note: Data shown for 1947 to 1966 for the Black population are for Black and other races. Data for 1947 to 1963 exclude kindergarten. Nursery school was first collected in 1964.

NA = Not available.

ʳ = Revised, controlled to 1990 census based population estimates; previous 1993 data controlled to 1980 census based population estimates.

Table A-10. Percentage of the Population 3 Years Old and Over Enrolled in School, by Age, Sex, Race, and Hispanic Origin, October 1947–2016—*Continued*

(Percent; civilian noninstitutionalized population.)

Year, sex, race, and Hispanic origin	Total enrolled 3 to 34 years old	Total enrolled 3 years old and over	3 and 4	5 and 6	7 to 9	10 to 13	14 and 15	16 and 17	18 and 19	20 and 21	22 to 24	25 to 29	30 to 34	35 and over
1954	50.0	NA	NA	77.3	99.2	99.5	95.8	78.0	32.4	------11.2------		4.1	1.5	NA
1953	48.8	NA	NA	55.7	99.4	99.4	96.5	74.7	31.2	------11.1------		2.9	1.7	NA
1952	46.8	NA	NA	54.7	98.7	98.9	96.2	73.4	28.7	------9.5------		2.6	1.1	NA
1951	45.4	NA	NA	54.5	99.0	99.2	94.8	75.1	26.3	------8.3------		2.5	NA	NA
1950	44.2	NA	NA	58.2	98.9	98.6	94.7	71.3	29.4	------9.0------		3.0	NA	NA
1949	43.9	NA	NA	59.3	98.5	98.7	93.5	69.5	25.3	------9.2------		3.8	1.1	NA
1948	43.1	NA	NA	56.0	98.3	98.0	92.7	71.2	26.9	------9.7------		2.6	0.9	NA
1947	42.3	NA	NA	58.0	98.4	98.6	91.6	67.6	24.3	------10.2------		3.0	1.0	NA
Male														
2016	54.8	25.6	54.1	92.7	97.5	98.3	98.7	92.7	68.2	51.4	27.6	11.8	5.5	1.2
2015	54.9	25.7	53.6	93.5	97.5	98.3	97.9	93.1	65.7	50.2	27.5	11.7	5.5	1.2
2014	54.8	25.9	53.5	94.0	97.5	96.9	97.5	92.1	64.9	49.1	28.1	12.2	5.3	1.4
2013	55.2	26.2	53.2	93.8	97.9	98.1	98.2	93.3	65.1	48.5	27.6	12.2	5.3	1.4
2012	55.9	26.6	52.7	93.2	97.7	98.2	98.3	95.7	65.8	49.5	29.4	11.9	5.8	1.3
2011	56.2	27.2	52.8	95.1	98.1	98.6	98.4	95.4	68.8	49.2	30.3	12.9	6.4	1.5
2010	55.9	27.1	53.0	93.7	97.6	97.9	98.0	94.9	66.9	49.2	27.0	13.5	6.7	1.6
2009	55.7	26.9	51.6	93.9	97.6	98.6	97.6	94.5	65.0	48.7	29.0	11.7	6.9	1.5
2008	55.6	26.9	52.3	93.8	98.0	98.7	99.0	94.9	64.0	47.4	26.3	12.1	6.3	1.4
2007	55.4	26.9	54.4	94.0	98.1	98.4	98.4	94.4	66.3	43.7	25.4	10.2	6.4	1.5
2006	55.5	27.0	56.0	94.4	98.1	98.2	98.2	94.1	63.6	44.0	25.0	10.4	5.9	1.5
2005	55.8	27.4	52.8	94.8	98.2	98.4	97.5	95.1	66.5	45.3	25.2	9.6	5.9	1.5
2004	55.0	27.6	54.7	95.5	97.8	98.5	98.7	94.9	60.3	46.6	24.1	11.5	5.6	1.6
2003	55.9	27.8	55.9	94.7	97.9	98.3	97.5	95.0	62.4	43.4	26.1	10.8	6.3	1.5
2002	55.8	27.9	54.6	95.3	98.1	98.3	98.4	94.0	61.8	44.8	23.8	10.7	5.5	1.7
2001	55.4	27.8	51.6	95.2	98.5	98.1	98.1	93.0	58.9	44.0	23.8	10.3	5.7	1.5
2000	55.8	28.0	50.8	95.1	98.0	98.3	98.7	92.7	58.3	41.0	23.9	10.0	5.6	1.5
1999	56.6	28.6	53.3	95.9	98.3	98.7	98.0	93.7	60.3	44.7	23.6	10.7	5.8	1.6
1998	55.9	28.6	53.3	95.2	98.7	99.0	98.3	93.5	60.1	42.7	24.6	10.9	5.5	1.6
1997	55.8	28.8	51.9	96.7	98.6	99.4	99.1	94.2	60.6	44.4	25.4	11.7	4.7	1.6
1996	54.4	28.5	46.9	93.8	97.2	98.0	98.5	93.2	60.8	43.9	25.2	11.4	4.9	1.8
1995	54.3	28.7	49.4	95.3	98.9	99.1	99.0	94.5	59.5	44.7	22.8	11.0	5.4	1.8
1994	53.7	28.7	47.6	97.0	99.2	99.4	98.8	94.3	60.4	42.7	24.2	10.5	5.9	1.7
1993ʳ	52.6	NA	41.1	95.5	99.5	99.6	99.0	94.9	61.1	42.3	25.3	9.6	5.2	NA
1993	52.6	27.9	41.5	95.5	99.5	99.6	99.0	95.0	61.6	42.6	25.5	9.6	5.2	1.6
1992	51.9	27.7	40.3	95.7	99.5	99.5	99.2	95.4	61.6	41.7	23.8	9.1	5.2	1.5
1991	51.5	27.9	39.9	95.0	99.7	99.8	99.1	93.7	59.8	41.8	24.0	10.6	5.6	1.6
1990	50.9	27.7	43.9	96.5	99.7	99.6	99.1	92.7	58.2	40.3	22.3	9.2	4.8	1.5
1989	49.7	27.3	38.8	95.1	99.3	99.2	99.2	93.2	56.6	37.3	20.4	9.3	5.0	1.4
1988	49.6	27.6	38.3	95.9	99.6	99.7	98.9	92.1	56.2	39.0	20.5	8.1	5.5	1.5
1987	49.9	27.9	40.0	95.7	99.7	99.7	98.7	92.3	57.9	41.2	18.7	9.1	5.0	1.3
1986	49.3	27.8	38.8	96.0	99.4	98.9	97.6	92.3	57.1	33.4	19.0	9.4	5.6	1.3
1985	49.2	27.9	36.8	95.3	99.1	99.2	98.3	92.4	52.2	36.5	18.8	9.4	5.4	1.3
1984	49.1	28.0	35.9	94.0	98.8	99.3	97.5	91.8	52.4	36.2	20.1	9.6	5.8	1.1
1983	49.7	28.6	38.1	95.1	98.8	99.3	98.4	91.8	50.4	35.2	19.4	10.7	5.8	1.2
1982	49.7	28.8	36.4	94.7	99.2	99.0	98.7	91.3	48.9	35.2	18.5	10.1	5.6	1.2
1981	50.2	29.3	36.8	94.2	98.9	99.2	98.2	90.7	50.5	32.1	19.2	9.6	6.2	1.2
1980	50.9	29.6	37.8	95.0	99.0	99.4	98.7	89.1	47.0	32.6	17.8	9.8	5.9	1.2
1979	51.8	30.2	34.6	96.3	99.0	98.9	98.3	90.8	46.6	31.6	17.6	10.4	6.0	1.3
1978	52.9	31.0	34.0	95.1	99.1	98.8	98.4	89.5	47.8	31.7	19.1	10.9	6.5	1.3
1977	54.3	NA	32.1	94.7	99.5	99.2	98.7	90.0	48.4	34.6	19.7	12.6	7.1	NA
1976	55.1	33.6	30.9	95.6	98.9	99.1	98.6	90.5	48.2	33.6	20.7	13.0	6.8	3.6
1975	56.0	NA	30.6	94.3	99.2	98.9	98.4	90.7	49.9	35.3	20.0	13.1	7.7	NA
1974	56.0	NA	28.1	94.4	99.1	99.3	98.0	88.6	45.8	34.8	19.4	12.7	6.7	NA
1973	56.1	NA	24.5	92.2	99.0	99.2	97.9	89.4	47.9	34.4	19.1	11.8	5.6	NA
1972	57.8	NA	24.4	91.7	98.9	99.3	97.7	90.2	51.2	37.3	21.3	12.1	5.8	NA
1971	59.3	NA	20.0	90.9	99.0	98.8	98.7	91.7	55.4	38.9	23.3	11.9	6.3	NA
1970	59.7	NA	21.2	88.9	99.3	98.8	98.2	91.3	54.4	42.7	21.2	11.0	5.3	NA
1969	60.5	NA	15.5	87.7	99.0	98.9	98.1	91.6	59.4	46.5	22.9	11.4	5.9	NA
1968	60.4	NA	15.4	87.3	98.9	98.9	98.2	91.7	60.4	45.0	20.5	10.8	5.0	NA
1967	60.0	NA	14.2	86.6	99.4	98.9	98.3	91.0	56.3	44.3	21.0	9.9	5.4	NA
1966	59.7	NA	12.3	84.5	99.2	99.1	98.7	89.9	57.8	41.4	21.3	9.6	3.8	NA
1965	58.8	NA	10.2	84.4	99.3	99.0	98.0	88.0	55.6	37.6	21.1	9.4	4.5	NA
1964	57.5	NA	8.9	83.4	98.7	98.9	99.0	89.8	50.9	34.4	16.1	8.1	3.6	NA
1963	62.3	NA	NA	82.7	99.2	99.0	98.7	89.4	51.0	33.6	19.5	7.8	3.7	NA
1962	61.7	NA	NA	82.6	99.1	99.2	98.7	87.1	51.2	31.3	17.7	8.5	3.9	NA

Note: Data shown for 1947 to 1966 for the Black population are for Black and other races. Data for 1947 to 1963 exclude kindergarten. Nursery school was first collected in 1964.
NA = Not available.
ʳ = Revised, controlled to 1990 census based population estimates; previous 1993 data controlled to 1980 census based population estimates.

Table A-10. Percentage of the Population 3 Years Old and Over Enrolled in School, by Age, Sex, Race, and Hispanic Origin, October 1947–2016—*Continued*

(Percent; civilian noninstitutionalized population.)

Year, sex, race, and Hispanic origin	Total enrolled 3 to 34 years old	Total enrolled 3 years old and over	3 and 4	5 and 6	7 to 9	10 to 13	14 and 15	16 and 17	18 and 19	20 and 21	22 to 24	25 to 29	30 to 34	35 and over
1961	60.4	NA	NA	82.0	99.5	99.2	98.1	84.7	48.6	29.5	13.9	7.1	2.9	NA
1960	60.0	NA	NA	80.8	99.6	99.4	97.9	84.5	47.8	27.1	15.0	8.4	3.7	NA
1959	59.1	NA	NA	79.5	99.2	99.4	97.8	84.8	45.6	28.3	13.7	8.9	3.3	NA
1958	58.7	NA	NA	80.6	99.6	99.4	96.9	83.8	47.5	------21.0------		9.5	2.9	NA
1957	57.5	NA	NA	78.3	99.4	99.6	98.0	82.8	43.3	------21.3------		9.5	2.6	NA
1956	56.3	NA	NA	77.1	99.2	99.1	97.1	79.9	45.1	------20.6------		8.9	2.7	NA
1955	54.9	NA	NA	78.1	99.1	99.4	95.7	81.1	42.5	------18.1------		7.0	2.1	NA
1954	54.0	NA	NA	76.3	99.0	99.4	96.1	80.9	40.6	------19.1------		6.7	1.9	NA
1953	50.2	NA	NA	55.0	99.3	99.1	96.4	76.5	37.7	------18.5------		5.5	2.0	NA
1952	49.4	NA	NA	54.8	98.6	98.9	96.2	73.9	37.2	------16.9------		4.7	1.7	NA
1951	56.8	NA	NA	55.1	99.1	99.1	95.1	74.3	32.4	------14.3------		4.2	NA	NA
1950	54.8	NA	NA	56.8	98.8	98.7	95.2	72.8	35.7	------14.3------		5.9	NA	NA
1949	45.8	NA	NA	60.1	98.5	98.6	93.9	70.8	31.6	------15.4------		6.8	1.9	NA
1948	44.8	NA	NA	55.1	99.5	98.1	92.0	72.1	34.3	------16.5------		5.1	1.5	NA
1947	44.3	NA	NA	57.4	98.5	98.7	90.3	67.6	31.4	------17.0------		5.8	1.7	NA
Female														
2016	55.6	24.7	53.5	93.8	98.1	98.7	97.3	93.3	70.7	59.7	30.0	14.7	7.2	1.7
2015	55.6	24.9	51.8	94.9	97.2	97.6	98.1	94.4	71.4	56.5	30.1	14.6	7.7	1.9
2014	55.7	25.2	55.5	92.8	97.9	98.1	98.2	93.8	72.1	53.9	31.0	14.0	7.4	2.1
2013	56.4	25.7	56.7	93.7	97.9	98.2	98.6	94.1	69.2	57.3	31.7	14.4	8.1	2.3
2012	57.4	26.2	54.4	93.3	98.4	97.8	98.2	95.9	72.3	58.3	32.1	16.0	9.2	2.3
2011	57.4	26.5	52.1	95.2	97.9	98.4	98.9	96.0	73.5	56.4	32.0	16.8	8.9	2.4
2010	57.4	26.7	53.4	95.3	98.0	98.6	98.3	97.3	71.5	56.0	30.8	15.8	9.9	2.6
2009	57.3	26.6	53.2	94.4	97.9	98.4	98.5	94.7	72.9	54.9	31.8	15.3	9.3	2.7
2008	56.7	26.3	53.3	93.7	98.7	99.2	98.2	95.4	68.1	53.0	30.1	14.3	8.3	2.5
2007	56.8	26.3	54.7	95.3	98.1	98.7	99.0	94.1	67.2	53.3	29.2	14.7	7.9	2.4
2006	56.6	26.3	55.4	94.8	98.3	98.4	98.4	95.0	67.4	51.1	28.5	13.0	8.5	2.3
2005	57.2	26.8	54.4	96.1	99.0	98.9	98.4	95.1	68.8	52.3	29.2	14.2	7.9	2.4
2004	56.5	26.8	53.2	95.3	98.5	98.7	98.3	94.1	68.5	51.3	28.4	14.4	7.7	2.5
2003	56.4	26.6	54.1	94.4	98.3	98.6	97.5	94.8	66.6	52.9	29.5	12.8	7.3	2.2
2002	56.4	26.8	54.4	95.1	97.9	98.7	98.5	94.7	65.0	50.9	27.3	13.5	7.7	2.5
2001	55.9	26.7	52.9	95.4	97.8	98.8	98.2	93.8	63.2	46.9	26.5	13.0	7.9	2.5
2000	56.0	26.9	53.4	96.1	98.2	98.3	98.6	92.9	64.2	47.3	25.3	12.7	7.7	2.3
1999	55.5	27.0	55.2	96.1	98.7	98.9	98.3	93.5	60.9	45.8	25.4	11.4	6.6	2.4
1998	55.6	27.3	50.9	95.9	98.8	99.1	98.5	94.3	64.4	47.2	25.2	12.9	7.7	2.6
1997	55.4	27.6	53.2	96.4	99.1	99.3	98.7	94.4	62.4	47.4	27.4	11.9	6.6	2.9
1996	53.8	27.1	49.8	94.3	97.3	98.2	97.5	92.4	62.2	44.8	24.5	12.5	7.3	2.8
1995	53.2	27.0	48.1	96.8	98.5	99.1	98.8	92.6	59.2	45.1	23.6	12.2	6.5	2.7
1994	52.9	27.2	46.9	96.4	99.5	99.4	98.7	94.4	60.0	47.0	23.9	11.1	7.5	2.8
1993ʳ	51.1	NA	39.0	95.2	99.4	99.5	98.7	92.8	61.7	42.8	21.7	10.8	6.6	NA
1993	51.0	25.9	39.3	95.2	99.4	99.5	98.7	92.9	61.7	42.9	21.8	10.8	6.6	2.6
1992	51.0	26.1	39.1	95.2	99.2	99.2	99.1	92.7	61.2	46.1	23.6	10.5	7.0	2.6
1991	49.9	26.0	41.1	95.8	99.5	99.6	98.4	92.8	59.4	42.2	20.4	9.8	6.8	2.8
1990	49.5	25.9	44.9	96.4	99.6	99.7	98.9	92.4	56.3	39.2	19.9	10.2	6.9	2.7
1989	48.4	25.5	39.5	95.2	99.2	99.6	98.4	92.2	55.5	39.7	19.5	9.3	6.4	2.5
1988	47.7	25.5	38.1	96.0	99.6	99.7	98.8	91.2	55.2	39.1	16.2	8.6	6.4	2.6
1987	47.4	25.3	36.6	94.5	99.5	99.2	98.4	91.1	53.4	36.4	16.5	9.0	6.7	2.2
1986	47.1	25.4	39.0	94.6	99.2	99.3	97.5	92.3	52.1	32.7	16.8	8.2	6.4	2.2
1985	47.4	25.7	41.2	97.0	99.2	99.4	97.9	90.9	51.0	34.1	15.1	9.1	6.8	2.1
1984	46.6	25.3	36.7	95.1	99.3	99.4	98.2	91.2	48.0	31.7	14.6	8.6	6.7	1.9
1983	47.0	25.7	36.9	95.8	99.0	99.5	98.2	91.6	50.3	29.9	13.9	8.5	7.0	2.0
1982	47.5	26.1	36.4	95.3	99.2	99.3	98.3	89.9	46.8	32.9	15.1	9.0	6.9	1.9
1981	47.7	26.6	35.2	93.8	99.5	99.4	97.7	90.5	47.5	31.2	13.9	8.4	7.5	2.0
1980	48.5	26.9	35.5	96.4	99.2	99.4	97.7	88.8	45.8	29.5	14.9	8.8	7.0	1.9
1979	49.0	27.3	35.6	95.2	99.4	99.4	97.9	87.6	43.4	28.9	14.1	8.8	6.7	2.0
1978	49.5	27.8	34.5	95.5	99.5	99.2	98.4	88.8	43.0	27.5	13.6	7.9	6.2	2.0
1977	50.7	NA	32.0	96.9	99.5	99.6	98.3	87.7	44.0	29.1	13.6	9.1	6.7	NA
1976	51.0	29.8	31.6	95.5	99.4	99.3	97.8	87.7	44.4	30.6	13.8	7.3	5.2	4.2
1975	51.5	NA	32.4	95.2	99.5	99.6	98.0	87.2	44.2	27.4	12.6	7.2	5.6	NA
1974	51.3	NA	29.5	93.9	99.2	99.7	97.9	87.1	40.7	26.0	11.1	6.7	4.6	NA
1973	50.9	NA	23.8	92.9	99.3	99.2	97.1	87.2	38.2	26.3	10.2	5.4	3.6	NA
1972	52.0	NA	24.4	92.2	99.1	99.4	97.5	87.6	41.8	26.3	8.9	5.3	3.6	NA
1971	53.2	NA	22.4	92.3	99.2	99.5	98.5	88.7	43.4	26.8	8.4	4.4	3.6	NA
1970	53.2	NA	19.8	90.2	99.3	99.5	98.0	88.6	41.6	23.6	9.4	4.3	3.1	NA
1969	53.6	NA	16.8	89.1	99.6	99.4	98.2	87.7	41.8	25.3	9.1	4.6	3.8	NA
1968	53.2	NA	16.1	88.0	99.3	99.3	97.8	88.7	41.3	21.5	8.3	3.4	2.9	NA

Note: Data shown for 1947 to 1966 for the Black population are for Black and other races. Data for 1947 to 1963 exclude kindergarten. Nursery school was first collected in 1964.

NA = Not available.

ʳ = Revised, controlled to 1990 census based population estimates; previous 1993 data controlled to 1980 census based population estimates.

Table A-10. Percentage of the Population 3 Years Old and Over Enrolled in School, by Age, Sex, Race, and Hispanic Origin, October 1947–2016—*Continued*

(Percent; civilian noninstitutionalized population.)

Year, sex, race, and Hispanic origin	Total enrolled 3 to 34 years old	Total enrolled 3 years old and over	Age 3 and 4	5 and 6	7 to 9	10 to 13	14 and 15	16 and 17	18 and 19	20 and 21	22 to 24	25 to 29	30 to 34	35 and over
1967	53.3	NA	14.1	88.2	99.5	99.3	98.2	86.7	40.3	24.9	7.4	3.6	2.8	NA
1966	52.7	NA	12.7	85.7	99.4	99.5	98.4	87.1	37.7	20.9	6.6	3.6	1.7	NA
1965	52.3	NA	10.9	84.4	99.3	99.5	98.7	86.9	37.7	19.5	6.5	3.1	2.1	NA
1964	51.5	NA	10.2	83.2	99.3	99.2	98.2	85.6	33.7	19.5	4.4	2.6	1.6	NA
1963	54.9	NA	NA	82.6	99.6	99.6	98.0	84.8	32.3	17.8	4.4	2.4	1.5	NA
1962	54.0	NA	NA	81.7	99.3	99.4	97.3	81.5	33.7	16.1	3.9	1.8	1.4	NA
1961	53.4	NA	NA	81.4	99.3	99.4	97.2	82.4	28.6	14.9	3.7	1.9	1.2	NA
1960	52.8	NA	NA	80.6	99.6	99.5	97.6	80.6	30.0	13.1	3.4	1.8	1.2	NA
1959	52.0	NA	NA	80.5	99.6	99.5	97.1	81.0	29.2	11.1	4.4	1.7	1.3	NA
1958	51.0	NA	NA	80.2	99.4	99.5	96.9	77.3	29.4	------7.3------		2.2	1.5	NA
1957	50.0	NA	NA	79.0	99.6	99.5	96.2	78.1	28.1	------8.2------		1.9	1.1	NA
1956	48.7	NA	NA	78.2	99.5	99.4	96.8	76.9	27.4	------6.8------		1.7	1.2	NA
1955	47.0	NA	NA	78.1	99.3	99.0	96.1	73.8	22.5	------6.1------		1.8	1.1	NA
1954	46.3	NA	NA	78.3	99.5	99.7	95.4	75.2	25.4	------6.0------		1.7	1.1	NA
1953	43.0	NA	NA	56.6	99.5	99.7	96.6	72.9	25.9	------6.4------		0.5	1.4	NA
1952	41.9	NA	NA	54.6	98.9	98.9	96.6	72.9	22.1	------4.9------		0.6	0.7	NA
1951	49.1	NA	NA	54.0	98.9	99.3	94.5	75.4	21.3	------4.3------		1.0	NA	NA
1950	48.4	NA	NA	59.5	99.0	98.4	94.3	69.8	24.3	------4.6------		0.4	NA	NA
1949	39.2	NA	NA	58.4	98.5	98.8	93.1	68.2	19.9	------3.7------		1.1	0.4	NA
1948	38.4	NA	NA	56.8	98.2	97.8	93.5	70.3	20.3	------3.4------		0.4	0.4	NA
1947	38.0	NA	NA	58.7	98.4	98.5	92.8	67.5	18.5	------3.9------		0.4	0.3	NA

WHITE ALONE

Both Sexes

Year, sex, race, and Hispanic origin	Total enrolled 3 to 34 years old	Total enrolled 3 years old and over	Age 3 and 4	5 and 6	7 to 9	10 to 13	14 and 15	16 and 17	18 and 19	20 and 21	22 to 24	25 to 29	30 to 34	35 and over
2016	54.7	23.6	53.7	93.8	98.0	98.4	98.4	92.4	69.4	56.2	27.5	12.7	5.9	1.3
2015	54.6	23.8	52.2	94.1	97.5	97.8	97.8	93.8	68.6	53.8	27.7	12.8	6.1	1.4
2014	54.6	24.0	53.6	93.6	97.6	97.5	97.7	93.5	68.3	53.0	28.6	12.4	5.9	1.5
2013	55.0	24.3	54.0	93.9	98.1	98.2	98.4	93.6	67.6	52.2	28.9	12.2	6.4	1.6
2012	55.8	24.8	54.0	93.3	98.2	97.7	98.3	96.0	68.7	54.4	29.5	13.4	6.5	1.6
2011	56.2	25.5	51.4	95.7	98.2	98.6	98.6	95.5	70.3	53.8	30.9	14.0	6.9	1.7
2010	55.8	25.4	52.1	94.2	97.7	98.1	98.0	96.2	70.0	51.6	28.1	13.9	7.8	1.9
2009	55.7	25.3	51.1	94.0	97.9	98.7	98.1	94.4	68.7	52.6	28.9	12.9	7.3	1.9
2008	55.5	25.3	52.0	94.0	98.2	98.9	98.7	95.4	67.1	51.2	28.1	12.3	6.2	1.8
2007	55.5	25.3	54.1	94.8	98.0	98.7	98.7	94.6	67.1	50.1	26.3	11.5	6.6	1.8
2006	55.5	25.3	55.6	95.0	98.4	98.4	98.4	95.0	64.9	48.2	25.5	11.3	6.7	1.7
2005	55.9	25.7	54.2	95.3	98.6	98.7	98.3	95.4	68.0	49.3	26.0	11.3	6.2	1.8
2004	55.5	25.7	52.8	95.5	98.1	98.3	98.5	94.2	64.9	49.3	25.3	12.2	6.4	1.8
2003[1]	55.4	25.8	55.3	94.7	98.0	98.4	97.3	95.0	64.4	48.2	26.7	11.0	6.2	1.8
2002	55.4	26.0	53.9	95.1	98.0	98.5	98.5	94.6	63.8	47.4	24.6	11.4	5.9	2.0
2001	54.8	25.8	51.7	94.8	98.3	98.7	98.2	93.5	60.4	45.9	23.3	10.7	6.0	1.8
2000	55.1	26.1	50.2	95.3	98.2	98.3	98.4	92.8	61.3	44.9	23.7	10.4	6.0	1.8
1999	55.2	26.4	53.7	95.6	98.5	98.8	98.2	93.5	60.5	45.6	24.1	10.5	5.8	1.9
1998	55.0	26.6	50.7	95.4	98.8	99.1	98.6	94.1	61.9	44.8	24.1	11.0	6.2	2.0
1997	54.8	26.8	50.9	96.8	98.8	99.3	98.4	94.5	61.5	46.4	25.8	11.3	5.4	2.2
1996	53.4	26.4	47.9	94.8	97.1	98.2	98.0	92.8	62.5	44.9	24.6	11.3	5.7	2.2
1995	53.2	26.6	49.6	96.2	98.9	99.0	98.8	93.7	59.3	46.2	23.1	11.5	5.5	2.1
1994	52.6	26.6	47.0	96.6	99.2	99.3	98.7	94.3	60.9	46.2	23.5	10.4	6.6	2.2
1993[r]	51.2	NA	40.4	95.4	99.5	99.5	98.9	93.9	61.4	43.7	23.1	9.7	5.9	NA
1993	51.1	25.7	40.8	95.5	99.5	99.5	98.9	94.1	61.7	44.0	23.3	9.8	5.9	2.1
1992	50.7	NA	40.1	95.4	99.4	99.3	99.2	94.2	61.7	45.3	23.3	9.6	6.0	NA
1991	50.0	NA	41.3	95.3	99.6	99.7	98.7	93.3	59.7	43.2	21.7	9.9	6.0	NA
1990	49.5	NA	44.9	96.5	99.7	99.6	99.1	92.5	57.1	41.0	20.2	9.9	5.9	NA
1989	48.4	NA	39.4	95.2	99.2	99.4	98.8	92.3	56.4	39.5	20.0	9.4	5.6	NA
1988	48.0	NA	38.9	96.1	99.7	99.7	98.8	91.4	55.8	40.2	18.6	8.2	5.9	NA
1987	47.7	NA	38.2	94.8	99.6	99.4	98.5	91.8	55.3	39.6	17.3	8.7	5.7	NA
1986	47.7	NA	39.1	95.3	99.3	97.8	99.0	92.2	55.3	33.9	17.7	9.1	6.2	NA
1985	47.8	NA	38.6	96.4	99.3	99.3	98.1	91.6	52.4	36.1	17.0	9.2	5.9	NA
1984	47.3	NA	36.0	94.6	99.0	99.4	97.8	91.2	51.1	34.3	17.2	9.1	6.2	NA
1983	47.7	NA	37.6	95.7	98.9	99.3	98.4	91.4	50.9	33.4	16.4	9.4	6.1	NA
1982	47.9	NA	35.9	94.9	99.2	99.2	98.6	90.3	47.3	35.1	16.2	9.6	6.2	NA
1981	48.2	NA	35.6	93.9	99.3	99.3	98.1	90.4	48.5	32.6	16.2	8.5	6.1	NA
1980	48.9	NA	36.3	95.8	99.0	99.4	98.3	88.6	46.3	31.9	16.4	9.2	6.3	NA
1979	49.6	NA	33.9	95.8	99.2	99.2	98.2	89.0	44.5	31.1	15.7	9.7	6.3	NA
1978	50.3	NA	32.7	95.4	99.3	99.0	98.4	88.7	44.9	29.6	16.1	9.4	6.2	NA

Note: Data shown for 1947 to 1966 for the Black population are for Black and other races. Data for 1947 to 1963 exclude kindergarten. Nursery school was first collected in 1964.

NA = Not available.

[1]Starting in 2003, respondents could identify more than one race. Except as noted, the race data in this table from 2003 onward represent those respondents who indicated only one race category.

r = Revised, controlled to 1990 census based population estimates; previous 1993 data controlled to 1980 census based population estimates.

Table A-10. Percentage of the Population 3 Years Old and Over Enrolled in School, by Age, Sex, Race, and Hispanic Origin, October 1947–2016—*Continued*

(Percent; civilian noninstitutionalized population.)

Year, sex, race, and Hispanic origin	Total enrolled 3 to 34 years old	Total enrolled 3 years old and over	Age											
			3 and 4	5 and 6	7 to 9	10 to 13	14 and 15	16 and 17	18 and 19	20 and 21	22 to 24	25 to 29	30 to 34	35 and over
1977	51.6	NA	31.1	95.6	99.5	99.4	98.5	88.5	45.5	31.8	16.3	10.6	6.6	NA
1976	52.3	NA	30.4	95.8	99.1	99.2	98.1	89.1	45.4	32.5	17.0	10.0	5.7	NA
1975	53.1	NA	30.9	94.8	99.4	99.3	98.3	89.3	46.5	31.8	16.8	10.0	6.6	NA
1974	53.0	NA	28.6	94.4	99.2	99.4	98.1	87.9	42.6	30.7	15.2	9.6	5.5	NA
1973	53.1	NA	23.2	93.0	99.1	99.3	97.6	88.3	43.4	31.3	14.6	8.7	4.5	NA
1972	54.4	NA	23.8	92.2	99.1	99.3	97.6	88.9	46.6	32.6	15.0	8.7	4.5	NA
1971	55.8	NA	20.9	91.9	99.1	99.2	98.7	90.5	49.4	32.7	15.9	8.1	4.8	NA
1970	56.2	NA	19.9	90.3	99.3	99.1	98.2	90.6	48.7	33.1	15.7	7.7	4.2	NA
1969	56.8	NA	15.1	89.2	99.4	99.2	98.2	90.2	50.9	35.4	16.2	8.2	5.0	NA
1968	56.6	NA	15.0	88.5	99.1	99.1	98.1	90.8	50.9	32.8	14.5	7.4	3.9	NA
1967	56.5	NA	13.3	88.2	99.5	99.2	98.5	89.5	48.4	34.7	14.1	6.7	4.1	NA
1966	56.1	NA	12.3	85.7	99.3	99.3	98.8	89.0	48.2	32.2	14.0	6.9	2.7	NA
1965	55.5	NA	10.3	85.3	99.4	99.4	99.0	87.8	47.1	29.4	14.1	6.5	3.2	NA
1964	54.4	NA	9.3	84.0	99.0	99.0	98.8	88.3	42.3	27.8	10.6	5.4	2.6	NA
1963	58.4	NA	NA	83.7	99.5	99.3	98.5	87.8	41.0	26.2	12.2	5.2	2.6	NA
1962	57.9	NA	NA	83.2	99.3	99.4	98.2	85.9	43.0	24.1	10.9	5.2	2.7	NA
1961	56.9	NA	NA	82.2	99.6	99.5	98.0	84.5	39.0	22.4	9.0	4.6	2.1	NA
1960	56.4	NA	NA	82.0	99.7	99.5	98.1	83.3	38.9	20.6	9.3	5.2	2.6	NA
1959	55.5	NA	NA	81.0	99.5	99.5	97.9	83.8	37.3	19.9	8.9	5.4	2.3	NA
1958	54.9	NA	NA	81.4	----99.6----		----90.0----		38.1	----14.1----		5.9	2.3	NA
1957	53.7	NA	NA	79.3	----99.7----		----90.1----		34.6	----14.7----		5.7	1.9	NA
1956	52.5	NA	NA	78.4	----99.4----		----89.2----		35.9	----13.4----		5.4	2.1	NA
1955	50.8	NA	NA	79.2	----99.3----		----87.5----		32.1	----11.6----		4.2	1.6	NA
1954	50.2	NA	NA	78.6	----99.6----		----88.3----		33.6	----12.0----		4.0	1.5	NA
1953	46.6	NA	NA	67.1	----99.7----		----86.4----		31.7	----11.9----		3.1	1.8	NA
1952	45.4	NA	NA	54.8	----99.1----		----86.1----		28.9	----9.8----		2.7	1.2	NA
1951	52.8	NA	NA	54.5	----99.3----		----86.3----		26.9	----8.8----		2.8	NA	NA
1950	51.6	NA	NA	----------89.0----------			----84.4----		30.5	----9.5----		3.0	NA	NA
1949	42.6	NA	NA	----------88.8----------			----83.0----		25.9	----9.6----		4.0	1.2	NA
1948	41.8	NA	NA	----------87.8----------			----83.9----		27.3	----10.0----		2.8	0.9	NA
1947	41.2	NA	NA	----------88.7----------			----80.2----		24.8	----10.5----		3.0	1.1	NA
Male														
2016	54.0	23.9	55.6	93.8	97.9	98.2	98.8	92.2	67.9	51.2	25.8	10.9	4.9	1.0
2015	53.9	24.0	53.0	93.5	97.5	98.0	97.5	92.9	65.1	50.8	25.7	11.5	5.3	1.1
2014	53.9	24.2	52.3	93.7	97.2	96.8	97.3	92.5	64.8	50.4	26.8	11.6	5.0	1.2
2013	54.1	24.4	52.2	93.7	98.0	98.2	98.3	92.8	66.0	47.2	26.1	11.1	5.3	1.2
2012	54.9	24.9	52.9	93.1	98.0	98.0	98.3	95.8	66.0	48.5	28.3	11.6	5.5	1.2
2011	55.5	25.8	52.0	95.5	98.4	98.6	98.5	95.5	67.6	50.3	30.1	12.3	6.0	1.4
2010	54.9	25.5	51.8	93.2	97.3	97.6	98.0	95.0	67.5	48.2	25.9	13.0	6.5	1.5
2009	54.8	25.4	50.0	93.7	97.7	98.9	97.9	94.1	64.6	48.8	28.3	11.2	6.4	1.4
2008	54.8	25.5	51.8	93.8	97.9	98.7	99.0	94.9	64.3	48.4	26.5	11.5	5.5	1.3
2007	54.4	25.4	52.9	94.1	97.9	98.6	98.3	94.5	66.4	44.6	24.2	9.6	5.7	1.4
2006	54.6	25.5	55.9	94.8	98.3	98.4	98.2	94.7	62.7	43.8	24.0	10.2	5.5	1.3
2005	54.9	25.9	53.1	94.6	98.2	98.6	98.3	95.1	66.1	45.1	24.4	8.9	5.5	1.4
2004	54.8	26.0	53.4	95.8	97.9	98.2	98.8	94.5	60.0	46.0	23.3	11.2	5.5	1.4
2003[1]	54.8	26.2	56.2	95.0	97.6	98.2	97.2	95.3	61.7	43.2	25.6	9.9	5.6	1.4
2002	54.9	26.5	54.0	95.0	98.0	98.3	98.4	94.2	62.5	44.1	23.5	10.2	5.0	1.6
2001	54.3	26.2	51.8	94.7	98.6	98.4	98.0	92.8	58.2	43.6	21.5	9.8	5.0	1.4
2000	54.8	26.5	49.1	94.8	97.8	98.3	98.4	93.1	58.5	41.8	23.2	9.5	4.9	1.4
1999	55.5	27.1	53.5	95.4	98.5	98.6	98.2	93.1	60.0	44.5	23.7	10.3	5.4	1.5
1998	54.9	27.1	52.4	94.9	98.8	99.1	98.7	93.3	59.7	42.1	24.5	10.2	5.2	1.6
1997	54.7	27.3	50.4	97.4	98.5	99.4	99.1	94.2	60.0	45.0	24.9	10.8	4.3	1.5
1996	53.3	27.0	46.5	94.6	96.9	98.0	98.6	93.0	60.9	43.6	25.4	10.6	4.3	1.7
1995	53.5	27.3	49.6	95.5	99.0	99.0	98.8	94.2	59.4	46.3	22.7	11.3	5.0	1.7
1994	52.7	27.2	46.2	97.0	99.1	99.3	98.7	94.3	61.3	43.4	23.6	9.9	5.8	1.7
1993[r]	51.6	NA	41.2	95.1	99.5	99.5	98.9	95.0	60.1	44.4	24.5	9.1	5.2	NA
1993	51.6	26.4	41.7	95.2	99.5	99.5	99.0	95.1	60.6	44.8	24.9	9.1	5.2	1.5
1992	50.8	NA	39.8	95.1	99.5	99.5	99.0	99.5	60.7	44.0	23.6	8.6	5.2	NA
1991	50.4	NA	40.6	94.9	99.7	99.8	98.9	94.2	58.4	42.4	23.3	10.0	5.4	NA
1990	50.0	NA	44.9	96.7	99.7	99.6	99.2	92.3	57.3	41.2	21.8	9.4	4.9	NA
1989	48.9	NA	38.7	95.4	99.3	99.2	99.3	92.6	57.3	39.3	20.4	9.3	5.0	NA
1988	48.7	NA	39.0	96.1	99.7	99.6	98.9	91.6	56.5	40.9	20.7	7.8	5.4	NA
1987	48.8	NA	39.8	95.2	99.6	99.7	98.8	92.5	57.3	42.1	18.4	8.6	5.0	NA
1986	48.6	NA	39.3	95.6	99.4	99.0	99.1	92.1	57.5	34.2	19.2	9.6	5.7	NA

Note: Data shown for 1947 to 1966 for the Black population are for Black and other races. Data for 1947 to 1963 exclude kindergarten. Nursery school was first collected in 1964.
NA = Not available.
[1]Starting in 2003, respondents could identify more than one race. Except as noted, the race data in this table from 2003 onward represent those respondents who indicated only one race category.
r = Revised, controlled to 1990 census based population estimates; previous 1993 data controlled to 1980 census based population estimates.

Table A-10. Percentage of the Population 3 Years Old and Over Enrolled in School, by Age, Sex, Race, and Hispanic Origin, October 1947–2016—*Continued*

(Percent; civilian noninstitutionalized population.)

Year, sex, race, and Hispanic origin	Total enrolled 3 to 34 years old	Total enrolled 3 years old and over	Age: 3 and 4	5 and 6	7 to 9	10 to 13	14 and 15	16 and 17	18 and 19	20 and 21	22 to 24	25 to 29	30 to 34	35 and over
1985	48.5	NA	37.3	95.7	99.3	99.2	98.2	92.5	51.9	37.2	19.0	9.5	5.4	NA
1984	48.3	NA	35.8	94.1	98.7	99.3	97.6	91.5	52.6	36.3	20.2	9.2	5.4	NA
1983	48.9	NA	38.2	95.1	98.8	99.3	98.3	91.6	50.7	36.6	19.2	10.4	5.6	NA
1982	48.9	NA	36.3	94.8	99.2	99.1	98.8	91.0	48.5	36.5	18.0	10.2	5.4	NA
1981	49.2	NA	36.8	94.3	99.1	99.2	98.3	90.5	49.2	33.3	19.1	9.1	5.5	NA
1980	50.0	NA	38.0	95.2	98.8	99.4	98.7	88.8	47.5	33.7	18.2	9.6	5.6	NA
1979	50.7	NA	33.5	96.3	99.0	99.0	98.3	90.3	46.1	32.2	17.6	10.5	5.9	NA
1978	51.9	NA	33.1	95.3	99.2	98.9	98.3	88.9	47.2	32.0	19.2	10.9	6.4	NA
1977	53.3	NA	31.7	94.3	99.6	99.3	98.7	89.5	47.7	34.7	19.4	12.6	6.8	NA
1976	54.2	NA	29.9	95.8	98.8	99.1	98.5	90.6	46.9	34.2	20.4	12.9	6.5	NA
1975	55.4	NA	30.8	94.3	99.2	99.0	98.5	91.0	49.6	36.3	20.5	13.1	7.5	NA
1974	55.2	NA	27.7	94.8	99.1	99.2	98.2	88.2	45.5	35.0	19.2	12.8	6.4	NA
1973	55.6	NA	23.5	92.7	99.0	99.3	98.0	89.4	48.4	35.7	19.6	12.1	5.4	NA
1972	57.3	NA	23.4	91.7	98.9	99.2	97.7	90.4	51.5	38.4	21.6	12.5	5.8	NA
1971	59.0	NA	20.1	91.2	99.0	98.9	98.9	92.0	55.9	39.7	24.6	12.1	6.2	NA
1970	59.6	NA	20.7	89.7	99.3	98.8	98.3	92.2	56.0	45.0	22.6	11.2	5.4	NA
1969	60.5	NA	14.5	88.5	99.1	98.9	98.2	92.2	60.9	48.9	24.2	12.2	6.2	NA
1968	60.4	NA	14.8	87.9	99.0	99.0	98.2	92.1	61.5	47.8	21.9	11.4	5.0	NA
1967	60.0	NA	13.6	87.5	99.5	99.0	98.5	91.4	57.2	46.9	22.0	10.5	5.4	NA
1966	59.8	NA	12.2	85.0	99.2	99.1	98.8	90.3	59.0	44.9	23.0	10.3	3.8	NA
1965	59.0	NA	10.4	84.8	99.3	99.3	99.1	88.6	56.6	39.9	23.3	10.0	4.5	NA
1964	57.6	NA	8.8	84.0	98.8	98.9	99.0	90.4	52.4	36.6	17.7	8.3	3.6	NA
1963	62.3	NA	NA	84.1	99.4	99.0	98.8	89.8	51.6	35.2	21.1	8.2	3.8	NA
1962	61.9	NA	NA	83.9	99.1	99.3	98.7	88.5	52.7	33.7	18.8	8.9	4.2	NA
1961	60.4	NA	NA	82.6	99.7	99.4	98.3	85.5	49.6	31.1	15.0	7.5	3.1	NA
1960	60.3	NA	NA	82.3	99.7	99.5	98.1	85.2	49.5	29.2	16.3	8.9	4.0	NA
1959	59.2	NA	NA	80.1	99.3	99.4	98.1	85.9	47.1	30.8	14.1	9.5	3.4	NA
1958	58.8	NA	NA	81.5	------99.6------		------91.1------		48.1	------22.3------		9.9	3.0	NA
1957	57.7	NA	NA	79.1	------99.7------		------91.9------		44.0	------22.9------		9.9	2.7	NA
1956	56.5	NA	NA	78.2	------99.4------		------90.1------		46.4	------21.8------		9.3	2.9	NA
1955	54.9	NA	NA	79.0	------99.4------		------89.1------		43.9	------19.3------		7.1	2.2	NA
1954	54.3	NA	NA	78.0	------99.4------		------89.6------		43.3	------20.5------		6.5	1.9	NA
1953	50.5	NA	NA	56.8	------99.4------		------87.9------		38.1	------20.3------		5.7	2.2	NA
1952	49.4	NA	NA	55.2	------99.1------		------87.0------		38.3	------17.8------		5.0	1.6	NA
1951	56.8	NA	NA	55.4	------99.3------		------86.6------		33.8	------14.9------		4.2	NA	NA
1950	54.7	NA	NA	-----------88.6-----------			------85.0------		37.3	------14.6------		5.9	NA	NA
1949	45.9	NA	NA	-----------89.1-----------			------84.1------		32.1	------15.7------		7.1	2.0	NA
1948	45.3	NA	NA	-----------87.6-----------			------84.4------		35.9	------17.2------		5.3	1.5	NA
1947	44.4	NA	NA	-----------88.6-----------			------79.6------		32.6	------17.4------		5.9	1.8	NA
Female														
2016	55.3	23.4	51.7	93.7	98.0	98.7	97.9	92.7	71.0	61.3	29.3	14.6	7.0	1.5
2015	55.2	23.5	51.4	94.9	97.4	97.5	98.0	94.8	72.2	56.9	29.8	14.1	6.8	1.7
2014	55.4	23.8	55.0	93.6	97.9	98.3	98.1	94.5	72.0	56.1	30.3	13.2	6.9	1.8
2013	55.9	24.3	55.8	94.0	98.1	98.2	98.5	94.5	69.2	57.5	31.6	13.3	7.5	2.0
2012	56.7	24.7	55.1	93.6	98.3	97.4	98.4	96.1	71.6	60.1	30.7	15.2	7.5	2.0
2011	56.9	25.2	50.8	96.0	97.9	98.5	98.8	95.6	73.2	57.5	31.7	15.8	7.9	2.0
2010	56.8	25.3	52.5	95.1	98.0	98.5	98.1	97.4	72.5	55.5	30.2	14.9	9.0	2.2
2009	56.7	25.2	52.2	94.3	98.1	98.4	98.4	94.8	73.0	56.6	29.5	14.7	8.3	2.4
2008	56.3	25.1	52.3	94.2	98.6	99.1	98.5	95.9	69.9	54.3	29.8	13.1	6.9	2.3
2007	56.7	25.2	55.4	95.6	98.1	98.8	99.2	94.7	67.8	55.7	28.5	13.6	7.6	2.2
2006	56.3	25.1	55.3	95.2	98.5	98.5	98.7	95.3	67.2	52.6	27.1	12.4	8.0	2.1
2005	57.0	25.6	55.4	96.0	98.9	98.8	98.4	95.7	70.1	53.8	27.7	13.8	7.0	2.2
2004	56.2	25.4	52.0	95.2	98.4	98.5	98.2	93.9	69.8	52.6	27.4	13.3	7.2	2.2
2003¹	55.9	25.4	54.3	94.4	98.4	98.6	97.4	94.8	67.3	53.1	27.8	12.1	6.8	2.1
2002	55.8	25.6	53.7	95.1	98.0	98.7	98.5	95.0	65.1	50.8	25.7	12.7	6.9	2.3
2001	55.3	25.4	51.5	94.9	97.9	98.9	98.4	94.3	62.7	48.2	25.1	11.7	7.0	2.2
2000	55.4	25.7	51.4	95.8	98.5	98.4	98.3	92.5	64.2	48.2	24.2	11.3	7.1	2.2
1999	55.0	25.8	53.9	95.8	98.7	98.9	98.3	93.8	60.9	46.8	24.5	10.7	6.3	2.3
1998	55.0	26.0	49.0	96.0	98.8	99.2	98.5	94.9	64.2	47.9	23.8	11.9	7.2	2.4
1997	54.9	26.3	51.3	96.2	99.1	99.2	98.6	94.8	63.1	47.9	26.7	11.8	6.4	2.8
1996	53.5	25.9	49.3	95.0	97.4	98.3	97.3	92.7	64.1	46.1	23.6	12.0	7.1	2.6
1995	52.9	25.8	49.6	96.9	98.8	99.1	98.8	93.3	59.2	46.0	23.6	11.7	6.0	2.6
1994	52.6	26.0	47.9	96.1	99.4	99.4	98.8	94.4	60.5	49.0	23.5	11.0	7.4	2.7
1993ʳ	50.7	NA	39.5	95.7	99.5	99.5	98.9	92.8	62.8	43.0	21.7	10.4	6.5	NA
1993	50.6	24.9	39.9	95.8	99.5	99.5	98.9	93.0	62.9	43.3	21.8	10.4	6.5	2.6

Note: Data shown for 1947 to 1966 for the Black population are for Black and other races. Data for 1947 to 1963 exclude kindergarten. Nursery school was first collected in 1964.

NA = Not available.

¹Starting in 2003, respondents could identify more than one race. Except as noted, the race data in this table from 2003 onward represent those respondents who indicated only one race category.

ʳ = Revised, controlled to 1990 census based population estimates; previous 1993 data controlled to 1980 census based population estimates.

Table A-10. Percentage of the Population 3 Years Old and Over Enrolled in School, by Age, Sex, Race, and Hispanic Origin, October 1947–2016—*Continued*

(Percent; civilian noninstitutionalized population.)

Year, sex, race, and Hispanic origin	Total enrolled 3 to 34 years old	Total enrolled 3 years old and over	Age											
			3 and 4	5 and 6	7 to 9	10 to 13	14 and 15	16 and 17	18 and 19	20 and 21	22 to 24	25 to 29	30 to 34	35 and over
1992	50.5	NA	40.4	95.7	99.2	99.1	99.4	92.8	62.7	46.6	22.9	10.6	6.7	NA
1991	49.5	NA	42.0	95.7	99.5	99.6	98.5	92.5	60.9	43.9	20.2	9.7	6.7	NA
1990	49.0	NA	44.8	96.4	99.7	99.7	98.9	92.8	57.0	40.9	18.7	10.4	6.9	NA
1989	47.8	NA	40.2	94.9	99.2	99.6	98.1	92.1	55.6	39.7	19.6	9.6	6.3	NA
1988	47.2	NA	38.8	96.1	99.6	99.8	98.8	91.1	55.1	39.6	16.5	8.6	6.3	NA
1987	46.7	NA	36.4	94.4	99.5	99.2	98.3	91.0	53.3	37.3	16.2	8.7	6.4	NA
1986	46.8	NA	39.0	94.9	99.1	99.3	98.8	92.2	53.0	33.7	16.2	8.7	6.7	NA
1985	47.0	NA	39.9	97.1	99.3	99.3	97.9	90.8	52.9	35.0	15.0	9.0	6.4	NA
1984	46.3	NA	36.1	95.2	99.3	99.4	98.0	91.0	49.6	32.3	14.2	8.9	6.9	NA
1983	46.6	NA	36.0	96.5	99.0	99.4	98.4	91.2	51.1	30.5	13.6	8.5	6.7	NA
1982	46.9	NA	35.5	95.0	99.2	99.4	98.4	89.6	47.4	33.7	14.5	9.0	6.9	NA
1981	47.1	NA	34.3	93.5	99.5	99.4	97.8	90.4	47.8	31.9	13.4	7.9	6.7	NA
1980	47.9	NA	34.6	96.4	99.2	99.4	97.8	88.4	45.1	30.2	14.8	8.9	7.0	NA
1979	48.4	NA	34.4	95.3	99.5	99.5	98.1	87.7	43.0	30.0	13.9	9.0	6.7	NA
1978	48.7	NA	32.2	95.6	99.5	99.2	98.5	88.4	42.7	27.4	13.0	7.9	6.0	NA
1977	49.9	NA	30.5	96.9	99.5	99.6	98.4	87.4	43.4	29.0	13.3	8.8	6.3	NA
1976	50.4	NA	31.0	95.8	99.5	99.3	97.6	87.7	44.0	30.9	13.7	7.1	4.8	NA
1975	50.9	NA	30.9	95.3	99.5	99.6	98.1	87.5	43.5	27.5	12.2	7.0	5.7	NA
1974	50.9	NA	29.5	94.0	99.3	99.7	97.9	87.6	39.9	26.6	11.4	6.5	4.6	NA
1973	50.5	NA	22.9	93.2	99.3	99.3	97.1	87.3	38.7	27.4	9.9	5.4	3.6	NA
1972	51.5	NA	24.4	92.7	99.2	99.4	97.5	87.3	41.9	27.5	8.9	5.1	3.2	NA
1971	52.6	NA	21.7	92.6	99.3	99.5	98.4	88.9	43.2	27.0	8.1	4.3	3.5	NA
1970	52.9	NA	19.1	90.9	99.3	99.5	98.1	89.0	41.8	24.1	9.7	4.4	3.1	NA
1969	53.2	NA	15.8	89.8	99.6	99.5	98.2	88.2	41.8	25.8	9.4	4.5	3.7	NA
1968	52.9	NA	15.2	89.0	99.3	99.3	98.0	89.4	41.3	22.3	8.2	3.7	2.8	NA
1967	53.0	NA	13.1	89.0	99.6	99.4	98.5	87.4	41.0	25.6	7.5	3.3	2.9	NA
1966	52.5	NA	12.4	86.4	99.5	99.5	98.7	87.6	38.6	22.3	6.6	3.9	1.7	NA
1965	52.2	NA	10.3	85.7	99.4	99.5	98.9	87.0	38.3	20.9	6.3	3.2	2.0	NA
1964	51.3	NA	9.9	83.9	99.2	99.1	98.6	86.1	33.7	20.3	4.5	2.6	1.6	NA
1963	54.7	NA	NA	83.8	99.7	99.5	98.2	85.7	32.1	18.6	4.4	2.4	1.5	NA
1962	54.0	NA	NA	82.4	99.5	99.5	97.6	83.3	34.6	16.3	4.1	1.8	1.4	NA
1961	53.4	NA	NA	81.7	99.5	99.5	97.7	83.5	29.7	15.3	3.8	2.1	1.3	NA
1960	52.7	NA	NA	81.6	99.7	99.6	98.1	81.4	29.7	13.5	3.5	1.8	1.2	NA
1959	52.0	NA	NA	81.9	99.7	99.6	97.7	81.6	28.8	11.1	4.6	1.7	1.3	NA
1958	51.1	NA	NA	81.2	------99.6------		------88.9------		29.9	------7.5------		2.2	1.6	NA
1957	49.8	NA	NA	79.5	------99.7------		------88.2------		27.0	------8.3------		1.7	1.1	NA
1956	48.6	NA	NA	78.6	------99.5------		------88.2------		27.3	------7.0------		1.8	1.3	NA
1955	46.9	NA	NA	79.5	------99.3------		------85.9------		22.4	------6.2------		1.5	1.0	NA
1954	46.4	NA	NA	79.1	------99.8------		------87.0------		25.3	------6.4------		1.7	1.1	NA
1953	42.9	NA	NA	57.4	------99.9------		------84.9------		26.5	------6.5------		0.6	1.5	NA
1952	41.7	NA	NA	54.3	------99.1------		------85.3------		21.1	------4.3------		0.6	0.7	NA
1951	49.0	NA	NA	53.6	------99.4------		------86.0------		21.7	------4.3------		0.9	NA	NA
1950	48.6	NA	NA	----------89.4----------			------83.7------		24.2	------4.8------		0.4	NA	NA
1949	39.4	NA	NA	----------88.6----------			------81.9------		20.5	------3.8------		1.2	0.4	NA
1948	38.4	NA	NA	----------87.9----------			------83.4------		19.7	------3.5------		0.4	0.4	NA
1947	38.1	NA	NA	----------88.9----------			------80.8------		18.3	------4.1------		0.4	0.4	NA
WHITE ALONE NON-HISPANIC														
Both Sexes														
2016	54.1	21.5	55.5	93.9	98.0	98.5	98.7	92.2	70.4	57.3	27.7	13.3	6.6	1.2
2015	54.4	21.8	56.0	94.1	97.5	98.1	98.3	94.4	70.1	55.5	28.9	13.1	6.5	1.3
2014	54.4	21.9	57.6	93.4	97.3	97.5	97.8	93.4	69.3	56.1	29.9	12.9	6.3	1.4
2013	54.7	22.3	57.4	93.6	97.9	98.5	98.4	93.6	69.6	55.2	29.1	12.9	6.5	1.6
2012	55.6	22.7	56.5	93.8	98.1	97.5	98.2	96.4	68.8	55.9	30.2	14.6	6.6	1.6
2011	56.4	23.6	56.2	95.8	98.2	98.5	98.9	95.9	72.1	56.2	32.9	15.2	7.8	1.7
2010	56.1	23.6	56.1	94.2	97.4	98.3	98.0	96.2	71.0	55.5	29.1	14.6	8.5	1.8
2009	56.8	23.9	55.5	94.1	98.4	98.9	98.3	95.0	72.4	56.4	31.1	14.0	8.1	1.9
2008	56.7	23.9	56.0	94.9	98.8	98.9	98.8	95.9	70.0	55.8	30.3	13.3	6.9	1.8
2007	56.6	23.9	56.3	95.0	98.6	98.6	98.8	95.6	69.7	54.5	28.4	12.5	7.4	1.8
2006	56.8	24.0	58.2	95.6	98.5	98.6	98.4	95.9	67.9	52.9	27.4	12.5	7.4	1.7
2005	57.6	24.6	58.5	95.9	99.0	99.0	98.6	96.1	71.6	54.4	27.8	12.5	6.9	1.8
2004	56.9	24.5	56.0	96.2	98.3	98.6	98.5	95.1	68.1	54.0	27.0	13.5	6.7	1.8
2003[1]	57.0	24.7	58.8	95.8	98.2	98.5	97.5	95.6	67.9	51.8	29.4	12.5	6.8	1.8
2002	56.8	24.9	57.8	95.3	98.1	98.6	98.6	95.3	67.1	53.1	27.3	12.2	6.3	1.9
2001	56.2	24.7	55.1	95.3	98.5	98.8	98.2	94.6	64.2	50.8	25.5	11.7	6.4	1.8

Note: Data shown for 1947 to 1966 for the Black population are for Black and other races. Data for 1947 to 1963 exclude kindergarten. Nursery school was first collected in 1964.
NA = Not available.
[1]Starting in 2003, respondents could identify more than one race. Except as noted, the race data in this table from 2003 onward represent those respondents who indicated only one race category.

Table A-10. Percentage of the Population 3 Years Old and Over Enrolled in School, by Age, Sex, Race, and Hispanic Origin, October 1947–2016—*Continued*

(Percent; civilian noninstitutionalized population.)

Year, sex, race, and Hispanic origin	Total enrolled 3 to 34 years old	Total enrolled 3 years old and over	Age											
			3 and 4	5 and 6	7 to 9	10 to 13	14 and 15	16 and 17	18 and 19	20 and 21	22 to 24	25 to 29	30 to 34	35 and over
2000	56.0	25.0	54.6	95.5	98.4	98.5	98.9	94.0	63.9	49.2	24.9	11.1	6.1	1.8
1999	56.2	25.4	58.6	96.0	98.5	98.9	98.4	94.5	64.1	50.0	26.3	10.9	5.9	1.9
1998	55.9	25.6	54.0	96.1	98.8	99.2	98.9	95.1	66.6	49.2	26.1	11.5	6.3	2.0
1997	55.6	25.9	54.9	96.9	98.9	99.2	98.9	95.1	64.1	49.9	27.8	12.2	5.6	2.2
1996	54.0	25.5	50.3	96.1	97.3	98.3	98.2	93.6	65.5	48.9	25.9	11.8	5.8	2.2
1995	53.8	25.9	52.3	96.6	99.0	99.0	98.8	94.4	61.8	49.7	24.4	12.3	5.7	2.1
1994	54.5	25.9	50.1	96.7	99.2	99.3	99.2	95.1	62.6	50.1	24.9	10.8	6.7	2.2
1993	51.4	25.0	43.1	95.7	99.5	99.5	99.1	95.0	63.6	46.1	24.9	10.2	6.0	2.1
Male														
2016	53.8	21.9	56.6	94.2	98.0	98.3	98.8	91.9	69.4	52.8	26.8	11.7	5.5	1.0
2015	54.1	22.1	57.1	93.2	97.8	98.3	98.3	93.8	67.2	53.3	26.9	12.3	5.9	1.0
2014	54.1	22.3	56.5	93.7	96.9	96.8	97.1	92.7	66.0	55.3	28.3	12.1	5.8	1.1
2013	54.1	22.4	55.2	93.7	97.8	98.4	98.4	92.8	68.6	51.0	26.2	11.4	5.6	1.1
2012	55.0	22.9	55.6	93.6	97.7	97.7	97.9	96.0	65.4	49.7	29.6	13.0	6.1	1.2
2011	56.1	23.9	56.4	95.5	98.3	98.5	98.4	95.8	69.9	53.0	33.1	13.2	7.0	1.3
2010	55.5	23.9	55.9	93.3	97.1	97.7	98.0	94.7	67.8	52.1	27.8	13.8	7.2	1.4
2009	56.2	24.2	54.9	93.3	98.2	99.0	97.9	94.7	68.4	53.2	30.8	12.4	7.1	1.4
2008	56.5	24.3	57.2	94.7	98.5	98.7	99.1	95.5	66.8	52.4	29.1	12.6	6.2	1.3
2007	56.0	24.2	53.8	94.0	98.5	98.5	98.3	95.2	69.3	49.9	26.9	10.6	6.7	1.3
2006	56.4	24.4	58.3	95.9	98.5	98.6	97.9	95.5	65.4	49.2	26.2	11.9	6.3	1.3
2005	57.1	24.9	56.8	95.4	98.9	99.1	98.4	95.9	69.8	50.5	26.4	10.2	6.5	1.3
2004	56.7	25.0	57.2	96.2	98.2	98.4	98.7	95.6	63.8	50.6	25.1	12.7	6.2	1.4
2003[1]	57.1	25.4	60.6	96.2	97.7	98.2	97.4	96.1	65.4	47.9	28.9	11.7	6.3	1.4
2002	56.8	25.5	57.8	94.9	98.1	98.5	98.5	95.2	66.3	49.2	27.6	11.1	5.5	1.6
2001	56.0	25.2	54.4	94.8	98.8	98.4	97.8	94.0	62.7	49.1	23.7	10.8	5.3	1.3
2000	55.8	25.5	54.1	94.5	98.1	98.2	98.8	94.7	61.2	45.8	25.0	10.5	4.7	1.4
1999	56.7	26.2	59.2	96.1	98.4	98.7	98.2	94.3	63.7	48.9	26.8	10.7	5.8	1.5
1998	55.7	26.3	54.8	95.5	98.8	99.0	99.0	94.4	65.2	46.4	27.4	10.9	5.3	1.6
1997	55.9	26.5	54.9	97.4	98.8	99.3	99.0	94.5	63.3	48.5	27.5	12.0	4.6	1.5
1996	54.2	26.1	48.0	95.5	97.2	98.1	98.8	93.5	63.7	48.7	27.3	11.4	4.3	1.6
1995	54.2	26.6	51.1	95.9	99.0	99.0	98.9	95.0	61.9	50.0	24.1	12.2	5.0	1.6
1994	53.5	26.6	49.0	97.1	99.2	99.4	99.4	95.4	62.5	47.6	25.5	10.3	6.0	1.6
1993	52.2	25.9	44.1	95.4	99.5	99.6	99.3	96.2	62.5	47.0	26.7	9.9	5.2	1.5
Female														
2016	54.4	21.1	54.3	93.5	97.9	98.8	98.6	92.5	71.6	62.0	28.5	14.9	7.8	1.4
2015	54.6	21.4	54.8	95.1	97.2	97.9	98.4	95.0	73.1	57.7	30.9	14.0	7.1	1.6
2014	54.7	21.6	58.8	93.1	97.7	98.1	98.5	94.1	72.9	57.0	31.4	13.6	6.9	1.7
2013	55.4	22.1	59.7	93.5	98.0	98.5	98.4	94.5	70.8	59.6	31.9	14.3	7.4	2.0
2012	56.2	22.5	57.4	94.0	98.5	97.3	98.4	96.8	72.3	61.7	30.8	16.2	7.1	2.0
2011	56.8	23.3	56.1	96.1	98.1	98.5	99.3	95.9	74.3	59.5	32.7	17.3	8.5	2.0
2010	56.7	23.4	56.3	95.2	97.7	98.9	98.1	97.8	74.3	59.2	30.4	15.4	9.8	2.2
2009	57.4	23.7	56.2	95.0	98.7	98.7	98.7	95.4	76.5	59.8	31.4	15.6	9.0	2.4
2008	57.0	23.5	54.8	95.0	99.1	99.2	98.4	96.3	73.4	59.5	31.5	14.0	7.6	2.2
2007	57.3	23.7	58.9	96.0	98.8	98.7	99.2	96.0	70.1	59.2	29.9	14.4	8.0	2.2
2006	57.1	23.7	58.1	95.3	98.6	98.5	99.0	96.2	70.5	56.5	28.7	13.2	8.5	2.1
2005	58.0	24.3	60.3	96.3	99.0	98.8	98.7	96.3	73.5	58.5	29.1	14.7	7.4	2.2
2004	57.1	24.1	54.7	96.2	98.5	98.7	98.3	94.5	72.5	57.4	28.8	14.4	7.2	2.1
2003[1]	57.0	24.1	56.9	95.3	98.6	98.8	97.6	95.1	70.3	55.6	29.9	13.2	7.3	2.1
2002	56.8	24.3	57.7	95.6	98.0	98.6	98.6	95.5	67.9	57.0	27.0	13.4	7.2	2.2
2001	56.4	24.2	55.9	95.9	98.3	99.1	98.6	95.3	65.8	52.4	27.3	12.5	7.4	2.2
2000	56.1	24.6	55.2	96.4	98.6	98.8	99.0	93.3	66.7	52.7	24.8	11.8	7.4	2.1
1999	55.7	24.7	57.9	96.0	98.5	99.1	98.6	94.8	64.6	51.1	25.7	11.0	6.1	2.3
1998	55.7	25.0	53.1	96.7	98.7	99.3	98.8	95.7	68.0	52.2	24.8	12.1	7.3	2.4
1997	55.2	25.4	55.0	96.4	99.0	99.1	98.8	95.7	64.9	51.3	28.1	12.4	6.6	2.9
1996	53.8	25.0	52.9	96.7	97.3	98.6	97.7	93.7	67.3	49.0	24.5	12.1	7.3	2.6
1995	53.4	25.1	53.5	97.4	98.9	99.0	98.7	93.8	61.8	49.3	24.8	12.3	6.3	2.5
1994	52.9	25.3	51.3	96.3	99.3	99.3	98.9	94.8	62.7	52.4	24.3	11.4	7.3	2.7
1993	50.6	24.3	42.0	96.0	99.5	99.5	98.9	93.7	64.8	45.2	23.1	10.5	6.7	2.6
BLACK ALONE														
Both Sexes														
2016	55.4	29.2	50.8	93.5	97.4	98.6	96.1	94.9	67.2	48.2	28.0	12.7	8.7	2.9
2015	55.3	29.2	52.7	93.7	95.4	98.3	98.7	94.4	64.5	43.7	27.5	13.1	8.2	2.8
2014	56.0	30.2	57.5	94.5	98.8	97.7	98.9	91.8	65.2	41.1	24.5	14.6	9.1	3.8

Note: Data shown for 1947 to 1966 for the Black population are for Black and other races. Data for 1947 to 1963 exclude kindergarten. Nursery school was first collected in 1964.
NA = Not available.
[1]Starting in 2003, respondents could identify more than one race. Except as noted, the race data in this table from 2003 onward represent those respondents who indicated only one race category.

Table A-10. Percentage of the Population 3 Years Old and Over Enrolled in School, by Age, Sex, Race, and Hispanic Origin, October 1947–2016—*Continued*

(Percent; civilian noninstitutionalized population.)

| Year, sex, race, and Hispanic origin | Total enrolled 3 to 34 years old | Total enrolled 3 years old and over | Age | | | | | | | | | | | |
			3 and 4	5 and 6	7 to 9	10 to 13	14 and 15	16 and 17	18 and 19	20 and 21	22 to 24	25 to 29	30 to 34	35 and over
2013	57.2	30.7	57.2	94.4	96.7	97.8	98.7	92.8	64.2	47.9	27.0	16.7	8.6	3.1
2012	58.3	31.4	53.1	91.5	97.2	98.9	97.3	94.2	68.6	49.4	27.9	16.1	12.2	3.2
2011	58.4	32.3	55.2	92.0	97.1	98.5	98.5	95.7	74.1	41.1	31.2	18.1	11.4	3.8
2010	58.4	32.5	56.2	94.3	97.1	98.6	98.5	95.5	62.7	50.2	29.0	16.0	10.9	4.0
2009	58.5	32.4	57.7	93.6	97.4	98.6	97.8	94.1	65.2	44.7	31.9	14.6	11.0	3.7
2008	57.8	31.7	54.6	93.1	98.9	99.0	97.9	94.2	59.2	40.3	24.9	14.7	11.5	2.8
2007	58.4	32.2	58.5	94.0	98.2	97.9	99.0	93.4	61.7	38.7	28.0	15.0	9.4	3.0
2006	58.1	32.3	59.2	92.6	97.1	97.2	97.5	93.3	64.7	39.1	27.2	11.8	8.6	3.1
2005	58.4	32.7	52.2	95.9	98.6	98.6	95.8	93.1	62.8	37.6	28.0	11.7	10.0	3.1
2004	59.0	33.4	59.6	94.1	97.5	99.4	99.0	95.7	59.2	40.0	25.1	14.3	7.2	3.3
2003[1]	59.2	33.4	55.5	94.4	98.3	98.2	97.9	94.3	61.9	41.4	27.4	12.2	8.6	2.8
2002	59.6	34.1	57.5	95.7	98.1	98.1	98.2	93.3	57.7	43.5	23.5	13.6	9.8	3.1
2001	59.5	34.3	58.8	96.0	97.8	97.0	97.6	92.1	59.6	37.2	26.0	12.2	11.5	3.2
2000	59.0	34.0	59.9	96.3	97.5	98.4	99.6	91.4	57.2	36.6	24.2	14.3	9.6	2.6
1999	58.1	33.7	56.3	97.5	98.2	98.7	98.2	93.3	57.4	39.4	21.7	10.4	7.8	2.5
1998	58.9	34.6	58.5	95.3	98.7	98.6	98.9	92.9	60.2	39.2	21.5	13.6	8.5	2.6
1997	58.4	34.6	60.0	95.8	99.2	99.4	99.2	93.4	58.2	35.9	25.4	10.7	6.5	2.8
1996	56.2	33.8	49.9	90.5	97.4	97.4	98.9	92.1	52.8	37.0	21.0	13.7	7.1	3.0
1995	56.1	33.9	47.5	95.5	97.7	99.2	99.0	92.9	57.4	37.4	19.9	10.0	7.8	2.7
1994	56.4	34.4	51.9	97.2	99.7	99.6	99.2	95.4	54.0	34.9	22.6	10.5	7.2	2.9
1993[r]	53.8	NA	39.8	94.5	99.0	99.8	98.5	94.8	57.6	30.1	18.0	10.4	5.5	NA
1993	53.6	32.4	39.8	94.6	99.0	99.8	98.5	94.7	57.7	30.0	18.1	10.4	5.5	2.6
1992	53.0	NA	38.6	95.9	99.4	99.7	99.4	93.0	56.2	33.3	20.3	7.9	5.3	NA
1991	52.5	NA	37.2	95.8	99.6	100.0	99.1	91.7	55.6	30.0	18.2	8.7	6.5	NA
1990	51.9	NA	41.6	96.3	99.9	99.9	99.2	91.7	55.2	28.4	20.0	6.1	4.4	NA
1989	51.3	NA	38.9	94.9	99.0	99.4	99.4	93.7	50.2	30.7	17.2	6.4	4.9	NA
1988	50.6	NA	33.4	95.5	99.7	99.7	98.9	91.5	50.3	28.1	13.2	7.2	5.6	NA
1987	51.7	NA	36.8	95.8	99.7	99.8	98.3	91.5	53.2	28.7	15.0	9.3	6.0	NA
1986	51.6	NA	38.6	95.4	99.8	99.0	98.3	93.9	50.7	25.6	17.1	8.0	6.2	NA
1985	50.9	NA	42.7	95.7	98.4	99.5	97.9	91.7	44.1	27.7	13.7	7.5	5.9	NA
1984	50.1	NA	38.2	94.1	99.5	99.3	97.9	92.4	44.3	27.7	15.7	7.4	5.1	NA
1983	50.8	NA	36.2	94.7	99.1	99.7	97.8	92.6	46.1	23.4	15.6	7.4	6.5	NA
1982	51.6	NA	38.6	95.4	99.2	98.9	98.1	91.6	43.6	24.3	17.0	7.8	7.6	NA
1981	52.5	NA	36.7	94.5	98.8	99.4	97.1	91.3	48.2	23.4	14.7	8.4	7.0	NA
1980	53.9	NA	38.2	95.4	99.4	99.4	97.9	90.6	45.7	23.4	13.6	8.8	6.8	NA
1979	55.0	NA	40.8	96.0	99.4	98.7	97.4	90.8	46.6	23.7	15.0	7.9	6.8	NA
1978	56.3	NA	41.3	93.9	99.5	98.9	98.5	91.2	46.2	25.6	15.0	8.7	7.9	NA
1977	57.7	NA	35.2	96.5	99.3	99.0	98.8	90.8	48.3	29.5	15.2	11.3	9.0	NA
1976	57.9	NA	34.5	94.0	99.3	98.8	99.0	89.0	50.4	28.2	16.4	9.4	8.1	NA
1975	57.7	NA	33.5	94.3	99.3	99.2	97.4	86.9	47.1	27.1	14.2	9.4	7.1	NA
1974	57.3	NA	29.1	92.8	99.2	99.8	97.0	87.1	44.0	23.4	12.1	8.9	6.9	NA
1973	55.8	NA	28.9	89.9	99.2	99.0	96.7	87.7	37.8	20.5	12.4	6.1	5.0	NA
1972	57.8	NA	28.3	90.0	98.7	99.3	97.4	89.5	42.8	22.0	13.1	6.5	5.9	NA
1971	58.6	NA	21.5	89.8	99.0	98.8	98.4	89.2	46.6	27.3	11.4	6.2	5.2	NA
1970	57.4	NA	22.7	84.9	99.3	98.3	97.6	85.7	40.1	22.8	8.0	4.8	3.4	NA
1969	57.8	NA	21.2	84.1	98.8	99.1	97.9	85.8	44.5	23.3	8.6	4.3	3.4	NA
1968	57.4	NA	18.7	82.7	99.2	99.0	97.7	86.4	45.4	18.2	7.9	3.1	3.3	NA
1967	56.8	NA	17.7	82.2	99.1	98.7	86.1	84.1	40.7	21.2	7.2	5.0	2.4	NA
1966	55.5	NA	13.7	80.8	99.2	99.2	97.4	85.2	37.7	11.6	6.1	2.3	2.3	NA
1965	55.6	NA	11.8	79.1	98.9	99.3	98.1	83.9	39.6	12.8	6.2	2.1	2.4	NA
1964	54.5	NA	10.5	80.3	99.0	99.0	96.9	82.4	35.6	14.0	3.8	3.1	2.9	NA
1963	58.8	NA	NA	76.6	98.5	99.5	97.6	82.0	39.8	16.2	5.5	3.3	2.0	NA
1962	57.1	NA	NA	76.0	98.6	98.8	97.1	73.2	33.4	14.9	6.1	3.8	1.5	NA
1961	56.8	NA	NA	79.1	98.0	98.3	95.1	76.8	30.6	15.9	4.3	2.4	1.1	NA
1960	55.9	NA	NA	73.3	99.3	99.0	95.9	76.9	34.6	11.9	4.4	2.9	1.0	NA
1959	55.1	NA	NA	74.3	98.9	99.1	93.9	76.3	33.6	11.6	6.3	2.8	1.3	NA
1958	54.0	NA	NA	73.9	------98.8------		------82.8-----		34.3	-------8.7------		3.9	1.3	NA
1957	53.5	NA	NA	74.3	------98.2-----		------84.8-----		36.7	-------8.8-----		4.6	1.2	NA
1956	51.5	NA	NA	72.8	------98.4-----		------81.2-----		31.8	-------8.7-----		3.1	0.7	NA
1955	50.7	NA	NA	71.1	------98.2-----		------82.8-----		27.6	-------7.2-----		4.9	1.8	NA
1954	48.6	NA	NA	68.8	------98.0-----		------78.8-----		24.0	-------5.8-----		4.8	1.4	NA
1953	45.5	NA	NA	46.3	------97.3-----		------82.3-----		27.6	-------5.4-----		1.7	0.8	NA
1952	46.4	NA	NA	54.0	------96.4-----		------77.3-----		--------------6.3--------------------					NA
1951	53.4	NA	NA	54.9	------97.3-----		------77.1-----		20.8	-------6.2-----		2.7	NA	NA
1950	51.2	NA	NA	--------------86.8-----------			------75.5-----		23.3	-------6.3-----		3.0	NA	NA

Note: Data shown for 1947 to 1966 for the Black population are for Black and other races. Data for 1947 to 1963 exclude kindergarten. Nursery school was first collected in 1964.

NA = Not available.

[1] Starting in 2003, respondents could identify more than one race. Except as noted, the race data in this table from 2003 onward represent those respondents who indicated only one race category.

[r] = Revised, controlled to 1990 census based population estimates; previous 1993 data controlled to 1980 census based population estimates.

Table A-10. Percentage of the Population 3 Years Old and Over Enrolled in School, by Age, Sex, Race, and Hispanic Origin, October 1947–2016—*Continued*

(Percent; civilian noninstitutionalized population.)

Year, sex, race, and Hispanic origin	Total enrolled 3 to 34 years old	Total enrolled 3 years old and over	3 and 4	5 and 6	7 to 9	10 to 13	14 and 15	16 and 17	18 and 19	20 and 21	22 to 24	25 to 29	30 to 34	35 and over
1949	40.9	NA	NA		83.7		69.5		20.0	6.2		1.8	0.5	NA
1948	39.2	NA	NA		80.1		66.8		24.6	6.3		1.5	0.6	NA
1947	41.0	NA	NA		84.8		71.9		20.2	6.9		2.5	0.5	NA
Male														
2016	56.0	30.5	46.6	91.2	96.1	98.6	98.9	95.7	66.6	46.2	26.8	12.9	7.4	2.3
2015	55.6	30.3	51.0	92.1	95.8	99.2	99.5	94.7	63.3	39.6	30.4	10.1	4.5	1.8
2014	56.2	31.2	58.0	96.1	98.6	97.3	98.7	92.6	60.3	41.8	22.2	11.6	7.0	2.7
2013	56.8	31.5	54.1	94.4	96.5	97.8	98.8	94.3	59.9	43.2	25.2	13.1	5.2	2.4
2012	58.1	31.9	51.1	92.1	97.0	98.9	98.5	95.5	60.5	48.8	26.8	11.5	7.3	1.9
2011	57.9	33.0	53.4	92.4	97.5	98.5	97.8	94.0	72.6	38.0	29.8	14.2	7.5	2.7
2010	57.9	33.1	55.5	93.7	97.5	98.4	97.7	93.5	60.8	44.5	28.5	13.2	6.5	2.7
2009	58.0	32.9	56.3	93.7	96.8	98.5	96.4	95.2	60.5	42.2	26.6	11.7	7.9	2.2
2008	58.0	32.7	53.3	95.5	98.5	98.5	98.9	94.0	57.9	37.8	23.2	10.6	8.5	1.5
2007	59.5	33.9	59.6	93.9	98.3	97.2	99.2	95.2	61.9	37.8	28.0	10.4	9.4	2.0
2006	58.7	33.7	56.6	93.5	97.2	96.8	97.7	91.8	63.9	38.0	24.2	9.3	6.9	2.5
2005	58.9	34.0	54.0	94.8	97.7	97.7	93.6	93.6	67.2	35.1	23.4	9.3	6.3	2.4
2004	59.2	34.6	61.1	93.7	96.7	99.2	98.8	96.5	58.1	37.8	20.2	8.7	4.0	2.2
2003[1]	60.0	34.9	56.5	92.4	98.8	98.1	98.3	94.0	61.5	34.3	23.5	9.7	7.4	1.9
2002	60.2	35.4	57.5	96.2	99.1	97.9	97.6	92.9	54.9	39.5	16.6	10.1	7.5	2.1
2001	60.1	35.7	55.4	95.6	98.3	96.0	99.0	93.2	57.3	36.2	22.7	8.2	8.3	2.3
2000	59.5	35.3	57.6	95.8	98.3	98.7	99.6	89.1	52.4	30.5	21.8	11.3	8.3	2.2
1999	59.9	35.8	53.0	98.4	97.7	99.0	97.9	94.4	60.3	42.3	16.1	9.0	6.5	2.0
1998	60.1	36.2	57.8	95.0	98.5	98.6	97.7	93.9	58.2	40.7	15.1	12.6	5.6	1.8
1997	59.5	36.2	57.3	94.2	98.7	99.1	99.6	93.9	56.7	34.1	21.5	10.5	5.6	2.0
1996	57.8	35.7	47.0	90.1	98.1	97.2	98.1	93.7	55.2	39.0	18.6	12.8	5.4	2.4
1995	58.3	36.2	51.5	94.7	98.2	99.5	99.6	95.2	59.1	36.1	20.3	6.1	6.7	2.3
1994	58.4	36.5	56.8	97.1	99.6	99.5	99.7	95.3	53.4	33.7	21.3	10.8	5.7	2.1
1993[1]	56.0	NA	41.6	96.8	99.3	100.0	99.0	96.1	63.4	23.7	19.6	10.4	3.1	NA
1993	55.8	34.8	41.7	96.9	99.3	100.0	99.0	96.0	63.6	23.9	19.6	10.3	3.1	2.0
1992	54.8	NA	41.3	97.6	99.9	99.7	99.9	94.5	60.7	27.1	18.7	7.6	3.3	NA
1991	54.5	NA	35.2	95.4	99.8	100.0	100.0	90.4	62.2	30.1	19.3	8.6	4.8	NA
1990	53.9	NA	38.3	96.1	99.9	99.9	99.7	93.2	60.7	31.1	20.0	4.6	2.3	NA
1989	52.6	NA	40.2	92.9	98.9	98.8	99.3	95.6	51.0	23.2	15.5	5.5	3.2	NA
1988	52.4	NA	34.5	96.0	99.6	100.0	99.1	93.2	49.7	20.7	14.7	6.3	4.1	NA
1987	54.0	NA	39.0	97.4	100.0	99.8	98.1	91.8	58.7	30.3	15.5	8.4	3.4	NA
1986	53.8	NA	38.7	97.1	99.6	98.8	98.4	94.7	54.1	25.4	17.3	7.1	5.9	NA
1985	52.6	NA	34.6	94.6	98.2	99.1	98.2	91.8	49.5	29.7	13.2	6.9	5.7	NA
1984	52.6	NA	37.2	92.8	99.5	99.1	96.9	93.2	48.6	29.7	17.5	5.7	3.9	NA
1983	52.9	NA	37.1	95.8	98.9	99.4	98.4	91.8	46.6	23.5	17.2	9.1	6.6	NA
1982	53.2	NA	37.4	93.9	99.3	98.4	97.8	92.2	46.5	20.9	17.4	8.5	7.1	NA
1981	54.5	NA	34.8	94.5	98.5	99.2	97.3	92.1	51.9	20.6	14.7	8.4	5.6	NA
1980	56.1	NA	36.6	94.1	99.5	99.4	98.5	90.8	42.8	23.0	13.3	10.6	7.3	NA
1979	57.8	NA	40.4	96.6	99.0	98.4	98.5	94.6	48.0	26.9	14.6	8.1	6.3	NA
1978	58.7	NA	37.9	93.2	99.4	98.8	99.0	92.8	50.5	25.2	14.7	9.5	7.8	NA
1977	60.3	NA	32.4	96.0	99.1	98.6	99.0	92.5	50.5	31.0	18.5	12.1	9.2	NA
1976	61.1	NA	36.3	94.4	99.5	98.8	99.5	90.9	54.9	28.0	18.7	11.0	8.8	NA
1975	60.3	NA	29.5	94.6	99.3	99.0	97.6	88.2	49.9	28.7	14.7	11.8	8.6	NA
1974	60.7	NA	30.3	91.8	99.5	99.6	96.1	90.1	46.1	27.7	16.0	10.4	9.7	NA
1973	58.6	NA	29.2	89.0	99.2	99.1	96.9	89.0	43.5	24.5	13.9	6.9	6.5	NA
1972	60.9	NA	32.1	90.8	98.4	99.4	97.6	88.9	47.7	27.1	18.4	7.3	5.2	NA
1971	60.4	NA	19.0	88.7	99.1	98.1	97.7	90.0	50.7	31.3	12.9	8.5	6.4	NA
1970	59.5	NA	22.3	84.2	99.2	99.1	98.0	85.4	41.3	27.8	9.6	6.1	3.6	NA
1969	60.0	NA	21.3	83.1	98.3	98.9	98.0	87.4	49.5	28.4	10.7	2.8	2.9	NA
1968	60.0	NA	16.9	84.1	98.8	98.4	98.5	88.5	53.1	23.4	7.5	5.2	3.4	NA
1967	59.2	NA	17.0	81.0	99.0	98.3	96.5	86.7	48.6	24.5	9.0	3.5	3.5	NA
1966	58.1	NA	12.7	80.0	99.1	99.0	98.2	87.4	46.3	14.4	9.1	2.6	2.7	NA
1965	57.7	NA	9.5	81.0	99.3	99.4	98.7	82.2	47.5	18.5	4.3	2.6	2.3	NA
1964	56.8	NA	9.4	80.7	98.2	98.7	98.8	84.3	39.9	14.2	3.8	3.5	4.0	NA
1963	61.9	NA	NA	74.3	97.7	99.2	98.2	85.9	46.5	21.7	7.1	4.7	2.7	NA
1962	60.4	NA	NA	74.5	98.9	98.6	99.1	77.1	40.3	15.0	10.1	5.8	1.7	NA
1961	60.0	NA	NA	78.7	98.4	97.6	96.6	78.6	41.7	19.9	6.1	4.0	1.9	NA
1960	58.3	NA	NA	71.8	99.4	98.7	97.0	79.1	36.9	13.7	6.3	3.9	1.0	NA
1959	58.0	NA	NA	76.0	98.7	99.1	95.8	76.3	35.5	12.5	10.6	4.5	1.8	NA

Note: Data shown for 1947 to 1966 for the Black population are for Black and other races. Data for 1947 to 1963 exclude kindergarten. Nursery school was first collected in 1964.
NA = Not available.
[1]Starting in 2003, respondents could identify more than one race. Except as noted, the race data in this table from 2003 onward represent those respondents who indicated only one race category.
r = Revised, controlled to 1990 census based population estimates; previous 1993 data controlled to 1980 census based population estimates.

Table A-10. Percentage of the Population 3 Years Old and Over Enrolled in School, by Age, Sex, Race, and Hispanic Origin, October 1947–2016—*Continued*

(Percent; civilian noninstitutionalized population.)

Year, sex, race, and Hispanic origin	Total enrolled 3 to 34 years old	Total enrolled 3 years old and over	3 and 4	5 and 6	7 to 9	10 to 13	14 and 15	16 and 17	18 and 19	20 and 21	22 to 24	25 to 29	30 to 34	35 and over
1958	58.0	NA	NA	74.2	------98.8------		------87.6------		43.4	------11.8------		6.3	2.4	NA
1957	55.9	NA	NA	73.1	------98.2------		------84.7------		38.5	------10.3------		6.0	1.2	NA
1956	54.3	NA	NA	70.4	------97.6------		------81.3------		36.8	------12.5------		5.3	0.9	NA
1955	54.4	NA	NA	72.8	------98.2------		------85.2------		32.9	------9.8------		6.2	1.9	NA
1954	52.0	NA	NA	64.7	------97.5------		------82.8------		21.6	------10.1------		7.9	1.9	NA
1953	47.8	NA	NA	41.6	------97.1------		------79.1------		34.6	------5.8------		3.3	0.9	NA
1952	49.7	NA	NA	51.4	------96.0------		------72.5------		------------6.0------------					NA
1951	56.9	NA	NA	52.8	------98.0------		------74.9------		23.6	------9.0------		4.3	NA	NA
1950	56.0	NA	NA	----------87.0----------			------79.3------		19.9	------11.1------		6.1	NA	NA
1949	45.0	NA	NA	----------83.1----------			------68.8------		26.1	------11.8------		3.3	1.1	NA
1948	40.4	NA	NA	----------78.9----------			------63.9------		24.0	------10.5------		2.5	1.4	NA
1947	45.1	NA	NA	----------84.6----------			------72.6------		20.7	------12.3------		5.1	0.8	NA
Female														
2016	54.9	28.0	55.1	95.9	98.7	98.6	93.2	94.0	67.8	50.3	29.0	12.5	9.8	3.4
2015	55.0	28.3	54.6	95.3	94.9	97.4	97.8	94.1	65.6	47.7	24.8	15.7	11.2	3.6
2014	55.7	29.4	57.0	92.9	98.9	98.0	99.1	91.0	70.1	40.5	26.8	17.2	10.8	4.6
2013	57.6	30.0	60.2	94.4	96.8	97.8	98.6	91.3	68.3	52.1	28.7	19.8	11.5	3.6
2012	58.6	30.9	55.1	90.9	97.3	98.9	96.1	92.8	76.6	50.0	28.9	20.0	16.1	4.2
2011	58.9	31.7	57.1	91.5	96.8	98.6	99.3	97.3	75.6	44.6	32.2	21.7	14.7	4.8
2010	58.8	31.9	56.8	95.0	96.8	98.8	99.3	97.5	64.5	55.4	29.6	18.5	14.6	4.9
2009	58.9	31.9	59.0	93.6	98.0	98.8	99.3	92.9	69.7	47.3	36.2	17.2	13.5	4.8
2008	57.6	30.9	55.8	90.8	99.4	99.4	96.9	94.4	60.5	42.6	26.3	18.3	13.8	3.8
2007	57.4	30.8	57.3	94.2	98.1	98.6	98.8	91.7	61.6	39.5	27.9	18.9	9.4	3.8
2006	57.6	31.1	61.5	91.7	96.9	97.6	97.2	94.7	65.4	40.2	30.0	14.0	9.9	3.6
2005	57.9	31.5	50.6	97.1	99.5	99.5	98.0	92.5	58.5	40.1	31.8	13.8	13.0	3.6
2004	58.7	32.3	57.7	94.5	98.2	99.6	99.1	94.8	60.2	41.9	29.5	19.0	9.8	4.2
2003[1]	58.4	32.1	54.5	96.4	97.7	98.3	97.5	94.6	62.2	47.4	30.8	14.2	9.6	3.5
2002	59.1	33.0	57.4	95.2	97.2	98.3	98.8	93.7	60.6	47.1	28.8	16.3	11.7	3.8
2001	58.9	33.1	62.1	96.5	97.2	98.1	96.2	91.0	62.0	37.9	29.0	15.3	14.0	3.9
2000	58.7	32.9	62.3	96.8	96.8	98.2	99.6	93.8	61.5	41.3	26.4	16.5	10.7	2.9
1999	56.5	32.0	59.1	96.5	98.7	98.6	98.5	92.1	54.7	36.9	25.9	11.5	8.9	2.9
1998	57.8	33.2	59.1	95.6	98.9	98.7	100.0	91.8	62.2	37.8	26.2	14.4	10.9	3.2
1997	57.4	33.3	62.9	97.2	99.8	99.7	98.9	92.9	59.6	37.3	28.7	10.8	7.2	3.5
1996	54.7	32.2	52.6	90.8	96.7	97.6	99.6	90.4	50.5	35.5	23.2	14.4	8.6	3.5
1995	54.1	31.9	43.6	96.3	97.2	99.0	98.3	90.4	55.9	38.5	19.5	13.0	8.7	3.0
1994	54.4	32.5	47.0	97.2	99.7	99.7	98.6	95.5	54.6	35.9	23.6	10.3	8.5	3.4
1993[r]	51.6	NA	37.9	92.0	98.7	99.7	97.9	93.4	52.0	35.3	16.6	10.5	7.4	NA
1993	51.6	30.4	37.8	92.1	98.7	99.7	97.9	93.4	51.9	35.1	16.7	10.5	7.5	3.0
1992	51.3	NA	35.8	94.1	98.9	99.6	98.8	91.5	51.8	38.6	21.6	8.2	6.9	NA
1991	50.6	NA	39.5	96.1	99.5	100.0	98.2	93.1	49.4	29.9	17.3	8.8	7.9	NA
1990	50.1	NA	45.0	96.5	99.8	99.8	98.7	90.2	50.0	26.0	20.1	7.3	6.2	NA
1989	50.1	NA	37.6	97.1	99.2	99.9	99.5	91.7	49.4	37.3	18.6	7.1	6.3	NA
1988	49.0	NA	32.3	94.9	99.8	99.3	98.6	89.8	50.9	34.3	11.9	7.9	6.9	NA
1987	49.6	NA	34.4	94.1	99.3	99.7	98.6	91.2	48.2	27.4	14.6	10.0	8.1	NA
1986	49.5	NA	38.6	93.7	100.0	99.3	98.2	93.1	47.6	25.7	16.9	8.6	6.5	NA
1985	49.4	NA	50.2	97.1	98.7	99.9	97.6	91.6	39.0	26.0	14.1	7.9	6.1	NA
1984	47.8	NA	39.2	95.3	99.5	99.4	99.0	91.7	40.3	25.9	14.1	8.8	6.2	NA
1983	48.8	NA	35.2	93.6	99.3	100.0	97.1	93.4	45.7	23.3	14.2	6.0	6.5	NA
1982	50.2	NA	39.8	97.0	99.1	99.5	98.3	91.0	41.0	27.2	16.6	7.2	8.0	NA
1981	50.6	NA	38.7	94.4	99.1	99.6	97.0	90.5	44.9	25.7	14.7	8.4	8.1	NA
1980	52.0	NA	39.7	96.7	99.3	99.3	97.4	90.4	48.2	23.7	13.9	7.4	6.5	NA
1979	52.5	NA	41.2	95.5	99.7	99.0	96.4	87.1	45.4	21.1	15.3	7.7	7.3	NA
1978	54.1	NA	44.8	94.7	99.6	99.1	98.0	89.6	42.4	26.0	15.2	8.1	8.0	NA
1977	55.4	NA	38.1	97.0	99.4	99.4	98.5	89.1	46.3	28.2	12.6	10.7	8.9	NA
1976	55.0	NA	32.6	93.6	99.1	98.8	98.4	87.0	46.4	28.4	14.5	8.1	7.6	NA
1975	55.3	NA	37.6	93.9	99.3	99.4	97.2	85.6	44.7	25.8	13.8	7.5	5.9	NA
1974	54.2	NA	28.0	93.8	98.9	100.0	97.9	84.2	42.1	20.1	9.0	7.7	4.8	NA
1973	53.3	NA	28.5	90.9	99.2	98.9	96.5	86.4	32.8	17.3	11.1	5.5	3.8	NA
1972	54.9	NA	24.5	89.1	99.0	99.3	97.3	90.1	38.7	17.9	8.5	5.9	6.5	NA
1971	56.9	NA	24.1	90.9	98.9	99.4	99.0	88.4	43.1	24.1	10.1	4.2	4.2	NA
1970	55.5	NA	23.2	85.7	99.5	99.5	97.2	85.9	38.9	18.9	6.7	3.6	3.3	NA
1969	55.8	NA	21.1	85.0	99.4	99.2	97.7	84.3	40.1	19.6	6.9	5.5	3.7	NA
1968	54.9	NA	20.5	81.3	99.7	99.5	96.9	84.3	38.6	14.5	8.3	1.5	3.2	NA
1967	54.6	NA	18.5	83.4	99.2	99.0	95.8	81.6	34.0	18.5	5.6	6.1	1.5	NA

Note: Data shown for 1947 to 1966 for the Black population are for Black and other races. Data for 1947 to 1963 exclude kindergarten. Nursery school was first collected in 1964.

NA = Not available.

[1]Starting in 2003, respondents could identify more than one race. Except as noted, the race data in this table from 2003 onward represent those respondents who indicated only one race category.

r = Revised, controlled to 1990 census based population estimates; previous 1993 data controlled to 1980 census based population estimates.

Table A-10. Percentage of the Population 3 Years Old and Over Enrolled in School, by Age, Sex, Race, and Hispanic Origin, October 1947–2016—*Continued*

(Percent; civilian noninstitutionalized population.)

Year, sex, race, and Hispanic origin	Total enrolled 3 to 34 years old	Total enrolled 3 years old and over	3 and 4	5 and 6	7 to 9	10 to 13	14 and 15	16 and 17	18 and 19	20 and 21	22 to 24	25 to 29	30 to 34	35 and over
1966	53.2	NA	14.7	81.6	99.3	99.4	96.5	83.1	30.3	9.3	3.6	2.0	2.0	NA
1965	53.6	NA	14.1	77.3	98.6	99.2	97.6	85.6	32.5	8.0	7.8	1.7	2.4	NA
1964	52.5	NA	11.7	79.9	99.9	99.3	95.0	80.6	31.7	13.7	3.8	2.8	2.0	NA
1963	56.0	NA	NA	79.0	99.2	99.8	96.9	78.2	33.9	11.5	4.3	2.2	1.5	NA
1962	54.1	NA	NA	77.5	98.3	99.1	95.2	69.5	27.3	14.9	3.0	2.2	1.3	NA
1961	53.8	NA	NA	79.5	97.6	99.0	93.5	75.1	20.6	12.4	2.7	1.0	0.4	NA
1960	53.7	NA	NA	74.9	99.1	99.3	94.8	74.7	32.2	10.4	2.8	2.1	1.0	NA
1959	52.4	NA	NA	72.5	99.2	99.1	92.0	76.4	31.9	10.8	2.7	1.4	1.0	NA
1958	50.3	NA	NA	73.7	------98.7------		------78.1------		26.4	------6.0------		1.9	0.4	NA
1957	51.3	NA	NA	75.6	------98.2------		------85.0------		35.1	------7.6------		3.5	1.1	NA
1956	49.0	NA	NA	75.2	------99.1------		------81.1------		27.5	------5.7------		1.3	0.6	NA
1955	47.4	NA	NA	69.4	------98.1------		------80.5------		23.1	------5.5------		3.8	1.7	NA
1954	45.6	NA	NA	73.0	------98.6------		------74.7------		25.7	------2.9------		2.3	0.9	NA
1953	43.5	NA	NA	51.1	------97.6------		------85.5------		21.6	------5.0------		0.3	0.7	NA
1952	43.6	NA	NA	56.3	------97.0------		------82.3------		------------------6.4--------------------					NA
1951	50.3	NA	NA	57.1	------96.5------		------79.2------		17.9	------4.3------		1.5	NA	NA
1950	47.0	NA	NA	--------------86.5-------------			------71.9------		25.7	------3.0------		0.6	NA	NA
1949	37.3	NA	NA	--------------84.5-------------			------70.0------		14.5	------1.9------		0.7	*	NA
1948	38.2	NA	NA	--------------81.3-------------			------69.6------		25.2	------2.7------		0.6	*	NA
1947	37.3	NA	NA	--------------84.9-------------			------71.3------		19.9	------2.5------		0.3	0.3	NA

ASIAN[2]

Both Sexes

Year														
2016	54.7	25.9	62.8	89.5	97.8	98.5	97.9	94.2	77.1	75.6	46.5	21.0	6.4	1.4
2015	56.4	26.6	56.2	95.4	97.4	98.3	99.7	86.8	83.7	83.8	49.7	20.2	8.6	1.5
2014	55.8	26.9	53.9	90.5	96.3	97.5	95.5	94.5	88.1	75.8	56.5	19.2	5.4	1.9
2013	56.6	27.4	57.5	91.7	96.9	98.8	98.8	96.8	83.8	81.7	47.3	18.9	8.0	2.1
2012	57.2	27.6	54.1	93.5	99.9	98.3	98.7	97.3	81.0	74.6	53.0	18.8	8.6	1.8
2011	56.8	26.9	51.8	96.7	97.4	96.7	97.9	97.2	84.5	79.0	42.6	16.4	8.3	2.0
2010	58.6	27.9	61.8	96.5	98.5	98.4	97.6	95.3	82.3	80.2	46.5	20.9	10.3	1.8
2009	57.8	26.9	52.4	94.7	96.4	95.4	96.2	96.6	94.1	73.0	56.7	19.3	10.8	2.0
2008	57.3	27.4	55.8	90.8	98.0	99.5	98.7	92.4	85.4	81.1	43.1	23.4	11.5	2.4
2007	55.6	26.9	53.4	94.3	98.2	99.2	99.8	92.6	86.5	66.5	47.4	19.0	9.9	1.7
2006	54.7	26.9	48.3	96.7	99.1	99.2	99.5	92.2	83.0	74.7	44.8	17.8	8.7	2.2
2005	55.6	28.2	55.0	94.7	99.5	97.6	98.8	98.3	88.3	80.5	42.7	21.0	9.3	2.2
2004	56.8	29.3	58.3	97.2	99.9	99.1	97.5	98.6	82.6	79.7	46.8	21.5	9.5	2.6
2003[1]	56.8	29.3	54.5	89.4	99.0	99.3	99.0	97.6	87.3	79.8	48.1	22.5	9.2	2.2
2002	57.3	30.8	56.1	95.6	96.9	98.8	98.4	94.9	78.9	72.8	49.5	18.3	8.3	2.4
2001	57.7	31.7	41.9	99.4	96.3	99.6	98.4	95.7	84.0	72.6	50.8	22.6	7.8	2.2
2000	58.3	32.6	56.0	97.6	97.8	97.6	99.6	98.4	78.8	66.2	45.3	18.7	8.9	2.8
1999	60.9	34.3	55.8	98.9	99.6	100.0	95.8	97.3	78.5	61.7	45.6	20.3	7.8	3.0
1998	59.9	34.2	53.4	97.9	97.9	98.1	95.3	95.6	83.3	70.6	49.0	21.3	8.7	2.6
1997	60.6	34.6	60.2	94.0	97.7	100.0	99.4	94.7	80.2	73.2	41.8	24.2	9.6	2.7
1996	58.6	35.0	50.4	95.7	98.9	99.3	96.8	94.3	78.3	65.8	39.5	18.6	9.9	3.6
1995	57.3	32.5	42.1	95.9	99.5	99.8	100.0	95.9	83.1	63.4	46.7	21.2	11.1	3.2
1994	60.9	33.1	42.3	97.8	99.5	99.7	100.0	97.3	81.8	67.4	53.5	23.8	8.4	2.7
1993	62.2	34.7	39.6	97.1	99.7	100.0	99.9	91.1	82.5	76.1	55.3	21.0	8.6	3.4

Male

Year														
2016	56.2	27.8	60.5	86.4	98.0	98.8	98.8	91.7	75.1	77.6	51.4	22.3	7.0	1.7
2015	57.1	27.6	60.4	97.8	97.6	98.4	99.7	85.3	80.5	81.8	47.2	20.2	8.4	1.1
2014	57.4	28.7	53.9	91.2	97.8	97.2	94.7	93.3	87.5	74.0	62.2	22.0	3.7	1.8
2013	58.4	29.0	60.1	94.5	97.7	99.0	98.0	95.2	83.0	86.6	48.4	22.3	6.1	1.7
2012	57.9	28.8	48.7	93.0	99.7	97.9	97.5	97.4	83.1	74.8	52.8	19.9	7.0	1.5
2011	57.7	28.0	51.6	96.9	96.8	98.2	98.4	96.5	89.2	80.5	39.4	15.8	8.1	1.3
2010	59.8	29.4	63.2	97.5	98.8	97.8	97.1	96.0	77.6	82.9	42.7	22.8	10.8	1.8
2009	58.0	28.2	51.9	94.2	95.6	94.5	97.3	95.1	92.6	71.8	56.9	19.6	9.5	2.3
2008	57.1	27.9	54.2	91.1	96.8	99.1	100.0	96.0	89.0	74.1	38.0	25.2	10.3	1.9
2007	57.2	28.6	56.7	96.9	99.0	99.0	99.7	93.5	91.8	67.6	46.0	18.1	10.3	1.9
2006	55.5	28.3	56.7	96.8	98.3	98.8	99.4	91.0	79.7	76.1	42.2	16.3	8.5	2.4
2005	56.9	29.7	53.2	96.8	99.8	96.9	97.8	97.8	85.2	84.0	42.6	21.1	10.3	2.0
2004	59.3	31.9	58.3	96.0	99.7	99.8	96.5	99.0	85.9	84.2	49.8	24.1	11.4	2.9
2003[1]	59.6	31.8	53.3	90.8	97.9	99.9	97.8	100.0	90.4	77.0	47.8	28.9	11.9	2.3
2002	58.7	32.3	54.1	97.7	95.6	98.4	99.5	94.3	80.0	70.2	50.1	20.6	9.5	2.4

Note: Data shown for 1947 to 1966 for the Black population are for Black and other races. Data for 1947 to 1963 exclude kindergarten. Nursery school was first collected in 1964.

NA = Not available.

[1]Starting in 2003, respondents could identify more than one race. Except as noted, the race data in this table from 2003 onward represent those respondents who indicated only one race category.

[2]The data shown prior to 2003 consists of those identifying themselves as "Asian or Pacific Islanders."

Table A-10. Percentage of the Population 3 Years Old and Over Enrolled in School, by Age, Sex, Race, and Hispanic Origin, October 1947–2016—*Continued*

(Percent; civilian noninstitutionalized population.)

Year, sex, race, and Hispanic origin	Total enrolled 3 to 34 years old	Total enrolled 3 years old and over	Age											
			3 and 4	5 and 6	7 to 9	10 to 13	14 and 15	16 and 17	18 and 19	20 and 21	22 to 24	25 to 29	30 to 34	35 and over
2001	59.1	33.6	35.9	99.6	96.0	100.0	97.1	94.5	83.3	74.9	58.9	22.9	10.6	1.7
2000	60.5	35.0	56.0	96.8	99.5	97.0	99.3	97.8	75.5	67.2	49.1	16.0	10.2	2.7
1999	62.0	35.8	53.5	97.9	99.2	100.0	93.7	98.7	74.4	59.6	50.5	21.4	10.6	3.1
1998	60.8	35.2	51.5	100.0	97.9	98.5	95.0	96.8	74.8	68.0	51.3	21.4	11.1	2.2
1997	63.4	36.6	61.3	89.7	99.4	100.0	98.6	95.5	88.2	71.6	46.9	31.0	10.6	2.5
1996	62.1	38.0	51.0	94.0	99.0	99.6	97.9	93.7	81.0	70.7	37.3	24.4	14.4	3.6
1995	60.0	35.6	38.0	94.5	98.9	99.6	100.0	96.9	81.9	60.3	47.8	24.8	15.7	3.5
1994	64.7	35.8	45.5	98.2	99.0	100.0	100.0	96.9	81.5	70.9	57.0	31.3	10.7	2.1
1993	65.9	37.9	43.0	95.9	99.8	99.9	100.0	93.4	79.4	78.5	65.4	21.0	11.2	3.4
Female														
2016	53.3	24.2	65.4	92.8	97.5	98.2	97.1	96.3	79.3	73.7	41.2	19.5	5.9	1.2
2015	55.7	25.7	51.9	92.6	97.1	98.2	99.7	88.2	86.9	85.6	52.5	20.1	8.9	1.9
2014	54.2	25.4	53.8	89.8	94.9	97.8	96.3	95.5	88.7	77.8	50.7	16.7	7.0	2.0
2013	54.9	26.0	54.6	88.8	96.2	98.5	99.6	98.0	84.6	76.3	46.0	15.7	9.6	2.5
2012	56.5	26.6	59.0	94.0	100.0	98.6	100.0	97.3	78.7	74.4	53.3	17.7	10.0	2.1
2011	55.9	25.9	52.0	96.5	98.0	95.3	97.3	98.0	79.2	77.5	46.0	17.0	8.5	2.5
2010	57.3	26.5	60.5	95.6	98.2	99.0	98.1	94.3	87.2	77.8	50.3	19.1	9.9	1.8
2009	57.5	25.8	53.1	95.3	97.3	96.2	94.5	98.3	95.8	74.1	56.5	19.1	12.0	1.8
2008	57.4	26.8	57.8	90.4	99.0	100.0	97.5	88.7	81.8	89.5	47.5	21.7	12.7	2.9
2007	54.0	25.3	49.1	91.9	97.3	99.5	100.0	91.7	81.0	65.4	48.5	19.8	9.6	1.5
2006	53.8	25.6	39.1	96.5	100.0	99.5	99.0	93.3	87.3	72.9	47.0	19.1	8.9	2.0
2005	54.4	26.8	56.8	92.3	99.3	98.3	100.0	98.8	91.7	75.9	42.9	20.9	8.4	2.4
2004	54.1	26.9	58.4	99.1	100.0	98.2	98.5	98.1	79.0	74.7	43.9	19.1	7.6	2.4
2003[1]	54.0	27.1	55.8	87.4	100.0	98.4	100.0	94.9	84.6	82.5	48.3	16.6	6.7	2.1
2002	56.1	29.5	58.1	93.4	97.9	99.2	97.5	95.5	77.9	75.8	48.9	16.1	7.2	2.3
2001	56.2	29.9	47.7	99.1	96.6	99.2	100.0	97.2	84.6	70.0	42.5	22.3	5.1	2.6
2000	56.0	30.4	55.9	98.6	96.2	98.2	100.0	99.1	82.0	65.1	41.7	20.6	7.5	2.9
1999	59.8	32.9	57.8	100.0	100.0	100.0	97.6	95.8	82.0	63.7	42.2	19.4	5.2	2.9
1998	59.0	33.2	55.0	95.6	97.8	97.7	95.6	94.4	91.5	73.6	46.6	21.2	6.5	3.0
1997	57.9	32.7	59.5	98.4	95.5	100.0	100.0	93.8	71.6	74.3	36.5	17.4	8.8	2.9
1996	54.9	32.0	49.5	97.9	98.8	99.0	95.5	95.0	75.4	80.8	42.2	13.5	6.1	3.7
1995	54.5	29.6	46.0	98.1	100.0	100.0	100.0	94.8	84.4	67.0	46.2	17.8	6.8	3.1
1994	57.3	30.6	39.0	97.4	100.0	99.4	100.0	97.7	81.9	64.2	49.3	16.9	6.7	3.2
1993	58.6	31.9	36.1	98.5	99.6	100.0	99.8	88.7	87.0	74.5	43.4	20.9	6.3	3.4
HISPANIC (OF ANY RACE)														
Both Sexes														
2016	56.8	32.9	49.5	93.0	97.0	98.4	97.6	93.6	68.4	51.7	26.7	11.3	4.7	1.6
2015	55.8	32.7	44.1	93.7	97.9	97.1	96.7	92.6	65.2	48.8	25.2	11.2	4.6	1.7
2014	55.4	33.1	45.5	94.4	98.2	97.3	97.1	92.2	64.7	44.7	24.0	10.7	5.3	1.9
2013	55.5	33.4	45.4	93.9	98.4	97.7	98.3	93.9	59.3	43.9	26.7	10.4	5.7	2.0
2012	56.4	34.2	46.3	92.1	98.1	98.3	98.5	94.8	68.1	49.5	27.1	9.4	6.2	1.8
2011	55.6	34.0	41.6	95.6	98.2	98.5	98.2	94.6	65.2	45.7	23.6	10.5	4.5	1.6
2010	55.1	33.8	44.2	94.3	98.5	97.3	97.9	96.0	66.2	37.0	23.8	11.4	5.7	2.3
2009	52.8	32.3	41.9	93.7	96.5	98.0	97.9	92.6	57.1	37.2	20.4	9.5	5.6	2.2
2008	51.9	31.9	43.6	91.8	97.1	98.6	98.7	93.8	55.1	32.1	19.8	9.2	4.2	2.2
2007	51.7	32.1	48.2	94.3	96.3	99.0	98.4	90.6	57.2	32.3	18.8	8.3	4.5	2.1
2006	51.3	31.9	48.8	93.4	98.1	98.2	98.4	91.1	53.4	30.6	17.9	7.3	5.3	1.8
2005	50.9	32.1	43.0	93.8	97.4	97.9	97.3	92.6	54.3	30.0	19.5	7.8	4.2	2.0
2004	50.7	32.4	43.9	93.9	97.2	97.5	99.0	89.2	43.9	30.6	17.2	6.7	3.3	1.5
2003	49.6	31.6	43.7	91.6	97.5	98.3	96.7	92.1	50.5	33.7	16.1	6.2	4.6	1.8
2002	49.9	32.3	41.0	94.4	97.9	98.1	98.1	90.9	50.6	24.6	15.3	8.4	4.4	2.4
2001	49.5	32.4	39.7	93.6	97.4	98.3	97.8	88.2	45.5	27.9	15.5	7.7	4.4	2.5
2000	51.3	32.6	35.9	94.3	97.5	97.4	96.2	87.0	49.5	26.1	18.2	7.4	5.6	2.0
1999	51.1	32.9	36.9	93.9	99.0	98.3	97.6	88.1	44.5	22.6	15.0	9.1	5.6	2.3
1998	50.4	32.6	36.7	98.2	98.8	99.1	96.8	89.1	40.3	25.6	16.3	8.7	5.5	2.3
1997	50.8	32.7	36.6	96.6	98.6	99.6	96.8	98.4	91.1	49.4	28.9	16.4	7.3	3.7
1996	50.3	32.8	38.1	89.5	96.6	97.6	96.6	88.7	47.0	25.3	17.6	8.6	5.0	2.5
1995	49.7	32.9	36.9	93.9	98.5	99.2	98.9	88.2	46.1	27.1	15.6	7.1	4.7	2.7
1994	49.0	32.6	30.8	96.1	99.2	99.4	96.1	88.3	51.4	24.9	15.1	8.1	5.7	2.7
1993[r]	48.6	NA	26.8	93.6	99.6	99.2	97.6	88.1	50.0	31.8	13.8	7.7	5.1	NA
1993	48.9	31.6	26.8	93.8	99.6	99.2	97.6	88.3	50.0	31.8	13.7	7.7	5.1	1.9

Note: Data shown for 1947 to 1966 for the Black population are for Black and other races. Data for 1947 to 1963 exclude kindergarten. Nursery school was first collected in 1964.

NA = Not available.

[1] Starting in 2003, respondents could identify more than one race. Except as noted, the race data in this table from 2003 onward represent those respondents who indicated only one race category.

r = Revised, controlled to 1990 census based population estimates; previous 1993 data controlled to 1980 census based population estimates.

Table A-10. Percentage of the Population 3 Years Old and Over Enrolled in School, by Age, Sex, Race, and Hispanic Origin, October 1947–2016—*Continued*

(Percent; civilian noninstitutionalized population.)

Year, sex, race, and Hispanic origin	Total enrolled 3 to 34 years old	Total enrolled 3 years old and over	Age											
			3 and 4	5 and 6	7 to 9	10 to 13	14 and 15	16 and 17	18 and 19	20 and 21	22 to 24	25 to 29	30 to 34	35 and over
1992	49.2	NA	28.8	96.0	99.5	99.1	98.8	87.2	53.7	30.1	14.5	6.7	6.0	NA
1991	47.9	NA	30.6	92.4	99.9	99.4	97.2	82.6	47.9	26.4	11.6	6.9	5.9	NA
1990	47.4	NA	29.8	94.8	99.6	99.2	99.0	85.4	44.1	27.2	9.9	6.3	3.1	NA
1989	45.8	NA	23.8	92.8	98.0	99.3	96.5	86.4	44.6	18.8	12.0	6.6	3.5	NA
1988	46.0	NA	24.5	95.7	99.6	99.8	98.8	78.8	44.1	16.7	12.1	5.8	6.2	NA
1987	47.2	NA	30.7	93.0	99.2	99.4	97.6	87.1	39.1	26.5	12.3	7.5	4.9	NA
1986	48.2	NA	28.8	93.7	99.4	99.3	97.2	84.0	46.0	21.4	13.7	9.2	5.6	NA
1985	47.7	NA	27.0	94.5	98.4	99.4	96.1	84.5	41.8	24.0	11.6	8.6	5.6	NA
1984	47.7	NA	24.2	93.9	98.7	99.4	94.9	85.7	39.9	28.1	11.3	6.6	7.5	NA
1983	49.3	NA	23.5	95.1	98.5	99.7	96.0	88.6	44.3	24.0	12.5	7.1	5.7	NA
1982	49.4	NA	21.8	92.2	98.7	98.8	96.9	85.5	39.2	22.7	10.4	8.2	4.4	NA
1981	49.0	NA	24.5	90.4	99.2	99.1	94.0	82.8	37.8	20.6	12.3	8.0	4.7	NA
1980	49.8	NA	28.5	94.5	98.4	99.7	94.3	81.8	37.8	19.5	11.7	6.9	4.1	NA
1979	48.6	NA	22.5	92.5	98.7	99.0	96.3	82.3	39.9	22.6	10.0	7.8	7.1	NA
1978	48.3	NA	22.5	91.4	99.5	98.0	95.2	83.0	35.7	16.8	11.8	8.0	4.1	NA
1977	50.8	NA	19.5	93.7	99.0	99.3	97.6	83.6	40.6	23.1	10.8	9.3	5.6	NA
1976	51.8	NA	22.2	95.0	97.5	99.1	95.4	81.3	45.2	24.0	14.8	7.9	2.7	NA
1975	54.8	NA	27.3	92.1	99.6	99.2	95.6	86.2	44.0	27.5	14.1	8.3	4.1	NA
1974	54.3	NA	25.3	92.1	98.8	99.2	96.1	78.3	45.2	23.2	11.3	6.7	2.2	NA
1973	52.8	NA	18.8	90.7	98.7	99.1	94.4	80.2	39.2	21.5	10.0	6.8	1.3	NA
1972	53.0	NA	20.5	90.0	98.7	99.1	96.7	83.9	41.4	17.0	9.9	5.2	3.5	NA
Male														
2016	55.4	32.6	50.7	91.8	96.3	98.1	98.4	93.4	66.3	46.0	23.4	9.3	3.6	1.3
2015	54.4	32.4	44.3	93.6	97.5	97.3	96.0	91.7	59.9	44.4	24.2	9.2	3.3	1.6
2014	53.6	32.6	43.1	94.6	97.8	96.7	97.8	89.3	61.6	37.4	21.5	10.0	3.2	1.9
2013	54.0	33.1	44.2	93.6	98.6	97.7	97.9	93.5	55.4	38.0	24.4	10.8	3.9	1.6
2012	54.7	33.9	45.4	92.2	98.2	98.6	98.9	95.1	65.7	44.4	24.7	7.4	3.3	1.8
2011	54.1	33.9	43.6	95.9	98.8	98.8	98.7	94.6	61.0	43.1	21.0	9.9	3.4	1.6
2010	52.9	32.8	43.3	93.4	98.1	96.9	97.5	96.0	64.9	34.0	18.6	9.6	4.9	1.9
2009	50.9	31.3	39.4	94.1	96.2	98.8	98.1	92.5	51.8	32.1	18.6	7.8	5.2	1.6
2008	50.0	31.1	40.5	91.0	96.7	98.6	98.6	93.1	54.7	30.8	16.6	8.2	4.1	1.6
2007	49.4	31.1	50.7	94.1	96.4	99.0	97.8	91.1	55.2	24.6	14.4	6.7	3.1	1.8
2006	49.0	30.9	49.1	91.7	97.7	97.9	99.0	91.7	51.5	24.1	16.0	5.4	3.5	1.2
2005	48.4	31.0	43.0	92.4	96.0	97.2	97.8	92.5	51.8	25.2	17.5	5.6	2.6	1.6
2004	48.5	31.5	43.8	93.9	97.2	97.5	99.0	89.2	43.9	30.6	17.2	6.7	3.3	1.5
2003	47.3	30.8	42.9	91.3	97.5	98.4	96.7	90.4	47.0	27.2	13.3	4.9	3.8	1.3
2002	48.1	31.9	41.7	95.1	97.8	97.6	98.2	88.8	48.4	24.5	11.5	7.0	3.1	2.2
2001	48.4	32.2	42.9	94.9	97.9	98.6	98.4	87.8	40.0	24.4	14.6	6.5	3.5	2.2
2000	50.5	32.5	31.9	95.4	96.6	98.4	96.9	85.7	48.0	24.2	15.2	5.1	5.7	1.4
1999	50.3	32.9	33.5	92.8	98.8	98.5	98.1	87.9	45.3	21.5	11.2	8.6	3.9	2.0
1998	49.0	32.4	44.9	92.8	98.8	99.3	97.0	88.0	33.7	24.6	12.9	6.9	4.7	1.8
1997	49.0	32.3	35.5	97.7	97.7	99.8	99.5	92.5	45.4	27.6	14.0	5.9	2.7	1.6
1996	49.2	33.0	39.6	91.0	95.4	97.9	98.0	90.4	46.8	19.5	16.2	6.8	4.3	2.6
1995	49.1	33.1	40.8	93.6	98.8	98.8	98.4	88.4	47.4	24.8	14.8	5.6	4.5	2.1
1994	48.0	32.5	32.6	96.5	98.6	99.3	94.6	86.6	54.2	23.7	14.0	7.1	4.2	2.3
1993[r]	46.6	NA	26.9	93.4	99.8	98.8	96.9	88.7	47.8	31.6	13.0	5.5	5.4	NA
1993	47.4	31.5	27.0	93.6	99.8	98.8	96.9	89.1	47.7	31.6	12.8	5.5	5.4	1.5
1992	47.9	NA	24.9	96.5	100.0	99.2	98.1	89.2	52.6	24.3	13.8	5.3	3.5	NA
1991	46.4	NA	30.7	92.3	99.8	99.7	97.8	83.6	42.1	20.8	9.9	6.8	3.3	NA
1990	47.1	NA	27.3	95.6	99.5	99.0	99.1	85.5	40.7	21.7	11.2	4.6	4.0	NA
1989	45.8	NA	21.3	92.5	97.7	98.6	99.0	88.7	44.2	17.1	12.2	7.3	4.1	NA
1988	46.2	NA	27.9	96.7	99.2	100.0	98.1	80.9	44.7	21.6	12.5	4.5	5.0	NA
1987	47.8	NA	30.5	92.8	99.7	100.0	98.1	90.9	42.3	30.1	11.4	7.8	5.1	NA
1986	47.3	NA	29.4	93.0	100.0	99.4	96.8	85.0	45.8	19.2	13.0	9.1	4.4	NA
1985	47.5	NA	26.4	95.3	98.9	99.1	96.2	88.9	38.6	20.3	12.6	8.7	3.8	NA
1984	48.6	NA	20.0	93.6	98.2	100.0	95.7	85.1	38.8	27.5	12.3	8.2	4.0	NA
1983	50.7	NA	25.0	91.9	98.8	99.6	97.8	88.2	40.4	26.2	15.1	6.9	4.6	NA
1982	50.4	NA	25.2	90.3	99.6	98.4	96.8	87.8	39.7	21.6	11.2	10.8	3.1	NA
1981	49.6	NA	25.5	89.6	98.8	99.0	92.3	84.5	36.0	24.4	11.4	8.3	4.3	NA
1980	49.9	NA	30.1	94.0	97.7	99.4	96.7	81.5	36.9	21.4	10.7	6.8	6.2	NA
1979	51.0	NA	22.8	93.8	98.7	99.0	96.6	85.1	42.6	24.0	12.4	8.7	6.1	NA
1978	50.5	NA	22.6	93.2	99.1	97.8	94.0	80.4	40.0	18.1	13.6	9.5	4.4	NA
1977	54.2	NA	23.2	91.4	100.0	98.7	99.1	89.4	43.1	22.8	16.0	13.1	6.4	NA
1976	55.0	NA	22.1	94.6	97.4	98.5	97.3	85.5	46.3	27.1	18.6	11.4	5.6	NA
1975	58.1	NA	26.7	89.7	99.6	98.8	97.4	88.3	51.9	31.3	15.9	11.9	7.2	NA
1974	56.0	NA	23.5	93.1	98.3	98.5	97.9	78.6	46.8	22.3	14.5	8.4	7.4	NA

Note: Data shown for 1947 to 1966 for the Black population are for Black and other races. Data for 1947 to 1963 exclude kindergarten. Nursery school was first collected in 1964.

NA = Not available.

[r] = Revised, controlled to 1990 census based population estimates; previous 1993 data controlled to 1980 census based population estimates.

Table A-10. Percentage of the Population 3 Years Old and Over Enrolled in School, by Age, Sex, Race, and Hispanic Origin, October 1947–2016—*Continued*

(Percent; civilian noninstitutionalized population.)

Year, sex, race, and Hispanic origin	Total enrolled 3 to 34 years old	Total enrolled 3 years old and over	Age											
			3 and 4	5 and 6	7 to 9	10 to 13	14 and 15	16 and 17	18 and 19	20 and 21	22 to 24	25 to 29	30 to 34	35 and over
1973	55.5	NA	23.1	92.4	99.1	99.1	96.5	86.6	45.8	23.8	10.8	9.9	6.7	NA
1972	54.7	NA	20.4	90.3	98.8	99.1	98.1	87.8	40.5	20.0	13.9	5.8	2.5	NA
Female														
2016	58.3	33.2	48.2	94.2	97.6	98.8	96.8	93.9	70.5	57.5	30.2	13.3	5.9	1.9
2015	55.7	32.9	44.0	93.9	98.4	96.9	97.4	93.7	70.1	53.2	26.3	13.2	5.9	1.8
2014	57.4	33.6	47.8	94.2	98.6	97.9	96.4	95.3	67.8	53.8	26.3	11.5	7.6	2.0
2013	57.0	33.7	46.7	94.1	98.2	97.7	98.8	94.3	63.2	50.6	29.1	10.0	7.6	2.3
2012	58.2	34.5	47.1	92.1	98.1	98.0	98.1	94.5	70.7	55.0	29.7	11.5	9.3	1.9
2011	57.2	34.1	39.6	95.3	97.6	98.2	97.6	94.6	70.3	48.8	26.6	11.2	5.8	1.6
2010	57.4	34.8	45.0	95.2	98.9	97.7	98.3	96.0	67.6	40.5	29.2	13.6	6.6	2.7
2009	55.0	33.3	44.4	93.2	96.7	97.2	97.6	92.6	62.5	43.1	22.2	11.6	6.0	2.8
2008	53.9	32.8	46.9	92.6	97.4	98.7	98.8	94.5	55.5	33.5	23.4	10.4	4.4	2.7
2007	54.3	33.1	45.6	94.5	96.2	99.0	99.1	90.0	59.2	41.0	23.7	10.3	6.1	2.3
2006	53.9	33.1	48.5	95.3	98.5	98.6	97.7	90.4	55.4	37.5	20.1	9.7	7.3	2.3
2005	58.0	33.3	43.0	95.3	98.8	98.6	96.7	92.6	57.2	35.3	21.8	10.4	6.1	2.4
2004	53.1	33.3	44.0	92.2	97.9	97.5	97.5	91.3	56.9	34.0	22.0	9.7	7.5	2.8
2003	52.2	32.5	44.7	92.0	97.5	98.2	96.8	93.8	54.4	41.1	19.4	7.9	5.6	2.2
2002	51.8	32.8	40.3	93.8	98.1	98.7	97.9	92.8	53.2	24.6	20.2	9.9	6.0	2.7
2001	50.6	32.6	36.3	92.4	96.9	98.1	97.2	88.7	51.1	31.6	16.7	9.1	5.3	2.8
2000	52.2	32.8	40.0	93.1	98.4	96.4	95.4	88.3	51.1	28.1	21.6	9.5	5.5	2.6
1999	52.1	32.8	40.5	95.0	99.3	98.0	96.9	88.3	43.6	23.6	19.2	9.5	7.3	2.7
1998	51.9	32.8	34.3	93.7	98.8	98.9	96.7	90.5	46.8	26.8	20.0	10.6	6.5	2.8
1997	52.7	33.0	37.7	95.7	99.6	99.5	97.3	89.6	53.9	30.4	19.2	8.8	4.9	2.0
1996	51.4	32.7	36.8	87.8	97.9	97.4	95.0	86.9	47.2	31.1	19.3	10.5	5.7	2.5
1995	50.3	32.7	32.7	94.3	98.2	99.6	99.4	88.0	44.8	29.2	16.6	8.7	4.9	3.2
1994	50.2	32.7	28.9	95.7	99.8	99.4	97.6	90.2	48.6	26.4	16.5	9.1	7.3	3.0
1993ʳ	50.7	NA	26.7	93.9	99.4	99.6	98.2	87.3	51.9	31.9	14.7	10.2	4.7	NA
1993	50.6	31.6	26.7	93.9	99.4	99.6	98.2	87.4	51.9	32.0	14.5	10.2	4.8	2.2
1992	50.6	NA	32.7	95.4	99.0	99.1	99.6	85.0	54.9	35.6	15.4	8.2	6.0	NA
1991	49.5	NA	30.5	92.6	100.0	99.2	96.6	81.5	53.7	32.0	13.6	7.0	5.9	NA
1990	47.7	NA	32.3	93.9	99.7	99.4	98.8	85.3	47.2	33.1	8.4	8.1	3.1	NA
1989	45.9	NA	26.5	93.3	98.3	100.0	95.1	83.7	45.0	20.8	11.9	5.8	3.5	NA
1988	45.8	NA	20.7	94.6	100.0	99.6	99.6	76.6	43.5	11.2	11.5	7.2	6.2	NA
1987	46.5	NA	30.8	93.2	98.7	98.9	97.1	82.6	36.2	22.0	13.2	7.3	4.9	NA
1986	49.0	NA	28.2	94.4	98.7	99.2	97.5	83.0	46.2	23.7	14.5	9.2	5.6	NA
1985	47.9	NA	27.7	93.7	98.0	99.7	96.0	80.0	44.7	27.4	10.4	8.6	5.6	NA
1984	46.8	NA	28.2	94.2	99.2	98.7	94.0	86.3	40.8	28.7	10.4	4.9	7.5	NA
1983	48.0	NA	22.0	98.3	98.1	99.8	94.1	89.1	47.6	21.7	10.1	7.4	5.7	NA
1982	48.4	NA	16.3	93.9	97.8	99.2	97.1	82.8	38.7	23.7	9.7	5.7	4.4	NA
1981	48.4	NA	23.4	91.3	99.6	99.3	95.7	80.8	39.4	16.8	13.1	7.7	4.7	NA
1980	49.8	NA	26.6	94.9	99.0	99.1	92.1	82.2	38.8	17.6	12.6	6.9	4.1	NA
1979	46.3	NA	22.3	91.1	98.7	98.9	95.9	79.5	37.1	21.5	7.8	7.0	7.1	NA
1978	46.2	NA	22.5	89.4	100.0	98.2	96.6	86.2	31.9	15.7	10.1	6.5	4.1	NA
1977	47.6	NA	15.8	96.3	97.9	99.9	95.9	77.4	38.5	23.4	6.2	5.9	5.6	NA
1976	48.8	NA	22.3	95.5	97.6	99.7	93.6	77.6	44.2	21.4	12.1	4.8	2.7	NA
1975	51.7	NA	27.9	94.4	99.5	99.7	93.8	84.0	37.1	24.3	12.5	5.3	4.1	NA
1974	52.5	NA	27.4	91.1	99.2	100.0	94.1	77.9	43.7	23.9	8.4	4.9	2.2	NA
1973	50.1	NA	14.0	88.9	98.3	99.1	92.5	74.9	32.9	19.4	9.2	3.9	1.3	NA
1972	51.4	NA	20.5	89.7	98.5	99.0	95.4	80.0	42.4	14.6	6.8	4.7	3.5	NA
WHITE ALONE OR IN COMBINATION														
Both Sexes														
2016	55.2	24.2	53.8	93.7	98.0	98.5	98.4	92.6	69.7	56.0	27.4	12.7	5.9	1.3
2015	55.2	24.4	52.1	94.2	97.6	97.9	97.9	94.0	68.5	53.4	27.7	12.7	6.1	1.4
2014	55.1	24.6	54.0	93.4	97.7	97.5	97.7	93.4	68.1	52.3	28.6	12.3	5.9	1.5
2013	55.5	25.0	54.4	93.9	98.2	98.2	98.5	93.7	67.0	52.3	29.1	12.2	6.3	1.6
2012	56.2	25.4	53.6	93.7	98.1	97.8	98.3	96.1	68.4	54.0	29.5	13.3	6.7	1.7
2011	56.5	25.9	51.6	95.6	98.2	98.6	98.7	95.7	70.2	53.7	30.8	14.1	7.0	1.7
2010	56.1	25.8	52.3	94.3	97.8	98.1	98.1	96.2	70.0	51.4	28.0	14.0	7.7	1.9
2009	56.0	25.7	51.3	94.2	98.0	98.7	98.1	94.6	68.4	52.5	28.8	13.0	7.4	1.9
2008	55.9	25.7	52.4	94.0	98.2	98.9	98.7	95.5	67.0	51.0	28.1	12.4	6.3	1.8
2007	55.7	25.7	54.0	94.8	98.0	98.7	98.7	94.6	67.1	49.7	26.2	16.2	9.4	1.8
2006	55.8	25.7	55.5	94.8	98.4	98.5	98.4	94.9	65.0	47.9	25.6	11.4	6.8	1.7

Note: Data shown for 1947 to 1966 for the Black population are for Black and other races. Data for 1947 to 1963 exclude kindergarten. Nursery school was first collected in 1964.

NA = Not available.

ʳ = Revised, controlled to 1990 census based population estimates; previous 1993 data controlled to 1980 census based population estimates.

Table A-10. Percentage of the Population 3 Years Old and Over Enrolled in School, by Age, Sex, Race, and Hispanic Origin, October 1947–2016—*Continued*

(Percent; civilian noninstitutionalized population.)

Year, sex, race, and Hispanic origin	Total enrolled 3 to 34 years old	Total enrolled 3 years old and over	Age											
			3 and 4	5 and 6	7 to 9	10 to 13	14 and 15	16 and 17	18 and 19	20 and 21	22 to 24	25 to 29	30 to 34	35 and over
2005	56.2	26.1	53.9	95.3	98.6	98.7	98.3	95.3	67.7	49.3	26.2	11.3	6.2	1.8
2004	55.7	26.1	52.7	95.5	98.2	98.4	98.5	94.0	64.8	49.4	25.2	12.2	6.4	1.8
2003	55.6	26.1	55.2	94.8	98.0	98.4	97.4	95.0	64.2	48.3	26.8	11.0	6.3	1.7
Male														
2016	54.5	24.5	55.3	93.7	97.9	98.2	98.7	92.2	68.4	51.0	25.7	10.7	4.9	1.0
2015	54.6	24.7	53.4	93.4	97.7	98.1	97.6	93.2	65.3	50.6	25.4	11.5	5.3	1.1
2014	54.4	24.9	52.6	93.8	97.4	96.8	97.3	92.4	64.6	49.4	26.7	11.5	5.1	1.2
2013	54.7	25.1	52.7	93.9	98.1	98.2	98.4	93.0	65.4	47.4	26.6	11.2	5.2	1.2
2012	55.3	25.5	52.8	93.6	97.8	98.1	98.2	95.9	65.6	48.2	28.2	11.5	5.6	1.3
2011	55.9	26.3	52.5	95.6	98.4	98.7	98.5	95.6	67.4	50.3	30.1	12.5	6.2	1.4
2010	55.2	26.0	52.2	93.4	97.4	97.7	98.1	95.0	67.5	48.2	25.9	13.1	6.4	1.5
2009	55.1	25.8	50.5	93.8	97.8	98.9	97.8	94.3	64.3	49.2	27.9	11.3	6.5	1.4
2008	55.2	25.9	52.1	93.6	97.9	98.7	99.0	95.0	64.4	48.1	26.4	11.6	5.7	1.3
2007	54.6	25.8	53.2	94.0	97.9	98.6	98.3	94.4	66.4	44.1	24.0	12.9	9.4	1.4
2006	54.9	25.9	56.0	94.5	98.3	98.4	98.2	94.7	62.7	43.5	24.1	10.3	5.6	1.3
2005	55.2	26.2	52.6	94.7	98.2	98.6	98.3	95.2	65.7	45.1	24.6	8.9	5.4	1.4
2004	55.0	26.3	53.4	95.8	98.0	98.2	98.8	94.3	59.9	46.5	23.2	11.1	5.5	1.4
2003	55.0	26.5	55.9	95.2	97.7	98.2	97.3	95.1	61.6	43.4	25.5	9.8	5.7	1.4
Female														
2016	55.9	24.0	52.3	93.7	98.2	98.8	98.0	93.0	71.0	61.2	29.0	14.8	6.9	1.5
2015	55.7	24.2	50.9	95.1	97.6	97.6	98.1	94.8	71.8	56.2	30.0	14.0	6.9	1.7
2014	55.8	24.3	55.4	92.9	98.0	98.2	98.1	94.4	71.7	55.7	30.3	13.1	6.8	1.8
2013	56.4	24.9	56.1	94.0	98.3	98.3	98.6	94.5	68.8	57.6	31.7	13.2	7.4	2.0
2012	57.2	25.3	54.5	93.8	98.4	97.5	98.5	96.3	71.4	59.6	31.0	15.1	7.8	2.0
2011	57.2	25.6	50.7	95.7	98.0	98.5	98.8	95.7	73.1	57.4	31.6	15.9	7.9	2.0
2010	57.1	25.7	52.5	95.2	98.1	98.5	98.1	97.4	72.5	55.0	30.1	15.0	9.1	2.3
2009	57.0	25.7	52.1	94.5	98.1	98.4	98.4	94.8	72.7	56.0	29.7	14.8	8.3	2.4
2008	56.6	25.5	52.7	94.4	98.6	99.1	98.5	96.0	69.7	54.0	29.8	13.2	7.0	2.3
2007	56.9	25.6	54.9	95.6	98.1	98.7	99.2	94.9	67.9	55.5	28.4	19.2	9.4	2.2
2006	56.6	25.5	55.0	95.2	98.5	98.5	98.6	95.2	67.3	52.4	27.1	12.4	8.1	2.1
2005	57.4	26.0	55.3	96.0	98.9	98.8	98.4	95.5	70.0	53.8	27.9	13.8	7.1	2.3
2004	56.5	25.8	51.9	95.3	98.4	98.5	98.2	93.8	69.7	52.4	27.1	13.4	7.3	2.2
2003	56.3	25.7	54.4	94.5	98.3	98.7	97.5	94.9	66.8	53.1	28.1	12.2	7.0	2.1
BLACK ALONE OR IN COMBINATION														
Both Sexes														
2016	57.1	31.1	52.4	93.2	97.7	98.8	96.3	95.0	67.2	47.6	27.2	12.6	8.7	2.9
2015	56.6	31.0	51.2	93.7	96.2	98.5	98.3	95	64.7	42.4	26.8	12.6	8.3	2.8
2014	57.1	31.8	56.9	94.6	98.8	97.8	98.7	91.7	64.8	39.7	24.7	14.2	9.0	3.7
2013	58.5	32.5	58.4	94.3	97.1	98.0	98.7	92.9	64.0	49.1	27.4	16.7	8.2	3.0
2012	59.5	33.2	51.8	92.4	96.7	99.0	97.6	94.6	68.7	49.6	29.3	15.7	12.2	3.3
2011	59.3	33.6	53.9	92.1	97.3	98.5	98.7	96.0	74.1	41.8	31.0	18.1	11.3	3.8
2010	59.2	33.6	55.8	94.8	97.5	98.7	98.6	95.7	63.2	49.9	28.9	16.0	10.8	3.9
2009	59.4	33.5	57.1	93.8	97.4	98.6	97.7	94.4	64.7	44.2	31.6	14.7	11.1	3.7
2008	58.8	33.0	54.5	92.9	98.8	99.1	98.1	94.5	59.7	40.4	24.8	15.1	11.4	2.8
2007	59.0	33.2	58.2	94.2	98.2	98.0	99.1	93.7	62.0	38.1	27.3	15.3	9.6	3.0
2006	58.8	33.3	59.0	92.4	96.9	97.2	97.4	93.2	64.9	38.9	27.8	11.9	8.9	3.2
2005	59.0	33.5	51.3	96.1	98.5	98.6	95.9	92.9	62.5	38.1	27.8	11.7	9.9	3.1
2004	59.6	34.3	58.6	94.5	97.4	99.4	98.6	95.3	59.7	40.8	25.3	14.8	7.0	3.3
2003	59.8	34.2	56.5	94.6	98.1	98.3	98.0	94.2	60.9	42.1	27.2	12.4	8.4	2.8
Male														
2016	57.4	32.4	48.1	90.8	96.6	98.8	98.5	95.4	66.9	44.2	25.8	12.3	7.3	2.2
2015	57.2	32.2	50.6	92.4	96.5	99.3	99.1	95.2	64.6	39.4	29.3	9.7	4.6	1.8
2014	57.4	32.8	56.4	95.7	98.8	97.8	98.4	91.7	61.1	39.2	21.9	11.6	7.2	2.6
2013	58.5	33.5	55.4	94.6	97.0	97.8	98.6	95.0	59.4	44.6	26.2	13.7	4.9	2.4
2012	59.0	33.7	48.8	93.5	95.8	99.1	98.7	95.6	61.4	49.4	27.2	11.1	7.2	2.1
2011	59.0	34.5	52.8	92.8	97.5	98.6	97.9	94.5	71.6	38.9	30.0	14.1	7.7	2.7
2010	58.8	34.4	55.0	94.2	97.7	98.6	97.8	93.8	62.0	44.9	28.0	12.9	6.3	2.7
2009	58.9	34.0	57.4	93.8	97.2	98.3	95.9	95.6	60.4	42.3	25.7	11.5	8.1	2.2
2008	58.8	34.0	53.1	94.0	98.3	98.7	99.0	94.3	58.0	38.1	22.7	11.0	8.6	1.6
2007	60.1	35.0	60.5	93.9	98.1	97.5	99.2	95.2	61.5	37.8	27.8	10.7	9.7	2.0
2006	59.5	34.8	57.0	92.5	97.0	97.1	97.8	91.9	64.1	38.8	25.6	9.5	7.0	2.5
2005	59.2	34.6	52.5	95.1	97.5	97.9	93.8	93.8	66.2	34.9	23.9	9.3	6.1	2.3

Note: Data shown for 1947 to 1966 for the Black population are for Black and other races. Data for 1947 to 1963 exclude kindergarten. Nursery school was first collected in 1964.

Table A-10. Percentage of the Population 3 Years Old and Over Enrolled in School, by Age, Sex, Race, and Hispanic Origin, October 1947–2016—*Continued*

(Percent; civilian noninstitutionalized population.)

Year, sex, race, and Hispanic origin	Total enrolled 3 to 34 years old	Total enrolled 3 years old and over	Age											
			3 and 4	5 and 6	7 to 9	10 to 13	14 and 15	16 and 17	18 and 19	20 and 21	22 to 24	25 to 29	30 to 34	35 and over
2004	59.7	35.3	59.9	93.9	96.8	99.2	98.8	96.3	57.9	38.2	21.0	9.3	3.9	2.2
2003	60.6	35.7	57.6	93.2	98.8	98.2	98.3	93.8	61.1	35.6	23.4	9.4	7.2	1.9
Female														
2016	56.8	29.9	56.6	95.6	98.9	98.8	93.9	94.6	67.6	51.1	28.5	12.8	9.9	3.4
2015	56.1	29.9	51.9	94.9	95.8	97.6	97.6	94.8	64.8	45.2	24.6	15.1	11.5	3.6
2014	56.8	31.0	57.4	93.6	98.9	97.9	99.1	91.6	68.4	40.1	27.5	16.4	10.5	4.5
2013	58.6	31.7	61.2	94.0	97.3	98.1	98.8	91.0	68.4	53.1	28.6	19.1	10.9	3.5
2012	59.9	32.7	54.7	91.3	97.7	99.0	96.5	93.7	76.4	49.7	31.2	19.6	16.3	4.3
2011	59.5	32.8	55.0	91.3	97.2	98.4	99.4	97.5	76.5	45.0	31.7	21.7	14.4	4.7
2010	59.6	33.0	56.7	95.4	97.2	98.8	99.4	97.6	64.3	54.2	29.7	18.7	14.5	4.9
2009	59.8	33.0	56.9	93.9	97.6	98.9	99.4	93.1	68.9	46.1	36.5	17.5	13.5	4.8
2008	58.8	32.1	55.7	91.7	99.4	99.5	97.2	94.7	61.3	42.5	26.6	18.6	13.8	3.8
2007	57.9	31.7	55.7	94.5	98.2	98.4	98.9	92.2	62.6	38.5	26.8	19.4	9.5	3.8
2006	58.2	32.0	60.9	92.3	96.9	97.4	97.0	94.6	65.6	39.0	29.8	14.0	10.5	3.6
2005	58.8	32.4	50.0	97.1	99.4	99.3	97.8	92.0	59.1	41.3	31.1	13.8	12.8	3.7
2004	59.6	33.4	57.0	95.0	98.1	99.6	98.4	94.2	61.3	43.1	29.3	19.3	9.5	4.2
2003	59.1	32.9	55.3	95.9	97.3	98.4	97.6	94.5	60.7	47.5	30.7	14.7	9.4	3.5
ASIAN ALONE OR IN COMBINATION														
Both Sexes														
2016	57.0	28.6	63.2	90.7	98.1	98.8	98.2	94.0	78.4	73.7	46.7	20.6	6.4	1.4
2015	58.0	28.8	59.9	95.6	97.8	98.2	98.2	88.1	83.3	83.1	48.4	19.8	9.0	1.5
2014	57.4	29.4	54.2	89.3	97.0	97.7	96.3	93.8	85.9	73.7	53.9	19.5	5.6	2.0
2013	58.7	30.3	57.4	92.5	97.7	98.5	99.0	97.4	83.0	80.3	46.2	18.1	7.8	2.2
2012	59.1	30.1	56.7	93.9	99.9	98.6	99.0	97.8	79.4	72.8	52.2	18.5	8.4	1.8
2011	58.8	29.7	55.4	96.6	97.9	97.4	98.2	97.6	80.4	77.1	41.4	17.2	9.1	2.1
2010	60.5	30.6	62.4	96.7	98.9	98.4	98.0	96.1	81.9	76.9	46.5	21.3	10.1	1.8
2009	59.3	29.0	55.3	95.6	97.2	95.8	96.8	97.0	90.1	73.6	53.5	18.7	10.8	2.1
2008	59.2	29.5	57.4	92.6	98.3	99.6	98.8	93.5	85.9	79.4	43.0	23.0	11.9	2.5
2007	57.0	28.8	54.1	93.9	98.4	99.3	99.7	93.4	86.3	64.3	45.9	14.9	9.5	1.8
2006	56.3	29.0	51.5	94.6	99.0	99.3	99.6	92.0	82.3	72.2	43.1	17.3	8.8	2.2
2005	57.6	30.5	54.4	95.5	99.6	97.5	98.7	98.2	86.2	77.1	44.4	20.9	9.4	2.3
2004	58.5	31.4	57.7	97.6	99.9	99.2	98.0	97.1	79.9	77.7	46.2	20.8	9.3	2.7
2003	58.2	31.3	51.4	89.3	99.2	99.4	99.1	95.7	87.1	77.0	48.1	21.6	9.4	2.2
Male														
2016	58.7	30.6	60.1	87.5	98.2	98.9	99.0	91.1	76.3	76.9	52.1	21.4	7.2	1.6
2015	58.5	29.8	65.2	96.6	98.0	98.6	97.9	87.5	81.4	82.3	44.7	19.8	8.4	1.1
2014	59.0	31.1	55.3	92.0	98.3	97.7	95.6	94.0	85.2	71.3	59.2	21.6	4.1	1.9
2013	59.6	31.3	57.8	94.1	98.2	98.3	98.3	96.1	82.4	84.2	47.9	20.4	5.6	1.6
2012	59.5	31.2	57.8	94.2	99.8	98.3	98.0	97.8	82.3	72.6	49.4	19.6	6.3	1.5
2011	59.4	30.7	55.9	97.4	97.3	98.6	98.6	96.9	83.3	79.5	39.1	17.0	9.5	1.4
2010	61.5	32.2	63.1	97.9	99.0	98.0	97.6	96.5	78.1	80.7	43.1	23.5	10.3	1.7
2009	59.5	30.5	54.9	95.3	96.6	95.3	97.8	96.1	91.4	74.3	51.5	17.9	9.7	2.3
2008	59.4	30.2	56.1	92.8	97.3	99.2	100.0	96.4	89.7	74.2	39.0	24.5	11.3	2.0
2007	58.6	30.4	58.9	95.4	99.1	99.1	99.7	93.5	90.6	62.7	47.0	19.5	9.8	2.1
2006	57.0	30.2	60.4	94.7	98.2	99.0	100.0	90.1	78.1	74.6	43.0	14.9	8.5	2.4
2005	58.3	31.7	51.1	97.4	99.7	96.5	98.0	97.3	83.6	82.1	42.2	20.2	9.9	2.0
2004	60.8	33.9	57.2	96.5	99.8	99.9	97.1	96.9	83.5	83.6	49.6	23.0	10.9	2.9
2003	60.2	33.4	49.3	91.9	98.2	99.9	98.2	95.9	89.6	74.0	47.3	27.9	12.1	2.4
Female														
2016	55.3	26.8	66.4	94.0	98.0	98.6	97.6	96.7	80.4	70.6	40.4	19.7	5.8	1.2
2015	57.4	28.0	54.4	94.4	97.5	97.8	98.5	88.7	85.2	83.8	52.5	19.8	9.6	1.9
2014	55.8	27.9	53.2	86.4	95.6	97.8	97.1	93.6	86.5	76.2	48.6	17.6	7.0	2.0
2013	57.8	29.4	57.0	90.5	97.2	98.7	99.7	98.4	83.6	76.0	44.4	15.8	9.6	2.7
2012	58.7	29.2	55.5	93.7	100.0	98.8	100.0	97.9	76.3	72.9	55.3	17.5	10.2	2.1
2011	58.3	28.7	54.9	95.7	98.5	96.2	97.9	98.3	77.1	74.8	44.0	17.4	8.7	2.6
2010	59.4	29.1	61.7	95.5	98.7	98.9	98.4	95.7	86.2	73.1	50.0	19.1	9.9	2.0
2009	59.2	27.7	55.8	95.9	97.8	96.3	95.2	98.1	88.8	73.0	55.6	19.5	11.9	1.9
2008	58.9	28.8	59.1	92.3	99.2	100.0	97.5	90.8	82.4	85.7	46.8	21.7	12.5	2.9
2007	55.5	27.4	48.3	92.5	97.6	99.5	99.7	93.2	82.2	66.1	45.0	19.7	9.2	1.5
2006	55.7	27.9	41.4	94.5	100.0	99.6	99.1	93.6	87.8	69.4	43.2	19.4	9.0	2.1
2005	57.0	29.3	57.5	93.2	99.5	98.5	99.7	99.1	89.2	71.2	46.2	21.6	8.9	2.5
2004	56.1	29.0	58.4	99.2	99.9	98.5	98.9	97.2	76.3	71.5	42.9	18.8	7.8	2.5
2003	56.2	29.3	54.2	86.0	100.0	98.7	100.0	95.4	85.1	79.7	48.8	15.8	6.9	2.1

Note: Data shown for 1947 to 1966 for the Black population are for Black and other races. Data for 1947 to 1963 exclude kindergarten. Nursery school was first collected in 1964.

Table A-11. Population 6 to 17 Years Old Enrolled Below Modal Grade, 1971–2016

(Numbers in thousands; percent; civilian noninstitutionalized population.)

Year, sex, race, and Hispanic origin	Percent below modal grade				Dropout rate, 15 to 17 years	Population in age group			
	6 to 8 years	9 to 11 years	12 to 14 years	15 to 17 years		6 to 8 years	9 to 11 years	12 to 14 years	15 to 17 years
ALL RACES									
Both Sexes									
2016	23.9	29.6	29.6	30.2	3.8	12,152	12,497	12,326	12,663
2015	23.3	29.1	30.3	30.5	3.2	12,182	12,520	12,361	12,663
2014	22.6	28.0	29.9	31.0	4.1	12,320	12,286	12,433	12,502
2013	22.4	26.0	30.4	31.5	3.7	12,405	12,246	12,448	12,422
2012	23.5	27.6	30.2	33.3	2.4	12,185	12,236	12,435	12,554
2011	22.4	28.3	29.4	31.4	2.3	12,643	12,408	11,834	12,282
2010	18.2	24.6	28.6	28.9	2.2	12,618	12,190	11,963	12,273
2009	18.9	26.3	29.7	29.5	3.0	12,305	11,819	12,030	12,391
2008	19.8	27.0	31.0	30.5	2.7	12,104	11,793	12,128	12,746
2007	20.1	26.2	27.9	30.0	2.9	12,011	11,805	12,398	12,857
2006	20.1	26.1	27.9	30.5	3.0	11,776	11,902	12,473	12,926
2005	20.7	25.4	28.3	30.6	2.8	11,784	11,998	12,689	13,204
2004	21.7	25.4	28.2	32.0	3.5	11,799	12,034	12,870	12,766
2003	21.3	28.1	28.8	30.6	3.2	11,866	12,124	12,951	12,753
2002	18.0	25.5	27.1	30.1	3.3	12,029	12,421	12,592	12,187
2001	18.6	23.7	25.9	29.7	3.8	11,972	12,738	12,357	12,031
2000	19.2	24.0	27.8	30.2	4.3	12,079	12,713	12,003	11,933
1999	17.4	25.3	26.5	30.8	4.0	12,159	12,537	11,921	12,048
1998	19.0	23.8	26.7	31.9	3.8	12,165	11,960	11,600	11,314
1997	18.6	24.2	28.5	32.1	3.6	12,325	11,866	11,650	11,953
1996	17.9	23.3	28.8	31.0	4.8	12,191	11,845	11,653	11,617
1995	17.5	25.6	30.8	32.8	4.1	11,728	11,812	11,582	11,401
1994	18.9	26.2	31.3	30.9	3.8	11,601	11,528	11,462	10,560
1993ʳ	18.7	28.1	31.0	32.3	3.8	11,363	11,283	10,981	10,247
1993	18.7	28.0	30.8	32.0	3.7	11,363	11,283	10,981	10,247
1992	19.4	28.4	30.9	30.5	3.6	11,260	11,183	10,723	10,114
1991	21.2	26.9	29.6	30.0	4.6	11,120	11,099	10,440	9,923
1990	21.5	27.6	31.0	30.1	4.7	11,015	10,914	10,152	9,912
1989	21.4	29.0	31.8	28.0	4.5	11,007	10,673	9,928	10,020
1988	20.4	28.4	28.7	26.2	5.1	10,906	10,350	9,869	10,379
1987	20.9	26.7	27.6	24.8	5.1	10,702	10,053	9,795	10,944
1986	19.2	26.5	27.3	25.8	4.9	10,389	9,959	9,908	11,149
1985	17.9	24.9	25.7	25.5	5.1	10,076	9,673	10,442	11,024
1984	16.6	23.9	27.0	24.6	5.3	9,707	9,594	10,858	10,711
1983	15.4	24.4	24.8	23.7	5.2	9,605	9,730	11,123	10,768
1982	16.6	22.8	23.9	23.0	5.4	9,492	10,169	10,989	11,131
1981	14.4	23.3	23.0	23.8	6.1	9,519	10,657	10,712	11,757
1980	14.3	20.3	22.6	22.5	6.6	9,350	10,681	10,537	11,835
1979	13.0	20.2	20.3	21.6	6.5	9,804	10,545	10,886	12,190
1978	12.4	19.5	19.2	21.8	6.5	10,246	10,448	11,391	12,346
1977	10.7	18.9	18.9	21.2	6.4	10,449	10,537	11,826	12,472
1976	10.6	18.1	19.8	22.2	6.3	10,334	10,872	12,137	12,550
1975	11.1	17.4	21.3	22.5	6.4	10,256	11,343	12,372	12,531
1974	10.3	17.8	21.7	21.6	7.1	10,343	11,789	12,415	12,566
1973	10.7	18.4	21.5	21.3	7.1	10,614	11,946	12,542	12,309
1972	10.7	19.6	21.9	22.3	6.6	11,119	12,152	12,451	12,283
1971	11.1	19.7	22.0	22.5	5.7	11,938	12,648	12,429	11,906
Male									
2016	25.1	30.8	33.0	33.5	4.1	6,197	6,358	6,296	6,413
2015	24.0	30.6	30.8	33.8	3.3	6,201	6,398	6,302	6,464
2014	24.1	29.5	32.1	33.5	4.7	6,269	6,316	6,346	6,375
2013	23.7	29.5	33.2	35.2	3.9	6,264	6,272	6,347	6,328
2012	25.8	30.4	34.3	37.1	2.6	6,252	5,251	6,347	6,423
2011	24.6	31.9	32.1	35.8	2.4	6,478	6,326	6,067	6,256
2010	20.0	27.4	30.7	31.5	2.4	6,451	6,213	6,104	6,300
2009	20.0	29.7	32.4	33.2	3.2	6,260	6,058	6,144	6,334
2008	22.0	28.3	34.0	33.3	2.8	6,174	6,005	6,220	6,502
2007	23.0	28.1	29.8	33.7	2.9	6,159	6,031	6,310	6,572
2006	21.7	28.2	31.1	35.0	3.3	5,991	6,115	6,374	6,574
2005	23.2	28.6	30.7	34.3	3.0	6,014	6,126	6,523	6,645
2004	23.9	28.2	31.7	36.8	3.5	6,075	6,120	6,685	6,395
2003	23.9	32.0	31.8	35.1	3.4	6,198	6,331	6,426	6,569
2002	20.3	29.2	31.0	35.6	3.5	6,156	6,349	6,436	6,210
2001	22.1	26.1	28.7	34.0	4.3	6,147	6,540	6,311	6,182
2000	22.1	27.2	31.3	34.3	4.5	6,181	6,504	6,148	6,136
1999	18.8	28.9	30.2	36.2	3.9	6,211	6,471	6,048	6,195
1998	21.4	26.6	30.4	37.4	4.1	6,234	6,125	5,897	5,791
1997	21.9	27.7	33.4	37.8	3.7	6,295	6,112	5,932	6,126
1996	20.7	26.0	33.9	36.9	4.5	6,268	6,043	5,934	5,985
1995	20.2	28.0	35.2	38.5	3.5	5,999	6,027	5,930	5,840

ʳ = Revised, controlled to 1990 census based population estimates; previous 1993 data controlled to 1980 census based population estimates.

Table A-11. Population 6 to 17 Years Old Enrolled Below Modal Grade, 1971–2016—*Continued*

(Numbers in thousands; percent; civilian noninstitutionalized population.)

Year, sex, race, and Hispanic origin	Percent below modal grade				Dropout rate, 15 to 17 years	Population in age group			
	6 to 8 years	9 to 11 years	12 to 14 years	15 to 17 years		6 to 8 years	9 to 11 years	12 to 14 years	15 to 17 years
1994	21.1	28.0	35.6	35.7	3.9	5,894	6,026	5,874	5,640
1993ʳ	21.2	32.1	35.4	40.3	3.3	5,837	5,736	5,629	5,262
1993	21.1	32.0	35.0	38.7	3.1	5,837	5,736	5,629	5,262
1992	21.6	32.6	37.0	35.2	2.7	5,738	5,742	5,502	5,166
1991	24.0	30.7	34.7	35.5	4.3	5,674	5,704	5,343	5,085
1990	23.9	32.0	36.2	35.3	4.6	5,629	5,603	5,200	5,078
1989	25.1	32.9	36.7	33.4	4.3	5,632	5,472	5,088	5,151
1988	23.5	33.2	33.7	30.6	4.8	5,580	5,298	5,065	5,286
1987	23.7	31.8	31.8	29.2	4.6	5,496	5,147	5,036	5,535
1986	22.9	30.4	32.2	30.2	4.9	5,311	5,113	5,066	5,697
1985	20.6	28.3	29.0	30.2	4.9	5,159	4,946	5,340	5,623
1984	18.8	27.7	31.1	30.2	5.5	4,963	4,905	5,521	5,469
1983	17.8	28.7	30.3	28.5	5.3	4,913	4,974	5,690	5,463
1982	19.2	26.4	28.0	27.9	5.2	4,852	5,198	5,566	5,688
1981	17.2	27.9	25.6	28.1	6.2	4,866	5,447	5,510	5,914
1980	16.4	23.4	27.3	26.8	6.4	4,774	5,453	5,282	6,067
1979	15.5	23.4	24.1	27.4	5.9	5,004	5,379	5,555	6,174
1978	14.7	22.9	22.9	26.2	6.7	5,227	5,326	5,797	6,265
1977	12.5	22.4	22.6	25.3	6.1	5,327	5,371	6,044	6,297
1976	12.5	20.9	23.4	27.5	5.7	5,265	5,540	6,185	6,356
1975	12.6	21.2	25.8	26.8	5.7	5,223	5,782	6,336	6,309
1974	12.2	21.2	25.9	26.3	7.0	5,267	6,011	6,329	6,352
1973	12.8	20.8	25.2	26.4	6.8	5,403	6,082	6,397	6,215
1972	12.5	23.3	26.8	26.8	6.2	5,662	6,188	6,322	6,232
1971	13.5	22.8	26.1	27.2	5.0	6,088	6,440	6,293	6,019
Female									
2016	22.6	28.3	26.1	26.7	3.5	5,955	6,140	6,030	6,250
2015	22.5	27.6	29.9	27.0	3.0	5,981	6,123	6,060	6,199
2014	21.1	26.4	27.6	28.4	3.4	6,050	5,970	6,087	6,126
2013	21.1	22.3	27.6	27.5	3.4	6,141	5,974	6,100	6,095
2012	21.0	24.6	25.8	29.3	2.1	5,933	5,985	6,087	6,132
2011	20.0	24.7	26.6	26.9	2.1	6,165	6,082	5,767	6,026
2010	16.4	21.7	26.4	26.1	1.5	6,166	5,977	5,860	5,973
2009	17.8	22.8	26.9	25.6	2.8	6,046	5,761	5,886	6,057
2008	17.5	25.6	27.7	27.7	2.4	5,930	5,787	5,908	6,244
2007	17.2	24.1	25.9	26.2	2.9	5,852	5,773	6,088	6,285
2006	18.4	23.9	24.6	25.9	2.6	5,785	5,787	6,099	6,352
2005	18.2	22.0	25.8	26.8	2.6	5,769	5,872	6,167	6,559
2004	19.4	22.5	24.4	27.1	3.5	5,724	5,914	6,185	6,371
2003	18.5	23.8	25.8	25.8	3.0	5,668	5,793	6,524	6,184
2002	15.6	21.7	23.0	24.4	3.1	5,872	6,072	6,156	5,977
2001	14.9	21.3	23.0	25.2	3.3	5,825	6,197	6,046	5,849
2000	16.1	20.6	24.2	25.8	4.2	5,897	6,209	5,855	5,797
1999	16.1	21.6	22.7	25.1	4.2	5,948	6,066	5,872	5,852
1998	16.5	20.9	22.8	26.2	3.5	5,931	5,835	5,703	5,523
1997	15.1	20.4	23.3	26.1	3.5	6,030	5,754	5,718	5,827
1996	14.9	20.4	23.4	24.7	5.3	5,923	5,802	5,719	5,632
1995	14.6	23.1	26.0	26.7	4.4	5,728	5,786	5,653	5,552
1994	16.5	24.2	26.7	24.8	3.6	5,705	5,644	5,666	5,384
1993ʳ	16.3	24.0	26.4	26.4	4.4	5,526	5,545	5,353	4,984
1993	16.1	23.9	26.2	24.9	4.3	5,526	5,545	5,353	4,984
1992	17.1	23.5	24.6	25.6	4.5	5,523	5,441	5,220	4,947
1991	18.2	22.8	24.6	24.2	5.1	5,445	5,395	5,098	4,838
1990	19.1	23.2	25.7	24.7	4.7	5,387	5,312	4,951	4,834
1989	18.1	22.6	26.6	22.3	4.6	5,375	5,201	4,840	4,869
1988	17.3	23.6	23.4	21.7	5.4	5,327	5,052	4,803	5,093
1987	17.8	21.5	23.2	20.2	5.6	5,206	4,906	4,759	5,408
1986	15.2	22.4	22.1	21.1	4.9	5,078	4,846	4,842	5,452
1985	15.1	21.4	22.1	20.6	5.5	4,917	4,727	5,102	5,401
1984	14.2	19.8	22.9	18.7	5.1	4,744	4,689	5,337	5,242
1983	12.9	19.9	19.1	18.6	5.2	4,692	4,756	5,433	5,305
1982	13.8	19.0	19.7	17.9	5.7	4,640	4,971	5,423	5,443
1981	11.6	18.4	20.1	19.6	6.1	4,653	5,210	5,202	5,843
1980	12.1	17.0	17.8	18.0	6.7	4,576	5,228	5,255	5,768
1979	10.4	16.9	16.4	15.6	7.1	4,800	5,166	5,331	6,016
1978	10.1	16.0	15.3	17.2	6.4	5,019	5,122	5,594	6,081
1977	8.9	15.2	15.0	17.1	6.6	5,122	5,166	5,782	6,175
1976	8.6	15.1	16.0	16.8	7.0	5,069	5,332	5,952	6,194
1975	9.4	13.5	16.7	18.2	7.2	5,033	5,561	6,036	6,222
1974	8.3	14.4	17.4	16.8	7.1	5,076	5,778	6,086	6,214
1973	8.7	15.8	16.5	16.1	7.4	5,211	5,864	6,145	6,094
1972	8.9	15.7	17.0	17.7	7.1	5,457	5,964	6,129	6,051
1971	8.7	12.3	17.8	17.6	6.5	5,850	6,208	6,136	5,887

ʳ = Revised, controlled to 1990 census based population estimates; previous 1993 data controlled to 1980 census based population estimates.

Table A-11. Population 6 to 17 Years Old Enrolled Below Modal Grade, 1971–2016—*Continued*

(Numbers in thousands; percent; civilian noninstitutionalized population.)

Year, sex, race, and Hispanic origin	Percent below modal grade				Dropout rate, 15 to 17 years	Population in age group			
	6 to 8 years	9 to 11 years	12 to 14 years	15 to 17 years		6 to 8 years	9 to 11 years	12 to 14 years	15 to 17 years
WHITE ALONE									
Both Sexes									
2016............................	24.5	29.7	30.1	30.4	4.1	8,772	9,060	9,073	9,267
2015............................	23.9	29.5	30.6	30.5	3.2	8,865	9,038	9,095	9,271
2014............................	23.2	27.7	29.1	30.3	3.9	8,983	9,035	9,181	9,220
2013............................	22.7	26.6	31.1	31.8	3.7	9,014	9,034	9,236	9,228
2012............................	23.9	27.7	30.7	32.7	2.4	9,006	9,067	9,247	9,291
2011............................	23.1	28.3	30.2	31.4	2.2	9,488	9,401	9,020	9,337
2010............................	19.1	24.7	28.3	28.5	2.3	9,455	9,276	9,110	9,344
2009............................	19.1	26.2	29.0	28.6	3.3	9,377	9,006	9,167	9,495
2008............................	20.3	27.1	29.4	29.7	2.6	9,288	8,967	9,250	9,658
2007............................	21.3	26.2	27.6	28.3	2.8	9,118	9,021	9,432	9,834
2006............................	20.6	25.5	26.8	29.9	3.0	8,981	9,074	9,542	9,813
2005............................	21.4	23.8	28.0	29.5	2.6	8,929	9,194	9,680	10,131
2004............................	22.4	25.6	27.6	30.7	3.8	9,051	9,173	9,853	9,784
2003[1]......................	21.5	27.6	28.3	29.4	3.2	9,102	9,112	9,875	9,889
2002............................	18.1	25.7	26.2	29.6	3.1	9,230	9,682	9,832	9,520
2001............................	19.2	22.7	25.2	28.9	3.8	9,330	9,826	9,651	9,480
2000............................	19.4	23.7	26.3	29.7	4.5	9,404	9,937	9,368	9,449
1999............................	18.3	24.6	25.8	30.0	4.2	9,539	9,768	9,323	9,428
1998............................	19.5	23.5	25.8	30.5	3.8	9,481	9,413	9,130	8,926
1997............................	18.8	24.0	27.9	30.3	3.5	9,555	9,390	9,167	9,352
1996............................	18.1	22.6	27.6	30.1	4.9	9,458	9,420	9,184	9,135
1995............................	17.7	24.9	29.2	31.0	3.9	9,221	9,340	9,130	8,933
1994............................	19.4	25.8	30.1	29.6	3.7	9,087	9,261	9,121	8,668
1993[r]......................	18.8	27.3	29.4	31.2	3.9	9,018	8,967	8,728	8,160
1993............................	18.7	27.2	29.2	29.7	3.6	9,074	9,017	8,783	8,159
1992............................	19.5	27.5	29.6	28.1	3.5	8,956	8,996	8,520	8,031
1991............................	21.3	25.7	27.7	27.2	4.7	8,874	8,840	8,328	7,903
1990............................	21.9	26.8	28.4	27.3	4.6	8,860	8,752	8,140	7,909
1989............................	22.4	26.8	29.9	25.7	4.6	8,858	8,527	7,994	8,026
1988............................	21.0	27.6	27.2	23.9	5.4	8,758	8,323	7,929	8,353
1987............................	21.1	25.9	26.0	22.7	5.1	8,606	8,117	7,846	8,887
1986............................	19.1	25.1	25.3	23.7	5.0	8,395	8,000	8,054	9,037
1985............................	18.0	23.3	23.3	23.0	5.3	8,136	7,840	8,429	9,045
1984............................	16.3	22.1	24.7	22.7	5.6	7,915	7,781	8,827	8,853
1983............................	15.5	22.4	23.1	21.1	5.4	7,821	7,906	9,152	8,831
1982............................	16.4	21.8	22.1	21.1	5.6	7,729	8,294	9,035	9,184
1981............................	14.7	22.2	21.0	21.6	6.1	7,782	8,741	8,813	9,762
1980............................	14.1	19.0	21.1	19.3	6.7	7,635	8,823	8,739	10,132
1979............................	12.9	18.4	18.5	19.4	6.5	8,041	8,747	9,026	10,239
1978............................	12.4	18.0	17.9	19.3	6.8	8,460	8,686	9,522	10,358
1977............................	10.6	17.7	17.5	19.3	6.6	8,675	8,771	9,918	10,510
1976............................	10.5	17.2	18.7	19.7	6.3	8,612	9,066	10,187	10,622
1975............................	11.0	16.0	20.0	20.4	6.3	8,566	9,486	10,466	10,583
1974............................	10.2	16.5	19.7	19.4	6.9	8,656	9,912	10,508	10,678
1973............................	10.6	17.3	19.9	19.1	7.0	8,929	10,117	10,704	10,481
1972............................	10.3	18.2	20.1	20.0	6.6	9,359	10,313	10,606	10,506
1971............................	10.5	18.3	20.4	19.9	5.5	9,988	10,692	10,682	10,231
Male									
2016............................	26.4	30.6	32.9	34.6	4.3	4,486	4,637	4,639	4,737
2015............................	25.5	31.0	31.3	33.8	3.6	4,535	4,628	4,650	4,742
2014............................	24.7	29.3	31.1	33.2	4.5	4,600	4,629	4,703	4,721
2013............................	25.1	30.1	33.9	35.3	4.2	4,618	4,626	4,733	4,726
2012............................	25.6	30.3	35.4	36.9	2.8	4,615	4,642	4,741	4,764
2011............................	25.7	31.6	32.9	36.5	2.2	4,861	4,816	4,626	4,809
2010............................	21.3	27.2	30.3	31.2	3.0	4,825	4,746	4,666	4,805
2009............................	20.4	29.5	31.7	31.9	3.5	4,816	4,611	4,697	4,866
2008............................	22.5	29.3	32.6	32.9	2.7	4,764	4,568	4,748	4,966
2007............................	24.3	28.4	29.5	31.8	2.9	4,671	4,620	4,851	5,022
2006............................	22.5	27.0	29.8	34.2	3.3	4,596	4,652	4,900	5,011
2005............................	24.3	27.4	31.0	33.2	2.7	4,576	4,715	4,995	5,116
2004............................	24.9	28.0	31.4	35.2	3.8	4,706	4,647	5,168	4,905
2003[1]......................	24.4	31.6	31.2	34.0	3.4	4,785	4,795	4,961	5,026
2002............................	21.7	29.5	30.4	34.7	3.2	4,737	4,965	5,044	4,875
2001............................	22.7	25.3	28.3	32.8	4.4	4,789	5,040	4,949	4,862
2000............................	22.5	27.6	29.6	34.0	4.4	4,815	5,094	4,798	4,861
1999............................	19.9	28.2	29.7	35.8	4.2	4,883	5,009	4,777	4,851
1998............................	21.9	26.4	30.2	36.2	4.4	4,851	4,823	4,686	4,571
1997............................	22.3	27.8	32.7	37.0	3.8	4,897	4,819	4,702	4,821

[1]Starting in 2003, respondents could identify more than one race. Except as noted, the race data in this table from 2003 onward represent those respondents who indicated only one race category.

[r] = Revised, controlled to 1990 census based population estimates; previous 1993 data controlled to 1980 census based population estimates.

Table A-11. Population 6 to 17 Years Old Enrolled Below Modal Grade, 1971–2016—*Continued*

(Numbers in thousands; percent; civilian noninstitutionalized population.)

Year, sex, race, and Hispanic origin	Percent below modal grade				Dropout rate, 15 to 17 years	Population in age group			
	6 to 8 years	9 to 11 years	12 to 14 years	15 to 17 years		6 to 8 years	9 to 11 years	12 to 14 years	15 to 17 years
1996	20.8	25.9	32.3	36.5	4.5	4,849	4,836	4,706	4,694
1995	20.5	28.0	33.4	36.5	3.8	4,727	4,797	4,680	4,592
1994	22.0	27.9	34.4	35.2	4.0	4,659	4,758	4,679	4,457
1993ʳ	21.4	31.8	33.8	37.6	3.2	4,625	4,601	4,476	4,178
1993	21.4	31.6	33.6	36.1	3.1	4,662	4,614	4,485	4,178
1992	21.5	31.8	35.8	32.4	2.8	4,602	4,607	4,359	4,115
1991	24.4	29.1	32.5	32.5	4.2	4,556	4,568	4,270	4,047
1990	24.6	31.3	33.3	32.6	4.8	4,555	4,482	4,186	4,054
1989	26.0	32.1	35.0	30.8	4.6	4,544	4,378	4,112	4,107
1988	24.7	32.8	32.2	28.8	5.1	4,493	4,272	4,062	4,281
1987	24.6	30.5	30.4	26.6	4.5	4,415	4,167	4,069	4,504
1986	22.9	28.9	30.1	27.9	5.2	4,307	4,108	4,125	4,624
1985	21.1	26.5	26.7	28.0	4.9	4,175	4,024	4,307	4,634
1984	18.1	25.8	28.7	28.1	5.8	4,061	3,994	4,501	4,542
1983	18.1	26.3	28.0	26.3	5.6	4,002	4,054	4,697	4,481
1982	19.3	26.2	26.2	26.1	5.3	3,956	4,260	4,591	4,711
1981	17.3	26.9	24.2	25.4	6.3	3,990	4,480	4,556	4,937
1980	16.3	21.9	25.7	23.9	6.7	3,907	4,517	4,399	5,066
1979	15.4	20.8	22.3	24.8	6.2	4,114	4,475	4,616	5,201
1978	14.7	21.2	22.0	23.1	7.2	4,328	4,441	4,843	5,287
1977	12.5	21.1	21.2	23.5	6.3	4,436	4,484	5,079	5,325
1976	12.6	20.2	22.1	24.8	5.6	4,402	4,632	5,200	5,398
1975	12.9	19.7	24.7	24.7	5.4	4,376	4,848	5,385	5,332
1974	12.1	19.5	23.7	23.8	7.0	4,422	5,066	5,383	5,402
1973	12.5	19.6	23.1	24.0	6.6	4,559	5,165	5,469	5,319
1972	12.2	21.9	24.6	24.3	6.1	4,778	5,266	5,410	5,340
1971	12.6	21.6	23.9	24.4	4.6	5,106	5,461	5,455	5,185
Female									
2016	22.5	28.8	27.1	26.0	3.9	4,286	4,423	4,434	4,530
2015	22.1	27.8	29.9	27.0	2.7	4,330	4,410	4,445	4,529
2014	21.7	26.0	27.0	27.3	3.4	4,383	4,406	4,479	4,500
2013	20.2	23.0	28.2	28.0	3.1	4,397	4,408	4,502	4,502
2012	22.0	24.9	25.7	28.2	2.0	4,392	4,425	4,506	4,527
2011	20.4	24.8	27.4	26.1	2.2	4,627	4,585	4,394	4,528
2010	16.9	22.1	26.1	25.7	1.4	4,630	4,530	4,444	4,539
2009	17.8	22.8	26.2	25.1	3.0	4,561	4,394	4,470	4,629
2008	18.0	24.8	26.0	26.3	2.4	4,524	4,398	4,502	4,692
2007	18.2	23.9	25.7	24.6	2.7	4,447	4,401	4,582	4,812
2006	18.6	24.0	23.8	25.5	2.6	4,385	4,422	4,643	4,801
2005	18.3	20.1	24.8	25.8	2.5	4,353	4,479	4,685	5,015
2004	19.7	23.3	23.4	26.1	3.8	4,345	4,527	4,686	4,878
2003[1]	18.3	23.1	25.3	24.7	3.0	4,317	4,317	4,914	4,863
2002	14.4	21.7	21.9	24.3	3.0	4,493	4,717	4,788	4,645
2001	15.5	20.0	21.8	24.9	3.1	4,541	4,786	4,701	4,618
2000	16.1	19.7	22.9	25.2	4.5	4,587	4,843	4,570	4,588
1999	16.7	20.7	21.8	23.9	4.1	4,655	4,579	4,546	4,578
1998	16.9	20.5	21.2	24.4	3.2	4,629	4,589	4,444	4,355
1997	15.1	20.0	22.7	23.2	3.3	4,658	4,571	4,464	4,530
1996	15.3	19.2	22.7	23.2	5.3	4,609	4,583	4,477	4,441
1995	14.7	21.6	24.8	25.0	4.1	4,494	4,543	4,449	4,342
1994	16.7	23.5	25.7	23.6	3.4	4,427	4,504	4,443	4,212
1993ʳ	15.9	22.6	24.8	24.4	4.3	4,393	4,366	4,252	3,982
1993	15.8	22.5	24.6	23.1	4.2	4,412	4,404	4,298	3,982
1992	17.3	22.9	23.2	23.6	4.3	4,354	4,389	4,161	3,916
1991	18.1	22.1	22.6	21.5	5.2	4,318	4,272	4,058	3,856
1990	19.0	22.2	23.2	21.8	4.5	4,305	4,270	3,954	3,855
1989	18.6	21.3	24.5	20.3	4.7	4,314	4,149	3,882	3,919
1988	17.1	22.2	21.9	18.8	5.6	4,265	4,051	3,867	4,072
1987	17.3	21.0	21.3	18.7	5.8	4,191	3,950	3,777	4,383
1986	15.0	21.1	20.2	19.3	4.8	4,088	3,892	3,929	4,413
1985	14.8	19.9	19.7	17.6	5.7	3,961	3,816	4,122	4,411
1984	14.3	18.3	20.5	17.0	5.4	3,854	3,787	4,326	4,311
1983	12.7	18.3	17.9	15.8	5.2	3,819	3,852	4,455	4,350
1982ʳ	13.4	17.2	17.8	15.8	6.0	3,773	4,034	4,444	4,473
1981	11.9	17.3	17.6	17.6	5.9	3,792	4,261	4,257	4,825
1980	11.7	16.0	16.5	14.7	6.6	3,728	4,306	4,340	5,066
1979	10.3	15.8	14.5	13.8	6.9	3,927	4,272	4,410	5,038
1978	10.0	14.7	13.7	15.2	6.4	4,132	4,245	4,679	5,071
1977	8.5	14.1	13.7	14.9	6.8	4,239	4,287	4,839	5,185
1976	8.4	14.1	15.1	14.5	6.9	4,210	4,434	4,987	5,224
1975	9.1	12.2	15.1	16.0	7.1	4,190	4,638	5,081	5,251
1974	8.2	13.4	15.5	15.0	6.7	4,234	4,846	5,125	5,276

[1]Starting in 2003, respondents could identify more than one race. Except as noted, the race data in this table from 2003 onward represent those respondents who indicated only one race category.

ʳ = Revised, controlled to 1990 census based population estimates; previous 1993 data controlled to 1980 census based population estimates.

Table A-11. Population 6 to 17 Years Old Enrolled Below Modal Grade, 1971–2016—*Continued*

(Numbers in thousands; percent; civilian noninstitutionalized population.)

Year, sex, race, and Hispanic origin	Percent below modal grade				Dropout rate, 15 to 17 years	Population in age group			
	6 to 8 years	9 to 11 years	12 to 14 years	15 to 17 years		6 to 8 years	9 to 11 years	12 to 14 years	15 to 17 years
1973............................	8.5	14.8	16.5	14.0	7.4	4,370	4,952	5,235	5,162
1972............................	8.3	14.2	15.4	15.5	7.2	4,581	5,047	5,196	5,166
1971............................	8.4	14.9	16.6	15.2	6.3	4,882	5,231	5,227	5,046
WHITE ALONE NON-HISPANIC									
Both Sexes									
2016............................	24.9	29.3	30.4	29.6	4.4	6,038	6,340	6,533	6,757
2015............................	24.9	29.4	30.2	29.5	2.7	6,185	6,411	6,574	6,806
2014............................	23.9	28.0	28.7	29.2	4.0	6,300	6,443	6,656	6,829
2013............................	22.7	25.4	30.4	30.7	3.6	6,287	6,489	6,752	6,865
2012............................	24.6	27.4	30.8	31.4	2.2	6,366	6,552	6,812	6,916
2011............................	24.5	28.5	30.6	29.9	1.8	6,648	6,765	6,750	7,033
2010............................	20.3	24.7	28.0	26.8	2.2	6,707	6,836	6,821	7,243
2009............................	19.4	26.3	29.3	27.8	2.8	6,768	6,755	6,989	7,437
2008............................	21.2	27.7	29.4	28.4	2.2	6,798	6,768	7,008	7,534
2007............................	21.3	25.3	26.5	26.8	2.1	6,763	6,783	7,182	7,784
2006............................	20.5	24.5	25.1	28.6	2.3	6,748	6,887	7,368	7,827
2005............................	22.4	23.2	26.3	29.0	2.1	6,728	7,052	7,584	8,150
2004............................	22.7	25.1	27.0	29.8	3.3	6,878	7,090	7,768	7,892
2003[1].........................	21.8	27.1	27.3	28.7	2.8	7,006	7,102	7,889	7,980
2002............................	18.9	24.9	25.8	28.1	2.5	7,118	7,627	7,913	7,803
2001............................	19.9	23.1	25.3	28.1	3.1	7,325	7,726	7,773	7,829
2000............................	19.4	23.7	26.1	28.8	3.5	7,418	8,045	7,727	7,852
1999............................	18.9	24.2	25.3	28.9	3.6	7,717	7,938	7,669	7,879
1998............................	20.5	23.7	26.0	28.9	3.0	7,755	7,794	7,697	7,859
1997............................	19.7	24.6	27.3	28.4	3.2	7,729	7,775	7,789	7,866
1996............................	18.8	22.7	26.2	28.6	4.2	7,803	7,792	7,731	7,716
1995............................	18.2	24.5	28.0	29.2	3.4	7,853	8,000	7,872	7,795
1994............................	19.8	25.6	30.0	28.0	3.1	7,779	7,864	7,845	7,490
1993............................	18.8	27.2	28.8	29.5	3.0	7,736	7,802	7,600	7,022
Male									
2016............................	27.5	31.3	32.8	32.9	4.9	3,086	3,251	3,360	3,467
2015............................	27.6	31.8	30.7	32.7	2.9	3,150	3,289	3,390	3,479
2014............................	25.0	28.9	31.1	31.5	4.6	3,218	3,303	3,412	3,487
2013............................	25.0	28.4	33.0	34.9	4.2	3,232	3,320	3,474	3,515
2012............................	25.9	30.8	31.4	32.5	2.2	3,264	3,371	3,518	3,545
2011............................	28.1	32.4	33.8	35.8	1.9	3,394	3,473	3,472	3,619
2010............................	23.3	27.7	30.6	30.5	3.1	3,414	3,498	3,487	3,728
2009............................	21.8	30.1	31.9	32.0	3.1	3,489	3,453	3,593	3,793
2008............................	24.4	29.9	33.2	31.8	2.4	3,485	3,459	3,599	3,862
2007............................	24.1	28.4	28.1	30.3	2.2	3,457	3,473	3,715	3,970
2006............................	23.1	26.0	27.6	32.4	2.9	3,449	3,537	3,775	3,984
2005............................	25.4	26.8	28.2	32.5	2.2	3,450	3,618	3,902	4,136
2004............................	25.0	27.9	30.6	35.0	3.4	3,548	3,605	4,054	3,994
2003[1].........................	24.6	31.7	30.7	33.4	2.9	3,668	3,725	3,960	4,101
2002............................	22.7	29.0	30.7	33.6	2.4	3,667	3,969	4,005	4,038
2001............................	23.1	26.2	28.5	31.6	3.7	3,808	3,971	3,920	4,020
2000............................	22.5	27.7	30.0	33.4	3.4	3,795	4,135	3,970	4,034
1999............................	20.3	27.7	29.7	35.1	3.5	3,955	4,076	3,913	4,058
1998............................	23.1	26.5	30.8	34.3	3.6	4,016	4,003	3,894	3,981
1997............................	24.1	29.0	32.5	35.3	3.8	3,977	3,971	3,996	4,020
1996............................	22.5	25.9	30.8	35.1	4.1	3,964	4,035	3,957	3,959
1995............................	22.1	27.3	31.9	34.9	3.1	4,038	4,094	4,017	4,010
1994............................	22.8	28.0	34.3	33.6	2.9	3,993	4,010	4,030	3,866
1993............................	22.0	31.5	33.2	35.6	2.4	3,952	4,021	3,889	3,578
Female									
2016............................	22.3	27.3	27.9	26.1	3.9	2,952	3,089	3,173	3,290
2015............................	22.2	26.7	29.6	26.1	2.6	3,035	3,122	3,184	3,327
2014............................	22.7	27.0	26.2	26.8	3.3	3,082	3,141	3,245	3,342
2013............................	20.3	22.1	27.6	26.2	3.0	3,055	3,169	3,279	3,350
2012............................	23.3	23.8	25.0	26.2	2.8	3,102	3,181	3,295	3,371
2011............................	20.8	24.4	27.3	23.6	1.7	3,254	3,292	3,278	3,414
2010............................	17.2	21.5	25.3	23.0	1.3	3,294	3,338	3,334	3,515
2009............................	16.9	22.4	26.6	23.5	2.4	3,280	3,301	3,396	3,644
2008............................	18.0	25.3	25.4	24.9	2.1	3,313	3,309	3,408	3,673
2007............................	18.4	22.0	24.7	23.1	2.0	3,306	3,310	3,467	3,814
2006............................	17.6	22.8	22.6	24.6	1.8	3,299	3,350	3,593	3,843
2005............................	19.2	19.4	24.2	25.3	2.0	3,277	3,434	3,682	4,014
2004............................	20.3	22.2	23.1	24.5	3.3	3,330	3,485	3,714	3,898

[1]Starting in 2003, respondents could identify more than one race. Except as noted, the race data in this table from 2003 onward represent those respondents who indicated only one race category.

Table A-11. Population 6 to 17 Years Old Enrolled Below Modal Grade, 1971–2016—*Continued*

(Numbers in thousands; percent; civilian noninstitutionalized population.)

Year, sex, race, and Hispanic origin	Percent below modal grade				Dropout rate, 15 to 17 years	Population in age group			
	6 to 8 years	9 to 11 years	12 to 14 years	15 to 17 years		6 to 8 years	9 to 11 years	12 to 14 years	15 to 17 years
2003[1]	18.6	22.2	24.0	23.7	2.6	3,337	3,377	3,929	3,878
2002	14.8	20.4	20.9	22.2	2.6	3,451	3,658	3,908	3,765
2001	16.4	19.8	22.0	24.4	2.6	3,517	3,755	3,853	3,809
2000	16.2	19.6	21.9	23.9	3.7	3,623	3,910	3,757	3,818
1999	17.4	20.5	20.8	22.3	3.6	3,761	3,864	3,757	3,840
1998	17.6	20.8	21.2	23.5	2.5	3,740	3,791	3,803	3,878
1997	15.0	19.9	21.8	21.3	2.6	3,752	3,804	3,793	3,846
1996	15.0	19.3	21.3	21.7	4.3	3,839	3,757	3,773	3,757
1995	14.1	21.5	23.8	23.1	3.8	3,815	3,906	3,854	3,784
1994	16.6	23.1	25.5	22.1	3.2	3,786	3,854	3,814	3,624
1993	15.4	22.6	24.2	23.1	3.6	3,784	3,782	3,710	3,444
BLACK ALONE									
Both Sexes									
2016	23.5	33.0	30.6	31.4	2.8	1,877	1,878	1,817	1,895
2015	21.2	28.2	31.7	34.1	3.1	1,794	1,913	1,831	1,899
2014	21.8	31.5	34.8	35.8	5.2	1,772	1,822	1,871	1,869
2013	23.9	27.4	31.5	34.1	4.6	1,885	1,781	1,892	1,865
2012	24.5	28.0	34.9	36.6	2.6	1,719	1,828	1,897	1,879
2011	20.2	30.0	28.9	32.4	2.7	1,882	1,831	1,773	1,855
2010	16.7	26.3	33.0	31.5	2.2	1,871	1,710	1,809	1,911
2009	20.1	30.7	32.7	34.8	2.7	1,692	1,814	1,801	1,943
2008	18.6	27.3	40.9	37.8	3.1	1,781	1,797	1,851	1,994
2007	17.7	28.1	33.0	39.2	3.0	1,797	1,770	1,937	2,021
2006	19.1	29.9	35.7	35.7	3.1	1,813	1,811	1,960	2,059
2005	20.8	35.6	34.1	38.8	4.2	1,806	1,826	2,011	2,085
2004	19.8	27.4	34.1	40.1	2.3	1,775	1,906	2,034	1,992
2003[1]	22.7	34.2	33.9	37.4	3.7	1,760	2,043	2,110	1,950
2002	19.6	28.6	32.8	36.2	3.9	2,017	2,048	2,036	1,943
2001	17.3	29.7	31.1	35.6	4.0	1,937	2,144	1,998	1,823
2000	19.6	26.9	37.8	34.6	4.7	1,976	2,082	1,961	1,852
1999	16.1	30.2	31.7	34.8	3.5	1,948	2,108	1,912	1,911
1998	18.3	26.6	31.4	38.4	3.6	2,019	1,934	1,840	1,801
1997	18.4	26.1	33.5	40.0	3.8	2,061	1,908	1,845	1,938
1996	18.4	29.2	36.8	36.9	4.8	2,054	1,847	1,839	1,858
1995	16.8	31.1	38.3	41.3	4.1	1,909	1,890	1,822	1,851
1994	18.4	35.1	36.1	37.7	3.3	1,912	1,795	1,835	1,809
1993[r]	20.0	33.6	34.8	45.1	3.6	1,767	1,763	1,747	1,641
1993	19.9	33.4	38.8	43.3	3.6	1,709	1,710	1,695	1,642
1992	20.6	28.7	38.0	40.6	4.2	1,761	1,635	1,686	1,621
1991	21.0	34.3	40.7	43.4	5.3	1,674	1,701	1,643	1,574
1990	21.9	33.1	46.1	42.9	5.2	1,645	1,712	1,574	1,571
1989	19.6	34.0	41.3	39.3	3.9	1,642	1,682	1,554	1,618
1988	18.6	33.1	37.6	38.4	4.7	1,680	1,629	1,545	1,637
1987	19.8	33.1	35.6	35.3	5.1	1,679	1,554	1,552	1,654
1986	12.7	34.6	38.5	38.3	4.6	1,611	1,542	1,530	1,692
1985	18.0	33.9	37.9	37.7	4.6	1,568	1,498	1,635	1,627
1984	17.9	32.3	38.1	34.6	4.1	1,445	1,442	1,652	1,536
1983	15.3	34.9	34.4	35.8	4.7	1,429	1,450	1,601	1,617
1982	17.2	27.1	32.5	32.6	4.6	1,765	1,874	1,953	1,947
1981	13.9	26.2	33.7	36.1	6.3	1,437	1,594	1,615	1,679
1980	14.9	27.8	30.5	37.6	5.1	1,460	1,606	1,568	1,728
1979	12.5	29.5	29.2	34.3	6.4	1,515	1,576	1,636	1,722
1978	12.6	27.8	26.6	35.4	5.7	1,557	1,523	1,664	1,764
1977	11.3	24.9	26.3	32.2	5.4	1,552	1,558	1,698	1,754
1976	10.5	23.2	26.1	35.6	6.7	1,493	1,633	1,724	1,726
1975	11.9	26.1	29.2	34.9	8.0	1,489	1,656	1,720	1,760
1974	11.6	26.2	33.2	34.4	8.2	1,509	1,684	1,750	1,682
1973	12.0	25.8	31.7	35.4	8.2	1,525	1,650	1,671	1,671
1972	13.2	30.5	33.1	37.3	6.6	1,585	1,638	1,691	1,636
1971	14.2	27.9	34.7	40.2	7.0	1,794	1,787	1,638	1,533
Male									
2016	21.1	35.2	36.4	30.0	2.4	962	931	918	952
2015	17.9	29.6	33.4	38.0	2.2	903	971	927	954
2014	23.0	33.4	37.2	38.0	4.6	883	959	948	939
2013	21.2	29.9	35.7	40.3	3.8	921	905	961	936
2012	28.5	33.1	36.9	39.1	1.4	918	911	963	943
2011	20.9	35.2	32.2	34.5	4.1	977	902	898	927
2010	16.8	30.9	34.7	35.0	3.0	954	856	912	961
2009	19.2	34.6	34.4	42.3	2.6	805	954	911	980
2008	19.4	26.2	46.3	41.3	3.4	917	908	934	992

[1]Starting in 2003, respondents could identify more than one race. Except as noted, the race data in this table from 2003 onward represent those respondents who indicated only one race category.

[r] = Revised, controlled to 1990 census based population estimates; previous 1993 data controlled to 1980 census based population estimates.

Table A-11. Population 6 to 17 Years Old Enrolled Below Modal Grade, 1971–2016—*Continued*

(Numbers in thousands; percent; civilian noninstitutionalized population.)

Year, sex, race, and Hispanic origin	Percent below modal grade				Dropout rate, 15 to 17 years	Population in age group			
	6 to 8 years	9 to 11 years	12 to 14 years	15 to 17 years		6 to 8 years	9 to 11 years	12 to 14 years	15 to 17 years
2007	22.7	31.6	35.4	43.5	2.2	946	886	964	1,027
2006	20.3	35.1	40.3	43.9	3.3	929	920	991	1,032
2005	22.6	37.9	35.8	43.0	5.2	912	913	1,011	1,041
2004	21.0	31.4	37.8	46.5	2.0	885	992	1,012	1,009
2003[1]	23.6	36.8	38.7	43.4	3.9	927	1,059	975	1,047
2002	17.5	32.5	37.0	44.7	5.0	1,044	1,036	1,012	973
2001	21.1	31.1	33.3	42.8	3.5	978	1,108	1,010	924
2000	20.8	27.5	43.3	37.0	6.4	1,003	1,057	994	941
1999	15.9	34.2	36.3	37.6	3.0	964	1,085	969	992
1998	20.9	29.3	33.3	41.9	3.0	1,027	973	926	928
1997	21.3	29.3	39.4	43.8	3.1	1,019	994	934	979
1996	21.3	30.4	45.1	43.2	4.5	1,054	925	931	943
1995	18.8	31.2	45.0	47.5	2.9	982	944	922	952
1994	19.4	30.3	39.9	39.8	3.2	951	928	928	898
1993[r]	21.8	36.5	44.3	53.0	2.5	903	884	891	832
1993	21.6	36.5	44.2	51.8	2.5	864	857	867	832
1992	24.5	28.7	44.5	47.0	2.8	864	862	860	813
1991	22.9	39.6	46.2	50.6	5.4	846	878	839	798
1990	23.2	37.3	52.7	49.1	4.3	828	877	791	795
1989	21.7	38.8	44.8	46.7	2.8	831	858	785	828
1988	18.9	37.2	43.7	41.4	4.1	851	828	780	828
1987	21.6	41.1	39.7	42.3	4.9	861	779	802	818
1986	15.0	39.0	45.2	45.9	4.0	806	792	770	855
1985	19.5	38.2	41.4	40.3	5.4	778	775	830	816
1984	24.1	38.1	42.5	42.8	4.2	729	727	832	769
1983	16.8	42.0	43.1	40.6	4.4	721	723	808	799
1982	18.8	27.5	36.2	36.9	4.8	898	937	975	977
1981	17.7	34.2	33.3	42.4	5.4	723	811	814	832
1980	16.8	31.8	36.2	43.3	4.9	736	807	770	876
1979	14.7	37.3	33.8	43.6	4.0	762	796	828	853
1978	15.4	33.0	30.3	43.1	4.1	774	767	847	870
1977	12.1	29.8	31.1	35.3	4.8	776	782	858	868
1976	11.5	26.1	30.9	43.3	5.7	755	816	870	855
1975	12.8	30.7	32.5	40.2	7.6	743	849	845	879
1974	13.5	31.0	40.9	41.1	7.2	747	858	861	849
1973	14.1	29.5	38.0	42.0	8.5	752	831	837	824
1972	14.5	36.8	41.3	43.8	6.6	787	828	836	818
1971	18.1	30.9	38.5	47.6	7.4	890	900	810	757
Female									
2016	26.0	31.0	24.7	32.9	3.3	915	947	899	943
2015	24.4	26.8	30.0	30.2	3.9	891	942	905	945
2014	20.6	29.5	32.5	33.7	5.8	890	863	923	930
2013	26.4	24.8	27.2	27.9	5.4	964	877	931	929
2012	20.0	22.8	32.8	34.0	3.9	801	917	934	935
2011	19.5	25.0	25.4	30.4	1.4	905	930	875	928
2010	16.5	21.6	31.4	28.0	1.4	917	853	897	951
2009	20.9	26.4	30.9	27.1	2.8	887	860	891	963
2008	17.7	28.4	35.5	34.2	2.9	864	889	917	1,003
2007	12.2	24.7	30.5	34.5	3.9	851	885	972	993
2006	17.7	24.7	31.0	27.5	2.8	884	891	968	1,027
2005	19.0	33.3	32.4	34.7	3.3	893	913	999	1,044
2004	18.6	23.1	30.5	33.4	2.6	890	914	1,022	983
2003[1]	21.7	31.5	39.8	30.3	3.4	833	983	1,135	903
2002	22.0	24.7	28.7	27.8	2.8	973	1,012	1,024	970
2001	13.3	28.2	29.0	27.9	4.5	959	1,036	988	900
2000	18.2	26.4	32.0	32.3	2.9	974	1,025	968	911
1999	16.3	25.8	27.0	31.6	4.0	984	1,022	944	919
1998	15.6	23.8	29.6	34.6	4.3	992	960	914	873
1997	15.9	22.8	27.4	36.0	4.5	1,041	915	911	959
1996	13.4	28.1	28.4	30.3	4.9	1,000	922	909	915
1995	14.8	23.6	30.9	34.6	5.3	928	946	901	898
1994	17.5	29.1	32.3	35.4	3.6	961	867	908	911
1993[r]	18.0	30.8	33.1	36.6	4.7	864	879	856	809
1993	18.1	30.3	33.2	34.6	4.7	844	854	828	809
1992	16.7	28.7	31.2	34.2	5.6	897	773	826	808
1991	19.0	28.6	35.0	36.0	5.2	828	823	804	776
1990	20.7	28.7	39.3	36.6	6.1	817	835	783	776
1989	17.5	29.0	37.7	31.5	5.1	811	824	769	790
1988	18.2	28.8	31.4	35.2	5.3	829	801	765	809
1987	18.0	25.2	31.3	28.5	5.3	818	775	750	836
1985	16.6	29.3	34.2	35.1	3.8	790	723	805	811
1984	11.5	26.4	33.5	26.3	4.0	716	715	820	767

[1]Starting in 2003, respondents could identify more than one race. Except as noted, the race data in this table from 2003 onward represent those respondents who indicated only one race category.
[r] = Revised, controlled to 1990 census based population estimates; previous 1993 data controlled to 1980 census based population estimates.

Table A-11. Population 6 to 17 Years Old Enrolled Below Modal Grade, 1971–2016—*Continued*

(Numbers in thousands; percent; civilian noninstitutionalized population.)

Year, sex, race, and Hispanic origin	Percent below modal grade				Dropout rate, 15 to 17 years	Population in age group			
	6 to 8 years	9 to 11 years	12 to 14 years	15 to 17 years		6 to 8 years	9 to 11 years	12 to 14 years	15 to 17 years
1983	13.8	27.8	25.5	31.2	5.0	708	727	793	818
1982	15.5	26.7	28.7	28.1	4.3	867	937	978	970
1981	10.1	17.9	34.2	29.9	7.1	714	783	801	847
1980	12.8	23.8	25.1	31.7	5.3	724	799	798	852
1979	10.4	21.5	24.5	25.2	8.7	753	780	808	869
1978	9.8	22.6	22.6	27.9	7.2	783	756	817	894
1977	10.6	20.0	21.3	29.1	6.0	776	776	840	886
1976	9.5	20.3	21.2	28.1	7.7	738	817	854	871
1975	11.0	21.3	25.9	29.6	8.3	746	807	875	881
1974	9.7	21.3	25.8	27.5	9.2	762	826	889	833
1973	10.0	22.1	25.4	28.9	7.9	773	819	834	847
1972	11.9	24.1	25.1	30.9	6.6	798	810	855	818
1971	10.4	24.9	31.0	33.1	6.7	904	887	828	776
ASIAN ALONE[2]									
Both Sexes									
2016	21.0	22.2	22.7	26.0	2.9	642	700	628	681
2015	24.5	21.8	22.3	23.2	4.8	605	691	619	644
2014	12.5	24.3	25.7	26.9	1.4	618	611	625	650
2013	14.5	14.7	20.9	18.4	1.2	606	630	542	615
2012	16.8	18.9	17.3	29.7	1.6	590	560	591	624
2011	16.8	23.1	24.3	25.6	2.4	602	582	481	536
2010	8.9	20.3	22.3	18.9	3.1	618	575	495	424
2009	8.8	11.7	25.5	20.0	1.5	522	491	448	421
2008	17.2	22.7	26.7	18.8	4.4	491	517	482	507
2007	11.3	21.9	17.0	24.2	3.7	545	534	497	463
2006	15.2	19.7	20.9	23.0	3.2	425	472	490	476
2005	12.8	12.2	16.3	19.1	1.2	502	429	486	457
2004	12.1	11.4	20.9	23.6	1.7	417	468	490	491
2003[1]	7.5	13.6	19.7	24.5	1.6	486	453	459	458
2002	11.1	12.3	20.4	18.6	2.7	602	490	530	553
2001	11.9	17.9	20.3	21.0	2.8	503	565	523	565
2000	10.7	15.5	17.5	22.2	0.6	524	490	490	475
1999	7.5	16.5	17.9	25.5	3.2	533	496	560	555
Male									
2016	23.2	27.9	24.9	27.5	3.3	337	360	313	307
2015	21.8	20.5	17.0	23.6	4.9	299	352	285	327
2014	18.0	24.6	30.1	28.9	2.9	316	306	323	303
2013	12.7	17.9	23.6	20.9	1.4	297	298	281	287
2012	18.7	19.3	16.6	29.2	2.4	300	259	307	327
2011	16.5	25.3	24.9	28.6	2.3	324	293	249	266
2010	8.0	20.0	24.1	20.7	2.6	327	296	247	237
2009	9.2	12.7	25.2	21.3	0.7	272	232	227	233
2008	23.8	20.4	24.3	17.4	2.4	227	257	249	253
2007	7.6	20.5	18.2	26.0	4.0	278	272	240	246
2006	14.3	18.4	23.5	21.7	3.3	206	256	264	227
2005	12.3	13.8	13.2	18.1	1.6	261	202	265	228
2004	10.9	16.0	20.9	23.5	2.4	220	216	282	231
2003[1]	7.3	15.9	20.3	19.3	*	226	223	261	231
2002	9.6	12.4	23.3	18.9	1.7	274	239	267	287
2001	15.2	16.6	19.0	22.2	4.9	265	294	256	313
2000	14.7	14.2	16.1	30.3	1.0	286	243	267	261
1999	8.4	16.4	17.6	30.3	2.2	277	269	246	276
Female									
2016	18.5	16.2	20.5	24.7	2.5	305	340	315	374
2015	27.0	23.1	26.8	22.8	4.8	305	339	334	318
2014	6.7	24.0	21.0	25.1	0.1	302	306	302	346
2013	16.2	11.9	18.1	16.1	1.0	309	332	262	327
2012	14.9	18.7	18.1	30.3	0.7	290	301	284	296
2011	17.1	20.9	23.7	22.7	2.6	278	289	232	270
2010	10.0	20.6	20.6	16.6	3.7	290	279	248	187
2009	8.5	10.9	25.9	18.5	2.4	251	259	220	188
2008	11.5	25.0	29.3	20.3	6.5	264	260	233	254
2007	15.2	23.5	15.8	22.2	3.4	268	263	257	217
2006	16.1	21.2	17.9	24.2	3.1	218	216	226	249
2005	13.4	10.8	20.0	20.1	0.9	241	227	221	229
2004	13.5	7.3	20.8	23.7	1.1	196	253	208	260
2003[1]	7.6	11.3	18.8	29.9	3.2	259	230	198	227

[1] Starting in 2003, respondents could identify more than one race. Except as noted, the race data in this table from 2003 onward represent those respondents who indicated only one race category.
[2] The data shown prior to 2003 consists of those identifying themselves as "Asian or Pacific Islanders."

Table A-11. Population 6 to 17 Years Old Enrolled Below Modal Grade, 1971–2016—*Continued*

(Numbers in thousands; percent; civilian noninstitutionalized population.)

Year, sex, race, and Hispanic origin	Percent below modal grade				Dropout rate, 15 to 17 years	Population in age group			
	6 to 8 years	9 to 11 years	12 to 14 years	15 to 17 years		6 to 8 years	9 to 11 years	12 to 14 years	15 to 17 years
2002	12.4	12.2	17.5	18.2	3.7	327	251	263	266
2001	8.3	19.3	21.4	19.6	0.2	238	270	268	252
2000	5.9	16.7	19.2	12.3	0.1	239	247	224	215
1999	6.6	16.7	18.5	20.6	4.0	256	227	314	278
HISPANIC (OF ANY RACE)									
Both Sexes									
2016	23.1	29.2	28.3	32.8	3.0	3,104	3,173	2,956	2,978
2015	20.7	30.3	30.3	32.4	4.0	3,134	3,165	2,909	2,871
2014	21.4	26.9	29.5	32.4	4.5	3,159	2,967	2,901	2,703
2013	22.0	29.3	32.2	34.3	3.6	3,117	2,926	2,868	2,662
2012	22.4	28.0	28.6	36.7	3.0	3,025	2,954	2,791	2,661
2011	19.8	28.0	28.6	36.1	3.3	3,161	2,847	2,496	2,502
2010	15.6	23.4	27.9	34.3	2.5	3,046	2,681	2,494	2,307
2009	18.1	26.0	28.3	32.1	4.7	2,893	2,524	2,418	2,254
2008	17.8	25.2	29.1	34.2	3.5	2,690	2,402	2,422	2,321
2007	20.9	28.9	31.1	34.0	5.7	2,541	2,414	2,418	2,211
2006	20.6	29.2	32.6	35.3	5.7	2,441	2,382	2,361	2,165
2005	18.1	26.2	33.2	32.1	4.9	2,390	2,317	2,322	2,202
2004	21.5	28.1	30.0	34.6	6.1	2,382	2,250	2,283	2,072
2003	20.2	28.7	31.3	32.7	5.2	2,280	2,221	2,167	2,063
2002	15.5	28.4	27.9	35.6	5.9	2,258	2,204	2,079	1,841
2001	16.7	22.1	25.0	34.6	6.9	2,143	2,198	2,011	1,733
2000	19.4	23.2	27.3	34.4	8.8	2,067	1,965	1,744	1,671
1999	15.7	25.9	27.9	36.5	7.3	1,902	1,922	1,734	1,653
1998	15.4	23.2	24.6	33.8	7.6	1,903	1,740	1,542	1,424
1997	15.2	21.5	31.0	41.4	5.5	1,909	1,666	1,444	1,575
1996	14.9	22.9	35.5	39.0	8.4	1,711	1,680	1,550	1,478
1995	14.4	26.1	38.5	43.6	7.4	1,597	1,628	1,496	1,373
1994	16.8	28.4	32.3	39.9	8.8	1,526	1,593	1,442	1,347
1993[r]	18.9	29.2	33.2	42.2	8.2	1,390	1,255	1,204	1,225
1993	18.9	29.2	32.7	38.3	7.9	1,455	1,295	1,243	1,226
1992	16.2	25.3	34.3	39.9	8.1	1,272	1,371	1,141	1,110
1991	21.8	30.7	35.8	38.4	11.3	1,290	1,356	1,088	1,023
1990	21.5	34.8	37.7	39.8	9.0	1,270	1,230	1,095	1,062
1989	21.9	33.8	39.9	39.5	10.6	1,257	1,154	1,079	1,001
1988	23.2	37.0	45.0	36.8	13.7	1,248	1,107	1,052	953
1987	16.9	31.2	38.9	37.3	9.1	1,181	1,054	1,063	981
1986	19.1	33.3	42.5	35.5	11.0	1,067	1,119	1,025	1,018
1985	18.7	32.4	35.8	35.7	11.3	1,035	1,047	957	946
1984	20.2	32.7	34.7	38.5	10.7	901	829	806	816
1983	20.2	32.7	39.5	38.0	8.3	903	909	949	860
1982	21.9	32.6	37.3	37.0	10.9	923	875	924	883
1981	17.9	34.7	34.9	34.9	13.3	882	939	866	963
1980	20.8	26.1	34.8	35.8	12.6	881	949	863	889
1979	18.2	33.6	33.0	30.3	10.9	729	712	697	755
1978	19.8	29.1	33.6	37.8	12.3	723	684	666	751
1977	13.0	24.1	25.1	35.2	11.0	676	693	662	773
Male									
2016	24.2	27.9	31.5	39.2	2.7	1,570	1,620	1,507	1,530
2015	20.1	30.7	30.6	35.0	4.6	1,595	1,608	1,492	1,512
2014	23.2	30.3	30.5	35.4	5.5	1,594	1,510	1,481	1,402
2013	24.0	34.2	34.3	36.5	4.0	1,579	1,507	1,458	1,373
2012	26.1	29.0	31.7	39.1	2.7	1,571	1,513	1,408	1,382
2011	29.3	20.7	30.5	30.0	3.0	1,605	1,465	1,290	1,294
2010	16.3	24.2	28.4	33.6	3.1	1,544	1,381	1,290	1,178
2009	16.4	27.7	31.8	32.5	4.9	1,458	1,322	1,216	1,165
2008	17.8	26.6	30.9	36.3	3.7	1,377	1,218	1,233	1,198
2007	24.3	28.5	34.1	37.4	5.9	1,302	1,252	1,217	1,130
2006	20.0	31.0	37.7	40.6	4.9	1,251	1,214	1,208	1,111
2005	20.5	29.2	39.2	37.0	4.7	1,219	1,192	1,202	1,087
2004	25.2	28.8	34.3	36.6	6.4	1,247	1,142	1,202	1,001
2003	23.0	31.2	32.3	35.9	6.2	1,205	1,178	1,081	1,020
2002	17.4	31.6	28.7	38.5	7.4	1,140	1,090	1,137	911
2001	21.2	23.4	27.8	40.8	7.7	1,065	1,128	1,093	895
2000	23.1	26.7	27.7	36.9	9.0	1,048	993	875	872
1999	17.9	29.5	29.7	38.9	7.6	973	990	893	854
1998	16.8	26.6	26.9	44.9	8.1	933	887	841	792
1997	15.3	22.3	33.7	45.8	3.7	969	863	735	836

[r] = Revised, controlled to 1990 census based population estimates; previous 1993 data controlled to 1980 census based population estimates.

Table A-11. Population 6 to 17 Years Old Enrolled Below Modal Grade, 1971–2016—*Continued*

(Numbers in thousands; percent; civilian noninstitutionalized population.)

Year, sex, race, and Hispanic origin	Percent below modal grade				Dropout rate, 15 to 17 years	Population in age group			
	6 to 8 years	9 to 11 years	12 to 14 years	15 to 17 years		6 to 8 years	9 to 11 years	12 to 14 years	15 to 17 years
1996	13.5	25.8	40.5	45.1	6.8	914	808	798	764
1995	11.4	31.1	42.4	47.6	7.5	794	839	776	697
1994	16.4	27.5	36.3	45.1	11.4	778	845	721	676
1993ʳ	19.1	35.1	37.2	50.4	7.6	722	612	618	658
1993	19.1	34.3	36.9	46.0	7.3	778	637	648	658
1992	15.6	27.2	42.5	46.2	6.8	636	687	602	576
1991	22.7	31.5	43.9	42.6	10.7	651	691	544	521
1990	22.2	36.4	40.2	43.8	9.0	676	616	590	564
1989	23.7	36.1	40.0	45.2	7.8	642	584	560	511
1988	26.9	42.0	53.8	40.5	12.4	676	566	470	523
1987	19.8	31.7	44.8	38.7	6.4	600	524	569	517
1986	22.2	38.0	49.3	37.8	10.8	544	555	535	471
1985	16.7	36.8	38.4	43.4	7.8	521	527	502	449
1984	18.3	35.7	33.1	42.8	10.0	443	420	423	432
1983	22.2	38.8	45.7	41.8	8.2	445	479	479	428
1982	23.1	36.4	39.1	43.4	10.1	428	426	466	477
1981	19.9	39.8	38.0	40.0	14.3	438	480	439	495
1980	22.5	29.9	40.5	40.7	13.5	418	481	415	445
1979	19.0	34.6	36.4	31.3	8.8	368	358	349	386
1978	23.5	29.9	33.9	37.3	13.6	388	335	339	413
1977	11.5	31.4	23.3	38.4	6.7	365	325	330	406
Female									
2016	22.1	30.6	24.9	26.0	3.3	1,534	1,553	1,449	1,448
2015	21.3	29.8	29.9	29.6	3.4	1,539	1,556	1,417	1,359
2014	19.7	23.4	28.4	29.2	3.5	1,565	1,457	1,420	1,301
2013	20.0	24.0	30.0	32.0	3.0	1,539	1,420	1,410	1,289
2012	18.4	27.0	25.4	34.1	3.3	1,454	1,441	1,382	1,279
2011	19.0	25.3	27.1	34.2	3.7	1,556	1,382	1,206	1,209
2010	15.0	22.6	27.3	35.1	2.0	1,502	1,301	1,204	1,129
2009	19.9	24.0	24.8	31.6	4.6	1,435	1,202	1,202	1,089
2008	17.8	23.7	27.2	32.1	3.2	1,313	1,184	1,189	1,123
2007	17.3	29.4	28.2	30.5	5.4	1,239	1,162	1,202	1,080
2006	21.3	27.4	27.3	29.5	6.5	1,190	1,168	1,153	1,054
2005	15.6	23.0	26.7	27.3	5.1	1,171	1,126	1,119	1,115
2004	17.6	27.3	25.1	32.8	5.7	1,135	1,108	1,080	1,070
2003	17.1	25.7	30.3	29.7	4.3	1,075	1,043	1,086	1,042
2002	13.6	25.3	27.0	32.7	4.5	1,118	1,115	942	930
2001	12.2	20.8	21.6	28.0	6.0	1,078	1,070	918	838
2000	15.7	19.7	26.9	31.8	8.6	1,020	974	869	800
1999	13.5	22.0	26.1	33.8	6.9	930	932	841	800
1998	14.1	19.7	21.8	31.1	7.0	970	853	701	632
1997	15.0	20.4	28.8	36.1	7.4	939	803	710	739
1996	16.6	20.3	30.4	32.4	10.4	798	871	753	712
1995	17.5	20.6	34.5	39.5	7.2	802	789	721	677
1994	17.2	29.2	28.5	34.9	6.1	748	747	722	671
1993ʳ	18.9	24.2	29.0	32.3	8.7	667	643	586	567
1993	18.7	24.3	28.3	29.3	8.6	678	658	597	567
1992	16.8	23.4	25.0	33.1	9.6	636	684	539	534
1991	20.8	29.8	27.6	34.1	12.0	639	665	544	502
1990	20.7	33.2	34.9	35.3	9.0	594	614	505	498
1989	20.0	31.4	39.7	33.5	13.5	615	570	519	490
1988	18.7	31.8	37.8	32.3	15.3	572	541	582	430
1987	13.8	30.8	32.2	35.8	12.1	581	530	494	464
1986	15.9	28.7	35.1	33.5	11.2	523	564	490	547
1985	20.8	27.9	33.0	28.8	14.5	514	520	455	497
1984	22.1	29.6	36.6	33.6	11.5	458	409	383	384
1983	18.1	25.8	33.2	34.3	8.3	458	430	470	432
1982	20.8	29.0	35.6	29.6	11.8	495	449	458	406
1981	16.0	29.4	31.6	29.5	12.2	444	459	427	468
1980	19.2	22.2	29.5	30.9	11.7	463	468	448	444
1979	17.5	32.5	29.6	29.3	13.0	361	354	348	369
1978	15.5	28.4	33.3	38.5	10.7	335	349	327	338
1977	14.8	17.7	26.8	31.6	15.8	311	368	332	367
WHITE ALONE OR IN COMBINATION									
Both Sexes									
2016	24.2	29.4	30.0	30.3	4.0	9,274	9,615	9,586	9,779
2015	23.8	29.7	30.5	30.4	3.1	9,492	9,632	9,658	9,802
2014	23.5	27.6	29.0	30.5	3.9	9,623	9,586	9,679	9,679
2013	22.7	26.8	30.7	31.6	3.6	9,664	9,574	9,754	9,681
2012	23.8	27.8	30.2	32.5	2.4	9,607	9,630	9,685	9,740
2011	23.1	28.4	30.0	31.5	2.1	9,956	9,824	9,378	9,652

ʳ = Revised, controlled to 1990 census based population estimates; previous 1993 data controlled to 1980 census based population estimates.

Table A-11. Population 6 to 17 Years Old Enrolled Below Modal Grade, 1971–2016—*Continued*

(Numbers in thousands; percent; civilian noninstitutionalized population.)

Year, sex, race, and Hispanic origin	Percent below modal grade				Dropout rate, 15 to 17 years	Population in age group			
	6 to 8 years	9 to 11 years	12 to 14 years	15 to 17 years		6 to 8 years	9 to 11 years	12 to 14 years	15 to 17 years
2010	19.0	24.7	28.1	28.5	2.2	9,935	9,712	9,435	9,699
2009	19.2	26.3	29.2	28.7	3.2	9,887	9,345	9,515	9,832
2008	20.2	27.1	29.2	29.6	2.5	9,680	9,298	9,577	10,043
2007	21.1	26.1	27.4	28.5	2.8	9,502	9,326	9,734	10,169
2006	20.6	25.6	26.7	29.9	3.0	9,346	9,444	9,850	10,175
2005	21.1	23.9	27.9	29.4	2.6	9,314	9,588	10,026	10,479
2004	22.4	25.6	27.4	30.5	3.9	9,422	9,506	10,175	10,079
2003	21.7	27.4	28.1	29.4	3.2	9,447	9,446	10,194	10,151
Male									
2016	26.0	30.3	32.9	34.4	4.3	4,731	4,923	4,922	4,998
2015	25.4	31.4	31.1	33.9	3.4	4,855	4,935	4,968	5,003
2014	24.8	29.0	31.1	33.4	4.6	4,945	4,931	4,960	4,948
2013	25.1	30.5	33.2	35.0	4.1	4,911	4,940	4,965	4,951
2012	25.9	30.4	35.0	36.6	2.8	4,898	4,966	4,935	4,979
2011	25.8	31.6	32.6	36.4	2.1	5,089	5,042	4,820	4,956
2010	21.2	27.3	30.1	31.0	3.0	5,039	4,970	4,824	4,996
2009	20.6	29.5	32.3	31.8	3.4	5,072	4,776	4,866	5,039
2008	22.3	29.1	32.3	32.4	2.7	4,963	4,744	4,934	5,163
2007	24.0	28.2	29.1	32.0	2.9	4,857	4,770	4,997	5,203
2006	22.4	27.2	29.6	34.1	3.4	4,769	4,842	5,042	5,193
2005	23.9	27.3	30.9	33.1	2.7	4,751	4,925	5,151	5,268
2004	24.9	28.1	31.2	35.1	3.9	4,876	4,823	5,318	5,043
2003	24.5	31.6	31.0	33.8	3.4	4,965	4,946	5,108	5,172
Female									
2016	22.3	28.4	26.9	26.0	3.7	4,543	4,692	4,664	4,782
2015	22.1	28.0	29.9	26.8	2.8	4,636	4,697	4,690	4,799
2014	22.2	26.1	26.9	27.6	3.2	4,678	4,655	4,718	4,731
2013	20.2	22.9	28.0	28.1	3.1	4,753	4,633	4,789	4,729
2012	21.7	25.1	25.2	28.3	1.9	4,709	4,664	4,751	4,761
2011	20.4	25.0	27.2	26.4	2.2	4,867	4,782	4,558	4,696
2010	16.8	21.9	26.0	25.9	1.4	4,896	4,743	4,610	4,703
2009	17.7	22.9	26.0	25.4	2.9	4,815	4,569	4,649	4,792
2008	17.9	25.0	26.0	26.6	2.4	4,717	4,554	4,643	4,880
2007	18.1	23.9	25.5	24.7	2.7	4,646	4,555	4,737	4,966
2006	18.7	23.8	23.6	25.5	2.6	4,577	4,602	4,808	4,982
2005	18.2	20.2	24.7	25.7	2.6	4,563	4,663	4,875	5,211
2004	19.6	23.0	23.2	25.9	3.9	4,545	4,683	4,857	5,037
2003	18.6	22.7	25.2	24.8	3.0	4,482	4,500	5,086	4,979
BLACK ALONE OR IN COMBINATION									
Both Sexes									
2016	23.5	32.7	30.3	31.1	2.8	2,217	2,212	2,130	2,238
2015	21.4	29.8	31.7	34.3	2.7	2,146	2,321	2,148	2,144
2014	22.6	31.1	34.5	35.6	5.2	2,157	2,130	2,131	2,133
2013	23.5	27.6	30.2	33.9	4.5	2,235	2,055	2,163	2,145
2012	25.1	28.2	33.2	36.6	2.4	2,066	2,094	2,139	2,113
2011	21.0	30.1	28.1	33.1	2.5	2,186	2,061	1,945	2,003
2010	16.9	25.9	32.4	31.6	2.1	2,122	1,938	1,971	2,067
2009	20.7	30.2	32.6	34.8	2.5	1,939	2,006	2,001	2,116
2008	18.3	26.8	39.4	37.1	3.0	2,026	2,002	2,036	2,179
2007	17.6	27.3	32.1	38.8	2.8	1,998	1,950	2,071	2,146
2006	18.9	28.3	34.8	35.0	3.1	1,982	1,988	2,074	2,202
2005	20.3	34.8	33.4	37.9	4.4	1,970	1,982	2,137	2,194
2004	20.3	27.0	33.2	39.1	2.5	1,950	2,022	2,174	2,107
2003	23.2	33.5	33.4	36.8	3.8	1,921	2,183	2,220	2,034
Male									
2016	21.4	35.2	35.2	30.6	2.7	1,138	1,093	1,083	1,135
2015	19.4	30.5	32.8	38.1	2.0	1,058	1,187	1,105	1,075
2014	22.4	33.1	37.4	37.7	5.3	1,055	1,122	1,097	1,053
2013	21.2	31.0	34.2	38.6	3.3	1,088	1,050	1,100	1,061
2012	30.1	31.6	35.5	38.3	1.4	1,095	1,061	1,085	1,047
2011	22.9	35.0	31.6	35.1	3.8	1,135	1,017	991	994
2010	16.7	30.4	34.1	34.2	3.0	1,085	961	978	1,041
2009	21.2	33.0	35.9	41.5	2.4	934	1,042	1,006	1,059
2008	19.8	25.6	44.8	39.7	3.3	1,026	1,020	1,032	1,090
2007	21.7	29.9	34.4	42.6	2.1	1,053	983	1,034	1,086
2006	20.0	33.5	39.0	42.8	3.5	1,013	1,018	1,050	1,094
2005	22.1	37.0	35.5	41.8	5.0	981	999	1,061	1,082
2004	21.1	30.6	37.3	45.3	1.9	966	1,042	1,065	1,056
2003	24.2	36.6	38.5	42.9	4.0	1,014	1,116	1,033	1,083

Table A-11. Population 6 to 17 Years Old Enrolled Below Modal Grade, 1971–2016—*Continued*

(Numbers in thousands; percent; civilian noninstitutionalized population.)

Year, sex, race, and Hispanic origin	Percent below modal grade				Dropout rate, 15 to 17 years	Population in age group			
	6 to 8 years	9 to 11 years	12 to 14 years	15 to 17 years		6 to 8 years	9 to 11 years	12 to 14 years	15 to 17 years
Female									
2016	25.7	30.2	25.2	31.5	2.8	1,079	1,119	1,047	1,103
2015	23.4	29.1	30.5	30.4	3.5	1,088	1,134	1,044	1,069
2014	22.9	28.9	31.4	33.6	5.1	1,102	1,008	1,033	1,080
2013	25.7	24.0	26.1	29.4	5.6	1,147	1,005	1,063	1,085
2012	19.6	24.6	30.8	34.9	3.4	971	1,032	1,054	1,066
2011	18.8	25.4	24.4	31.2	1.3	1,051	1,044	954	1,009
2010	17.0	21.4	30.7	28.9	1.3	1,037	977	993	1,026
2009	20.3	27.1	29.3	28.1	2.5	1,004	965	995	1,058
2008	16.8	28.1	34.0	34.5	2.7	1,000	982	1,004	1,089
2007	13.2	24.6	29.9	34.8	3.6	945	967	1,037	1,061
2006	17.8	23.0	30.6	27.3	2.7	969	969	1,024	1,108
2005	18.6	32.6	31.4	34.1	3.7	990	983	1,076	1,112
2004	17.8	23.0	30.6	27.3	2.7	969	969	1,024	1,108
2003	22.0	30.4	29.0	29.8	3.4	907	1,067	1,187	951
ASIAN ALONE OR IN COMBINATION									
Both Sexes									
2016	22.6	21.0	22.3	24.0	3.0	784	890	761	813
2015	25.5	23.3	21.6	22.1	4.5	761	793	765	772
2014	15.0	23.2	24.7	26.8	1.3	801	783	756	760
2013	16.6	16.2	21.0	18.5	1.0	825	772	693	734
2012	16.8	19.1	17.5	30.2	1.3	751	707	738	768
2011	16.9	22.1	25.2	27.1	2.0	744	718	614	650
2010	10.6	19.6	22.2	19.1	2.5	779	728	603	532
2009	9.2	13.2	25.7	19.3	1.2	690	563	513	508
2008	16.4	23.5	24.7	19.7	3.9	599	587	558	603
2007	11.4	20.6	15.6	25.3	3.6	650	613	600	548
2006	15.0	19.9	19.2	22.2	3.2	528	574	574	603
2005	13.0	12.3	16.5	18.4	1.2	600	531	576	581
2004	13.9	12.4	20.3	24.6	2.6	494	576	585	599
2003	8.8	14.9	18.4	23.5	2.4	579	548	552	543
Male									
2016	24.0	26.4	24.6	24.3	3.9	411	460	389	382
2015	23.5	21.9	16.9	23.0	4.1	377	402	358	388
2014	19.9	20.8	28.7	30.1	2.5	414	395	373	348
2013	15.9	19.0	22.0	20.6	1.2	383	373	339	343
2012	18.5	20.5	17.2	32.0	2.0	376	341	368	397
2011	17.0	22.6	26.7	29.9	2.0	380	368	324	300
2010	9.5	19.3	24.9	20.9	2.1	397	385	309	291
2009	10.1	16.4	25.6	20.1	0.6	363	269	271	285
2008	21.3	22.6	20.4	15.5	2.1	285	291	299	289
2007	8.4	20.2	16.7	28.4	4.3	316	307	287	289
2006	15.4	15.4	15.4	15.4	4.1	259	311	291	285
2005	12.5	13.2	14.5	16.5	1.6	318	254	307	286
2004	12.4	16.2	19.3	22.3	3.6	254	278	324	286
2003	9.3	19.8	19.4	19.2	1.8	263	268	299	277
Female									
2016	21.0	15.2	19.9	23.8	2.2	373	430	372	432
2015	27.5	24.6	25.7	21.1	4.9	383	392	407	384
2014	9.7	25.6	20.8	24.0	0.3	388	389	383	411
2013	17.2	13.6	20.0	16.6	0.8	442	400	354	391
2012	15.0	17.8	17.9	28.3	0.5	376	366	370	371
2011	16.9	21.5	23.6	24.7	2.0	364	350	290	350
2010	11.8	19.9	19.3	16.9	2.0	382	344	294	242
2009	8.2	10.2	25.9	18.3	2.1	326	293	242	223
2008	12.0	24.3	29.6	23.6	5.5	314	295	259	314
2007	14.3	21.1	14.6	21.8	2.9	334	306	314	259
2006	14.6	20.6	15.4	22.2	2.4	269	263	283	318
2005	13.7	11.5	18.8	20.2	0.9	282	276	269	295
2004	15.5	8.8	21.6	26.7	1.6	241	298	261	313
2003	8.4	10.3	17.2	28.0	3.1	316	280	253	266

Table A-12. Annual High School Dropout Rates of 15 to 24 Year Olds by Sex, Race, Grade, and Hispanic Origin, October 1967–2016

(Numbers in thousands; percent; civilian noninstitutionalized population.)

Year, grade, race, and Hispanic origin	Total[1] Total students	Dropouts	Dropout rate	Male Total students	Dropouts	Dropout rate	Female Total students	Dropouts	Dropout rate
ALL RACES									
Grades 10–12									
2016	11,807	532	4.5	5,939	305	5.1	5,868	227	3.9
2015	11,646	535	4.6	5,894	283	4.8	5,752	252	4.4
2014	11,634	567	4.9	5,932	300	5.1	5,702	267	4.7
2013	11,495	508	4.4	5,844	267	4.6	5,651	241	4.3
2012	11,962	386	3.2	5,997	201	3.4	5,965	184	3.1
2011	11,726	375	3.2	6,010	206	3.4	5,716	169	2.9
2010	11,647	326	2.8	6,006	172	2.9	5,641	154	2.7
2009	11,651	373	3.2	5,798	189	3.3	5,853	184	3.1
2008	11,750	390	3.3	5,999	174	2.9	5,751	216	3.8
2007	11,584	383	3.3	5,879	206	3.5	5,705	177	3.1
2006	11,604	407	3.5	5,932	227	3.8	5,672	180	3.2
2005	11,494	414	3.6	5,843	233	4.0	5,651	181	3.2
2004	11,166	486	4.4	5,624	266	4.7	5,542	220	4.0
2003	11,378	429	3.8	5,705	225	4.0	5,674	203	3.6
2002	10,989	367	3.3	5,504	193	3.5	5,484	174	3.2
2001	10,777	507	4.7	5,534	293	5.3	5,243	214	4.1
2000	10,773	488	4.5	5,417	280	5.2	5,356	208	3.9
1999	11,067	520	4.7	5,659	243	4.3	5,411	277	5.1
1998	10,791	479	4.4	5,486	237	4.3	5,305	243	4.6
1997	10,645	454	4.3	5,330	251	4.7	5,313	203	3.8
1996	10,249	485	4.7	5,175	240	4.6	5,072	244	4.8
1995	10,106	544	5.4	5,161	297	5.8	4,946	247	5.0
1994	9,922	497	5.0	5,048	249	4.9	4,873	247	5.1
1993[r]	9,430	404	4.3	4,787	211	4.4	4,640	192	4.1
1993	9,021	382	4.2	4,570	199	4.4	4,452	183	4.1
1992	8,939	384	4.3	4,580	175	3.8	4,357	207	4.8
1991	8,612	348	4.0	4,380	167	3.8	4,231	180	4.3
1990	8,679	347	4.0	4,356	177	4.1	4,323	170	3.9
1989	8,974	404	4.5	4,519	203	4.5	4,453	199	4.5
1988	9,590	461	4.8	4,960	256	5.2	4,628	206	4.5
1987	9,802	403	4.1	4,921	215	4.4	4,879	187	3.8
1986	9,829	421	4.3	4,910	213	4.3	4,917	208	4.2
1985	9,704	504	5.2	4,831	259	5.4	4,874	245	5.0
1984	10,041	507	5.0	4,986	268	5.4	5,054	238	4.7
1983	10,331	535	5.2	5,130	294	5.7	5,200	241	4.6
1982	10,611	577	5.4	5,310	305	5.7	5,301	271	5.1
1981	10,868	639	5.9	5,379	322	6.0	5,487	316	5.8
1980	10,891	658	6.0	5,445	362	6.6	5,448	296	5.4
1979	11,136	744	6.7	5,479	369	6.7	5,658	377	6.7
1978	11,116	743	6.7	5,558	415	7.5	5,558	328	5.9
1977	11,300	734	6.5	5,657	392	6.9	5,643	342	6.1
1976	10,996	644	5.9	5,534	360	6.5	5,463	285	5.2
1975	11,033	639	5.8	5,485	296	5.4	5,548	343	6.2
1974	11,026	742	6.7	5,421	402	7.4	5,605	340	6.1
1973	10,851	683	6.3	5,407	370	6.8	5,444	313	5.7
1972	10,664	659	6.2	5,305	317	6.0	5,358	341	6.4
1971	10,451	562	5.4	5,193	297	5.7	5,258	266	5.1
1970	10,281	588	5.7	5,145	288	5.6	5,138	302	5.9
1969	10,212	551	5.4	5,069	273	5.4	5,142	278	5.4
1968	9,814	506	5.2	4,831	247	5.1	4,983	259	5.2
1967	9,350	486	5.2	4,605	237	5.1	4,745	249	5.2
Grade 10									
2016	3,985	69	1.7	2,013	36	1.8	1,972	33	1.7
2015	3,994	61	1.5	2,016	24	1.2	1,979	37	1.9
2014	4,026	73	1.8	2,095	58	2.8	1,931	16	0.8
2013	3,971	35	0.9	1,996	19	0.9	1,976	16	0.8
2012	4,226	34	0.8	2,104	20	1.0	2,122	14	0.7
2011	3,998	48	1.2	2,009	26	1.3	1,989	22	1.1
2010	3,983	27	0.7	2,008	17	0.8	1,976	10	0.5
2009	3,983	50	1.2	1,993	28	1.4	1,989	22	1.1
2008	4,154	56	1.4	2,104	25	1.2	2,050	31	1.5
2007	4,064	63	1.6	2,027	32	1.6	2,037	31	1.5
2006	4,179	31	0.7	2,053	19	0.9	2,126	12	0.5
2005	4,483	72	1.6	2,244	49	2.2	2,239	23	1.0
2004	4,028	99	2.5	2,096	56	2.7	1,931	42	2.2
2003	4,107	64	1.6	2,111	26	1.2	1,995	37	1.9
2002	3,896	55	1.4	1,963	36	1.8	1,934	19	1.0

[1]Starting in 2003 respondents could identify more than one race. Except as noted, the race data in this table from 2003 onward represent those respondents who indicated only one race category.

[r] = Revised, controlled to 1990 census based population estimates; previous 1993 data controlled to 1980 census based population estimates.

Table A-12. Annual High School Dropout Rates of 15 to 24 Year Olds by Sex, Race, Grade, and Hispanic Origin, October 1967–2016—*Continued*

(Numbers in thousands; percent; civilian noninstitutionalized population.)

Year, grade, race, and Hispanic origin	Total[1]			Male			Female		
	Total students	Dropouts	Dropout rate	Total students	Dropouts	Dropout rate	Total students	Dropouts	Dropout rate
2001	3,900	90	2.3	1,988	50	2.5	1,913	41	2.1
2000	3,957	77	1.9	2,036	48	2.4	1,920	28	1.5
1999	3,910	104	2.7	2,036	54	2.7	1,875	50	2.7
1998	3,883	90	2.3	1,971	36	1.8	1,911	54	2.8
1997	3,738	79	2.1	1,894	44	2.3	1,843	35	1.9
1996	3,691	94	2.5	1,906	50	2.6	1,784	43	2.4
1995	3,552	88	2.5	1,823	40	2.2	1,728	47	2.7
1994	3,474	76	2.2	1,793	45	2.5	1,681	31	1.8
1993[r]	3,265	86	2.6	1,696	52	3.1	1,567	33	2.1
1993	3,139	81	2.6	1,627	50	3.1	1,513	31	2.0
1992	3,197	81	2.5	1,657	37	2.2	1,539	43	2.8
1991	3,132	105	3.4	1,571	46	2.9	1,561	59	3.8
1990	3,215	90	2.8	1,660	43	2.6	1,555	47	3.0
1989	3,071	99	3.2	1,567	56	3.6	1,504	43	2.9
1988	3,308	112	3.4	1,716	63	3.7	1,592	49	3.1
1987	3,492	106	3.0	1,818	45	2.5	1,674	61	3.6
1986	3,555	119	3.3	1,820	56	3.1	1,734	63	3.6
1985	3,491	143	4.1	1,797	74	4.1	1,695	69	4.1
1984	3,415	135	4.0	1,735	76	4.4	1,680	59	3.5
1983	3,468	129	3.7	1,755	70	4.0	1,713	59	3.4
1982	3,540	144	4.1	1,792	69	3.9	1,747	74	4.2
1981	3,735	144	3.9	1,816	65	3.6	1,918	78	4.1
1980	3,817	166	4.3	1,957	95	4.9	1,861	71	3.8
1979	3,920	217	5.5	1,985	102	5.1	1,934	114	5.9
1978	3,878	185	4.8	1,943	96	4.9	1,935	89	4.6
1977	3,970	177	4.5	2,021	96	4.8	1,949	81	4.2
1976	3,914	145	3.7	1,960	79	4.0	1,955	67	3.4
1975	3,983	183	4.6	2,017	87	4.3	1,967	97	4.9
1974	3,901	223	5.7	1,951	122	6.3	1,949	101	5.2
1973	3,899	210	5.4	1,930	112	5.8	1,969	98	5.0
1972	3,868	203	5.2	1,940	106	5.5	1,928	97	5.0
1971	3,762	174	4.6	1,925	95	4.9	1,838	79	4.3
1970	3,686	186	5.0	1,865	90	4.8	1,822	97	5.3
1969	3,485	159	4.6	1,756	84	4.8	1,729	75	4.3
1968	3,615	151	4.2	1,849	75	4.1	1,767	76	4.3
1967	3,370	129	3.8	1,726	64	3.7	1,644	65	4.0
Grade 11									
2016	4,261	126	3.0	2,191	78	3.6	2,070	48	2.3
2015	4,338	137	3.2	2,198	63	2.9	2,140	74	3.4
2014	4,274	151	3.5	2,189	89	4.1	2,085	63	3.0
2013	4,232	149	3.5	2,172	89	4.1	2,060	60	2.9
2012	4,378	66	1.5	2,228	28	1.2	2,150	39	1.8
2011	4,358	84	1.9	2,234	52	2.3	2,124	32	1.5
2010	4,247	84	2.0	2,201	50	2.3	2,046	34	1.7
2009	4,444	106	2.4	2,226	51	2.3	2,218	55	2.5
2008	4,186	96	2.3	2,113	60	2.9	2,073	36	1.7
2007	4,388	118	2.7	2,280	64	2.8	2,108	55	2.6
2006	4,324	112	2.6	2,209	62	2.7	2,053	50	2.4
2005	4,080	72	1.8	2,184	46	2.1	1,896	26	1.4
2004	4,010	141	3.5	2,012	76	3.8	1,998	65	3.3
2003	4,327	117	2.7	2,158	68	3.2	2,169	49	2.3
2002	4,137	99	2.4	2,111	54	2.6	2,026	45	2.2
2001	4,114	139	3.4	2,134	72	3.4	1,979	67	3.4
2000	3,833	170	4.4	1,933	78	4.0	1,901	93	4.9
1999	4,036	150	3.7	2,052	69	3.4	1,984	81	4.0
1998	3,735	110	2.9	1,902	55	2.9	1,833	55	3.0
1997	3,882	142	3.7	1,957	71	3.6	1,925	71	3.7
1996	3,606	138	3.8	1,828	76	4.2	1,778	62	3.5
1995	3,568	159	4.5	1,846	89	4.8	1,724	71	4.1
1994	3,587	132	3.7	1,864	61	3.3	1,722	70	4.1
1993[r]	3,375	106	3.1	1,725	43	2.5	1,650	63	3.8
1993	3,218	100	3.1	1,643	40	2.4	1,575	60	3.8
1992	3,213	120	3.7	1,642	52	3.2	1,570	67	4.3
1991	3,083	101	3.3	1,598	42	2.6	1,484	58	3.9
1990	2,976	98	3.3	1,462	57	3.9	1,514	41	2.7
1989	3,302	125	3.8	1,683	67	4.0	1,618	57	3.5
1988	3,447	161	4.7	1,819	89	4.9	1,627	72	4.4
1987	3,566	122	3.4	1,766	71	4.0	1,800	51	2.8

[1]Starting in 2003 respondents could identify more than one race. Except as noted, the race data in this table from 2003 onward represent those respondents who indicated only one race category.

[r] = Revised, controlled to 1990 census based population estimates; previous 1993 data controlled to 1980 census based population estimates.

Table A-12. Annual High School Dropout Rates of 15 to 24 Year Olds by Sex, Race, Grade, and Hispanic Origin, October 1967–2016—*Continued*

(Numbers in thousands; percent; civilian noninstitutionalized population.)

Year, grade, race, and Hispanic origin	Total[1]			Male			Female		
	Total students	Dropouts	Dropout rate	Total students	Dropouts	Dropout rate	Total students	Dropouts	Dropout rate
1986	3,433	116	3.4	1,700	51	3.0	1,733	65	3.8
1985	3,274	139	4.2	1,618	70	4.3	1,656	69	4.2
1984	3,328	163	4.9	1,682	87	5.2	1,646	76	4.6
1983	3,601	162	4.5	1,825	87	4.8	1,775	75	4.2
1982	3,694	218	5.9	1,872	122	6.5	1,822	96	5.3
1981	3,787	262	6.9	1,937	144	7.4	1,850	118	6.4
1980	3,670	225	6.1	1,832	120	6.6	1,839	105	5.7
1979	3,718	229	6.2	1,840	102	5.5	1,879	128	6.8
1978	3,708	230	6.2	1,905	113	5.9	1,803	117	6.5
1977	3,832	244	6.4	1,964	133	6.8	1,867	110	5.9
1976	3,786	227	6.0	1,955	123	6.3	1,831	104	5.7
1975	3,596	230	6.4	1,828	103	5.6	1,767	126	7.1
1974	3,721	237	6.4	1,819	123	6.8	1,902	114	6.0
1973	3,631	237	6.5	1,877	126	6.7	1,754	111	6.3
1972	3,581	241	6.7	1,825	107	5.9	1,756	134	7.6
1971	3,585	185	5.2	1,772	82	4.6	1,811	103	5.7
1970	3,456	198	5.7	1,750	96	5.5	1,706	102	6.0
1969	3,489	190	5.4	1,779	100	5.6	1,710	90	5.3
1968	3,255	179	5.5	1,640	91	5.5	1,614	88	5.5
1967	3,068	169	5.5	1,557	76	4.9	1,511	93	6.2
Grade 12									
2016	3,561	337	9.5	1,735	191	11.0	1,826	146	8.0
2015	3,315	337	10.2	1,680	196	11.7	1,634	141	8.6
2014	3,334	343	10.3	1,648	154	9.3	1,686	189	11.2
2013	3,291	325	9.9	1,675	159	9.5	1,615	166	10.3
2012	3,358	285	8.5	1,665	154	9.2	1,693	131	7.7
2011	3,370	243	7.2	1,767	129	7.3	1,603	114	7.1
2010	3,417	215	6.3	1,798	106	5.9	1,620	110	6.8
2009	3,224	217	6.7	1,578	109	6.9	1,646	108	6.5
2008	3,409	237	7.0	1,781	89	5.0	1,628	149	9.1
2007	3,133	202	6.4	1,572	111	7.0	1,561	91	5.8
2006	3,101	265	8.5	1,608	146	9.1	1,492	119	8.0
2005	2,931	270	9.2	1,415	138	9.7	1,516	132	8.7
2004	3,130	247	7.9	1,516	133	8.8	1,614	114	7.1
2003	2,945	248	8.4	1,435	131	9.1	1,510	117	7.7
2002	2,956	214	7.2	1,432	104	7.3	1,524	110	7.2
2001	2,762	277	10.0	1,411	171	12.1	1,351	106	7.8
2000	2,983	241	8.1	1,447	154	10.6	1,535	87	5.7
1999	3,121	266	8.5	1,571	120	7.6	1,552	146	9.4
1998	3,173	279	8.8	1,613	146	9.0	1,560	133	8.5
1997	3,025	233	7.7	1,479	136	9.2	1,545	97	6.3
1996	2,952	253	8.6	1,441	114	7.9	1,510	139	9.2
1995	2,986	297	9.9	1,492	168	11.3	1,494	129	8.6
1994	2,861	289	10.1	1,391	143	10.3	1,470	146	9.9
1993[r]	2,790	212	7.6	1,366	116	8.5	1,423	96	6.7
1993	2,664	201	7.5	1,300	109	8.4	1,364	92	6.7
1992	2,529	183	7.2	1,281	86	6.7	1,248	97	7.8
1991	2,397	142	5.9	1,211	79	6.5	1,186	63	5.3
1990	2,488	159	6.4	1,234	77	6.2	1,254	82	6.5
1989	2,601	180	6.9	1,269	80	6.3	1,331	99	7.4
1988	2,835	188	6.6	1,425	104	7.3	1,409	85	6.0
1987	2,744	175	6.4	1,337	99	7.4	1,405	75	5.3
1986	2,841	186	6.5	1,390	106	7.6	1,450	80	5.5
1985	2,939	222	7.6	1,416	115	8.1	1,523	107	7.0
1984	3,298	209	6.3	1,569	105	6.7	1,728	103	6.0
1983	3,262	244	7.5	1,550	137	8.8	1,712	107	6.3
1982	3,377	215	6.4	1,646	114	6.9	1,732	101	5.8
1981	3,346	233	7.0	1,626	113	6.9	1,719	120	7.0
1980	3,404	267	7.8	1,656	147	8.9	1,748	120	6.9
1979	3,498	298	8.5	1,654	164	9.9	1,845	135	7.3
1978	3,530	328	9.3	1,710	206	12.0	1,820	122	6.7
1977	3,498	313	8.9	1,672	163	9.7	1,827	151	8.3
1976	3,296	272	8.3	1,619	158	9.8	1,677	114	6.8
1975	3,454	226	6.5	1,640	106	6.5	1,814	120	6.6
1974	3,404	282	8.3	1,651	157	9.5	1,754	125	7.1
1973	3,321	236	7.1	1,600	132	8.3	1,721	104	6.0
1972	3,215	215	6.7	1,540	104	6.8	1,674	110	6.6
1971	3,104	203	6.5	1,496	120	8.0	1,609	84	5.2

[1]Starting in 2003 respondents could identify more than one race. Except as noted, the race data in this table from 2003 onward represent those respondents who indicated only one race category.
[r] = Revised, controlled to 1990 census based population estimates; previous 1993 data controlled to 1980 census based population estimates.

Table A-12. Annual High School Dropout Rates of 15 to 24 Year Olds by Sex, Race, Grade, and Hispanic Origin, October 1967–2016—*Continued*

(Numbers in thousands; percent; civilian noninstitutionalized population.)

Year, grade, race, and Hispanic origin	Total[1]			Male			Female		
	Total students	Dropouts	Dropout rate	Total students	Dropouts	Dropout rate	Total students	Dropouts	Dropout rate
1970	3,139	204	6.5	1,530	102	6.7	1,610	103	6.4
1969	3,238	202	6.2	1,534	89	5.8	1,703	113	6.6
1968	2,944	176	6.0	1,342	81	6.0	1,602	95	5.9
1967	2,912	188	6.5	1,322	97	7.3	1,590	91	5.7
WHITE ALONE									
Grades 10–12									
2016	8,541	371	4.3	4,303	211	4.9	4,238	159	3.8
2015	8,605	369	4.3	4,382	213	4.9	4,223	156	3.7
2014	8,594	434	5.0	4,379	218	5.0	4,215	216	5.1
2013	8,501	386	4.5	4,391	216	4.9	4,110	171	4.2
2012	8,767	207	2.4	4,479	126	2.8	4,288	81	1.9
2011	8,815	261	3.0	4,559	145	3.2	4,256	116	2.7
2010	8,793	221	2.5	4,592	127	2.8	4,201	94	2.2
2009	8,886	269	3.0	4,459	146	3.3	4,427	123	2.8
2008	8,942	246	2.8	4,588	123	2.7	4,353	123	2.8
2007	8,927	246	2.8	4,518	126	2.8	4,409	120	2.7
2006	8,924	311	3.5	4,568	177	3.9	4,355	133	3.1
2005	8,855	271	3.1	4,472	151	3.4	4,382	120	2.7
2004	8,585	359	4.2	4,344	211	4.9	4,241	148	3.5
2003[1]	8,781	321	3.7	4,434	172	3.9	4,347	148	3.4
2002	8,636	259	3.0	4,371	133	3.0	4,265	126	3.0
2001	8,490	388	4.6	4,363	230	5.3	4,126	158	3.8
2000	8,540	371	4.3	4,368	204	4.7	4,172	167	4.0
1999	8,665	380	4.4	4,426	180	4.1	4,238	198	4.7
1998	8,487	371	4.4	4,306	188	4.4	4,181	183	4.4
1997	8,402	355	4.2	4,220	208	4.9	4,180	145	3.5
1996	8,005	361	4.5	4,077	198	4.8	3,928	163	4.1
1995	7,926	402	5.1	4,079	220	5.4	3,849	183	4.8
1994	7,862	371	4.7	4,014	184	4.6	3,848	188	4.9
1993[r]	7,442	306	4.1	3,790	157	4.1	3,654	150	4.1
1993	7,152	290	4.1	3,623	147	4.1	3,530	143	4.1
1992	7,077	292	4.1	3,646	140	3.8	3,430	151	4.4
1991	6,856	254	3.7	3,514	127	3.6	3,343	128	3.8
1990	6,984	266	3.8	3,522	144	4.1	3,462	122	3.5
1989	7,243	286	3.9	3,653	149	4.1	3,589	136	3.8
1988	7,727	362	4.7	4,016	203	5.1	3,712	161	4.3
1987	7,979	299	3.7	4,023	163	4.1	3,953	135	3.4
1986	8,011	333	4.2	4,007	168	4.2	4,007	166	4.1
1985	7,967	384	4.8	3,963	195	4.9	4,003	188	4.7
1984	8,221	410	5.0	4,119	220	5.3	4,101	190	4.6
1983	8,531	410	4.8	4,264	232	5.4	4,264	177	4.2
1982	8,769	444	5.1	4,381	231	5.3	4,390	214	4.9
1981	9,067	478	5.3	4,532	254	5.6	4,536	224	4.9
1980	9,177	517	5.6	4,624	294	6.4	4,554	224	4.9
1979	9,437	588	6.2	4,694	311	6.6	4,742	277	5.8
1978	9,360	574	6.1	4,747	329	6.9	4,611	244	5.3
1977	9,536	594	6.2	4,766	327	6.9	4,770	267	5.6
1976	9,362	532	5.7	4,708	297	6.3	4,654	235	5.0
1975	9,440	507	5.4	4,709	234	5.0	4,732	274	5.8
1974	9,403	566	6.0	4,650	326	7.0	4,754	241	5.1
1973	9,359	537	5.7	4,708	288	6.1	4,649	248	5.3
1972	9,173	520	5.7	4,588	247	5.4	4,583	272	5.9
1971	9,140	470	5.1	4,577	244	5.3	4,562	226	5.0
1970	8,959	449	5.0	4,496	212	4.7	4,462	237	5.3
1969	8,878	429	4.8	4,438	208	4.7	4,439	221	5.0
1968	8,580	387	4.5	4,246	190	4.5	4,331	196	4.5
1967	8,186	379	4.6	4,060	189	4.7	4,126	190	4.6
WHITE ALONE, NON-HISPANIC									
Grades 10–12									
2016	6,230	273	4.4	3,234	164	5.1	2,996	109	3.6
2015	6,382	233	3.6	3,289	145	4.4	3,092	87	2.8
2014	6,397	285	4.5	3,288	154	4.7	3,109	131	4.2
2013	6,268	256	4.1	3,236	144	4.5	3,031	112	3.7
2012	6,436	95	1.5	3,257	61	1.9	3,179	34	1.1

[1]Starting in 2003 respondents could identify more than one race. Except as noted, the race data in this table from 2003 onward represent those respondents who indicated only one race category.

[r] = Revised, controlled to 1990 census based population estimates; previous 1993 data controlled to 1980 census based population estimates.

Table A-12. Annual High School Dropout Rates of 15 to 24 Year Olds by Sex, Race, Grade, and Hispanic Origin, October 1967–2016—*Continued*

(Numbers in thousands; percent; civilian noninstitutionalized population.)

Year, grade, race, and Hispanic origin	Total[1]			Male			Female		
	Total students	Dropouts	Dropout rate	Total students	Dropouts	Dropout rate	Total students	Dropouts	Dropout rate
2011	6,647	171	2.6	3,404	89	2.6	3,243	82	2.5
2010	6,851	150	2.2	3,568	97	2.7	3,284	53	1.6
2009	6,944	160	2.3	3,491	91	2.6	3,453	68	2.0
2008	7,079	156	2.2	3,638	83	2.3	3,441	73	2.1
2007	7,274	155	2.1	3,684	82	2.2	3,590	73	2.0
2006	7,171	200	2.8	3,693	120	3.2	3,478	80	2.3
2005	7,227	196	2.7	3,652	103	2.8	3,575	93	2.6
2004	7,015	245	3.5	3,582	130	3.6	3,434	115	3.4
2003[1]	7,139	214	3.0	3,665	116	3.2	3,474	98	2.8
2002	7,124	173	2.4	3,620	84	2.3	3,504	89	2.6
2001	7,070	272	3.8	3,647	173	4.7	3,423	98	2.9
2000	7,159	276	3.9	3,648	150	4.1	3,511	126	3.6
1999	7,265	274	3.8	3,744	130	3.5	3,523	145	4.1
1998	7,174	266	3.7	3,605	130	3.6	3,570	137	3.8
1997	7,090	242	3.4	3,533	140	4.0	3,558	103	2.9
1996	6,850	267	3.9	3,511	145	4.1	3,337	121	3.6
1995	6,905	296	4.3	3,564	164	4.6	3,341	131	3.9
1994	6,839	274	4.0	3,496	137	3.9	3,343	137	4.1
1993	6,277	237	3.8	3,229	128	4.0	3,047	108	3.5
BLACK ALONE									
Grades 10–12									
2016	1,815	98	5.4	919	49	5.3	897	49	5.5
2015	1,735	112	6.4	842	49	5.8	893	63	7
2014	1,757	83	4.7	905	44	4.9	852	39	4.5
2013	1,791	88	4.9	859	37	4.3	931	51	5.5
2012	1,949	124	6.4	897	49	5.5	1,052	75	7.1
2011	1,944	78	4.0	965	54	5.6	978	24	2.4
2010	1,898	62	3.2	946	36	3.8	952	26	2.7
2009	1,797	81	4.5	870	38	4.4	927	42	4.6
2008	1,868	114	6.1	925	42	4.6	943	72	7.6
2007	1,781	76	4.3	914	45	4.9	867	31	3.6
2006	1,767	65	3.7	902	29	3.2	864	37	4.3
2005	1,763	122	6.9	943	71	7.5	820	51	6.2
2004	1,716	90	5.2	833	40	4.8	883	50	5.7
2003[1]	1,698	76	4.5	812	33	4.1	886	43	4.9
2002	1,664	73	4.4	782	40	5.1	882	33	3.8
2001	1,655	95	5.7	828	51	6.2	827	45	5.4
2000	1,706	96	5.6	819	62	7.6	888	34	3.8
1999	1,794	107	6.0	925	48	5.2	870	59	6.8
1998	1,759	88	5.0	918	42	4.6	841	46	5.5
1997	1,678	80	4.8	813	33	4.1	866	49	5.7
1996	1,704	107	6.3	803	37	4.6	901	70	7.8
1995	1,598	97	6.1	797	63	7.9	802	35	4.4
1994	1,559	96	6.1	763	50	6.5	795	45	5.7
1993[r]	1,499	80	5.3	740	43	5.8	758	37	4.9
1993	1,447	78	5.4	724	41	5.7	722	36	5.0
1992	1,422	70	4.9	702	23	3.3	720	48	6.7
1991	1,366	85	6.2	685	38	5.5	683	48	7.0
1990	1,303	66	5.1	636	26	4.1	666	40	6.0
1989	1,384	106	7.7	684	47	6.9	701	60	8.6
1988	1,468	93	6.3	751	50	6.7	717	43	6.0
1987	1,463	93	6.4	730	45	6.2	732	47	6.4
1986	1,449	68	4.7	711	34	4.8	737	34	4.6
1985	1,422	110	7.7	703	58	8.3	719	52	7.2
1984	1,524	88	5.8	711	44	6.2	813	43	5.3
1983	1,498	103	6.9	687	48	7.0	810	55	6.8
1982	1,553	121	7.8	786	71	9.0	767	50	6.5
1981	1,516	146	9.6	704	66	9.4	815	83	10.2
1980	1,496	124	8.3	714	57	8.0	781	66	8.5
1979	1,479	142	9.6	679	51	7.5	802	92	11.5
1978	1,542	160	10.4	706	78	11.0	835	81	9.7
1977	1,588	133	8.4	746	62	8.3	789	71	9.0
1976	1,449	105	7.2	729	62	8.5	721	45	6.2
1975	1,416	123	8.7	673	56	8.3	743	67	9.0
1974	1,441	167	11.6	679	73	10.8	761	93	12.2
1973	1,372	138	10.1	650	78	12.0	725	61	8.4
1972	1,373	133	9.7	644	65	10.1	756	68	9.0
1971	1,195	87	7.3	552	51	9.2	643	37	5.8

[1]Starting in 2003 respondents could identify more than one race. Except as noted, the race data in this table from 2003 onward represent those respondents who indicated only one race category.
[r] = Revised, controlled to 1990 census based population estimates; previous 1993 data controlled to 1980 census based population estimates.

Table A-12. Annual High School Dropout Rates of 15 to 24 Year Olds by Sex, Race, Grade, and Hispanic Origin, October 1967–2016—*Continued*

(Numbers in thousands; percent; civilian noninstitutionalized population.)

Year, grade, race, and Hispanic origin	Total[1]			Male			Female		
	Total students	Dropouts	Dropout rate	Total students	Dropouts	Dropout rate	Total students	Dropouts	Dropout rate
1970..............................	1,192	133	11.2	587	74	12.6	606	60	9.9
1969..............................	1,209	113	9.3	562	58	10.3	646	55	8.5
1968..............................	1,123	113	10.1	523	52	9.9	600	61	10.2
1967..............................	1,066	106	9.9	485	47	9.7	578	58	10.0
ASIAN[2]									
Grades 10–12									
2016..............................	594	20	3.3	281	11	3.9	313	9	2.8
2015..............................	552	34	6.2	263	20	7.5	288	14	5.0
2014..............................	566	5	0.9	259	3	1.2	307	2	0.6
2013..............................	604	10	1.7	279	4	1.5	324	6	1.8
2012..............................	592	19	3.2	331	9	2.7	261	10	3.8
2011..............................	495	17	3.5	272	4	1.5	223	13	6.0
2010..............................	419	12	2.8	220	6	2.9	199	5	2.6
2009..............................	426	7	1.7	215	2	0.8	210	5	2.6
2008..............................	429	17	3.9	219	-	0.2	210	16	7.8
2007..............................	404	30	7.5	202	13	6.6	202	17	8.3
2006..............................	445	19	4.2	237	11	4.5	208	8	3.7
2005..............................	425	6	1.5	219	5	2.4	206	1	0.5
2004..............................	452	4	0.9	233	-	-	219	4	1.9
2003[1]..............................	457	11	2.4	237	3	1.4	221	7	3.4
2002..............................	515	12	2.3	266	8	3.0	249	4	1.6
2001..............................	470	10	2.1	274	9	3.3	197	1	0.5
2000..............................	399	13	3.3	178	12	6.7	221	1	0.5
1999..............................	523	25	4.8	269	13	4.8	253	12	4.7
HISPANIC ORIGIN (OF ANY RACE)									
Grades 10–12									
2016..............................	2,747	118	4.3	1,331	67	5.1	1,416	51	3.6
2015..............................	2,599	148	5.7	1,314	67	5.1	1,285	80	6.3
2014..............................	2,490	179	7.2	1,254	86	6.8	1,236	93	7.5
2013..............................	2,509	132	5.3	1,291	71	5.5	1,218	61	5.0
2012..............................	2,671	136	5.1	1,377	76	5.5	1,294	60	4.6
2011..............................	2,376	100	4.2	1,260	56	4.4	1,116	44	4.0
2010..............................	2,130	80	3.8	1,113	30	2.7	1,018	51	5.0
2009..............................	2,129	114	5.3	1,039	55	5.3	1,090	59	5.4
2008..............................	2,062	101	4.9	1,052	44	4.2	1,011	57	5.6
2007..............................	1,785	99	5.5	904	49	5.5	882	49	5.6
2006..............................	1,923	124	6.4	958	61	6.3	965	63	6.6
2005..............................	1,814	86	4.7	910	51	5.6	904	35	3.9
2004..............................	1,723	138	8.0	842	97	11.5	881	40	4.6
2003..............................	1,792	116	6.5	846	65	7.7	945	51	5.4
2002..............................	1,614	86	5.3	801	50	6.2	814	36	4.4
2001..............................	1,487	121	8.1	755	57	7.5	732	64	8.7
2000..............................	1,465	100	6.8	761	54	7.1	704	46	6.5
1999..............................	1,482	105	7.1	729	50	6.9	751	55	7.3
1998..............................	1,368	115	8.4	731	63	8.6	637	52	8.2
1997..............................	1,377	119	8.6	710	74	10.4	668	45	6.7
1996..............................	1,195	100	8.4	588	54	9.2	608	46	7.6
1995..............................	1,251	145	11.6	644	70	10.9	608	76	12.5
1994..............................	1,179	109	9.2	607	51	8.4	572	58	10.1
1993[r]..............................	1,061	69	6.5	488	25	5.1	573	44	7.5
1993..............................	943	60	6.4	436	21	4.8	508	39	7.7
1992..............................	917	72	7.9	468	27	5.8	441	38	8.6
1991..............................	809	59	7.3	396	41	10.4	417	20	4.8
1990..............................	811	65	8.0	379	33	8.7	428	31	7.2
1989..............................	762	59	7.7	394	30	7.6	366	28	7.7
1988..............................	730	77	10.5	398	49	12.3	333	28	8.4
1987..............................	769	43	5.6	380	19	5.0	389	24	6.2
1986..............................	764	91	11.9	376	44	11.7	388	48	12.4
1985..............................	729	71	9.7	333	31	9.3	396	39	9.8
1984..............................	706	77	10.9	311	38	12.2	396	40	10.1
1983..............................	691	68	9.8	351	48	13.7	340	21	6.2
1982..............................	692	65	9.4	370	35	9.5	321	29	9.0

[1]Starting in 2003 respondents could identify more than one race. Except as noted, the race data in this table from 2003 onward represent those respondents who indicated only one race category.
[2]The data shown prior to 2003 consists of those identifying themselves as "Asian or Pacific Islanders."
[r] = Revised, controlled to 1990 census based population estimates; previous 1993 data controlled to 1980 census based population estimates.

Table A-12. Annual High School Dropout Rates of 15 to 24 Year Olds by Sex, Race, Grade, and Hispanic Origin, October 1967–2016—*Continued*

(Numbers in thousands; percent; civilian noninstitutionalized population.)

Year, grade, race, and Hispanic origin	Total[1]			Male			Female		
	Total students	Dropouts	Dropout rate	Total students	Dropouts	Dropout rate	Total students	Dropouts	Dropout rate
1981	717	77	10.7	350	37	10.6	367	40	10.9
1980	646	74	11.5	295	50	16.9	350	24	6.9
1979	593	58	9.8	295	30	10.2	298	27	9.1
1978	567	70	12.3	295	46	15.6	271	23	8.5
1977	627	50	8.0	341	35	10.3	287	15	5.2
1976	638	46	7.2	300	22	7.3	336	23	6.8
1975	614	67	10.9	317	32	10.1	294	34	11.6
1974	547	53	9.7	271	34	12.5	278	20	7.2
1973	499	50	10.0	240	19	7.9	259	31	12.0
1972	498	55	11.0	253	28	11.1	247	27	10.9
WHITE ALONE OR IN COMBINATION									
Grades 10–12									
2016	9,054	385	4.3	4,566	224	4.9	4,488	161	3.6
2015	9,037	378	4.2	4,610	213	4.6	4,427	165	3.7
2014	9,005	446	5.0	4,580	229	5.0	4,424	217	4.9
2013	8,854	404	4.6	4,577	226	4.9	4,276	178	4.2
2012	9,101	220	2.4	4,629	137	3.0	4,473	83	1.9
2011	9,087	272	3.0	4,696	145	3.1	4,391	127	2.9
2010	9,112	242	2.7	4,764	130	2.7	4,348	112	2.6
2009	9,216	280	3.0	4,610	148	3.2	4,606	132	2.9
2008	9,277	257	2.8	4,766	129	2.7	4,511	128	2.8
2007	9,199	251	2.7	4,664	131	2.8	4,535	120	2.7
2006	9,212	320	3.5	4,695	185	3.9	4,517	136	3.0
2005	9,158	281	3.1	4,610	155	3.4	4,548	126	2.8
2004	8,821	382	4.3	4,464	222	5.0	4,357	160	3.7
2003	9,045	335	3.7	4,573	183	4.0	4,471	151	3.4
BLACK ALONE OR IN COMBINATION									
Grades 10–12									
2016	2,142	106	4.9	1,077	56	5.2	1,066	49	4.6
2015	1,950	112	5.7	951	49	5.1	999	63	6.3
2014	2,012	95	4.7	1,019	55	5.4	993	40	4.0
2013	1,989	98	4.9	962	42	4.3	1,027	56	5.4
2012	2,124	129	6.1	976	52	5.3	1,148	77	6.7
2011	2,051	82	4.0	1,024	54	5.3	1,027	28	2.8
2010	2,038	76	3.7	1,021	38	3.7	1,017	39	3.8
2009	1,985	86	4.3	958	40	4.2	1,026	46	4.5
2008	2,033	121	5.9	1,012	46	4.5	1,021	75	7.3
2007	1,900	78	4.1	977	47	4.8	923	31	3.4
2006	1,891	66	3.5	952	29	3.0	939	38	4.0
2005	1,870	129	6.9	979	71	7.3	890	58	6.5
2004	1,797	99	5.5	869	40	4.6	928	59	6.3
2003	1,808	79	4.4	853	36	4.2	955	43	4.5
ASIAN ALONE OR IN COMBINATION									
Grades 10–12									
2016	731	25	3.4	353	16	4.4	378	9	2.3
2015	661	38	5.7	312	20	6.3	349	18	5.2
2014	660	5	0.8	300	3	1.0	361	2	0.5
2013	744	10	1.4	339	4	1.2	405	6	1.5
2012	696	19	2.7	368	9	2.5	328	10	3.1
2011	579	17	3.0	303	4	1.3	275	13	4.9
2010	520	16	3.2	270	6	2.4	250	10	4.0
2009	525	8	1.4	255	2	0.8	270	5	2.0
2008	511	17	3.3	256	-	0.2	255	16	6.4
2007	483	30	6.2	233	13	5.8	250	17	6.7
2006	542	23	4.2	279	15	5.4	263	8	3.0
2005	525	8	1.5	270	6	2.3	255	2	0.6
2004	516	8	1.6	273	3	1.2	243	5	2.1
2003	533	17	3.1	278	8	3.0	254	8	3.3

[1]Starting in 2003 respondents could identify more than one race. Except as noted, the race data in this table from 2003 onward represent those respondents who indicated only one race category.

Table A-13. Population 14 to 24 Years Old, by High School Graduate Status, College Enrollment, Attainment, Sex, Race, and Hispanic Origin, October 1967–2016

(Numbers in thousands; percent; civilian noninstitutionalized population.)

| Year, race, and Hispanic origin | Population 18 to 24 years old | | | | | | | | High school graduates, 14 to 24 years old | | |
| | High school graduates | | | Percent | | | High school dropouts | | | Percent | |
	Total	Total	Enrolled in college	High school graduates	Enrolled in college	High school graduate enrolled in college	Number	Percent	All graduates	Enrolled in college	Enrolled or completed some college
ALL RACES											
Both Sexes											
2016	29,893	26,123	12,320	87.4	41.2	47.2	1,911	6.4	26,571	47.3	72.3
2015	30,037	26,248	12,152	87.4	40.5	46.3	1,917	6.4	26,673	46.4	72.2
2014	30,304	26,311	12,132	86.8	40.0	46.1	2,090	6.9	26,700	46.3	72.0
2013	30,556	26,317	12,202	86.1	39.9	46.4	2,215	7.3	26,734	46.8	71.8
2012	30,377	25,866	12,456	85.1	41.0	48.2	2,319	7.6	26,255	48.5	72.9
2011	29,943	25,435	12,570	84.9	42.0	49.4	2,481	8.3	25,765	49.6	73.1
2010	29,659	25,224	12,213	85.0	41.2	48.4	2,590	8.7	25,564	48.7	72.6
2009	29,223	24,647	12,073	84.3	41.3	49.0	2,733	9.4	25,015	49.1	72.0
2008	28,950	24,568	11,466	84.9	39.6	46.7	2,702	9.3	24,922	47.0	70.6
2007	28,778	24,146	11,161	83.9	38.8	46.2	2,937	10.2	24,491	46.3	69.7
2006	28,372	23,430	10,586	82.6	37.3	45.2	3,128	11.0	23,800	45.4	69.3
2005	27,855	23,103	10,834	82.9	38.9	46.9	3,154	11.3	23,445	47.0	69.8
2004	27,948	23,086	10,611	82.6	38.0	46.0	3,836	12.1	23,379	46.2	69.0
2003	27,404	22,603	10,364	82.5	37.8	45.9	3,228	11.8	22,898	45.9	68.8
2002	27,367	22,319	10,033	81.6	36.7	45.0	3,375	12.3	22,639	45.2	67.6
2001	26,965	21,836	9,629	81.0	35.7	44.1	3,519	13.0	22,136	44.1	66.7
2000	26,658	21,822	9,452	81.9	35.5	43.3	3,315	12.4	22,080	43.5	66.7
1999	26,041	21,127	9,259	81.1	35.6	43.8	3,413	13.1	21,390	44.0	67.2
1998	25,507	20,567	9,322	80.6	36.6	45.3	3,544	13.9	20,775	45.5	68.0
1997	24,973	20,338	9,204	81.4	36.9	45.2	3,236	13.0	20,577	45.6	67.3
1996	24,671	20,131	8,767	81.6	35.5	43.5	3,147	12.8	20,465	44.0	67.2
1995	24,900	20,125	8,539	80.8	34.3	42.4	3,471	13.9	20,359	42.7	67.1
1994	25,254	20,581	8,729	81.5	34.6	42.4	3,365	13.3	20,779	42.7	66.9
1993ʳ	25,522	20,844	8,630	81.7	33.8	41.4	3,349	13.1	21,060	41.6	65.3
1993	24,100	19,772	8,193	82.0	34.0	41.4	3,070	12.7	19,979	41.6	65.4
1992	24,278	19,921	8,343	82.1	34.4	41.9	3,083	12.7	20,194	42.3	65.6
1991	24,572	19,883	8,172	80.9	33.3	41.1	3,486	14.2	20,065	41.4	60.7
1990	24,852	20,311	7,964	82.3	32.0	39.1	3,379	13.6	20,571	39.6	58.9
1989	25,261	20,461	7,804	81.0	30.9	38.1	3,644	14.4	20,749	38.5	57.9
1988	25,733	20,900	7,791	81.2	30.3	37.3	3,749	14.6	21,204	37.6	57.4
1987	25,950	21,118	7,693	81.4	29.6	36.4	3,751	14.5	21,477	36.9	56.2
1986	26,512	21,768	7,477	82.1	28.2	34.3	3,687	13.9	22,086	34.8	55.0
1985	27,122	22,349	7,537	82.4	27.8	33.7	3,687	13.9	22,722	34.3	54.3
1984	28,031	22,870	7,591	81.6	27.1	33.2	4,142	14.8	23,252	33.7	53.0
1983	28,580	22,988	7,477	80.4	26.2	32.5	4,410	15.4	23,359	33.1	52.8
1982	28,846	23,291	7,678	80.7	26.6	33.0	4,500	15.6	23,708	33.5	52.7
1981	28,965	23,343	7,575	80.6	26.2	32.5	4,520	15.6	23,705	32.9	51.7
1980	28,957	23,413	7,400	80.9	25.6	31.6	4,515	15.6	23,856	32.1	51.1
1979	27,974	22,421	6,991	80.1	25.0	31.2	4,560	16.3	22,911	31.9	51.6
1978	27,647	22,309	6,995	80.7	25.3	31.4	4,388	15.9	22,759	31.9	51.4
1977	27,331	22,008	7,142	80.5	26.1	32.5	4,313	15.8	22,499	33.0	52.0
1976	26,919	21,677	7,181	80.5	26.7	33.1	4,276	15.9	22,158	33.7	53.4
1975	26,387	21,326	6,935	80.8	26.3	32.5	4,110	15.6	21,824	33.1	52.5
1974	25,670	20,725	6,316	80.7	24.6	30.5	4,070	15.9	21,267	31.2	51.3
1973	25,237	20,377	6,055	80.7	24.0	29.7	3,973	15.7	20,895	30.4	50.7
1972	24,579	19,618	6,257	79.8	25.5	31.9	4,068	16.6	20,107	32.6	52.9
1971	23,668	18,691	6,210	79.0	26.2	33.2	4,025	17.0	19,130	33.9	53.1
1970	22,552	17,768	5,805	78.8	25.7	32.7	3,908	17.3	18,218	33.5	52.3
1969	21,362	16,703	5,840	78.2	27.3	35.0	3,769	17.6	17,152	35.7	52.5
1968	20,562	15,683	5,356	76.3	26.0	34.2	3,929	19.1	16,165	35.2	51.5
1967	20,009	15,114	5,100	75.5	25.5	33.7	3,967	19.8	15,642	34.9	50.5
Male											
2016	15,042	12,851	5,800	85.4	38.6	45.1	1,134	7.5	13,014	45.2	68.1
2015	15,074	13,031	5,694	86.5	37.8	43.7	1,034	6.9	13,256	43.8	68.0
2014	15,234	13,019	5,676	85.5	37.3	43.6	1,132	7.4	13,225	43.9	67.7
2013	15,379	13,051	5,630	84.9	36.6	43.1	1,183	7.7	13,254	43.6	67.0
2012	15,252	12,753	5,731	83.6	37.6	44.9	1,300	8.5	12,940	45.3	68.4
2011	15,211	12,659	5,953	83.2	39.1	47.0	1,374	9.0	12,834	47.2	69.0

Note: The change in the educational attainment question and the college completion categories from "4 or more years of college" to "at least some college," in 1992 caused an increase in the proportion of 14-to-24-year-old high school graduates enrolled in college or completed some college, of approximately 5 percentage points. High school graduates are people who have completed 4 years of high school or more, for 1967 to 1991. Beginning in 1992, they were people whose highest degree was a high school diploma (including equivalency) or higher.

ʳ = Revised, controlled to 1990 census based population estimates; previous 1993 data controlled to 1980 census based population estimates.

Table A-13. Population 14 to 24 Years Old, by High School Graduate Status, College Enrollment, Attainment, Sex, Race, and Hispanic Origin, October 1967–2016—*Continued*

(Numbers in thousands; percent; civilian noninstitutionalized population.)

Year, race, and Hispanic origin	Population 18 to 24 years old								High school graduates, 14 to 24 years old		
	High school graduates			Percent			High school dropouts			Percent	
	Total	Total	Enrolled in college	High school graduates	Enrolled in college	High school graduate enrolled in college	Number	Percent	All graduates	Enrolled in college	Enrolled or completed some college
2010	14,887	12,371	5,698	83.1	38.3	46.1	1,473	9.9	12,540	46.2	68.4
2009	14,677	12,111	5,640	82.5	38.4	46.6	1,568	10.7	12,277	46.7	68.5
2008	14,559	12,181	5,383	83.7	37.0	44.2	1,445	9.9	12,374	44.6	66.7
2007	14,515	11,825	5,156	81.5	35.5	43.6	1,680	11.6	11,972	43.7	66.0
2006	14,300	11,508	4,874	80.5	34.1	42.4	1,741	12.2	11,659	42.5	65.1
2005	14,077	11,182	4,973	79.4	35.3	44.5	1,852	13.2	11,330	44.4	65.9
2004	14,018	11,258	4,865	80.3	34.7	43.2	1,942	13.9	11,364	43.5	65.0
2003	13,681	10,919	4,697	79.8	34.3	43.0	1,875	13.7	11,040	43.1	65.0
2002	13,744	10,823	4,629	78.7	33.7	42.8	1,925	14.0	10,975	42.9	64.6
2001	13,434	10,461	4,437	77.9	33.0	42.4	2,028	15.1	10,587	42.4	63.9
2000	13,338	10,622	4,343	79.6	32.6	40.9	1,837	13.8	10,736	41.0	63.1
1999	12,905	10,201	4,396	79.1	34.0	43.1	1,818	14.9	10,331	43.3	64.5
1998	12,764	9,915	4,403	77.7	34.5	44.4	2,018	15.8	10,006	44.5	64.9
1997	12,513	9,933	4,374	79.4	35.0	44.0	1,765	14.1	10,025	44.2	64.9
1996	12,285	9,815	4,187	80.0	34.1	42.6	1,628	13.2	9,960	43.0	65.6
1995	12,351	9,789	4,089	79.3	33.1	41.8	1,791	14.5	9,884	42.1	64.2
1994	12,557	9,970	4,152	79.4	33.1	41.6	1,804	14.4	10,051	41.9	64.9
1993ʳ	12,712	10,142	4,237	79.8	33.3	41.8	1,745	13.7	10,229	42.0	63.9
1993	11,898	9,541	3,994	80.2	33.6	41.9	1,575	13.2	9,625	42.0	64.1
1992	11,965	9,576	3,912	80.0	32.7	40.9	1,617	13.5	9,706	41.3	64.1
1991	12,036	9,493	3,954	78.9	32.9	41.7	1,810	15.0	9,564	41.9	59.2
1990	12,134	9,778	3,922	80.6	32.3	40.1	1,689	13.9	9,894	40.5	58.0
1989	12,325	9,700	3,717	78.7	30.2	38.3	1,941	15.7	9,810	38.6	57.2
1988	12,491	9,832	3,770	78.7	30.2	38.3	1,950	15.6	9,947	38.5	56.5
1987	12,626	10,030	3,867	79.4	30.6	38.6	1,948	15.4	10,207	39.0	56.0
1986	12,921	10,338	3,702	80.0	28.7	35.8	1,924	14.9	10,465	36.2	54.4
1985	13,199	10,614	3,749	80.4	28.4	35.3	2,015	15.3	10,784	36.0	54.6
1984	13,744	10,914	3,929	79.4	28.6	36.0	2,184	15.9	11,052	36.4	53.6
1983	14,003	10,906	3,820	77.9	27.3	35.0	2,379	17.0	10,959	35.5	52.7
1982	14,083	11,120	3,837	79.0	27.2	34.5	2,329	16.5	11,295	35.0	53.0
1981	14,127	11,052	3,833	78.2	27.1	34.7	2,424	17.2	11,203	35.1	52.1
1980	14,107	11,125	3,717	78.9	26.3	33.4	2,390	16.9	11,309	33.7	51.4
1979	13,571	10,657	3,508	78.5	25.8	32.9	2,320	17.1	10,838	33.6	52.4
1978	13,385	10,614	3,621	79.3	27.1	34.1	2,200	16.4	10,789	34.5	52.6
1977	13,218	10,440	3,712	79.0	28.1	35.6	2,170	16.4	10,626	36.0	54.2
1976	13,012	10,312	3,673	79.2	28.2	35.6	2,109	16.2	10,492	36.0	55.7
1975	12,724	10,214	3,693	80.3	29.0	36.2	1,928	15.2	10,415	36.7	56.1
1974	12,315	9,835	3,411	79.9	27.7	34.7	1,958	15.9	10,073	35.3	55.6
1973	12,111	9,716	3,360	80.2	27.7	34.6	1,853	15.3	9,908	35.1	55.4
1972	11,712	9,247	3,534	79.0	30.2	38.2	1,898	16.2	9,461	38.8	59.0
1971	11,092	8,669	3,599	78.2	32.4	41.5	1,865	16.8	8,855	42.1	60.1
1970	10,385	8,087	3,331	77.9	32.1	41.2	1,746	16.8	8,279	41.8	59.2
1969	9,649	7,445	3,392	77.2	35.2	45.6	1,640	17.0	7,609	46.2	61.2
1968	9,251	6,864	3,152	74.2	34.1	45.9	1,777	19.2	8,038	46.7	61.1
1967	8,999	6,678	2,982	74.2	33.1	44.7	1,804	20.0	6,829	45.1	58.8
Female											
2016	14,851	13,273	6,521	89.4	43.9	49.1	778	5.2	13,557	49.3	76.4
2015	14,963	13,217	6,459	88.3	43.2	48.9	883	5.9	13,418	49.0	76.3
2014	15,070	13,293	6,456	88.2	42.8	48.6	958	6.4	13,475	48.7	76.3
2013	15,177	13,266	6,573	87.4	43.3	49.5	1,033	6.8	13,480	49.9	76.6
2012	15,125	13,113	6,725	86.7	44.5	51.3	1,019	6.7	13,316	51.6	77.2
2011	14,732	12,776	6,617	86.7	44.9	51.8	1,107	7.5	12,930	51.9	77.2
2010	14,772	12,854	6,515	87.0	44.1	50.7	1,116	7.6	13,024	51.1	76.7
2009	14,546	12,536	6,432	86.2	44.2	51.3	1,165	8.0	12,738	51.4	75.5
2008	14,391	12,387	6,083	86.1	42.3	49.1	1,257	8.7	12,548	49.3	74.5
2007	14,263	12,321	6,005	86.4	42.1	48.7	1,256	8.8	12,519	48.8	73.3
2006	14,073	11,922	5,712	84.7	40.6	47.9	1,387	9.9	12,141	48.1	73.3
2005	13,778	11,921	5,861	86.5	42.5	49.2	1,302	9.5	12,115	49.4	73.4
2004	13,930	11,828	5,746	84.9	41.2	48.6	1,444	10.4	12,015	48.8	72.8
2003	13,724	11,684	5,667	85.1	41.3	48.5	1,354	9.9	11,858	48.5	72.2
2002	13,623	11,496	5,404	84.4	39.7	47.0	1,450	10.6	11,664	47.3	70.3

Note: The change in the educational attainment question and the college completion categories from "4 or more years of college" to "at least some college," in 1992 caused an increase in the proportion of 14-to-24-year-old high school graduates enrolled in college or completed some college, of approximately 5 percentage points. High school graduates are people who have completed 4 years of high school or more, for 1967 to 1991. Beginning in 1992, they were people whose highest degree was a high school diploma (including equivalency) or higher.

ʳ = Revised, controlled to 1990 census based population estimates; previous 1993 data controlled to 1980 census based population estimates.

Table A-13. Population 14 to 24 Years Old, by High School Graduate Status, College Enrollment, Attainment, Sex, Race, and Hispanic Origin, October 1967–2016—*Continued*

(Numbers in thousands; percent; civilian noninstitutionalized population.)

	Population 18 to 24 years old								High school graduates, 14 to 24 years old		
		High school graduates			Percent			High school dropouts		Percent	
Year, race, and Hispanic origin	Total	Total	Enrolled in college	High school graduates	Enrolled in college	High school graduate enrolled in college	Number	Percent	All graduates	Enrolled in college	Enrolled or completed some college
2001	13,531	11,375	5,192	84.1	38.4	45.7	1,491	11.0	11,549	45.7	69.4
2000	13,319	11,200	5,109	84.1	38.4	45.6	1,478	11.1	11,344	45.8	70.1
1999	13,136	10,926	4,863	83.2	37.0	44.5	1,594	12.1	11,058	44.6	69.8
1998	12,743	10,651	4,919	83.6	38.6	46.2	1,526	12.0	10,768	46.4	70.7
1997	12,460	10,403	4,829	83.5	38.8	46.4	1,471	11.8	10,549	46.8	69.6
1996	12,386	10,317	4,582	83.3	37.0	44.4	1,519	12.3	10,507	44.9	68.6
1995	12,548	10,338	4,452	82.4	35.5	43.1	1,679	13.4	10,477	43.4	69.8
1994	12,696	10,611	4,576	83.6	36.0	43.1	1,561	12.3	10,729	43.4	68.7
1993ʳ	12,810	10,702	4,393	83.5	34.3	41.0	1,604	12.5	10,831	41.3	66.6
1993	12,202	10,232	4,199	83.9	34.4	41.0	1,494	12.2	10,355	41.2	66.7
1992	12,313	10,344	4,429	84.0	36.0	42.8	1,466	11.9	10,486	43.3	66.9
1991	12,536	10,391	4,218	82.9	33.6	40.6	1,676	13.4	10,502	41.0	62.1
1990	12,718	10,533	4,042	82.8	31.8	38.4	1,690	13.3	10,676	38.7	59.8
1989	12,936	10,758	4,085	83.2	31.6	38.0	1,702	13.2	10,936	38.4	58.6
1988	13,242	11,068	4,021	83.6	30.4	36.3	1,799	13.5	11,257	36.8	58.2
1987	13,324	11,086	3,826	83.2	28.7	34.5	1,803	13.5	11,268	35.0	56.4
1986	13,591	11,430	3,775	84.1	27.8	33.0	1,751	12.9	11,623	33.5	55.5
1985	13,923	11,736	3,788	84.3	27.2	32.3	1,804	13.0	11,937	32.8	54.0
1984	14,287	11,956	3,662	83.7	25.6	30.6	1,958	13.7	12,199	31.3	52.4
1983	14,577	12,082	3,657	82.9	25.1	30.3	2,031	13.9	12,294	31.0	52.8
1982	14,763	12,171	3,841	82.4	26.0	31.6	2,171	14.7	12,411	32.1	52.4
1981	14,838	12,290	3,741	82.8	25.2	30.4	2,097	14.1	12,503	31.0	51.3
1980	14,851	12,287	3,682	82.7	24.8	30.0	2,124	14.3	12,547	30.6	50.8
1979	14,403	11,763	3,482	81.7	24.2	29.6	2,240	15.6	12,074	30.4	50.8
1978	14,262	11,694	3,373	82.0	23.7	28.8	2,188	15.3	11,969	29.6	50.3
1977	14,113	11,569	3,431	82.0	24.3	29.7	2,143	15.2	11,875	30.3	50.0
1976	13,907	11,365	3,508	81.7	25.2	30.9	2,168	15.6	11,666	31.6	51.4
1975	13,663	11,113	3,243	81.3	23.7	29.2	2,181	16.0	11,407	29.9	49.2
1974	13,355	10,889	2,905	81.5	21.8	26.7	2,112	15.8	11,194	27.4	47.5
1973	13,126	10,663	2,696	81.2	20.5	25.3	2,119	16.1	10,986	26.1	46.5
1972	12,867	10,371	2,724	80.6	21.2	26.3	2,170	16.9	10,644	27.0	47.4
1971	12,576	10,020	2,610	79.7	20.8	26.0	2,159	17.2	10,272	26.9	47.1
1970	12,167	9,680	2,474	79.6	20.3	25.6	2,163	17.8	9,908	26.3	46.6
1969	11,713	9,259	2,448	79.0	20.9	26.4	2,128	18.2	9,499	27.1	45.7
1968	11,311	8,820	2,205	78.0	19.5	25.0	2,150	19.0	9,072	25.9	44.4
1967	11,011	8,436	2,117	76.6	19.2	25.1	2,162	19.6	8,694	26.0	44.7
WHITE ALONE											
Both Sexes											
2016	22,018	19,373	9,106	88.0	41.4	47.0	1,381	6.3	19,673	47.1	72.7
2015	22,244	19,451	8,969	87.4	40.3	46.1	1,430	6.4	19,747	46.2	72.6
2014	22,507	19,541	9,077	86.8	40.3	46.4	1,599	7.1	19,786	46.6	72.1
2013	22,658	19,660	9,049	86.8	39.9	46.0	1,599	7.1	19,985	46.5	72.1
2012	22,712	19,555	9,302	86.1	41.0	47.6	1,641	7.2	19,831	47.9	73.5
2011	23,089	19,760	9,813	85.6	42.5	49.7	1,885	8.2	20,007	49.8	74.0
2010	22,851	19,517	9,325	85.4	40.8	47.8	1,941	8.5	19,741	48.0	73.0
2009	22,606	19,241	9,327	85.1	41.3	48.5	2,059	9.1	19,512	48.6	72.1
2008	22,530	19,334	9,141	85.8	40.6	47.3	1,991	8.8	19,586	47.5	71.6
2007	22,392	18,913	8,780	84.5	39.2	46.4	2,248	10.0	19,170	46.5	70.3
2006	22,169	18,489	8,298	83.4	37.4	44.9	2,399	10.8	18,751	45.1	69.9
2005	21,777	18,130	8,498	83.3	39.0	46.9	2,466	11.3	18,352	46.9	70.0
2004	21,896	18,213	8,351	82.6	38.0	45.9	2,599	11.9	18,414	46.1	69.1
2003¹	21,502	17,901	8,150	83.3	37.9	45.5	2,489	11.6	18,123	45.5	69.1
2002	21,704	17,793	7,921	82.0	36.5	44.5	2,641	12.2	17,995	44.6	67.5
2001	21,372	17,348	7,548	81.2	35.3	43.5	2,865	13.4	17,547	43.5	67.0
2000	21,257	17,512	7,566	82.4	35.6	43.2	2,598	12.2	17,714	43.4	66.9
1999	20,866	17,052	7,447	81.7	35.7	43.7	2,680	12.8	17,220	43.8	67.5
1998	20,465	16,701	7,541	81.6	36.9	45.2	2,810	13.7	16,855	45.3	68.3
1997	20,020	16,557	7,495	82.7	37.4	45.3	2,476	12.4	16,733	45.6	67.7
1996	19,676	16,199	7,123	82.3	36.2	44.0	2,458	12.5	16,436	44.3	68.4

Note: The change in the educational attainment question and the college completion categories from "4 or more years of college" to "at least some college," in 1992 caused an increase in the proportion of 14-to-24-year-old high school graduates enrolled in college or completed some college, of approximately 5 percentage points. High school graduates are people who have completed 4 years of high school or more, for 1967 to 1991. Beginning in 1992, they were people whose highest degree was a high school diploma (including equivalency) or higher.

¹Starting in 2003 respondents could identify more than one race. Except as noted, the race data in this table from 2003 onward represent those respondents who indicated only one race category.

ʳ = Revised, controlled to 1990 census based population estimates; previous 1993 data controlled to 1980 census based population estimates.

Table A-13. Population 14 to 24 Years Old, by High School Graduate Status, College Enrollment, Attainment, Sex, Race, and Hispanic Origin, October 1967–2016—*Continued*

(Numbers in thousands; percent; civilian noninstitutionalized population.)

| | Population 18 to 24 years old | | | | | | | | High school graduates, 14 to 24 years old | | |
| | High school graduates | | | Percent | | | High school dropouts | | | Percent | |
Year, race, and Hispanic origin	Total	Total	Enrolled in college	High school graduates	Enrolled in college	High school graduate enrolled in college	Number	Percent	All graduates	Enrolled in college	Enrolled or completed some college
1995	19,866	16,269	7,011	81.9	35.3	43.1	2,711	13.6	16,439	43.4	68.3
1994	20,171	16,670	7,118	82.6	35.3	42.7	2,553	12.7	16,814	42.9	67.6
1993ʳ	20,493	16,989	7,074	82.9	34.5	41.6	2,595	12.7	17,161	41.8	66.5
1993	19,430	16,196	6,763	83.4	34.8	41.8	2,369	12.2	16,361	41.9	66.7
1992	19,671	16,379	6,916	83.3	35.2	42.2	2,398	12.2	16,586	42.7	67.0
1991	19,980	16,324	6,813	81.7	34.1	41.7	2,845	14.2	16,467	42.0	62.3
1990	20,393	16,823	6,635	82.5	32.5	39.4	2,751	13.5	17,022	39.8	60.1
1989	20,825	17,089	6,631	82.1	31.8	38.8	2,926	14.1	17,329	39.1	58.9
1988	21,261	17,491	6,659	82.3	31.3	38.1	3,012	14.2	17,720	38.4	58.5
1987	21,493	17,689	6,483	82.3	30.2	36.6	3,042	14.2	17,982	37.1	56.8
1986	22,020	18,291	6,307	83.1	28.6	34.5	2,961	13.4	18,554	34.9	55.5
1985	22,632	18,916	6,500	83.6	28.7	34.4	3,050	13.5	19,229	35.0	55.3
1984	23,347	19,373	6,256	83.0	28.0	33.7	3,281	14.1	19,686	34.2	53.8
1983	23,899	19,643	6,463	82.2	27.0	32.9	3,428	14.3	19,948	33.5	53.4
1982	24,206	19,944	6,694	82.4	27.2	33.1	3,523	14.6	20,292	33.6	53.1
1981	24,486	20,123	6,549	82.2	26.7	32.5	3,590	14.7	20,439	33.0	52.1
1980	24,482	20,214	6,423	82.6	26.2	31.8	3,525	14.4	20,583	32.3	51.4
1979	23,895	19,616	6,120	82.1	25.6	31.2	3,571	14.9	20,033	31.8	51.7
1978	23,650	19,526	6,077	82.6	25.7	31.1	3,464	14.6	19,911	31.7	51.3
1977	23,430	19,291	6,209	82.3	26.5	32.2	3,445	14.7	19,712	32.6	52.1
1976	23,119	19,045	6,276	82.4	27.1	33.0	3,407	14.7	19,462	33.5	53.5
1975	22,703	18,883	6,116	83.2	26.9	32.4	3,149	13.9	19,298	33.0	52.7
1974	22,141	18,318	5,589	82.7	25.2	30.5	3,212	14.5	18,794	31.2	51.7
1973	21,766	18,023	5,438	82.8	25.0	30.2	3,085	14.2	18,470	30.8	51.6
1972	21,315	17,410	5,624	81.7	26.4	32.3	3,241	15.2	17,838	33.0	53.9
1971	20,533	16,593	5,594	81.3	27.2	33.5	3,156	15.4	17,087	34.2	54.1
1970	19,608	15,960	5,305	81.4	27.1	33.2	2,974	15.2	16,334	33.9	53.4
1969	18,606	15,031	5,347	80.8	28.7	35.6	2,915	15.7	15,383	36.2	53.5
1968	17,951	14,127	4,929	78.7	27.5	34.9	3,107	17.3	14,506	35.7	52.5
1967	17,500	13,657	4,708	78.0	26.9	34.5	3,141	17.9	14,022	35.2	51.4
Male											
2016	11,139	9,614	4,267	86.3	38.3	44.4	818	7.3	9,734	44.4	67.7
2015	11,251	9,714	4,189	86.3	37.2	43.1	791	7.0	9,875	43.2	67.6
2014	11,397	9,781	4,296	85.8	37.7	43.9	866	7.6	9,904	44.1	67.4
2013	11,475	9,792	4,131	85.3	36.0	42.2	855	7.5	9,956	42.6	66.7
2012	11,499	9,692	4,261	84.3	37.1	44.0	937	8.1	9,810	44.3	68.0
2011	11,850	9,928	4,685	83.8	39.5	47.2	1,077	9.1	10,061	47.3	70.0
2010	11,579	9,651	4,369	83.3	37.7	45.3	1,124	9.7	9,754	45.4	68.6
2009	11,449	9,535	4,404	83.3	38.5	46.2	1,201	10.5	9,662	46.4	68.3
2008	11,432	9,646	4,340	84.4	38.0	45.0	1,122	9.8	9,784	45.2	67.8
2007	11,387	9,311	4,040	81.8	35.5	43.4	1,333	11.7	9,430	43.5	66.0
2006	11,264	9,139	3,842	81.1	34.1	42.0	1,396	12.4	9,237	42.2	66.0
2005	11,116	8,885	3,924	79.9	35.3	44.1	1,469	13.2	8,986	44.1	65.9
2004	11,107	9,001	3,855	81.0	34.7	42.8	1,524	13.7	9,067	43.1	64.4
2003¹	10,885	8,763	3,726	80.5	34.2	42.5	1,452	13.3	8,862	42.6	65.1
2002	10,986	8,717	3,701	79.4	33.7	42.5	1,506	13.7	8,833	42.5	64.6
2001	10,817	8,490	3,521	78.5	32.6	41.5	1,659	15.3	8,582	41.5	64.0
2000	10,739	8,603	3,522	80.1	32.8	40.9	1,450	13.5	8,690	41.1	63.5
1999	10,532	8,382	3,585	79.6	34.0	42.7	1,462	13.9	8,457	42.8	64.8
1998	10,400	8,194	3,634	78.8	34.9	44.3	1,628	15.7	8,256	44.4	65.5
1997	10,173	8,204	3,633	80.6	35.7	44.3	1,406	13.8	8,274	44.5	65.3
1996	9,897	8,000	3,419	80.8	34.5	42.7	1,275	12.9	8,104	43.0	66.0
1995	9,980	8,001	3,398	80.2	34.0	42.5	1,430	14.3	8,067	42.7	65.3
1994	10,123	8,168	3,406	80.7	33.6	41.7	1,377	13.6	8,227	41.9	65.4
1993ʳ	10,294	8,338	3,498	81.0	34.0	42.0	1,388	13.5	8,411	42.1	65.1
1993	9,641	7,857	3,313	81.5	34.4	42.2	1,379	12.9	7,926	42.3	65.4
1992	9,744	7,911	3,291	81.2	33.8	41.6	1,300	13.3	8,016	42.1	65.8
1991	9,896	7,843	3,270	79.3	33.0	41.7	1,520	15.4	7,899	41.9	59.9
1990	10,053	8,157	3,292	81.1	32.7	40.3	1,430	14.2	8,246	40.7	58.8
1989	10,240	8,177	3,223	79.9	31.5	39.4	1,572	15.4	8,271	39.7	58.5

Note: The change in the educational attainment question and the college completion categories from "4 or more years of college" to "at least some college," in 1992 caused an increase in the proportion of 14-to-24-year-old high school graduates enrolled in college or completed some college, of approximately 5 percentage points. High school graduates are people who have completed 4 years of high school or more, for 1967 to 1991. Beginning in 1992, they were people whose highest degree was a high school diploma (including equivalency) or higher.

¹Starting in 2003 respondents could identify more than one race. Except as noted, the race data in this table from 2003 onward represent those respondents who indicated only one race category.

ʳ = Revised, controlled to 1990 census based population estimates; previous 1993 data controlled to 1980 census based population estimates.

Table A-13. Population 14 to 24 Years Old, by High School Graduate Status, College Enrollment, Attainment, Sex, Race, and Hispanic Origin, October 1967–2016—*Continued*

(Numbers in thousands; percent; civilian noninstitutionalized population.)

Year, race, and Hispanic origin	Population 18 to 24 years old								High school graduates, 14 to 24 years old		
		High school graduates		Percent			High school dropouts			Percent	
	Total	Total	Enrolled in college	High school graduates	Enrolled in college	High school graduate enrolled in college	Number	Percent	All graduates	Enrolled in college	Enrolled or completed some college
1988	10,380	8,268	3,260	79.7	31.4	39.4	1,594	15.4	8,365	39.6	57.8
1987	10,549	8,498	3,289	80.6	31.2	38.7	1,593	15.1	8,647	39.2	56.4
1986	10,814	8,780	3,168	81.2	29.3	36.1	1,575	14.6	8,886	36.4	55.1
1985	11,108	9,077	3,254	81.7	29.3	35.8	1,637	14.7	9,229	36.6	55.5
1984	11,521	9,348	3,406	81.1	29.6	36.4	1,744	15.1	9,459	36.8	54.2
1983	11,787	9,411	3,335	79.8	28.3	35.4	1,865	15.8	9,534	35.9	53.5
1982	11,874	9,611	3,308	80.9	27.9	34.4	1,810	15.2	9,761	34.9	53.2
1981	12,040	9,619	3,340	79.9	27.7	34.7	1,960	16.3	9,754	35.1	52.8
1980	12,011	9,686	3,275	80.6	27.3	33.8	1,883	15.7	9,838	34.1	51.8
1979	11,721	9,457	3,104	80.7	26.5	32.8	1,830	15.6	9,615	33.4	52.7
1978	11,572	9,438	3,195	81.6	27.6	33.9	1,722	14.9	9,582	34.3	52.5
1977	11,445	9,263	3,286	80.9	28.7	35.5	1,779	15.5	9,422	35.8	54.5
1976	11,279	9,186	3,250	81.4	28.8	35.4	1,691	15.0	9,340	35.7	55.9
1975	11,050	9,139	3,326	82.7	30.1	36.4	1,490	13.5	9,310	36.9	56.6
1974	10,722	8,768	3,035	81.8	28.3	34.6	1,579	14.7	8,980	35.2	55.9
1973	10,511	8,637	3,032	82.2	28.8	35.1	1,453	13.8	8,817	35.6	56.5
1972	10,212	8,278	3,195	81.1	31.3	38.6	1,506	14.7	8,462	39.2	60.1
1971	9,653	7,807	3,284	80.9	34.0	42.1	1,429	14.8	7,978	42.6	61.4
1970	9,053	7,324	3,096	80.9	34.2	42.3	1,297	14.3	7,496	42.9	60.9
1969	8,420	6,740	3,146	80.0	37.4	46.7	1,248	14.8	6,882	47.3	62.8
1968	8,084	6,221	2,949	77.0	36.5	47.4	1,401	17.3	6,372	48.1	62.7
1967	7,864	6,073	2,761	77.2	35.1	45.5	1,391	17.7	6,210	45.9	60.0
Female											
2016	10,879	9,759	4,839	89.7	44.5	49.6	563	5.2	9,939	49.8	77.5
2015	10,993	9,736	4,780	88.6	43.5	49.1	639	5.8	9,872	49.1	77.5
2014	11,110	9,760	4,780	87.9	43.0	49.0	733	6.6	9,882	49.2	76.8
2013	11,183	9,868	4,919	88.2	44.0	49.8	744	6.7	10,029	50.2	77.5
2012	11,214	9,863	5,041	88.0	45.0	51.1	704	6.3	10,021	51.5	78.8
2011	11,238	9,832	5,128	87.5	45.6	51.8	808	7.2	9,946	52.2	78.0
2010	11,271	9,867	4,956	87.5	44.0	50.2	817	7.2	9,987	50.6	77.3
2009	11,157	9,706	4,923	87.0	44.1	50.7	858	7.7	9,850	50.8	75.8
2008	11,098	9,688	4,801	87.3	43.3	49.6	869	7.8	9,802	49.9	75.4
2007	11,005	9,603	4,741	87.3	43.1	49.4	915	8.3	9,741	49.5	74.4
2006	10,905	9,350	4,456	85.7	40.9	47.7	1,003	9.2	9,513	47.9	73.7
2005	10,661	9,245	4,574	86.7	42.9	49.5	997	9.4	9,366	49.7	73.9
2004	10,789	9,212	4,496	85.4	41.7	48.8	1,075	10.0	9,347	49.0	73.5
2003[1]	10,617	9,138	4,424	86.1	41.7	48.4	1,037	9.8	9,260	48.3	72.9
2002	10,718	9,075	4,220	84.7	39.4	46.5	1,135	10.6	9,162	46.6	70.4
2001	10,555	8,859	4,027	83.9	38.1	45.5	1,206	11.4	8,965	45.5	69.8
2000	10,517	8,909	4,044	84.7	38.5	45.4	1,148	10.9	9,024	45.6	70.2
1999	10,334	8,671	3,862	83.9	37.4	44.5	1,218	11.8	8,763	44.7	70.1
1998	10,065	8,507	3,907	84.5	38.8	45.9	1,181	11.7	8,599	46.2	71.0
1997	9,847	8,352	3,863	84.8	39.2	46.3	1,072	10.9	8,458	46.6	70.1
1996	9,778	8,200	3,705	83.9	37.9	45.2	1,182	12.1	8,333	45.6	70.7
1995	9,886	8,271	3,615	83.7	36.6	43.7	1,281	13.0	8,376	44.0	71.3
1994	10,048	8,503	3,714	84.6	37.0	43.7	1,175	11.7	8,588	43.9	69.7
1993[r]	10,199	8,651	3,576	84.8	35.1	41.3	1,207	11.8	8,750	41.5	67.9
1993	9,790	8,339	3,450	85.2	35.2	41.4	1,125	11.5	8,435	41.6	68.0
1992	9,928	8,468	3,625	85.3	36.5	42.8	1,098	11.1	8,569	43.2	68.1
1991	10,119	8,481	3,544	83.8	35.0	41.8	1,324	13.1	8,568	42.1	64.5
1990	10,340	8,666	3,344	83.8	32.3	38.6	1,322	12.8	8,775	38.9	61.4
1989	10,586	8,913	3,409	84.2	32.2	38.2	1,354	12.8	9,059	38.6	59.2
1988	10,881	9,223	3,399	84.8	31.2	36.9	1,418	13.0	9,355	37.3	59.1
1987	10,944	9,189	3,192	84.0	29.2	34.7	1,449	13.2	9,334	36.2	57.2
1986	11,205	9,509	3,139	84.9	28.0	33.0	1,388	12.4	9,667	33.6	55.8
1985	11,524	9,840	3,247	85.4	28.2	33.0	1,413	12.3	10,001	33.6	55.2
1984	11,826	10,026	3,120	84.8	26.4	31.1	1,535	13.0	10,089	31.8	53.4
1983	12,112	10,233	3,129	84.5	25.8	30.6	1,563	12.9	10,233	31.3	53.4
1982	12,332	10,333	3,285	83.8	26.6	31.8	1,713	13.0	10,530	32.3	52.9

Note: The change in the educational attainment question and the college completion categories from "4 or more years of college" to "at least some college," in 1992 caused an increase in the proportion of 14-to-24-year-old high school graduates enrolled in college or completed some college, of approximately 5 percentage points. High school graduates are people who have completed 4 years of high school or more, for 1967 to 1991. Beginning in 1992, they were people whose highest degree was a high school diploma (including equivalency) or higher.

[1] Starting in 2003 respondents could identify more than one race. Except as noted, the race data in this table from 2003 onward represent those respondents who indicated only one race category.

[r] = Revised, controlled to 1990 census based population estimates; previous 1993 data controlled to 1980 census based population estimates.

Table A-13. Population 14 to 24 Years Old, by High School Graduate Status, College Enrollment, Attainment, Sex, Race, and Hispanic Origin, October 1967–2016—*Continued*

(Numbers in thousands; percent; civilian noninstitutionalized population.)

Year, race, and Hispanic origin	Population 18 to 24 years old								High school graduates, 14 to 24 years old		
		High school graduates		Percent			High school dropouts			Percent	
	Total	Total	Enrolled in college	High school graduates	Enrolled in college	High school graduate enrolled in college	Number	Percent	All graduates	Enrolled in college	Enrolled or completed some college
1981	12,446	10,504	3,208	84.4	25.8	30.5	1,629	13.1	10,687	31.1	51.6
1980	12,471	10,528	3,147	84.4	25.2	29.9	1,642	13.2	10,749	30.6	50.9
1979	12,174	10,157	3,015	83.4	24.8	29.7	1,741	14.3	10,417	30.3	50.8
1978	12,078	10,088	2,882	83.5	23.9	28.6	1,742	14.4	10,327	29.3	50.3
1977	11,985	10,029	2,923	83.7	24.4	29.1	1,666	13.9	10,292	29.7	50.0
1976	11,840	9,860	3,026	83.3	25.6	30.7	1,717	14.5	10,118	31.4	51.3
1975	11,653	9,743	2,790	83.6	23.9	28.6	1,658	14.2	9,986	29.4	49.1
1974	11,419	9,551	2,555	83.6	22.4	26.8	1,633	14.3	9,811	27.5	47.8
1973	11,255	9,387	2,406	83.4	21.4	25.6	1,632	14.5	9,653	26.4	47.1
1972	11,103	9,132	2,428	82.2	21.9	26.6	1,735	15.6	9,377	27.4	48.3
1971	10,880	8,887	2,310	81.7	21.2	26.0	1,726	15.9	9,107	26.8	47.7
1970	10,555	8,634	2,209	81.8	20.9	25.6	1,675	15.9	8,837	26.3	47.2
1969	10,186	8,291	2,200	81.4	21.6	26.5	1,668	16.4	8,501	27.2	46.3
1968	9,866	7,906	1,980	80.1	20.1	25.0	1,706	17.3	8,135	26.0	45.1
1967	9,637	7,586	1,949	78.7	20.2	25.7	1,750	18.2	7,815	26.6	45.7
WHITE ALONE NON-HISPANIC											
Both Sexes											
2016	16,363	14,641	6,895	89.5	42.1	47.1	822	5.0	14,816	47.1	74.6
2015	16,615	14,812	6,938	89.1	41.8	46.8	816	4.9	15,025	46.9	74.6
2014	16,723	14,877	7,054	89.0	42.2	47.4	890	5.3	15,066	47.6	74.9
2013	16,962	15,135	7,065	89.2	41.6	46.7	876	5.2	15,394	47.1	75.0
2012	17,072	15,216	7,189	89.1	42.1	47.2	819	4.8	15,421	47.6	75.0
2011	17,627	15,565	7,882	88.3	44.7	50.6	1,002	5.7	15,752	50.7	76.2
2010	17,693	15,761	7,663	89.1	43.3	48.6	1,003	5.7	15,927	48.8	75.4
2009	17,750	15,839	7,983	89.2	45.0	50.4	1,029	5.8	16,051	50.5	75.2
2008	17,839	16,038	7,894	89.9	44.2	49.2	960	5.4	16,224	49.4	74.2
2007	17,669	15,727	7,533	89.0	42.6	47.9	1,064	6.0	15,921	48.0	72.9
2006	17,565	15,452	7,200	88.0	41.0	46.6	1,189	6.8	15,642	46.8	72.5
2005	17,293	15,187	7,393	87.8	42.8	48.7	1,216	7.0	15,368	48.7	72.6
2004	17,326	15,224	7,228	87.9	41.7	47.5	1,313	7.6	15,382	47.7	71.8
2003[1]	17,158	15,070	7,129	87.8	41.6	47.3	1,267	7.4	15,255	47.3	71.5
2002	17,131	14,910	7,004	87.0	40.9	47.0	1,289	7.5	15,089	47.1	70.4
2001	16,721	14,480	6,565	86.6	39.3	45.3	1,390	8.3	14,646	45.3	69.7
2000	17,327	15,187	6,709	87.7	38.7	44.2	1,316	7.6	15,344	44.3	69.0
1999	17,080	14,812	6,735	86.7	39.4	45.5	1,404	8.2	14,952	45.6	70.2
1998	16,634	14,402	6,757	86.6	40.6	46.9	1,491	9.0	14,542	47.0	70.6
1997	16,575	14,414	6,728	87.0	40.6	46.7	1,432	8.6	14,527	46.9	70.0
1996	16,339	14,288	6,447	87.5	39.5	45.1	1,303	8.0	14,501	45.5	70.7
1995	16,867	14,523	6,393	86.1	37.9	44.0	1,647	9.8	14,672	44.3	70.2
1994	17,114	14,916	6,521	87.2	38.1	43.7	1,505	8.8	15,049	44.0	69.2
1993	16,895	14,665	6,221	86.8	36.8	42.4	1,524	9.0	14,801	42.6	68.1
Male											
2016	8,259	7,279	3,288	88.1	39.8	45.2	463	5.6	7,348	45.2	69.6
2015	8,401	7,396	3,284	88.0	39.1	44.4	451	5.4	7,512	44.4	69.7
2014	8,446	7,426	3,391	87.9	40.2	45.7	485	5.7	7,526	45.8	70.5
2013	8,562	7,526	3,260	87.9	38.1	43.3	462	5.4	7,658	43.8	70.2
2012	8,598	7,552	3,290	87.8	38.3	43.6	455	5.3	7,637	43.9	69.5
2011	8,864	7,697	3,754	86.8	42.4	48.8	554	6.2	7,794	48.9	72.7
2010	8,919	7,808	3,617	87.5	40.6	46.3	569	6.4	7,884	46.4	70.9
2009	8,957	7,818	3,787	87.3	42.3	48.4	632	7.1	7,915	48.5	71.9
2008	9,032	8,028	3,766	88.9	41.7	46.9	546	6.0	8,126	47.1	70.4
2007	8,940	7,786	3,541	87.1	39.6	45.5	622	7.0	7,883	45.5	68.8
2006	8,842	7,660	3,354	86.6	37.9	43.8	647	7.3	7,734	43.9	68.4
2005	8,700	7,443	3,429	85.5	39.4	46.1	685	7.9	7,526	46.0	68.6
2004	8,644	7,527	3,322	87.1	38.4	44.1	691	8.0	7,576	44.4	66.7
2003[2]	8,538	7,325	3,291	85.8	38.5	44.9	721	8.4	7,401	45.0	68.5
2002	8,453	7,244	3,287	85.7	38.9	45.4	668	7.9	7,352	45.5	67.9

Note: The change in the educational attainment question and the college completion categories from "4 or more years of college" to "at least some college," in 1992 caused an increase in the proportion of 14-to-24-year-old high school graduates enrolled in college or completed some college, of approximately 5 percentage points. High school graduates are people who have completed 4 years of high school or more, for 1967 to 1991. Beginning in 1992, they were people whose highest degree was a high school diploma (including equivalency) or higher.
[1]Starting in 2003 respondents could identify more than one race. Except as noted, the race data in this table from 2003 onward represent those respondents who indicated only one race category.
[2]The data shown prior to 2003 consists of those identifying themselves as "Asian or Pacific Islanders."

Table A-13. Population 14 to 24 Years Old, by High School Graduate Status, College Enrollment, Attainment, Sex, Race, and Hispanic Origin, October 1967–2016—*Continued*

(Numbers in thousands; percent; civilian noninstitutionalized population.)

| Year, race, and Hispanic origin | Population 18 to 24 years old | | | | | | | | High school graduates, 14 to 24 years old | | |
| | | High school graduates | | Percent | | | High school dropouts | | | Percent | |
	Total	Total	Enrolled in college	High school graduates	Enrolled in college	High school graduate enrolled in college	Number	Percent	All graduates	Enrolled in college	Enrolled or completed some college
2001	8,343	7,112	3,094	85.3	37.1	43.4	741	8.9	7,191	43.4	67.1
2000	8,670	7,493	3,136	86.4	36.2	41.9	677	7.8	7,556	42.0	65.4
1999	8,580	7,301	3,284	85.1	38.3	45.0	753	8.8	7,369	45.0	67.7
1998	8,380	7,094	3,300	84.7	39.4	46.5	826	9.9	7,151	46.6	68.2
1997	8,326	7,112	3,276	85.4	39.3	46.1	797	9.6	7,154	46.3	68.1
1996	8,168	7,050	3,130	86.3	38.3	44.4	651	8.0	7,143	44.7	68.6
1995	8,399	7,089	3,105	84.4	37.0	43.8	883	10.5	7,147	44.0	67.3
1994	8,457	7,261	3,126	85.9	37.0	43.1	777	9.2	7,317	43.3	67.0
1993	8,403	7,138	3,071	84.9	36.6	43.0	811	9.7	7,191	43.2	67.1
Female											
2016	8,104	7,362	3,606	90.8	44.5	49.0	360	4.4	7,468	49.0	79.5
2015	8,215	7,416	3,654	90.3	44.5	49.3	365	4.4	7,513	49.3	79.5
2014	8,278	7,451	3,663	90.0	44.2	49.2	404	4.9	7,541	49.3	79.3
2013	8,400	7,609	3,804	90.6	45.3	50.0	414	4.9	7,736	50.4	79.8
2012	8,474	7,664	3,899	90.4	46.0	50.9	364	4.3	7,784	51.2	80.5
2011	8,763	7,868	4,128	89.8	47.1	52.5	448	5.1	7,958	52.5	79.6
2010	8,774	7,953	4,046	90.6	46.1	50.9	434	4.9	8,044	51.2	79.8
2009	8,793	8,021	4,195	91.2	47.7	52.3	398	4.5	8,136	52.4	78.3
2008	8,808	8,010	4,127	90.9	46.9	51.5	414	4.7	8,099	51.7	78.0
2007	8,728	7,941	3,992	91.0	45.7	50.3	442	5.1	8,039	50.4	76.9
2006	8,724	7,791	3,846	89.3	44.1	49.4	542	6.2	7,908	49.5	76.4
2005	8,593	7,744	3,964	90.1	46.1	51.2	531	6.2	7,842	51.4	76.4
2004	8,628	7,697	3,906	89.2	45.3	50.7	622	7.2	7,805	50.9	76.8
2003[1]	8,620	7,745	3,838	89.9	44.5	49.6	546	6.3	7,854	49.5	74.4
2002	8,678	7,666	3,717	88.3	42.8	48.5	621	7.2	7,736	48.6	72.8
2001	8,378	7,368	3,471	87.9	41.4	47.2	648	7.7	7,455	47.2	72.3
2000	8,657	7,693	3,573	88.9	41.3	46.4	638	7.4	7,789	46.6	72.5
1999	8,500	7,510	3,451	88.4	40.6	46.0	651	7.7	7,583	46.2	72.5
1998	8,254	7,308	3,457	88.5	41.9	47.3	665	8.1	7,391	47.5	73.0
1997	8,249	7,302	3,452	88.5	41.9	47.3	636	7.7	7,373	47.5	71.9
1996	8,171	7,238	3,317	88.6	40.6	45.8	652	8.0	7,358	46.3	72.8
1995	8,467	7,433	3,288	87.8	38.8	44.2	764	9.0	7,525	44.6	73.1
1994	8,657	7,655	3,395	88.4	39.2	44.4	728	8.4	7,732	44.6	71.3
1993	8,492	7,527	3,150	88.6	37.1	41.9	714	8.4	7,610	42.0	69.1
BLACK ALONE											
Both Sexes											
2016	4,551	3,857	1,644	84.7	36.1	42.6	314	6.9	3,937	42.5	65.6
2015	4,635	3,971	1,636	85.7	35.3	41.2	347	7.5	4,019	41.3	64.5
2014	4,704	3,993	1,528	84.9	32.5	38.3	345	7.3	4,061	39.0	65.9
2013	4,746	3,885	1,600	81.9	33.7	41.2	393	8.3	3,929	41.5	65.7
2012	4,714	3,754	1,689	79.6	35.8	45.0	467	9.9	3,816	45.0	66.6
2011	4,503	3,649	1,639	81.0	36.4	44.9	399	8.9	3,702	45.3	66.3
2010	4,457	3,669	1,692	82.3	38.0	46.1	450	10.1	3,731	46.2	66.2
2009	4,346	3,458	1,604	79.6	36.9	46.4	505	11.6	3,532	46.4	67.5
2008	4,265	3,387	1,349	79.4	31.6	40.0	548	12.1	3,445	40.2	60.7
2007	4,182	3,423	1,396	81.8	33.4	40.8	425	10.2	3,483	40.9	61.4
2006	4,085	3,156	1,321	77.3	32.3	41.9	532	13.0	3,224	41.9	60.8
2005	3,964	3,137	1,297	79.1	32.7	41.3	512	12.9	3,212	41.3	63.5
2004	3,940	3,050	1,238	77.4	31.4	40.6	596	15.1	3,112	41.1	63.2
2003[1]	3,837	2,948	1,225	76.8	31.9	41.6	545	14.2	2,997	41.8	62.5
2002	3,924	3,040	1,226	77.5	31.3	40.3	571	14.5	3,117	41.1	61.2
2001	3,916	3,016	1,206	77.0	30.8	40.0	540	13.8	3,095	40.0	59.0
2000	4,013	3,090	1,216	77.0	30.3	39.4	615	15.3	3,129	39.5	61.0
1999	3,827	2,911	1,145	76.1	29.9	39.4	613	16.0	2,985	39.9	60.4
1998	3,745	2,747	1,116	73.4	29.8	40.6	642	17.1	2,790	40.8	61.8
1997	3,650	2,725	1,085	74.7	29.7	39.8	611	16.7	2,762	40.2	60.0
1996	3,637	2,738	983	75.3	27.0	35.9	581	16.0	2,805	36.6	54.6
1995	3,625	2,788	988	76.9	27.3	35.4	522	14.4	2,828	35.8	58.0
1994	3,661	2,818	1,001	77.0	27.3	35.5	568	15.5	2,859	36.3	59.2

Note: The change in the educational attainment question and the college completion categories from "4 or more years of college" to "at least some college," in 1992 caused an increase in the proportion of 14-to-24-year-old high school graduates enrolled in college or completed some college, of approximately 5 percentage points. High school graduates are people who have completed 4 years of high school or more, for 1967 to 1991. Beginning in 1992, they were people whose highest degree was a high school diploma (including equivalency) or higher.
[1]Starting in 2003 respondents could identify more than one race. Except as noted, the race data in this table from 2003 onward represent those respondents who indicated only one race category.

Table A-13. Population 14 to 24 Years Old, by High School Graduate Status, College Enrollment, Attainment, Sex, Race, and Hispanic Origin, October 1967–2016—*Continued*

(Numbers in thousands; percent; civilian noninstitutionalized population.)

| Year, race, and Hispanic origin | Population 18 to 24 years old | | | | | | | | High school graduates, 14 to 24 years old | | |
| | | High school graduates | | Percent | | | High school dropouts | | | Percent | |
	Total	Total	Enrolled in college	High school graduates	Enrolled in college	High school graduate enrolled in college	Number	Percent	All graduates	Enrolled in college	Enrolled or completed some college
1993^r	3,666	2,747	897	74.9	24.5	32.7	600	16.4	2,771	32.8	54.0
1993	3,516	2,629	861	74.8	24.5	32.8	578	16.4	2,653	32.9	53.9
1992	3,521	2,625	886	74.6	25.2	33.8	575	16.3	2,668	34.3	53.3
1991	3,504	2,630	828	75.1	23.6	31.5	545	15.6	2,658	31.8	46.0
1990	3,520	2,710	894	77.0	25.4	33.0	530	15.1	2,759	33.7	48.0
1989	3,559	2,708	835	76.1	23.5	30.8	583	16.4	2,750	31.5	49.2
1988	3,568	2,680	752	75.1	21.1	28.1	631	17.7	2,741	28.6	46.3
1987	3,603	2,739	823	76.0	22.8	30.0	611	17.0	2,790	30.6	48.1
1986	3,653	2,795	812	76.5	22.2	29.1	617	16.8	2,837	29.3	47.8
1985	3,716	2,810	734	75.6	19.8	26.1	655	17.6	2,848	26.5	43.8
1984	3,862	2,885	786	74.7	20.4	27.2	712	18.4	2,950	28.0	45.2
1983	3,865	2,740	741	70.9	19.2	27.0	832	21.5	2,790	27.7	45.0
1982	3,872	2,744	767	70.9	19.8	28.0	851	22.0	2,793	28.2	45.5
1981	3,778	2,678	750	70.9	19.9	28.0	821	21.7	2,718	28.7	44.8
1980	3,721	2,592	715	69.7	19.2	27.6	876	23.5	2,656	28.1	45.9
1979	3,510	2,356	696	67.1	19.8	29.5	895	25.5	2,415	30.6	48.4
1978	3,452	2,340	694	67.8	20.1	29.7	850	24.6	2,396	30.6	47.8
1977	3,387	2,286	721	67.5	21.3	31.5	808	23.9	2,342	32.4	46.9
1976	3,315	2,239	749	67.5	22.6	33.5	803	24.2	2,291	34.2	50.4
1975	3,213	2,081	665	64.8	20.7	32.0	877	27.3	2,149	32.6	48.1
1974	3,105	2,083	555	67.1	17.9	26.6	780	25.1	2,145	27.5	44.8
1973	3,114	2,079	498	66.8	16.0	24.0	826	26.5	2,139	25.0	41.6
1972	2,986	1,992	540	66.7	18.1	27.1	782	26.2	2,044	28.0	42.0
1971	2,866	1,789	522	62.4	18.2	29.2	825	28.8	1,833	30.0	42.3
1970	2,692	1,602	416	59.5	15.5	26.0	897	33.3	1,635	26.7	39.4
1969	2,542	1,497	407	58.9	16.0	27.2	828	32.6	1,547	27.5	40.1
1968	2,421	1,399	352	57.8	14.5	25.2	799	33.0	1,432	26.0	38.1
1967	2,283	1,276	297	55.9	13.0	23.3	788	34.5	1,316	23.7	35.0
Male											
2016	2,218	1,774	728	80.0	32.8	41.0	204	9.2	1,795	41.2	61.4
2015	2,257	1,923	779	85.2	34.5	40.5	165	7.3	1,947	40.6	63.3
2014	2,289	1,889	633	82.5	27.6	33.5	166	7.3	1,934	34.7	61.1
2013	2,303	1,847	690	80.2	30.0	37.4	221	9.6	1,865	38.0	61.7
2012	2,278	1,787	760	78.4	33.4	42.5	258	11.3	1,820	42.7	63.8
2011	2,165	1,701	717	78.6	33.1	42.2	205	9.5	1,732	42.7	60.9
2010	2,140	1,692	734	79.1	34.3	43.4	258	12.1	1,730	43.2	61.4
2009	2,082	1,592	673	76.5	32.3	42.3	289	13.9	1,617	42.0	63.5
2008	2,045	1,641	595	80.2	29.1	36.3	210	10.2	1,668	36.9	54.8
2007	2,011	1,622	649	80.6	32.3	40.0	202	10.0	1,642	40.1	59.3
2006	1,959	1,488	541	76.0	27.6	36.4	219	11.2	1,519	36.3	53.4
2005	1,897	1,393	530	73.4	27.9	38.0	280	14.8	1,420	37.9	58.4
2004	1,852	1,341	479	72.4	25.9	35.7	331	17.9	1,363	36.1	60.9
2003^1	1,801	1,331	499	73.9	27.7	37.5	300	16.7	1,346	37.8	57.1
2002	1,843	1,354	475	73.5	25.8	35.1	311	16.9	1,372	35.6	56.1
2001	1,818	1,287	470	70.8	25.8	36.4	308	16.9	1,310	36.4	53.1
2000	1,885	1,389	470	73.7	24.9	33.8	329	17.4	1,409	34.1	53.5
1999	1,747	1,292	501	73.9	28.7	38.8	285	16.3	1,336	40.2	57.7
1998	1,724	1,163	445	67.5	25.8	38.2	354	20.5	1,186	38.5	57.5
1997	1,701	1,214	425	71.4	25.0	35.0	297	17.5	1,232	35.1	56.3
1996	1,682	1,199	422	71.3	25.1	35.2	292	17.4	1,225	35.8	53.7
1995	1,660	1,247	430	75.1	25.9	34.4	235	14.2	1,262	35.1	56.2
1994	1,733	1,277	440	73.7	25.4	34.5	303	17.5	1,293	35.3	57.9
1993^r	1,703	1,240	387	72.8	22.7	31.2	266	15.6	1,247	31.4	50.1
1993	1,659	1,207	379	72.8	22.8	31.4	258	15.6	1,214	31.5	50.0
1992	1,676	1,211	356	72.3	21.2	29.4	259	15.5	1,226	29.7	49.4
1991	1,635	1,174	378	71.8	23.1	32.2	252	15.4	1,188	32.4	47.0
1990	1,634	1,240	426	75.9	26.1	34.4	223	13.6	1,260	35.1	48.8
1989	1,654	1,195	324	72.2	19.6	27.1	307	18.6	1,207	27.5	45.8
1988	1,653	1,189	297	71.9	18.0	25.0	312	18.9	1,205	25.1	42.5
1987	1,666	1,188	377	71.3	22.6	31.7	312	18.7	1,209	32.3	48.0
1986	1,687	1,220	349	72.3	20.7	28.6	300	17.8	1,239	29.1	44.4

Note: The change in the educational attainment question and the college completion categories from "4 or more years of college" to "at least some college," in 1992 caused an increase in the proportion of 14-to-24-year-old high school graduates enrolled in college or completed some college, of approximately 5 percentage points. High school graduates are people who have completed 4 years of high school or more, for 1967 to 1991. Beginning in 1992, they were people whose highest degree was a high school diploma (including equivalency) or higher.

[1] Starting in 2003 respondents could identify more than one race. Except as noted, the race data in this table from 2003 onward represent those respondents who indicated only one race category.

^r = Revised, controlled to 1990 census based population estimates; previous 1993 data controlled to 1980 census based population estimates.

Table A-13. Population 14 to 24 Years Old, by High School Graduate Status, College Enrollment, Attainment, Sex, Race, and Hispanic Origin, October 1967–2016—*Continued*

(Numbers in thousands; percent; civilian noninstitutionalized population.)

Year, race, and Hispanic origin	Population 18 to 24 years old								High school graduates, 14 to 24 years old		
		High school graduates		Percent			High school dropouts			Percent	
	Total	Total	Enrolled in college	High school graduates	Enrolled in college	High school graduate enrolled in college	Number	Percent	All graduates	Enrolled in college	Enrolled or completed some college
1985	1,720	1,244	345	72.3	20.1	27.7	323	18.8	1,258	28.2	43.6
1984	1,811	1,272	367	70.2	20.3	28.9	362	20.2	1,295	29.6	45.2
1983	1,807	1,202	331	66.5	18.3	27.5	435	24.1	1,228	27.9	43.6
1982	1,786	1,171	331	65.6	18.5	28.3	458	25.6	1,188	28.6	44.5
1981	1,730	1,154	325	66.7	18.8	28.2	419	24.2	1,165	28.5	42.3
1980	1,690	1,115	293	66.0	17.3	26.3	440	26.0	1,141	26.9	44.1
1979	1,577	973	304	61.7	19.3	31.2	457	29.0	988	32.0	46.7
1978	1,554	956	305	61.5	19.6	31.9	451	29.0	981	32.4	49.3
1977	1,528	970	309	63.5	20.2	31.9	369	24.1	991	33.0	47.6
1976	1,503	936	331	62.3	22.0	35.4	393	26.1	952	35.9	50.3
1975	1,451	897	294	61.8	20.3	32.8	404	27.8	923	33.4	50.5
1974	1,396	919	280	65.8	20.1	30.5	346	24.8	941	31.1	47.3
1973	1,434	952	266	66.4	18.5	27.9	371	25.9	962	28.4	44.2
1972	1,373	870	287	63.4	20.9	33.0	373	27.2	897	34.0	47.4
1971	1,318	769	262	58.3	19.9	34.1	416	31.6	783	34.9	45.8
1970	1,220	668	192	54.8	15.7	28.7	436	35.7	684	29.5	41.4
1969	1,141	631	202	55.3	17.7	32.0	383	33.6	653	32.5	44.6
1968	1,087	582	170	53.5	15.6	29.2	370	34.0	600	30.3	43.2
1967	1,032	525	167	50.9	16.2	31.8	397	38.5	539	32.3	41.6
Female											
2016	2,333	2,083	916	89.3	39.3	44.0	111	4.7	2,142	43.6	69.1
2015	2,378	2,048	857	86.1	36.1	41.9	182	7.7	2,071	42.0	65.6
2014	2,415	2,104	895	87.2	37.1	42.5	179	7.4	2,128	42.9	70.2
2013	2,442	2,038	909	83.4	37.2	44.6	173	7.1	2,064	44.7	69.3
2012	2,436	1,967	929	80.8	38.1	47.2	209	8.6	1,996	47.0	69.2
2011	2,339	1,949	921	83.3	39.4	47.3	194	8.3	1,970	47.6	71.0
2010	2,317	1,977	958	85.3	41.3	48.4	192	8.3	2,001	48.8	70.4
2009	2,263	1,865	931	82.4	41.1	49.9	216	9.5	1,915	50.1	70.9
2008	2,220	1,746	754	78.7	34.0	43.2	304	13.7	1,777	43.3	66.2
2007	2,171	1,801	747	82.9	34.4	41.5	223	10.3	1,841	41.5	63.3
2006	2,126	1,668	780	78.5	36.7	46.7	313	14.7	1,705	46.9	67.3
2005	2,067	1,745	767	84.4	37.1	44.0	232	11.2	1,793	44.0	67.5
2004	2,088	1,709	759	81.8	36.3	44.4	266	12.7	1,749	44.9	65.0
2003¹	2,035	1,618	726	79.5	35.7	44.9	245	12.0	1,652	45.1	66.8
2002	2,081	1,686	751	81.0	36.1	44.5	260	12.5	1,745	45.5	65.2
2001	2,098	1,729	736	82.4	35.1	42.7	232	11.0	1,785	42.7	63.3
2000	2,128	1,700	747	79.9	35.1	43.9	287	13.5	1,720	43.9	67.1
1999	2,080	1,619	644	77.9	31.0	39.8	327	15.7	1,650	39.6	62.6
1998	2,021	1,584	671	78.4	33.2	42.4	288	14.3	1,604	42.4	65.0
1997	1,949	1,511	659	77.5	33.8	43.6	314	16.1	1,529	43.1	63.0
1996	1,956	1,539	561	78.7	28.7	36.4	288	14.7	1,580	37.3	55.3
1995	1,965	1,541	558	78.4	28.4	36.2	287	14.6	1,566	36.3	59.5
1994	1,928	1,542	561	80.0	29.1	36.4	265	13.7	1,567	37.1	60.3
1993ʳ	1,965	1,508	511	76.7	26.0	33.9	337	17.2	1,526	34.1	57.2
1993	1,857	1,425	484	76.7	26.1	34.0	319	17.2	1,441	34.1	57.1
1992	1,845	1,417	531	76.8	28.8	37.5	315	17.1	1,446	38.2	56.6
1991	1,869	1,455	450	77.8	24.1	30.9	296	15.8	1,468	31.4	45.2
1990	1,886	1,468	467	77.8	24.8	31.8	306	16.2	1,498	32.4	47.3
1989	1,905	1,511	511	79.3	26.8	33.8	277	14.5	1,541	34.7	51.8
1988	1,915	1,492	455	77.9	23.8	30.5	318	16.6	1,538	31.3	49.2
1987	1,937	1,550	445	80.0	23.0	28.7	298	15.4	1,579	29.4	48.9
1986	1,966	1,574	462	80.1	23.5	29.4	306	15.6	1,598	29.3	50.4
1985	1,996	1,565	389	78.4	19.5	24.9	332	16.6	1,592	25.1	44.0
1984	2,052	1,613	419	78.6	20.4	26.0	349	17.0	1,655	26.8	45.1
1983	2,058	1,539	411	74.8	20.0	26.7	398	19.3	1,561	27.5	46.3
1982	2,086	1,572	436	75.4	20.9	27.7	393	18.8	1,604	27.9	46.3
1981	2,049	1,526	424	74.5	20.7	27.8	402	19.6	1,554	28.8	46.6
1980	2,031	1,475	422	72.6	20.8	28.6	436	21.5	1,511	29.1	47.4
1979	1,934	1,383	392	71.5	20.3	28.3	439	22.7	1,426	29.7	49.8
1978	1,897	1,384	390	73.0	20.6	28.2	398	21.0	1,415	29.3	46.7

Note: The change in the educational attainment question and the college completion categories from "4 or more years of college" to "at least some college," in 1992 caused an increase in the proportion of 14-to-24-year-old high school graduates enrolled in college or completed some college, of approximately 5 percentage points. High school graduates are people who have completed 4 years of high school or more, for 1967 to 1991. Beginning in 1992, they were people whose highest degree was a high school diploma (including equivalency) or higher.

¹Starting in 2003 respondents could identify more than one race. Except as noted, the race data in this table from 2003 onward represent those respondents who indicated only one race category.

ʳ = Revised, controlled to 1990 census based population estimates; previous 1993 data controlled to 1980 census based population estimates.

Table A-13. Population 14 to 24 Years Old, by High School Graduate Status, College Enrollment, Attainment, Sex, Race, and Hispanic Origin, October 1967–2016—*Continued*

(Numbers in thousands; percent; civilian noninstitutionalized population.)

Year, race, and Hispanic origin	Population 18 to 24 years old								High school graduates, 14 to 24 years old		
		High school graduates		Percent			High school dropouts			Percent	
	Total	Total	Enrolled in college	High school graduates	Enrolled in college	High school graduate enrolled in college	Number	Percent	All graduates	Enrolled in college	Enrolled or completed some college
1977...........................	1,859	1,317	413	70.8	22.2	31.4	439	23.6	1,354	31.9	46.2
1976...........................	1,813	1,302	417	71.8	23.0	32.0	410	22.6	1,338	32.9	50.3
1975...........................	1,761	1,182	372	67.1	21.1	31.5	473	26.9	1,224	32.0	46.4
1974...........................	1,709	1,167	277	68.3	16.2	23.7	434	25.4	1,207	24.8	42.9
1973...........................	1,681	1,125	231	66.9	13.7	20.5	456	27.1	1,177	22.2	39.4
1972...........................	1,613	1,123	253	69.6	15.7	22.5	408	25.3	1,150	23.2	37.9
1971...........................	1,547	1,019	259	65.9	16.7	25.4	409	26.4	1,049	26.4	39.8
1970...........................	1,471	935	225	63.6	15.3	24.1	461	31.3	955	24.7	39.3
1969...........................	1,402	867	206	61.8	14.7	23.8	444	31.7	896	24.0	38.6
1968...........................	1,334	819	183	61.4	13.7	22.3	430	32.2	834	22.9	35.9
1967...........................	1,249	751	130	60.1	10.4	17.3	391	31.3	778	17.9	33.2
ASIAN ALONE[2]											
Both Sexes											
2016...........................	1,768	1,628	1,003	92.1	56.7	61.6	53	3.0	1,661	61.5	87.7
2015...........................	1,634	1,514	1,026	92.6	62.8	67.8	38	2.3	1,560	67.1	91.9
2014...........................	1,590	1,504	1,023	94.6	64.3	68.0	17	1.1	1,541	67.6	91.7
2013...........................	1,639	1,495	1,001	91.2	61.1	66.9	61	3.7	1,530	67.4	86.8
2012...........................	1,537	1,385	915	90.1	59.5	66.0	54	3.5	1,418	66.3	84.9
2011...........................	1,252	1,123	748	89.8	59.7	66.5	65	5.2	1,149	66.9	88.1
2010...........................	1,303	1,193	811	91.5	62.2	68.0	64	4.9	1,232	68.4	89.8
2009...........................	1,181	1,080	768	91.4	65.0	71.1	26	2.2	1,096	71.0	91.8
2008...........................	1,113	1,021	655	91.8	58.9	64.1	42	3.8	1,056	64.6	90.4
2007...........................	1,165	1,010	658	86.7	56.4	65.1	86	7.4	1,026	65.1	91.6
2006...........................	1,148	1,046	661	91.1	57.6	63.2	46	4.0	1,064	63.0	87.0
2005...........................	1,145	1,072	693	93.6	60.5	64.6	34	3.0	1,098	65.1	87.0
2004...........................	1,152	1,066	695	92.5	60.3	65.2	49	4.3	1,090	65.7	89.1
2003[1].......................	1,144	1,030	693	90.1	60.6	67.3	56	4.9	1,046	67.7	88.2
2002...........................	1,339	1,230	803	91.8	60.0	65.3	57	4.2	1,265	65.7	86.9
2001...........................	1,312	1,197	794	91.2	60.5	66.5	47	3.6	1,218	66.5	87.6
2000...........................	1,143	1,038	639	90.8	55.9	61.6	52	4.6	1,053	61.8	83.9
1999...........................	1,130	1,019	626	90.2	55.4	61.4	58	5.1	1,035	62.0	85.5
Male											
2016...........................	914	842	533	92.1	58.3	63.3	21	2.3	854	63.0	87.1
2015...........................	819	758	493	92.6	60.2	65.0	24	2.9	783	64.2	90.0
2014...........................	809	771	549	95.3	67.9	71.2	13	1.6	793	71.0	91.1
2013...........................	859	795	534	92.5	62.2	67.2	18	2.1	806	67.2	86.1
2012...........................	776	695	455	89.6	58.6	65.4	21	2.6	713	65.9	84.7
2011...........................	639	573	379	89.6	59.3	66.2	30	4.7	582	66.1	87.6
2010...........................	651	597	390	91.7	59.9	65.3	29	4.5	619	65.7	87.5
2009...........................	590	546	383	92.4	64.9	70.2	7	1.2	559	69.9	90.1
2008...........................	547	487	295	89.1	53.9	60.5	21	3.9	510	62.0	89.9
2007...........................	560	481	318	85.8	56.9	66.3	38	6.8	483	66.4	91.8
2006...........................	591	525	338	88.8	57.2	64.4	34	5.8	536	64.0	84.0
2005...........................	590	552	366	93.5	62.0	66.3	17	2.9	565	66.4	88.2
2004...........................	586	549	373	93.7	63.6	67.9	15	2.5	561	68.4	88.2
2003[1].......................	543	483	337	88.9	62.0	69.8	43	7.8	486	69.9	90.0
2002...........................	707	637	417	90.0	59.0	65.5	38	5.4	652	65.3	86.7
2001...........................	661	583	417	88.1	63.1	72.0	35	5.3	594	72.0	88.9
2000...........................	571	521	337	91.1	58.9	64.7	34	6.0	527	64.7	85.6
1999...........................	505	443	284	87.8	56.2	64.0	39	7.7	454	64.9	82.5
Female											
2016...........................	854	787	469	92.2	55.0	59.7	32	3.8	808	60.0	88.3
2015...........................	816	756	533	92.6	65.4	70.6	14	1.7	776	70.0	93.8
2014...........................	780	732	473	93.9	60.6	64.6	4	0.5	748	63.9	92.3
2013...........................	780	700	467	89.8	59.8	66.6	43	5.5	723	67.5	87.5
2012...........................	761	690	460	90.7	60.4	66.6	33	4.3	704	66.8	85.1
2011...........................	612	551	369	89.9	60.2	66.9	35	5.8	567	67.8	88.7

Note: The change in the educational attainment question and the college completion categories from "4 or more years of college" to "at least some college," in 1992 caused an increase in the proportion of 14-to-24-year-old high school graduates enrolled in college or completed some college, of approximately 5 percentage points. High school graduates are people who have completed 4 years of high school or more, for 1967 to 1991. Beginning in 1992, they were people whose highest degree was a high school diploma (including equivalency) or higher.
[1] Starting in 2003 respondents could identify more than one race. Except as noted, the race data in this table from 2003 onward represent those respondents who indicated only one race category.
[2] The data shown prior to 2003 consists of those identifying themselves as "Asian or Pacific Islanders."

Table A-13. Population 14 to 24 Years Old, by High School Graduate Status, College Enrollment, Attainment, Sex, Race, and Hispanic Origin, October 1967–2016—*Continued*

(Numbers in thousands; percent; civilian noninstitutional population.)

Year, race, and Hispanic origin	Population 18 to 24 years old								High school graduates, 14 to 24 years old		
		High school graduates			Percent			High school dropouts		Percent	
	Total	Total	Enrolled in college	High school graduates	Enrolled in college	High school graduate enrolled in college	Number	Percent	All graduates	Enrolled in college	Enrolled or completed some college
2010	653	596	422	91.3	64.6	70.7	35	5.3	614	71.2	92.1
2009	591	534	384	90.4	65.1	72.0	19	3.3	538	72.2	93.7
2008	566	534	360	94.4	63.7	67.5	21	3.6	546	67.0	90.9
2007	605	529	339	87.4	56.0	64.1	48	7.9	543	63.9	91.5
2006	557	521	324	93.6	58.1	62.2	11	2.1	528	61.9	90.0
2005	555	521	327	93.8	58.9	62.8	17	3.0	533	63.7	85.8
2004	567	517	323	91.3	56.9	62.4	35	6.1	529	62.8	90.0
2003[1]	601	547	356	91.2	59.3	65.1	13	2.2	561	65.9	86.7
2002	632	593	386	93.8	61.0	65.1	19	2.9	613	66.1	87.2
2001	651	614	377	94.3	57.9	61.3	12	1.8	625	61.3	86.3
2000	572	517	302	90.4	52.9	58.5	18	3.1	526	58.9	82.3
1999	626	576	342	92.1	54.7	59.4	19	3.1	582	59.7	87.8

HISPANIC (OF ANY RACE)

Both Sexes

Year, race, and Hispanic origin	Total	Total	Enrolled in college	High school graduates	Enrolled in college	High school graduate enrolled in college	Number	Percent	All graduates	Enrolled in college	Enrolled or completed some college
2016	6,539	5,477	2,565	83.8	39.2	46.8	648	9.9	5,608	47.3	67.2
2015	6,464	5,366	2,368	83.0	36.6	44.1	669	10.3	5,460	44.2	66.6
2014	6,568	5,324	2,282	81.1	34.7	42.9	777	11.8	5,409	43.1	62.8
2013	6,489	5,118	2,193	78.9	33.8	42.8	889	13.7	5,190	43.1	62.3
2012	6,416	4,902	2,403	76.4	37.5	49.0	972	15.1	4,987	49.4	68.1
2011	5,974	4,569	2,079	76.5	34.8	45.5	975	16.3	4,630	45.7	65.4
2010	5,685	4,138	1,814	72.8	31.9	43.8	1,050	18.5	4,199	44.2	63.2
2009	5,332	3,747	1,465	70.3	27.5	39.1	1,112	20.8	3,813	39.6	57.8
2008	5,176	3,618	1,338	69.9	25.8	37.0	1,155	22.3	3,691	37.7	58.7
2007	5,175	3,487	1,375	67.4	26.6	39.4	1,310	25.3	3,553	39.9	58.0
2006	5,006	3,301	1,182	65.9	23.6	35.8	1,313	26.2	3,379	36.6	57.2
2005	4,898	3,230	1,215	66.0	24.8	37.6	1,335	27.3	3,280	38.0	57.3
2004	4,941	3,244	1,221	65.6	24.7	37.7	1,386	28.0	3,287	37.9	55.9
2003	4,754	3,096	1,115	65.1	23.5	36.0	1,353	28.4	3,135	36.0	56.5
2002	4,918	3,078	979	62.6	19.9	31.8	1,479	30.1	3,109	32.0	53.1
2001	4,892	3,031	1,035	62.0	21.1	34.2	1,548	31.7	3,068	34.2	52.8
2000	4,134	2,462	899	59.6	21.7	36.5	1,335	32.3	2,509	36.8	53.1
1999	3,953	2,325	739	58.8	18.7	31.8	1,340	33.9	2,359	31.7	49.6
1998	4,014	2,403	820	59.8	20.4	34.1	1,383	34.4	2,419	34.3	53.2
1997	3,606	2,236	806	62.0	22.4	36.0	1,103	30.6	2,302	37.1	54.3
1996	3,510	2,019	706	57.5	20.1	35.0	1,210	34.5	2,046	34.5	52.5
1995	3,603	2,112	745	58.6	20.7	35.3	1,250	34.7	2,142	35.7	55.8
1994	3,523	1,995	662	56.6	18.8	33.2	1,224	34.7	2,009	33.4	54.3
1993[r]	3,363	2,049	728	60.9	21.6	35.5	1,103	32.8	2,081	35.8	55.6
1993	2,772	1,682	602	60.7	21.7	35.8	907	32.7	1,712	36.0	55.8
1992	2,754	1,579	586	57.3	21.3	37.1	936	33.9	1,603	37.6	55.0
1991	2,874	1,498	516	52.1	18.0	34.4	1,139	39.6	1,519	34.6	47.6
1990	2,749	1,498	435	54.5	15.8	29.0	1,025	37.3	1,523	29.4	44.7
1989	2,818	1,576	453	55.9	16.1	28.7	1,062	37.7	1,600	29.4	43.6
1988	2,642	1,458	450	55.2	17.0	30.9	1,046	39.6	1,481	31.3	47.0
1987	2,592	1,597	455	61.6	17.6	28.5	849	32.8	1,612	28.7	44.0
1986	2,514	1,507	458	59.9	18.2	30.4	864	34.4	1,535	30.9	45.6
1985	2,221	1,396	375	62.9	16.9	26.9	700	31.5	1,419	27.6	46.7
1984	2,018	1,212	362	60.1	17.9	29.9	691	34.2	1,223	30.0	46.0
1983	2,025	1,110	349	54.8	17.2	31.4	759	37.5	1,134	32.3	48.4
1982	2,001	1,153	337	57.6	16.8	29.2	740	37.0	1,173	30.0	47.3
1981	2,052	1,144	342	55.8	16.7	29.9	790	38.5	1,166	30.5	45.8
1980	2,033	1,099	327	54.1	16.1	29.8	820	40.3	1,117	30.1	47.3
1979	1,754	968	292	55.2	16.6	30.2	687	39.2	1,001	31.2	45.7
1978	1,672	935	254	55.9	15.2	27.2	656	39.2	965	28.0	43.2
1977	1,609	880	277	54.7	17.2	31.5	622	38.7	900	32.4	43.8
1976	1,551	862	309	55.6	19.9	35.8	566	36.5	891	36.3	48.9

Note: The change in the educational attainment question and the college completion categories from "4 or more years of college" to "at least some college," in 1992 caused an increase in the proportion of 14-to-24-year-old high school graduates enrolled in college or completed some college, of approximately 5 percentage points. High school graduates are people who have completed 4 years of high school or more, for 1967 to 1991. Beginning in 1992, they were people whose highest degree was a high school diploma (including equivalency) or higher.

[1]Starting in 2003 respondents could identify more than one race. Except as noted, the race data in this table from 2003 onward represent those respondents who indicated only one race category.

[r] = Revised, controlled to 1990 census based population estimates; previous 1993 data controlled to 1980 census based population estimates.

Table A-13. Population 14 to 24 Years Old, by High School Graduate Status, College Enrollment, Attainment, Sex, Race, and Hispanic Origin, October 1967–2016—*Continued*

(Numbers in thousands; percent; civilian noninstitutionalized population.)

Year, race, and Hispanic origin	Population 18 to 24 years old								High school graduates, 14 to 24 years old		
		High school graduates		Percent			High school dropouts			Percent	
	Total	Total	Enrolled in college	High school graduates	Enrolled in college	High school graduate enrolled in college	Number	Percent	All graduates	Enrolled in college	Enrolled or completed some college
1975	1,446	832	295	57.5	20.4	35.5	505	34.9	849	36.5	50.8
1974	1,506	842	272	55.9	18.1	32.3	558	37.1	858	33.1	47.8
1973	1,285	709	206	55.2	16.0	29.1	500	38.9	732	30.3	43.0
1972	1,338	694	179	51.9	13.4	25.8	541	40.4	709	27.2	36.7
Male											
2016	3,291	2,674	1,148	81.3	34.9	42.9	395	12.0	2,729	43.1	63.0
2015	3,246	2,661	1,063	82.0	32.8	40.0	360	11.1	2,711	40.1	61.3
2014	3,354	2,667	1,016	79.5	30.3	38.1	429	12.8	2,700	38.1	57.7
2013	3,329	2,564	968	77.0	29.1	37.7	491	14.7	2,597	38.0	55.7
2012	3,311	2,455	1,109	74.1	33.5	45.2	560	16.9	2,496	45.5	63.2
2011	3,250	2,421	1,006	74.5	31.0	41.6	568	17.5	2,458	41.9	60.2
2010	2,930	2,034	819	69.4	27.9	40.2	623	21.3	2,065	40.6	58.5
2009	2,741	1,894	663	69.1	24.2	35.0	616	22.5	1,925	35.6	51.3
2008	2,675	1,797	615	67.2	23.0	34.2	649	24.3	1,841	35.1	54.4
2007	2,706	1,689	560	62.4	20.7	33.1	790	29.2	1,711	33.6	52.2
2006	2,618	1,600	523	61.1	20.0	32.7	812	31.0	1,628	33.2	53.2
2005	2,613	1,569	540	60.1	20.7	34.4	838	32.1	1,589	34.6	52.4
2004	2,648	1,597	574	60.3	21.7	36.0	888	33.5	1,614	35.9	53.0
2003	2,541	1,548	465	60.9	18.3	30.0	805	31.7	1,571	30.0	48.7
2002	2,707	1,562	439	57.7	16.2	28.1	914	33.8	1,572	28.1	48.4
2001	2,596	1,455	449	56.1	17.3	31.0	962	37.1	1,468	31.0	48.1
2000	2,171	1,172	401	54.0	18.5	34.2	800	36.8	1,197	34.5	50.8
1999	2,045	1,122	322	54.9	15.8	28.7	746	36.4	1,131	28.7	45.7
1998	2,109	1,146	346	54.3	16.4	30.2	838	39.7	1,153	30.0	47.2
1997	1,937	1,140	371	58.9	19.2	32.5	643	33.2	1,168	33.0	49.2
1996	1,815	994	300	54.8	16.5	30.2	657	36.2	1,005	30.6	48.8
1995	1,907	1,106	356	58.0	18.7	32.2	653	34.2	1,022	36.2	52.3
1994	1,896	1,021	312	53.8	16.5	30.6	685	36.1	1,026	30.7	52.7
1993ʳ	1,710	1,005	338	58.8	19.8	33.6	591	34.6	1,023	33.7	51.2
1993	1,354	786	266	58.1	19.6	33.8	470	34.7	803	33.9	51.1
1992	1,384	720	247	52.0	17.8	34.3	531	38.4	736	34.8	52.2
1991	1,503	719	211	47.8	14.0	29.3	668	44.4	728	29.7	42.2
1990	1,403	753	214	53.7	15.3	28.4	559	39.8	770	29.4	46.5
1989	1,439	756	211	52.5	14.7	27.9	580	40.3	767	28.2	42.7
1988	1,375	724	228	52.7	16.6	31.5	553	40.2	736	32.2	48.3
1987	1,337	795	247	59.5	18.5	31.1	461	34.5	803	31.1	45.1
1986	1,339	769	233	57.4	17.4	30.3	499	37.3	776	30.5	44.4
1985	1,132	659	168	58.2	14.8	25.5	405	35.8	675	26.4	44.9
1984	956	549	154	57.4	16.1	28.1	338	35.4	554	28.2	45.7
1983	968	476	152	49.2	15.7	31.9	396	40.9	489	33.1	47.4
1982	944	519	141	55.0	14.9	27.2	347	36.8	525	28.0	44.8
1981	988	498	164	50.4	16.6	32.9	428	43.3	506	33.6	48.6
1980	1,012	518	160	51.2	15.8	30.9	431	42.6	521	31.1	49.5
1979	837	454	153	54.2	18.3	33.7	328	39.2	469	34.3	49.5
1978	781	420	126	53.8	16.1	30.0	313	40.1	438	30.4	46.3
1977	754	396	139	52.5	18.4	35.1	295	39.1	404	35.9	46.5
1976	701	378	150	53.9	21.4	39.7	253	36.1	403	39.8	51.8
1975	678	383	145	56.5	21.4	37.9	221	32.6	390	37.9	55.4
1974	720	390	141	54.2	19.6	36.2	279	38.8	401	36.7	51.4
1973	625	348	105	55.7	16.8	30.2	228	36.5	361	32.1	45.4
1972	609	301	92	49.4	15.1	30.6	253	41.5	309	32.0	44.3
Female											
2016	3,248	2,803	1,417	86.3	43.6	50.6	253	7.8	2,879	51.3	71.2
2015	3,218	2,704	1,305	84.0	40.5	48.2	309	9.6	2,750	48.2	71.9
2014	3,214	2,657	1,265	82.7	39.4	47.6	348	10.8	2,709	48.2	67.9
2013	3,160	2,554	1,225	80.8	38.8	48.0	398	12.6	2,593	48.1	69.0
2012	3,105	2,447	1,294	78.8	41.7	52.9	411	13.2	2,491	53.3	72.9
2011	2,724	2,147	1,073	78.8	39.4	50.0	407	15.0	2,173	50.0	71.4
2010	2,755	2,104	995	76.4	36.1	47.3	426	15.5	2,134	47.7	67.8

Note: The change in the educational attainment question and the college completion categories from "4 or more years of college" to "at least some college," in 1992 caused an increase in the proportion of 14-to-24-year-old high school graduates enrolled in college or completed some college, of approximately 5 percentage points. High school graduates are people who have completed 4 years of high school or more, for 1967 to 1991. Beginning in 1992, they were people whose highest degree was a high school diploma (including equivalency) or higher.
ʳ = Revised, controlled to 1990 census based population estimates; previous 1993 data controlled to 1980 census based population estimates.

Table A-13. Population 14 to 24 Years Old, by High School Graduate Status, College Enrollment, Attainment, Sex, Race, and Hispanic Origin, October 1967–2016—*Continued*

(Numbers in thousands; percent; civilian noninstitutional population.)

Year, race, and Hispanic origin	Population 18 to 24 years old								High school graduates, 14 to 24 years old		
		High school graduates		Percent			High school dropouts			Percent	
	Total	Total	Enrolled in college	High school graduates	Enrolled in college	High school graduate enrolled in college	Number	Percent	All graduates	Enrolled in college	Enrolled or completed some college
2009	2,591	1,853	803	71.5	31.0	43.3	496	19.1	1,888	43.6	64.5
2008	2,501	1,821	723	72.8	28.9	39.7	506	20.2	1,850	40.3	63.1
2007	2,469	1,798	816	72.8	33.0	45.4	520	21.1	1,842	45.6	63.4
2006	2,388	1,701	660	71.2	27.6	38.8	501	21.0	1,751	39.7	61.0
2005	2,285	1,661	675	72.7	29.5	40.6	498	21.8	1,691	41.2	62.0
2004	2,293	1,647	647	71.8	28.2	39.3	498	21.7	1,673	39.8	58.6
2003	2,213	1,548	651	69.9	29.4	42.1	548	24.7	1,563	41.9	64.4
2002	2,211	1,516	540	68.6	24.4	35.6	565	25.6	1,537	35.9	57.9
2001	2,296	1,576	585	68.6	25.5	37.1	586	25.5	1,600	37.1	57.0
2000	1,963	1,290	498	65.7	25.4	38.6	535	27.3	1,312	38.9	55.2
1999	1,908	1,203	417	63.0	21.8	34.7	593	31.1	1,228	34.4	53.3
1998	1,906	1,257	474	66.0	24.9	37.7	545	28.6	1,266	38.2	58.7
1997	1,669	1,097	436	65.7	26.1	39.7	460	27.6	1,135	41.4	59.6
1996	1,694	1,026	406	60.6	24.0	39.6	554	32.7	1,043	40.4	56.0
1995	1,696	1,011	389	59.6	22.9	38.4	598	35.4	1,022	38.6	59.6
1994	1,628	973	350	59.8	21.5	36.0	539	33.1	983	36.2	55.9
1993 ʳ	1,652	1,045	390	63.3	23.6	37.3	510	30.9	1,059	37.8	60.1
1993	1,418	895	336	63.1	23.7	37.5	439	31.0	907	38.0	60.4
1992	1,369	860	339	62.8	24.8	39.4	405	29.6	867	39.9	57.4
1991	1,372	780	305	56.9	22.2	39.1	473	34.5	791	39.2	52.5
1990	1,346	745	221	55.3	16.4	29.7	465	34.5	753	29.5	43.0
1989	1,377	823	244	59.8	17.7	29.6	482	35.0	836	30.5	44.5
1988	1,267	736	224	58.1	17.7	30.4	492	38.8	747	30.5	45.8
1987	1,256	801	208	63.8	16.6	26.0	387	30.8	808	26.4	43.2
1986	1,175	739	226	62.9	19.2	30.6	365	31.1	759	31.4	46.8
1985	1,091	734	205	67.3	18.8	27.9	295	27.0	743	28.4	48.0
1984	1,061	661	207	62.3	19.5	31.3	353	33.2	667	31.5	46.6
1983	1,057	634	198	60.0	18.7	31.2	363	34.3	644	31.8	49.7
1982	1,056	634	196	60.0	18.6	30.9	393	37.2	648	31.8	49.2
1981	1,064	646	178	60.7	16.7	27.6	362	34.0	662	28.2	43.4
1980	1,021	579	165	56.7	16.2	28.5	389	38.1	595	29.1	45.4
1979	917	516	140	56.3	15.3	27.1	358	39.0	534	28.1	42.3
1978	891	516	128	57.9	14.4	24.8	343	38.5	528	25.8	40.0
1977	855	483	139	56.5	16.3	28.8	326	38.1	495	29.7	41.6
1976	850	483	160	56.8	18.8	33.1	313	36.8	489	33.5	46.5
1975	769	449	150	58.4	19.5	33.4	283	36.8	460	34.8	46.7
1974	786	451	129	57.4	16.4	28.6	280	35.6	459	29.2	43.4
1973	658	362	102	55.0	15.5	28.2	272	41.3	372	28.8	41.1
1972	728	394	88	54.1	12.1	22.3	288	39.6	402	23.6	31.1
WHITE ALONE OR IN COMBINATION											
Both Sexes											
2016	22,830	20,100	9,446	88.0	41.4	47.0	1,419	6.2	20,416	47.2	72.6
2015	23,067	20,193	9,268	87.5	40.2	45.9	1,464	6.3	20,507	46.0	72.5
2014	23,327	20,258	9,329	86.8	40.0	46.1	1,638	7.0	20,520	46.2	72.0
2013	23,539	20,436	9,422	86.8	40.0	46.1	1,679	7.1	20,773	46.5	72.1
2012	23,516	20,257	9,614	86.1	40.9	47.5	1,710	7.3	20,546	47.8	73.4
2011	23,679	20,256	10,043	85.5	42.4	49.6	1,941	8.2	20,504	49.7	73.9
2010	23,381	19,949	9,524	85.3	40.7	47.7	2,013	8.6	20,180	48.0	72.9
2009	23,256	19,784	9,562	85.1	41.1	48.3	2,127	9.1	20,060	48.5	72.0
2008	23,120	19,810	9,360	85.7	40.5	47.2	2,072	9.0	20,067	47.5	71.6
2007	22,928	19,330	8,958	84.3	39.1	46.3	2,338	10.2	19,595	46.5	70.3
2006	22,670	18,882	8,465	83.3	37.3	44.8	2,458	10.8	19,153	45.1	69.9
2005	22,345	18,583	8,721	83.2	39.0	47.1	2,539	11.4	18,818	47.0	70.0
2004	22,411	18,663	8,544	83.3	38.1	45.8	2,639	11.8	18,868	46.0	69.0
2003	22,029	18,335	8,358	83.2	37.9	45.6	2,558	11.6	18,565	45.6	69.0
Male											
2016	11,534	9,967	4,432	86.4	38.4	44.5	845	7.3	10,093	44.5	67.9
2015	11,635	10,059	4,319	86.5	37.1	42.9	812	7.0	10,224	43.0	67.6

Note: The change in the educational attainment question and the college completion categories from "4 or more years of college" to "at least some college," in 1992 caused an increase in the proportion of 14-to-24-year-old high school graduates enrolled in college or completed some college, of approximately 5 percentage points. High school graduates are people who have completed 4 years of high school or more, for 1967 to 1991. Beginning in 1992, they were people whose highest degree was a high school diploma (including equivalency) or higher.
ʳ = Revised, controlled to 1990 census based population estimates; previous 1993 data controlled to 1980 census based population estimates.

Table A-13. Population 14 to 24 Years Old, by High School Graduate Status, College Enrollment, Attainment, Sex, Race, and Hispanic Origin, October 1967–2016—*Continued*

(Numbers in thousands; percent; civilian noninstitutionalized population.)

Year, race, and Hispanic origin	Population 18 to 24 years old								High school graduates, 14 to 24 years old		
		High school graduates		Percent			High school dropouts			Percent	
	Total	Total	Enrolled in college	High school graduates	Enrolled in college	High school graduate enrolled in college	Number	Percent	All graduates	Enrolled in college	Enrolled or completed some college
2014	11,801	10,108	4,397	85.7	37.3	43.5	900	7.6	10,237	43.7	67.4
2013	11,921	10,185	4,323	85.4	36.3	42.4	896	7.5	10,357	42.9	66.7
2012	11,925	10,045	4,399	84.2	36.9	43.8	991	8.3	10,174	44.2	68.1
2011	12,153	10,175	4,789	83.7	39.4	47.1	1,105	9.1	10,308	47.2	69.7
2010	11,832	9,869	4,472	83.4	37.8	45.3	1,152	9.7	9,976	45.4	68.5
2009	11,774	9,824	4,513	83.4	38.3	45.9	1,224	10.4	9,952	46.1	68.3
2008	11,738	9,891	4,444	84.3	37.9	44.9	1,165	9.9	10,031	45.2	67.8
2007	11,670	9,511	4,116	81.5	35.3	43.3	1,397	12.0	9,634	43.4	66.0
2006	11,502	9,331	3,923	81.1	34.1	42.0	1,427	12.4	9,435	42.2	66.1
2005	11,394	9,086	4,018	79.7	35.3	43.5	1,519	13.3	9,193	44.2	60.0
2004	11,371	9,227	3,956	81.1	34.8	42.9	1,548	13.6	9,296	43.1	64.4
2003	11,147	8,967	3,815	80.4	34.2	42.5	1,493	13.4	9,070	42.6	65.1
Female											
2016	11,296	10,133	5,014	89.7	44.4	49.5	574	5.1	10,323	49.7	77.3
2015	11,433	10,134	4,949	88.6	43.3	48.8	653	5.7	10,283	48.9	77.4
2014	11,526	10,151	4,932	88.1	42.8	48.6	739	6.4	10,283	48.8	76.5
2013	11,617	10,251	5,099	88.2	43.9	49.7	783	6.7	10,415	50.1	77.4
2012	11,590	10,212	5,215	88.1	45.0	51.1	719	6.2	10,372	51.4	78.5
2011	11,525	10,081	5,254	87.5	45.6	52.1	836	7.3	10,196	52.1	78.1
2010	11,549	10,080	5,052	87.3	43.7	50.1	861	7.5	10,204	50.5	77.1
2009	11,482	9,960	5,049	86.7	44.0	50.7	903	7.9	10,108	50.8	75.6
2008	11,381	9,919	4,916	87.2	43.2	49.6	908	8.0	10,036	49.9	75.4
2007	11,258	9,820	4,842	87.2	43.0	49.3	941	8.4	9,960	49.4	74.4
2006	11,168	9,551	4,542	85.5	40.7	47.6	1,032	9.2	9,718	47.8	73.6
2005	10,952	9,497	4,702	86.7	42.9	49.4	1,020	9.3	9,625	49.7	73.9
2004	11,040	9,436	4,588	85.5	41.6	48.6	1,091	9.9	9,572	48.8	73.5
2003	10,882	9,367	4,543	86.1	41.7	48.5	1,065	9.8	9,495	48.5	72.7
BLACK ALONE OR IN COMBINATION											
Both Sexes											
2016	4,978	4,216	1,782	84.7	35.8	42.3	342	6.9	4,305	42.2	65.5
2015	5,032	4,316	1,741	85.8	34.6	40.3	359	7.1	4,367	40.5	64.2
2014	5,121	4,352	1,645	85.0	32.1	37.8	366	7.1	4,426	38.4	65.7
2013	5,199	4,297	1,806	82.7	34.7	42.0	422	8.1	4,345	42.4	66.4
2012	5,142	4,119	1,891	80.1	36.8	45.9	500	9.7	4,187	45.9	67.2
2011	4,793	3,902	1,759	81.4	36.7	45.1	424	8.8	3,955	45.5	67.3
2010	4,745	3,898	1,808	82.1	38.1	46.4	493	10.4	3,965	46.6	66.7
2009	4,623	3,688	1,699	79.8	36.8	46.1	532	11.5	3,766	46.0	67.2
2008	4,531	3,588	1,435	79.2	31.7	40.0	548	12.1	3,646	40.3	60.9
2007	4,425	3,603	1,468	81.4	33.2	40.7	477	10.8	3,671	40.9	61.8
2006	4,264	3,287	1,387	77.1	32.5	42.2	560	13.1	3,359	42.2	61.1
2005	4,158	3,303	1,371	79.4	33.0	31.7	530	12.7	3,378	41.5	63.5
2004	4,115	3,190	1,318	77.5	32.0	41.3	620	15.1	3,253	41.8	63.5
2003	4,016	3,091	1,285	77.0	32.0	41.6	563	14.0	3,141	41.9	62.0
Male											
2016	2,407	1,924	777	79.9	32.3	40.4	226	9.4	1,948	40.6	61.2
2015	2,421	2,067	833	85.4	34.4	40.3	172	7.1	2,094	40.5	63.2
2014	2,451	2,008	660	81.9	26.9	32.8	183	7.4	2,055	34.0	60.6
2013	2,491	2,020	780	81.1	31.3	38.6	230	9.2	2,042	39.3	62.5
2012	2,500	1,972	859	78.9	34.4	43.6	279	11.2	2,009	43.8	65.0
2011	2,289	1,800	762	78.6	33.3	42.4	218	9.5	1,831	42.9	61.4
2010	2,250	1,781	779	79.2	34.6	43.7	269	11.9	1,823	43.7	61.9
2009	2,211	1,702	712	76.9	32.2	41.9	301	13.6	1,726	41.6	63.7
2008	2,190	1,743	633	79.6	28.9	36.3	235	10.7	1,770	36.9	54.9
2007	2,132	1,703	686	79.9	32.2	40.3	234	11.0	1,728	40.4	59.6
2006	2,032	1,545	577	76.0	28.4	37.3	225	11.0	1,576	37.2	54.5
2005	1,988	1,466	557	73.7	28.0	42.5	290	14.6	1,492	37.9	58.2
2004	1,951	1,418	521	72.7	26.7	36.7	347	17.8	1,442	37.0	61.3
2003	1,868	1,382	525	74.0	28.1	38.0	311	16.6	1,397	38.3	57.4

Note: The change in the educational attainment question and the college completion categories from "4 or more years of college" to "at least some college," in 1992 caused an increase in the proportion of 14-to-24-year-old high school graduates enrolled in college or completed some college, of approximately 5 percentage points. High school graduates are people who have completed 4 years of high school or more, for 1967 to 1991. Beginning in 1992, they were people whose highest degree was a high school diploma (including equivalency) or higher.

Table A-13. Population 14 to 24 Years Old, by High School Graduate Status, College Enrollment, Attainment, Sex, Race, and Hispanic Origin, October 1967–2016—*Continued*

(Numbers in thousands; percent; civilian noninstitutionalized population.)

Year, race, and Hispanic origin	Population 18 to 24 years old								High school graduates, 14 to 24 years old		
		High school graduates		Percent			High school dropouts			Percent	
	Total	Total	Enrolled in college	High school graduates	Enrolled in college	High school graduate enrolled in college	Number	Percent	All graduates	Enrolled in college	Enrolled or completed some college
Female											
2016	2,571	2,292	1,004	89.1	39.1	43.8	116	4.5	2,357	43.5	69.1
2015	2,612	2,249	908	86.1	34.8	40.4	188	7.2	2,273	40.6	65.2
2014	2,670	2,344	985	87.8	36.9	42.0	183	6.9	2,371	42.3	70.1
2013	2,708	2,277	1,026	84.1	37.9	45.0	192	7.1	2,303	45.1	69.9
2012	2,642	2,147	1,032	81.3	39.1	48.1	221	8.4	2,178	47.9	69.4
2011	2,504	2,102	997	84.0	39.8	47.4	206	8.2	2,124	47.7	72.3
2010	2,495	2,117	1,029	84.8	41.3	48.6	224	9.0	2,142	49.0	70.7
2009	2,411	1,987	987	82.4	40.9	49.7	231	9.6	2,040	49.8	70.1
2008	2,341	1,845	802	78.8	34.2	43.5	313	13.4	1,876	43.5	66.5
2007	2,293	1,900	782	82.9	34.1	41.2	243	10.6	1,942	41.3	63.7
2006	2,232	1,742	810	78.1	36.3	46.5	335	15.0	1,783	46.5	66.8
2005	2,170	1,837	814	84.7	37.5	21.2	240	11.1	1,885	44.3	67.7
2004	2,164	1,772	797	81.9	36.8	45.0	272	12.6	1,811	45.5	65.3
2003	2,148	1,708	760	79.5	35.4	44.5	252	11.7	1,744	44.7	65.7
ASIAN ALONE OR IN COMBINATION											
Both Sexes											
2016	2,025	1,867	1,161	92.2	57.3	62.2	61	3.0	1,903	62.1	87.3
2015	1,889	1,747	1,182	92.5	62.6	67.7	52	2.8	1,795	67.0	91.5
2014	1,844	1,737	1,132	94.2	61.4	65.2	17	0.9	1,781	64.6	90.2
2013	1,947	1,765	1,156	90.6	59.4	65.5	70	3.6	1,801	65.9	86.5
2012	1,780	1,610	1,043	90.5	58.6	64.8	61	3.4	1,650	65.2	85.2
2011	1,435	1,295	833	90.2	58.0	64.3	67	4.6	1,149	66.9	88.1
2010	1,465	1,338	904	91.3	61.7	67.6	80	5.5	1,382	68.0	88.9
2009	1,345	1,231	844	91.5	62.8	68.5	29	2.1	1,249	68.5	90.8
2008	1,251	1,153	738	92.1	59.0	64.0	42	3.4	1,188	64.4	89.7
2007	1,293	1,126	720	87.1	55.7	63.9	94	7.3	1,143	63.9	90.3
2006	1,270	1,158	705	91.2	55.5	60.9	49	3.9	1,180	60.6	86.1
2005	1,299	1,214	773	93.5	59.5	63.7	38	2.9	1,243	64.2	86.0
2004	1,263	1,167	750	92.5	59.4	64.3	53	4.2	1,191	64.6	87.6
2003	1,280	1,162	774	90.8	60.5	66.6	56	4.4	1,184	66.9	87.8
Male											
2016	1,045	969	624	92.7	59.7	64.4	25	2.3	984	64.1	87.3
2015	937	869	561	92.8	59.9	64.6	30	3.2	896	63.9	89.2
2014	932	882	600	94.6	64.3	68.0	13	1.4	904	67.9	89.8
2013	1,009	927	612	91.9	60.7	66.1	22	2.2	939	66.1	84.8
2012	900	807	510	89.7	56.7	63.2	28	3.1	832	63.9	84.5
2011	747	673	429	90.1	57.4	63.7	31	4.2	582	66.1	87.6
2010	750	685	453	91.4	60.4	66.1	40	5.3	711	66.5	87.4
2009	673	624	418	92.8	62.2	67.0	7	1.1	637	66.8	89.8
2008	626	560	340	89.4	54.4	60.8	22	3.4	582	62.2	89.2
2007	560	481	318	85.8	56.9	66.3	38	6.8	483	66.4	91.8
2006	649	578	362	89.1	55.8	62.7	34	5.3	591	62.3	83.8
2005	653	603	392	92.4	59.9	65.0	20	3.1	621	65.1	86.3
2004	634	588	398	92.8	62.7	67.7	18	2.9	601	68.0	87.8
2003	609	545	370	89.5	60.8	67.9	43	7.1	551	67.7	88.7
Female											
2016	980	898	536	91.6	54.7	59.7	36	3.7	919	60.0	87.3
2015	952	878	621	92.2	65.2	70.7	22	2.3	899	70.2	93.8
2014	911	855	533	93.8	58.5	62.3	4	0.5	877	61.3	90.6
2013	938	838	544	89.3	58.0	64.9	48	5.1	861	65.7	88.4
2012	880	803	533	91.2	60.6	66.4	33	3.7	817	66.5	85.8
2011	688	622	403	90.4	58.7	64.9	35	5.1	567	67.8	88.7
2010	715	652	451	91.2	63.1	69.1	41	5.7	671	69.7	90.4
2009	673	607	426	90.3	63.3	70.1	21	3.2	611	70.2	91.8
2008	625	593	397	94.9	63.6	67.0	21	3.3	605	66.5	90.3
2007	605	529	339	87.4	56.0	64.1	48	7.9	543	63.9	91.5
2006	621	580	343	93.4	55.3	59.2	14	2.3	589	58.8	88.5
2005	645	610	381	94.6	59.1	62.5	17	2.7	622	63.3	85.8
2004	628	579	352	92.1	56.0	60.8	35	5.5	591	61.2	87.5
2003	671	617	404	92.0	60.2	65.5	13	1.9	633	66.3	87.0

Table A-14. Population 18 and 19 Years Old, by School Enrollment Status, Sex, Race, and Hispanic Origin, October 1967–2016

(Numbers in thousands; percent; civilian noninstitutionalized population.)

| Year, race, and Hispanic origin | Total | Population 18 and 19 years old | | | | | | | |
		Still in high school	Percent	Dropped out	Percent	High school graduate only	Percent	In college	Percent
ALL RACES									
Both Sexes									
2016	8,266	1,570	19.0	532	6.4	1,993	24.1	4,171	50.5
2015	8,158	1,613	19.8	611	7.5	1,957	24.0	3,978	48.8
2014	8,261	1,618	19.6	588	7.1	2,019	24.4	4,036	48.9
2013	8,473	1,736	20.5	529	6.2	2,257	26.6	3,951	46.6
2012	8,484	1,840	21.7	605	7.1	2,025	23.9	4,015	47.3
2011	8,465	1,775	21.0	545	6.4	1,903	22.5	4,242	50.1
2010	8,529	1,540	18.1	622	7.3	2,003	23.5	4,364	51.2
2009	8,615	1,645	19.1	736	8.5	1,944	22.6	4,289	49.8
2008	8,492	1,481	17.4	750	8.8	2,134	25.1	4,126	48.6
2007	8,338	1,491	17.9	675	8.1	2,097	25.2	4,075	48.9
2006	8,102	1,560	19.3	743	9.2	2,053	25.3	3,746	46.2
2005	7,559	1,372	18.1	661	8.7	1,694	22.4	3,832	50.7
2004	7,701	1,266	16.4	840	10.9	1,910	24.8	3,685	47.8
2003	7,533	1,345	17.9	817	10.8	1,859	24.7	3,512	46.6
2002	7,907	1,427	18.0	884	11.2	2,015	25.5	3,581	45.3
2001	7,985	1,394	17.5	1,034	12.9	2,079	26.0	3,478	43.6
2000	8,045	1,327	16.5	1,012	12.6	2,107	26.2	3,599	44.7
1999	7,991	1,321	16.5	1,047	13.1	2,103	26.3	3,520	44.0
1998	7,902	1,244	15.7	1,104	14.0	1,884	23.8	3,670	46.4
1997	7,510	1,256	16.7	1,038	13.8	1,854	24.7	3,362	44.8
1996	7,376	1,230	16.7	940	12.7	1,897	25.7	3,309	44.9
1995	7,198	1,173	16.3	1,051	14.6	1,873	26.0	3,101	43.1
1994	6,946	1,129	16.3	929	13.4	1,837	26.4	3,051	43.9
1993	6,594	1,137	17.2	778	11.8	1,753	26.6	2,926	44.4
1992	6,535	1,121	17.2	780	11.9	1,742	26.7	2,892	44.3
1991	6,664	1,040	15.6	889	13.3	1,806	27.1	2,929	44.0
1990	7,064	1,024	14.5	1,003	14.2	2,018	28.6	3,019	42.7
1989	7,361	1,058	14.4	1,033	14.0	2,204	29.9	3,066	41.7
1988	7,294	1,013	13.9	1,063	14.6	2,172	29.8	3,046	41.8
1987	7,160	937	13.1	954	13.3	2,224	31.1	3,045	42.5
1986	7,095	930	13.1	872	12.3	2,351	33.1	2,942	41.5
1985	7,204	809	11.2	1,031	14.3	2,457	34.1	2,907	40.4
1984	7,428	857	11.5	1,129	15.2	2,575	34.7	2,867	38.6
1983	7,819	999	12.8	1,132	14.5	2,748	35.1	2,940	37.6
1982	8,023	908	11.3	1,336	16.7	2,850	35.5	2,929	36.5
1981	8,115	932	11.5	1,299	16.0	2,840	35.0	3,044	37.5
1980	8,160	855	10.5	1,284	15.7	3,088	37.8	2,933	35.9
1979	8,214	849	10.3	1,382	16.8	3,139	38.2	2,844	34.6
1978	8,153	801	9.8	1,361	16.7	3,092	37.9	2,899	35.6
1977	8,151	849	10.4	1,355	16.6	3,034	37.2	2,913	35.7
1976	8,148	831	10.2	1,355	16.6	3,025	37.1	2,937	36.0
1975	8,024	822	10.2	1,286	16.0	2,973	37.1	2,943	36.7
1974	7,822	777	9.9	1,302	16.6	3,146	40.2	2,597	33.2
1973	7,649	766	10.0	1,228	16.1	3,138	41.0	2,517	32.9
1972	7,462	778	10.4	1,100	14.7	2,904	38.9	2,680	35.9
1971	7,231	830	11.5	1,108	15.3	2,567	35.5	2,726	37.7
1970	6,958	728	10.5	1,125	16.2	2,511	36.1	2,594	37.3
1969	6,677	749	11.2	1,007	15.1	2,320	34.7	2,601	39.0
1968	6,587	816	12.4	1,033	15.7	2,237	34.0	2,501	38.0
1967	6,358	741	11.7	1,086	17.1	2,245	35.3	2,286	36.0
Male									
2016	4,192	916	21.9	303	7.2	1,028	24.5	1,944	46.4
2015	4,106	860	20.9	359	8.7	1,050	25.6	1,838	44.7
2014	4,183	935	22.4	323	7.7	1,146	27.4	1,779	42.5
2013	4,319	1,004	23.2	272	6.3	1,235	28.6	1,809	41.9
2012	4,310	1,023	23.7	359	8.3	1,114	25.9	1,803	41.8
2011	4,341	1,038	23.9	293	6.8	1,060	24.4	1,949	44.9
2010	4,296	867	20.2	347	8.1	1,073	25.0	2,009	46.8
2009	4,352	899	20.7	410	9.4	1,114	25.6	1,928	44.3
2008	4,289	834	19.5	376	8.8	1,169	27.3	1,909	44.5
2007	4,222	895	21.2	354	8.4	1,070	25.3	1,903	45.1
2006	4,103	907	22.1	414	10.1	1,079	26.3	1,703	41.5
2005	3,880	899	23.2	392	10.1	914	23.6	1,675	43.2
2004	3,861	714	18.5	522	13.5	1,015	26.3	1,610	41.7
2003	3,764	781	20.7	480	12.8	935	24.8	1,568	41.7
2002	4,042	862	21.3	523	12.9	1,022	25.3	1,635	40.5
2001	4,027	801	19.9	614	15.2	1,042	25.9	1,570	39.0
2000	4,037	783	19.4	571	14.1	1,113	27.6	1,570	38.9

Note: High school graduates are people who have completed 4 years of high school or more, for 1967 to 1991. Beginning in 1992, they were people whose highest degree was a high school diploma (including equivalency) or higher.

Table A-14. Population 18 and 19 Years Old, by School Enrollment Status, Sex, Race, and Hispanic Origin, October 1967–2016—*Continued*

(Numbers in thousands; percent; civilian noninstitutionalized population.)

Year, race, and Hispanic origin	Total	Still in high school	Percent	Dropped out	Percent	High school graduate only	Percent	In college	Percent
						Population 18 and 19 years old			
1999	4,026	780	19.4	550	13.7	1,048	26.0	1,648	40.9
1998	3,994	732	18.3	611	15.3	984	24.6	1,667	41.7
1997	3,816	750	19.7	585	15.3	920	24.1	1,561	40.9
1996	3,711	769	20.7	488	13.2	965	26.0	1,489	40.1
1995	3,611	719	19.9	532	14.7	929	25.7	1,431	39.6
1994	3,485	688	19.7	499	14.3	882	25.3	1,416	40.6
1993	3,329	712	21.4	403	12.1	877	26.3	1,337	40.2
1992	3,275	694	21.2	400	12.2	856	26.1	1,325	40.5
1991	3,307	650	19.7	453	13.7	878	26.5	1,326	40.1
1990	3,503	595	17.0	512	14.6	953	27.2	1,443	41.2
1989	3,640	640	17.6	531	14.6	1,047	28.8	1,422	39.1
1988	3,618	666	18.4	566	15.6	1,021	28.2	1,365	37.7
1987	3,537	564	15.9	493	13.9	997	28.2	1,483	41.9
1986	3,502	594	17.0	459	13.1	1,045	29.8	1,404	40.1
1985	3,550	503	14.2	580	16.3	1,118	31.5	1,349	38.0
1984	3,674	551	15.0	594	16.2	1,156	31.5	1,373	37.4
1983	3,877	616	15.9	630	16.2	1,291	33.3	1,340	34.6
1982	3,961	562	14.2	709	17.9	1,314	33.2	1,376	34.7
1981	3,996	567	14.2	706	17.7	1,273	31.9	1,450	36.3
1980	3,993	510	12.8	673	16.9	1,441	36.1	1,369	34.3
1979	4,023	533	13.2	739	18.4	1,410	35.0	1,341	33.3
1978	3,975	511	12.9	692	17.4	1,381	34.7	1,391	35.0
1977	3,961	522	13.2	702	17.7	1,341	33.9	1,396	35.2
1976	3,957	516	13.0	684	17.3	1,366	34.5	1,391	35.2
1975	3,891	514	13.2	603	15.5	1,348	34.6	1,426	36.6
1974	3,782	469	12.4	706	18.7	1,345	35.6	1,262	33.4
1973	3,720	490	13.2	589	15.8	1,348	36.2	1,293	34.8
1972	3,630	492	13.6	555	15.3	1,217	33.5	1,366	37.6
1971	3,503	496	14.2	551	15.7	1,012	28.9	1,444	41.2
1970	3,349	485	14.5	537	16.0	981	29.3	1,346	40.2
1969	3,173	489	15.4	473	14.9	814	25.7	1,397	44.0
1968	3,133	535	17.1	485	15.5	756	24.1	1,357	43.3
1967	2,908	438	15.1	500	17.2	772	26.5	1,198	41.2
Female									
2016	4,075	654	16.0	229	5.6	965	23.7	2,227	54.7
2015	4,052	752	18.6	252	6.2	907	22.4	2,141	52.8
2014	4,079	683	16.7	265	6.5	873	21.4	2,257	55.3
2013	4,154	732	17.6	257	6.2	1,022	24.6	2,142	51.6
2012	4,174	788	18.9	245	5.9	911	21.8	2,212	53.0
2011	4,124	737	17.9	252	6.1	843	20.4	2,293	55.6
2010	4,233	673	15.9	275	6.5	930	22.0	2,355	55.6
2009	4,263	746	17.5	325	7.6	830	19.5	2,361	55.4
2008	4,203	647	15.4	374	8.9	965	23.0	2,217	52.7
2007	4,116	595	14.5	321	7.8	1,027	25.0	2,172	52.8
2006	3,999	654	16.3	328	8.2	974	24.4	2,043	51.1
2005	3,679	472	12.8	269	7.3	886	24.1	2,052	55.8
2004	3,840	553	14.4	318	8.3	895	23.3	2,074	54.0
2003	3,769	565	15.0	337	8.9	923	24.5	1,944	51.6
2002	3,865	565	14.6	361	9.3	993	25.7	1,946	50.3
2001	3,958	594	15.0	420	10.6	1,037	26.2	1,907	48.2
2000	4,008	544	13.6	440	11.0	995	24.8	2,029	50.6
1999	3,965	540	13.6	497	12.5	1,056	26.6	1,872	47.2
1998	3,908	513	13.1	492	12.6	900	23.0	2,003	51.3
1997	3,694	506	13.7	453	12.3	934	25.3	1,801	48.8
1996	3,665	460	12.6	452	12.3	932	25.4	1,821	49.7
1995	3,587	453	12.6	519	14.5	944	26.3	1,671	46.6
1994	3,461	440	12.7	430	12.4	956	27.6	1,635	47.2
1993	3,265	425	13.0	375	11.5	877	26.9	1,588	48.6
1992	3,260	428	13.1	380	11.7	886	27.2	1,566	48.0
1991	3,357	389	11.6	436	13.0	929	27.7	1,603	47.8
1990	3,561	429	12.0	491	13.8	1,065	29.9	1,576	44.3
1989	3,721	421	11.3	501	13.5	1,156	31.1	1,643	44.2
1988	3,676	346	9.4	497	13.5	1,151	31.3	1,682	45.8
1987	3,623	374	10.3	461	12.7	1,226	33.8	1,562	43.1
1986	3,593	337	9.4	413	11.5	1,306	36.3	1,537	42.8
1985	3,654	304	8.3	451	12.3	1,340	36.7	1,559	42.7
1984	3,754	306	8.2	535	14.3	1,419	37.8	1,494	39.8
1983	3,942	383	9.7	502	12.7	1,457	37.0	1,600	40.6

Note: High school graduates are people who have completed 4 years of high school or more, for 1967 to 1991. Beginning in 1992, they were people whose highest degree was a high school diploma (including equivalency) or higher.

Table A-14. Population 18 and 19 Years Old, by School Enrollment Status, Sex, Race, and Hispanic Origin, October 1967–2016—*Continued*

(Numbers in thousands; percent; civilian noninstitutionalized population.)

| Year, race, and Hispanic origin | Total | Population 18 and 19 years old | | | | | | | |
		Still in high school	Percent	Dropped out	Percent	High school graduate only	Percent	In college	Percent
1982	4,062	346	8.5	627	15.4	1,536	37.8	1,553	38.2
1981	4,119	364	8.8	594	14.4	1,567	38.0	1,594	38.7
1980	4,167	345	8.3	611	14.7	1,646	39.5	1,565	37.6
1979	4,191	317	7.6	643	15.3	1,728	41.2	1,503	35.9
1978	4,178	291	7.0	669	16.0	1,711	41.0	1,507	36.1
1977	4,190	326	7.8	654	15.6	1,693	40.4	1,517	36.2
1976	4,191	314	7.5	672	16.0	1,659	39.6	1,546	36.9
1975	4,133	308	7.5	683	16.5	1,625	39.3	1,517	36.7
1974	4,040	309	7.6	596	14.8	1,800	44.6	1,335	33.0
1973	3,929	276	7.0	638	16.2	1,791	45.6	1,224	31.2
1972	3,832	287	7.5	545	14.2	1,686	44.0	1,314	34.3
1971	3,728	337	9.0	556	14.9	1,554	41.7	1,281	34.4
1970	3,609	253	7.0	589	16.3	1,519	42.1	1,248	34.6
1969	3,504	260	7.4	534	15.2	1,506	43.0	1,204	34.4
1968	3,454	281	8.1	548	15.9	1,481	42.9	1,144	33.1
1967	3,450	302	8.8	586	17.0	1,474	42.7	1,088	31.5
WHITE									
Both Sexes									
2016	6,144	1,097	17.9	370	6.0	1,506	24.5	3,170	51.6
2015	6,147	1,159	18.9	474	7.7	1,456	23.7	3,057	49.7
2014	6,213	1,182	19.0	451	7.3	1,517	24.4	3,064	49.3
2013	6,294	1,219	19.4	390	6.2	1,652	26.2	3,033	48.2
2012	6,372	1,278	20.1	418	6.6	1,575	24.7	3,077	48.3
2011	6,501	1,274	19.6	449	6.9	1,480	22.8	3,298	50.7
2010	6,523	1,168	17.9	435	6.7	1,522	23.3	3,398	52.1
2009	6,594	1,194	18.1	526	8.0	1,536	23.3	3,337	50.6
2008	6,589	1,067	16.2	558	8.5	1,611	24.4	3,353	50.9
2007	6,446	1,083	16.8	517	8.0	1,605	24.9	3,242	50.3
2006	6,321	1,121	17.7	600	9.5	1,619	25.6	2,982	47.2
2005	5,893	1,023	17.4	515	8.7	1,383	23.5	2,972	50.4
2004	6,043	963	15.9	634	10.5	1,500	24.8	2,946	48.8
2003[1]	5,915	979	16.6	659	11.1	1,444	24.4	2,833	47.9
2002	6,252	1,096	17.5	663	10.6	1,602	25.6	2,891	46.2
2001	6,254	1,022	16.3	843	13.5	1,634	26.1	2,755	44.1
2000	6,399	1,010	15.8	795	12.4	1,680	26.3	2,914	45.5
1999	6,383	1,009	15.8	810	12.7	1,715	26.9	2,849	44.6
1998	6,266	884	14.1	848	13.5	1,540	24.6	2,994	47.8
1997	5,995	896	14.9	816	13.6	1,491	24.9	2,792	46.6
1996	5,833	914	15.7	735	12.6	1,453	24.9	2,731	46.8
1995	5,698	803	14.1	809	14.2	1,509	26.5	2,577	45.2
1994	5,559	817	14.7	681	12.3	1,493	26.9	2,568	46.2
1993	5,252	786	15.0	628	12.0	1,382	26.3	2,456	46.8
1992	5,203	793	15.2	582	11.2	1,409	27.1	2,419	46.5
1991	5,358	709	13.2	722	13.5	1,440	26.9	2,487	46.4
1990	5,725	724	12.6	799	14.0	1,654	28.9	2,548	44.5
1989	6,013	744	12.4	819	13.6	1,802	30.0	2,648	44.0
1988	5,981	699	11.7	855	14.3	1,788	29.9	2,639	44.1
1987	5,845	667	11.4	762	13.0	1,852	31.7	2,564	43.9
1986	5,825	669	11.5	693	11.9	1,940	33.3	2,523	43.3
1985	5,922	566	9.6	815	13.8	2,002	33.8	2,539	42.9
1984	6,139	594	9.7	913	14.9	2,091	34.1	2,541	41.4
1983	6,452	688	10.7	884	13.7	2,283	35.4	2,597	40.3
1982	6,666	647	9.7	1,051	15.8	2,419	36.3	2,549	38.2
1981	6,794	656	9.7	1,054	15.5	2,445	36.0	2,639	38.8
1980	6,913	621	9.0	1,032	14.9	2,682	38.8	2,578	37.3
1979	6,980	607	8.7	1,115	16.0	2,760	39.5	2,498	35.8
1978	6,933	560	8.1	1,082	15.6	2,738	39.5	2,553	36.8
1977	6,944	581	8.4	1,103	15.9	2,681	38.6	2,579	37.1
1976	6,951	581	8.4	1,131	16.3	2,662	38.3	2,577	37.1
1975	6,855	572	8.3	1,005	14.7	2,665	38.9	2,613	38.1
1974	6,707	551	8.2	1,045	15.6	2,803	41.8	2,308	34.4
1973	6,559	568	8.7	962	14.7	2,748	41.9	2,281	34.8
1972	6,424	582	9.1	857	13.3	2,574	40.1	2,411	37.5
1971	6,243	596	9.5	875	14.0	2,287	36.6	2,485	39.8
1970	6,009	563	9.4	845	14.1	2,240	37.3	2,361	39.3
1969	5,762	557	9.7	772	13.4	2,056	35.7	2,377	41.3

Note: High school graduates are people who have completed 4 years of high school or more, for 1967 to 1991. Beginning in 1992, they were people whose highest degree was a high school diploma (including equivalency) or higher.

[1]Starting in 2003 respondents could identify more than one race. Except as noted, the race data in this table from 2003 onward represent those respondents who indicated only one race category.

Table A-14. Population 18 and 19 Years Old, by School Enrollment Status, Sex, Race, and Hispanic Origin, October 1967–2016—*Continued*

(Numbers in thousands; percent; civilian noninstitutionalized population.)

Year, race, and Hispanic origin	Total	Population 18 and 19 years old							
		Still in high school	Percent	Dropped out	Percent	High school graduate only	Percent	In college	Percent
1968............................	5,692	614	10.8	822	14.4	1,972	34.6	2,284	40.1
1967............................	5,506	558	10.1	875	15.9	1,968	35.7	2,105	38.2
Male									
2016............................	3,119	649	20.8	202	6.5	798	25.6	1,470	47.1
2015............................	3,123	621	19.9	282	9.0	806	25.8	1,414	45.3
2014............................	3,165	653	20.6	236	7.5	879	27.8	1,397	44.1
2013............................	3,212	732	22.8	196	6.1	898	27.9	1,386	43.2
2012............................	3,259	753	23.1	237	7.3	872	26.8	1,387	42.6
2011............................	3,352	748	22.3	240	7.2	845	25.2	1,520	45.3
2010............................	3,316	667	20.1	246	7.4	830	25.0	1,573	47.4
2009............................	3,349	652	19.5	291	8.7	894	26.7	1,511	45.1
2008............................	3,350	589	17.6	299	8.9	896	26.7	1,566	46.7
2007............................	3,277	668	20.4	281	8.6	819	25.0	1,508	46.0
2006............................	3,211	645	20.1	351	10.9	848	26.4	1,367	42.6
2005............................	3,049	665	21.8	304	10.0	737	24.2	1,343	44.1
2004............................	3,062	524	17.1	406	13.3	824	26.9	1,308	42.7
2003[1].......................	3,003	594	19.8	381	12.7	770	25.6	1,258	41.9
2002............................	3,186	661	20.7	366	11.5	830	26.1	1,329	41.7
2001............................	3,192	585	18.3	494	15.5	840	26.3	1,273	39.9
2000............................	3,248	612	18.8	447	13.8	900	27.7	1,289	39.7
1999............................	3,242	609	18.8	423	13.0	874	27.0	1,336	41.2
1998............................	3,197	533	16.7	472	14.8	816	25.5	1,376	43.0
1997............................	3,060	523	17.1	473	15.5	750	24.5	1,314	42.9
1996............................	2,953	575	19.5	382	12.9	773	26.2	1,223	41.4
1995............................	2,886	519	18.0	408	14.1	764	26.5	1,195	41.4
1994............................	2,813	512	18.2	355	12.6	734	26.1	1,212	43.1
1993............................	2,641	497	18.8	338	12.8	703	26.6	1,103	41.8
1992............................	2,608	482	18.5	304	11.7	720	27.6	1,102	42.3
1991............................	2,677	451	16.8	381	14.2	733	27.4	1,112	41.5
1990............................	2,852	416	14.6	421	14.8	797	27.9	1,218	42.7
1989............................	2,997	463	15.4	433	14.4	848	28.3	1,253	41.8
1988............................	2,976	487	16.4	461	15.5	834	28.0	1,194	40.1
1987............................	2,906	404	13.9	400	13.8	842	29.0	1,260	43.4
1986............................	2,888	411	14.2	370	12.8	866	30.0	1,241	43.0
1985............................	2,937	349	11.9	478	16.3	934	31.8	1,176	40.0
1984............................	3,047	378	12.4	480	15.8	965	31.7	1,224	40.2
1983............................	3,216	434	13.5	500	15.5	1,085	33.7	1,197	37.2
1982............................	3,301	412	12.5	549	16.6	1,151	34.9	1,189	36.0
1981............................	3,356	394	11.7	599	17.8	1,104	32.9	1,259	37.5
1980............................	3,407	385	11.3	549	16.1	1,241	36.4	1,232	36.2
1979............................	3,445	395	11.5	610	17.7	1,248	36.2	1,192	34.6
1978............................	3,405	368	10.8	554	16.3	1,244	36.5	1,239	36.4
1977............................	3,396	348	10.2	577	17.0	1,199	35.3	1,272	37.5
1976............................	3,393	348	10.3	582	17.2	1,219	35.9	1,244	36.7
1975............................	3,343	374	11.2	458	13.7	1,228	36.7	1,283	38.4
1974............................	3,265	343	10.5	568	17.4	1,211	37.1	1,143	35.0
1973............................	3,208	375	11.7	454	14.2	1,202	37.5	1,177	36.7
1972............................	3,137	374	11.9	423	13.5	1,098	35.0	1,242	39.6
1971............................	3,035	367	12.1	432	14.2	908	29.9	1,328	43.8
1970............................	2,901	374	12.9	384	13.2	892	30.7	1,251	43.1
1969............................	2,745	374	13.6	345	12.6	728	26.5	1,298	47.3
1968............................	2,710	403	14.9	387	14.3	658	24.3	1,262	46.6
1967............................	2,511	340	13.5	386	15.4	688	27.4	1,097	43.7
Female									
2016............................	3,025	448	14.8	168	5.6	709	23.4	1,700	56.2
2015............................	3,024	538	17.8	192	6.3	650	21.5	1,644	54.4
2014............................	3,049	529	17.4	215	7.1	638	20.9	1,667	54.7
2013............................	3,083	487	15.8	195	6.3	754	24.5	1,646	53.4
2012............................	3,113	525	16.9	181	5.8	702	22.6	1,690	54.3
2011............................	3,148	526	16.7	209	6.6	635	20.2	1,779	56.5
2010............................	3,206	501	15.6	188	5.9	692	21.6	1,825	56.9
2009............................	3,245	542	16.7	235	7.2	642	19.8	1,826	56.3
2008............................	3,239	478	14.8	259	8.0	715	22.1	1,787	55.2
2007............................	3,169	414	13.1	235	7.4	785	24.8	1,734	54.7
2006............................	3,111	476	15.3	249	8.0	771	24.8	1,615	51.9
2005............................	2,844	358	12.6	210	7.4	647	22.7	1,629	57.3
2004............................	2,980	440	14.7	227	7.6	675	22.7	1,638	55.0

Note: High school graduates are people who have completed 4 years of high school or more, for 1967 to 1991. Beginning in 1992, they were people whose highest degree was a high school diploma (including equivalency) or higher.

[1]Starting in 2003 respondents could identify more than one race. Except as noted, the race data in this table from 2003 onward represent those respondents who indicated only one race category.

Table A-14. Population 18 and 19 Years Old, by School Enrollment Status, Sex, Race, and Hispanic Origin, October 1967–2016—*Continued*

(Numbers in thousands; percent; civilian noninstitutionalized population.)

Year, race, and Hispanic origin	Total	Population 18 and 19 years old								
		Still in high school	Percent	Dropped out	Percent	High school graduate only	Percent	In college	Percent
2003[1]	2,913	385	13.2	279	9.6	674	23.1	1,575	54.1
2002	3,066	435	14.2	297	9.7	772	25.2	1,562	50.9
2001	3,062	438	14.3	349	11.4	794	25.9	1,481	48.4
2000	3,151	397	12.6	348	11.0	781	24.8	1,625	51.6
1999	3,141	400	12.7	387	12.3	841	26.8	1,513	48.2
1998	3,069	351	11.4	376	12.3	724	23.6	1,618	52.7
1997	2,934	371	12.6	344	11.7	740	25.2	1,479	50.4
1996	2,879	338	11.7	353	12.3	680	23.6	1,508	52.4
1995	2,812	283	10.1	401	14.3	745	26.5	1,383	49.2
1994	2,746	305	11.1	325	11.8	759	27.6	1,357	49.4
1993	2,611	289	11.1	290	11.1	679	26.0	1,353	51.8
1992	2,595	311	12.0	278	10.7	689	26.6	1,317	50.8
1991	2,681	259	9.7	341	12.7	706	26.3	1,375	51.3
1990	2,873	307	10.7	378	13.2	857	29.8	1,331	46.3
1989	3,016	281	9.3	386	12.8	954	31.6	1,395	46.3
1988	3,005	212	7.1	394	13.1	954	31.7	1,445	48.1
1987	2,939	263	8.9	362	12.3	1,010	34.4	1,304	44.4
1986	2,937	257	8.8	323	11.0	1,074	36.6	1,283	43.7
1985	2,985	217	7.3	337	11.3	1,068	35.8	1,363	45.7
1984	3,092	216	7.0	432	14.0	1,127	36.4	1,317	42.6
1983	3,236	255	7.9	383	11.8	1,198	37.0	1,400	43.3
1982	3,365	234	7.0	502	14.9	1,269	37.7	1,360	40.4
1981	3,438	262	7.6	454	13.2	1,342	39.0	1,380	40.1
1980	3,506	237	6.8	483	13.8	1,440	41.1	1,346	38.4
1979	3,535	213	6.0	505	14.3	1,511	42.7	1,306	36.9
1978	3,528	193	5.5	528	15.0	1,493	42.3	1,314	37.2
1977	3,548	232	6.5	526	14.8	1,483	41.8	1,307	36.8
1976	3,558	230	6.5	550	15.5	1,444	40.6	1,334	37.5
1975	3,512	199	5.7	547	15.6	1,436	40.9	1,330	37.9
1974	3,442	207	6.0	477	13.9	1,592	46.3	1,166	33.9
1973	3,351	192	5.7	508	15.2	1,547	46.2	1,104	32.9
1972	3,287	208	6.3	434	13.2	1,476	44.9	1,169	35.6
1971	3,208	229	7.1	442	13.8	1,380	43.0	1,157	36.1
1970	3,108	190	6.1	460	14.8	1,348	43.4	1,110	35.7
1969	3,017	183	6.1	427	14.2	1,328	44.0	1,079	35.8
1968	2,981	210	7.0	435	14.6	1,314	44.1	1,022	34.3
1967	2,996	218	7.3	489	16.3	1,280	42.7	1,009	33.7
WHITE NON-HISPANIC									
Both Sexes									
2016	4,563	775	17.0	242	5.3	1,106	24.2	2,439	53.5
2015	4,575	839	18.3	305	6.7	1,063	23.2	2,368	51.8
2014	4,555	860	18.9	290	6.4	1,106	24.3	2,299	50.5
2013	4,645	856	18.4	248	5.3	1,162	25.0	2,379	51.2
2012	4,748	883	18.6	249	5.2	1,232	26.0	2,363	49.8
2011	4,889	937	19.2	291	5.9	1,074	22.0	2,588	52.9
2010	4,935	804	16.3	277	5.6	1,156	23.4	2,699	54.7
2009	5,068	826	16.3	288	5.7	1,112	21.9	2,842	56.1
2008	5,185	780	15.0	296	5.7	1,258	24.3	2,850	55.0
2007	5,067	793	15.7	283	5.6	1,252	24.7	2,739	54.1
2006	5,018	843	16.8	361	7.2	1,251	24.9	2,564	51.1
2005	4,770	790	16.6	297	6.2	1,065	22.3	2,618	54.9
2004	4,885	731	15.0	363	7.4	1,195	24.5	2,596	53.1
2003[1]	4,780	758	15.9	379	7.9	1,157	24.2	2,486	52.0
2002	5,016	817	16.3	369	7.4	1,281	25.5	2,549	50.8
2001	4,928	780	15.8	467	9.5	1,298	26.3	2,383	48.4
2000	5,221	757	14.5	500	9.6	1,384	26.5	2,580	49.4
1999	5,228	779	14.9	491	9.4	1,384	26.5	2,574	49.2
1998	5,080	691	13.6	475	9.4	1,211	23.8	2,703	53.2
Male									
2016	2,351	463	19.7	123	5.2	597	25.4	1,168	49.7
2015	2,350	460	19.6	181	7.7	589	25.1	1,121	47.7
2014	2,334	490	21.0	147	6.3	646	27.7	1,050	45.0
2013	2,392	516	21.6	123	5.2	629	26.3	1,124	47.0
2012	2,412	517	21.4	124	5.1	710	29.4	1,051	43.6
2011	2,470	543	22.0	145	5.9	599	24.2	1,184	47.9

Note: High school graduates are people who have completed 4 years of high school or more, for 1967 to 1991. Beginning in 1992, they were people whose highest degree was a high school diploma (including equivalency) or higher.
[1]Starting in 2003 respondents could identify more than one race. Except as noted, the race data in this table from 2003 onward represent those respondents who indicated only one race category.

Table A-14. Population 18 and 19 Years Old, by School Enrollment Status, Sex, Race, and Hispanic Origin, October 1967–2016—*Continued*

(Numbers in thousands; percent; civilian noninstitutionalized population.)

Year, race, and Hispanic origin	Total	Population 18 and 19 years old							
		Still in high school	Percent	Dropped out	Percent	High school graduate only	Percent	In college	Percent
2010.............................	2,516	470	18.7	166	6.6	645	25.6	1,236	49.1
2009.............................	2,573	473	18.4	173	6.7	641	24.9	1,286	50.0
2008.............................	2,649	423	16.0	170	6.4	709	26.8	1,346	50.8
2007.............................	2,587	496	19.2	150	5.8	643	24.9	1,298	50.2
2006.............................	2,553	501	19.6	204	8.0	679	26.6	1,168	45.7
2005.............................	2,449	515	21.0	168	6.9	573	23.4	1,193	48.7
2004.............................	2,443	408	16.7	204	8.4	681	27.9	1,150	47.1
2003[1].........................	2,407	460	19.1	230	9.6	602	25.0	1,115	46.3
2002.............................	2,502	481	19.2	182	7.3	660	26.4	1,179	47.1
2001.............................	2,526	453	17.9	257	10.2	685	27.1	1,131	44.8
2000.............................	2,628	471	17.9	274	10.4	745	28.3	1,138	43.3
1999.............................	2,648	473	17.9	255	9.6	706	26.7	1,214	45.8
1998.............................	2,613	432	16.5	254	9.7	653	25.0	1,274	48.8
Female									
2016.............................	2,212	312	14.1	119	5.4	510	23.1	1,271	57.5
2015.............................	2,225	379	17.1	124	5.6	474	21.3	1,248	56.1
2014.............................	2,222	370	16.6	143	6.4	460	20.7	1,249	56.2
2013.............................	2,253	340	15.1	125	5.5	533	23.7	1,254	55.7
2012.............................	2,336	366	15.7	125	5.3	522	22.3	1,312	56.2
2011.............................	2,470	543	22.0	145	5.9	599	24.2	1,184	47.9
2010.............................	2,419	334	13.8	111	4.6	511	21.1	1,463	60.5
2009.............................	2,495	353	14.1	115	4.6	471	18.9	1,556	62.4
2008.............................	2,536	357	14.1	126	5.0	549	21.7	1,504	59.3
2007.............................	2,480	298	12.0	132	5.3	609	24.6	1,441	58.1
2006.............................	2,466	341	13.8	157	6.4	571	23.2	1,396	56.6
2005.............................	2,321	275	11.9	129	5.6	491	21.2	1,425	61.4
2004.............................	2,441	323	13.2	159	6.5	513	21.0	1,446	59.2
2003[1].........................	2,373	298	12.6	149	6.3	555	23.4	1,371	57.8
2002.............................	2,514	336	13.4	187	7.4	621	24.7	1,370	54.5
2001.............................	2,402	328	13.7	209	8.7	613	25.5	1,252	52.1
2000.............................	2,593	286	11.0	225	8.7	639	24.6	1,443	55.6
1999.............................	2,580	307	11.9	236	9.1	677	26.2	1,360	52.7
1998.............................	2,467	259	10.5	221	9.0	558	22.6	1,429	57.9
BLACK									
Both Sexes									
2016.............................	1,244	305	24.5	87	7.0	321	25.8	530	42.6
2015.............................	1,233	286	23.2	84	6.8	354	28.7	509	41.3
2014.............................	1,251	307	24.5	94	7.5	341	27.3	510	40.7
2013.............................	1,305	386	29.6	92	7.1	375	28.8	451	34.6
2012.............................	1,356	396	29.2	110	8.1	315	23.2	531	39.1
2011.............................	1,316	396	30.1	60	4.5	281	21.3	580	44.0
2010.............................	1,336	271	20.3	144	10.8	355	26.5	567	42.4
2009.............................	1,346	319	23.7	180	13.4	288	21.4	559	41.5
2008.............................	1,335	311	23.3	145	10.8	400	30.0	479	35.9
2007.............................	1,284	300	23.4	112	8.7	380	29.6	492	38.3
2006.............................	1,230	332	27.0	103	8.3	332	27.0	464	37.7
2005.............................	1,126	256	22.7	110	9.8	309	27.4	451	40.0
2004.............................	1,112	218	19.6	162	14.5	292	26.3	440	39.6
2003[1].........................	1,052	277	26.3	128	12.2	273	26.0	374	35.6
2002.............................	1,181	251	21.3	180	15.2	320	27.1	430	36.4
2001.............................	1,246	299	24.0	152	12.2	351	28.2	444	35.6
2000.............................	1,251	262	20.9	187	14.9	348	27.8	454	36.3
1999.............................	1,199	259	21.6	190	15.8	320	26.7	430	35.9
1998.............................	1,246	290	23.3	224	18.0	271	21.7	461	37.0
1997.............................	1,133	278	24.5	172	15.2	302	26.7	381	33.6
1996.............................	1,161	268	23.1	175	15.1	373	32.1	345	29.7
1995.............................	1,099	287	26.1	177	16.1	291	26.5	344	31.3
1994.............................	1,017	239	23.5	199	19.6	269	26.5	310	30.5
1993.............................	1,040	290	27.9	133	12.8	306	29.4	311	29.9
1992.............................	1,007	275	27.3	166	16.5	275	27.3	291	28.9
1991.............................	1,041	276	26.5	146	14.0	316	30.4	303	29.1
1990.............................	1,079	246	22.8	178	16.5	306	28.4	349	32.3
1989.............................	1,078	239	22.2	194	18.0	343	31.8	302	28.0
1988.............................	1,057	251	23.7	189	17.9	336	31.8	281	26.6
1987.............................	1,043	213	20.4	166	15.9	323	31.0	341	32.7
1986.............................	1,048	212	20.2	156	14.9	374	35.7	306	29.2

Note: High school graduates are people who have completed 4 years of high school or more, for 1967 to 1991. Beginning in 1992, they were people whose highest degree was a high school diploma (including equivalency) or higher.
[1]Starting in 2003 respondents could identify more than one race. Except as noted, the race data in this table from 2003 onward represent those respondents who indicated only one race category.

Table A-14. Population 18 and 19 Years Old, by School Enrollment Status, Sex, Race, and Hispanic Origin, October 1967–2016—*Continued*

(Numbers in thousands; percent; civilian noninstitutionalized population.)

Year, race, and Hispanic origin	Total	Population 18 and 19 years old							
		Still in high school	Percent	Dropped out	Percent	High school graduate only	Percent	In college	Percent
1985...........................	1,072	213	19.9	186	17.4	414	38.6	259	24.2
1984...........................	1,092	218	20.0	186	17.0	423	38.7	265	24.3
1983...........................	1,134	265	23.4	199	17.5	412	36.3	258	22.8
1982...........................	1,146	226	19.7	253	22.1	393	34.3	274	23.9
1981...........................	1,128	238	21.1	218	19.3	366	32.4	306	27.1
1980...........................	1,081	211	19.5	229	21.2	358	33.1	283	26.2
1979...........................	1,072	221	20.6	246	22.9	326	30.4	279	26.0
1978...........................	1,065	221	20.8	258	24.2	316	29.7	270	25.4
1977...........................	1,072	249	23.2	235	21.9	319	29.8	269	25.1
1976...........................	1,055	230	21.8	211	20.0	312	29.6	302	28.6
1975...........................	1,030	225	21.8	262	25.4	283	27.5	260	25.2
1974...........................	1,004	209	20.8	235	23.4	327	32.6	233	23.2
1973...........................	997	182	18.3	252	25.3	369	37.0	194	19.5
1972...........................	958	181	18.9	229	23.9	319	33.3	229	23.9
1971...........................	908	219	24.1	219	24.1	266	29.3	204	22.5
1970...........................	878	161	18.3	274	31.2	252	28.7	191	21.8
1969...........................	837	179	21.4	227	27.1	238	28.4	193	23.1
1968...........................	830	195	23.5	202	24.3	251	30.2	182	21.9
1967...........................	780	175	22.4	203	26.0	261	33.5	141	18.1
Male									
2016...........................	612	193	31.5	56	9.2	148	24.2	215	35.1
2015...........................	606	155	25.5	49	8.0	173	28.6	229	37.8
2014...........................	617	197	31.9	56	9.1	189	30.6	175	28.4
2013...........................	646	201	31.1	58	8.9	201	31.1	186	28.9
2012...........................	673	201	29.9	87	12.9	179	26.6	206	30.6
2011...........................	645	226	35.0	39	6.0	138	21.4	242	37.6
2010...........................	654	159	24.4	83	12.6	174	26.5	238	36.4
2009...........................	659	174	26.4	102	15.5	158	24.0	225	34.1
2008...........................	653	173	26.5	53	8.1	222	34.0	205	31.4
2007...........................	628	161	25.7	54	8.6	186	29.6	227	36.2
2006...........................	600	210	35.0	42	7.0	174	29.0	174	28.9
2005...........................	552	178	32.2	60	10.9	121	21.9	193	35.0
2004...........................	519	137	26.4	91	17.6	126	24.3	165	31.7
2003[1]...........................	502	143	28.5	77	15.3	116	23.1	166	33.1
2002...........................	608	155	25.5	123	20.2	151	24.8	179	29.4
2001...........................	624	179	28.7	97	15.5	169	27.1	179	28.7
2000...........................	593	148	25.0	105	17.7	177	29.8	163	27.5
1999...........................	586	144	24.6	97	16.6	136	23.2	209	35.7
1998...........................	613	163	26.6	128	20.9	128	20.9	194	31.6
1997...........................	554	172	31.0	90	16.2	150	27.1	142	25.6
1996...........................	564	167	29.6	90	16.0	162	28.7	145	25.7
1995...........................	519	162	31.2	94	18.1	118	22.7	145	27.9
1994...........................	497	134	27.0	116	23.3	115	23.1	132	26.6
1993...........................	517	181	35.0	53	10.3	135	26.1	148	28.6
1992...........................	499	180	36.1	82	16.4	114	22.8	123	24.6
1991...........................	504	176	34.9	62	12.3	129	25.6	137	27.2
1990...........................	520	152	29.2	80	15.4	124	23.8	164	31.5
1989...........................	516	137	26.6	90	17.4	163	31.6	126	24.4
1988...........................	510	145	28.4	92	18.0	165	32.4	108	21.2
1987...........................	501	140	27.9	80	16.0	127	25.3	154	30.7
1986...........................	506	149	29.4	74	14.6	165	32.6	118	23.3
1985...........................	518	135	26.1	92	17.8	170	32.8	121	23.4
1984...........................	524	143	27.3	103	19.7	166	31.7	112	21.4
1983...........................	539	158	29.3	106	19.7	182	33.8	93	17.3
1982...........................	549	132	24.0	145	26.4	148	27.0	124	22.6
1981...........................	538	145	27.0	102	19.0	158	29.4	133	24.7
1980...........................	503	118	23.5	114	22.7	173	34.4	98	19.5
1979...........................	497	128	25.8	122	24.5	137	27.6	110	22.1
1978...........................	493	135	27.4	127	25.8	117	23.7	114	23.1
1977...........................	496	161	32.5	118	23.8	127	25.6	90	18.1
1976...........................	499	153	30.7	96	19.2	129	25.9	121	24.2
1975...........................	476	127	26.7	132	27.7	106	22.3	111	23.3
1974...........................	474	116	24.5	128	27.0	128	27.0	102	21.5
1973...........................	467	106	22.7	130	27.8	135	28.9	96	20.6
1972...........................	445	110	24.7	121	27.2	112	25.2	102	22.9
1971...........................	423	120	28.4	110	26.0	99	23.4	94	22.2
1970...........................	414	98	23.7	151	36.5	92	22.2	73	17.6
1969...........................	394	109	27.7	124	31.5	75	19.0	86	21.8

Note: High school graduates are people who have completed 4 years of high school or more, for 1967 to 1991. Beginning in 1992, they were people whose highest degree was a high school diploma (including equivalency) or higher.
[1]Starting in 2003 respondents could identify more than one race. Except as noted, the race data in this table from 2003 onward represent those respondents who indicated only one race category.

Table A-14. Population 18 and 19 Years Old, by School Enrollment Status, Sex, Race, and Hispanic Origin, October 1967–2016—*Continued*

(Numbers in thousands; percent; civilian noninstitutionalized population.)

| Year, race, and Hispanic origin | Total | Population 18 and 19 years old | | | | | | | |
		Still in high school	Percent	Dropped out	Percent	High school graduate only	Percent	In college	Percent
1968	390	124	31.8	93	23.8	90	23.1	83	21.3
1967	356	95	26.7	109	30.6	74	20.8	78	21.9
Female									
2016	631	112	17.8	31	4.9	173	27.4	316	50.0
2015	627	131	20.9	36	5.7	180	28.8	280	44.6
2014	635	110	17.4	38	6.0	152	24.0	334	52.7
2013	659	186	28.2	35	5.2	174	26.4	265	40.1
2012	683	195	28.5	23	3.4	136	20.0	325	47.6
2011	671	170	25.4	21	3.1	143	21.3	337	50.3
2010	682	111	16.3	61	9.0	181	26.5	329	48.2
2009	687	145	21.1	78	11.3	130	19.0	334	48.6
2008	681	138	20.3	92	13.5	178	26.1	274	40.2
2007	655	139	21.2	58	8.8	194	29.6	265	40.4
2006	631	122	19.3	60	9.6	158	25.0	291	46.1
2005	574	78	13.6	49	8.6	189	32.9	258	44.9
2004	593	81	13.7	70	11.9	167	28.2	275	46.5
2003[1]	550	133	24.2	51	9.3	157	28.5	209	38.0
2002	574	97	16.9	57	9.9	169	29.4	251	43.7
2001	623	122	19.6	54	8.7	182	29.2	265	42.5
2000	658	113	17.2	82	12.5	172	26.1	291	44.2
1999	613	114	18.6	94	15.3	184	30.0	221	36.1
1998	633	127	20.1	96	15.2	143	22.6	267	42.2
1997	579	107	18.5	82	14.2	152	26.3	238	41.1
1996	597	102	17.1	85	14.2	211	35.3	199	33.3
1995	581	126	21.7	83	14.3	173	29.8	199	34.3
1994	520	105	20.2	83	16.0	154	29.6	178	34.2
1993	523	108	20.7	80	15.3	172	32.9	163	31.2
1992	508	95	18.7	84	16.5	161	31.7	168	33.1
1991	537	99	18.4	85	15.8	187	34.8	166	30.9
1990	559	95	17.0	98	17.5	181	32.4	185	33.1
1989	562	102	18.1	104	18.5	180	32.0	176	31.3
1988	547	105	19.2	97	17.7	172	31.4	173	31.6
1987	542	75	13.8	85	15.7	196	36.2	186	34.3
1986	542	62	11.4	83	15.3	209	38.6	188	34.7
1985	554	78	14.1	94	17.0	244	44.0	138	24.9
1984	568	76	13.4	82	14.4	257	45.2	153	26.9
1983	595	108	18.2	93	15.6	230	38.7	164	27.6
1982	597	95	15.9	108	18.1	244	40.9	150	25.1
1981	590	93	15.8	116	19.7	209	35.4	172	29.2
1980	578	93	16.1	115	19.9	185	32.0	185	32.0
1979	576	93	16.1	125	21.7	189	32.8	169	29.3
1978	572	88	15.4	130	22.7	199	34.8	155	27.1
1977	576	88	15.3	117	20.3	192	33.3	179	31.1
1976	556	77	13.8	115	20.7	183	32.9	181	32.6
1975	553	97	17.5	130	23.5	176	31.8	150	27.1
1974	530	92	17.4	107	20.2	200	37.7	131	24.7
1973	530	77	14.5	122	23.0	234	44.2	97	18.3
1972	513	71	13.8	108	21.1	207	40.4	127	24.8
1971	485	100	20.6	109	22.5	167	34.4	109	22.5
1970	464	62	13.4	124	26.7	160	34.5	118	25.4
1969	443	70	15.8	102	23.0	163	36.8	108	24.4
1968	439	69	15.7	109	24.8	161	36.7	100	22.8
1967	424	81	19.1	93	21.9	187	44.1	63	14.9
ASIAN ALONE[2]									
Both Sexes									
2016	405	57	14.1	16	4.1	76	18.9	255	63.0
2015	358	65	18.1	17	4.7	41	11.5	235	65.6
2014	352	40	11.3	*	*	42	11.9	270	76.8
2013	442	68	15.5	4	0.9	68	15.3	302	68.3
2012	388	61	15.7	23	5.8	51	13.1	253	65.3
2011	337	44	13.2	13	3.7	40	11.8	240	71.3
2010	331	38	11.5	12	3.7	46	14.0	234	70.8
2009	327	64	19.7	2	0.7	17	5.2	243	74.4
2008	259	49	19.0	7	2.7	31	12.0	172	66.4
2007	296	55	18.4	12	4.2	27	9.3	201	68.1
2006	297	43	14.4	9	3.0	41	14.0	204	68.6

Note: High school graduates are people who have completed 4 years of high school or more, for 1967 to 1991. Beginning in 1992, they were people whose highest degree was a high school diploma (including equivalency) or higher.
[1]Starting in 2003 respondents could identify more than one race. Except as noted, the race data in this table from 2003 onward represent those respondents who indicated only one race category.
[2]The data shown prior to 2003 consists of those identifying themselves as "Asian or Pacific Islanders."
* = Quantity zero or rounds to zero.

Table A-14. Population 18 and 19 Years Old, by School Enrollment Status, Sex, Race, and Hispanic Origin, October 1967–2016—*Continued*

(Numbers in thousands; percent; civilian noninstitutionalized population.)

Year, race, and Hispanic origin	Total	Population 18 and 19 years old							
		Still in high school	Percent	Dropped out	Percent	High school graduate only	Percent	In college	Percent
2005............	251	34	13.4	4	1.5	25	10.0	188	74.9
2004............	257	31	11.9	10	3.8	34	13.2	182	70.7
2003[1]...........	286	41	14.3	3	1.0	33	11.5	209	73.1
2002............	353	42	11.9	14	4.0	61	17.3	236	66.9
2001............	353	50	14.2	18	5.1	38	10.8	247	70.0
2000............	326	45	13.8	17	5.2	52	16.0	212	65.0
1999............	339	43	12.7	22	6.5	51	15.0	223	65.8
Male									
2016............	215	27	12.6	10	4.4	44	20.5	135	62.5
2015............	178	31	17.4	14	8.0	20	11.5	112	63.1
2014............	177	19	11.0	*	*	22	12.5	136	76.5
2013............	230	37	16.2	1	0.3	38	16.7	154	66.9
2012............	200	37	18.7	14	7.1	20	9.7	129	64.5
2011............	178	28	15.4	*	*	19	10.8	131	73.7
2010............	170	16	9.6	8	5.0	30	17.4	116	68.1
2009............	178	31	17.6	*	*	13	7.4	134	75.0
2008............	128	39	30.2	6	5.1	8	5.9	75	58.9
2007............	150	33	22.1	2	1.1	11	7.1	104	69.7
2006............	167	20	12.2	8	4.7	26	15.7	113	67.5
2005............	131	21	16.3	3	2.0	17	13.0	90	68.9
2004............	133	22	16.7	1	0.7	18	13.5	92	69.3
2003[1]...........	129	14	10.9	3	2.3	9	7.0	103	79.8
2002............	179	22	12.3	10	5.6	26	14.5	121	67.6
2001............	168	27	16.1	14	8.3	14	8.3	113	67.3
2000............	162	14	8.6	14	8.6	26	16.0	108	66.7
1999............	156	23	14.7	17	10.9	23	14.7	93	59.6
Female									
2016............	189	30	15.7	7	3.6	32	17.0	120	63.6
2015............	180	34	18.7	3	1.5	21	11.6	123	68.2
2014............	175	20	11.6	*	*	20	11.3	134	77.0
2013............	212	31	14.8	3	1.6	29	13.8	148	69.8
2012............	188	24	12.6	8	4.5	32	16.8	124	66.2
2011............	158	17	10.7	13	7.9	20	12.8	109	68.6
2010............	161	22	13.6	4	2.4	17	10.4	118	73.6
2009............	149	33	22.2	2	1.6	4	2.7	109	73.6
2008............	132	11	8.0	*	0.4	24	17.9	97	73.7
2007............	146	21	14.6	11	7.5	17	11.5	97	66.4
2006............	130	23	17.3	1	0.9	15	11.8	91	70.0
2005............	120	12	10.3	1	0.9	9	7.5	98	81.4
2004............	124	8	6.8	9	7.1	18	14.5	89	72.2
2003[1]...........	157	26	16.6	*	*	24	15.3	107	68.2
2002............	173	20	11.6	3	1.7	35	20.2	115	66.5
2001............	185	23	12.4	4	2.2	24	13.0	134	72.4
2000............	164	30	18.3	4	2.4	26	15.9	104	63.4
1999............	183	20	10.9	5	2.7	28	15.3	130	71.0
HISPANIC (OF ANY RACE)									
Both Sexes									
2016............	1,825	364	19.9	146	8.0	430	23.6	884	48.5
2015............	1,760	372	21.1	181	10.3	432	24.5	776	44.1
2014............	1,908	377	19.8	183	9.6	491	25.7	857	44.9
2013............	1,889	393	20.8	184	9.7	585	31.0	727	38.5
2012............	1,871	445	23.8	222	11.9	374	20.0	827	44.2
2011............	1,743	371	21.3	166	9.5	441	25.3	765	43.9
2010............	1,768	389	22.0	179	10.1	418	23.6	783	44.3
2009............	1,680	409	24.3	261	15.5	460	27.4	550	32.7
2008............	1,539	320	20.8	296	19.3	395	25.7	528	34.3
2007............	1,523	311	20.4	254	16.7	399	26.2	559	36.7
2006............	1,406	307	21.8	253	18.0	402	28.6	444	31.6
2005............	1,253	272	21.7	227	18.1	348	27.8	406	32.4
2004............	1,270	244	19.2	296	23.3	346	27.2	384	30.2
2003[1]...........	1,214	229	18.9	291	24.0	315	25.9	379	31.2
2002............	1,309	303	23.1	310	23.7	336	25.7	360	27.5
2001............	1,391	246	17.7	399	28.7	359	25.8	387	27.8
2000............	1,248	268	21.5	311	24.9	320	25.6	349	28.0

Note: High school graduates are people who have completed 4 years of high school or more, for 1967 to 1991. Beginning in 1992, they were people whose highest degree was a high school diploma (including equivalency) or higher.

[1]Starting in 2003 respondents could identify more than one race. Except as noted, the race data in this table from 2003 onward represent those respondents who indicated only one race category.

* = Quantity zero or rounds to zero.

Table A-14. Population 18 and 19 Years Old, by School Enrollment Status, Sex, Race, and Hispanic Origin, October 1967–2016—*Continued*

(Numbers in thousands; percent; civilian noninstitutionalized population.)

Year, race, and Hispanic origin	Total	Population 18 and 19 years old							
		Still in high school	Percent	Dropped out	Percent	High school graduate only	Percent	In college	Percent
1999	1,220	246	20.2	337	27.6	340	27.9	297	24.3
1998	1,209	199	16.5	402	33.3	320	26.5	288	23.8
1997	1,087	221	20.3	274	25.2	276	25.4	316	29.1
1996	1,000	229	22.9	295	29.5	236	23.6	240	24.0
1995	1,012	203	20.1	312	30.8	233	23.0	264	26.1
1994	925	250	27.0	237	25.6	213	23.0	225	24.3
1993	710	159	22.4	201	28.3	155	21.8	195	27.5
1992	778	188	24.2	197	25.3	163	21.0	230	29.6
1991	823	206	25.0	269	32.7	160	19.4	188	22.8
1990	746	181	24.3	255	34.2	162	21.7	148	19.8
1989	733	150	20.5	205	28.0	201	27.4	177	24.1
1988	734	121	16.5	229	31.2	181	24.7	203	27.7
1987	699	121	17.3	195	27.9	231	33.0	152	21.7
1986	614	114	18.6	164	26.7	171	27.9	165	26.9
1985	570	111	19.5	175	30.7	157	27.5	127	22.3
1984	561	88	15.7	146	26.0	191	34.0	136	24.2
1983	573	119	20.8	166	29.0	154	26.9	134	23.4
1982	600	92	15.3	198	33.0	167	27.8	143	23.8
1981	606	100	16.5	220	36.3	157	25.9	129	21.3
1980	597	89	14.9	233	39.0	138	23.1	137	22.9
1979	507	78	15.4	157	31.0	148	29.2	124	24.5
1978	478	61	12.8	183	38.3	125	26.2	109	22.8
1977	515	86	16.7	168	32.6	138	26.8	123	23.9
1976	534	98	18.4	164	30.7	129	24.2	143	26.8
1975	489	97	19.8	147	30.1	127	26.0	118	24.1
1974	467	99	21.2	139	29.8	117	25.1	112	24.0
1973	387	70	18.1	142	36.7	93	24.0	82	21.2
1972	381	88	23.1	117	30.7	106	27.8	70	18.4
Male									
2016	894	210	23.4	90	10.0	212	23.7	383	42.8
2015	849	194	22.8	108	12.8	232	27.3	315	37.1
2014	958	206	21.5	105	10.9	263	27.4	385	40.2
2013	953	233	24.4	98	10.3	326	34.2	295	31.0
2012	950	252	26.5	143	15.1	183	19.2	372	39.2
2011	952	229	24.1	102	10.7	269	28.3	351	36.9
2010	896	201	22.4	97	10.9	217	24.2	381	42.5
2009	853	200	23.4	129	15.2	282	33.0	242	28.4
2008	779	190	24.4	141	18.1	212	27.2	236	30.3
2007	780	185	23.7	145	18.5	205	26.3	246	31.5
2006	708	152	21.4	150	21.2	193	27.3	213	30.1
2005	663	166	25.1	144	21.7	180	27.1	173	26.2
2004	668	117	17.5	214	32.0	166	24.9	171	25.6
2003	635	142	22.4	161	25.4	179	28.2	153	24.1
2002	716	191	26.7	200	27.9	169	23.6	156	21.8
2001	701	131	18.7	254	36.2	167	23.8	149	21.3
2000	656	154	23.5	183	27.9	159	24.2	160	24.4
1999	642	148	23.1	180	28.0	171	26.6	143	22.3
1998	598	104	17.4	234	39.1	163	27.3	97	16.2
1997	579	130	22.5	162	28.0	154	26.6	133	23.0
1996	506	139	27.5	154	30.4	115	22.7	98	19.4
1995	535	132	24.7	145	27.1	137	25.6	121	22.6
1994	454	157	34.6	118	26.0	90	19.8	89	19.6
1993	325	86	26.5	105	32.3	65	20.0	69	21.2
1992	385	110	28.6	99	25.7	83	21.6	93	24.2
1991	416	107	25.7	161	38.7	80	19.2	68	16.3
1990	358	76	21.2	141	39.4	71	19.8	70	19.6
1989	371	89	24.0	96	25.9	111	29.9	75	20.2
1988	364	88	24.2	128	35.2	73	20.1	75	20.6
1987	333	66	19.8	105	31.5	86	25.8	76	22.8
1986	326	58	17.8	95	29.1	86	26.4	87	26.7
1985	275	62	22.5	116	42.2	53	19.3	44	16.0
1984	249	55	22.1	65	26.1	87	34.9	42	16.9
1983	266	66	24.8	87	32.7	72	27.1	41	15.4
1982	304	69	22.7	106	34.9	77	25.3	52	17.1
1981	288	47	16.3	127	44.1	57	19.8	57	19.8
1980	310	46	14.8	134	43.2	62	20.0	68	21.9
1979	256	42	16.4	89	34.8	58	22.7	67	26.2
1978	221	35	15.8	81	36.7	52	23.5	53	24.0
1977	238	49	20.6	80	33.6	55	23.1	54	22.7
1976	258	51	19.8	82	31.8	56	21.7	69	26.7
1975	229	66	28.8	60	26.2	50	21.8	53	23.1

Note: High school graduates are people who have completed 4 years of high school or more, for 1967 to 1991. Beginning in 1992, they were people whose highest degree was a high school diploma (including equivalency) or higher.

Table A-14. Population 18 and 19 Years Old, by School Enrollment Status, Sex, Race, and Hispanic Origin, October 1967–2016—*Continued*

(Numbers in thousands; percent; civilian noninstitutionalized population.)

Year, race, and Hispanic origin	Total	Population 18 and 19 years old							
		Still in high school	Percent	Dropped out	Percent	High school graduate only	Percent	In college	Percent
1974..........................	222	49	22.1	78	35.1	40	18.0	55	24.8
1973..........................	190	48	25.3	62	32.6	41	21.6	39	20.5
1972..........................	190	49	25.8	67	35.3	46	24.2	28	14.7
Female									
2016..........................	930	154	16.6	56	6.1	218	23.5	501	53.9
2015..........................	912	179	19.6	72	7.9	200	21.9	461	50.5
2014..........................	950	172	18.1	78	8.2	228	24.0	472	49.7
2013..........................	936	160	17.1	86	9.1	259	27.6	432	46.2
2012..........................	921	193	21.0	79	8.6	191	20.7	454	49.3
2011..........................	791	142	17.9	64	8.1	172	21.7	414	52.4
2010..........................	872	188	21.5	82	9.4	201	23.0	402	46.1
2009..........................	827	209	25.3	132	15.9	179	21.6	308	37.2
2008..........................	760	130	17.1	156	20.5	183	24.0	292	38.4
2007..........................	743	126	17.0	109	14.7	193	26.1	313	42.2
2006..........................	698	156	22.3	102	14.7	209	30.0	231	33.1
2005..........................	591	105	17.8	83	14.0	171	28.9	232	39.3
2004..........................	602	127	21.1	82	13.6	180	29.9	213	35.4
2003..........................	579	87	15.0	130	22.5	136	23.5	226	39.0
2002..........................	593	112	18.9	110	18.5	167	28.2	204	34.4
2001..........................	691	116	16.8	145	21.0	192	27.8	238	34.4
2000..........................	591	114	19.3	128	21.7	161	27.2	188	31.8
1999..........................	577	99	17.2	157	27.2	168	29.1	153	26.5
1998..........................	611	95	15.5	169	27.7	156	25.5	191	31.3
1997..........................	508	91	17.9	112	22.0	122	24.0	183	36.0
1996..........................	494	91	18.4	140	28.3	121	24.5	142	28.7
1995..........................	478	71	14.9	167	34.9	97	20.3	143	29.9
1994..........................	471	93	19.7	119	25.3	123	26.1	136	28.9
1993..........................	385	74	19.2	96	24.9	89	23.1	126	32.7
1992..........................	393	78	19.8	98	24.9	80	20.4	137	34.9
1991..........................	407	98	24.1	109	26.8	80	19.7	120	29.5
1990..........................	388	105	27.1	114	29.4	91	23.5	78	20.1
1989..........................	362	60	16.6	108	29.8	91	25.1	103	28.5
1988..........................	370	32	8.6	101	27.3	108	29.2	129	34.9
1987..........................	367	58	15.8	89	24.3	144	39.2	76	20.7
1986..........................	288	54	18.8	69	24.0	86	29.9	79	27.4
1985..........................	296	51	17.2	59	19.9	104	35.1	82	27.7
1984..........................	311	33	10.6	81	26.0	103	33.1	94	30.2
1983..........................	307	53	17.3	79	25.7	82	26.7	93	30.3
1982..........................	296	23	7.8	92	31.1	90	30.4	91	30.7
1981..........................	318	53	16.7	93	29.2	100	31.4	72	22.6
1980..........................	287	44	15.3	99	34.5	76	26.5	68	23.7
1979..........................	251	35	13.9	68	27.1	90	35.9	58	23.1
1978..........................	257	26	10.1	102	39.7	73	28.4	56	21.8
1977..........................	277	37	13.4	88	31.8	82	29.6	70	25.3
1976..........................	276	49	17.8	81	29.3	72	26.1	74	26.8
1975..........................	261	32	12.3	87	33.3	77	29.5	65	24.9
1974..........................	245	50	20.4	62	25.3	77	31.4	56	22.9
1973..........................	197	21	10.7	80	40.6	52	26.4	44	22.3
1972..........................	191	37	19.4	50	26.2	61	31.9	43	22.5
WHITE ALONE OR IN COMBINATION									
Both Sexes									
2016..........................	6,392	1,139	17.8	383	6.0	1,554	24.3	3,316	51.9
2015..........................	6,376	1,204	18.9	489	7.7	1,519	23.8	3,163	49.6
2014..........................	6,450	1,238	19.2	467	7.2	1,592	24.7	3,154	48.9
2013..........................	6,502	1,235	19.0	414	6.4	1,728	26.6	3,124	48.0
2012..........................	6,539	1,306	20.0	437	6.7	1,627	24.9	3,144	48.1
2011..........................	6,686	1,309	19.6	455	6.8	1,540	23.0	3,381	50.6
2010..........................	6,679	1,195	17.9	450	6.7	1,556	23.3	3,478	52.1
2009..........................	6,780	1,227	18.1	538	7.9	1,601	23.6	3,414	50.3
2008..........................	6,762	1,093	16.2	581	8.6	1,647	24.4	3,440	50.9
2007..........................	6,595	1,108	16.8	525	8.0	1,644	24.9	3,318	50.3
2006..........................	6,466	1,160	17.9	615	9.5	1,648	25.5	3,043	47.1
2005..........................	6,078	1,064	17.5	537	8.8	1,442	23.7	3,035	49.9
2004..........................	6,191	988	16.0	643	10.4	1,548	25.0	3,012	48.7
2003..........................	6,093	994	16.3	675	11.1	1,519	24.9	2,905	47.7
Male									
2016..........................	3,233	664	20.5	209	6.5	813	25.1	1,547	47.8
2015..........................	3,232	639	19.8	289	8.9	832	25.7	1,472	45.5

Note: High school graduates are people who have completed 4 years of high school or more, for 1967 to 1991. Beginning in 1992, they were people whose highest degree was a high school diploma (including equivalency) or higher.

Table A-14. Population 18 and 19 Years Old, by School Enrollment Status, Sex, Race, and Hispanic Origin, October 1967–2016—*Continued*

(Numbers in thousands; percent; civilian noninstitutionalized population.)

Year, race, and Hispanic origin	Total	Population 18 and 19 years old							
		Still in high school	Percent	Dropped out	Percent	High school graduate only	Percent	In college	Percent
2014............................	3,292	694	21.1	252	7.7	913	27.7	1,433	43.5
2013............................	3,327	743	22.3	209	6.3	943	28.3	1,433	43.1
2012............................	3,364	769	22.9	254	7.5	902	26.8	1,429	42.5
2011............................	3,457	776	22.4	247	7.1	881	25.5	1,554	44.9
2010............................	3,396	674	19.8	251	7.4	852	25.1	1,620	47.7
2009............................	3,422	665	19.4	297	8.7	925	27.0	1,535	44.9
2008............................	3,435	605	17.6	305	8.9	917	26.7	1,607	46.8
2007............................	3,350	684	20.4	284	8.5	842	25.1	1,540	46.0
2006............................	3,278	657	20.0	357	10.9	864	26.4	1,399	42.7
2005............................	3,149	692	22.0	321	10.2	358	11.4	1,778	56.5
2004............................	3,129	538	17.2	415	13.3	845	27.0	1,331	42.5
2003............................	3,078	604	19.6	390	12.7	801	26.0	1,283	41.7
Female									
2016............................	3,159	475	15.0	174	5.5	741	23.5	1,770	56.0
2015............................	3,144	565	18.0	200	6.4	687	21.9	1,691	53.8
2014............................	3,159	544	17.2	215	6.8	679	21.5	1,720	54.5
2013............................	3,174	492	15.5	206	6.5	786	24.7	1,691	53.3
2012............................	3,175	537	16.9	183	5.8	725	22.8	1,715	54.0
2011............................	3,228	533	16.5	209	6.5	659	20.4	1,828	56.6
2010............................	3,282	521	15.9	200	6.1	704	21.4	1,858	56.6
2009............................	3,358	562	16.7	242	7.2	676	20.1	1,879	55.9
2008............................	3,328	488	14.7	277	8.3	730	21.9	1,833	55.1
2007............................	3,245	424	13.1	241	7.4	801	24.7	1,779	54.8
2006............................	3,188	503	15.8	258	8.1	784	24.6	1,643	51.5
2005............................	2,929	372	12.7	216	7.4	669	22.8	1,672	57.1
2004............................	3,062	450	14.7	228	7.4	702	22.9	1,682	54.9
2003............................	3,015	390	12.9	284	9.4	719	23.8	1,622	53.8
BLACK ALONE OR IN COMBINATION									
Both Sexes									
2016............................	1,399	338	24.2	99	7.1	360	25.7	602	43.1
2015............................	1,370	326	23.8	90	6.5	394	28.8	560	40.8
2014............................	1,384	345	24.9	106	7.7	380	27.5	553	39.9
2013............................	1,420	399	28.1	101	7.1	411	29.0	509	35.9
2012............................	1,461	422	28.9	117	8.0	340	23.3	579	39.6
2011............................	1,381	409	29.6	65	4.7	292	21.2	615	44.5
2010............................	1,439	287	20.0	158	11.0	371	25.8	622	43.2
2009............................	1,450	335	23.1	191	13.1	321	22.1	604	41.7
2008............................	1,431	339	23.7	155	10.8	422	29.5	515	36.0
2007............................	1,347	306	22.7	116	8.6	395	29.3	530	39.3
2006............................	1,287	343	26.6	111	8.6	341	26.5	492	38.2
2005............................	1,195	266	22.3	112	9.4	336	28.1	481	40.2
2004............................	1,163	229	19.7	163	14.0	305	26.2	466	40.1
2003............................	1,129	288	25.5	131	11.6	310	27.5	400	35.4
Male									
2016............................	686	208	30.4	64	9.3	163	23.8	250	36.5
2015............................	661	167	25.3	49	7.4	186	28.1	259	39.2
2014............................	679	222	32.8	66	9.7	198	29.2	192	28.4
2013............................	700	206	29.4	62	8.9	222	31.7	210	30.0
2012............................	744	213	28.6	94	12.6	194	26.0	244	32.7
2011............................	681	238	35.0	44	6.5	149	21.9	250	36.6
2010............................	700	170	24.3	86	12.3	180	25.7	264	37.7
2009............................	708	182	25.8	110	15.5	171	24.1	245	34.6
2008............................	706	191	27.0	58	8.3	238	33.7	219	31.1
2007............................	657	164	25.0	56	8.5	197	30.0	240	36.5
2006............................	623	213	34.3	45	7.3	178	28.6	186	29.8
2005............................	586	187	31.8	62	10.7	136	23.2	201	34.3
2004............................	549	142	25.9	93	17.0	139	25.3	175	31.9
2003............................	525	146	27.8	81	15.4	123	23.4	175	33.3
Female									
2016............................	713	130	18.2	35	4.9	197	27.6	352	49.3
2015............................	709	159	22.4	41	5.8	209	29.5	300	42.3

Note: High school graduates are people who have completed 4 years of high school or more, for 1967 to 1991. Beginning in 1992, they were people whose highest degree was a high school diploma (including equivalency) or higher.

Table A-14. Population 18 and 19 Years Old, by School Enrollment Status, Sex, Race, and Hispanic Origin, October 1967–2016—*Continued*

(Numbers in thousands; percent; civilian noninstitutionalized population.)

Year, race, and Hispanic origin	Total	Population 18 and 19 years old							
		Still in high school	Percent	Dropped out	Percent	High school graduate only	Percent	In college	Percent
2014.............................	705	122	17.3	41	5.7	182	25.8	360	51.1
2013.............................	720	193	26.8	38	5.3	189	26.3	299	41.6
2012.............................	717	209	29.1	23	3.2	146	20.4	335	46.7
2011.............................	699	170	24.3	21	3.0	143	20.5	365	52.2
2010.............................	739	117	15.9	72	9.8	192	25.9	358	48.4
2009.............................	742	152	20.5	81	11.3	150	20.2	359	48.4
2008.............................	724	148	20.5	96	13.3	184	25.4	296	40.8
2007.............................	690	142	20.6	61	8.8	198	28.6	290	42.0
2006.............................	665	130	19.5	66	9.9	163	24.5	307	46.1
2005.............................	609	80	13.1	49	8.1	200	32.8	280	45.9
2004.............................	615	86	14.0	70	11.4	169	27.5	290	47.2
2003.............................	604	142	23.5	51	8.4	186	30.8	225	37.3
ASIAN ALONE OR IN COMBINATION									
Both Sexes									
2016.............................	487	69	14.2	17	3.6	88	18.1	313	64.2
2015.............................	430	71	16.5	24	5.6	48	11.1	287	66.8
2014.............................	407	53	13.0	*	*	58	14.1	296	72.8
2013.............................	529	89	16.7	9	1.7	81	15.4	350	66.2
2012.............................	436	71	16.4	23	5.2	67	15.4	274	63.0
2011.............................	399	55	13.6	13	3.1	66	16.4	267	66.8
2010.............................	369	39	10.5	13	3.6	53	14.4	264	71.5
2009.............................	384	74	19.3	3	0.9	35	9.0	271	70.8
2008.............................	309	52	16.8	7	2.3	37	11.8	214	69.1
2007.............................	336	58	17.2	12	3.7	34	10.0	232	69.1
2006.............................	318	47	14.8	9	2.8	47	14.9	215	67.5
2005.............................	286	42	14.7	4	1.3	36	12.6	204	71.5
2004.............................	299	36	12.0	14	4.5	46	15.4	203	67.9
2003.............................	320	43	13.4	3	1.1	38	11.9	236	73.8
Male									
2016.............................	244	27	11.2	10	3.9	48	19.8	159	65.2
2015.............................	213	32	15.1	18	8.3	22	10.3	141	66.3
2014.............................	206	29	14.3	*	*	30	14.8	146	71.0
2013.............................	265	48	18.0	1	0.2	46	17.3	171	64.5
2012.............................	225	42	18.6	14	6.3	26	11.4	143	63.7
2011.............................	214	33	15.5	*	*	36	16.7	145	67.9
2010.............................	196	17	8.6	9	4.6	34	17.2	136	69.5
2009.............................	188	34	18.3	1	0.3	16	8.3	138	73.2
2008.............................	150	41	27.6	6	4.3	9	6.0	93	62.1
2007.............................	161	33	20.7	2	1.0	14	8.4	113	69.9
2006.............................	179	22	12.4	8	4.3	31	17.5	118	65.8
2005.............................	152	30	19.5	3	1.7	22	14.5	97	64.1
2004.............................	149	27	18.1	5	3.2	20	13.4	97	65.1
2003.............................	144	17	11.8	3	2.3	12	8.3	112	77.8
Female									
2016.............................	243	42	17.2	8	3.2	40	16.3	153	63.3
2015.............................	217	39	18.0	6	2.9	26	11.9	146	67.3
2014.............................	201	24	11.8	*	*	27	13.5	150	74.7
2013.............................	263	41	15.5	8	3.1	35	13.4	179	68.0
2012.............................	210	30	14.1	8	4.0	41	19.7	131	62.2
2011.............................	186	21	11.6	13	6.8	30	16.1	122	65.6
2010.............................	174	22	12.6	4	2.5	20	11.3	128	73.7
2009.............................	196	40	20.4	3	1.5	19	9.7	134	68.4
2008.............................	159	11	6.6	*	0.3	28	17.3	121	75.8
2007.............................	174	24	13.9	11	6.3	20	11.5	119	68.3
2006.............................	139	25	18.0	1	0.8	16	11.4	97	69.7
2005.............................	134	12	9.2	1	0.9	14	10.4	107	80.0
2004.............................	150	8	5.3	9	5.9	27	18.0	106	70.7
2003.............................	176	25	14.2	*	*	27	15.3	124	70.5

Note: High school graduates are people who have completed 4 years of high school or more, for 1967 to 1991. Beginning in 1992, they were people whose highest degree was a high school diploma (including equivalency) or higher.
* = Quantity zero or rounds to zero.

Table A-15. Age Distribution of College Students 14 Years Old and Over, by Sex, Selected Years, October 1947–2016

(Numbers in thousands; civilian noninstitutionalized population.)

Year, sex, race, and Hispanic origin	All students								Male							
	Total	14 to 17 years	18 and 19 years	20 and 21 years	22 to 24 years	25 to 29 years	30 to 34 years	35 years and over	Total	14 to 17 years	18 and 19 years	20 and 21 years	22 to 24 years	25 to 29 years	30 to 34 years	35 years and over
ALL RACES																
2016	19,196	241	4,171	4,417	3,733	2,882	1,336	2,417	8,644	80	1,944	2,085	1,771	1,264	574	927
2015	19,101	222	3,978	4,505	3,669	2,805	1,370	2,551	8,484	108	1,838	2,113	1,743	1,238	565	878
2014	19,175	234	4,036	4,218	3,878	2,722	1,267	2,820	8,629	126	1,779	2,090	1,808	1,283	509	1,036
2013	19,467	308	3,951	4,326	3,925	2,715	1,351	2,891	8,536	148	1,809	2,001	1,819	1,253	522	983
2012	19,930	269	4,015	4,562	3,879	2,817	1,516	2,871	8,602	130	1,803	2,049	1,878	1,194	576	971
2011	20,397	203	4,242	4,459	3,869	3,066	1,551	3,007	9,132	108	1,949	2,127	1,877	1,343	643	1,084
2010	20,275	229	4,364	4,348	3,501	2,992	1,632	3,210	9,007	94	2,009	2,108	1,580	1,396	659	1,160
2009	19,764	206	4,289	4,034	3,749	2,769	1,524	3,193	8,642	89	1,928	1,943	1,770	1,194	649	1,069
2008	18,632	241	4,126	3,920	3,420	2,657	1,356	2,911	8,311	133	1,909	1,908	1,566	1,229	577	989
2007	17,956	186	4,075	3,794	3,292	2,496	1,342	2,772	7,826	76	1,903	1,729	1,524	1,029	596	968
2006	17,232	212	3,746	3,675	3,166	2,312	1,346	2,776	7,506	79	1,703	1,682	1,489	1,033	537	982
2005	17,472	181	3,727	3,945	3,162	2,291	1,309	2,857	7,539	62	1,675	1,878	1,420	923	562	1,019
2004	17,383	198	3,685	3,777	3,149	2,403	1,287	2,884	7,575	75	1,610	1,811	1,444	1,068	533	1,033
2003[1]	16,638	150	3,512	3,533	3,320	2,164	1,330	2,630	7,318	61	1,568	1,551	1,578	982	607	970
2002	16,497	195	3,581	3,525	2,927	2,093	1,308	2,867	7,240	80	1,635	1,640	1,354	918	542	1,071
2001	15,873	138	3,478	3,421	2,731	2,084	1,337	2,685	6,875	54	1,570	1,579	1,287	917	559	908
2000	15,314	149	3,599	3,169	2,683	1,962	1,244	2,507	6,682	61	1,570	1,472	1,300	844	517	918
1999	15,203	151	3,520	3,120	2,620	1,940	1,155	2,697	6,956	78	1,648	1,525	1,224	911	547	1,023
1998	15,546	123	3,670	3,092	2,561	2,148	1,266	2,685	6,905	48	1,667	1,517	1,219	979	521	953
1997	15,436	171	3,362	3,143	2,699	2,154	1,116	2,791	6,843	59	1,561	1,521	1,292	1,052	457	899
1996	15,226	237	3,309	2,907	2,551	2,215	1,228	2,778	6,820	97	1,489	1,379	1,319	1,038	485	1,013
1995	14,715	158	3,101	2,940	2,498	2,143	1,206	2,669	6,703	68	1,431	1,423	1,235	1,008	553	985
1994[2]	15,022	150	3,051	3,028	2,650	2,026	1,393	2,725	6,764	65	1,416	1,414	1,322	972	617	958
1993[r]	14,394	130	3,070	2,892	2,668	1,914	1,226	2,493	6,599	55	1,407	1,405	1,425	892	534	880
1993	13,898	123	2,926	2,734	2,533	1,867	1,227	2,488	6,324	52	1,337	1,312	1,345	872	534	873
1992	14,035	205	2,892	2,938	2,512	1,829	1,296	2,364	6,192	97	1,325	1,344	1,243	845	547	789
1991	14,057	132	2,929	2,939	2,304	1,983	1,302	2,468	6,439	49	1,326	1,390	1,238	1,018	587	832
1990	13,621	178	3,019	2,767	2,178	1,927	1,235	2,319	6,192	86	1,443	1,364	1,115	910	502	772
1989	13,180	183	3,066	2,570	2,168	1,889	1,192	2,112	5,950	73	1,422	1,228	1,067	926	517	716
1988	13,116	182	3,046	2,681	2,064	1,735	1,228	2,179	5,950	58	1,365	1,295	1,110	835	560	727
1987	12,719	239	3,045	2,642	2,006	1,826	1,159	1,802	6,030	116	1,483	1,350	1,034	921	500	625
1986	12,651	201	2,967	2,374	2,136	1,860	1,245	1,867	5,957	82	1,421	1,161	1,120	968	577	628
1985	12,524	262	2,907	2,616	2,014	1,884	1,180	1,661	5,906	131	1,349	1,313	1,087	942	522	561
1984	12,304	253	2,867	2,597	2,127	1,857	1,158	1,445	5,989	91	1,373	1,337	1,219	965	527	476
1983	12,320	260	2,940	2,495	2,042	1,921	1,167	1,495	6,010	108	1,340	1,310	1,170	1,055	521	506
1982	12,308	254	2,929	2,689	2,060	1,859	1,129	1,389	5,899	112	1,376	1,346	1,115	968	492	490
1981	12,127	232	3,044	2,545	1,986	1,717	1,211	1,393	5,825	96	1,450	1,239	1,144	909	533	453
1980	11,387	249	2,933	2,423	1,870	1,641	1,062	1,207	5,430	96	1,369	1,246	989	853	472	405
1979	11,380	311	2,844	2,353	1,794	1,679	996	1,402	5,480	129	1,341	1,192	975	893	463	487
1978	11,141	274	2,899	2,298	1,798	1,619	950	1,303	5,580	106	1,391	1,202	1,028	922	474	457
1977	11,546	274	2,913	2,430	1,799	1,809	992	1,329	5,889	112	1,396	1,280	1,036	1,035	511	520
1976	11,139	281	2,937	2,398	1,846	1,686	803	1,189	5,785	105	1,391	1,209	1,073	1,067	451	489
1975	10,880	293	2,943	2,313	1,679	1,616	853	1,183	5,911	128	1,426	1,256	1,011	1,025	496	569
1974	9,852	309	2,597	2,192	1,527	1,482	720	1,025	5,402	145	1,262	1,206	943	951	420	476
1973	8,966	295	2,517	2,073	1,465	1,278	551	787	5,048	121	1,293	1,130	937	867	329	371
1972	9,096	295	2,680	2,116	1,461	1,229	531	783	5,218	141	1,366	1,170	998	848	330	365
1971	8,087	284	2,726	1,997	1,487	1,067	527	NA	4,850	129	1,444	1,090	1,065	787	334	NA
1970	7,413	260	2,594	1,857	1,354	939	410	NA	4,401	130	1,346	1,083	902	684	256	NA
1969	7,435	242	2,601	1,945	1,294	918	435	NA	4,448	120	1,397	1,112	883	671	265	NA
1968	6,801	281	2,501	1,826	1,029	790	373	NA	4,124	134	1,357	1,093	702	603	236	NA
1967	6,401	239	2,286	1,816	998	707	356	NA	3,841	96	1,198	1,066	718	524	239	NA
1966	6,085	254	2,440	1,472	987	679	254	NA	3,749	105	1,355	899	722	494	174	NA
1965	5,675	264	2,215	1,326	940	614	316	NA	3,503	113	1,218	804	699	458	211	NA
1964	4,643	291	1,616	1,287	670	523	256	NA	2,888	165	866	769	510	396	182	NA
1963	4,336	180	1,504	1,212	717	482	241	NA	2,742	99	796	734	574	365	174	NA
1962	4,208	233	1,612	996	630	486	251	NA	2,742	125	891	617	508	406	195	NA
1961	3,731	213	1,470	892	507	437	212	NA	2,356	84	834	554	393	337	154	NA
1960	3,570	222	1,299	790	509	491	259	NA	2,339	99	734	503	411	399	193	NA
1959	3,340	210	1,175	739	489	503	224	NA	2,187	92	651	501	355	422	166	NA
1958	3,242	167	1,114	-----1,221----		534	206	NA	2,129	73	621	-----850-----		439	146	NA
1957	3,138	176	989	-----1,236----		553	184	NA	2,028	77	538	-----827-----		459	127	NA
1956	2,883	167	934	-----1,105----		494	183	NA	1,932	77	512	-----781-----		429	133	NA
1955	2,379	147	745	-------931----		406	150	NA	1,579	57	432	-----647-----		337	107	NA

NA = Not available.

[1]Starting in 2003, respondents could identify more than one race. Except as noted, the race data in this table from 2003 onward represent those respondents who indicated only one race category.

[2]Before 1994, total enrolled does not include the 35 and over population.

r = Revised, controlled to 1990 census based population estimates; previous 1993 data controlled to 1980 census based population estimates.

Table A-15. Age Distribution of College Students 14 Years Old and Over, by Sex, Selected Years, October 1947–2016—*Continued*

(Numbers in thousands; civilian noninstitutionalized population.)

Year, sex, race, and Hispanic origin				Female				
	Total	14 to 17 years	18 and 19 years	20 and 21 years	22 to 24 years	25 to 29 years	30 to 34 years	35 years and over
ALL RACES								
2016........................	10,551	161	2,227	2,331	1,962	1,618	762	1,490
2015........................	10,617	113	2,141	2,392	1,927	1,567	805	1,673
2014........................	10,546	108	2,257	2,128	2,070	1,439	758	1,784
2013........................	10,931	159	2,142	2,325	2,105	1,462	829	1,908
2012........................	11,327	139	2,212	2,513	2,001	1,623	940	1,899
2011........................	11,266	95	2,293	2,333	1,992	1,722	908	1,923
2010........................	11,268	135	2,355	2,240	1,920	1,596	973	2,049
2009........................	11,123	116	2,361	2,091	1,980	1,575	875	2,124
2008........................	10,321	108	2,217	2,013	1,854	1,428	779	1,922
2007........................	10,130	109	2,172	2,065	1,768	1,466	746	1,804
2006........................	9,726	133	2,043	1,993	1,677	1,278	809	1,793
2005........................	9,934	119	2,052	2,067	1,742	1,368	747	1,838
2004........................	9,808	123	2,074	1,966	1,705	1,335	753	1,850
2003[1].....................	9,319	89	1,944	1,982	1,742	1,181	723	1,660
2002........................	9,258	116	1,946	1,885	1,573	1,175	766	1,797
2001........................	8,998	84	1,907	1,841	1,444	1,167	778	1,776
2000........................	8,631	88	2,029	1,697	1,383	1,118	728	1,589
1999........................	8,247	73	1,872	1,595	1,396	1,029	608	1,674
1998........................	8,641	74	2,003	1,574	1,342	1,170	745	1,732
1997........................	8,593	112	1,801	1,622	1,406	1,102	658	1,892
1996........................	8,406	140	1,821	1,528	1,233	1,177	743	1,765
1995........................	8,013	90	1,671	1,518	1,263	1,135	653	1,684
1994[2].....................	8,258	85	1,635	1,613	1,328	1,054	776	1,766
1993[r].....................	7,795	75	1,663	1,487	1,243	1,022	692	1,613
1993........................	7,574	71	1,588	1,422	1,189	995	693	1,616
1992........................	7,844	107	1,566	1,594	1,269	984	748	1,575
1991........................	7,618	83	1,603	1,549	1,066	965	715	1,636
1990........................	7,429	91	1,576	1,403	1,063	1,017	732	1,546
1989........................	7,231	110	1,643	1,342	1,100	964	675	1,396
1988........................	7,166	124	1,682	1,386	953	900	668	1,452
1987........................	6,689	123	1,562	1,292	972	905	659	1,176
1986........................	6,694	120	1,546	1,213	1,016	892	667	1,240
1985........................	6,618	129	1,559	1,303	926	941	658	1,100
1984........................	6,315	161	1,494	1,260	908	892	630	970
1983........................	6,310	153	1,600	1,185	872	865	645	989
1982........................	6,410	141	1,553	1,343	945	891	637	900
1981........................	6,303	136	1,594	1,305	842	808	677	940
1980........................	5,957	153	1,565	1,178	882	788	590	802
1979........................	5,900	183	1,503	1,161	818	786	533	914
1978........................	5,559	168	1,507	1,096	770	697	476	845
1977........................	5,657	162	1,517	1,151	763	774	481	809
1976........................	5,354	176	1,546	1,189	773	619	352	700
1975........................	4,969	164	1,517	1,058	668	590	357	614
1974........................	4,449	165	1,335	986	584	531	300	548
1973........................	3,918	174	1,224	944	528	411	222	416
1972........................	3,877	153	1,314	946	464	381	200	418
1971........................	3,236	154	1,281	906	423	280	192	NA
1970........................	3,013	130	1,248	774	452	255	154	NA
1969........................	2,987	122	1,204	833	411	247	171	NA
1968........................	2,677	147	1,144	733	328	187	138	NA
1967........................	2,560	143	1,088	749	280	183	117	NA
1966........................	2,337	149	1,085	573	265	185	80	NA
1965........................	2,172	151	997	522	241	156	105	NA
1964........................	1,755	126	750	518	160	127	74	NA
1963........................	1,594	81	708	478	143	117	67	NA
1962........................	1,466	108	721	379	122	80	56	NA
1961........................	1,375	129	636	338	114	100	58	NA
1960........................	1,231	123	565	287	98	92	66	NA
1959........................	1,153	118	524	238	134	81	58	NA
1958........................	1,113	94	493	-----371-----		95	60	NA
1957........................	1,110	99	451	-----409-----		94	57	NA
1956........................	951	90	422	-----324-----		65	50	NA
1955........................	800	90	313	-----285-----		69	43	NA

NA = Not available.
[1]Starting in 2003, respondents could identify more than one race. Except as noted, the race data in this table from 2003 onward represent those respondents who indicated only one race category.
[2]Before 1994, total enrolled does not include the 35 and over population.
[r] = Revised, controlled to 1990 census based population estimates; previous 1993 data controlled to 1980 census based population estimates.

Table A-15. Age Distribution of College Students 14 Years Old and Over, by Sex, Selected Years, October 1947–2016—*Continued*

(Numbers in thousands; civilian noninstitutionalized population.)

Year, sex, race, and Hispanic origin	All students								Male							
	Total	14 to 17 years	18 and 19 years	20 and 21 years	22 to 24 years	25 to 29 years	30 to 34 years	35 years and over	Total	14 to 17 years	18 and 19 years	20 and 21 years	22 to 24 years	25 to 29 years	30 to 34 years	35 years and over
1950	2,175	180	733	------939----		324	NA	NA	1,474	74	395	-----692-----		314	NA	NA
1947	2,311	188	620	----1,088----		321	94	NA	1,687	87	343	-----872-----		301	84	NA
WHITE ALONE																
2016	13,901	166	3,170	3,289	2,647	2,041	925	1,663	6,222	55	1,470	1,549	1,247	872	385	644
2015	13,859	149	3,057	3,308	2,604	2,021	945	1,776	6,253	78	1,414	1,586	1,189	920	415	651
2014	13,953	148	3,064	3,232	2,781	1,942	888	1,898	6,398	67	1,397	1,621	1,278	927	374	733
2013	14,240	234	3,033	3,160	2,857	1,879	970	2,107	6,241	115	1,386	1,452	1,292	867	406	721
2012	14,628	204	3,077	3,427	2,798	2,048	1,002	2,072	6,392	87	1,387	1,497	1,377	892	428	725
2011	15,412	141	3,298	3,545	2,970	2,254	1,085	2,120	7,054	78	1,520	1,679	1,486	1,013	470	808
2010	15,258	154	3,398	3,297	2,629	2,217	1,197	2,366	6,883	59	1,573	1,624	1,172	1,051	511	893
2009	15,027	160	3,337	3,205	2,784	2,066	1,097	2,377	6,681	77	1,511	1,533	1,360	904	483	814
2008	14,405	171	3,353	3,119	2,669	1,952	907	2,234	6,570	85	1,566	1,524	1,250	938	413	794
2007	13,835	141	3,242	3,053	2,485	1,817	952	2,144	6,050	62	1,508	1,359	1,172	770	413	766
2006	13,273	161	2,982	2,958	2,358	1,740	985	2,090	5,829	57	1,367	1,344	1,131	799	396	734
2005	13,466	116	2,972	3,176	2,350	1,708	939	2,205	5,843	38	1,343	1,488	1,092	685	420	777
2004	13,381	134	2,946	3,016	2,389	1,776	974	2,146	5,944	49	1,308	1,437	1,110	837	421	782
2003[1]	12,870	100	2,833	2,796	2,521	1,585	960	2,075	5,714	48	1,258	1,236	1,232	723	435	783
2002	12,781	109	2,891	2,810	2,220	1,582	933	2,236	5,719	57	1,329	1,306	1,066	712	394	855
2001	12,208	88	2,755	2,774	2,019	1,514	956	2,103	5,383	36	1,273	1,305	943	693	401	731
2000	11,999	117	2,914	2,590	2,062	1,433	906	1,978	5,311	47	1,289	1,225	1,008	662	367	713
1999	12,053	87	2,849	2,520	2,077	1,475	870	2,174	5,562	33	1,336	1,226	1,024	715	414	816
1998	12,401	93	2,994	2,537	2,011	1,604	964	2,199	5,602	30	1,376	1,256	1,002	746	396	795
1997	12,442	127	2,792	2,602	2,101	1,666	856	2,298	5,552	48	1,314	1,289	1,030	802	345	725
1996	12,189	167	2,731	2,362	2,030	1,704	940	2,254	5,453	70	1,223	1,117	1,079	797	357	811
1995	12,021	116	2,577	2,437	1,997	1,745	941	2,208	5,535	44	1,195	1,201	1,002	857	432	804
1994[2]	12,222	101	2,568	2,459	2,091	1,592	1,143	2,267	5,524	44	1,212	1,140	1,054	749	512	815
1993[r]	11,735	103	2,566	2,356	2,152	1,507	1,003	2,049	5,403	44	1,157	1,196	1,145	705	451	705
1993	11,434	98	2,456	2,243	2,064	1,490	1,015	2,068	5,222	41	1,103	1,120	1,090	699	457	711
1992	11,710	158	2,419	2,466	2,031	1,512	1,070	2,053	5,210	82	1,102	1,162	1,027	689	471	678
1991	11,686	104	2,487	2,449	1,877	1,598	1,063	2,107	5,304	41	1,112	1,146	1,012	809	480	703
1990	11,488	132	2,548	2,341	1,746	1,638	1,060	2,023	5,235	63	1,218	1,151	923	782	434	665
1989	11,243	147	2,648	2,170	1,813	1,611	986	1,868	5,136	63	1,253	1,070	900	789	438	623
1988	11,140	137	2,639	2,270	1,750	1,425	1,023	1,896	5,078	50	1,194	1,114	952	685	470	613
1987	10,731	194	2,564	2,254	1,665	1,483	985	1,584	5,104	97	1,260	1,156	873	740	436	541
1986	10,707	173	2,549	2,015	1,743	1,580	1,037	1,609	5,074	69	1,254	982	932	835	475	528
1985	10,781	229	2,539	2,257	1,704	1,590	1,014	1,448	5,103	120	1,176	1,137	941	812	449	468
1984	10,520	209	2,541	2,206	1,779	1,566	967	1,252	5,111	73	1,224	1,143	1,039	796	434	402
1983	10,565	214	2,597	2,161	1,705	1,603	961	1,324	5,162	87	1,197	1,149	989	875	421	444
1982	10,551	216	2,549	2,348	1,697	1,581	938	1,222	5,077	95	1,189	1,188	931	831	415	428
1981	10,353	197	2,639	2,239	1,671	1,390	1,027	1,190	5,010	86	1,259	1,104	977	745	448	391
1980	9,925	212	2,578	2,131	1,625	1,413	915	1,051	4,804	79	1,232	1,114	878	735	400	366
1979	9,956	256	2,498	2,079	1,543	1,474	859	1,247	4,823	110	1,192	1,058	854	788	398	423
1978	9,661	229	2,553	1,993	1,531	1,399	808	1,148	4,913	90	1,239	1,056	900	810	413	405
1977	9,962	227	2,579	2,099	1,531	1,550	827	1,149	5,156	91	1,272	1,124	890	907	433	439
1976	9,679	237	2,577	2,108	1,591	1,458	673	1,035	5,084	89	1,244	1,073	933	936	382	427
1975	9,546	252	2,613	2,042	1,461	1,410	737	1,031	5,263	111	1,283	1,134	909	911	426	489
1974	8,689	271	2,308	1,940	1,341	1,308	613	908	4,782	128	1,143	1,067	825	855	350	414
1973	8,014	253	2,281	1,865	1,292	1,152	481	690	4,218	111	1,177	1,017	838	789	286	NA
1972	7,458	259	2,411	1,917	1,296	1,119	456	NA	4,395	120	1,242	1,062	891	784	296	NA
1971	7,273	251	2,485	1,758	1,351	965	463	NA	4,407	117	1,328	964	992	712	293	NA
1970	6,759	230	2,361	1,684	1,260	853	371	NA	4,066	117	1,251	995	850	622	231	NA
1969	6,827	222	2,377	1,762	1,208	855	404	NA	4,146	110	1,298	1,021	827	637	252	NA
1968	6,255	251	2,284	1,691	954	741	333	NA	3,843	117	1,262	1,021	666	564	213	NA
1967	5,905	220	2,105	1,688	915	646	329	NA	3,560	88	1,097	998	666	494	217	NA
1966	5,708	233	2,293	----2,313----		----869-----		NA	3,536	93	1,281	----1,541----		------621----		NA
1965	5,317	233	2,074	----2,139-----		----871-----		NA	3,326	104	1,152	----1,441----		------629----		NA
1964	4,337	257	1,519	----1,850-----		----711-----		NA	2,720	147	823	----1,226----		------524----		NA
1963	4,050	171	1,391	----1,817-----		----671-----		NA	2,593	94	746	----1,246----		------507----		NA
1962	3,934	217	1,509	----1,517-----		----691-----		NA	2,586	120	836	----1,066----		------564----		NA
1961	3,498	204	1,388	----1,296-----		----610-----		NA	2,208	79	786	------883----		------460----		NA
1960	3,342	214	1,211	----1,209-----		----709-----		NA	2,214	97	691	------859----		------567----		NA
1959	3,118	193	1,101	----1,134-----		----690-----		NA	2,067	88	620	------798----		------561----		NA

NA = Not available.

[1]Starting in 2003, respondents could identify more than one race. Except as noted, the race data in this table from 2003 onward represent those respondents who indicated only one race category.

[2]Before 1994, total enrolled does not include the 35 and over population.

[r] = Revised, controlled to 1990 census based population estimates; previous 1993 data controlled to 1980 census based population estimates.

Table A-15. Age Distribution of College Students 14 Years Old and Over, by Sex, Selected Years, October 1947–2016—*Continued*

(Numbers in thousands; civilian noninstitutionalized population.)

Year, sex, race, and Hispanic origin	Female							
	Total	14 to 17 years	18 and 19 years	20 and 21 years	22 to 24 years	25 to 29 years	30 to 34 years	35 years and over
1950	701	106	338	-----247-----		10	NA	NA
1947	624	101	277	-----216-----		20	10	NA
WHITE ALONE								
2016	7,678	112	1,700	1,740	1,400	1,169	540	1,019
2015	7,607	71	1,644	1,721	1,415	1,101	530	1,124
2014	7,555	81	1,667	1,611	1,502	1,015	514	1,165
2013	7,999	119	1,646	1,707	1,565	1,011	564	1,386
2012	8,236	117	1,690	1,930	1,421	1,156	574	1,347
2011	8,358	63	1,779	1,866	1,484	1,241	615	1,311
2010	8,375	95	1,825	1,673	1,458	1,166	686	1,472
2009	8,346	84	1,826	1,672	1,424	1,162	614	1,564
2008	7,835	85	1,787	1,595	1,419	1,014	493	1,440
2007	7,785	80	1,734	1,694	1,313	1,047	539	1,378
2006	7,445	104	1,615	1,613	1,227	941	588	1,355
2005	7,624	79	1,629	1,688	1,258	1,024	519	1,428
2004	7,438	86	1,638	1,579	1,279	939	553	1,364
2003[1]	7,155	53	1,575	1,560	1,289	862	525	1,291
2002	7,062	52	1,562	1,504	1,154	870	539	1,381
2001	6,826	52	1,481	1,468	1,077	820	555	1,372
2000	6,689	70	1,625	1,365	1,054	770	539	1,266
1999	6,491	55	1,513	1,296	1,053	760	455	1,359
1998	6,799	63	1,618	1,281	1,008	858	567	1,405
1997	6,890	79	1,479	1,313	1,071	864	511	1,573
1996	6,735	97	1,508	1,246	951	906	583	1,443
1995	6,486	72	1,383	1,237	995	887	508	1,404
1994[2]	6,698	57	1,357	1,320	1,037	844	631	1,453
1993[r]	6,331	59	1,409	1,160	1,007	802	552	1,344
1993	6,212	57	1,353	1,123	974	791	558	1,357
1992	6,499	76	1,317	1,303	1,005	823	599	1,376
1991	6,382	63	1,375	1,304	865	789	583	1,404
1990	6,253	69	1,331	1,190	823	856	627	1,358
1989	6,107	84	1,395	1,101	913	822	548	1,245
1988	6,063	87	1,445	1,156	798	740	554	1,283
1987	5,627	97	1,304	1,097	791	743	550	1,044
1986	5,632	105	1,295	1,033	811	745	562	1,081
1985	5,679	110	1,363	1,120	764	778	565	979
1984	5,410	136	1,317	1,063	740	770	533	851
1983	5,404	127	1,400	1,012	717	728	540	880
1982	5,472	120	1,360	1,159	766	749	523	795
1981	5,342	111	1,380	1,134	694	646	578	799
1980	5,121	133	1,346	1,017	747	678	514	686
1979	5,131	146	1,306	1,021	688	686	461	823
1978	4,748	139	1,314	937	631	590	395	742
1977	4,806	135	1,307	975	641	643	394	711
1976	4,593	147	1,334	1,034	658	521	291	608
1975	4,284	141	1,330	908	552	500	311	542
1974	3,907	143	1,166	873	516	453	263	493
1973	3,107	142	1,104	848	454	363	196	NA
1972	3,061	138	1,169	855	404	334	160	NA
1971	2,867	134	1,157	794	359	252	170	NA
1970	2,693	113	1,110	689	410	231	140	NA
1969	2,681	112	1,079	741	380	218	151	NA
1968	2,412	134	1,022	670	288	177	120	NA
1967	2,345	133	1,009	690	250	152	112	NA
1966	2,172	140	1,012	-----772-----		-----248-----		NA
1965	1,991	129	922	-----698-----		-----242-----		NA
1964	1,617	110	696	-----624-----		-----187-----		NA
1963	1,457	77	645	-----571-----		-----164-----		NA
1962	1,348	97	673	-----451-----		-----127-----		NA
1961	1,290	125	602	-----413-----		-----150-----		NA
1960	1,128	117	520	-----350-----		-----142-----		NA
1959	1,051	105	481	-----336-----		-----129-----		NA

NA = Not available.

[1]Starting in 2003, respondents could identify more than one race. Except as noted, the race data in this table from 2003 onward represent those respondents who indicated only one race category.

[2]Before 1994, total enrolled does not include the 35 and over population.

[r] = Revised, controlled to 1990 census based population estimates; previous 1993 data controlled to 1980 census based population estimates.

Table A-15. Age Distribution of College Students 14 Years Old and Over, by Sex, Selected Years, October 1947–2016—*Continued*

(Numbers in thousands; civilian noninstitutionalized population.)

Year, sex, race, and Hispanic origin	All students Total	14 to 17 years	18 and 19 years	20 and 21 years	22 to 24 years	25 to 29 years	30 to 34 years	35 years and over	Male Total	14 to 17 years	18 and 19 years	20 and 21 years	22 to 24 years	25 to 29 years	30 to 34 years	35 years and over
1958	3,030	155	1,044	----1,136-----		-----695-----		NA	1,999	68	577	------802----		------552----		NA
1957	2,932	161	921	----1,165-----		-----685-----		NA	1,938	68	510	------797----		------563----		NA
1956	2,687	152	869	----1,025-----		-----641-----		NA	1,808	68	474	------733----		------533----		NA
1955	2,224	125	715	------880-----		-----504-----		NA	1,495	47	418	------621----		------409----		NA

WHITE ALONE NON-HISPANIC

Year, sex, race, and Hispanic origin	All students Total	14 to 17 years	18 and 19 years	20 and 21 years	22 to 24 years	25 to 29 years	30 to 34 years	35 years and over	Male Total	14 to 17 years	18 and 19 years	20 and 21 years	22 to 24 years	25 to 29 years	30 to 34 years	35 years and over
2016	10,749	82	2,439	2,465	1,990	1,615	789	1,368	4,879	30	1,168	1,168	952	702	327	531
2015	10,904	106	2,368	2,517	2,053	1,593	777	1,489	4,970	54	1,121	1,234	930	744	353	534
2014	11,068	113	2,299	2,545	2,209	1,545	742	1,613	5,115	58	1,050	1,310	1,031	728	337	600
2013	11,348	193	2,379	2,456	2,230	1,529	764	1,798	4,944	97	1,124	1,135	1,001	668	322	597
2012	11,650	150	2,363	2,620	2,207	1,734	778	1,799	5,074	61	1,051	1,126	1,113	761	356	606
2011	12,703	105	2,588	2,867	2,427	1,892	936	1,888	5,731	55	1,184	1,349	1,221	817	417	689
2010	12,613	114	2,699	2,813	2,152	1,818	996	2,022	5,673	39	1,236	1,395	986	854	416	747
2009	12,826	120	2,842	2,755	2,385	1,736	913	2,074	5,709	54	1,286	1,327	1,174	765	397	706
2008	12,324	121	2,850	2,734	2,309	1,625	779	1,906	5,602	58	1,346	1,322	1,098	766	347	664
2007	11,867	104	2,739	2,677	2,117	1,509	816	1,904	5,269	45	1,298	1,223	1,021	639	370	674
2006	11,485	114	2,564	2,606	2,030	1,494	830	1,848	5,085	41	1,168	1,208	979	702	347	640
2005	11,715	93	2,618	2,769	2,006	1,445	806	1,977	5,114	30	1,193	1,308	928	590	373	692
2004	11,571	111	2,596	2,618	2,014	1,513	814	1,905	5,146	44	1,150	1,242	930	710	372	698
2003[1]	11,295	90	2,486	2,419	2,225	1,371	832	1,872	5,067	41	1,115	1,082	1,094	639	386	710
2002	11,236	97	2,549	2,525	1,931	1,317	812	2,007	5,060	57	1,179	1,162	947	596	350	770
2001	10,602	74	2,383	2,450	1,732	1,283	827	1,854	4,691	30	1,131	1,170	794	587	348	632
2000	10,636	92	2,580	2,333	1,796	1,275	770	1,790	4,716	35	1,138	1,109	890	603	296	646
1999	10,818	80	2,574	2,324	1,837	1,283	755	1,965	5,033	30	1,214	1,141	929	627	368	722
1998	11,109	84	2,715	2,281	1,760	1,408	840	2,020	5,084	30	1,280	1,123	897	668	348	738
1997	11,246	81	2,491	2,361	1,876	1,504	779	2,153	5,024	33	1,184	1,161	930	732	314	669
1996	11,034	147	2,504	2,156	1,788	1,514	834	2,091	4,961	61	1,136	1,039	955	727	303	740
1995	11,024	103	2,372	2,226	1,796	1,618	859	2,051	5,068	36	1,111	1,103	892	799	380	749
1994[2]	11,178	93	2,362	2,255	1,904	1,444	1,018	2,101	5,053	41	1,132	1,039	955	689	457	741
1993	10,554	83	2,270	2,026	1,924	1,367	923	1,960	4,838	36	1,038	1,016	1,017	663	399	670

BLACK

Year, sex, race, and Hispanic origin	All students Total	14 to 17 years	18 and 19 years	20 and 21 years	22 to 24 years	25 to 29 years	30 to 34 years	35 years and over	Male Total	14 to 17 years	18 and 19 years	20 and 21 years	22 to 24 years	25 to 29 years	30 to 34 years	35 years and over
2016	2,885	30	530	572	542	405	247	559	1,217	12	215	276	237	192	97	188
2015	2,826	25	509	575	553	404	223	537	1,147	12	229	252	298	145	57	154
2014	2,934	54	510	537	482	414	242	695	1,132	38	175	244	214	162	79	220
2013	2,857	32	451	633	515	461	225	539	1,116	18	186	268	236	172	54	182
2012	3,038	27	531	636	522	443	326	553	1,152	18	206	316	238	142	85	148
2011	3,146	38	580	489	570	511	307	651	1,212	23	242	243	232	189	92	191
2010	3,083	33	567	622	503	438	277	643	1,185	14	238	262	234	180	77	180
2009	2,889	34	559	495	550	410	253	587	1,058	5	225	237	212	151	81	147
2008	2,481	36	479	463	408	377	269	451	919	21	205	217	174	115	82	106
2007	2,501	27	492	436	468	400	229	449	1,016	10	227	213	209	126	102	130
2006	2,334	30	464	416	441	303	199	480	896	10	174	182	186	112	70	163
2005	2,217	28	431	393	435	282	217	430	832	6	182	178	153	99	64	150
2004	2,301	40	440	398	400	352	170	501	776	13	165	169	146	92	41	151
2003[1]	2,144	28	374	415	435	289	214	388	798	10	166	153	180	100	84	105
2002	2,278	56	430	418	379	301	241	454	802	14	179	175	121	97	83	133
2001	2,230	33	444	383	379	283	279	429	781	7	179	137	153	88	90	126
2000	2,164	19	454	375	387	325	242	361	815	10	163	137	169	110	92	133
1999	1,998	45	430	389	325	254	199	354	833	34	210	193	98	93	79	123
1998	2,016	22	461	354	300	328	211	340	770	12	194	162	88	140	67	105
1997	1,903	24	381	321	383	258	165	372	723	7	142	137	146	110	65	117
1996	1,901	45	345	346	292	337	182	354	764	17	145	155	122	142	64	120
1995	1,772	24	344	339	305	233	193	334	710	13	145	142	143	65	80	122
1994	1,800	36	310	347	344	256	184	323	745	16	132	161	147	118	72	99
1993[r]	1,599	13	322	311	264	253	143	293	652	4	151	109	127	118	36	107
1993	1,545	13	311	297	253	245	141	284	636	4	148	107	124	116	36	102
1992	1,424	28	291	316	279	170	132	208	527	8	123	114	119	73	37	54
1991	1,477	18	303	302	223	216	157	257	629	7	137	138	103	99	55	90
1990	1,393	35	349	287	258	150	108	207	587	16	164	151	111	52	26	65
1989	1,287	32	302	290	243	156	119	146	480	8	126	104	94	65	37	47
1988	1,321	33	281	273	198	188	142	206	494	6	108	90	99	75	48	68

NA = Not available.

[1] Starting in 2003, respondents could identify more than one race. Except as noted, the race data in this table from 2003 onward represent those respondents who indicated only one race category.

[2] Before 1994, total enrolled does not include the 35 and over population.

r = Revised, controlled to 1990 census based population estimates; previous 1993 data controlled to 1980 census based population estimates.

Table A-15. Age Distribution of College Students 14 Years Old and Over, by Sex, Selected Years, October 1947–2016—*Continued*

(Numbers in thousands; civilian noninstitutionalized population.)

Year, sex, race, and Hispanic origin				Female				
	Total	14 to 17 years	18 and 19 years	20 and 21 years	22 to 24 years	25 to 29 years	30 to 34 years	35 years and over
1958........................	1,031	87	467	-----334-----		-----143-----		NA
1957........................	994	93	411	-----368-----		-----122-----		NA
1956........................	879	84	395	-----292-----		-----108-----		NA
1955........................	729	78	297	-----259-----		------95-----		NA
WHITE ALONE NON-HISPANIC								
2016........................	5,870	52	1,271	1,297	1,038	913	463	837
2015........................	5,934	52	1,248	1,283	1,123	849	424	954
2014........................	5,953	55	1,249	1,235	1,179	817	405	1,013
2013........................	6,404	95	1,254	1,321	1,229	861	442	1,201
2012........................	6,575	88	1,312	1,494	1,094	973	422	1,193
2011........................	6,972	50	1,404	1,517	1,206	1,075	519	1,199
2010........................	6,940	75	1,463	1,417	1,166	964	581	1,275
2009........................	7,116	66	1,556	1,429	1,211	971	516	1,368
2008........................	6,722	63	1,504	1,412	1,211	859	432	1,242
2007........................	6,598	59	1,441	1,455	1,096	870	447	1,230
2006........................	6,400	73	1,396	1,398	1,051	792	483	1,208
2005........................	6,601	63	1,425	1,461	1,078	855	433	1,285
2004........................	6,425	67	1,446	1,375	1,085	803	442	1,207
2003[1]....................	6,228	49	1,371	1,337	1,130	732	446	1,163
2002........................	6,177	40	1,370	1,364	984	721	462	1,237
2001........................	5,912	44	1,252	1,280	938	695	479	1,222
2000........................	5,921	57	1,443	1,224	906	672	474	1,145
1999........................	5,785	49	1,360	1,183	908	656	387	1,241
1998........................	6,025	54	1,435	1,158	863	740	493	1,282
1997........................	6,222	48	1,307	1,200	946	771	465	1,485
1996........................	6,073	86	1,367	1,117	833	787	531	1,352
1995........................	5,956	67	1,261	1,123	904	819	479	1,302
1994[2]....................	6,124	53	1,229	1,216	950	755	561	1,361
1993........................	5,715	48	1,232	1,010	907	704	524	1,290
BLACK								
2016........................	1,669	18	316	296	305	212	151	372
2015........................	1,679	13	280	323	255	259	166	383
2014........................	1,802	17	334	293	268	252	164	475
2013........................	1,740	14	265	365	280	289	171	357
2012........................	1,886	10	325	320	284	301	241	406
2011........................	1,934	16	337	246	338	322	215	460
2010........................	1,898	20	329	360	269	258	199	463
2009........................	1,831	29	334	258	338	259	172	441
2008........................	1,562	15	274	246	234	261	188	345
2007........................	1,485	18	265	223	259	274	127	320
2006........................	1,438	20	291	234	255	191	130	318
2005........................	1,385	22	249	215	282	183	153	281
2004........................	1,525	27	275	229	254	259	130	350
2003[1]....................	1,346	19	209	262	255	188	130	283
2002........................	1,476	42	251	243	257	204	158	321
2001........................	1,449	26	265	245	226	195	190	302
2000........................	1,349	9	291	238	218	215	150	228
1999........................	1,164	10	221	196	227	161	120	229
1998........................	1,247	9	267	192	212	188	144	234
1997........................	1,180	17	238	184	237	149	100	255
1996........................	1,136	28	199	192	170	195	119	234
1995........................	1,062	11	199	197	162	168	113	212
1994........................	1,054	21	178	186	197	138	112	224
1993[r]....................	947	9	172	202	137	135	107	186
1993........................	909	8	163	191	130	129	106	182
1992........................	897	21	168	202	161	97	95	154
1991........................	848	11	166	164	120	118	102	167
1990........................	807	19	185	136	146	98	82	141
1989........................	807	24	176	186	149	91	82	99
1988........................	827	27	173	183	99	113	94	138

NA = Not available.

[1]Starting in 2003, respondents could identify more than one race. Except as noted, the race data in this table from 2003 onward represent those respondents who indicated only one race category.

[2]Before 1994, total enrolled does not include the 35 and over population.

[r] = Revised, controlled to 1990 census based population estimates; previous 1993 data controlled to 1980 census based population estimates.

Table A-15. Age Distribution of College Students 14 Years Old and Over, by Sex, Selected Years, October 1947–2016—*Continued*

(Numbers in thousands; civilian noninstitutionalized population.)

Year, sex, race, and Hispanic origin	All students								Male							
	Total	14 to 17 years	18 and 19 years	20 and 21 years	22 to 24 years	25 to 29 years	30 to 34 years	35 years and over	Total	14 to 17 years	18 and 19 years	20 and 21 years	22 to 24 years	25 to 29 years	30 to 34 years	35 years and over
1987	1,351	32	341	264	218	220	121	155	587	13	154	124	99	99	37	62
1986	1,359	19	308	242	262	187	143	198	580	12	120	111	118	81	64	74
1985	1,263	21	259	274	201	183	112	213	552	10	121	140	84	64	40	93
1984	1,332	40	265	274	247	182	131	193	618	16	112	129	126	99	62	74
1983	1,273	31	258	242	241	179	151	171	560	12	93	112	126	91	64	62
1982	1,294	22	274	242	251	196	142	167	544	9	124	92	115	91	51	62
1981	1,335	31	306	232	212	219	132	203	566	7	133	92	100	115	57	62
1980	1,163	30	283	225	180	176	113	156	476	14	98	101	79	92	53	39
1979	1,156	43	279	224	193	150	112	155	498	12	110	110	84	71	47	64
1978	1,175	38	270	238	186	167	121	155	504	13	114	106	85	82	52	52
1977	1,284	37	269	262	190	210	136	180	571	18	90	115	104	101	62	81
1976	1,217	34	302	252	195	171	109	154	551	11	121	113	97	90	57	62
1975	1,099	34	260	237	168	151	97	152	523	14	111	107	76	82	53	80
1974	930	34	233	190	132	136	88	117	485	13	102	100	78	70	60	62
1973	781	37	194	164	140	89	60	97	358	7	96	93	77	49	36	NA
1972	727	32	229	168	143	87	68	NA	384	18	102	91	94	49	30	NA
1971	680	29	204	199	119	79	50	NA	363	11	94	106	62	58	31	NA
1970	522	21	191	152	73	54	31	NA	253	10	73	81	38	33	19	NA
1969	492	19	193	149	65	39	26	NA	236	10	86	75	41	15	10	NA
1968	434	20	182	112	58	33	29	NA	221	12	83	61	26	27	13	NA
1967	370	16	141	105	51	42	15	NA	199	7	78	57	32	15	11	NA
1966	282	17	112	-----112-----		------41----		NA	154	10	47	-----72-----		-----25-----		NA
1965	274	30	111	------99-----		------34-----		NA	126	8	52	------47-----		------19-----		NA
1964	234	30	78	------79-----		------47-----		NA	120	16	35	------36-----		------33-----		NA
1963	286	9	113	-----112-----		------52-----		NA	149	5	50	------62-----		------32-----		NA
1962	274	16	103	-----109-----		------46-----		NA	156	5	55	------59-----		------37-----		NA
1961	233	9	82	-----103-----		------39-----		NA	148	5	48	------64-----		------31-----		NA
1960	227	8	88	------90-----		------41-----		NA	125	2	43	------55-----		------25-----		NA
1959	222	17	74	------94-----		------37-----		NA	120	4	31	------58-----		------27-----		NA
1958	212	12	70	------85-----		------45-----		NA	130	5	44	------48-----		------33-----		NA
1957	206	15	68	------71-----		------52-----		NA	90	9	28	------30-----		------23-----		NA
1956	196	15	65	------80-----		------36-----		NA	124	9	38	------48-----		------29-----		NA
1955	155	21	31	------51-----		------52-----		NA	84	9	15	------25-----		------35-----		NA
BLACK ALONE NON-HISPANIC[3]																
2005	2,217	28	431	393	435	282	217	430	832	6	182	178	153	99	64	150
2004	2,231	40	430	392	379	344	163	483	760	13	161	166	143	92	38	147
2003[1]	2,090	28	368	399	423	282	205	385	773	10	166	145	177	93	80	102
2002	2,217	56	428	410	358	293	233	439	782	14	177	174	113	95	83	126
2001	2,173	33	430	373	375	263	275	423	759	7	174	137	150	78	90	123
2000	2,119	19	439	373	370	321	242	355	798	10	154	137	164	110	92	130
1999	1,952	45	413	390	320	250	192	342	811	35	192	193	99	91	76	125
1998	1,971	22	453	351	282	322	211	331	752	12	194	159	83	134	67	102
1997	1,868	21	371	314	378	253	161	369	712	7	138	137	143	105	65	117
1996	1,863	41	342	342	281	329	176	350	750	17	142	155	122	134	64	117
1995	1,745	24	332	337	302	231	189	330	699	13	136	142	143	65	80	120
1994	1,783	36	308	347	342	253	182	314	734	16	131	161	145	116	72	93
1993	1,505	13	310	291	246	232	134	279	615	4	149	105	121	104	33	100
ASIAN[4]																
2016	1,585	19	255	358	390	328	108	127	835	4	135	177	222	177	53	68
2015	1,616	20	235	421	370	291	135	143	752	10	112	193	188	138	61	49
2014	1,543	19	270	305	447	273	80	148	797	14	136	158	255	149	26	59
2013	1,576	30	302	340	359	261	111	174	789	8	154	188	193	151	38	58
2012	1,447	26	253	289	372	247	116	143	700	15	129	140	185	131	44	55
2011	1,204	21	240	281	227	189	99	147	567	6	131	141	107	92	45	45
2010	1,322	32	234	308	269	237	117	126	647	17	116	150	124	126	58	57
2009	1,231	11	243	216	308	197	114	141	613	8	134	97	153	96	53	73
2008	1,220	27	172	247	236	245	137	156	567	22	75	123	96	132	61	58
2007	1,103	10	201	204	252	206	123	105	533	2	104	106	108	98	60	54
2006	1,084	8	204	215	242	187	103	125	535	5	113	121	104	80	51	61
2005	1,184	22	188	272	234	226	114	129	605	10	90	163	113	110	61	58

NA = Not available.
[1]Starting in 2003, respondents could identify more than one race. Except as noted, the race data in this table from 2003 onward represent those respondents who indicated only one race category.
[3]This series was discontinued in 2006.
[4]The data shown before 2003 consists of those identifying themselves as "Asian or Pacific Islanders."

Table A-15. Age Distribution of College Students 14 Years Old and Over, by Sex, Selected Years, October 1947–2016—*Continued*

(Numbers in thousands; civilian noninstitutionalized population.)

Year, sex, race, and Hispanic origin		Female						
	Total	14 to 17 years	18 and 19 years	20 and 21 years	22 to 24 years	25 to 29 years	30 to 34 years	35 years and over
1987	764	19	186	140	119	121	84	93
1986	779	7	187	131	144	106	79	124
1985	712	11	138	134	117	119	72	121
1984	714	24	153	145	121	83	69	119
1983	714	19	164	131	116	88	87	109
1982	750	12	150	150	136	105	92	105
1981	769	24	172	140	112	105	75	141
1980	686	16	185	124	101	84	60	116
1979	659	31	169	114	109	79	66	91
1978	671	25	155	133	102	85	68	103
1977	712	19	179	147	87	108	74	98
1976	665	23	181	139	97	81	52	92
1975	577	20	150	130	92	69	44	72
1974	448	22	131	91	55	66	28	55
1973	325	30	97	71	63	40	24	NA
1972	343	14	127	77	49	38	38	NA
1971	317	18	109	93	57	21	19	NA
1970	269	11	118	71	36	22	11	NA
1969	256	9	108	74	24	25	17	NA
1968	213	8	100	51	32	7	15	NA
1967	171	9	63	48	19	27	4	NA
1966	128	7	65	-----40-----		-----16-----		NA
1965	148	22	59	-----52-----		-----15-----		NA
1964	114	14	43	-----43-----		-----14-----		NA
1963	137	4	63	-----50-----		-----20-----		NA
1962	118	11	48	-----50-----		-----9-----		NA
1961	85	4	34	-----39-----		-----8-----		NA
1960	102	6	45	-----35-----		-----16-----		NA
1959	102	13	43	-----36-----		-----10-----		NA
1958	82	7	26	-----37-----		-----12-----		NA
1957	116	6	40	-----41-----		-----29-----		NA
1956	72	6	27	-----32-----		-----7-----		NA
1955	71	12	16	-----26-----		-----17-----		NA
BLACK ALONE NON-HISPANIC[3]								
2005	1,385	22	249	215	282	183	153	281
2004	1,471	27	268	227	237	251	125	336
2003[1]	1,317	19	202	254	246	188	125	283
2002	1,435	42	251	237	244	198	150	313
2001	1,414	26	256	236	226	186	185	300
2000	1,321	9	285	235	206	211	150	225
1999	1,141	10	221	196	221	159	117	218
1998	1,219	9	259	192	199	188	144	229
1997	1,156	14	233	177	235	149	96	252
1996	1,113	25	199	188	160	195	113	234
1995	1,046	11	196	195	159	167	109	210
1994	1,049	21	178	186	197	138	109	221
1993	890	8	161	186	125	128	102	179
ASIAN[4]								
2016	749	15	120	181	168	151	55	59
2015	864	10	123	229	182	153	74	94
2014	746	5	134	147	192	124	55	89
2013	787	22	148	152	166	110	73	116
2012	747	11	124	148	187	116	72	88
2011	637	16	109	140	120	97	54	101
2010	676	15	118	158	145	111	59	69
2009	619	4	109	120	155	101	61	68
2008	653	5	97	123	140	113	76	98
2007	569	8	97	98	144	108	63	51
2006	549	3	91	94	139	107	52	64
2005	579	12	98	109	120	116	53	71

NA = Not available.
[1]Starting in 2003, respondents could identify more than one race. Except as noted, the race data in this table from 2003 onward represent those respondents who indicated only one race category.
[3]This series was discontinued in 2006.
[4]The data shown before 2003 consists of those identifying themselves as "Asian or Pacific Islanders."

Table A-15. Age Distribution of College Students 14 Years Old and Over, by Sex, Selected Years, October 1947–2016—*Continued*

(Numbers in thousands; civilian noninstitutionalized population.)

Year, sex, race, and Hispanic origin	All students								Male							
	Total	14 to 17 years	18 and 19 years	20 and 21 years	22 to 24 years	25 to 29 years	30 to 34 years	35 years and over	Total	14 to 17 years	18 and 19 years	20 and 21 years	22 to 24 years	25 to 29 years	30 to 34 years	35 years and over
2004........................	1,191	20	182	245	269	217	113	146	636	11	92	135	145	116	65	71
2003[1]......................	1,162	16	209	219	264	228	108	116	606	3	103	104	130	141	67	59
2002........................	1,258	28	236	269	299	182	105	140	649	8	121	137	160	101	56	67
2001........................	1,280	17	247	245	302	265	90	115	664	10	113	127	177	134	63	40
2000........................	1,049	12	212	200	227	188	81	130	517	4	108	109	120	66	51	60
1999........................	1,041	16	223	192	211	187	71	142	506	11	93	95	96	97	47	67
HISPANIC (OF ANY RACE)																
2016........................	3,661	89	884	948	732	491	191	326	1,582	28	383	437	327	210	76	120
2015........................	3,374	43	776	930	663	459	189	315	1,484	23	315	421	327	192	69	136
2014........................	3,295	52	857	797	628	441	189	332	1,441	11	385	356	275	222	47	144
2013........................	3,219	43	727	773	692	417	222	345	1,438	19	295	352	321	237	84	130
2012........................	3,400	61	827	912	664	365	257	313	1,510	26	372	421	316	155	72	148
2011........................	2,953	36	765	740	574	407	175	256	1,438	23	351	376	279	212	67	130
2010........................	2,879	41	783	517	514	424	228	373	1,302	19	381	242	196	197	108	159
2009........................	2,434	43	550	482	433	373	217	336	1,080	23	242	221	200	159	108	127
2008........................	2,227	53	528	407	402	359	141	337	1,042	31	236	210	169	186	76	135
2007........................	2,172	41	559	412	404	332	155	269	880	16	246	154	160	145	57	102
2006........................	1,968	54	444	386	353	271	190	271	808	19	213	146	164	109	64	94
2005........................	1,942	31	406	420	389	288	150	257	804	10	173	183	183	111	52	92
2004........................	1,975	23	384	431	407	280	179	271	852	5	171	212	191	131	53	89
2003........................	1,714	12	379	407	329	224	156	207	703	7	153	167	145	93	61	77
2002........................	1,656	15	360	303	316	274	140	249	705	3	156	151	132	118	49	97
2001........................	1,700	14	387	342	306	255	136	260	731	6	149	145	156	116	57	102
2000........................	1,426	24	349	268	282	167	142	194	619	12	160	118	123	61	75	70
1999........................	1,307	7	297	197	247	207	127	225	568	2	143	84	96	94	54	95
1998........................	1,363	9	288	263	269	206	130	198	550	*	97	139	110	86	54	64
1997........................	1,260	49	316	254	236	174	80	151	555	15	133	132	106	78	31	60
1996........................	1,223	22	240	213	253	198	112	184	529	8	98	78	124	79	54	90
1995........................	1,207	20	264	245	236	153	97	193	568	14	121	111	124	71	55	73
1994[2]......................	1,187	9	225	230	207	180	132	205	529	3	89	115	108	73	55	86
1993[r]......................	1,169	17	222	299	207	178	106	139	539	7	81	154	103	71	67	56
1993........................	995	15	195	241	166	149	100	129	442	6	69	118	79	57	63	51
1992........................	918	17	230	200	156	124	90	102	388	9	93	80	74	57	35	40
1991........................	830	10	188	203	125	124	72	109	347	5	68	79	64	64	30	37
1990........................	748	13	148	188	99	109	59	130	364	12	70	80	64	39	30	67
1989........................	754	17	177	134	142	112	58	114	353	5	75	66	70	63	31	42
1988........................	747	13	203	110	137	118	73	93	355	9	75	76	77	48	29	43
1987........................	739	8	152	155	148	137	67	73	390	3	76	100	71	77	42	21
1986........................	794	16	171	146	141	164	67	89	377	4	92	67	74	80	26	34
1985........................	580	16	127	128	120	111	78	NA	279	10	44	53	71	72	29	NA
1984........................	524	5	136	133	93	100	57	NA	231	2	42	63	49	49	26	NA
1983........................	521	17	134	124	91	114	41	NA	253	10	41	61	50	74	17	NA
1982........................	494	16	143	104	90	94	47	NA	216	6	52	47	42	49	20	NA
1981........................	510	15	129	123	90	103	50	NA	258	6	57	68	39	55	33	NA
1980........................	443	10	137	94	84	69	49	NA	222	2	68	52	34	36	30	NA
1979........................	439	18	124	95	73	73	56	NA	225	8	67	43	43	39	25	NA
1978........................	377	15	109	68	77	78	30	NA	196	7	53	30	43	49	14	NA
1977........................	417	14	123	95	59	81	45	NA	224	6	54	45	40	56	23	NA
1976........................	426	13	143	83	83	73	31	NA	223	3	69	39	42	50	20	NA
1975........................	411	13	118	101	76	68	35	NA	218	3	53	52	40	45	25	NA
1974........................	354	11	112	96	64	39	32	NA	195	6	55	44	42	24	24	NA
1973........................	289	15	82	69	55	45	23	NA	168	11	39	37	29	32	20	NA
1972........................	242	14	70	60	49	34	15	NA	126	7	28	35	29	20	7	NA

NA = Not available.

[1] Starting in 2003, respondents could identify more than one race. Except as noted, the race data in this table from 2003 onward represent those respondents who indicated only one race category.

[2] Before 1994, total enrolled does not include the 35 and over population.

[r] = Revised, controlled to 1990 census based population estimates; previous 1993 data controlled to 1980 census based population estimates.

Table A-15. Age Distribution of College Students 14 Years Old and Over, by Sex, Selected Years, October 1947–2016—*Continued*

(Numbers in thousands; civilian noninstitutionalized population.)

Year, sex, race, and Hispanic origin	Female							
	Total	14 to 17 years	18 and 19 years	20 and 21 years	22 to 24 years	25 to 29 years	30 to 34 years	35 years and over
2004	556	9	89	110	124	101	48	75
2003[1]	556	13	107	115	134	88	42	57
2002	609	19	115	132	139	82	49	73
2001	616	6	134	118	125	131	27	75
2000	532	8	104	91	107	122	30	69
1999	534	5	130	97	115	89	24	74
HISPANIC (OF ANY RACE)								
2016	2,079	60	501	511	405	281	115	206
2015	1,890	20	461	508	336	267	120	179
2014	1,855	40	472	441	352	219	142	188
2013	1,781	24	432	421	371	180	138	215
2012	1,890	35	454	491	348	211	185	166
2011	1,515	13	414	364	294	196	108	126
2010	1,576	21	402	275	319	227	119	213
2009	1,354	20	308	261	234	214	108	209
2008	1,185	23	292	197	233	173	65	202
2007	1,292	25	313	258	244	187	98	167
2006	1,161	36	231	240	189	162	126	177
2005	1,137	21	232	237	206	178	98	165
2004	1,123	19	213	219	216	150	126	182
2003	1,011	5	226	240	185	131	95	130
2002	951	12	204	152	184	156	92	152
2001	969	8	238	197	150	139	80	157
2000	807	13	188	150	160	106	67	124
1999	739	5	154	113	151	113	73	130
1998	814	9	191	124	159	120	77	134
1997	704	34	183	123	130	96	49	91
1996	693	15	142	136	128	119	59	95
1995	639	6	143	134	112	82	42	120
1994[2]	659	6	136	115	99	106	78	119
1993[r]	630	10	141	145	104	107	40	83
1993	553	9	126	123	87	93	38	78
1992	530	7	137	120	82	67	55	62
1991	483	5	120	124	61	59	42	72
1990	384	1	78	108	35	70	29	63
1989	401	11	103	69	72	49	27	71
1988	391	4	129	35	60	70	43	51
1987	349	5	76	56	76	60	25	51
1986	417	12	79	80	67	84	41	54
1985	299	6	82	75	48	39	49	NA
1984	292	3	94	70	43	51	31	NA
1983	270	7	93	64	41	40	25	NA
1982	278	10	91	57	48	45	27	NA
1981	252	9	72	55	51	48	17	NA
1980	221	8	63	42	50	33	20	NA
1979	215	10	58	52	30	34	31	NA
1978	181	8	56	38	34	29	16	NA
1977	194	8	70	50	19	25	22	NA
1976	203	9	74	45	41	23	11	NA
1975	193	10	65	49	36	23	10	NA
1974	157	5	56	51	22	15	8	NA
1973	123	5	44	33	25	13	3	NA
1972	117	7	43	25	20	14	8	NA

NA = Not available.
[1] Starting in 2003, respondents could identify more than one race. Except as noted, the race data in this table from 2003 onward represent those respondents who indicated only one race category.
[2] Before 1994, total enrolled does not include the 35 and over population.
[r] = Revised, controlled to 1990 census based population estimates; previous 1993 data controlled to 1980 census based population estimates.

Table A-15. Age Distribution of College Students 14 Years Old and Over, by Sex, Selected Years, October 1947–2016—*Continued*

(Numbers in thousands; civilian noninstitutionalized population.)

Year, sex, race, and Hispanic origin	Total	All students							Male							
		14 to 17 years	18 and 19 years	20 and 21 years	22 to 24 years	25 to 29 years	30 to 34 years	35 years and over	Total	14 to 17 years	18 and 19 years	20 and 21 years	22 to 24 years	25 to 29 years	30 to 34 years	35 years and over
WHITE ALONE OR IN COMBINATION																
2016	14,355	180	3,316	3,418	2,712	2,099	942	1,687	6,415	60	1,547	1,602	1,284	876	396	651
2015	14,295	165	3,163	3,416	2,689	2,072	972	1,818	6,425	81	1,472	1,627	1,220	942	423	658
2014	14,310	154	3,154	3,299	2,877	1,982	910	1,935	6,549	73	1,433	1,646	1,318	947	385	748
2013	14,743	246	3,124	3,292	3,005	1,942	988	2,145	6,500	123	1,433	1,521	1,369	905	411	738
2012	15,117	216	3,144	3,574	2,897	2,099	1,058	2,130	6,612	98	1,429	1,547	1,423	915	442	759
2011	15,785	141	3,381	3,631	3,031	2,316	1,124	2,160	7,239	78	1,554	1,719	1,517	1,046	496	830
2010	15,586	157	3,478	3,359	2,687	2,287	1,220	2,399	7,030	60	1,620	1,656	1,196	1,080	516	902
2009	15,391	160	3,414	3,289	2,859	2,125	1,133	2,411	6,848	77	1,535	1,591	1,387	930	501	826
2008	14,738	175	3,440	3,181	2,738	2,003	936	2,264	6,730	87	1,607	1,550	1,286	966	426	807
2007	14,114	147	3,318	3,111	2,529	1,857	978	2,174	6,169	64	1,540	1,390	1,186	789	425	774
2006	13,564	166	3,043	3,006	2,416	1,791	1,016	2,125	5,966	61	1,399	1,363	1,161	827	411	744
2005	13,791	125	3,043	3,244	2,433	1,740	954	2,251	5,978	43	1,371	1,519	1,128	696	424	796
2004	13,668	135	3,012	3,106	2,425	1,807	989	2,192	6,068	49	1,331	1,494	1,131	847	425	792
2003	13,164	106	2,905	2,868	2,584	1,613	989	2,099	5,837	48	1,283	1,274	1,257	730	446	798
BLACK ALONE OR IN COMBINATION																
2016	3,079	35	602	607	572	430	261	572	1,283	14	250	280	247	195	102	194
2015	2,985	28	560	602	580	421	244	551	1,216	14	259	269	305	150	63	156
2014	3,099	56	553	562	530	432	259	707	1,181	40	192	244	223	173	88	220
2013	3,118	36	509	716	581	499	228	550	1,238	22	210	306	263	192	54	190
2012	3,335	33	579	721	592	465	348	598	1,292	22	244	353	263	149	89	174
2011	3,317	39	615	540	605	533	321	665	1,279	23	250	264	249	196	100	198
2010	3,250	38	622	653	533	463	286	655	1,241	19	264	271	244	186	78	180
2009	3,030	34	604	520	574	428	268	601	1,109	5	245	250	217	155	88	149
2008	2,619	36	515	490	429	400	278	470	983	21	219	229	184	127	85	116
2007	2,630	33	530	459	479	432	243	455	1,077	12	240	229	217	139	110	130
2006	2,444	30	492	423	471	318	217	493	951	10	186	186	206	120	74	170
2005	2,387	31	481	428	462	299	229	458	895	9	201	189	167	109	66	154
2004	2,412	40	466	436	416	371	170	512	827	13	175	187	159	100	41	153
2003	2,227	30	400	440	445	303	214	395	826	10	175	165	186	100	84	107
ASIAN ALONE OR IN COMBINATION																
2016	1,780	22	313	421	427	346	118	133	937	7	159	211	254	178	59	70
2015	1,821	21	287	488	407	315	156	147	840	11	141	218	202	151	67	49
2014	1,712	19	296	347	490	310	90	161	878	14	146	175	278	166	30	68
2013	1,766	31	350	394	412	274	117	188	872	8	171	221	221	153	38	60
2012	1,617	33	274	348	421	266	124	151	774	21	143	165	202	140	44	58
2011	1,356	21	267	323	243	220	121	161	658	6	145	162	123	110	60	53
2010	1,467	37	264	343	298	268	125	133	740	20	136	177	141	149	61	57
2009	1,334	11	271	242	330	207	122	150	656	8	138	115	165	98	57	76
2008	1,340	27	214	265	259	260	149	167	632	22	93	134	113	135	70	65
2007	1,204	11	232	220	268	232	126	116	592	2	113	116	123	113	61	64
2006	1,154	9	215	227	263	198	110	131	566	6	118	122	122	81	55	62
2005	1,297	25	204	292	277	240	122	137	640	13	97	170	124	113	63	60
2003	1,262	19	236	248	290	232	117	121	649	3	112	115	143	142	72	61

Table A-15. Age Distribution of College Students 14 Years Old and Over, by Sex, Selected Years, October 1947–2016—*Continued*

(Numbers in thousands; civilian noninstitutionalized population.)

Year, sex, race, and Hispanic origin	Female							
	Total	14 to 17 years	18 and 19 years	20 and 21 years	22 to 24 years	25 to 29 years	30 to 34 years	35 years and over
WHITE ALONE OR IN COMBINATION								
2016.........................	7,940	121	1,770	1,816	1,428	1,224	546	1,036
2015.........................	7,870	84	1,691	1,789	1,469	1,129	548	1,160
2014.........................	7,761	81	1,720	1,653	1,559	1,036	525	1,187
2013.........................	8,243	123	1,691	1,771	1,637	1,037	577	1,407
2012.........................	8,505	119	1,715	2,027	1,473	1,184	615	1,372
2011.........................	8,545	63	1,828	1,912	1,514	1,270	627	1,330
2010.........................	8,556	97	1,858	1,702	1,491	1,207	703	1,497
2009.........................	8,544	84	1,879	1,698	1,473	1,195	631	1,585
2008.........................	8,008	88	1,833	1,631	1,452	1,037	510	1,457
2007.........................	7,945	82	1,779	1,721	1,343	1,068	553	1,400
2006.........................	7,598	105	1,643	1,643	1,255	964	605	1,382
2005.........................	7,813	82	1,672	1,725	1,305	1,044	530	1,454
2004.........................	7,600	86	1,682	1,612	1,295	960	564	1,401
2003.........................	7,328	57	1,622	1,594	1,327	883	543	1,302
BLACK ALONE OR IN COMBINATION								
2016.........................	1,797	21	352	328	325	234	159	378
2015.........................	1,770	14	300	332	275	271	181	396
2014.........................	1,919	17	360	318	307	259	171	486
2013.........................	1,880	14	299	409	317	306	174	360
2012.........................	2,043	11	335	368	329	316	259	424
2011.........................	2,037	16	365	276	356	337	221	467
2010.........................	2,009	20	358	383	289	277	208	474
2009.........................	1,921	29	359	270	357	274	180	451
2008.........................	1,636	15	296	261	245	272	193	354
2007.........................	1,553	20	290	230	263	292	133	325
2006.........................	1,493	20	307	238	265	198	143	323
2005.........................	1,493	22	280	239	295	190	164	303
2004.........................	1,584	27	290	249	258	271	130	359
2003.........................	1,401	20	225	275	260	203	130	288
ASIAN ALONE OR IN COMBINATION								
2016.........................	843	15	153	209	174	169	60	63
2015.........................	981	10	146	270	205	164	88	98
2014.........................	834	5	150	171	212	145	60	92
2013.........................	894	22	179	173	191	121	78	128
2012.........................	843	11	131	183	219	126	80	94
2011.........................	697	16	122	161	121	110	61	108
2010.........................	727	17	128	166	157	119	63	76
2009.........................	678	4	134	127	165	109	65	74
2008.........................	708	5	121	131	146	125	79	102
2007.........................	612	9	119	104	145	118	65	52
2006.........................	588	3	97	105	141	117	55	69
2005.........................	657	12	107	122	153	128	59	77
2003.........................	613	16	124	133	147	89	44	60

Table A-16. College Enrollment of Students 14 Years Old and Over, by Type of College, Attendance Status, Age, and Sex, October 1970–2016

(Numbers in thousands; civilian noninstitutionalized population.)

Year and type of college	Total	All students 14 to 19 years	All students 20 to 21 years	All students 22 to 24 years	All students 25 to 34 years	All students 35 years and over	Public	Private	Male Total	Male Full-time	Male Part-time	Female Total	Female Full-time	Female Part-time
ALL UNDERGRADUATES														
2016	15,497	4,369	4,295	2,916	2,489	1,427	12,523	2,974	7,075	5,630	1,445	8,422	6,486	1,936
2015	15,433	4,165	4,371	2,774	2,570	1,553	12,762	2,671	7,002	5,477	1,525	8,431	6,438	1,992
2014	15,498	4,249	4,075	2,978	2,438	1,759	12,877	2,620	7,071	5,713	1,358	8,427	6,524	1,903
2013	15,738	4,202	4,159	3,052	2,598	1,727	13,129	2,609	7,097	5,606	1,492	8,641	6,507	2,133
2012	16,170	4,236	4,420	3,025	2,783	1,706	13,451	2,719	7,107	5,603	1,505	9,063	6,789	2,274
2011	16,625	4,435	4,368	3,000	3,019	1,802	13,816	2,809	7,515	5,830	1,685	9,110	6,908	2,202
2010	16,354	4,546	4,225	2,671	2,912	2,000	13,701	2,653	7,300	5,582	1,718	9,054	6,773	2,282
2009	16,012	4,463	3,965	2,849	2,737	1,999	13,356	2,656	7,121	5,632	1,488	8,891	6,686	2,205
2008	14,955	4,347	3,862	2,600	2,430	1,716	12,340	2,616	6,737	5,220	1,517	8,218	6,158	2,060
2007	14,365	4,237	3,732	2,513	2,277	1,605	11,811	2,554	6,405	5,053	1,353	7,959	5,813	2,146
2006	13,854	3,940	3,591	2,437	2,178	1,709	11,269	2,585	6,135	4,686	1,450	7,719	5,695	2,024
2005	14,169	3,901	3,847	2,588	2,142	1,690	11,292	2,876	6,189	4,799	1,391	7,979	5,852	2,127
2004	14,004	3,863	3,700	2,431	2,257	1,753	11,384	2,620	6,156	4,714	1,442	7,848	5,704	2,144
2003	13,370	3,633	3,449	2,687	2,094	1,506	10,980	2,389	5,902	4,476	1,425	7,468	5,391	2,077
2002	13,426	3,743	3,457	2,355	2,106	1,764	10,830	2,595	5,929	4,462	1,467	7,497	5,273	2,223
2001	12,552	3,568	3,329	2,136	1,979	1,540	10,188	2,364	5,522	4,057	1,464	7,030	4,949	2,082
2000	12,401	3,710	3,093	2,113	1,988	1,498	10,044	2,357	5,520	4,059	1,461	6,881	4,832	2,049
1999	12,046	3,625	3,043	2,000	1,885	1,493	9,689	2,357	5,554	4,143	1,411	6,492	4,548	1,945
1998	12,509	3,749	3,019	2,025	2,101	1,616	10,100	2,410	5,621	4,051	1,570	6,888	4,765	2,123
1997	12,409	3,504	3,080	2,137	1,970	1,718	10,074	2,335	5,539	4,165	1,375	6,870	4,752	2,118
1996	12,305	3,526	2,856	2,017	2,226	1,680	10,121	2,183	5,533	4,032	1,502	6,772	4,502	2,269
1995	11,966	3,251	2,881	2,033	2,151	1,651	9,570	2,396	5,413	3,911	1,501	6,554	4,433	2,121
1994	12,410	3,192	3,006	2,099	2,281	1,832	9,983	2,427	5,526	3,969	1,557	6,883	4,480	2,404
1993ʳ	11,959	3,197	2,879	2,131	2,118	1,634	9,706	2,253	5,442	4,020	1,422	6,517	4,346	2,171
1993	11,507	3,045	2,721	2,020	2,088	1,633	9,330	2,176	5,194	3,812	1,382	6,313	4,182	2,130
1992	11,643	3,097	2,902	2,004	2,090	1,550	9,519	2,124	5,091	3,724	1,365	6,553	4,338	2,214
1991	11,374	3,061	2,902	1,757	2,120	1,534	9,257	2,117	5,120	3,724	1,395	6,254	4,145	2,109
1990	11,108	3,194	2,740	1,681	2,067	1,425	9,031	2,076	5,030	3,628	1,402	6,077	3,967	2,109
1989	10,661	3,250	2,529	1,658	1,921	1,304	8,633	2,027	4,730	3,436	1,295	5,931	3,880	2,051
1988	10,605	3,229	2,645	1,600	1,865	1,266	8,617	1,988	4,763	3,441	1,322	5,842	3,816	2,026
1987	10,304	3,283	2,585	1,512	1,848	1,076	8,306	1,998	4,878	3,476	1,403	5,426	3,445	1,981
1986	10,036	3,158	2,298	1,583	1,932	1,065	7,955	2,081	4,663	3,350	1,312	5,373	3,474	1,899
1985	10,097	3,169	2,586	1,475	1,884	984	8,042	2,055	4,667	3,454	1,213	5,430	3,578	1,852
1984	9,910	3,120	2,564	1,547	1,826	852	7,944	1,966	4,725	3,573	1,152	5,185	3,419	1,766
1983	9,925	3,200	2,464	1,475	1,873	914	7,808	2,117	4,759	3,472	1,287	5,166	3,424	1,742
1982	9,952	3,183	2,657	1,526	1,745	843	7,908	2,044	4,703	3,485	1,218	5,249	3,480	1,769
1981	9,969	3,276	2,511	1,458	1,808	916	7,789	2,180	4,724	3,452	1,273	5,245	3,490	1,755
1980	9,279	3,182	2,393	1,316	1,598	791	NA	NA	4,353	3,247	1,105	4,927	3,210	1,717
1979	9,193	3,156	2,308	1,297	1,526	905	7,331	1,861	4,387	3,219	1,168	4,805	3,163	1,642
1978	8,947	3,173	2,246	1,233	1,505	790	7,008	1,939	4,445	3,269	1,176	4,502	3,031	1,471
1977¹	8,408	3,184	2,376	1,206	1,640	NA	6,683	1,724	4,372	3,304	1,068	4,027	3,002	1,025
1976	8,988	3,216	2,358	1,224	1,472	718	7,196	1,787	4,569	3,353	1,213	4,419	3,166	1,253
1975	8,108	3,237	2,255	1,072	1,546	NA	6,598	1,510	4,393	3,394	999	3,715	2,902	813
1974	7,338	2,906	2,131	1,028	1,272	NA	5,843	1,494	4,030	3,128	902	3,307	2,561	746
1973	6,794	2,812	2,031	924	1,028	NA	5,279	1,516	3,791	3,035	756	3,004	2,423	581
1972	6,992	2,974	2,065	944	1,011	NA	5,460	1,532	3,982	3,231	751	3,010	2,445	565
1971	6,895	3,008	1,936	1,019	931	NA	5,472	1,423	4,017	3,240	777	2,878	2,348	530
1970	6,274	2,854	1,803	866	750	NA	4,910	1,363	3,627	3,045	582	2,646	2,164	482
TWO-YEAR COLLEGE STUDENTS														
2016	4,346	1,363	876	692	903	512	4,054	293	2,040	1,350	690	2,306	1,432	875
2015	4,717	1,433	1,104	632	912	637	4,344	373	2,124	1,379	745	2,593	1,669	924
2014	4,841	1,432	989	734	973	714	4,410	431	2,056	1,363	693	2,786	1,839	946
2013	5,270	1,502	1,052	938	1,008	770	4,920	350	2,390	1,617	772	2,881	1,865	1,016
2012	5,830	1,624	1,307	892	1,205	802	5,377	453	2,509	1,665	844	3,321	2,119	1,201
2011	5,705	1,596	1,187	845	1,237	840	5,265	440	2,453	1,664	790	3,252	2,053	1,199
2010	5,904	1,754	1,230	836	1,170	915	5,450	454	2,693	1,803	890	3,211	2,066	1,144
2009	5,551	1,636	960	813	1,221	920	5,095	456	2,363	1,573	790	3,188	2,060	1,128
2008	5,345	1,731	1,001	726	1,095	792	5,006	339	2,331	1,487	844	3,014	1,910	1,104
2007	4,814	1,496	856	774	963	725	4,418	396	2,061	1,322	739	2,753	1,666	1,087
2006	4,294	1,367	788	573	836	731	3,878	416	1,788	1,169	620	2,506	1,531	975
2005	4,327	1,259	833	603	882	751	3,890	437	1,866	1,197	669	2,462	1,436	1,026

NA = Not available.

¹Data for 1970–1975 and 1977 do not include people ages 35 and over.

ʳ = Revised, controlled to 1990 census based population estimates; previous 1993 data controlled to 1980 census based population estimates.

Table A-16. College Enrollment of Students 14 Years Old and Over, by Type of College, Attendance Status, Age, and Sex, October 1970–2016—*Continued*

(Numbers in thousands; civilian noninstitutionalized population.)

Year and type of college	Full time Total	14 to 19 years	20 to 21 years	22 to 24 years	25 to 34 years	35 years and over	Part time Total	14 to 19 years	20 to 21 years	22 to 24 years	25 to 34 years	35 years and over
ALL UNDERGRADUATES												
2016	12,116	4,011	3,757	2,314	1,398	637	3,381	359	539	602	1,091	790
2015	11,915	3,751	3,848	2,170	1,424	722	3,518	414	523	604	1,146	831
2014	12,237	3,943	3,620	2,338	1,542	794	3,260	306	455	640	895	964
2013	12,113	3,823	3,627	2,250	1,608	805	3,625	379	532	802	990	922
2012	12,391	3,820	3,804	2,369	1,675	723	3,779	416	616	655	1,109	983
2011	12,738	4,059	3,855	2,235	1,758	832	3,887	376	514	766	1,261	970
2010	12,354	4,032	3,653	2,071	1,674	924	4,000	514	572	599	1,237	1,077
2009	12,318	4,128	3,534	2,276	1,547	833	3,694	335	431	573	1,189	1,165
2008	11,378	3,999	3,445	2,017	1,240	676	3,577	347	417	583	1,190	1,040
2007	10,866	3,879	3,282	1,858	1,285	562	3,499	358	450	656	992	1,043
2006	10,380	3,567	3,150	1,810	1,242	612	3,474	373	441	627	936	1,097
2005	10,651	3,540	3,369	1,977	1,139	625	3,518	360	479	611	1,003	1,065
2004	10,418	3,533	3,251	1,836	1,150	648	3,586	330	449	595	1,107	1,105
2003	9,868	3,299	2,992	1,948	1,081	547	3,502	334	457	739	1,013	959
2002	9,735	3,356	3,058	1,737	1,073	511	3,690	387	399	619	1,033	1,253
2001	9,006	3,190	2,840	1,524	976	476	3,546	378	489	612	1,003	1,064
2000	8,891	3,368	2,658	1,479	930	457	3,510	342	435	633	1,058	1,041
1999	8,691	3,280	2,625	1,485	888	412	3,355	345	418	514	997	1,081
1998	8,816	3,327	2,619	1,461	956	452	3,693	421	400	563	1,145	1,164
1997	8,917	3,144	2,704	1,576	960	532	3,492	360	376	560	1,010	1,186
1996	8,534	3,131	2,460	1,516	990	437	3,771	394	396	501	1,236	1,243
1995	8,344	2,902	2,462	1,444	1,004	533	3,622	349	419	589	1,147	1,118
1994	8,449	2,843	2,585	1,455	981	586	3,961	350	421	644	1,300	1,245
1993'	8,366	2,866	2,513	1,513	941	533	3,593	332	366	619	1,176	1,102
1993	7,994	2,732	2,380	1,429	927	527	3,513	314	342	590	1,161	1,106
1992	8,063	2,838	2,506	1,427	834	458	3,580	259	396	578	1,255	1,092
1991	7,869	2,809	2,534	1,248	878	400	3,505	252	368	509	1,242	1,134
1990	7,597	2,912	2,333	1,165	824	363	3,511	282	408	515	1,244	1,062
1989	7,314	2,989	2,209	1,122	655	341	3,346	260	321	536	1,266	963
1988	7,257	2,925	2,275	1,079	691	285	3,348	303	371	521	1,173	981
1987	6,920	2,892	2,179	1,005	610	235	3,384	391	406	507	1,238	841
1986	6,825	2,880	1,973	1,055	680	237	3,212	278	324	528	1,254	828
1985	7,033	2,900	2,237	1,017	701	178	3,065	269	349	457	1,184	806
1984	6,992	2,846	2,221	1,067	689	170	2,918	274	344	480	1,139	683
1983	6,896	2,895	2,124	993	718	166	3,029	305	340	482	1,153	748
1982	6,965	2,880	2,286	979	662	159	2,987	302	372	547	1,083	684
1981	6,942	2,983	2,157	986	613	202	3,027	293	353	471	1,195	715
1980	6,457	2,897	2,107	810	500	142	2,822	283	287	505	1,098	649
1979	6,383	2,892	1,994	815	523	158	2,810	264	314	482	1,003	748
1978	6,300	2,872	1,918	820	559	132	2,647	302	328	412	947	658
1977[1]	6,304	2,855	2,075	775	598	NA	2,104	329	301	431	1,042	NA
1976	6,519	2,963	2,033	821	563	138	2,466	253	325	403	909	577
1975	6,296	2,987	1,958	696	655	NA	1,812	250	297	376	891	NA
1974	5,689	2,661	1,842	697	488	NA	1,649	245	289	331	784	NA
1973	5,460	2,629	1,801	630	398	NA	1,334	183	230	294	630	NA
1972	5,678	2,797	1,845	624	412	NA	1,314	177	220	320	599	NA
1971	5,588	2,801	1,729	700	357	NA	1,307	207	207	319	574	NA
1970	5,208	2,685	1,628	591	301	NA	1,066	169	175	275	449	NA
TWO-YEAR COLLEGE STUDENTS												
2016	2,782	1,125	587	416	446	207	1,565	238	290	276	457	304
2015	3,048	1,142	792	403	457	254	1,669	291	312	229	454	383
2014	3,202	1,225	665	474	559	279	1,639	207	324	259	415	434
2013	3,482	1,254	748	571	535	374	1,788	249	305	367	472	396
2012	3,784	1,312	938	568	631	336	2,046	312	369	324	574	466
2011	3,716	1,341	882	458	672	363	1,989	255	306	387	564	477
2010	3,870	1,422	868	554	654	372	2,034	332	362	282	516	542
2009	3,633	1,409	689	540	641	354	1,918	227	271	274	580	566
2008	3,397	1,450	763	455	466	263	1,948	281	239	271	628	529
2007	2,988	1,276	627	425	443	219	1,826	221	230	349	520	506
2006	2,699	1,145	600	312	401	241	1,595	221	188	261	435	490
2005	2,632	1,031	605	373	393	231	1,695	228	228	230	489	520

NA = Not available.

[1] Data for 1970–1975 and 1977 do not include people ages 35 and over.

' = Revised, controlled to 1990 census based population estimates; previous 1993 data controlled to 1980 census based population estimates.

Table A-16. College Enrollment of Students 14 Years Old and Over, by Type of College, Attendance Status, Age, and Sex, October 1970–2016—*Continued*

(Numbers in thousands; civilian noninstitutionalized population.)

Year and type of college	All students Total	14 to 19 years	20 to 21 years	22 to 24 years	25 to 34 years	35 years and over	Public	Private	Male Total	Male Full-time	Male Part-time	Female Total	Female Full-time	Female Part-time
2004	4,340	1,243	802	568	898	829	3,939	401	1,756	1,141	615	2,584	1,461	1,123
2003	4,384	1,178	746	843	834	784	3,999	385	1,782	1,055	726	2,603	1,507	1,095
2002	4,378	1,227	777	656	880	838	3,948	431	1,884	1,102	783	2,494	1,363	1,131
2001	4,159	1,200	776	605	832	746	3,749	410	1,802	1,057	745	2,357	1,252	1,105
2000	3,881	1,232	710	525	673	741	3,590	291	1,655	969	686	2,226	1,224	1,002
1999	3,794	1,187	715	460	683	749	3,482	312	1,637	949	688	2,157	1,157	1,000
1998	4,234	1,301	701	619	839	774	3,865	369	1,845	1,049	796	2,389	1,287	1,103
1997	4,078	1,178	760	528	806	807	3,780	298	1,663	983	680	2,415	1,307	1,108
1996	4,174	1,223	669	515	922	845	3,890	284	1,752	974	778	2,423	1,235	1,187
1995	3,882	1,028	608	593	892	761	3,553	330	1,626	898	728	2,256	1,124	1,132
1994	4,208	1,063	623	621	1,011	890	3,846	362	1,704	937	766	2,504	1,234	1,270
1993ʳ	4,345	1,131	745	648	978	843	4,024	321	1,825	1,061	764	2,520	1,317	1,203
1993	4,196	1,077	696	614	965	844	3,884	311	1,748	1,006	742	2,448	1,268	1,179
1992	4,239	1,084	789	581	988	797	3,937	302	1,688	936	751	2,551	1,268	1,283
1991	4,277	1,120	732	560	1,084	781	4,025	252	1,798	973	825	2,479	1,239	1,239
1990	3,965	1,059	689	475	967	775	3,689	276	1,624	849	775	2,340	1,103	1,237
1989	3,627	1,048	557	467	880	676	3,382	245	1,464	777	688	2,163	949	1,214
1988	3,837	1,134	665	497	879	662	3,609	228	1,542	847	695	2,295	1,054	1,241
1987	3,648	1,111	624	457	851	605	3,405	243	1,522	780	742	2,127	937	1,190
1986	3,391	1,023	506	427	875	559	3,089	302	1,466	752	714	1,924	856	1,068
1985	3,289	959	558	403	851	518	3,009	281	1,336	702	634	1,954	914	1,040
1984	3,172	994	525	442	795	417	2,875	298	1,436	834	601	1,738	829	909
1983	3,416	1,050	595	405	882	485	3,136	280	1,498	807	691	1,919	897	1,022
1982	3,448	1,088	604	494	826	437	3,164	283	1,477	854	623	1,971	961	1,011
1981	3,347	1,144	566	414	768	455	3,091	255	1,475	837	638	1,872	909	963
1980	3,107	1,079	450	417	721	441	NA	NA	1,331	768	563	1,777	798	979
1979	2,897	933	403	407	664	490	2,710	187	1,251	684	567	1,646	725	921
1978	2,904	966	427	391	670	451	2,686	218	1,368	698	669	1,537	701	835
1977¹	2,510	933	455	380	741	NA	2,362	148	1,253	681	572	1,256	691	565
1976	2,854	907	444	367	718	419	2,688	165	1,400	760	640	1,454	743	711
1975	2,561	1,024	431	354	752	NA	2,437	123	1,412	850	562	1,148	717	431
1974	2,072	834	369	305	565	NA	1,917	154	1,172	709	463	899	528	371
1973	1,797	816	278	254	449	NA	1,669	128	1,012	629	383	785	471	314
1972	1,910	883	334	267	426	NA	1,816	94	1,125	770	355	785	484	301
1971	1,830	928	307	263	331	NA	1,726	105	1,087	726	361	743	473	270
1970	1,692	895	281	234	283	NA	1,559	133	1,001	726	275	691	452	239
GRADUATE STUDENTS														
2016	3,699	42	121	817	1,729	990	2,448	1,251	1,569	1,071	498	2,130	1,234	896
2015	3,668	35	134	895	1,605	998	2,413	1,255	1,482	1,043	439	2,186	1,278	908
2014	3,677	22	143	900	1,551	1,061	2,447	1,230	1,559	957	602	2,119	1,205	913
2013	3,729	57	168	873	1,468	1,164	2,385	1,344	1,439	933	506	2,291	1,182	1,108
2012	3,760	48	142	854	1,550	1,165	2,327	1,433	1,495	910	585	2,265	1,301	964
2011	3,773	11	91	868	1,598	1,205	2,318	1,454	1,617	905	712	2,156	1,261	895
2010	3,921	47	123	830	1,712	1,209	2,453	1,468	1,708	1,050	658	2,214	1,196	1,017
2009	3,752	32	70	901	1,556	1,194	2,366	1,386	1,521	852	669	2,232	1,194	1,038
2008	3,676	20	58	819	1,583	1,195	2,399	1,277	1,574	880	694	2,103	987	1,116
2007	3,591	24	62	779	1,560	1,166	2,261	1,330	1,420	819	601	2,171	971	1,200
2006	3,378	18	84	729	1,480	1,067	2,197	1,181	1,371	692	678	2,007	998	1,009
2005	3,304	7	98	574	1,458	1,167	2,143	1,161	1,349	711	638	1,955	875	1,079
2004	3,378	20	77	718	1,433	1,131	2,267	1,111	1,419	726	693	1,959	845	1,114
2003	3,268	29	84	632	1,399	1,123	2,129	1,139	1,416	774	643	1,852	849	1,003
2002	3,072	33	68	572	1,296	1,104	2,003	1,068	1,311	632	679	1,761	774	987
2001	3,321	48	91	595	1,442	1,145	2,233	1,088	1,353	614	739	1,968	784	1,184
2000	2,913	38	77	571	1,218	1,009	1,965	948	1,162	546	616	1,750	722	1,028
1999	3,157	45	77	620	1,211	1,205	1,970	1,188	1,403	699	703	1,755	722	1,033
1998	3,037	45	73	536	1,313	1,070	1,884	1,153	1,284	614	669	1,753	758	995
1997	3,027	30	63	562	1,299	1,073	2,016	1,010	1,304	651	653	1,723	668	1,055
1996	2,922	21	52	534	1,217	1,098	1,893	1,029	1,288	650	638	1,634	655	979
1995	2,749	8	60	465	1,198	1,018	1,802	947	1,290	646	644	1,459	554	905
1994	2,613	9	21	551	1,138	893	1,710	902	1,238	619	619	1,375	505	870
1993ʳ	2,435	3	14	537	1,022	859	1,611	824	1,156	601	555	1,278	458	820
1993	2,391	3	13	514	1,006	856	1,580	812	1,130	579	551	1,261	446	815
1992	2,392	*	36	508	1,035	814	1,546	846	1,102	606	496	1,291	521	770
1991	2,683	*	37	547	1,165	934	1,824	859	1,320	688	631	1,364	491	872

NA = Not available.
¹Data for 1970–1975 and 1977 do not include people ages 35 and over.
* = Quantity zero or rounds to zero.
ʳ = Revised, controlled to 1990 census based population estimates; previous 1993 data controlled to 1980 census based population estimates.

Table A-16. College Enrollment of Students 14 Years Old and Over, by Type of College, Attendance Status, Age, and Sex, October 1970–2016—*Continued*

(Numbers in thousands; civilian noninstitutionalized population.)

Year and type of college		Full time						Part time				
	Total	14 to 19 years	20 to 21 years	22 to 24 years	25 to 34 years	35 years and over	Total	14 to 19 years	20 to 21 years	22 to 24 years	25 to 34 years	35 years and over
2004	2,602	1,027	553	327	425	269	1,738	216	249	241	472	560
2003	2,563	973	516	386	429	258	1,822	205	230	457	404	526
2002	2,464	975	571	344	374	200	1,914	252	206	312	506	638
2001	2,310	951	529	301	307	222	1,850	250	247	304	524	525
2000	2,193	993	507	278	230	184	1,688	239	202	247	444	557
1999	2,105	955	498	261	230	161	1,688	231	217	199	453	588
1998	2,336	1,024	495	331	302	184	1,899	277	206	288	537	591
1997	2,290	947	522	283	327	212	1,788	231	238	245	479	595
1996	2,209	995	457	271	315	171	1,965	227	212	244	607	674
1995	2,022	810	397	298	321	195	1,860	218	211	295	571	565
1994	2,172	848	407	319	341	256	2,036	215	216	302	669	634
1993ʳ	2,378	891	515	348	365	259	1,967	240	230	300	613	585
1993	2,274	850	483	325	360	256	1,922	227	213	288	605	588
1992	2,205	897	528	287	304	188	2,034	187	261	294	683	609
1991	2,212	915	476	269	361	191	2,065	205	256	291	723	589
1990	1,953	847	408	227	310	160	2,012	212	281	247	657	615
1989	1,725	860	368	160	210	128	1,902	188	189	307	669	548
1988	1,901	926	410	209	227	128	1,936	207	256	288	651	534
1987	1,716	839	368	192	212	105	1,932	272	256	264	639	500
1986	1,608	814	296	170	223	105	1,783	209	210	257	652	454
1985	1,615	779	341	174	244	78	1,674	180	217	229	607	440
1984	1,663	812	330	190	247	84	1,509	182	195	252	548	333
1983	1,703	855	374	159	250	65	1,713	195	221	245	631	420
1982	1,814	883	381	214	260	77	1,634	205	223	280	566	356
1981	1,745	927	357	170	188	102	1,601	217	209	243	579	353
1980	1,566	884	287	160	167	67	1,542	195	163	256	554	374
1979	1,408	749	251	156	185	68	1,489	184	152	251	480	423
1978	1,400	776	243	157	167	57	1,505	190	184	234	503	394
1977[1]	1,372	718	283	162	208	NA	1,138	216	172	218	533	NA
1976	1,503	764	261	177	228	74	1,351	143	183	190	490	346
1975	1,567	865	274	155	274	NA	994	159	157	199	478	NA
1974	1,237	702	233	151	152	NA	835	132	136	154	413	NA
1973	1,100	702	164	121	111	NA	697	114	113	133	338	NA
1972	1,255	772	223	134	126	NA	655	111	111	133	300	NA
1971	1,199	797	209	124	70	NA	631	131	98	139	261	NA
1970	1,177	786	197	114	80	NA	515	109	84	120	203	NA
GRADUATE STUDENTS												
2016	2,305	42	95	693	1,103	372	1,394	*	26	123	627	618
2015	2,321	35	105	749	1,051	381	1,347	*	29	146	555	617
2014	2,163	22	111	739	911	380	1,515	*	32	161	640	682
2013	2,115	38	143	702	866	366	1,614	18	25	171	602	798
2012	2,211	45	122	699	924	420	1,549	3	21	155	625	745
2011	2,165	6	77	684	955	444	1,607	5	14	185	643	761
2010	2,246	35	120	697	1,027	367	1,675	12	4	133	685	842
2009	2,046	26	49	704	916	351	1,707	6	20	197	641	843
2008	1,867	20	53	646	851	296	1,810	*	5	173	732	899
2007	1,790	23	59	569	815	324	1,801	1	4	210	745	842
2006	1,690	16	70	542	809	254	1,688	3	14	187	671	813
2005	1,587	4	98	423	767	294	1,717	3	*	150	691	873
2004	1,571	20	76	548	675	252	1,807	*	1	170	757	878
2003	1,622	26	76	479	738	304	1,646	3	8	153	662	820
2002	1,406	31	61	432	631	251	1,666	2	6	140	666	852
2001	1,398	38	77	455	630	197	1,923	10	14	139	812	947
2000	1,268	32	67	414	544	211	1,645	6	10	156	674	798
1999	1,421	38	71	487	539	287	1,736	8	6	133	672	918
1998	1,372	45	58	429	579	262	1,665	*	15	107	734	808
1997	1,319	26	57	401	605	229	1,708	3	6	160	694	844
1996	1,305	18	42	420	570	254	1,617	3	9	114	647	844
1995	1,199	8	43	352	571	225	1,550	*	17	112	627	793
1994	1,124	9	19	377	544	175	1,489	*	2	174	594	718
1993ʳ	1,059	3	11	376	482	186	1,376	*	3	161	540	673
1993	1,025	3	10	358	469	184	1,366	*	3	156	536	672
1992	1,126	*	33	387	478	228	1,266	*	3	120	557	586
1991	1,180	*	29	423	539	188	1,504	*	8	124	626	746

NA = Not available.

[1]Data for 1970–1975 and 1977 do not include people ages 35 and over.

* = Quantity zero or rounds to zero.

ʳ = Revised, controlled to 1990 census based population estimates; previous 1993 data controlled to 1980 census based population estimates.

Table A-16. College Enrollment of Students 14 Years Old and Over, by Type of College, Attendance Status, Age, and Sex, October 1970–2016—*Continued*

(Numbers in thousands; civilian noninstitutionalized population.)

Year and type of college	All students								Male			Female		
	Total	14 to 19 years	20 to 21 years	22 to 24 years	25 to 34 years	35 years and over	Public	Private	Total	Full-time	Part-time	Total	Full-time	Part-time
1990	2,514	2	27	497	1,095	893	1,722	792	1,162	569	593	1,352	531	820
1989	2,520	*	40	509	1,161	809	1,662	857	1,219	626	594	1,300	515	786
1988	2,511	*	36	464	1,098	913	1,716	795	1,187	522	666	1,324	435	889
1987	2,415	1	57	494	1,137	725	1,655	760	1,152	579	573	1,263	462	801
1986	2,365	*	44	530	1,057	732	1,624	741	1,184	596	589	1,181	479	702
1985	2,427	*	31	540	1,179	678	1,652	775	1,239	607	632	1,188	395	793
1984	2,395	*	32	580	1,190	594	1,648	747	1,263	654	610	1,132	440	692
1983	2,442	*	32	568	1,214	629	1,614	829	1,279	665	614	1,163	438	725
1982	2,393	1	31	534	1,244	584	1,587	806	1,216	626	590	1,178	421	756
1981	2,205	*	34	528	1,120	523	1,478	726	1,127	546	581	1,078	347	731
1980	2,173	2	31	554	1,104	481	NA	NA	1,106	526	581	1,066	372	694
1979	2,214	*	45	497	1,149	523	1,537	678	1,105	503	602	1,109	355	754
1978	2,217	*	51	565	1,064	536	1,454	762	1,149	516	633	1,068	366	702
1977	1,810	2	53	593	1,161	NA	1,241	568	995	548	447	813	338	475
1976	2,152	*	40	622	1,017	472	1,516	634	1,216	576	638	937	292	644
1975	1,590	*	59	607	923	NA	1,105	484	949	542	407	640	267	373
1974	1,490	*	61	499	930	NA	1,061	428	897	457	440	593	205	388
1973	1,385	*	42	541	801	NA	945	439	887	467	420	498	163	335
1972	1,320	1	52	517	749	NA	877	443	872	481	391	450	155	295
1971	1,192	1	60	468	663	NA	799	393	833	480	353	359	136	223
1970	1,140	*	54	488	599	NA	789	351	774	432	342	366	123	243

NA = Not available.
[1]Data for 1970–1975 and 1977 do not include people ages 35 and over.
* = Quantity zero or rounds to zero.

Table A-16. College Enrollment of Students 14 Years Old and Over, by Type of College, Attendance Status, Age, and Sex, October 1970–2016—*Continued*

(Numbers in thousands; civilian noninstitutionalized population.)

Year and type of college	Full time						Part time					
	Total	14 to 19 years	20 to 21 years	22 to 24 years	25 to 34 years	35 years and over	Total	14 to 19 years	20 to 21 years	22 to 24 years	25 to 34 years	35 years and over
1990	1,100	2	25	376	518	180	1,413	*	2	121	577	714
1989	1,140	*	33	375	525	208	1,380	*	7	135	637	601
1988	956	*	31	304	465	157	1,555	*	5	160	634	756
1987	1,041	1	52	343	477	167	1,374	*	5	151	660	558
1986	1,074	*	40	412	465	157	1,291	*	4	120	593	575
1985	1,002	*	27	385	449	141	1,424	*	4	155	728	537
1984	1,093	*	27	427	544	95	1,302	*	6	153	644	498
1983	1,103	*	32	420	530	121	1,339	*	*	148	685	507
1982	1,047	*	28	381	522	116	1,346	1	4	153	721	467
1981	893	*	28	355	447	64	1,312	*	6	173	673	459
1980	898	2	24	403	403	66	1,275	*	6	152	702	415
1979	858	*	32	358	397	72	1,356	*	14	140	752	451
1978	882	*	38	396	376	71	1,335	*	14	169	688	465
1977	886	2	43	382	459	NA	922	*	10	211	702	NA
1976	869	*	35	405	355	73	1,282	*	5	217	662	398
1975	809	*	43	382	386	NA	780	*	16	225	537	NA
1974	662	*	41	289	330	NA	828	*	20	210	600	NA
1973	630	*	33	350	248	NA	755	*	9	191	553	NA
1972	636	1	44	332	262	NA	686	*	8	185	487	NA
1971	616	1	57	299	261	NA	576	*	3	169	402	NA
1970	555	*	42	304	212	NA	585	*	12	184	387	NA

NA = Not available.
[1]Data for 1970–1975 and 1977 do not include people ages 35 and over.
* = Quantity zero or rounds to zero.

PART A

NATIONAL EDUCATION STATISTICS

■ **Attainment Tables**

Table A-17. Educational Attainment of the Population 18 Years Old and Over, by Age, Sex, Race, and Hispanic Origin, 2017

(Numbers in thousands; civilian noninstitutionalized population.[1])

Age, sex, race, and Hispanic origin	Total	None	1st to 4th grade	5th to 6th grade	7th to 8th grade	9th grade	10th grade	11th grade[2]	High school graduate
ALL RACES									
Both Sexes									
18 years old and over	246,325	770	1,555	3,214	3,648	3,484	4,267	10,245	71,170
18 to 24 years old	29,404	53	64	80	182	231	604	3,427	8,658
25 years old and over	216,921	717	1,490	3,133	3,467	3,253	3,663	6,817	62,512
25 to 29 years old	22,745	18	71	114	172	224	351	761	6,076
30 to 34 years old	21,505	51	78	208	238	298	277	620	5,418
35 to 39 years old	20,773	53	102	325	280	385	306	623	5,152
40 to 44 years old	19,273	53	119	328	297	316	253	581	4,646
45 to 49 years old	20,662	46	111	330	268	335	279	641	5,753
50 to 54 years old	21,364	80	146	307	267	311	366	661	6,553
55 to 59 years old	21,837	76	125	313	260	278	358	699	7,125
60 to 64 years old	19,488	73	157	318	271	229	313	560	5,892
65 to 69 years old	16,750	56	147	295	287	239	273	490	4,830
70 to 74 years old	12,462	53	138	191	310	198	279	367	3,863
75 years old and over	20,062	158	297	405	816	440	607	813	7,206
Male									
18 years old and over	119,170	360	793	1,639	1,849	1,738	2,211	5,321	36,161
18 to 24 years old	14,845	24	40	54	122	111	333	1,892	4,865
25 years old and over	104,324	337	753	1,585	1,727	1,627	1,878	3,430	31,296
25 to 29 years old	11,410	13	43	77	90	113	190	439	3,398
30 to 34 years old	10,711	29	50	114	109	141	168	359	3,059
35 to 39 years old	10,281	20	66	203	162	186	166	326	2,939
40 to 44 years old	9,454	25	75	176	153	159	125	333	2,509
45 to 49 years old	10,118	20	55	162	133	174	162	348	3,107
50 to 54 years old	10,449	44	89	165	151	163	206	363	3,477
55 to 59 years old	10,587	35	50	167	134	144	195	366	3,648
60 to 64 years old	9,154	48	77	154	105	117	153	268	2,778
65 to 69 years old	7,907	19	68	138	142	110	134	221	2,111
70 to 74 years old	5,759	22	55	77	180	110	133	141	1,600
75 years old and over	8,493	61	126	153	368	209	246	266	2,672
Female									
18 years old and over	127,155	410	761	1,575	1,800	1,746	2,056	4,923	35,010
18 to 24 years old	14,559	29	24	27	59	120	271	1,536	3,794
25 years old and over	112,597	380	737	1,548	1,740	1,626	1,785	3,388	31,216
25 to 29 years old	11,335	5	29	37	82	110	161	323	2,678
30 to 34 years old	10,795	22	28	94	129	157	110	261	2,359
35 to 39 years old	10,492	33	35	122	118	199	140	297	2,213
40 to 44 years old	9,819	28	43	152	145	156	128	249	2,137
45 to 49 years old	10,543	25	56	167	135	161	117	293	2,646
50 to 54 years old	10,915	36	57	142	117	148	161	298	3,075
55 to 59 years old	11,250	41	75	146	126	133	162	333	3,477
60 to 64 years old	10,334	25	80	163	167	112	160	292	3,114
65 to 69 years old	8,843	37	79	157	146	129	139	269	2,719
70 to 74 years old	6,702	31	83	114	130	88	145	226	2,263
75 years old and over	11,569	98	171	252	448	231	361	547	4,533
WHITE ALONE									
Both Sexes									
18 years old and over	192,667	487	1,206	2,614	2,885	2,750	3,100	7,331	55,566
18 to 24 years old	21,620	32	47	66	147	164	401	2,505	6,358
25 years old and over	171,046	455	1,159	2,549	2,738	2,586	2,699	4,826	49,209
25 to 29 years old	16,667	17	50	93	140	184	265	518	4,356
30 to 34 years old	16,101	30	54	176	196	247	198	445	4,109
35 to 39 years old	15,738	32	94	288	253	312	237	441	3,886
40 to 44 years old	14,581	35	89	301	250	252	197	408	3,476
45 to 49 years old	16,065	28	93	289	228	284	209	472	4,444
50 to 54 years old	16,881	56	117	263	211	258	272	471	5,085
55 to 59 years old	17,561	43	111	255	216	204	251	482	5,699
60 to 64 years old	15,828	49	125	248	179	175	214	368	4,699
65 to 69 years old	13,869	40	107	211	187	179	203	315	3,904
70 to 74 years old	10,503	33	95	142	229	153	198	256	3,252
75 years old and over	17,251	90	222	282	649	338	455	651	6,299
Male									
18 years old and over	94,277	254	613	1,373	1,513	1,395	1,646	3,890	28,512
18 to 24 years old	10,979	17	30	43	101	88	233	1,413	3,658

[1]Civilian noninstitutionalized population, plus armed forces living off post or with their families on post.
[2]Population who attained the 12th grade but received no diploma are included in this category.

Table A-17. Educational Attainment of the Population 18 Years Old and Over, by Age, Sex, Race, and Hispanic Origin, 2017—*Continued*

(Numbers in thousands; civilian noninstitutionalized population.[1])

Age, sex, race, and Hispanic origin	Educational attainment						
	Some college, no degree	Associate's degree, occupational	Associate's degree, academic	Bachelor's degree	Master's degree	Professional degree	Doctoral degree
ALL RACES							
Both Sexes							
18 years old and over......................	46,445	10,081	13,990	49,368	20,797	3,196	4,096
18 to 24 years old	10,990	672	1088	3,105	205	25	20
25 years old and over......................	35,455	9,408	12,902	46,262	20,592	3,172	4,077
25 to 29 years old	4,462	918	1,463	6,028	1,675	197	214
30 to 34 years old	3,680	893	1,376	5,356	2,197	357	458
35 to 39 years old	3,209	914	1,284	4,984	2,438	283	434
40 to 44 years old	2,890	941	1,197	4,622	2,273	325	432
45 to 49 years old	3,149	907	1,300	4,612	2,198	323	410
50 to 54 years old	3,338	1,020	1,473	4,247	1,937	264	394
55 to 59 years old	3,515	1,024	1,426	4,235	1,715	337	353
60 to 64 years old	3,393	892	1,196	3,658	1,859	319	358
65 to 69 years old	2,805	780	875	3,295	1,707	312	358
70 to 74 years old	1,951	511	577	2,308	1247	200	270
75 years old and over....................	3,063	609	735	2,918	1,346	254	396
Male							
18 years old and over......................	22,198	4,682	5,711	23,223	9,117	1,770	2,396
18 to 24 years old	5,268	308	434	1,317	68	6	4
25 years old and over......................	16,930	4,374	5,277	21,906	9,049	1,765	2,392
25 to 29 years old	2,335	426	631	2,765	706	87	98
30 to 34 years old	1,820	412	642	2,492	903	190	223
35 to 39 years old	1,564	468	549	2,335	935	121	241
40 to 44 years old	1,445	474	502	2,134	959	154	232
45 to 49 years old	1,563	409	503	2,155	965	142	221
50 to 54 years old	1,550	455	546	1,996	878	143	224
55 to 59 years old	1,656	488	552	2,004	744	189	215
60 to 64 years old	1,597	437	451	1,703	856	193	217
65 to 69 years old	1255	375	375	1692	812	207	250
70 to 74 years old	869	184	247	1,180	606	164	191
75 years old and over....................	1,276	247	280	1,450	686	175	279
Female							
18 years old and over......................	24,247	5,399	8,278	26,145	11,680	1,426	1,700
18 to 24 years old	5,721	364	654	1,788	137	19	16
25 years old and over......................	18,525	5,035	7,624	24,357	11,543	1,407	1,685
25 to 29 years old	2,126	492	832	3,264	969	110	116
30 to 34 years old	1,860	481	734	2,864	1,294	167	235
35 to 39 years old	1,645	447	735	2,650	1,503	162	192
40 to 44 years old	1,444	467	696	2,487	1,315	171	200
45 to 49 years old	1,587	498	797	2,456	1,233	182	189
50 to 54 years old	1,788	565	927	2,251	1,058	121	170
55 to 59 years old	1,859	536	874	2,231	971	148	137
60 to 64 years old	1,796	455	745	1,954	1,003	126	140
65 to 69 years old	1,550	405	500	1,603	895	105	108
70 to 74 years old	1,082	327	330	1128	641	36	79
75 years old and over....................	1,788	361	455	1,468	660	79	117
WHITE ALONE							
Both Sexes							
18 years old and over......................	35,609	8,342	11,171	39,672	16,169	2,655	3,109
18 to 24 years old	7,929	540	839	2,438	130	13	12
25 years old and over......................	27,680	7,802	10,332	37,234	16,039	2,642	3,096
25 to 29 years old	3,158	698	1,127	4,633	1,134	139	155
30 to 34 years old	2,623	674	1,019	4,182	1,535	281	331
35 to 39 years old	2,394	723	1,003	3,810	1,707	225	334
40 to 44 years old	2,159	746	918	3,554	1,654	260	283
45 to 49 years old	2,418	725	1,024	3,670	1,631	265	286
50 to 54 years old	2,596	888	1,171	3,482	1,518	205	288
55 to 59 years old	2,802	880	1,187	3,466	1,437	284	245
60 to 64 years old	2,807	773	975	3,045	1,608	279	283
65 to 69 years old	2,321	701	766	2,829	1499	285	323
70 to 74 years old	1,672	442	484	2,018	1,122	185	222
75 years old and over....................	2,731	552	658	2,545	1,194	235	347
Male							
18 years old and over......................	17,162	3,961	4,567	18,917	7,097	1,549	1,829
18 to 24 years old	3,749	251	322	1025	40	6	4

[1]Civilian noninstitutionalized population, plus armed forces living off post or with their families on post.

Table A-17. Educational Attainment of the Population 18 Years Old and Over, by Age, Sex, Race, and Hispanic Origin, 2017—Continued

(Numbers in thousands; civilian noninstitutionalized population.[1])

Age, sex, race, and Hispanic origin	Total	None	1st to 4th grade	5th to 6th grade	7th to 8th grade	9th grade	10th grade	11th grade[2]	High school graduate
25 years old and over	83,298	237	583	1,330	1,412	1,307	1,413	2,477	24,854
25 to 29 years old	8,449	13	31	61	75	87	152	329	2,524
30 to 34 years old	8,144	19	32	96	99	108	108	260	2,409
35 to 39 years old	7,978	8	62	179	143	141	127	233	2,266
40 to 44 years old	7,273	18	57	165	130	131	102	236	1,932
45 to 49 years old	8,019	13	43	148	117	150	130	261	2,441
50 to 54 years old	8,381	33	74	136	126	134	151	267	2,739
55 to 59 years old	8,598	22	44	144	108	117	140	258	2,932
60 to 64 years old	7,525	34	62	134	77	91	111	177	2,233
65 to 69 years old	6,621	12	43	103	88	87	100	141	1,707
70 to 74 years old	4,913	18	40	54	140	90	106	98	1,332
75 years old and over	7,397	47	95	110	309	171	185	215	2,341
Female									
18 years old and over	98,390	233	593	1,242	1,373	1,356	1,453	3,441	27,054
18 to 24 years old	10,641	15	17	23	46	77	168	1,092	2,700
25 years old and over	87,749	218	576	1,219	1,327	1,279	1,285	2,349	24,354
25 to 29 years old	8,218	4	19	32	66	97	114	189	1,832
30 to 34 years old	7,958	11	22	80	98	139	89	185	1,700
35 to 39 years old	7,760	24	32	109	110	171	110	208	1,620
40 to 44 years old	7,308	17	32	136	120	121	95	172	1,545
45 to 49 years old	8,046	15	50	141	111	133	78	211	2,003
50 to 54 years old	8,500	24	43	127	85	124	121	204	2,346
55 to 59 years old	8,964	21	67	111	108	88	111	223	2,767
60 to 64 years old	8,303	15	64	114	102	84	102	191	2,466
65 to 69 years old	7,248	28	64	108	100	91	103	173	2,197
70 to 74 years old	5,590	16	55	89	89	64	92	158	1,920
75 years old and over	9,854	44	127	173	340	167	271	436	3,959
BLACK ALONE									
Both Sexes									
18 years old and over	30,847	128	116	236	421	450	802	1,989	10,249
18 to 24 years old	4,392	10	5	7	20	46	133	553	1,527
25 years old and over	26,455	117	111	229	401	403	669	1,436	8,722
25 to 29 years old	3,434	1	13	14	13	25	43	170	1186
30 to 34 years old	2,921	9	4	7	9	27	63	125	821
35 to 39 years old	2,776	10	1	5	7	43	52	123	853
40 to 44 years old	2,536	6	6	12	25	30	41	111	757
45 to 49 years old	2,639	6	3	17	24	28	47	109	831
50 to 54 years old	2,712	14	6	8	26	32	70	144	981
55 to 59 years old	2,626	12	*	20	25	38	66	154	996
60 to 64 years old	2,249	10	10	29	43	42	61	149	791
65 to 69 years old	1,775	7	21	27	57	41	55	133	613
70 to 74 years old	1171	8	18	24	54	25	59	93	387
75 years old and over	1,615	34	28	67	119	71	114	125	505
Male									
18 years old and over	14,038	51	75	116	196	208	412	943	5,071
18 to 24 years old	2,140	3	4	5	15	22	73	273	798
25 years old and over	11,898	47	71	111	181	186	338	670	4,273
25 to 29 years old	1,657	*	11	14	9	15	24	73	603
30 to 34 years old	1,360	*	4	4	1	16	50	71	402
35 to 39 years old	1,256	7	*	4	5	26	34	56	449
40 to 44 years old	1,146	3	3	5	8	12	17	65	377
45 to 49 years old	1,193	2	3	8	10	12	27	56	434
50 to 54 years old	1,240	7	3	3	12	19	36	71	531
55 to 59 years old	1,185	7	*	7	18	15	37	78	500
60 to 64 years old	1003	6	5	9	7	20	21	65	374
65 to 69 years old	759	2	16	14	33	12	27	62	262
70 to 74 years old	497	2	10	11	33	11	19	35	164
75 years old and over	602	10	16	31	46	27	48	38	176
Female									
18 years old and over	16,808	77	42	120	225	242	390	1,045	5,177
18 to 24 years old	2,252	7	1	3	5	24	59	280	728
25 years old and over	14,557	70	40	118	221	218	331	765	4,449
25 to 29 years old	1,777	1	2	*	4	10	19	97	583
30 to 34 years old	1,561	9	*	3	9	12	13	54	420
35 to 39 years old	1,521	3	1	1	2	16	18	67	404

[1]Civilian noninstitutionalized population, plus armed forces living off post or with their families on post.
[2]Population who attained the 12th grade but received no diploma are included in this category.
* = Quantity zero or rounds to zero.

Table A-17. Educational Attainment of the Population 18 Years Old and Over, by Age, Sex, Race, and Hispanic Origin, 2017—*Continued*

(Numbers in thousands; civilian noninstitutionalized population.[1])

Age, sex, race, and Hispanic origin	Educational attainment						
	Some college, no degree	Associate's degree, occupational	Associate's degree, academic	Bachelor's degree	Master's degree	Professional degree	Doctoral degree
25 years old and over	13,413	3,710	4,245	17,892	7,056	1,543	1,825
25 to 29 years old	1,634	333	492	2,123	459	71	65
30 to 34 years old	1,337	322	468	1,960	605	156	164
35 to 39 years old	1,221	382	433	1,829	667	105	183
40 to 44 years old	1,083	407	399	1,648	677	137	151
45 to 49 years old	1,258	326	397	1,723	738	121	152
50 to 54 years old	1,231	392	436	1,701	695	110	156
55 to 59 years old	1,364	437	449	1,653	609	167	155
60 to 64 years old	1,332	383	378	1,437	738	167	169
65 to 69 years old	1070	335	325	1497	699	190	223
70 to 74 years old	755	165	211	1,041	551	155	158
75 years old and over	1128	228	257	1,281	617	165	248
Female							
18 years old and over	18,447	4,381	6,604	20,755	9,072	1,106	1,280
18 to 24 years old	4,180	289	517	1,413	90	8	8
25 years old and over	14,267	4,092	6,087	19,342	8,982	1,098	1,271
25 to 29 years old	1,524	365	635	2,511	675	68	90
30 to 34 years old	1,286	352	552	2,222	930	125	167
35 to 39 years old	1,173	341	570	1,980	1,040	120	151
40 to 44 years old	1,077	339	519	1,906	977	123	132
45 to 49 years old	1,160	399	627	1,947	893	144	134
50 to 54 years old	1,364	496	735	1,781	824	95	132
55 to 59 years old	1,437	443	738	1,814	828	117	90
60 to 64 years old	1,475	390	597	1,608	870	112	113
65 to 69 years old	1,252	366	441	1332	799	95	99
70 to 74 years old	917	276	273	978	570	30	64
75 years old and over	1,603	324	401	1,264	576	70	100
BLACK ALONE							
Both Sexes							
18 years old and over	6,857	1,194	1,743	4,301	1,872	194	297
18 to 24 years old	1,534	80	148	299	27	3	1
25 years old and over	5,323	1,114	1,595	4,002	1,845	191	296
25 to 29 years old	878	148	179	581	136	28	18
30 to 34 years old	732	147	221	484	218	27	26
35 to 39 years old	536	133	177	521	284	21	11
40 to 44 years old	503	144	172	466	211	14	36
45 to 49 years old	502	122	192	424	278	16	39
50 to 54 years old	533	82	185	392	177	30	30
55 to 59 years old	497	112	147	368	127	20	46
60 to 64 years old	395	83	148	284	154	14	36
65 to 69 years old	351	62	61	202	120	8	17
70 to 74 years old	187	49	62	119	61	6	19
75 years old and over	208	32	50	160	78	6	18
Male							
18 years old and over	3,017	486	703	1,891	672	64	135
18 to 24 years old	719	33	67	114	12	*	*
25 years old and over	2,298	453	636	1,776	660	64	135
25 to 29 years old	449	53	69	276	52	3	7
30 to 34 years old	325	57	116	217	75	9	13
35 to 39 years old	210	62	69	241	85	3	3
40 to 44 years old	247	49	69	206	68	*	15
45 to 49 years old	206	60	75	190	96	*	13
50 to 54 years old	223	39	64	144	53	19	16
55 to 59 years old	182	37	58	169	47	10	18
60 to 64 years old	181	41	54	126	66	8	19
65 to 69 years old	115	34	24	83	60	4	11
70 to 74 years old	74	13	20	62	24	5	15
75 years old and over	85	6	18	62	32	2	6
Female							
18 years old and over	3,840	708	1,040	2,410	1,199	130	162
18 to 24 years old	815	47	81	184	14	3	1
25 years old and over	3,025	661	959	2,226	1,185	127	161
25 to 29 years old	429	95	111	305	84	25	11
30 to 34 years old	408	89	105	267	143	18	13
35 to 39 years old	326	70	108	280	198	18	9

[1]Civilian noninstitutionalized population, plus armed forces living off post or with their families on post.
* = Quantity zero or rounds to zero.

Table A-17. Educational Attainment of the Population 18 Years Old and Over, by Age, Sex, Race, and Hispanic Origin, 2017—*Continued*

(Numbers in thousands; civilian noninstitutionalized population.[1])

Age, sex, race, and Hispanic origin	Total	None	1st to 4th grade	5th to 6th grade	7th to 8th grade	9th grade	10th grade	11th grade[2]	High school graduate
40 to 44 years old	1,390	3	3	7	16	18	25	45	380
45 to 49 years old	1,446	4	*	9	14	16	20	53	396
50 to 54 years old	1,472	7	4	4	14	14	34	74	450
55 to 59 years old	1,441	5	*	13	7	22	29	76	496
60 to 64 years old	1,246	4	5	20	36	22	40	84	418
65 to 69 years old	1,016	5	4	13	24	29	28	70	351
70 to 74 years old	674	5	8	13	21	14	40	58	223
75 years old and over	1,013	24	12	36	73	44	67	87	329
ASIAN ALONE									
Both Sexes									
18 years old and over	15,005	112	146	238	236	123	178	361	2,960
18 to 24 years old	1,821	8	9	3	5	9	31	130	291
25 years old and over	13,183	104	137	235	231	114	148	231	2,668
25 to 29 years old	1,708	*	7	6	11	4	12	15	248
30 to 34 years old	1,617	3	13	4	21	6	5	19	230
35 to 39 years old	1,506	6	5	5	9	16	15	22	237
40 to 44 years old	1,476	3	8	6	18	8	10	36	203
45 to 49 years old	1,381	9	3	18	16	10	8	14	306
50 to 54 years old	1,214	10	6	14	23	14	8	17	313
55 to 59 years old	1123	17	13	29	10	13	21	27	251
60 to 64 years old	948	10	11	34	35	5	23	21	246
65 to 69 years old	776	8	14	47	26	9	7	29	213
70 to 74 years old	546	12	19	23	26	15	11	10	134
75 years old and over	886	26	37	49	36	15	28	21	288
Male									
18 years old and over	7,073	32	50	78	82	51	68	178	1,367
18 to 24 years old	914	3	5	3	3	*	9	62	156
25 years old and over	6,159	29	45	76	78	51	59	115	1,211
25 to 29 years old	877	*	*	*	3	2	5	10	143
30 to 34 years old	762	*	8	2	6	5	2	5	117
35 to 39 years old	679	*	3	3	5	12	4	12	114
40 to 44 years old	707	*	6	*	11	2	2	16	96
45 to 49 years old	661	3	2	4	6	4	2	9	141
50 to 54 years old	546	4	1	8	9	6	7	9	117
55 to 59 years old	538	4	5	12	3	3	10	15	114
60 to 64 years old	422	7	3	9	13	*	12	13	104
65 to 69 years old	364	4	4	16	10	5	3	13	95
70 to 74 years old	244	2	5	11	7	7	3	5	70
75 years old and over	360	4	10	10	5	5	8	10	101
Female									
18 years old and over	7,931	80	96	159	155	72	110	183	1,593
18 to 24 years old	907	5	4	*	2	9	21	68	135
25 years old and over	7,024	74	92	159	152	64	89	116	1,458
25 to 29 years old	831	*	7	5	8	2	7	5	105
30 to 34 years old	855	3	5	2	15	1	3	14	113
35 to 39 years old	828	6	2	2	4	4	11	10	123
40 to 44 years old	769	3	2	5	7	6	7	21	107
45 to 49 years old	720	6	1	14	10	5	5	6	165
50 to 54 years old	668	6	5	6	13	8	1	7	196
55 to 59 years old	585	12	8	18	7	10	11	12	137
60 to 64 years old	527	3	8	25	22	5	11	8	142
65 to 69 years old	413	4	10	31	15	4	4	16	118
70 to 74 years old	303	10	15	12	20	8	8	6	64
75 years old and over	525	21	27	39	31	10	20	10	187
HISPANIC (OF ANY RACE)									
Both Sexes									
18 years old and over	39,170	411	1,097	2,414	1,504	1,626	1,087	2,809	12,291
18 to 24 years old	6,511	16	21	67	63	93	165	904	2,165
25 years old and over	32,660	395	1,076	2,347	1,441	1,533	923	1,905	10,126
25 to 29 years old	4,639	6	62	95	89	105	147	300	1,547
30 to 34 years old	4,404	32	57	186	143	198	107	258	1,405
35 to 39 years old	4,321	29	81	304	189	247	121	251	1,404
40 to 44 years old	3,910	34	102	298	210	224	111	223	1,206
45 to 49 years old	3,560	27	106	293	172	225	66	255	1,136

[1]Civilian noninstitutionalized population, plus armed forces living off post or with their families on post.
[2]Population who attained the 12th grade but received no diploma are included in this category.
* = Quantity zero or rounds to zero.

Table A-17. Educational Attainment of the Population 18 Years Old and Over, by Age, Sex, Race, and Hispanic Origin, 2017—*Continued*

(Numbers in thousands; civilian noninstitutionalized population.[1])

Age, sex, race, and Hispanic origin	Educational attainment						
	Some college, no degree	Associate's degree, occupational	Associate's degree, academic	Bachelor's degree	Master's degree	Professional degree	Doctoral degree
40 to 44 years old	257	95	103	261	143	14	21
45 to 49 years old	296	62	118	234	183	16	26
50 to 54 years old	310	43	121	248	124	11	14
55 to 59 years old	315	75	89	198	80	10	28
60 to 64 years old	214	42	93	158	87	6	17
65 to 69 years old	236	28	37	120	60	4	6
70 to 74 years old	113	36	42	58	37	2	4
75 years old and over	122	26	32	97	46	4	12
ASIAN ALONE							
Both Sexes							
18 years old and over	2,171	294	623	4,297	2,365	281	620
18 to 24 years old	926	31	41	281	42	9	6
25 years old and over	1,245	263	582	4,016	2,323	272	614
25 to 29 years old	228	33	87	625	361	30	42
30 to 34 years old	155	39	74	542	379	36	93
35 to 39 years old	116	27	54	505	377	37	76
40 to 44 years old	115	32	74	480	346	36	101
45 to 49 years old	127	39	49	430	247	33	74
50 to 54 years old	116	26	68	289	212	26	73
55 to 59 years old	114	19	55	337	138	26	52
60 to 64 years old	95	12	51	274	80	18	33
65 to 69 years old	67	9	32	214	68	16	17
70 to 74 years old	40	13	18	143	51	6	24
75 years old and over	72	15	20	178	63	10	29
Male							
18 years old and over	1140	126	256	1,915	1,206	139	386
18 to 24 years old	482	12	18	146	15	*	*
25 years old and over	658	114	238	1,770	1,191	139	386
25 to 29 years old	146	14	44	290	181	13	26
30 to 34 years old	79	16	30	236	194	19	44
35 to 39 years old	53	14	30	208	164	13	44
40 to 44 years old	66	10	19	220	187	13	58
45 to 49 years old	70	18	20	200	117	18	46
50 to 54 years old	49	13	26	109	124	14	51
55 to 59 years old	59	8	26	150	80	12	36
60 to 64 years old	41	7	12	115	47	14	26
65 to 69 years old	38	3	16	89	42	10	15
70 to 74 years old	19	4	10	61	21	4	16
75 years old and over	38	7	5	92	34	7	24
Female							
18 years old and over	1,032	168	367	2,382	1,159	142	234
18 to 24 years old	444	19	23	135	27	9	6
25 years old and over	587	150	344	2,247	1,132	133	227
25 to 29 years old	81	19	44	335	180	17	16
30 to 34 years old	76	23	43	305	184	17	49
35 to 39 years old	62	14	24	297	213	23	32
40 to 44 years old	49	21	55	261	159	22	43
45 to 49 years old	57	21	29	229	130	15	28
50 to 54 years old	67	13	42	180	89	12	22
55 to 59 years old	55	11	30	187	58	14	16
60 to 64 years old	55	5	39	159	33	4	6
65 to 69 years old	29	6	15	125	25	6	3
70 to 74 years old	21	9	8	81	30	2	9
75 years old and over	34	7	15	86	30	2	5
HISPANIC (OF ANY RACE)							
Both Sexes							
18 years old and over	6,978	1,239	1,721	4,330	1,281	147	235
18 to 24 years old	2,279	153	208	360	15	*	2
25 years old and over	4,699	1,086	1,513	3,970	1,266	147	232
25 to 29 years old	1,002	180	247	681	144	16	18
30 to 34 years old	774	153	227	648	179	12	27
35 to 39 years old	595	165	208	499	197	16	15
40 to 44 years old	474	126	180	485	182	19	36
45 to 49 years old	406	126	142	418	130	24	34

[1]Civilian noninstitutionalized population, plus armed forces living off post or with their families on post.
* = Quantity zero or rounds to zero.

Table A-17. Educational Attainment of the Population 18 Years Old and Over, by Age, Sex, Race, and Hispanic Origin, 2017—*Continued*

(Numbers in thousands; civilian noninstitutionalized population.[1])

Age, sex, race, and Hispanic origin	Total	Educational attainment							
		None	1st to 4th grade	5th to 6th grade	7th to 8th grade	9th grade	10th grade	11th grade[2]	High school graduate
50 to 54 years old	3,172	46	113	261	115	138	106	191	960
55 to 59 years old	2,595	42	90	234	128	136	88	132	787
60 to 64 years old	2,001	44	127	219	98	75	63	105	557
65 to 69 years old	1,573	29	98	163	107	67	52	93	430
70 to 74 years old	966	21	85	101	55	48	18	40	287
75 years old and over	1,518	84	156	193	135	71	42	58	407
Male									
18 years old and over	19,487	213	585	1,262	756	802	564	1,516	6,531
18 to 24 years old	3,292	10	18	45	43	54	84	497	1,207
25 years old and over	16,195	202	568	1,218	713	748	479	1019	5,325
25 to 29 years old	2,406	6	43	64	57	50	78	168	904
30 to 34 years old	2,280	23	38	99	69	88	62	154	781
35 to 39 years old	2,224	16	55	191	116	107	62	136	785
40 to 44 years old	1,945	17	67	162	105	108	63	134	625
45 to 49 years old	1,764	15	53	144	82	118	30	132	610
50 to 54 years old	1,598	25	71	133	61	84	52	110	502
55 to 59 years old	1,253	21	32	127	58	72	53	63	371
60 to 64 years old	969	29	64	112	35	32	32	56	248
65 to 69 years old	716	10	44	70	47	32	26	37	202
70 to 74 years old	417	9	32	32	30	24	2	13	129
75 years old and over	623	31	70	82	53	32	20	17	171
Female									
18 years old and over	19,684	199	512	1,152	748	824	524	1,293	5,760
18 to 24 years old	3,219	6	4	22	20	39	80	406	958
25 years old and over	16,464	193	508	1,130	728	785	443	886	4,801
25 to 29 years old	2,233	*	19	31	32	55	69	132	643
30 to 34 years old	2,125	9	19	87	74	109	45	104	625
35 to 39 years old	2,098	13	27	113	72	141	59	115	619
40 to 44 years old	1,966	17	35	136	106	116	48	89	581
45 to 49 years old	1,796	12	53	148	90	107	36	123	526
50 to 54 years old	1,574	21	42	127	54	54	54	82	458
55 to 59 years old	1,342	21	59	107	70	64	35	69	416
60 to 64 years old	1032	15	63	106	63	42	31	48	309
65 to 69 years old	857	19	54	93	60	35	26	56	229
70 to 74 years old	549	12	53	69	25	24	16	26	158
75 years old and over	894	53	86	111	82	38	22	41	236

[1]Civilian noninstitutionalized population, plus armed forces living off post or with their families on post.
[2]Population who attained the 12th grade but received no diploma are included in this category.
* = Quantity zero or rounds to zero.

Table A-17. Educational Attainment of the Population 18 Years Old and Over, by Age, Sex, Race, and Hispanic Origin, 2017—*Continued*

(Numbers in thousands; civilian noninstitutionalized population.[1])

Age, sex, race, and Hispanic origin	Educational attainment						
	Some college, no degree	Associate's degree, occupational	Associate's degree, academic	Bachelor's degree	Master's degree	Professional degree	Doctoral degree
50 to 54 years old	430	115	182	354	134	7	21
55 to 59 years old	350	63	121	297	94	7	26
60 to 64 years old	242	49	88	219	84	15	15
65 to 69 years old	191	44	58	165	41	17	18
70 to 74 years old	105	39	32	83	42	2	8
75 years old and over	129	26	29	121	40	13	14
Male							
18 years old and over	3,311	535	725	1,962	538	76	110
18 to 24 years old	1064	63	78	121	8	*	*
25 years old and over	2,247	472	647	1,842	530	76	110
25 to 29 years old	507	66	104	292	56	9	3
30 to 34 years old	372	68	114	330	62	7	13
35 to 39 years old	280	79	102	218	70	2	6
40 to 44 years old	230	55	76	209	70	8	17
45 to 49 years old	191	61	51	184	62	13	18
50 to 54 years old	195	54	66	170	62	1	11
55 to 59 years old	179	26	51	141	43	5	10
60 to 64 years old	123	23	32	124	38	12	7
65 to 69 years old	76	18	24	84	28	9	11
70 to 74 years old	50	13	10	43	20	2	6
75 years old and over	44	8	16	46	19	9	6
Female							
18 years old and over	3,667	704	997	2,368	742	71	125
18 to 24 years old	1,215	90	130	240	7	*	2
25 years old and over	2,452	614	866	2,129	735	71	122
25 to 29 years old	495	114	143	389	88	7	16
30 to 34 years old	402	85	113	318	117	4	13
35 to 39 years old	315	86	105	282	127	14	9
40 to 44 years old	244	71	104	276	113	11	19
45 to 49 years old	216	65	91	234	68	11	16
50 to 54 years old	235	60	115	184	72	5	10
55 to 59 years old	171	37	70	156	50	2	16
60 to 64 years old	120	27	55	95	46	3	8
65 to 69 years old	115	26	35	81	13	8	7
70 to 74 years old	55	27	21	40	21	*	2
75 years old and over	85	18	13	75	21	5	7

[1]Civilian noninstitutionalized population, plus armed forces living off post or with their families on post.
* = Quantity zero or rounds to zero.

Table A-18. Percent of People 25 Years and Over Who Have Completed High School or College, by Race, Hispanic Origin, and Sex, Selected Years, 1940–2017

(Percent; civilian noninstitutionalized population.)

Age and Year	All races Total	All races Male	All races Female	White Total	White Male	White Female	Non-Hispanic White Total	Non-Hispanic White Male	Non-Hispanic White Female	Black[1] Total	Black[1] Male	Black[1] Female	Asian Total	Asian Male	Asian Female
25 YEARS AND OLDER															
Completed 4 Years of High School or More															
2017	89.6	89.1	90.0	90.1	89.5	90.6	94.1	93.7	94.5	87.3	86.5	87.9	90.9	92.6	89.4
2016	89.1	88.5	89.6	89.5	88.8	90.1	93.8	93.4	94.3	87.1	86.4	87.7	90.3	91.9	89.0
2015	88.4	88.0	88.8	88.8	88.3	89.3	93.3	93.0	93.5	87.0	86.4	87.6	89.1	91.0	87.4
2014	88.3	87.7	88.9	88.8	88.0	89.6	93.1	92.5	93.7	85.8	85.3	86.2	89.5	91.9	87.4
2013	88.2	87.6	88.6	88.6	88.0	89.2	92.9	92.7	93.2	85.1	84.1	86.0	90.1	91.5	89.0
2012[2]	87.6	87.3	88.0	88.1	87.6	88.5	92.5	92.2	92.7	85.0	84.3	85.5	88.9	90.4	87.6
2011	87.6	87.1	88.0	88.1	87.4	88.6	92.4	92.0	92.8	84.5	83.8	85.0	88.6	90.4	87.1
2010	87.1	86.6	87.6	87.6	86.9	88.2	92.1	91.8	92.3	84.2	83.6	84.6	88.9	91.2	87.0
2009	86.7	86.2	87.1	87.1	86.5	87.7	91.6	91.4	91.9	84.1	84.0	84.1	88.2	90.4	86.2
2008	86.6	85.9	87.2	87.1	86.3	87.8	91.5	91.1	91.8	83.0	81.8	84.0	88.7	90.8	86.9
2007	85.7	85.0	86.4	86.2	85.3	87.1	90.6	90.2	91.0	82.3	81.9	82.6	87.8	89.8	85.9
2006	85.5	85.0	85.9	86.1	85.5	86.7	90.5	90.2	90.8	80.7	80.1	81.2	87.4	89.6	85.5
2005	85.2	84.9	85.5	85.8	85.2	86.2	90.1	89.9	90.3	81.1	81.0	81.2	87.6	90.4	85.2
2004	85.2	84.8	85.4	85.8	85.3	86.3	90.0	89.9	90.1	80.6	80.4	80.8	86.8	88.7	85.0
2003[3]	84.6	84.1	85.0	85.1	84.5	85.7	89.4	89.0	89.7	80.0	79.6	80.3	87.6	89.5	86.0
2002	84.1	83.8	84.4	84.8	84.3	85.2	88.7	88.5	88.9	78.7	78.5	78.9	NA	NA	NA
2001[4]	84.1	84.1	84.2	84.8	84.4	85.1	88.6	88.6	88.6	78.8	79.2	78.5	NA	NA	NA
2000	84.1	84.2	84.0	84.9	84.8	85.0	88.4	88.5	88.4	78.5	78.7	78.3	NA	NA	NA
1999	83.4	83.4	83.4	84.3	84.2	84.3	87.7	87.7	87.7	77.0	76.7	77.2	NA	NA	NA
1998	82.8	82.8	82.9	83.7	83.6	83.8	87.1	87.1	87.1	76.0	75.2	76.7	NA	NA	NA
1997	82.1	82.0	82.2	83.0	82.9	83.2	86.3	86.3	86.3	74.9	73.5	76.0	NA	NA	NA
1996	81.7	81.9	81.6	82.8	82.7	82.8	86.0	86.1	85.9	74.3	74.3	74.2	NA	NA	NA
1995	81.7	81.7	81.6	83.0	83.0	83.0	85.9	86.0	85.8	73.8	73.4	74.1	NA	NA	NA
1994	80.9	81.0	80.7	82.0	82.1	81.9	84.9	85.1	84.7	72.9	71.7	73.8	NA	NA	NA
1993	80.2	80.5	80.0	81.5	81.8	81.3	84.1	84.5	83.8	70.4	69.6	71.1	NA	NA	NA
1992[5]	79.4	79.7	79.2	80.9	81.1	80.7	NA	NA	NA	67.7	67.0	68.2	NA	NA	NA
1991	78.4	78.5	78.3	79.9	79.8	79.9	NA	NA	NA	66.7	66.7	66.7	NA	NA	NA
1990	77.6	77.7	77.5	79.1	79.1	79.0	NA	NA	NA	66.2	65.8	66.5	NA	NA	NA
1989	76.9	77.2	76.6	78.4	78.6	78.2	NA	NA	NA	64.6	64.2	65.0	NA	NA	NA
1988	76.2	76.4	76.0	77.7	77.7	77.6	NA	NA	NA	63.5	63.7	63.4	NA	NA	NA
1987	75.6	76.0	75.3	77.0	77.3	76.7	NA	NA	NA	63.4	63.0	63.7	NA	NA	NA
1986	74.7	75.1	74.4	76.2	76.5	75.9	NA	NA	NA	62.3	61.5	63.0	NA	NA	NA
1985	73.9	74.4	73.5	75.5	76.0	75.1	NA	NA	NA	59.8	58.4	60.8	NA	NA	NA
1984	73.3	73.7	73.0	75.0	75.4	74.6	NA	NA	NA	58.5	57.1	59.7	NA	NA	NA
1983	72.1	72.7	71.5	73.8	74.4	73.3	NA	NA	NA	56.8	56.5	57.1	NA	NA	NA
1982	71.0	71.7	70.3	72.8	73.4	72.3	NA	NA	NA	54.9	55.7	54.3	NA	NA	NA
1981	69.7	70.3	69.1	71.6	72.1	71.2	NA	NA	NA	52.9	53.2	52.6	NA	NA	NA
1980	68.6	69.2	68.1	70.5	71.0	70.1	NA	NA	NA	51.2	51.1	51.3	NA	NA	NA
1979	67.7	68.4	67.1	69.7	70.3	69.2	NA	NA	NA	49.4	49.2	49.5	NA	NA	NA
1978	65.9	66.8	65.2	67.9	68.6	67.2	NA	NA	NA	47.6	47.9	47.3	NA	NA	NA
1977	64.9	65.6	64.4	67.0	67.5	66.5	NA	NA	NA	45.5	45.6	45.4	NA	NA	NA
1976	64.1	64.7	63.5	66.1	66.7	65.5	NA	NA	NA	43.8	42.3	45.0	NA	NA	NA
1975	62.5	63.1	62.1	64.5	65.0	64.1	NA	NA	NA	42.5	41.6	43.3	NA	NA	NA
1974	61.2	61.6	60.9	63.3	63.6	63.0	NA	NA	NA	40.8	39.9	41.5	NA	NA	NA
1973	59.8	60.0	59.6	61.9	62.1	61.7	NA	NA	NA	39.2	38.2	40.1	NA	NA	NA
1972	58.2	58.2	58.2	60.4	60.3	60.5	NA	NA	NA	36.6	35.7	37.2	NA	NA	NA
1971	56.4	56.3	56.6	58.6	58.4	58.8	NA	NA	NA	34.7	33.8	35.4	NA	NA	NA
1970	55.2	55.0	55.4	57.4	57.2	57.6	NA	NA	NA	33.7	32.4	34.8	NA	NA	NA
1969	54.0	53.6	54.4	56.3	55.7	56.7	NA	NA	NA	32.3	31.9	32.6	NA	NA	NA
1968	52.6	52.0	53.2	54.9	54.3	55.5	NA	NA	NA	30.1	28.9	31.0	NA	NA	NA
1967	51.1	50.5	51.7	53.4	52.8	53.8	NA	NA	NA	29.5	27.1	31.5	NA	NA	NA
1966	49.9	49.0	50.8	52.2	51.3	53.0	NA	NA	NA	27.8	25.8	29.5	NA	NA	NA
1965	49.0	48.0	49.9	51.3	50.2	52.2	NA	NA	NA	27.2	25.8	28.4	NA	NA	NA
1964	48.0	47.0	48.9	50.3	49.3	51.2	NA	NA	NA	25.7	23.7	27.4	NA	NA	NA
1962	46.3	45.0	47.5	48.7	47.4	49.9	NA	NA	NA	24.8	23.2	26.2	NA	NA	NA
1959	43.7	42.2	45.2	46.1	44.5	47.7	NA	NA	NA	20.7	19.6	21.6	NA	NA	NA
1957	41.6	39.7	43.3	43.2	41.1	45.1	NA	NA	NA	18.4	16.9	19.7	NA	NA	NA

Note: Starting in 2001, data are from the expanded CPS sample.

[1]Data in the column labeled "Black" include Black and other races from 1940 to 1962: from 1963 to 2003, data are for the Black population only.

[2]Starting in 2012, data were calculated using population controls based on the 2010 Census.

[3]Starting in 2003, respondents could choose more than one race. The race data in this table for White, non-Hispanic White, Black, and Asian from 2003 onward represent those respondents who indicated only one racial identity. Prior to 2003, Asians were grouped with Pacific Islanders.

[4]Starting in 2001, data were calculated using population controls based on Census 2000.

[5]Begining with data for 1992, a new question results in different categories than for earlier years: Data shown as 'Completed 4 Years of High School or more' is now collected in the category 'High School Graduate.' Data shown as 'College 1 to 3 years' is now collected in the 'Some college' and the two 'Associate degree' categories. Data shown as 'Completed 4 Years of College or more' is now collected in the categories 'Bachelor's degree,' 'Master's degree,' 'Doctorate degree,' and 'Professional degree.' Due to the change in question format, median years of schooling cannot be derived.

Table A-18. Percent of People 25 Years and Over Who Have Completed High School or College, by Race, Hispanic Origin, and Sex, Selected Years, 1940–2017—*Continued*

(Percent; civilian noninstitutionalized population.)

Age and Year	Hispanic (of any race)			White alone or in combination			Non-Hispanic White alone or in combination			Black alone or in combination			Asian alone or in combination		
	Total	Male	Female	Total	Male	Female	Total	Male	Female	Total	Male	Female	Total	Male	Female
25 YEARS AND OLDER															
Completed 4 Years of High School or More															
2017	70.5	69.5	71.6	90.0	89.4	90.5	94.1	93.7	94.5	87.2	86.3	88.0	91.1	92.7	89.7
2016	68.5	67.2	69.7	89.4	88.8	90.1	93.8	93.4	94.3	87.2	86.5	87.7	90.6	92.0	89.4
2015	66.7	65.5	67.8	88.7	88.2	89.2	93.3	93.0	93.5	87.1	86.4	87.6	89.3	91.1	87.7
2014	66.5	65.1	67.9	88.7	87.9	89.5	93.1	92.6	93.7	85.8	85.2	86.3	89.9	92.2	87.9
2013	66.2	64.6	67.9	88.6	88.0	89.2	92.9	92.7	93.1	85.1	84.1	85.9	90.3	91.6	89.2
2012[2]	65.0	64.0	66.0	88.1	87.6	88.5	92.5	92.2	92.7	85.1	84.5	85.6	89.0	90.5	87.8
2011	64.3	63.6	65.1	88.0	87.4	88.6	92.4	92.0	92.7	84.6	83.9	85.1	88.9	90.6	87.4
2010	62.9	61.4	64.4	87.6	86.8	88.2	92.0	91.7	92.3	84.2	83.5	84.8	89.1	91.2	87.3
2009	61.9	60.6	63.3	87.1	86.4	87.7	91.6	91.4	91.8	84.1	83.9	84.2	88.3	90.6	86.4
2008	62.3	60.9	63.7	87.1	86.3	87.8	91.4	91.1	91.8	83.2	81.9	84.1	89.0	90.9	87.2
2007	60.3	58.2	62.5	86.2	85.3	87.0	90.6	90.2	91.0	82.4	82.0	82.6	87.8	89.2	86.5
2006	59.3	58.5	60.1	86.1	85.5	86.7	90.5	90.2	90.8	80.8	80.3	81.2	87.6	89.6	85.8
2005	58.5	57.9	59.1	85.7	85.2	86.2	90.1	89.9	90.3	81.3	81.2	81.3	87.9	90.5	85.6
2004	58.4	57.3	59.5	85.8	85.3	86.2	90.0	89.9	90.1	80.6	80.3	80.9	86.9	88.8	85.2
2003[3]	57.0	56.3	57.8	85.1	84.5	85.7	89.4	89.0	89.6	80.0	79.5	80.3	87.8	89.7	86.1
2002	57.0	56.1	57.9	NA	NA	NA	NA	NA	NA	NA	NA	NA	NA	NA	NA
2001[4]	56.8	55.5	58.0	NA	NA	NA	NA	NA	NA	NA	NA	NA	NA	NA	NA
2000	57.0	56.6	57.5	NA	NA	NA	NA	NA	NA	NA	NA	NA	NA	NA	NA
1999	56.1	56.0	56.3	NA	NA	NA	NA	NA	NA	NA	NA	NA	NA	NA	NA
1998	55.5	55.7	55.3	NA	NA	NA	NA	NA	NA	NA	NA	NA	NA	NA	NA
1997	54.7	54.9	54.6	NA	NA	NA	NA	NA	NA	NA	NA	NA	NA	NA	NA
1996	53.1	53.0	53.3	NA	NA	NA	NA	NA	NA	NA	NA	NA	NA	NA	NA
1995	53.4	52.9	53.8	NA	NA	NA	NA	NA	NA	NA	NA	NA	NA	NA	NA
1994	53.3	53.4	53.2	NA	NA	NA	NA	NA	NA	NA	NA	NA	NA	NA	NA
1993	53.1	52.9	53.2	NA	NA	NA	NA	NA	NA	NA	NA	NA	NA	NA	NA
1992[5]	52.6	53.7	51.5	NA	NA	NA	NA	NA	NA	NA	NA	NA	NA	NA	NA
1991	51.3	51.4	51.2	NA	NA	NA	NA	NA	NA	NA	NA	NA	NA	NA	NA
1990	50.8	50.3	51.3	NA	NA	NA	NA	NA	NA	NA	NA	NA	NA	NA	NA
1989	50.9	51.0	50.7	NA	NA	NA	NA	NA	NA	NA	NA	NA	NA	NA	NA
1988	51.0	52.0	50.0	NA	NA	NA	NA	NA	NA	NA	NA	NA	NA	NA	NA
1987	50.9	51.8	50.0	NA	NA	NA	NA	NA	NA	NA	NA	NA	NA	NA	NA
1986	48.5	49.2	47.8	NA	NA	NA	NA	NA	NA	NA	NA	NA	NA	NA	NA
1985	47.9	48.5	47.4	NA	NA	NA	NA	NA	NA	NA	NA	NA	NA	NA	NA
1984	47.1	48.6	45.7	NA	NA	NA	NA	NA	NA	NA	NA	NA	NA	NA	NA
1983	46.2	48.6	44.2	NA	NA	NA	NA	NA	NA	NA	NA	NA	NA	NA	NA
1982	45.9	48.1	44.1	NA	NA	NA	NA	NA	NA	NA	NA	NA	NA	NA	NA
1981	44.5	45.5	43.6	NA	NA	NA	NA	NA	NA	NA	NA	NA	NA	NA	NA
1980	45.3	46.4	44.1	NA	NA	NA	NA	NA	NA	NA	NA	NA	NA	NA	NA
1979	42.0	42.3	41.7	NA	NA	NA	NA	NA	NA	NA	NA	NA	NA	NA	NA
1978	40.8	42.2	39.6	NA	NA	NA	NA	NA	NA	NA	NA	NA	NA	NA	NA
1977	39.6	42.3	37.2	NA	NA	NA	NA	NA	NA	NA	NA	NA	NA	NA	NA
1976	39.3	41.4	37.3	NA	NA	NA	NA	NA	NA	NA	NA	NA	NA	NA	NA
1975	37.9	39.5	36.7	NA	NA	NA	NA	NA	NA	NA	NA	NA	NA	NA	NA
1974	36.5	38.3	34.9	NA	NA	NA	NA	NA	NA	NA	NA	NA	NA	NA	NA
1973	NA	NA	NA	NA	NA	NA	NA	NA	NA	NA	NA	NA	NA	NA	NA
1972	NA	NA	NA	NA	NA	NA	NA	NA	NA	NA	NA	NA	NA	NA	NA
1971	NA	NA	NA	NA	NA	NA	NA	NA	NA	NA	NA	NA	NA	NA	NA
1970	NA	NA	NA	NA	NA	NA	NA	NA	NA	NA	NA	NA	NA	NA	NA
1969	NA	NA	NA	NA	NA	NA	NA	NA	NA	NA	NA	NA	NA	NA	NA
1968	NA	NA	NA	NA	NA	NA	NA	NA	NA	NA	NA	NA	NA	NA	NA
1967	NA	NA	NA	NA	NA	NA	NA	NA	NA	NA	NA	NA	NA	NA	NA
1966	NA	NA	NA	NA	NA	NA	NA	NA	NA	NA	NA	NA	NA	NA	NA
1965	NA	NA	NA	NA	NA	NA	NA	NA	NA	NA	NA	NA	NA	NA	NA
1964	NA	NA	NA	NA	NA	NA	NA	NA	NA	NA	NA	NA	NA	NA	NA
1962	NA	NA	NA	NA	NA	NA	NA	NA	NA	NA	NA	NA	NA	NA	NA
1959	NA	NA	NA	NA	NA	NA	NA	NA	NA	NA	NA	NA	NA	NA	NA
1957	NA	NA	NA	NA	NA	NA	NA	NA	NA	NA	NA	NA	NA	NA	NA

Note: Starting in 2001, data are from the expanded CPS sample.

[1] Data in the column labeled "Black" include Black and other races from 1940 to 1962: from 1963 to 2003, data are for the Black population only.

[2] Starting in 2012, data were calculated using population controls based on the 2010 Census.

[3] Starting in 2003, respondents could choose more than one race. The race data in this table for White, non-Hispanic White, Black, and Asian from 2003 onward represent those respondents who indicated only one racial identity. Prior to 2003, Asians were grouped with Pacific Islanders.

[4] Starting in 2001, data were calculated using population controls based on Census 2000.

[5] Begining with data for 1992, a new question results in different categories than for earlier years: Data shown as 'Completed 4 Years of High School or more' is now collected in the category 'High School Graduate.' Data shown as 'College 1 to 3 years' is now collected in the 'Some college' and the two 'Associate degree' categories. Data shown as 'Completed 4 Years of College or more' is now collected in the categories 'Bachelor's degree,' 'Master's degree,' 'Doctorate degree,' and 'Professional degree.' Due to the change in question format, median years of schooling cannot be derived.

Table A-18. Percent of People 25 Years and Over Who Have Completed High School or College, by Race, Hispanic Origin, and Sex, Selected Years, 1940–2017—*Continued*

(Percent; civilian noninstitutionalized population.)

Age and Year	All races			White			Non-Hispanic White			Black[1]			Asian		
	Total	Male	Female	Total	Male	Female	Total	Male	Female	Total	Male	Female	Total	Male	Female
1952	38.8	36.9	40.5	NA	NA	NA	NA	NA	NA	15.0	14.0	15.7	NA	NA	NA
1950	34.3	32.6	36.0	NA	NA	NA	NA	NA	NA	13.7	12.5	14.7	NA	NA	NA
1947	33.1	31.4	34.7	35.0	33.2	36.7	NA	NA	NA	13.6	12.7	14.5	NA	NA	NA
1940	24.5	22.7	26.3	26.1	24.2	28.1	NA	NA	NA	7.7	6.9	8.4	NA	NA	NA
Completed 4 Years of College or More															
2017	34.2	33.7	34.6	34.5	34.0	35.0	38.1	37.8	38.3	23.9	22.1	25.4	54.8	56.6	53.2
2016	33.4	33.2	33.7	33.7	33.4	34.0	37.3	37.2	37.3	23.3	21.7	24.6	55.9	58.8	53.4
2015	32.5	32.3	32.7	32.8	32.6	32.9	36.2	36.3	36.1	22.5	20.6	24.0	53.9	56.8	51.5
2014	32.0	31.9	32.0	32.3	32.3	32.3	35.6	35.9	35.3	22.2	20.4	23.7	52.3	54.7	50.3
2013	31.7	32.0	31.4	32.0	32.4	31.6	35.2	36.0	34.4	21.8	19.8	23.3	53.2	56.1	50.8
2012	30.9	31.4	30.6	31.3	31.9	30.8	34.5	35.5	33.5	21.2	19.2	22.9	51.0	53.7	48.8
2011	30.4	30.8	30.1	31.0	31.5	30.5	34.0	35.0	33.1	19.9	18.0	21.4	50.3	53.4	47.7
2010	29.9	30.3	29.6	30.3	30.8	29.9	33.2	34.2	32.4	19.8	17.7	21.4	52.4	55.6	49.5
2009	29.5	30.1	29.1	29.9	30.6	29.3	32.9	33.9	31.9	19.3	17.8	20.6	52.3	55.7	49.3
2008	29.4	30.1	28.8	29.8	30.5	29.1	32.6	33.8	31.5	19.6	18.7	20.4	52.6	55.8	49.8
2007	28.7	29.5	28.0	29.1	29.9	28.3	31.8	33.2	30.6	18.5	18.0	19.0	52.1	55.2	49.3
2006	28.0	29.2	26.9	28.4	29.7	27.1	31.0	32.8	29.3	18.5	17.2	19.4	49.7	52.5	47.1
2005	27.7	28.9	26.5	28.1	29.4	26.8	30.6	32.4	28.9	17.6	16.0	18.8	50.2	54.0	46.8
2004	27.7	29.4	26.1	28.2	30.0	26.4	30.6	32.9	28.4	17.6	16.6	18.5	49.4	53.7	45.6
2003	27.2	28.9	25.7	27.6	29.4	25.9	30.0	32.3	27.9	17.3	16.7	17.8	49.8	53.9	46.1
2002	26.7	28.5	25.1	27.2	29.1	25.4	29.4	31.7	27.3	17.0	16.4	17.5	NA	NA	NA
2001	26.2	28.2	24.3	26.6	28.7	24.6	28.7	31.3	26.3	15.7	15.3	16.1	NA	NA	NA
2000	25.6	27.8	23.6	26.1	28.5	23.9	28.1	30.8	25.5	16.5	16.3	16.7	NA	NA	NA
1999	25.2	27.5	23.1	25.9	28.5	23.5	27.7	30.6	25.0	15.4	14.2	16.4	NA	NA	NA
1998	24.4	26.5	22.4	25.0	27.3	22.8	26.6	29.3	24.1	14.7	13.9	15.4	NA	NA	NA
1997	23.9	26.2	21.7	24.6	27.0	22.3	26.2	29.0	23.7	13.3	12.5	13.9	NA	NA	NA
1996	23.6	26.0	21.4	24.3	26.9	21.8	25.9	28.8	23.2	13.6	12.4	14.6	NA	NA	NA
1995	23.0	26.0	20.2	24.0	27.2	21.0	25.4	28.9	22.1	13.2	13.6	12.9	NA	NA	NA
1994	22.2	25.1	19.6	22.9	26.1	20.0	24.3	27.8	21.1	12.9	12.8	13.0	NA	NA	NA
1993	21.9	24.8	19.2	22.6	25.7	19.7	23.8	27.2	20.7	12.2	11.9	12.4	NA	NA	NA
1992	21.4	24.3	18.6	22.1	25.2	19.1	NA	NA	NA	11.9	11.9	12.0	NA	NA	NA
1991	21.4	24.3	18.8	22.2	25.4	19.3	NA	NA	NA	11.5	11.4	11.6	NA	NA	NA
1990	21.3	24.4	18.4	22.0	25.3	19.0	NA	NA	NA	11.3	11.9	10.8	NA	NA	NA
1989	21.1	24.5	18.1	21.8	25.4	18.5	NA	NA	NA	11.8	11.7	11.9	NA	NA	NA
1988	20.3	24.0	17.0	20.9	25.0	17.3	NA	NA	NA	11.2	11.1	11.4	NA	NA	NA
1987	19.9	23.6	16.5	20.5	24.5	16.9	NA	NA	NA	10.7	11.0	10.4	NA	NA	NA
1986	19.4	23.2	16.1	20.1	24.1	16.4	NA	NA	NA	10.9	11.2	10.7	NA	NA	NA
1985	19.4	23.1	16.0	20.0	24.0	16.3	NA	NA	NA	11.1	11.2	11.0	NA	NA	NA
1984	19.1	22.9	15.7	19.8	23.9	16.0	NA	NA	NA	10.4	10.4	10.4	NA	NA	NA
1983	18.8	23.0	15.1	19.5	24.0	15.4	NA	NA	NA	9.5	10.0	9.2	NA	NA	NA
1982	17.7	21.9	14.0	18.5	23.0	14.4	NA	NA	NA	8.8	9.1	8.5	NA	NA	NA
1981	17.1	21.1	13.4	17.8	22.2	13.8	NA	NA	NA	8.2	8.2	8.2	NA	NA	NA
1980	17.0	20.9	13.6	17.8	22.1	14.0	NA	NA	NA	7.9	7.7	8.1	NA	NA	NA
1979	16.4	20.4	12.9	17.2	21.4	13.3	NA	NA	NA	7.9	8.3	7.5	NA	NA	NA
1978	15.7	19.7	12.2	16.4	20.7	12.6	NA	NA	NA	7.2	7.3	7.1	NA	NA	NA
1977	15.4	19.2	12.0	16.1	20.2	12.4	NA	NA	NA	7.2	7.0	7.4	NA	NA	NA
1976	14.7	18.6	11.3	15.4	19.6	11.6	NA	NA	NA	6.6	6.3	6.8	NA	NA	NA
1975	13.9	17.6	10.6	14.5	18.4	11.0	NA	NA	NA	6.4	6.7	6.2	NA	NA	NA
1974	13.3	16.9	10.1	14.0	17.7	10.6	NA	NA	NA	5.5	5.7	5.3	NA	NA	NA
1973	12.6	16.0	9.6	13.1	16.8	9.9	NA	NA	NA	6.0	5.9	6.0	NA	NA	NA
1972	12.0	15.4	9.0	12.6	16.2	9.4	NA	NA	NA	5.1	5.5	4.8	NA	NA	NA
1971	11.4	14.6	8.5	12.0	15.5	8.9	NA	NA	NA	4.5	4.7	4.3	NA	NA	NA
1970	11.0	14.1	8.2	11.6	15.0	8.6	NA	NA	NA	4.5	4.6	4.4	NA	NA	NA
1969	10.7	13.6	8.1	11.2	14.3	8.5	NA	NA	NA	4.6	4.8	4.5	NA	NA	NA
1968	10.5	13.3	8.0	11.0	14.1	8.3	NA	NA	NA	4.3	3.7	4.8	NA	NA	NA
1967	10.1	12.8	7.6	10.6	13.6	7.9	NA	NA	NA	4.0	3.4	4.4	NA	NA	NA
1966	9.8	12.5	7.4	10.4	13.3	7.7	NA	NA	NA	3.8	3.9	3.7	NA	NA	NA
1965	9.4	12.0	7.1	9.9	12.7	7.3	NA	NA	NA	4.7	4.9	4.5	NA	NA	NA
1964	9.1	11.7	6.8	9.6	12.3	7.1	NA	NA	NA	3.9	4.5	3.4	NA	NA	NA
1962	8.9	11.4	6.7	9.5	12.2	7.0	NA	NA	NA	4.0	3.9	4.0	NA	NA	NA
1959	8.1	10.3	6.0	8.6	11.0	6.2	NA	NA	NA	3.3	3.8	2.9	NA	NA	NA
1957	7.6	9.6	5.8	8.0	10.1	6.0	NA	NA	NA	2.9	2.7	3.0	NA	NA	NA
1952	7.0	8.3	5.8	NA	NA	NA	NA	NA	NA	2.4	2.0	2.7	NA	NA	NA
1950	6.2	7.3	5.2	NA	NA	NA	NA	NA	NA	2.3	2.1	2.4	NA	NA	NA

Note: Starting in 2001, data are from the expanded CPS sample.
[1] Data in the column labeled "Black" include Black and other races from 1940 to 1962: from 1963 to 2003, data are for the Black population only.

Table A-18. Percent of People 25 Years and Over Who Have Completed High School or College, by Race, Hispanic Origin, and Sex, Selected Years, 1940–2017—*Continued*

(Percent; civilian noninstitutionalized population.)

Age and Year	Hispanic (of any race)			White alone or in combination			Non-Hispanic White alone or in combination			Black alone or in combination			Asian alone or in combination		
	Total	Male	Female	Total	Male	Female	Total	Male	Female	Total	Male	Female	Total	Male	Female
1952	NA	NA	NA	NA	NA	NA	NA	NA	NA	NA	NA	NA	NA	NA	NA
1950	NA	NA	NA	NA	NA	NA	NA	NA	NA	NA	NA	NA	NA	NA	NA
1947	NA	NA	NA	NA	NA	NA	NA	NA	NA	NA	NA	NA	NA	NA	NA
1940	NA	NA	NA	NA	NA	NA	NA	NA	NA	NA	NA	NA	NA	NA	NA
Completed 4 Years of College or More															
2017	17.2	15.8	18.6	34.4	33.9	34.9	38	37.8	38.3	24.2	22.3	25.7	54.4	55.9	53.2
2016	16.4	15.4	17.4	33.6	33.3	33.9	37.2	37.1	37.3	23.5	21.8	24.9	55.4	57.9	53.3
2015	15.5	14.3	16.6	32.7	32.5	32.9	36.2	36.2	36.1	22.7	20.7	24.2	53.7	56.2	51.5
2014	15.2	14.2	16.1	32.2	32.2	32.3	35.5	35.8	35.3	22.7	20.6	24.3	52.2	54.2	50.4
2013	15.1	13.9	16.2	31.9	32.3	31.5	35.1	35.9	34.4	22.0	20.0	23.6	52.8	55.5	50.5
2012	14.5	13.3	15.8	31.2	31.8	30.7	34.4	35.4	33.4	21.4	19.4	22.9	50.4	52.6	48.6
2011	14.1	13.1	15.2	30.9	31.4	30.5	33.9	34.9	33.1	20.1	18.2	21.6	49.9	52.8	47.3
2010	13.9	12.9	14.9	30.2	30.7	29.8	33.2	34.1	32.3	19.9	17.7	21.6	51.8	54.7	49.3
2009	13.2	12.5	14.0	29.8	30.4	29.3	32.8	33.8	31.8	19.4	17.8	20.7	51.8	54.8	49.2
2008	13.3	12.6	14.1	29.7	30.3	29.0	32.5	33.6	31.4	19.8	18.8	20.5	52.0	54.6	49.8
2007	12.7	11.8	13.7	29.0	29.8	28.3	31.7	33.0	30.5	18.7	18.2	19.1	47.1	49.1	45.4
2006	12.4	11.9	12.9	28.3	29.6	27.0	30.9	32.7	29.2	18.7	17.4	19.7	49.0	51.4	46.8
2005	12.0	11.8	12.1	28.0	29.3	26.7	30.5	32.3	28.9	17.6	16.0	18.9	49.8	53.3	46.6
2004	12.1	11.8	12.3	28.0	29.9	26.3	30.5	32.8	28.3	17.7	16.5	18.6	48.9	52.8	45.4
2003	11.4	11.2	11.6	27.5	29.3	25.8	29.9	32.2	27.9	17.5	16.8	18.0	49.2	52.7	46.0
2002	11.1	11.0	11.2	NA	NA	NA	NA	NA	NA	NA	NA	NA	NA	NA	NA
2001	11.1	10.8	11.4	NA	NA	NA	NA	NA	NA	NA	NA	NA	NA	NA	NA
2000	10.6	10.7	10.6	NA	NA	NA	NA	NA	NA	NA	NA	NA	NA	NA	NA
1999	10.9	10.7	11.0	NA	NA	NA	NA	NA	NA	NA	NA	NA	NA	NA	NA
1998	11.0	11.1	10.9	NA	NA	NA	NA	NA	NA	NA	NA	NA	NA	NA	NA
1997	10.3	10.6	10.1	NA	NA	NA	NA	NA	NA	NA	NA	NA	NA	NA	NA
1996	9.3	10.3	8.3	NA	NA	NA	NA	NA	NA	NA	NA	NA	NA	NA	NA
1995	9.3	10.1	8.4	NA	NA	NA	NA	NA	NA	NA	NA	NA	NA	NA	NA
1994	9.1	9.6	8.6	NA	NA	NA	NA	NA	NA	NA	NA	NA	NA	NA	NA
1993	9.0	9.5	8.5	NA	NA	NA	NA	NA	NA	NA	NA	NA	NA	NA	NA
1992	9.3	10.2	8.5	NA	NA	NA	NA	NA	NA	NA	NA	NA	NA	NA	NA
1991	9.7	10.0	9.4	NA	NA	NA	NA	NA	NA	NA	NA	NA	NA	NA	NA
1990	9.2	9.8	8.7	NA	NA	NA	NA	NA	NA	NA	NA	NA	NA	NA	NA
1989	9.9	11.0	8.8	NA	NA	NA	NA	NA	NA	NA	NA	NA	NA	NA	NA
1988	10.1	12.3	8.1	NA	NA	NA	NA	NA	NA	NA	NA	NA	NA	NA	NA
1987	8.6	9.7	7.5	NA	NA	NA	NA	NA	NA	NA	NA	NA	NA	NA	NA
1986	8.4	9.5	7.4	NA	NA	NA	NA	NA	NA	NA	NA	NA	NA	NA	NA
1985	8.5	9.7	7.3	NA	NA	NA	NA	NA	NA	NA	NA	NA	NA	NA	NA
1984	8.2	9.5	7.0	NA	NA	NA	NA	NA	NA	NA	NA	NA	NA	NA	NA
1983	7.9	9.2	6.8	NA	NA	NA	NA	NA	NA	NA	NA	NA	NA	NA	NA
1982	7.8	9.6	6.2	NA	NA	NA	NA	NA	NA	NA	NA	NA	NA	NA	NA
1981	7.7	9.7	5.9	NA	NA	NA	NA	NA	NA	NA	NA	NA	NA	NA	NA
1980	7.9	9.7	6.2	NA	NA	NA	NA	NA	NA	NA	NA	NA	NA	NA	NA
1979	6.7	8.2	5.3	NA	NA	NA	NA	NA	NA	NA	NA	NA	NA	NA	NA
1978	7.0	8.6	5.7	NA	NA	NA	NA	NA	NA	NA	NA	NA	NA	NA	NA
1977	6.2	8.1	4.4	NA	NA	NA	NA	NA	NA	NA	NA	NA	NA	NA	NA
1976	6.1	8.6	4.0	NA	NA	NA	NA	NA	NA	NA	NA	NA	NA	NA	NA
1975	6.3	8.3	4.6	NA	NA	NA	NA	NA	NA	NA	NA	NA	NA	NA	NA
1974	5.5	7.1	4.0	NA	NA	NA	NA	NA	NA	NA	NA	NA	NA	NA	NA
1973	NA	NA	NA	NA	NA	NA	NA	NA	NA	NA	NA	NA	NA	NA	NA
1972	NA	NA	NA	NA	NA	NA	NA	NA	NA	NA	NA	NA	NA	NA	NA
1971	NA	NA	NA	NA	NA	NA	NA	NA	NA	NA	NA	NA	NA	NA	NA
1970	NA	NA	NA	NA	NA	NA	NA	NA	NA	NA	NA	NA	NA	NA	NA
1969	NA	NA	NA	NA	NA	NA	NA	NA	NA	NA	NA	NA	NA	NA	NA
1968	NA	NA	NA	NA	NA	NA	NA	NA	NA	NA	NA	NA	NA	NA	NA
1967	NA	NA	NA	NA	NA	NA	NA	NA	NA	NA	NA	NA	NA	NA	NA
1966	NA	NA	NA	NA	NA	NA	NA	NA	NA	NA	NA	NA	NA	NA	NA
1965	NA	NA	NA	NA	NA	NA	NA	NA	NA	NA	NA	NA	NA	NA	NA
1964	NA	NA	NA	NA	NA	NA	NA	NA	NA	NA	NA	NA	NA	NA	NA
1962	NA	NA	NA	NA	NA	NA	NA	NA	NA	NA	NA	NA	NA	NA	NA
1959	NA	NA	NA	NA	NA	NA	NA	NA	NA	NA	NA	NA	NA	NA	NA
1957	NA	NA	NA	NA	NA	NA	NA	NA	NA	NA	NA	NA	NA	NA	NA
1952	NA	NA	NA	NA	NA	NA	NA	NA	NA	NA	NA	NA	NA	NA	NA
1950	NA	NA	NA	NA	NA	NA	NA	NA	NA	NA	NA	NA	NA	NA	NA

Note: Starting in 2001, data are from the expanded CPS sample.

Table A-18. Percent of People 25 Years and Over Who Have Completed High School or College, by Race, Hispanic Origin, and Sex, Selected Years, 1940–2017—*Continued*

(Percent; civilian noninstitutionalized population.)

Age and Year	All races Total	All races Male	All races Female	White Total	White Male	White Female	Non-Hispanic White Total	Non-Hispanic White Male	Non-Hispanic White Female	Black[1] Total	Black[1] Male	Black[1] Female	Asian Total	Asian Male	Asian Female
1947	5.4	6.2	4.7	5.7	6.6	4.9	NA	NA	NA	2.5	2.4	2.6	NA	NA	NA
1940	4.6	5.5	3.8	4.9	5.9	4.0	NA	NA	NA	1.3	1.4	1.2	NA	NA	NA

25 TO 29 YEARS

Completed 4 Years of High School or More

Age and Year	All races Total	All races Male	All races Female	White Total	White Male	White Female	Non-Hispanic White Total	Non-Hispanic White Male	Non-Hispanic White Female	Black[1] Total	Black[1] Male	Black[1] Female	Asian Total	Asian Male	Asian Female
2017	92.5	91.5	93.4	92.4	91.2	93.7	95.6	94.8	96.4	91.8	91.2	92.4	96.8	97.7	95.9
2016	91.7	90.9	92.5	91.6	90.6	92.7	95.2	94.8	95.7	90.6	90.8	90.4	96.5	95.9	97.1
2015	91.2	90.5	91.8	90.8	90.0	91.7	95.4	95.1	95.8	92.2	91.4	93.0	95.5	96.3	94.7
2014	90.8	90.1	91.5	90.9	90.2	91.7	95.6	95.4	95.9	89.8	90.2	89.4	96.7	96.3	97.2
2013	89.9	88.3	91.5	89.5	88.0	91.1	94.1	93.3	94.9	89.8	87.3	92.1	94.7	93.6	95.7
2012	89.7	88.4	91.1	89.6	88.3	90.9	94.6	93.8	95.3	88.5	87.1	89.7	95.7	96.2	95.3
2011	89.0	87.5	90.7	88.9	87.1	90.8	94.4	93.4	95.5	87.7	87.6	87.8	95.2	93.6	96.7
2010	88.8	87.4	90.2	88.5	87.3	89.9	94.5	94.6	94.4	89.0	86.7	91.0	93.2	92.3	94.1
2009	88.6	87.5	89.8	88.4	87.0	89.9	94.6	94.4	94.8	88.9	88.6	89.1	95.2	95.6	94.9
2008	87.8	85.8	89.9	87.6	85.5	89.8	93.7	92.6	94.7	87.4	85.4	89.2	95.6	95.4	95.7
2007	87.0	84.9	89.1	86.5	84.2	89.0	93.5	92.7	94.2	87.4	87.0	87.8	97.2	95.8	98.5
2006	86.4	84.4	88.5	86.1	84.1	88.3	93.4	92.3	94.6	85.6	83.1	87.8	96.6	97.2	96.0
2005	86.2	85.0	87.4	85.7	84.3	87.1	92.8	91.8	93.8	86.5	86.4	86.6	95.5	96.7	94.5
2004	86.6	85.2	88.0	85.9	83.7	88.1	93.3	92.1	94.5	87.9	90.1	86.1	96.2	96.9	95.4
2003	86.5	84.9	88.2	85.7	83.8	87.6	93.7	92.8	94.5	87.6	86.4	88.5	97.1	97.4	96.8
2002	86.4	84.7	88.1	85.9	84.1	87.7	93.0	92.1	93.8	86.6	85.0	88.0	NA	NA	NA
2001	86.8	85.3	88.3	86.4	84.6	88.3	93.4	93.1	93.7	86.3	85.4	87.0	NA	NA	NA
2000	88.1	86.7	89.4	88.3	86.6	90.0	94.0	92.9	95.2	85.9	86.6	85.3	NA	NA	NA
1999	87.8	86.1	89.5	87.6	85.8	89.3	93.0	91.9	94.1	88.2	87.7	88.6	NA	NA	NA
1998	88.1	86.6	89.6	88.1	86.3	90.0	93.6	92.5	94.6	87.6	87.6	87.6	NA	NA	NA
1997	87.4	85.8	88.9	87.6	85.8	89.4	92.9	91.7	94.0	86.2	85.2	87.1	NA	NA	NA
1996	87.3	86.5	88.1	87.5	86.3	88.8	92.6	92.0	93.1	85.6	87.2	84.2	NA	NA	NA
1995	86.8	86.3	87.4	87.4	86.6	88.2	92.5	92.0	93.0	86.5	88.1	85.1	NA	NA	NA
1994	86.1	84.5	87.6	86.5	84.7	88.3	91.1	90.0	92.3	84.1	82.9	85.0	NA	NA	NA
1993	86.7	86.0	87.4	87.3	86.1	88.5	91.2	90.6	91.8	82.8	85.0	80.9	NA	NA	NA
1992	86.3	86.1	86.5	87.0	86.5	87.6	NA	NA	NA	80.9	82.5	79.5	NA	NA	NA
1991	85.4	84.9	85.8	85.8	85.1	86.6	NA	NA	NA	81.7	83.5	80.1	NA	NA	NA
1990	85.7	84.4	87.0	86.3	84.6	88.1	NA	NA	NA	81.7	81.5	81.8	NA	NA	NA
1989	85.5	84.4	86.5	86.0	84.8	87.1	NA	NA	NA	82.2	80.6	83.6	NA	NA	NA
1988	85.7	84.4	87.0	86.5	84.8	88.2	NA	NA	NA	80.7	80.6	80.7	NA	NA	NA
1987	86.0	85.5	86.4	86.3	85.6	87.0	NA	NA	NA	83.3	84.8	82.1	NA	NA	NA
1986	86.1	85.9	86.4	86.5	85.6	87.4	NA	NA	NA	83.4	86.5	80.6	NA	NA	NA
1985	86.1	85.9	86.4	86.8	86.4	87.3	NA	NA	NA	80.6	80.8	80.4	NA	NA	NA
1984	85.9	85.6	86.3	86.9	86.8	87.0	NA	NA	NA	78.9	75.9	81.5	NA	NA	NA
1983	86.0	86.0	86.0	86.9	86.9	86.9	NA	NA	NA	79.4	78.9	79.8	NA	NA	NA
1982	86.2	86.3	86.1	86.9	87.0	86.8	NA	NA	NA	80.9	80.5	81.3	NA	NA	NA
1981	86.3	86.5	86.1	87.6	87.6	87.6	NA	NA	NA	77.3	78.4	76.4	NA	NA	NA
1980	85.4	85.4	85.5	86.9	86.8	87.0	NA	NA	NA	76.6	74.8	78.1	NA	NA	NA
1979	85.6	86.3	84.9	87.0	87.7	86.4	NA	NA	NA	74.8	73.9	75.4	NA	NA	NA
1978	85.3	86.0	84.6	86.3	86.8	85.8	NA	NA	NA	77.3	78.5	76.3	NA	NA	NA
1977	85.4	86.6	84.2	86.8	87.6	86.0	NA	NA	NA	74.4	77.5	72.0	NA	NA	NA
1976	84.7	86.0	83.5	85.9	87.3	84.6	NA	NA	NA	73.8	72.5	74.9	NA	NA	NA
1975	83.1	84.5	81.8	84.4	85.7	83.2	NA	NA	NA	71.0	72.2	70.1	NA	NA	NA
1974	81.9	83.1	80.8	83.4	84.1	82.7	NA	NA	NA	68.2	71.1	66.0	NA	NA	NA
1973	80.2	80.6	79.8	82.0	82.4	81.6	NA	NA	NA	64.2	63.1	64.9	NA	NA	NA
1972	79.8	80.5	79.2	81.5	82.3	80.8	NA	NA	NA	64.1	61.8	66.2	NA	NA	NA
1971	77.2	78.1	76.4	79.5	80.8	78.3	NA	NA	NA	57.5	54.1	60.7	NA	NA	NA
1970	75.4	76.6	74.2	77.8	79.2	76.4	NA	NA	NA	56.2	54.5	57.9	NA	NA	NA
1969	74.7	75.6	73.8	77.0	77.5	76.6	NA	NA	NA	55.8	59.8	52.3	NA	NA	NA
1968	73.2	73.7	72.7	75.3	75.5	75.0	NA	NA	NA	55.8	58.1	53.6	NA	NA	NA
1967	72.5	72.1	72.9	74.8	74.3	75.3	NA	NA	NA	53.4	51.7	55.0	NA	NA	NA
1966	71.0	70.9	71.2	73.8	73.2	74.4	NA	NA	NA	47.9	48.9	47.0	NA	NA	NA
1965	70.3	70.5	70.1	72.8	72.7	72.8	NA	NA	NA	50.3	50.3	50.4	NA	NA	NA
1964	69.2	68.8	69.5	72.1	71.8	72.4	NA	NA	NA	45.0	41.6	47.9	NA	NA	NA
1962	65.9	65.8	66.1	69.2	69.2	69.3	NA	NA	NA	41.6	38.9	43.8	NA	NA	NA
1959	63.9	63.9	64.0	67.2	66.9	67.4	NA	NA	NA	39.5	40.6	38.6	NA	NA	NA
1957	60.2	57.9	62.4	63.3	60.7	65.7	NA	NA	NA	31.6	27.4	35.2	NA	NA	NA
1952	57.1	55.3	58.7	NA	NA	NA	NA	NA	NA	28.1	27.9	28.3	NA	NA	NA
1950	52.8	50.6	55.0	NA	NA	NA	NA	NA	NA	23.6	21.3	25.5	NA	NA	NA

Note: Starting in 2001, data are from the expanded CPS sample.
[1]Data in the column labeled "Black" include Black and other races from 1940 to 1962: from 1963 to 2003, data are for the Black population only.

Table A-18. Percent of People 25 Years and Over Who Have Completed High School or College, by Race, Hispanic Origin, and Sex, Selected Years, 1940–2017—*Continued*

(Percent; civilian noninstitutionalized population.)

Age and Year	Hispanic (of any race) Total	Male	Female	White alone or in combination Total	Male	Female	Non-Hispanic White alone or in combination Total	Male	Female	Black alone or in combination Total	Male	Female	Asian alone or in combination Total	Male	Female
1947	NA	NA	NA	NA	NA	NA	NA	NA	NA	NA	NA	NA	NA	NA	NA
1940	NA	NA	NA	NA	NA	NA	NA	NA	NA	NA	NA	NA	NA	NA	NA

25 TO 29 YEARS

Completed 4 Years of High School or More

Age and Year	Total	Male	Female	Total	Male	Female	Total	Male	Female	Total	Male	Female	Total	Male	Female
2017	82.7	80.7	84.8	92.3	91.2	93.5	95.6	94.8	96.3	91.8	90.9	92.6	96.9	97.9	95.9
2016	80.6	78.3	83.2	91.7	90.7	92.7	95.2	94.9	95.6	90.7	91	90.5	96.7	96.2	97.2
2015	77.1	75.7	78.6	90.8	90.0	91.6	95.4	95.2	95.6	92.2	91.5	92.8	95.5	95.8	95.1
2014	74.7	72.4	77.4	90.8	89.9	91.7	95.6	95.4	95.9	89.1	88.9	89.3	96.9	96.3	97.4
2013	75.8	73.1	78.8	89.6	88.1	91.1	94.2	93.4	95.0	89.5	87.0	91.7	94.9	94.0	95.9
2012	75.0	73.3	76.9	89.6	88.2	91.0	94.6	93.8	95.4	88.4	86.8	89.8	95.5	96.1	94.8
2011	71.5	69.2	74.3	88.9	87.1	90.8	94.4	93.3	95.5	87.9	87.6	88.3	94.7	92.8	96.5
2010	69.4	65.7	74.1	88.5	87.3	89.8	94.4	94.5	94.3	89.9	86.5	91.0	93.1	92.3	93.9
2009	68.9	66.2	72.5	88.4	87.0	89.9	94.5	94.4	94.6	88.8	88.5	89.1	95.1	95.7	94.6
2008	68.3	65.6	71.9	87.6	85.5	89.8	93.7	92.6	94.8	87.7	85.6	89.4	95.7	95.5	95.9
2007	65.0	60.5	70.7	86.5	84.2	88.8	93.4	92.7	94.1	87.4	87.0	87.8	96.3	95.8	96.8
2006	63.3	60.6	66.7	86.0	83.9	88.2	93.3	92.2	94.5	85.6	83.2	87.7	96.0	96.4	95.7
2005	63.3	63.2	63.4	85.6	84.2	87.0	92.8	91.7	93.8	86.6	86.4	86.7	95.5	96.7	94.4
2004	62.4	60.1	65.2	85.9	83.9	87.9	93.2	92.1	94.4	87.8	89.9	86.2	95.7	97.0	94.5
2003	61.7	59.6	64.2	85.7	83.9	87.6	93.6	92.8	94.4	87.4	86.4	88.5	97.2	97.5	97.0
2002	62.4	60.2	65.0	NA	NA	NA	NA	NA	NA	NA	NA	NA	NA	NA	NA
2001	62.4	58.3	67.3	NA	NA	NA	NA	NA	NA	NA	NA	NA	NA	NA	NA
2000	62.8	59.2	66.4	NA	NA	NA	NA	NA	NA	NA	NA	NA	NA	NA	NA
1999	61.6	57.4	66.0	NA	NA	NA	NA	NA	NA	NA	NA	NA	NA	NA	NA
1998	62.8	59.9	66.3	NA	NA	NA	NA	NA	NA	NA	NA	NA	NA	NA	NA
1997	61.8	59.2	64.9	NA	NA	NA	NA	NA	NA	NA	NA	NA	NA	NA	NA
1996	61.1	59.7	62.9	NA	NA	NA	NA	NA	NA	NA	NA	NA	NA	NA	NA
1995	57.1	55.7	58.7	NA	NA	NA	NA	NA	NA	NA	NA	NA	NA	NA	NA
1994	60.3	58.0	63.0	NA	NA	NA	NA	NA	NA	NA	NA	NA	NA	NA	NA
1993	60.9	58.3	64.0	NA	NA	NA	NA	NA	NA	NA	NA	NA	NA	NA	NA
1992	60.9	61.1	60.6	NA	NA	NA	NA	NA	NA	NA	NA	NA	NA	NA	NA
1991	56.7	56.4	57.1	NA	NA	NA	NA	NA	NA	NA	NA	NA	NA	NA	NA
1990	58.2	56.6	59.9	NA	NA	NA	NA	NA	NA	NA	NA	NA	NA	NA	NA
1989	61.0	61.0	61.0	NA	NA	NA	NA	NA	NA	NA	NA	NA	NA	NA	NA
1988	62.0	59.4	65.0	NA	NA	NA	NA	NA	NA	NA	NA	NA	NA	NA	NA
1987	59.8	58.6	61.0	NA	NA	NA	NA	NA	NA	NA	NA	NA	NA	NA	NA
1986	59.1	58.2	60.0	NA	NA	NA	NA	NA	NA	NA	NA	NA	NA	NA	NA
1985	60.9	58.6	63.1	NA	NA	NA	NA	NA	NA	NA	NA	NA	NA	NA	NA
1984	58.6	56.8	60.2	NA	NA	NA	NA	NA	NA	NA	NA	NA	NA	NA	NA
1983	58.3	57.8	58.9	NA	NA	NA	NA	NA	NA	NA	NA	NA	NA	NA	NA
1982	60.9	60.7	61.2	NA	NA	NA	NA	NA	NA	NA	NA	NA	NA	NA	NA
1981	59.8	59.1	60.4	NA	NA	NA	NA	NA	NA	NA	NA	NA	NA	NA	NA
1980	58.6	58.3	58.8	NA	NA	NA	NA	NA	NA	NA	NA	NA	NA	NA	NA
1979	57.0	55.5	58.5	NA	NA	NA	NA	NA	NA	NA	NA	NA	NA	NA	NA
1978	56.6	58.5	54.7	NA	NA	NA	NA	NA	NA	NA	NA	NA	NA	NA	NA
1977	58.1	62.1	54.8	NA	NA	NA	NA	NA	NA	NA	NA	NA	NA	NA	NA
1976	58.1	57.6	58.4	NA	NA	NA	NA	NA	NA	NA	NA	NA	NA	NA	NA
1975	51.7	51.1	52.1	NA	NA	NA	NA	NA	NA	NA	NA	NA	NA	NA	NA
1974	52.5	55.1	49.9	NA	NA	NA	NA	NA	NA	NA	NA	NA	NA	NA	NA
1973	NA	NA	NA	NA	NA	NA	NA	NA	NA	NA	NA	NA	NA	NA	NA
1972	NA	NA	NA	NA	NA	NA	NA	NA	NA	NA	NA	NA	NA	NA	NA
1971	NA	NA	NA	NA	NA	NA	NA	NA	NA	NA	NA	NA	NA	NA	NA
1970	NA	NA	NA	NA	NA	NA	NA	NA	NA	NA	NA	NA	NA	NA	NA
1969	NA	NA	NA	NA	NA	NA	NA	NA	NA	NA	NA	NA	NA	NA	NA
1968	NA	NA	NA	NA	NA	NA	NA	NA	NA	NA	NA	NA	NA	NA	NA
1967	NA	NA	NA	NA	NA	NA	NA	NA	NA	NA	NA	NA	NA	NA	NA
1966	NA	NA	NA	NA	NA	NA	NA	NA	NA	NA	NA	NA	NA	NA	NA
1965	NA	NA	NA	NA	NA	NA	NA	NA	NA	NA	NA	NA	NA	NA	NA
1964	NA	NA	NA	NA	NA	NA	NA	NA	NA	NA	NA	NA	NA	NA	NA
1962	NA	NA	NA	NA	NA	NA	NA	NA	NA	NA	NA	NA	NA	NA	NA
1959	NA	NA	NA	NA	NA	NA	NA	NA	NA	NA	NA	NA	NA	NA	NA
1957	NA	NA	NA	NA	NA	NA	NA	NA	NA	NA	NA	NA	NA	NA	NA
1952	NA	NA	NA	NA	NA	NA	NA	NA	NA	NA	NA	NA	NA	NA	NA
1950	NA	NA	NA	NA	NA	NA	NA	NA	NA	NA	NA	NA	NA	NA	NA

Note: Starting in 2001, data are from the expanded CPS sample.

Table A-18. Percent of People 25 Years and Over Who Have Completed High School or College, by Race, Hispanic Origin, and Sex, Selected Years, 1940–2017—*Continued*

(Percent; civilian noninstitutionalized population.)

Age and Year	All races			White			Non-Hispanic White			Black[1]			Asian		
	Total	Male	Female	Total	Male	Female	Total	Male	Female	Total	Male	Female	Total	Male	Female
1947	51.4	49.4	53.3	54.9	52.9	56.8	NA	NA	NA	22.3	19.6	24.7	NA	NA	NA
1940	38.1	36.0	40.1	41.2	38.9	43.4	NA	NA	NA	12.3	10.6	13.6	NA	NA	NA
Completed 4 Years of College or More															
2017	35.7	32.0	39.3	36.4	32.2	40.7	42.1	37.7	46.5	22.2	20.4	23.9	61.9	58.1	65.9
2016	36.1	32.7	39.5	37.0	33.6	40.5	42.9	39.5	46.3	22.7	20.2	25	64.7	60.3	68.8
2015	35.6	32.4	38.9	36.7	33.2	40.3	43.0	39.5	46.6	20.5	16.5	24.2	65.0	62.8	67.2
2014	34.0	30.9	37.2	34.8	31.6	38.2	40.8	37.7	43.9	21.5	19.5	23.4	61.7	56.3	66.5
2013	33.6	30.2	37.0	34.3	30.8	37.9	40.4	37.1	43.8	20.1	16.8	23.1	59.0	54.3	63.2
2012	33.5	29.8	37.2	33.7	29.9	37.6	39.8	36.0	43.6	22.7	18.5	26.2	60.8	56.8	64.5
2011	32.2	28.4	36.1	33.1	29.2	37.4	39.2	35.5	43.0	19.6	16.1	22.8	56.2	51.5	60.6
2010	31.7	27.8	35.7	32.7	28.8	37.0	38.6	34.8	42.4	19.0	14.8	22.9	55.4	52.0	58.6
2009	30.6	26.6	34.8	31.3	27.0	36.0	37.2	32.6	42.0	19.0	15.2	22.4	59.3	58.0	60.6
2008	30.8	26.8	34.9	31.1	26.7	35.9	37.1	32.6	41.7	20.6	18.7	22.3	59.4	55.1	63.5
2007	29.6	26.3	33.0	29.8	25.8	34.0	35.5	31.9	39.2	18.9	17.9	19.9	60.9	59.8	62.0
2006	28.4	25.3	31.6	28.3	25.0	31.7	34.3	31.4	37.2	18.6	14.9	21.6	60.9	59.8	61.9
2005	28.8	25.5	32.2	28.9	25.3	32.7	34.5	30.7	38.2	17.4	14.1	20.1	61.6	60.5	62.5
2004	28.7	26.1	31.4	28.9	25.8	32.1	34.5	31.4	37.5	16.9	13.4	19.7	61.4	62.0	60.9
2003	28.4	26.0	30.9	28.3	25.3	31.5	34.2	31.4	37.1	17.2	17.5	17.0	61.6	60.9	62.3
2002	29.3	26.9	31.8	29.7	26.5	33.1	35.9	32.6	39.2	17.5	17.4	17.7	NA	NA	NA
2001	28.4	25.5	31.3	28.5	25.1	32.1	33.7	30.4	36.9	16.8	15.6	17.9	NA	NA	NA
2000	29.1	27.9	30.1	29.6	27.8	31.3	34.0	32.3	35.8	17.5	18.1	17.0	NA	NA	NA
1999	28.2	26.8	29.5	29.3	27.6	30.9	33.6	32.0	35.1	15.0	13.1	16.5	NA	NA	NA
1998	27.3	25.6	29.0	28.4	26.5	30.4	32.3	30.5	34.2	15.8	14.2	17.0	NA	NA	NA
1997	27.8	26.3	29.3	28.9	27.2	30.7	32.6	31.2	34.1	14.4	12.1	16.4	NA	NA	NA
1996	27.1	26.1	28.2	28.1	27.2	29.1	31.6	30.9	32.3	14.6	12.4	16.4	NA	NA	NA
1995	24.7	24.5	24.9	26.0	25.4	26.6	28.8	28.4	29.2	15.3	17.2	13.6	NA	NA	NA
1994	23.3	22.5	24.0	24.2	23.6	24.8	27.1	26.8	27.4	13.7	11.7	15.4	NA	NA	NA
1993	23.7	23.4	23.9	24.7	24.4	25.1	27.2	27.2	27.1	13.2	12.6	13.8	NA	NA	NA
1992	23.6	23.2	24.0	25.0	24.2	25.7	NA	NA	NA	11.3	12.0	10.6	NA	NA	NA
1991	23.2	23.0	23.4	24.6	24.1	25.0	NA	NA	NA	11.0	11.5	10.6	NA	NA	NA
1990	23.2	23.7	22.8	24.2	24.2	24.3	NA	NA	NA	13.4	15.1	11.9	NA	NA	NA
1989	23.4	23.9	22.9	24.4	24.8	24.0	NA	NA	NA	12.7	12.0	13.3	NA	NA	NA
1988	22.5	23.2	21.9	23.5	24.0	22.9	NA	NA	NA	12.2	12.6	11.9	NA	NA	NA
1987	22.0	22.3	21.7	23.0	23.3	22.8	NA	NA	NA	11.4	11.6	11.1	NA	NA	NA
1986	22.4	22.9	21.9	23.5	24.1	22.9	NA	NA	NA	11.8	10.1	13.3	NA	NA	NA
1985	22.2	23.1	21.3	23.2	24.2	22.2	NA	NA	NA	11.5	10.3	12.6	NA	NA	NA
1984	21.9	23.2	20.7	23.1	24.3	21.9	NA	NA	NA	11.6	12.9	10.5	NA	NA	NA
1983	22.5	23.9	21.1	23.4	25.0	21.8	NA	NA	NA	12.9	13.1	12.8	NA	NA	NA
1982	21.7	23.3	20.2	22.7	24.5	20.9	NA	NA	NA	12.6	11.8	13.2	NA	NA	NA
1981	21.3	23.1	19.6	22.4	24.3	20.5	NA	NA	NA	11.6	12.1	11.1	NA	NA	NA
1980	22.5	24.0	21.0	23.7	25.5	22.0	NA	NA	NA	11.6	10.5	12.5	NA	NA	NA
1979	23.1	25.6	20.5	24.3	27.1	21.5	NA	NA	NA	12.4	13.3	11.7	NA	NA	NA
1978	23.3	26.0	20.6	24.5	27.6	21.4	NA	NA	NA	11.8	10.7	12.6	NA	NA	NA
1977	24.0	27.0	21.1	25.3	28.5	22.1	NA	NA	NA	12.6	12.8	12.4	NA	NA	NA
1976	23.7	27.5	20.1	24.6	28.7	20.6	NA	NA	NA	13.0	12.0	13.6	NA	NA	NA
1975	21.9	25.1	18.7	22.8	26.3	19.4	NA	NA	NA	10.7	11.4	10.1	NA	NA	NA
1974	20.7	23.9	17.6	22.0	25.3	18.8	NA	NA	NA	7.9	8.8	7.2	NA	NA	NA
1973	19.0	21.6	16.4	19.9	22.8	17.0	NA	NA	NA	8.1	7.1	8.8	NA	NA	NA
1972	19.0	22.0	16.0	19.9	23.1	16.7	NA	NA	NA	8.3	7.1	9.4	NA	NA	NA
1971	16.9	20.1	13.8	17.9	21.3	14.6	NA	NA	NA	6.4	6.4	6.5	NA	NA	NA
1970	16.4	20.0	12.9	17.3	21.3	13.3	NA	NA	NA	7.3	6.7	8.0	NA	NA	NA
1969	16.0	19.4	12.8	17.0	20.6	13.4	NA	NA	NA	6.7	8.1	5.5	NA	NA	NA
1968	14.7	18.0	11.6	15.6	19.1	12.3	NA	NA	NA	5.3	5.3	5.3	NA	NA	NA
1967	14.6	17.2	12.1	15.5	18.3	12.7	NA	NA	NA	5.4	4.2	6.3	NA	NA	NA
1966	14.0	16.8	11.3	14.7	17.9	11.8	NA	NA	NA	5.9	5.4	6.4	NA	NA	NA
1965	12.4	15.6	9.5	13.0	16.4	9.8	NA	NA	NA	6.8	7.3	6.8	NA	NA	NA
1964	12.8	16.6	9.2	13.6	17.5	9.9	NA	NA	NA	5.5	7.5	3.9	NA	NA	NA
1962	13.1	17.2	9.2	14.3	18.7	10.0	NA	NA	NA	4.2	5.7	3.0	NA	NA	NA
1959	11.1	14.8	7.6	11.9	15.9	8.1	NA	NA	NA	4.6	5.6	3.7	NA	NA	NA
1957	10.4	13.5	7.5	11.1	14.5	7.8	NA	NA	NA	4.1	3.3	5.0	NA	NA	NA
1952	10.1	13.8	6.7	NA	NA	NA	NA	NA	NA	4.6	3.2	5.8	NA	NA	NA
1950	7.7	9.6	5.9	NA	NA	NA	NA	NA	NA	2.9	2.4	3.2	NA	NA	NA
1947	5.6	5.8	5.4	5.9	6.2	5.7	NA	NA	NA	2.8	2.6	2.9	NA	NA	NA
1940	5.9	6.9	4.9	6.4	7.5	5.3	NA	NA	NA	1.6	1.5	1.7	NA	NA	NA

Note: Starting in 2001, data are from the expanded CPS sample.
[1] Data in the column labeled "Black" include Black and other races from 1940 to 1962: from 1963 to 2003, data are for the Black population only.

Table A-18. Percent of People 25 Years and Over Who Have Completed High School or College, by Race, Hispanic Origin, and Sex, Selected Years, 1940–2017—*Continued*

(Percent; civilian noninstitutionalized population.)

Age and Year	Hispanic (of any race)			White alone or in combination			Non-Hispanic White alone or in combination			Black alone or in combination			Asian alone or in combination		
	Total	Male	Female	Total	Male	Female	Total	Male	Female	Total	Male	Female	Total	Male	Female
1947	NA	NA	NA	NA	NA	NA	NA	NA	NA	NA	NA	NA	NA	NA	NA
1940	NA	NA	NA	NA	NA	NA	NA	NA	NA	NA	NA	NA	NA	NA	NA
Completed 4 Years of College or More															
2017	18.5	15.0	22.4	36.2	32.1	40.4	41.8	37.5	46.3	22.4	20.6	24.1	61.2	56.9	65.7
2016	18.7	16.2	21.5	36.7	33.2	40.4	42.5	38.9	46.1	22.9	20.1	25.4	63.2	58.3	67.8
2015	16.4	14.5	18.5	36.4	33.0	40.0	42.6	39.1	46.3	20.7	17.0	24.1	63.5	60.6	66.3
2014	15.1	12.4	18.3	34.5	31.2	38.0	40.6	37.4	43.8	21.4	18.7	23.9	60.0	54.4	65.3
2013	15.7	13.1	18.6	34.1	30.6	37.7	40.1	36.8	43.5	19.8	16.6	22.8	58.1	53.7	62.2
2012	14.8	12.5	17.4	33.5	29.8	37.4	39.6	35.9	43.4	22.8	18.1	27.0	59.6	55.7	63.4
2011	12.8	9.6	16.8	33.0	29.0	37.1	39.0	35.4	42.7	19.8	16.3	22.9	55.7	52.0	59.1
2010	13.5	10.8	16.8	32.6	28.6	36.8	38.4	34.6	42.3	19.3	14.8	23.5	53.7	49.6	57.6
2009	12.2	11.0	13.8	31.1	26.8	35.9	37.1	32.4	41.9	19.0	15.0	22.6	58.0	56.7	59.3
2008	12.4	10.0	15.5	31.0	26.6	35.8	36.9	32.4	41.5	20.9	19.3	22.3	57.4	52.9	61.8
2007	11.6	8.6	15.4	29.7	25.7	33.8	35.3	31.7	39.0	19.1	18.1	19.9	59.0	57.8	60.1
2006	9.5	6.9	12.8	28.1	24.8	31.6	34.1	31.2	37.0	18.9	15.0	22.3	59.4	58.4	60.5
2005	11.2	10.2	12.4	28.8	25.3	32.5	34.3	30.6	38.1	17.6	14.6	20.3	60.3	59.0	61.5
2004	10.9	9.6	12.4	28.7	25.7	31.8	34.2	31.2	37.2	16.8	13.4	19.5	59.9	61.1	58.9
2003	10.0	8.4	12.0	28.2	25.2	31.4	34.0	31.2	36.9	17.3	17.4	17.3	60.3	58.8	61.7
2002	8.9	8.3	9.7	NA	NA	NA	NA	NA	NA	NA	NA	NA	NA	NA	NA
2001	10.5	8.2	13.3	NA	NA	NA	NA	NA	NA	NA	NA	NA	NA	NA	NA
2000	9.7	8.3	11.0	NA	NA	NA	NA	NA	NA	NA	NA	NA	NA	NA	NA
1999	8.9	7.5	10.4	NA	NA	NA	NA	NA	NA	NA	NA	NA	NA	NA	NA
1998	10.4	9.5	11.3	NA	NA	NA	NA	NA	NA	NA	NA	NA	NA	NA	NA
1997	11.0	9.6	10.1	NA	NA	NA	NA	NA	NA	NA	NA	NA	NA	NA	NA
1996	10.0	10.2	9.8	NA	NA	NA	NA	NA	NA	NA	NA	NA	NA	NA	NA
1995	8.9	7.8	10.1	NA	NA	NA	NA	NA	NA	NA	NA	NA	NA	NA	NA
1994	8.0	6.6	9.8	NA	NA	NA	NA	NA	NA	NA	NA	NA	NA	NA	NA
1993	8.3	7.1	9.8	NA	NA	NA	NA	NA	NA	NA	NA	NA	NA	NA	NA
1992	9.5	8.8	10.3	NA	NA	NA	NA	NA	NA	NA	NA	NA	NA	NA	NA
1991	9.2	8.1	10.4	NA	NA	NA	NA	NA	NA	NA	NA	NA	NA	NA	NA
1990	8.1	7.3	9.1	NA	NA	NA	NA	NA	NA	NA	NA	NA	NA	NA	NA
1989	10.1	9.6	10.6	NA	NA	NA	NA	NA	NA	NA	NA	NA	NA	NA	NA
1988	11.4	12.1	10.6	NA	NA	NA	NA	NA	NA	NA	NA	NA	NA	NA	NA
1987	8.7	9.2	8.2	NA	NA	NA	NA	NA	NA	NA	NA	NA	NA	NA	NA
1986	9.0	8.9	9.1	NA	NA	NA	NA	NA	NA	NA	NA	NA	NA	NA	NA
1985	11.1	10.9	11.2	NA	NA	NA	NA	NA	NA	NA	NA	NA	NA	NA	NA
1984	10.6	9.6	11.6	NA	NA	NA	NA	NA	NA	NA	NA	NA	NA	NA	NA
1983	10.4	9.6	11.1	NA	NA	NA	NA	NA	NA	NA	NA	NA	NA	NA	NA
1982	9.7	10.7	8.7	NA	NA	NA	NA	NA	NA	NA	NA	NA	NA	NA	NA
1981	7.5	8.6	6.5	NA	NA	NA	NA	NA	NA	NA	NA	NA	NA	NA	NA
1980	7.7	8.4	6.9	NA	NA	NA	NA	NA	NA	NA	NA	NA	NA	NA	NA
1979	7.3	7.9	6.8	NA	NA	NA	NA	NA	NA	NA	NA	NA	NA	NA	NA
1978	9.6	9.6	9.7	NA	NA	NA	NA	NA	NA	NA	NA	NA	NA	NA	NA
1977	6.7	7.2	6.4	NA	NA	NA	NA	NA	NA	NA	NA	NA	NA	NA	NA
1976	7.4	10.3	4.8	NA	NA	NA	NA	NA	NA	NA	NA	NA	NA	NA	NA
1975	8.8	10.0	7.3	NA	NA	NA	NA	NA	NA	NA	NA	NA	NA	NA	NA
1974	5.7	7.2	4.6	NA	NA	NA	NA	NA	NA	NA	NA	NA	NA	NA	NA
1973	NA	NA	NA	NA	NA	NA	NA	NA	NA	NA	NA	NA	NA	NA	NA
1972	NA	NA	NA	NA	NA	NA	NA	NA	NA	NA	NA	NA	NA	NA	NA
1971	NA	NA	NA	NA	NA	NA	NA	NA	NA	NA	NA	NA	NA	NA	NA
1970	NA	NA	NA	NA	NA	NA	NA	NA	NA	NA	NA	NA	NA	NA	NA
1969	NA	NA	NA	NA	NA	NA	NA	NA	NA	NA	NA	NA	NA	NA	NA
1968	NA	NA	NA	NA	NA	NA	NA	NA	NA	NA	NA	NA	NA	NA	NA
1967	NA	NA	NA	NA	NA	NA	NA	NA	NA	NA	NA	NA	NA	NA	NA
1966	NA	NA	NA	NA	NA	NA	NA	NA	NA	NA	NA	NA	NA	NA	NA
1965	NA	NA	NA	NA	NA	NA	NA	NA	NA	NA	NA	NA	NA	NA	NA
1964	NA	NA	NA	NA	NA	NA	NA	NA	NA	NA	NA	NA	NA	NA	NA
1962	NA	NA	NA	NA	NA	NA	NA	NA	NA	NA	NA	NA	NA	NA	NA
1959	NA	NA	NA	NA	NA	NA	NA	NA	NA	NA	NA	NA	NA	NA	NA
1957	NA	NA	NA	NA	NA	NA	NA	NA	NA	NA	NA	NA	NA	NA	NA
1952	NA	NA	NA	NA	NA	NA	NA	NA	NA	NA	NA	NA	NA	NA	NA
1950	NA	NA	NA	NA	NA	NA	NA	NA	NA	NA	NA	NA	NA	NA	NA
1947	NA	NA	NA	NA	NA	NA	NA	NA	NA	NA	NA	NA	NA	NA	NA
1940	NA	NA	NA	NA	NA	NA	NA	NA	NA	NA	NA	NA	NA	NA	NA

Note: Starting in 2001, data are from the expanded CPS sample.

Table A-19. Educational Attainment of the Population 25 Years Old and Over, by Marital Status and Sex, 2017

(Numbers in thousands; percent; civilian noninstitutionalized population.[1])

Sex and marital status	Educational attainment									
	Total		None to 8th grade		9th to 11th grade		High school graduate		Some college, no degree	
	Number	Percent	Number	Percent	Number	Percent	Number	Percent	Number	Percent
BOTH SEXES										
Total	216,921	100.0	8,807	100.0	13,734	100.0	62,512	100.0	35,455	100.0
Married spouse present	124,378	57.3	4,615	52.4	6,302	45.9	33,478	53.6	18,554	52.3
Married spouse absent, not separated	3,660	1.7	351	4.0	276	2.0	1,116	1.8	527	1.5
Separated	4,802	2.2	329	3.7	599	4.4	1,613	2.6	824	2.3
Widowed	14,914	6.9	1,269	14.4	1,542	11.2	5,526	8.8	2,352	6.6
Divorced	25,300	11.7	677	7.7	1,666	12.1	7,921	12.7	5,337	15.1
Never married	43,867	20.2	1,566	17.8	3,347	24.4	12,857	20.6	7,861	22.2
MALE										
Total	104,324	100.0	4,402	100.0	6,934	100.0	31,296	100.0	16,930	100.0
Married spouse present	62,446	59.9	2,531	57.5	3,384	48.8	17,141	54.8	9,371	55.4
Married spouse absent, not separated	1,942	1.9	221	5.0	129	1.9	597	1.9	238	1.4
Separated	2,070	2.0	140	3.2	250	3.6	762	2.4	307	1.8
Widowed	3,258	3.1	272	6.2	350	5.0	1,156	3.7	542	3.2
Divorced	10,829	10.4	357	8.1	822	11.9	3,915	12.5	2,189	12.9
Never married	23,780	22.8	881	20.0	1,999	28.8	7,726	24.7	4,282	25.3
FEMALE										
Total	112,597	100.0	4,406	100.0	6,799	100.0	31,216	100.0	18,525	100.0
Married spouse present	61,932	55.0	2,084	47.3	2,918	42.9	16,337	52.3	9,182	49.6
Married spouse absent, not separated	1,718	1.5	130	3.0	147	2.2	520	1.7	289	1.6
Separated	2,732	2.4	190	4.3	349	5.1	852	2.7	518	2.8
Widowed	11,656	10.4	997	22.6	1,192	17.5	4,370	14.0	1,809	9.8
Divorced	14,471	12.9	319	7.2	844	12.4	4,006	12.8	3,148	17.0
Never married	20,087	17.8	685	15.5	1,349	19.8	5,131	16.4	3,579	19.3

[1]Plus armed forces living off post or with their families on post.

Table A-19. Educational Attainment of the Population 25 Years Old and Over, by Marital Status and Sex, 2017—*Continued*

(Numbers in thousands; percent; civilian noninstitutionalized population.[1])

Sex and marital status	Educational attainment									
	Associate's degree		Bachelor's degree		Master's degree		Professional degree		Doctoral degree	
	Number	Percent	Number	Percent	Number	Percent	Number	Percent	Number	Percent
BOTH SEXES										
Total	22,310	100.0	46,262	100.0	20,592	100.0	3,172	100.0	4,077	100.0
Married spouse present	13,283	59.5	29,229	63.2	13,736	66.7	2,225	70.1	2,956	72.5
Married spouse absent, not separated	252	1.1	649	1.4	351	1.7	69	2.2	70	1.7
Separated	445	2.0	601	1.3	286	1.4	52	1.6	51	1.3
Widowed	1,233	5.5	1,927	4.2	814	4.0	115	3.6	135	3.3
Divorced	3,038	13.6	4,250	9.2	1,926	9.4	227	7.2	257	6.3
Never married	4,060	18.2	9,606	20.8	3,479	16.9	483	15.2	607	14.9
MALE										
Total	9,651	100.0	21,906	100.0	9,049	100.0	1,765	100.0	2,392	100.0
Married spouse present	6,059	62.8	14,209	64.9	6,510	71.9	1,336	75.7	1,904	79.6
Married spouse absent, not separated	113	1.2	371	1.7	178	2.0	39	2.2	54	2.3
Separated	137	1.4	286	1.3	132	1.5	39	2.2	18	0.8
Widowed	239	2.5	451	2.1	168	1.9	41	2.3	40	1.7
Divorced	1,094	11.3	1,688	7.7	581	6.4	89	5.0	93	3.9
Never married	2,010	20.8	4,900	22.4	1,481	16.4	221	12.5	282	11.8
FEMALE										
Total	12,659	100.0	24,357	100.0	11,543	100.0	1,407	100.0	1,685	100.0
Married spouse present	7,224	57.1	15,020	61.7	7,226	62.6	888	63.1	1,052	62.4
Married spouse absent, not separated	139	1.1	277	1.1	173	1.5	30	2.1	15	0.9
Separated	308	2.4	315	1.3	154	1.3	14	1.0	32	1.9
Widowed	994	7.9	1,476	6.1	647	5.6	74	5.3	95	5.6
Divorced	1,945	15.4	2,562	10.5	1,345	11.7	138	9.8	164	9.7
Never married	2,050	16.2	4,706	19.3	1,998	17.3	263	18.7	326	19.3

[1]Plus armed forces living off post or with their families on post.

Table A-20. Educational Attainment of the Population 25 Years Old and Over, by Household Relationship and Sex, 2017

(Numbers in thousands; percent; civilian noninstitutionalized population.[1])

Sex and household relationship	Educational attainment									
	Total		None to 8th grade		9th to 11th grade		High school graduate		Some college, no degree	
	Number	Percent	Number	Percent	Number	Percent	Number	Percent	Number	Percent
BOTH SEXES										
Total	216,921	100.0	8,807	100.0	13,734	100.0	62,512	100.0	35,455	100.0
Family householder										
Married spouse present	59,853	27.6	1,939	22.0	2,863	20.8	14,956	23.9	9,599	27.1
Other family householder	19,842	9.1	880	10.0	1,781	13.0	6,123	9.8	4,144	11.7
Nonfamily householder										
Living alone	33,894	15.6	1,266	14.4	2,441	17.8	9,913	15.9	6,103	17.2
Living with nonrelatives	6,557	3.0	151	1.7	357	2.6	1,514	2.4	1,208	3.4
Relative of householder										
Spouse	59,761	27.5	2,043	23.2	3,031	22.1	16,739	26.8	8,367	23.6
Other	24,876	11.5	1,983	22.5	2,446	17.8	9,435	15.1	4,087	11.5
Nonrelative	12,138	5.6	546	6.2	815	5.9	3,832	6.1	1,948	5.5
MALE										
Total	104,324	100.0	4,402	100.0	6,934	100.0	31,296	100.0	16,930	100.0
Family householder										
Married spouse present	36,137	34.6	1,262	28.7	1,674	24.1	9,194	29.4	5,597	33.1
Other family householder	5,508	5.3	286	6.5	476	6.9	1,893	6.0	1,091	6.4
Nonfamily householder										
Living alone	15,050	14.4	559	12.7	1,128	16.3	4,541	14.5	2,769	16.4
Living with nonrelatives	3,943	3.8	105	2.4	226	3.3	1012	3.2	715	4.2
Relative of householder										
Spouse	23,901	22.9	950	21.6	1,491	21.5	7,047	22.5	3,464	20.5
Other	13,249	12.7	865	19.7	1,472	21.2	5,360	17.1	2,265	13.4
Nonrelative	6,536	6.3	376	8.5	467	6.7	2,248	7.2	1029	6.1
FEMALE										
Total	112,597	100.0	4,406	100.0	6,799	100.0	31,216	100.0	18,525	100.0
Family householder										
Married spouse present	23,716	21.1	678	15.4	1,190	17.5	5,762	18.5	4,002	21.6
Other family householder	14,333	12.7	594	13.5	1,305	19.2	4,230	13.6	3,053	16.5
Nonfamily householder										
Living alone	18,844	16.7	707	16.0	1,313	19.3	5,372	17.2	3,334	18.0
Living with nonrelatives	2,614	2.3	46	1.0	130	1.9	503	1.6	493	2.7
Relative of householder										
Spouse	35,860	31.8	1,093	24.8	1,540	22.7	9,692	31.0	4,902	26.5
Other	11,627	10.3	1,118	25.4	973	14.3	4,074	13.1	1,822	9.8
Nonrelative	5,601	5.0	170	3.9	348	5.1	1,584	5.1	919	5.0

Note. Percentages may not sum to total because of rounding.
[1] Civilian noninstitutionalized population, plus armed forces living off post or with their families on post.

Table A-20. Educational Attainment of the Population 25 Years Old and Over, by Household Relationship and Sex, 2017—*Continued*

(Numbers in thousands; percent; civilian noninstitutionalized population.[1])

Sex and household relationship	Educational attainment									
	Associate degree		Bachelor's degree		Master's degree		Professional degree		Doctoral degree	
	Number	Percent	Number	Percent	Number	Percent	Number	Percent	Number	Percent
BOTH SEXES										
Total	22,310	100.0	46,262	100.0	20,592	100.0	3,172	100.0	4,077	100.0
Family householder..........................										
Married spouse present	6,396	28.7	14,368	31.1	7,079	34.4	1,060	33.4	1,593	39.1
Other family householder......................	2,340	10.5	3,073	6.6	1196	5.8	143	4.5	161	3.9
Nonfamily householder										
Living alone..........................	3,266	14.6	6,536	14.1	3,295	16.0	493	15.5	583	14.3
Living with nonrelatives	669	3.0	1,717	3.7	716	3.5	85	2.7	141	3.5
Relative of householder										
Spouse..........................	6,501	29.1	14,201	30.7	6,445	31.3	1,126	35.5	1,307	32.1
Other..........................	2,073	9.3	3,627	7.8	976	4.7	133	4.2	117	2.9
Nonrelative..........................	1,065	4.8	2,740	5.9	885	4.3	132	4.2	175	4.3
MALE										
Total	9,651	100.0	21,906	100.0	9,049	100.0	1,765	100.0	2,392	100.0
Family householder..........................										
Married spouse present	3,545	36.7	8,694	39.7	4,204	46.5	753	42.7	1,215	50.8
Other family householder......................	565	5.9	873	4.0	234	2.6	39	2.2	51	2.1
Nonfamily householder										
Living alone..........................	1,313	13.6	3,062	14.0	1219	13.5	219	12.4	241	10.1
Living with nonrelatives	350	3.6	1023	4.7	362	4.0	60	3.4	91	3.8
Relative of householder										
Spouse..........................	2,356	24.4	5,186	23.7	2,201	24.3	555	31.4	651	27.2
Other..........................	960	9.9	1,750	8.0	430	4.8	78	4.4	67	2.8
Nonrelative..........................	561	5.8	1,319	6.0	399	4.4	60	3.4	77	3.2
FEMALE										
Total	12,659	100.0	24,357	100.0	11,543	100.0	1,407	100.0	1,685	100.0
Family householder..........................										
Married spouse present	2,851	22.5	5,674	23.3	2,875	24.9	307	21.8	378	22.4
Other family householder......................	1,775	14.0	2,200	9.0	962	8.3	104	7.4	111	6.6
Nonfamily householder										
Living alone..........................	1,953	15.4	3,475	14.3	2,076	18.0	274	19.5	342	20.3
Living with nonrelatives	319	2.5	694	2.8	354	3.1	25	1.8	51	3.0
Relative of householder										
Spouse..........................	4,145	32.7	9,015	37.0	4,245	36.8	571	40.6	656	38.9
Other..........................	1,113	8.8	1,877	7.7	546	4.7	54	3.8	50	3.0
Nonrelative..........................	504	4.0	1,421	5.8	485	4.2	72	5.1	98	5.8

Note. Percentages may not sum to total because of rounding.
[1] Civilian noninstitutionalized population, plus armed forces living off post or with their families on post.

Table A-21. Educational Attainment of the Population 25 Years Old and Over, by Labor Force Status and Sex, 2017

(Numbers in thousands; percent; civilian noninstitutionalized population.[1])

Sex and labor force status	Total	Educational attainment								
		None to 8th grade	9th to 11th grade	High school graduate	Some college, no degree	Associate's degree	Bachelor's degree	Master's degree	Professional degree	Doctoral degree
BOTH SEXES										
Total	216,921	8,807	13,734	62,512	35,455	22,310	46,262	20,592	3,172	4,077
Employed	133,718	3,564	5,822	34,196	21,678	14,988	32,982	14,934	2,423	3,133
Unemployed	5,478	254	577	1,867	946	511	901	339	29	54
Unemployment rate	3.9	6.7	9.0	5.2	4.2	3.3	2.7	2.2	1.2	1.7
Not in civilian labor force ..	77,725	4,990	7,335	26,450	12,831	6,812	12,379	5,319	720	890
Percent	35.8	56.7	53.4	42.3	36.2	30.5	26.8	25.8	22.7	21.8
MALE										
Total	104,324	4,402	6,934	31,296	16,930	9,651	21,906	9,049	1,765	2,392
Employed	70,824	2,338	3,609	19,983	11,244	6,971	16,668	6,850	1,361	1,800
Unemployed	3,021	172	346	1,079	531	226	455	168	18	26
Unemployment rate	4.1	6.9	8.7	5.1	4.5	3.1	2.7	2.4	1.3	1.4
Not in civilian labor force ..	30,479	1,892	2,979	10,234	5,155	2,454	4,783	2,031	386	566
Percent	29.2	43.0	43.0	32.7	30.4	25.4	21.8	22.4	21.9	23.7
FEMALE										
Total	112,597	4,406	6,799	31,216	18,525	12,659	24,357	11,543	1,407	1,685
Employed	62,894	1,226	2,213	14,213	10,434	8,016	16,314	8,084	1,062	1,332
Unemployed	2,456	81	231	788	415	285	446	171	12	29
Unemployment rate	3.8	6.2	9.5	5.3	3.8	3.4	2.7	2.1	1.1	2.1
Not in civilian labor force ..	47,246	3,098	4,356	16,216	7,676	4,358	7,597	3,288	334	324
Percent	42.0	70.3	64.1	51.9	41.4	34.4	31.2	28.5	23.7	19.2

Note. Percentages may not sum to total because of rounding.
[1]Civilian noninstitutionalized population, plus armed forces living off post or with their families on post. May be of any race.

Table A-22. Educational Attainment of Employed Civilians 25 Years Old and Over, by Occupation and Sex, 2017

(Numbers in thousands; percent; civilian noninstitutionalized population.[1])

Occupation and sex	Total	Percent	Educational attainment							
			None to 8th grade	Percent	9th to 11th grade	Percent	High school graduate	Percent	Some college, no degree	Percent
BOTH SEXES										
Total Employed Civilians	133,718	100.0	3,564	2.7	5,822	4.4	34,196	25.6	21,678	16.2
Occupation										
Management, business, and financial occupations	24,172	18.1	175	4.9	353	6.1	3,621	10.6	3,373	15.6
Professional and related occupations	33,264	24.9	45	1.3	121	2.1	2,082	6.1	2,942	13.6
Service occupations..	20,759	15.5	1,215	34.1	1,836	31.5	7,800	22.8	4,057	18.7
Sales and related occupations...........................	12,557	9.4	147	4.1	460	7.9	3,397	9.9	2,554	11.8
Office and administrative occupations	15,137	11.3	121	3.4	376	6.5	4,839	14.2	3,725	17.2
Farming, forestry, and fishing occupations	936	0.7	198	5.6	137	2.4	364	1.1	113	0.5
Construction and extraction occupations..........	6,901	5.2	718	20.1	831	14.3	3,048	8.9	1,110	5.1
Installation, maintenance, and repair occupations	4,488	3.4	119	3.3	314	5.4	1,898	5.6	922	4.3
Production occupations	7,418	5.5	471	13.2	723	12.4	3,366	9.8	1,308	6.0
Transportation and material moving occupations	8,086	6.0	356	10.0	670	11.5	3,781	11.1	1,572	7.3
MALE										
Total Employed Civilians	70,824	100.0	2,338	100.0	3,609	100.0	19,983	100.0	11,244	100.0
Occupation										
Management, business, and financial occupations	13,440	19.0	128	5.5	250	6.9	2,140	10.7	1,805	16.1
Professional and related occupations	14,173	20.0	21	0.9	53	1.5	898	4.5	1,152	10.2
Service occupations..	8,854	12.5	565	24.2	743	20.6	3,264	16.3	1,726	15.4
Sales and related occupations...........................	6,607	9.3	52	2.2	167	4.6	1,637	8.2	1,295	11.5
Office and administrative occupations	4,027	5.7	61	2.6	127	3.5	1,262	6.3	1003	8.9
Farming, forestry, and fishing occupations	687	1.0	153	6.5	116	3.2	271	1.4	75	0.7
Construction and extraction occupations..........	6,708	9.5	708	30.3	814	22.6	2,975	14.9	1,079	9.6
Installation, maintenance, and repair occupations	4,325	6.1	116	5.0	304	8.4	1,850	9.3	890	7.9
Production occupations	5,294	7.5	253	10.8	482	13.4	2,489	12.5	932	8.3
Transportation and material moving occupations	6,711	9.5	280	12.0	554	15.4	3,196	16.0	1,287	11.4
FEMALE										
Total Employed Civilians	62,894	100.0	1,226	100.0	2,213	100.0	14,213	100.0	10,434	100.0
Occupation										
Management, business, and financial occupations	10,733	17.1	47	3.8	103	4.7	1,481	10.4	1,568	15.0
Professional and related occupations	19,091	30.4	23	1.9	68	3.1	1,184	8.3	1,790	17.2
Service occupations..	11,905	18.9	650	53.0	1,093	49.4	4,536	31.9	2,331	22.3
Sales and related occupations...........................	5,950	9.5	95	7.7	293	13.2	1,760	12.4	1,259	12.1
Office and administrative occupations	11,110	17.7	60	4.9	250	11.3	3,577	25.2	2,722	26.1
Farming, forestry, and fishing occupations	249	0.4	45	3.7	21	0.9	92	0.6	37	0.4
Construction and extraction occupations........	193	0.3	10	0.8	17	0.8	72	0.5	31	0.3
Installation, maintenance, and repair occupations	163	0.3	2	0.2	10	0.5	49	0.3	33	0.3
Production occupations	2,124	3.4	218	17.8	241	10.9	877	6.2	377	3.6
Transportation and material moving occupations	1,375	2.2	75	6.1	117	5.3	585	4.1	286	2.7

Note. Percentages may not sum to total because of rounding.
[1]Civilian noninstitutionalized population plus armed forces living off post or with their families on post.

Table A-22. Educational Attainment of Employed Civilians 25 Years Old and Over, by Occupation and Sex, 2017—*Continued*

(Numbers in thousands; percent; civilian noninstitutionalized population.[1])

Occupation and sex	Educational attainment									
	Associate's degree	Percent	Bachelor's degree	Percent	Master's degree	Percent	Professional degree	Percent	Doctoral degree	Percent
BOTH SEXES										
Total Employed Civilians	14,988	11.2	32,982	24.7	14,934	11.2	2,423	1.8	3,133	2.3
Occupation										
Management, business, and financial occupations	2,133	14.2	9,323	28.3	4,491	30.1	313	12.9	390	12.4
Professional and related occupations	3,665	24.5	11,904	36.1	8,028	53.8	1,920	79.2	2,556	81.6
Service occupations..	2,617	17.5	2,626	8.0	498	3.3	56	2.3	54	1.7
Sales and related occupations.........................	1,401	9.3	3,682	11.2	810	5.4	47	1.9	58	1.9
Office and administrative occupations	2,161	14.4	3,170	9.6	676	4.5	44	1.8	24	0.8
Farming, forestry, and fishing occupations	44	0.3	66	0.2	11	0.1	*	*	5	0.2
Construction and extraction occupations.........	658	4.4	443	1.3	73	0.5	14	0.6	5	0.2
Installation, maintenance, and repair occupations	789	5.3	361	1.1	66.0	0.4	4	0.2	15	0.5
Production occupations	777	5.2	596	1.8	145.0	1.0	14	0.6	17	0.5
Transportation and material moving occupations	742	5.0	812	2.5	135.0	0.9	10	0.4	8	0.3
MALE										
Total Employed Civilians	6,971	100.0	16,668	100.0	6,850	100.0	1,361	100.0	1,800	100.0
Occupation										
Management, business, and financial occupations	1,070	15.3	5,243	31.5	2,390	34.9	172	12.6	242	13.4
Professional and related occupations	1,196	17.2	5,126	30.8	3,195	46.6	1,071	78.7	1,461	81.2
Service occupations..	968	13.9	1,310	7.9	228	3.3	29	2.1	20	1.1
Sales and related occupations.........................	697	10.0	2,177	13.1	504	7.4	36	2.6	40	2.2
Office and administrative occupations	410	5.9	931	5.6	213	3.1	13	1.0	7	0.4
Farming, forestry, and fishing occupations	30	0.4	34	0.2	7	0.1	*	*	*	*
Construction and extraction occupations.........	644	9.2	397	2.4	70	1.0	14	1.0	5	0.3
Installation, maintenance, and repair occupations	759	10.9	338	2.0	53	0.8	4	0.3	11	0.6
Production occupations	588	8.4	442	2.7	87	1.3	13	1.0	9	0.5
Transportation and material moving occupations	608	8.7	669	4.0	103	1.5	10	0.7	4	0.2
FEMALE										
Total Employed Civilians	8,016	100.0	16,314	100.0	8,084	100.0	1,062	100.0	1,332	100.0
Occupation										
Management, business, and financial occupations	1,064	13.3	4,080	25.0	2,101	26.0	141	13.3	148	11.1
Professional and related occupations	2,469	30.8	6,778	41.5	4,833	59.8	849	79.9	1,096	82.3
Service occupations..	1,649	20.6	1,316	8.1	270	3.3	27	2.5	33	2.5
Sales and related occupations.........................	704	8.8	1,505	9.2	306	3.8	11	1.0	18	1.4
Office and administrative occupations	1,751	21.8	2,238	13.7	463	5.7	32	3.0	17	1.3
Farming, forestry, and fishing occupations	14	0.2	32	0.2	4	*	*	*	5	0.4
Construction and extraction occupations.........	13	0.2	46	0.3	3	*	*	*	*	*
Installation, maintenance, and repair occupations	30	0.4	23	0.1	13	0.2	*	*	4	0.3
Production occupations	189	2.4	155	1.0	58	0.7	2	0.2	8	0.6
Transportation and material moving occupations	133	1.7	143	0.9	32	0.4	*	*	4	0.3

Note. Percentages may not sum to total because of rounding.
* = Quantity zero or rounds to zero.
[1]Civilian noninstitutionalized population plus armed forces living off post or with their families on post.

Table A-23. Educational Attainment of the Population 25 Years Old and Older, by Industry and Sex, 2017

(Numbers in thousands; percent; civilian noninstitutionalized population.[1])

Industry and sex	Total	Percent	None to 8th grade	Percent	9th to 11th grade	Percent	High school graduate	Percent	Some college, no degree	Percent
BOTH SEXES										
Total Employed Civilians	133,718	100.0	3,564	100.0	5,822	100.0	34,196	100.0	21,678	100.0
Industry										
Agriculture, forestry, fishing, and hunting	2,147	1.6	278	7.8	199	3.4	772	2.3	305	1.4
Mining	693	0.5	14	0.4	30	0.5	233	0.7	138	0.6
Construction	9,514	7.1	703	19.7	930	16.0	3,891	11.4	1,539	7.1
Manufacturing	13,940	10.4	525	14.7	736	12.6	4,736	13.8	2,239	10.3
Wholesale and retail trade	16,250	12.2	325	9.1	843	14.5	5,485	16.0	3,302	15.2
Transportation and utilities	7,428	5.6	166	4.7	364	6.3	2,806	8.2	1,649	7.6
Information	2,596	1.9	2	0.1	46	0.8	384	1.1	390	1.8
Financial activities	9,798	7.3	65	1.8	124	2.1	1,617	4.7	1,797	8.3
Professional and business services	16,904	12.6	472	13.2	674	11.6	2,980	8.7	2,091	9.6
Educational and health services	32,001	23.9	253	7.1	617	10.6	4,933	14.4	4,091	18.9
Leisure and hospitality	9,419	7.0	479	13.4	811	13.9	3,199	9.4	1,832	8.5
Other services	6,533	4.9	265	7.4	393	6.8	2,038	6.0	1,089	5.0
Public administration	6,495	4.9	16	0.4	55	0.9	1,121	3.3	1,215	5.6
MALE										
Total Employed Civilians	70,824	100.0	2,338	100.0	3,609	100.0	19,983	100.0	11,244	100.0
Industry										
Agriculture, forestry, fishing, and hunting	1,595	2.3	220	9.4	169	4.7	618	3.1	200	1.8
Mining	603	0.9	14	0.6	28	0.8	220	1.1	115	1.0
Construction	8,531	12.0	683	29.2	903	25.0	3,578	17.9	1,362	12.1
Manufacturing	9,755	13.8	298	12.7	487	13.5	3,436	17.2	1,547	13.8
Wholesale and retail trade	9,032	12.8	191	8.2	481	13.3	2,995	15.0	1,848	16.4
Transportation and utilities	5,681	8.0	145	6.2	290	8.0	2,221	11.1	1,195	10.6
Information	1,565	2.2	2	0.1	25	0.7	273	1.4	242	2.2
Financial activities	4,617	6.5	54	2.3	73	2.0	566	2.8	671	6.0
Professional and business services	9,843	13.9	300	12.8	391	10.8	1,729	8.7	1,084	9.6
Educational and health services	8,110	11.5	44	1.9	125	3.5	1076	5.4	816	7.3
Leisure and hospitality	4,791	6.8	262	11.2	388	10.8	1,629	8.2	917	8.2
Other services	3,151	4.4	117	5.0	217	6.0	1,053	5.3	519	4.6
Public administration	3,548	5.0	8	0.3	31	0.9	588	2.9	726	6.5
FEMALE										
Total Employed Civilians	62,894	100.0	1,226	100.0	2,213	100.0	14,213	100.0	10,434	100.0
Industry										
Agriculture, forestry, fishing, and hunting	552	0.9	57	4.6	30	1.4	154	1.1	105	1.0
Mining	90	0.1	*	*	2	0.1	13	0.1	23	0.2
Construction	983	1.6	20	1.6	28	1.3	313	2.2	177	1.7
Manufacturing	4,185	6.7	227	18.5	248	11.2	1,300	9.1	692	6.6
Wholesale and retail trade	7,217	11.5	135	11.0	362	16.4	2,490	17.5	1,454	13.9
Transportation and utilities	1,747	2.8	21	1.7	74	3.3	585	4.1	453	4.3
Information	1,030	1.6	*	*	21	0.9	111	0.8	148	1.4
Financial activities	5,181	8.2	11	0.9	51	2.3	1,051	7.4	1,125	10.8
Professional and business services	7,061	11.2	172	14.0	283	12.8	1,251	8.8	1,007	9.7
Educational and health services	23,891	38.0	210	17.1	492	22.2	3,858	27.1	3,275	31.4
Leisure and hospitality	4,628	7.4	218	17.8	423	19.1	1,571	11.1	915	8.8
Other services	3,382	5.4	148	12.1	175	7.9	985	6.9	570	5.5
Public administration	2,947	4.7	7	0.6	24	1.1	532	3.7	488	4.7

Note. Percentages may not sum to total because of rounding.
* = Quantity zero or rounds to zero.
[1] Civilian noninstitutionalized population plus armed forces living off post or with their families on post.

Table A-23. Educational Attainment of the Population 25 Years Old and Older, by Industry and Sex, 2017—*Continued*

(Numbers in thousands; percent; civilian noninstitutionalized population.[1])

Industry and sex	Educational attainment									
	Associate's degree	Percent	Bachelor's degree	Percent	Master's degree	Percent	Professional degree	Percent	Doctoral degree	Percent
BOTH SEXES										
Total Employed Civilians	14,988	100.0	32,982	100.0	14,934	100.0	2,423	100.0	3,133	100.0
Industry										
Agriculture, forestry, fishing, and hunting	182	1.2	324	1.0	77	0.5	1	*	10	0.3
Mining	71	0.5	128	0.4	69	0.5	*	*	11	0.4
Construction	968	6.5	1,203	3.6	229	1.5	29	1.2	22	0.7
Manufacturing	1,501	10.0	2,911	8.8	1,064	7.1	56	2.3	172	5.5
Wholesale and retail trade	1,775	11.8	3,545	10.7	742	5.0	91	3.8	140	4.5
Transportation and utilities	868	5.8	1,209	3.7	332	2.2	19	0.8	16	0.5
Information	253	1.7	1,051	3.2	415	2.8	17	0.7	38	1.2
Financial activities	1013	6.8	3,767	11.4	1,201	8.0	125	5.2	87	2.8
Professional and business services	1,565	10.4	5,423	16.4	2,408	16.1	701	28.9	592	18.9
Educational and health services	4,183	27.9	8,568	26.0	6,500	43.5	1,045	43.1	1,810	57.8
Leisure and hospitality	867	5.8	1,750	5.3	425	2.8	30	1.2	26	0.8
Other services	911	6.1	1,172	3.6	533	3.6	68	2.8	64	2.0
Public administration	833	5.6	1,931	5.9	939	6.3	241	9.9	146	4.7
MALE										
Total Employed Civilians	6,971	100.0	16,668	100.0	6,850	100.0	1,361	100.0	1,800	100.0
Industry										
Agriculture, forestry, fishing, and hunting	121	1.7	213	1.3	47	0.7	1	0.1	6	0.3
Mining	57	0.8	100	0.6	63	0.9	*	*	6	0.3
Construction	841	12.1	964	5.8	165	2.4	21	1.5	15	0.8
Manufacturing	1081	15.5	2,016	12.1	730	10.7	38	2.8	122	6.8
Wholesale and retail trade	954	13.7	2,017	12.1	410	6.0	55	4.0	82	4.6
Transportation and utilities	677	9.7	897	5.4	233	3.4	14	1.0	9	0.5
Information	155	2.2	618	3.7	212	3.1	9	0.7	29	1.6
Financial activities	345	4.9	2,059	12.4	717	10.5	71	5.2	60	3.3
Professional and business services	754	10.8	3,196	19.2	1,531	22.4	460	33.8	398	22.1
Educational and health services	695	10.0	2,091	12.5	1,795	26.2	531	39.0	938	52.1
Leisure and hospitality	429	6.2	932	5.6	210	3.1	12	0.9	14	0.8
Other services	400	5.7	495	3.0	276	4.0	32	2.4	43	2.4
Public administration	465	6.7	1,071	6.4	461	6.7	119	8.7	79	4.4
FEMALE										
Total Employed Civilians	8,016	100.0	16,314	100.0	8,084	100.0	1,062	100.0	1,332	100.0
Industry										
Agriculture, forestry, fishing, and hunting	61	0.8	112	0.7	30	0.4	*	*	4	0.3
Mining	14	0.2	28	0.2	6	0.1	*	*	5	0.4
Construction	126	1.6	239	1.5	65	0.8	8	0.8	7	0.5
Manufacturing	420	5.2	896	5.5	335	4.1	18	1.7	50	3.8
Wholesale and retail trade	821	10.2	1,529	9.4	332	4.1	36	3.4	57	4.3
Transportation and utilities	191	2.4	311	1.9	99	1.2	6	0.6	7	0.5
Information	98	1.2	433	2.7	203	2.5	7	0.7	9	0.7
Financial activities	669	8.3	1,708	10.5	484	6.0	54	5.1	28	2.1
Professional and business services	811	10.1	2,227	13.7	876	10.8	241	22.7	193	14.5
Educational and health services	3,488	43.5	6,477	39.7	4,705	58.2	514	48.4	872	65.5
Leisure and hospitality	438	5.5	818	5.0	215	2.7	19	1.8	11	0.8
Other services	511	6.4	677	4.1	257	3.2	36	3.4	22	1.7
Public administration	368	4.6	860	5.3	478	5.9	122	11.5	67	5.0

Note. Percentages may not sum to total because of rounding.
* = Quantity zero or rounds to zero.
[1]Civilian noninstitutionalized population plus armed forces living off post or with their families on post.

Table A-24. Educational Attainment of the Population 25 Years Old and Over, by Citizenship, Nativity, Period of Entry, and Sex, 2017

(Numbers in thousands; percent; civilian noninstitutionalized population.[1])

Citizenship, nativity, period of entry, and sex	Total		None to 8th grade		9th to 11th grade		High school graduate		Some college, no degree	
	Number	Percent	Number	Percent	Number	Percent	Number	Percent	Number	Percent
BOTH SEXES										
Total	216,922	100.0	8,808	4.1	13,733	6.3	62,512	28.8	35,455	16.3
Native	178,913	82.5	3,155	1.8	10,003	5.6	52,418	29.3	31,814	17.8
Foreign-born	38,009	17.5	5,653	14.9	3,730	9.8	10,094	26.6	3,641	9.6
Native										
Native parentage[2]	162,239	74.8	2,720	30.9	9,054	65.9	48,295	77.3	28,836	81.3
Foreign or mixed parentage[3]	16,673	7.7	435	4.9	949	6.9	4,123	6.6	2,978	8.4
Foreign-born										
Naturalized citizen	18,891	8.7	1,757	19.9	1,179	8.6	4,934	7.9	2,226	6.3
Not a citizen	19,117	8.8	3,896	44.2	2,551	18.6	5,161	8.3	1,416	4.0
Year of entry										
2000 or later	16,240	7.5	2,165	24.6	1,620	11.8	4,166	6.7	1,377	3.9
1990-1999	9,224	4.3	1,478	16.8	1,045	7.6	2,486	4.0	932	2.6
1980-1989	6,538	3.0	1,047	11.9	636	4.6	1,790	2.9	657	1.9
1970-1979	3,633	1.7	636	7.2	289	2.1	958	1.5	371	1.0
Before 1970	2,373	1.1	326	3.7	141	1.0	694	1.1	304	0.9
MALE										
Total	104,325	100.0	4,402	4.2	6,934	6.6	31,296	30.0	16,930	16.2
Native	86,009	82.4	1,650	37.5	5,068	73.1	26,413	84.4	15,227	89.9
Foreign-born	18,316	17.6	2,752	62.5	1,866	26.9	4,883	15.6	1,703	10.1
Native										
Native parentage[2]	77,718	74.5	1,425	32.4	4,571	65.9	24,339	77.8	13,694	80.9
Foreign or mixed parentage[3]	8,291	7.9	225	5.1	497	7.2	2,074	6.6	1,533	9.1
Foreign-born										
Naturalized citizen	8,640	8.3	783	17.8	556	8.0	2,215	7.1	999	5.9
Not a citizen	9,676	9.3	1,969	44.7	1,310	18.9	2,668	8.5	704	4.2
Year of entry										
2000 or later	7,845	7.5	1,069	24.3	783	11.3	2,090	6.7	595	3.5
1990-1999	4,500	4.3	722	16.4	540	7.8	1,203	3.8	484	2.9
1980-1989	3,271	3.1	550	12.5	340	4.9	877	2.8	331	2.0
1970-1979	1,694	1.6	286	6.5	132	1.9	429	1.4	167	1.0
Before 1970	1,007	1.0	126	2.9	71	1.0	284	0.9	125	0.7
FEMALE										
Total	112,597	100.0	4,405	3.9	6,799	6.0	31,216	27.7	18,526	16.5
Native	92,904	82.5	1,505	34.2	4,935	72.6	26,004	83.3	16,587	89.5
Foreign-born	19,693	17.5	2,900	65.8	1,864	27.4	5,212	16.7	1,939	10.5
Native										
Native parentage[2]	84,522	75.1	1,296	29.4	4,483	65.9	23,955	76.7	15,142	81.7
Foreign or mixed parentage[3]	8,382	7.4	210	4.8	452	6.6	2,049	6.6	1,445	7.8
Foreign-born										
Naturalized citizen	10,251	9.1	974	22.1	623	9.2	2,719	8.7	1,227	6.6
Not a citizen	9,442	8.4	1,926	43.7	1,241	18.3	2,493	8.0	712	3.8
Year of entry										
2000 or later	8,395	7.5	1,097	24.9	837	12.3	2,076	6.7	782	4.2
1990-1999	4,724	4.2	756	17.2	504	7.4	1,283	4.1	448	2.4
1980-1989	3,267	2.9	497	11.3	295	4.3	913	2.9	326	1.8
1970-1979	1,940	1.7	350	7.9	157	2.3	529	1.7	204	1.1
Before 1970	1,366	1.2	200	4.5	70	1.0	410	1.3	179	1.0

[1]Civilian noninstitutionalized population plus armed forces living off post or with their families on post.
[2]Native parentage: Both parents born in the United States. Percent: percent of native citizens.
[3]Foreign or mixed parentage: One or both parents born outside of the United States.

Table A-24. Educational Attainment of the Population 25 Years Old and Over, by Citizenship, Nativity, Period of Entry, and Sex, 2017—*Continued*

(Numbers in thousands; percent; civilian noninstitutionalized population.[1])

Citizenship, nativity, period of entry, and sex	Educational attainment									
	Associate degree		Bachelor's degree		Master's degree		Professional degree		Doctoral degree	
	Number	Percent	Number	Percent	Number	Percent	Number	Percent	Number	Percent
BOTH SEXES										
Total	22,310	10.3	46,262	21.3	20,592	9.5	3,172	1.5	4,077	1.9
Native................................	19,951	11.2	39,066	21.8	16,811	9.4	2,680	1.5	3,015	1.7
Foreign-born	2,359	6.2	7,196	18.9	3,781	9.9	492	1.3	1062	2.8
Native................................										
Native parentage[2]	18,138	81.3	35,152	76.0	15,073	73.2	2,305	72.7	2,666	65.4
Foreign or mixed parentage[3]	1,813	8.1	3,914	8.5	1,738	8.4	375	11.8	350	8.6
Foreign-born										
Naturalized citizen	1,573	7.1	4,250	9.2	2,028	9.8	335	10.6	611	15.0
Not a citizen	787	3.5	2,947	6.4	1,753	8.5	157	4.9	451	11.1
Year of entry										
2000 or later	868	3.9	3,381	7.3	2,015	9.8	167	5.3	480	11.8
1990-1999	586	2.6	1,570	3.4	766	3.7	112	3.5	249	6.1
1980-1989	434	1.9	1,181	2.6	509	2.5	106	3.3	179	4.4
1970-1979	235	1.1	671	1.5	303	1.5	75	2.4	94	2.3
Before 1970	237	1.1	394	0.9	188	0.9	30	0.9	59	1.4
MALE										
Total	9,651	9.3	21,906	21.0	9,049	8.7	1,765	1.7	2,392	2.3
Native................................	8,691	90.1	18,594	84.9	7,125	78.7	1,516	85.9	1,725	72.1
Foreign-born	960	9.9	3,312	15.1	1,924	21.3	249	14.1	667	27.9
Native................................										
Native parentage[2]	7,846	81.3	16,612	75.8	6,386	70.6	1,321	74.8	1,523	63.7
Foreign or mixed parentage[3]	845	8.8	1,982	9.0	739	8.2	195	11.0	202	8.4
Foreign-born										
Naturalized citizen	614	6.4	1,914	8.7	1002	11.1	174	9.9	383	16.0
Not a citizen	346	3.6	1,398	6.4	922	10.2	75	4.2	284	11.9
Year of entry										
2000 or later	350	3.6	1,524	7.0	1074	11.9	75	4.2	285	11.9
1990-1999	244	2.5	750	3.4	356	3.9	55	3.1	146	6.1
1980-1989	177	1.8	558	2.5	252	2.8	59	3.3	127	5.3
1970-1979	103	1.1	316	1.4	155	1.7	38	2.2	67	2.8
Before 1970	86	0.9	165	0.8	87	1.0	21	1.2	42	1.8
FEMALE										
Total	12,659	11.2	24,357	21.6	11,543	10.3	1,407	1.2	1,685	1.5
Native................................	11,260	88.9	20,472	84.0	9,686	83.9	1,164	82.7	1,290	76.6
Foreign-born	1,399	11.1	3,885	16.0	1,857	16.1	243	17.3	395	23.4
Native................................										
Native parentage[2]	10,292	81.3	18,540	76.1	8,688	75.3	984	69.9	1,142	67.8
Foreign or mixed parentage[3]	968	7.6	1,932	7.9	999	8.7	180	12.8	148	8.8
Foreign-born										
Naturalized citizen	959	7.6	2,336	9.6	1,026	8.9	161	11.4	228	13.5
Not a citizen	440	3.5	1,549	6.4	831	7.2	82	5.8	167	9.9
Year of entry										
2000 or later	518	4.1	1,857	7.6	941	8.2	92	6.5	195	11.6
1990-1999	343	2.7	820	3.4	410	3.6	57	4.1	103	6.1
1980-1989	256	2.0	623	2.6	257	2.2	47	3.3	52	3.1
1970-1979	131	1.0	355	1.5	149	1.3	37	2.6	28	1.7
Before 1970	151	1.2	229	0.9	101	0.9	9	0.6	17	1.0

[1]Civilian noninstitutionalized population plus armed forces living off post or with their families on post.
[2]Native parentage: Both parents born in the United States. Percent: percent of native citizens.
[3]Foreign or mixed parentage: One or both parents born outside of the United States.

Table A-25. Years of School Completed by People 25 Years Old and Over, by Age and Sex, Selected Years, 1940–2017

(Numbers in thousands; civilian noninstitutionalized population, except where noted.)

Year, sex, and age	Total	Elementary 0 to 4 years	Elementary 5 to 8 years	High school 1 to 3 years	High school 4 years	College 1 to 3 years	College 4 years or more	Median years
25 YEARS OLD AND OVER								
Both Sexes								
2017	216,921	2,208	6,600	13,734	62,512	57,765	74,103	NA
2016	215,015	2,414	7,078	13,961	62,002	57,660	71,900	NA
2015	212,132	2,601	7,295	14,686	62,575	56,031	68,945	NA
2014	209,287	2,525	7,388	14,545	62,240	55,709	66,879	NA
2013	206,899	2,344	7,578	14,595	61,704	55,173	65,506	NA
2012	204,579	2,484	7,800	14,993	62,113	53,900	63,291	NA
2011	201,543	2,589	7,688	14,763	61,911	53,249	61,343	NA
2010	199,928	2,615	7,836	15,260	62,456	51,920	59,840	NA
2009	198,285	2,785	8,043	15,587	61,626	51,670	58,574	NA
2008	196,305	2,599	8,226	15,516	61,183	50,994	57,787	NA
2007	194,318	2,830	8,462	16,451	61,490	49,243	55,842	NA
2006	191,884	2,951	8,791	16,154	60,898	49,371	53,720	NA
2005	189,367	2,983	8,935	16,099	60,893	48,076	52,381	NA
2004	186,876	2,858	8,888	15,999	59,811	47,571	51,749	NA
2003	185,183	2,915	9,361	16,323	59,292	46,910	50,383	NA
2002	182,142	2,902	9,668	16,378	58,456	46,042	48,696	NA
2001	180,389	2,810	9,518	16,279	58,272	46,281	47,228	NA
2000	175,230	2,742	9,438	15,674	58,086	44,445	44,845	NA
1999	173,754	2,742	9,655	15,674	57,935	43,176	43,803	NA
1998	172,211	2,834	9,948	16,776	58,174	42,506	41,973	NA
1997	170,581	2,840	10,472	17,211	57,586	41,774	40,697	NA
1996	168,323	3,027	10,595	17,102	56,559	41,372	39,668	NA
1995	166,438	3,074	10,873	16,566	56,450	41,249	38,226	NA
1994	164,512	3,156	11,359	16,925	56,515	40,014	36,544	NA
1993	162,826	3,380	11,747	17,067	57,589	37,451	35,590	NA
1992	160,827	3,449	11,989	17,672	57,860	35,520	34,337	NA
1991	158,694	3,803	13,046	17,379	61,272	29,170	34,026	12.7
1990	156,538	3,833	13,758	17,461	60,119	28,075	33,291	12.7
1989	154,155	3,861	14,061	17,719	59,336	26,614	32,565	12.7
1988	151,635	3,714	14,550	17,847	58,940	25,799	30,787	12.7
1987	149,144	3,640	15,301	17,417	57,669	25,479	29,637	12.7
1986	146,606	3,894	15,672	17,484	56,338	24,729	28,489	12.6
1985	143,524	3,873	16,020	17,553	54,866	23,405	27,808	12.6
1984	140,794	3,884	16,258	17,433	54,073	22,281	26,862	12.6
1983	138,020	4,119	16,714	17,681	52,060	21,531	25,915	12.6
1982	135,526	4,119	17,232	18,006	51,426	20,692	24,050	12.6
1981	132,899	4,358	17,868	18,041	49,915	20,042	22,674	12.5
1980	130,409	4,390	18,426	18,086	47,934	19,379	22,193	12.5
1979	125,295	4,324	18,504	17,559	45,915	18,393	20,579	12.5
1978	123,019	4,445	19,309	18,175	44,381	17,379	19,332	12.4
1977	120,870	4,509	19,567	18,318	43,602	16,247	18,627	12.4
1976	118,848	4,601	19,912	18,204	43,157	15,477	17,496	12.4
1975	116,897	4,912	20,633	18,237	42,353	14,518	16,244	12.3
1974	115,005	5,106	21,200	18,274	41,460	13,665	15,300	12.3
1973	112,866	5,100	21,838	18,420	40,448	12,831	14,228	12.3
1972	111,133	5,124	22,503	18,855	39,171	12,117	13,364	12.2
1971	110,627	5,574	24,029	18,601	38,029	11,782	12,612	12.2
1970	109,310	5,747	24,519	18,682	37,134	11,164	12,062	12.2
1969	107,750	6,014	24,976	18,527	36,133	10,564	11,535	12.1
1968	106,469	6,248	25,467	18,724	34,603	10,254	11,171	12.1
1967	104,864	6,400	26,178	18,647	33,173	9,914	10,550	12.0
1966	103,876	6,705	26,478	18,859	32,391	9,235	10,212	12.0
1965	103,245	6,982	27,063	18,617	31,703	9,139	9,742	11.8
1964	102,421	7,295	27,551	18,419	30,728	9,085	9,345	11.7
1962	100,664	7,826	28,438	17,751	28,477	9,170	9,002	11.4
1960	99,465	8,303	31,218	19,140	24,440	8,747	7,617	10.6
1959	97,478	7,816	28,490	17,520	26,219	7,888	7,734	11.0
1957	95,630	8,561	29,316	16,951	24,832	6,985	7,172	10.6
1952	88,358	8,004	30,274	15,228	21,074	6,714	6,118	10.1

Note: Starting in 2012, data were created using population controls based on 2010 Census data. Starting in 2001, data were created using population controls based on Census 2000 data. Also starting in 2001, data are from the expanded CPS sample. Begining with data for 1992, a new question results in different categories than for earlier years. Data shown as 'High School, 4 years' are now collected in the category 'High School Graduate.' Data shown as 'College 1 to 3 years' are now collected in the 'Some college' and the two 'Associate degree' categories. Data shown as 'College 4 years or more,' are now collected in the categories, 'Bachelor's degree,' 'Master's degree,' 'Doctorate degree,' and 'Professional degree.' Due to the change in question format, median years of schooling cannot be derived. Total includes persons who did not report on years of school completed.
NA = Not available.

Table A-25. Years of School Completed by People 25 Years Old and Over, by Age and Sex, Selected Years, 1940–2017—*Continued*

(Numbers in thousands; civilian noninstitutionalized population, except where noted.)

Year, sex, and age	Total	Elementary 0 to 4 years	Elementary 5 to 8 years	High school 1 to 3 years	High school 4 years	College 1 to 3 years	College 4 years or more	Median years
1950	87,484	9,491	31,617	14,817	17,625	6,246	5,272	9.3
1947	82,578	8,611	32,308	13,487	16,926	5,533	4,424	9.0
1940	74,776	10,105	34,413	11,182	10,552	4,075	3,407	8.6
Male								
2017	104,324	1,090	3,312	6,934	31,296	26,581	35,112	NA
2016	103,372	1,183	3,513	7,144	30,780	26,468	34,283	NA
2015	101,887	1,243	3,669	7,278	30,997	25,778	32,923	NA
2014	100,592	1,184	3,761	7,403	30,718	25,430	32,095	NA
2013	99,305	1,127	3,836	7,314	30,014	25,283	31,731	NA
2012	98,119	1,237	3,879	7,388	30,216	24,632	30,766	NA
2011	97,220	1,234	3,883	7,443	30,370	24,319	29,971	NA
2010	96,325	1,279	3,931	7,705	30,682	23,570	29,158	NA
2009	95,518	1,372	4,027	7,754	30,025	23,634	28,706	NA
2008	94,470	1,310	4,136	7,853	29,491	23,247	28,433	NA
2007	93,421	1,458	4,249	8,294	29,604	22,219	27,596	NA
2006	92,233	1,472	4,395	7,940	29,380	22,136	26,910	NA
2005	90,899	1,505	4,402	7,787	29,151	21,794	26,259	NA
2004	89,558	1,496	4,308	7,766	27,889	21,763	26,336	NA
2003	88,597	1,482	4,566	8,026	27,356	21,568	25,598	NA
2002	86,996	1,457	4,743	7,894	26,947	21,127	24,828	NA
2001	86,096	1,419	4,673	7,615	26,956	21,120	24,313	NA
2000	83,611	1,341	4,577	7,298	26,651	20,493	23,252	NA
1999	82,917	1,339	4,651	7,736	26,368	20,043	22,782	NA
1998	82,376	1,431	4,727	8,017	26,575	19,792	21,832	NA
1997	81,620	1,454	5,023	8,212	26,226	19,332	21,374	NA
1996	80,339	1,537	5,067	7,930	25,649	19,301	20,854	NA
1995	79,463	1,598	5,231	7,691	25,378	18,933	20,631	NA
1994	78,539	1,669	5,427	7,789	25,404	18,544	19,705	NA
1993	77,644	1,709	5,594	7,821	25,766	17,521	19,234	NA
1992	76,579	1,737	5,726	8,085	25,774	16,631	18,627	NA
1991	75,487	2,018	6,299	7,887	27,189	13,720	18,373	12.8
1990	74,421	2,004	6,557	8,000	26,426	13,271	18,164	12.8
1989	73,225	1,956	6,659	8,076	25,897	12,725	17,913	12.8
1988	71,911	1,852	6,849	8,247	25,638	12,057	17,268	12.7
1987	70,677	1,794	7,259	7,909	24,998	12,062	16,654	12.7
1986	69,503	1,978	7,446	7,872	24,260	11,856	16,091	12.7
1985	67,756	1,947	7,629	7,783	23,552	11,164	15,682	12.7
1984	66,350	1,945	7,688	7,837	22,990	10,678	15,211	12.7
1983	65,004	2,103	7,750	7,867	22,048	10,310	14,926	12.7
1982	63,764	2,074	7,987	7,960	21,749	10,020	13,974	12.6
1981	62,509	2,141	8,322	8,084	21,019	9,734	13,208	12.6
1980	61,389	2,212	8,627	8,046	20,080	9,593	12,832	12.6
1979	58,986	2,190	8,785	7,636	19,250	9,100	12,025	12.6
1978	57,922	2,230	9,195	7,821	18,620	8,657	11,398	12.5
1977	56,917	2,296	9,330	7,969	18,290	8,104	10,926	12.5
1976	55,902	2,371	9,463	7,923	18,048	7,699	10,397	12.5
1975	55,036	2,568	9,760	7,985	17,769	7,274	9,679	12.4
1974	54,167	2,637	10,186	7,966	17,488	6,756	9,135	12.4
1973	53,067	2,598	10,488	8,120	17,011	6,376	8,473	12.3
1972	52,351	2,634	10,854	8,413	16,424	5,972	8,055	12.3
1971	52,357	2,933	11,703	8,264	16,008	5,798	7,653	12.2
1970	51,784	3,031	11,925	8,355	15,571	5,580	7,321	12.2
1969	51,031	3,095	12,182	8,398	15,177	5,263	6,917	12.1
1968	50,510	3,261	12,407	8,564	14,613	4,945	6,721	12.1
1967	49,756	3,417	12,736	8,463	14,015	4,755	6,372	12.0
1966	49,410	3,614	12,992	8,611	13,672	4,342	6,180	11.8
1965	49,242	3,774	13,308	8,529	13,334	4,370	5,923	11.7
1964	48,975	3,959	13,467	8,537	12,902	4,394	5,714	11.5
1962	48,283	4,213	13,927	8,399	11,932	4,315	5,497	11.1
1960	47,997	4,522	15,562	8,988	10,175	4,127	4,626	10.3
1959	47,041	4,257	14,039	8,326	10,870	3,801	4,765	10.7
1957	46,208	4,610	14,634	8,003	10,230	3,347	4,359	10.3
1952	42,368	4,396	14,876	7,048	8,760	3,164	3,480	9.7

Note: Starting in 2012, data were created using population controls based on 2010 Census data. Starting in 2001, data were created using population controls based on Census 2000 data. Also starting in 2001, data are from the expanded CPS sample. Begining with data for 1992, a new question results in different categories than for earlier years. Data shown as 'High School, 4 years' are now collected in the category 'High School Graduate.' Data shown as 'College 1 to 3 years' are now collected in the 'Some college' and the two 'Associate degree' categories. Data shown as 'College 4 years or more,' are now collected in the categories, 'Bachelor's degree,' 'Master's degree,' 'Doctorate degree,' and 'Professional degree.' Due to the change in question format, median years of schooling cannot be derived. Total includes persons who did not report on years of school completed.
NA = Not available.

Table A-25. Years of School Completed by People 25 Years Old and Over, by Age and Sex, Selected Years, 1940–2017—*Continued*

(Numbers in thousands; civilian noninstitutionalized population, except where noted.)

Year, sex, and age	Total	Elementary		High school		College		Median years
		0 to 4 years	5 to 8 years	1 to 3 years	4 years	1 to 3 years	4 years or more	
1950	42,627	5,074	15,852	6,974	7,511	2,888	3,008	9.0
1947	40,483	4,615	16,086	6,535	7,353	2,625	2,478	8.9
1940	37,463	5,550	17,639	5,333	4,507	1,824	2,021	8.6
Female								
2017	112,597	1,117	3,288	6,799	31,216	31,185	38,991	NA
2016	111,643	1,231	3,565	6,817	31,221	31,192	37,617	NA
2015	110,245	1,358	3,626	7,408	31,578	30,253	36,021	NA
2014	108,695	1,341	3,627	7,142	31,522	30,279	34,784	NA
2013	107,594	1,217	3,741	7,282	31,690	29,890	33,775	NA
2012	106,460	1,246	3,920	7,604	31,898	29,267	32,524	NA
2011	104,323	1,355	3,806	7,320	31,541	28,930	31,372	NA
2010	103,603	1,336	3,904	7,555	31,774	28,350	30,683	NA
2009	102,767	1,413	4,016	7,833	31,601	28,036	29,868	NA
2008	101,835	1,289	4,090	7,663	31,692	27,747	29,354	NA
2007	100,897	1,371	4,213	8,157	31,887	27,024	28,245	NA
2006	99,651	1,479	4,395	8,215	31,518	27,234	26,810	NA
2005	98,467	1,477	4,532	8,311	31,742	26,283	26,122	NA
2004	97,319	1,363	4,580	8,233	31,921	25,808	25,413	NA
2003	96,586	1,433	4,795	8,297	31,936	25,342	24,784	NA
2002	95,146	1,445	4,926	8,484	31,509	24,915	23,868	NA
2001	94,293	1,392	4,845	8,664	31,316	25,161	22,915	NA
2000	91,620	1,400	4,861	8,378	31,435	23,953	21,594	NA
1999	90,837	1,404	5,004	8,707	31,566	23,133	21,021	NA
1998	89,835	1,403	5,220	8,758	31,599	22,714	20,142	NA
1997	88,961	1,387	5,450	8,999	31,360	22,442	19,323	NA
1996	87,984	1,491	5,528	9,171	30,911	22,071	18,813	NA
1995	86,975	1,476	5,642	8,874	31,072	22,317	17,594	NA
1994	85,973	1,487	5,932	9,135	31,111	21,470	16,838	NA
1993	85,181	1,672	6,154	9,246	31,823	19,930	16,357	NA
1992	84,248	1,712	6,263	9,587	32,086	18,889	15,709	NA
1991	83,207	1,784	6,747	9,491	34,083	15,449	15,652	12.7
1990	82,116	1,829	7,200	9,462	33,693	14,806	15,126	12.7
1989	80,930	1,904	7,402	9,643	33,440	13,888	14,652	12.6
1988	79,724	1,862	7,700	9,599	33,303	13,741	13,519	12.6
1987	78,467	1,846	8,042	9,508	32,671	13,417	12,983	12.6
1986	77,102	1,916	8,226	9,612	32,078	12,874	12,399	12.6
1985	75,768	1,926	8,390	9,770	31,314	12,242	12,126	12.6
1984	74,444	1,939	8,571	9,596	31,083	11,603	11,651	12.6
1983	73,016	2,015	8,964	9,814	30,012	11,220	10,990	12.5
1982	71,762	2,045	9,245	10,046	29,677	10,673	10,076	12.5
1981	70,390	2,217	9,545	9,957	28,896	10,309	9,466	12.5
1980	69,020	2,178	9,800	10,040	27,854	9,786	9,362	12.4
1979	66,309	2,133	9,720	9,945	26,665	9,293	8,554	12.4
1978	65,097	2,214	10,114	10,353	25,761	8,721	7,934	12.4
1977	63,953	2,213	10,236	10,349	25,312	8,142	7,701	12.4
1976	62,946	2,230	10,449	10,281	25,109	7,779	7,098	12.3
1975	61,861	2,344	10,871	10,252	24,584	7,243	6,565	12.3
1974	60,838	2,469	11,015	10,308	23,972	6,910	6,165	12.3
1973	59,799	2,502	11,350	10,300	23,437	6,454	5,755	12.2
1972	58,782	2,490	11,649	10,442	22,746	6,145	5,309	12.2
1971	58,270	2,641	12,327	10,339	22,021	5,984	4,959	12.2
1970	57,527	2,716	12,595	10,327	21,563	5,584	4,743	12.1
1969	56,719	2,919	12,796	10,131	20,955	5,301	4,619	12.1
1968	55,959	2,987	13,060	10,160	19,991	5,309	4,450	12.1
1967	55,107	2,985	13,439	10,185	19,157	5,162	4,178	12.0
1966	54,467	3,090	13,488	10,246	18,719	4,892	4,032	12.0
1965	54,004	3,207	13,753	10,085	18,369	4,767	3,820	12.0
1964	53,447	3,333	14,086	9,881	17,825	4,686	3,629	11.8
1962	52,381	3,613	14,511	9,352	16,545	4,855	3,505	11.6
1960	51,468	3,781	15,656	10,151	14,267	4,620	2,991	10.9
1959	50,437	3,559	14,451	9,194	15,349	4,087	2,969	11.2
1957	49,422	3,951	14,682	8,948	14,602	3,638	2,813	10.9
1952	45,990	3,608	15,398	8,180	12,314	3,550	2,638	10.4

Note: Starting in 2012, data were created using population controls based on 2010 Census data. Starting in 2001, data were created using population controls based on Census 2000 data. Also starting in 2001, data are from the expanded CPS sample. Begining with data for 1992, a new question results in different categories than for earlier years. Data shown as 'High School, 4 years' are now collected in the category 'High School Graduate.' Data shown as 'College 1 to 3 years' are now collected in the 'Some college' and the two 'Associate degree' categories. Data shown as 'College 4 years or more,' are now collected in the categories, 'Bachelor's degree,' Master's degree,' 'Doctorate degree,' and 'Professional degree.' Due to the change in question format, median years of schooling cannot be derived. Total includes persons who did not report on years of school completed.
NA = Not available.

Table A-25. Years of School Completed by People 25 Years Old and Over, by Age and Sex, Selected Years, 1940–2017—*Continued*

(Numbers in thousands; civilian noninstitutionalized population, except where noted.)

Year, sex, and age	Total	Years of school completed						Median years
		Elementary		High school		College		
		0 to 4 years	5 to 8 years	1 to 3 years	4 years	1 to 3 years	4 years or more	
1950..................................	44,857	4,417	15,824	7,843	10,114	3,358	2,264	9.6
1947..................................	42,095	3,996	16,222	6,952	9,573	2,908	1,946	8.9
1940..................................	37,313	4,554	16,773	5,849	6,044	2,251	1,386	8.7
25 TO 34 YEARS								
Both Sexes								
2017..................................	44,250	218	732	2,532	11,494	12,792	16,482	NA
2016..................................	43,763	210	858	2,656	11,224	12,609	16,207	NA
2015..................................	43,006	292	863	2,938	10,965	12,420	15,528	NA
2014..................................	42,466	286	946	3,018	11,040	12,178	14,997	NA
2013..................................	41,797	260	1,035	3,116	10,950	11,955	14,481	NA
2012..................................	41,219	273	1,063	3,079	10,974	11,765	14,065	NA
2011..................................	41,584	318	1,140	3,098	11,250	12,046	13,731	NA
2010..................................	41,085	323	1,169	3,271	11,186	11,655	13,480	NA
2009..................................	40,520	321	1,226	3,202	11,351	11,409	13,010	NA
2008..................................	40,146	282	1,189	3,296	11,297	11,113	12,969	NA
2007..................................	39,868	380	1,283	3,462	11,408	10,961	12,375	NA
2006..................................	39,481	359	1,410	3,375	11,302	11,229	11,806	NA
2005..................................	39,310	414	1,375	3,422	11,269	10,865	11,965	NA
2004..................................	39,201	430	1,399	3,239	11,244	11,044	11,844	NA
2003..................................	39,242	370	1,370	3,336	11,392	10,986	11,791	NA
2002..................................	38,670	433	1,393	3,245	10,988	10,776	11,834	NA
2001..................................	38,865	380	1,317	3,202	11,294	11,146	11,526	NA
2000..................................	37,786	287	1,135	3,052	11,546	10,700	11,066	NA
1999..................................	38,474	280	1,142	3,296	11,826	10,893	11,040	NA
1998..................................	39,354	319	1,207	3,228	12,569	11,220	10,811	NA
1997..................................	40,256	334	1,163	3,624	12,710	11,524	10,892	NA
1996..................................	40,919	418	1,169	3,780	13,087	11,624	10,841	NA
1995..................................	41,388	394	1,264	3,667	14,061	11,659	10,342	NA
1994..................................	41,946	367	1,297	4,057	14,483	11,913	9,829	NA
1993..................................	41,864	382	1,223	3,894	15,036	11,361	9,968	NA
1992..................................	42,493	433	1,250	4,071	16,021	10,860	9,861	NA
1991..................................	42,905	465	1,322	4,178	17,503	9,283	10,153	12.9
1990..................................	43,240	505	1,413	4,041	17,635	9,320	10,326	12.9
1989..................................	43,240	446	1,352	4,013	17,901	9,072	10,454	12.9
1988..................................	42,953	430	1,308	4,095	17,887	9,076	10,155	12.9
1987..................................	42,635	390	1,360	3,995	17,539	9,157	10,196	12.9
1986..................................	42,053	387	1,359	3,797	17,311	9,104	10,094	12.9
1985..................................	40,858	362	1,328	3,703	16,748	8,980	9,737	12.9
1984..................................	40,173	404	1,371	3,638	16,431	8,555	9,771	12.9
1983..................................	39,342	376	1,324	3,664	15,804	8,567	9,605	12.9
1982..................................	38,703	337	1,371	3,598	15,893	8,304	9,200	12.9
1981..................................	37,828	337	1,428	3,665	15,419	8,198	8,782	12.9
1980..................................	36,615	362	1,424	3,571	14,481	7,942	8,836	12.9
1979..................................	34,053	370	1,381	3,452	13,338	7,415	8,096	12.9
1978..................................	33,120	325	1,459	3,515	12,993	7,008	7,821	12.9
1977..................................	32,284	269	1,383	3,715	12,845	6,398	7,676	12.8
1976..................................	31,148	247	1,508	3,619	12,920	5,813	7,041	12.8
1975..................................	30,092	313	1,644	3,743	12,544	5,403	6,443	12.7
1974..................................	28,972	352	1,654	3,763	12,362	5,056	5,785	12.7
1973..................................	27,793	333	1,850	3,915	12,194	4,454	5,047	12.6
1972..................................	26,517	285	1,791	3,981	11,635	4,090	4,734	12.6
1971..................................	25,545	327	2,011	3,986	11,232	3,822	4,169	12.6
1970..................................	24,865	329	1,937	4,251	10,929	3,491	3,926	12.5
1969..................................	24,072	359	2,086	4,140	10,592	3,202	3,693	12.5
1968..................................	23,285	350	2,246	4,129	10,157	2,989	3,413	12.5
1967..................................	22,388	319	2,293	4,017	9,645	2,946	3,169	12.5
1966..................................	22,023	430	2,208	4,158	9,546	2,647	3,037	12.4
1965..................................	21,980	543	2,437	4,058	9,500	2,561	2,880	12.4
1964..................................	21,997	502	2,591	4,176	9,370	2,529	2,830	12.4
1962..................................	22,130	597	2,936	4,371	8,815	2,552	2,859	12.4
1960..................................	22,821	709	3,738	5,135	8,166	2,572	2,499	12.4
1959..................................	22,922	761	3,348	4,741	8,979	2,398	2,480	12.3
1957..................................	23,437	750	3,971	4,965	8,927	2,275	2,351	12.2

Note: Starting in 2012, data were created using population controls based on 2010 Census data. Starting in 2001, data were created using population controls based on Census 2000 data. Also starting in 2001, data are from the expanded CPS sample. Begining with data for 1992, a new question results in different categories than for earlier years. Data shown as 'High School, 4 years' are now collected in the category 'High School Graduate.' Data shown as 'College 1 to 3 years' are now collected in the 'Some college' and the two 'Associate degree' categories. Data shown as 'College 4 years or more,' are now collected in the categories, 'Bachelor's degree,' Master's degree,' 'Doctorate degree,' and 'Professional degree.' Due to the change in question format, median years of schooling cannot be derived. Total includes persons who did not report on years of school completed.
NA = Not available.

Table A-25. Years of School Completed by People 25 Years Old and Over, by Age and Sex, Selected Years, 1940–2017—*Continued*

(Numbers in thousands; civilian noninstitutionalized population, except where noted.)

Year, sex, and age	Total	Years of school completed						Median years
		Elementary		High school		College		
		0 to 4 years	5 to 8 years	1 to 3 years	4 years	1 to 3 years	4 years or more	
1952............................	23,138	844	4,362	4,898	8,620	2,220	2,052	12.2
1950............................	23,626	1,147	5,308	5,050	7,660	2,198	1,252	11.9
1947............................	22,627	1,015	5,523	4,997	7,630	1,908	1,378	11.9
1940............................	21,339	1,377	7,676	4,553	4,702	1,554	1,288	10.0
Male								
2017............................	22,121	135	390	1,410	6,456	6,267	7,464	NA
2016............................	21,845	116	468	1,427	6,386	6,015	7,432	NA
2015............................	21,427	166	488	1,584	6,198	5,920	7,071	NA
2014............................	21,217	151	512	1,611	6,323	5,910	6,710	NA
2013............................	20,816	161	582	1,747	6,058	5,749	6,519	NA
2012............................	20,464	161	579	1,707	6,127	5,619	6,270	NA
2011............................	20,985	190	657	1,791	6,444	5,750	6,151	NA
2010............................	20,689	186	641	1,866	6,458	5,587	5,951	NA
2009............................	20,440	184	695	1,806	6,495	5,508	5,752	NA
2008............................	20,210	172	714	1,874	6,356	5,277	5,816	NA
2007............................	20,024	246	757	1,930	6,361	5,137	5,593	NA
2006............................	19,827	218	834	1,835	6,233	5,336	5,371	NA
2005............................	19,677	241	769	1,827	6,216	5,198	5,426	NA
2004............................	19,598	280	793	1,723	6,020	5,286	5,495	NA
2003............................	19,564	216	771	1,831	6,028	5,252	5,466	NA
2002............................	19,234	280	809	1,782	5,751	5,131	5,480	NA
2001............................	19,330	233	748	1,677	6,099	5,161	5,411	NA
2000............................	18,563	155	593	1,637	5,989	4,870	5,318	NA
1999............................	18,294	157	616	1,724	6,114	5,052	5,260	NA
1998............................	19,526	190	654	1,735	6,592	5,233	5,125	NA
1997............................	20,039	193	629	2,007	6,482	5,477	5,249	NA
1996............................	20,390	225	601	2,055	6,701	5,536	5,274	NA
1995............................	20,589	229	708	1,930	7,176	5,373	5,174	NA
1994............................	20,873	230	716	2,134	7,408	5,510	4,873	NA
1993............................	20,856	237	679	1,986	7,604	5,308	5,041	NA
1992............................	21,125	231	682	2,057	8,113	5,116	4,927	NA
1991............................	21,319	270	694	2,095	8,810	4,441	5,009	12.9
1990............................	21,462	295	759	2,153	8,649	4,392	5,215	12.9
1989............................	21,461	251	698	2,129	8,659	4,391	5,335	12.9
1988............................	21,277	237	651	2,227	8,569	4,273	5,319	12.9
1987............................	21,142	223	698	2,030	8,544	4,384	5,263	12.9
1986............................	20,956	227	715	1,887	8,359	4,488	5,279	12.9
1985............................	20,184	194	700	1,823	7,955	4,433	5,080	12.9
1984............................	19,876	231	721	1,739	7,798	4,238	5,150	12.9
1983............................	19,438	213	659	1,724	7,351	4,284	5,207	13.0
1982............................	19,090	182	659	1,654	7,380	4,162	5,053	13.0
1981............................	18,625	176	733	1,679	6,991	4,185	4,863	13.0
1980............................	18,051	198	699	1,639	6,393	4,166	4,957	13.0
1979............................	16,719	197	695	1,476	5,852	3,862	4,637	13.0
1978............................	16,263	154	717	1,526	5,701	3,698	4,471	13.1
1977............................	15,863	134	672	1,625	5,634	3,403	4,396	13.0
1976............................	15,266	134	724	1,566	5,672	3,085	4,087	12.9
1975............................	14,776	177	815	1,605	5,508	2,915	3,757	12.9
1974............................	14,222	211	859	1,617	5,491	2,672	3,372	12.8
1973............................	13,638	204	966	1,760	5,363	2,416	2,927	12.7
1972............................	13,030	157	927	1,796	5,150	2,191	2,809	12.7
1971............................	12,596	170	1,092	1,771	5,049	2,005	2,506	12.6
1970............................	12,236	189	1,063	1,896	4,833	1,842	2,412	12.6
1969............................	11,788	204	1,121	1,849	4,652	1,719	2,241	12.6
1968............................	11,381	193	1,192	1,880	4,473	1,505	2,136	12.5
1967............................	10,876	170	1,209	1,814	4,187	1,522	1,973	12.5
1966............................	10,701	241	1,162	1,839	4,191	1,374	1,894	12.5
1965............................	10,693	325	1,240	1,802	4,188	1,316	1,822	12.5
1964............................	10,729	297	1,344	1,962	4,008	1,306	1,812	12.4
1962............................	10,762	334	1,569	2,008	3,700	1,309	1,842	12.4
1960............................	11,184	420	2,026	2,441	3,356	1,316	1,624	12.2
1959............................	11,226	416	1,822	2,238	3,682	1,256	1,658	12.3
1957............................	11,368	423	2,097	2,446	3,542	1,181	1,556	12.2
1952............................	10,936	502	2,202	2,268	3,458	1,118	1,268	12.1

Note: Starting in 2012, data were created using population controls based on 2010 Census data. Starting in 2001, data were created using population controls based on Census 2000 data. Also starting in 2001, data are from the expanded CPS sample. Begining with data for 1992, a new question results in different categories than for earlier years. Data shown as 'High School, 4 years' are now collected in the category 'High School Graduate.' Data shown as 'College 1 to 3 years' are now collected in the 'Some college' and the two 'Associate degree' categories. Data shown as 'College 4 years or more,' are now collected in the categories, 'Bachelor's degree,' 'Master's degree,' 'Doctorate degree,' and 'Professional degree.' Due to the change in question format, median years of schooling cannot be derived. Total includes persons who did not report on years of school completed.
NA = Not available.

Table A-25. Years of School Completed by People 25 Years Old and Over, by Age and Sex, Selected Years, 1940–2017—*Continued*

(Numbers in thousands; civilian noninstitutionalized population, except where noted.)

Year, sex, and age	Total	Years of school completed						Median years
		Elementary		High school		College		
		0 to 4 years	5 to 8 years	1 to 3 years	4 years	1 to 3 years	4 years or more	
1950.................................	11,454	631	2,705	2,426	3,250	1,117	1,037	11.5
1947.................................	10,894	544	2,665	2,494	3,337	993	738	11.7
1940.................................	10,521	779	3,932	2,220	2,049	692	744	9.7
Female								
2017.................................	22,129	84	342	1,122	5,037	6,526	9,018	NA
2016.................................	21,918	93	390	1,229	4,838	6,594	8,774	NA
2015.................................	21,579	126	375	1,354	4,767	6,500	8,457	NA
2014.................................	21,248	135	435	1,407	4,717	6,267	8,287	NA
2013.................................	20,981	99	454	1,369	4,892	6,205	7,962	NA
2012.................................	20,755	112	484	1,372	4,847	6,145	7,795	NA
2011.................................	20,599	128	483	1,307	4,806	6,296	7,580	NA
2010.................................	20,396	137	527	1,405	4,728	6,068	7,530	NA
2009.................................	20,079	137	531	1,395	4,856	5,901	7,258	NA
2008.................................	19,937	111	475	1,421	4,941	5,836	7,153	NA
2007.................................	19,843	134	527	1,532	5,047	5,824	6,781	NA
2006.................................	19,654	140	577	1,538	5,069	5,894	6,435	NA
2005.................................	19,633	173	607	1,594	5,053	5,667	6,539	NA
2004.................................	19,603	150	606	1,516	5,224	5,758	6,349	NA
2003.................................	19,679	153	598	1,503	5,364	5,734	6,325	NA
2002.................................	19,436	153	584	1,463	5,237	5,645	6,353	NA
2001.................................	19,536	147	569	1,525	5,195	5,985	6,115	NA
2000.................................	19,222	130	542	1,415	5,557	5,831	5,750	NA
1999.................................	19,551	122	525	1,572	5,712	5,842	5,779	NA
1998.................................	19,828	130	553	1,493	5,977	5,986	5,688	NA
1997.................................	20,217	149	533	1,615	6,227	6,047	5,643	NA
1996.................................	20,528	195	569	1,734	6,386	6,090	5,568	NA
1995.................................	20,800	165	556	1,738	6,885	6,286	5,170	NA
1994.................................	21,073	138	581	1,923	7,075	6,404	4,953	NA
1993.................................	21,007	143	543	1,907	7,432	6,054	4,928	NA
1992.................................	21,368	203	567	2,014	7,908	5,744	4,933	NA
1991.................................	21,586	195	629	2,085	8,693	4,841	5,143	12.9
1990.................................	21,779	209	653	1,889	8,986	4,927	5,112	12.9
1989.................................	21,777	195	654	1,885	9,242	4,681	5,119	12.9
1988.................................	21,675	193	657	1,869	9,319	4,801	4,836	12.9
1987.................................	21,494	168	662	1,965	8,995	4,772	4,932	12.9
1986.................................	21,097	160	644	1,910	8,952	4,616	4,813	12.9
1985.................................	20,673	168	627	1,880	8,794	4,547	4,657	12.9
1984.................................	20,297	173	649	1,904	8,634	4,319	4,621	12.9
1983.................................	19,903	161	665	1,941	8,452	4,285	4,398	12.9
1982.................................	19,614	155	713	1,942	8,512	4,140	4,148	12.8
1981.................................	19,203	161	698	1,986	8,427	4,013	3,918	12.8
1980.................................	18,565	164	725	1,932	8,087	3,777	3,879	12.8
1979.................................	17,334	173	685	1,977	7,486	3,553	3,460	12.8
1978.................................	16,857	172	742	1,989	7,292	3,311	3,351	12.6
1977.................................	16,421	136	710	2,088	7,212	2,995	3,280	12.7
1976.................................	15,882	112	784	2,054	7,248	2,731	2,954	12.7
1975.................................	15,316	135	833	2,139	7,037	2,489	2,686	12.6
1974.................................	14,750	142	796	2,145	6,871	2,383	2,413	12.6
1973.................................	14,155	129	884	2,154	6,830	2,037	2,121	12.6
1972.................................	13,487	128	862	2,184	6,485	1,899	1,926	12.5
1971.................................	12,950	156	919	2,212	6,183	1,816	1,663	12.5
1970.................................	12,629	140	876	2,355	6,096	1,648	1,512	12.5
1969.................................	12,285	155	965	2,291	5,941	1,481	1,451	12.4
1968.................................	11,904	157	1,053	2,246	5,684	1,484	1,278	12.4
1967.................................	11,512	149	1,084	2,200	5,458	1,426	1,195	12.4
1966.................................	11,322	186	1,047	2,319	5,355	1,273	1,134	12.4
1965.................................	11,284	218	1,197	2,256	5,310	1,244	1,060	12.4
1964.................................	11,269	202	1,248	2,216	5,362	1,221	1,018	12.4
1962.................................	11,368	263	1,367	2,363	5,115	1,243	1,017	12.3
1960.................................	11,637	289	1,712	2,694	4,810	1,256	875	12.2
1959.................................	11,696	345	1,526	2,503	5,297	1,142	822	12.3
1957.................................	12,069	327	1,874	2,519	5,385	1,094	795	12.2
1952.................................	12,202	342	2,160	2,630	5,162	1,102	784	12.2
1950.................................	12,172	516	2,603	2,624	4,410	1,081	714	12.1

Note: Starting in 2012, data were created using population controls based on 2010 Census data. Starting in 2001, data were created using population controls based on Census 2000 data. Also starting in 2001, data are from the expanded CPS sample. Begining with data for 1992, a new question results in different categories than for earlier years. Data shown as 'High School, 4 years' are now collected in the category 'High School Graduate.' Data shown as 'College 1 to 3 years' are now collected in the 'Some college' and the two 'Associate degree' categories. Data shown as 'College 4 years or more,' are now collected in the categories, 'Bachelor's degree,' 'Master's degree,' 'Doctorate degree,' and 'Professional degree.' Due to the change in question format, median years of schooling cannot be derived. Total includes persons who did not report on years of school completed.
NA = Not available.

Table A-25. Years of School Completed by People 25 Years Old and Over, by Age and Sex, Selected Years, 1940–2017—*Continued*

(Numbers in thousands; civilian noninstitutionalized population, except where noted.)

Year, sex, and age	Total	Elementary 0 to 4 years	Elementary 5 to 8 years	High school 1 to 3 years	High school 4 years	College 1 to 3 years	College 4 years or more	Median years
1947	11,733	471	2,858	2,503	4,293	915	640	12.0
1940	10,818	598	3,744	2,333	2,653	862	544	10.3
35 TO 54 YEARS								
Both Sexes								
2017	82,072	709	2,403	5,059	22,103	21,621	30,176	NA
2016	82,571	799	2,636	5,296	22,298	22,070	29,473	NA
2015	82,715	862	2,742	5,471	23,153	21,826	28,660	NA
2014	82,687	875	2,612	5,433	23,238	22,472	28,057	NA
2013	83,324	778	2,611	5,437	23,708	22,831	27,959	NA
2012	83,883	863	2,762	5,569	24,608	22,792	27,288	NA
2011	83,796	899	2,474	5,682	25,039	22,796	26,907	NA
2010	84,834	852	2,549	5,937	26,145	22,911	26,440	NA
2009	85,688	909	2,716	6,046	26,121	23,384	26,513	NA
2008	86,067	905	2,742	5,882	26,108	23,504	26,926	NA
2007	86,224	874	2,720	6,310	26,675	22,777	26,869	NA
2006	85,918	965	2,769	6,274	26,636	23,317	25,958	NA
2005	85,311	954	2,757	5,892	27,232	23,129	25,347	NA
2004	84,642	963	2,582	5,938	26,649	23,093	25,417	NA
2003	84,308	957	2,620	6,112	26,346	23,039	25,234	NA
2002	83,829	941	2,636	5,874	26,740	23,148	24,489	NA
2001	83,286	886	2,612	5,899	26,356	23,271	24,262	NA
2000	81,435	932	2,521	5,702	26,481	22,618	23,183	NA
1999	79,976	872	2,535	6,052	26,367	21,561	22,589	NA
1998	78,520	890	2,613	6,164	26,079	21,267	21,506	NA
1997	76,973	867	2,686	6,045	26,054	20,684	20,635	NA
1996	74,661	968	2,710	5,803	24,924	20,105	20,152	NA
1995	73,028	927	2,561	5,664	24,070	19,926	19,878	NA
1994	71,049	987	2,680	5,415	23,804	19,210	18,956	NA
1993	68,845	942	2,486	5,538	23,927	17,984	17,970	NA
1992	66,594	899	2,608	5,845	23,442	16,658	17,144	NA
1991	64,351	995	3,057	5,522	24,815	13,348	16,614	12.9
1990	62,499	980	3,104	5,529	24,434	12,553	15,899	12.9
1989	60,494	999	3,315	5,800	23,334	11,627	15,417	12.9
1988	58,555	958	3,272	5,889	23,049	11,017	14,369	12.8
1987	56,650	842	3,398	5,656	22,820	10,523	13,409	12.8
1986	55,170	896	3,614	5,769	22,151	10,110	12,629	12.8
1985	53,697	899	3,639	5,978	21,600	9,217	12,363	12.8
1984	52,297	893	3,754	6,158	21,290	8,702	11,500	12.7
1983	50,956	973	4,044	6,313	20,788	8,045	10,795	12.7
1982	49,722	963	4,320	6,657	20,445	7,580	9,756	12.6
1981	48,680	1,038	4,531	6,773	20,032	7,115	9,181	12.6
1980	48,124	1,034	4,676	7,063	19,584	6,943	8,822	12.6
1979	47,437	1,030	4,895	7,132	19,488	6,655	8,237	12.5
1978	46,921	1,107	5,262	7,590	19,012	6,286	7,667	12.5
1977	46,409	1,192	5,445	7,781	18,781	6,013	7,196	12.5
1976	46,271	1,245	5,729	7,671	18,893	5,957	6,776	12.5
1975	46,193	1,296	5,942	7,765	19,010	5,673	6,506	12.4
1974	46,217	1,293	6,244	7,896	19,038	5,375	6,372	12.4
1973	45,910	1,344	6,519	8,001	18,651	5,318	6,076	12.4
1972	45,956	1,367	7,004	8,521	18,400	5,074	5,589	12.3
1971	46,294	1,439	7,588	8,393	18,334	5,082	5,460	12.3
1970	46,319	1,461	7,935	8,555	18,200	4,875	5,294	12.3
1969	46,255	1,644	8,313	8,586	17,773	4,749	5,190	12.3
1968	46,396	1,654	8,698	8,838	17,362	4,642	5,200	12.2
1967	46,321	1,771	9,036	9,138	16,906	4,525	4,947	12.2
1966	46,313	1,837	9,528	9,309	16,605	4,230	4,805	12.1
1965	46,296	1,827	9,812	9,266	16,359	4,384	4,647	12.1
1964	46,089	1,905	10,259	9,289	15,760	4,397	4,482	12.1
1962	45,287	2,181	10,795	8,938	14,668	4,452	4,253	12.0
1960	44,742	2,424	12,536	9,502	12,517	4,123	3,639	11.3
1959	43,989	2,303	11,657	8,719	13,244	3,715	3,709	11.8
1957	42,645	2,658	12,349	8,384	12,041	3,248	3,360	11.3
1952	39,014	2,606	13,274	7,348	9,374	3,148	2,802	10.5
1950	38,432	3,404	14,420	6,976	7,262	2,878	2,516	9.7

Note: Starting in 2012, data were created using population controls based on 2010 Census data. Starting in 2001, data were created using population controls based on Census 2000 data. Also starting in 2001, data are from the expanded CPS sample. Begining with data for 1992, a new question results in different categories than for earlier years. Data shown as 'High School, 4 years' are now collected in the category 'High School Graduate.' Data shown as 'College 1 to 3 years' are now collected in the 'Some college' and the two 'Associate degree' categories. Data shown as 'College 4 years or more,' are now collected in the categories, 'Bachelor's degree,' 'Master's degree,' 'Doctorate degree,' and 'Professional degree.' Due to the change in question format, median years of schooling cannot be derived. Total includes persons who did not report on years of school completed.

NA = Not available.

Table A-25. Years of School Completed by People 25 Years Old and Over, by Age and Sex, Selected Years, 1940–2017—*Continued*

(Numbers in thousands; civilian noninstitutionalized population, except where noted.)

Year, sex, and age	Total	Elementary		High school		College		Median years
		0 to 4 years	5 to 8 years	1 to 3 years	4 years	1 to 3 years	4 years or more	
1947..................................	36,717	3,203	15,184	6,311	6,715	2,622	2,221	9.0
1940..................................	33,845	4,549	16,270	4,972	4,217	1,836	1,540	8.6
Male								
2017..................................	40,303	395	1,305	2,711	12,032	10,026	13,834	NA
2016..................................	40,539	443	1,336	2,903	12,021	10,217	13,620	NA
2015..................................	40,565	469	1,416	2,987	12,401	9,996	13,296	NA
2014..................................	40,525	489	1,459	2,992	12,246	10,199	13,139	NA
2013..................................	40,868	409	1,464	2,962	12,417	10,473	13,142	NA
2012..................................	41,167	462	1,525	2,927	12,869	10,439	12,944	NA
2011..................................	41,209	447	1,292	3,027	13,250	10,339	12,854	NA
2010..................................	41,858	446	1,367	3,227	13,824	10,311	12,682	NA
2009..................................	42,263	500	1,458	3,278	13,644	10,670	12,713	NA
2008..................................	42,419	507	1,490	3,228	13,625	10,711	12,858	NA
2007..................................	42,476	491	1,433	3,480	13,737	10,359	12,976	NA
2006..................................	42,344	549	1,472	3,356	13,660	10,608	12,701	NA
2005..................................	42,024	547	1,476	3,063	14,017	10,429	12,491	NA
2004..................................	41,612	577	1,323	3,157	13,238	10,636	12,682	NA
2003..................................	41,340	538	1,372	3,282	12,903	10,622	12,622	NA
2002..................................	41,154	513	1,333	3,063	13,133	10,739	12,373	NA
2001..................................	40,858	488	1,368	2,974	12,784	10,827	12,417	NA
2000..................................	40,024	479	1,288	2,845	12,845	10,716	11,854	NA
1999..................................	39,300	470	1,290	3,101	12,544	10,233	11,664	NA
1998..................................	38,654	486	1,333	3,284	12,239	10,098	11,214	NA
1997..................................	37,912	486	1,370	3,143	12,326	9,713	10,870	NA
1996..................................	36,596	520	1,319	2,877	11,749	9,514	10,526	NA
1995..................................	35,994	529	1,368	2,781	11,223	9,305	10,784	NA
1994..................................	34,998	545	1,383	2,621	11,009	9,073	10,369	NA
1993..................................	33,751	478	1,316	2,660	10,983	8,624	9,687	NA
1992..................................	32,619	472	1,368	2,750	10,670	7,968	9,389	NA
1991..................................	31,460	530	1,624	2,612	11,092	6,430	9,169	13.0
1990..................................	30,623	527	1,658	2,573	10,790	6,169	8,905	13.0
1989..................................	29,597	504	1,762	2,628	10,235	5,719	8,749	13.0
1988..................................	28,645	498	1,725	2,654	10,100	5,327	8,340	12.9
1987..................................	27,680	412	1,801	2,617	9,781	5,173	7,895	12.9
1986..................................	26,925	475	1,919	2,699	9,393	5,013	7,426	12.9
1985..................................	26,181	501	1,928	2,726	9,210	4,502	7,314	12.9
1984..................................	25,460	506	2,014	2,831	8,926	4,257	6,929	12.8
1983..................................	24,796	548	2,108	2,862	8,795	3,884	6,601	12.8
1982..................................	24,164	530	2,302	2,989	8,609	3,757	5,977	12.7
1981..................................	23,646	572	2,425	3,112	8,431	3,519	5,588	12.7
1980..................................	23,373	590	2,492	3,202	8,278	3,442	5,370	12.7
1979..................................	22,976	545	2,612	3,194	8,232	3,306	5,090	12.6
1978..................................	22,719	609	2,779	3,377	8,001	3,136	4,817	12.6
1977..................................	22,445	661	2,889	3,554	7,822	3,000	4,520	12.5
1976..................................	22,403	730	3,004	3,473	7,904	2,969	4,323	12.5
1975..................................	22,358	763	3,100	3,510	7,952	2,879	4,153	12.5
1974..................................	22,367	733	3,286	3,532	8,004	2,730	4,081	12.6
1973..................................	22,166	716	3,413	3,586	7,836	2,714	3,901	12.4
1972..................................	22,200	749	3,674	3,917	7,663	2,564	3,631	12.4
1971..................................	22,474	849	3,985	3,823	7,674	2,578	3,567	12.3
1970..................................	22,475	834	4,208	3,876	7,612	2,555	3,390	12.3
1969..................................	22,420	889	4,359	4,012	7,427	2,456	3,277	12.3
1968..................................	22,521	931	4,487	4,160	7,324	2,364	3,257	12.2
1967..................................	22,482	1,000	4,700	4,270	7,143	2,244	3,128	12.2
1966..................................	22,508	1,085	4,886	4,455	6,990	2,029	3,063	12.1
1965..................................	22,534	1,081	5,076	4,462	6,815	2,161	2,937	12.1
1964..................................	22,457	1,158	5,226	4,416	6,657	2,212	2,789	12.2
1962..................................	22,081	1,235	5,545	4,359	6,202	2,142	2,598	11.9
1960..................................	21,919	1,397	6,415	4,579	5,364	1,957	2,206	11.1
1959..................................	21,511	1,350	5,781	4,329	5,604	1,827	2,250	11.5
1957..................................	20,873	1,491	6,293	3,987	5,195	1,558	1,972	11.0
1952..................................	18,888	1,466	6,512	3,462	4,040	1,518	1,576	10.3
1950..................................	18,896	1,834	7,338	3,339	3,151	1,271	1,403	9.6

Note: Starting in 2012, data were created using population controls based on 2010 Census data. Starting in 2001, data were created using population controls based on Census 2000 data. Also starting in 2001, data are from the expanded CPS sample. Begining with data for 1992, a new question results in different categories than for earlier years. Data shown as 'High School, 4 years' are now collected in the category 'High School Graduate.' Data shown as 'College 1 to 3 years' are now collected in the 'Some college' and the two 'Associate degree' categories. Data shown as 'College 4 years or more,' are now collected in the categories, 'Bachelor's degree,' Master's degree,' 'Doctorate degree,' and 'Professional degree.' Due to the change in question format, median years of schooling cannot be derived. Total includes persons who did not report on years of school completed.
NA = Not available.

Table A-25. Years of School Completed by People 25 Years Old and Over, by Age and Sex, Selected Years, 1940–2017—*Continued*

(Numbers in thousands; civilian noninstitutionalized population, except where noted.)

Year, sex, and age	Total	Elementary		High school		College		Median years
		0 to 4 years	5 to 8 years	1 to 3 years	4 years	1 to 3 years	4 years or more	
1947	18,165	1,678	7,765	3,102	2,907	1,168	1,258	8.6
1940	17,127	2,480	8,458	2,388	1,798	819	917	8.5
Female								
2017	41,769	314	1,098	2,348	10,072	11,595	16,342	NA
2016	42,031	356	1,300	2,393	10,276	11,853	15,853	NA
2015	42,150	394	1,326	2,484	10,752	11,830	15,364	NA
2014	42,163	385	1,153	2,440	10,993	12,273	14,919	NA
2013	42,456	369	1,147	2,475	11,290	12,358	14,817	NA
2012	42,716	400	1,237	2,642	11,739	12,352	14,345	NA
2011	42,587	452	1,183	2,654	11,789	12,457	14,053	NA
2010	42,976	406	1,181	2,710	12,321	12,600	13,758	NA
2009	43,424	409	1,258	2,768	12,476	12,713	13,800	NA
2008	43,648	398	1,253	2,654	12,483	12,792	14,067	NA
2007	43,748	382	1,288	2,830	12,938	12,419	13,892	NA
2006	43,573	417	1,298	2,915	12,976	12,710	13,255	NA
2005	43,287	407	1,280	2,829	13,215	12,700	12,856	NA
2004	43,030	386	1,259	2,781	13,411	12,458	12,736	NA
2003	42,968	419	1,248	2,830	13,443	12,417	12,611	NA
2002	42,675	428	1,303	2,811	13,607	12,410	12,116	NA
2001	42,428	398	1,244	2,926	13,572	12,444	11,844	NA
2000	41,411	452	1,235	2,858	13,635	11,905	11,330	NA
1999	40,676	402	1,248	2,950	13,825	11,326	10,925	NA
1998	39,866	403	1,279	2,879	13,841	11,168	10,293	NA
1997	39,061	381	1,319	2,902	13,726	10,969	9,766	NA
1996	38,065	449	1,301	2,924	13,174	10,592	9,623	NA
1995	37,034	396	1,192	2,881	12,846	10,623	9,096	NA
1994	36,051	443	1,298	2,792	12,795	10,140	8,587	NA
1993	35,093	462	1,169	2,877	12,944	9,358	8,283	NA
1992	33,975	427	1,240	3,096	12,770	8,687	7,756	NA
1991	32,891	464	1,431	2,910	13,723	6,919	7,443	12.8
1990	31,876	454	1,448	2,955	13,643	6,383	6,997	12.8
1989	30,898	498	1,552	3,171	13,099	5,908	6,669	12.8
1988	29,908	462	1,547	3,234	12,949	5,689	6,029	12.7
1987	28,969	430	1,598	3,039	13,038	5,349	5,513	12.7
1986	28,244	420	1,694	3,071	12,759	5,098	5,202	12.7
1985	27,516	398	1,710	3,252	12,391	4,715	5,049	12.7
1984	26,838	389	1,740	3,331	12,364	4,444	4,570	12.6
1983	26,161	427	1,935	3,450	11,993	4,161	4,193	12.6
1982	25,555	433	2,017	3,666	11,833	3,827	3,778	12.6
1981	25,034	467	2,105	3,661	11,599	3,605	3,595	12.5
1980	24,751	444	2,186	3,862	11,307	3,501	3,452	12.5
1979	24,461	486	2,282	3,935	11,258	3,353	3,147	12.5
1978	24,202	497	2,483	4,212	11,012	3,149	2,849	12.5
1977	23,964	534	2,557	4,227	10,959	3,014	2,678	12.4
1976	23,868	517	2,721	4,198	10,989	2,988	2,455	12.4
1975	23,835	533	2,842	4,256	11,058	2,793	2,352	12.4
1974	23,850	559	2,956	4,364	11,033	2,647	2,290	12.4
1973	23,744	628	3,106	4,415	10,815	2,603	2,174	12.3
1972	23,756	618	3,330	4,604	10,736	2,509	1,958	12.3
1971	23,821	590	3,604	4,570	10,660	2,505	1,894	12.3
1970	23,845	629	3,728	4,679	10,588	2,318	1,903	12.3
1969	23,834	755	3,953	4,575	10,349	2,293	1,913	12.3
1968	23,874	725	4,212	4,676	10,038	2,281	1,943	12.2
1967	23,839	773	4,334	4,868	9,762	2,282	1,819	12.2
1966	23,806	752	4,644	4,853	9,615	2,200	1,741	12.2
1965	23,765	746	4,735	4,803	9,545	2,223	1,712	12.2
1964	23,632	748	5,033	4,871	9,103	2,183	1,691	12.1
1962	23,206	946	5,250	4,579	8,466	2,310	1,655	12.1
1960	22,823	1,027	6,121	4,923	7,153	2,166	1,433	11.6
1959	22,478	953	5,876	4,390	7,640	1,888	1,459	12.0
1957	21,772	1,167	6,056	4,397	6,846	1,690	1,388	11.5
1952	20,126	1,140	6,762	3,886	5,334	1,630	1,226	10.7
1950	19,536	1,570	7,082	3,637	4,111	1,607	1,113	9.7

Note: Starting in 2012, data were created using population controls based on 2010 Census data. Starting in 2001, data were created using population controls based on Census 2000 data. Also starting in 2001, data are from the expanded CPS sample. Begining with data for 1992, a new question results in different categories than for earlier years. Data shown as 'High School, 4 years' are now collected in the category 'High School Graduate.' Data shown as 'College 1 to 3 years' are now collected in the 'Some college' and the two 'Associate degree' categories. Data shown as 'College 4 years or more,' are now collected in the categories, 'Bachelor's degree,' Master's degree,' 'Doctorate degree,' and 'Professional degree.' Due to the change in question format, median years of schooling cannot be derived. Total includes persons who did not report on years of school completed.

NA = Not available.

Table A-25. Years of School Completed by People 25 Years Old and Over, by Age and Sex, Selected Years, 1940–2017—*Continued*

(Numbers in thousands; civilian noninstitutionalized population, except where noted.)

Year, sex, and age	Total	Years of school completed						Median years
		Elementary		High school		College		
		0 to 4 years	5 to 8 years	1 to 3 years	4 years	1 to 3 years	4 years or more	
1947	18,552	1,525	7,419	3,209	3,808	1,454	963	9.3
1940	16,718	2,070	7,812	2,584	2,419	1,017	623	8.7
55 YEARS AND OVER								
Both Sexes								
2017	90,599	1,280	3,465	6,143	28,916	23,351	27,444	NA
2016	88,682	1,406	3,584	6,009	28,481	22,981	26,221	NA
2015	86,411	1,447	3,690	6,276	28,457	21,785	24,756	NA
2014	84,134	1,365	3,829	6,094	27,962	21,059	23,825	NA
2013	81,778	1,306	3,931	6,043	27,046	20,387	23,066	NA
2012	79,478	1,348	3,974	6,344	26,531	19,343	21,937	NA
2011	76,163	1,372	4,073	5,983	25,622	18,408	20,705	NA
2010	74,008	1,440	4,118	6,051	25,125	17,354	19,920	NA
2009	72,077	1,555	4,101	6,338	24,154	16,877	19,051	NA
2008	70,092	1,411	4,294	6,338	23,779	16,378	17,892	NA
2007	68,226	1,576	4,458	6,680	23,408	15,505	16,599	NA
2006	66,485	1,628	4,610	6,508	22,961	14,824	15,956	NA
2005	64,745	1,614	4,803	6,784	22,392	14,083	15,069	NA
2004	63,034	1,465	4,907	6,821	21,918	13,434	14,488	NA
2003	61,633	1,589	5,372	6,876	21,554	12,884	13,358	NA
2002	59,644	1,528	5,639	7,258	20,728	12,117	12,374	NA
2001	58,238	1,544	5,589	7,178	20,622	11,864	11,440	NA
2000	56,008	1,524	5,780	6,921	20,059	11,126	10,598	NA
1999	55,303	1,589	5,978	7,096	19,742	10,722	10,174	NA
1998	54,337	1,624	6,126	7,385	19,526	10,022	9,654	NA
1997	53,352	1,628	6,622	7,543	18,823	9,565	9,169	NA
1996	52,742	1,642	6,716	7,520	18,549	9,642	8,677	NA
1995	52,022	1,755	7,048	7,232	18,320	9,662	8,005	NA
1994	51,516	1,802	7,382	7,454	18,228	8,890	7,761	NA
1993	52,117	2,058	8,038	7,637	18,626	8,106	7,652	NA
1992	51,740	2,118	8,133	7,756	18,397	8,005	7,332	NA
1991	51,439	2,341	8,668	7,675	18,954	6,540	7,258	12.6
1990	50,798	2,349	9,239	7,893	18,050	6,202	7,064	12.3
1989	50,421	2,412	9,395	7,907	18,102	5,914	6,693	12.3
1988	50,128	2,325	9,969	7,860	18,004	5,705	6,263	12.3
1987	49,858	2,408	10,544	7,766	17,310	5,799	6,033	12.2
1986	49,383	2,611	10,699	7,917	16,876	5,515	5,767	12.2
1985	48,969	2,612	11,052	7,872	16,516	5,208	5,708	12.2
1984	48,324	2,584	11,131	7,636	16,353	5,026	5,593	12.2
1983	47,723	2,769	11,348	7,703	15,470	4,915	5,514	12.1
1982	47,102	2,818	11,541	7,751	15,091	4,807	5,095	12.1
1981	46,391	2,983	11,909	7,600	14,464	4,721	4,711	12.0
1980	45,670	2,994	12,326	7,451	13,869	4,494	4,535	12.1
1979	43,806	2,924	12,230	6,999	13,088	4,321	4,245	12.0
1978	42,977	3,013	12,593	7,069	12,376	4,086	3,843	11.6
1977	42,176	3,047	12,740	6,823	11,977	3,835	3,754	11.3
1976	41,429	3,107	12,674	6,915	11,346	3,709	3,677	11.1
1975	40,613	3,303	13,045	6,730	10,798	3,442	3,295	10.8
1974	39,817	3,461	13,302	6,615	10,060	3,233	3,145	10.4
1973	39,163	3,424	13,467	6,504	9,604	3,060	3,105	10.2
1972	38,659	3,471	13,706	6,351	9,136	2,952	3,042	10.0
1971	38,787	3,808	14,430	6,225	8,463	2,878	2,982	9.6
1970	38,126	3,957	14,647	5,877	8,005	2,797	2,843	9.2
1969	37,424	4,012	14,576	5,801	7,768	2,615	2,653	9.1
1968	36,789	4,244	14,522	5,760	7,085	2,624	2,558	8.9
1967	36,155	4,310	14,849	5,495	6,622	2,443	2,434	8.7
1966	35,540	4,438	14,742	5,392	6,240	2,358	2,370	8.6
1965	34,969	4,612	14,814	5,293	5,844	2,194	2,215	8.5
1964	34,335	4,888	14,701	4,954	5,598	2,159	2,033	8.3
1962	33,247	5,048	14,707	4,442	4,994	2,166	1,890	8.1
1960	31,902	5,169	14,944	4,503	3,757	2,051	1,479	8.5
1959	30,567	4,752	13,485	4,060	3,996	1,775	1,545	8.1
1957	29,548	5,153	12,996	3,602	3,864	1,462	1,461	8.0
1952	26,206	4,554	12,638	2,982	3,080	1,346	1,264	7.7
1950	25,427	4,940	11,947	2,791	2,704	1,170	1,005	8.3

Note: Starting in 2012, data were created using population controls based on 2010 Census data. Starting in 2001, data were created using population controls based on Census 2000 data. Also starting in 2001, data are from the expanded CPS sample. Begining with data for 1992, a new question results in different categories than for earlier years. Data shown as 'High School, 4 years' are now collected in the category 'High School Graduate.' Data shown as 'College 1 to 3 years' are now collected in the 'Some college' and the two 'Associate degree,' categories. Data shown as 'College 4 years or more,' are now collected in the categories, 'Bachelor's degree,' 'Master's degree,' 'Doctorate degree,' and 'Professional degree.' Due to the change in question format, median years of schooling cannot be derived. Total includes persons who did not report on years of school completed.
NA = Not available.

Table A-25. Years of School Completed by People 25 Years Old and Over, by Age and Sex, Selected Years, 1940–2017—*Continued*

(Numbers in thousands; civilian noninstitutionalized population, except where noted.)

Year, sex, and age	Total	Elementary		High school		College		Median years
		0 to 4 years	5 to 8 years	1 to 3 years	4 years	1 to 3 years	4 years or more	
1947	23,234	4,393	11,601	2,179	2,581	1,003	825	7.5
1940	19,592	4,178	10,467	1,656	1,633	685	579	8.2
Male								
2017	41,901	561	1,617	2,813	12,808	10,288	13,814	NA
2016	40,988	624	1,708	2,814	12,374	10,236	13,231	NA
2015	39,895	608	1,765	2,707	12,398	9,863	12,556	NA
2014	38,850	544	1,790	2,800	12,150	9,320	12,246	NA
2013	37,621	557	1,790	2,605	11,539	9,060	12,070	NA
2012	36,489	614	1,775	2,754	11,220	8,574	11,552	NA
2011	35,027	597	1,934	2,625	10,676	8,230	10,966	NA
2010	33,778	647	1,923	2,611	10,399	7,672	10,525	NA
2009	32,814	689	1,874	2,669	9,886	7,456	10,241	NA
2008	31,841	631	1,932	2,751	9,510	7,259	9,759	NA
2007	30,920	721	2,060	2,884	9,505	6,723	9,026	NA
2006	30,060	705	2,090	2,784	9,488	6,193	8,837	NA
2005	29,198	717	2,157	2,896	8,918	6,167	8,341	NA
2004	28,347	639	2,192	2,885	8,631	5,841	8,159	NA
2003	27,694	729	2,423	2,912	8,425	5,694	7,510	NA
2002	26,608	664	2,601	3,048	8,063	5,257	6,975	NA
2001	25,908	697	2,558	2,964	8,073	5,131	6,485	NA
2000	25,023	706	2,696	2,817	7,816	4,906	6,079	NA
1999	24,694	712	2,746	2,911	7,712	4,756	5,856	NA
1998	24,197	755	2,740	3,000	7,745	4,461	5,496	NA
1997	23,668	773	3,026	3,060	7,417	4,139	5,255	NA
1996	23,352	795	3,058	2,998	7,198	4,254	5,055	NA
1995	22,881	839	3,153	2,980	6,980	4,254	4,675	NA
1994	22,669	894	3,327	3,037	6,987	3,962	4,462	NA
1993	23,038	992	3,595	3,174	7,178	3,587	4,508	NA
1992	22,836	1,033	3,676	3,277	6,991	3,549	4,312	NA
1991	22,708	1,217	3,980	3,183	7,287	2,850	4,193	12.4
1990	22,337	1,182	4,141	3,274	6,986	2,707	4,046	12.4
1989	22,167	1,202	4,198	3,317	7,003	2,616	3,829	12.3
1988	21,989	1,117	4,471	3,366	6,968	2,455	3,609	12.3
1987	21,855	1,160	4,762	3,261	6,673	2,504	3,496	12.3
1986	21,622	1,275	4,813	3,286	6,509	2,355	3,385	12.2
1985	21,391	1,252	5,001	3,234	6,387	2,229	3,289	12.2
1984	21,014	1,209	4,951	3,270	6,265	2,185	3,132	12.2
1983	20,769	1,343	4,986	3,282	5,906	2,141	3,117	12.1
1982	20,508	1,362	5,026	3,313	5,759	2,102	2,946	12.1
1981	20,237	1,394	5,165	3,292	5,597	2,032	2,758	12.0
1980	19,967	1,424	5,436	3,206	5,409	1,986	2,506	11.9
1979	19,292	1,446	5,479	2,964	5,167	1,935	2,301	11.8
1978	18,939	1,467	5,701	2,919	4,919	1,824	2,110	11.4
1977	18,608	1,502	5,770	2,787	4,835	1,700	2,011	11.2
1976	18,233	1,507	5,733	2,884	4,473	1,646	1,989	11.0
1975	17,903	1,628	5,845	2,871	4,308	1,480	1,768	10.5
1974	17,579	1,693	6,042	2,817	3,993	1,356	1,682	10.1
1973	17,263	1,678	6,111	2,774	3,811	1,245	1,645	9.9
1972	17,120	1,728	6,252	2,698	3,612	1,215	1,614	9.6
1971	17,288	1,913	6,629	2,668	3,285	1,214	1,579	9.1
1970	17,074	2,011	6,655	2,583	3,127	1,182	1,516	9.0
1969	16,822	2,003	6,701	2,536	3,099	1,086	1,397	8.8
1968	16,609	2,137	6,728	2,523	2,816	1,078	1,328	8.7
1967	16,398	2,247	6,827	2,379	2,685	989	1,271	8.5
1966	16,201	2,288	6,944	2,317	2,491	939	1,223	8.3
1965	16,015	2,368	6,992	2,265	2,331	893	1,164	8.2
1964	15,789	2,504	6,897	2,159	2,237	876	1,113	8.1
1962	15,440	2,644	6,813	2,032	2,030	864	1,057	8.0
1960	14,895	2,704	7,121	1,969	1,453	853	796	8.4
1959	14,304	2,491	6,436	1,759	1,584	718	857	7.9
1957	13,967	2,696	6,244	1,570	1,493	608	831	7.7
1952	12,544	2,428	6,162	1,318	1,262	528	636	7.5
1950	12,277	2,609	5,808	1,209	1,111	500	569	8.2
1947	11,424	2,393	5,656	939	1,109	464	482	7.3
1940	9,815	2,293	5,249	724	660	313	361	8.1

Note: Starting in 2012, data were created using population controls based on 2010 Census data. Starting in 2001, data were created using population controls based on Census 2000 data. Also starting in 2001, data are from the expanded CPS sample. Begining with data for 1992, a new question results in different categories than for earlier years. Data shown as 'High School, 4 years' are now collected in the category 'High School Graduate.' Data shown as 'College 1 to 3 years' are now collected in the 'Some college' and the two 'Associate degree' categories. Data shown as 'College 4 years or more,' are now collected in the categories, 'Bachelor's degree,' Master's degree,' 'Doctorate degree,' and 'Professional degree.' Due to the change in question format, median years of schooling cannot be derived. Total includes persons who did not report on years of school completed.
NA = Not available.

Table A-25. Years of School Completed by People 25 Years Old and Over, by Age and Sex, Selected Years, 1940–2017—*Continued*

(Numbers in thousands; civilian noninstitutionalized population, except where noted.)

Year, sex, and age	Total	Elementary		High school		College		Median years
		0 to 4 years	5 to 8 years	1 to 3 years	4 years	1 to 3 years	4 years or more	
Female								
2017	48,698	719	1,849	3,329	16,107	13,063	13,630	NA
2016	47,694	782	1,875	3,195	16,107	12,745	12,990	NA
2015	46,516	839	1,925	3,570	16,059	11,922	12,201	NA
2014	45,284	821	2,039	3,295	15,812	11,739	11,578	NA
2013	44,158	749	2,141	3,438	15,507	11,327	10,996	NA
2012	42,989	734	2,199	3,590	15,311	10,769	10,384	NA
2011	41,136	775	2,140	3,358	14,946	10,178	9,739	NA
2010	40,230	793	2,195	3,440	14,725	9,682	9,395	NA
2009	39,263	867	2,228	3,669	14,268	9,421	8,810	NA
2008	38,251	780	2,362	3,588	14,269	9,119	8,133	NA
2007	37,306	855	2,398	3,796	13,902	8,781	7,573	NA
2006	36,425	922	2,521	3,761	13,472	8,630	7,119	NA
2005	35,547	897	2,645	3,887	13,474	7,916	6,728	NA
2004	34,687	826	2,715	3,936	13,287	7,593	6,329	NA
2003	33,939	860	2,949	3,964	13,129	7,190	5,848	NA
2002	33,035	864	3,038	4,210	12,664	6,860	5,399	NA
2001	32,329	847	3,032	4,213	12,549	6,733	4,956	NA
2000	30,985	817	3,085	4,105	12,243	6,218	4,517	NA
1999	30,609	879	3,232	4,186	12,031	5,965	4,319	NA
1998	30,140	868	3,386	4,386	11,780	5,560	4,160	NA
1997	29,684	855	3,596	4,483	11,407	5,427	3,916	NA
1996	29,390	848	3,659	4,523	11,350	5,387	3,623	NA
1995	29,142	915	3,894	4,255	11,340	5,410	3,330	NA
1994	28,848	909	4,054	4,419	11,242	4,926	3,298	NA
1993	29,080	1,066	4,442	4,462	11,447	4,519	3,149	NA
1992	28,904	1,084	4,456	4,478	11,409	4,455	3,021	NA
1991	28,729	1,125	4,687	4,495	11,667	3,690	3,066	12.3
1990	28,461	1,167	5,098	4,619	11,063	3,495	3,019	12.3
1989	28,255	1,211	5,195	4,587	11,099	3,300	2,863	12.3
1988	28,139	1,208	5,498	4,495	11,034	3,250	2,655	12.3
1987	28,004	1,248	5,782	4,504	10,637	3,294	2,539	12.2
1986	27,762	1,336	5,886	4,630	10,367	3,160	2,382	12.2
1985	27,578	1,360	6,052	4,638	10,129	2,979	2,420	12.2
1984	27,309	1,377	6,183	4,363	10,086	2,843	2,459	12.2
1983	26,954	1,428	6,364	4,423	9,567	2,774	2,398	12.1
1982	26,593	1,458	6,511	4,435	9,330	2,705	2,150	12.1
1981	26,152	1,589	6,742	4,308	8,868	2,690	1,954	12.0
1980	25,703	1,571	6,889	4,245	8,460	2,509	2,030	12.0
1979	24,514	1,474	6,750	4,034	7,920	2,389	1,944	12.0
1978	24,038	1,545	6,889	4,149	7,457	2,263	1,733	11.6
1977	23,568	1,546	6,972	4,034	7,141	2,135	1,742	11.0
1976	23,196	1,602	6,942	4,029	6,871	2,063	1,690	11.0
1975	22,710	1,675	7,198	3,858	6,490	1,962	1,527	10.9
1974	22,238	1,762	7,261	3,799	6,068	1,880	1,463	10.7
1973	21,900	1,746	7,359	3,729	5,790	1,814	1,461	10.5
1972	21,539	1,743	7,455	3,654	5,526	1,737	1,425	10.3
1971	21,500	1,896	7,805	3,556	5,179	1,665	1,402	9.9
1970	21,052	1,946	7,993	3,292	4,879	1,615	1,327	9.5
1969	20,601	2,009	7,878	3,264	4,669	1,526	1,255	9.4
1968	20,180	2,106	7,795	3,237	4,269	1,544	1,229	9.2
1967	19,756	2,063	8,021	3,117	3,937	1,454	1,164	8.9
1966	19,339	2,152	7,797	3,074	3,749	1,419	1,147	8.9
1965	18,955	2,243	7,821	3,026	3,514	1,300	1,048	8.7
1964	18,546	2,383	7,805	2,794	3,360	1,282	920	8.5
1962	17,807	2,404	7,894	2,410	2,964	1,302	833	8.3
1960	17,007	2,465	7,823	2,534	2,304	1,198	683	8.6
1959	16,263	2,261	7,049	2,301	2,412	1,057	688	8.3
1957	15,581	2,457	6,752	2,032	2,371	854	630	8.2
1952	13,662	2,126	6,476	1,664	1,818	818	628	7.9
1950	13,150	2,331	6,139	1,582	1,593	670	436	8.4
1947	11,810	2,000	5,945	1,240	1,472	539	343	7.6
1940	9,777	1,886	5,217	932	973	372	219	8.3

Note: Starting in 2012, data were created using population controls based on 2010 Census data. Starting in 2001, data were created using population controls based on Census 2000 data. Also starting in 2001, data are from the expanded CPS sample. Begining with data for 1992, a new question results in different categories than for earlier years. Data shown as 'High School, 4 years' are now collected in the category 'High School Graduate.' Data shown as 'College 1 to 3 years' are now collected in the 'Some college' and the two 'Associate degree' categories. Data shown as 'College 4 years or more,' are now collected in the categories, 'Bachelor's degree,' 'Master's degree,' 'Doctorate degree,' and 'Professional degree.' Due to the change in question format, median years of schooling cannot be derived. Total includes persons who did not report on years of school completed.
NA = Not available.

Table A-26. Detailed Years of School Completed by People 25 Years and Over, by Sex, Age Groups, Race, and Hispanic Origin, 2017

(Numbers in thousands; civilian noninstitutionalized population.[1])

Detailed years of school	All races Number	All races Percent	Males Number	Males Percent	Females Number	Females Percent	25 to 34 years old Number	25 to 34 years old Percent	35 to 54 years old Number	35 to 54 years old Percent
Total	216,921	100.0	104,325	100.0	112,597	100.0	44,250	100.0	82,072	100.0
Elementary or High school, no diploma										
Less than 1 year, no diploma	717	0.3	337	0.3	380	0.3	70	0.2	231	0.3
1st-4th grade, no diploma..................................	1,490	0.7	753	0.7	737	0.7	149	0.3	478	0.6
5th-6th grade, no diploma..................................	3,133	1.4	1,585	1.5	1,548	1.4	322	0.7	1,290	1.6
7th-8th grade, no diploma	3,467	1.6	1,727	1.7	1,740	1.6	410	0.9	1,113	1.4
9th grade, no diploma......................................	3,253	1.5	1,627	1.6	1,626	1.4	522	1.2	1,347	1.6
10th grade, no diploma....................................	3,663	1.7	1,878	1.8	1,785	1.6	629	1.4	1,205	1.5
11th grade, no diploma....................................	4,056	1.9	1,990	1.9	2,066	1.8	796	1.8	1,466	1.8
12th grade, no diploma....................................	2,762	1.3	1,440	1.4	1,322	1.2	586	1.3	1,041	1.3
Elementary or High school, GED										
Less than 1 year, GED	39	*	20	*	19	*	8	*	17	*
1st-4th grade, GED	104	0.1	57	0.1	47	*	43	0.1	26	*
5th-6th grade, GED	51	*	27	*	23	*	4	*	14	*
7th-8th grade, GED	370	0.2	187	0.2	184	0.2	47	0.1	121	0.2
9th grade, GED..	633	0.3	312	0.3	320	0.3	125	0.3	214	0.3
10th grade, GED..	1,359	0.6	743	0.7	616	0.6	309	0.7	539	0.7
11th grade, GED..	2,177	1.0	1,265	1.2	912	0.8	514	1.2	848	1.0
12th grade, GED..	1,463	0.7	836	0.8	627	0.6	290	0.7	667	0.8
High school diploma	56,316	26.0	27,849	26.7	28,467	25.3	10,153	23.0	19,658	24.0
College, no degree										
Less than 1 year college, no degree......................	4,673	2.2	2,233	2.1	2,440	2.2	1,080	2.4	1,582	1.9
One year of college, no degree...........................	11,375	5.2	5,204	5.0	6,171	5.5	2,597	5.9	4,045	4.9
Two years of college, no degree...........................	14,354	6.6	6,823	6.5	7,531	6.7	3,005	6.8	5,126	6.3
Three years of college, no degree	3,472	1.6	1,826	1.8	1,646	1.5	1,007	2.3	1,232	1.5
Four or more years of college, no degree..............	1,580	0.7	844	0.8	736	0.7	454	1.0	601	0.7
Associate's degree, vocational										
Less than 1 year college, vocational/associate's ...	471	0.2	201	0.2	270	0.2	103	0.2	174	0.2
One year of college, vocational/associate's	1,227	0.6	536	0.5	691	0.6	273	0.6	458	0.6
Two years of college, vocational/associate's	5,960	2.8	2,850	2.7	3,109	2.8	1,073	2.4	2,431	3.0
Three years of college, vocational/associate's.......	865	0.4	319	0.3	546	0.5	187	0.4	346	0.4
Four or more years of college, vocational/ associate's	886	0.4	467	0.5	418	0.4	175	0.4	373	0.5
Associate's degree, academic										
Less than 1 year college, academic/associate's	117	0.1	63	*	54	0.1	19	*	50	0.1
One year of college, academic/associate's	654	0.3	280	0.3	375	0.3	155	0.4	238	0.3
Two years of college, academic/associate's	8,847	4.1	3,606	3.5	5,242	4.7	1,830	4.1	3,579	4.4
Three years of college, academic/associate's........	1,744	0.8	759	0.7	985	0.9	415	0.9	754	0.9
Four or more years of college, academic/ associate's	1,539	0.7	570	0.6	969	0.9	421	1.0	633	0.8
Bachelor's degree.....................................	46,262	21.3	21,906	21.0	24,357	21.6	11,384	25.7	18,465	22.5
Master's degree[2]	20,592	9.5	9,049	8.7	11,543	10.3	3,872	8.8	8,846	10.8
Professional degree	3,172	1.5	1,765	1.7	1,407	1.3	554	1.3	1,196	1.5
Doctorate degree..	4,077	1.9	2,392	2.3	1,685	1.5	672	1.5	1,669	2.0

[1]Excluding members of the Armed Forces living in barracks.
[2]Detail on graduate school attendance and length of master's degree program, available in previous years, discontinued due to questionnaire changes in 2015.
* = Quantity zero or rounds to zero.

Table A-26. Detailed Years of School Completed by People 25 Years and Over, by Sex, Age Groups, Race, and Hispanic Origin, 2017—*Continued*

(Numbers in thousands; civilian noninstitutionalized population.[1])

Detailed years of school	55 years and older Number	Percent	White Number	Percent	Non-Hispanic White Number	Percent	Black Number	Percent	Asian Number	Percent	Hispanic (of any race) Number	Percent
Total	90,599	100.0	171,046	100.0	141,860	100.0	26,455	100.0	13,183	100.0	32,660	100.0
Elementary or High school, no diploma												
Less than 1 year, no diploma	416	0.5	455	0.3	116	0.1	117	0.4	104	0.8	395	1.2
1st-4th grade, no diploma.........................	864	1.0	1,159	0.7	190	0.1	111	0.4	137	1.0	1,076	3.3
5th-6th grade, no diploma	1,521	1.7	2,549	1.5	366	0.3	229	0.9	235	1.8	2,347	7.2
7th-8th grade, no diploma	1,944	2.2	2,738	1.6	1,415	1.0	401	1.5	231	1.8	1,441	4.4
9th grade, no diploma.............................	1,384	1.5	2,586	1.5	1,194	0.8	403	1.5	114	0.8	1,533	4.7
10th grade, no diploma............................	1,829	2.0	2,699	1.6	1,878	1.3	669	2.5	148	1.1	923	2.8
11th grade, no diploma............................	1,794	2.0	2,891	1.7	2,035	1.4	890	3.4	70	0.5	968	3.0
12th grade, no diploma............................	1,135	1.3	1,936	1.1	1,134	0.8	545	2.0	161	1.2	937	2.9
Elementary or High school, GED												
Less than 1 year, GED	14	*	30	*	19	*	9	*	*	*	11	*
1st-4th grade, GED	35	*	81	1.0	60	*	15	0.1	2	*	22	0.1
5th-6th grade, GED	32	*	47	*	24	*	3	*	*	*	23	0.1
7th-8th grade, GED.................................	203	0.2	312	0.2	243	0.2	31	0.1	2	*	80	0.2
9th grade, GED......................................	293	0.3	526	0.3	412	0.3	48	0.2	14	0.1	125	0.4
10th grade, GED.....................................	512	0.6	1,148	0.7	1,010	0.7	138	0.5	20	0.2	149	0.5
11th grade, GED.....................................	814	0.9	1,688	1.0	1,456	1.0	356	1.4	26	0.2	271	0.8
12th grade, GED.....................................	507	0.6	1,072	0.6	796	0.6	236	0.9	70	0.5	327	1.0
High school diploma	26,505	29.3	44,304	25.9	36,133	25.5	7,886	29.8	2,534	19.2	9,118	27.9
College, no degree												
Less than 1 year college, no degree..........	2,012	2.2	3,815	2.2	3,281	2.3	639	2.4	79	0.6	588	1.8
One year of college, no degree..................	4,734	5.2	9,113	5.3	7,837	5.5	1,628	6.2	241	1.8	1,464	4.5
Two years of college, no degree................	6,223	6.9	10,985	6.4	9,288	6.6	2,253	8.5	622	4.7	1,944	6.0
Three years of college, no degree	1,233	1.4	2,611	1.5	2,164	1.5	562	2.1	184	1.4	488	1.5
Four or more years of college, no degree...	526	0.6	1,157	0.7	967	0.7	241	0.9	120	0.9	216	0.7
Associate's degree, vocational												
Less than 1 year college, vocational/associate's..	194	0.2	387	0.2	335	0.2	53	0.2	16	0.1	55	0.2
One year of college, vocational/associate's	497	0.6	1,006	0.6	853	0.6	163	0.6	32	0.2	165	0.5
Two years of college, vocational/associate's..	2,456	2.7	4,969	2.9	4,415	3.1	713	2.7	139	1.0	616	1.9
Three years of college, vocational/associate's..	331	0.4	724	0.4	590	0.4	96	0.4	30	0.2	141	0.4
Four or more years of college, vocational/associate's..	337	0.4	715	0.4	620	0.4	88	0.3	46	0.4	110	0.3
Associate's degree, academic												
Less than 1 year college, academic/associate's..	49	0.1	69	*	54	*	42	0.2	4	*	19	0.1
One year of college, academic/associate's .	261	0.3	533	0.3	457	0.3	80	0.3	33	0.3	87	0.3
Two years of college, academic/associate's	3,439	3.8	7,161	4.2	6,321	4.5	1,073	4.1	375	2.8	956	3.0
Three years of college, academic/associate's..	575	0.6	1,365	0.8	1,148	0.8	220	0.8	83	0.6	247	0.8
Four or more years of college, academic/associate's..	485	0.5	1,205	0.7	1,034	0.7	181	0.7	87	0.7	204	0.6
Bachelor's degree............................	16,414	18.1	37,234	21.8	33,687	23.8	4,002	15.1	4,016	30.5	3,970	12.2
Master's degree[2]	7,874	8.7	16,039	9.4	14,924	10.5	1,845	7.0	2,323	17.6	1,266	3.9
Professional degree	1,422	1.6	2,642	1.5	2,501	1.8	191	0.7	272	2.0	147	0.5
Doctorate degree....................................	1,735	1.9	3,096	1.8	2,905	2.1	296	1.1	614	4.7	232	0.7

[1]Excluding members of the Armed Forces living in barracks.
[2]Detail on graduate school attendance and length of master's degree program, available in previous years, discontinued due to questionnaire changes in 2015.
* = Quantity zero or rounds to zero.

PART A

NATIONAL EDUCATION STATISTICS

■ **Historical Attainment Tables**

Table A-27. Mean Earnings of Workers 18 Years Old and Over, by Educational Attainment, Race, Hispanic Origin, and Sex, 1975–2016

(Dollars except as noted)

Race, sex, year, and Hispanic origin	Total		Not a high school graduate		High school graduate	
	Mean earnings	Number of workers (thousands)	Mean earnings	Number of workers (thousands)	Mean earnings	Number of workers (thousands)
ALL RACES						
Both Sexes						
2016...........................	51,893	162,218	27,800	12,281	36,702	42,897
2015...........................	49,994	161,074	25,315	13,159	35,615	42,404
2014...........................	47,653	158,000	25,236	13,197	34,099	42,529
2013...........................	46,187	156,031	23,755	12,961	32,881	42,433
2012...........................	45,598	155,148	21,622	13,030	32,630	41,915
2011[2]	44,729	152,711	21,107	13,594	32,493	42,129
2010...........................	42,922	151,498	20,911	13,345	31,003	42,599
2009...........................	42,469	152,707	20,241	14,083	30,627	44,396
2008...........................	42,588	155,989	21,023	15,217	31,283	45,182
2007...........................	42,064	155,738	21,484	15,330	31,286	45,393
2006...........................	41,412	154,438	20,873	16,652	31,071	45,936
2005...........................	39,579	152,215	19,915	16,317	29,448	45,652
2004...........................	37,899	150,095	19,182	16,372	28,631	45,571
2003[3]	37,046	148,660	18,734	16,282	27,915	45,064
2002...........................	36,308	148,492	18,826	16,931	27,280	45,407
2001...........................	35,805	147,829	18,793	17,293	26,795	45,641
2000[4]	34,514	147,966	17,738	17,425	25,692	45,977
1999...........................	32,356	144,640	16,121	16,737	24,572	46,082
1998...........................	30,928	142,053	16,053	16,742	23,594	45,987
1997...........................	29,514	140,367	16,124	16,962	22,895	45,976
1996...........................	28,106	138,703	15,011	17,075	22,154	45,908
1995...........................	26,792	136,221	14,013	16,990	21,431	44,546
1994...........................	25,852	135,096	13,697	16,479	20,248	44,614
1993...........................	24,674	133,119	12,820	16,575	19,422	44,779
1992...........................	23,227	130,860	12,809	16,612	18,737	45,340
1991...........................	22,332	130,371	12,613	17,553	18,261	46,508
1990...........................	21,793	130,080	12,582	18,698	17,820	51,977
1989...........................	21,414	129,094	12,242	19,137	17,594	51,846
1988...........................	20,060	127,564	11,889	19,635	16,750	51,297
1987...........................	19,016	124,874	11,824	19,748	15,939	50,815
1986...........................	18,149	122,757	11,203	19,665	15,120	50,104
1985...........................	17,181	120,651	10,726	19,692	14,457	49,674
1984...........................	16,083	118,183	10,384	20,206	13,893	48,452
1983...........................	15,137	115,095	9,853	20,020	13,044	47,560
1982...........................	14,351	113,451	9,387	20,789	12,560	46,584
1981...........................	13,624	113,301	9,357	22,296	12,109	47,332
1980...........................	12,665	111,919	8,845	23,028	11,314	46,795
1979...........................	11,795	110,826	8,420	23,783	10,624	45,497
1978...........................	10,812	106,436	7,759	23,787	9,834	43,510
1977...........................	9,887	103,119	7,066	24,854	9,013	41,696
1976...........................	9,180	100,510	6,720	25,035	8,393	40,570
1975...........................	8,552	97,881	6,198	24,916	7,843	39,827
Male						
2016...........................	61,232	85,718	32,463	7,695	43,534	24,908
2015...........................	58,944	85,263	30,230	8,210	41,942	24,647
2014...........................	56,701	83,402	29,618	8,256	39,874	24,468
2013...........................	54,658	82,576	27,586	8,286	37,763	24,327
2012...........................	54,118	81,979	24,955	8,183	38,454	23,783
2011[2]	52,273	80,502	25,155	8,359	38,679	23,800
2010...........................	50,645	80,284	24,413	8,382	36,181	24,230
2009...........................	50,186	80,799	23,036	8,851	35,468	25,143
2008...........................	51,148	82,727	24,831	9,596	36,753	25,290
2007...........................	50,110	82,932	24,985	9,780	36,839	25,396
2006...........................	49,647	82,310	24,072	10,541	37,356	25,489
2005...........................	48,034	81,258	23,222	10,273	35,248	25,348
2004...........................	46,008	79,765	22,537	10,188	34,050	25,209
2003[3]	44,726	78,869	21,447	10,173	33,266	24,292
2002...........................	44,310	78,757	22,091	10,526	32,673	24,174
2001...........................	43,648	78,342	21,508	10,572	32,363	24,239
2000[4]	42,772	78,319	21,007	10,535	31,446	24,439
1999...........................	40,257	76,233	18,855	9,917	30,414	24,235
1998...........................	38,134	75,213	19,155	10,085	28,742	24,155

[2]Starting in 2011, earnings data were created using population controls based on Census 2010 data.
[3]Starting in 2003, respondents could choose more than one race. The race data in this table from 2003 onward represent respondents who indicated only one race.
[4]Beginning in 2000, earnings data are from the expanded Current Population Survey (CPS) sample and were calculated using population controls based on Census 2000.

Table A-27. Mean Earnings of Workers 18 Years Old and Over, by Educational Attainment, Race, Hispanic Origin, and Sex, 1975–2016—*Continued*

(Dollars except as noted)

Race, sex, year, and Hispanic origin	Some college or associate's degree[1]		Bachelor's degree[1]		Advanced degree[1]	
	Mean earnings	Number of workers (thousands)	Mean earnings	Number of workers (thousands)	Mean earnings	Number of workers (thousands)
ALL RACES						
Both Sexes						
2016	40,201	48,128	67,267	37,272	95,203	21,639
2015	38,943	47,961	65,482	36,348	92,525	21,199
2014	37,945	47,023	62,466	35,305	88,056	19,944
2013	36,428	46,952	59,661	34,422	90,304	19,261
2012	35,943	47,469	60,159	33,948	89,253	18,783
2011[2]	35,585	45,999	59,415	33,188	87,981	17,800
2010	34,366	45,643	57,621	32,429	83,841	17,481
2009	34,773	45,239	56,665	32,127	85,818	16,860
2008	34,808	46,663	58,613	31,890	83,144	17,035
2007	35,138	46,577	57,181	31,832	80,977	16,604
2006	34,650	45,073	56,788	31,006	82,320	15,769
2005	33,496	45,434	54,689	29,658	79,946	15,152
2004	32,010	44,387	51,568	29,004	78,224	14,713
2003[3]	31,498	44,048	51,206	28,672	74,602	14,592
2002	31,046	43,776	51,194	28,257	72,824	14,119
2001	30,782	43,214	50,623	27,980	72,869	13,700
2000[4]	29,939	43,874	49,595	27,488	71,194	13,200
1999	28,403	42,860	45,678	26,215	67,697	12,749
1998	27,566	41,412	43,782	25,818	63,473	12,095
1997	26,235	40,802	40,478	25,035	63,229	11,591
1996	25,181	40,410	38,112	24,028	61,317	11,281
1995	23,862	40,142	36,980	23,285	56,667	11,258
1994	22,226	40,135	37,224	22,712	56,105	11,155
1993	21,539	39,429	35,121	21,815	55,789	10,521
1992	20,867	37,339	32,629	21,091	48,652	10,479
1991	20,551	35,732	31,323	20,475	46,039	10,103
1990	20,694	28,993	31,112	18,128	41,458	12,285
1989	20,255	28,078	30,736	17,767	41,019	12,265
1988	19,066	27,217	28,344	17,308	37,724	12,109
1987	18,054	26,404	26,919	16,497	35,968	11,411
1986	17,073	26,113	26,511	15,788	34,787	11,087
1985	16,349	25,402	24,877	15,373	32,909	10,510
1984	14,936	24,463	23,072	14,653	30,192	10,410
1983	14,245	23,208	21,532	13,929	28,333	10,377
1982	13,503	22,602	20,272	13,425	26,915	10,051
1981	13,176	21,759	19,006	12,579	25,281	9,336
1980	12,409	21,384	18,075	12,175	23,308	8,535
1979	11,377	21,174	16,514	11,751	21,874	8,621
1978	10,357	20,121	15,291	11,001	20,173	8,017
1977	9,607	18,905	14,207	10,357	19,077	7,309
1976	8,813	17,786	13,033	10,132	17,911	6,985
1975	8,388	16,917	12,332	9,764	16,725	6,457
Male						
2016	48,123	23,891	82,089	18,627	116,617	10,595
2015	46,154	23,578	79,927	18,287	113,279	10,539
2014	46,137	23,057	76,169	17,725	110,645	9,895
2013	43,841	23,112	72,124	17,203	115,282	9,647
2012	43,593	23,267	72,546	17,175	110,501	9,570
2011[2]	43,239	22,469	71,162	16,769	109,063	9,102
2010	40,935	22,150	69,623	16,595	103,359	8,925
2009	41,773	21,895	69,479	16,226	105,636	8,683
2008	42,221	22,830	72,868	16,100	103,980	8,909
2007	41,709	22,916	70,898	16,109	100,550	8,730
2006	41,521	21,952	69,818	15,769	101,441	8,556
2005	40,995	22,173	67,980	15,217	100,379	8,245
2004	39,509	21,473	63,753	14,860	97,855	8,032
2003[3]	38,451	21,534	63,084	14,849	91,831	8,019
2002	38,377	21,599	63,503	14,667	90,761	7,788
2001	37,429	21,390	63,354	14,507	90,130	7,631
2000[4]	37,372	21,526	62,609	14,375	88,077	7,442
1999	35,326	21,173	57,706	13,683	84,051	7,225
1998	34,179	20,545	55,057	13,486	77,217	6,942

[1]For data prior to 1991, "Some college/Associate degree" equals 1 to 3 years of college completed; "Bachelor's degree" equals 4 years of college; "Advanced degree" equals 5 or more years of college completed.
[2]Starting in 2011, earnings data were created using population controls based on Census 2010 data.
[3]Starting in 2003, respondents could choose more than one race. The race data in this table from 2003 onward represent respondents who indicated only one race.
[4]Beginning in 2000, earnings data are from the expanded Current Population Survey (CPS) sample and were calculated using population controls based on Census 2000.

Table A-27. Mean Earnings of Workers 18 Years Old and Over, by Educational Attainment, Race, Hispanic Origin, and Sex, 1975–2016—*Continued*

(Dollars except as noted)

Race, sex, year, and Hispanic origin	Total		Not a high school graduate		High school graduate	
	Mean earnings	Number of workers (thousands)	Mean earnings	Number of workers (thousands)	Mean earnings	Number of workers (thousands)
1997	36,556	74,596	19,575	10,348	28,307	24,152
1996	34,705	73,955	17,826	10,583	27,642	23,966
1995	33,251	72,634	16,748	10,312	26,333	23,473
1994	32,087	72,246	16,633	9,981	25,038	23,418
1993	30,568	71,183	14,946	10,151	23,973	23,388
1992	28,448	70,409	14,934	10,335	22,978	23,610
1991	27,494	70,145	15,056	10,679	22,663	24,110
1990	27,164	70,218	14,991	11,412	22,378	26,753
1989	27,025	69,798	14,727	11,774	22,508	26,469
1988	25,344	69,006	14,551	11,993	21,481	26,080
1987	24,015	67,951	14,544	12,117	20,364	25,981
1986	23,057	67,189	13,703	12,208	19,453	25,562
1985	21,823	66,439	13,124	12,137	18,575	25,496
1984	20,452	65,005	12,775	12,325	18,016	24,827
1983	19,175	63,816	12,052	12,376	16,728	24,449
1982	18,244	63,489	11,513	12,868	16,160	24,059
1981	17,542	63,547	11,668	13,701	15,900	24,435
1980	16,382	62,825	11,042	14,273	15,002	24,023
1979	15,430	62,464	10,628	14,711	14,317	23,318
1978	14,154	60,586	9,894	14,550	13,188	22,650
1977	12,888	59,441	8,939	15,369	12,092	21,846
1976	11,923	58,419	8,522	15,634	11,189	21,499
1975	11,091	57,297	7,843	15,613	10,475	21,347
Female						
2016	41,429	76,500	19,974	4,586	27,242	17,988
2015	39,929	75,811	17,162	4,949	26,832	17,756
2014	37,538	74,597	17,915	4,941	26,275	18,060
2013	36,664	73,454	16,964	4,675	26,322	18,106
2012	36,404	57,409	15,250	3,682	25,487	14,107
2011[2]	35,205	72,209	14,643	5,234	24,460	18,328
2010	34,216	71,214	14,995	4,962	24,172	18,368
2009	33,797	71,907	15,514	5,232	24,304	19,253
2008	32,922	73,262	14,521	5,621	24,329	19,892
2007	32,899	72,805	15,315	5,550	24,234	19,997
2006	32,015	72,128	15,352	6,110	23,236	20,447
2005	29,897	70,956	14,294	6,044	22,208	20,304
2004	28,691	70,285	13,655	6,183	21,923	20,361
2003[3]	28,367	69,790	14,214	6,108	21,659	20,772
2002	27,271	69,735	13,459	6,404	21,141	21,233
2001	26,962	69,487	14,524	6,720	20,489	21,402
2000[4]	25,228	69,647	12,739	6,890	19,162	21,538
1999	23,551	68,409	12,145	6,819	18,092	21,847
1998	22,818	66,840	11,353	6,657	17,898	21,832
1997	21,528	65,771	10,725	6,614	16,906	21,824
1996	20,570	64,748	10,421	6,492	16,161	21,942
1995	19,414	63,587	9,790	6,678	15,970	21,073
1994	18,684	62,850	9,189	6,498	14,955	21,195
1993	17,900	61,937	9,462	6,425	14,446	21,391
1992	17,145	60,451	9,311	6,277	14,128	21,730
1991	16,320	60,226	8,818	6,875	13,523	22,398
1990	15,493	59,862	8,808	7,286	12,986	25,224
1989	14,809	59,296	8,268	7,363	12,468	25,377
1988	13,833	58,558	7,711	7,642	11,857	25,217
1987	13,049	56,923	7,504	7,631	11,309	24,834
1986	12,214	55,568	7,109	7,457	10,606	24,542
1985	11,493	54,212	6,874	7,555	10,115	24,178
1984	10,742	53,178	6,644	7,881	9,561	23,625
1983	10,111	51,279	6,292	7,644	9,147	23,111
1982	9,403	49,962	5,932	7,921	8,715	22,525
1981	8,619	49,754	5,673	8,595	8,063	22,897
1980	7,909	49,094	5,263	8,755	7,423	22,772
1979	7,099	48,362	4,840	9,072	6,741	22,179
1978	6,396	45,850	4,397	9,237	6,192	20,860
1977	5,804	43,678	4,032	9,485	5,624	19,850

[2]Starting in 2011, earnings data were created using population controls based on Census 2010 data.
[3]Starting in 2003, respondents could choose more than one race. The race data in this table from 2003 onward represent respondents who indicated only one race.
[4]Beginning in 2000, earnings data are from the expanded Current Population Survey (CPS) sample and were calculated using population controls based on Census 2000.

Table A-27. Mean Earnings of Workers 18 Years Old and Over, by Educational Attainment, Race, Hispanic Origin, and Sex, 1975–2016—*Continued*

(Dollars except as noted)

Race, sex, year, and Hispanic origin	Some college or associate's degree[1]		Bachelor's degree[1]		Advanced degree[1]	
	Mean earnings	Number of workers (thousands)	Mean earnings	Number of workers (thousands)	Mean earnings	Number of workers (thousands)
1997	32,641	20,359	50,056	13,008	78,032	6,728
1996	31,426	20,208	46,702	12,562	74,406	6,636
1995	29,851	19,918	46,111	12,251	69,588	6,679
1994	27,636	19,859	46,278	12,324	67,032	6,663
1993	26,614	19,532	43,499	11,810	68,221	6,302
1992	25,660	18,768	40,039	11,353	58,324	6,344
1991	25,345	18,076	38,484	11,126	54,449	6,154
1990	26,120	14,844	38,901	9,807	49,768	7,402
1989	25,555	14,384	38,692	9,737	50,144	7,434
1988	23,827	14,019	35,906	9,466	45,677	7,449
1987	22,781	13,433	33,677	9,286	43,140	7,134
1986	21,784	13,502	33,376	8,908	41,836	7,009
1985	20,698	13,385	31,433	8,794	39,768	6,627
1984	18,863	12,818	29,203	8,387	35,804	6,648
1983	18,052	12,261	27,239	8,010	33,635	6,719
1982	17,108	12,103	25,758	7,865	32,109	6,594
1981	16,870	11,784	24,353	7,393	30,072	6,235
1980	15,871	11,663	23,340	7,132	27,846	5,733
1979	14,716	11,781	21,482	6,889	26,411	5,765
1978	13,382	11,352	19,861	6,611	24,274	5,422
1977	12,393	10,848	18,187	6,341	22,786	5,038
1976	11,376	10,282	16,714	6,135	21,202	4,868
1975	10,805	9,851	15,758	5,960	19,672	4,526
Female						
2016	32,391	24,236	52,461	18,645	74,656	11,043
2015	31,970	24,382	50,856	18,061	72,006	10,660
2014	30,064	23,966	48,650	17,580	65,814	10,049
2013	29,242	23,840	47,209	17,218	65,242	9,614
2012	28,861	18,881	47,596	13,383	66,934	7,355
2011[2]	28,275	23,529	47,418	16,419	65,915	8,697
2010	28,173	23,492	45,044	15,834	63,482	8,556
2009	28,207	23,344	43,589	15,900	64,771	8,176
2008	27,708	23,833	44,078	15,789	60,301	8,126
2007	28,773	23,660	43,127	15,722	59,273	7,873
2006	28,126	23,121	43,302	15,237	59,636	7,213
2005	26,348	23,260	40,684	14,440	55,553	6,906
2004	24,983	22,914	38,776	14,143	54,623	6,680
2003[3]	24,848	22,514	38,447	13,823	53,579	6,572
2002	23,905	22,176	37,909	13,589	50,756	6,330
2001	24,268	21,824	36,913	13,472	51,160	6,068
2000[4]	22,779	22,348	35,328	13,113	49,368	5,757
1999	21,644	22,687	32,546	12,533	46,307	5,523
1998	21,056	20,867	31,452	12,332	44,954	5,153
1997	19,856	20,442	30,119	12,027	42,744	4,863
1996	18,933	20,202	28,701	11,466	42,625	4,646
1995	17,962	20,224	26,841	11,034	37,813	4,578
1994	16,928	20,276	26,483	10,388	39,905	4,493
1993	16,555	19,897	25,232	10,005	37,212	4,218
1992	16,023	18,571	23,991	9,738	33,814	4,135
1991	15,643	17,657	22,802	9,348	32,929	3,948
1990	15,002	14,149	21,933	8,321	28,862	4,883
1989	14,688	13,694	21,089	8,030	26,977	4,831
1988	14,009	13,198	19,216	7,842	25,010	4,660
1987	13,158	12,971	18,217	7,211	24,004	4,277
1986	12,029	12,611	17,623	6,880	22,672	4,078
1985	11,504	12,017	16,114	6,579	21,202	3,883
1984	10,614	11,645	14,865	6,266	20,275	3,762
1983	9,981	10,947	13,808	5,919	18,593	3,658
1982	9,348	10,499	12,511	5,560	17,009	3,457
1981	8,811	9,975	11,384	5,186	15,647	3,101
1980	8,256	9,721	10,628	5,043	14,022	2,802
1979	7,190	9,393	9,474	4,862	12,717	2,856
1978	6,441	8,769	8,408	4,390	11,603	2,595
1977	5,856	8,057	7,923	4,016	10,848	2,271

[1]For data prior to 1991, "Some college/Associate degree" equals 1 to 3 years of college completed; "Bachelor's degree" equals 4 years of college; "Advanced degree" equals 5 or more years of college completed.
[2]Starting in 2011, earnings data were created using population controls based on Census 2010 data.
[3]Starting in 2003, respondents could choose more than one race. The race data in this table from 2003 onward represent respondents who indicated only one race.
[4]Beginning in 2000, earnings data are from the expanded Current Population Survey (CPS) sample and were calculated using population controls based on Census 2000.

Table A-27. Mean Earnings of Workers 18 Years Old and Over, by Educational Attainment, Race, Hispanic Origin, and Sex, 1975–2016—*Continued*

(Dollars except as noted)

Race, sex, year, and Hispanic origin	Total		Not a high school graduate		High school graduate	
	Mean earnings	Number of workers (thousands)	Mean earnings	Number of workers (thousands)	Mean earnings	Number of workers (thousands)
1976............................	5,373	42,091	3,723	9,401	5,240	19,071
1975............................	4,968	40,584	3,438	9,303	4,802	18,480
WHITE						
Both Sexes						
2016............................	53,178	127,241	28,489	9,615	38,326	33,491
2015............................	51,183	127,291	26,441	10,404	37,106	33,342
2014............................	48,971	125,227	26,065	10,553	35,528	33,616
2013............................	47,452	124,663	24,363	10,220	34,192	33,746
2012............................	46,844	124,316	22,048	10,491	33,928	33,498
2011[2]........................	46,053	123,044	21,704	10,891	33,719	33,803
2010............................	44,142	123,870	21,471	10,820	32,067	34,611
2009............................	43,337	125,151	20,457	11,507	31,429	36,125
2008............................	43,666	127,552	21,590	12,379	32,126	36,819
2007............................	43,139	127,413	22,289	12,363	32,223	37,058
2006............................	42,395	126,570	21,464	13,582	32,083	37,362
2005............................	40,717	124,870	20,264	13,157	30,569	37,122
2004............................	38,946	123,452	19,367	13,289	29,605	37,114
2003[3]........................	38,053	122,599	19,110	13,094	28,708	36,951
2002............................	37,376	122,699	19,264	13,740	28,145	37,380
2001............................	36,844	122,930	19,120	14,012	27,700	37,969
2000[4]........................	35,527	123,039	18,285	14,172	26,444	38,133
1999............................	33,326	120,916	16,623	13,585	25,270	38,428
1998............................	32,057	119,201	16,474	13,531	24,409	38,397
1997............................	30,515	117,985	16,596	13,780	23,618	38,409
1996............................	28,844	117,230	15,358	13,972	22,782	38,463
1995............................	27,556	115,636	14,234	13,869	22,154	37,802
1994............................	26,696	114,586	13,941	13,119	20,911	37,562
1993............................	25,440	113,342	13,171	13,480	19,918	37,826
1992............................	23,932	112,120	13,193	13,494	19,265	38,692
1991............................	22,998	111,830	12,914	14,041	18,766	39,764
1990............................	22,401	111,972	12,773	15,191	18,257	44,635
1989............................	22,035	111,243	12,654	15,628	18,011	44,726
1988............................	20,616	110,159	12,236	16,042	17,183	44,399
1987............................	19,599	108,407	12,502	16,165	16,339	44,235
1986............................	18,698	106,384	11,605	16,094	15,514	43,593
1985............................	17,709	104,818	11,115	16,149	14,815	43,347
1984............................	16,546	103,022	10,732	16,559	14,274	42,547
1983............................	15,556	101,035	10,239	16,568	13,357	42,007
1982............................	14,767	99,488	9,719	17,132	12,854	41,157
1981............................	14,027	99,510	9,737	18,298	12,355	42,080
1980............................	13,040	98,358	9,743	18,925	11,524	41,600
1979............................	12,155	97,544	8,827	19,504	10,431	40,458
1978............................	11,135	94,002	8,135	19,516	10,020	38,915
1977............................	10,191	91,254	7,415	20,492	9,173	37,521
1976............................	9,469	89,099	7,018	20,625	8,559	36,523
1975............................	8,815	86,894	6,438	20,696	8,005	35,799
Male						
2016............................	62,680	68,496	33,153	6,255	45,390	19,941
2015............................	60,652	68,610	31,336	6,755	43,711	19,807
2014............................	58,387	67,466	30,342	6,858	41,492	19,815
2013............................	56,215	67,148	28,253	6,773	39,191	19,796
2012............................	55,802	66,906	25,725	6,809	40,070	19,390
2011[2]........................	55,013	66,151	25,819	6,917	40,247	19,524
2010............................	52,304	66,887	25,100	7,011	37,477	20,018
2009............................	51,287	67,464	23,353	7,426	36,418	20,855
2008............................	52,672	68,816	25,386	8,113	37,852	20,899
2007............................	51,781	69,099	25,886	8,170	38,214	21,129
2006............................	51,013	68,752	24,579	8,932	38,833	21,090
2005............................	49,611	67,874	23,556	8,582	36,753	20,914
2004............................	47,404	66,677	22,598	8,591	35,360	20,781
2003[3]........................	46,114	66,199	21,791	8,500	34,224	20,238
2002............................	45,793	66,202	22,539	8,841	33,920	20,156
2001............................	45,071	66,216	22,006	8,833	33,545	20,465
2000[4]........................	44,181	66,222	21,561	8,859	32,528	20,553

[2]Starting in 2011, earnings data were created using population controls based on Census 2010 data.
[3]Starting in 2003, respondents could choose more than one race. The race data in this table from 2003 onward represent respondents who indicated only one race.
[4]Beginning in 2000, earnings data are from the expanded Current Population Survey (CPS) sample and were calculated using population controls based on Census 2000.

Table A-27. Mean Earnings of Workers 18 Years Old and Over, by Educational Attainment, Race, Hispanic Origin, and Sex, 1975–2016—*Continued*

(Dollars except as noted)

Race, sex, year, and Hispanic origin	Some college or associate's degree[1]		Bachelor's degree[1]		Advanced degree[1]	
	Mean earnings	Number of workers (thousands)	Mean earnings	Number of workers (thousands)	Mean earnings	Number of workers (thousands)
1976............................	5,301	7,504	7,383	3,997	10,345	2,117
1975............................	5,019	7,066	6,963	3,804	9,818	1,931
WHITE						
Both Sexes						
2016............................	41,583	37,481	68,538	29,950	95,647	16,701
2015............................	39,959	37,686	66,926	29,216	92,640	16,640
2014............................	39,590	36,920	63,422	28,313	88,835	15,823
2013............................	37,528	37,388	60,962	27,869	91,369	15,439
2012............................	36,493	37,706	61,527	27,651	90,948	14,967
2011[2]	36,204	36,861	61,253	27,096	90,060	14,391
2010............................	35,180	37,071	59,188	26,950	85,070	14,415
2009............................	35,634	37,035	57,762	26,595	86,188	13,887
2008............................	35,622	37,891	59,866	26,487	84,739	13,973
2007............................	35,685	37,988	58,652	26,310	82,384	13,692
2006............................	35,338	36,878	57,932	25,763	83,185	12,983
2005............................	34,326	37,409	55,785	24,652	81,697	12,527
2004............................	32,751	36,547	52,877	24,061	79,071	12,397
2003[3]	32,346	36,318	52,259	24,010	75,638	12,226
2002............................	31,878	36,023	52,479	23,638	73,870	11,916
2001............................	31,482	35,722	51,631	23,531	74,398	11,694
2000[4]	30,638	36,334	50,969	23,110	71,983	11,288
1999............................	29,105	35,634	46,894	22,322	68,910	10,949
1998............................	28,318	34,540	44,852	22,266	65,379	10,467
1997............................	26,906	34,274	41,439	21,528	65,058	9,994
1996............................	25,511	34,087	38,936	20,846	61,779	9,861
1995............................	24,349	33,850	37,711	20,203	57,054	9,914
1994............................	22,648	34,006	37,996	19,917	56,475	9,981
1993............................	21,924	33,728	35,846	18,922	56,964	9,386
1992............................	21,357	32,014	33,092	18,555	49,347	9,363
1991............................	21,013	30,973	31,837	18,033	46,498	9,019
1990............................	21,095	25,105	31,626	15,993	41,908	11,049
1989............................	20,678	24,212	31,266	15,723	41,610	10,952
1988............................	19,384	23,643	28,886	15,221	38,129	10,854
1987............................	18,265	23,083	27,741	14,624	36,175	10,300
1986............................	17,371	22,653	27,061	14,055	35,265	9,987
1985............................	16,701	22,131	25,376	13,670	33,401	9,522
1984............................	15,197	21,451	23,472	13,056	30,515	9,409
1983............................	14,486	20,452	21,914	12,577	28,532	9,430
1982............................	13,799	19,967	20,760	12,103	27,040	9,127
1981............................	13,424	19,102	19,389	11,450	25,564	8,582
1980............................	12,677	18,888	18,434	11,067	23,466	7,876
1979............................	11,574	18,835	16,758	10,807	22,085	7,940
1978............................	10,504	18,022	15,463	10,171	20,531	7,376
1977............................	9,771	16,968	14,462	9,534	19,337	6,739
1976............................	8,958	16,127	13,279	9,325	18,153	6,498
1975............................	8,525	15,423	12,597	8,955	16,920	6,021
Male						
2016............................	50,063	18,951	84,069	15,136	116,854	8,211
2015............................	47,900	18,905	82,495	14,884	115,094	8,257
2014............................	48,405	18,518	78,348	14,409	112,351	7,864
2013............................	45,403	18,729	74,018	14,113	117,959	7,735
2012............................	45,049	18,825	74,594	14,268	114,150	7,612
2011[2]	44,155	18,279	73,630	13,978	112,515	7,451
2010............................	42,151	18,362	71,958	14,077	105,869	7,417
2009............................	42,884	18,273	71,286	13,740	106,571	7,168
2008............................	43,463	18,849	75,053	13,596	107,099	7,356
2007............................	42,903	18,995	73,477	13,577	103,293	7,227
2006............................	42,684	18,340	71,735	13,326	103,340	7,063
2005............................	42,206	18,583	69,852	12,900	103,144	6,893
2004............................	40,639	17,990	65,652	12,555	100,084	6,758
2003[3]	39,594	18,060	65,264	12,665	94,017	6,734
2002............................	39,605	18,068	65,439	12,512	92,733	6,623
2001............................	38,501	17,957	65,046	12,396	92,304	6,562
2000[4]	38,476	18,179	64,831	12,271	89,812	6,359

[1]For data prior to 1991, "Some college/Associate degree" equals 1 to 3 years of college completed; "Bachelor's degree" equals 4 years of college; "Advanced degree" equals 5 or more years of college completed.
[2]Starting in 2011, earnings data were created using population controls based on Census 2010 data.
[3]Starting in 2003, respondents could choose more than one race. The race data in this table from 2003 onward represent respondents who indicated only one race.
[4]Beginning in 2000, earnings data are from the expanded Current Population Survey (CPS) sample and were calculated using population controls based on Census 2000.

Table A-27. Mean Earnings of Workers 18 Years Old and Over, by Educational Attainment, Race, Hispanic Origin, and Sex, 1975–2016—*Continued*

(Dollars except as noted)

Race, sex, year, and Hispanic origin	Total Mean earnings	Total Number of workers (thousands)	Not a high school graduate Mean earnings	Not a high school graduate Number of workers (thousands)	High school graduate Mean earnings	High school graduate Number of workers (thousands)
1999	41,598	64,856	19,320	8,286	31,279	20,526
1998	39,638	64,181	19,632	8,430	29,782	20,388
1997	37,933	63,738	20,071	8,670	29,298	20,426
1996	35,821	63,532	18,246	8,899	28,591	20,329
1995	34,276	62,520	17,032	8,660	27,467	19,982
1994	33,292	62,029	16,835	8,133	26,125	19,833
1993	31,719	61,356	15,295	8,430	24,781	19,835
1992	29,515	60,919	15,414	8,487	23,844	20,259
1991	28,516	60,770	15,499	8,720	23,475	20,765
1990	28,105	60,676	15,319	9,476	23,135	23,088
1989	28,013	60,877	15,217	9,805	23,291	23,029
1988	26,184	60,221	14,943	10,008	22,216	22,707
1987	24,898	59,468	15,303	10,132	21,012	22,682
1986	23,892	58,932	14,168	10,239	20,128	22,392
1985	22,604	58,385	13,579	10,163	19,203	22,357
1984	21,174	57,362	13,248	10,280	18,681	21,989
1983	19,812	56,641	12,573	10,387	17,281	21,733
1982	18,859	56,364	11,952	10,816	16,662	21,436
1981	18,141	56,397	12,094	11,523	16,352	21,809
1980	16,945	55,772	11,539	11,937	15,382	21,453
1979	15,971	55,556	11,127	12,291	13,916	20,834
1978	14,627	54,113	10,358	12,141	13,534	20,328
1977	13,329	53,174	9,366	12,903	12,377	19,773
1976	12,342	52,312	8,867	13,117	11,497	19,446
1975	11,448	51,510	8,110	13,191	10,726	19,361
Female						
2016	42,098	58,744	19,807	3,360	27,929	13,549
2015	40,112	58,680	17,379	3,649	27,440	13,535
2014	37,971	57,761	18,129	3,695	26,965	13,800
2013	37,222	57,515	16,718	3,446	27,097	13,949
2012	36,404	57,409	15,250	3,682	25,487	14,107
2011[2]	35,635	56,892	14,541	3,974	24,793	14,279
2010	34,561	56,982	14,791	3,808	24,645	14,593
2009	34,040	57,687	15,187	4,080	24,615	15,270
2008	33,115	58,735	14,370	4,265	24,610	15,919
2007	32,899	58,313	15,278	4,192	24,276	15,929
2006	32,148	57,818	15,483	4,650	23,334	16,272
2005	30,125	56,995	14,086	4,575	22,590	16,208
2004	28,966	56,705	13,459	4,703	22,260	16,358
2003[3]	28,591	56,400	14,149	4,593	22,028	16,712
2002	27,512	56,496	13,354	4,898	21,388	17,224
2001	27,240	56,714	14,197	5,178	20,866	17,503
2000[4]	25,441	56,816	12,823	5,313	19,330	17,579
1999	23,756	56,061	12,405	5,299	18,381	17,902
1998	23,213	55,020	11,255	5,102	18,327	18,009
1997	21,779	54,247	10,700	5,111	17,166	17,983
1996	20,590	53,697	10,290	5,073	16,270	18,134
1995	19,647	53,117	9,582	5,208	16,196	17,820
1994	18,912	52,557	9,220	4,987	15,078	17,729
1993	18,028	51,986	9,624	5,050	14,557	17,991
1992	17,289	51,200	9,428	5,007	14,233	18,434
1991	16,431	51,060	8,677	5,321	13,621	18,999
1990	15,559	50,905	8,725	5,715	13,031	21,547
1989	14,810	50,366	8,338	5,823	12,406	21,697
1988	13,902	49,938	7,747	6,034	11,915	21,692
1987	13,161	48,939	7,798	6,033	11,421	21,553
1986	12,247	47,452	7,123	5,855	10,641	21,201
1985	11,555	46,433	6,931	5,986	10,142	20,990
1984	10,732	45,660	6,614	6,279	9,561	20,558
1983	10,126	44,394	6,317	6,181	9,150	20,274
1982	9,419	43,124	5,896	6,316	8,714	19,721
1981	8,646	43,113	5,727	6,775	8,054	20,271
1980	7,926	42,586	6,675	6,988	7,415	20,147
1979	7,105	41,988	4,909	7,213	6,731	19,624
1978	6,398	39,889	4,476	7,375	6,176	18,587
1977	5,808	38,080	4,097	7,589	5,604	17,748

[2] Starting in 2011, earnings data were created using population controls based on Census 2010 data.
[3] Starting in 2003, respondents could choose more than one race. The race data in this table from 2003 onward represent respondents who indicated only one race.
[4] Beginning in 2000, earnings data are from the expanded Current Population Survey (CPS) sample and were calculated using population controls based on Census 2000.

Table A-27. Mean Earnings of Workers 18 Years Old and Over, by Educational Attainment, Race, Hispanic Origin, and Sex, 1975–2016—*Continued*

(Dollars except as noted)

Race, sex, year, and Hispanic origin	Some college or associate's degree[1]		Bachelor's degree[1]		Advanced degree[1]	
	Mean earnings	Number of workers (thousands)	Mean earnings	Number of workers (thousands)	Mean earnings	Number of workers (thousands)
1999	36,518	17,928	59,606	11,851	85,345	6,265
1998	35,277	17,407	56,620	11,874	79,734	6,083
1997	33,691	17,423	51,678	11,340	80,322	5,879
1996	32,238	17,418	48,014	11,065	75,481	5,821
1995	30,529	17,136	47,016	10,851	70,155	5,891
1994	28,240	17,091	47,575	10,992	67,629	5,979
1993	27,297	16,959	44,505	10,452	70,000	5,680
1992	26,387	16,335	40,893	10,118	59,329	5,720
1991	26,090	15,873	39,547	9,893	55,257	5,519
1990	26,841	13,003	39,780	8,770	50,385	6,731
1989	26,260	12,582	39,654	8,750	51,031	6,710
1988	24,462	12,277	36,637	8,467	46,181	6,762
1987	23,310	11,771	34,865	8,384	43,440	6,499
1986	22,303	11,846	34,273	8,041	42,480	6,413
1985	21,240	11,831	32,165	7,970	40,358	6,064
1984	19,344	11,387	29,781	7,624	36,219	6,081
1983	18,388	10,974	27,726	7,379	33,981	6,168
1982	17,571	10,822	26,404	7,242	32,266	6,047
1981	17,303	10,448	24,943	6,824	30,396	5,794
1980	16,313	10,400	23,803	6,618	27,991	5,363
1979	15,043	10,572	21,785	6,464	26,645	5,395
1978	13,589	10,350	20,085	6,205	24,635	5,088
1977	12,657	9,853	18,521	5,941	23,093	4,704
1976	11,616	9,394	16,995	5,765	21,490	4,589
1975	11,028	9,096	16,079	5,587	19,858	4,275
Female						
2016	32,911	18,530	52,669	14,814	75,138	8,490
2015	31,966	18,781	50,759	14,332	70,520	8,382
2014	30,718	18,401	47,954	13,904	65,599	7,959
2013	29,622	18,658	47,565	13,755	64,670	7,704
2012	28,861	18,881	47,596	13,383	66,934	7,355
2011[2]	28,383	18,581	48,064	13,117	65,952	6,940
2010	28,339	18,709	45,223	12,873	63,021	6,997
2009	28,573	16,762	43,309	12,855	64,441	6,718
2008	27,859	19,041	43,848	12,891	59,877	6,616
2007	28,466	18,993	42,846	12,733	59,006	6,464
2006	28,069	18,537	43,142	12,437	59,141	5,920
2005	26,547	18,825	40,344	11,751	55,461	5,634
2004	25,104	18,556	38,898	11,445	53,895	5,641
2003[3]	25,177	18,258	37,739	11,344	53,102	5,492
2002	24,101	17,954	37,903	11,126	50,270	5,293
2001	24,387	17,764	36,698	11,135	51,499	5,131
2000[4]	22,790	18,155	35,273	10,838	48,982	4,929
1999	21,598	17,705	32,507	10,471	45,741	4,684
1998	21,246	17,132	31,406	10,393	45,462	4,384
1997	19,892	16,852	30,041	10,188	43,236	4,114
1996	18,482	16,669	28,667	9,781	42,049	4,041
1995	18,011	16,714	26,916	9,352	37,864	4,022
1994	16,998	16,915	26,198	8,925	39,816	4,002
1993	16,490	16,769	25,161	8,470	36,988	3,705
1992	16,116	15,679	23,738	8,437	33,675	3,643
1991	15,677	15,100	22,471	8,140	32,687	3,500
1990	14,922	12,102	21,725	7,223	28,694	4,318
1989	14,640	11,630	20,741	6,973	26,709	4,242
1988	13,898	11,366	19,169	6,754	24,824	4,092
1987	13,015	11,312	18,170	6,240	23,753	3,801
1986	11,964	10,807	17,418	6,014	22,320	3,574
1985	11,488	10,300	15,883	5,700	21,202	3,458
1984	10,504	10,064	14,617	5,432	20,092	3,328
1983	9,969	9,478	13,664	5,198	18,230	3,262
1982	9,336	9,145	12,352	4,861	16,779	3,080
1981	8,740	8,654	11,196	4,626	15,523	2,788
1980	8,221	8,488	10,447	4,449	13,809	2,513
1979	7,135	8,263	9,275	4,343	12,420	2,545
1978	6,342	7,672	8,231	3,966	11,404	2,288
1977	5,774	7,115	7,750	3,593	10,655	2,035

[1]For data prior to 1991, "Some college/Associate degree" equals 1 to 3 years of college completed; "Bachelor's degree" equals 4 years of college; "Advanced degree" equals 5 or more years of college completed.
[2]Starting in 2011, earnings data were created using population controls based on Census 2010 data.
[3]Starting in 2003, respondents could choose more than one race. The race data in this table from 2003 onward represent respondents who indicated only one race.
[4]Beginning in 2000, earnings data are from the expanded Current Population Survey (CPS) sample and were calculated using population controls based on Census 2000.

Table A-27. Mean Earnings of Workers 18 Years Old and Over, by Educational Attainment, Race, Hispanic Origin, and Sex, 1975–2016—*Continued*

(Dollars except as noted)

Race, sex, year, and Hispanic origin	Total		Not a high school graduate		High school graduate	
	Mean earnings	Number of workers (thousands)	Mean earnings	Number of workers (thousands)	Mean earnings	Number of workers (thousands)
1976............................	5,383	36,787	3,788	7,508	5,214	17,077
1975............................	4,982	35,384	3,500	7,505	4,800	16,438
NON-HISPANIC WHITE						
Both Sexes						
2016............................	56,574	103,334	27,014	3,981	39,265	25,971
2015............................	54,352	103,957	26,974	4,394	38,588	25,921
2014............................	52,171	102,756	29,080	4,344	36,826	26,583
2013............................	50,604	102,814	26,750	4,136	35,595	27,119
2012............................	49,981	102,974	23,126	4,503	35,399	26,822
2011[2]	49,147	102,365	22,642	4,849	35,365	27,313
2010............................	46,878	103,829	22,557	4,877	33,279	28,369
2009............................	45,939	105,137	21,229	5,216	32,562	29,860
2008............................	46,179	107,294	21,765	5,798	33,159	30,598
2007............................	45,542	107,434	23,015	5,908	33,094	30,855
2006............................	44,813	106,828	22,206	6,876	32,931	31,345
2005............................	42,963	106,337	21,134	6,603	31,445	31,484
2004............................	40,943	105,505	19,742	6,754	30,197	31,793
2003[3]	40,094	105,214	19,769	6,768	29,571	31,831
2002............................	39,220	105,706	19,423	7,380	28,756	32,365
2001............................	38,711	106,384	19,659	7,812	28,426	33,050
2000[4]	37,346	106,709	19,147	7,957	27,122	33,231
1999............................	34,838	106,573	16,957	8,219	25,847	34,121
1998............................	33,336	105,523	16,837	8,488	24,801	34,344
Male						
2016............................	67,180	54,893	31,668	2,543	46,416	15,315
2015............................	64,884	56,124	33,003	2,862	45,533	15,559
2014............................	63,100	54,432	35,105	2,752	43,312	15,583
2013............................	60,804	54,529	32,329	2,717	40,991	15,819
2012............................	60,396	54,569	28,026	2,784	42,157	15,388
2011[2]	59,584	54,244	27,872	2,978	42,772	15,644
2010............................	56,417	55,094	27,375	3,030	39,284	16,186
2009............................	55,318	55,638	25,695	3,187	38,160	17,015
2008............................	56,538	56,822	26,479	3,654	39,405	17,206
2007............................	55,662	57,080	27,874	3,716	39,764	17,309
2006............................	54,843	56,843	26,100	4,289	40,180	17,470
2005............................	53,263	56,675	25,511	4,127	38,134	17,507
2004............................	50,597	55,930	23,590	4,203	36,324	17,568
2003[3]	49,386	55,774	22,957	4,224	35,589	17,225
2002............................	48,817	55,994	23,250	4,580	34,909	17,218
2001............................	47,973	56,528	23,096	4,749	34,627	17,672
2000[4]	47,084	56,675	23,296	4,763	33,669	17,733
1999............................	44,032	56,575	20,256	4,842	32,321	18,047
1998............................	41,612	56,246	20,781	5,152	30,429	18,048
Female						
2016............................	44,556	48,441	18,777	1,437	28,989	10,656
2015............................	42,070	48,771	15,942	1,595	28,315	10,646
2014............................	39,860	48,324	18,662	1,591	27,637	10,999
2013............................	39,084	48,284	16,062	1,418	28,041	11,300
2012............................	38,240	48,405	15,189	1,718	26,303	11,433
2011[2]	37,382	48,120	14,314	1,870	25,435	11,669
2010............................	36,093	48,735	14,649	1,846	25,300	12,183
2009............................	35,396	49,498	14,216	2,029	25,147	12,845
2008............................	34,517	50,471	13,730	2,144	25,133	13,391
2007............................	34,069	50,353	14,779	2,192	24,570	13,546
2006............................	33,407	49,984	15,751	2,857	23,805	13,875
2005............................	31,208	49,661	13,837	2,476	23,004	13,977
2004............................	30,051	49,575	13,401	2,550	22,631	14,224
2003[3]	29,613	49,439	14,475	2,543	22,473	14,605
2002............................	28,410	49,712	13,163	2,800	21,762	15,146
2001............................	28,210	49,856	14,328	3,062	21,301	15,378
2000[4]	26,315	50,034	12,962	3,194	19,631	15,498

[2]Starting in 2011, earnings data were created using population controls based on Census 2010 data.
[3]Starting in 2003, respondents could choose more than one race. The race data in this table from 2003 onward represent respondents who indicated only one race.
[4]Beginning in 2000, earnings data are from the expanded Current Population Survey (CPS) sample and were calculated using population controls based on Census 2000.

Table A-27. Mean Earnings of Workers 18 Years Old and Over, by Educational Attainment, Race, Hispanic Origin, and Sex, 1975–2016—*Continued*

(Dollars except as noted)

Race, sex, year, and Hispanic origin	Some college or associate's degree[1]		Bachelor's degree[1]		Advanced degree[1]	
	Mean earnings	Number of workers (thousands)	Mean earnings	Number of workers (thousands)	Mean earnings	Number of workers (thousands)
1976.............................	5,250	6,733	7,262	3,560	10,131	1,909
1975.............................	4,926	6,327	6,822	3,368	9,728	1,746
NON-HISPANIC WHITE						
Both Sexes						
2016.............................	42,932	30,953	70,220	26,916	96,689	15,510
2015.............................	40,812	31,693	67,636	26,508	93,599	15,438
2014.............................	40,487	31,236	64,462	25,783	89,735	14,808
2013.............................	38,371	31,688	61,913	25,437	92,569	14,432
2012.............................	37,942	32,362	62,537	25,246	91,627	14,039
2011[2].............................	36,992	31,780	62,389	24,891	90,659	13,529
2010.............................	35,903	32,184	60,119	24,823	85,840	13,574
2009.............................	36,249	32,430	58,487	24,533	86,770	13,095
2008.............................	36,158	33,221	60,866	24,445	85,017	13,230
2007.............................	36,290	33,431	59,727	24,366	82,900	12,871
2006.............................	35,872	32,403	58,917	23,855	83,785	12,347
2005.............................	34,866	33,355	56,462	23,013	82,205	11,879
2004.............................	33,192	33,200	53,411	22,544	79,166	11,961
2003[3].............................	32,825	32,460	52,856	22,474	76,200	11,680
2002.............................	32,318	32,344	53,185	22,221	74,122	11,395
2001.............................	31,905	32,118	52,300	22,204	74,932	11,198
2000[4].............................	31,217	32,836	51,351	21,824	72,356	10,859
1999.............................	29,557	32,454	47,401	21,272	68,910	10,507
1998.............................	23,897	31,459	45,342	21,175	65,461	10,059
Male						
2016.............................	51,782	15,718	86,312	13,676	118,068	7,639
2015.............................	48,967	16,271	83,328	13,664	116,296	7,766
2014.............................	49,712	15,606	80,075	13,117	113,515	7,372
2013.............................	46,713	15,873	75,345	12,910	120,004	7,208
2012.............................	46,477	16,175	75,826	13,080	115,598	7,139
2011[2].............................	45,443	15,675	75,168	12,900	113,244	7,045
2010.............................	43,272	15,846	73,149	13,010	107,125	7,019
2009.............................	43,802	15,981	72,305	12,708	107,872	6,746
2008.............................	44,237	16,439	76,613	12,562	107,498	6,960
2007.............................	43,835	16,684	75,214	12,597	104,317	6,772
2006.............................	43,589	16,024	73,376	12,321	104,031	6,738
2005.............................	43,137	16,456	70,932	12,048	104,107	6,535
2004.............................	41,490	16,259	66,527	11,739	100,220	6,527
2003[3].............................	40,316	16,048	66,390	11,849	95,029	6,427
2002.............................	40,368	16,121	66,638	11,764	93,686	6,309
2001.............................	39,133	16,114	66,196	11,692	92,954	6,299
2000[4].............................	39,379	16,435	65,459	11,594	90,150	6,149
1999.............................	37,224	16,343	60,384	11,307	85,918	6,036
1998.............................	29,555	15,849	57,346	11,335	79,524	5,862
Female						
2016.............................	33,801	15,235	53,598	13,240	75,942	7,871
2015.............................	32,304	15,772	51,126	13,009	71,035	7,746
2014.............................	31,276	15,630	48,291	12,665	66,161	7,436
2013.............................	29,999	15,815	48,070	12,526	65,190	7,223
2012.............................	29,413	16,187	48,247	12,165	66,824	6,900
2011[2].............................	28,766	16,105	48,640	11,990	66,120	6,484
2010.............................	28,755	16,337	45,767	11,812	63,047	6,555
2009.............................	28,911	16,448	43,636	11,825	64,351	6,349
2008.............................	28,244	16,781	44,220	11,883	60,063	6,270
2007.............................	28,772	16,746	43,150	11,769	59,121	6,099
2006.............................	28,322	16,379	43,473	11,534	59,458	5,608
2005.............................	26,812	16,899	40,562	10,964	55,422	5,344
2004.............................	25,228	16,940	39,161	10,805	53,875	5,433
2003[3].............................	25,499	16,411	37,761	10,624	53,164	5,253
2002.............................	24,318	16,222	38,049	10,457	49,845	5,085
2001.............................	24,628	16,004	36,844	10,512	51,756	4,898
2000[4].............................	23,038	16,401	35,362	10,230	49,126	4,710

[1]For data prior to 1991, "Some college/Associate degree" equals 1 to 3 years of college completed; "Bachelor's degree" equals 4 years of college; "Advanced degree" equals 5 or more years of college completed.
[2]Starting in 2011, earnings data were created using population controls based on Census 2010 data.
[3]Starting in 2003, respondents could choose more than one race. The race data in this table from 2003 onward represent respondents who indicated only one race.
[4]Beginning in 2000, earnings data are from the expanded Current Population Survey (CPS) sample and were calculated using population controls based on Census 2000.

Table A-27. Mean Earnings of Workers 18 Years Old and Over, by Educational Attainment, Race, Hispanic Origin, and Sex, 1975–2016—*Continued*

(Dollars except as noted)

Race, sex, year, and Hispanic origin	Total		Not a high school graduate		High school graduate	
	Mean earnings	Number of workers (thousands)	Mean earnings	Number of workers (thousands)	Mean earnings	Number of workers (thousands)
1999..............................	24,436	49,998	12,227	3,378	18,579	16,074
1998..............................	23,891	49,277	10,746	3,336	18,568	16,295
BLACK						
Both Sexes						
2016..............................	40,767	19,755	24,054	1,496	30,131	6,150
2015..............................	39,394	19,150	19,783	1,582	29,211	6,015
2014..............................	37,012	18,657	22,353	1,420	28,439	5,905
2013..............................	35,817	18,023	21,403	1,590	26,670	5,689
2012..............................	34,800	17,838	18,889	1,486	26,625	5,639
2011[2]..........................	34,755	17,295	17,488	1,613	27,562	5,539
2010..............................	32,808	16,840	17,644	1,559	25,757	5,518
2009..............................	33,362	16,744	18,936	1,618	26,970	5,803
2008..............................	32,874	17,509	18,123	1,748	27,265	6,060
2007..............................	33,333	17,453	17,439	1,854	27,179	5,996
2006..............................	32,443	17,234	17,823	1,943	26,368	6,159
2005..............................	30,472	17,000	17,216	2,025	23,904	6,101
2004..............................	29,096	16,631	17,827	2,044	23,498	6,138
2003[3]..........................	28,838	16,389	16,201	2,095	23,777	5,941
2002..............................	28,179	16,352	16,516	2,148	22,823	5,822
2001..............................	27,031	16,683	17,248	2,382	21,743	5,729
2000[4]..........................	26,204	16,756	15,201	2,434	21,789	6,020
1999..............................	24,979	16,936	13,569	2,393	20,991	6,112
1998..............................	22,829	16,201	13,672	2,402	19,236	6,053
1997..............................	21,909	15,873	13,185	2,437	18,980	5,964
1996..............................	21,978	15,255	13,110	2,383	18,722	5,844
1995..............................	20,537	14,847	12,956	2,389	17,072	5,453
1994..............................	19,772	14,754	12,705	2,290	16,446	5,596
1993..............................	18,614	14,315	11,065	2,352	16,122	5,521
1992..............................	17,416	13,836	11,077	2,451	15,260	5,379
1991..............................	16,809	13,865	11,248	2,860	15,060	5,512
1990..............................	16,627	13,731	11,184	2,853	14,794	6,049
1989..............................	16,072	13,600	10,066	2,883	14,613	5,894
1988..............................	15,318	13,356	10,202	2,970	13,835	5,760
1987..............................	14,136	13,023	9,976	3,015	12,862	5,699
1986..............................	13,494	12,729	9,365	3,028	12,276	5,470
1985..............................	12,926	12,427	9,116	3,009	11,791	5,223
1984..............................	12,002	11,948	8,725	3,127	10,882	4,927
1983..............................	11,299	11,296	7,867	3,035	10,557	4,692
1982..............................	10,612	11,081	7,799	3,188	10,287	4,591
1981..............................	10,117	11,088	7,520	3,514	9,994	4,388
1980..............................	11,085	5,576	8,421	2,054	11,563	2,119
1979..............................	8,720	10,856	6,424	3,776	8,723	4,267
1978..............................	7,981	10,420	5,918	3,841	8,152	3,944
1977..............................	7,271	10,014	5,406	3,946	7,553	3,604
1976..............................	6,716	9,744	5,304	4,008	6,805	3,515
1975..............................	6,190	9,368	4,989	3,922	6,281	3,495
Male						
2016..............................	46,686	9,231	26,919	769	34,968	3,235
2015..............................	43,781	8,979	23,846	796	33,881	3,158
2014..............................	42,454	8,645	25,516	746	32,836	3,036
2013..............................	40,785	8,348	26,346	843	29,893	2,887
2012..............................	38,244	8,293	19,497	800	30,276	2,891
2011[2]..........................	38,633	7,951	21,035	812	31,219	2,811
2010..............................	35,598	7,735	19,452	829	29,478	2,878
2009..............................	37,553	7,657	21,828	861	30,723	2,996
2008..............................	36,057	8,116	22,344	866	30,985	3,166
2007..............................	35,668	8,088	19,705	985	29,640	2,994
2006..............................	36,045	7,932	21,294	982	30,122	3,067
2005..............................	34,165	7,836	19,890	1,056	27,360	3,050
2004..............................	33,020	7,668	22,796	1,029	26,608	3,119
2003[3]..........................	32,545	7,469	17,915	1,039	28,102	2,910
2002..............................	31,790	7,483	19,294	1,072	25,582	2,832
2001..............................	30,502	7,727	18,543	1,210	25,037	2,759
2000[4]..........................	30,109	7,700	17,992	1,235	25,219	2,942

[2]Starting in 2011, earnings data were created using population controls based on Census 2010 data.
[3]Starting in 2003, respondents could choose more than one race. The race data in this table from 2003 onward represent respondents who indicated only one race.
[4]Beginning in 2000, earnings data are from the expanded Current Population Survey (CPS) sample and were calculated using population controls based on Census 2000.

Table A-27. Mean Earnings of Workers 18 Years Old and Over, by Educational Attainment, Race, Hispanic Origin, and Sex, 1975–2016—*Continued*

(Dollars except as noted)

Race, sex, year, and Hispanic origin	Some college or associate's degree[1]		Bachelor's degree[1]		Advanced degree[1]	
	Mean earnings	Number of workers (thousands)	Mean earnings	Number of workers (thousands)	Mean earnings	Number of workers (thousands)
1999............................	21,779	16,112	32,667	9,964	45,943	4,470
1998............................	18,198	15,610	31,516	9,840	45,805	4,196
BLACK						
Both Sexes						
2016............................	34,740	6,841	57,409	3,394	80,903	1,873
2015............................	34,653	6,606	55,506	3,220	80,976	1,725
2014............................	32,074	6,605	51,983	3,084	72,257	1,642
2013............................	32,137	6,228	49,904	2,997	72,496	1,517
2012............................	31,730	6,398	48,972	2,854	68,329	1,459
2011[2]	32,891	5,964	45,477	2,796	70,140	1,380
2010............................	30,351	5,927	44,311	2,596	71,000	1,237
2009............................	30,520	5,577	47,799	2,583	66,923	1,162
2008............................	30,248	5,933	46,527	2,550	66,198	1,216
2007............................	32,787	5,813	46,502	2,682	64,247	1,107
2006............................	31,234	5,581	47,903	2,503	64,834	1,045
2005............................	28,848	5,390	47,101	2,412	63,664	1,071
2004............................	27,779	5,191	42,342	2,348	65,538	909
2003[3]	27,187	5,119	42,968	2,321	64,164	911
2002............................	27,626	5,255	42,285	2,275	59,944	851
2001............................	26,907	5,481	40,165	2,212	55,771	877
2000[4]	26,324	5,431	41,513	2,060	52,373	809
1999............................	25,176	5,417	37,422	2,140	52,437	873
1998............................	23,927	4,559	36,373	1,897	44,760	764
1997............................	22,899	4,902	32,062	1,846	42,791	724
1996............................	23,628	4,783	31,955	1,655	48,731	590
1995............................	21,824	4,727	29,666	1,684	46,654	595
1994............................	19,631	4,610	30,938	1,679	48,653	579
1993............................	18,867	4,279	29,953	1,638	41,221	525
1992............................	18,719	4,054	27,457	1,429	41,439	523
1991............................	17,850	3,581	25,630	1,383	38,002	528
1990............................	18,209	3,004	26,448	1,217	32,962	607
1989............................	17,385	3,008	25,357	1,121	32,740	694
1988............................	16,760	2,802	23,689	1,204	30,802	621
1987............................	15,491	2,617	20,805	1,097	29,163	596
1986............................	14,743	2,662	21,403	1,004	27,503	564
1985............................	13,805	2,615	20,533	1,046	26,246	535
1984............................	12,890	2,396	19,330	937	24,072	561
1983............................	12,426	2,206	17,207	828	23,506	535
1982............................	11,119	2,067	15,152	747	22,959	488
1981............................	11,456	2,078	14,587	708	19,463	398
1980............................	12,393	964	15,616	283	19,960	353
1979............................	9,895	1,826	13,473	622	18,182	366
1978............................	9,026	1,689	12,870	557	15,076	389
1977............................	8,321	1,578	11,088	532	14,749	354
1976............................	7,331	1,370	10,331	547	15,013	305
1975............................	7,212	1,193	9,473	517	12,333	241
Male						
2016............................	39,407	3,004	70,026	1,531	103,465	691
2015............................	39,459	2,874	63,477	1,466	88,699	683
2014............................	37,116	2,831	60,458	1,376	91,652	653
2013............................	38,126	2,696	57,304	1,312	88,641	608
2012............................	36,043	2,804	53,983	1,210	81,253	585
2011[2]	38,029	2,654	49,390	1,155	85,528	518
2010............................	33,905	2,473	48,068	1,075	81,199	477
2009............................	35,889	2,301	55,655	1,030	78,574	467
2008............................	34,209	2,505	51,691	1,059	73,948	518
2007............................	34,035	2,492	53,029	1,155	74,351	459
2006............................	34,750	2,334	52,569	1,086	74,507	460
2005............................	33,544	2,273	52,070	1,011	77,210	444
2004............................	32,367	2,176	47,746	956	79,168	386
2003[3]	31,556	2,156	45,635	966	76,871	397
2002............................	32,764	2,283	47,018	974	75,050	321
2001............................	31,084	2,457	46,511	943	67,007	356
2000[4]	30,966	2,291	49,270	880	60,207	349

[1]For data prior to 1991, "Some college/Associate degree" equals 1 to 3 years of college completed; "Bachelor's degree" equals 4 years of college; "Advanced degree" equals 5 or more years of college completed.
[2]Starting in 2011, earnings data were created using population controls based on Census 2010 data.
[3]Starting in 2003, respondents could choose more than one race. The race data in this table from 2003 onward represent respondents who indicated only one race.
[4]Beginning in 2000, earnings data are from the expanded Current Population Survey (CPS) sample and were calculated using population controls based on Census 2000.

Table A-27. Mean Earnings of Workers 18 Years Old and Over, by Educational Attainment, Race, Hispanic Origin, and Sex, 1975–2016—*Continued*

(Dollars except as noted)

Race, sex, year, and Hispanic origin	Total		Not a high school graduate		High school graduate	
	Mean earnings	Number of workers (thousands)	Mean earnings	Number of workers (thousands)	Mean earnings	Number of workers (thousands)
1999	28,821	7,806	16,391	1,199	25,849	2,934
1998	26,090	7,488	16,013	1,190	22,698	2,974
1997	25,080	7,370	15,423	1,304	22,440	2,862
1996	25,067	7,125	15,461	1,290	22,267	2,836
1995	23,876	7,090	14,877	1,280	19,514	2,812
1994	22,614	7,009	15,984	1,191	18,527	2,818
1993	21,108	6,833	13,074	1,305	18,668	2,775
1992	19,278	6,822	12,661	1,457	16,978	2,683
1991	18,607	6,830	15,714	1,624	17,352	2,731
1990	18,859	6,781	13,031	1,563	17,046	3,013
1989	18,108	6,654	11,827	1,614	16,658	2,848
1988	17,782	6,593	12,439	1,671	16,345	2,795
1987	16,171	6,505	11,899	1,711	14,800	2,769
1986	15,441	6,326	11,248	1,691	14,214	2,666
1985	14,932	6,237	10,802	1,716	13,721	2,572
1984	13,560	5,899	10,216	1,780	12,382	2,339
1983	12,789	5,707	9,094	1,768	11,956	2,312
1982	12,203	5,535	9,153	1,798	11,952	2,213
1981	11,937	5,651	9,266	1,925	11,905	2,191
1980	11,085	5,576	8,421	2,054	11,563	2,119
1979	10,403	5,581	7,938	2,138	10,662	2,087
1978	9,651	5,350	7,423	2,156	9,869	1,982
1977	8,710	5,220	6,648	2,230	9,332	1,770
1976	7,991	5,156	6,670	2,289	8,056	1,766
1975	7,541	4,864	6,364	2,247	7,847	1,684
Female						
2016	35,576	10,524	21,023	727	24,763	2,915
2015	35,521	10,170	15,665	786	24,047	2,856
2014	32,313	10,012	18,852	674	23,785	2,868
2013	31,531	9,675	15,831	747	23,349	2,801
2012	31,808	9,544	18,178	685	22,783	2,747
2011[2]	31,455	9,343	13,893	801	23,795	2,728
2010	30,438	9,104	15,589	730	21,700	2,640
2009	29,831	9,087	15,644	756	22,964	2,806
2008	29,734	9,392	13,976	881	23,195	2,893
2007	31,317	9,365	14,869	868	24,724	3,001
2006	29,371	9,302	14,277	961	22,643	3,092
2005	27,314	9,163	14,300	968	20,449	3,051
2004	25,738	8,962	12,785	1,014	20,284	3,019
2003[3]	25,735	8,919	14,513	1,056	19,623	3,030
2002	25,131	8,868	13,748	1,075	20,209	2,989
2001	24,036	8,956	15,912	1,172	18,683	2,970
2000[4]	22,884	9,056	12,321	1,198	18,510	3,078
1999	21,694	9,130	10,734	1,194	16,506	3,178
1998	20,026	8,713	11,372	1,212	15,892	3,078
1997	19,161	8,503	10,607	1,132	15,789	3,102
1996	19,271	8,129	10,337	1,094	15,379	3,008
1995	17,485	7,757	10,739	1,108	14,473	2,641
1994	17,200	7,745	9,150	1,099	14,333	2,777
1993	16,336	7,481	8,562	1,048	13,550	2,746
1992	15,605	7,014	8,756	995	13,550	2,696
1991	15,065	7,034	9,151	1,237	12,810	2,781
1990	14,449	6,950	8,946	1,290	12,560	3,036
1989	14,122	6,946	7,827	1,269	12,701	3,046
1988	12,916	6,763	7,325	1,299	11,469	2,965
1987	12,106	6,518	7,452	1,304	11,030	2,930
1986	11,571	6,403	6,984	1,337	10,434	2,804
1985	10,904	6,190	6,879	1,293	9,918	2,651
1984	10,482	6,049	6,754	1,347	9,527	2,588
1983	9,778	5,589	6,154	1,267	9,197	2,380
1982	9,024	5,546	6,047	1,390	8,737	2,378
1981	8,225	5,437	5,404	1,589	8,088	2,197

[2]Starting in 2011, earnings data were created using population controls based on Census 2010 data.
[3]Starting in 2003, respondents could choose more than one race. The race data in this table from 2003 onward represent respondents who indicated only one race.
[4]Beginning in 2000, earnings data are from the expanded Current Population Survey (CPS) sample and were calculated using population controls based on Census 2000.

Table A-27. Mean Earnings of Workers 18 Years Old and Over, by Educational Attainment, Race, Hispanic Origin, and Sex, 1975–2016—*Continued*

(Dollars except as noted)

Race, sex, year, and Hispanic origin	Some college or associate's degree[1]		Bachelor's degree[1]		Advanced degree[1]	
	Mean earnings	Number of workers (thousands)	Mean earnings	Number of workers (thousands)	Mean earnings	Number of workers (thousands)
1999	28,442	2,338	42,530	971	59,587	365
1998	26,586	2,215	42,539	792	51,198	318
1997	27,215	2,108	35,792	818	49,940	278
1996	26,365	2,047	35,558	700	65,981	253
1995	26,846	2,047	36,026	659	57,186	293
1994	23,748	1,959	34,073	758	52,829	281
1993	21,734	1,804	35,147	721	47,372	228
1992	22,697	1,796	30,989	643	48,968	244
1991	20,548	1,570	26,075	650	43,927	255
1990	21,152	1,372	29,471	564	39,104	269
1989	20,253	1,352	27,493	515	38,166	326
1988	19,265	1,311	28,506	533	36,452	283
1987	18,081	1,250	23,345	482	34,073	294
1986	17,419	1,226	23,412	480	31,054	263
1985	16,415	1,230	23,818	477	31,947	243
1984	14,960	1,106	21,986	424	27,893	250
1983	15,113	996	20,370	363	25,466	268
1982	12,926	953	17,658	319	26,452	253
1981	13,740	1,002	16,624	327	21,082	205
1980	12,393	964	15,616	283	23,346	156
1979	11,971	931	16,161	259	21,092	166
1978	11,197	770	16,009	260	18,083	181
1977	10,023	799	12,978	234	16,385	188
1976	8,688	726	12,246	233	17,859	143
1975	8,505	599	11,318	213	13,720	121
Female						
2016	31,087	3,837	47,036	1,862	67,707	1,182
2015	30,951	3,732	48,842	1,753	75,911	1,041
2014	28,290	3,773	45,149	1,707	59,429	988
2013	27,564	3,531	44,139	1,684	61,698	909
2012	28,363	3,593	25,282	1,644	59,675	874
2011[2]	28,771	3,310	42,721	1,640	60,889	862
2010	27,805	3,453	41,653	1,520	64,586	759
2009	26,748	3,276	42,587	1,552	59,073	694
2008	27,354	3,428	42,858	1,491	60,430	697
2007	31,850	3,320	41,560	1,526	57,076	647
2006	28,706	3,246	44,326	1,417	57,206	584
2005	25,422	3,116	43,516	1,401	54,044	626
2004	24,468	3,015	38,626	1,391	55,436	522
2003[3]	24,007	2,963	41,066	1,355	54,346	514
2002	23,679	2,972	38,741	1,301	50,766	529
2001	23,511	3,023	35,448	1,269	48,080	521
2000[4]	22,937	3,140	35,719	1,179	46,416	459
1999	22,699	3,080	33,184	1,170	47,358	509
1998	20,371	2,870	31,952	1,105	40,214	448
1997	19,643	2,794	29,091	1,027	38,392	448
1996	21,581	2,736	29,311	954	35,785	337
1995	17,985	2,679	25,577	1,025	36,585	304
1994	16,589	2,651	28,356	921	44,618	297
1993	16,778	2,475	25,865	917	36,485	296
1992	15,553	2,256	24,572	786	34,902	281
1991	15,743	2,010	25,235	733	32,467	273
1990	15,734	1,632	23,837	653	28,074	338
1989	15,044	1,656	23,541	606	27,933	368
1988	14,557	1,491	19,862	671	26,072	338
1987	13,123	1,367	18,815	615	24,383	302
1986	12,459	1,436	19,562	524	24,400	301
1985	11,488	1,385	17,779	569	21,502	292
1984	11,115	1,290	17,134	513	21,000	311
1983	10,215	1,210	14,738	465	21,539	267
1982	9,574	1,114	13,284	428	19,198	235
1981	9,329	1,076	12,839	381	17,743	193

[1]For data prior to 1991, "Some college/Associate degree" equals 1 to 3 years of college completed; "Bachelor's degree" equals 4 years of college; "Advanced degree" equals 5 or more years of college completed.
[2]Starting in 2011, earnings data were created using population controls based on Census 2010 data.
[3]Starting in 2003, respondents could choose more than one race. The race data in this table from 2003 onward represent respondents who indicated only one race.
[4]Beginning in 2000, earnings data are from the expanded Current Population Survey (CPS) sample and were calculated using population controls based on Census 2000.

Table A-27. Mean Earnings of Workers 18 Years Old and Over, by Educational Attainment, Race, Hispanic Origin, and Sex, 1975–2016—*Continued*

(Dollars except as noted)

Race, sex, year, and Hispanic origin	Total		Not a high school graduate		High school graduate	
	Mean earnings	Number of workers (thousands)	Mean earnings	Number of workers (thousands)	Mean earnings	Number of workers (thousands)
1980.............................	7,684	...	4,685	...	7,508	...
1979.............................	6,940	5,275	4,448	1,638	6,866	2,180
ASIAN						
Both Sexes						
2016.............................	63,650	9,941	28,588	536	32,548	1,758
2015.............................	61,603	9,439	23,418	571	34,215	1,533
2014.............................	57,351	9,170	21,969	577	29,809	1,571
2013.............................	54,752	8,732	24,616	588	30,996	1,616
2012.............................	55,151	8,469	23,994	521	30,149	1,445
2011[2].............................	51,500	8,014	21,640	563	28,302	1,478
2010.............................	49,894	7,244	20,922	534	28,579	1,374
2009.............................	53,419	7,158	20,461	487	29,312	1,367
2008.............................	51,063	7,118	21,200	540	29,390	1,213
2007.............................	49,571	7,137	21,305	512	28,773	1,241
2006.............................	50,940	7,073	20,573	599	29,426	1,301
2005.............................	45,751	6,684	22,909	598	27,082	1,304
2004.............................	44,361	6,369	19,684	497	28,289	1,192
2003[3].............................	42,163	6,190	19,558	539	25,704	1,162
2002.............................	40,793	6,086	16,746	536	24,900	1,138
Male						
2016.............................	75,610	5,258	36,311	267	37,255	933
2015.............................	71,362	5,014	26,616	303	39,038	814
2014.............................	66,326	4,817	26,516	279	33,374	823
2013.............................	64,019	4,690	24,897	288	35,882	881
2012.............................	64,502	4,455	24,256	251	32,794	748
2011[2].............................	60,397	4,195	25,534	298	32,500	754
2010.............................	57,937	3,814	24,355	280	31,783	695
2009.............................	62,328	3,811	21,167	255	33,080	695
2008.............................	60,007	3,776	23,814	279	34,904	606
2007.............................	57,890	3,731	24,213	244	33,607	630
2006.............................	60,516	3,757	23,311	298	32,528	710
2005.............................	54,257	3,564	28,150	307	30,547	721
2004.............................	52,544	3,440	20,691	235	31,710	676
2003[3].............................	48,890	3,333	23,745	291	28,522	582
2002.............................	48,934	3,272	17,659	298	29,547	578
Female						
2016.............................	50,220	4,683	20,875	268	27,217	824
2015.............................	50,544	4,424	19,791	267	28,748	718
2014.............................	47,419	4,353	17,691	297	25,886	748
2013.............................	43,995	4,041	24,346	300	25,129	734
2012.............................	44,770	4,013	23,751	270	27,308	697
2011[2].............................	41,727	3,819	17,263	265	23,926	723
2010.............................	40,952	3,430	17,142	254	25,295	678
2009.............................	43,270	3,346	19,684	232	25,420	672
2008.............................	40,954	3,341	18,395	260	23,886	607
2007.............................	40,455	3,405	18,643	267	23,785	611
2006.............................	40,089	3,315	17,855	300	25,696	590
2005.............................	36,033	3,119	17,383	291	22,789	582
2004.............................	34,748	2,928	18,780	262	23,802	515
2003[3].............................	34,315	2,857	14,614	247	22,876	580
2002.............................	31,328	2,814	15,595	237	20,094	559
HISPANIC[5]						
Both Sexes						
2016.............................	38,276	26,936	29,264	6,260	34,751	8,477
2015.............................	37,083	26,263	25,697	6,630	31,647	8,240
2014.............................	33,944	25,254	23,747	6,819	30,329	7,869
2013.............................	32,368	24,393	22,431	6,704	28,415	7,313
2012.............................	31,596	23,811	21,087	6,545	28,097	7,462
2011[2].............................	30,739	23,027	20,953	6,583	26,681	7,176
2010.............................	29,917	21,566	20,534	6,301	26,381	6,750
2009.............................	29,565	21,551	19,816	6,667	25,998	6,753
2008.............................	30,291	21,853	21,310	6,972	27,020	6,702

[2]Starting in 2011, earnings data were created using population controls based on Census 2010 data.
[3]Starting in 2003, respondents could choose more than one race. The race data in this table from 2003 onward represent respondents who indicated only one race.
[5]May be of any race.
... = Not available.

Table A-27. Mean Earnings of Workers 18 Years Old and Over, by Educational Attainment, Race, Hispanic Origin, and Sex, 1975–2016—*Continued*

(Dollars except as noted)

Race, sex, year, and Hispanic origin	Some college or associate's degree[1]		Bachelor's degree[1]		Advanced degree[1]	
	Mean earnings	Number of workers (thousands)	Mean earnings	Number of workers (thousands)	Mean earnings	Number of workers (thousands)
1980............................	8,544	...	12,389	...	17,278	...
1979............................	7,735	895	11,555	363	15,766	200
ASIAN						
Both Sexes						
2016............................	37,793	1,996	68,610	3,022	105,557	2,627
2015............................	36,914	1,847	65,558	3,056	101,667	2,429
2014............................	32,524	1,792	64,864	3,106	97,309	2,123
2013............................	34,638	1,767	57,841	2,755	96,266	2,003
2012............................	33,239	1,744	59,507	2,717	93,772	2,040
2011[2]	35,034	1,582	57,150	2,645	87,205	1,743
2010............................	31,273	1,432	57,183	2,338	84,657	1,565
2009............................	32,958	1,356	55,730	2,376	98,871	1,569
2008............................	32,671	1,466	58,524	2,298	83,721	1,600
2007............................	34,423	1,456	54,451	2,354	81,943	1,572
2006............................	33,238	1,350	56,197	2,268	88,408	1,553
2005............................	31,460	1,337	51,064	2,108	80,145	1,335
2004............................	29,524	1,364	47,912	2,118	81,259	1,196
2003[3]	27,209	1,355	48,333	1,878	74,046	1,254
2002............................	27,340	1,325	46,628	1,911	72,852	1,174
Male						
2016............................	44,013	1,022	78,528	1,520	124,668	1,513
2015............................	39,272	894	74,452	1,587	116,397	1,414
2014............................	36,790	903	71,685	1,581	112,262	1,229
2013............................	37,731	936	66,653	1,417	112,837	1,166
2012............................	38,417	871	69,657	1,361	105,017	1,222
2011[2]	42,378	810	65,740	1,316	98,812	1,015
2010............................	35,347	741	65,448	1,181	96,699	915
2009............................	37,691	722	62,561	1,198	113,711	940
2008............................	37,283	773	67,088	1,186	97,068	931
2007............................	41,876	773	60,356	1,156	93,604	926
2006............................	37,263	658	67,144	1,150	101,676	939
2005............................	35,401	675	60,739	1,048	92,552	811
2004............................	33,798	679	56,998	1,078	90,870	770
2003[3]	31,775	673	52,508	992	83,098	793
2002............................	32,750	664	55,198	971	82,170	758
Female						
2016............................	31,258	973	58,567	1,501	79,613	1,114
2015............................	34,704	953	55,956	1,469	81,135	1,015
2014............................	28,185	888	57,793	1,525	76,741	893
2013............................	31,154	831	48,505	1,337	73,159	836
2012............................	28,077	873	49,308	1,355	76,942	817
2011[2]	27,328	772	48,647	1,329	71,001	727
2010............................	26,899	690	48,745	1,157	67,690	649
2009............................	27,574	634	48,783	1,178	76,637	628
2008............................	27,528	693	49,380	1,111	65,148	669
2007............................	25,992	683	48,748	1,197	65,206	645
2006............................	29,415	692	44,932	1,118	68,084	613
2005............................	27,439	662	41,494	1,059	60,934	524
2004............................	25,280	684	38,488	1,040	63,894	426
2003[3]	22,703	682	43,655	885	58,489	461
2002............................	21,912	661	37,766	939	55,851	415
HISPANIC[5]						
Both Sexes						
2016............................	35,288	7,404	53,283	3,421	79,831	1,373
2015............................	35,780	6,887	58,152	3,096	82,499	1,409
2014............................	33,822	6,541	52,143	2,852	73,952	1,171
2013............................	32,153	6,524	50,673	2,759	74,926	1,090
2012............................	30,694	6,042	50,592	2,707	77,985	1,054
2011[2]	31,423	5,773	47,873	2,528	78,606	966
2010............................	30,708	5,327	47,980	2,290	71,647	896
2009............................	31,004	5,036	49,017	2,256	74,675	837
2008............................	31,644	5,149	48,081	2,225	77,630	802

[1]For data prior to 1991, "Some college/Associate degree" equals 1 to 3 years of college completed; "Bachelor's degree" equals 4 years of college; "Advanced degree" equals 5 or more years of college completed.
[2]Starting in 2011, earnings data were created using population controls based on Census 2010 data.
[3]Starting in 2003, respondents could choose more than one race. The race data in this table from 2003 onward represent respondents who indicated only one race.
[5]May be of any race.

Table A-27. Mean Earnings of Workers 18 Years Old and Over, by Educational Attainment, Race, Hispanic Origin, and Sex, 1975–2016—*Continued*

(Dollars except as noted)

Race, sex, year, and Hispanic origin	Total		Not a high school graduate		High school graduate	
	Mean earnings	Number of workers (thousands)	Mean earnings	Number of workers (thousands)	Mean earnings	Number of workers (thousands)
2007	29,910	21,561	21,303	6,888	27,604	6,682
2006	29,155	21,209	20,581	7,134	27,508	6,495
2005	27,760	20,025	19,294	6,995	25,659	6,080
2004	27,263	19,343	19,025	6,935	25,823	5,740
2003[3]	25,810	18,786	18,349	6,767	23,472	5,517
2002	25,824	18,409	18,981	6,748	24,163	5,499
2001	24,786	17,575	18,334	6,533	22,866	5,265
2000[4]	23,855	17,161	17,156	6,428	22,009	5,145
1999	22,096	15,122	16,106	5,601	20,704	4,539
1998	22,117	14,372	15,832	5,281	20,978	4,219
1997	20,766	13,972	15,069	5,238	19,558	4,082
1996	19,439	13,365	13,287	5,062	18,528	3,783
1995	18,262	12,434	13,068	4,784	18,333	3,594
1994	18,568	12,035	13,733	4,686	17,323	3,444
1993	17,102	11,644	11,852	4,425	16,591	3,367
1992	16,824	10,171	11,836	3,962	16,714	2,991
1991	16,300	10,006	11,335	3,906	16,142	3,045
1990	15,943	9,729	10,368	3,929	15,417	3,282
1989	15,714	9,570	11,500	3,985	14,901	3,188
1988	15,007	9,226	11,045	3,824	14,667	2,953
1987	14,695	8,817	10,961	3,457	13,958	2,982
1986	13,558	8,393	9,896	3,379	13,389	2,835
1985	13,120	7,840	9,956	3,223	13,044	2,661
1984	12,583	7,349	9,671	3,129	12,858	2,457
1983	11,901	6,222	9,473	2,674	12,077	2,030
1982	11,307	5,914	8,498	2,583	11,539	1,967
1981	10,872	5,930	8,645	2,648	11,046	1,966
1980	10,062	5,723	8,119	2,649	10,182	1,824
1979	9,248	5,545	7,683	2,533	9,338	1,812
1978	8,460	4,898	7,138	2,345	8,512	1,554
1977	7,761	4,752	6,547	2,306	8,079	1,461
1976	7,081	4,303	5,984	2,107	7,580	1,309
1975	6,567	4,078	5,462	2,028	6,759	1,293
Male						
2016	44,237	15,189	33,701	4,124	41,541	5,136
2015	41,556	14,962	29,719	4,327	36,549	4,982
2014	38,152	14,478	27,032	4,478	34,347	4,686
2013	35,990	13,980	25,151	4,475	32,070	4,366
2012	35,423	13,622	24,012	4,379	32,313	4,460
2011[2]	34,135	13,134	24,189	4,277	29,872	4,272
2010	32,981	12,644	23,384	4,218	29,620	4,143
2009	32,279	12,643	21,588	4,486	28,908	4,109
2008	34,240	12,857	24,340	4,720	30,618	3,990
2007	33,040	12,885	23,923	4,726	30,932	4,111
2006	32,532	12,711	23,060	4,920	32,148	3,884
2005	31,008	12,015	21,623	4,744	29,471	3,667
2004	30,828	11,562	21,606	4,633	29,694	3,439
2003[3]	28,806	11,195	20,637	4,556	26,652	3,234
2002	29,084	10,979	21,611	4,506	27,992	3,205
2001	27,964	10,258	20,614	4,289	26,745	2,985
2000[4]	27,253	9,996	19,501	4,236	25,629	2,940
1999	24,970	8,713	18,020	3,592	23,736	2,597
1998	25,534	8,288	17,756	3,428	24,739	2,413
1997	23,520	8,261	17,447	3,444	22,253	2,391
1996	21,870	7,975	14,986	3,382	21,593	2,116
1995	20,312	7,337	14,774	3,140	20,882	2,039
1994	21,288	7,117	16,355	3,111	19,667	1,937
1993	19,460	6,957	13,572	2,928	18,765	1,954
1992	18,842	6,034	13,313	2,633	19,357	1,665
1991	18,516	5,932	13,133	2,548	18,582	1,705
1990	18,320	5,745	13,182	2,562	18,100	1,812
1989	18,087	5,641	13,167	2,632	17,579	1,711
1988	17,357	5,477	12,836	2,517	17,446	1,621
1987	17,048	5,248	12,823	2,281	16,774	1,616
1986	15,624	5,037	11,262	2,262	15,948	1,546

[2]Starting in 2011, earnings data were created using population controls based on Census 2010 data.
[3]Starting in 2003, respondents could choose more than one race. The race data in this table from 2003 onward represent respondents who indicated only one race.
[4]Beginning in 2000, earnings data are from the expanded Current Population Survey (CPS) sample and were calculated using population controls based on Census 2000.

Table A-27. Mean Earnings of Workers 18 Years Old and Over, by Educational Attainment, Race, Hispanic Origin, and Sex, 1975–2016—*Continued*

(Dollars except as noted)

Race, sex, year, and Hispanic origin	Some college or associate's degree[1]		Bachelor's degree[1]		Advanced degree[1]	
	Mean earnings	Number of workers (thousands)	Mean earnings	Number of workers (thousands)	Mean earnings	Number of workers (thousands)
2007............	31,040	5,000	44,696	2,114	73,111	874
2006............	31,380	4,863	45,371	2,038	70,432	678
2005............	29,836	4,467	45,933	1,775	70,916	705
2004............	29,260	4,369	45,166	1,669	69,839	629
2003[3]............	28,494	4,235	43,676	1,663	62,794	603
2002............	27,757	4,024	40,949	1,568	67,679	569
2001............	27,523	3,842	40,586	1,416	62,194	517
2000[4]............	25,276	3,737	44,661	1,395	63,908	455
1999............	24,577	3,392	36,212	1,117	55,352	472
1998............	23,091	3,289	35,014	1,156	62,583	425
1997............	22,001	3,075	33,465	1,140	58,571	437
1996............	22,209	3,096	32,955	1,027	49,873	398
1995............	19,923	2,856	30,602	866	45,612	334
1994............	21,041	2,723	29,165	844	51,898	337
1993............	19,043	2,728	30,359	799	45,034	325
1992............	19,778	2,242	28,260	702	46,736	274
1991............	19,123	2,080	26,623	665	40,154	311
1990............	19,206	1,534	25,703	601	38,075	382
1989............	18,707	1,513	28,157	535	39,273	349
1988............	18,101	1,511	23,745	596	33,843	340
1987............	16,899	1,400	23,105	644	34,413	335
1986............	16,523	1,411	22,707	471	28,316	295
1985............	15,318	1,226	20,878	458	28,357	273
1984............	14,359	1,116	19,924	381	26,327	265
1983............	13,371	976	17,972	320	24,352	222
1982............	13,108	873	18,186	303	28,167	186
1981............	12,971	834	16,114	320	24,082	161
1980............	11,891	808	15,676	283	21,910	157
1979............	10,181	768	14,940	240	18,273	190
1978............	9,575	661	13,985	213	17,333	125
1977............	8,172	656	12,572	210	16,660	118
1976............	7,252	592	11,242	177	14,000	118
1975............	7,154	474	10,573	173	15,756	111
Male						
2016............	42,172	3,652	62,670	1,643	98,834	633
2015............	40,672	3,426	69,600	1,570	95,226	655
2014............	40,192	3,331	59,791	1,439	92,887	542
2013............	37,245	3,222	59,368	1,360	89,624	555
2012............	36,238	2,949	60,552	1,308	89,780	528
2011[2]............	36,660	2,928	54,936	1,200	96,359	456
2010............	35,406	2,729	56,774	1,136	82,797	416
2009............	36,071	2,485	58,570	1,122	84,368	439
2008............	37,864	2,615	56,980	1,109	96,976	422
2007............	35,861	2,510	50,805	1,057	87,195	478
2006............	36,217	2,500	51,336	1,066	87,835	340
2005............	34,754	2,326	54,700	896	84,033	380
2004............	34,447	2,241	53,567	915	84,152	331
2003[3]............	34,157	2,193	49,298	867	71,446	344
2002............	32,935	2,112	46,115	815	73,836	338
2001............	32,595	1,962	45,445	748	75,746	272
2000[4]............	30,155	1,873	55,050	722	81,447	223
1999............	29,387	1,698	42,733	577	66,745	250
1998............	26,483	1,652	40,889	569	83,754	226
1997............	25,923	1,598	37,963	557	68,097	272
1996............	26,682	1,687	38,130	531	49,307	259
1995............	22,171	1,475	35,109	466	50,802	215
1994............	24,517	1,410	33,797	450	60,858	210
1993............	22,417	1,444	37,554	438	52,441	194
1992............	23,033	1,193	33,430	380	53,645	164
1991............	21,974	1,131	31,699	356	45,873	193
1990............	22,376	852	31,485	314	47,479	205
1989............	22,374	810	32,767	292	49,088	196
1988............	21,631	811	26,935	333	40,916	194
1987............	19,414	758	26,581	383	39,014	211
1986............	19,675	778	27,427	274	32,538	176

[1]For data prior to 1991, "Some college/Associate degree" equals 1 to 3 years of college completed; "Bachelor's degree" equals 4 years of college; "Advanced degree" equals 5 or more years of college completed.
[2]Starting in 2011, earnings data were created using population controls based on Census 2010 data.
[3]Starting in 2003, respondents could choose more than one race. The race data in this table from 2003 onward represent respondents who indicated only one race.
[4]Beginning in 2000, earnings data are from the expanded Current Population Survey (CPS) sample and were calculated using population controls based on Census 2000.

Table A-27. Mean Earnings of Workers 18 Years Old and Over, by Educational Attainment, Race, Hispanic Origin, and Sex, 1975–2016—*Continued*

(Dollars except as noted)

Race, sex, year, and Hispanic origin	Total		Not a high school graduate		High school graduate	
	Mean earnings	Number of workers (thousands)	Mean earnings	Number of workers (thousands)	Mean earnings	Number of workers (thousands)
1985............................	15,293	4,702	11,671	2,111	15,602	1,491
1984............................	14,957	4,344	11,441	2,022	15,763	1,319
1983............................	14,265	3,577	11,353	1,678	14,584	1,074
1982............................	13,484	3,480	10,108	1,622	13,883	1,083
1981[2]........................	13,052	3,504	10,447	1,686	13,513	1,037
1980............................	12,310	3,401	9,825	1,707	13,108	961
1979............................	11,332	3,269	9,393	1,615	11,714	952
1978............................	10,473	2,915	8,836	1,498	10,940	815
1977............................	9,655	2,833	8,192	1,460	10,386	776
1976............................	8,787	2,571	7,440	1,321	9,640	712
1975............................	8,162	2,456	6,745	1,287	8,546	691
Female						
2016............................	30,569	11,747	20,694	2,135	24,313	3,340
2015............................	31,160	11,301	18,138	2,302	24,151	3,258
2014............................	28,291	10,775	17,461	2,340	24,412	3,183
2013............................	27,504	10,412	16,971	2,229	22,999	2,946
2012............................	26,479	10,189	15,174	2,166	21,832	3,001
2011[2]........................	26,230	9,892	14,949	2,305	21,988	2,904
2010............................	25,574	8,921	14,763	2,083	21,234	2,607
2009............................	25,713	8,907	16,170	2,180	21,473	2,644
2008............................	24,646	8,995	14,960	2,552	21,725	2,712
2007............................	25,262	8,676	15,574	2,162	22,283	2,570
2006............................	24,104	8,497	15,072	2,214	20,608	2,611
2005............................	22,887	8,009	14,365	2,250	19,864	2,413
2004............................	21,967	7,781	13,830	2,302	20,037	2,300
2003[3]........................	21,391	7,591	13,632	2,210	18,967	2,283
2002............................	21,008	7,430	13,694	2,241	18,810	2,293
2001............................	20,330	7,316	13,976	2,243	17,786	2,279
2000[4]........................	19,115	7,164	12,622	2,191	17,180	2,204
1999............................	18,187	6,409	12,684	2,010	16,653	1,943
1998............................	17,461	6,804	12,273	1,854	15,952	1,806
1997............................	16,781	5,711	10,503	1,794	15,747	1,691
1996............................	15,841	5,390	9,867	1,680	14,635	1,667
1995............................	15,310	5,096	9,809	1,644	14,989	1,555
1994............................	14,631	4,918	8,559	1,576	14,313	1,508
1993............................	13,602	4,687	8,489	1,498	13,584	1,413
1992............................	13,880	4,137	8,913	1,330	13,396	1,326
1991............................	13,069	4,072	4,809	1,358	13,043	1,339
1990............................	12,516	3,984	5,093	1,367	12,109	1,470
1989............................	12,307	3,929	8,256	1,353	11,799	1,477
1988............................	11,573	3,749	7,597	1,307	11,284	1,332
1987............................	11,234	3,569	7,350	1,176	10,627	1,366
1986............................	10,457	3,356	7,130	1,117	10,319	1,289
1985............................	9,865	3,138	6,699	1,112	9,784	1,170
1984............................	9,150	3,005	6,438	1,107	9,492	1,138
1983............................	8,704	2,645	6,305	996	9,261	956
1982............................	8,195	2,434	5,781	961	8,668	884
1981............................	7,723	2,426	5,486	962	8,292	929
1980............................	6,770	2,322	5,028	942	6,923	863
1979............................	6,255	2,276	4,675	918	6,708	860
1978............................	5,501	1,983	4,135	847	5,834	739
1977............................	4,964	1,919	3,707	846	5,466	685
1976............................	4,548	1,732	3,537	786	5,124	597
1975............................	4,152	1,622	3,233	741	4,708	602
WHITE ALONE OR IN COMBINATION						
Both Sexes						
2016............................	52,885	129,984	28,492	9,901	38,170	34,183
2015............................	50,981	129,762	26,268	10,609	36,948	33,995
2014............................	48,772	127,557	25,894	10,790	35,354	34,216
2013............................	47,280	127,029	24,264	10,470	34,101	34,391
2012............................	46,650	126,527	22,019	10,696	33,803	34,058
2011[2]........................	45,898	125,256	21,648	11,080	33,584	34,425
2010............................	44,023	125,712	21,388	11,004	31,990	35,140
2009............................	43,213	127,001	20,468	11,708	31,351	36,656

[2]Starting in 2011, earnings data were created using population controls based on Census 2010 data.
[3]Starting in 2003, respondents could choose more than one race. The race data in this table from 2003 onward represent respondents who indicated only one race.
[4]Beginning in 2000, earnings data are from the expanded Current Population Survey (CPS) sample and were calculated using population controls based on Census 2000.

Table A-27. Mean Earnings of Workers 18 Years Old and Over, by Educational Attainment, Race, Hispanic Origin, and Sex, 1975–2016—*Continued*

(Dollars except as noted)

Race, sex, year, and Hispanic origin	Some college or associate's degree[1]		Bachelor's degree[1]		Advanced degree[1]	
	Mean earnings	Number of workers (thousands)	Mean earnings	Number of workers (thousands)	Mean earnings	Number of workers (thousands)
1985................................	18,168	678	24,723	267	32,831	155
1984................................	17,261	611	23,835	223	30,727	168
1983................................	16,626	514	21,911	170	28,680	141
1982................................	15,560	495	22,565	153	34,474	125
1981................................	15,432	489	19,201	177	27,619	114
1980................................	14,331	451	19,224	167	24,642	114
1979................................	12,489	441	18,923	142	21,299	118
1978................................	11,545	393	16,898	127	20,702	82
1977................................	9,924	391	15,189	120	19,025	85
1976................................	8,843	342	13,650	114	16,184	81
1975................................	8,807	279	12,881	113	17,991	86
Female						
2016................................	28,587	3,752	44,608	1,778	63,592	740
2015................................	30,937	3,460	46,372	1,525	71,443	754
2014................................	27,210	3,209	44,347	1,412	57,642	629
2013................................	27,184	3,302	42,216	1,398	59,686	535
2012................................	25,408	3,093	41,277	1,398	66,273	528
2011[2]	26,032	2,844	41,483	1,327	62,746	510
2010................................	25,771	2,597	39,321	1,153	61,967	479
2009................................	26,065	2,550	39,566	1,134	64,405	398
2008................................	25,226	2,534	39,231	1,115	56,175	380
2007................................	26,179	2,489	38,584	1,057	56,129	396
2006................................	26,260	2,362	38,825	971	52,896	337
2005................................	24,493	2,141	37,003	879	55,554	324
2004................................	23,796	2,127	34,949	753	53,887	297
2003[3]	22,411	2,042	37,550	795	51,294	258
2002................................	22,035	1,911	35,357	753	58,623	230
2001................................	22,229	1,879	35,142	668	47,176	245
2000[4]	20,372	1,864	33,489	672	47,057	232
1999................................	19,754	1,694	29,249	540	42,503	222
1998................................	20,460	1,639	29,317	587	38,422	200
1997................................	17,759	1,477	29,173	584	43,051	165
1996................................	16,856	1,409	27,407	495	50,960	139
1995................................	17,521	1,380	25,338	399	36,255	118
1994................................	17,309	1,313	23,867	393	37,269	127
1993................................	15,250	1,284	21,627	361	34,001	131
1992................................	16,076	1,049	22,160	322	34,551	110
1991................................	15,721	948	20,791	309	30,721	117
1990................................	15,245	682	19,378	287	27,184	177
1989................................	14,482	703	22,617	243	26,700	153
1988................................	14,012	700	19,707	263	24,444	146
1987................................	13,929	642	18,003	261	26,584	124
1986................................	12,648	633	16,142	197	22,071	119
1985................................	11,791	548	15,503	191	22,480	118
1984................................	10,848	505	14,404	158	18,706	97
1983................................	9,750	462	13,507	150	16,817	81
1982................................	9,896	378	13,719	150	15,244	61
1981................................	9,483	345	12,292	143	15,503	47
1980................................	8,808	357	10,568	116	14,668	43
1979................................	7,069	327	9,168	98	13,313	72
1978................................	6,686	268	9,684	86	10,908	43
1977................................	5,588	265	9,082	90	10,569	33
1976................................	5,075	250	6,884	63	9,218	37
1975................................	4,790	195	6,226	60	8,067	25
WHITE ALONE OR IN COMBINATION						
Both Sexes						
2016................................	41,339	38,480	68,292	30,471	95,331	16,947
2015................................	39,835	38,596	66,733	29,682	92,570	16,877
2014................................	39,403	37,756	63,404	28,754	88,614	16,039
2013................................	37,330	38,164	60,859	28,374	91,349	15,627
2012................................	36,751	38,544	61,399	28,072	90,761	15,154
2011[2]	36,139	37,718	61,173	27,455	89,895	14,575
2010................................	35,139	37,717	59,055	27,266	84,972	14,582
2009................................	35,540	37,684	57,662	26,920	86,067	14,031

[1]For data prior to 1991, "Some college/Associate degree" equals 1 to 3 years of college completed; "Bachelor's degree" equals 4 years of college; "Advanced degree" equals 5 or more years of college completed.
[2]Starting in 2011, earnings data were created using population controls based on Census 2010 data.
[3]Starting in 2003, respondents could choose more than one race. The race data in this table from 2003 onward represent respondents who indicated only one race.
[4]Beginning in 2000, earnings data are from the expanded Current Population Survey (CPS) sample and were calculated using population controls based on Census 2000.

Table A-27. Mean Earnings of Workers 18 Years Old and Over, by Educational Attainment, Race, Hispanic Origin, and Sex, 1975–2016—*Continued*

(Dollars except as noted)

Race, sex, year, and Hispanic origin	Total		Not a high school graduate		High school graduate	
	Mean earnings	Number of workers (thousands)	Mean earnings	Number of workers (thousands)	Mean earnings	Number of workers (thousands)
2008............................	43,550	129,419	21,483	12,630	32,072	37,299
2007............................	43,000	129,203	22,245	12,568	32,126	37,570
2006............................	42,249	128,366	21,389	13,800	31,998	37,915
2005............................	40,592	126,882	20,225	13,424	30,494	37,723
2004............................	38,855	125,387	19,365	13,539	29,595	37,639
2003[3]........................	37,958	124,456	18,734	16,282	27,915	45,064
2002............................	37,290	124,337	19,278	13,957	28,107	37,863
Male						
2016............................	62,320	69,912	33,197	6,429	45,231	20,309
2015............................	60,364	69,837	31,168	6,866	43,502	20,177
2014............................	58,148	68,611	30,224	6,989	41,291	20,145
2013............................	55,973	68,402	28,083	6,948	39,102	20,165
2012............................	55,544	68,068	25,701	6,940	39,910	19,715
2011[2]........................	54,835	67,254	25,719	7,030	40,105	19,864
2010............................	52,152	67,831	25,023	7,117	37,378	20,333
2009............................	51,133	68,426	23,327	7,561	36,321	21,162
2008............................	52,502	69,829	25,254	8,263	37,740	21,192
2007............................	51,599	70,073	25,848	8,305	38,072	21,436
2006............................	50,826	69,702	24,524	9,055	38,699	21,401
2005............................	49,437	68,987	23,526	8,740	36,608	21,289
2004............................	47,275	67,758	22,576	8,751	35,348	21,073
2003[3]........................	45,989	67,198	21,787	8,682	34,225	20,534
2002............................	45,682	67,082	22,601	8,977	33,846	20,430
Female						
2016............................	41,905	60,071	19,780	3,472	27,833	13,873
2015............................	40,046	59,924	17,281	3,743	27,376	13,817
2014............................	37,859	58,945	17,930	3,801	26,854	14,070
2013............................	37,138	58,627	16,731	3,522	27,011	14,226
2012............................	36,293	58,458	15,217	3,756	25,408	14,343
2011[2]........................	35,534	58,001	14,581	4,050	24,687	14,561
2010............................	34,497	57,881	14,733	3,887	24,593	14,807
2009............................	33,961	58,574	15,254	4,146	24,561	15,494
2008............................	33,060	59,590	14,345	4,366	24,615	16,107
2007............................	32,810	59,130	15,226	4,263	24,226	16,134
2006............................	32,059	58,663	15,408	4,745	23,313	16,514
2005............................	30,053	57,895	14,066	4,684	22,574	16,434
2004............................	28,954	57,629	13,498	4,788	22,277	16,565
2003[3]........................	28,532	57,257	14,086	4,684	22,029	16,926
2002............................	27,457	57,254	13,286	4,979	21,381	17,433
NON-HISPANIC WHITE ALONE OR IN COMBINATION						
Both Sexes						
2016............................	56,249	105,396	27,150	4,117	39,070	26,546
2015............................	54,138	105,849	26,738	4,515	38,446	26,400
2014............................	51,984	104,543	28,791	4,447	36,673	27,032
2013............................	50,424	104,642	26,562	4,238	35,470	27,636
2012............................	48,727	104,714	23,002	4,588	35,260	27,261
2011[2]........................	48,950	104,217	22,468	4,960	35,205	27,811
2010............................	46,754	105,350	22,413	4,982	33,207	28,787
2009............................	45,813	106,618	21,241	5,331	32,478	30,276
2008............................	46,050	108,823	21,579	5,959	33,105	30,982
2007............................	45,393	108,929	22,945	6,040	32,992	31,288
2006............................	44,652	108,297	22,094	6,995	32,844	31,802
2005............................	42,839	107,945	21,088	6,744	31,367	31,951
2004............................	40,847	107,086	19,667	6,892	30,195	32,216
2003[3]........................	39,989	106,658	19,764	6,906	29,561	32,225
2002............................	39,135	107,050	19,491	7,516	28,714	32,758
Male						
2016............................	66,808	55,923	32,056	2,622	46,245	15,570
2015............................	64,884	56,124	33,003	2,862	45,533	15,559
2014............................	62,883	55,277	34,929	2,799	43,134	15,831
2013............................	60,564	55,448	32,072	2,770	40,829	16,130
2012............................	60,103	55,462	27,899	2,824	41,984	15,644

[2]Starting in 2011, earnings data were created using population controls based on Census 2010 data.
[3]Starting in 2003, respondents could choose more than one race. The race data in this table from 2003 onward represent respondents who indicated only one race.

Table A-27. Mean Earnings of Workers 18 Years Old and Over, by Educational Attainment, Race, Hispanic Origin, and Sex, 1975–2016—*Continued*

(Dollars except as noted)

Race, sex, year, and Hispanic origin	Some college or associate's degree[1]		Bachelor's degree[1]		Advanced degree[1]	
	Mean earnings	Number of workers (thousands)	Mean earnings	Number of workers (thousands)	Mean earnings	Number of workers (thousands)
2008............................	35,528	38,593	59,824	26,784	84,687	14,111
2007............................	35,565	38,664	58,565	26,583	82,309	13,816
2006............................	35,276	37,530	57,807	26,035	83,002	13,084
2005............................	34,279	38,149	55,758	24,919	81,437	12,665
2004............................	32,736	37,287	52,790	24,361	78,747	12,560
2003[3]	31,498	44,048	51,206	28,672	74,601	14,592
2002............................	31,767	36,639	52,509	23,865	73,773	12,011
Male						
2016............................	49,685	19,464	83,750	15,397	116,488	8,312
2015............................	47,616	19,353	82,230	15,086	115,139	8,353
2014............................	48,193	18,921	78,225	14,611	112,251	7,943
2013............................	45,088	19,129	73,958	14,346	117,941	7,813
2012............................	44,814	19,246	74,396	14,465	113,877	7,700
2011[2]	44,135	18,674	73,557	14,163	112,265	7,521
2010............................	42,130	18,666	71,793	14,222	105,700	7,492
2009............................	42,760	18,567	71,166	13,886	106,451	7,248
2008............................	43,307	19,210	75,024	13,734	107,065	7,428
2007............................	42,760	19,343	73,390	13,697	103,214	7,291
2006............................	42,605	18,686	71,602	13,443	103,097	7,116
2005............................	42,139	18,954	69,821	13,045	102,904	6,957
2004............................	40,627	18,361	65,498	12,728	99,534	6,842
2003[3]	39,555	18,421	65,237	12,774	93,792	6,785
2002............................	39,439	18,377	65,548	12,621	92,575	6,675
Female						
2016............................	32,797	19,015	52,505	15,074	74,966	8,635
2015............................	32,010	19,243	50,716	14,596	70,453	8,523
2014............................	30,572	18,835	48,092	14,143	65,422	8,095
2013............................	29,534	19,035	47,464	14,028	64,762	7,814
2012............................	28,709	19,298	47,584	13,607	66,881	7,454
2011[2]	28,299	19,044	47,976	13,292	66,041	7,053
2010............................	28,290	19,051	45,165	13,044	63,069	7,090
2009............................	28,528	19,116	43,275	13,034	64,283	6,782
2008............................	27,819	19,383	43,826	13,050	59,814	6,683
2007............................	28,362	19,321	42,807	12,886	58,951	6,525
2006............................	28,008	18,844	43,078	12,591	59,042	5,968
2005............................	25,518	19,194	40,306	11,873	55,273	5,707
2004............................	25,079	18,925	38,886	11,632	53,859	5,717
2003[3]	25,093	18,616	37,750	11,476	53,021	5,552
2002............................	24,046	18,261	37,872	11,243	50,255	5,336
NON-HISPANIC WHITE ALONE OR IN COMBINATION						
Both Sexes						
2016............................	42,644	31,746	69,962	27,347	96,379	15,729
2015............................	40,705	32,404	67,469	26,896	93,459	15,633
2014............................	40,306	31,919	64,462	26,162	89,586	14,981
2013............................	38,177	32,311	61,814	25,858	92,592	14,598
2012............................	37,275	33,054	62,395	25,607	91,442	14,202
2011[2]	36,916	32,528	62,300	25,217	90,442	13,699
2010............................	35,855	32,746	59,993	25,101	85,771	13,732
2009............................	36,163	32,964	58,398	24,814	86,674	13,231
2008............................	36,042	33,806	60,818	24,717	84,996	13,358
2007............................	36,176	33,994	59,637	24,622	82,840	12,983
2006............................	35,795	32,962	58,785	24,103	83,629	12,433
2005............................	34,824	33,991	56,441	23,253	81,944	12,003
2004............................	33,192	33,200	53,335	22,814	79,166	11,961
2003[3]	32,732	33,062	52,823	22,686	76,029	11,777
2002............................	32,210	32,876	53,244	22,415	74,011	11,482
Male						
2016............................	51,344	16,121	86,032	13,879	117,742	7,730
2015............................	48,967	16,271	83,328	13,664	116,296	7,766
2014............................	49,537	15,922	80,000	13,283	113,429	7,439
2013............................	46,426	16,176	75,330	13,088	119,984	7,282
2012............................	46,207	16,520	75,609	13,257	115,320	7,215

[1]For data prior to 1991, "Some college/Associate degree" equals 1 to 3 years of college completed; "Bachelor's degree" equals 4 years of college; "Advanced degree" equals 5 or more years of college completed.
[2]Starting in 2011, earnings data were created using population controls based on Census 2010 data.
[3]Starting in 2003, respondents could choose more than one race. The race data in this table from 2003 onward represent respondents who indicated only one race.

Table A-27. Mean Earnings of Workers 18 Years Old and Over, by Educational Attainment, Race, Hispanic Origin, and Sex, 1975–2016—*Continued*

(Dollars except as noted)

Race, sex, year, and Hispanic origin	Total		Not a high school graduate		High school graduate	
	Mean earnings	Number of workers (thousands)	Mean earnings	Number of workers (thousands)	Mean earnings	Number of workers (thousands)
2011[2]	59,346	55,152	27,620	3,049	42,612	15,908
2010	56,252	55,855	27,218	3,086	39,192	16,430
2009	55,161	56,390	25,612	3,262	38,049	17,253
2008	56,357	57,636	26,226	3,743	39,288	17,435
2007	55,457	57,886	27,810	3,800	39,602	17,567
2006	54,624	57,615	25,996	4,358	40,034	17,723
2005	53,084	57,553	25,469	4,213	38,034	17,787
2004	50,488	56,761	23,520	4,287	36,323	17,817
2003[3]	49,227	56,549	22,947	4,313	35,550	17,549
2002	48,700	56,714	23,426	4,663	34,830	17,446
Female						
2016	44,314	49,473	18,546	1,495	28,808	10,886
2015	42,009	49,725	15,893	1,653	28,275	10,840
2014	39,755	49,266	18,362	1,647	27,542	11,201
2013	38,994	49,193	16,163	1,468	27,957	11,505
2012	38,106	49,251	15,161	1,763	26,205	11,617
2011[2]	37,264	49,065	14,246	1,910	25,304	11,902
2010	36,034	49,495	14,590	1,895	25,249	12,356
2009	35,318	50,227	14,347	2,068	25,096	13,022
2008	34,445	51,187	13,726	2,215	25,148	13,547
2007	33,979	51,043	14,690	2,239	24,530	13,721
2006	33,316	50,682	15,642	2,636	23,794	14,079
2005	31,139	50,391	13,793	2,530	22,994	14,163
2004	29,972	50,324	13,325	2,605	22,613	14,399
2003[3]	29,564	50,108	14,469	2,592	22,479	14,765
2002	28,359	50,335	13,060	2,853	21,745	15,312
BLACK ALONE OR IN COMBINATION						
Both Sexes						
2016	40,580	20,976	24,895	1,638	30,186	6,459
2015	39,326	20,228	19,655	1,677	29,060	6,260
2014	36,922	19,750	22,204	1,514	28,241	6,204
2013	35,571	19,045	20,951	1,726	26,594	5,960
2012	34,798	18,798	18,964	1,599	26,408	5,885
2011[2]	34,640	18,098	17,330	1,701	27,323	5,766
2010	32,934	17,524	17,406	1,641	25,842	5,709
2009	33,294	17,389	18,841	1,691	26,805	5,972
2008	32,878	18,157	18,049	1,826	27,123	6,220
2007	33,318	18,023	17,555	1,903	27,096	6,149
2006	32,384	17,721	17,842	1,995	26,290	6,305
2005	30,521	17,540	17,264	2,097	23,810	6,246
2004	29,031	17,109	17,821	2,085	23,458	6,298
2003[3]	28,854	16,871	16,238	2,177	23,956	6,082
2002	28,255	16,833	17,114	2,217	22,762	5,940
Male						
2016	46,496	9,842	28,803	868	35,148	3,389
2015	43,773	9,472	23,797	848	33,581	3,287
2014	42,302	9,139	25,531	802	32,701	3,179
2013	40,318	8,860	25,377	934	29,742	3,044
2012	38,147	8,772	19,877	869	29,982	3,033
2011[2]	38,722	8,350	20,704	861	31,081	2,927
2010	35,899	8,067	19,116	875	29,746	2,974
2009	37,500	7,963	21,585	912	30,541	3,087
2008	36,386	8,442	21,894	913	30,690	3,263
2007	35,669	8,405	19,932	1,019	29,508	3,083
2006	36,026	8,170	21,361	1,006	29,973	3,146
2005	34,258	8,127	19,996	1,093	27,189	3,142
2004	32,919	7,884	22,755	1,049	26,575	3,202
2003[3]	32,574	7,689	17,982	1,088	28,323	2,981
2002	31,967	7,734	20,537	1,114	25,510	2,902
Female						
2016	35,351	11,134	20,483	769	24,709	3,069
2015	35,411	10,756	15,420	829	24,060	2,972

[2]Starting in 2011, earnings data were created using population controls based on Census 2010 data.
[3]Starting in 2003, respondents could choose more than one race. The race data in this table from 2003 onward represent respondents who indicated only one race.

Table A-27. Mean Earnings of Workers 18 Years Old and Over, by Educational Attainment, Race, Hispanic Origin, and Sex, 1975–2016—*Continued*

(Dollars except as noted)

Race, sex, year, and Hispanic origin	Some college or associate's degree[1]		Bachelor's degree[1]		Advanced degree[1]	
	Mean earnings	Number of workers (thousands)	Mean earnings	Number of workers (thousands)	Mean earnings	Number of workers (thousands)
2011[2]	45,417	16,018	75,075	13,067	112,884	7,108
2010	43,238	16,108	72,990	13,140	106,988	7,088
2009	43,680	16,218	72,222	12,834	107,782	6,821
2008	44,075	16,739	76,560	12,692	107,540	7,025
2007	43,707	16,973	75,109	12,715	104,236	6,830
2006	43,491	16,320	73,244	12,424	103,794	6,787
2005	43,083	16,769	70,891	12,187	103,850	6,593
2004	41,490	16,259	66,467	11,869	100,220	6,527
2003[3]	40,196	16,358	66,368	11,946	94,830	6,471
2002	40,195	16,390	66,776	11,859	100,412	6,510
Female						
2016	33,667	15,625	53,401	13,468	75,732	7,998
2015	32,372	16,132	51,092	13,232	70,913	7,866
2014	31,118	15,997	48,436	12,879	66,065	7,541
2013	29,907	16,135	47,960	12,769	65,324	7,315
2012	29,250	16,534	48,210	12,349	66,783	6,986
2011[2]	28,668	16,510	48,561	12,150	66,241	6,591
2010	28,707	16,637	45,715	11,960	63,134	6,644
2009	28,882	16,745	43,589	11,980	64,211	6,409
2008	28,163	17,067	44,203	12,025	59,983	6,332
2007	28,665	17,020	43,115	11,907	59,092	6,153
2006	28,248	16,641	43,402	11,678	59,389	5,646
2005	26,782	17,222	40,527	11,065	55,242	5,409
2004	25,228	16,940	39,092	10,945	53,875	5,433
2003[3]	25,422	16,704	37,757	10,739	53,102	5,306
2002	24,271	16,485	38,042	10,556	49,827	5,127
BLACK ALONE OR IN COMBINATION						
Both Sexes						
2016	34,166	7,299	57,751	3,598	79,881	1,981
2015	34,345	7,059	55,584	3,393	81,381	1,837
2014	31,932	7,047	52,652	3,257	71,738	1,725
2013	31,867	6,541	49,351	3,229	72,413	1,587
2012	31,438	6,743	49,385	3,021	69,209	1,548
2011[2]	32,580	6,274	45,809	2,922	70,880	1,433
2010	30,521	6,172	44,519	2,712	71,305	1,288
2009	30,451	5,823	47,773	2,696	67,075	1,205
2008	30,266	6,207	46,983	2,654	66,247	1,248
2007	32,580	6,056	46,555	2,761	64,714	1,152
2006	31,175	5,759	47,740	2,580	64,563	1,080
2005	28,817	5,576	47,641	2,501	63,065	1,118
2004	27,801	5,369	42,131	2,414	64,545	941
2003[3]	27,095	5,296	42,991	2,374	63,966	940
2002	27,582	5,441	42,099	2,348	60,458	884
Male						
2016	38,631	3,230	70,663	1,626	101,400	727
2015	39,238	3,084	63,992	1,537	90,477	714
2014	37,034	3,034	60,583	1,446	91,907	675
2013	37,568	2,852	56,800	1,387	88,936	640
2012	35,733	2,973	54,486	1,270	81,457	625
2011[2]	37,776	2,799	50,163	1,218	87,635	543
2010	34,307	2,592	48,406	1,117	81,533	507
2009	35,842	2,409	55,824	1,068	79,551	485
2008	34,159	2,631	52,773	1,103	73,362	530
2007	33,845	2,621	52,951	1,200	75,355	480
2006	34,784	2,417	52,382	1,124	74,769	475
2005	33,449	2,380	53,556	1,049	76,407	462
2004	32,466	2,258	47,448	976	77,648	398
2003[3]	31,591	2,233	45,705	982	76,954	402
2002	32,696	2,375	46,942	1,009	76,003	332
Female						
2016	30,622	4,069	47,094	1,971	67,406	1,254
2015	30,548	3,974	48,620	1,855	75,598	1,123

[1]For data prior to 1991, "Some college/Associate degree" equals 1 to 3 years of college completed; "Bachelor's degree" equals 4 years of college; "Advanced degree" equals 5 or more years of college completed.
[2]Starting in 2011, earnings data were created using population controls based on Census 2010 data.
[3]Starting in 2003, respondents could choose more than one race. The race data in this table from 2003 onward represent respondents who indicated only one race.

Table A-27. Mean Earnings of Workers 18 Years Old and Over, by Educational Attainment, Race, Hispanic Origin, and Sex, 1975–2016—*Continued*

(Dollars except as noted)

Race, sex, year, and Hispanic origin	Total		Not a high school graduate		High school graduate	
	Mean earnings	Number of workers (thousands)	Mean earnings	Number of workers (thousands)	Mean earnings	Number of workers (thousands)
2014............................	32,288	10,611	18,457	712	23,553	3,025
2013............................	31,442	10,185	15,723	791	23,309	2,916
2012............................	31,867	10,026	17,876	730	22,606	2,851
2011[2].........................	31,144	9,748	13,869	840	23,449	2,839
2010............................	30,405	9,456	15,449	765	21,597	2,735
2009............................	29,740	9,426	15,631	779	22,805	2,884
2008............................	29,829	9,715	14,204	913	23,187	2,957
2007............................	31,263	9,618	14,816	884	24,669	3,065
2006............................	29,268	9,551	14,257	988	22,622	3,159
2005............................	27,295	9,413	14,289	1,003	20,389	3,104
2004............................	25,707	9,224	12,818	1,035	20,236	3,096
2003[3].........................	25,739	9,182	14,495	1,089	19,765	3,100
2002............................	25,099	9,098	13,656	1,103	20,137	3,038
ASIAN ALONE OR IN COMBINATION						
Both Sexes						
2016............................	62,413	10,599	27,996	567	32,276	1,866
2015............................	60,892	10,057	23,340	591	33,847	1,652
2014............................	56,577	9,805	21,960	610	29,376	1,703
2013............................	54,320	9,367	24,499	613	31,088	1,726
2012............................	54,277	9,067	23,974	543	30,241	1,555
2011[2].........................	50,943	8,587	21,649	592	28,304	1,609
2010............................	49,145	7,711	20,791	555	28,544	1,468
2009............................	61,575	4,022	20,995	267	32,985	747
2008............................	50,622	7,553	21,195	569	29,163	1,300
2007............................	48,865	7,563	21,399	530	28,524	1,331
2006............................	50,094	7,501	20,142	631	29,502	1,413
2005............................	45,269	7,131	22,330	629	27,059	1,413
2004............................	43,856	6,771	19,536	524	27,946	1,292
2003[3].........................	41,563	6,560	19,548	564	25,554	1,256
2002............................	40,323	6,424	16,969	559	25,038	1,221
Male						
2016............................	74,131	5,602	34,904	289	37,283	984
2015............................	70,202	5,322	26,205	315	38,246	886
2014............................	65,545	5,124	26,738	294	32,798	887
2013............................	63,189	5,032	24,585	302	36,133	951
2012............................	63,269	4,759	24,720	262	32,762	819
2011[2].........................	59,326	4,489	25,638	318	32,392	828
2010............................	56,907	4,048	24,137	292	31,788	741
2009............................	61,575	4,022	20,995	267	32,985	747
2008............................	59,565	4,007	23,204	297	34,568	655
2007............................	56,990	3,945	24,261	254	33,105	685
2006............................	59,328	3,980	22,631	318	32,716	783
2005............................	53,761	3,797	27,107	328	30,490	790
2004............................	52,032	3,633	20,799	251	31,194	730
2003[3].........................	48,062	3,522	23,122	308	28,514	635
2002............................	48,128	3,469	18,101	312	29,493	633
Female						
2016............................	49,273	4,996	20,803	277	26,695	882
2015............................	50,426	4,734	20,074	276	28,752	765
2014............................	46,761	4,681	17,496	315	25,652	815
2013............................	44,026	4,335	24,416	311	24,895	775
2012............................	44,342	4,307	23,277	280	27,432	735
2011[2].........................	41,759	4,097	17,012	274	23,973	781
2010............................	40,566	3,663	17,055	262	25,230	726
2009............................	42,848	3,561	20,121	239	25,448	713
2008............................	40,518	3,546	18,999	272	23,665	644
2007............................	40,002	3,617	18,753	275	23,660	645
2006............................	39,652	3,520	17,610	313	25,508	630
2005............................	35,593	3,333	17,122	301	22,703	622
2004............................	34,387	3,137	18,375	273	23,721	561
2003[3].........................	34,031	3,038	15,233	255	22,530	621
2002............................	31,157	2,954	15,536	247	20,242	588

[2]Starting in 2011, earnings data were created using population controls based on Census 2010 data.
[3]Starting in 2003, respondents could choose more than one race. The race data in this table from 2003 onward represent respondents who indicated only one race.

Table A-27. Mean Earnings of Workers 18 Years Old and Over, by Educational Attainment, Race, Hispanic Origin, and Sex, 1975–2016—*Continued*

(Dollars except as noted)

Race, sex, year, and Hispanic origin	Some college or associate's degree[1]		Bachelor's degree[1]		Advanced degree[1]	
	Mean earnings	Number of workers (thousands)	Mean earnings	Number of workers (thousands)	Mean earnings	Number of workers (thousands)
2014...........................	28,073	4,013	46,315	1,810	58,757	1,050
2013...........................	27,457	3,688	43,738	1,841	61,233	946
2012...........................	28,051	3,769	45,688	1,751	60,912	923
2011[2]	28,395	3,475	42,696	1,704	60,632	889
2010...........................	27,779	3,579	41,796	1,595	64,662	781
2009...........................	26,646	3,414	42,487	1,627	58,664	719
2008...........................	27,399	3,575	42,861	1,550	60,996	718
2007...........................	31,614	3,435	41,636	1,561	57,105	672
2006...........................	28,565	3,342	44,157	1,456	56,541	605
2005...........................	25,366	3,195	43,369	1,452	53,669	656
2004...........................	24,415	3,111	38,522	1,438	54,931	543
2003[3]	23,816	3,063	41,073	1,391	54,265	538
2002...........................	23,621	3,066	38,447	1,339	51,101	552
ASIAN ALONE OR IN COMBINATION						
Both Sexes						
2016...........................	37,279	2,246	67,706	3,189	104,680	2,729
2015...........................	38,217	2,051	64,314	3,259	101,782	2,501
2014...........................	32,506	1,974	64,665	3,294	96,335	2,222
2013...........................	33,613	1,984	58,218	2,948	96,346	2,094
2012...........................	32,728	1,989	58,891	2,865	93,791	2,113
2011[2]	34,825	1,796	57,118	2,784	87,273	1,804
2010...........................	30,951	1,608	56,521	2,459	84,367	1,621
2009...........................	37,106	793	62,504	1,237	113,267	976
2008...........................	32,577	1,630	58,179	2,403	84,523	1,649
2007...........................	33,846	1,630	54,204	2,454	81,694	1,615
2006...........................	33,050	1,495	55,827	2,375	87,887	1,585
2005...........................	31,332	1,504	51,750	2,204	79,229	1,379
2004...........................	29,377	1,490	47,711	2,226	81,310	1,237
2003[3]	27,083	1,495	47,945	1,948	73,812	1,295
2002...........................	27,146	1,456	46,218	1,984	72,943	1,202
Male						
2016...........................	43,483	1,171	77,744	1,604	124,132	1,554
2015...........................	39,357	1,004	73,370	1,671	117,211	1,444
2014...........................	37,109	998	71,395	1,677	112,206	1,266
2013...........................	36,128	1,060	67,355	1,521	113,152	1,196
2012...........................	37,917	981	68,713	1,439	104,757	1,256
2011[2]	41,887	918	65,569	1,392	98,425	1,032
2010...........................	34,995	827	64,573	1,253	96,286	933
2009...........................	37,106	793	62,504	1,237	113,267	976
2008...........................	37,228	865	66,880	1,228	98,718	959
2007...........................	40,965	875	60,606	1,187	93,566	942
2006...........................	37,104	736	66,740	1,191	101,474	950
2005...........................	35,583	758	62,247	1,097	92,170	823
2004...........................	34,237	736	56,581	1,126	91,406	788
2003[3]	31,430	746	52,179	1,024	83,131	807
....	32,427	744	54,683	1,006	82,134	772
Female						
2016...........................	30,524	1,075	57,544	1,584	78,963	1,175
2015...........................	37,124	1,046	54,785	1,588	80,694	1,056
2014...........................	27,803	976	57,684	1,617	75,320	956
2013...........................	30,727	924	48,470	1,426	73,960	898
2012...........................	27,683	1,008	48,971	1,425	77,697	856
2011[2]	27,441	878	48,660	1,391	72,373	772
2010...........................	26,667	780	48,151	1,205	68,200	687
2009...........................	27,565	717	48,655	1,241	76,052	650
2008...........................	27,315	764	49,076	1,174	64,802	690
2007...........................	25,597	755	48,200	1,266	65,098	673
2006...........................	29,116	759	44,846	1,183	67,514	634
2005...........................	27,007	745	41,350	1,107	60,077	556
2004...........................	24,634	754	38,618	1,099	63,553	448
2003[3]	22,750	748	43,252	924	58,391	487
2002...........................	21,615	711	37,507	978	56,417	429

[1]For data prior to 1991, "Some college/Associate degree" equals 1 to 3 years of college completed; "Bachelor's degree" equals 4 years of college; "Advanced degree" equals 5 or more years of college completed.
[2]Starting in 2011, earnings data were created using population controls based on Census 2010 data.
[3]Starting in 2003, respondents could choose more than one race. The race data in this table from 2003 onward represent respondents who indicated only one race.

Table A-28. Median Annual Earnings, Number, and Percentage of Full-Time Year-Round Workers 25 Years Old and Over, by Highest Level of Educational Attainment and Sex, 1990–2015

(Dollars except as noted; people 25 years old and over as of March of the following year; income in current and 2015 CPI-U-RS adjusted dollars.)

Sex and year	Total			Elementary/secondary		
				Less than 9th Grade		
	Number of persons with earnings who worked full time, year round (thousands)	Median annual earnings		Number of persons with earnings who worked full time, year round (thousands)	Median annual earnings	
		Current dollars	2015 dollars		Current dollars	2015 dollars
Male						
2015	59,690	52,310	52,310	2,008	27,160	27,160
2014	58,435	51,400	51,460	1,994	26,580	26,610
2013	56,703	51,120	52,010	1,944	26,160	26,620
2012	55,208	50,950	52,600	1,793	25,130	25,940
2011	54,279	50,660	53,370	1,848	25,220	26,580
2010	52,890	50,360	54,740	1,600	24,450	26,580
2009	52,445	49,990	55,230	1,561	23,950	26,450
2008	55,655	49,000	53,940	1,982	24,260	26,700
2007	58,147	47,000	53,730	2,142	23,380	26,720
2006	58,109	45,760	53,800	2,361	22,710	26,700
2005	56,717	43,320	52,570	2,425	22,330	27,100
2004	55,469	42,090	52,810	2,427	21,660	27,180
2003	54,253	41,940	54,040	2,209	21,220	27,340
2002	54,108	41,150	54,230	2,154	20,920	27,560
2001	54,013	41,620	55,710	2,207	21,360	28,590
2000	54,065	41,060	56,510	1,968	20,790	28,610
1999	53,062	40,330	57,390	1,993	20,430	29,070
1998	52,381	37,910	55,120	1,870	19,380	28,180
1997	50,807	36,680	54,160	1,914	19,290	28,480
1996	49,764	35,620	53,830	2,041	17,960	27,140
1995	48,500	34,550	53,740	1,946	18,350	28,550
1994	47,566	33,440	53,470	1,895	17,530	28,030
1993	45,873	32,360	53,090	1,790	16,860	27,670
1992	44,752	32,060	54,150	1,815	17,290	29,210
1991	44,199	31,610	55,020	1,807	17,620	30,670
1990	44,406	30,730	55,750	2,250	17,390	31,550
Female						
2015	44,012	41,680	41,680	823	21,050	21,050
2014	42,957	40,830	40,880	796	20,990	21,020
2013	42,021	40,610	41,320	788	19,840	20,190
2012	41,319	39,980	41,270	690	20,060	20,710
2011	40,885	38,910	41,000	779	20,100	21,180
2010	40,196	38,290	41,620	732	18,240	19,820
2009	40,376	37,260	41,170	776	18,480	20,420
2008	40,979	36,700	40,400	814	18,630	20,510
2007	42,196	36,090	41,250	823	18,260	20,870
2006	41,311	35,100	41,260	934	18,130	21,320
2005	40,021	33,080	40,140	902	16,140	19,590
2004	39,072	31,990	40,140	917	17,020	21,360
2003	38,681	31,570	40,670	882	16,910	21,780
2002	38,510	31,010	40,860	858	16,510	21,750
2001	38,228	31,360	41,970	927	16,690	22,340
2000	37,762	30,330	41,740	930	15,800	21,740
1999	37,091	28,840	41,040	886	15,100	21,480
1998	35,628	27,960	40,650	814	14,470	21,040
1997	34,624	26,970	39,830	791	14,160	20,910
1996	33,549	25,810	39,000	750	14,410	21,780
1995	32,673	24,880	38,690	774	13,580	21,120
1994	31,379	24,400	39,010	696	12,430	19,880
1993	30,683	23,630	38,770	765	12,420	20,370
1992	30,346	23,140	39,090	734	12,960	21,890
1991	29,474	22,040	38,360	733	12,070	21,000
1990	28,636	21,370	38,770	847	12,250	22,220

Table A-28. Median Annual Earnings, Number, and Percentage of Full-Time Year-Round Workers 25 Years Old and Over, by Highest Level of Educational Attainment and Sex, 1990–2015—*Continued*

(Dollars except as noted; people 25 years old and over as of March of the following year; income in current and 2015 CPI-U-RS adjusted dollars.

	Elementary/secondary					
	Some high school, no diploma[1]			High school completion (includes equivalency)[2]		
Sex and year	Number of persons with earnings who worked full time, year round (thousands)	Median annual earnings		Number of persons with earnings who worked full time, year round (thousands)	Median annual earnings	
		Current dollars	2015 dollars		Current dollars	2015 dollars
Male						
2015	2,984	32,140	32,140	16,286	41,570	41,570
2014	3,012	30,840	30,870	16,429	40,930	40,980
2013	2,910	30,570	31,100	16,034	40,290	40,990
2012	2,671	30,330	31,310	15,295	40,350	41,660
2011	2,715	30,420	32,060	15,335	40,450	42,620
2010	2,615	29,440	31,990	15,104	40,060	43,540
2009	2,795	28,020	30,960	15,258	39,480	43,610
2008	3,118	29,680	32,670	16,195	39,010	42,940
2007	3,451	29,320	33,510	17,224	37,860	43,270
2006	3,872	27,650	32,510	17,369	37,030	43,540
2005	3,652	27,190	33,000	17,266	36,300	44,060
2004	3,468	26,280	32,970	17,067	35,730	44,830
2003	3,369	26,470	34,100	16,285	35,410	45,630
2002	3,680	25,900	34,130	16,005	33,210	43,750
2001	3,503	26,210	35,080	16,314	34,720	46,480
2000	3,354	25,100	34,540	16,834	34,300	47,210
1999	3,295	25,040	35,620	16,589	33,180	47,220
1998	3,613	23,960	34,840	16,442	31,480	45,770
1997	3,548	24,730	36,510	16,225	31,220	46,090
1996	3,441	22,720	34,330	15,840	30,710	46,400
1995	3,335	22,190	34,510	15,331	29,510	45,900
1994	3,057	22,050	35,260	15,109	28,040	44,830
1993	3,083	21,750	35,690	14,604	27,370	44,910
1992	3,009	21,270	35,940	14,722	27,280	46,080
1991	3,083	21,400	37,250	15,025	26,780	46,600
1990	3,315	20,900	37,920	16,394	26,650	48,350
Female						
2015	1,308	22,670	22,670	9,739	31,250	31,250
2014	1,356	21,990	22,010	9,802	30,650	30,680
2013	1,309	22,250	22,640	9,990	30,800	31,340
2012	1,351	21,390	22,080	9,870	30,410	31,390
2011	1,380	21,110	22,250	10,040	30,010	31,620
2010	1,371	20,880	22,700	10,117	29,860	32,450
2009	1,519	21,230	23,450	10,467	29,150	32,200
2008	1,568	20,410	22,460	10,851	28,380	31,240
2007	1,649	20,400	23,320	11,447	27,240	31,140
2006	1,802	20,130	23,670	11,652	26,740	31,440
2005	1,740	20,130	24,420	11,419	26,290	31,910
2004	1,797	19,160	24,050	11,392	26,030	32,660
2003	1,739	18,940	24,400	11,587	26,070	33,590
2002	1,841	19,310	25,440	11,687	25,180	33,180
2001	1,869	19,160	25,640	11,690	25,300	33,870
2000	1,950	17,920	24,660	11,789	24,970	34,370
1999	1,883	17,020	24,210	11,824	23,060	32,810
1998	1,878	16,480	23,970	11,613	22,780	33,120
1997	1,765	16,700	24,650	11,475	22,070	32,580
1996	1,751	16,950	25,620	11,363	21,180	32,000
1995	1,763	15,830	24,610	11,064	20,460	31,830
1994	1,675	15,130	24,200	10,785	20,370	32,580
1993	1,576	15,390	25,240	10,513	19,960	32,750
1992	1,659	14,560	24,590	11,039	19,430	32,820
1991	1,819	14,460	25,160	10,959	18,840	32,780
1990	1,861	14,430	26,170	11,810	18,320	33,230

[1] Includes 1 to 3 years of high school for 1990.
[2] Includes 4 years of high school for 1990.

Table A-28. Median Annual Earnings, Number, and Percentage of Full-Time Year-Round Workers 25 Years Old and Over, by Highest Level of Educational Attainment and Sex, 1990–2015—*Continued*

(Dollars except as noted; people 25 years old and over as of March of the following year; income in current and 2015 CPI-U-RS adjusted dollars.)

	College					
	Some college, no degree[3]			Associate's degree		
	Number of persons with earnings who worked full time, year round (thousands)	Median annual earnings		Number of persons with earnings who worked full time, year round (thousands)	Median annual earnings	
Sex and year		Current dollars	2015 dollars		Current dollars	2015 dollars
Male						
2015	9,445	49,670	49,670	5,907	52,070	52,070
2014	9,281	46,900	46,950	5,622	51,110	51,170
2013	8,960	47,650	48,480	5,605	51,000	51,890
2012	8,974	47,190	48,710	5,423	50,960	52,610
2011	8,752	47,070	49,600	5,206	50,930	53,660
2010	8,541	46,430	50,470	5,042	50,280	54,650
2009	8,609	47,100	52,030	4,828	50,300	55,570
2008	9,515	45,820	50,440	5,020	50,150	55,200
2007	9,867	44,900	51,320	5,244	49,040	56,060
2006	9,493	43,830	51,540	5,110	47,070	55,340
2005	9,532	42,420	51,480	5,022	47,180	57,260
2004	9,257	41,900	52,570	4,913	44,400	55,720
2003	9,340	41,350	53,270	4,696	42,870	55,240
2002	9,603	40,850	53,830	4,399	42,860	56,470
2001	9,494	41,050	54,940	4,714	42,780	57,260
2000	9,792	40,340	55,520	4,729	41,950	57,740
1999	9,684	39,220	55,810	4,359	41,640	59,250
1998	9,375	36,930	53,700	4,347	40,270	58,560
1997	9,170	35,950	53,080	4,086	38,020	56,140
1996	9,173	34,850	52,650	3,931	37,130	56,110
1995	8,908	33,880	52,700	3,926	35,200	54,750
1994	8,783	32,280	51,620	3,735	35,790	57,240
1993	8,493	32,080	52,630	3,557	33,690	55,280
1992	8,067	32,100	54,230	3,203	33,430	56,470
1991	8,034	31,660	55,100	2,899	33,820	58,850
1990	9,113	31,730	57,570	[6]	[6]	[6]
Female						
2015	7,525	36,140	36,140	5,507	40,190	40,190
2014	7,241	34,380	34,420	5,426	37,480	37,520
2013	7,070	35,240	35,860	5,253	37,700	38,360
2012	6,899	35,060	36,190	5,246	37,320	38,530
2011	6,989	34,590	36,450	5,131	39,290	41,400
2010	7,150	33,400	36,310	4,999	37,770	41,060
2009	7,164	34,090	37,660	4,924	37,270	41,170
2008	7,456	32,630	35,920	4,955	36,760	40,470
2007	7,916	32,840	37,540	4,891	36,330	41,530
2006	7,613	31,950	37,570	4,760	35,160	41,340
2005	7,452	31,400	38,110	4,751	33,940	41,190
2004	7,330	30,820	38,670	4,505	33,480	42,010
2003	7,341	30,140	38,840	4,397	32,250	41,560
2002	7,354	29,400	38,740	4,285	31,630	41,670
2001	7,283	30,420	40,720	4,190	32,150	43,040
2000	7,391	28,700	39,500	4,118	31,070	42,770
1999	7,453	27,760	39,500	3,804	30,920	43,990
1998	7,070	27,420	39,870	3,527	29,920	43,510
1997	6,628	26,340	38,890	3,538	28,810	42,540
1996	6,582	25,170	38,030	3,468	28,080	42,440
1995	6,329	24,000	37,330	3,336	27,310	42,480
1994	6,256	23,510	37,600	3,210	25,940	41,480
1993	6,279	23,060	37,830	3,067	25,880	42,470
1992	5,904	23,160	39,120	2,655	25,620	43,280
1991	5,633	22,140	38,540	2,523	25,000	43,510
1990	6,462	22,230	40,320	[6]	[6]	[6]

[3]Includes 1 to 3 years of college and associate's degrees for 1990.
[6]Not reported separately for 1990.

Table A-28. Median Annual Earnings, Number, and Percentage of Full-Time Year-Round Workers 25 Years Old and Over, by Highest Level of Educational Attainment and Sex, 1990–2015—*Continued*

(Dollars except as noted; people 25 years old and over as of March of the following year; income in current and 2015 CPI-U-RS adjusted dollars.)

	College					
	Bachelor's or higher degree[4]					
	Total			Bachelor's degree[5]		
	Number of persons with earnings who worked full time, year round (thousands)	Median annual earnings		Number of persons with earnings who worked full time, year round (thousands)	Median annual earnings	
Sex and year		Current dollars	2015 dollars		Current dollars	2015 dollars
Male						
2015	23,059	79,320	79,320	14,469	71,390	71,390
2014	22,098	75,910	76,000	13,969	68,160	68,240
2013	21,249	76,110	77,430	13,378	67,240	68,410
2012	21,052	75,320	77,750	13,315	66,150	68,290
2011	20,423	73,850	77,820	13,013	66,200	69,750
2010	19,990	71,780	78,020	12,836	63,740	69,280
2009	19,395	71,470	78,950	12,290	62,440	68,990
2008	19,825	72,220	79,500	12,609	65,800	72,440
2007	20,218	70,400	80,480	12,962	62,090	70,970
2006	19,903	66,930	78,690	12,764	60,910	71,610
2005	18,820	66,170	80,300	12,032	60,020	72,840
2004	18,338	62,800	78,800	11,701	57,220	71,800
2003	18,354	62,080	79,980	11,846	56,500	72,800
2002	18,267	61,700	81,300	11,829	56,080	73,890
2001	17,780	62,220	83,290	11,479	55,930	74,870
2000	17,387	61,870	85,160	11,395	56,330	77,540
1999	17,142	60,200	85,660	11,142	52,990	75,390
1998	16,733	56,520	82,190	11,058	51,410	74,740
1997	15,864	53,450	78,920	10,349	48,620	71,790
1996	15,339	51,440	77,730	9,898	45,850	69,280
1995	15,054	50,480	78,520	9,597	45,270	70,410
1994	14,987	49,230	78,720	9,636	43,660	69,820
1993	14,346	47,740	78,330	9,178	42,760	70,150
1992	13,937	45,800	77,370	8,719	41,360	69,850
1991	13,350	45,140	78,550	8,456	40,910	71,190
1990	13,334	42,670	77,410	7,569	39,240	71,180
Female						
2015	19,109	57,220	57,220	11,751	51,680	51,680
2014	18,336	55,940	56,010	11,420	51,350	51,410
2013	17,611	55,720	56,700	11,124	50,750	51,630
2012	17,263	53,690	55,420	10,961	50,170	51,790
2011	16,566	52,140	54,940	10,537	49,110	51,740
2010	15,826	51,940	56,460	9,903	47,440	51,560
2009	15,526	51,880	57,310	10,066	46,830	51,740
2008	15,335	51,410	56,590	9,856	47,030	51,770
2007	15,469	50,400	57,610	9,931	45,770	52,320
2006	14,549	49,570	58,280	9,645	45,410	53,390
2005	13,758	46,950	56,980	9,074	42,170	51,180
2004	13,131	45,910	57,610	8,664	41,680	52,300
2003	12,735	45,120	58,130	8,330	41,330	53,250
2002	12,484	43,250	56,980	8,229	40,850	53,830
2001	12,269	44,780	59,940	8,257	40,990	54,870
2000	11,584	42,710	58,780	7,899	40,420	55,630
1999	11,242	41,750	59,400	7,607	37,990	54,060
1998	10,725	39,790	57,850	7,288	36,560	53,160
1997	10,427	38,040	56,170	7,173	35,380	52,240
1996	9,636	36,460	55,100	6,689	33,530	50,660
1995	9,406	35,260	54,840	6,434	32,050	49,850
1994	8,756	35,380	56,570	5,901	31,740	50,750
1993	8,483	34,310	56,290	5,735	31,200	51,190
1992	8,355	32,300	54,570	5,604	30,330	51,230
1991	7,807	31,310	54,490	5,263	29,080	50,610
1990	7,655	30,380	55,100	4,704	28,020	50,820

[4]Includes 4 or more years of college for 1990.
[5]Includes 4 years of college for 1990.

Table A-28. Median Annual Earnings, Number, and Percentage of Full-Time Year-Round Workers 25 Years Old and Over, by Highest Level of Educational Attainment and Sex, 1990–2015—*Continued*

(Dollars except as noted; people 25 years old and over as of March of the following year; income in current and 2015 CPI-U-RS adjusted dollars.)

	College								
	Bachelor's or higher degree[4]								
	Master's degree			Professional degree			Doctor's degree		
	Number of	Median annual earnings		Number of	Median annual earnings		Number of	Median annual earnings	
Sex and year	persons with earnings who worked full time, year round (thousands)	Current dollars	2015 dollars	persons with earnings who worked full time, year round (thousands)	Current dollars	2015 dollars	persons with earnings who worked full time, year round (thousands)	Current dollars	2015 dollars
Male									
2015	5,883	86,740	86,740	1,256	131,190	131,190	1,451	102,340	102,340
2014	5,401	84,760	84,860	1,359	121,750	121,900	1,369	100,710	100,830
2013	5,146	86,310	87,810	1,249	126,730	128,930	1,476	105,280	107,120
2012	5,003	85,120	87,870	1,301	116,350	120,120	1,433	106,470	109,910
2011	4,839	83,030	87,490	1,300	119,470	125,890	1,271	100,770	106,180
2010	4,670	80,960	88,000	1,237	115,300	125,320	1,246	101,220	110,020
2009	4,575	79,340	87,660	1,319	123,240	136,160	1,212	100,740	111,300
2008	4,709	80,960	89,130	1,388	100,000	110,090	1,119	100,000	110,090
2007	4,800	76,280	87,200	1,332	100,000	114,310	1,125	92,090	105,270
2006	4,542	75,430	88,690	1,425	100,000	117,570	1,172	100,000	117,570
2005	4,275	75,030	91,050	1,369	100,000	121,370	1,144	85,860	104,210
2004	4,243	71,530	89,760	1,305	100,000	125,480	1,088	82,400	103,400
2003	4,124	70,640	91,010	1,348	100,000	128,840	1,037	87,130	112,260
2002	4,065	67,280	88,650	1,308	100,000	131,770	1,065	83,310	109,770
2001	3,961	70,900	94,900	1,298	100,000	133,860	1,041	86,970	116,410
2000	3,680	68,320	94,040	1,274	99,410	136,830	1,038	80,250	110,460
1999	3,725	66,240	94,260	1,267	100,000	142,290	1,008	81,690	116,230
1998	3,414	62,240	90,500	1,264	94,740	137,750	998	75,080	109,160
1997	3,228	61,690	91,090	1,321	85,010	125,530	966	76,230	112,570
1996	3,272	60,510	91,430	1,277	85,960	129,900	893	71,230	107,630
1995	3,395	55,220	85,880	1,208	79,670	123,910	853	65,340	101,620
1994	3,225	53,500	85,550	1,258	75,010	119,940	868	61,920	99,010
1993	3,131	51,870	85,100	1,231	80,550	132,160	808	63,150	103,610
1992	3,178	49,970	84,410	1,295	76,220	128,750	745	57,420	96,990
1991	3,073	49,730	86,550	1,147	74,000	128,780	674	57,190	99,520
1990	6	6	6	6	6	6	6	6	6
Female									
2015	5,562	62,380	62,380	784	82,470	82,470	1,012	82,310	82,310
2014	5,310	60,830	60,900	776	91,810	91,920	830	80,540	80,640
2013	4,963	61,280	62,350	793	85,400	86,880	732	75,090	76,400
2012	4,887	60,930	62,900	670	94,470	97,530	745	77,900	80,420
2011	4,700	60,300	63,540	635	80,720	85,050	694	77,460	81,620
2010	4,576	59,100	64,240	622	76,740	83,410	725	77,390	84,120
2009	4,261	61,070	67,470	606	83,910	92,700	592	76,580	84,610
2008	4,176	57,510	63,310	753	71,300	78,490	550	74,030	81,490
2007	4,389	55,430	63,360	666	71,100	81,270	484	68,990	78,860
2006	3,746	52,440	61,650	662	76,240	89,640	497	70,520	82,910
2005	3,591	51,410	62,400	657	80,460	97,650	437	66,850	81,140
2004	3,451	51,320	64,390	564	75,040	94,160	452	68,880	86,430
2003	3,376	50,160	64,630	567	66,490	85,670	462	67,210	86,600
2002	3,281	48,890	64,420	572	57,020	75,130	402	65,720	86,590
2001	3,089	50,670	67,820	531	61,750	82,650	392	62,120	83,160
2000	2,823	50,140	69,010	509	58,960	81,150	353	57,080	78,570
1999	2,818	48,100	68,440	470	59,900	85,240	346	60,080	85,490
1998	2,639	45,280	65,840	468	57,570	83,700	329	57,800	84,040
1997	2,448	44,950	66,370	488	61,050	90,150	318	53,040	78,320
1996	2,213	41,900	63,320	413	57,620	87,080	322	56,270	85,030
1995	2,268	40,260	62,630	421	50,000	77,770	283	48,140	74,880
1994	2,174	39,460	63,090	398	50,620	80,940	283	51,120	81,740
1993	2,166	38,610	63,350	323	50,210	82,380	260	47,250	77,520
1992	2,192	36,040	60,870	334	46,260	78,140	225	45,790	77,350
1991	2,025	34,950	60,820	312	46,740	81,350	206	43,300	75,360
1990	6	6	6	6	6	6	6	6	6

[4]Includes 4 or more years of college for 1990.
[6]Not reported separately for 1990.

Table A-29. Total Fall Enrollment in Degree-Granting Institutions, by Attendance Status, Sex of Student, and Control of Institution, Selected Years, 1947–2015

(Number; percent.)

Year	Total enrolled	Attendance status			Sex of student			Control of institution			
									Private		
		Full-time	Part-time	Percent part-time	Male	Female	Percent Female	Public	Total	Not-for-profit	For-profit
2015	19,977,270	12,290,829	7,686,441	38.2	8,721,403	11,255,867	57.0	14,568,103	5,409,167	4,063,372	1,345,795
2014	20,207,369	12,453,975	7,753,394	38.2	8,797,061	11,410,308	57.0	14,655,015	5,552,354	3,996,089	1,556,265
2013	20,376,677	12,596,610	7,780,067	38.2	8,861,197	11,515,480	56.5	14,746,848	5,629,829	3,971,390	1,658,439
2012	20,644,478	12,734,404	7,910,074	38.3	8,919,006	11,725,472	56.8	14,884,667	5,759,811	3,951,388	1,808,423
2011	21,010,590	13,002,531	8,008,059	38.1	9,034,256	11,976,334	57.0	15,116,303	5,894,287	3,926,819	1,967,468
2010	21,019,438	13,087,182	7,932,256	37.7	9,045,759	11,973,679	57.0	15,142,171	5,877,267	3,854,482	2,022,785
2009	20,313,594	12,605,355	7,708,239	37.9	8,732,953	11,580,641	57.0	14,810,768	5,502,826	3,767,672	1,735,154
2008	19,102,814	11,747,743	7,355,071	38.5	8,188,895	10,913,919	57.1	13,972,153	5,130,661	3,661,519	1,469,142
2007	18,248,128	11,269,892	6,978,236	38.2	7,815,914	10,432,214	57.2	13,490,780	4,757,348	3,571,150	1,186,198
2006	17,758,870	10,957,305	6,801,565	38.3	7,574,815	10,184,055	57.3	13,180,133	4,578,737	3,512,866	1,065,871
2005	17,487,475	10,797,011	6,690,464	38.3	7,455,925	10,031,550	57.4	13,021,834	4,465,641	3,454,692	1,010,949
2004	17,272,044	10,610,177	6,661,867	38.6	7,387,262	9,884,782	57.2	12,980,112	4,291,932	3,411,685	880,247
2003	16,911,481	10,326,133	6,585,348	38.9	7,260,264	9,651,217	57.1	12,858,698	4,052,783	3,341,048	711,735
2002	16,611,711	9,946,359	6,665,352	40.1	7,202,116	9,409,595	56.6	12,751,993	3,859,718	3,265,476	594,242
2001	15,927,987	9,447,502	6,480,485	40.7	6,960,815	8,967,172	56.3	12,233,156	3,694,831	3,167,330	527,501
2000	15,312,289	9,009,600	6,302,689	41.2	6,721,769	8,590,520	56.1	11,752,786	3,559,503	3,109,419	450,084
1999	14,849,691	8,803,139	6,046,552	40.7	6,515,164	8,334,527	56.1	11,375,739	3,473,952	3,055,029	418,923
1998	14,506,967	8,563,338	5,943,629	41.0	6,369,265	8,137,702	56.1	11,137,769	3,369,198	3,004,925	364,273
1997	14,502,334	8,438,062	6,064,272	41.8	6,396,028	8,106,306	55.9	11,196,119	3,306,215	2,977,614	328,601
1996	14,367,520	8,302,953	6,064,567	42.2	6,352,825	8,014,695	55.8	11,120,499	3,247,021	2,942,556	304,465
1995	14,261,781	8,128,802	6,132,979	43.0	6,342,539	7,919,242	55.5	11,092,374	3,169,407	2,929,044	240,363
1994	14,278,790	8,137,776	6,141,014	43.0	6,371,898	7,906,892	55.4	11,133,680	3,145,110	2,910,107	235,003
1993	14,304,803	8,127,618	6,177,185	43.2	6,427,450	7,877,353	55.1	11,189,088	3,115,715	2,888,897	226,818
1992	14,487,359	8,162,118	6,325,241	43.7	6,523,989	7,963,370	55.0	11,384,567	3,102,792	2,872,523	230,269
1991	14,358,953	8,115,329	6,243,624	43.5	6,501,844	7,857,109	54.7	11,309,563	3,049,390	2,819,041	230,349
1990	13,818,637	7,820,985	5,997,652	43.4	6,283,909	7,534,728	54.5	10,844,717	2,973,920	2,760,227	213,693
1989	13,538,560	7,660,950	5,877,610	43.4	6,190,015	7,348,545	54.3	10,577,963	2,960,597	2,731,174	229,423
1988	13,055,337	7,436,768	5,618,569	43.0	6,001,896	7,053,441	54.0	10,161,388	2,893,949	2,673,567	220,382
1987	12,766,642	7,231,085	5,535,557	43.4	5,932,056	6,834,586	53.5	9,973,254	2,793,388	2,602,350	191,038 3
1986	12,503,511	7,119,550	5,383,961	43.1	5,884,515	6,618,996	52.9	9,713,893	2,789,618	2,572,479	217,139 3
1985	12,247,055	7,075,221	5,171,834	42.2	5,818,450	6,428,605	52.5	9,479,273	2,767,782	2,571,791	195,991
1984	12,241,940	7,098,388	5,143,552	42.0	5,863,574	6,378,366	52.1	9,477,370	2,764,570	2,574,419	190,151
1983	12,464,661	7,261,050	5,203,611	41.7	6,023,725	6,440,936	51.7	9,682,734	2,781,927	2,589,187	192,740
1982	12,425,780	7,220,618	5,205,162	41.9	6,031,384	6,394,396	51.5	9,696,087	2,729,693	2,552,739	176,954 2
1981	12,371,672	7,181,250	5,190,422	42.0	5,975,056	6,396,616	51.7	9,647,032	2,724,640	2,572,405	152,235 2
1980	12,096,895	7,097,958	4,998,937	41.3	5,874,374	6,222,521	51.4	9,457,394	2,639,501	2,527,787	152,235 2
1979	11,569,899	6,794,039	4,775,860	41.3	5,682,877	5,887,022	50.9	9,036,822	2,533,077	2,461,773	71,304
1978	11,260,092	6,667,657	4,592,435	40.8	5,640,998	5,619,094	49.9	8,785,893	2,474,199	2,408,331	65,868
1977	11,285,787	6,792,925	4,492,862	39.8	5,789,016	5,496,771	48.7	8,846,993	2,438,794	2,386,652	52,142
1976	11,012,137	6,717,058	4,295,079	39.0	5,810,828	5,201,309	47.2	8,653,477	2,358,660	2,314,298	44,362
1975	11,184,859	6,841,334	4,343,525	38.8	6,148,997	5,035,862	45.0	8,834,508	2,350,351	2,311,448	38,903
1974	10,223,729	6,370,273	3,853,456	37.7	5,622,429	4,601,300	45.0	7,988,500	2,235,229	2,200,963	34,266
1973	9,602,123	6,189,493	3,412,630	35.5	5,371,052	4,231,071	44.1	7,419,516	2,182,607	2,148,784	33,823
1972	9,214,860	6,072,389	3,142,471	34.1	5,238,757	3,976,103	43.1	7,070,635	2,144,225	2,123,245	20,980
1971	8,948,644	6,077,232	2,871,412	32.1	5,207,004	3,741,640	41.8	6,804,309	2,144,335	2,121,913	22,422
1970	8,580,887	5,816,290	2,764,597	32.2	5,043,642	3,537,245	41.2	6,428,134	2,152,753	2,134,420	18,333
1969	8,004,660	5,498,883	2,505,777	31.3	4,746,201	3,258,459	40.7	5,896,868	2,107,792	2,087,653	20,139
1968	7,513,091	5,210,155	2,302,936	30.7	4,477,649	3,035,442	40.4	5,430,652	2,082,439	2,061,211	21,228
1967[1]	6,911,748	4,793,128	2,118,620	30.7	4,132,800	2,778,948	40.2	4,816,028	2,095,720	2,074,041	21,679
1966[1]	6,389,872	4,438,606	1,951,266	30.5	3,856,216	2,533,656	39.7	4,348,917	2,040,955	NA	NA
1965[1]	5,920,864	4,095,728	1,825,136	30.8	3,630,020	2,290,844	38.7	3,969,596	1,951,268	NA	NA
1964[1]	5,280,020	3,573,238	1,706,782	32.3	3,248,713	2,031,307	38.5	3,467,708	1,812,312	NA	NA
1963[1]	4,779,609	3,183,833	1,595,776	33.4	2,961,540	1,818,069	38.0	3,081,279	1,698,330	NA	NA
1961[1]	4,145,065	2,785,133	1,359,932	32.8	2,585,821	1,559,244	37.6	2,561,447	1,583,618	NA	NA

Note: Data through 1995 are for institutions of higher education, while later data are for degree-granting institutions. Degree-granting institutions grant associate's or higher degrees and participate in Title IV federal financial aid programs. The degree-granting classification is very similar to the earlier higher education classification, but it includes more 2-year colleges and excludes a few higher education institutions that did not grant degrees. Some data have been revised from previously published figures.
NA = Not available.
[1] Includes part-time resident students and all extension students (students attending courses at sites separate from the primary reporting campus).
[2] Degree-credit enrollment only.

Table A-29. Total Fall Enrollment in Degree-Granting Institutions, by Attendance Status, Sex of Student, and Control of Institution, Selected Years, 1947–2015—*Continued*

(Number; percent.)

Year	Total enrolled	Attendance status			Sex of student			Control of institution			
		Full-time	Part-time	Percent part-time	Male	Female	Percent Female	Public	Private		
									Total	Not-for-profit	For-profit
1959[1]	3,639,847	2,421,016	1,218,831	33.5	2,332,617	1,307,230	35.9	2,180,982	1,458,865	NA	NA
1957	3,323,783	NA	NA	NA	2,170,765	1,153,018	34.7	1,972,673	1,351,110	NA	NA
1956[2]	2,918,212	NA	NA	NA	1,911,458	1,006,754	34.5	1,656,402	1,261,810	NA	NA
1955[2]	2,653,034	NA	NA	NA	1,733,184	919,850	34.7	1,476,282	1,176,752	NA	NA
1954[2]	2,446,693	NA	NA	NA	1,563,382	883,311	36.1	1,353,531	1,093,162	NA	NA
1953[2]	2,231,054	NA	NA	NA	1,422,598	808,456	36.2	1,185,876	1,045,178	NA	NA
1952[2]	2,134,242	NA	NA	NA	1,380,357	753,885	35.3	1,101,240	1,033,002	NA	NA
1951[2]	2,101,962	NA	NA	NA	1,390,740	711,222	33.8	1,037,938	1,064,024	NA	NA
1950[2]	2,281,298	NA	NA	NA	1,560,392	720,906	31.6	1,139,699	1,141,599	NA	NA
1949[2]	2,444,900	NA	NA	NA	1,721,572	723,328	29.6	1,207,151	1,237,749	NA	NA
1948[2]	2,403,396	NA	NA	NA	1,709,367	694,029	28.9	1,185,588	1,217,808	NA	NA
1947[2]	2,338,226	NA	NA	NA	1,659,249	678,977	29.0	1,152,377	1,185,849	NA	NA

Note: Data through 1995 are for institutions of higher education, while later data are for degree-granting institutions. Degree-granting institutions grant associate's or higher degrees and participate in Title IV federal financial aid programs. The degree-granting classification is very similar to the earlier higher education classification, but it includes more 2-year colleges and excludes a few higher education institutions that did not grant degrees. Some data have been revised from previously published figures.
NA = Not available.
[1] Includes part-time resident students and all extension students (students attending courses at sites separate from the primary reporting campus).
[2] Degree-credit enrollment only.

Table A-30. Total Fall Enrollment in Degree-Granting Institutions, by Control and Type of Institution, 1970–2016

(Numbers in thousands.)

Year	All institutions			Public institutions			Private institutions		
	Total	4-year	2-year	Total	4-year	2-year	Total	4-year	2-year
2016	19,841	13,751	6,090	14,583	8,742	5,841	5,258	5,009	249
2015	19,988	13,489	6,499	14,573	8,349	6,224	5,415	5,140	275
2014	20,209	13,494	6,715	14,655	8,257	6,398	5,554	5,237	317
2013	20,377	13,406	6,971	14,747	8,120	6,626	5,630	5,286	344
2012	20,644	13,477	7,168	14,885	8,093	6,792	5,760	5,384	376
2011	21,011	13,499	7,511	15,116	8,048	7,068	5,894	5,451	443
2010	21,019	13,336	7,684	15,142	7,924	7,218	5,877	5,412	466
2009	20,314	12,791	7,523	14,811	7,709	7,102	5,503	5,082	421
2008	19,103	12,131	6,971	13,972	7,332	6,640	5,131	4,800	331
2007	18,248	11,630	6,618	13,491	7,167	6,324	4,757	4,464	294
2006	17,759	11,240	6,519	13,180	6,955	6,225	4,579	4,285	293
2005	17,487	10,999	6,488	13,022	6,838	6,184	4,466	4,162	304
2004	17,272	10,726	6,546	12,980	6,737	6,244	4,292	3,990	302
2003	16,911	10,417	6,494	12,859	6,649	6,209	4,053	3,768	285
2002	16,612	10,082	6,529	12,752	6,482	6,270	3,860	3,601	259
2001	15,928	9,677	6,251	12,233	6,236	5,997	3,695	3,441	254
2000	15,312	9,364	5,948	11,753	6,055	5,697	3,560	3,308	251
1999	14,850	9,196	5,654	11,376	5,978	5,398	3,474	3,218	255
1998	14,507	9,018	5,489	11,138	5,892	5,246	3,369	3,126	243
1997	14,502	8,897	5,606	11,196	5,835	5,361	3,306	3,061	245
1996	14,368	8,804	5,563	11,120	5,806	5,314	3,247	2,998	249
1995	14,262	8,769	5,493	11,092	5,815	5,278	3,169	2,955	215
1994	14,279	8,749	5,530	11,134	5,825	5,308	3,145	2,924	221
1993	14,305	8,739	5,566	11,189	5,852	5,337	3,116	2,887	229
1992	14,487	8,765	5,722	11,385	5,900	5,485	3,103	2,865	238
1991	14,359	8,707	5,652	11,310	5,905	5,405	3,049	2,802	247
1990	13,819	8,579	5,240	10,845	5,848	4,996	2,974	2,730	244
1989	13,539	8,388	5,151	10,578	5,694	4,884	2,961	2,693	267
1988	13,055	8,180	4,875	10,161	5,546	4,615	2,894	2,634	260
1987	12,767	7,990	4,776	9,973	5,432	4,541	2,793	2,558	235
1986	12,504	7,824	4,680	9,714	5,300	4,414	2,790	2,524	265
1985	12,247	7,716	4,531	9,479	5,210	4,270	2,768	2,506	261
1984	12,242	7,711	4,531	9,477	5,198	4,279	2,765	2,513	252
1983	12,465	7,741	4,723	9,683	5,223	4,459	2,782	2,518	264
1982	12,426	7,654	4,772	9,696	5,176	4,520	2,730	2,478	264[1]
1981	12,372	7,655	4,716	9,647	5,166	4,481	2,725	2,489	264[1]
1980	12,097	7,571	4,526	9,457	5,129	4,329	2,640	2,442	264[1]
1979	11,570	7,353	4,217	9,037	4,980	4,057	2,533	2,373	160
1978	11,260	7,232	4,028	8,786	4,912	3,874	2,474	2,319	155
1977	11,286	7,243	4,043	8,847	4,945	3,902	2,439	2,298	141
1976	11,012	7,129	3,883	8,653	4,902	3,752	2,359	2,227	132
1975	11,185	7,215	3,970	8,835	4,998	3,836	2,350	2,217	134
1974	10,224	6,820	3,404	7,989	4,703	3,285	2,235	2,117	119
1973	9,602	6,590	3,012	7,420	4,530	2,890	2,183	2,060	122
1972	9,215	6,459	2,756	7,071	4,430	2,641	2,144	2,029	115
1971	8,949	6,369	2,579	6,804	4,347	2,457	2,144	2,022	122
1970	8,581	6,262	2,319	6,428	4,233	2,195	2,153	2,029	124

Note: Data through 1995 are for institutions of higher education, while later data are for degree-granting institutions. Degree-granting institutions grant associate's or higher degrees and participate in Title IV federal financial aid programs. The degree-granting classification is very similar to the earlier higher education classification, but it includes more 2-year colleges and excludes a few higher education institutions that did not grant degrees. A university is an institution of higher education consisting of a liberal arts college, a diverse graduate program, and usually two or more professional schools or faculties. It is empowered to confer degrees in various fields of study; for purposes of maintaining trend data in this publication, the selection of university institutions has not been revised since 1982. Some data have been revised from previously published figures.

[1]Large increases are due to the addition of schools accredited by the Accrediting Commission of Career Schools and Colleges of Technology.

Table A-31. Total Fall Enrollment in Degree-Granting Postsecondary Institutions, by Level of Enrollment, Control and Type of Institution, Age, and Attendance Status of Student, 2015

(Number; percent.)

| Age of student and attendance status | Total | Percent | Undergraduate | | | | | | | | | | | |
| | | | Public | | | | | | Private, nonprofit | | | | | |
			Total	Percent	4-year	Percent	2-year	Percent	Total	Percent	4-year	Percent	2-year	Percent
All students	17,036,778	100.0	13,145,720	100.0	6,930,054	100.0	6,215,666	100.0	2,819,174	100.0	2,769,125	100.0	50,049	100.0
Under 18	1,055,371	6.2	952,202	7.2	309,725	4.5	642,477	10.3	97,966	3.5	96,702	3.5	1,264	2.5
18 and 19	4,341,399	25.5	3,430,770	26.1	2,000,360	28.9	1,430,410	23.0	838,714	29.8	831,301	30.0	7,413	14.8
20 and 21	4,041,207	23.7	3,097,399	23.6	2,024,958	29.2	1,072,441	17.3	842,115	29.9	834,810	30.1	7,305	14.6
22 to 24	2,682,977	15.7	2,161,692	16.4	1,277,876	18.4	883,816	14.2	369,471	13.1	361,327	13.0	8,144	16.3
25 to 29	1,843,292	10.8	1,398,873	10.6	601,730	8.7	797,143	12.8	210,548	7.5	201,801	7.3	8,747	17.5
30 to 34	1,038,342	6.1	726,939	5.5	272,570	3.9	454,369	7.3	137,559	4.9	132,332	4.8	5,227	10.4
35 to 39	685,459	4.0	460,509	3.5	161,107	2.3	299,402	4.8	102,900	3.7	99,238	3.6	3,662	7.3
40 to 49	832,617	4.9	550,883	4.2	182,086	2.6	368,797	5.9	138,179	4.9	133,684	4.8	4,495	9.0
50 to 64	434,424	2.5	305,115	2.3	86,003	1.2	219,112	3.5	68,044	2.4	65,504	2.4	2,540	5.1
65 and over	54,723	0.3	46,998	0.4	9,816	0.1	37,182	0.6	4,037	0.1	3,865	0.1	172	0.3
Age unknown	26,967	0.2	14,340	0.1	3,823	0.1	10,517	0.2	9,641	0.3	8,561	0.3	1,080	2.2
Full-time	10,604,992	100.0	7,553,732	100.0	5,280,550	100.0	2,273,182	100.0	2,301,160	100.0	2,265,093	100.0	36,067	100.0
Under 18	207,463	2.0	165,722	2.2	89,219	1.7	76,503	3.4	39,356	1.7	39,069	1.7	287	0.8
18 and 19	3,612,756	34.1	2,736,447	36.2	1,855,824	35.1	880,623	38.7	811,834	35.3	805,247	35.6	6,587	18.3
20 and 21	3,208,201	30.3	2,314,304	30.6	1,820,168	34.5	494,136	21.7	809,775	35.2	803,699	35.5	6,076	16.8
22 to 24	1,641,624	15.5	1,227,358	16.2	943,616	17.9	283,742	12.5	301,295	13.1	295,228	13.0	6,067	16.8
25 to 29	846,359	8.0	555,809	7.4	323,622	6.1	232,187	10.2	126,278	5.5	120,158	5.3	6,120	17.0
30 to 34	419,782	4.0	232,973	3.1	114,549	2.2	118,424	5.2	70,926	3.1	67,397	3.0	3,529	9.8
35 to 39	253,482	2.4	127,155	1.7	56,999	1.1	70,156	3.1	48,609	2.1	46,229	2.0	2,380	6.6
40 to 49	280,755	2.6	130,801	1.7	54,458	1.0	76,343	3.4	61,343	2.7	58,582	2.6	2,761	7.7
50 to 64	117,245	1.1	56,083	0.7	20,049	0.4	36,034	1.6	26,121	1.1	24,615	1.1	1,506	4.2
65 and over	7,175	0.1	3,510	*	1,108	*	2,402	0.1	1,030	*	916	*	114	0.3
Age unknown	10,150	0.1	3,570	*	938	*	2,632	0.1	4,593	0.2	3,953	0.2	640	1.8
Part-time	6,431,786	100.0	5,591,988	100.0	1,649,504	100.0	3,942,484	100.0	518,014	100.0	504,032	100.0	13,982	100.0
Under 18	847,908	13.2	786,480	14.1	220,506	13.4	565,974	14.4	58,610	11.3	57,633	11.4	977	7.0
18 and 19	728,643	11.3	694,323	12.4	144,536	8.8	549,787	13.9	26,880	5.2	26,054	5.2	826	5.9
20 and 21	833,006	13.0	783,095	14.0	204,790	12.4	578,305	14.7	32,340	6.2	31,111	6.2	1,229	8.8
22 to 24	1,041,353	16.2	934,334	16.7	334,260	20.3	600,074	15.2	68,176	13.2	66,099	13.1	2,077	14.9
25 to 29	996,933	15.5	843,064	15.1	278,108	16.9	564,956	14.3	84,270	16.3	81,643	16.2	2,627	18.8
30 to 34	618,560	9.6	493,966	8.8	158,021	9.6	335,945	8.5	66,633	12.9	64,935	12.9	1,698	12.1
35 to 39	431,977	6.7	333,354	6.0	104,108	6.3	229,246	5.8	54,291	10.5	53,009	10.5	1,282	9.2
40 to 49	551,862	8.6	420,082	7.5	127,628	7.7	292,454	7.4	76,836	14.8	75,102	14.9	1,734	12.4
50 to 64	317,179	4.9	249,032	4.5	65,954	4.0	183,078	4.6	41,923	8.1	40,889	8.1	1,034	7.4
65 and over	47,548	0.7	43,488	0.8	8,708	0.5	34,780	0.9	3,007	0.6	2,949	0.6	58	0.4
Age unknown	16,817	0.3	10,770	0.2	2,885	0.2	7,885	0.2	5,048	1.0	4,608	0.9	440	3.1

Note: Degree-granting institutions grant associate's or higher degrees and participate in Title IV federal financial aid programs. Details may not sum to totals because of rounding.
* = Quantity zero or equals zero.

Table A-31. Total Fall Enrollment in Degree-Granting Postsecondary Institutions, by Level of Enrollment, Control and Type of Institution, Age, and Attendance Status of Student, 2015—Continued

(Number; percent.)

Age of student and attendance status	Undergraduate						Postbaccalaureate							
	Total	Percent	Private, for-profit				Total	Percent	Public	Percent	Private, non-profit	Percent	Private, for-profit	Percent
			4-year	Percent	2-year	Percent								
All students	1,071,884	100.0	846,671	100.0	225,213	100.0	2,940,492	100.0	1,422,383	100.0	1,244,198	100.0	273,911	100.0
Under 18	5,203	0.5	3,998	0.5	1,205	0.5	255	*	104	*	136	*	15	*
18 and 19	71,915	6.7	46,050	5.4	25,865	11.5	975	*	541	*	417	*	17	*
20 and 21	101,693	9.5	68,129	8.0	33,564	14.9	36,560	1.2	18,946	1.3	17,115	1.4	499	0.2
22 to 24	151,814	14.2	110,754	13.1	41,060	18.2	641,346	21.8	352,312	24.8	275,245	22.1	13,789	5.0
25 to 29	233,871	21.8	186,377	22.0	47,494	21.1	933,409	31.7	481,833	33.9	402,436	32.3	49,140	17.9
30 to 34	173,844	16.2	146,097	17.3	27,747	12.3	471,521	16.0	229,898	16.2	191,887	15.4	49,736	18.2
35 to 39	122,050	11.4	103,957	12.3	18,093	8.0	285,464	9.7	126,797	8.9	114,504	9.2	44,163	16.1
40 to 49	143,555	13.4	123,553	14.6	20,002	8.9	355,007	12.1	139,652	9.8	145,078	11.7	70,277	25.7
50 to 64	61,265	5.7	52,717	6.2	8,548	3.8	191,283	6.5	66,663	4.7	81,430	6.5	43,190	15.8
65 and over	3,688	0.3	3,305	0.4	383	0.2	12,112	0.4	4,574	0.3	4,946	0.4	2,592	0.9
Age unknown	2,986	0.3	1,734	0.2	1,252	0.6	12,560	0.4	1,063	0.1	11,004	0.9	493	0.2
Full-time	750,100	100.0	548,128	100.0	201,972	100.0	1,685,837	100.0	800,943	100.0	747,972	100.0	136,922	100.0
Under 18	2,385	0.3	1,238	0.2	1,147	0.6	110	*	69	*	36	*	5	*
18 and 19	64,475	8.6	39,502	7.2	24,973	12.4	788	*	494	0.1	282	*	12	*
20 and 21	84,122	11.2	52,844	9.6	31,278	15.5	33,015	2.0	17,207	2.1	15,410	2.1	398	0.3
22 to 24	112,971	15.1	76,005	13.9	36,966	18.3	515,543	30.6	282,963	35.3	223,567	29.9	9,013	6.6
25 to 29	164,272	21.9	122,280	22.3	41,992	20.8	596,975	35.4	299,585	37.4	270,881	36.2	26,509	19.4
30 to 34	115,883	15.4	91,557	16.7	24,326	12.0	230,597	13.7	106,107	13.2	99,995	13.4	24,495	17.9
35 to 39	77,718	10.4	62,026	11.3	15,692	7.8	115,175	6.8	44,290	5.5	49,383	6.6	21,502	15.7
40 to 49	88,611	11.8	71,419	13.0	17,192	8.5	123,590	7.3	36,089	4.5	53,859	7.2	33,642	24.6
50 to 64	35,041	4.7	27,995	5.1	7,046	3.5	60,092	3.6	13,336	1.7	26,913	3.6	19,843	14.5
65 and over	2,635	0.4	2,331	0.4	304	0.2	3,402	0.2	637	0.1	1,584	0.2	1,181	0.9
Age unknown	1,987	0.3	931	0.2	1,056	0.5	6,550	0.4	166	*	6,062	0.8	322	0.2
Part-time	321,784	100.0	298,543	100.0	23,241	100.0	1,254,655	100.0	621,440	100.0	496,226	100.0	136,989	100.0
Under 18	2,818	0.9	2,760	0.9	58	0.2	145	*	35	*	100	*	10	*
18 and 19	7,440	2.3	6,548	2.2	892	3.8	187	*	47	*	135	*	5	*
20 and 21	17,571	5.5	15,285	5.1	2,286	9.8	3,545	0.3	1,739	0.3	1,705	0.3	101	0.1
22 to 24	38,843	12.1	34,749	11.6	4,094	17.6	125,803	10.0	69,349	11.2	51,678	10.4	4,776	3.5
25 to 29	69,599	21.6	64,097	21.5	5,502	23.7	336,434	26.8	182,248	29.3	131,555	26.5	22,631	16.5
30 to 34	57,961	18.0	54,540	18.3	3,421	14.7	240,924	19.2	123,791	19.9	91,892	18.5	25,241	18.4
35 to 39	44,332	13.8	41,931	14.0	2,401	10.3	170,289	13.6	82,507	13.3	65,121	13.1	22,661	16.5
40 to 49	54,944	17.1	52,134	17.5	2,810	12.1	231,417	18.4	103,563	16.7	91,219	18.4	36,635	26.7
50 to 64	26,224	8.1	24,722	8.3	1,502	6.5	131,191	10.5	53,327	8.6	54,517	11.0	23,347	17.0
65 and over	1,053	0.3	974	0.3	79	0.3	8,710	0.7	3,937	0.6	3,362	0.7	1,411	1.0
Age unknown	999	0.3	803	0.3	196	0.8	6,010	0.5	897	0.1	4,942	1.0	171	0.1

Note: Degree-granting institutions grant associate's or higher degrees and participate in Title IV federal financial aid programs. Details may not sum to totals because of rounding.
* = Quantity zero or equals zero.

Table A-32. Unemployment Rates of Persons 16 to 64 Years Old, by Age Group and Highest Level of Educational Attainment, Selected Years, 1975–2016

(Number; percent.)

Year	16 to 19 years old				20 to 24 years old				
	Unemployment rate for all education levels	Less than high school completion	High school completion	At least some college	Unemployment rate for all education levels	Less than high school completion	High school completion	At least some college	Bachelor's or higher degree
2016...............	20.2	21.6	22.0	11.8	10.5	17.3	12.2	9.9	4.9
2015...............	22.5	25.6	23.3	13.2	12.3	19.9	15.8	9.6	5.1
2014...............	22.9	22.9	25.0	15.1	14.9	25.3	18.9	12.2	6.7
2013...............	29.4	36.3	29.2	16.2	15.2	29.2	17.5	12.2	7.0
2012...............	30.6	41.1	28.7	19.6	15.5	27.6	18.3	12.7	6.0
2011...............	28.8	35.1	28.9	16.2	18.1	30.1	21.6	14.0	8.7
2010...............	31.9	41.7	29.6	18.1	18.8	32.3	22.3	14.2	7.9
2009...............	30.3	38.9	29.1	18.1	17.0	29.0	20.3	12.1	7.9
2008...............	20.9	30.8	17.2	11.3	10.7	19.2	13.0	6.8	4.5
2007...............	19.5	28.6	15.1	8.9	9.3	18.6	9.4	7.2	3.4
2006...............	20.6	25.8	17.6	17.7	9.3	15.7	10.4	7.1	3.9
2005...............	22.8	30.3	19.1	15.8	10.9	18.9	12.0	7.3	5.4
2000...............	17.2	21.4	15.3	‡	9.2	16.6	10.0	5.2	5.0
1995...............	21.0	30.3	15.1	12.4	10.7	19.5	12.0	7.3	4.1
1990...............	17.0	26.2	11.7	‡	8.2	17.4	7.8	4.8	3.1
1985...............	NA	NA	NA	NA	NA	NA	NA	NA	NA
1980...............	NA	NA	NA	NA	NA	NA	NA	NA	NA
1975...............	NA	NA	NA	NA	NA	NA	NA	NA	NA

NA = Not available.
‡ = Reporting standards not met.

Table A-32. Unemployment Rates of Persons 16 to 64 Years Old, by Age Group and Highest Level of Educational Attainment, Selected Years, 1975–2016—*Continued*

(Number; percent.)

Year	25 to 34 years old					35 to 44 years old				
	Unemployment rate for all education levels	Less than high school completion	High school completion	At least some college	Bachelor's or higher degree	Unemployment rate for all education levels	Less than high school completion	High school completion	At least some college	Bachelor's or higher degree
2016.........................	5.6	13.1	8.6	5.6	2.4	4.1	6.2	6.6	4.5	2.0
2015.........................	5.9	12.5	8.9	6.5	2.4	4.4	8.4	6.3	4.5	2.1
2014.........................	7.4	13.7	10.5	7.8	3.7	5.7	11.5	7.4	6.1	2.8
2013.........................	8.0	15.1	12.1	8.0	3.6	6.4	11.5	8.5	6.7	3.6
2012.........................	9.2	16.8	12.8	10.1	4.1	7.1	14.1	9.1	7.4	3.6
2011.........................	10.0	19.7	14.3	10.1	4.3	8.2	15.9	11.3	7.5	4.6
2010.........................	10.8	20.3	15.9	10.6	4.5	9.2	17.8	11.9	9.2	4.6
2009.........................	10.1	19.9	14.1	9.8	4.5	7.9	15.3	10.6	7.2	4.2
2008.........................	5.9	14.2	8.5	5.0	2.2	4.3	9.1	6.0	3.8	1.9
2007.........................	4.9	10.3	6.2	4.6	2.2	3.7	9.3	4.8	3.0	1.5
2006.........................	5.5	11.0	6.5	5.3	2.8	4.1	8.6	5.1	3.7	2.0
2005.........................	5.8	11.6	7.7	5.4	2.6	4.2	8.7	5.2	3.9	2.0
2000.........................	4.0	10.3	4.8	3.6	1.6	3.5	8.4	3.9	3.1	1.8
1995.........................	5.8	12.9	6.8	5.0	2.7	4.6	10.5	5.1	4.7	2.2
1990.........................	4.8	12.0	5.1	3.8	1.9	3.3	8.3	3.7	2.8	1.6
1985.........................	7.3	15.5	9.1	5.4	2.8	5.6	12.4	6.1	4.8	2.2
1980.........................	6.8	13.7	7.9	6.0	2.5	4.3	9.0	4.2	3.1	1.6
1975.........................	8.6	17.2	9.4	6.7	2.9	6.4	11.2	5.7	4.6	2.3

Table A-32. Unemployment Rates of Persons 16 to 64 Years Old, by Age Group and Highest Level of Educational Attainment, Selected Years, 1975–2016—*Continued*

(Number; percent.)

Year	45 to 54 years old					55 to 64 years old				
	Unemployment rate for all education levels	Less than high school completion	High school completion	At least some college	Bachelor's or higher degree	Unemployment rate for all education levels	Less than high school completion	High school completion	At least some college	Bachelor's or higher degree
2016..................	3.7	6.6	5.0	3.4	2.3	3.9	6.5	4.1	4.1	3.2
2015..................	4.1	8.6	5.2	4.1	2.2	4.2	6.9	4.4	4.3	3.3
2014..................	4.9	8.0	6.1	4.8	3.2	5.2	8.2	5.6	5.5	4.0
2013..................	6.0	12.3	7.8	5.2	3.8	5.7	11.2	6.4	5.8	4.2
2012..................	6.8	13.5	7.8	6.9	3.9	6.6	11.5	7.1	7.1	4.8
2011..................	7.5	16.3	9.3	7.1	4.0	6.9	10.0	8.4	7.3	4.9
2010..................	8.4	15.6	11.0	7.6	4.8	7.3	10.1	9.3	7.7	5.0
2009..................	7.4	13.6	8.8	7.5	4.3	6.7	12.7	7.8	7.0	4.3
2008..................	3.9	8.9	4.7	4.0	1.9	3.3	5.6	3.4	3.7	2.4
2007..................	3.5	7.3	4.0	3.7	1.8	3.1	5.3	3.7	3.5	1.8
2006..................	3.4	5.9	3.9	3.4	2.3	2.9	6.0	2.9	3.1	2.0
2005..................	3.9	7.0	4.6	3.7	2.5	3.7	7.5	4.3	3.5	2.3
2000..................	2.4	6.1	2.7	2.4	1.3	2.8	5.2	3.1	2.8	1.4
1995..................	3.9	7.9	4.0	3.9	2.4	3.9	6.7	3.4	3.2	3.3
1990..................	2.5	4.7	2.3	2.6	1.4	2.8	3.9	3.0	2.2	1.8
1985..................	5.4	10.2	5.4	3.2	2.1	4.6	7.1	4.5	3.0	2.2
1980..................	3.9	6.6	3.4	3.0	1.3	3.2	5.2	2.7	2.0	‡
1975..................	5.9	8.5	5.6	4.7	2.0	5.5	7.1	5.1	4.1	1.5

‡ = Reporting standards not met.

This page is intentionally left blank

Table A-33. Total Undergraduate Fall Enrollment in Degree-Granting Institutions, by Attendance Status and Sex of Student, Selected Years, 1970–2016

(Number.)

Year	Total	Full-time	Part-time	Males	Females	Males Full-time	Males Part-time
2016[1]	17,269,000	10,723,000	6,546,000	7,619,000	9,650,000	4,911,000	2,708,000
2015	17,036,778	10,604,992	6,431,786	7,499,837	9,536,941	4,810,564	2,689,273
2014	17,292,787	10,783,802	6,508,985	7,585,910	9,706,877	4,876,952	2,708,958
2013	17,474,835	10,938,494	6,536,341	7,659,626	9,815,209	4,949,572	2,710,054
2012	17,735,638	11,097,092	6,638,546	7,714,938	10,020,700	4,984,389	2,730,549
2011	18,077,303	11,365,175	6,712,128	7,822,992	10,254,311	5,070,553	2,752,439
2010	18,082,427	11,457,040	6,625,387	7,836,282	10,246,145	5,118,975	2,717,307
2009	17,464,179	11,038,275	6,425,904	7,563,176	9,901,003	4,942,120	2,621,056
2008	16,365,738	10,254,930	6,110,808	7,066,623	9,299,115	4,577,431	2,489,192
2007	15,603,771	9,840,978	5,762,793	6,727,600	8,876,171	4,396,868	2,330,732
2006	15,184,302	9,571,079	5,613,223	6,513,756	8,670,546	4,264,606	2,249,150
2005	14,963,964	9,446,430	5,517,534	6,408,871	8,555,093	4,200,863	2,208,008
2004	14,780,630	9,284,336	5,496,294	6,340,048	8,440,582	4,140,628	2,199,420
2003	14,480,364	9,045,253	5,435,111	6,227,372	8,252,992	4,048,682	2,178,690
2002	14,257,077	8,734,252	5,522,825	6,192,390	8,064,687	3,934,168	2,258,222
2001	13,715,610	8,327,640	5,387,970	6,004,431	7,711,179	3,768,630	2,235,801
2000	13,155,393	7,922,926	5,232,467	5,778,268	7,377,125	3,588,246	2,190,022
1999	12,739,445	7,753,548	4,985,897	5,584,234	7,155,211	3,524,586	2,059,648
1998	12,436,937	7,538,711	4,898,226	5,446,133	6,990,804	3,428,161	2,017,972
1997	12,450,587	7,418,598	5,031,989	5,468,532	6,982,055	3,379,597	2,088,935
1996	12,326,948	7,298,839	5,028,109	5,420,672	6,906,276	3,339,108	2,081,564
1995	12,231,719	7,145,268	5,086,451	5,401,130	6,830,589	3,296,610	2,104,520
1994	12,262,608	7,168,706	5,093,902	5,422,113	6,840,495	3,341,591	2,080,522
1993	12,323,959	7,179,482	5,144,477	5,483,682	6,840,277	3,381,997	2,101,685
1992	12,537,700	7,244,442	5,293,258	5,582,936	6,954,764	3,424,739	2,158,197
1991	12,439,287	7,221,412	5,217,875	5,571,003	6,868,284	3,435,526	2,135,477
1990	11,959,106	6,976,030	4,983,076	5,379,759	6,579,347	3,336,535	2,043,224
1989	11,742,531	6,840,696	4,901,835	5,310,990	6,431,541	3,278,647	2,032,343
1988	11,316,548	6,642,428	4,674,120	5,137,644	6,178,904	3,206,442	1,931,202
1987	11,046,235	6,462,549	4,583,686	5,068,457	5,977,778	3,163,676	1,904,781
1986	10,797,975	6,352,073	4,445,902	5,017,505	5,780,470	3,146,330	1,871,175
1985	10,596,674	6,319,592	4,277,082	4,962,080	5,634,594	3,156,446	1,805,634
1984	10,618,071	6,347,653	4,270,418	5,006,813	5,611,258	3,194,930	1,811,883
1983	10,845,995	6,514,034	4,331,961	5,158,300	5,687,695	3,304,247	1,854,053
1982	10,825,062	6,483,805	4,341,257	5,170,494	5,654,568	3,299,436	1,871,058
1981	10,754,522	6,449,068	4,305,454	5,108,271	5,646,251	3,260,473	1,847,798
1980	10,475,055	6,361,744	4,113,311	5,000,177	5,474,878	3,226,857	1,773,320
1975	9,679,455	6,168,396	3,511,059	5,257,005	4,422,450	3,459,328	1,797,677
1970	7,368,644	5,280,064	2,088,580	4,249,702	3,118,942	3,096,371	1,153,331

Note: Data include unclassified undergraduate students. Data through 1995 are for institutions of higher education, while later data are for degree-granting institutions. Degree-granting institutions grant associate's or higher degrees and participate in Title IV federal financial aid programs. The degree-granting classification is very similar to the earlier higher education classification, but it includes more 2-year colleges and excludes a few higher education institutions that did not grant degrees. Some data have been revised from previously published figures. Details may not sum to totals because of rounding.
[1] Projected.

Table A-33. Total Undergraduate Fall Enrollment in Degree-Granting Institutions, by Attendance Status and Sex of Student, Selected Years, 1970–2016—*Continued*

(Number.)

| Year | Females | | Public | Private | | |
	Full-time	Part-time		Total	Nonprofit	For-profit
2016[1]	5,813,000	3,838,000	13,433,000	3,836,000	NA	NA
2015	5,794,428	3,742,513	13,145,720	3,891,058	2,819,174	1,071,884
2014	5,906,850	3,800,027	13,244,837	4,047,950	2,771,341	1,276,609
2013	5,988,922	3,826,287	13,347,002	4,127,833	2,757,447	1,370,386
2012	6,112,703	3,907,997	13,478,100	4,257,538	2,744,400	1,513,138
2011	6,294,622	3,959,689	13,694,899	4,382,404	2,718,923	1,663,481
2010	6,338,065	3,908,080	13,703,000	4,379,427	2,652,993	1,726,434
2009	6,096,155	3,804,848	13,386,375	4,077,804	2,595,171	1,482,633
2008	5,677,499	3,621,616	12,591,217	3,774,521	2,536,532	1,237,989
2007	5,444,110	3,432,061	12,137,583	3,466,188	2,470,327	995,861
2006	5,306,473	3,364,073	11,847,426	3,336,876	2,448,240	888,636
2005	5,245,567	3,309,526	11,697,730	3,266,234	2,418,368	847,866
2004	5,143,708	3,296,874	11,650,580	3,130,050	2,389,366	740,684
2003	4,996,571	3,256,421	11,523,103	2,957,261	2,346,673	610,588
2002	4,800,084	3,264,603	11,432,855	2,824,222	2,306,091	518,131
2001	4,559,010	3,152,169	10,985,871	2,729,739	2,257,718	472,021
2000	4,334,680	3,042,445	10,539,322	2,616,071	2,213,180	402,891
1999	4,228,962	2,926,249	10,174,228	2,565,217	2,185,290	379,927
1998	4,110,550	2,880,254	9,950,212	2,486,725	2,152,655	334,070
1997	4,039,001	2,943,054	10,007,479	2,443,108	2,139,824	303,284
1996	3,959,731	2,946,545	9,935,283	2,391,665	2,112,318	279,347
1995	3,848,658	2,981,931	9,903,626	2,328,093	2,104,693	223,400
1994	3,827,115	3,013,380	9,945,128	2,317,480	2,100,465	217,015
1993	3,797,485	3,042,792	10,011,787	2,312,172	2,099,197	212,975
1992	3,819,703	3,135,061	10,216,297	2,321,403	2,101,721	219,682
1991	3,785,886	3,082,398	10,147,957	2,291,330	2,072,354	218,976
1990	3,639,495	2,939,852	9,709,596	2,249,510	2,043,407	206,103
1989	3,562,049	2,869,492	9,487,742	2,254,789	NA	NA
1988	3,435,986	2,742,918	9,103,146	2,213,402	NA	NA
1987	3,298,873	2,678,905	8,918,589	2,127,646	1,939,942	187,704
1986	3,205,743	2,574,727	8,660,716	2,137,259	1,928,294	208,965
1985	3,163,146	2,471,448	8,477,125	2,119,549	1,928,996	190,553
1984	3,152,723	2,458,535	8,493,491	2,124,580	1,940,310	184,270
1983	3,209,787	2,477,908	8,697,118	2,148,877	1,961,076	187,801
1982	3,184,369	2,470,199	8,713,073	2,111,989	1,939,389	172,600
1981	3,188,595	2,457,656	8,648,363	2,106,159	1,958,848	147,311
1980	3,134,887	2,339,991	8,441,955	2,033,100	1,926,703	106,397
1975	2,709,068	1,713,382	7,826,032	1,853,423	1,814,844	38,579
1970	2,183,693	935,249	5,620,255	1,748,389	1,730,133	18,256

Note: Data include unclassified undergraduate students. Data through 1995 are for institutions of higher education, while later data are for degree-granting institutions. Degree-granting institutions grant associate's or higher degrees and participate in Title IV federal financial aid programs. The degree-granting classification is very similar to the earlier higher education classification, but it includes more 2-year colleges and excludes a few higher education institutions that did not grant degrees. Some data have been revised from previously published figures. Details may not sum to totals because of rounding.
NA = Not available.
[1]Projected.

Table A-34. Total Postbaccalaureate Fall Enrollment in Degree-Granting Institutions, by Attendance Status, Sex of Student, and Control of Institution, 1967–2016

(Number.)

Year	Total	Full-time	Part-time	Males	Females	Males Full-time	Males Part-time
2016[1]	2,916,000	1,673,000	1,243,000	1,236,000	1,680,000	768,000	468,000
2015	2,940,492	1,685,837	1,254,655	1,221,566	1,718,926	749,971	471,595
2014	2,914,582	1,670,173	1,244,409	1,211,151	1,703,431	742,439	468,712
2013	2,900,954	1,658,618	1,242,336	1,201,160	1,699,794	732,594	468,566
2012	2,908,840	1,637,312	1,271,528	1,204,068	1,704,772	724,017	480,051
2011	2,933,287	1,637,356	1,295,931	1,211,264	1,722,023	722,265	488,999
2010	2,937,011	1,630,142	1,306,869	1,209,477	1,727,534	719,408	490,069
2009	2,849,415	1,567,080	1,282,335	1,169,777	1,679,638	689,977	479,800
2008	2,737,076	1,492,813	1,244,263	1,122,272	1,614,804	656,926	465,346
2007	2,644,357	1,428,914	1,215,443	1,088,314	1,556,043	632,576	455,738
2006	2,574,568	1,386,226	1,188,342	1,061,059	1,513,509	614,709	446,350
2005	2,523,511	1,350,581	1,172,930	1,047,054	1,476,457	602,525	444,529
2004	2,491,414	1,325,841	1,165,573	1,047,214	1,444,200	598,727	448,487
2003	2,431,117	1,280,880	1,150,237	1,032,892	1,398,225	589,190	443,702
2002	2,354,634	1,212,107	1,142,527	1,009,726	1,344,908	566,930	442,796
2001	2,212,377	1,119,862	1,092,515	956,384	1,255,993	531,260	425,124
2000	2,156,896	1,086,674	1,070,222	943,501	1,213,395	522,847	420,654
1999	2,110,246	1,049,591	1,060,655	930,930	1,179,316	508,930	422,000
1998	2,070,030	1,024,627	1,045,403	923,132	1,146,898	505,492	417,640
1997	2,051,747	1,019,464	1,032,283	927,496	1,124,251	510,845	416,651
1996	2,040,572	1,004,114	1,036,458	932,153	1,108,419	512,100	420,053
1995	2,030,062	983,534	1,046,528	941,409	1,088,653	510,782	430,627
1994	2,016,182	969,070	1,047,112	949,785	1,066,397	513,592	436,193
1993	1,980,844	948,136	1,032,708	943,768	1,037,076	508,574	435,194
1992	1,949,659	917,676	1,031,983	941,053	1,008,606	502,166	438,887
1991	1,919,666	893,917	1,025,749	930,841	988,825	493,849	436,992
1990	1,859,531	844,955	1,014,576	904,150	955,381	471,217	432,933
1989	1,796,029	820,254	975,775	879,025	917,004	461,596	417,429
1988	1,738,789	794,340	944,449	864,252	874,537	455,337	408,915
1987	1,720,407	768,536	951,871	863,599	856,808	447,212	416,387
1986	1,705,536	767,477	938,059	867,010	838,526	452,717	414,293
1985	1,650,381	755,629	894,752	856,370	794,011	451,274	405,096
1984	1,623,869	750,735	873,134	856,761	767,108	452,579	404,182
1983	1,618,666	747,016	871,650	865,425	753,241	455,540	409,885
1982	1,600,718	736,813	863,905	860,890	739,828	453,519	407,371
1981	1,617,150	732,182	884,968	866,785	750,365	452,364	414,421
1980	1,621,840	736,214	885,626	874,197	747,643	462,387	411,810
1979	1,571,922	714,624	857,298	862,754	709,168	456,197	406,557
1978	1,575,693	704,831	870,862	879,931	695,762	458,865	421,066
1977	1,569,084	698,902	870,182	891,819	677,265	462,038	429,781
1976	1,577,546	683,825	893,721	904,551	672,995	459,286	445,265
1975	1,505,404	672,938	832,466	891,992	613,412	467,425	424,567
1974	1,425,001	643,927	781,074	856,847	568,154	454,706	402,141
1973	1,342,452	610,935	731,517	833,453	508,999	444,219	389,234
1972	1,272,421	583,299	689,122	810,164	462,257	436,533	373,631
1971	1,204,390	564,236	640,154	789,131	415,259	428,167	360,964
1970	1,212,243	536,226	676,017	793,940	418,303	407,724	386,216
1969	1,120,175	506,833	613,342	738,673	381,502	383,630	355,043
1968	1,037,377	469,747	567,630	696,649	340,728	358,686	337,963
1967	896,065	448,238	447,827	630,701	265,364	354,628	276,073

Note: Data include unclassified graduate students. Data through 1995 are for institutions of higher education, while later data are for degree-granting institutions. Degree-granting institutions grant associate's or higher degrees and participate in Title IV federal financial aid programs. The degree-granting classification is very similar to the earlier higher education classification, but it includes more 2-year colleges and excludes a few higher education institutions that did not grant degrees. Some data have been revised from previously published figures.
[1] Projected.

Table A-34. Total Postbaccalaureate Fall Enrollment in Degree-Granting Institutions, by Attendance Status, Sex of Student, and Control of Institution, 1967–2016—*Continued*

(Number.)

| Year | Females | | Public | Private | | |
	Full-time	Part-time		Total	Nonprofit	For-profit
2016[1]	905,000	775,000	1,411,000	1,504,000	NA	NA
2015	935,866	783,060	1,422,383	1,518,109	1,244,198	273,911
2014	927,734	775,697	1,410,178	1,504,404	1,224,748	279,656
2013	926,024	773,770	1,398,556	1,502,398	1,216,557	285,841
2012	913,295	791,477	1,406,567	1,502,273	1,206,988	295,285
2011	915,091	806,932	1,421,404	1,511,883	1,207,896	303,987
2010	910,734	816,800	1,439,171	1,497,840	1,201,489	296,351
2009	877,103	802,535	1,424,393	1,425,022	1,172,501	252,521
2008	835,887	778,917	1,380,936	1,356,140	1,124,987	231,153
2007	796,338	759,705	1,353,197	1,291,160	1,100,823	190,337
2006	771,517	741,992	1,332,707	1,241,861	1,064,626	177,235
2005	748,056	728,401	1,324,104	1,199,407	1,036,324	163,083
2004	727,114	717,086	1,329,532	1,161,882	1,022,319	139,563
2003	691,690	706,535	1,335,595	1,095,522	994,375	101,147
2002	645,177	699,731	1,319,138	1,035,496	959,385	76,111
2001	588,602	667,391	1,247,285	965,092	909,612	55,480
2000	563,827	649,568	1,213,464	943,432	896,239	47,193
1999	540,661	638,655	1,201,511	908,735	869,739	38,996
1998	519,135	627,763	1,187,557	882,473	852,270	30,203
1997	508,619	615,632	1,188,640	863,107	837,790	25,317
1996	492,014	616,405	1,185,216	855,356	830,238	25,118
1995	472,752	615,901	1,188,748	841,314	824,351	16,963
1994	455,478	610,919	1,188,552	827,630	809,642	17,988
1993	439,562	597,514	1,177,301	803,543	789,700	13,843
1992	415,510	593,096	1,168,270	781,389	770,802	10,587
1991	400,068	588,757	1,161,606	758,060	746,687	11,373
1990	373,738	581,643	1,135,121	724,410	716,820	7,590
1989	358,658	558,346	1,090,221	705,808	NA	NA
1988	339,003	535,534	1,058,242	680,547	NA	NA
1987	321,324	535,484	1,054,665	665,742	662,408	3,334
1986	314,760	523,766	1,053,177	652,359	644,185	8,174
1985	304,355	489,656	1,002,148	648,233	642,795	5,438
1984	298,156	468,952	983,879	639,990	634,109	5,881
1983	291,476	461,765	985,616	633,050	628,111	4,939
1982	283,294	456,534	983,014	617,704	613,350	4,354
1981	279,818	470,547	998,669	618,481	613,557	4,924
1980	273,827	473,816	1,015,439	606,401	601,084	5,317
1979	258,427	450,741	989,991	581,931	578,425	3,506
1978	245,966	449,796	998,608	577,085	573,563	3,522
1977	236,864	440,401	1,004,013	565,071	561,384	3,687
1976	224,539	448,456	1,033,115	544,431	541,064	3,367
1975	205,513	407,899	1,008,476	496,928	496,604	324
1974	189,221	378,933	956,770	468,231	467,950	281
1973	166,716	342,283	897,104	445,348	445,205	143
1972	146,766	315,491	848,031	424,390	424,278	112
1971	136,069	279,190	796,516	407,874	407,804	70
1970	128,502	289,801	807,879	404,364	404,287	77
1969	123,203	258,299	738,551	381,624	381,558	66
1968	111,061	229,667	648,657	388,720	388,681	39
1967	93,610	171,754	522,623	373,442	373,336	106

Note: Data include unclassified graduate students. Data through 1995 are for institutions of higher education, while later data are for degree-granting institutions. Degree-granting institutions grant associate's or higher degrees and participate in Title IV federal financial aid programs. The degree-granting classification is very similar to the earlier higher education classification, but it includes more 2-year colleges and excludes a few higher education institutions that did not grant degrees. Some data have been revised from previously published figures.
NA = Not available.
[1]Projected.

Table A-35. Total Fall Enrollment in Degree-Granting Institutions, by Race/Ethnicity, Sex, Attendance Status, and Level of Student, Selected Years, 1976–2015

(Nnumbers in thousands; percent.)

Race/ethnicity, sex, attendance status, and level of student	1976 Number	1976 Percent	1990 Number	1990 Percent	2000 Number	2000 Percent	2010 Number	2010 Percent
All students, total	10,985.6	100.0	13,818.6	100.0	15,312.3	100.0	21,019.4	100.0
White	9,076.1	84.3	10,722.5	79.9	10,462.1	70.8	12,720.8	62.6
Total, selected races/ethnicities	1,690.8	15.7	2,704.7	20.1	4,321.5	29.2	7,591.0	37.4
Black	1,033.0	9.6	1,247.0	9.3	1,730.3	11.7	3,039.0	15.0
Hispanic	383.8	3.6	782.4	5.8	1,461.8	9.9	2,748.8	13.5
Asian/Pacific Islander	197.9	1.8	572.4	4.3	978.2	6.6	1,281.6	6.3
Asian	NA	NA	NA	NA	NA	NA	1,217.6	6.0
Pacific Islander	NA	NA	NA	NA	NA	NA	64.0	0.3
American Indian/Alaska Native	76.1	0.7	102.8	0.8	151.2	1.0	196.2	1.0
Two or more races	NA	NA	NA	NA	NA	NA	325.4	1.6
Nonresident alien	218.7	X	391.5	X	528.7	X	707.7	X
Male	5,794.4	100.0	6,283.9	100.0	6,721.8	100.0	9,045.8	100.0
White	4,813.7	85.3	4,861.0	80.5	4,634.6	72.1	5,605.8	64.7
Total, selected races/ethnicities	826.6	14.7	1,176.6	19.5	1,789.8	27.9	3,060.3	35.3
Black	469.9	8.3	484.7	8.0	635.3	9.9	1,089.0	12.6
Hispanic	209.7	3.7	353.9	5.9	627.1	9.8	1,157.6	13.4
Asian/Pacific Islander	108.4	1.9	294.9	4.9	465.9	7.3	600.6	6.9
Asian	NA	NA	NA	NA	NA	NA	572.1	6.6
Pacific Islander	NA	NA	NA	NA	NA	NA	28.5	0.3
American Indian/Alaska Native	38.5	0.7	43.1	0.7	61.4	1.0	78.7	0.9
Two or more races	NA	NA	NA	NA	NA	NA	134.4	1.6
Nonresident alien	154.1	X	246.3	X	297.3	X	379.6	X
Female	5,191.2	100.0	7,534.7	100.0	8,590.5	100.0	11,973.7	100.0
White	4,262.4	83.1	5,861.5	79.3	5,827.5	69.7	7,115.0	61.1
Total, selected races/ethnicities	864.2	16.9	1,528.1	20.7	2,531.7	30.3	4,530.7	38.9
Black	563.1	11.0	762.3	10.3	1,095.0	13.1	1,949.9	16.7
Hispanic	174.1	3.4	428.5	5.8	834.7	10.0	1,591.2	13.7
Asian/Pacific Islander	89.4	1.7	277.5	3.8	512.3	6.1	681.0	5.8
Asian	NA	NA	NA	NA	NA	NA	645.5	5.5
Pacific Islander	NA	NA	NA	NA	NA	NA	35.5	0.3
American Indian/Alaska Native	37.6	0.7	59.7	0.8	89.7	1.1	117.5	1.0
Two or more races	NA	NA	NA	NA	NA	NA	191.0	1.6
Nonresident alien	64.6	X	145.2	X	231.4	X	328.0	X
Full-time	6,703.6	100.0	7,821.0	100.0	9,009.6	100.0	13,087.2	100.0
White	5,512.6	84.2	6,016.5	79.9	6,231.1	72.5	8,053.5	64.3
Total, selected races/ethnicities	1,030.9	15.8	1,514.9	20.1	2,368.5	27.5	4,468.5	35.7
Black	659.2	10.1	718.3	9.5	982.6	11.4	1,811.3	14.5
Hispanic	211.1	3.2	394.7	5.2	710.3	8.3	1,501.0	12.0
Asian/Pacific Islander	117.7	1.8	347.4	4.6	591.2	6.9	820.8	6.6
Asian	NA	NA	NA	NA	NA	NA	783.0	6.3
Pacific Islander	NA	NA	NA	NA	NA	NA	37.8	0.3
American Indian/Alaska Native	43.0	0.7	54.4	0.7	84.4	1.0	118.3	0.9
Two or more races	NA	NA	NA	NA	NA	NA	217.2	1.7
Nonresident alien	160.0	X	289.6	X	410.0	X	565.2	X
Part-time	4,282.1	100.0	5,997.7	100.0	6,302.7	100.0	7,932.3	100.0
White	3,563.5	84.4	4,706.0	79.8	4,231.0	68.4	4,667.3	59.9
Total, selected races/ethnicities	659.9	15.6	1,189.8	20.2	1,953.0	31.6	3,122.5	40.1
Black	373.8	8.9	528.7	9.0	747.7	12.1	1,227.7	15.8
Hispanic	172.7	4.1	387.7	6.6	751.5	12.2	1,247.9	16.0
Asian/Pacific Islander	80.2	1.9	225.1	3.8	387.1	6.3	460.8	5.9
Asian	NA	NA	NA	NA	NA	NA	434.6	5.6
Pacific Islander	NA	NA	NA	NA	NA	NA	26.2	0.3
American Indian/Alaska Native	33.1	0.8	48.4	0.8	66.8	1.1	78.0	1.0
Two or more races	NA	NA	NA	NA	NA	NA	108.2	1.4
Nonresident alien	58.7	X	101.8	X	118.7	X	142.5	X
Undergraduate, total	9,419.0	100.0	11,959.1	100.0	13,155.4	100.0	18,082.4	100.0
White	7,740.5	83.4	9,272.6	79.0	8,983.5	69.8	10,895.9	61.6
Total, selected races/ethnicities	1,535.3	16.6	2,467.7	21.0	3,884.0	30.2	6,788.1	38.4

Note: Race categories exclude persons of Hispanic ethnicity. Because of underreporting and nonreporting of racial/ethnic data, some figures are slightly lower than corresponding data in other tables. Data through 1990 are for institutions of higher education, while later data are for degree-granting institutions. Degree-granting institutions grant associate's or higher degrees and participate in Title IV federal financial aid programs. The degree-granting classification is very similar to the earlier higher education classification, but it includes more 2-year colleges and excludes a few higher education institutions that did not grant degrees. Some data have been revised from previously published figures. Details may not sum to totals because of rounding.
NA = Not available.
X = Not applicable.

Table A-35. Total Fall Enrollment in Degree-Granting Institutions, by Race/Ethnicity, Sex, Attendance Status, and Level of Student, Selected Years, 1976–2015—*Continued*

(Nnumbers in thousands; percent.)

Race/ethnicity, sex, attendance status, and level of student	2013 Number	2013 Percent	2014 Number	2014 Percent	2015 Number	2015 Percent
All students, total....................................	20,375.8	100.0	20,207.4	100.0	19,977.3	100.0
White	11,590.7	59.3	11,237.4	58.3	10,937.1	57.6
Total, selected races/ethnicities....................	7,944.8	40.7	8,051.0	41.7	8,057.1	42.4
Black	2,872.1	14.7	2,791.9	14.5	2,675.4	14.1
Hispanic	3,091.1	15.8	3,191.7	16.5	3,292.2	17.3
Asian/Pacific Islander........................	1,259.6	6.4	1,272.4	6.6	1,283.8	6.8
Asian	1,198.5	6.1	1,213.6	6.3	1,228.3	6.5
Pacific Islander	61.1	0.3	58.8	0.3	55.5	0.3
American Indian/Alaska Native..............	162.6	0.8	152.9	0.8	146.2	0.8
Two or more races	559.4	2.9	642.1	3.3	659.6	3.5
Nonresident alien	840.3	X	918.9	X	983.1	X
Male..	8,860.8	100.0	8,797.1	100.0	8,721.4	100.0
White	5,133.1	61.1	4,973.7	60.0	4,848.0	59.3
Total, selected races/ethnicities....................	3,267.6	38.9	3,312.9	40.0	3,324.4	40.7
Black	1,065.0	12.7	1,034.7	12.5	997.7	12.2
Hispanic	1,306.5	15.6	1,347.9	16.3	1,387.3	17.0
Asian/Pacific Islander........................	594.3	7.1	599.2	7.2	602.8	7.4
Asian	567.0	6.7	573.0	6.9	577.5	7.1
Pacific Islander	27.3	0.3	26.3	0.3	25.4	0.3
American Indian/Alaska Native..............	64.8	0.8	61.3	0.7	58.2	0.7
Two or more races	236.9	2.8	269.7	3.3	278.4	3.4
Nonresident alien	460.1	X	510.5	X	548.9	X
Female	11,515.0	100.0	11,410.3	100.0	11,255.9	100.0
White	6,457.6	58.0	6,263.7	56.9	6,089.0	56.3
Total, selected races/ethnicities....................	4,677.2	42.0	4,738.1	43.1	4,732.7	43.7
Black	1,807.1	16.2	1,757.2	16.0	1,677.7	15.5
Hispanic	1,784.6	16.0	1,843.8	16.8	1,904.9	17.6
Asian/Pacific Islander........................	665.3	6.0	673.2	6.1	681.0	6.3
Asian	631.5	5.7	640.6	5.8	650.8	6.0
Pacific Islander	33.8	0.3	32.6	0.3	30.2	0.3
American Indian/Alaska Native..............	97.7	0.9	91.6	0.8	88.0	0.8
Two or more races	322.5	2.9	372.4	3.4	381.1	3.5
Nonresident alien	380.2	X	408.4	X	434.2	X
Full-time...	12,597.1	100.0	12,454.0	100.0	12,290.8	100.0
White	7,239.2	60.8	6,982.4	59.7	6,786.6	59.1
Total, selected races/ethnicities....................	4,662.5	39.2	4,708.5	40.3	4,690.9	40.9
Black	1,669.3	14.0	1,600.0	13.7	1,536.3	13.4
Hispanic	1,700.3	14.3	1,748.3	15.0	1,786.5	15.6
Asian/Pacific Islander........................	821.3	6.9	832.1	7.1	844.5	7.4
Asian	785.5	6.6	798.1	6.8	812.8	7.1
Pacific Islander	35.7	0.3	34.0	0.3	31.7	0.3
American Indian/Alaska Native..............	94.5	0.8	88.0	0.8	82.8	0.7
Two or more races	377.2	3.2	440.1	3.8	440.8	3.8
Nonresident alien	695.3	X	763.1	X	813.3	X
Part-time...	7,778.7	100.0	7,753.4	100.0	7,686.4	100.0
White	4,351.5	57.0	4,255.0	56.0	4,150.5	55.2
Total, selected races/ethnicities....................	3,282.2	43.0	3,342.6	44.0	3,366.2	44.8
Black	1,202.9	15.8	1,191.9	15.7	1,139.1	15.2
Hispanic	1,390.8	18.2	1,443.4	19.0	1,505.6	20.0
Asian/Pacific Islander........................	438.3	5.7	440.3	5.8	439.4	5.8
Asian	413.0	5.4	415.5	5.5	415.5	5.5
Pacific Islander	25.3	0.3	24.8	0.3	23.9	0.3
American Indian/Alaska Native..............	68.1	0.9	64.9	0.9	63.3	0.8
Two or more races	182.1	2.4	202.0	2.7	218.8	2.9
Nonresident alien	145.0	X	155.8	X	169.8	X
Undergraduate, total..............................	17,474.8	100.0	17,292.8	100.0	17,036.8	100.0
White	9,899.2	58.3	9,581.5	57.2	9,302.4	56.5
Total, selected races/ethnicities....................	7,092.3	41.7	7,180.9	42.8	7,168.5	43.5

Note: Race categories exclude persons of Hispanic ethnicity. Because of underreporting and nonreporting of racial/ethnic data, some figures are slightly lower than corresponding data in other tables. Data through 1990 are for institutions of higher education, while later data are for degree-granting institutions. Degree-granting institutions grant associate's or higher degrees and participate in Title IV federal financial aid programs. The degree-granting classification is very similar to the earlier higher education classification, but it includes more 2-year colleges and excludes a few higher education institutions that did not grant degrees. Some data have been revised from previously published figures. Details may not sum to totals because of rounding.

X = Not applicable.

Table A-35. Total Fall Enrollment in Degree-Granting Institutions, by Race/Ethnicity, Sex, Attendance Status, and Level of Student, Selected Years, 1976–2015—*Continued*

(Nnumbers in thousands; percent.)

Race/ethnicity, sex, attendance status, and level of student	1976 Number	1976 Percent	1990 Number	1990 Percent	2000 Number	2000 Percent	2010 Number	2010 Percent
Black	943.4	10.2	1,147.2	9.8	1,548.9	12.0	2,677.1	15.1
Hispanic	352.9	3.8	724.6	6.2	1,351.0	10.5	2,551.0	14.4
Asian/Pacific Islander	169.3	1.8	500.5	4.3	845.5	6.6	1,087.3	6.1
Asian	NA	NA	NA	NA	NA	NA	1,029.8	5.8
Pacific Islander	NA	NA	NA	NA	NA	NA	57.5	0.3
American Indian/Alaska Native	69.7	0.8	95.5	0.8	138.5	1.1	179.1	1.0
Two or more races	NA	NA	NA	NA	NA	NA	293.7	1.7
Nonresident alien	143.2	X	218.7	X	288.0	X	398.4	X
Male	4,896.8	100.0	5,379.8	100.0	5,778.3	100.0	7,836.3	100.0
White	4,052.2	84.4	4,184.4	79.6	4,010.1	71.3	4,861.0	63.7
Total, selected races/ethnicities	748.2	15.6	1,069.3	20.4	1,618.0	28.7	2,773.8	36.3
Black	430.7	9.0	448.0	8.5	577.0	10.3	982.9	12.9
Hispanic	191.7	4.0	326.9	6.2	582.6	10.4	1,082.9	14.2
Asian/Pacific Islander	91.1	1.9	254.5	4.8	401.9	7.1	513.4	6.7
Asian	NA	NA	NA	NA	NA	NA	487.4	6.4
Pacific Islander	NA	NA	NA	NA	NA	NA	26.0	0.3
American Indian/Alaska Native	34.8	0.7	39.9	0.8	56.4	1.0	72.3	0.9
Two or more races	NA	NA	NA	NA	NA	NA	122.3	1.6
Nonresident alien	96.4	X	126.1	X	150.2	X	201.5	X
Female	4,522.1	100.0	6,579.3	100.0	7,377.1	100.0	10,246.1	100.0
White	3,688.3	82.4	5,088.2	78.4	4,973.3	68.7	6,035.0	60.1
Total, selected races/ethnicities	787.0	17.6	1,398.5	21.6	2,266.0	31.3	4,014.3	39.9
Black	512.7	11.5	699.2	10.8	971.9	13.4	1,694.2	16.9
Hispanic	161.2	3.6	397.6	6.1	768.4	10.6	1,468.1	14.6
Asian/Pacific Islander	78.2	1.7	246.0	3.8	443.6	6.1	573.9	5.7
Asian	NA	NA	NA	NA	NA	NA	542.4	5.4
Pacific Islander	NA	NA	NA	NA	NA	NA	31.5	0.3
American Indian/Alaska Native	34.9	0.8	55.5	0.9	82.1	1.1	106.8	1.1
Two or more races	NA	NA	NA	NA	NA	NA	171.3	1.7
Nonresident alien	46.8	X	92.6	X	137.8	X	196.9	X
Postbaccalaureate, total	1,566.6	100.0	1,859.5	100.0	2,156.9	100.0	2,937.0	100.0
White	1,335.6	89.6	1,449.8	86.0	1,478.6	77.2	1,824.9	69.4
Total, selected races/ethnicities	155.5	10.4	237.0	14.0	437.5	22.8	802.8	30.6
Black	89.7	6.0	99.8	5.9	181.4	9.5	361.9	13.8
Hispanic	30.9	2.1	57.9	3.4	110.8	5.8	197.8	7.5
Asian/Pacific Islander	28.6	1.9	72.0	4.3	132.7	6.9	194.3	7.4
Asian	NA	NA	NA	NA	NA	NA	187.8	7.1
Pacific Islander	NA	NA	NA	NA	NA	NA	6.5	0.2
American Indian/Alaska Native	6.4	0.4	7.3	0.4	12.6	0.7	17.1	0.7
Two or more races	NA	NA	NA	NA	NA	NA	31.7	1.2
Nonresident alien	75.5	X	172.7	X	240.7	X	309.3	X
Male	897.6	100.0	904.2	100.0	943.5	100.0	1,209.5	100.0
White	761.6	90.7	676.6	86.3	624.5	78.4	744.9	72.2
Total, selected races/ethnicities	78.4	9.3	107.4	13.7	171.9	21.6	286.5	27.8
Black	39.2	4.7	36.7	4.7	58.3	7.3	106.1	10.3
Hispanic	18.1	2.2	27.0	3.4	44.5	5.6	74.7	7.2
Asian/Pacific Islander	17.4	2.1	40.4	5.2	64.0	8.0	87.2	8.5
Asian	NA	NA	NA	NA	NA	NA	84.7	8.2
Pacific Islander	NA	NA	NA	NA	NA	NA	2.5	0.2
American Indian/Alaska Native	3.7	0.4	3.2	0.4	5.0	0.6	6.4	0.6
Two or more races	NA	NA	NA	NA	NA	NA	12.0	1.2
Nonresident alien	57.7	X	120.2	X	147.1	X	178.2	X
Female	669.1	100.0	955.4	100.0	1,213.4	100.0	1,727.5	100.0
White	574.1	88.1	773.2	85.6	854.1	76.3	1,080.0	67.7
Total, selected races/ethnicities	77.2	11.9	129.6	14.4	265.7	23.7	516.4	32.3
Black	50.5	7.7	63.1	7.0	123.1	11.0	255.8	16.0
Hispanic	12.8	2.0	30.9	3.4	66.3	5.9	123.1	7.7
Asian/Pacific Islander	11.2	1.7	31.5	3.5	68.7	6.1	107.0	6.7
Asian	NA	NA	NA	NA	NA	NA	103.1	6.5
Pacific Islander	NA	NA	NA	NA	NA	NA	3.9	0.2
American Indian/Alaska Native	2.7	0.4	4.1	0.5	7.6	0.7	10.7	0.7
Two or more races	NA	NA	NA	NA	NA	NA	19.7	1.2
Nonresident alien	17.8	X	52.5	X	93.6	X	131.1	X

Note: Race categories exclude persons of Hispanic ethnicity. Because of underreporting and nonreporting of racial/ethnic data, some figures are slightly lower than corresponding data in other tables. Data through 1990 are for institutions of higher education, while later data are for degree-granting institutions. Degree-granting institutions grant associate's or higher degrees and participate in Title IV federal financial aid programs. The degree-granting classification is very similar to the earlier higher education classification, but it includes more 2-year colleges and excludes a few higher education institutions that did not grant degrees. Some data have been revised from previously published figures. Details may not sum to totals because of rounding.
NA = Not available.
X = Not applicable.

Table A-35. Total Fall Enrollment in Degree-Granting Institutions, by Race/Ethnicity, Sex, Attendance Status, and Level of Student, Selected Years, 1976–2015—*Continued*

(Nnumbers in thousands; percent.)

Race/ethnicity, sex, attendance status, and level of student	2013 Number	2013 Percent	2014 Number	2014 Percent	2015 Number	2015 Percent
Black	2,504.8	14.7	2,425.8	14.5	2,311.1	14.0
Hispanic	2,870.2	16.9	2,961.9	17.7	3,049.6	18.5
Asian/Pacific Islander	1,064.4	6.3	1,075.0	6.4	1,083.4	6.6
Asian	1,010.1	5.9	1,022.7	6.1	1,033.9	6.3
Pacific Islander	54.2	0.3	52.3	0.3	49.5	0.3
American Indian/Alaska Native	147.8	0.9	138.6	0.8	132.3	0.8
Two or more races	505.2	3.0	579.5	3.5	592.2	3.6
Nonresident alien	483.4	X	530.4	X	565.8	X
Male	7,659.6	100.0	7,585.9	100.0	7,499.8	100.0
White	4,439.6	60.0	4,298.9	58.9	4,187.9	58.2
Total, selected races/ethnicities	2,961.6	40.0	2,999.6	41.1	3,004.5	41.8
Black	955.4	12.9	924.6	12.7	887.0	12.3
Hispanic	1,222.9	16.5	1,261.4	17.3	1,296.4	18.0
Asian/Pacific Islander	507.4	6.9	511.7	7.0	514.9	7.2
Asian	482.9	6.5	488.1	6.7	491.9	6.8
Pacific Islander	24.5	0.3	23.6	0.3	23.1	0.3
American Indian/Alaska Native	59.5	0.8	56.0	0.8	53.2	0.7
Two or more races	216.3	2.9	245.9	3.4	252.9	3.5
Nonresident alien	258.4	X	287.5	X	307.4	X
Female	9,815.2	100.0	9,706.9	100.0	9,536.9	100.0
White	5,459.6	56.9	5,282.6	55.8	5,114.5	55.1
Total, selected races/ethnicities	4,130.6	43.1	4,181.3	44.2	4,164.1	44.9
Black	1,549.4	16.2	1,501.3	15.9	1,424.1	15.3
Hispanic	1,647.2	17.2	1,700.5	18.0	1,753.2	18.9
Asian/Pacific Islander	556.9	5.8	563.3	6.0	568.5	6.1
Asian	527.3	5.5	534.6	5.6	542.0	5.8
Pacific Islander	29.7	0.3	28.7	0.3	26.5	0.3
American Indian/Alaska Native	88.2	0.9	82.5	0.9	79.1	0.9
Two or more races	288.8	3.0	333.6	3.5	339.2	3.7
Nonresident alien	225.0	X	243.0	X	258.4	X
Postbaccalaureate, total	2,901.0	100.0	2,914.6	100.0	2,940.5	100.0
White	1,691.5	66.5	1,655.9	65.6	1,634.6	64.8
Total, selected races/ethnicities	852.5	33.5	870.2	34.4	888.6	35.2
Black	367.3	14.4	366.0	14.5	364.3	14.4
Hispanic	221.0	8.7	229.8	9.1	242.6	9.6
Asian/Pacific Islander	195.2	7.7	197.4	7.8	200.4	7.9
Asian	188.4	7.4	190.9	7.6	194.4	7.7
Pacific Islander	6.8	0.3	6.5	0.3	6.0	0.2
American Indian/Alaska Native	14.8	0.6	14.3	0.6	13.9	0.6
Two or more races	54.2	2.1	62.6	2.5	67.4	2.7
Nonresident alien	356.9	X	388.5	X	417.3	X
Male	1,201.2	100.0	1,211.2	100.0	1,221.6	100.0
White	693.5	69.4	674.8	68.3	660.1	67.4
Total, selected races/ethnicities	306.0	30.6	313.3	31.7	320.0	32.6
Black	109.6	11.0	110.1	11.1	110.7	11.3
Hispanic	83.6	8.4	86.5	8.8	90.9	9.3
Asian/Pacific Islander	86.9	8.7	87.5	8.9	87.9	9.0
Asian	84.2	8.4	84.9	8.6	85.6	8.7
Pacific Islander	2.7	0.3	2.7	0.3	2.3	0.2
American Indian/Alaska Native	5.3	0.5	5.3	0.5	5.0	0.5
Two or more races	20.6	2.1	23.8	2.4	25.5	2.6
Nonresident alien	201.7	X	223.0	X	241.5	X
Female	1,699.8	100.0	1,703.4	100.0	1,718.9	100.0
White	998.0	64.6	981.1	63.8	974.5	63.2
Total, selected races/ethnicities	546.5	35.4	556.9	36.2	568.6	36.8
Black	257.7	16.7	255.9	16.6	253.6	16.4
Hispanic	137.4	8.9	143.3	9.3	151.7	9.8
Asian/Pacific Islander	108.4	7.0	109.9	7.1	112.5	7.3
Asian	104.2	6.7	106.0	6.9	108.8	7.1
Pacific Islander	4.1	0.3	3.9	0.3	3.7	0.2
American Indian/Alaska Native	9.5	0.6	9.0	0.6	8.9	0.6
Two or more races	33.6	2.2	38.8	2.5	41.9	2.7
Nonresident alien	155.2	X	165.5	X	175.8	X

Note: Race categories exclude persons of Hispanic ethnicity. Because of underreporting and nonreporting of racial/ethnic data, some figures are slightly lower than corresponding data in other tables. Data through 1990 are for institutions of higher education, while later data are for degree-granting institutions. Degree-granting institutions grant associate's or higher degrees and participate in Title IV federal financial aid programs. The degree-granting classification is very similar to the earlier higher education classification, but it includes more 2-year colleges and excludes a few higher education institutions that did not grant degrees. Some data have been revised from previously published figures. Details may not sum to totals because of rounding.

X = Not applicable.

Table A-36. Total Fall Enrollment in Degree-Granting Institutions, by Race/Ethnicity of Student and Type and Control of Institution, Selected Years, 1976–2015

(Numbers in thousands; percent.)

Race/ethnicity of student and type and control of institution	1976 Number	1976 Percent	1990 Number	1990 Percent	2000 Number	2000 Percent	2010 Number	2010 Percent
All students, total.................................	10,986	100.0	13,819	100.0	15,312	100.0	21,019	100.0
White	9,076	84.3	10,722	79.9	10,462	70.8	12,721	62.6
Total, selected races/ethnicities...........	1,691	15.7	2,705	20.1	4,321	29.2	7,591	37.4
Black	1,033	9.6	1,247	9.3	1,730	11.7	3,039	15.0
Hispanic	384	3.6	782	5.8	1,462	9.9	2,749	13.5
Asian/Pacific Islander....................	198	1.8	572	4.3	978	6.6	1,282	6.3
Asian	NA	NA	NA	NA	NA	NA	1,218	6.0
Pacific Islander	NA	NA	NA	NA	NA	NA	64	0.3
American Indian/Alaska Native..........	76	0.7	103	0.8	151	1.0	196	1.0
Two or more races	NA	NA	NA	NA	NA	NA	325	1.6
Nonresident alien	219	X	391	X	529	X	708	X
Public..	8,641	78.7	10,845	78.5	11,753	76.8	15,142	72.0
White	7,095	83.5	8,385	79.2	7,963	69.8	9,182	62.5
Total, selected races/ethnicities...........	1,401	16.5	2,199	20.8	3,446	30.2	5,507	37.5
Black	831	9.8	976	9.2	1,319	11.6	1,989	13.5
Hispanic	337	4.0	671	6.3	1,229	10.8	2,164	14.7
Asian/Pacific Islander....................	166	2.0	461	4.4	771	6.8	969	6.6
Asian	NA	NA	NA	NA	NA	NA	925	6.3
Pacific Islander	NA	NA	NA	NA	NA	NA	44	0.3
American Indian/Alaska Native..........	68	0.8	90	0.9	127	1.1	151	1.0
Two or more races	NA	NA	NA	NA	NA	NA	235	1.6
Nonresident alien	145	X	260	X	343	X	453	X
Private...	2,345	21.3	2,974	21.5	3,560	23.2	5,877	28.0
White	1,982	87.3	2,337	82.2	2,499	74.1	3,539	62.9
Total, selected races/ethnicities...........	290	12.7	505	17.8	875	25.9	2,084	37.1
Black	202	8.9	271	9.5	411	12.2	1,050	18.7
Hispanic	47	2.1	111	3.9	233	6.9	585	10.4
Asian/Pacific Islander....................	32	1.4	111	3.9	208	6.2	313	5.6
Asian	NA	NA	NA	NA	NA	NA	293	5.2
Pacific Islander	NA	NA	NA	NA	NA	NA	20	0.4
American Indian/Alaska Native..........	9	0.4	12	0.4	24	0.7	45	0.8
Two or more races	NA	NA	NA	NA	NA	NA	90	1.6
Nonresident alien	73	X	131	X	186	X	255	X
4-year, total.....................................	7,107	64.7	8,579	62.1	9,364	61.2	13,336	63.4
White	5,999	86.6	6,768	82.0	6,658	74.6	8,400	66.0
Total, selected races/ethnicities...........	931	13.4	1,486	18.0	2,266	25.4	4,328	34.0
Black	604	8.7	723	8.8	995	11.2	1,840	14.5
Hispanic	174	2.5	358	4.3	618	6.9	1,356	10.7
Asian/Pacific Islander....................	119	1.7	357	4.3	576	6.5	818	6.4
Asian	NA	NA	NA	NA	NA	NA	782	6.1
Pacific Islander	NA	NA	NA	NA	NA	NA	36	0.3
American Indian/Alaska Native..........	35	0.5	48	0.6	76	0.9	109	0.9
Two or more races	NA	NA	NA	NA	NA	NA	205	1.6
Nonresident alien	177	X	324	X	440	X	608	X
Public..	4,893	68.9	5,848	68.2	6,055	64.7	7,924	59.4
White	4,120	86.1	4,606	81.5	4,311	74.4	5,070	67.0
Total, selected races/ethnicities...........	667	13.9	1,046	18.5	1,486	25.6	2,497	33.0
Black	422	8.8	495	8.8	628	10.8	913	12.1
Hispanic	129	2.7	263	4.6	420	7.2	870	11.5
Asian/Pacific Islander....................	87	1.8	251	4.4	381	6.6	523	6.9
Asian	NA	NA	NA	NA	NA	NA	505	6.7
Pacific Islander	NA	NA	NA	NA	NA	NA	18	0.2
American Indian/Alaska Native..........	28	0.6	38	0.7	57	1.0	69	0.9
Two or more races	NA	NA	NA	NA	NA	NA	122	1.6
Nonresident alien	106	X	196	X	258	X	358	X
Private...	2,214	31.1	2,730	31.8	3,308	35.3	5,412	40.6
White	1,879	87.7	2,163	83.1	2,347	75.1	3,330	64.5
Total, selected races/ethnicities...........	264	12.3	440	16.9	780	24.9	1,831	35.5
Black	182	8.5	228	8.7	368	11.8	927	18.0
Hispanic	44	2.1	96	3.7	198	6.3	486	9.4
Asian/Pacific Islander....................	31	1.5	107	4.1	195	6.2	296	5.7

Note: Race categories exclude persons of Hispanic ethnicity. Because of underreporting and nonreporting of racial/ethnic data, some figures are slightly lower than corresponding data in other tables. Data through 1990 are for institutions of higher education, while later data are for degree-granting institutions. Degree-granting institutions grant associate's or higher degrees and participate in Title IV federal financial aid programs. The degree-granting classification is very similar to the earlier higher education classification, but it includes more 2-year colleges and excludes a few higher education institutions that did not grant degrees. Some data have been revised from previously published figures. Details may not sum to totals because of rounding.
NA = Not available.
X = Not applicable.

Table A-36. Total Fall Enrollment in Degree-Granting Institutions, by Race/Ethnicity of Student and Type and Control of Institution, Selected Years, 1976–2015—*Continued*

(Numbers in thousands; percent.)

Race/ethnicity of student and type and control of institution	2013 Number	2013 Percent	2014 Number	2014 Percent	2015 Number	2015 Percent
All students, total...................................	20,376	100.0	20,207	100.0	19,977	100.0
White	11,591	59.3	11,237	58.3	10,937	57.6
Total, selected races/ethnicities..................	7,945	40.7	8,051	41.7	8,057	42.4
Black...	2,872	14.7	2,792	14.5	2,675	14.1
Hispanic..	3,091	15.8	3,192	16.5	3,292	17.3
Asian/Pacific Islander...............................	1,260	6.4	1,272	6.6	1,284	6.8
Asian..	1,199	6.1	1,214	6.3	1,228	6.5
Pacific Islander....................................	61	0.3	59	0.3	56	0.3
American Indian/Alaska Native...................	163	0.8	153	0.8	146	0.8
Two or more races	559	2.9	642	3.3	660	3.5
Nonresident alien	840	X	919	X	983	X
Public...	14,746	72.4	14,655	72.5	14,568	72.9
White	8,364	58.9	8,119	57.7	7,913	56.8
Total, selected races/ethnicities..................	5,847	41.1	5,947	42.3	6,027	43.2
Black...	1,887	13.3	1,840	13.1	1,770	12.7
Hispanic..	2,477	17.4	2,580	18.3	2,689	19.3
Asian/Pacific Islander...............................	945	6.6	956	6.8	969	7.0
Asian..	906	6.4	919	6.5	934	6.7
Pacific Islander....................................	39	0.3	38	0.3	36	0.3
American Indian/Alaska Native...................	125	0.9	118	0.8	114	0.8
Two or more races	413	2.9	453	3.2	484	3.5
Nonresident alien	534	X	588	X	628	X
Private..	5,630	27.6	5,552	27.5	5,409	27.1
White	3,227	60.6	3,118	59.7	3,024	59.8
Total, selected races/ethnicities..................	2,098	39.4	2,104	40.3	2,030	40.2
Black...	985	18.5	952	18.2	905	17.9
Hispanic..	614	11.5	611	11.7	603	11.9
Asian/Pacific Islander...............................	315	5.9	316	6.1	315	6.2
Asian..	293	5.5	295	5.7	295	5.8
Pacific Islander....................................	22	0.4	21	0.4	20	0.4
American Indian/Alaska Native...................	38	0.7	35	0.7	32	0.6
Two or more races	146	2.7	189	3.6	175	3.5
Nonresident alien	306	X	331	X	355	X
4-year, total..	13,407	65.8	13,493	66.8	13,486	67.5
White	7,955	62.8	7,828	61.8	7,712	61.2
Total, selected races/ethnicities..................	4,704	37.2	4,843	38.2	4,896	38.8
Black...	1,799	14.2	1,778	14.0	1,740	13.8
Hispanic..	1,600	12.6	1,671	13.2	1,742	13.8
Asian/Pacific Islander...............................	844	6.7	865	6.8	883	7.0
Asian..	806	6.4	828	6.5	847	6.7
Pacific Islander....................................	38	0.3	37	0.3	35	0.3
American Indian/Alaska Native...................	92	0.7	87	0.7	83	0.7
Two or more races	370	2.9	442	3.5	448	3.6
Nonresident alien	748	X	823	X	878	X
Public...	8,120	60.6	8,257	61.2	8,352	61.9
White	4,867	63.4	4,834	62.3	4,793	61.2
Total, selected races/ethnicities..................	2,809	36.6	2,929	37.7	3,033	38.8
Black...	909	11.8	915	11.8	916	11.7
Hispanic..	1,064	13.9	1,133	14.6	1,200	15.3
Asian/Pacific Islander...............................	545	7.1	563	7.3	580	7.4
Asian..	526	6.9	545	7.0	562	7.2
Pacific Islander....................................	19	0.2	19	0.2	17	0.2
American Indian/Alaska Native...................	58	0.8	56	0.7	55	0.7
Two or more races	233	3.0	262	3.4	283	3.6
Nonresident alien	445	X	495	X	526	X
Private..	5,287	39.4	5,236	38.8	5,134	38.1
White	3,088	62.0	2,994	61.0	2,919	61.0
Total, selected races/ethnicities..................	1,895	38.0	1,913	39.0	1,863	39.0
Black...	890	17.9	864	17.6	823	17.2
Hispanic..	536	10.8	538	11.0	542	11.3
Asian/Pacific Islander...............................	299	6.0	301	6.1	303	6.3

Note: Race categories exclude persons of Hispanic ethnicity. Because of underreporting and nonreporting of racial/ethnic data, some figures are slightly lower than corresponding data in other tables. Data through 1990 are for institutions of higher education, while later data are for degree-granting institutions. Degree-granting institutions grant associate's or higher degrees and participate in Title IV federal financial aid programs. The degree-granting classification is very similar to the earlier higher education classification, but it includes more 2-year colleges and excludes a few higher education institutions that did not grant degrees. Some data have been revised from previously published figures. Details may not sum to totals because of rounding.
X = Not applicable.

Table A-36. Total Fall Enrollment in Degree-Granting Institutions, by Race/Ethnicity of Student and Type and Control of Institution, Selected Years, 1976–2015—*Continued*

(Numbers in thousands; percent.)

Race/ethnicity of student and type and control of institution	1976		1990		2000		2010	
	Number	Percent	Number	Percent	Number	Percent	Number	Percent
Asian	NA	NA	NA	NA	NA	NA	278	5.4
Pacific Islander	NA	NA	NA	NA	NA	NA	18	0.3
American Indian/Alaska Native	7	0.3	10	0.4	19	0.6	40	0.8
Two or more races	NA	NA	NA	NA	NA	NA	82	1.6
Nonresident alien	70	X	128	X	182	X	251	X
2-year, total	3,879	35.3	5,240	37.9	5,948	38.8	7,684	36.6
White	3,077	80.2	3,954	76.4	3,804	64.9	4,321	57.0
Total, selected races/ethnicities	760	19.8	1,219	23.6	2,055	35.1	3,263	43.0
Black	429	11.2	524	10.1	735	12.5	1,199	15.8
Hispanic	210	5.5	424	8.2	844	14.4	1,393	18.4
Asian/Pacific Islander	79	2.1	215	4.2	402	6.9	463	6.1
Asian	NA	NA	NA	NA	NA	NA	435	5.7
Pacific Islander	NA	NA	NA	NA	NA	NA	28	0.4
American Indian/Alaska Native	41	1.1	55	1.1	75	1.3	87	1.1
Two or more races	NA	NA	NA	NA	NA	NA	121	1.6
Nonresident alien	42	X	67	X	89	X	99	X
Public	3,748	96.6	4,996	95.4	5,697	95.8	7,218	93.9
White	2,974	80.2	3,780	76.6	3,652	65.1	4,113	57.7
Total, selected races/ethnicities	735	19.8	1,153	23.4	1,960	34.9	3,010	42.3
Black	409	11.0	481	9.8	691	12.3	1,076	15.1
Hispanic	208	5.6	409	8.3	809	14.4	1,294	18.2
Asian/Pacific Islander	78	2.1	210	4.3	389	6.9	446	6.3
Asian	NA	NA	NA	NA	NA	NA	420	5.9
Pacific Islander	NA	NA	NA	NA	NA	NA	26	0.4
American Indian/Alaska Native	39	1.1	52	1.1	70	1.2	81	1.1
Two or more races	NA	NA	NA	NA	NA	NA	113	1.6
Nonresident alien	39	X	64	X	85	X	95	X
Private	131	3.4	244	4.6	251	4.2	466	6.1
White	103	80.3	174	72.7	152	61.4	209	45.2
Total, selected races/ethnicities	25	19.7	66	27.3	95	38.6	253	54.8
Black	20	15.5	43	17.9	44	17.6	123	26.6
Hispanic	3	2.1	15	6.4	35	14.0	99	21.4
Asian/Pacific Islander	1	0.7	5	2.0	13	5.1	17	3.7
Asian	NA	NA	NA	NA	NA	NA	15	3.2
Pacific Islander	NA	NA	NA	NA	NA	NA	2	0.5
American Indian/Alaska Native	2	1.4	3	1.1	5	1.8	6	1.3
Two or more races	NA	NA	NA	NA	NA	NA	8	1.8
Nonresident alien	3	X	3	X	4	X	4	X

Note: Race categories exclude persons of Hispanic ethnicity. Because of underreporting and nonreporting of racial/ethnic data, some figures are slightly lower than corresponding data in other tables. Data through 1990 are for institutions of higher education, while later data are for degree-granting institutions. Degree-granting institutions grant associate's or higher degrees and participate in Title IV federal financial aid programs. The degree-granting classification is very similar to the earlier higher education classification, but it includes more 2-year colleges and excludes a few higher education institutions that did not grant degrees. Some data have been revised from previously published figures. Details may not sum to totals because of rounding.
NA = Not available.
X = Not applicable.

Table A-36. Total Fall Enrollment in Degree-Granting Institutions, by Race/Ethnicity of Student and Type and Control of Institution, Selected Years, 1976–2015—*Continued*

(Numbers in thousands; percent.)

Race/ethnicity of student and type and control of institution	2013		2014		2015	
	Number	Percent	Number	Percent	Number	Percent
Asian	280	5.6	283	5.8	285	6.0
Pacific Islander	19	0.4	19	0.4	18	0.4
American Indian/Alaska Native	33	0.7	31	0.6	29	0.6
Two or more races	136	2.7	180	3.7	165	3.5
Nonresident alien	303	X	328	X	352	X
2-year, total	6,969	34.2	6,714	33.2	6,491	32.5
White	3,636	52.9	3,410	51.5	3,225	50.5
Total, selected races/ethnicities	3,241	47.1	3,208	48.5	3,161	49.5
Black	1,073	15.6	1,014	15.3	936	14.6
Hispanic	1,491	21.7	1,521	23.0	1,550	24.3
Asian/Pacific Islander	416	6.0	408	6.2	401	6.3
Asian	392	5.7	386	5.8	381	6.0
Pacific Islander	23	0.3	21	0.3	20	0.3
American Indian/Alaska Native	71	1.0	66	1.0	63	1.0
Two or more races	190	2.8	200	3.0	211	3.3
Nonresident alien	92	X	96	X	105	X
Public	6,625	95.1	6,398	95.3	6,216	95.8
White	3,497	53.5	3,286	52.1	3,120	51.0
Total, selected races/ethnicities	3,038	46.5	3,018	47.9	2,994	49.0
Black	978	15.0	925	14.7	854	14.0
Hispanic	1,414	21.6	1,447	23.0	1,490	24.4
Asian/Pacific Islander	400	6.1	393	6.2	390	6.4
Asian	379	5.8	374	5.9	371	6.1
Pacific Islander	21	0.3	19	0.3	18	0.3
American Indian/Alaska Native	66	1.0	62	1.0	59	1.0
Two or more races	180	2.8	191	3.0	201	3.3
Nonresident alien	90	X	94	X	102	X
Private	344	4.9	317	4.7	275	4.2
White	139	40.7	124	39.4	105	38.7
Total, selected races/ethnicities	202	59.3	190	60.6	167	61.3
Black	95	27.9	89	28.2	82	30.0
Hispanic	77	22.7	74	23.5	61	22.2
Asian/Pacific Islander	16	4.6	15	4.7	11	4.1
Asian	13	3.8	12	3.9	10	3.5
Pacific Islander	3	0.8	3	0.8	2	0.6
American Indian/Alaska Native	4	1.3	4	1.3	4	1.3
Two or more races	10	2.8	9	2.9	10	3.7
Nonresident alien	2	X	3	X	3	X

Note: Race categories exclude persons of Hispanic ethnicity. Because of underreporting and nonreporting of racial/ethnic data, some figures are slightly lower than corresponding data in other tables. Data through 1990 are for institutions of higher education, while later data are for degree-granting institutions. Degree-granting institutions grant associate's or higher degrees and participate in Title IV federal financial aid programs. The degree-granting classification is very similar to the earlier higher education classification, but it includes more 2-year colleges and excludes a few higher education institutions that did not grant degrees. Some data have been revised from previously published figures. Details may not sum to totals because of rounding.
X = Not applicable.

Table A-37. Degrees Conferred by Postsecondary Institutions, by Level of Degree and Sex of Student, 1970–1971 through 2015–2016

(Number.)

Degree conferred, level of degree, and sex of student (when available)	1970-71	1971-72	1972-73	1973-74	1974-75	1975-76	1976-77	1977-78	1978-79
Agriculture and Natural Resources									
Bachelor's degrees, total	12,672	13,516	14,756	16,253	17,528	19,402	21,467	22,650	23,134
Male	12,136	12,779	13,661	14,684	15,061	15,845	16,690	17,069	16,854
Female	536	737	1,095	1,569	2,467	3,557	4,777	5,581	6,280
Master's degrees, total	2,457	2,680	2,807	2,928	3,067	3,340	3,724	4,023	3,994
Male	2,313	2,490	2,588	2,640	2,703	2,862	3,177	3,268	3,187
Female	144	190	219	288	364	478	547	755	807
Doctor's degrees, total	1,086	971	1,059	930	991	928	893	971	950
Male	1,055	945	1,031	897	958	867	831	909	877
Female	31	26	28	33	33	61	62	62	73
Architecture and Related Services									
Bachelor's degrees, total	5,570	6,440	6,962	7,822	8,226	9,146	9,222	9,250	9,273
Male	4,906	5,667	6,042	6,665	6,791	7,396	7,249	7,054	6,876
Female	664	773	920	1,157	1,435	1,750	1,973	2,196	2,397
Master's degrees, total	1,705	1,899	2,307	2,702	2,938	3,215	3,213	3,115	3,113
Male	1,469	1,626	1,943	2,208	2,343	2,545	2,489	2,304	2,226
Female	236	273	364	494	595	670	724	811	887
Doctor's degrees, total	36	50	58	69	69	82	73	73	96
Male	33	43	54	65	58	69	62	57	74
Female	3	7	4	4	11	13	11	16	22
Biological and Biomedical Sciences									
Bachelor's degrees, total	35,705	37,269	42,207	48,244	51,609	54,154	53,464	51,360	48,713
Male	25,319	26,314	29,625	33,217	34,580	35,498	34,178	31,673	29,173
Female	10,386	10,955	12,582	15,027	17,029	18,656	19,286	19,687	19,540
Master's degrees, total	5,625	5,989	6,156	6,408	6,429	6,457	6,953	6,651	6,638
Male	3,782	4,056	4,317	4,512	4,554	4,466	4,670	4,353	4,198
Female	1,843	1,933	1,839	1,896	1,875	1,991	2,283	2,298	2,440
Doctor's degrees, total	3,603	3,587	3,583	3,358	3,334	3,347	3,335	3,255	3,459
Male	3,018	2,981	2,892	2,684	2,612	2,631	2,627	2,481	2,593
Female	585	606	691	674	722	716	708	774	866
Biology, Microbiology, and Zoology									
Biology, general									
Bachelor's degree	26,294	27,473	31,185	36,188	38,748	40,163	39,530	37,598	35,962
Master's degree	2,665	2,943	2,959	3,186	3,109	3,177	3,322	3,094	3,093
Doctor's degree	536	580	627	657	637	624	608	664	663
Microbiology									
Bachelor's degree	1,475	1,548	1,940	2,311	2,767	2,927	2,884	2,695	2,670
Master's degree	456	470	517	505	552	585	659	615	597
Doctor's degree	365	351	344	384	345	364	325	353	395
Zoology									
Bachelor's degree	5,721	5,518	5,763	6,128	6,110	6,077	5,574	5,096	4,738
Master's degree	1,027	1,040	1,042	1,091	1,039	976	985	958	946
Doctor's degree	878	836	803	677	697	645	696	624	669
Business									
Bachelor's degrees, total	115,396	121,917	126,717	132,304	133,639	143,171	152,010	160,775	172,392
Male	104,936	110,331	113,337	115,363	111,983	114,986	116,394	117,103	119,765
Female	10,460	11,586	13,380	16,941	21,656	28,185	35,616	43,672	52,627
Master's degrees, total	26,490	30,509	31,208	32,691	36,315	42,592	46,505	48,347	50,397
Male	25,458	29,317	29,689	30,557	33,274	37,654	39,852	40,224	40,766
Female	1,032	1,192	1,519	2,134	3,041	4,938	6,653	8,123	9,631
Doctor's degrees, total	774	876	917	922	939	906	839	834	852
Male	753	857	864	873	900	856	785	760	752
Female	21	19	53	49	39	50	54	74	100
Communication, Journalism, and Related Programs in Communications Technologies									
Bachelor's degrees, total	10,802	12,340	14,317	17,096	19,248	21,282	23,214	25,400	26,457
Male	6,989	7,964	9,074	10,536	11,455	12,458	12,932	13,480	13,266
Female	3,813	4,376	5,243	6,560	7,793	8,824	10,282	11,920	13,191
Master's degrees, total	1,856	2,200	2,406	2,640	2,794	3,126	3,091	3,296	2,882
Male	1,214	1,443	1,546	1,668	1,618	1,818	1,719	1,673	1,483
Female	642	757	860	972	1,176	1,308	1,372	1,623	1,399
Doctor's degrees, total	145	111	139	175	165	204	171	191	192

Note: Data are for postsecondary institutions participating in Title IV federal financial aid programs.

Table A-37. Degrees Conferred by Postsecondary Institutions, by Level of Degree and Sex of Student, 1970–1971 through 2015–2016—*Continued*

(Number.)

Degree conferred, level of degree, and sex of student (when available)	1979-80	1980-81	1981-82	1982-83	1983-84	1984-85	1985-86	1986-87	1987-88
Agriculture and Natural Resources									
Bachelor's degrees, total	22,802	21,886	21,029	20,909	19,317	18,107	16,823	14,991	14,222
Male	16,045	15,154	14,443	14,085	13,206	12,477	11,544	10,314	9,744
Female	6,757	6,732	6,586	6,824	6,111	5,630	5,279	4,677	4,478
Master's degrees, total	3,976	4,003	4,163	4,254	4,178	3,928	3,801	3,522	3,479
Male	3,082	3,061	3,114	3,129	2,989	2,846	2,701	2,460	2,427
Female	894	942	1,049	1,125	1,189	1,082	1,100	1,062	1,052
Doctor's degrees, total	991	1,067	1,079	1,149	1,172	1,213	1,158	1,049	1,142
Male	879	940	925	1,004	1,001	1,036	966	871	926
Female	112	127	154	145	171	177	192	178	216
Architecture and Related Services									
Bachelor's degrees, total	9,132	9,455	9,728	9,823	9,186	9,325	9,119	8,950	8,603
Male	6,596	6,800	6,825	6,403	5,895	6,019	5,824	5,617	5,271
Female	2,536	2,655	2,903	3,420	3,291	3,306	3,295	3,333	3,332
Master's degrees, total	3,139	3,153	3,327	3,357	3,223	3,275	3,260	3,163	3,159
Male	2,245	2,234	2,242	2,224	2,197	2,148	2,129	2,086	2,042
Female	894	919	1,085	1,133	1,026	1,127	1,131	1,077	1,117
Doctor's degrees, total	79	93	80	97	84	89	73	92	98
Male	66	73	58	74	62	66	56	66	66
Female	13	20	22	23	22	23	17	26	32
Biological and Biomedical Sciences									
Bachelor's degrees, total	46,254	43,078	41,501	39,924	38,593	38,354	38,395	38,074	36,688
Male	26,797	24,124	22,722	21,572	20,565	20,071	20,000	19,684	18,267
Female	19,457	18,954	18,779	18,352	18,028	18,283	18,395	18,390	18,421
Master's degrees, total	6,339	5,766	5,679	5,711	5,489	5,109	5,064	4,995	4,871
Male	4,042	3,602	3,384	3,298	3,123	2,775	2,733	2,646	2,530
Female	2,297	2,164	2,295	2,413	2,366	2,334	2,331	2,349	2,341
Doctor's degrees, total	3,568	3,640	3,662	3,386	3,496	3,465	3,405	3,469	3,688
Male	2,651	2,620	2,611	2,306	2,416	2,335	2,273	2,268	2,389
Female	917	1,020	1,051	1,080	1,080	1,130	1,132	1,201	1,299
Biology, Microbiology, and Zoology									
Biology, general									
Bachelor's degree	33,523	31,323	29,651	28,022	27,379	27,593	27,618	27,465	26,838
Master's degree	2,911	2,598	2,579	2,354	2,313	2,130	2,173	2,022	1,981
Doctor's degree	718	734	678	521	617	658	574	537	576
Microbiology									
Bachelor's degree	2,631	2,414	2,377	2,324	2,349	2,207	2,257	2,159	2,061
Master's degree	596	482	470	499	505	471	392	451	404
Doctor's degree	376	370	350	358	388	319	362	380	442
Zoology									
Bachelor's degree	4,301	3,873	3,615	3,407	3,231	3,069	2,894	2,791	2,537
Master's degree	922	881	868	738	700	664	618	623	629
Doctor's degree	639	613	625	533	521	508	548	464	492
Business									
Bachelor's degrees, total	186,264	200,521	215,190	226,442	229,013	232,282	236,700	240,346	242,859
Male	123,639	126,798	130,693	131,451	129,296	127,467	128,415	128,506	129,467
Female	62,625	73,723	84,497	94,991	99,717	104,815	108,285	111,840	113,392
Master's degrees, total	55,008	57,888	61,251	64,741	66,129	66,981	66,676	67,093	69,230
Male	42,744	43,411	44,230	45,987	46,167	46,199	45,927	44,913	45,980
Female	12,264	14,477	17,021	18,754	19,962	20,782	20,749	22,180	23,250
Doctor's degrees, total	767	808	826	770	926	827	923	1,062	1,063
Male	650	686	676	638	727	685	720	808	810
Female	117	122	150	132	199	142	203	254	253
Communication, Journalism, and Related Programs in Communications Technologies									
Bachelor's degrees, total	28,616	31,282	34,222	38,647	40,203	42,102	43,145	45,521	46,916
Male	13,656	14,179	14,917	16,213	16,662	17,233	17,681	18,201	18,672
Female	14,960	17,103	19,305	22,434	23,541	24,869	25,464	27,320	28,244
Master's degrees, total	3,082	3,105	3,327	3,600	3,620	3,657	3,808	3,881	3,916
Male	1,527	1,448	1,578	1,660	1,578	1,574	1,603	1,584	1,568
Female	1,555	1,657	1,749	1,940	2,042	2,083	2,205	2,297	2,348
Doctor's degrees, total	193	182	200	208	216	232	218	275	233

Note: Data are for postsecondary institutions participating in Title IV federal financial aid programs.

Table A-37. Degrees Conferred by Postsecondary Institutions, by Level of Degree and Sex of Student, 1970–1971 through 2015–2016—*Continued*

(Number.)

Degree conferred, level of degree, and sex of student (when available)	1970-71	1971-72	1972-73	1973-74	1974-75	1975-76	1976-77	1977-78	1978-79
Male	126	96	114	146	119	154	130	138	138
Female	19	15	25	29	46	50	41	53	54
Computer and Information Sciences									
Bachelor's degrees, total	2,388	3,402	4,304	4,756	5,033	5,652	6,407	7,201	8,719
Male	2,064	2,941	3,664	3,976	4,080	4,534	4,876	5,349	6,272
Female	324	461	640	780	953	1,118	1,531	1,852	2,447
Master's degrees, total	1,588	1,977	2,113	2,276	2,299	2,603	2,798	3,038	3,055
Male	1,424	1,752	1,888	1,983	1,961	2,226	2,332	2,471	2,480
Female	164	225	225	293	338	377	466	567	575
Doctor's degrees, total	128	167	196	198	213	244	216	196	236
Male	125	155	181	189	199	221	197	181	206
Female	3	12	15	9	14	23	19	15	30
Education									
Bachelor's degrees, total	176,307	190,880	193,984	184,907	166,758	154,437	143,234	135,821	125,873
Male	44,896	49,344	51,300	48,997	44,463	42,004	39,867	37,410	33,743
Female	131,411	141,536	142,684	135,910	122,295	112,433	103,367	98,411	92,130
Master's degrees, total	87,666	96,668	103,777	110,402	117,841	126,061	124,267	116,916	109,866
Male	38,365	41,141	43,298	44,112	44,430	44,831	42,308	37,662	34,410
Female	49,301	55,527	60,479	66,290	73,411	81,230	81,959	79,254	75,456
Doctor's degrees, total	6,041	6,648	6,857	6,757	6,975	7,202	7,338	7,018	7,170
Male	4,771	5,104	5,191	4,974	4,856	4,826	4,832	4,281	4,174
Female	1,270	1,544	1,666	1,783	2,119	2,376	2,506	2,737	2,996
Engineering and Engineering Technologies									
Bachelor's degrees, total	50,182	51,258	51,384	50,412	47,131	46,676	49,482	56,150	62,898
Male	49,775	50,726	50,766	49,611	46,105	45,184	47,238	52,353	57,603
Female	407	532	618	801	1,026	1,492	2,244	3,797	5,295
Master's degrees, total	16,947	17,299	16,988	15,851	15,837	16,800	16,659	16,887	16,012
Male	16,734	17,009	16,694	15,470	15,426	16,174	15,891	15,940	14,971
Female	213	290	294	381	411	626	768	947	1,041
Doctor's degrees, total	3,688	3,708	3,513	3,374	3,181	2,874	2,622	2,483	2,545
Male	3,663	3,685	3,459	3,318	3,113	2,805	2,547	2,424	2,459
Female	25	23	54	56	68	69	75	59	86
Chemical, Civil, Electrical, and Mechanical Engineering									
Chemical engineering									
Bachelor's degree	3,579	3,625	3,578	3,399	3,070	3,140	3,524	4,569	5,568
Master's degree	1,100	1,154	1,051	1,044	990	1,031	1,086	1,235	1,149
Doctor's degree	406	394	397	400	346	308	291	259	304
Civil engineering									
Bachelor's degree	6,526	6,803	7,390	8,017	7,651	7,923	8,228	9,135	9,809
Master's degree	2,425	2,487	2,627	2,652	2,769	2,999	2,964	2,685	2,646
Doctor's degree	446	415	397	368	356	370	309	277	253
Electrical, electronics, and communications engineering									
Bachelor's degree	12,198	12,101	12,313	11,316	10,161	9,791	9,936	11,133	12,338
Master's degree	4,282	4,206	3,895	3,499	3,469	3,774	3,788	3,740	3,591
Doctor's degree	879	824	791	705	701	649	566	503	586
Mechanical engineering									
Bachelor's degree	8,858	8,530	8,523	7,677	6,890	6,800	7,703	8,875	10,107
Master's degree	2,237	2,282	2,141	1,843	1,858	1,907	1,952	1,942	1,877
Doctor's degree	438	411	370	385	340	305	283	279	271
English Language and Literature/Letters									
Bachelor's degrees, total	63,914	63,707	60,607	54,190	47,062	41,452	37,343	34,799	33,218
Male	22,005	22,580	22,022	20,082	17,689	15,898	14,135	12,972	12,085
Female	41,909	41,127	38,585	34,108	29,373	25,554	23,208	21,827	21,133
Master's degrees, total	10,441	10,412	10,035	9,573	9,178	8,599	7,824	7,444	6,503
Male	4,126	4,066	3,988	3,824	3,463	3,290	2,907	2,623	2,307
Female	6,315	6,346	6,047	5,749	5,715	5,309	4,917	4,821	4,196
Doctor's degrees, total	1,554	1,734	1,817	1,755	1,595	1,514	1,373	1,272	1,186
Male	1,107	1,173	1,189	1,142	974	895	768	698	639
Female	447	561	628	613	621	619	605	574	547
Foreign Languages and Literatures									
Bachelor's degrees, total	20,988	19,890	20,170	20,197	19,103	17,068	15,496	14,334	13,211

Note: Data are for postsecondary institutions participating in Title IV federal financial aid programs.

Table A-37. Degrees Conferred by Postsecondary Institutions, by Level of Degree and Sex of Student, 1970–1971 through 2015–2016—*Continued*

(Number.)

Degree conferred, level of degree, and sex of student (when available)	1979-80	1980-81	1981-82	1982-83	1983-84	1984-85	1985-86	1986-87	1987-88
Male	121	107	136	123	129	141	116	158	133
Female	72	75	64	85	87	91	102	117	100
Computer and Information Sciences									
Bachelor's degrees, total	11,154	15,121	20,267	24,565	32,439	39,121	42,337	39,767	34,651
Male	7,782	10,202	13,218	15,641	20,416	24,737	27,208	25,962	23,414
Female	3,372	4,919	7,049	8,924	12,023	14,384	15,129	13,805	11,237
Master's degrees, total	3,647	4,218	4,935	5,321	6,190	7,101	8,070	8,481	9,197
Male	2,883	3,247	3,625	3,813	4,379	5,064	5,658	5,985	6,726
Female	764	971	1,310	1,508	1,811	2,037	2,412	2,496	2,471
Doctor's degrees, total	240	252	251	262	251	248	344	374	428
Male	213	227	230	228	225	223	299	322	380
Female	27	25	21	34	26	25	45	52	48
Education									
Bachelor's degrees, total	118,038	108,074	100,932	97,908	92,310	88,078	87,147	86,788	90,928
Male	30,901	27,039	24,380	23,651	22,200	21,254	20,982	20,705	20,947
Female	87,137	81,035	76,552	74,257	70,110	66,824	66,165	66,083	69,981
Master's degrees, total	101,819	96,713	91,601	83,254	75,700	74,667	74,816	72,619	75,270
Male	30,300	27,548	25,339	22,824	21,164	20,539	20,302	18,955	18,777
Female	71,519	69,165	66,262	60,430	54,536	54,128	54,514	53,664	56,493
Doctor's degrees, total	7,314	7,279	6,999	7,063	6,914	6,614	6,610	5,905	5,568
Male	4,100	3,843	3,612	3,550	3,448	3,174	3,088	2,745	2,530
Female	3,214	3,436	3,387	3,513	3,466	3,440	3,522	3,160	3,038
Engineering and Engineering Technologies									
Bachelor's degrees, total	69,387	75,355	80,632	89,811	95,295	97,099	97,122	93,560	89,406
Male	62,877	67,573	71,305	78,673	82,841	83,991	84,050	80,543	76,886
Female	6,510	7,782	9,327	11,138	12,454	13,108	13,072	13,017	12,520
Master's degrees, total	16,765	17,216	18,475	19,949	21,197	22,124	22,146	23,101	23,839
Male	15,535	15,761	16,747	18,038	18,916	19,688	19,545	20,137	20,815
Female	1,230	1,455	1,728	1,911	2,281	2,436	2,601	2,964	3,024
Doctor's degrees, total	2,546	2,608	2,676	2,871	3,032	3,269	3,456	3,854	4,237
Male	2,447	2,499	2,532	2,742	2,864	3,055	3,220	3,585	3,941
Female	99	109	144	129	168	214	236	269	296
Chemical, Civil, Electrical, and Mechanical Engineering									
Chemical engineering									
Bachelor's degree	6,320	6,527	6,740	7,185	7,475	7,146	5,877	4,991	3,917
Master's degree	1,270	1,267	1,285	1,368	1,514	1,544	1,361	1,184	1,088
Doctor's degree	284	300	311	319	330	418	446	497	579
Civil engineering									
Bachelor's degree	10,326	10,678	10,524	9,989	9,693	9,162	8,679	8,147	7,488
Master's degree	2,683	2,891	2,995	3,074	3,146	3,172	2,926	2,901	2,836
Doctor's degree	270	325	329	340	369	377	395	451	481
Electrical, electronics, and communications engineering									
Bachelor's degree	13,821	14,938	16,455	18,049	19,943	21,691	23,742	24,547	23,597
Master's degree	3,836	3,901	4,462	4,531	5,078	5,153	5,534	6,183	6,688
Doctor's degree	525	535	526	550	585	660	722	724	860
Mechanical engineering									
Bachelor's degree	11,808	13,329	13,922	15,675	16,629	16,794	16,194	15,450	14,900
Master's degree	2,060	2,291	2,399	2,511	2,797	3,053	3,075	3,198	3,329
Doctor's degree	281	276	333	299	319	409	426	528	596
English Language and Literature/Letters									
Bachelor's degrees, total	32,187	31,922	33,078	31,327	32,296	32,686	34,083	35,667	38,106
Male	11,237	11,082	11,300	10,699	11,007	11,195	11,657	12,133	12,687
Female	20,950	20,840	21,778	20,628	21,289	21,491	22,426	23,534	25,419
Master's degrees, total	6,026	5,742	5,593	4,866	4,814	4,987	5,335	5,298	5,366
Male	2,181	2,026	1,916	1,653	1,681	1,723	1,811	1,819	1,796
Female	3,845	3,716	3,677	3,213	3,133	3,264	3,524	3,479	3,570
Doctor's degrees, total	1,196	1,040	986	877	899	915	895	853	858
Male	635	497	467	419	413	414	390	367	380
Female	561	543	519	458	486	501	505	486	478
Foreign Languages and Literatures									
Bachelor's degrees, total	12,480	11,638	11,175	11,170	10,985	11,436	11,550	11,706	11,515

Note: Data are for postsecondary institutions participating in Title IV federal financial aid programs.

Table A-37. Degrees Conferred by Postsecondary Institutions, by Level of Degree and Sex of Student, 1970–1971 through 2015–2016—*Continued*

(Number.)

Degree conferred, level of degree, and sex of student (when available)	1970-71	1971-72	1972-73	1973-74	1974-75	1975-76	1976-77	1977-78	1978-79
Male	5,508	5,196	5,119	5,063	4,723	4,270	3,965	3,684	3,391
Female	15,480	14,694	15,051	15,134	14,380	12,798	11,531	10,650	9,820
Master's degrees, total	5,480	5,283	5,068	4,851	4,721	4,432	4,056	3,624	3,248
Male	1,961	1,919	1,909	1,788	1,672	1,581	1,365	1,194	1,092
Female	3,519	3,364	3,159	3,063	3,049	2,851	2,691	2,430	2,156
Doctor's degrees, total	1,084	1,134	1,347	1,248	1,220	1,245	1,103	1,002	960
Male	714	742	829	703	665	643	574	490	471
Female	370	392	518	545	555	602	529	512	489
French, German, Italian, and Spanish Language and Literature									
French									
Bachelor's degree	7,306	6,822	6,705	6,263	5,745	4,783	4,228	3,708	3,558
Master's degree	1,437	1,421	1,277	1,195	1,077	914	875	692	576
Doctor's degree	192	193	203	213	200	190	177	155	143
German									
Bachelor's degree	2,601	2,477	2,520	2,425	2,289	1,983	1,820	1,647	1,524
Master's degree	690	608	598	550	480	471	394	357	344
Doctor's degree	144	167	176	149	147	164	126	101	106
Italian									
Bachelor's degree	201	287	313	292	329	342	325	301	236
Master's degree	87	104	78	81	100	85	89	58	60
Doctor's degree	10	19	27	19	13	19	16	19	14
Spanish									
Bachelor's degree	7,068	6,847	7,209	7,250	6,719	5,984	5,359	4,832	4,563
Master's degree	1,456	1,421	1,298	1,217	1,228	1,080	930	822	720
Doctor's degree	168	152	206	203	202	176	153	113	118
Arabic, Chinese, Korean, and Russian Language and Literature									
Arabic									
Bachelor's degree	15	10	12	20	13	10	7	8	4
Master's degree	6	4	3	5	11	7	15	3	4
Doctor's degree	4	0	1	1	2	2	1	1	5
Chinese									
Bachelor's degree	89	103	98	121	141	150	112	116	91
Master's degree	22	20	29	37	26	23	32	23	22
Doctor's degree	8	11	13	5	12	6	6	4	12
Korean									
Bachelor's degree	NA	NA	NA	NA	NA	NA	NA	NA	NA
Master's degree	NA	NA	NA	NA	NA	NA	NA	NA	NA
Doctor's degree	NA	NA	NA	NA	NA	NA	NA	NA	NA
Russian									
Bachelor's degree	715	658	622	624	598	531	528	442	465
Master's degree	110	150	120	100	106	81	66	50	51
Doctor's degree	14	15	27	27	20	13	19	12	9
Health Professions and Related Programs									
Bachelor's degrees, total	25,223	28,611	33,562	41,421	49,002	53,885	57,222	59,445	62,095
Male	5,785	7,005	7,752	9,347	10,844	11,386	11,896	11,600	11,214
Female	19,438	21,606	25,810	32,074	38,158	42,499	45,326	47,845	50,881
Master's degrees, total	5,330	6,811	7,978	9,232	10,277	12,164	12,627	14,027	15,110
Male	2,165	2,749	3,189	3,444	3,686	3,837	3,865	3,972	4,155
Female	3,165	4,062	4,789	5,788	6,591	8,327	8,762	10,055	10,955
Doctor's degrees, total	15,988	16,538	18,215	20,094	22,191	25,267	24,972	26,516	27,766
Male	14,863	15,373	16,870	18,287	19,808	21,980	21,022	21,622	22,194
Female	1,125	1,165	1,345	1,807	2,383	3,287	3,950	4,894	5,572
Mathematics and Statistics									
Bachelor's degrees, total	24,801	23,713	23,067	21,635	18,181	15,984	14,196	12,569	11,806
Male	15,369	14,454	13,796	12,791	10,586	9,475	8,303	7,398	6,899
Female	9,432	9,259	9,271	8,844	7,595	6,509	5,893	5,171	4,907
Master's degrees, total	5,191	5,198	5,028	4,834	4,327	3,857	3,695	3,373	3,036
Male	3,673	3,655	3,525	3,337	2,905	2,547	2,396	2,228	1,985
Female	1,518	1,543	1,503	1,497	1,422	1,310	1,299	1,145	1,051
Doctor's degrees, total	1,199	1,128	1,068	1,031	975	856	823	805	730

Note: Data are for postsecondary institutions participating in Title IV federal financial aid programs.
NA = Not available.

Table A-37. Degrees Conferred by Postsecondary Institutions, by Level of Degree and Sex of Student, 1970–1971 through 2015–2016—*Continued*

(Number.)

Degree conferred, level of degree, and sex of student (when available)	1979-80	1980-81	1981-82	1982-83	1983-84	1984-85	1985-86	1986-87	1987-88
Male	3,226	3,013	2,919	3,048	3,098	3,186	3,374	3,374	3,223
Female	9,254	8,625	8,256	8,122	7,887	8,250	8,176	8,332	8,292
Master's degrees, total	3,067	2,934	2,892	2,706	2,814	2,708	2,690	2,574	2,680
Male	1,026	1,039	997	1,001	984	932	878	847	931
Female	2,041	1,895	1,895	1,705	1,830	1,776	1,812	1,727	1,749
Doctor's degrees, total	857	931	869	790	779	761	768	769	725
Male	412	460	407	362	353	342	338	332	330
Female	445	471	462	428	426	419	430	437	395
French, German, Italian, and Spanish Language and Literature									
French									
Bachelor's degree	3,285	3,178	3,054	2,871	2,876	2,991	3,015	3,062	3,082
Master's degree	513	460	485	360	418	385	409	421	437
Doctor's degree	128	115	92	106	86	74	86	85	89
German									
Bachelor's degree	1,466	1,286	1,327	1,367	1,292	1,411	1,396	1,366	1,350
Master's degree	309	294	324	281	241	240	249	234	244
Doctor's degree	94	79	76	68	63	58	73	70	71
Italian									
Bachelor's degree	272	205	208	224	206	190	240	219	224
Master's degree	49	65	55	45	41	44	42	53	45
Doctor's degree	9	13	14	18	13	9	10	17	7
Spanish									
Bachelor's degree	4,331	3,870	3,633	3,349	3,254	3,415	3,385	3,450	3,416
Master's degree	685	592	568	506	537	505	521	504	553
Doctor's degree	103	131	140	129	102	115	95	104	93
Arabic, Chinese, Korean, and Russian Language and Literature									
Arabic									
Bachelor's degree	13	6	15	12	6	9	5	8	9
Master's degree	2	7	4	4	2	4	4	1	4
Doctor's degree	5	0	4	1	0	0	0	1	0
Chinese									
Bachelor's degree	79	73	68	92	115	97	87	110	103
Master's degree	33	20	14	15	14	21	23	16	31
Doctor's degree	7	6	10	7	10	3	11	10	9
Korean									
Bachelor's degree	NA	NA	NA	NA	NA	NA	NA	NA	NA
Master's degree	NA	NA	NA	NA	NA	NA	NA	NA	NA
Doctor's degree	NA	NA	NA	NA	NA	NA	NA	NA	NA
Russian									
Bachelor's degree	402	409	324	342	340	432	493	502	472
Master's degree	60	68	49	33	39	47	33	54	54
Doctor's degree	6	8	7	5	3	6	3	8	8
Health Professions and Related Programs									
Bachelor's degrees, total	63,848	63,665	63,660	65,642	65,305	65,331	65,309	63,963	61,614
Male	11,330	10,531	10,110	10,247	10,068	9,741	9,629	9,137	8,955
Female	52,518	53,134	53,550	55,395	55,237	55,590	55,680	54,826	52,659
Master's degrees, total	15,374	16,176	16,212	16,941	17,351	17,442	18,603	18,442	18,774
Male	4,060	4,024	3,743	4,138	4,124	4,046	4,355	3,818	4,004
Female	11,314	12,152	12,469	12,803	13,227	13,396	14,248	14,624	14,770
Doctor's degrees, total	28,190	29,595	30,096	30,800	31,655	31,493	31,922	29,500	30,060
Male	22,157	22,792	22,968	22,920	22,851	22,045	22,069	19,686	19,853
Female	6,033	6,803	7,128	7,880	8,804	9,448	9,853	9,814	10,207
Mathematics and Statistics									
Bachelor's degrees, total	11,378	11,078	11,599	12,294	13,087	15,009	16,122	16,257	15,712
Male	6,562	6,342	6,593	6,888	7,290	8,080	8,623	8,673	8,408
Female	4,816	4,736	5,006	5,406	5,797	6,929	7,499	7,584	7,304
Master's degrees, total	2,860	2,567	2,727	2,810	2,723	2,859	3,131	3,283	3,413
Male	1,828	1,692	1,821	1,838	1,773	1,858	2,028	1,995	2,052
Female	1,032	875	906	972	950	1,001	1,103	1,288	1,361
Doctor's degrees, total	724	728	681	697	695	699	742	723	750

Note: Data are for postsecondary institutions participating in Title IV federal financial aid programs.
NA = Not available.

Table A-37. Degrees Conferred by Postsecondary Institutions, by Level of Degree and Sex of Student, 1970–1971 through 2015–2016—*Continued*

(Number.)

Degree conferred, level of degree, and sex of student (when available)	1970-71	1971-72	1972-73	1973-74	1974-75	1975-76	1976-77	1977-78	1978-79
Male	1,106	1,039	966	931	865	762	714	681	608
Female	93	89	102	100	110	94	109	124	122
Physical Sciences and Science Technologies									
Bachelor's degrees, total	21,410	20,743	20,692	21,170	20,770	21,458	22,482	22,975	23,197
Male	18,457	17,661	17,622	17,669	16,986	17,349	17,985	18,083	17,976
Female	2,953	3,082	3,070	3,501	3,784	4,109	4,497	4,892	5,221
Master's degrees, total	6,336	6,268	6,230	6,019	5,782	5,428	5,281	5,507	5,418
Male	5,495	5,390	5,388	5,157	4,949	4,622	4,411	4,583	4,438
Female	841	878	842	862	833	806	870	924	980
Doctor's degrees, total	4,324	4,075	3,961	3,558	3,577	3,388	3,295	3,073	3,061
Male	4,082	3,805	3,698	3,312	3,284	3,097	2,981	2,763	2,717
Female	242	270	263	246	293	291	314	310	344
Chemistry, Geology and Earth Science, and Physics									
Chemistry									
Bachelor's degree	11,061	10,588	10,124	10,430	10,541	11,015	11,200	11,304	11,499
Master's degree	2,244	2,229	2,198	2,082	1,961	1,745	1,717	1,832	1,724
Doctor's degree	2,093	1,943	1,827	1,755	1,773	1,578	1,522	1,461	1,475
Geology and earth science[1]									
Bachelor's degree	3,312	3,766	4,117	4,526	4,566	4,677	5,280	5,648	5,753
Master's degree	1,074	1,233	1,296	1,479	1,320	1,384	1,446	1,633	1,596
Doctor's degree	408	433	430	416	433	445	480	419	414
Physics[2]									
Bachelor's degree	5,071	4,634	4,259	3,952	3,706	3,544	3,420	3,330	3,337
Master's degree	2,188	2,033	1,747	1,655	1,574	1,451	1,319	1,294	1,319
Doctor's degree	1,482	1,344	1,338	1,115	1,080	997	945	873	918
Psychology									
Bachelor's degrees, total	38,187	43,433	47,940	52,139	51,245	50,278	47,861	44,879	42,697
Male	21,227	23,352	25,117	25,868	24,284	22,898	20,627	18,422	16,540
Female	16,960	20,081	22,823	26,271	26,961	27,380	27,234	26,457	26,157
Master's degrees, total	5,717	6,764	7,619	8,796	9,394	10,167	10,859	10,282	10,132
Male	3,395	3,934	4,325	4,983	5,035	5,136	5,293	4,670	4,405
Female	2,322	2,830	3,294	3,813	4,359	5,031	5,566	5,612	5,727
Doctor's degrees, total	2,144	2,277	2,550	2,872	2,913	3,157	3,386	3,164	3,228
Male	1,629	1,694	1,797	1,987	1,979	2,115	2,127	1,974	1,895
Female	515	583	753	885	934	1,042	1,259	1,190	1,333
Public Administration and Social Services									
Bachelor's degrees, total	5,466	7,508	10,690	11,966	13,661	15,440	16,136	16,607	17,328
Male	1,726	2,588	3,998	4,266	4,630	5,706	5,544	5,096	4,938
Female	3,740	4,920	6,692	7,700	9,031	9,734	10,592	11,511	12,390
Master's degrees, total	7,785	8,756	10,068	11,415	13,617	15,209	17,026	17,337	17,306
Male	3,893	4,537	5,271	6,028	7,200	7,969	8,810	8,513	8,051
Female	3,892	4,219	4,797	5,387	6,417	7,240	8,216	8,824	9,255
Doctor's degrees, total	174	193	198	201	257	292	292	357	315
Male	132	150	160	154	192	192	197	237	215
Female	42	43	38	47	65	100	95	120	100
Social Sciences and History									
Bachelor's degrees, total	155,324	158,060	155,970	150,320	135,190	126,396	117,040	112,952	108,059
Male	98,173	100,895	99,735	95,650	84,826	78,691	71,128	67,217	62,852
Female	57,151	57,165	56,235	54,670	50,364	47,705	45,912	45,735	45,207
Master's degrees, total	16,539	17,445	17,477	17,293	16,977	15,953	15,533	14,718	12,963
Male	11,833	12,540	12,605	12,321	11,875	10,918	10,413	9,845	8,395
Female	4,706	4,905	4,872	4,972	5,102	5,035	5,120	4,873	4,568
Doctor's degrees, total	3,660	4,081	4,234	4,124	4,212	4,157	3,802	3,594	3,371
Male	3,153	3,483	3,573	3,383	3,334	3,262	2,957	2,722	2,501
Female	507	598	661	741	878	895	845	872	870
Economics, History, Political Science and Government, and Sociology									
Economics									
Bachelor's degree	15,758	15,231	14,770	14,285	14,046	14,741	15,296	15,661	16,409

Note: Data are for postsecondary institutions participating in Title IV federal financial aid programs.
[1] Includes geology/earth science, general; geochemistry; geophysics; paleontology; hydrology; oceanography; and geological and earth sciences, other.
[2] Includes physics, general; atomic/molecular physics; elementary particle physics; nuclear physics; optics; acoustics; theoretical physics; and physics, other.

Table A-37. Degrees Conferred by Postsecondary Institutions, by Level of Degree and Sex of Student, 1970–1971 through 2015–2016—*Continued*

(Number.)

Degree conferred, level of degree, and sex of student (when available)	1979-80	1980-81	1981-82	1982-83	1983-84	1984-85	1985-86	1986-87	1987-88
Male	624	614	587	581	569	590	618	598	625
Female	100	114	94	116	126	109	124	125	125
Physical Sciences and Science Technologies									
Bachelor's degrees, total	23,407	23,936	24,045	23,374	23,645	23,694	21,711	20,060	17,797
Male	17,861	18,052	17,861	16,988	17,112	17,065	15,750	14,365	12,385
Female	5,546	5,884	6,184	6,386	6,533	6,629	5,961	5,695	5,412
Master's degrees, total	5,167	5,246	5,446	5,250	5,541	5,752	5,860	5,586	5,696
Male	4,210	4,172	4,274	4,131	4,249	4,425	4,443	4,193	4,300
Female	957	1,074	1,172	1,119	1,292	1,327	1,417	1,393	1,396
Doctor's degrees, total	3,044	3,105	3,246	3,214	3,269	3,349	3,521	3,629	3,758
Male	2,669	2,733	2,804	2,767	2,789	2,808	2,946	3,004	3,085
Female	375	372	442	447	480	541	575	625	673
Chemistry, Geology and Earth Science, and Physics									
Chemistry									
Bachelor's degree	11,229	11,331	11,058	10,789	10,698	10,472	10,110	9,660	9,043
Master's degree	1,671	1,616	1,683	1,582	1,632	1,675	1,712	1,695	1,671
Doctor's degree	1,500	1,586	1,682	1,691	1,707	1,735	1,878	1,932	1,944
Geology and earth science[1]									
Bachelor's degree	5,785	6,332	6,650	6,981	7,524	7,194	5,760	3,943	3,204
Master's degree	1,623	1,702	1,848	1,784	1,747	1,927	2,036	1,835	1,722
Doctor's degree	440	404	452	406	408	401	395	399	462
Physics[2]									
Bachelor's degree	3,396	3,441	3,472	3,793	3,907	4,097	4,180	4,318	4,100
Master's degree	1,192	1,294	1,284	1,369	1,532	1,523	1,501	1,543	1,675
Doctor's degree	830	866	873	873	953	951	1,010	1,074	1,093
Psychology									
Bachelor's degrees, total	42,093	41,068	41,212	40,460	39,955	39,900	40,628	43,152	45,371
Male	15,440	14,332	13,645	13,131	12,812	12,706	12,605	13,395	13,579
Female	26,653	26,736	27,567	27,329	27,143	27,194	28,023	29,757	31,792
Master's degrees, total	9,938	10,223	9,947	9,981	9,525	9,891	9,845	11,000	10,488
Male	4,096	4,066	3,823	3,647	3,400	3,452	3,347	3,516	3,256
Female	5,842	6,157	6,124	6,334	6,125	6,439	6,498	7,484	7,232
Doctor's degrees, total	3,395	3,576	3,461	3,602	3,535	3,447	3,593	4,062	3,973
Male	1,921	2,002	1,856	1,838	1,774	1,739	1,724	1,801	1,783
Female	1,474	1,574	1,605	1,764	1,761	1,708	1,869	2,261	2,190
Public Administration and Social Services									
Bachelor's degrees, total	16,644	16,707	16,495	14,414	12,570	11,754	11,887	12,328	12,385
Male	4,451	4,248	4,176	3,343	2,998	2,829	2,966	2,993	2,923
Female	12,193	12,459	12,319	11,071	9,572	8,925	8,921	9,335	9,462
Master's degrees, total	17,560	17,803	17,416	16,046	15,060	15,575	15,692	16,432	16,424
Male	7,866	7,460	6,975	5,961	5,634	5,573	5,594	5,673	5,631
Female	9,694	10,343	10,441	10,085	9,426	10,002	10,098	10,759	10,793
Doctor's degrees, total	342	362	372	347	420	431	382	398	470
Male	216	212	205	184	230	213	171	216	238
Female	126	150	167	163	190	218	211	182	232
Social Sciences and History									
Bachelor's degrees, total	103,662	100,513	99,705	95,228	93,323	91,570	93,840	96,342	100,460
Male	58,511	56,131	55,196	52,771	52,154	51,226	52,724	53,949	56,377
Female	45,151	44,382	44,509	42,457	41,169	40,344	41,116	42,393	44,083
Master's degrees, total	12,176	11,945	12,002	11,205	10,577	10,503	10,564	10,506	10,412
Male	7,794	7,457	7,468	6,974	6,551	6,475	6,419	6,373	6,310
Female	4,382	4,488	4,534	4,231	4,026	4,028	4,145	4,133	4,102
Doctor's degrees, total	3,230	3,122	3,061	2,931	2,911	2,851	2,955	2,916	2,781
Male	2,357	2,274	2,237	2,042	2,030	1,933	1,970	2,026	1,849
Female	873	848	824	889	881	918	985	890	932
Economics, History, Political Science and Government, and Sociology									
Economics									
Bachelor's degree	17,863	18,753	19,876	20,517	20,719	20,711	21,602	22,378	22,911

Note: Data are for postsecondary institutions participating in Title IV federal financial aid programs.

[1] Includes geology/earth science, general; geochemistry; geophysics; paleontology; hydrology; oceanography; and geological and earth sciences, other.

[2] Includes physics, general; atomic/molecular physics; elementary particle physics; nuclear physics; optics; acoustics; theoretical physics; and physics, other.

Table A-37. Degrees Conferred by Postsecondary Institutions, by Level of Degree and Sex of Student, 1970–1971 through 2015–2016—*Continued*

(Number.)

Degree conferred, level of degree, and sex of student (when available)	1970-71	1971-72	1972-73	1973-74	1974-75	1975-76	1976-77	1977-78	1978-79
Master's degree..	1,995	2,224	2,225	2,141	2,127	2,087	2,158	1,995	1,955
Doctor's degree..	721	794	845	788	815	763	758	706	712
History									
Bachelor's degree..	44,663	43,695	40,943	37,049	31,470	28,400	25,433	23,004	21,019
Master's degree..	5,157	5,217	5,030	4,533	4,226	3,658	3,393	3,033	2,536
Doctor's degree..	991	1,133	1,140	1,114	1,117	1,014	921	813	756
Political science and government.....................									
Bachelor's degree..	27,482	28,135	30,100	30,744	29,126	28,302	26,411	26,069	25,628
Master's degree..	2,318	2,451	2,398	2,448	2,333	2,191	2,222	2,069	2,037
Doctor's degree..	700	758	747	766	680	723	641	636	563
Sociology									
Bachelor's degree..	33,263	35,216	35,436	35,491	31,488	27,634	24,713	22,750	20,285
Master's degree..	1,808	1,944	1,923	2,196	2,112	2,009	1,830	1,611	1,415
Doctor's degree..	574	636	583	632	693	729	714	599	612
Visual and Performing Arts									
Bachelor's degrees, total.................................	30,394	33,831	36,017	39,730	40,782	42,138	41,793	40,951	40,969
Male	12,256	13,580	14,267	15,821	15,532	16,491	16,166	15,572	15,380
Female	18,138	20,251	21,750	23,909	25,250	25,647	25,627	25,379	25,589
Master's degrees, total....................................	6,675	7,537	7,254	8,001	8,362	8,817	8,636	9,036	8,524
Male	3,510	4,049	4,005	4,325	4,448	4,507	4,211	4,327	3,933
Female	3,165	3,488	3,249	3,676	3,914	4,310	4,425	4,709	4,591
Doctor's degrees, total.....................................	621	572	616	585	649	620	662	708	700
Male	483	428	449	440	446	447	447	448	454
Female	138	144	167	145	203	173	215	260	246

Note: Data are for postsecondary institutions participating in Title IV federal financial aid programs.

Table A-37. Degrees Conferred by Postsecondary Institutions, by Level of Degree and Sex of Student, 1970–1971 through 2015–2016—*Continued*

(Number.)

Degree conferred, level of degree, and sex of student (when available)	1979-80	1980-81	1981-82	1982-83	1983-84	1984-85	1985-86	1986-87	1987-88
Master's degree	1,821	1,911	1,964	1,972	1,891	1,992	1,937	1,855	1,847
Doctor's degree	677	727	677	734	729	749	789	750	770
History									
Bachelor's degree	19,301	18,301	17,146	16,467	16,643	16,049	16,415	16,997	18,207
Master's degree	2,367	2,237	2,210	2,041	1,940	1,921	1,961	2,021	2,093
Doctor's degree	712	643	636	575	561	468	497	534	517
Political science and government									
Bachelor's degree	25,457	24,977	25,658	25,791	25,719	25,834	26,439	26,817	27,207
Master's degree	1,938	1,875	1,954	1,829	1,769	1,500	1,704	1,618	1,579
Doctor's degree	535	484	513	435	457	441	439	435	391
Sociology									
Bachelor's degree	18,881	17,272	16,042	14,105	13,145	11,968	12,271	12,239	13,024
Master's degree	1,341	1,240	1,145	1,112	1,008	1,022	965	950	984
Doctor's degree	583	610	558	522	520	480	504	451	452
Visual and Performing Arts									
Bachelor's degrees, total	40,892	40,479	40,422	39,804	40,131	38,285	37,241	36,873	37,150
Male	15,065	14,798	14,819	14,695	15,089	14,518	14,236	13,980	14,225
Female	25,827	25,681	25,603	25,109	25,042	23,767	23,005	22,893	22,925
Master's degrees, total	8,708	8,629	8,746	8,763	8,526	8,720	8,420	8,508	7,939
Male	4,067	4,056	3,866	4,013	3,897	3,896	3,775	3,756	3,442
Female	4,641	4,573	4,880	4,750	4,629	4,824	4,645	4,752	4,497
Doctor's degrees, total	655	654	670	692	730	696	722	793	727
Male	413	396	380	404	406	407	396	447	424
Female	242	258	290	288	324	289	326	346	303

Note: Data are for postsecondary institutions participating in Title IV federal financial aid programs.

Table A-37. Degrees Conferred by Postsecondary Institutions, by Level of Degree and Sex of Student, 1970–1971 through 2015–2016—*Continued*

(Number.)

Degree conferred, level of degree, and sex of student (when available)	1988-89	1989-90	1990-91	1991-92	1992-93	1993-94	1994-95	1995-96	1996-97
Agriculture and Natural Resources									
Bachelor's degrees, total	13,492	12,900	13,124	15,113	16,769	18,056	19,832	21,425	22,597
Male	9,298	8,822	8,832	9,867	11,079	11,746	12,686	13,531	13,791
Female	4,194	4,078	4,292	5,246	5,690	6,310	7,146	7,894	8,806
Master's degrees, total	3,245	3,382	3,295	3,730	3,959	4,110	4,234	4,551	4,505
Male	2,231	2,239	2,160	2,409	2,474	2,512	2,541	2,642	2,601
Female	1,014	1,143	1,135	1,321	1,485	1,598	1,693	1,909	1,904
Doctor's degrees, total	1,183	1,295	1,185	1,205	1,159	1,262	1,256	1,259	1,202
Male	950	1,038	953	955	869	969	955	926	875
Female	233	257	232	250	290	293	301	333	327
Architecture and Related Services									
Bachelor's degrees, total	9,150	9,364	9,781	8,753	9,167	8,975	8,756	8,352	7,944
Male	5,545	5,703	5,788	5,805	5,940	5,764	5,741	5,340	5,090
Female	3,605	3,661	3,993	2,948	3,227	3,211	3,015	3,012	2,854
Master's degrees, total	3,383	3,499	3,490	3,640	3,808	3,943	3,923	3,993	4,034
Male	2,192	2,228	2,244	2,271	2,376	2,428	2,310	2,361	2,336
Female	1,191	1,271	1,246	1,369	1,432	1,515	1,613	1,632	1,698
Doctor's degrees, total	86	103	135	132	148	161	141	141	135
Male	63	73	101	93	105	111	95	96	93
Female	23	30	34	39	43	50	46	45	42
Biological and Biomedical Sciences									
Bachelor's degrees, total	36,068	37,304	39,482	42,892	47,009	51,296	55,983	61,014	63,973
Male	17,998	18,363	19,418	20,816	22,870	25,071	26,734	28,921	29,562
Female	18,070	18,941	20,064	22,076	24,139	26,225	29,249	32,093	34,411
Master's degrees, total	5,034	4,941	4,834	4,862	5,026	5,462	5,873	6,593	6,986
Male	2,598	2,509	2,417	2,437	2,540	2,681	2,920	3,212	3,419
Female	2,436	2,432	2,417	2,425	2,486	2,781	2,953	3,381	3,567
Doctor's degrees, total	3,617	3,922	4,152	4,442	4,749	4,891	5,069	5,250	5,313
Male	2,299	2,478	2,618	2,749	2,866	2,910	3,012	3,062	3,014
Female	1,318	1,444	1,534	1,693	1,883	1,981	2,057	2,188	2,299
Biology, Microbiology, and Zoology									
Biology, general									
Bachelor's degree	26,229	27,213	29,285	31,909	34,932	38,103	41,658	44,818	46,632
Master's degree	2,097	1,998	1,956	1,995	2,000	2,178	2,350	2,606	2,742
Doctor's degree	527	551	632	657	671	665	729	768	693
Microbiology									
Bachelor's degree	1,833	1,973	1,788	1,750	1,798	1,872	1,992	2,220	2,530
Master's degree	449	403	343	372	367	359	326	364	363
Doctor's degree	423	441	443	532	621	591	572	606	612
Zoology									
Bachelor's degree	2,549	2,473	2,641	2,811	3,036	3,162	3,149	3,463	3,438
Master's degree	634	548	551	530	559	658	586	677	720
Doctor's degree	466	545	516	494	465	503	487	501	474
Business									
Bachelor's degrees, total	246,262	248,568	249,165	256,298	256,473	246,265	233,895	226,623	225,934
Male	131,098	132,284	131,557	135,263	135,368	128,946	121,663	116,545	116,023
Female	115,164	116,284	117,608	121,035	121,105	117,319	112,232	110,078	109,911
Master's degrees, total	73,065	76,676	78,255	84,517	89,425	93,285	93,540	93,554	97,204
Male	48,540	50,585	50,883	54,609	57,504	59,223	58,931	58,400	59,333
Female	24,525	26,091	27,372	29,908	31,921	34,062	34,609	35,154	37,871
Doctor's degrees, total	1,100	1,093	1,185	1,242	1,346	1,364	1,391	1,366	1,336
Male	800	818	876	953	969	980	1,011	972	947
Female	300	275	309	289	377	384	380	394	389
Communication, Journalism, and Related Programs in Communications Technologies									
Bachelor's degrees, total	48,889	51,572	53,047	55,144	54,907	52,033	48,969	48,173	47,894
Male	19,357	20,374	20,806	21,601	22,154	21,484	20,501	19,868	19,771
Female	29,532	31,198	32,241	33,543	32,753	30,549	28,468	28,305	28,123
Master's degrees, total	4,249	4,353	4,327	4,463	5,179	5,388	5,559	5,561	5,552
Male	1,734	1,705	1,711	1,692	1,969	2,088	2,086	2,153	1,989
Female	2,515	2,648	2,616	2,771	3,210	3,300	3,473	3,408	3,563
Doctor's degrees, total	248	272	272	255	301	345	321	345	300

Note: Data are for postsecondary institutions participating in Title IV federal financial aid programs.

Table A-37. Degrees Conferred by Postsecondary Institutions, by Level of Degree and Sex of Student, 1970–1971 through 2015–2016—*Continued*

(Number.)

Degree conferred, level of degree, and sex of student (when available)	1997-98	1998-99	1999-2000	2000-01	2001-02	2002-03	2003-04	2004-05	2005-06
Agriculture and Natural Resources									
Bachelor's degrees, total	23,276	24,179	24,238	23,370	23,331	23,348	22,835	23,002	23,053
Male	13,806	14,045	13,843	12,840	12,630	12,343	11,889	11,987	12,063
Female	9,470	10,134	10,395	10,530	10,701	11,005	10,946	11,015	10,990
Master's degrees, total	4,464	4,376	4,360	4,272	4,503	4,492	4,783	4,746	4,640
Male	2,545	2,360	2,356	2,251	2,340	2,232	2,306	2,288	2,280
Female	1,919	2,016	2,004	2,021	2,163	2,260	2,477	2,458	2,360
Doctor's degrees, total	1,290	1,249	1,168	1,127	1,148	1,229	1,185	1,173	1,194
Male	924	869	803	741	760	790	758	763	710
Female	366	380	365	386	388	439	427	410	484
Architecture and Related Services									
Bachelor's degrees, total	7,652	8,245	8,462	8,480	8,808	9,056	8,838	9,237	9,515
Male	4,966	5,145	5,193	5,086	5,224	5,331	5,059	5,222	5,414
Female	2,686	3,100	3,269	3,394	3,584	3,725	3,779	4,015	4,101
Master's degrees, total	4,347	4,235	4,268	4,302	4,566	4,925	5,424	5,674	5,743
Male	2,537	2,435	2,508	2,515	2,606	2,832	3,049	3,180	3,165
Female	1,810	1,800	1,760	1,787	1,960	2,093	2,375	2,494	2,578
Doctor's degrees, total	131	119	129	153	183	152	173	179	201
Male	80	76	85	83	117	83	94	110	108
Female	51	43	44	70	66	69	79	69	93
Biological and Biomedical Sciences									
Bachelor's degrees, total	65,917	65,310	63,630	60,576	60,309	61,294	62,624	65,915	70,607
Male	29,663	28,507	26,579	24,600	23,694	23,356	23,691	25,104	27,183
Female	36,254	36,803	37,051	35,976	36,615	37,938	38,933	40,811	43,424
Master's degrees, total	6,848	6,966	6,850	7,017	7,011	7,050	7,732	8,284	8,781
Male	3,336	3,279	3,171	3,075	3,033	3,015	3,271	3,361	3,709
Female	3,512	3,687	3,679	3,942	3,978	4,035	4,461	4,923	5,072
Doctor's degrees, total	5,474	5,250	5,463	5,225	5,104	5,268	5,538	5,935	6,162
Male	3,123	3,010	3,068	2,923	2,836	2,866	2,975	3,025	3,138
Female	2,351	2,240	2,395	2,302	2,268	2,402	2,563	2,910	3,024
Biology, Microbiology, and Zoology									
Biology, general									
Bachelor's degree	47,054	46,172	44,982	42,310	42,281	42,699	43,465	45,540	48,855
Master's degree	2,617	2,616	2,599	2,582	2,424	2,340	2,529	2,564	2,719
Doctor's degree	809	718	727	780	689	680	681	712	776
Microbiology									
Bachelor's degree	2,926	2,885	3,049	2,779	2,622	2,455	2,365	2,318	2,243
Master's degree	401	406	383	334	325	297	350	390	372
Doctor's degree	585	544	551	553	538	507	599	610	612
Zoology									
Bachelor's degree	3,653	3,508	3,226	3,045	2,979	2,488	2,454	2,159	2,140
Master's degree	685	606	616	560	578	379	367	384	384
Doctor's degree	465	462	481	380	413	355	245	268	254
Business									
Bachelor's degrees, total	232,079	239,924	256,070	263,515	278,217	293,391	307,149	311,574	318,042
Male	119,379	121,741	128,521	132,275	138,343	145,075	152,513	155,940	159,683
Female	112,700	118,183	127,549	131,240	139,874	148,316	154,636	155,634	158,359
Master's degrees, total	101,652	106,830	111,532	115,602	119,725	127,685	139,347	142,617	146,406
Male	62,357	64,271	67,078	68,471	70,463	75,239	80,858	82,151	83,550
Female	39,295	42,559	44,454	47,131	49,262	52,446	58,489	60,466	62,856
Doctor's degrees, total	1,290	1,216	1,194	1,180	1,156	1,252	1,481	1,498	1,711
Male	885	848	812	783	746	820	960	901	1,049
Female	405	368	382	397	410	432	521	597	662
Communication, Journalism, and Related Programs in Communications Technologies									
Bachelor's degrees, total	50,263	52,397	57,058	59,191	64,036	69,828	73,002	75,238	76,936
Male	20,103	20,943	22,152	22,542	23,692	25,338	25,813	26,926	28,142
Female	30,160	31,454	34,906	36,649	40,344	44,490	47,189	48,312	48,794
Master's degrees, total	6,097	5,582	5,525	5,645	5,980	6,495	6,900	7,195	7,745
Male	2,369	2,001	2,030	1,964	2,169	2,301	2,329	2,535	2,611
Female	3,728	3,581	3,495	3,681	3,811	4,194	4,571	4,660	5,134
Doctor's degrees, total	359	348	357	370	383	398	426	468	464

Note: Data are for postsecondary institutions participating in Title IV federal financial aid programs.

Table A-37. Degrees Conferred by Postsecondary Institutions, by Level of Degree and Sex of Student, 1970–1971 through 2015–2016—*Continued*

(Number.)

Degree conferred, level of degree, and sex of student (when available)	1988-89	1989-90	1990-91	1991-92	1992-93	1993-94	1994-95	1995-96	1996-97
Male	137	145	150	132	146	174	162	190	155
Female	111	127	122	123	155	171	159	155	145
Computer and Information Sciences									
Bachelor's degrees, total	30,560	27,347	25,159	24,821	24,519	24,527	24,737	24,506	25,422
Male	21,143	19,159	17,771	17,685	17,606	17,528	17,684	17,757	18,527
Female	9,417	8,188	7,388	7,136	6,913	6,999	7,053	6,749	6,895
Master's degrees, total	9,414	9,677	9,324	9,655	10,353	10,568	10,595	10,579	10,513
Male	6,775	6,960	6,563	6,980	7,557	7,836	7,805	7,729	7,526
Female	2,639	2,717	2,761	2,675	2,796	2,732	2,790	2,850	2,987
Doctor's degrees, total	551	627	676	772	805	810	887	869	857
Male	466	534	584	669	689	685	726	743	721
Female	85	93	92	103	116	125	161	126	136
Education									
Bachelor's degrees, total	96,740	105,112	110,807	107,836	107,578	107,440	105,929	105,384	105,116
Male	21,643	23,007	23,417	22,655	23,199	24,424	25,619	26,214	26,242
Female	75,097	82,105	87,390	85,181	84,379	83,016	80,310	79,170	78,874
Master's degrees, total	79,793	84,890	87,352	91,225	94,497	97,427	99,835	104,936	108,720
Male	19,616	20,469	20,448	20,897	21,857	22,656	23,511	24,955	25,518
Female	60,177	64,421	66,904	70,328	72,640	74,771	76,324	79,981	83,202
Doctor's degrees, total	5,884	6,503	6,189	6,423	6,581	6,450	6,475	6,246	6,297
Male	2,522	2,776	2,614	2,652	2,712	2,555	2,490	2,404	2,367
Female	3,362	3,727	3,575	3,771	3,869	3,895	3,985	3,842	3,930
Engineering and Engineering Technologies									
Bachelor's degrees, total	85,982	82,480	79,751	78,036	78,619	78,580	78,483	77,997	75,659
Male	74,020	70,859	68,482	67,086	67,214	66,867	66,157	65,362	62,994
Female	11,962	11,621	11,269	10,950	11,405	11,713	12,326	12,635	12,665
Master's degrees, total	25,066	25,294	25,450	26,373	29,103	30,102	29,949	28,843	27,016
Male	21,731	21,753	21,780	22,397	24,721	25,394	25,028	23,840	22,047
Female	3,335	3,541	3,670	3,976	4,382	4,708	4,921	5,003	4,969
Doctor's degrees, total	4,572	5,030	5,330	5,499	5,870	5,954	6,108	6,354	6,166
Male	4,160	4,576	4,834	4,967	5,300	5,288	5,378	5,559	5,408
Female	412	454	496	532	570	666	730	795	758
Chemical, Civil, Electrical, and Mechanical Engineering									
Chemical engineering									
Bachelor's degree	3,663	3,430	3,444	3,754	4,459	5,163	5,901	6,319	6,564
Master's degree	1,093	1,035	903	956	990	1,032	1,085	1,176	1,131
Doctor's degree	602	562	611	590	595	604	571	670	650
Civil engineering									
Bachelor's degree	7,312	7,252	7,314	8,034	8,868	9,479	9,927	10,607	10,437
Master's degree	2,903	2,812	2,927	3,113	3,610	3,873	4,077	3,905	3,833
Doctor's degree	505	516	536	540	577	651	625	616	640
Electrical, electronics, and communications engineering									
Bachelor's degree	21,908	20,711	19,320	17,958	17,281	15,823	14,929	13,900	13,336
Master's degree	7,028	7,225	7,095	7,360	7,870	7,791	7,693	7,103	6,393
Doctor's degree	998	1,162	1,220	1,282	1,413	1,470	1,543	1,591	1,512
Mechanical engineering									
Bachelor's degree	14,843	14,336	13,977	14,067	14,464	15,030	14,794	14,177	13,493
Master's degree	3,498	3,424	3,516	3,653	3,982	4,099	4,213	3,881	3,608
Doctor's degree	633	742	757	851	871	887	890	940	913
English Language and Literature/Letters									
Bachelor's degrees, total	41,786	46,803	51,064	54,250	55,289	53,150	51,170	49,928	48,641
Male	13,729	15,437	16,891	18,314	19,007	18,214	17,581	17,007	16,325
Female	28,057	31,366	34,173	35,936	36,282	34,936	33,589	32,921	32,316
Master's degrees, total	5,716	6,317	6,784	7,215	7,537	7,611	7,612	7,657	7,487
Male	1,930	2,125	2,203	2,441	2,570	2,620	2,672	2,727	2,650
Female	3,786	4,192	4,581	4,774	4,967	4,991	4,940	4,930	4,837
Doctor's degrees, total	929	986	1,056	1,142	1,201	1,205	1,393	1,395	1,431

Note: Data are for postsecondary institutions participating in Title IV federal financial aid programs.

Table A-37. Degrees Conferred by Postsecondary Institutions, by Level of Degree and Sex of Student, 1970–1971 through 2015–2016—*Continued*

(Number.)

Degree conferred, level of degree, and sex of student (when available)	1997-98	1998-99	1999-2000	2000-01	2001-02	2002-03	2003-04	2004-05	2005-06
Male	171	182	168	190	168	179	186	195	207
Female	188	166	189	180	215	219	240	273	257
Computer and Information Sciences									
Bachelor's degrees, total	27,829	30,552	37,788	44,142	50,365	57,433	59,488	54,111	47,480
Male	20,372	22,289	27,185	31,923	36,462	41,950	44,585	42,125	37,705
Female	7,457	8,263	10,603	12,219	13,903	15,483	14,903	11,986	9,775
Master's degrees, total	11,765	12,843	14,990	16,911	17,173	19,509	20,143	18,416	17,055
Male	8,343	8,866	9,978	11,195	11,447	13,267	13,868	13,136	12,470
Female	3,422	3,977	5,012	5,716	5,726	6,242	6,275	5,280	4,585
Doctor's degrees, total	858	806	779	768	752	816	909	1,119	1,416
Male	718	656	648	632	581	648	709	905	1,109
Female	140	150	131	136	171	168	200	214	307
Education									
Bachelor's degrees, total	105,833	107,372	108,034	105,458	106,295	105,845	106,278	105,451	107,238
Male	26,285	26,321	26,103	24,580	24,049	22,604	22,802	22,513	22,448
Female	79,548	81,051	81,931	80,878	82,246	83,241	83,476	82,938	84,790
Master's degrees, total	113,374	118,226	123,045	127,829	135,189	147,883	162,345	167,490	174,620
Male	26,814	28,077	29,081	29,997	31,907	34,033	37,843	38,863	40,700
Female	86,560	90,149	93,964	97,832	103,282	113,850	124,502	128,627	133,920
Doctor's degrees, total	6,261	6,471	6,409	6,284	6,549	6,832	7,088	7,681	7,584
Male	2,334	2,297	2,295	2,237	2,211	2,314	2,403	2,557	2,664
Female	3,927	4,174	4,114	4,047	4,338	4,518	4,685	5,124	4,920
Engineering and Engineering Technologies									
Bachelor's degrees, total	74,557	72,796	73,323	72,869	74,588	77,231	78,079	79,544	81,406
Male	61,880	59,859	59,668	59,489	60,417	62,821	63,401	65,033	66,866
Female	12,677	12,937	13,655	13,380	14,171	14,410	14,678	14,511	14,540
Master's degrees, total	27,244	26,689	26,648	27,187	26,987	30,583	35,053	34,988	33,389
Male	21,800	21,348	21,047	21,341	21,212	24,097	27,561	27,049	25,568
Female	5,444	5,341	5,601	5,846	5,775	6,486	7,492	7,939	7,821
Doctor's degrees, total	5,966	5,413	5,367	5,547	5,181	5,252	5,859	6,467	7,318
Male	5,230	4,643	4,539	4,630	4,285	4,353	4,821	5,263	5,848
Female	736	770	828	917	896	899	1,038	1,204	1,470
Chemical, Civil, Electrical, and Mechanical Engineering									
Chemical engineering									
Bachelor's degree	6,319	6,038	5,807	5,611	5,462	5,109	4,742	4,397	4,326
Master's degree	1,128	1,130	1,078	1,083	973	1,065	1,165	1,183	1,116
Doctor's degree	652	575	590	610	605	542	623	773	819
Civil engineering									
Bachelor's degree	9,926	9,178	8,136	7,588	7,665	7,836	7,827	8,186	9,090
Master's degree	3,795	3,656	3,433	3,310	3,295	3,596	3,790	3,834	3,768
Doctor's degree	610	534	543	571	574	599	636	713	750
Electrical, electronics, and communications engineering									
Bachelor's degree	12,995	12,606	12,930	13,091	13,056	13,627	14,123	14,171	13,966
Master's degree	6,737	6,708	6,926	6,815	6,587	7,621	9,511	9,054	8,123
Doctor's degree	1,458	1,309	1,392	1,417	1,235	1,256	1,440	1,566	1,860
Mechanical engineering									
Bachelor's degree	13,071	12,753	12,807	12,817	13,058	13,693	14,050	14,609	15,850
Master's degree	3,441	3,268	3,273	3,371	3,391	3,695	4,420	4,637	4,443
Doctor's degree	933	788	776	849	772	747	787	915	1,096
English Language and Literature/Letters									
Bachelor's degrees, total	49,016	49,877	50,106	50,569	52,375	53,699	53,984	54,379	55,096
Male	16,280	16,332	16,124	15,997	16,457	16,738	16,792	17,154	17,316
Female	32,736	33,545	33,982	34,572	35,918	36,961	37,192	37,225	37,780
Master's degrees, total	7,587	7,326	7,022	6,763	7,097	7,428	7,956	8,468	8,845
Male	2,568	2,452	2,315	2,160	2,270	2,433	2,459	2,615	2,860
Female	5,019	4,874	4,707	4,603	4,827	4,995	5,497	5,853	5,985
Doctor's degrees, total	1,489	1,412	1,470	1,330	1,291	1,246	1,207	1,212	1,254

Note: Data are for postsecondary institutions participating in Title IV federal financial aid programs.

Table A-37. Degrees Conferred by Postsecondary Institutions, by Level of Degree and Sex of Student, 1970–1971 through 2015–2016—*Continued*

(Number.)

Degree conferred, level of degree, and sex of student (when available)	1988-89	1989-90	1990-91	1991-92	1992-93	1993-94	1994-95	1995-96	1996-97
Male	405	444	469	484	495	512	589	535	610
Female	524	542	587	658	706	693	804	860	821
Foreign Languages and Literatures									
Bachelor's degrees, total	12,403	13,133	13,937	14,634	15,305	15,242	14,558	14,832	14,487
Male	3,432	3,625	4,008	4,225	4,435	4,573	4,496	4,514	4,388
Female	8,971	9,508	9,929	10,409	10,870	10,669	10,062	10,318	10,099
Master's degrees, total	2,837	3,018	3,049	3,229	3,513	3,612	3,439	3,443	3,361
Male	955	987	1,018	1,074	1,182	1,199	1,124	1,141	1,104
Female	1,882	2,031	2,031	2,155	2,331	2,413	2,315	2,302	2,257
Doctor's degrees, total	727	816	889	984	977	1,033	1,081	1,020	1,064
Male	317	348	396	434	417	418	479	446	450
Female	410	468	493	550	560	615	602	574	614
French, German, Italian, and Spanish Language and Literature									
French									
Bachelor's degree	3,297	3,259	3,355	3,371	3,280	3,094	2,764	2,655	2,468
Master's degree	444	478	480	465	513	479	470	446	414
Doctor's degree	83	115	98	112	98	104	118	113	119
German									
Bachelor's degree	1,428	1,437	1,543	1,616	1,572	1,580	1,352	1,290	1,214
Master's degree	263	253	242	273	317	298	278	305	281
Doctor's degree	59	67	58	85	86	61	83	75	80
Italian									
Bachelor's degree	239	247	253	238	274	264	271	232	234
Master's degree	45	38	36	55	50	47	69	44	49
Doctor's degree	17	19	21	18	13	24	31	22	18
Spanish									
Bachelor's degree	3,748	4,176	4,480	4,768	5,233	5,505	5,602	5,995	6,161
Master's degree	552	573	609	647	667	691	709	769	677
Doctor's degree	101	108	125	143	145	160	161	151	175
Arabic, Chinese, Korean, and Russian Language and Literature									
Arabic									
Bachelor's degree	6	4	9	13	8	8	10	8	9
Master's degree	2	0	0	0	3	2	1	3	3
Doctor's degree	1	1	1	0	2	0	1	2	0
Chinese									
Bachelor's degree	138	144	150	183	129	112	107	136	152
Master's degree	27	33	24	36	54	48	63	42	31
Doctor's degree	8	8	9	14	8	18	16	19	15
Korean									
Bachelor's degree	NA	NA	NA	NA	NA	NA	NA	NA	NA
Master's degree	NA	NA	NA	NA	NA	NA	NA	NA	NA
Doctor's degree	NA	NA	NA	NA	NA	NA	NA	NA	NA
Russian									
Bachelor's degree	469	549	593	629	612	611	572	494	455
Master's degree	55	52	70	68	68	71	66	58	46
Doctor's degree	6	5	6	7	4	3	3	7	9
Health Professions and Related Programs									
Bachelor's degrees, total	59,850	58,983	59,875	62,779	68,434	75,890	81,596	86,087	87,997
Male	8,878	9,075	9,619	10,330	11,605	13,377	14,812	15,942	16,440
Female	50,972	49,908	50,256	52,449	56,829	62,513	66,784	70,145	71,557
Master's degrees, total	19,493	20,406	21,354	23,671	26,190	28,442	31,770	33,920	36,162
Male	4,197	4,486	4,423	4,794	5,249	5,813	6,718	7,017	7,536
Female	15,296	15,920	16,931	18,877	20,941	22,629	25,052	26,903	28,626
Doctor's degrees, total	30,546	30,101	29,842	31,479	31,089	30,959	32,124	32,678	34,971
Male	19,893	19,118	18,492	19,362	18,446	17,988	18,463	18,495	19,619
Female	10,653	10,983	11,350	12,117	12,643	12,971	13,661	14,183	15,352
Mathematics and Statistics									
Bachelor's degrees, total	15,017	14,276	14,393	14,468	14,384	14,171	13,494	12,713	12,401
Male	8,081	7,674	7,580	7,668	7,566	7,594	7,154	6,847	6,649
Female	6,936	6,602	6,813	6,800	6,818	6,577	6,340	5,866	5,752
Master's degrees, total	3,405	3,624	3,549	3,558	3,644	3,682	3,820	3,651	3,504
Male	2,061	2,172	2,096	2,151	2,151	2,237	2,289	2,178	2,055

Note: Data are for postsecondary institutions participating in Title IV federal financial aid programs.
NA = Not available.

Table A-37. Degrees Conferred by Postsecondary Institutions, by Level of Degree and Sex of Student, 1970–1971 through 2015–2016—*Continued*

(Number.)

Degree conferred, level of degree, and sex of student (when available)	1997-98	1998-99	1999-2000	2000-01	2001-02	2002-03	2003-04	2004-05	2005-06
Male	611	554	611	533	532	492	479	494	510
Female	878	858	859	797	759	754	728	718	744
Foreign Languages and Literatures									
Bachelor's degrees, total	15,279	15,835	15,886	16,128	16,258	16,912	17,754	18,386	19,410
Male	4,585	4,738	4,616	4,695	4,685	4,996	5,215	5,370	5,842
Female	10,694	11,097	11,270	11,433	11,573	11,916	12,539	13,016	13,568
Master's degrees, total	3,181	3,109	3,037	3,035	3,075	3,049	3,124	3,407	3,539
Male	1,033	976	944	969	958	874	957	1,056	1,049
Female	2,148	2,133	2,093	2,066	2,117	2,175	2,167	2,351	2,490
Doctor's degrees, total	1,118	1,049	1,086	1,078	1,003	1,042	1,031	1,027	1,074
Male	473	443	446	420	418	424	410	410	436
Female	645	606	640	658	585	618	621	617	638
French, German, Italian, and Spanish Language and Literature									
French									
Bachelor's degree	2,530	2,565	2,514	2,371	2,396	2,294	2,362	2,394	2,410
Master's degree	389	365	343	376	356	348	361	356	395
Doctor's degree	104	115	129	115	89	75	85	80	84
German									
Bachelor's degree	1,181	1,237	1,125	1,143	1,092	1,097	1,031	1,103	1,106
Master's degree	209	242	184	242	208	188	153	180	172
Doctor's degree	94	78	76	73	64	77	30	56	48
Italian									
Bachelor's degree	252	257	237	286	263	307	279	277	321
Master's degree	60	41	48	42	46	54	49	70	94
Doctor's degree	25	12	13	11	15	20	31	12	17
Spanish									
Bachelor's degree	6,595	6,992	7,031	7,164	7,243	7,619	7,991	8,304	8,690
Master's degree	781	697	718	716	792	791	833	919	981
Doctor's degree	160	153	175	185	193	190	199	190	192
Arabic, Chinese, Korean, and Russian Language and Literature									
Arabic									
Bachelor's degree	16	13	6	7	13	13	13	21	26
Master's degree	2	3	4	2	2	3	3	5	4
Doctor's degree	1	1	5	3	2	0	1	0	2
Chinese									
Bachelor's degree	161	178	183	183	189	190	186	208	241
Master's degree	21	20	18	13	16	12	15	21	20
Doctor's degree	13	14	15	7	12	9	5	8	10
Korean									
Bachelor's degree	NA	NA	NA	NA	NA	5	9	8	17
Master's degree	NA	NA	NA	NA	NA	0	2	0	4
Doctor's degree	NA	NA	NA	NA	NA	0	1	0	3
Russian									
Bachelor's degree	383	398	340	335	277	271	301	298	279
Master's degree	49	29	33	24	34	16	21	18	28
Doctor's degree	9	4	10	7	5	6	3	0	7
Health Professions and Related Programs									
Bachelor's degrees, total	86,843	84,989	80,863	75,933	72,887	71,261	73,934	80,685	91,973
Male	15,700	15,191	13,342	12,514	10,869	10,096	10,017	10,858	12,914
Female	71,143	69,798	67,521	63,419	62,018	61,165	63,917	69,827	79,059
Master's degrees, total	39,567	40,628	42,593	43,623	43,560	42,748	44,939	46,703	51,380
Male	8,644	9,152	9,500	9,711	9,588	9,280	9,670	9,816	10,630
Female	30,923	31,476	33,093	33,912	33,972	33,468	35,269	36,887	40,750
Doctor's degrees, total	35,369	35,939	37,829	39,019	39,435	39,799	41,861	44,201	45,677
Male	19,370	19,673	19,984	20,260	19,760	19,493	19,587	19,697	19,640
Female	15,999	16,266	17,845	18,759	19,675	20,306	22,274	24,504	26,037
Mathematics and Statistics									
Bachelor's degrees, total	11,795	12,011	11,418	11,171	11,950	12,505	13,327	14,351	14,770
Male	6,247	6,206	5,955	5,791	6,333	6,784	7,203	7,937	8,115
Female	5,548	5,805	5,463	5,380	5,617	5,721	6,124	6,414	6,655
Master's degrees, total	3,409	3,304	3,208	3,209	3,350	3,620	4,191	4,477	4,730
Male	1,985	1,912	1,749	1,857	1,913	1,996	2,302	2,525	2,712

Note: Data are for postsecondary institutions participating in Title IV federal financial aid programs.
NA = Not available.

Table A-37. Degrees Conferred by Postsecondary Institutions, by Level of Degree and Sex of Student, 1970–1971 through 2015–2016—*Continued*

(Number.)

Degree conferred, level of degree, and sex of student (when available)	1988-89	1989-90	1990-91	1991-92	1992-93	1993-94	1994-95	1995-96	1996-97
Female	1,344	1,452	1,453	1,407	1,493	1,445	1,531	1,473	1,449
Doctor's degrees, total	866	917	978	1,048	1,138	1,125	1,181	1,158	1,134
Male	700	754	790	825	867	880	919	919	861
Female	166	163	188	223	271	245	262	239	273
Physical Sciences and Science Technologies									
Bachelor's degrees, total	17,179	16,056	16,334	16,970	17,577	18,474	19,247	19,716	19,594
Male	12,071	11,026	11,170	11,443	11,853	12,271	12,556	12,634	12,285
Female	5,108	5,030	5,164	5,527	5,724	6,203	6,691	7,082	7,309
Master's degrees, total	5,691	5,410	5,281	5,397	5,392	5,718	5,798	5,910	5,616
Male	4,180	3,996	3,823	3,935	3,840	4,069	4,058	4,031	3,799
Female	1,511	1,414	1,458	1,462	1,552	1,649	1,740	1,879	1,817
Doctor's degrees, total	3,795	4,116	4,248	4,378	4,372	4,652	4,486	4,589	4,501
Male	3,046	3,328	3,417	3,433	3,426	3,657	3,443	3,543	3,479
Female	749	788	831	945	946	995	1,043	1,046	1,022
Chemistry, Geology and Earth Science, and Physics									
Chemistry									
Bachelor's degree	8,618	8,122	8,311	8,629	8,903	9,417	9,706	10,395	10,609
Master's degree	1,742	1,643	1,637	1,746	1,822	1,968	2,062	2,214	2,203
Doctor's degree	1,974	2,135	2,196	2,233	2,216	2,298	2,211	2,228	2,202
Geology and earth science[1]									
Bachelor's degree	2,847	2,372	2,367	2,784	3,123	3,456	4,032	4,019	4,023
Master's degree	1,609	1,399	1,336	1,245	1,195	1,221	1,280	1,288	1,258
Doctor's degree	492	562	600	549	626	577	539	555	564
Physics[2]									
Bachelor's degree	4,352	4,155	4,236	4,098	4,063	4,001	3,823	3,679	3,376
Master's degree	1,736	1,831	1,725	1,834	1,777	1,945	1,817	1,678	1,496
Doctor's degree	1,112	1,192	1,209	1,337	1,277	1,465	1,424	1,462	1,410
Psychology									
Bachelor's degrees, total	49,083	53,952	58,655	63,683	66,931	69,419	72,233	73,416	74,308
Male	14,265	15,336	16,067	17,062	17,942	18,668	19,570	19,836	19,408
Female	34,818	38,616	42,588	46,621	48,989	50,751	52,663	53,580	54,900
Master's degrees, total	11,329	10,730	11,349	11,659	12,518	13,723	15,378	15,152	15,769
Male	3,465	3,377	3,329	3,335	3,380	3,763	4,210	4,090	4,155
Female	7,864	7,353	8,020	8,324	9,138	9,960	11,168	11,062	11,614
Doctor's degrees, total	4,143	3,811	3,932	3,814	4,100	4,021	4,252	4,141	4,507
Male	1,773	1,566	1,520	1,490	1,570	1,497	1,562	1,380	1,495
Female	2,370	2,245	2,412	2,324	2,530	2,524	2,690	2,761	3,012
Public Administration and Social Services									
Bachelor's degrees, total	13,162	13,908	14,350	15,987	16,775	17,815	18,586	19,849	20,649
Male	3,214	3,334	3,215	3,479	3,801	3,919	3,935	4,205	4,177
Female	9,948	10,574	11,135	12,508	12,974	13,896	14,651	15,644	16,472
Master's degrees, total	17,020	17,399	17,905	19,243	20,634	21,833	23,501	24,229	24,781
Male	5,615	5,634	5,679	5,769	6,105	6,406	6,870	6,927	6,957
Female	11,405	11,765	12,226	13,474	14,529	15,427	16,631	17,302	17,824
Doctor's degrees, total	428	508	430	432	459	519	556	499	518
Male	210	235	190	204	215	238	274	220	243
Female	218	273	240	228	244	281	282	279	275
Social Sciences and History									
Bachelor's degrees, total	108,151	118,083	125,107	133,974	135,703	133,680	128,154	126,479	124,891
Male	60,121	65,887	68,701	73,001	73,589	72,006	68,139	65,872	64,115
Female	48,030	52,196	56,406	60,973	62,114	61,674	60,015	60,607	60,776
Master's degrees, total	11,023	11,634	12,233	12,702	13,471	14,561	14,845	15,012	14,787
Male	6,599	6,898	7,016	7,237	7,671	8,152	8,207	8,093	7,830
Female	4,424	4,736	5,217	5,465	5,800	6,409	6,638	6,919	6,957
Doctor's degrees, total	2,885	3,010	3,012	3,218	3,460	3,627	3,725	3,760	3,989
Male	1,949	2,019	1,956	2,126	2,203	2,317	2,319	2,339	2,479
Female	936	991	1,056	1,092	1,257	1,310	1,406	1,421	1,510
Economics, History, Political Science and Government, and Sociology									
Economics									
Bachelor's degree	23,454	23,923	23,488	23,423	21,321	19,496	17,673	16,674	16,539

Note: Data are for postsecondary institutions participating in Title IV federal financial aid programs.
[1] Includes geology/earth science, general; geochemistry; geophysics; paleontology; hydrology; oceanography; and geological and earth sciences, other.
[2] Includes physics, general; atomic/molecular physics; elementary particle physics; nuclear physics; optics; acoustics; theoretical physics; and physics, other.

Table A-37. Degrees Conferred by Postsecondary Institutions, by Level of Degree and Sex of Student, 1970–1971 through 2015–2016—*Continued*

(Number.)

Degree conferred, level of degree, and sex of student (when available)	1997-98	1998-99	1999-2000	2000-01	2001-02	2002-03	2003-04	2004-05	2005-06
Female	1,424	1,392	1,459	1,352	1,437	1,624	1,889	1,952	2,018
Doctor's degrees, total	1,215	1,107	1,075	997	923	1,007	1,060	1,176	1,293
Male	903	812	803	715	658	734	762	841	911
Female	312	295	272	282	265	273	298	335	382
Physical Sciences and Science Technologies									
Bachelor's degrees, total	19,454	18,448	18,427	18,025	17,890	18,038	18,131	19,104	20,522
Male	11,999	11,119	11,019	10,628	10,349	10,625	10,577	11,065	11,978
Female	7,455	7,329	7,408	7,397	7,541	7,413	7,554	8,039	8,544
Master's degrees, total	5,411	5,241	4,888	5,134	5,082	5,196	5,714	5,823	6,063
Male	3,484	3,454	3,167	3,276	3,186	3,284	3,470	3,569	3,666
Female	1,927	1,787	1,721	1,858	1,896	1,912	2,244	2,254	2,397
Doctor's degrees, total	4,592	4,229	4,017	3,968	3,824	3,939	3,937	4,248	4,642
Male	3,451	3,206	3,002	2,914	2,766	2,854	2,855	3,071	3,258
Female	1,141	1,023	1,015	1,054	1,058	1,085	1,082	1,177	1,384
Chemistry, Geology and Earth Science, and Physics									
Chemistry									
Bachelor's degree	10,528	10,109	9,989	9,466	9,084	9,013	9,016	9,664	10,606
Master's degree	2,108	2,019	1,857	1,952	1,823	1,777	2,009	1,879	2,044
Doctor's degree	2,291	2,175	2,028	2,056	1,984	2,092	2,033	2,148	2,403
Geology and earth science[1]									
Bachelor's degree	3,866	3,570	3,516	3,495	3,449	3,381	3,312	3,276	3,322
Master's degree	1,227	1,196	1,186	1,220	1,263	1,323	1,389	1,420	1,476
Doctor's degree	588	533	492	472	494	466	463	476	505
Physics[2]									
Bachelor's degree	3,441	3,200	3,342	3,418	3,627	3,900	4,118	4,182	4,541
Master's degree	1,371	1,326	1,232	1,365	1,344	1,438	1,625	1,785	1,846
Doctor's degree	1,393	1,257	1,208	1,169	1,096	1,089	1,119	1,254	1,341
Psychology									
Bachelor's degrees, total	74,107	73,747	74,194	73,645	76,775	78,650	82,098	85,614	88,134
Male	18,976	18,376	17,451	16,585	17,284	17,514	18,193	19,000	19,865
Female	55,131	55,371	56,743	57,060	59,491	61,136	63,905	66,614	68,269
Master's degrees, total	15,142	15,560	15,740	16,539	16,357	17,161	17,898	18,830	19,770
Male	3,978	3,959	3,821	3,892	3,814	3,839	3,789	3,900	4,079
Female	11,164	11,601	11,919	12,647	12,543	13,322	14,109	14,930	15,691
Doctor's degrees, total	4,541	4,678	4,731	5,091	4,759	4,835	4,827	5,106	4,921
Male	1,470	1,528	1,529	1,598	1,503	1,483	1,496	1,466	1,347
Female	3,071	3,150	3,202	3,493	3,256	3,352	3,331	3,640	3,574
Public Administration and Social Services									
Bachelor's degrees, total	20,408	20,323	20,185	19,447	19,392	19,900	20,552	21,769	21,986
Male	3,881	3,799	3,816	3,670	3,706	3,726	3,793	4,209	4,126
Female	16,527	16,524	16,369	15,777	15,686	16,174	16,759	17,560	17,860
Master's degrees, total	25,144	25,038	25,594	25,268	25,448	25,903	28,250	29,552	30,510
Male	7,025	6,621	6,808	6,544	6,505	6,391	7,001	7,370	7,572
Female	18,119	18,417	18,786	18,724	18,943	19,512	21,249	22,182	22,938
Doctor's degrees, total	499	534	537	574	571	599	649	673	704
Male	223	240	227	263	250	265	275	272	285
Female	276	294	310	311	321	334	374	401	419
Social Sciences and History									
Bachelor's degrees, total	125,040	124,815	127,101	128,036	132,874	143,256	150,357	156,892	161,485
Male	63,537	61,843	62,062	61,749	64,170	69,517	73,834	77,702	80,799
Female	61,503	62,972	65,039	66,287	68,704	73,739	76,523	79,190	80,686
Master's degrees, total	14,938	14,396	14,066	13,791	14,112	14,630	16,110	16,952	17,369
Male	7,960	7,440	7,024	6,816	6,941	7,202	7,810	8,256	8,415
Female	6,978	6,956	7,042	6,975	7,171	7,428	8,300	8,696	8,954
Doctor's degrees, total	4,127	3,873	4,095	3,930	3,902	3,850	3,811	3,819	3,914
Male	2,445	2,290	2,407	2,302	2,219	2,196	2,188	2,184	2,218
Female	1,682	1,583	1,688	1,628	1,683	1,654	1,623	1,635	1,696
Economics, History, Political Science and Government, and Sociology									
Economics									
Bachelor's degree	17,074	17,577	18,441	19,437	20,927	23,007	24,069	24,217	23,807

Note: Data are for postsecondary institutions participating in Title IV federal financial aid programs.
[1] Includes geology/earth science, general; geochemistry; geophysics; paleontology; hydrology; oceanography; and geological and earth sciences, other.
[2] Includes physics, general; atomic/molecular physics; elementary particle physics; nuclear physics; optics; acoustics; theoretical physics; and physics, other.

Table A-37. Degrees Conferred by Postsecondary Institutions, by Level of Degree and Sex of Student, 1970–1971 through 2015–2016—*Continued*

(Number.)

Degree conferred, level of degree, and sex of student (when available)	1988-89	1989-90	1990-91	1991-92	1992-93	1993-94	1994-95	1995-96	1996-97
Master's degree....................................	1,886	1,950	1,951	2,106	2,292	2,521	2,400	2,533	2,433
Doctor's degree....................................	827	806	802	866	879	869	910	916	968
History									
Bachelor's degree.............................	20,159	22,476	24,541	26,966	27,774	27,503	26,598	26,005	25,214
Master's degree................................	2,121	2,369	2,591	2,754	2,952	3,009	3,091	2,898	2,901
Doctor's degree.................................	487	570	606	644	690	752	816	805	873
Political science and government.....................									
Bachelor's degree.............................	30,450	33,560	35,737	37,805	37,931	36,097	33,013	30,775	28,969
Master's degree................................	1,598	1,580	1,772	1,908	1,943	2,147	2,019	2,024	1,909
Doctor's degree.................................	452	480	468	535	529	616	637	634	686
Sociology									
Bachelor's degree.............................	14,435	16,035	17,550	19,568	20,896	22,368	22,886	24,071	24,672
Master's degree................................	1,135	1,198	1,260	1,347	1,521	1,639	1,748	1,772	1,731
Doctor's degree.................................	451	432	465	501	536	530	546	527	591
Visual and Performing Arts									
Bachelor's degrees, total	38,420	39,934	42,186	46,522	47,761	49,053	48,690	49,296	50,083
Male	14,698	15,189	15,761	17,616	18,610	19,538	19,781	20,126	20,729
Female	23,722	24,745	26,425	28,906	29,151	29,515	28,909	29,170	29,354
Master's degrees, total................................	8,267	8,481	8,657	9,353	9,440	9,925	10,277	10,280	10,627
Male	3,611	3,706	3,830	4,078	4,099	4,229	4,374	4,361	4,470
Female	4,656	4,775	4,827	5,275	5,341	5,696	5,903	5,919	6,157
Doctor's degrees, total	753	849	838	906	882	1,054	1,080	1,067	1,060
Male	446	472	466	504	478	585	545	524	525
Female	307	377	372	402	404	469	535	543	535

Note: Data are for postsecondary institutions participating in Title IV federal financial aid programs.

Table A-37. Degrees Conferred by Postsecondary Institutions, by Level of Degree and Sex of Student, 1970–1971 through 2015–2016—*Continued*

(Number.)

Degree conferred, level of degree, and sex of student (when available)	1997-98	1998-99	1999-2000	2000-01	2001-02	2002-03	2003-04	2004-05	2005-06
Master's degree	2,435	2,332	2,168	2,139	2,330	2,582	2,824	3,092	2,941
Doctor's degree	928	819	851	851	826	836	849	973	930
History									
Bachelor's degree	25,726	24,742	25,247	25,090	26,001	27,757	29,808	31,398	33,153
Master's degree	2,895	2,618	2,573	2,365	2,420	2,521	2,522	2,893	2,992
Doctor's degree	937	931	984	931	924	861	855	819	852
Political science and government									
Bachelor's degree	28,044	27,476	27,635	27,792	29,354	33,205	35,581	38,107	39,409
Master's degree	1,957	1,667	1,627	1,596	1,641	1,664	1,869	1,983	2,054
Doctor's degree	705	694	693	688	625	671	618	636	649
Sociology									
Bachelor's degree	24,806	24,979	25,598	25,268	25,202	26,095	26,939	28,473	28,467
Master's degree	1,737	1,940	1,996	1,845	1,928	1,897	2,009	1,499	1,547
Doctor's degree	596	521	595	546	534	591	558	527	562
Visual and Performing Arts									
Bachelor's degrees, total	52,077	54,446	58,791	61,148	66,773	71,482	77,181	80,955	83,297
Male	21,483	22,270	24,003	24,967	27,130	27,922	30,037	31,355	32,117
Female	30,594	32,176	34,788	36,181	39,643	43,560	47,144	49,600	51,180
Master's degrees, total	11,145	10,762	10,918	11,404	11,595	11,982	12,906	13,183	13,530
Male	4,596	4,544	4,672	4,788	4,912	4,975	5,531	5,646	5,801
Female	6,549	6,218	6,246	6,616	6,683	7,007	7,375	7,537	7,729
Doctor's degrees, total	1,163	1,117	1,127	1,167	1,114	1,293	1,282	1,278	1,383
Male	566	567	537	568	490	613	572	594	639
Female	597	550	590	599	624	680	710	684	744

Note: Data are for postsecondary institutions participating in Title IV federal financial aid programs.

Table A-37. Degrees Conferred by Postsecondary Institutions, by Level of Degree and Sex of Student, 1970–1971 through 2015–2016—*Continued*

(Number.)

Degree conferred, level of degree, and sex of student (when available)	2006-07	2007-08	2008-09	2009-10	2010-11	2011-12	2012-13	2013-14	2014-15	2015-16
Agriculture and Natural Resources										
Bachelor's degrees, total	23,133	24,113	24,982	26,343	28,630	30,972	33,592	35,125	36,278	37,005
Male	12,309	12,634	13,096	13,524	14,678	15,485	16,618	17,254	17,585	17,622
Female	10,824	11,479	11,886	12,819	13,952	15,487	16,974	17,871	18,693	19,383
Master's degrees, total	4,623	4,684	4,878	5,215	5,766	6,390	6,336	6,544	6,426	6,681
Male	2,174	2,180	2,328	2,512	2,746	3,026	2,912	2,966	2,904	2,955
Female	2,449	2,504	2,550	2,703	3,020	3,364	3,424	3,578	3,522	3,726
Doctor's degrees, total	1,272	1,257	1,328	1,149	1,246	1,333	1,411	1,407	1,561	1,508
Male	768	742	741	626	675	721	767	739	811	816
Female	504	515	587	523	571	612	644	668	750	692
Architecture and Related Services										
Bachelor's degrees, total	9,717	9,805	10,119	10,051	9,831	9,727	9,757	9,149	9,090	8,823
Male	5,393	5,579	5,797	5,694	5,698	5,566	5,581	5,174	5,116	4,854
Female	4,324	4,226	4,322	4,357	4,133	4,161	4,176	3,975	3,974	3,969
Master's degrees, total	5,951	6,065	6,587	7,280	7,788	8,448	8,095	8,048	8,006	7,986
Male	3,304	3,252	3,657	4,012	4,265	4,504	4,261	4,122	4,147	4,163
Female	2,647	2,813	2,930	3,268	3,523	3,944	3,834	3,926	3,859	3,823
Doctor's degrees, total	178	199	212	210	205	255	247	247	272	236
Male	104	103	113	116	110	147	134	134	145	122
Female	74	96	99	94	95	108	113	113	127	114
Biological and Biomedical Sciences										
Bachelor's degrees, total	76,832	79,829	82,828	86,391	89,984	95,850	100,397	104,657	109,904	113,749
Male	30,600	32,401	33,707	35,866	36,888	39,542	41,556	43,440	45,104	45,579
Female	46,232	47,428	49,121	50,525	53,096	56,308	58,841	61,217	64,800	68,170
Master's degrees, total	8,898	9,689	10,018	10,730	11,324	12,419	13,300	13,964	14,655	15,714
Male	3,639	4,094	4,250	4,612	4,869	5,378	5,783	6,073	6,252	6,705
Female	5,259	5,595	5,768	6,118	6,455	7,041	7,517	7,891	8,403	9,009
Doctor's degrees, total	6,764	7,400	7,499	7,672	7,693	7,935	7,939	8,302	8,053	7,914
Male	3,440	3,645	3,549	3,603	3,648	3,708	3,689	3,884	3,763	3,723
Female	3,324	3,755	3,950	4,069	4,045	4,227	4,250	4,418	4,290	4,191
Biology, Microbiology, and Zoology										
Biology, general										
Bachelor's degree	52,527	54,384	55,859	58,700	61,236	64,616	66,692	69,425	71,622	73,041
Master's degree	2,679	2,935	2,987	3,087	3,283	3,494	3,479	3,465	3,432	3,445
Doctor's degree	788	866	896	919	935	964	1,003	1,053	976	942
Microbiology										
Bachelor's degree	2,347	2,458	2,480	2,449	2,466	2,532	2,582	2,572	2,567	2,637
Master's degree	369	353	291	303	337	395	402	465	510	524
Doctor's degree	667	734	716	767	739	687	704	674	688	642
Zoology										
Bachelor's degree	2,223	2,235	2,140	2,147	2,062	2,174	2,246	2,269	2,250	2,316
Master's degree	416	381	347	360	338	346	416	464	421	501
Doctor's degree	263	281	297	243	230	258	231	217	230	271
Business										
Bachelor's degrees, total	327,531	335,254	348,056	358,119	365,133	367,235	360,887	358,132	363,741	371,694
Male	166,350	170,978	177,924	183,272	187,116	190,180	187,843	188,468	191,288	196,312
Female	161,181	164,276	170,132	174,847	178,017	177,055	173,044	169,664	172,453	175,382
Master's degrees, total	150,211	155,637	168,404	177,748	187,178	191,606	188,617	189,364	185,236	186,834
Male	84,115	86,258	91,991	96,742	101,440	103,250	101,599	101,061	98,593	99,491
Female	66,096	69,379	76,413	81,006	85,738	88,356	87,018	88,303	86,643	87,343
Doctor's degrees, total	2,029	2,084	2,123	2,249	2,286	2,538	2,828	3,039	3,116	3,323
Male	1,188	1,250	1,302	1,338	1,357	1,461	1,605	1,722	1,716	1,931
Female	841	834	821	911	929	1,077	1,223	1,317	1,400	1,392
Communication, Journalism, and Related Programs in Communications Technologies										
Bachelor's degrees, total	78,420	81,048	83,084	86,062	88,089	88,754	89,805	92,603	95,793	97,378
Male	29,009	30,384	31,207	32,048	33,018	33,525	33,670	34,393	35,220	35,538
Female	49,411	50,664	51,877	54,014	55,071	55,229	56,135	58,210	60,573	61,840
Master's degrees, total	7,272	7,546	7,517	8,093	8,804	9,502	9,337	9,930	10,135	10,167
Male	2,485	2,580	2,446	2,656	2,819	3,068	3,021	3,131	3,111	3,104

Note: Data are for postsecondary institutions participating in Title IV federal financial aid programs.

Table A-37. Degrees Conferred by Postsecondary Institutions, by Level of Degree and Sex of Student, 1970–1971 through 2015–2016—*Continued*

(Number.)

Degree conferred, level of degree, and sex of student (when available)	2006-07	2007-08	2008-09	2009-10	2010-11	2011-12	2012-13	2013-14	2014-15	2015-16
Female	4,787	4,966	5,071	5,437	5,985	6,434	6,316	6,799	7,024	7,063
Doctor's degrees, total	480	496	535	573	578	567	612	614	644	633
Male	188	209	225	225	207	242	246	267	259	258
Female	292	287	310	348	371	325	366	347	385	375
Computer and Information Sciences										
Bachelor's degrees, total	42,170	38,476	37,992	39,593	43,066	47,406	50,961	55,271	59,586	64,405
Male	34,342	31,694	31,213	32,414	35,477	38,796	41,874	45,320	48,844	52,333
Female	7,828	6,782	6,779	7,179	7,589	8,610	9,087	9,951	10,742	12,072
Master's degrees, total	16,232	17,087	17,907	17,955	19,516	20,925	22,782	24,514	31,475	40,128
Male	11,985	12,513	13,063	13,019	14,010	15,132	16,539	17,472	21,893	27,787
Female	4,247	4,574	4,844	4,936	5,506	5,793	6,243	7,042	9,582	12,341
Doctor's degrees, total	1,595	1,698	1,580	1,599	1,588	1,698	1,834	1,982	1,998	1,979
Male	1,267	1,323	1,226	1,250	1,267	1,332	1,480	1,566	1,548	1,582
Female	328	375	354	349	321	366	354	416	450	397
Education										
Bachelor's degrees, total	105,641	102,582	101,716	101,287	104,008	105,656	104,698	98,838	91,596	87,217
Male	22,516	21,828	21,163	20,739	21,206	21,714	21,824	20,357	18,467	17,427
Female	83,125	80,754	80,553	80,548	82,802	83,942	82,874	78,481	73,129	69,790
Master's degrees, total	176,572	175,880	178,538	182,165	185,127	179,047	164,652	154,655	146,581	145,781
Male	40,164	40,055	40,312	41,284	42,043	41,364	37,816	35,974	33,963	33,802
Female	136,408	135,825	138,226	140,881	143,084	137,683	126,836	118,681	112,618	111,979
Doctor's degrees, total	8,261	8,491	9,028	9,237	9,642	10,118	10,572	10,929	11,772	11,829
Male	2,681	2,773	2,956	3,023	3,070	3,262	3,418	3,464	3,838	3,692
Female	5,580	5,718	6,072	6,214	6,572	6,856	7,154	7,465	7,934	8,137
Engineering and Engineering Technologies										
Bachelor's degrees, total	81,854	83,608	84,404	88,735	93,097	98,654	102,997	108,976	115,105	124,009
Male	68,081	69,540	70,504	73,838	77,080	81,364	84,645	88,941	93,541	99,628
Female	13,773	14,068	13,900	14,897	16,017	17,290	18,352	20,035	21,564	24,381
Master's degrees, total	31,989	34,430	38,008	39,391	43,179	45,116	45,328	47,343	51,441	57,685
Male	24,746	26,461	29,458	30,554	33,372	34,712	34,496	35,791	38,453	43,177
Female	7,243	7,969	8,550	8,837	9,807	10,404	10,832	11,552	12,988	14,508
Doctor's degrees, total	7,928	7,977	7,803	7,773	8,425	8,856	9,467	10,117	10,362	10,342
Male	6,285	6,263	6,123	5,986	6,548	6,838	7,305	7,820	7,958	7,915
Female	1,643	1,714	1,680	1,787	1,877	2,018	2,162	2,297	2,404	2,427
Chemical, Civil, Electrical, and Mechanical Engineering										
Chemical engineering										
Bachelor's degree	4,492	4,795	5,036	5,740	6,311	7,027	7,529	8,104	8,980	9,916
Master's degree	957	933	994	1,043	1,283	1,389	1,450	1,518	1,626	1,698
Doctor's degree	835	853	789	830	831	823	835	992	1,015	1,002
Civil engineering										
Bachelor's degree	9,671	10,455	10,785	11,335	12,557	12,808	13,262	12,995	12,673	13,244
Master's degree	3,482	3,595	3,794	4,079	4,860	5,359	5,353	5,501	5,365	5,625
Doctor's degree	805	752	763	717	751	787	868	972	1,031	1,007
Electrical, electronics, and communications engineering										
Bachelor's degree	13,089	12,375	11,620	11,450	11,575	12,110	12,835	13,856	14,599	15,734
Master's degree	7,777	8,631	9,178	9,052	9,691	9,696	9,485	9,829	11,917	13,778
Doctor's degree	2,042	1,996	1,812	1,869	2,037	2,119	2,118	2,301	2,320	2,241
Mechanical engineering										
Bachelor's degree	16,601	17,367	17,352	18,498	19,171	20,541	21,990	24,301	26,394	29,214
Master's degree	4,294	4,497	4,620	4,818	5,802	5,840	5,872	6,182	6,841	7,558
Doctor's degree	1,106	1,109	1,142	996	1,106	1,213	1,321	1,387	1,526	1,463
English Language and Literature/Letters										
Bachelor's degrees, total	55,122	55,038	55,465	53,229	52,754	53,765	52,401	50,464	45,851	42,795
Male	17,475	17,681	17,973	17,050	16,917	16,976	16,508	15,831	14,055	12,776
Female	37,647	37,357	37,492	36,179	35,837	36,789	35,893	34,633	31,796	30,019
Master's degrees, total	8,742	9,161	9,262	9,202	9,475	9,938	9,755	9,294	8,928	8,577
Male	2,867	3,027	3,000	3,006	3,137	3,403	3,213	3,115	3,052	2,883
Female	5,875	6,134	6,262	6,196	6,338	6,535	6,542	6,179	5,876	5,694

Note: Data are for postsecondary institutions participating in Title IV federal financial aid programs.

Table A-37. Degrees Conferred by Postsecondary Institutions, by Level of Degree and Sex of Student, 1970–1971 through 2015–2016—*Continued*

(Number.)

Degree conferred, level of degree, and sex of student (when available)	2006-07	2007-08	2008-09	2009-10	2010-11	2011-12	2012-13	2013-14	2014-15	2015-16
Doctor's degrees, total	1,178	1,262	1,271	1,334	1,344	1,427	1,377	1,393	1,418	1,392
Male	478	453	464	523	529	548	554	557	554	517
Female	700	809	807	811	815	879	823	836	864	875
Foreign Languages and Literatures										
Bachelor's degrees, total	20,275	20,977	21,169	21,507	21,705	21,756	21,647	20,332	19,493	18,427
Male	6,173	6,254	6,305	6,607	6,719	6,629	6,842	6,266	6,066	5,755
Female	14,102	14,723	14,864	14,900	14,986	15,127	14,805	14,066	13,427	12,672
Master's degrees, total	3,443	3,565	3,592	3,756	3,727	3,827	3,708	3,482	3,566	3,405
Male	1,058	1,128	1,211	1,254	1,256	1,280	1,235	1,222	1,241	1,173
Female	2,385	2,437	2,381	2,502	2,471	2,547	2,473	2,260	2,325	2,232
Doctor's degrees, total	1,059	1,078	1,111	1,091	1,158	1,231	1,304	1,230	1,243	1,265
Male	437	431	426	446	477	497	531	498	532	510
Female	622	647	685	645	681	734	773	732	711	755
French, German, Italian, and Spanish Language and Literature										
French										
Bachelor's degree	2,462	2,432	2,450	2,488	2,490	2,358	2,278	2,043	1,916	1,750
Master's degree	364	359	386	391	366	341	332	308	270	306
Doctor's degree	95	102	86	87	81	96	115	107	110	93
German										
Bachelor's degree	1,055	1,085	1,058	1,028	1,019	1,001	931	878	828	809
Master's degree	158	173	163	143	156	130	102	123	115	88
Doctor's degree	56	51	47	46	43	67	52	44	52	64
Italian										
Bachelor's degree	280	359	341	336	313	332	284	271	231	191
Master's degree	97	88	76	73	83	72	73	58	55	34
Doctor's degree	20	25	34	23	28	35	27	29	23	26
Spanish										
Bachelor's degree	9,013	9,278	9,333	9,138	8,920	8,714	8,419	8,034	7,508	6,874
Master's degree	982	990	878	962	955	991	928	832	830	747
Doctor's degree	195	193	218	199	179	189	205	192	198	197
Arabic, Chinese, Korean, and Russian Language and Literature										
Arabic										
Bachelor's degree	68	57	85	121	141	143	167	165	169	155
Master's degree	2	8	14	10	5	8	12	6	4	18
Doctor's degree	0	1	1	6	1	7	1	0	2	1
Chinese										
Bachelor's degree	261	289	384	456	449	496	510	497	509	482
Master's degree	30	35	45	51	51	46	61	46	48	44
Doctor's degree	2	5	11	12	8	9	12	3	6	6
Korean										
Bachelor's degree	13	15	24	27	28	38	43	32	43	54
Master's degree	0	4	2	19	10	8	14	10	8	6
Doctor's degree	0	1	1	1	3	3	0	8	2	2
Russian										
Bachelor's degree	311	294	325	356	340	392	392	371	339	304
Master's degree	18	20	21	19	11	17	11	14	15	13
Doctor's degree	4	1	1	1	3	2	5	1	4	0
Health Professions and Related Programs										
Bachelor's degrees, total	101,810	111,478	120,420	129,623	143,463	163,675	181,149	198,777	216,228	228,896
Male	14,325	16,286	17,776	19,309	21,540	24,905	28,208	30,932	33,658	36,261
Female	87,485	95,192	102,644	110,314	121,923	138,770	152,941	167,845	182,570	192,635
Master's degrees, total	54,531	58,120	62,642	69,112	75,571	84,355	90,933	97,416	103,052	110,348
Male	10,636	11,010	11,848	12,874	14,034	15,675	16,747	17,751	18,793	20,423
Female	43,895	47,110	50,794	56,238	61,537	68,680	74,186	79,665	84,259	89,925
Doctor's degrees, total	48,943	51,675	54,846	57,750	60,221	62,097	64,192	67,447	71,004	73,682
Male	20,522	21,616	22,678	23,946	25,386	26,074	26,852	28,082	29,427	30,385
Female	28,421	30,059	32,168	33,804	34,835	36,023	37,340	39,365	41,577	43,297
Mathematics and Statistics										
Bachelor's degrees, total	14,954	15,192	15,507	16,029	17,182	18,841	20,449	20,987	21,854	22,777
Male	8,360	8,490	8,801	9,087	9,782	10,722	11,599	11,970	12,462	13,088
Female	6,594	6,702	6,706	6,942	7,400	8,119	8,850	9,017	9,392	9,689
Master's degrees, total	4,884	4,980	5,211	5,639	5,866	6,246	6,957	7,273	7,589	8,446

Note: Data are for postsecondary institutions participating in Title IV federal financial aid programs.

Table A-37. Degrees Conferred by Postsecondary Institutions, by Level of Degree and Sex of Student, 1970–1971 through 2015–2016—*Continued*

(Number.)

Degree conferred, level of degree, and sex of student (when available)	2006-07	2007-08	2008-09	2009-10	2010-11	2011-12	2012-13	2013-14	2014-15	2015-16
Male	2,859	2,860	3,064	3,378	3,459	3,695	4,178	4,256	4,508	4,920
Female	2,025	2,120	2,147	2,261	2,407	2,551	2,779	3,017	3,081	3,526
Doctor's degrees, total	1,351	1,360	1,535	1,596	1,586	1,669	1,823	1,863	1,801	1,850
Male	949	938	1,059	1,118	1,132	1,198	1,292	1,325	1,298	1,322
Female	402	422	476	478	454	471	531	538	503	528
Physical Sciences and Science Technologies										
Bachelor's degrees, total	21,291	22,179	22,691	23,381	24,705	26,664	28,053	29,307	30,042	30,477
Male	12,604	13,143	13,465	13,866	14,778	15,972	17,142	17,804	18,480	18,666
Female	8,687	9,036	9,226	9,515	9,927	10,692	10,911	11,503	11,562	11,811
Master's degrees, total	6,012	6,061	5,862	6,066	6,386	6,911	7,014	6,984	7,100	7,122
Male	3,675	3,762	3,576	3,654	3,907	4,299	4,377	4,312	4,438	4,427
Female	2,337	2,299	2,286	2,412	2,479	2,612	2,637	2,672	2,662	2,695
Doctor's degrees, total	5,041	4,994	5,237	5,065	5,295	5,370	5,514	5,806	5,823	6,016
Male	3,454	3,513	3,554	3,406	3,608	3,609	3,646	3,873	3,826	4,076
Female	1,587	1,481	1,683	1,659	1,687	1,761	1,868	1,933	1,997	1,940
Chemistry, Geology and Earth Science, and Physics										
Chemistry										
Bachelor's degree	10,994	11,568	11,852	12,107	12,656	13,473	13,814	14,443	14,447	14,477
Master's degree	2,097	2,194	2,085	2,123	2,272	2,435	2,396	2,357	2,425	2,455
Doctor's degree	2,514	2,410	2,556	2,470	2,599	2,537	2,617	2,796	2,792	2,877
Geology and earth science[1]										
Bachelor's degree	3,319	3,561	3,809	4,093	4,611	5,111	5,539	5,959	6,405	6,551
Master's degree	1,437	1,350	1,352	1,447	1,568	1,807	1,845	1,933	1,955	1,911
Doctor's degree	640	577	614	613	567	612	657	735	681	770
Physics[2]										
Bachelor's degree	4,843	4,862	4,824	4,984	5,199	5,531	6,082	6,263	6,658	6,949
Master's degree	1,777	1,791	1,653	1,793	1,769	1,873	1,975	1,866	1,926	1,949
Doctor's degree	1,442	1,507	1,580	1,571	1,670	1,752	1,740	1,768	1,840	1,833
Psychology										
Bachelor's degrees, total	90,039	92,587	94,273	97,215	100,906	109,099	114,446	117,312	117,573	117,440
Male	20,343	21,202	21,490	22,262	23,230	25,420	26,814	27,306	26,803	26,279
Female	69,696	71,385	72,783	74,953	77,676	83,679	87,632	90,006	90,770	91,161
Master's degrees, total	21,037	21,431	23,415	23,763	25,062	27,052	27,787	27,926	26,772	27,645
Male	4,265	4,356	4,789	4,799	5,127	5,482	5,715	5,729	5,538	5,571
Female	16,772	17,075	18,626	18,964	19,935	21,570	22,072	22,197	21,234	22,074
Doctor's degrees, total	5,153	5,296	5,477	5,540	5,851	5,936	6,326	6,634	6,583	6,532
Male	1,382	1,440	1,478	1,478	1,481	1,525	1,628	1,680	1,624	1,658
Female	3,771	3,856	3,999	4,062	4,370	4,411	4,698	4,954	4,959	4,874
Public Administration and Social Services										
Bachelor's degrees, total	23,147	23,493	23,852	25,421	26,799	29,695	31,950	33,483	34,364	34,432
Male	4,354	4,202	4,373	4,578	4,913	5,386	5,664	5,916	6,146	6,025
Female	18,793	19,291	19,479	20,843	21,886	24,309	26,286	27,567	28,218	28,407
Master's degrees, total	31,131	33,029	33,934	35,740	38,614	41,737	43,591	44,508	45,948	46,751
Male	7,758	8,140	8,346	8,868	9,791	10,494	10,864	10,834	11,181	11,181
Female	23,373	24,889	25,588	26,872	28,823	31,243	32,727	33,674	34,767	35,570
Doctor's degrees, total	726	760	812	838	851	890	979	1,047	1,123	1,065
Male	253	269	306	323	327	343	351	346	374	354
Female	473	491	506	515	524	547	628	701	749	711
Social Sciences and History										
Bachelor's degrees, total	164,183	167,363	168,517	172,782	177,169	178,534	177,767	173,132	166,971	161,230
Male	82,417	84,868	85,202	87,404	89,809	90,628	90,143	88,254	85,484	81,300
Female	81,766	82,495	83,315	85,378	87,360	87,906	87,624	84,878	81,487	79,930
Master's degrees, total	17,665	18,495	19,241	20,234	21,085	21,891	21,591	21,497	20,533	19,828
Male	8,577	9,349	9,605	9,967	10,578	10,987	10,811	10,764	10,318	9,990
Female	9,088	9,146	9,636	10,267	10,507	10,904	10,780	10,733	10,215	9,838
Doctor's degrees, total	3,844	4,059	4,234	4,238	4,390	4,597	4,610	4,724	4,828	4,667
Male	2,110	2,194	2,353	2,292	2,331	2,464	2,461	2,494	2,589	2,571
Female	1,734	1,865	1,881	1,946	2,059	2,133	2,149	2,230	2,239	2,096
Economics, History, Political Science and Government, and Sociology										
Economics										
Bachelor's degree	23,916	25,278	26,301	27,623	28,517	27,994	28,449	29,999	32,683	33,475

Note: Data are for postsecondary institutions participating in Title IV federal financial aid programs.

[1]Includes geology/earth science, general; geochemistry; geophysics; paleontology; hydrology; oceanography; and geological and earth sciences, other.

[2]Includes physics, general; atomic/molecular physics; elementary particle physics; nuclear physics; optics; acoustics; theoretical physics; and physics, other.

Table A-37. Degrees Conferred by Postsecondary Institutions, by Level of Degree and Sex of Student, 1970–1971 through 2015–2016—*Continued*

(Number.)

Degree conferred, level of degree, and sex of student (when available)	2006-07	2007-08	2008-09	2009-10	2010-11	2011-12	2012-13	2013-14	2014-15	2015-16
Master's degree..	2,962	3,187	3,233	3,358	3,731	3,890	3,872	4,115	3,993	3,933
Doctor's degree..	941	1,025	1,015	983	1,018	1,130	1,076	1,059	1,128	1,156
History...										
Bachelor's degree..	34,446	34,441	34,713	35,191	35,008	35,122	34,188	31,122	28,038	25,597
Master's degree..	3,144	3,403	3,543	3,858	4,003	4,155	4,083	3,955	3,703	3,455
Doctor's degree..	807	860	918	888	908	969	1,003	1,040	986	971
Political science and government.....................										
Bachelor's degree..	39,899	40,259	39,202	39,462	40,133	39,792	38,466	37,360	35,442	33,958
Master's degree..	2,102	2,156	2,171	2,252	2,488	2,510	2,332	2,294	2,082	1,980
Doctor's degree..	614	639	709	745	722	746	821	792	844	781
Sociology...										
Bachelor's degree..	28,960	28,815	28,735	28,650	29,281	30,136	30,531	30,070	29,000	28,001
Master's degree..	1,545	1,560	1,580	1,428	1,559	1,696	1,603	1,611	1,447	1,363
Doctor's degree..	569	585	628	603	656	626	615	674	722	639
Visual and Performing Arts										
Bachelor's degrees, total................................	85,186	87,703	89,143	91,798	93,939	95,806	97,799	97,414	95,840	92,979
Male...	32,729	33,862	35,055	35,768	36,342	37,164	38,063	38,177	38,024	36,710
Female..	52,457	53,841	54,088	56,030	57,597	58,642	59,736	59,237	57,816	56,269
Master's degrees, total...................................	13,767	14,164	14,918	15,562	16,277	17,307	17,869	17,869	17,756	18,048
Male...	5,910	5,998	6,325	6,531	6,881	7,320	7,610	7,712	7,643	7,677
Female..	7,857	8,166	8,593	9,031	9,396	9,987	10,259	10,157	10,113	10,371
Doctor's degrees, total..................................	1,364	1,453	1,569	1,599	1,646	1,728	1,814	1,778	1,793	1,808
Male...	625	675	726	700	770	790	850	869	837	857
Female..	739	778	843	899	876	938	964	909	956	951

Note: Data are for postsecondary institutions participating in Title IV federal financial aid programs.

NOTES AND DEFINITIONS: NATIONAL SCHOOL ENROLLMENT, EDUCATIONAL ATTAINMENT, AND POSTSECONDARY EDUCATION

ENROLLMENT TABLES A-1 THROUGH A-16

Source: U.S. Census Bureau. School Enrollment in the United States. *Current Population Survey (CPS) Report.*
https://www.census.gov/data/tables/2016/demo/school-enrollment/2016-cps.html and https://www.census.gov/data/tables/time-series/demo/school-enrollment/cps-historical-time-series.html.

ATTAINMENT TABLES A-17 THROUGH A-28

Source: U.S. Census Bureau. Educational Attainment in the United States: 2016. *Annual Social and Economic Supplement to the Current Population Survey.*
https://www.census.gov/data/tables/2016/demo/education-attainment/cps-detailed-tables.html.

POSTSECONDARY EDUCATION TABLES A-29 THROUGH A-37

Source: U.S. Department of Education, National Center for Education Statistics, Institute of Education Sciences, *Digest of Education Statistics 2016.*
https://www.census.gov/data/tables/time-series/demo/income-poverty/historical-income-people.html and https://nces.ed.gov/programs/digest/d16/.

SCHOOL ENROLLMENT AND EDUCATIONAL ATTAINMENT TABLES

The School Enrollment and Educational Attainment tables in Part A are derived from the Current Population Survey (CPS). The Census Bureau disseminated comparable tables in the P-20 series of *Current Population Reports* (CPR) for most years between 1947 and 1994. Since then, these tables have not been available in printed form. However, they can be found on the Census Bureau website at www.census.gov. In the historical series, data before 1992 are not strictly comparable to data after 1992. Before 1992, the CPS did not ask questions about degrees received; educational attainment was gauged only by years of school completed.

Age. Age classification is based on the age of the person at his or her last birthday.

Citizenship status. There are five categories of citizenship status: (1) born in the United States; (2) born in Puerto Rico or another outlying area of the United States; (3) born abroad to U.S. citizen parents; (4) naturalized citizens; and (5) non-citizens. Place of birth was asked for every household member and for the parents of every household member in the CPS sample. People born in the United States or its outlying areas, or whose parents were born in the United States or its outlying areas, were not asked citizenship questions. Citizenship statuses (1), (2), and (3) were assigned during the editing phase of data preparation, based on the place of birth of the household member or the place of birth of his or her parents. People born outside the United States and its outlying areas, whose parents were born outside the United States and its outlying areas, were asked, "Are you a citizen of the United States?" "Yes" answers were assigned to the "naturalized citizen" category (4), and "No" answers were assigned to the "not a citizen" category (5) during the editing process. People for whom no birthplace was provided were also assigned a citizenship status during the editing process; for example, the citizenship status of a child might have been assigned based on the citizenship status of his or her mother.

Dropouts. See School, dropout rate, annual high school.

Earnings. See Income.

Educational attainment. Data on educational attainment are derived from a single question that asks, "What is the highest grade of school . . . completed, or the highest degree . . . received?"

The single educational attainment question now in use was introduced into the CPS in January 1992. It is similar to the question used in the 1990 Decennial Census of Population and Housing. Consequently, data on educational attainment from the 1992 CPS are not directly comparable to CPS data from earlier years. The new question replaces the previous two-part question used in the CPS, which asked respondents to report the highest grade they attended and whether or not they completed that grade.

The question concerning educational attainment applies only to progress in "regular" schools. Such schools include graded public, private, and parochial elementary and high schools (both junior and senior high schools), colleges, universities, and professional schools, and both day schools and night schools. Thus, regular schooling is that which may advance a person toward an elementary school certificate, a high school diploma, or a college, university, or professional school degree. Non-regular schooling was counted only if the credits obtained were regarded as transferable to a school within the regular school system.

Family. A family is a group of two people or more residing together (including the householder) related by birth, marriage, or adoption; all such people (including related subfamily members) are considered members of one family. Beginning with the 1980 Current Population Survey, unrelated subfamilies (formerly referred to as secondary families) are no longer included in the count of families, nor are members of unrelated subfamilies included in the count of family members. The number of families is equal to the number of family households; however, the count of family members differs from

the count of family household members, as family household members include any non-relatives living in the household.

Family household. A family household is a household maintained by a householder within a family (as defined above). It includes any unrelated people (unrelated subfamily members and/or secondary individuals) residing in the household. The number of family households is equal to the number of families; however, the count of family household members differs from the count of family members. Family household members include all people living in the household, whereas family members include only the householder and his or her relatives. (See Family for more information.)

Hispanic origin. People of Hispanic origin were identified by a question that asked respondents to self-identify their origin or descent. Respondents were asked to select their origin (and the origin of other household members) from a "flash card" listing different ethnicities. People of Hispanic origin were those who indicated that their descent was of Mexican, Puerto Rican, Cuban, Central or South American, or some other Hispanic origin. It should be noted that people of Hispanic origin may be of any race.

People who were of non-Hispanic White origin were identified by crossing the responses to two self-identification questions: (1) origin or descent; and (2) race. Respondents were asked to select their race (and the race of other household members) from a "flash card" listing racial groups. Since March 1989, the population has been divided into five groups on the basis of race: White; Black; American Indian, Eskimo, or Aleut; Asian or Pacific Islander; and Other races. The last category includes any race other than the four indicated races. Respondents who identified their race as White and did not select one of the Hispanic origin subgroups (Mexican, Puerto Rican, Cuban, Central or South

American) were classified as non-Hispanic White.

Household. A household consists of all the people who occupy a housing unit. A house, apartment, group of rooms, or single room is regarded as a housing unit when it is occupied or intended for occupancy as separate living quarters (meaning that occupants do not live and eat with any other persons in the structure and have direct access to their dwelling from outside or through a common hall). A household includes related family members and all unrelated people—such as lodgers, foster children, wards, or employees—who share the housing unit. A person living alone in a housing unit, or a group of unrelated people sharing a dwelling (such as partners or roomers), are also counted as a household. The count of households excludes group quarters. There are two major categories of households: "family" and "nonfamily." (See Family household and Nonfamily household for more information.)

Householder. The householder is the person (or one of the people) in whose name the housing unit is owned or rented (maintained). If there is no such person, any adult member of the household—excluding roomers, boarders, and paid employees—can be counted as the householder. If a married couple jointly owns or rents the housing unit, the householder may be either the husband or the wife. The person designated as the householder is the "reference person" to whom the relationship of all other household members, if any, is recorded.

The number of householders is equal to the number of households. The number of family householders is also equal to the number of families.

Head versus householder. The Census Bureau discontinued the use of the terms "head of household" and "head of family" beginning with the 1980 CPS. Instead, the terms "householder" and "family householder" are used.

Recent social changes have resulted in a greater sharing of household responsibilities among the adult members. This has made the term "head" increasingly inappropriate in the analysis of household and family data. Specifically, beginning in 1980, the Census Bureau discontinued its longtime practice of always classifying the husband as the reference person (head of household) when he was living with his wife.

INCOME. Definitions of income and the types of income are found below.

Income, official definition of. For each person age 15 years and over in the sample, the CPS asks questions about the amount of money income received during the preceding calendar year from each of the following sources: earnings; unemployment compensation; workers' compensation; Social Security; Supplemental Security Income; public assistance or welfare payments; veterans' payments; survivor benefits; disability benefits; pension or retirement income; interest, dividends, rents, royalties, and estates and trusts; educational assistance; child support; alimony; financial assistance from outside the household; and other income.

Although the income statistics refer to receipts during the preceding calendar year, demographic characteristics such as age, labor force status, and family or household composition are as of the survey date. The income of the family/household does not include amounts received by members who were members of the family/household during all or part of the income year if these people no longer resided in the family/household at the time of interview. However, the CPS collects income data for people who are current residents, but who did not reside in the household during the income year.

Data on consumer income collected in the CPS by the Census Bureau cover money income (exclusive of certain money receipts, such as capital gains) received before payments for personal income taxes, Social Security, union dues, Medicare deductions, and so on. Therefore, money income does not reflect the fact that some families receive part of their income in the form of noncash benefits, such as food stamps, health benefits, rent-free housing, and goods produced and consumed on the farm. Money income also does not reflect the fact that noncash benefits are also received by some nonfarm residents. These benefits often take the form of the use of business transportation and facilities, full or partial payments by business for retirement programs, medical and educational expenses, and so on. Data users should consider these elements when comparing income levels. Moreover, readers should be aware that respondents in household surveys tend to underreport their income for many different reasons. Based on an analysis of independently derived income estimates, the Census Bureau determined that respondents report income earned from wages or salaries much more accurately than income earned from other sources of income, and that the reported wage and salary income is nearly equal to independent estimates of aggregate income.

The Census Bureau collects data for the following income sources:

Alimony. Alimony includes all periodic payments received from ex-spouses. It excludes one-time property settlements.

Child support. Child support includes all periodic payments received from an absent parent for the support of his or her children, even if these payments are made through a state or local government office.

Disability benefits. Disability benefits include payments people received due to a health problem or disability (other than those received from Social Security). Respondents can report payments from 10 sources, including workers' compensation,

companies or unions, federal government (civil service), military, state or local governments, railroad retirement, accident or disability insurance, Black Lung payments, state temporary sickness, or other disability payments.

Dividends. Dividends include income received from stock holdings and mutual fund shares. The CPS does not include capital gains from the sale of stock holdings as income.

Earnings. The Census Bureau classifies earnings from respondents' longest job (or self-employment) and other employment earnings into three types:

- Money wage or salary income, is the total income people receive for work performed as an employee during the income year. This category includes wages, salary, armed forces pay, commissions, tips, piece-rate payments, and cash bonuses earned, before deductions are made for items such as taxes, bonds, pensions, and union dues.

- Net income from nonfarm self-employment is the net money income (gross receipts minus expenses) from a respondent's own business, professional enterprise, or partnership. Gross receipts include the value of all goods sold and all services rendered. Expenses include items such as the costs of goods purchased; rent, heat, power, and depreciation charges; wages and salaries paid; and business taxes (but not personal income taxes). In general, the Census Bureau considers inventory changes in determining net income from nonfarm self-employment; replies based on income tax returns or other official records reflect inventory changes. However, when respondents do not report values of inventory changes, interviewers will accept net income figures exclusive of inventory changes. The Census Bureau does not include the value of saleable merchandise consumed by the proprietors of retail stores as part of net income.

- Net income from farm self-employment is the net money income (gross receipts minus operating expenses) from the operation of a farm by a person acting on their own account as owner, renter, or sharecropper. Gross receipts include the value of all products sold, payments from government farm programs, money received from renting farm equipment to others, rent received from farm property if payment is based on the percentage of crops produced, and incidental receipts from the sale of items such as wood, sand, and gravel.

- Operating expenses include items such as the cost of feed, fertilizer, seed, and other farming supplies; cash wages paid to farmhands; depreciation charges; cash rent; interest on farm mortgages; farm building repairs; and farm taxes (not state and federal personal income taxes). The Census Bureau does not include the value of fuel, food, or other farm products used for family living as part of net income, and only considers inventory changes in determining net income when they are accounted for in income tax returns or other official records. Otherwise, the Census Bureau does not take inventory changes into account.

Educational assistance. Educational assistance includes Pell Grants, other government educational assistance, scholarships or grants, and any financial assistance received from employers, friends, or relatives not residing in the student's household.

Financial assistance from outside the household. Financial assistance from outside the household includes periodic payments received from nonhousehold members. This type of assistance excludes gifts and sporadic assistance.

Government transfers. Government transfers include payments received from the following sources: unemployment compensation, state workers' compensation, Social Security, Supplemental Security Income (SSI), public assistance, veterans' payments, government survivor benefits, government disability benefits, government pensions, and government educational assistance.

Interest income. Interest income includes payments received or credited to accounts from bonds, treasury notes, individual retirement accounts (IRAs), certificates of deposit, interest-bearing savings and checking accounts, and all other interest-paying investments.

Other income. Other income includes any other unclassified payments received regularly. Some examples are state programs such as foster child payments, military family allotments, and income received from foreign government pensions.

Pension or retirement income. Pension or retirement income includes payments received from eight sources, including companies or unions; federal government (civil service); military; state or local governments; railroad retirement; annuities or paid-up insurance policies; IRAs, Keogh, or 401(k) payments; or other retirement income.

Public assistance or welfare payments. Public assistance or welfare payments include cash payments to low-income persons, including payments given under programs such as Aid to Families with Dependent Children (AFDC, ADC) and Temporary Assistance to Needy Families (TANF), emergency assistance, and other general assistance.

Rents, royalties, and estates and trusts. Rents, royalties, and estates and trusts include net income received from the rental of a house, a store, or other property; receipts from boarders or lodgers; net royalty income; and periodic payments from estate or trust funds.

Social Security. Social Security includes pensions, survivors' benefits, and permanent disability insurance payments made by the Social Security Administration prior to medical insurance deductions. The Census Bureau does not include Medicare reimbursements for health services as Social Security benefits.

Supplemental Security Income. Supplemental Security Income includes federal, state, and local welfare agency payments to low-income people age 65 years and over and to blind or disabled people of any age.

Survivor benefits. Survivor benefits include payments received from survivors' or widows' pensions, estates, trusts, annuities, or any other types of survivors' benefits. Respondents can report payments from 10 different sources, including private companies or unions, federal government (civil service), military, state or local governments, railroad retirement, workers' compensation, Black Lung payments, estates and trusts, annuities or paid-up insurance policies, and other survivor payments.

Unemployment compensation. Unemployment compensation includes payments made to the respondent from government unemployment agencies or private companies during periods of unemployment. It also accounts for any strike benefits the respondent received from union funds.

Veterans' payments. Veterans' payments include periodic payments from the Department of Veterans Affairs to disabled members of the armed forces or survivors of deceased veterans for education and on-the-job training. These payments also include means-tested assistance to veterans.

Workers' compensation. Workers' compensation includes periodic payments from public or private insurance companies for work-related injuries.

The Census Bureau does not count the following receipts as income: (1) capital gains (or losses) from the sale of property, including stocks, bonds, houses, or cars (unless the person was engaged in the business of selling such property, in which case the CPS counts the net proceeds as income from self-employment); (2) withdrawals of bank deposits; (3) money borrowed; (4) tax refunds; (5) gifts; and (6) lump-sum inheritances or insurance payments.

The Census Bureau combines all sources of income into two major types:

Total money earnings. Total money earnings is the algebraic sum of money wages, salary, and net income from farm and non-farm self-employment.

Income other than earnings. Income other than earnings is the algebraic sum of all sources of money income, except wages and salaries and income from self-employment.

Mean (average) income. Mean (average) income is the amount obtained by dividing the total aggregate income of a group by the number of units in that group. The means for households, families, and unrelated individuals are based respectively on all households, all families, and all unrelated individuals. The means (averages) for people are based on people age 15 years and over with income.

Median income. Median income is the amount that divides the income distribution into two equal groups. Half of all people have incomes above the median, and half of all people have incomes below the median. The medians for households, families, and unrelated individuals are respectively based on all households, all families, and all unrelated individuals. The medians for people are based on people age 15 years and over with income.

LABOR FORCE STATUS. Definitions of labor force characteristics are found below:

Civilian labor force. Consists of people classified as employed or unemployed. Excluded are institutionalized people and people on active duty in the United States

Armed Forces. The entire labor force consists of people classified as employed or unemployed and people in the armed forces.

Current job (basic data). A worker's current job is the job held during the reference week (the week before the survey). A person holding two or more jobs is classified as being in the job at which he or she spent the most hours during the reference week. The unemployed are classified according to their most recent full-time job of two weeks or more, or by the job (either the full-time or part-time job) from which they were laid off. The occupation/industry classification system for the 1990 Decennial Census of Population was first used to code CPS data for the January 1992 file. The occupation/industry classification system for the 2000 Decennial Census of Population was first used to code CPS data for the January 2003 file.

Employed. Employed persons include all civilians who, during the survey week, did any work at all (for at least one hour) as paid employees or in their own business or profession, or on their own farm, or who worked 15 hours or more as unpaid workers on a farm or a business operated by a member of the family; and all people who had jobs but were not working due to illness, bad weather, vacation, labor-management dispute, or personal reasons, whether or not they were seeking other jobs. Each employed person is counted only once. People who held two or more jobs are counted as working in the job at which they worked the greatest number of hours during the survey week. If a person worked an equal number of hours at two or more jobs, he or she is counted as working at the job that they have held the longest.

Labor force. Workers are classified as being in the labor force if they are employed, unemployed, or in the armed forces during the survey week. The "civilian labor force" includes all civilians classified as employed or unemployed. The file includes labor force data for civilians age 15 years and over.

However, the official definition of the civilian labor force consists of workers age 16 years and over.

Not in labor force. All civilians age 15 years and over who are not classified as employed or unemployed are considered not to be in the labor force. These people are further classified as being engaged in a major activity such as keeping house, going to school, unable to work because of long-term physical or mental illness, and "other," which is mostly composed of retired persons. Those who report doing unpaid work on a family-owned farm or in a family-owned business for less than 15 hours are also classified as not in the labor force.

For persons not in the labor force, questions about previous work experience, intentions to seek work again, current desire for a job, and reasons for not seeking work are only asked of households in the fourth and eighth months of the sample. These are the "outgoing" groups—those that were in the sample for three previous months and would not be in it for the subsequent month.

Finally, it should be noted that the unemployment rate represents the number of unemployed persons as a percentage of the civilian labor force age 16 years and over. This measure can be computed for groups within the labor force by sex, age, marital status, race, and so on. The job loser, job leaver, reentrant, and new entrant rates are each calculated as a percentage of the civilian labor force age 16 years and over; the sum of the rates for the four groups thus equals the total unemployment rate.

Unemployed. Unemployed persons are civilians who, during the survey week, had no employment but were available for work and had engaged in any specific job-seeking activity within the past four previous weeks, such as registering at a public or private employment office, meeting with prospective employers, checking with friends or relatives, placing and answering advertisements, writing letters of application, or being on a union or professional register. Others in this category were waiting to be called back to a job from which they had been laid off or were within 30 days of starting a new wage or salary job. This category consists of job leavers, job losers, new job entrants, and job reentrants.

Work experience. A person with work experience is one who did any work for pay or profit or worked without pay on a family-operated farm or business at any time during the preceding calendar year, on a part-time or full-time basis. A full-time worker is a worker who worked 35 hours or more per week during a majority of the weeks in the preceding calendar year. A year-round worker is a worker who worked for 50 weeks or more during the preceding calendar year. A full-time, year-round worker is a person who worked full-time (35 or more hours per week) for 50 or more weeks during the previous calendar year.

Level of school completed. The statistics on level of school completed indicate the number of persons enrolled at each of five levels: nursery school, kindergarten, elementary school (first to eighth grades), high school (ninth to twelfth grades), and college or professional school. The last group includes graduate students at colleges and universities. Those enrolled in elementary school, middle school, intermediate school, or junior high through eighth grade are classified as being in elementary school. All persons enrolled in ninth through twelfth grade are classified as being in high school.

Modal grade. See School, modal grade.

Nativity. There are two major categories of nativity, native born and foreign born. A person who is native is a citizen at birth. All people with the following citizenship status are native born: (1) born in the United States; (2) born in Puerto Rico or an outlying area of the United States; and (3) born abroad of American parents. (See Citizenship status

for more information.) All other people are classified as foreign born.

Nonfamily household. A nonfamily household consists of a householder living alone (a one-person household) or a household shared exclusively by unrelated people.

Population coverage. The sample for the CPS includes the civilian noninstitutional population of the United States, along with members of the armed forces in the United States living off post or with their families on post. It excludes all other members of the armed forces. The information on the Hispanic population from the CPS was collected in the 50 states and the District of Columbia and does not include residents of outlying areas or of U.S. territories such as Guam, Puerto Rico, and the U.S. Virgin Islands.

Race. The race of individuals was identified through a question requiring self-identification of the person's race. Respondents were asked to select their race from a "flash card" listing racial groups. Since March 1989, the population has been divided into five groups on the basis of race: White; Black; American Indian, Eskimo or Aleut; Asian or Pacific Islander; and Other races. The last category includes any other race except the five mentioned. In most of the published tables, "Other races" are included in the total population data line but are not shown individually.

Reference person. The reference person serves as the central point for determining relationships within the household. The household reference person is the person listed as the householder. (See Householder for more information.) The subfamily reference person is either the single parent or the husband or wife in a married-couple situation.

Rounding. Percentages are rounded to the nearest 10th of a percent; therefore, the percentages in a distribution do not always sum to exactly 100 percent.

School, dropout rate, annual high school. The annual high school dropout rate is an estimate of the proportion of students who drop out of school in a single year. This section briefly explains how the annual dropout rate is calculated; for further explanation and details of its derivation, see *Current Population Report (Series P-20, No. 413): "School Enrollment—Social and Economic Characteristics of Students: October 1983."*

Annual dropout rates for a single grade (X) are estimated as the ratio between the number of people enrolled in grade (X) in the year preceding the survey who did not complete grade (X) and are not currently enrolled in grade (X) at the start of the year preceding this survey. People reported as enrolled last year but not currently enrolled are presented by the highest grade completed in Table 8 of the *Current Population Report* on school enrollment. They are presumed to have dropped out of the succeeding grade (except for those who graduated this year). Thus, individuals counted as 10th grade dropouts are those whose highest grade completed is the 9th grade, but who are not currently enrolled in school. (The dropout classification also includes those people who finished the 9th grade in the spring preceding the survey and were not enrolled on the survey date.) These estimates form the numerator of the annual grade-specific dropout rate.

People currently enrolled in high school are presumed to have been enrolled in and have successfully completed the preceding grade during the preceding year. For example, those who have successfully completed the 10th grade would be enrolled in the 11th grade. Along with the people who dropped out of that grade, they comprise the denominator of the estimate of the annual grade-specific dropout rate:

$$\text{Dropout from Grade n} = \frac{\text{Not enrolled and highest grade completed} = \text{n}-1}{\left(\begin{array}{c}\text{Enrolled in n}+1 + \text{Not enrolled and} \\ \text{highest grade completed} = \text{n}-1\end{array}\right)}$$

It cannot be presumed that all 12th grade graduates will enroll in college. The estimate of the number of people enrolled in the 12th grade one year before the survey is constructed as the sum of the number of people reported to have graduated from high school "this year" (whether or not they are currently enrolled in college) and those not currently enrolled who were enrolled last year and whose highest grade completed is the 11th grade (dropouts). The annual dropout rate for all grades during one year can be obtained by summing the components of the rates for the individual grades—the sum of all people previously enrolled in the 10th, 11th, or 12th grade last year, but who are not currently enrolled and do not have a high school diploma.

In addition to the annual rate, two other estimates of dropouts are frequently used. The annual dropout rate is different from a "pool" (or status) measure, such as the proportion of high school dropouts within an age group. A third measure of dropouts is the "cohort measure," most commonly from a longitudinal study, in which the proportion of a specific group of people enrolled in a specific year is calculated. These people did not receive diplomas (and are no longer in school) some years later. For example, the proportion of a cohort enrolled in 9th grade in year X, who were not enrolled and had not received a diploma by year X equals 4.

School enrollment. The school enrollment statistics from the CPS are based on replies to inquiries concerning current regular school enrollment. Those counted as enrolled had attended a public, parochial, or other private school in the regular school system at any time during the current or previous school year. Such schools include nursery schools, kindergartens, elementary schools, high schools, colleges, universities, and professional schools. Attendance could have been on either a full-time or part-time basis during the day or night. Regular schooling is that which advances a person toward an elementary or high school diploma or toward a college, university, or professional school degree. Children enrolled in nursery schools and kindergarten are included in the enrollment figures for regular schools and are shown separately.

Enrollment in schools not in the regular school system, such as trade schools, business colleges, and schools for the mentally handicapped is not included, as these schools do not advance students toward regular school degrees.

People enrolled in classes not requiring their physical presence in school, such as correspondence courses or other courses of independent study, and those enrolled in training courses given directly on the job, are also excluded from the count of those enrolled in school, unless such courses are being counted for credit at a regular school.

School enrollment in the year preceding current survey. All respondents were asked to state their school enrollment status as of October of the preceding year. Before 1988, this question was only asked of people not currently attending regular school and people who were enrolled in college. In the tabulations of previous year's secondary school enrollment, those currently enrolled in high school were assumed to have been enrolled the previous year.

Comparability of enrollment data in previous years. Changes in the edit and tabulation packages used to process the October CPS school enrollment supplement caused some minor revisions to the estimates. The current edit and tabulation package began with 1987 data. The 1986 data published in the *Current Population Report (Series P-20 No. 429)* were reprocessed with the rewritten programs in order to clarify comparability. Time series tables usually show only the revised estimates for 1986. The previous edit and tabulation package was used from 1967 to 1986.

Major changes in the data caused by the 1987 edit revisions were: (1) Among 14- and 15-year-olds, an edit improvement allowed people with unreported enrollment data, who were previously imputed as "not enrolled," to be enrolled; (2) Revisions in the tabulation of enrollment in the previous year simplified the calculation of an annual high school dropout rate; (3) Edit improvements caused increases in college enrollment estimates, most notably above the age of 24. This age group was largely ignored in earlier edits; (4) Type of college is fully allocated (discussed earlier in the section); (5) Tabulations of type of college (2-year and 4-year colleges) were made available by race; (6) Dependent family members became consistently defined; (7) New tabulations of employment status, vocational course enrollment, college retention and re-entry, and families with children enrolled in public and private school became available beginning in 1987.

In the series of reports on school enrollment for 1987 to 1992, race and Hispanic origin were erroneously tabulated for a small percentage of children age 3 to 14 years. Race and Hispanic origin of an adult in the household were attributed to the child, rather than using the child's reported characteristics. In the vast majority of cases, these characteristics were the same for family members, but for a small percentage of children, they were different. The correction made the following proportional changes in the numbers of children in each group: White (-0.5 percent), Black (+3.1 percent), and Hispanic (-4.6 percent).

Published data on enrollment from the October CPS for 1981 to 1993 used population controls based on the 1980 census. Beginning in 1994, estimates used 1990 census–based population controls, including adjustment for undercount. Time series tables show two sets of data for 1993; the data labeled "1993r" were processed using population controls based on the 1990 census with adjustments for undercount. The change in 1994 from a paper-and-pencil survey to a computer-assisted survey had some affect on the data. Most notably, the enrollment question for children age 3 to 5 years was different from the question for older children—it included a reference to nursery school. In 1994, reported nursery school enrollment was significantly higher than in earlier years.

Attendance, full-time and part-time. College students are classified according to their attendance status. A student is categorized as attending college full-time if he or she was taking 12 or more hours of classes during the average school week, and part-time if he or she was taking less than 12 hours of classes per average school week.

College enrollment. The college enrollment statistics are based on reports of school enrollment, including the grade in which the respondent was enrolled. Students enrolled in college at any time during the current term or school year were counted as enrolled, except those who had left for the remainder of the term. Thus, regular college enrollment includes those attending two-year or four-year colleges, universities, or professional schools (such as medical or law schools) in courses that advance students toward a recognized college or university degree (such as a B.A. or an M.A.). Attendance may be full-time or part-time during the day or night. The college student need not be working toward a degree, but he or she must be enrolled in a class for which credit would be applied toward a degree. (See school enrollment for more information.) Students are classified by year of college, based on the academic year (not calendar year). The undergraduate years are the first through fourth year, or freshman through senior years. Graduate or professional school years include the fifth year and higher.

Two-year and four-year colleges. College students were asked if their school was a two-year college (junior or community college) or a four-year college or university. Students enrolled in the first four years of college (undergraduates) were classified by the type of school that they attended. Graduate students are shown as a separate group.

Vocational school enrollment. Vocational school enrollment includes enrollment in business, vocational, technical, secretarial, trade, or correspondence courses that are not counted as regular school enrollment. This category excludes recreation or adult education classes. Courses that counted as college enrollment are also excluded.

School, modal grade. Enrolled people are classified according to their relative progress in school and whether the grade or year in which they were enrolled was below, at, or above the modal (or typical) grade for students of their age at the time of the survey. The modal grade is the year of school in which the largest proportion of students of a given age were enrolled.

School, nursery. A nursery school is defined as a group or class that has been organized to provide educational experiences for children during the year or years preceding kindergarten. It includes instruction as an important and integral phase of its childcare program. Private homes, in which essentially custodial care is provided, are not considered nursery schools. Children attending nursery school are classified as attending for part of the day or for the full day. Part-day attendance refers to those who attend either in the morning or in the afternoon. Full-day attendance refers to those who attend in the morning and in the afternoon. Children enrolled in Head Start programs or similar local agency-sponsored programs that provide preschool education to young children are counted as being enrolled in nursery school.

School, public or private. A public school is defined as any educational institution operated by publicly elected or appointed school officials and supported by public funds. Private schools include educational institutions established and operated by religious bodies, as well as those that are under other private controls. In cases in which a school or college was both publicly and privately controlled or supported, enrollment was counted according to whether the school was primarily public or private.

Undocumented immigrants or illegal aliens. Since all residents of the United States living in households are represented in the sample of households interviewed by the CPS, undocumented immigrants or illegal aliens are probably included in CPS data. Because the CPS makes no attempt to ascertain the legal status of any person interviewed, these individuals cannot be identified from CPS data.

POSTSECONDARY EDUCATION TABLES

Tables A-29 through A-37 were adapted from the most current published tables from the National Center for Education Statistics, Institute of Education Sciences: *Digest of Education Statistics.*

Consumer Price Index. This price index measures the average change in the cost of a fixed market basket of goods and services purchased by consumers.

Control of institution describes whether an institution is operated by publicly elected or appointed officials (public control) or by privately elected or appointed officials and derives its major source of funds from private sources (private not-for-profit or private for-profit control). There are nine institutional categories resulting from dividing the universe according to control and level. Control categories are public, private not-for-profit, and private for-profit. Level categories are 4-year and higher (4 year), 2-but-less-than-4-year (2 year), and less than 2-year. For example: Public, 4-year is one of the institution sectors.

Fall enrollment. IPEDS collects data on the number of students enrolled in the fall at postsecondary institutions. Students reported are those enrolled in courses creditable toward a degree or other formal award;

students enrolled in courses that are part of a vocational or occupational program, including those enrolled in off-campus or extension centers; and high school students taking regular college courses for credit. Institutions report annually the number of full- and part-time students, by gender, race/ethnicity, and level (undergraduate, graduate, first-professional); the total number of undergraduate entering students (first-time, full- and part-time students, transfer-ins, and nondegree students); and retention rates. In even-numbered years, data are collected for state of residence of first-time students and for the number of those students who graduated from high school or received high school equivalent certificates in the past 12 months. Also in even-numbered years, 4-year institutions are required to provide enrollment data by gender, race/ethnicity, and level for selected fields of study. In odd-numbered years, data are collected for enrollment by age category by student level and gender.

Data through 1995 are for institutions of higher education, while later data are for degree-granting institutions. Degree-granting institutions grant associate's or higher degrees and participate in Title IV federal financial aid programs. The degree-granting classification is very similar to the earlier higher education classification, but it includes more 2-year colleges and excludes a few higher education institutions that did not grant degrees.

Nonresident alien is a person who is not a citizen or national of the United States and who is in this country on a visa or temporary basis and does not have the right to remain indefinitely.

A postbaccalaureate student is a student with a bachelor's degree who is enrolled in graduate-level or first-professional courses.

Price of attendance includes tuition and required fees, books and supplies, room and board charges, and other expenses. Amounts are institutional averages as reported by the institution, not average amounts paid by students (for example, charges are not weighted by enrollment). Out-of-state average tuition and required fees were used for private institutions that reported varying tuitions by residency. The 2,578 institutions with academic calendars that differ by program or allow continuous enrollment are not included. U.S. service academies are not included. All amounts from 2011–2012 were converted to 2013–2014 dollars using the average Consumer Price Index values for the 12-month periods ending in October 2011 and October 2013. On-campus average price is based on those institutions that offer on-campus housing and/or meal service. Off-campus average price is based on those institutions that do not require full-time, first-time students to live on campus. For public institutions, "in district" refers to the charges paid by a student who lives in the locality surrounding the institution, such as a county.

Race/ethnicity categories were developed in 1997 by the Office of Management and Budget (OMB) and are used to describe groups to which individuals belong, identify with, or belong in the eyes of the community. The categories do not denote scientific definitions of anthropological origins. The designations are used to categorize U.S. citizens, resident aliens, and other eligible non-citizens. Individuals are asked to first designate ethnicity as Hispanic/Latino or not Hispanic/Latino. Hispanic/Latino refers to a person of Cuban, Mexican, Puerto Rican, South or Central American, or other Spanish culture or origin, regardless of race. Second, individuals are asked to indicate all races that apply among the following:

American Indian or Alaska Native A person having origins in any of the original peoples of North and South America (including Central America) who maintains cultural identification through tribal affiliation or community attachment.

Asian A person having origins in any of the original peoples of the Far East, Southeast Asia, or the Indian Subcontinent, including, for example, Cambodia, China, India, Japan, Korea, Malaysia, Pakistan, the Philippine Islands, Thailand, and Vietnam.

Black or African American A person having origins in any of the black racial groups of Africa.

Native Hawaiian or Other Pacific Islander A person having origins in any of the original peoples of Hawaii, Guam, Samoa, or other Pacific Islands.

White A person having origins in any of the original peoples of Europe, the Middle East, or North Africa.

Before 1997, slightly different race/ethnicity categories were used and persons could identify with only one racial category.

Tuition and required fees is the amount of tuition and required fees covering a full academic year most frequently charged to students. These values represent what a typical student would be charged and may not be the same for all students at an institution. If tuition is charged on a per-credit-hour basis, the average full-time credit hour load for an entire academic year is used to estimate average tuition. Required fees include all fixed sum charges that are required of such a large proportion of all students that the student who does not pay the charges is an exception.

PART B

REGION AND STATE
EDUCATION STATISTICS

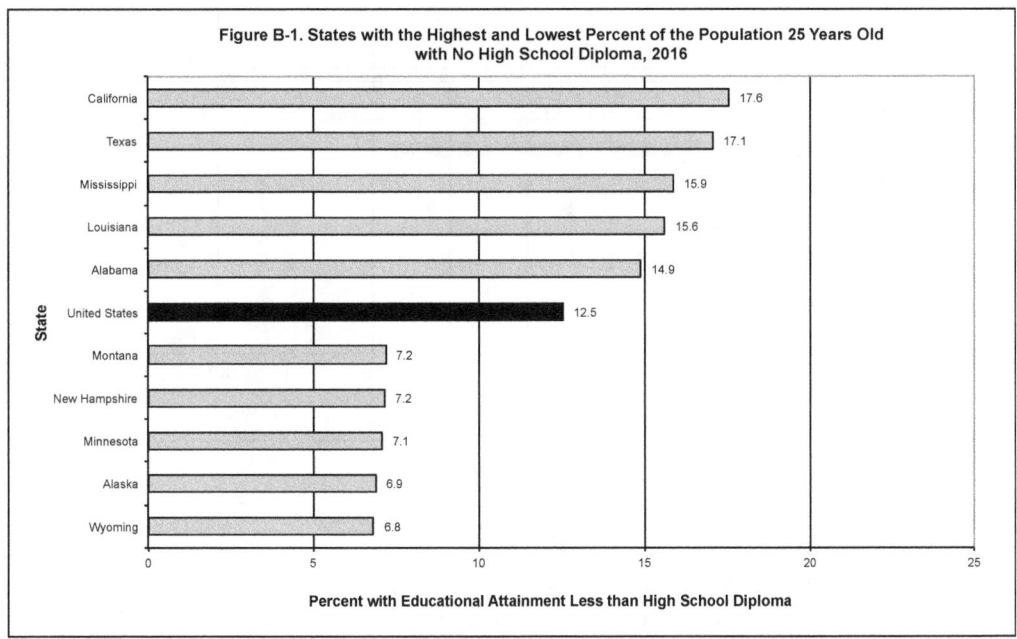

Figure B-1. States with the Highest and Lowest Percent of the Population 25 Years Old with No High School Diploma, 2016

In 2016, 87.5 percent of the U.S. population 25 years old and over had graduated from high school and/or a higher education establishment. The West region had the lowest average high-school attainment rate of 86.0 percent, followed by the South (86.2 percent), the Northeast (88.8 percent) and the Midwest (90.2 percent). All states had high-school attainment levels of more than 80 percent. California had the lowest level at 82.4 percent. Wyoming had the highest high-school graduation rate of 93.2 percent. (Table B-2)

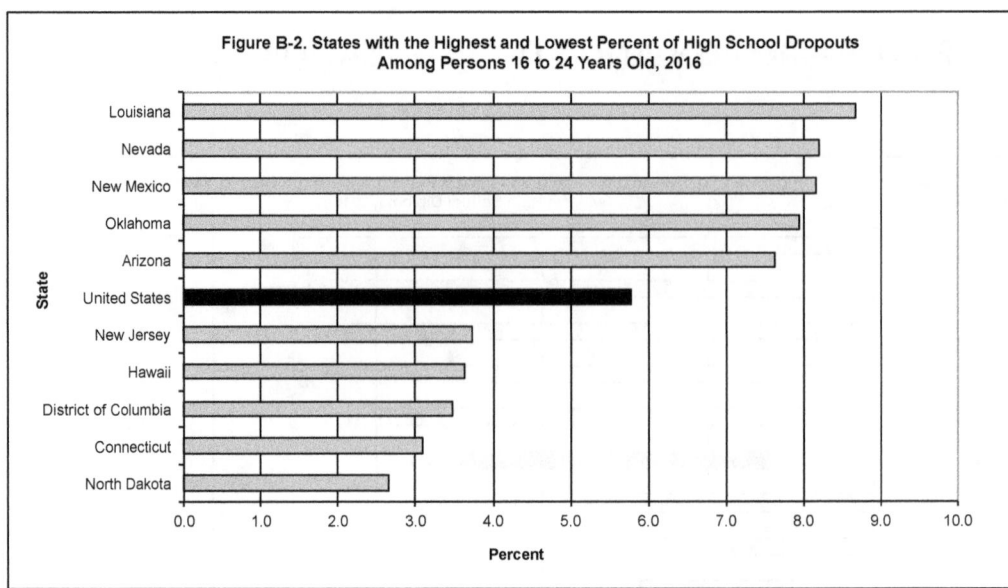

Figure B-2. States with the Highest and Lowest Percent of High School Dropouts Among Persons 16 to 24 Years Old, 2016

There are several ways to measure high school dropouts. "Event dropout rates" provide the state's estimate of students who have left their schools with no documented reason (for example, transfer, move, or illness). The American Community Survey can be used to estimate the state's proportion of young people who have not completed high school. In 2016, 5.8 percent of the population 16 to 24 years old were estimated to have dropped out of school before graduation because they are no longer enrolled in school and not high school graduates. Of the states, North Dakota had the lowest percentage of these dropouts (2.7 percent) and Louisiana had the highest percentage (8.7 percent). Among the regions, seven of the nine Northeast states ranked among the 14 lowest percentages of dropout students, all at 4.5 percent or below. The West had four of the top six states with the highest percentage of students not finishing high school, all of which had 7.5 percent high-school dropouts or higher. (Table B-11)The proportion of the U.S. population with a bachelor's degree or more has increased since 2011, rising from 28.5 percent to 29.1 percent in 2012 and 30.6 percent in 2015. In the District of Columbia, 56.7 percent of residents held a bachelor's degree or more, the highest rate in the nation. Among the states, 10 had proportions of college graduates exceeding 35 percent. Only West Virginia had a college attainment level of less than 20 percent. (Table B-1)

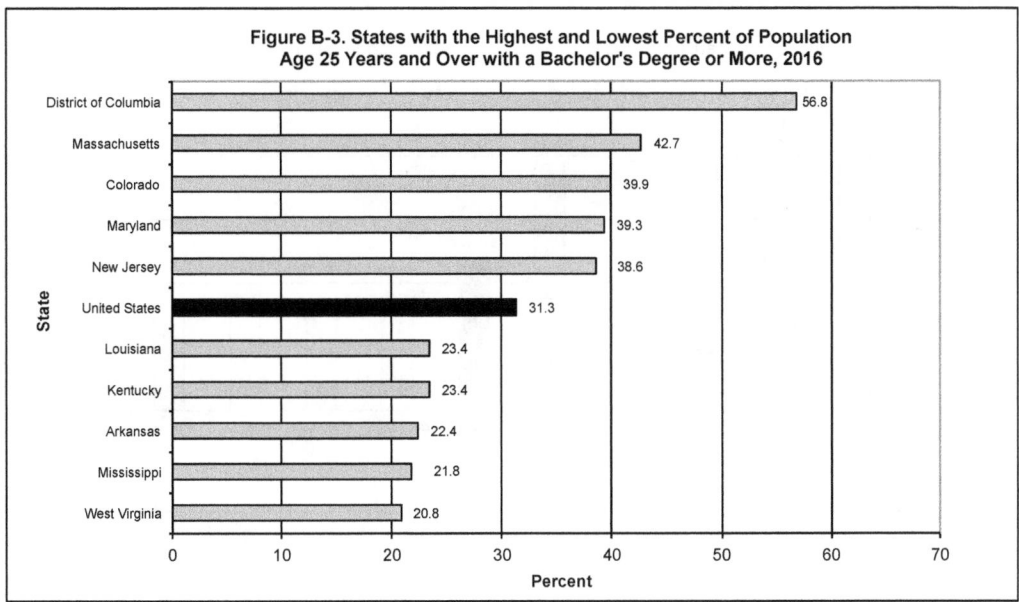

Figure B-3. States with the Highest and Lowest Percent of Population Age 25 Years and Over with a Bachelor's Degree or More, 2016

The proportion of the U.S. population with a bachelor's degree or more was 31.3 percent for the population age 25 and over in 2016. In the District of Columbia, 56.8 percent of residents held a bachelor's degree or more, the highest rate in the nation. Among the states, 11 had proportions of college graduates exceeding 35 percent. West Virginia had the lowest college attainment level of 20.8 percent. (Table B-2)

The Northeast region had the highest college attainment rate (35.9 percent), followed by the West (32.5 percent), the Midwest (29.9 percent), and the South (29.1 percent).

Among the races 25 years old and older, Asians had the highest college attainment (53.2 percent), followed by Whites (32.7 percent), Blacks (20.9 percent), and Hispanics (15.3 percent). The District of Columbia had the highest percent of all racial/ethnic groups with bachelor's degrees or more. Of the states, Massachusetts had the highest percent of Whites with bachelor's degrees or more (44.6 percent). Idaho had the largest proportion of Blacks with bachelor's degrees or more (30.1 percent). New Jersey had the highest percent of Asians with bachelor's degrees or more (68.9 percent), and Vermont had the highest percent of Hispanics with bachelor's degrees or more (35.5 percent). (Table B-2)

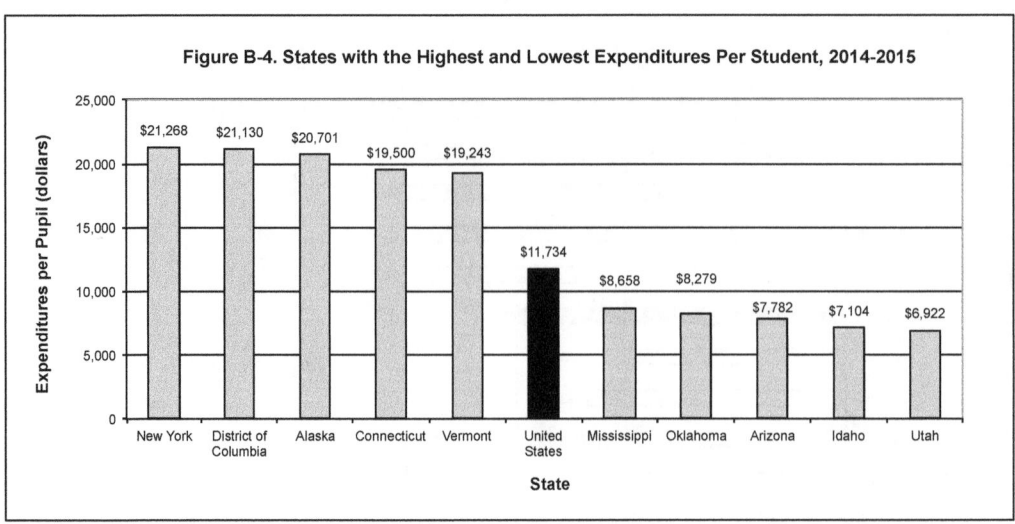

Figure B-4. States with the Highest and Lowest Expenditures Per Student, 2014-2015

Nationally, expenditures for 2014–2015 were 60.7 percent for instructional services, 35.1 percent for support services, and 4.2 percent for non-instruction services. New York had the highest proportion of instruction and instruction-related expenditures, at 70.2 percent. Arizona had the lowest, at 53.6 percent. The national average expenditure per student was $11,734 in 2014–2015. The state with the largest expenditure per student was New York, where the expenditure per pupil was $21,268 per student. Utah, the state with the smallest expenditure per student, spent less than one-third the amount New York did per student ($6,922). (Table B-10)

Schools can be divided into four locales: city, suburban, town, or rural. Nevada was the state with the most students in a city school in 2015–2016 (50.4 percent). New Jersey had the highest percent of students in suburban schools (79.7 percent), Wyoming had the largest percent of students attending schools located in towns (44.1 percent), and Vermont had the highest percent of students in rural schools (55.7 percent).

Nationally, the student-teacher ratio was 16.1 in Fall 2014. California, Utah, and Arizona all exceeded 23 students per teacher. North Dakota and Vermont had student-teacher ratios below 12 students per teacher. (Table B-9)

During the 2014–2015 school year, 51.8 percent of students nationwide were eligible for free or reduced-price lunch. The District of Columbia had the highest percent of students eligible for free or reduced-price lunch (92.4 percent), followed by Mississippi (73.7 percent), and Louisiana (63.6 percent). The state with the most English language learner students was California (21.0 percent), followed by Texas and Nevada, which both had 16.8 percent ELL students. (Table B-7)

Table B-1. Educational Attainment of the Population 18 Years and Over, by Region, Age, and Sex, 2016

(Number; percent.)

Characteristic	United States Number	United States Percent	Northeast Number	Northeast Percent	Midwest Number	Midwest Percent	South Number	South Percent	West Number	West Percent
Total...	249,489,772	100.0	44,397,615	17.8	52,372,880	21.0	93,934,682	37.7	58,784,595	23.6
18 to 24 years...............................	31,014,292	12.4	5,367,861	12.1	6,569,311	12.5	11,668,986	12.4	7,408,134	12.6
Less than 9th grade	460,303	1.5	79,602	1.5	92,294	1.4	186,149	1.6	102,258	1.4
9th to 12th grade, no diploma........	3,617,979	11.7	532,858	9.9	747,812	11.4	1,491,269	12.8	846,040	11.4
High school graduate (includes equivalency)	9,611,552	31.0	1,554,484	29.0	1,979,749	30.1	3,764,798	32.3	2,312,521	31.2
Some college, no degree................	12,359,971	39.9	2,107,829	39.3	2,668,029	40.6	4,529,977	38.8	3,054,136	41.2
Associate's degree	1,613,174	5.2	274,475	5.1	350,229	5.3	600,795	5.1	387,675	5.2
Bachelor's degree..........................	3,101,433	10.0	743,426	13.8	687,041	10.5	1,015,823	8.7	655,143	8.8
Graduate or professional degree..................	249,880	0.8	75,187	1.4	44,157	0.7	80,175	0.7	50,361	0.7
25 to 34 years...............................	44,390,248	17.8	7,638,169	17.2	8,902,015	17.0	16,627,861	17.7	11,222,203	19.1
Less than 9th grade	1,385,515	3.1	215,363	2.8	218,704	2.5	558,630	3.4	392,818	3.5
9th to 12th grade, no diploma........	2,999,252	6.8	403,917	5.3	506,195	5.7	1,275,569	7.7	813,571	7.2
High school graduate (includes equivalency)	10,512,436	23.7	1,717,012	22.5	2,029,323	22.8	4,263,357	25.6	2,502,744	22.3
Some college, no degree................	10,025,393	22.6	1,341,743	17.6	2,072,104	23.3	3,875,918	23.3	2,735,628	24.4
Associate's degree	3,973,128	9.0	624,121	8.2	915,724	10.3	1,470,169	8.8	963,114	8.6
Bachelor's degree..........................	10,808,609	24.3	2,213,049	29.0	2,246,697	25.2	3,608,081	21.7	2,740,782	24.4
Graduate or professional degree..................	4,685,915	10.6	1,122,964	14.7	913,268	10.3	1,576,137	9.5	1,073,546	9.6
35 to 44 years...............................	40,655,592	16.3	6,841,929	15.4	8,251,315	15.8	15,601,797	16.6	9,960,551	16.9
Less than 9th grade	2,028,427	5.0	283,644	4.1	270,091	3.3	779,052	5.0	695,640	7.0
9th to 12th grade, no diploma........	2,871,406	7.1	376,403	5.5	473,761	5.7	1,240,242	7.9	781,000	7.8
High school graduate (includes equivalency)	9,614,326	23.6	1,635,777	23.9	1,984,063	24.0	3,933,638	25.2	2,060,848	20.7
Some college, no degree................	8,131,705	20.0	1,094,713	16.0	1,758,504	21.3	3,207,891	20.6	2,070,597	20.8
Associate's degree	3,752,143	9.2	603,383	8.8	881,008	10.7	1,396,774	9.0	870,978	8.7
Bachelor's degree..........................	8,652,461	21.3	1,631,780	23.8	1,794,486	21.7	3,088,640	19.8	2,137,555	21.5
Graduate or professional degree..................	5,605,124	13.8	1,216,229	17.8	1,089,402	13.2	1,955,560	12.5	1,343,933	13.5
45 to 64 years...............................	84,214,475	33.8	15,502,655	34.9	18,071,393	34.5	31,426,053	33.5	19,214,374	32.7
Less than 9th grade	4,256,593	5.1	634,005	4.1	513,139	2.8	1,608,547	5.1	1,500,902	7.8
9th to 12th grade, no diploma........	5,767,241	6.8	923,469	6.0	1,053,167	5.8	2,486,252	7.9	1,304,353	6.8
High school graduate (includes equivalency)	23,708,815	28.2	4,640,377	29.9	5,588,125	30.9	9,187,273	29.2	4,293,040	22.3
Some college, no degree................	17,430,535	20.7	2,610,621	16.8	3,932,579	21.8	6,490,339	20.7	4,396,996	22.9
Associate's degree	7,590,901	9.0	1,407,305	9.1	1,818,931	10.1	2,683,262	8.5	1,681,403	8.8
Bachelor's degree..........................	15,605,855	18.5	3,076,911	19.8	3,246,148	18.0	5,565,478	17.7	3,717,318	19.3
Graduate or professional degree..................	9,854,535	11.7	2,209,967	14.3	1,919,304	10.6	3,404,902	10.8	2,320,362	12.1
65 years and over	49,215,165	19.7	9,047,001	20.4	10,578,846	20.2	18,609,985	19.8	10,979,333	18.7
Less than 9th grade	4,022,369	8.2	747,894	8.3	592,354	5.6	1,664,193	8.9	1,017,928	9.3
9th to 12th grade, no diploma........	4,081,431	8.3	772,028	8.5	852,352	8.1	1,747,681	9.4	709,370	6.5
High school graduate (includes equivalency)	15,538,203	31.6	3,162,863	35.0	3,946,326	37.3	5,803,645	31.2	2,625,369	23.9
Some college, no degree................	9,507,715	19.3	1,287,541	14.2	2,116,482	20.0	3,617,077	19.4	2,486,615	22.6
Associate's degree	2,943,669	6.0	530,354	5.9	579,042	5.5	1,056,257	5.7	778,016	7.1
Bachelor's degree..........................	7,175,470	14.6	1,269,993	14.0	1,385,497	13.1	2,620,171	14.1	1,899,809	17.3
Graduate or professional degree..................	5,946,308	12.1	1,276,328	14.1	1,106,793	10.5	2,100,961	11.3	1,462,226	13.3
Male	121,383,148	48.7	21,357,872	48.1	25,557,926	48.8	45,406,685	48.3	29,060,665	49.4
18 to 24 years...............................	15,916,664	13.1	2,720,977	12.7	3,368,035	13.2	5,995,305	13.2	3,832,347	13.2
Less than 9th grade	278,721	1.8	48,397	1.8	53,717	1.6	114,558	1.9	62,049	1.6
9th to 12th grade, no diploma........	2,093,314	13.2	304,839	11.2	435,990	12.9	864,067	14.4	488,418	12.7
High school graduate (includes equivalency)	5,435,902	34.2	860,246	31.6	1,122,609	33.3	2,132,342	35.6	1,320,705	34.5
Some college, no degree................	5,955,465	37.4	1,024,511	37.7	1,283,435	38.1	2,164,580	36.1	1,482,939	38.7
Associate's degree	734,976	4.6	130,104	4.8	163,310	4.8	269,573	4.5	171,989	4.5
Bachelor's degree..........................	1,320,304	8.3	324,038	11.9	290,802	8.6	422,081	7.0	283,383	7.4
Graduate or professional degree..................	97,982	0.6	28,842	1.1	18,172	0.5	28,104	0.5	22,864	0.6
25 to 34 years...............................	22,398,722	18.5	3,839,430	18.0	4,499,945	17.6	8,291,840	18.3	5,767,507	19.8
Less than 9th grade	801,483	3.6	120,066	3.1	122,693	2.7	333,357	4.0	225,367	3.9
9th to 12th grade, no diploma........	1,739,048	7.8	233,728	6.1	291,832	6.5	737,397	8.9	476,091	8.3
High school graduate (includes equivalency)	6,062,838	27.1	999,111	26.0	1,191,854	26.5	2,413,050	29.1	1,458,823	25.3
Some college, no degree................	5,063,328	22.6	694,308	18.1	1,058,977	23.5	1,896,379	22.9	1,413,664	24.5
Associate's degree	1,792,747	8.0	293,166	7.6	415,081	9.2	634,366	7.7	450,134	7.8
Bachelor's degree..........................	5,014,044	22.4	1,049,602	27.3	1,046,606	23.3	1,636,647	19.7	1,281,189	22.2
Graduate or professional degree..................	1,925,234	8.6	449,449	11.7	372,902	8.3	640,644	7.7	462,239	8.0
35 to 44 years...............................	20,215,641	16.7	3,371,430	15.8	4,130,705	16.2	7,688,905	16.9	5,024,601	17.3
Less than 9th grade	1,093,085	5.4	158,024	4.7	143,080	3.5	432,619	5.6	359,362	7.2
9th to 12th grade, no diploma........	1,622,560	8.0	211,096	6.3	269,629	6.5	708,371	9.2	433,464	8.6
High school graduate (includes equivalency)	5,417,417	26.8	923,093	27.4	1,166,200	28.2	2,184,824	28.4	1,143,300	22.8
Some college, no degree................	4,032,103	19.9	552,585	16.4	879,397	21.3	1,553,022	20.2	1,047,099	20.8
Associate's degree	1,619,706	8.0	258,426	7.7	382,277	9.3	587,836	7.6	391,167	7.8
Bachelor's degree..........................	3,979,661	19.7	752,667	22.3	823,614	19.9	1,377,895	17.9	1,025,485	20.4
Graduate or professional degree..................	2,451,109	12.1	515,539	15.3	466,508	11.3	844,338	11.0	624,724	12.4

Table B-1. Educational Attainment of the Population 18 Years and Over, by Region, Age, and Sex, 2016—*Continued*

(Number; percent.)

Characteristic	United States Number	United States Percent	Northeast Number	Northeast Percent	Midwest Number	Midwest Percent	South Number	South Percent	West Number	West Percent
45 to 64 years	41,091,683	33.9	7,522,017	35.2	8,889,173	34.8	15,210,815	33.5	9,469,678	32.6
Less than 9th grade	2,206,119	5.4	318,783	4.2	274,390	3.1	873,535	5.7	739,411	7.8
9th to 12th grade, no diploma	3,162,550	7.7	504,185	6.7	592,379	6.7	1,369,590	9.0	696,396	7.4
High school graduate (includes equivalency)	12,169,455	29.6	2,405,017	32.0	2,920,437	32.9	4,628,640	30.4	2,215,361	23.4
Some college, no degree	8,254,417	20.1	1,243,888	16.5	1,882,916	21.2	3,011,268	19.8	2,116,345	22.3
Associate's degree	3,145,293	7.7	566,968	7.5	760,318	8.6	1,080,098	7.1	737,909	7.8
Bachelor's degree	7,381,543	18.0	1,442,863	19.2	1,538,669	17.3	2,610,447	17.2	1,789,564	18.9
Graduate or professional degree	4,772,306	11.6	1,040,313	13.8	920,064	10.4	1,637,237	10.8	1,174,692	12.4
65 years and over	21,760,438	17.9	3,904,018	18.3	4,670,068	18.3	8,219,820	18.1	4,966,532	17.1
Less than 9th grade	1,720,803	7.9	305,894	7.8	270,914	5.8	733,319	8.9	410,676	8.3
9th to 12th grade, no diploma	1,671,006	7.7	322,471	8.3	364,104	7.8	701,339	8.5	283,092	5.7
High school graduate (includes equivalency)	5,950,428	27.3	1,171,971	30.0	1,543,452	33.0	2,219,024	27.0	1,015,981	20.5
Some college, no degree	4,160,821	19.1	569,009	14.6	930,190	19.9	1,576,860	19.2	1,084,762	21.8
Associate's degree	1,271,665	5.8	213,782	5.5	249,701	5.3	453,134	5.5	355,048	7.1
Bachelor's degree	3,655,559	16.8	637,346	16.3	698,510	15.0	1,356,686	16.5	963,017	19.4
Graduate or professional degree	3,330,156	15.3	683,545	17.5	613,197	13.1	1,179,458	14.3	853,956	17.2
Female	128,106,624	51.3	23,039,743	51.9	26,814,954	51.2	48,527,997	51.7	29,723,930	50.6
18 to 24 years	15,097,628	11.8	2,646,884	11.5	3,201,276	11.9	5,673,681	11.7	3,575,787	12.0
Less than 9th grade	181,582	1.2	31,205	1.2	38,577	1.2	71,591	1.3	40,209	1.1
9th to 12th grade, no diploma	1,524,665	10.1	228,019	8.6	311,822	9.7	627,202	11.1	357,622	10.0
High school graduate (includes equivalency)	4,175,650	27.7	694,238	26.2	857,140	26.8	1,632,456	28.8	991,816	27.7
Some college, no degree	6,404,506	42.4	1,083,318	40.9	1,384,594	43.3	2,365,397	41.7	1,571,197	43.9
Associate's degree	878,198	5.8	144,371	5.5	186,919	5.8	331,222	5.8	215,686	6.0
Bachelor's degree	1,781,129	11.8	419,388	15.8	396,239	12.4	593,742	10.5	371,760	10.4
Graduate or professional degree	151,898	1.0	46,345	1.8	25,985	0.8	52,071	0.9	27,497	0.8
25 to 34 years	21,991,526	17.2	3,798,739	16.5	4,402,070	16.4	8,336,021	17.2	5,454,696	18.4
Less than 9th grade	584,032	2.7	95,297	2.5	96,011	2.2	225,273	2.7	167,451	3.1
9th to 12th grade, no diploma	1,260,204	5.7	170,189	4.5	214,363	4.9	538,172	6.5	337,480	6.2
High school graduate (includes equivalency)	4,449,598	20.2	717,901	18.9	837,469	19.0	1,850,307	22.2	1,043,921	19.1
Some college, no degree	4,962,065	22.6	647,435	17.0	1,013,127	23.0	1,979,539	23.7	1,321,964	24.2
Associate's degree	2,180,381	9.9	330,955	8.7	500,643	11.4	835,803	10.0	512,980	9.4
Bachelor's degree	5,794,565	26.3	1,163,447	30.6	1,200,091	27.3	1,971,434	23.6	1,459,593	26.8
Graduate or professional degree	2,760,681	12.6	673,515	17.7	540,366	12.3	935,493	11.2	611,307	11.2
35 to 44 years	20,439,951	16.0	3,470,499	15.1	4,120,610	15.4	7,912,892	16.3	4,935,950	16.6
Less than 9th grade	935,342	4.6	125,620	3.6	127,011	3.1	346,433	4.4	336,278	6.8
9th to 12th grade, no diploma	1,248,846	6.1	165,307	4.8	204,132	5.0	531,871	6.7	347,536	7.0
High school graduate (includes equivalency)	4,196,909	20.5	712,684	20.5	817,863	19.8	1,748,814	22.1	917,548	18.6
Some college, no degree	4,099,602	20.1	542,128	15.6	879,107	21.3	1,654,869	20.9	1,023,498	20.7
Associate's degree	2,132,437	10.4	344,957	9.9	498,731	12.1	808,938	10.2	479,811	9.7
Bachelor's degree	4,672,800	22.9	879,113	25.3	970,872	23.6	1,710,745	21.6	1,112,070	22.5
Graduate or professional degree	3,154,015	15.4	700,690	20.2	622,894	15.1	1,111,222	14.0	719,209	14.6
45 to 64 years	43,122,792	33.7	7,980,638	34.6	9,182,220	34.2	16,215,238	33.4	9,744,696	32.8
Less than 9th grade	2,050,474	4.8	315,222	3.9	238,749	2.6	735,012	4.5	761,491	7.8
9th to 12th grade, no diploma	2,604,691	6.0	419,284	5.3	460,788	5.0	1,116,662	6.9	607,957	6.2
High school graduate (includes equivalency)	11,539,360	26.8	2,235,360	28.0	2,667,688	29.1	4,558,633	28.1	2,077,679	21.3
Some college, no degree	9,176,118	21.3	1,366,733	17.1	2,049,663	22.3	3,479,071	21.5	2,280,651	23.4
Associate's degree	4,445,608	10.3	840,337	10.5	1,058,613	11.5	1,603,164	9.9	943,494	9.7
Bachelor's degree	8,224,312	19.1	1,634,048	20.5	1,707,479	18.6	2,955,031	18.2	1,927,754	19.8
Graduate or professional degree	5,082,229	11.8	1,169,654	14.7	999,240	10.9	1,767,665	10.9	1,145,670	11.8
65 years and over	27,454,727	21.4	5,142,983	22.3	5,908,778	22.0	10,390,165	21.4	6,012,801	20.2
Less than 9th grade	2,301,566	8.4	442,000	8.6	321,440	5.4	930,874	9.0	607,252	10.1
9th to 12th grade, no diploma	2,410,425	8.8	449,557	8.7	488,248	8.3	1,046,342	10.1	426,278	7.1
High school graduate (includes equivalency)	9,587,775	34.9	1,990,892	38.7	2,402,874	40.7	3,584,621	34.5	1,609,388	26.8
Some college, no degree	5,346,894	19.5	718,532	14.0	1,186,292	20.1	2,040,217	19.6	1,401,853	23.3
Associate's degree	1,672,004	6.1	316,572	6.2	329,341	5.6	603,123	5.8	422,968	7.0
Bachelor's degree	3,519,911	12.8	632,647	12.3	686,987	11.6	1,263,485	12.2	936,792	15.6
Graduate or professional degree	2,616,152	9.5	592,783	11.5	493,596	8.4	921,503	8.9	608,270	10.1

Table B-2. Educational Attainment of the Population 25 Years Old and Over, by Sex, Race, Hispanic Origin, and Region or State, 2016

(Number; percent.)

Region or State	Population	Less than 9th grade	9th to 12th grade, no diploma	High school graduate (includes equivalency)	Some college, no degree	Associate degree	Bachelor's degree	Graduate or professional degree	High school graduate or higher (percent)	Bachelor's degree or higher (percent)
United States	218,475,480	11,692,904	15,719,330	59,373,780	45,095,348	18,259,841	42,242,395	26,091,882	87.5	31.3
Northeast Region	39,029,754	1,880,906	2,475,817	11,156,029	6,334,618	3,165,163	8,191,733	5,825,488	88.8	35.9
Midwest Region	45,803,569	1,594,288	2,885,475	13,547,837	9,879,669	4,194,705	8,672,828	5,028,767	90.2	29.9
South Region	82,265,696	4,610,422	6,749,744	23,187,913	17,191,225	6,606,462	14,882,370	9,037,560	86.2	29.1
West Region	51,376,461	3,607,288	3,608,294	11,482,001	11,689,836	4,293,511	10,495,464	6,200,067	86.0	32.5
Alabama	3,300,713	157,797	333,897	1,011,236	711,231	271,030	506,680	308,842	85.1	24.7
Alaska	478,951	10,392	22,585	133,928	129,650	40,819	90,861	50,716	93.1	29.6
Arizona	4,626,409	265,215	349,224	1,105,497	1,179,736	390,843	835,779	500,115	86.7	28.9
Arkansas	1,990,448	100,157	179,465	681,969	449,709	133,315	282,608	163,225	86.0	22.4
California	26,304,241	2,556,147	2,062,516	5,390,935	5,602,398	2,031,775	5,426,164	3,234,306	82.4	32.9
Colorado	3,745,506	128,209	192,377	822,144	787,366	322,529	934,273	558,608	91.4	39.9
Connecticut	2,467,737	100,513	133,422	678,776	415,150	186,288	541,369	412,219	90.5	38.6
Delaware	662,547	22,347	48,247	212,474	122,182	52,228	121,717	83,352	89.3	31.0
District of Columbia	480,158	17,097	28,646	85,248	62,206	14,086	115,097	157,778	90.5	56.8
Florida	14,703,671	762,762	1,092,451	4,249,733	2,961,148	1,429,121	2,675,907	1,532,549	87.4	28.6
Georgia	6,785,395	334,607	588,019	1,884,080	1,394,205	518,208	1,270,275	796,001	86.4	30.5
Hawaii	990,937	36,083	43,580	277,743	212,677	104,261	211,850	104,743	92.0	31.9
Idaho	1,087,265	34,434	69,695	302,866	275,485	104,375	203,363	97,047	90.4	27.6
Illinois	8,665,219	429,910	536,517	2,250,392	1,823,126	682,989	1,813,840	1,128,445	88.8	34.0
Indiana	4,392,576	164,742	346,757	1,481,882	900,213	374,136	716,293	408,553	88.4	25.6
Iowa	2,087,020	66,242	105,856	649,532	438,173	234,055	398,242	194,920	91.8	28.4
Kansas	1,891,936	68,491	110,352	496,294	438,343	157,030	390,861	230,565	90.5	32.8
Kentucky	2,995,509	170,725	257,735	968,299	640,040	256,369	419,081	283,260	85.7	23.4
Louisiana	3,115,020	160,929	325,509	1,059,273	654,115	187,288	473,299	254,607	84.4	23.4
Maine	966,569	25,640	48,498	318,369	187,940	94,984	181,434	109,704	92.3	30.1
Maryland	4,122,508	166,606	240,623	1,046,470	779,195	268,485	860,491	760,638	90.1	39.3
Massachusetts	4,727,515	212,315	240,370	1,156,496	734,632	363,356	1,124,295	896,051	90.4	42.7
Michigan	6,760,402	203,405	444,504	1,978,343	1,598,192	626,128	1,162,737	747,093	90.4	28.3
Minnesota	3,725,283	111,658	152,230	937,937	796,712	429,762	860,125	436,859	92.9	34.8
Mississippi	1,957,022	94,724	216,010	603,335	438,995	177,695	264,865	161,398	84.1	21.8
Missouri	4,121,014	137,315	292,624	1,265,386	927,795	325,244	729,511	443,139	89.6	28.5
Montana	712,616	13,453	37,785	206,415	168,223	66,134	148,944	71,662	92.8	31.0
Nebraska	1,243,820	51,410	61,935	328,348	281,360	129,795	261,931	129,041	90.9	31.4
Nevada	2,010,610	122,892	157,641	585,057	516,903	156,342	308,547	163,228	86.0	23.5
New Hampshire	947,586	20,623	47,275	256,245	179,277	97,488	213,461	133,217	92.8	36.6
New Jersey	6,171,172	317,182	343,494	1,706,073	1,024,289	400,332	1,460,518	919,284	89.3	38.6
New Mexico	1,391,381	84,515	118,426	370,508	323,025	116,674	215,691	162,542	85.4	27.2
New York	13,653,592	865,976	1,002,316	3,574,814	2,150,858	1,191,816	2,749,619	2,118,193	86.3	35.7
North Carolina	6,877,185	319,570	553,627	1,775,846	1,482,131	654,866	1,345,615	745,490	87.3	30.4
North Dakota	495,015	13,827	23,917	134,178	109,216	67,554	107,578	38,745	92.4	29.6
Ohio	7,922,061	222,209	568,107	2,639,028	1,630,529	682,507	1,362,205	817,476	90.0	27.5
Oklahoma	2,571,636	103,252	209,774	802,529	603,826	203,590	432,922	215,743	87.8	25.2
Oregon	2,857,952	106,021	171,461	655,893	745,532	244,515	572,508	362,022	90.3	32.7
Pennsylvania	8,921,975	289,165	591,181	3,132,444	1,431,231	730,217	1,676,971	1,070,766	90.1	30.8
Rhode Island	734,045	38,405	45,778	204,045	135,369	60,183	151,195	99,070	88.5	34.1
South Carolina	3,388,476	148,917	304,737	981,669	713,098	317,549	591,086	331,420	86.6	27.2
South Dakota	565,894	18,275	31,736	163,910	123,619	65,093	111,002	52,259	91.2	28.9
Tennessee	4,527,198	216,289	374,024	1,465,937	959,498	328,595	756,055	426,800	87.0	26.1
Texas	17,775,280	1,529,632	1,506,376	4,474,711	3,869,300	1,259,574	3,362,678	1,773,009	82.9	28.9
Utah	1,783,244	51,995	95,408	404,605	472,108	178,193	381,130	199,805	91.7	32.6
Vermont	439,563	11,087	23,483	128,767	75,872	40,499	92,871	66,984	92.1	36.4
Virginia	5,721,173	247,576	366,738	1,372,836	1,116,669	438,669	1,241,751	936,934	89.3	38.1
Washington	4,996,555	192,181	266,656	1,111,786	1,178,772	491,450	1,098,509	657,201	90.8	35.1
West Virginia	1,291,757	57,435	123,866	512,228	233,677	95,794	162,243	106,514	86.0	20.8
Wisconsin	3,933,329	106,804	210,940	1,222,607	812,391	420,412	758,503	401,672	91.9	29.5
Wyoming	390,794	5,751	20,940	114,624	97,961	45,601	67,845	38,072	93.2	27.1

Table B-2. Educational Attainment of the Population 25 Years Old and Over, by Sex, Race, Hispanic Origin, and Region or State, 2016—*Continued*

(Number; percent.)

Region or State		Male, age 25 years and over								
	Population	Less than 9th grade	9th to 12th grade, no diploma	High school graduate (includes equivalency)	Some college, no degree	Associate degree	Bachelor's degree	Graduate or professional degree	High school graduate or higher (percent)	Bachelor's degree or higher (percent)
United States..........	105,466,484	5,821,490	8,195,164	29,600,138	21,510,669	7,829,411	20,030,807	12,478,805	86.7	30.8
Northeast Region.........	18,636,895	902,767	1,271,480	5,499,192	3,059,790	1,332,342	3,882,478	2,688,846	88.3	35.3
Midwest Region...........	22,189,891	811,077	1,517,944	6,821,943	4,751,480	1,807,377	4,107,399	2,372,671	89.5	29.2
South Region..............	39,411,380	2,372,830	3,516,697	11,445,538	8,037,529	2,755,434	6,981,675	4,301,677	85.1	28.6
West Region................	25,228,318	1,734,816	1,889,043	5,833,465	5,661,870	1,934,258	5,059,255	3,115,611	85.6	32.4
Alabama......................	1,560,045	82,192	173,660	489,259	329,529	105,425	241,303	138,677	83.6	24.4
Alaska	247,350	5,059	12,401	75,546	69,508	20,551	38,870	25,415	92.9	26.0
Arizona.......................	2,263,051	132,055	182,136	548,375	558,940	183,367	408,669	249,509	86.1	29.1
Arkansas	953,641	53,974	91,540	343,934	208,824	51,433	129,954	73,982	84.7	21.4
California....................	12,859,902	1,213,765	1,072,508	2,717,268	2,721,438	904,152	2,611,917	1,618,854	82.2	32.9
Colorado	1,861,945	65,436	101,937	426,175	385,429	148,331	458,937	275,700	91.0	39.5
Connecticut.................	1,175,476	47,363	67,590	341,415	197,814	72,877	253,333	195,084	90.2	38.1
Delaware	313,606	12,148	26,499	102,241	56,590	20,110	55,559	40,459	87.7	30.6
District of Columbia......	226,729	8,139	13,341	41,159	27,041	6,051	56,069	74,929	90.5	57.8
Florida.......................	7,045,931	374,950	578,066	2,050,410	1,403,088	611,811	1,267,222	760,384	86.5	28.8
Georgia	3,213,631	179,739	304,422	933,069	642,745	210,975	585,938	356,743	84.9	29.3
Hawaii........................	488,721	14,375	23,213	145,542	109,835	47,253	98,240	50,263	92.3	30.4
Idaho.........................	534,801	18,049	35,653	153,930	128,056	47,933	97,467	53,713	90.0	28.3
Illinois.......................	4,179,051	217,560	286,210	1,124,607	862,649	300,763	864,429	522,833	87.9	33.2
Indiana.......................	2,117,365	85,175	176,467	738,708	427,500	157,512	339,781	192,222	87.6	25.1
Iowa..........................	1,019,726	36,216	57,044	336,775	211,320	98,725	183,541	96,105	90.9	27.4
Kansas	921,728	35,824	57,356	253,835	209,706	66,531	188,462	110,014	89.9	32.4
Kentucky	1,440,939	89,770	132,560	494,051	299,236	99,473	199,959	125,890	84.6	22.6
Louisiana	1,491,265	93,155	175,550	518,497	304,429	71,099	213,787	114,748	82.0	22.0
Maine.........................	463,729	13,993	28,083	164,040	90,345	39,451	78,669	49,148	90.9	27.6
Maryland.....................	1,949,460	87,994	126,767	508,352	354,587	113,063	401,255	357,442	89.0	38.9
Massachusetts.............	2,250,613	102,885	127,076	585,782	346,269	142,418	532,330	413,853	89.8	42.0
Michigan.....................	3,261,814	104,653	232,528	977,187	776,368	255,174	555,669	360,235	89.7	28.1
Minnesota	1,829,789	52,969	82,986	489,136	392,297	195,127	409,869	207,405	92.6	33.7
Mississippi..................	917,578	52,395	114,022	298,962	202,322	72,011	111,834	66,032	81.9	19.4
Missouri.....................	1,978,971	67,246	145,844	644,234	433,586	139,771	343,343	204,947	89.2	27.7
Montana......................	354,746	8,076	20,461	105,543	83,583	30,043	71,460	35,580	92.0	30.2
Nebraska	612,019	27,878	34,023	172,266	135,655	62,114	117,825	62,258	89.9	29.4
Nevada	998,377	62,474	80,526	301,424	254,737	72,426	146,233	80,557	85.7	22.7
New Hampshire.............	463,773	12,107	28,198	129,593	83,223	44,372	103,065	63,215	91.3	35.9
New Jersey	2,947,683	149,631	177,253	822,816	498,855	165,797	680,626	452,705	88.9	38.4
New Mexico	676,970	41,650	62,221	192,181	151,683	49,681	102,537	77,017	84.7	26.5
New York....................	6,484,900	409,984	501,963	1,750,826	1,058,454	516,642	1,310,195	936,836	85.9	34.7
North Carolina.............	3,256,354	169,216	293,077	884,171	684,238	261,646	620,321	343,685	85.8	29.6
North Dakota...............	252,446	7,536	14,323	72,981	56,389	34,161	49,390	17,666	91.3	26.6
Ohio..........................	3,806,328	110,872	292,413	1,304,562	785,432	274,413	654,330	384,306	89.4	27.3
Oklahoma....................	1,244,732	54,158	106,512	404,313	286,802	88,636	200,225	104,086	87.1	24.4
Oregon.......................	1,395,238	51,603	91,882	337,593	350,976	113,096	272,536	177,552	89.7	32.3
Pennsylvania...............	4,289,950	143,715	304,020	1,533,643	687,805	307,399	810,836	502,532	89.6	30.6
Rhode Island...............	348,142	17,116	23,280	102,325	61,779	26,604	71,714	45,324	88.4	33.6
South Carolina	1,600,416	79,421	158,385	486,849	326,989	124,204	277,398	147,170	85.1	26.5
South Dakota	280,106	10,327	17,113	85,933	61,409	30,947	50,441	23,936	90.2	26.6
Tennessee	2,158,282	113,501	192,103	723,545	443,089	137,210	355,398	193,436	85.8	25.4
Texas.........................	8,659,045	762,285	772,333	2,225,385	1,832,541	568,428	1,609,219	888,854	82.3	28.8
Utah..........................	886,906	25,812	52,009	197,980	228,450	77,027	183,627	122,001	91.2	34.5
Vermont......................	212,629	5,973	14,017	68,752	35,246	16,782	41,710	30,149	90.6	33.8
Virginia......................	2,754,728	128,408	190,128	685,632	527,275	178,585	578,508	466,192	88.4	37.9
Washington..................	2,462,437	93,372	143,204	568,571	571,404	219,787	536,032	330,067	90.4	35.2
West Virginia...............	624,998	31,385	67,732	255,709	108,204	35,274	77,726	48,968	84.1	20.3
Wisconsin	1,930,548	54,821	121,637	621,719	399,169	192,139	350,319	190,744	90.9	28.0
Wyoming	197,874	3,090	10,892	63,337	47,831	20,611	32,730	19,383	92.9	26.3

Table B-2. Educational Attainment of the Population 25 Years Old and Over, by Sex, Race, Hispanic Origin, and Region or State, 2016—*Continued*

(Number; percent.)

Region or State		Female, age 25 years and over								
	Population	Less than 9th grade	9th to 12th grade, no diploma	High school graduate (includes equivalency)	Some college, no degree	Associate degree	Bachelor's degree	Graduate or professional degree	High school graduate or higher (percent)	Bachelor's degree or higher (percent)
United States...........	113,008,996	5,871,414	7,524,166	29,773,642	23,584,679	10,430,430	22,211,588	13,613,077	88.1	31.7
Northeast Region.........	20,392,859	978,139	1,204,337	5,656,837	3,274,828	1,832,821	4,309,255	3,136,642	89.3	36.5
Midwest Region............	23,613,678	783,211	1,367,531	6,725,894	5,128,189	2,387,328	4,565,429	2,656,096	90.9	30.6
South Region	42,854,316	2,237,592	3,233,047	11,742,375	9,153,696	3,851,028	7,900,695	4,735,883	87.2	29.5
West Region.................	26,148,143	1,872,472	1,719,251	5,648,536	6,027,966	2,359,253	5,436,209	3,084,456	86.3	32.6
Alabama	1,740,668	75,605	160,237	521,977	381,702	165,605	265,377	170,165	86.5	25.0
Alaska	231,601	5,333	10,184	58,382	60,142	20,268	51,991	25,301	93.3	33.4
Arizona.......................	2,363,358	133,160	167,088	557,122	620,796	207,476	427,110	250,606	87.3	28.7
Arkansas	1,036,807	46,183	87,925	338,035	240,885	81,882	152,654	89,243	87.1	23.3
California.....................	13,444,339	1,342,382	990,008	2,673,667	2,880,960	1,127,623	2,814,247	1,615,452	82.7	32.9
Colorado	1,883,561	62,773	90,440	395,969	401,937	174,198	475,336	282,908	91.9	40.3
Connecticut..................	1,292,261	53,150	65,832	337,361	217,336	113,411	288,036	217,135	90.8	39.1
Delaware	348,941	10,199	21,748	110,233	65,592	32,118	66,158	42,893	90.8	31.3
District of Columbia	253,429	8,958	15,305	44,089	35,165	8,035	59,028	82,849	90.4	56.0
Florida........................	7,657,740	387,812	514,385	2,199,323	1,558,060	817,310	1,408,685	772,165	88.2	28.5
Georgia	3,571,764	154,868	283,597	951,011	751,460	307,233	684,337	439,258	87.7	31.5
Hawaii	502,216	21,708	20,367	132,201	102,842	57,008	113,610	54,480	91.6	33.5
Idaho..........................	552,464	16,385	34,042	148,936	147,429	56,442	105,896	43,334	90.9	27.0
Illinois........................	4,486,168	212,350	250,307	1,125,785	960,477	382,226	949,411	605,612	89.7	34.7
Indiana	2,275,211	79,567	170,290	743,174	472,713	216,624	376,512	216,331	89.0	26.1
Iowa...........................	1,067,294	30,026	48,812	312,757	226,853	135,330	214,701	98,815	92.6	29.4
Kansas	970,208	32,667	52,996	242,459	228,637	90,499	202,399	120,551	91.2	33.3
Kentucky	1,554,570	80,955	125,175	474,248	340,804	156,896	219,122	157,370	86.7	24.2
Louisiana	1,623,755	67,774	149,959	540,776	349,686	116,189	259,512	139,859	86.6	24.6
Maine..........................	502,840	11,647	20,415	154,329	97,595	55,533	102,765	60,556	93.6	32.5
Maryland......................	2,173,048	78,612	113,856	538,118	424,608	155,422	459,236	403,196	91.1	39.7
Massachusetts..............	2,476,902	109,430	113,294	570,714	388,363	220,938	591,965	482,198	91.0	43.4
Michigan......................	3,498,588	98,752	211,976	1,001,156	821,824	370,954	607,068	386,858	91.1	28.4
Minnesota	1,895,494	58,689	69,244	448,801	404,415	234,635	450,256	229,454	93.3	35.9
Mississippi...................	1,039,444	42,329	101,988	304,373	236,673	105,684	153,031	95,366	86.1	23.9
Missouri......................	2,142,043	70,069	146,780	621,152	494,209	185,473	386,168	238,192	89.9	29.1
Montana......................	357,870	5,377	17,324	100,872	84,640	36,091	77,484	36,082	93.7	31.7
Nebraska	631,801	23,532	27,912	156,082	145,705	67,681	144,106	66,783	91.9	33.4
Nevada........................	1,012,233	60,418	77,115	283,633	262,166	83,916	162,314	82,671	86.4	24.2
New Hampshire.............	483,813	8,516	19,077	126,652	96,054	53,116	110,396	70,002	94.3	37.3
New Jersey	3,223,489	167,551	166,241	883,257	525,434	234,535	779,892	466,579	89.6	38.7
New Mexico	714,411	42,865	56,205	178,327	171,342	66,993	113,154	85,525	86.1	27.8
New York......................	7,168,692	455,992	500,353	1,823,988	1,092,404	675,174	1,439,424	1,181,357	86.7	36.6
North Carolina..............	3,620,831	150,354	260,550	891,715	797,893	393,220	725,294	401,805	88.7	31.1
North Dakota.................	242,569	6,291	9,594	61,197	52,827	33,393	58,188	21,079	93.5	32.7
Ohio...........................	4,115,733	111,337	275,694	1,334,466	845,097	408,094	707,875	433,170	90.6	27.7
Oklahoma....................	1,326,904	49,094	103,262	398,216	317,024	114,954	232,697	111,657	88.5	26.0
Oregon........................	1,462,714	54,418	79,579	318,300	394,556	131,419	299,972	184,470	90.8	33.1
Pennsylvania................	4,632,025	145,450	287,161	1,598,801	743,426	422,818	866,135	568,234	90.7	31.0
Rhode Island................	385,903	21,289	22,498	101,720	73,590	33,579	79,481	53,746	88.7	34.5
South Carolina	1,788,060	69,496	146,352	494,820	386,109	193,345	313,688	184,250	87.9	27.8
South Dakota	285,788	7,948	14,623	77,977	62,210	34,146	60,561	28,323	92.1	31.1
Tennessee	2,368,916	102,788	181,921	742,392	516,409	191,385	400,657	233,364	88.0	26.8
Texas..........................	9,116,235	767,347	734,043	2,249,326	2,036,759	691,146	1,753,459	884,155	83.5	28.9
Utah...........................	896,338	26,183	43,399	206,625	243,658	101,166	197,503	77,804	92.2	30.7
Vermont.......................	226,934	5,114	9,466	60,015	40,626	23,717	51,161	36,835	93.6	38.8
Virginia.......................	2,966,445	119,168	176,610	687,204	589,394	260,084	663,243	470,742	90.0	38.2
Washington...................	2,534,118	98,809	123,452	543,215	607,368	271,663	562,477	327,134	91.2	35.1
West Virginia.................	666,759	26,050	56,134	256,519	125,473	60,520	84,517	57,546	87.7	21.3
Wisconsin	2,002,781	51,983	89,303	600,888	413,222	228,273	408,184	210,928	92.9	30.9
Wyoming	192,920	2,661	10,048	51,287	50,130	24,990	35,115	18,689	93.4	27.9

Table B-2. Educational Attainment of the Population 25 Years Old and Over, by Sex, Race, Hispanic Origin, and Region or State, 2016—*Continued*

(Number; percent.)

Region or State	White alone, age 25 years and over						
	Population	Less than a high school diploma	High school graduate (includes equivalency)	Some college or associate's degree	Bachelor's degree or higher	High school graduate or higher (percent)	Bachelor's degree or higher (percent)
United States..........	164,450,361	17,361,819	45,095,768	48,288,165	53,704,609	89.4	32.7
Northeast Region.........	29,492,641	2,538,381	8,566,062	7,226,471	11,161,727	91.4	37.8
Midwest Region..........	38,254,571	3,171,667	11,525,223	11,767,530	11,790,151	91.7	30.8
South Region..............	60,418,504	7,566,547	16,899,205	17,465,418	18,487,334	87.5	30.6
West Region................	36,284,645	4,085,224	8,105,278	11,828,746	12,265,397	88.7	33.8
Alabama.....................	2,343,981	310,541	706,813	695,076	631,551	86.8	26.9
Alaska........................	333,536	14,347	79,124	120,210	119,855	95.7	35.9
Arizona.......................	3,681,437	392,505	876,125	1,278,064	1,134,743	89.3	30.8
Arkansas....................	1,591,895	195,691	551,857	469,108	375,239	87.7	23.6
California....................	16,275,015	2,408,057	3,333,583	4,998,189	5,535,186	85.2	34.0
Colorado	3,228,969	234,464	686,558	963,345	1,344,602	92.7	41.6
Connecticut................	1,966,682	148,722	529,925	479,251	808,784	92.4	41.1
Delaware....................	482,121	47,691	150,268	127,755	156,407	90.1	32.4
District of Columbia	209,538	5,505	6,051	11,619	186,363	97.4	88.9
Florida.......................	11,584,929	1,275,514	3,330,883	3,490,918	3,487,614	89.0	30.1
Georgia	4,196,094	511,966	1,157,656	1,146,858	1,379,614	87.8	32.9
Hawaii........................	268,335	9,483	51,422	93,491	113,939	96.5	42.5
Idaho.........................	1,000,599	83,395	280,228	354,047	282,929	91.7	28.3
Illinois.......................	6,421,241	556,982	1,706,011	1,874,644	2,283,604	91.3	35.6
Indiana......................	3,788,926	401,153	1,301,469	1,087,296	999,008	89.4	26.4
Iowa..........................	1,933,496	139,507	613,248	633,360	547,381	92.8	28.3
Kansas	1,650,245	137,074	431,822	524,238	557,111	91.7	33.8
Kentucky....................	2,674,479	375,892	873,592	786,805	638,190	85.9	23.9
Louisiana	2,037,772	249,091	681,184	553,390	554,107	87.8	27.2
Maine.........................	926,882	68,697	308,486	269,042	280,657	92.6	30.3
Maryland....................	2,436,346	195,105	601,906	591,593	1,047,742	92.0	43.0
Massachusetts.............	3,842,201	286,545	935,233	906,374	1,714,049	92.5	44.6
Michigan....................	5,489,471	453,459	1,629,846	1,806,465	1,599,701	91.7	29.1
Minnesota..................	3,242,452	160,848	830,657	1,084,880	1,166,067	95.0	36.0
Mississippi.................	1,215,141	153,277	364,687	389,056	308,121	87.4	25.4
Missouri.....................	3,493,148	337,398	1,086,329	1,045,869	1,023,552	90.3	29.3
Montana.....................	652,363	43,392	188,660	213,168	207,143	93.3	31.8
Nebraska....................	1,124,773	86,760	300,034	376,596	361,383	92.3	32.1
Nevada......................	1,408,273	171,792	411,051	482,921	342,509	87.8	24.3
New Hampshire............	896,354	62,168	242,497	266,191	325,498	93.1	36.3
New Jersey	4,344,913	408,009	1,229,777	1,001,330	1,705,797	90.6	39.3
New Mexico	1,057,238	135,416	267,460	334,663	319,699	87.2	30.2
New York....................	9,009,259	834,962	2,340,494	2,247,625	3,586,178	90.7	39.8
North Carolina.............	4,954,652	531,449	1,239,192	1,538,142	1,645,869	89.3	33.2
North Dakota...............	444,563	29,277	119,910	158,648	136,728	93.4	30.8
Ohio	6,674,927	606,456	2,265,558	1,902,277	1,900,636	90.9	28.5
Oklahoma...................	1,975,808	215,031	611,305	622,204	527,268	89.1	26.7
Oregon	2,488,068	207,330	576,573	879,586	824,579	91.7	33.1
Pennsylvania...............	7,468,949	636,009	2,683,165	1,783,429	2,366,346	91.5	31.7
Rhode Island...............	617,580	61,074	172,130	163,037	221,339	90.1	35.8
South Carolina	2,387,052	262,424	639,796	736,299	748,533	89.0	31.4
South Dakota	501,633	33,480	146,315	168,131	153,707	93.3	30.6
Tennessee..................	3,646,786	447,986	1,191,522	1,023,653	983,625	87.7	27.0
Texas.........................	13,436,720	2,258,640	3,357,417	3,888,595	3,932,068	83.2	29.3
Utah..........................	1,570,964	94,816	348,840	594,740	532,568	94.0	33.9
Vermont.....................	419,821	32,195	124,355	110,192	153,079	92.3	36.5
Virginia......................	4,027,719	359,390	947,571	1,085,249	1,635,509	91.1	40.6
Washington.................	3,954,098	266,825	898,622	1,381,084	1,407,567	93.3	35.6
West Virginia...............	1,217,471	171,354	487,505	309,098	249,514	85.9	20.5
Wisconsin	3,489,696	229,273	1,094,024	1,105,126	1,061,273	93.4	30.4
Wyoming	365,750	23,402	107,032	135,238	100,078	93.6	27.4

Table B-2. Educational Attainment of the Population 25 Years Old and Over, by Sex, Race, Hispanic Origin, and Region or State, 2016—*Continued*

(Number; percent.)

Region or State	Black or African American alone, age 25 years and over						
	Population	Less than a high school diploma	High school graduate (includes equivalency)	Some college or associate's degree	Bachelor's degree or higher	High school graduate or higher (percent)	Bachelor's degree or higher (percent)
United States.............	25,944,692	3,827,071	8,113,148	8,590,059	5,414,414	85.2	20.9
Northeast Region	4,340,930	648,413	1,413,575	1,299,388	979,554	85.1	22.6
Midwest Region	4,342,521	632,280	1,336,737	1,577,480	796,024	85.4	18.3
South Region	14,938,431	2,293,120	4,789,678	4,770,402	3,085,231	84.6	20.7
West Region..................	2,322,810	253,258	573,158	942,789	553,605	89.1	23.8
Alabama	825,982	149,070	274,390	256,808	145,714	82.0	17.6
Alaska	14,926	1,031	4,909	7,164	1,822	93.1	12.2
Arizona...........................	182,951	19,552	40,953	79,120	43,326	89.3	23.7
Arkansas	281,785	49,304	99,810	87,579	45,092	82.5	16.0
California........................	1,523,493	164,252	363,328	625,382	370,531	89.2	24.3
Colorado	145,505	15,778	39,338	54,644	35,745	89.2	24.6
Connecticut.....................	241,134	33,351	86,486	74,220	47,077	86.2	19.5
Delaware	132,020	16,592	50,834	37,088	27,506	87.4	20.8
District of Columbia	217,411	29,591	73,660	58,472	55,688	86.4	25.6
Florida............................	2,082,501	388,942	683,844	629,576	380,139	81.3	18.3
Georgia	2,034,955	282,455	620,120	655,828	476,552	86.1	23.4
Hawaii	16,842	793	4,385	7,513	4,151	95.3	24.6
Idaho..............................	5,078	92	1,627	1,833	1,526	98.2	30.1
Illinois	1,154,328	159,104	322,252	423,174	249,798	86.2	21.6
Indiana	370,196	53,527	123,515	134,854	58,300	85.5	15.7
Iowa...............................	59,550	10,523	17,365	19,831	11,831	82.3	19.9
Kansas	102,119	12,142	30,163	38,961	20,853	88.1	20.4
Kentucky	223,064	32,635	71,899	86,088	32,442	85.4	14.5
Louisiana	930,771	201,658	337,341	254,355	137,417	78.3	14.8
Maine.............................	8,256	1,691	2,577	2,388	1,600	79.5	19.4
Maryland.........................	1,191,325	115,001	365,257	359,221	351,846	90.3	29.5
Massachusetts	316,115	47,289	96,942	92,916	78,968	85.0	25.0
Michigan	861,144	127,190	270,144	317,315	146,495	85.2	17.0
Minnesota	180,040	32,840	44,623	65,237	37,340	81.8	20.7
Mississippi......................	686,306	142,836	226,283	212,765	104,422	79.2	15.2
Missouri..........................	437,911	58,951	139,399	159,610	79,951	86.5	18.3
Montana..........................	2,967	726	944	517	780	75.5	26.3
Nebraska.........................	50,875	6,915	14,335	17,785	11,840	86.4	23.3
Nevada............................	166,410	15,585	54,482	65,564	30,779	90.6	18.5
New Hampshire...............	10,823	1,220	3,541	2,879	3,183	88.7	29.4
New Jersey	786,869	92,804	271,306	238,215	184,544	88.2	23.5
New Mexico	25,485	1,994	6,503	9,695	7,293	92.2	28.6
New York........................	2,045,692	337,591	624,624	601,960	481,517	83.5	23.5
North Carolina.................	1,407,993	216,014	426,794	479,176	286,009	84.7	20.3
North Dakota...................	10,632	1,000	4,521	4,087	1,024	90.6	9.6
Ohio	900,291	130,544	298,402	325,355	145,990	85.5	16.2
Oklahoma........................	173,789	20,410	57,762	62,175	33,442	88.3	19.2
Oregon	49,212	6,543	12,857	19,194	10,618	86.7	21.6
Pennsylvania...................	886,334	127,862	315,349	270,256	172,867	85.6	19.5
Rhode Island...................	41,620	6,216	12,099	14,618	8,687	85.1	20.9
South Carolina	860,249	160,854	307,572	256,834	134,989	81.3	15.7
South Dakota	7,354	2,104	1,982	2,030	1,238	71.4	16.8
Tennessee	696,665	105,533	234,354	221,364	135,414	84.9	19.4
Texas..............................	2,097,614	228,990	624,275	759,222	485,127	89.1	23.1
Utah	17,317	2,752	3,896	6,797	3,872	84.1	22.4
Vermont..........................	4,087	389	651	1,936	1,111	90.5	27.2
Virginia...........................	1,050,527	147,820	317,779	340,210	244,718	85.9	23.3
Washington.....................	169,496	23,954	38,704	64,139	42,699	85.9	25.2
West Virginia..................	45,474	5,415	17,704	13,641	8,714	88.1	19.2
Wisconsin	208,081	37,440	70,036	69,241	31,364	82.0	15.1
Wyoming	...	...	...	...	...	...	...

... = Not available.

Table B-2. Educational Attainment of the Population 25 Years Old and Over, by Sex, Race, Hispanic Origin, and Region or State, 2016—*Continued*

(Number; percent.)

Region or State	Population	Asian alone, age 25 years and over					
		Less than a high school diploma	High school graduate (includes equivalency)	Some college or associate's degree	Bachelor's degree or higher	High school graduate or higher (percent)	Bachelor's degree or higher (percent)
United States..........	12,334,122	1,652,736	1,842,042	2,280,769	6,558,575	86.6	53.2
Northeast Region	2,532,468	403,264	390,142	346,700	1,392,362	84.1	55.0
Midwest Region	1,366,245	183,268	177,594	216,028	789,355	86.6	57.8
South Region	2,792,441	348,152	408,854	472,855	1,562,580	87.5	56.0
West Region.................	5,642,968	718,052	865,452	1,245,186	2,814,278	87.3	49.9
Alabama	42,268	6,020	8,502	7,239	20,507	85.8	48.5
Alaska	31,070	4,083	9,366	9,491	8,130	86.9	26.2
Arizona	153,710	20,221	20,320	29,208	83,961	86.8	54.6
Arkansas	28,508	3,759	5,560	5,698	13,491	86.8	47.3
California.....................	4,086,920	531,667	565,037	874,567	2,115,649	87.0	51.8
Colorado	118,963	15,532	20,448	22,731	60,252	86.9	50.6
Connecticut.................	106,420	10,153	14,002	12,464	69,801	90.5	65.6
Delaware	25,509	1,762	3,129	4,300	16,318	93.1	64.0
District of Columbia	19,965	690	839	1,350	17,086	96.5	85.6
Florida.........................	402,415	55,382	67,599	77,849	201,585	86.2	50.1
Georgia	271,011	35,790	38,480	40,324	156,417	86.8	57.7
Hawaii	426,716	46,112	115,355	119,282	145,967	89.2	34.2
Idaho...........................	15,651	1,686	2,889	4,456	6,620	89.2	42.3
Illinois	478,425	44,267	49,195	73,495	311,468	90.7	65.1
Indiana	83,957	14,667	13,719	10,644	44,927	82.5	53.5
Iowa............................	44,570	7,675	7,242	6,196	23,457	82.8	52.6
Kansas	50,988	7,911	8,469	8,707	25,901	84.5	50.8
Kentucky	39,780	5,618	7,346	6,252	20,564	85.9	51.7
Louisiana	53,602	10,351	11,302	8,824	23,125	80.7	43.1
Maine..........................	12,254	1,599	2,261	3,231	5,163	87.0	42.1
Maryland......................	268,482	25,346	30,385	44,861	167,890	90.6	62.5
Massachusetts	294,451	43,920	40,375	35,954	174,202	85.1	59.2
Michigan	189,523	21,957	21,561	26,596	119,409	88.4	63.0
Minnesota	154,563	32,967	22,916	34,236	64,444	78.7	41.7
Mississippi...................	18,529	2,837	3,708	3,991	7,993	84.7	43.1
Missouri.......................	77,588	9,958	11,014	10,865	45,751	87.2	59.0
Montana.......................	5,326	233	1,167	933	2,993	95.6	56.2
Nebraska	23,787	6,219	3,608	3,869	10,091	73.9	42.4
Nevada	185,203	18,156	41,527	55,982	69,538	90.2	37.5
New Hampshire.............	21,475	2,132	4,977	2,593	11,773	90.1	54.8
New Jersey	599,087	42,200	63,242	80,711	412,934	93.0	68.9
New Mexico	23,167	2,172	5,026	4,358	11,611	90.6	50.1
New York......................	1,188,298	252,407	215,010	172,493	548,388	78.8	46.1
North Carolina..............	181,455	23,588	26,584	27,609	103,674	87.0	57.1
North Dakota................	4,905	996	1,111	507	2,291	79.7	46.7
Ohio	160,629	19,430	21,191	24,883	95,125	87.9	59.2
Oklahoma.....................	50,989	7,678	9,133	11,890	22,288	84.9	43.7
Oregon	119,827	17,370	17,282	24,263	60,912	85.5	50.8
Pennsylvania................	281,606	47,745	44,205	34,028	155,628	83.0	55.3
Rhode Island................	22,693	2,065	4,799	4,485	11,344	90.9	50.0
South Carolina	53,050	6,784	12,202	10,515	23,549	87.2	44.4
South Dakota	7,145	1,957	1,667	527	2,994	72.6	41.9
Tennessee	76,429	10,490	13,066	10,786	42,087	86.3	55.1
Texas...........................	883,132	109,589	122,187	150,634	500,722	87.6	56.7
Utah	46,290	6,414	8,276	9,725	21,875	86.1	47.3
Vermont.......................	6,184	1,043	1,271	741	3,129	83.1	50.6
Virginia........................	367,796	42,173	47,071	59,645	218,907	88.5	59.5
Washington	426,803	54,293	58,334	89,924	224,252	87.3	52.5
West Virginia................	9,521	295	1,761	1,088	6,377	96.9	67.0
Wisconsin	90,165	15,264	15,901	15,503	43,497	83.1	48.2
Wyoming	...	...	...	...	...	...	...

... = Not available.

Table B-2. Educational Attainment of the Population 25 Years Old and Over, by Sex, Race, Hispanic Origin, and Region or State, 2016—*Continued*

(Number; percent.)

Region or State	Hispanic or Latino,[1] age 25 years and over						
	Population	Less than a high school diploma	High school graduate (includes equivalency)	Some college or associate's degree	Bachelor's degree or higher	High school graduate or higher (percent)	Bachelor's degree or higher (percent)
United States...........	32,331,742	10,632,841	8,986,570	7,750,580	4,961,751	67.1	15.3
Northeast Region.........	4,726,621	1,399,328	1,417,268	1,074,955	835,070	70.4	17.7
Midwest Region...........	2,721,334	887,711	793,079	628,579	411,965	67.4	15.1
South Region..............	12,153,259	3,855,889	3,340,908	2,848,760	2,107,702	68.3	17.3
West Region................	12,730,528	4,489,913	3,435,315	3,198,286	1,607,014	64.7	12.6
Alabama......................	98,289	40,990	25,195	19,374	12,730	58.3	13.0
Alaska	26,133	4,690	7,716	10,175	3,552	82.1	13.6
Arizona.......................	1,153,404	358,867	324,376	323,282	146,879	68.9	12.7
Arkansas....................	101,002	44,152	30,679	16,427	9,744	56.3	9.6
California....................	8,703,787	3,251,528	2,257,233	2,137,583	1,057,443	62.6	12.1
Colorado	646,809	187,188	202,093	155,998	101,530	71.1	15.7
Connecticut.................	316,522	87,604	101,854	70,403	56,661	72.3	17.9
Delaware	45,728	14,725	15,566	8,065	7,372	67.8	16.1
District of Columbia	47,175	15,183	6,780	5,619	19,593	67.8	41.5
Florida........................	3,356,171	733,249	962,993	891,133	768,796	78.2	22.9
Georgia	499,428	200,510	123,338	91,603	83,977	59.9	16.8
Hawaii........................	73,497	6,626	25,782	28,868	12,221	91.0	16.6
Idaho..........................	99,188	35,622	31,166	23,339	9,061	64.1	9.1
Illinois	1,205,051	398,865	366,607	264,872	174,707	66.9	14.5
Indiana	224,064	74,424	67,126	52,773	29,741	66.8	13.3
Iowa...........................	85,565	33,457	22,997	18,473	10,638	60.9	12.4
Kansas	163,361	59,541	48,051	33,015	22,754	63.6	13.9
Kentucky	72,292	23,392	19,642	14,329	14,929	67.6	20.7
Louisiana....................	136,193	37,444	41,813	34,515	22,421	72.5	16.5
Maine.........................	11,366	1,261	3,255	3,701	3,149	88.9	27.7
Maryland.....................	329,396	115,734	80,431	64,231	69,000	64.9	20.9
Massachusetts	430,798	132,376	125,338	95,726	77,358	69.3	18.0
Michigan	247,726	69,873	65,860	68,574	43,419	71.8	17.5
Minnesota	141,538	52,959	36,462	30,639	21,478	62.6	15.2
Mississippi..................	41,837	14,795	11,356	10,313	5,373	64.6	12.8
Missouri......................	122,482	33,435	36,355	28,887	23,805	72.7	19.4
Montana......................	18,098	3,152	5,189	5,403	4,354	82.6	24.1
Nebraska....................	98,476	43,771	23,026	21,018	10,661	55.6	10.8
Nevada.......................	460,183	168,072	144,574	103,466	44,071	63.5	9.6
New Hampshire............	25,368	6,045	5,031	6,897	7,395	76.2	29.2
New Jersey	1,079,365	292,837	355,496	244,181	186,851	72.9	17.3
New Mexico	598,277	143,931	190,872	171,156	92,318	75.9	15.4
New York.....................	2,299,307	714,419	645,327	522,573	416,988	68.9	18.1
North Carolina..............	461,251	186,791	111,635	94,586	68,239	59.5	14.8
North Dakota................	12,173	2,951	3,816	3,538	1,868	75.8	15.3
Ohio	214,826	54,344	62,286	55,885	42,311	74.7	19.7
Oklahoma....................	190,584	74,031	52,528	42,076	21,949	61.2	11.5
Oregon........................	264,005	97,863	64,489	65,199	36,454	62.9	13.8
Pennsylvania...............	472,845	140,370	149,686	109,564	73,225	70.3	15.5
Rhode Island................	84,781	23,629	29,955	19,980	11,217	72.1	13.2
South Carolina	140,423	54,851	33,945	31,646	19,981	60.9	14.2
South Dakota	14,002	4,748	2,972	3,918	2,364	66.1	16.9
Tennessee	168,404	61,449	49,117	32,779	25,059	63.5	14.9
Texas.........................	6,024,554	2,114,662	1,667,265	1,387,185	855,442	64.9	14.2
Utah...........................	206,718	66,056	61,976	51,618	27,068	68.0	13.1
Vermont......................	6,269	787	1,326	1,930	2,226	87.4	35.5
Virginia.......................	426,580	120,461	104,470	100,934	100,715	71.8	23.6
Washington..................	450,014	158,880	110,910	111,515	68,709	64.7	15.3
West Virginia................	13,952	3,470	4,155	3,945	2,382	75.1	17.1
Wisconsin	192,070	59,343	57,521	46,987	28,219	69.1	14.7
Wyoming	30,415	7,438	8,939	10,684	3,354	75.5	11.0

[1]May be of any race.

Table B-3. Selected Characteristics of Children and the School-Age Population, by Region and State, 2016

(Number; dollars; percent.)

Region or State	Population			Median income for a family of four, (2016 inflation-adjusted dollars)	Poverty status	
	Total	5 to 17 years old	5 to 17 years old (percent)		Total children under 18 years old for whom poverty status is determined	Children under 18 years old in poverty (percent)
UNITED STATES	323,127,515	53,839,189	16.7	$86,877	72,452,603	19.5
Northeast Region	56,209,510	8,665,133	15.4	$102,931	11,613,157	17.3
Midwest Region	67,941,431	11,414,743	16.8	$88,755	15,286,446	17.9
South Region	122,319,574	20,743,534	17.0	$78,432	27,955,363	21.9
West Region........................	76,657,000	13,015,779	17.0	$87,097	17,597,637	18.5
Alabama.............................	4,863,300	812,874	16.7	$75,978	1,084,701	24.5
Alaska...............................	741,894	134,801	18.2	$102,997	183,790	14.1
Arizona..............................	6,931,071	1,195,100	17.2	$74,317	1,602,166	23.6
Arkansas............................	2,988,248	518,644	17.4	$69,807	693,626	23.8
California............................	39,250,017	6,610,827	16.8	$89,444	8,961,540	19.9
Colorado............................	5,540,545	925,441	16.7	$94,472	1,242,620	13.4
Connecticut........................	3,576,452	567,133	15.9	$117,344	743,032	12.9
Delaware............................	952,065	148,996	15.6	$90,892	201,224	17.4
District of Columbia	681,170	77,236	11.3	$98,864	118,383	25.8
Florida...............................	20,612,439	3,027,673	14.7	$72,958	4,080,165	21.0
Georgia	10,310,371	1,855,732	18.0	$78,368	2,472,797	22.9
Hawaii...............................	1,428,557	217,043	15.2	$97,849	301,115	10.1
Idaho................................	1,683,140	322,314	19.1	$72,299	430,772	17.7
Illinois..............................	12,801,539	2,153,229	16.8	$94,472	2,883,787	17.7
Indiana..............................	6,633,053	1,157,166	17.4	$79,296	1,544,329	19.5
Iowa.................................	3,134,693	529,480	16.9	$91,006	711,566	14.8
Kansas..............................	2,907,289	517,513	17.8	$83,723	704,613	14.1
Kentucky............................	4,436,974	739,508	16.7	$75,416	989,252	25.0
Louisiana	4,681,666	810,318	17.3	$76,237	1,096,646	28.6
Maine................................	1,331,479	191,010	14.3	$91,184	248,446	17.2
Maryland............................	6,016,447	983,257	16.3	$115,826	1,326,304	12.7
Massachusetts.....................	6,811,779	1,019,173	15.0	$121,280	1,357,280	13.6
Michigan	9,928,300	1,619,520	16.3	$87,070	2,150,156	20.7
Minnesota..........................	5,519,952	937,543	17.0	$105,651	1,266,718	12.7
Mississippi.........................	2,988,726	536,323	17.9	$62,564	711,595	29.7
Missouri.............................	6,093,000	1,018,532	16.7	$81,445	1,361,864	19.2
Montana.............................	1,042,520	167,531	16.1	$82,460	224,160	15.1
Nebraska............................	1,907,116	341,928	17.9	$85,885	463,863	14.2
Nevada	2,940,058	494,141	16.8	$75,783	665,164	19.1
New Hampshire....................	1,334,795	195,363	14.6	$113,508	255,309	7.9
New Jersey	8,944,469	1,464,269	16.4	$118,697	1,961,260	14.6
New Mexico	2,081,015	364,388	17.5	$62,509	482,338	30.1
New York............................	19,745,289	3,020,367	15.3	$96,527	4,100,325	20.7
North Carolina.....................	10,146,788	1,702,301	16.8	$76,382	2,259,252	21.7
North Dakota.......................	757,953	119,697	15.8	$95,893	170,455	12.4
Ohio	11,614,373	1,916,226	16.5	$83,515	2,558,132	20.5
Oklahoma...........................	3,923,561	697,860	17.8	$70,144	945,261	22.9
Oregon	4,093,465	633,664	15.5	$88,448	851,463	17.0
Pennsylvania.......................	12,784,227	1,965,102	15.4	$91,692	2,624,826	18.5
Rhode Island.......................	1,056,426	154,496	14.6	$105,447	206,562	17.0
South Carolina	4,961,119	809,952	16.3	$75,946	1,083,041	23.0
South Dakota	865,454	153,009	17.7	$86,452	210,420	16.9
Tennessee	6,651,194	1,099,084	16.5	$73,604	1,476,765	22.6
Texas................................	27,862,596	5,284,783	19.0	$76,933	7,211,897	22.4
Utah.................................	3,051,217	668,425	21.9	$81,794	910,019	11.1
Vermont.............................	624,594	88,220	14.1	$89,657	116,117	14.8
Virginia..............................	8,411,808	1,363,778	16.2	$101,389	1,835,772	14.3
Washington.........................	7,288,000	1,179,117	16.2	$100,282	1,604,190	13.7
West Virginia.......................	1,831,102	275,215	15.0	$72,767	368,682	24.0
Wisconsin	5,778,709	950,900	16.5	$93,500	1,260,543	15.7
Wyoming	585,501	102,987	17.6	$90,270	138,300	11.1

Table B-3. Selected Characteristics of Children and the School-Age Population, by Region and State, 2016—*Continued*

(Number; dollars; percent.)

Region or State	Health insurance		Language spoken at home					
	Total children under 18 years old	Children under 18 years with no health insurance (percent)	Population 5 to 17 years old	English only (percent)	Language other than English (percent)			
					Spanish	Other Indo-European Languages	Asian and Pacific Island Languages	Other languages
UNITED STATES	73,503,793	4.5	53,839,189	77.5	16.1	2.8	2.4	1.1
Northeast Region	11,784,890	2.9	8,665,133	76.2	13.0	6.2	3.0	1.7
Midwest Region	15,541,571	3.7	11,414,743	87.3	7.5	2.4	1.5	1.2
South Region	28,334,329	5.9	20,743,534	79.6	16.1	1.9	1.6	0.8
West Region........................	17,843,003	3.9	13,015,779	66.6	25.8	2.2	4.2	1.2
Alabama	1,098,052	2.4	812,874	93.2	5.1	0.5	0.7	0.4
Alaska	186,839	10.0	134,801	87.1	2.9	1.8	3.9	4.2
Arizona	1,629,040	7.3	1,195,100	70.9	24.5	1.0	1.3	2.3
Arkansas	705,155	3.6	518,644	90.3	8.0	0.5	1.0	0.2
California.............................	9,079,778	2.9	6,610,827	55.8	34.7	2.8	5.7	0.9
Colorado	1,258,167	4.0	925,441	79.2	16.7	1.5	1.7	0.9
Connecticut.........................	751,459	2.8	567,133	78.2	13.9	5.1	1.8	1.1
Delaware	203,704	3.1	148,996	86.1	10.2	1.5	1.3	0.9
District of Columbia	120,313	3.1	77,236	80.7	14.0	2.5	1.5	1.3
Florida	4,136,345	6.2	3,027,673	71.5	22.3	4.5	1.2	0.6
Georgia	2,506,326	6.5	1,855,732	84.4	11.1	2.0	1.6	0.8
Hawaii	307,561	2.2	217,043	79.8	2.1	0.8	16.6	0.7
Idaho	435,630	4.7	322,314	87.3	10.4	1.2	0.7	0.4
Illinois	2,919,863	2.4	2,153,229	76.1	17.1	3.9	1.8	1.0
Indiana	1,573,925	5.9	1,157,166	89.6	6.9	2.0	1.1	0.5
Iowa	724,997	2.5	529,480	90.2	5.8	1.7	1.3	1.0
Kansas	713,102	4.3	517,513	85.3	11.4	1.5	1.4	0.4
Kentucky	1,009,986	3.2	739,508	93.6	3.4	1.4	0.7	0.9
Louisiana	1,115,457	3.0	810,318	93.7	4.1	0.9	0.9	0.4
Maine	254,723	4.6	191,010	95.3	1.0	1.5	0.7	1.4
Maryland..............................	1,344,588	3.3	983,257	81.1	10.5	3.7	2.9	1.9
Massachusetts.....................	1,375,244	0.9	1,019,173	76.7	11.0	7.4	3.4	1.4
Michigan	2,187,554	2.9	1,619,520	89.4	4.3	2.5	1.4	2.5
Minnesota............................	1,286,323	3.4	937,543	86.1	5.9	1.5	3.6	2.9
Mississippi...........................	721,108	4.5	536,323	95.5	3.4	0.4	0.4	0.4
Missouri...............................	1,386,471	4.5	1,018,532	92.8	3.5	2.0	1.0	0.6
Montana...............................	227,631	4.7	167,531	96.9	1.4	0.6	0.1	1.1
Nebraska	472,689	5.0	341,928	85.9	10.8	0.9	1.5	0.9
Nevada	676,435	6.8	494,141	66.0	29.6	1.1	2.7	0.7
New Hampshire.....................	259,410	2.6	195,363	92.4	2.6	2.0	1.7	1.2
New Jersey	1,979,948	3.5	1,464,269	69.5	18.6	6.1	3.9	1.8
New Mexico..........................	488,598	5.3	364,388	70.4	23.4	1.1	0.8	4.4
New York..............................	4,170,786	2.4	3,020,367	68.7	16.8	8.3	3.8	2.4
North Carolina......................	2,292,483	4.5	1,702,301	84.5	11.7	1.4	1.4	0.9
North Dakota........................	174,130	7.8	119,697	95.6	2.7	0.9	0.3	0.4
Ohio	2,605,997	3.6	1,916,226	92.9	2.7	2.6	0.9	0.9
Oklahoma.............................	959,850	7.3	697,860	87.6	9.9	0.6	1.3	0.6
Oregon	866,585	3.3	633,664	79.9	14.7	2.2	2.4	0.7
Pennsylvania........................	2,666,701	4.4	1,965,102	87.4	6.4	3.7	1.7	0.8
Rhode Island........................	208,268	1.9	154,496	77.0	16.3	4.6	1.6	0.5
South Carolina	1,097,385	4.0	809,952	91.3	6.8	0.9	0.7	0.2
South Dakota	212,981	4.5	153,009	92.4	2.7	1.3	1.6	2.0
Tennessee	1,500,902	3.5	1,099,084	90.8	6.6	1.0	0.9	0.6
Texas...................................	7,282,033	9.2	5,284,783	64.3	31.4	1.4	2.1	0.7
Utah	918,971	5.8	668,425	84.9	11.8	1.1	1.5	0.7
Vermont...............................	118,351	1.6	88,220	94.7	0.9	2.7	0.8	0.9
Virginia................................	1,864,852	4.8	1,363,778	83.8	9.0	2.7	3.1	1.5
Washington..........................	1,627,304	2.5	1,179,117	77.5	13.1	3.5	4.1	1.7
West Virginia........................	375,790	2.1	275,215	97.8	1.2	0.5	0.3	0.2
Wisconsin	1,283,539	3.5	950,900	88.9	6.7	2.0	1.8	0.6
Wyoming	140,464	8.8	102,987	91.5	6.8	0.7	0.8	0.2

Table B-3. Selected Characteristics of Children and the School-Age Population, by Region and State, 2016—*Continued*

(Number; dollars; percent.)

Region or State	Total, children under 18 years old in households	White (percent)	Black (percent)	Hispanic or Latino (may be of any race) (percent)	Asian (percent)	Asian and Pacific Islander (percent)	American Indian, Alaska Native (percent)	Some other race (percent)	Two or more races (percent)
UNITED STATES	73,398,694	66.8	14.0	24.9	4.8	0.2	1.0	6.7	6.5
Northeast Region	11,754,234	66.5	13.3	19.9	6.3	-	0.3	7.5	6.1
Midwest Region	15,520,209	74.5	12.0	12.1	3.1	0.1	0.8	3.7	5.9
South Region	28,301,625	65.1	21.2	24.0	3.1	0.1	0.7	4.3	5.5
West Region........................	17,822,626	63.1	4.6	40.7	7.9	0.7	2.0	12.7	9.0
Alabama..............................	1,096,907	62.2	29.7	7.2	1.6	-	0.5	2.6	3.5
Alaska	186,569	53.7	2.8	9.2	5.4	1.9	18.2	1.4	16.5
Arizona...............................	1,627,645	68.2	4.9	43.8	2.7	0.2	5.8	10.9	7.3
Arkansas	703,794	69.7	17.7	12.0	1.2	0.5	0.7	4.8	5.3
California............................	9,069,929	55.2	5.4	52.0	11.3	0.4	0.8	18.0	8.9
Colorado.............................	1,256,943	79.1	4.8	31.1	3.1	0.2	0.9	5.3	6.6
Connecticut.........................	750,629	69.4	12.0	23.4	4.9	0.1	0.4	6.2	7.1
Delaware	203,603	60.8	26.6	15.5	3.4	0.4	0.4	2.1	6.2
District of Columbia.............	120,168	26.8	55.8	16.3	1.7	-	0.1	10.4	5.3
Florida................................	4,131,400	67.2	20.6	30.5	2.6	0.1	0.2	3.5	5.8
Georgia	2,504,491	52.3	34.2	14.2	3.5	0.1	0.4	4.3	5.2
Hawaii................................	306,816	18.1	1.4	18.0	25.5	13.2	0.2	0.9	40.7
Idaho..................................	435,166	85.8	1.0	18.1	1.3	0.2	1.8	5.7	4.2
Illinois................................	2,916,836	65.3	15.2	24.6	4.9	-	0.2	9.0	5.4
Indiana...............................	1,571,044	77.5	11.1	10.8	2.0	0.1	0.2	3.6	5.5
Iowa...................................	724,516	85.9	4.9	9.7	2.4	0.2	0.3	1.9	4.4
Kansas	712,523	79.8	6.0	18.1	2.3	0.1	0.7	3.5	7.5
Kentucky	1,008,572	82.5	9.4	6.0	1.5	0.1	0.2	1.3	5.0
Louisiana	1,114,733	55.1	36.9	6.4	1.4	-	0.6	1.9	4.1
Maine.................................	254,151	90.0	3.1	2.4	1.4	-	0.9	0.2	4.4
Maryland............................	1,343,111	50.1	31.5	14.5	5.6	-	0.2	5.2	7.4
Massachusetts.....................	1,371,574	71.5	9.3	17.7	6.7	-	0.2	5.8	6.5
Michigan............................	2,184,024	72.4	15.8	8.1	2.9	-	0.5	1.8	6.6
Minnesota	1,282,585	74.5	8.7	8.7	5.7	-	1.6	3.1	6.3
Mississippi..........................	720,367	51.6	43.1	4.5	0.9	-	0.6	1.5	2.3
Missouri.............................	1,384,053	76.8	13.2	6.5	1.8	0.2	0.6	2.0	5.3
Montana.............................	227,381	82.2	0.2	6.0	0.7	-	10.8	0.7	5.4
Nebraska............................	472,335	82.8	5.7	17.2	2.3	-	1.2	3.0	4.9
Nevada...............................	675,418	59.9	10.0	40.9	6.0	0.9	1.4	12.5	9.2
New Hampshire....................	258,845	90.3	1.5	5.9	2.9	-	0.1	0.8	4.3
New Jersey	1,978,978	62.7	13.9	26.3	9.4	0.1	0.3	8.1	5.5
New Mexico	487,224	69.8	2.0	60.3	1.3	-	11.3	10.4	5.2
New York............................	4,150,819	57.5	16.7	24.5	7.6	-	0.4	11.7	6.1
North Carolina.....................	2,289,203	61.8	23.1	15.7	2.9	-	1.3	4.9	6.0
North Dakota.......................	173,795	80.5	3.3	5.7	0.8	-	8.8	1.0	5.6
Ohio...................................	2,603,212	75.6	14.6	5.9	1.9	-	0.1	1.4	6.3
Oklahoma...........................	959,061	63.8	8.0	16.7	1.9	0.2	9.2	3.8	13.3
Oregon...............................	864,736	78.2	2.3	21.8	3.5	0.4	1.2	4.4	9.9
Pennsylvania.......................	2,663,213	73.9	13.2	11.6	3.4	-	0.2	3.2	6.1
Rhode Island.......................	207,806	71.8	8.0	24.7	3.8	0.1	0.4	8.8	7.1
South Carolina	1,096,303	60.7	29.9	9.1	1.5	0.1	0.4	2.3	5.3
South Dakota	212,617	75.6	2.2	6.3	2.0	-	13.9	1.0	5.3
Tennessee	1,499,076	71.9	19.0	9.3	1.8	0.1	0.3	2.2	4.7
Texas.................................	7,272,795	72.1	12.1	49.3	4.1	0.1	0.5	6.7	4.5
Utah	918,622	83.7	1.3	17.3	1.6	1.1	1.1	6.4	4.8
Vermont..............................	118,219	90.9	1.9	3.2	1.4	-	0.1	1.3	4.3
Virginia...............................	1,862,569	61.9	19.9	13.1	6.2	0.1	0.2	3.6	8.0
Washington.........................	1,626,051	67.9	4.2	20.9	6.8	0.8	1.7	7.2	11.4
West Virginia.......................	375,472	90.3	3.9	2.5	0.7	-	0.2	0.4	4.5
Wisconsin	1,282,669	77.8	8.4	11.6	3.3	-	1.1	3.5	6.0
Wyoming	140,126	88.0	1.1	13.9	1.6	-	3.2	1.1	5.0

- = Zero or rounds to zero.

Table B-4. Number and Percent of Students in City, Suburban, Town, and Rural Regular Public Elementary and Secondary Schools, by State, 2015–2016

(Number; percent.)

Region or State	Total number of operating schools[1]	Total number of students[2]	City Number of schools	City Percent of students	Suburban Number of schools	Suburban Percent of students	Town Number of schools	Town Percent of students	Rural Number of schools	Rural Percent of students
UNITED STATES	88,835	49,312,454	23,756	30.2	28,291	39.7	11,582	11.3	25,188	18.7
Alabama	1,315	740,713	289	23.7	232	21.9	195	14.6	599	39.7
Alaska	474	129,054	88	35.4	14	8.6	82	25.8	290	30.2
Arizona	1,910	1,090,144	895	48.6	476	31.3	243	10.3	296	9.8
Arkansas	1,052	491,390	227	28.6	120	14.2	233	23.6	472	33.6
California............................	8,788	6,044,665	3,592	42.7	3,592	45.8	632	5.7	972	5.8
Colorado	1,756	878,804	585	38.5	545	39.0	198	9.0	428	13.5
Connecticut........................	1,062	519,528	296	29.7	557	55.5	38	2.8	157	12.0
Delaware	196	124,161	36	13.3	99	52.8	31	16.7	30	17.3
District of Columbia	212	80,914	211	100.0	0	0.0	0	0.0	0	0.0
Florida................................	3,472	2,727,105	961	25.6	1,856	58.5	217	4.4	438	11.5
Georgia	2,237	1,753,296	406	15.8	847	46.4	270	10.5	714	27.3
Hawaii................................	288	181,870	68	23.9	107	45.2	72	21.8	41	9.1
Idaho..................................	635	286,447	114	23.3	119	27.8	143	23.9	258	24.8
Illinois................................	3,908	2,012,523	965	30.0	1,635	49.0	499	10.2	809	10.8
Indiana...............................	1,862	1,045,085	514	30.8	394	26.9	288	14.4	664	27.9
Iowa...................................	1,323	497,345	233	27.4	109	12.8	321	25.5	660	34.2
Kansas	1,311	488,382	249	28.3	148	17.4	321	26.3	593	28.1
Kentucky	1,221	676,793	159	16.0	224	22.1	307	25.5	531	36.5
Louisiana	1,337	714,923	367	29.5	324	29.0	231	14.2	415	27.3
Maine	581	176,396	48	12.7	66	16.6	77	17.1	390	53.6
Maryland............................	1,329	861,595	299	20.6	762	62.0	55	3.6	213	13.8
Massachusetts....................	1,793	914,148	328	17.7	1,226	72.0	39	1.4	200	8.8
Michigan	2,939	1,412,050	665	23.6	1,079	43.7	368	11.5	827	21.1
Minnesota...........................	1,666	832,485	329	21.4	426	36.2	325	20.6	586	21.7
Mississippi.........................	908	486,910	103	10.7	86	14.0	267	28.4	452	46.9
Missouri..............................	2,220	913,246	378	18.5	529	34.7	388	20.3	925	26.6
Montana..............................	817	145,240	64	25.2	11	2.0	138	36.7	604	36.1
Nebraska............................	1,001	316,014	211	38.8	85	14.8	190	21.0	515	25.4
Nevada	609	464,272	260	50.4	173	36.0	71	7.5	105	6.1
New Hampshire...................	488	181,307	49	14.8	133	36.9	71	14.1	235	34.2
New Jersey	2,374	1,337,561	232	10.4	1,884	79.7	63	2.1	195	7.8
New Mexico	834	330,429	219	34.4	83	13.6	227	27.3	305	24.7
New York	4,617	2,634,356	2,037	45.4	1,484	36.8	352	6.3	744	11.4
North Carolina....................	2,495	1,536,724	653	28.6	485	23.8	307	10.5	1,050	37.0
North Dakota.......................	471	106,372	61	27.7	24	11.6	64	21.5	322	39.2
Ohio...................................	3,479	1,708,484	751	19.1	1,288	45.3	506	13.3	934	22.3
Oklahoma...........................	1,791	692,546	279	23.7	219	22.2	388	23.6	905	30.5
Oregon...............................	1,207	562,870	326	34.7	254	27.0	291	23.8	336	14.5
Pennsylvania......................	2,921	1,692,726	569	20.8	1,344	51.3	286	9.0	722	18.8
Rhode Island......................	297	136,719	72	24.5	188	65.4	0	0.0	37	10.1
South Carolina	1,182	761,721	216	19.6	345	35.4	151	11.3	470	33.6
South Dakota	650	132,433	56	26.8	6	1.7	99	30.2	489	41.3
Tennessee	1,744	991,648	572	32.5	277	20.5	281	16.6	614	30.3
Texas	7,851	5,224,531	2,923	41.5	1,988	32.3	1,004	9.8	1,935	16.4
Utah	928	636,734	149	16.0	495	62.9	118	10.8	166	10.3
Vermont..............................	298	84,355	14	7.8	17	9.4	52	27.1	215	55.7
Virginia	1,846	1,281,866	429	23.0	676	45.4	161	7.0	580	24.5
Washington.........................	1,961	1,040,890	572	32.8	683	42.7	266	12.5	440	12.1
West Virginia......................	677	276,449	81	15.4	126	20.6	123	21.6	347	42.4
Wisconsin	2,145	861,518	504	29.2	445	28.1	419	19.7	777	23.0
Wyoming	358	94,717	52	25.0	6	2.0	114	44.1	186	28.9

[1]The total number of schools is limited to regular, operational schools with membership and excludes schools also reported by the Bureau of Indian Education (BIE). The number of operating schools shared with the BIE include one in Arizona, one in Michigan, and eight in North Dakota.
[2]Total number of students is the count of students enrolled on October 1 of the reported school year.

Table B-5. Population 3 Years and Over Enrolled in Public or Private School, by Selected Grade Levels and Region or State, 2016

(Number; percent.)

Region or State	Total enrolled population	Percent in public school	Percent in private school	Nursery school		
				Total enrolled	Percent in public school	Percent in private school
UNITED STATES	81,572,277	83.9	16.1	4,905,286	59.4	40.6
Northeast Region	13,721,454	76.9	23.1	874,189	53.9	46.1
Midwest Region	17,102,445	83.6	16.4	1,063,805	62.9	37.1
South Region	30,827,902	85.4	14.6	1,823,208	61.0	39.0
West Region	19,920,476	86.7	13.3	1,144,084	57.8	42.2
Alabama	1,186,076	85.2	14.8	64,446	57.0	43.0
Alaska	187,359	88.9	11.1	10,070	69.0	31.0
Arizona	1,761,534	88.8	11.2	85,986	62.8	37.2
Arkansas	739,490	88.2	11.8	47,061	71.6	28.4
California	10,490,279	86.5	13.5	604,873	59.4	40.6
Colorado	1,382,107	88.1	11.9	81,262	63.0	37.0
Connecticut	914,755	79.2	20.8	57,620	51.0	49.0
Delaware	227,224	84.2	15.8	14,297	62.5	37.5
District of Columbia	168,430	59.7	40.3	14,755	83.3	16.7
Florida	4,718,808	82.5	17.5	284,728	57.9	42.1
Georgia	2,747,236	85.4	14.6	168,465	64.2	35.8
Hawaii	331,540	78.2	21.8	23,628	35.4	64.6
Idaho	454,191	86.3	13.7	22,817	52.7	47.3
Illinois	3,286,606	81.7	18.3	224,254	60.8	39.2
Indiana	1,684,219	83.5	16.5	102,982	55.2	44.8
Iowa	804,741	84.9	15.1	55,658	70.6	29.4
Kansas	774,902	86.4	13.6	50,128	63.7	36.3
Kentucky	1,085,033	84.5	15.5	62,109	63.1	36.9
Louisiana	1,172,916	80.4	19.6	76,515	59.2	40.8
Maine	293,857	81.2	18.8	18,084	62.3	37.7
Maryland	1,540,625	81.9	18.1	93,322	52.5	47.5
Massachusetts	1,737,713	73.2	26.8	109,538	50.9	49.1
Michigan	2,488,397	87.4	12.6	144,413	71.5	28.5
Minnesota	1,392,956	84.4	15.6	93,562	62.9	37.1
Mississippi	781,666	86.9	13.1	45,452	69.6	30.4
Missouri	1,507,305	81.5	18.5	95,054	60.9	39.1
Montana	242,914	85.9	14.1	14,701	49.2	50.8
Nebraska	505,491	83.7	16.3	32,402	60.9	39.1
Nevada	700,680	89.3	10.7	36,133	67.5	32.5
New Hampshire	307,848	77.4	22.6	16,398	40.1	59.9
New Jersey	2,239,783	81.3	18.7	168,540	56.4	43.6
New Mexico	539,773	90.6	9.4	27,412	73.7	26.3
New York	4,843,659	76.3	23.7	293,971	57.3	42.7
North Carolina	2,523,926	85.6	14.4	133,211	54.1	45.9
North Dakota	181,543	87.7	12.3	10,253	68.8	31.2
Ohio	2,830,005	82.0	18.0	164,686	57.8	42.2
Oklahoma	1,004,589	89.5	10.5	64,323	79.8	20.2
Oregon	960,446	85.2	14.8	59,080	46.3	53.7
Pennsylvania	2,975,685	75.7	24.3	184,819	48.7	51.3
Rhode Island	264,768	72.5	27.5	15,314	52.6	47.4
South Carolina	1,209,286	85.7	14.3	63,614	55.8	44.2
South Dakota	218,239	87.2	12.8	14,308	65.4	34.6
Tennessee	1,578,309	83.0	17.0	90,286	60.1	39.9
Texas	7,603,170	89.1	10.9	455,348	66.2	33.8
Utah	973,643	86.2	13.8	59,491	55.6	44.4
Vermont	143,386	79.4	20.6	9,905	64.0	36.0
Virginia	2,146,237	82.9	17.1	125,494	41.0	59.0
Washington	1,744,806	85.2	14.8	110,123	46.8	53.2
West Virginia	394,881	90.0	10.0	19,782	78.3	21.7
Wisconsin	1,428,041	83.0	17.0	76,105	69.5	30.5
Wyoming	151,204	92.7	7.3	8,508	65.5	34.5

Table B-5. Population 3 Years and Over Enrolled in Public or Private School, by Selected Grade Levels and Region or State, 2016—*Continued*

(Number; percent.)

Region or State	Kindergarten			Elementary: grades 1-4		
	Total enrolled	Percent in public school	Percent in private school	Total enrolled	Percent in public school	Percent in private school
UNITED STATES	4,104,332	87.4	12.6	16,378,344	89.8	10.2
Northeast Region	656,733	84.5	15.5	2,591,956	87.5	12.5
Midwest Region	867,387	86.4	13.6	3,446,168	88.3	11.7
South Region	1,572,276	87.9	12.1	6,418,387	90.3	9.7
West Region	1,007,936	89.5	10.5	3,921,833	92.0	8.0
Alabama	63,979	83.8	16.2	249,965	88.3	11.7
Alaska	8,488	88.9	11.1	43,544	90.9	9.1
Arizona	90,003	90.4	9.6	369,162	93.1	6.9
Arkansas	43,117	90.6	9.4	157,750	90.8	9.2
California	534,972	90.6	9.4	1,927,600	92.1	7.9
Colorado	69,262	89.3	10.7	295,597	92.7	7.3
Connecticut	41,218	88.7	11.3	161,664	90.8	9.2
Delaware	12,111	85.0	15.0	42,859	86.8	13.2
District of Columbia	7,772	92.2	7.8	27,189	89.5	10.5
Florida	230,962	85.1	14.9	911,583	87.9	12.1
Georgia	139,268	86.9	13.1	566,516	91.0	9.0
Hawaii	16,245	82.2	17.8	61,052	89.7	10.3
Idaho	22,497	89.7	10.3	99,699	92.2	7.8
Illinois	160,333	85.1	14.9	648,117	89.6	10.4
Indiana	88,555	88.1	11.9	362,719	87.2	12.8
Iowa	41,695	88.5	11.5	160,955	90.4	9.6
Kansas	39,302	89.5	10.5	158,123	89.5	10.5
Kentucky	52,439	90.1	9.9	231,627	88.0	12.0
Louisiana	58,564	79.2	20.8	256,040	82.9	17.1
Maine	15,570	86.3	13.7	56,638	89.1	10.9
Maryland	70,421	85.8	14.2	301,667	88.7	11.3
Massachusetts	77,663	87.5	12.5	295,869	90.9	9.1
Michigan	121,028	88.6	11.4	476,222	89.8	10.2
Minnesota	71,027	87.6	12.4	286,128	89.6	10.4
Mississippi	43,885	86.9	13.1	171,783	88.5	11.5
Missouri	76,558	86.2	13.8	305,719	87.1	12.9
Montana	13,292	78.6	21.4	51,896	87.0	13.0
Nebraska	26,306	89.2	10.8	104,683	88.8	11.2
Nevada	35,613	89.1	10.9	148,060	92.3	7.7
New Hampshire	14,661	81.0	19.0	57,839	90.3	9.7
New Jersey	113,491	85.3	14.7	435,400	89.3	10.7
New Mexico	26,019	88.9	11.1	112,499	93.1	6.9
New York	238,285	82.8	17.2	931,590	86.1	13.9
North Carolina	119,125	89.2	10.8	528,880	90.3	9.7
North Dakota	9,812	94.3	5.7	37,799	88.3	11.7
Ohio	138,527	82.8	17.2	571,657	86.8	13.2
Oklahoma	55,363	92.8	7.2	224,052	92.9	7.1
Oregon	47,645	86.5	13.5	190,990	91.1	8.9
Pennsylvania	139,772	83.6	16.4	583,635	85.1	14.9
Rhode Island	9,289	81.9	18.1	42,496	89.9	10.1
South Carolina	70,763	85.5	14.5	251,036	91.3	8.7
South Dakota	12,853	88.6	11.4	47,408	89.5	10.5
Tennessee	80,594	88.1	11.9	322,272	89.1	10.9
Texas	398,036	91.1	8.9	1,669,632	93.3	6.7
Utah	54,478	91.2	8.8	212,139	93.9	6.1
Vermont	6,784	90.2	9.8	26,825	91.4	8.6
Virginia	104,673	87.0	13.0	422,751	89.6	10.4
Washington	81,422	85.8	14.2	374,121	89.6	10.4
West Virginia	21,204	92.2	7.8	82,785	93.0	7.0
Wisconsin	81,391	84.0	16.0	286,638	84.8	15.2
Wyoming	8,000	94.0	6.0	35,474	95.9	4.1

Table B-5. Population 3 Years and Over Enrolled in Public or Private School, by Selected Grade Levels and Region or State, 2016—*Continued*

(Number; percent.)

Region or State	Elementary: grades 5-8			High school: grades 9-12		
	Total enrolled	Percent in public school	Percent in private school	Total enrolled	Percent in public school	Percent in private school
UNITED STATES	16,469,946	89.6	10.4	17,108,087	90.3	9.7
Northeast Region	2,653,266	87.4	12.6	2,847,146	87.4	12.6
Midwest Region	3,480,037	88.3	11.7	3,622,410	90.1	9.9
South Region	6,363,557	89.6	10.4	6,506,004	90.3	9.7
West Region......................................	3,973,086	92.0	8.0	4,132,527	92.5	7.5
Alabama	240,980	87.9	12.1	256,949	88.7	11.3
Alaska	40,244	91.3	8.7	41,622	93.0	7.0
Arizona	364,468	92.7	7.3	380,417	92.8	7.2
Arkansas	153,826	92.0	8.0	160,153	92.0	8.0
California..	2,039,430	92.2	7.8	2,155,646	92.4	7.6
Colorado	279,243	92.8	7.2	281,381	93.7	6.3
Connecticut......................................	182,290	91.4	8.6	195,934	88.6	11.4
Delaware	47,488	88.5	11.5	47,757	88.9	11.1
District of Columbia	20,535	90.1	9.9	24,084	86.1	13.9
Florida..	931,475	87.0	13.0	992,412	88.7	11.3
Georgia	581,202	90.0	10.0	589,201	89.5	10.5
Hawaii	67,704	81.7	18.3	63,001	78.8	21.2
Idaho..	97,904	91.6	8.4	98,421	92.8	7.2
Illinois..	663,810	89.8	10.2	695,062	90.7	9.3
Indiana...	344,888	86.7	13.3	362,276	89.6	10.4
Iowa...	161,330	90.5	9.5	160,787	93.1	6.9
Kansas	160,069	89.2	10.8	158,802	90.5	9.5
Kentucky	228,054	86.8	13.2	234,080	87.8	12.2
Louisiana	252,347	82.4	17.6	252,067	82.9	17.1
Maine	55,118	92.2	7.8	63,819	87.8	12.2
Maryland...	298,780	85.8	14.2	308,860	86.2	13.8
Massachusetts..................................	320,077	89.8	10.2	349,101	89.3	10.7
Michigan...	496,766	90.0	10.0	534,098	90.8	9.2
Minnesota...	287,011	90.0	10.0	292,795	92.0	8.0
Mississippi..	162,536	87.1	12.9	166,355	89.2	10.8
Missouri..	311,460	87.1	12.9	323,125	87.8	12.2
Montana..	50,744	89.4	10.6	50,892	92.1	7.9
Nebraska...	104,418	89.2	10.8	102,098	89.1	10.9
Nevada..	153,517	94.2	5.8	158,488	93.7	6.3
New Hampshire..................................	60,543	90.7	9.3	65,094	88.6	11.4
New Jersey	450,278	89.7	10.3	475,089	88.9	11.1
New Mexico	110,125	93.4	6.6	113,805	94.1	5.9
New York	907,433	85.9	14.1	988,375	86.1	13.9
North Carolina...................................	510,991	89.6	10.4	545,590	91.5	8.5
North Dakota.....................................	35,713	88.0	12.0	31,717	93.5	6.5
Ohio...	582,402	86.4	13.6	616,194	88.1	11.9
Oklahoma..	211,273	91.9	8.1	206,405	92.5	7.5
Oregon..	192,242	90.4	9.6	196,608	91.2	8.8
Pennsylvania.....................................	601,353	84.8	15.2	629,804	86.7	13.3
Rhode Island.....................................	49,391	86.3	13.7	52,569	86.6	13.4
South Carolina	251,159	90.1	9.9	253,167	91.5	8.5
South Dakota	44,347	90.9	9.1	45,515	90.7	9.3
Tennessee...	342,310	88.2	11.8	346,212	87.2	12.8
Texas..	1,628,509	93.4	6.6	1,603,737	93.6	6.4
Utah...	197,278	93.8	6.2	200,629	95.0	5.0
Vermont..	26,783	90.4	9.6	27,361	89.3	10.7
Virginia...	417,362	89.0	11.0	436,168	91.0	9.0
Washington.......................................	349,397	90.2	9.8	362,881	92.5	7.5
West Virginia.....................................	84,730	93.3	6.7	82,807	92.8	7.2
Wisconsin	287,823	84.4	15.6	299,941	90.7	9.3
Wyoming	30,790	93.8	6.2	28,736	95.9	4.1

Table B-5. Population 3 Years and Over Enrolled in Public or Private School, by Selected Grade Levels and Region or State, 2016—*Continued*

(Number; percent.)

Region or State	College, undergraduate			Graduate, professional school		
	Total enrolled	Percent in public school	Percent in private school	Total enrolled	Percent in public school	Percent in private school
UNITED STATES	18,436,671	78.9	21.1	4,169,611	59.7	40.3
Northeast Region	3,238,772	64.3	35.7	859,392	42.4	57.6
Midwest Region	3,764,740	78.7	21.3	857,898	63.3	36.7
South Region	6,665,938	82.1	17.9	1,478,532	65.9	34.1
West Region	4,767,221	84.4	15.6	973,789	62.1	37.9
Alabama	260,766	85.7	14.3	48,991	74.3	25.7
Alaska	34,811	88.4	11.6	8,580	73.2	26.8
Arizona	390,943	87.5	12.5	80,555	63.9	36.1
Arkansas	149,413	84.0	16.0	28,170	78.4	21.6
California	2,702,025	84.5	15.5	525,733	56.7	43.3
Colorado	298,676	86.0	14.0	76,686	66.7	33.3
Connecticut	222,904	66.6	33.4	53,125	43.0	57.0
Delaware	50,404	84.4	15.6	12,308	63.1	36.9
District of Columbia	45,431	24.0	76.0	28,664	23.2	76.8
Florida	1,125,217	79.9	20.1	242,431	58.8	41.2
Georgia	576,421	81.7	18.3	126,163	64.3	35.7
Hawaii	80,763	80.4	19.6	19,147	68.3	31.7
Idaho	94,518	77.4	22.6	18,335	73.7	26.3
Illinois	695,704	73.1	26.9	199,326	48.5	51.5
Indiana	352,881	79.5	20.5	69,918	72.4	27.6
Iowa	185,622	76.2	23.8	38,694	62.4	37.6
Kansas	167,829	85.0	15.0	40,649	77.5	22.5
Kentucky	228,750	82.1	17.9	47,974	73.6	26.4
Louisiana	231,882	82.7	17.3	45,501	66.0	34.0
Maine	70,476	68.6	31.4	14,152	59.1	40.9
Maryland	356,897	82.6	17.4	110,678	61.9	38.1
Massachusetts	445,969	53.2	46.8	139,496	30.8	69.2
Michigan	594,533	86.2	13.8	121,337	75.9	24.1
Minnesota	299,600	77.8	22.2	62,833	59.1	40.9
Mississippi	162,789	90.2	9.8	28,866	71.1	28.9
Missouri	318,559	75.4	24.6	76,830	55.8	44.2
Montana	52,220	88.1	11.9	9,169	83.4	16.6
Nebraska	109,537	78.1	21.9	26,047	65.8	34.2
Nevada	139,241	86.3	13.7	29,628	67.5	32.5
New Hampshire	74,126	62.4	37.6	19,187	45.7	54.3
New Jersey	472,162	74.1	25.9	124,823	50.9	49.1
New Mexico	122,469	88.9	11.1	27,444	80.6	19.4
New York	1,175,025	65.7	34.3	308,980	40.5	59.5
North Carolina	560,939	82.5	17.5	125,190	67.1	32.9
North Dakota	46,544	87.2	12.8	9,705	80.6	19.4
Ohio	614,826	76.5	23.5	141,713	69.6	30.4
Oklahoma	204,557	85.0	15.0	38,616	75.5	24.5
Oregon	227,042	85.2	14.8	46,839	62.7	37.3
Pennsylvania	659,388	62.4	37.6	176,914	46.7	53.3
Rhode Island	79,802	54.8	45.2	15,907	39.1	60.9
South Carolina	267,422	80.8	19.2	52,125	71.8	28.2
South Dakota	45,375	84.9	15.1	8,433	82.7	17.3
Tennessee	323,679	77.9	22.1	72,956	58.1	41.9
Texas	1,525,151	84.9	15.1	322,757	73.2	26.8
Utah	211,447	73.1	26.9	38,181	70.4	29.6
Vermont	38,920	62.1	37.9	6,808	59.8	40.2
Virginia	509,829	80.1	19.9	129,960	61.9	38.1
Washington	380,910	83.6	16.4	85,952	69.6	30.4
West Virginia	86,391	84.7	15.3	17,182	82.5	17.5
Wisconsin	333,730	80.5	19.5	62,413	59.5	40.5
Wyoming	32,156	95.1	4.9	7,540	79.6	20.4

Table B-6. School Districts and Public Schools, by School Type, Title I Eligibility, and State, 2015–2016

(Number; percent.)

Region or state	Number of school districts	Type of school					Charter schools	Magnet schools	Title I status	
		Total schools	Regular schools	Special education schools	Vocational schools	Alternative schools			Title I eligible schools	Title I schoolwide schools
UNITED STATES	18,328	98,456	89,644	2,011	1,419	5,382	6,857	3,237	68,614	53,669
Alabama	180	1,509	1,326	34	68	81	0	40	‡	‡
Alaska	54	508	478	3	3	24	28	32	358	337
Arizona	692	2,284	1,963	20	242	59	552	0	1,724	1,306
Arkansas	289	1,088	1,052	4	26	6	65	30	988	924
California	1,163	10,303	8,936	151	74	1,142	1224	504	7,339	5,640
Colorado	265	1,862	1,756	6	6	94	226	28	690	539
Connecticut	205	1,369	1,062	168	17	122	24	85	608	270
Delaware	50	223	198	13	6	6	28	3	151	151
District of Columbia	64	228	216	3	0	9	115	6	186	181
Florida	76	4,322	3,716	174	53	379	653	536	3,109	2,950
Georgia	223	2,297	2,237	19	0	41	82	80	1,630	1,548
Hawaii	1	290	288	1	0	1	34	*	192	192
Idaho	159	744	635	18	14	77	54	19	576	504
Illinois	1052	4175	3929	108	0	138	64	105	3312	2095
Indiana	418	1,921	1,863	22	28	8	88	30	1,510	1,219
Iowa	345	1,349	1,324	3	0	22	3	0	923	512
Kansas	317	1,320	1,315	4	0	1	10	32	1137	873
Kentucky	186	1,541	1,230	8	121	182	*	66	1,119	1084
Louisiana	179	1,390	1,341	32	12	5	138	36	1,239	1,212
Maine	267	611	582	2	27	0	7	1	527	392
Maryland	25	1437	1329	37	27	44	50	97	800	704
Massachusetts	408	1862	1796	7	38	21	81	‡	1061	596
Michigan	902	3,468	2,962	187	4	315	370	386	2302	1523
Minnesota	564	2,478	1,686	292	9	491	216	80	965	454
Mississippi	157	1,076	915	2	91	68	2	17	738	736
Missouri	567	2,424	2,247	53	63	61	70	29	1887	1569
Montana	490	823	817	2	0	4	*	0	720	436
Nebraska	284	1,085	1,009	25	0	51	*	*	454	345
Nevada	19	662	610	14	0	38	47	44	349	347
New Hampshire..............................	299	490	490	0	0	0	31	1	434	164
New Jersey	694	2588	2384	64	56	84	89	0	1764	553
New Mexico	158	884	846	6	0	32	99	*	788	767
New York	989	4824	4618	131	21	54	256	‡	3578	2937
North Carolina...............................	297	2,603	2,498	24	7	74	158	123	2,112	1987
North Dakota	222	518	474	31	13	0	*	*	259	109
Ohio	1103	3,619	3,495	51	73	0	373	NA	2,887	2,267
Oklahoma......................................	605	1,800	1,791	4	0	5	45	*	1,602	1,112
Oregon	221	1242	1209	1	0	32	126	*	572	486
Pennsylvania	784	3,019	2,925	4	84	6	175	50	2,417	1,707
Rhode Island	64	313	297	1	10	5	29	*	241	154
South Carolina	102	1,248	1,185	9	42	12	68	111	587	587
South Dakota	168	698	651	12	3	32	0	*	588	329
Tennessee	146	1859	1806	16	15	22	100	126	1575	1516
Texas	1232	8826	7872	14	0	940	702	258	7080	6770
Utah	152	1,033	935	64	6	28	117	22	321	250
Vermont...	357	314	298	0	15	1	*	2	226	200
Virginia..	222	2,133	1,864	53	89	127	7	140	737	584
Washington....................................	330	2,427	1,998	96	20	313	9	NA	1,535	1,283
West Virginia.................................	57	744	682	3	30	29	*	0	350	348
Wisconsin	465	2255	2147	12	6	90	242	8	2205	833
Wyoming	60	370	361	3	0	6	0	0	162	87

* Not applicable. Some states/jurisdictions do not have charter school authorization and some states/jurisdictions do not designate magnet schools.
‡ Reporting standards not met. Data missing for more than 80 percent of schools in the state or jurisdiction.

Table B-7. Participation in Public School Services, by State, Selected Years

(Number; percent.)

State	Enrollment in public elementary and secondary schools (Fall 2015)	Percent of students eligible for free or reduced-price lunch (2014-2015)	Percent of students with IEP (2015-2016)	Number of English language learner students (Fall 2015)	Percent English language learner students (Fall 2015)	Percent homeless students (2014-2015)
UNITED STATES	50,438,043	51.8	13.2	4,794,994	9.5	2.5
Alabama...	743,789	51.8	11.3	20,228	2.7	2.6
Alaska...	132,477	43.1	13.9	15,203	11.5	3.1
Arizona..	1,109,040	43.0	12.0	67,195	6.1	2.6
Arkansas..	492,132	62.3	13.9	38,376	7.8	2.2
California..	6,305,347	58.7	11.5	1,307,804	21.0	3.7
Colorado..	899,112	41.6	10.6	104,289	11.6	2.7
Connecticut....................................	537,933	37.7	13.9	35,064	6.5	0.6
Delaware..	134,847	37.1	15.4	9,704	7.2	2.3
District of Columbia	84,024	92.4	14.6	6,215	7.4	4.4
Florida...	2,792,234	58.4	13.3	268,189	9.6	2.7
Georgia..	1,757,237	62.4	11.5	112,006	6.4	2.2
Hawaii...	181,995	50.1	10.6	13,619	7.5	1.9
Idaho...	292,277	48.5	10.2	13,492	4.6	2.5
Illinois..	2,041,779	54.1	14.5	194,040	9.5	2.6
Indiana..	1,046,757	49.2	16.4	50,717	4.8	1.8
Iowa..	508,014	40.7	12.6	27,300	5.4	1.4
Kansas...	495,884	49.9	14.3	52,789	10.6	2.0
Kentucky	686,598	56.9	14.5	22,067	3.2	4.0
Louisiana	718,711	63.6	11.7	23,924	3.3	2.8
Maine..	181,613	47.1	17.9	5,091	2.8	1.1
Maryland..	879,601	45.0	12.0	63,349	7.2	1.8
Massachusetts................................	964,026	39.9	17.4	82,779	8.6	2.0
Michigan..	1,536,231	46.6	12.8	89,597	5.8	2.7
Minnesota......................................	864,384	38.3	14.8	71,162	8.2	1.8
Mississippi.....................................	487,200	73.7	13.7	9,588	2.0	2.1
Missouri...	919,234	51.3	13.7	29,690	3.2	3.3
Montana...	145,319	43.6	12.0	3,202	2.2	2.1
Nebraska..	316,014	44.3	15.1	20,900	6.6	1.1
Nevada..	467,527	52.3	11.9	78,416	16.8	3.7
New Hampshire...............................	182,425	29.0	15.8	4,116	2.3	1.8
New Jersey	1,408,845	36.8	16.5	68,725	4.9	0.7
New Mexico	335,694	62.6	14.8	52,821	15.7	3.0
New York..	2,711,626	50.9	18.4	216,378	8.0	4.3
North Carolina................................	1,544,934	57.2	12.9	102,090	6.6	1.7
North Dakota..................................	108,644	29.2	12.8	3,171	3.0	2.5
Ohio..	1,716,585	45.1	14.8	51,441	3.0	1.6
Oklahoma.......................................	692,878	60.9	15.7	46,831	6.8	3.9
Oregon...	608,825	52.9	13.9	52,786	9.2	3.8
Pennsylvania...................................	1,717,414	45.6	17.7	52,624	3.1	1.3
Rhode Island...................................	142,014	46.8	16.6	10,550	7.4	0.7
South Carolina	763,533	55.9	13.3	42,574	5.6	1.8
South Dakota	134,253	39.5	14.5	4,598	3.4	1.6
Tennessee......................................	1,001,235	55.9	12.9	40,637	4.1	1.3
Texas..	5,301,477	58.8	8.7	892,082	16.8	2.2
Utah..	647,870	36.9	12.3	42,815	6.6	2.4
Vermont...	87,866	39.1	15.8	1,448	1.6	1.3
Virginia..	1,283,590	40.2	12.8	109,104	8.5	1.4
Washington.....................................	1,087,030	46.0	12.5	112,763	10.4	3.3
West Virginia..................................	277,452	46.1	16.3	2,812	1.0	3.2
Wisconsin	867,800	41.5	13.9	45,669	5.3	2.1
Wyoming	94,717	37.6	16.5	2,964	3.1	1.7

Table B-8. Number of Private Schools, Students, Teachers, High School Graduates, and Percent Change in Enrollment, by State, Fall 2015

State	Private schools				
	Number of private schools, Fall 2015	Total teachers, Fall 2015	High school graduates, 2014–2015	Enrollment in Pre-K to 12th grade, Fall 2015	Enrollment percent change, Fall 2005 to Fall 2015
UNITED STATES	34,580	481,560	343,250	5,750,520	-5.3
Alabama	350	5,870	4,710	75,070	-18.6
Alaska	50	480	220	5,540	-26.1
Arizona	320	4,110	3,030	56,610	-15.3
Arkansas	330	3,670	1,800	37,930	7.2
California	3,420	49,520	36,930	627,170	-15.0
Colorado	600	5,680	2,790	68,140	-3.7
Connecticut	420	7,770	7,140	66,710	-12.5
Delaware	100	1,650	1,180	19,660	-34.1
District of Columbia	90	2,050	1,500	17,110	-13.9
Florida	2,200	30,520	22,770	389,310	-1.9
Georgia	1,220	19,930	11,630	189,630	24.3
Hawaii	140	3,730	3,510	45,600	39.0
Idaho	260	1,420	640	20,230	32.0
Illinois	1,500	19,600	16800	280,440	-11.8
Indiana	1,660	11,940	7,130	171,570	23.1
Iowa	510	5,120	2,580	70,870	16.3
Kansas	210	3,210	2,550	42,270	-10.3
Kentucky	330	5,670	4,520	70,090	-11.1
Louisiana	580	12,640	11,420	166,560	20.5
Maine	140	2,020	2,700	18,600	-10.1
Maryland	760	13,810	9,130	142,630	-16.3
Massachusetts	760	14,440	9,270	123,230	-21.9
Michigan	890	13,550	10,960	172,130	3.1
Minnesota	470	5,860	4,430	75,630	-27.8
Mississippi	180	3,530	2,700	43,580	-24.8
Missouri	870	10,340	8,540	125,290	-9.1
Montana	120	980	400	11,690	NA
Nebraska	350	3,120	2,460	48,960	15.4
Nevada	150	1,540	1240	23,910	-17.9
New Hampshire	260	2,670	2,430	25,330	-23.8
New Jersey	1,270	19,170	14320	213,170	-16.8
New Mexico	170	2,010	1,440	22,230	-11.2
New York	1,940	46,140	35,600	520,660	1.9
North Carolina	650	11,830	7,490	124,030	5.8
North Dakota	50	630	370	7,830	7.4
Ohio	1,360	18,380	12,920	255,690	0.5
Oklahoma	180	2,740	1,570	32,160	-9.0
Oregon	410	4,210	3470	57,310	-17.7
Pennsylvania	2,740	26,350	19,640	315,830	-5.1
Rhode Island	130	1,900	1,460	20,620	-32.6
South Carolina	370	5,310	3,130	62,830	-10.5
South Dakota	70	830	380	10,740	-15.4
Tennessee	500	8,730	6,040	91,950	-12.6
Texas	2,400	30,430	16,540	351,270	15.5
Utah	160	1,800	1,490	21,140	-0.4
Vermont	110	1,280	1080	10,040	-12.9
Virginia	950	12,850	7,150	140,350	-9.6
Washington	640	7,680	5,650	100,140	-16.3
West Virginia	130	1,330	850	14,780	-8.3
Wisconsin	1,050	11,310	5,540	144,020	1.2
Wyoming	40	220	30	2,240	-3.0

Note: Includes special education, vocational/technical education, and alternative schools. Tabulation includes schools that offer kindergarten or higher grade. Includes enrollment of students in prekindergarten through grade 12 in schools that offer kindergarten or higher grade. Details may not sum to totals because of rounding.
NA = Not available.

Table B-9. Staff Employed by Public Elementary and Secondary School Systems, Fall 2014

State	Total staff	Pupil/ Teacher Ratio	Principals and assistant principals		School and library support staff		Teachers		Instructional aides		Guidance counselors	
			Number	Percent	Number	Percent	Number	Percent	Number	Percent	Number	Percent
UNITED STATES............	6,258,543	16.1	174,664	2.8	280,908	4.5	3,132,351	50.0	749,143	12.0	104,306	1.7
Alabama............................	87,454	17.4	3,837	4.4	2,873	3.3	42,737	48.9	6,200	7.1	1,643	1.9
Alaska	17,088	16.9	645	3.8	1,137	6.7	7,759	45.4	2,477	14.5	297	1.7
Arizona.............................	102,383	23.1	2,492	2.4	3,672	3.6	48,124	47.0	14,690	14.3	1,204	1.2
Arkansas...........................	74,107	13.9	1,789	2.4	3,018	4.1	35,430	47.8	8,830	11.9	1,317	1.8
California..........................	571,389	23.6	17,791	3.1	36,462	6.4	267,685	46.8	73,220	12.8	8,303	1.5
Colorado	108,671	17.3	3,160	2.9	5,496	5.1	51,388	47.3	16,719	15.4	2,320	2.1
Connecticut......................	94,058	12.9	2,216	2.4	3,543	3.8	42,062	44.7	15,525	16.5	1,164	1.2
Delaware	18,553	13.9	458	2.5	397	2.1	9,649	52.0	2,007	10.8	312	1.7
District of Columbia	13,617	12.3	755	5.5	689	5.1	6,565	48.2	1,758	12.9	225	1.6
Florida..............................	341,440	15.3	8,582	2.5	16,739	4.9	180,442	52.8	31,227	9.1	5,690	1.7
Georgia	221,926	15.6	6,262	2.8	9,951	4.5	111,470	50.2	23,911	10.8	3,604	1.6
Hawaii...............................	22,424	15.6	662	3.0	1,013	4.5	11,663	52.0	2,457	11.0	623	2.8
Idaho................................	27,451	18.6	678	2.5	1,218	4.4	15,609	56.9	3,052	11.1	477	1.7
Illinois..............................	261,922	15.5	8,226	3.1	10,681	4.1	132,456	50.6	25,929	9.9	3,089	1.2
Indiana.............................	139,587	18.5	3,246	2.3	8,018	5.7	56,547	40.5	16,737	12.0	1,925	1.4
Iowa.................................	72,129	14.2	1,758	2.4	2,756	3.8	35,684	49.5	11,754	16.3	1,209	1.7
Kansas..............................	71,175	13.2	1,899	2.7	2,642	3.7	37,659	52.9	9,139	12.8	1,051	1.5
Kentucky	97,269	16.6	3,424	3.5	5,746	5.9	41,586	42.8	12,961	13.3	1,521	1.6
Louisiana	85,371	15.5	3,009	3.5	3,351	3.9	46,340	54.3	10,958	12.8	1,532	1.8
Maine................................	32,225	12.2	905	2.8	1,502	4.7	14,937	46.4	5,764	17.9	579	1.8
Maryland...........................	117,238	14.8	3,578	3.1	6,415	5.5	59,194	50.5	11,017	9.4	2,369	2.0
Massachusetts...................	128,723	13.3	4,713	3.7	6,774	5.3	71,859	55.8	25,455	19.8	2,258	1.8
Michigan...........................	183,722	18.1	6,632	3.6	11,450	6.2	85,038	46.3	20,578	11.2	2,109	1.1
Minnesota.........................	115,999	15.4	2,322	2.0	4,632	4.0	55,690	48.0	18,462	15.9	1,186	1.0
Mississippi........................	68,000	15.2	1,994	2.9	2,500	3.7	32,311	47.5	8,225	12.1	1,120	1.6
Missouri............................	127,062	13.6	3,229	2.5	336	0.3	67,356	53.0	13,401	10.5	2,641	2.1
Montana............................	20,456	14.1	508	2.5	814	4.0	10,234	50.0	2,454	12.0	453	2.2
Nebraska...........................	46,931	13.6	1,073	2.3	1,930	4.1	22,988	49.0	6,771	14.4	807	1.7
Nevada	33,749	21.2	1,108	3.3	1,629	4.8	21,656	64.2	4,259	12.6	889	2.6
New Hampshire..................	31,851	12.5	513	1.6	761	2.4	14,773	46.4	7,007	22.0	812	2.5
New Jersey	235,231	12.2	5,075	2.2	10,819	4.6	115,067	48.9	36,595	15.6	3,781	1.6
New Mexico	46,921	15.2	1,366	2.9	4,123	8.8	22,411	47.8	6,160	13.1	755	1.6
New York..........................	356,055	13.5	5,130	1.4	7,017	2.0	203,781	57.2	43,136	12.1	4,314	1.2
North Carolina...................	191,323	15.6	5,700	3.0	7,288	3.8	99,320	51.9	22,601	11.8	4,098	2.1
North Dakota.....................	17,599	11.8	464	2.6	742	4.2	9,049	51.4	2,431	13.8	347	2.0
Ohio.................................	250,106	16.2	5,453	2.2	12,649	5.1	106,526	42.6	19,667	7.9	3,810	1.5
Oklahoma..........................	85,835	16.4	2,367	2.8	4,516	5.3	42,073	49.0	9,732	11.3	1,614	1.9
Oregon.............................	62,956	21.6	1,609	2.6	4,615	7.3	27,850	44.2	9,654	15.3	1,054	1.7
Pennsylvania......................	243,290	14.3	5,010	2.1	11,408	4.7	122,030	50.2	31,231	12.8	4,409	1.8
Rhode Island......................	15,716	15.0	523	3.3	637	4.1	9,471	60.3	1,967	12.5	336	2.1
South Carolina	75,718	15.3	2,901	3.8	1,854	2.4	49,475	65.3	9,713	12.8	2,049	2.7
South Dakota.....................	19,326	13.8	429	2.2	664	3.4	9,618	49.8	2,621	13.6	331	1.7
Tennessee	127,043	15.2	3,545	2.8	5,684	4.5	65,341	51.4	16,095	12.7	2,933	2.3
Texas................................	675,112	15.3	24,521	3.6	27,462	4.1	342,257	50.7	64,936	9.6	11,646	1.7
Utah.................................	55,355	23.2	1,427	2.6	2,737	4.9	27,374	49.5	8,668	15.7	929	1.7
Vermont............................	18,130	10.6	472	2.6	874	4.8	8,276	45.6	4,068	22.4	436	2.4
Virginia.............................	177,733	14.2	4,150	2.3	8,557	4.8	89,968	50.6	18,989	10.7	3,462	1.9
Washington.......................	111,696	18.0	3,063	2.7	5,164	4.6	59,555	53.3	11,201	10.0	2,230	2.0
West Virginia.....................	39,272	14.0	1,146	2.9	792	2.0	20,029	51.0	3,699	9.4	752	1.9
Wisconsin	103,208	14.9	2,468	2.4	4,178	4.0	58,376	56.6	10,648	10.3	1,865	1.8
Wyoming	16,946	12.4	383	2.3	984	5.8	7,615	44.9	2,389	14.1	429	2.5

- = Zero or rounds to zero.

Table B-9. Staff Employed by Public Elementary and Secondary School Systems, Fall 2014—*Continued*

| State | School staff | | School district staff | | | | | | | | | |
| | Librarians | | Officials and administrators | | Administrative support staff | | Instruction coordinators | | Student support staff | | Other support services staff | |
	Number	Percent	Number	Percent	Number	Percent	Number	Percent	Number	Percent	Number	Percent
UNITED STATES................	44,624	0.7	68,962	1.1	187,941	3.0	79,267	1.3	313,034	5.0	1,123,343	17.9
Alabama....................	984	1.1	770	0.9	754	0.9	182	0.2	3,079	3.5	24,395	27.9
Alaska.......................	141	0.8	638	3.7	789	4.6	203	1.2	613	3.6	2,389	14.0
Arizona......................	458	0.4	1,321	1.3	4,107	4.0	641	0.6	11,345	11.1	14,329	14.0
Arkansas	962	1.3	637	0.9	2,595	3.5	958	1.3	8,138	11.0	10,434	14.1
California...................	811	0.1	3,240	0.6	20,021	3.5	20,195	3.5	17,739	3.1	105,923	18.5
Colorado	601	0.6	1,275	1.2	4,583	4.2	2,865	2.6	6,130	5.6	14,134	13.0
Connecticut...............	742	0.8	2,151	2.3	1,703	1.8	4,759	5.1	2,910	3.1	17,282	18.4
Delaware	125	0.7	434	2.3	397	2.1	293	1.6	1,119	6.0	3,362	18.1
District of Columbia	94	0.7	638	4.7	715	5.2	224	1.6	1,185	8.7	769	5.7
Florida.......................	2,079	0.6	2,067	0.6	15,384	4.5	726	0.2	11,045	3.2	67,458	19.8
Georgia	2,104	0.9	2,435	1.1	2,669	1.2	2,861	1.3	8,072	3.6	48,588	21.9
Hawaii.......................	173	0.8	252	1.1	696	3.1	636	2.8	1,732	7.7	2,518	11.2
Idaho........................	49	0.2	131	0.5	663	2.4	228	0.8	542	2.0	4,805	17.5
Illinois	1,693	0.6	4,132	1.6	6,639	2.5	1,678	0.6	36,938	14.1	30,460	11.6
Indiana......................	703	0.5	548	0.4	740	0.5	3,384	2.4	9,542	6.8	38,196	27.4
Iowa..........................	440	0.6	1,253	1.7	1,990	2.8	549	0.8	4,373	6.1	10,365	14.4
Kansas......................	677	1.0	467	0.7	1,442	2.0	991	1.4	4,472	6.3	10,736	15.1
Kentucky...................	1,063	1.1	897	0.9	2,238	2.3	1,584	1.6	2,951	3.0	23,297	24.0
Louisiana..................	1,006	1.2	88	0.1	385	0.5	895	1.0	3,164	3.7	14,642	17.2
Maine........................	198	0.6	459	1.4	738	2.3	287	0.9	1,417	4.4	5,438	16.9
Maryland...................	1,170	1.0	3,606	3.1	2,193	1.9	1,591	1.4	4,930	4.2	21,175	18.1
Massachusetts...........	700	0.5	2,528	2.0	2,959	2.3	415	0.3	9,415	7.3	1,646	1.3
Michigan	500	0.3	4,138	2.3	1,121	0.6	1,287	0.7	13,457	7.3	37,413	20.4
Minnesota	622	0.5	2,338	2.0	2,272	2.0	2,550	2.2	13,101	11.3	12,825	11.1
Mississippi................	813	1.2	984	1.4	2,072	3.0	679	1.0	3,171	4.7	14,132	20.8
Missouri....................	1,390	1.1	868	0.7	6,737	5.3	1,437	1.1	5,043	4.0	24,624	19.4
Montana....................	363	1.8	405	2.0	678	3.3	203	1.0	682	3.3	3,662	17.9
Nebraska...................	551	1.2	629	1.3	1,126	2.4	817	1.7	1,551	3.3	8,690	18.5
Nevada......................	322	1.0	176	0.5	976	2.9	1,458	4.3	61	0.2	1,216	3.6
New Hampshire...........	318	1.0	742	2.3	716	2.2	256	0.8	706	2.2	5,248	16.5
New Jersey	1,477	0.6	1,428	0.6	5,628	2.4	3,973	1.7	13,445	5.7	37,944	16.1
New Mexico	236	0.5	886	1.9	114	0.2	638	1.4	3,316	7.1	6,917	14.7
New York....................	2,360	0.7	2,525	0.7	18,647	5.2	1,400	0.4	8,485	2.4	59,260	16.6
North Carolina............	2,178	1.1	1,643	0.9	5,485	2.9	1,161	0.6	10,824	5.7	31,024	16.2
North Dakota..............	196	1.1	502	2.8	277	1.6	215	1.2	850	4.8	2,527	14.4
Ohio..........................	911	0.4	2,507	1.0	13,814	5.5	1,593	0.6	23,209	9.3	59,967	24.0
Oklahoma..................	1,027	1.2	534	0.6	3,080	3.6	345	0.4	4,869	5.7	15,679	18.3
Oregon......................	130	0.2	449	0.7	2,627	4.2	442	0.7	2,734	4.3	11,791	18.7
Pennsylvania.............	1,734	0.7	2,479	1.0	6,991	2.9	1,544	0.6	7,248	3.0	49,206	20.2
Rhode Island..............	191	1.2	124	0.8	428	2.7	165	1.0	431	2.7	1,444	9.2
South Carolina	1,090	1.4	768	1.0	2,502	3.3	1,916	2.5	3,449	4.6	2	-
South Dakota	106	0.6	706	3.7	355	1.8	170	0.9	844	4.4	3,482	18.0
Tennessee	1,898	1.5	188	0.1	1,209	1.0	798	0.6	1,358	1.1	27,994	22.0
Texas........................	4,647	0.7	6,351	0.9	24,103	3.6	3,605	0.5	25,832	3.8	139,752	20.7
Utah	240	0.4	798	1.4	1,057	1.9	1,958	3.5	1,194	2.2	8,973	16.2
Vermont.....................	211	1.2	127	0.7	451	2.5	239	1.3	950	5.2	2,028	11.2
Virginia......................	1,709	1.0	1,741	1.0	4,370	2.5	1,796	1.0	4,773	2.7	38,219	21.5
Washington................	1,092	1.0	2,549	2.3	1,967	1.8	332	0.3	3,396	3.0	21,148	18.9
West Virginia..............	300	0.8	921	2.3	1,399	3.6	393	1.0	1,188	3.0	8,653	22.0
Wisconsin..................	936	0.9	1,088	1.1	2,861	2.8	1,388	1.3	5,302	5.1	14,098	13.7
Wyoming	107	0.6	400	2.4	479	2.8	360	2.1	716	4.2	3,085	18.2

- = Zero or rounds to zero.

Table B-10. Revenues and Expenditures for Public Elementary and Secondary Schools, by State, 2014–2015

(Dollars in thousands except as noted; percent.)

State	Revenues for public elementary and secondary schools, by source				Current expenditures for public elementary and secondary schools, by function				
	Total revenue (thousands of dollars)	Percent from:			Total current expenditures (thousands of dollars)	Current expenditure per pupil (dollars)	Percent for:		
		Federal government	State government	Local government			Instruction and instruction-related	Support services	Non-instruction
UNITED STATES	647,679,130	8.5	46.6	45.0	575,331,825	11,734	60.7	35.1	4.2
Alabama	7,435,758	11.2	55.5	33.2	6,806,467	9,378	56.9	36.0	7.1
Alaska	2,935,538	11.8	69.4	18.7	2,648,552	20,701	56.2	40.6	3.2
Arizona	9,860,167	13.0	44.1	43.0	8,370,884	7,782	53.6	41.0	5.4
Arkansas	5,283,244	11.5	51.5	37.0	4,813,321	10,052	56.1	38.3	5.6
California.........................	74,395,627	9.6	57.2	33.2	65,953,946	10,713	59.5	36.1	4.4
Colorado..........................	9,764,525	7.4	45.6	47.0	8,260,461	9,527	56.5	39.4	4.1
Connecticut......................	11,376,740	4.2	41.0	54.8	10,321,511	19,500	63.2	33.7	3.1
Delaware	2,077,887	8.7	57.7	33.6	1,860,732	14,232	61.8	34.7	3.5
District of Columbia	2,251,430	9.7	†	90.3	1,668,528	21,130	54.0	42.3	3.7
Florida.............................	26,789,374	11.9	39.8	48.3	25,123,548	9,343	61.4	33.7	5.0
Georgia	18,772,155	10.1	45.2	44.7	16,530,506	9,716	61.8	32.4	5.8
Hawaii.............................	2,699,827	9.6	88.2	2.2	2,344,496	13,179	58.8	35.7	5.6
Idaho...............................	2,294,497	10.7	65.0	24.3	2,015,654	7,104	59.5	35.3	5.3
Illinois	27,304,004	8.3	24.9	66.8	28,545,089	14,287	61.7	35.6	2.7
Indiana	12,103,344	8.2	56.1	35.8	9,970,350	9,770	57.5	37.7	4.8
Iowa................................	6,463,514	7.4	53.5	39.1	5,526,877	11,214	60.9	34.5	4.5
Kansas	6,225,153	8.9	64.3	26.8	5,136,532	10,590	59.9	35.3	4.8
Kentucky	7,453,976	11.5	54.9	33.6	6,583,287	9,801	57.5	36.1	6.4
Louisiana.........................	8,927,289	14.7	43.4	41.9	7,960,448	11,386	56.4	38.2	5.4
Maine...............................	2,737,132	7.0	39.4	53.6	2,538,313	14,330	58.8	37.1	4.2
Maryland..........................	14,521,045	5.7	43.5	50.8	12,620,036	14,795	62.5	34.7	2.9
Massachusetts	17,197,389	5.3	39.1	55.6	15,723,617	16,866	63.7	33.6	2.7
Michigan	19,452,849	9.2	60.2	30.6	16,849,135	11,233	57.5	38.8	3.7
Minnesota	12,183,690	5.7	66.7	27.5	10,222,017	12,226	64.8	30.6	4.6
Mississippi.......................	4,550,410	14.8	51.1	34.1	4,145,632	8,658	56.9	37.0	6.1
Missouri...........................	10,927,026	9.0	32.5	58.5	9,390,061	10,490	59.0	36.3	4.7
Montana...........................	1,805,295	12.2	47.9	40.0	1,601,097	11,358	58.8	36.6	4.6
Nebraska..........................	4,168,349	8.2	32.4	59.4	3,805,871	12,481	63.9	29.4	6.7
Nevada.............................	4,522,125	9.2	35.9	54.9	3,880,472	8,664	58.1	38.0	3.9
New Hampshire.................	2,992,501	5.6	33.4	61.0	2,764,233	15,347	63.5	33.9	2.5
New Jersey	28,489,659	4.2	42.1	53.7	25,993,208	19,028	60.2	36.8	3.0
New Mexico	3,986,781	14.0	69.5	16.5	3,309,622	9,969	57.1	38.0	4.9
New York	62,517,215	4.5	41.5	54.0	56,862,010	21,268	70.2	27.7	2.0
North Carolina..................	13,681,971	12.2	62.4	25.4	13,210,839	8,745	62.2	32.3	5.5
North Dakota....................	1,578,414	10.1	58.7	31.2	1,373,266	13,210	59.5	32.9	7.6
Ohio.................................	24,516,266	7.5	45.6	46.9	20,231,423	12,026	58.4	38.2	3.3
Oklahoma.........................	6,261,170	11.5	49.4	39.2	5,560,047	8,279	55.1	37.6	7.3
Oregon	7,077,486	8.0	52.0	40.0	5,969,321	10,721	58.3	38.0	3.7
Pennsylvania....................	28,983,071	6.9	37.1	55.9	25,109,991	14,769	61.5	34.7	3.8
Rhode Island....................	2,444,422	8.1	40.5	51.3	2,242,486	16,196	61.4	35.9	2.7
South Carolina	8,891,519	9.6	47.2	43.2	7,437,182	10,079	55.2	39.2	5.6
South Dakota	1,420,613	14.9	30.4	54.8	1,211,080	9,333	58.5	35.4	6.1
Tennessee	9,428,987	12.0	45.2	42.9	8,736,367	8,998	61.5	33.1	5.5
Texas...............................	56,127,791	10.8	40.6	48.6	47,527,971	9,310	57.8	36.4	5.8
Utah	5,127,846	8.8	54.6	36.6	4,290,876	6,922	63.2	31.0	5.8
Vermont...........................	1,758,461	6.0	90.1	3.9	1,638,720	19,243	63.3	33.7	3.0
Virginia............................	15,624,013	6.5	39.9	53.6	14,384,705	11,519	60.9	35.3	3.9
Washington.......................	13,606,501	7.6	61.0	31.4	11,470,245	10,953	57.6	38.1	4.3
West Virginia	3,525,371	10.3	57.5	32.2	3,226,918	11,803	57.2	36.5	6.3
Wisconsin	11,197,990	7.5	45.9	46.6	10,054,346	11,829	59.5	36.8	3.7
Wyoming	1,961,721	6.2	56.9	36.9	1,509,532	16,453	59.5	37.5	3.0

Table B-11. Percentage of High School Dropouts Among Persons 16 to 24 Years Old, by Race/Ethnicity and State, 2016

(Percent.)

State	Total	White	Black	Hispanic	Asian	Pacific Islander	American Indian/ Alaska Native	Two or more races
UNITED STATES	5.8	4.5	7.0	9.1	2.0	6.9	11.0	4.8
Alabama	6.9	6.7	6.5	12.4	NA	NA	NA	3.2
Alaska	5.6	1.9	NA	NA	NA	NA	19.0	10.1
Arizona	7.6	5.0	8.9	10.6	NA	NA	11.1	3.3
Arkansas	7.2	5.8	10.7	9.1	NA	NA	NA	8.2
California	5.3	3.0	5.7	7.7	1.6	NA	3.6	3.6
Colorado	6.4	3.5	9.0	12.5	2.5	NA	12.1	6.1
Connecticut	3.1	1.9	2.5	8.1	NA	NA	NA	NA
Delaware	7.1	3.4	10.3	18.0	NA	NA	NA	NA
District of Columbia	3.5	NA	6.0	6.4	NA	NA	NA	NA
Florida	6.6	5.4	7.1	8.7	2.2	NA	NA	5.2
Georgia	6.9	5.9	7.3	12.0	2.8	NA	NA	5.6
Hawaii	3.6	3.9	NA	5.0	1.2	9.0	NA	3.4
Idaho	4.1	3.6	NA	7.2	NA	NA	NA	NA
Illinois	4.8	3.2	7.4	7.5	2.1	NA	NA	5.4
Indiana	7.0	6.2	8.2	13.6	NA	NA	NA	5.0
Iowa	4.5	4.0	12.2	6.6	NA	NA	NA	NA
Kansas	5.3	4.6	5.2	10.4	NA	NA	NA	4.0
Kentucky	6.6	6.4	7.2	12.4	NA	NA	NA	NA
Louisiana	8.7	6.6	11.9	7.5	NA	NA	NA	7.0
Maine	4.1	4.2	NA	NA	NA	NA	NA	NA
Maryland	5.2	3.4	5.2	14.4	NA	NA	NA	4.8
Massachusetts	3.8	2.3	6.9	10.0	1.4	NA	NA	2.1
Michigan	6.1	5.6	9.0	7.3	1.1	NA	9.7	6.6
Minnesota	4.3	3.5	5.9	10.5	NA	NA	17.6	6.8
Mississippi	6.2	5.6	6.5	9.0	NA	NA	NA	NA
Missouri	5.8	4.8	7.9	11.9	NA	NA	NA	7.3
Montana	5.2	5.0	NA	NA	NA	NA	11.3	NA
Nebraska	5.1	3.6	12.4	13.1	NA	NA	NA	NA
Nevada	8.2	6.1	9.5	11.9	1.8	NA	NA	3.1
New Hampshire	3.9	3.5	NA	NA	NA	NA	NA	NA
New Jersey	3.7	2.1	4.9	7.3	1.4	NA	NA	2.5
New Mexico	8.2	5.4	NA	9.3	NA	NA	10.7	NA
New York	5.5	3.7	7.7	9.5	2.1	NA	NA	4.5
North Carolina	6.0	5.3	5.7	10.7	2.3	NA	11.1	5.3
North Dakota	2.7	2.2	NA	NA	NA	NA	NA	NA
Ohio	6.2	5.3	9.7	9.3	NA	NA	NA	9.1
Oklahoma	7.9	5.8	14.8	10.3	NA	NA	12.5	7.4
Oregon	5.5	5.2	NA	7.6	NA	NA	16.5	4.4
Pennsylvania	5.3	5.0	4.8	10.7	2.4	NA	NA	3.2
Rhode Island	4.1	2.6	NA	8.5	NA	NA	NA	NA
South Carolina	5.9	5.7	5.9	8.9	NA	NA	NA	6.1
South Dakota	5.1	3.1	NA	NA	NA	NA	22.0	NA
Tennessee	4.8	4.2	6.2	9.5	NA	NA	NA	NA
Texas	6.7	4.4	6.0	9.2	2.6	NA	5.3	2.1
Utah	4.7	3.7	NA	9.9	NA	NA	13.8	3.9
Vermont	4.5	4.8	NA	NA	NA	NA	NA	NA
Virginia	3.9	2.8	4.3	9.9	3.1	NA	NA	1.7
Washington	7.5	5.8	10.5	13.2	4.1	12.2	11.7	9.4
West Virginia	6.6	6.6	9.5	NA	NA	NA	NA	NA
Wisconsin	4.7	3.8	9.3	9.3	2.7	NA	NA	NA
Wyoming	5.2	5.2	NA	NA	NA	NA	NA	NA

Note: Dropouts are 16- to 24-year-olds who are not enrolled in school and who have not completed a high school program, regardless of when they left school. People who have received GED credentials are counted as high school completers. Data are based on sample surveys of the entire population in the given age range residing within the United States, including both noninstitutionalized persons (e.g., those living in households, college housing, or military housing located within the United States) and institutionalized persons (e.g., those living in prisons, nursing facilities, or other healthcare facilities). Totals include other racial/ethnic groups not separately shown. Race categories exclude persons of Hispanic ethnicity.
NA = Not available. Reporting standards not met.

Table B-12. Total Fall Enrollment in Degree-Granting Postsecondary Institutions, by Level and Control of School, and State, Fall 2015

(Number.)

State	Public				Private							
	Undergraduate			Post-baccalaureate	Undergraduate					Postbaccalaureate		
	Total	4-year	2-year		Total	Nonprofit 4-year	For-profit 4-year	Nonprofit 2-year	For-profit 2-year	Total	Nonprofit 4-year	For-profit 4-year
UNITED STATES	13,145,720	6,930,054	6,215,666	1,422,383	3,891,058	2,769,125	846,671	50,049	225,213	1,518,109	1,244,198	273,911
Alabama	212,968	131,503	81,465	34,483	44,682	20,938	21,000	436	2,308	10,826	4,593	6,233
Alaska	26,118	25,925	193	2,275	2,694	315	1,935	66	378	244	234	10
Arizona	330,531	134,476	196,055	30,445	210,846	5,012	197,019	0	8,815	77,910	4,594	73,316
Arkansas	132,725	82,087	50,638	17,440	15,905	14,309	559	1,017	20	2,332	2,228	104
California	2,095,116	617,777	1,477,339	107,978	321,357	166,925	114,442	1,785	38,205	163,904	135,703	28,201
Colorado	229,875	144,810	85,065	35,953	59,601	22,012	29,685	624	7,280	22,669	12,765	9,904
Connecticut	106,337	53,576	52,761	13,429	56,722	49,154	7,568	0	0	23,178	22,561	617
Delaware	36,514	23,043	13,471	4,097	11,467	11,067	247	153	0	8,314	8,235	79
District of Columbia	4,485	4,485	0	633	46,069	39,594	5,606	29	840	42,808	39,678	3,130
Florida	727,982	686,642	41,340	66,408	228,427	138,671	54,100	15,285	20,371	60,445	53,261	7,184
Georgia	374,330	252,947	121,383	44,123	82,458	51,376	22,750	1,441	6,891	30,388	21,289	9,099
Hawaii	50,011	23,234	26,777	5,745	11,355	9,088	1,757	0	510	2,220	1,498	722
Idaho	65,222	43,052	22,170	7,117	48,022	46,908	694	0	420	747	743	4
Illinois	459,770	143,615	316,155	49,334	190,820	134,754	49,923	389	5,754	102,319	86,199	16,120
Indiana	282,266	200,598	81,668	39,234	86,933	72,458	10,052	504	3,919	17,930	17,790	140
Iowa	156,026	63,560	92,466	14,979	80,986	41,564	38,989	0	433	23,115	12,515	10,600
Kansas	158,138	78,985	79,153	21,622	33,770	20,373	11,956	0	1,441	6,692	4,876	1,816
Kentucky	182,947	103,122	79,825	22,961	36,923	27,773	8,034	0	1,116	12,891	11,710	1,181
Louisiana	188,258	119,191	69,067	23,076	25,691	18,337	1,924	492	4,938	7,635	7,516	119
Maine	43,908	26,526	17,382	3,496	18,340	16,300	1,436	273	331	5,971	5,851	120
Maryland	260,457	130,862	129,595	43,097	33,281	26,873	3,899	0	2,509	27,096	26,191	905
Massachusetts	195,262	98,767	96,495	26,981	179,465	174,325	3,032	1,179	929	108,688	108,445	243
Michigan	435,931	257,960	177,971	66,350	79,883	75,348	3,607	0	928	18,039	17,631	408
Minnesota	232,013	109,001	123,012	24,174	78,253	49,030	28,556	68	599	93,317	21,568	71,749
Mississippi	138,411	65,503	72,908	14,889	13,093	11,215	212	0	1,666	5,743	5,645	98
Missouri	219,402	125,705	93,697	29,114	112,550	97,853	7,140	893	6,664	48,930	48,582	348
Montana	41,379	32,917	8,462	4,555	4,687	4,245	0	442	0	177	177	0
Nebraska	85,884	46,107	39,777	14,146	24,425	22,551	1,568	151	155	11,632	11,527	105
Nevada	96,451	85,366	11,085	7,967	8,390	8,390	3,261	417	3,827	3,289	2,912	377
New Hampshire	38,728	23,957	14,771	4,138	58,305	56,753	1,429	123	0	22,795	22,732	63
New Jersey	301,480	145,648	155,832	38,263	58,619	48,657	7,021	0	2,941	25,417	24,978	439
New Mexico	118,486	47,804	70,682	12,801	5,841	770	3,599	0	1,472	1,061	847	214
New York	641,936	329,523	312,413	67,207	406,136	361,252	27,111	2,509	15,264	170,141	167,036	3,105
North Carolina	403,516	180,376	223,140	44,539	86,834	72,260	10,991	705	2,878	27,553	24,719	2,834
North Dakota	41,888	34,929	6,959	6,309	4,686	4,083	603	0	0	957	957	0
Ohio	443,022	272,251	170,771	61,793	134,332	109,198	12,069	1,318	11,747	28,613	28,026	587
Oklahoma	158,646	100,266	58,380	20,362	26,686	19,689	2,990	1,155	2,852	5,210	5,152	58
Oregon	180,035	86,892	93,143	17,913	26,857	21,826	3,523	111	1,397	15,841	15,596	245
Pennsylvania	361,361	231,242	130,119	47,693	237,643	194,394	14,001	8,504	20,744	89,973	89,264	709
Rhode Island	37,282	21,087	16,195	4,038	34,690	34,690	0	0	0	6,282	6,282	0
South Carolina	181,885	91,269	90,616	20,602	41,785	30,260	8,297	771	2,457	5,382	3,575	1,807
South Dakota	38,450	32,328	6,122	5,804	8,451	6,093	2,188	170	0	959	958	1
Tennessee	199,752	113,071	86,681	23,659	76,996	60,862	7,694	736	7,704	23,092	21,387	1,705
Texas	1,231,190	548,513	682,677	148,086	150,844	99,171	25,259	3,005	23,409	40,494	37,884	2,610
Utah	158,396	129,046	29,350	12,829	101,144	94,787	3,836	2,153	368	21,158	20,069	1,089
Vermont	22,999	17,016	5,983	2,384	14,297	13,918	379	0	0	4,183	4,183	0
Virginia	349,238	170,096	179,142	44,972	125,294	89,041	29,548	923	5,782	50,255	45,074	5,181
Washington	290,496	206,044	84,452	24,010	38,397	30,570	3,728	1,760	2,339	12,509	12,267	242
West Virginia	74,091	55,662	18,429	12,251	53,521	7,449	43,586	0	2,486	10,880	1,216	9,664
Wisconsin	258,250	156,861	101,389	24,000	52,093	44,099	7,868	0	126	15,905	15,479	426
Wyoming	31,090	10,045	21,045	2,603	512	50	0	462	0	0	0	0

Note: Degree-granting institutions grant associate's or higher degrees and participate in Title IV federal financial aid programs.

Table B-13. Degrees Conferred by Institutions of Higher Education, by State, 2014–2015

(Number.)

State	Total degrees	Associate's degrees				Bachelor's degrees			
		Total	Public	Private not-for-profit	Private for-profit	Total	Public	Private not-for-profit	Private for-profit
UNITED STATES	3,846,160	1,013,971	821,874	58,622	133,475	1,894,934	1,209,438	553,534	131,962
Alabama	57,918	13,629	9,964	146	3,519	30,060	22,802	3,663	3,595
Alaska	4,399	1,715	1,331	20	364	1,932	1,803	70	59
Arizona	128,390	37,703	18,602	197	18,904	58,534	26,554	695	31,285
Arkansas	30,846	9,095	8,788	165	142	15,881	12,965	2,722	194
California	427,582	133,533	115,262	1,658	16,613	201,116	136,033	39,335	25,748
Colorado	65,143	13,992	9,058	634	4,300	33,626	25,020	4,171	4,435
Connecticut	41,217	7,026	5,840	872	314	22,344	11,362	10,031	951
Delaware	12,587	2,039	1,874	153	12	6,895	4,548	2,326	21
District of Columbia	24,836	741	276	248	217	9,272	335	8,476	461
Florida	237,779	94,688	72,804	12,387	9,497	100,521	68,522	23,748	8,251
Georgia	91,162	19,497	14,712	1,027	3,758	49,862	36,906	9,932	3,024
Hawaii	13,875	4,429	3,930	495	4	6,966	4,599	2,013	354
Idaho	18,382	5,152	3,247	1,621	284	10,886	6,532	4,247	107
Illinois	163,341	40,187	35,162	1,077	3,948	74,317	32,817	30,814	10,686
Indiana	83,072	17,243	12,449	1,474	3,320	48,082	32,390	14,882	810
Iowa	56,122	16,772	12,093	625	4,054	28,201	12,835	10,474	4,892
Kansas	41,166	12,043	9,780	716	1,547	20,081	14,870	4,045	1,166
Kentucky	47,072	13,055	10,411	384	2,260	22,608	17,467	4,605	536
Louisiana	39,234	7,146	5,767	263	1,116	22,247	18,295	3,625	327
Maine	13,215	3,211	2,670	120	421	7,418	4,158	3,125	135
Maryland	71,560	16,919	16,249	17	653	33,219	26,265	6,437	517
Massachusetts	118,348	14,356	12,195	1,487	674	59,625	20,382	38,768	475
Michigan	119,106	32,572	27,955	3,784	833	59,970	46,116	13,162	692
Minnesota	84,786	20,141	16,875	596	2,670	36,726	21,394	11,226	4,106
Mississippi	33,927	13,320	12,835	41	444	14,296	12,064	2,215	17
Missouri	86,102	18,831	12,647	3,427	2,757	41,161	22,092	18,149	920
Montana	10,391	2,477	2,311	166	0	6,156	5,347	809	0
Nebraska	26,603	5,712	5,057	229	426	14,080	8,578	5,345	157
Nevada	17,896	6,059	4,814	144	1,101	8,519	7,478	306	735
New Hampshire	21,138	3,034	2,019	789	226	11,832	5,279	6,291	262
New Jersey	83,964	23,154	21,692	143	1,319	42,016	31,446	9,776	794
New Mexico	23,389	10,533	9,817	0	716	8,791	7,994	132	665
New York	289,989	68,302	52,384	7,332	8,586	136,396	62,250	70,182	3,964
North Carolina	106,837	31,876	28,946	1,063	1,867	52,889	37,348	14,658	883
North Dakota	10,817	2,309	1,987	132	190	6,291	5,604	633	54
Ohio	132,758	33,386	24,934	2,996	5,456	69,635	47,294	21,298	1,043
Oklahoma	41,935	13,047	11,484	252	1,311	20,730	16,608	3,865	257
Oregon	48,654	13,679	12,822	108	749	22,656	17,071	5,172	413
Pennsylvania	167,233	27,624	16,533	3,487	7,604	93,050	48,106	43,240	1,704
Rhode Island	18,631	3,606	1,645	1,961	0	11,730	4,317	7,413	0
South Carolina	44,470	11,767	9,930	363	1,474	24,823	18,167	5,534	1,122
South Dakota	10,062	2,479	2,103	177	199	5,638	4,424	983	231
Tennessee	62,487	12,822	9,896	736	2,190	34,197	20,887	12,312	998
Texas	261,315	79,401	72,359	1,366	5,676	122,165	98,598	20,429	3,138
Utah	56,361	12,982	10,974	1,039	969	32,160	15,765	15,734	661
Vermont	10,021	1,156	946	141	69	6,160	3,368	2,743	49
Virginia	111,587	25,554	18,433	1,703	5,418	56,878	36,710	15,913	4,255
Washington	75,389	29,998	29,205	136	657	33,309	25,300	7,321	688
West Virginia	30,073	6,497	3,594	111	2,792	15,997	9,515	1,147	5,335
Wisconsin	63,897	14,510	12,398	257	1,855	37,555	27,427	9,338	790
Wyoming	5,683	2,972	2,815	157	0	2,026	2,022	4	0

Note: Data are for postsecondary institutions participating in Title IV federal financial aid programs.

Table B-13. Degrees Conferred by Institutions of Higher Education, by State, 2014–2015
—*Continued*

(Number.)

State	Master's degrees				Doctoral degrees[1]			
	Total	Public	Private not-for-profit	Private for-profit	Total	Public	Private not-for-profit	Private for-profit
UNITED STATES	758,708	351,119	336,182	71,407	178,547	90,252	80,092	8,203
Alabama	11,800	8,888	825	2,087	2,429	1,938	482	9
Alaska	703	640	55	8	49	41	8	0
Arizona	27,785	8,519	546	18,720	4,368	1,976	818	1,574
Arkansas	4,899	4,342	512	45	971	893	78	0
California	74,626	29,157	35,794	9,675	18,307	6,955	9,896	1,456
Colorado	14,685	7,579	4,043	3,063	2,840	1,851	567	422
Connecticut	9,732	3,133	6,389	210	2,115	787	1,328	0
Delaware	3,112	980	2,101	31	541	280	261	0
District of Columbia	11,439	116	10,786	537	3,384	68	3,316	0
Florida	33,360	17,608	13,320	2,432	9,210	4,846	3,795	569
Georgia	17,219	10,514	4,743	1,962	4,584	2,521	1,702	361
Hawaii	1,856	1,035	632	189	624	579	0	45
Idaho	1,957	1,651	294	12	387	366	21	0
Illinois	40,080	12,398	23,922	3,760	8,757	3,058	5,446	253
Indiana	14,099	9,193	4,785	121	3,648	2,768	880	0
Iowa	8,298	2,616	2,337	3,345	2,851	1,425	1,295	131
Kansas	7,344	5,258	1,506	580	1,698	1,482	216	0
Kentucky	9,314	5,690	3,136	488	2,095	1,602	368	125
Louisiana	7,332	5,128	2,099	105	2,509	1,579	930	0
Maine	2,046	843	1,184	19	540	159	381	0
Maryland	18,428	10,580	7,586	262	2,994	2,204	790	0
Massachusetts	35,958	6,005	29,836	117	8,409	759	7,650	0
Michigan	20,689	16,583	3,924	182	5,875	4,469	1,406	0
Minnesota	22,827	5,218	5,256	12,353	5,092	1,800	1,109	2,183
Mississippi	5,017	3,480	1,508	29	1,294	1,001	293	0
Missouri	21,313	7,862	13,293	158	4,797	1,633	3,164	0
Montana	1,300	1,210	90	0	458	458	0	0
Nebraska	5,228	2,761	2,445	22	1,583	859	724	0
Nevada	2,266	1,668	396	202	1,052	537	515	0
New Hampshire	5,775	1,192	4,549	34	497	185	312	0
New Jersey	15,773	8,918	6,726	129	3,021	2,116	905	0
New Mexico	3,371	3,003	246	122	694	694	0	0
New York	70,767	18,733	50,824	1,210	14,524	3,093	11,427	4
North Carolina	17,237	11,134	5,620	483	4,835	2,654	1,741	440
North Dakota	1,706	1,336	370	0	511	476	35	0
Ohio	23,581	15,571	7,744	266	6,156	4,572	1,584	0
Oklahoma	6,532	5,043	1,451	38	1,626	1,346	280	0
Oregon	10,353	4,225	6,078	50	1,966	1,019	947	0
Pennsylvania	36,579	11,780	24,503	296	9,980	3,394	6,586	0
Rhode Island	2,571	755	1,816	0	724	250	474	0
South Carolina	5,990	4,521	1,036	433	1,890	1,517	158	215
South Dakota	1,538	1,257	265	16	407	404	3	0
Tennessee	11,807	5,580	5,760	467	3,661	1,822	1,728	111
Texas	48,762	37,575	10,061	1,126	10,987	8,532	2,427	28
Utah	9,982	3,487	6,261	234	1,237	875	227	135
Vermont	2,311	478	1,833	0	394	224	170	0
Virginia	23,790	11,472	10,384	1,934	5,365	3,347	1,894	124
Washington	9,498	5,863	3,457	178	2,584	1,897	669	18
West Virginia	6,524	2,670	344	3,510	1,055	938	117	0
Wisconsin	9,082	5,404	3,511	167	2,750	1,781	969	0
Wyoming	463	463	0	0	222	222	0	0

Note: Data are for postsecondary institutions participating in Title IV federal financial aid programs.

[1] Includes Ph.D., Ed.D., and comparable degrees at the doctoral level. Includes most degrees formerly classified as first-professional, such as M.D., D.D.S., and law degrees.

Table B-14. Race/Ethnicity of Students Enrolled in Institutions of Higher Education, Fall 2016

(Number; percent.)

State	Total enrolled	U.S. residents							Nonresident alien (percent)
		White (percent)	Black (percent)	Hispanic or Latino (may be of any race) (percent)	Asian (percent)	Pacific Islander (percent)	American Indian/ Alaska Native (percent)	Two or more races (percent)	
UNITED STATES	19,841,014	54.0	13.0	17.3	6.3	0.3	0.7	3.4	5.0
Alabama...............................	304,052	62.0	26.7	3.4	1.9	0.1	0.7	2.3	3.0
Alaska..................................	28,446	60.4	3.3	7.9	5.9	0.8	10.9	8.8	1.9
Arizona................................	608,084	49.7	13.0	24.1	3.7	0.5	2.3	3.4	3.3
Arkansas..............................	167,320	68.3	16.0	6.1	1.7	0.1	0.8	3.2	3.8
California..............................	2,700,106	28.9	6.6	39.2	14.7	0.5	0.4	4.4	5.2
Colorado..............................	352,296	63.7	7.3	16.6	3.6	0.3	0.9	4.2	3.4
Connecticut..........................	198,011	58.2	12.7	14.7	5.3	0.1	0.2	2.7	6.0
Delaware..............................	61,139	55.7	21.6	6.8	3.5	0.1	0.5	2.5	9.1
District of Columbia..............	93,040	44.9	25.2	8.5	6.8	0.2	0.2	2.9	11.3
Florida.................................	1,075,496	44.6	18.0	26.1	3.5	0.2	0.3	3.0	4.2
Georgia................................	532,907	48.7	31.7	7.1	5.2	0.1	0.3	2.8	4.1
Hawaii..................................	65,858	16.9	2.2	11.2	31.1	6.8	0.3	25.6	6.0
Idaho...................................	123,796	76.2	1.1	8.5	1.5	0.6	0.8	3.9	7.5
Illinois.................................	777,720	54.2	13.0	17.7	6.6	0.2	0.2	2.5	5.5
Indiana.................................	419,203	71.8	9.5	6.1	3.0	0.1	0.2	2.9	6.5
Iowa....................................	266,513	73.1	9.2	7.1	2.7	0.2	0.5	2.3	4.9
Kansas.................................	214,301	68.5	8.6	9.5	2.7	0.2	1.3	3.2	6.0
Kentucky..............................	255,072	80.1	8.7	3.4	1.7	0.1	0.2	2.8	2.9
Louisiana.............................	239,287	55.6	30.5	5.2	2.5	0.1	0.6	2.5	3.1
Maine...................................	72,116	84.8	4.0	2.9	2.6	0.1	1.0	2.4	2.2
Maryland..............................	365,667	46.0	27.8	8.8	7.4	0.2	0.3	3.8	5.7
Massachusetts.......................	505,723	57.6	8.8	10.8	7.8	0.1	0.2	3.1	11.6
Michigan..............................	583,035	69.7	12.2	4.7	3.9	0.1	0.6	3.2	5.6
Minnesota............................	422,792	66.5	14.7	5.3	5.4	0.2	0.8	3.2	3.9
Mississippi...........................	172,712	55.3	37.1	2.3	1.2	0.1	0.4	1.6	2.1
Missouri...............................	401,094	71.0	12.2	4.9	3.1	0.2	0.5	3.0	5.1
Montana...............................	50,916	79.9	0.9	4.0	1.6	0.2	7.2	2.9	3.3
Nebraska..............................	136,102	74.0	5.3	9.7	2.9	0.2	0.7	2.9	4.3
Nevada.................................	116,030	45.5	7.7	26.0	10.6	1.2	0.7	6.2	2.0
New Hampshire......................	133,136	73.0	11.6	6.9	3.1	0.2	0.6	2.0	2.6
New Jersey...........................	421,377	48.0	14.2	20.7	9.2	0.3	0.3	2.1	5.2
New Mexico..........................	134,607	33.1	3.0	47.3	2.0	0.2	9.4	2.3	2.8
New York..............................	1,273,651	48.1	13.8	17.4	9.4	0.2	0.3	2.3	8.4
North Carolina.......................	561,496	58.4	23.1	7.4	3.3	0.1	1.1	3.1	3.5
North Dakota.........................	54,203	79.2	3.5	3.4	1.4	0.2	4.5	2.9	5.0
Ohio....................................	658,229	73.4	11.4	3.9	2.7	0.1	0.3	3.0	5.2
Oklahoma.............................	208,345	57.7	8.6	8.3	2.9	0.2	7.6	8.9	5.7
Oregon.................................	236,235	65.7	3.1	12.7	5.9	0.6	1.1	5.7	5.2
Pennsylvania........................	725,770	66.8	11.4	6.8	5.5	0.1	0.2	2.8	6.4
Rhode Island.........................	83,348	65.8	7.2	12.5	4.6	0.1	0.4	3.5	6.0
South Carolina......................	246,563	63.3	25.2	4.4	1.7	0.1	0.4	2.8	2.1
South Dakota........................	53,685	80.8	3.4	3.1	1.2	0.1	5.2	2.3	3.8
Tennessee............................	321,751	68.4	18.6	4.3	2.5	0.1	0.3	2.8	2.9
Texas...................................	1,603,259	37.3	12.6	36.7	5.9	0.2	0.4	2.5	4.4
Utah....................................	311,534	76.4	4.0	9.8	2.8	0.7	0.8	3.2	2.3
Vermont...............................	44,719	80.3	3.6	5.3	2.7	0.1	0.6	3.5	3.9
Virginia................................	557,461	57.2	20.0	8.3	6.4	0.2	0.4	3.9	3.5
Washington...........................	366,162	58.8	4.5	12.2	9.4	0.6	1.2	6.9	6.4
West Virginia........................	146,358	75.3	10.3	5.7	1.7	0.4	0.5	3.2	3.0
Wisconsin.............................	341,859	77.1	5.6	6.4	3.9	0.1	0.7	2.7	3.5
Wyoming..............................	33,365	81.9	1.2	8.2	0.9	0.2	1.4	2.8	3.3

Note: Includes special education, vocational/technical education, and alternative schools. Tabulation includes schools that offer kindergarten or higher grade. Includes enrollment of students in prekindergarten through grade 12 in schools that offer kindergarten or higher grade. Details may not sum to totals because of rounding.

Table B-15. Average Undergraduate Tuition, Fees, and Room and Board Rates for Full-Time College Students, by State, 2015–2016

(Dollars.)

| State | Public 4-year | | | | | Private 4-year | | | | Public 2-year, tuition and required fees | |
| | In-state | | | | Out-of-state tuition and required fees | Total | Tuition and required fees | Room | Board | In-state | Out-of-state |
	Total	Tuition and required fees	Room	Board							
UNITED STATES	19,189	8,778	5,850	4,561	24,354	39,529	27,951	6,463	5,116	3,038	7,409
Alabama..............................	18,509	9,179	5,228	4,101	23,261	24,648	15,359	4,690	4,599	4,289	8,464
Alaska.................................	16,701	6,880	5,678	4,142	20,463	26,388	19,957	3,323	3,108	3,340	3,340
Arizona...............................	20,621	9,884	6,555	4,182	24,161	22,245	12,667	5,076	4,501	2,061	8,255
Arkansas............................	15,976	7,577	4,836	3,562	18,306	28,827	20,936	3,997	3,894	3,105	4,638
California............................	22,151	9,070	7,310	5,771	31,526	41,182	29,519	6,495	5,168	1,246	6,968
Colorado............................	20,594	9,128	5,507	5,959	27,986	33,651	22,332	6,540	4,779	3,630	8,915
Connecticut........................	23,351	11,106	6,603	5,642	32,870	51,570	37,679	7,888	6,003	4,039	12,100
Delaware............................	23,566	11,670	7,139	4,757	28,962	25,511	14,200	5,637	5,674	3,215	6,548
District of Columbia	NA	5,251	NA	NA	11,233	53,572	38,901	9,590	5,081	NA	NA
Florida................................	14,457	4,438	5,871	4,148	17,656	33,973	22,793	6,231	4,948	2,387	8,862
Georgia..............................	17,292	7,011	5,989	4,291	23,167	37,464	25,754	6,544	5,166	3,181	7,929
Hawaii................................	20,098	9,263	5,484	5,351	27,911	27,895	15,561	5,398	6,936	2,935	7,930
Idaho..................................	14,211	6,915	3,464	3,832	20,624	13,069	6,006	2,574	4,489	3,108	7,959
Illinois................................	24,098	13,387	5,784	4,927	27,909	41,331	29,639	6,804	4,888	3,692	10,630
Indiana...............................	18,712	8,745	5,271	4,696	28,313	41,030	30,533	5,405	5,092	4,115	7,992
Iowa...................................	16,748	7,879	4,411	4,458	24,136	34,144	25,308	4,167	4,670	4,478	5,832
Kansas...............................	16,783	8,011	4,522	4,250	20,901	26,114	17,827	3,891	4,397	3,201	4,395
Kentucky............................	18,702	9,490	5,169	4,043	22,321	32,996	24,258	4,460	4,278	3,650	12,478
Louisiana............................	17,287	8,162	5,568	3,558	23,099	44,652	32,733	6,587	5,331	3,919	7,292
Maine..................................	18,767	9,186	4,820	4,761	25,598	46,578	34,277	6,134	6,167	3,648	6,396
Maryland.............................	20,076	8,942	6,371	4,763	21,768	52,013	38,352	7,699	5,962	3,816	9,147
Massachusetts.....................	23,389	11,670	7,205	4,514	27,736	55,024	40,761	8,196	6,067	4,559	9,944
Michigan.............................	21,380	11,708	4,766	4,907	34,863	30,954	22,018	4,288	4,648	3,179	6,590
Minnesota...........................	19,266	10,701	4,712	3,852	18,295	39,131	29,377	5,101	4,652	5,332	5,975
Mississippi..........................	16,434	7,175	5,297	3,962	18,516	24,034	16,438	3,923	3,673	2,645	4,810
Missouri..............................	17,418	8,178	5,457	3,783	19,860	31,692	22,416	5,166	4,110	3,016	5,814
Montana..............................	14,853	6,443	3,867	4,544	22,145	31,239	22,961	3,958	4,320	3,310	9,177
Nebraska............................	16,761	7,446	5,054	4,261	18,651	29,873	21,641	4,308	3,925	2,852	3,910
Nevada...............................	15,570	5,298	5,373	4,898	20,355	32,302	18,827	7,277	6,198	2,805	9,450
New Hampshire....................	26,008	14,986	6,595	4,427	26,795	44,945	31,979	7,987	4,978	6,999	15,204
New Jersey	25,544	13,021	7,653	4,870	27,358	46,835	34,040	7,511	5,284	4,223	7,462
New Mexico	15,029	6,262	4,492	4,275	15,842	30,395	20,532	5,562	4,301	1,553	4,909
New York............................	21,489	7,647	8,990	4,853	20,305	50,295	36,361	8,463	5,472	4,969	8,756
North Carolina.....................	16,364	6,944	5,302	4,119	23,309	40,532	29,307	5,782	5,443	2,391	8,300
North Dakota.......................	14,847	7,208	3,002	4,637	17,727	20,103	13,883	2,854	3,366	4,506	8,719
Ohio...................................	20,931	9,757	6,123	5,051	23,179	39,449	28,953	5,419	5,078	3,642	7,738
Oklahoma............................	14,677	6,680	4,127	3,871	18,458	32,303	23,658	4,337	4,309	3,349	8,019
Oregon...............................	20,516	9,406	6,515	4,595	28,676	46,262	35,034	5,789	5,439	4,148	7,874
Pennsylvania.......................	24,236	13,516	6,342	4,377	25,367	49,895	37,237	6,932	5,725	4,791	11,801
Rhode Island.......................	22,722	11,321	7,112	4,289	27,967	51,053	37,406	8,194	5,453	4,266	11,496
South Carolina	21,150	11,791	5,620	3,739	28,702	32,109	23,167	4,549	4,393	4,219	8,510
South Dakota	16,108	8,273	4,094	3,740	11,592	29,775	22,164	3,699	3,913	5,419	5,253
Tennessee..........................	17,735	8,932	4,730	4,073	24,554	34,621	25,053	5,343	4,224	3,940	15,346
Texas..................................	17,395	8,091	4,879	4,425	21,677	39,613	28,880	5,942	4,792	2,017	5,502
Utah...................................	13,344	6,140	3,109	4,094	18,501	15,221	7,571	3,838	3,813	3,569	11,337
Vermont..............................	25,910	15,062	6,862	3,986	36,475	51,862	39,518	6,842	5,502	6,054	11,958
Virginia...............................	21,889	11,669	5,734	4,486	31,559	30,916	21,016	5,312	4,589	4,793	10,867
Washington.........................	18,665	7,782	5,687	5,197	28,849	45,470	34,412	5,814	5,243	3,771	6,565
West Virginia.......................	16,426	6,900	5,105	4,422	18,833	20,186	11,721	4,163	4,302	3,825	9,077
Wisconsin...........................	16,194	8,504	4,558	3,132	21,327	39,363	29,777	5,465	4,121	4,382	7,336
Wyoming	13,942	4,178	4,310	5,454	12,770	NA	18,021	NA	NA	2,788	6,733

NA = Not applicable.

NOTES AND DEFINITIONS: REGION AND STATE EDUCATION STATISTICS

This section provides details about each item's source and relevant definitions. Internet references are provided when available. In some cases, the Internet reference will lead to a general website instead of to the precise data included in this volume. Additional data sources, such as the U.S. Census Bureau's online FERRET (Federal Electronic Research and Review Extraction Tool) and online databases from the National Center for Education Statistics (NCES), were often used.

TABLE B-1

EDUCATIONAL ATTAINMENT

Source: U.S. Census Bureau. *American Community Survey, 2016.* Table B15001. Educational Attainment of the Population 18 Years and Over, by Region, Sex, and Age, 2016. (ACS 5-Year Estimates) http://factfinder2.census.gov.

Statistics for educational attainment only include persons 25 years old and over. Respondents are classified according to the highest degree or the highest level of school completed. The question includes instructions for people currently enrolled in school to report the level of the previous grade attended or the highest degree received.

High school graduate or more. This category includes persons who have received a high school diploma or its equivalent, and those who reported any level higher than a high school diploma.

Bachelor's degree or more. This category includes persons who have received bachelor's degrees, master's degrees, professional school degrees (such as law school or medical school degrees), and doctoral degrees.

TABLE B-2

Source: U.S. Census Bureau. *American Community Survey*, 2016. 1-year estimates. Tables C15002, C15002A, C15002B, C15002D, and C15002H. Attainment of the Population 25 Over, by Region, State, Sex, Race, and Hispanic Origin, 2016. http://factfinder2.census.gov.

Tables B-1 and B-2 are from the American Community Survey (ACS), the sample survey that has replaced the long form of the decennial census. The sample data are estimates of the actual figures that would have been obtained from a complete count. Estimates derived from a sample are expected to be different from the 100-percent figures because they are subject to sampling and nonsampling errors. Sampling error in data arises from the selection of people and housing units included in the sample. Nonsampling error affects both sample and 100-percent data. It is introduced as a result of errors that may occur during the data collection and processing phases of the census. Conclusions should not be based on small numbers or small differences and users should consult the ACS website to determine the appropriate margins of error. The ACS is ongoing and data are released on an annual basis for all regions and states.

For additional information about the American Community Survey, see www.census.gov/acs/www/.

Educational attainment. In the ACS, respondents are classified according to the highest degree or the highest level of school completed. The question includes instructions for people currently enrolled in school to report the level of the previous grade attended or the highest degree received.

High school graduate or higher. This category includes persons who have received a high school diploma or its equivalent (for example, GED), and those who reported any level higher than a high school diploma.

Bachelor's degree or higher. This category includes persons who have received bachelor's degrees, master's degrees, professional school degrees (such as law school or medical school degrees), and doctoral degrees.

Geographic Definitions

Data are presented for the four major regions of the United States. These groups of states are as follows:

Northeast: Connecticut, Maine, Massachusetts, New Hampshire, New Jersey, New York, Pennsylvania, Rhode Island, and Vermont

Midwest: Illinois, Indiana, Iowa, Kansas, Michigan, Minnesota, Missouri, Nebraska, North Dakota, Ohio, South Dakota, and Wisconsin

South: Alabama, Arkansas, Delaware, District of Columbia, Florida, Georgia, Kentucky, Louisiana, Maryland, Mississippi, North Carolina, Oklahoma, South Carolina, Tennessee, Texas, Virginia, and West Virginia

West: Alaska, Arizona, California, Colorado, Hawaii, Idaho, Montana, Nevada, New Mexico, Oregon, Utah, Washington, and Wyoming

TABLE B-3

POPULATION

Source: U.S. Census Bureau. *Population Estimates Program.* www.census.gov/popest/states/ and the 2016 American Community Survey. https://factfinder.census.gov

The population data for 2016 are U.S. Census Bureau estimates of the resident population as of July 1, 2015.

INCOME, POVERTY, AND HEALTH INSURANCE

Source: U.S. Census Bureau. American Community Survey, 2016 1-Year Estimates.

The Census Bureau reports income from several major household surveys and programs. Each of these surveys differs from the others in some way, such as the length and detail of its questionnaire, the number of households included (sample size), and the methodology used to collect and process the data. The American Community Survey (ACS) is preferred for subnational data on income and poverty by detailed demographic characteristics, because of its large sample size. The Census Bureau recommends using the ACS for single-year estimates of income and poverty at the state level.

The median income for a family of four is from ACS table B19119 on American FactFinder. "Total income" is the sum of the amounts reported separately for wages, salary, commissions, bonuses, or tips; self-employment income from own nonfarm or farm businesses, including proprietorships and partnerships; interest, dividends, net rental income, royalty income, or income from estates and trusts; Social Security or Railroad Retirement income; Supplemental Security Income (SSI); any public assistance or welfare payments from the state or local welfare office; retirement, survivor, or disability pensions; and any other sources of income received regularly such as Veterans' (VA) payments, unemployment compensation, child support, or alimony. Receipts not counted as income include various "lump sum" payments, such as capital gains or inheritances. The total represents the amount of income received before deductions for personal income taxes, Social Security, bond purchases, union dues, Medicare deductions, and the like.

Poverty status is based on the definition prescribed by the U.S. Office of Management and Budget as the standard to be used by federal agencies for statistical purposes.

Persons lacking health insurance coverage include those not covered by a private health plan or by Medicaid, Medicare, or a military health plan.

LANGUAGE SPOKEN AT HOME
Source: U.S. Census Bureau, *American Community Survey*, 2016. 1-year estimates. Tables S1601 and S1603. http://factfinder2.census.gov.

RACE AND ETHNICITY ORIGIN
Source: U.S. Census Bureau, *American Community Survey*, 2016. 1-year estimates. Table S0901. http://factfinder2.census.gov.

TABLE B-4

CITY, SUBURBAN, TOWN, OR RURAL SCHOOLS
Source: U.S. Department of Education, National Center for Education Statistics (NCES), Common Core of Data (CCD), "Public Elementary/Secondary School Universe Survey," Provisional Version 1a, and the NCES Education Demographic and Geographic Estimates (EDGE), "Public Elementary/Secondary School Universe - Geographic Data," 2015–16. Table 4. https://nces.ed.gov/pubs2018/2018052/tables/table_04.asp.

The locales of "city," "suburban," "town," and "rural" are a collapse of the 12 category, urban-centric locale code.

TABLE B-5

SCHOOL ENROLLMENT OF RESIDENT POPULATION
Source: U.S. Census Bureau. American Community Survey, 2016 1-Year Estimates.

Tables C14002 and B14004 from American FactFinder.

School enrollment is enrollment in a regular school, either public or private, including nursery schools, kindergarten, and elementary schools, as well as schooling that leads to a high school diploma or college degree.

Schools supported and controlled primarily by the federal, state, or local government are defined as public schools (including tribal schools). Schools primarily supported and controlled by religious organizations or other private groups are considered private schools.

TABLE B-6

NUMBER AND TYPE OF SCHOOLS
Sources: U.S. Department of Education. National Center for Education Statistics. *Common Core of Data, 2015–2016; Public Elementary/Secondary School Universe Survey, SY 2015–16 Provisional Version 1a;* nces.ed.gov/ccd.

The state data are from the CCD school universe. Almost 99,000 schools are represented, including all those that were operating in 2015–2016.

Regular schools do not focus primarily on special, vocational, or alternative education, though they may offer these programs in addition to the regular curriculum. Special education schools focus primarily on special education, with materials and instructional approaches adapted to meet students' needs. Vocational education schools focus on vocational, technical, or career education. They provide education or training in at least one semi-skilled or technical occupation. Alternative education schools address students' needs that typically cannot be met in a regular school setting. These schools provide nontraditional educational experiences.

A charter school is a school that provides free public elementary and/or secondary education to eligible students under a specific charter granted by the state legislature or other appropriate authority; the school must have also been designated as a charter school by these authorities. Charter schools can be administered by regular school districts, State Education Agencies (SEAs), or chartering organizations.

A magnet school or program is a special school or program designed to attract students of different racial and ethnic backgrounds for the purpose of reducing, preventing, or eliminating racial isolation and/or to provide an academic or social focus on a particular theme.

A Title I eligible school is a school designated under appropriate state and federal regulations as being high poverty and eligible for participation in programs (such as remedial reading or remedial math) authorized by Title I of P.L. 107–110. A Title I school is one in which the percentage of children from low-income families is at least as high as the percentage of children from low-income families served by the LEA as a whole, or a school designated by the LEA as Title I eligible because 35 percent or more of the children are from low-income families. A Title I schoolwide school is a school in which all the students are designated under appropriate state and federal regulations as eligible for participation in Title I programs authorized by Title I of P.L. 107–110. The number of students who received Title I services is from the Public School Data File of the Schools and Staffing Survey.

TABLE B-7

STUDENTS WHO ARE ELIGIBLE FOR FREE OR REDUCED-PRICE LUNCH

Sources: U.S. Department of Education. National Center for Education Statistics. *Common Core of Data, Public Elementary/ Secondary School Universe Survey, 2015– 2016 v.1a;* nces.ed.gov/ccd/pubschuniv.asp. Accessed through the Elementary/Secondary Information System (ELSI).

The Free and Reduced-Price Lunch Program is a program under the National School Lunch Act that provides cash subsidies for free or reduced-price meals to students based on family size and income criteria. Participation in the Free and Reduced-Price Lunch Program depends on income, and

eligibility is often used to estimate student needs.

STUDENTS WITH INDIVIDUAL EDUCATION PROGRAMS

Sources: U.S. Department of Education. National Center for Education Statistics. *Common Core of Data, Local Education Agency Universe Survey, 2015–2016 v.1a.* nces. ed.gov/ccd/pubagency.asp. Accessed through the Elementary/Secondary Information System (ELSI).

An Individualized Education Program (IEP) is a written instructional plan for students with disabilities who are designated as special education students under IDEA (Individuals with Disabilities Education Act). An IEP includes a statement of present levels of educational performance of a child; a statement of annual goals, including short-term instructional objectives; a statement of specific educational services to be provided and the extent to which the child will be able to participate in regular educational programs; a projected date for initiation and the anticipated duration of services; appropriate objectives, criteria, and evaluation procedures; and schedules for determining, on at least an annual basis, whether instructional objectives are being achieved.

STUDENTS WHO ARE ENGLISH-LANGUAGE LEARNERS

Sources: U.S. Department of Education. National Center for Education Statistics. *Local Education Agency Universe Survey, 2015–2016 v.1a;* nces.ed.gov/ccd/pubagency. asp. Accessed through the Elementary/Secondary Information System (ELSI).

This category includes the number of students who are served in appropriate programs of language assistance (e.g., English as a Second Language, High Intensity Language Training, and bilingual education). This designation changed from Limited-English Proficient (LEP) to English-Language

Learners (ELL) in the 2001–2002 school year.

TABLE B-8

PRIVATE SCHOOLS
Sources: U.S. Department of Education, National Center for Education Statistics, Private School Universe Survey (PSS), 2005-06 through 2015–16. Table 205.80. https://nces.ed.gov/programs/digest/d16/tables/dt16_205.80.asp.

Since 1989, the Census Bureau has conducted the biennial Private School Universe Survey (PSS) for NCES. The PSS is designed to generate biennial data on the total number of private schools, students, and teachers and to build a universe of private schools in all of the states and the District of Columbia to serve as a sampling frame of private schools for NCES sample surveys. The target population for the PSS is every school in all of the states and the District of Columbia that are not primarily supported by public funds, provide instruction for one or more grades between kindergarten and grade 12 (or comparable ungraded levels), and have one or more teachers. Organizations or institutions that provide support for home schooling, but do not provide classroom instruction, are not included. Although the PSS has begun to collect limited data on the many private schools for which kindergarten is the highest grade, the data in this volume are for (traditional) schools that include at least one grade between grades 1 and 12.

A private school is controlled by an individual or agency other than a state, a subdivision of a state, or the federal government; is usually supported primarily by nonpublic funds; and the operation of its program does not rest with publicly elected or appointed officials. Private schools include both nonprofit and proprietary institutions.

Data for private schools in Arkansas, Kansas, and Missouri should be interpreted with caution. The coefficient of variation for these estimates is larger than 25 percent. Reporting standards were not met for private high school graduates in Iowa, North Dakota and Wyoming.

TABLE B-9

PUBLIC SCHOOL STAFF
Source: U.S. Department of Education, National Center for Education Statistics, Common Core of Data (CCD), "State Non-fiscal Survey of Public Elementary/ Secondary Education," 2013–14. Table 213.30. https://nces.ed.gov/programs/digest/d16/tables/dt16_213.30.asp.

The number of teachers represents full-time equivalent teachers employed within the state. Instructional aides directly assist teachers in providing instruction. Instructional coordinators help teachers through curriculum development and in-service training. Support staff includes those involved with food, health, library, maintenance, transportation, security, and other services in public schools. School administrators are principals and assistant principals. School district administrators include the Local Education Agency (LEA) superintendents, deputies, assistant superintendents, and other persons with district-wide responsibilities.

TABLE B-10

REVENUES
Source: U.S. Department of Education. National Center for Education Statistics. "National Public Education Financial Survey (State Fiscal)" (FY 2015).

The state data include adjustments made by NCES. Values that were missing and not reported elsewhere in the survey were imputed based on corresponding proportions in reporting states. Other adjustments were made when a single value was reported that included two or more categories. NCES distributed portions of the single reported value to the missing items. In Nebraska and Wyoming, the fiscal data do not include prekindergarten. In Illinois and Wisconsin, revenues for charter schools are not included. In addition to these adjustments, the NPEFS may also include state-run education programs. Consequently, these numbers may differ from the state totals in Table C, which are derived from a different survey.

Revenues from federal sources include direct grants-in-aid from the federal government, federal grants-in-aid through the state or an intermediate agency, and other revenue in lieu of taxes to compensate a school district for nontaxable federal institutions within a district's boundaries.

State revenues include revenues that can be used without restriction, revenues for categorical purposes, and revenues in lieu of taxation. Also included are revenues from payments made by a state for the benefit of the Local Education Agency (LEA) or contributions of equipment or supplies. Such revenues include the payment of a pension fund by the state on behalf of an LEA employee for services rendered and contributions of fixed assets (property, plant, or equipment), such as school buses and textbooks.

Revenues from local sources include local property and non-property tax revenues, taxes levied or assessed by an LEA, revenues from a local government to the LEA, tuition received, transportation fees, earnings on investments from LEA holdings, net revenues from food services (gross receipts less gross expenditures), net revenues from student activities (gross receipts less gross expenditures), and other revenues (textbook sales, donations, and property rentals). Intermediate revenues were included in local revenue totals. Intermediate revenues are derived from sources other than Local or State Education Agencies; these sources operate at an intermediate level between Local and State Education Agencies and

possess independent fundraising capabilities (such as county or municipal agencies).

EXPENDITURES
Source: U.S. Department of Education. National Center for Education Statistics. "National Public Education Financial Survey (State Fiscal)" (FY 2015).

The state data include adjustments made by NCES. Values that were missing and not reported elsewhere in the survey were imputed based on proportions in reporting states. Other adjustments were made when a single value was reported that included two or more categories. NCES distributed portions of the single reported value to the missing items. In Nebraska and Wyoming, the fiscal data do not include prekindergarten. In Illinois and Wisconsin, expenditures for charter schools are not included. In addition to these adjustments, the NPEFS may include state-run education programs. Consequently, these numbers may differ from the state totals in Table C, which come from a different survey.

Current expenditures consist of expenditures for the categories of instruction, support services, and non-instructional services for salaries; employee benefits; purchased services and supplies; and payments by the state made for or on behalf of school systems. These expenditures do not include expenditures for debt service, capital outlay, and property (e.g., equipment), or direct costs (e.g., Head Start, adult education, community colleges, etc.) and community services expenditures.

Instructional and instruction-related expenses comprise current expenditures for activities that deal directly with the interaction between students and teachers. These expenditures include teacher salaries and benefits, supplies (such as textbooks), instructional staff support (for example, salaries for librarians and instructional specialists), and purchased instructional services.

Support services expenditures consist of current expenditures for activities supporting instruction. These services include operation and maintenance of buildings, school administration, student support services (e.g., nurses, therapists, and guidance counselors), student transportation, school district administration, business services, research, and data processing.

Noninstructional expenditures are mostly for food service, but also consist of expenditures for enterprise operations, such as bookstores and interscholastic athletics.

TABLE B-11

DROPOUTS
Source: U.S Department of Commerce, Census Bureau, American Community Survey (ACS), 1-year sample, 2016. NCES, *Digest of Education Statistics*, Table 219.85a. https://nces.ed.gov/programs/digest/d17/tables/dt17_219.85a.asp.

"Status" dropouts are 16- to 24-year-olds who are not enrolled in school and who have not completed a high school program, regardless of when they left school. People who have received GED credentials are counted as high school completers. Data are based on sample surveys of the entire population in the given age range residing within the United States, including both noninstitutionalized persons (e.g., those living in households, college housing, or military housing located within the United States) and institutionalized persons (e.g., those living in prisons, nursing facilities, or other healthcare facilities). Totals include other racial/ethnic groups not separately shown. Race categories exclude persons of Hispanic ethnicity.

TABLES B-12 TO B-15

HIGHER EDUCATION
Sources: U.S. Department of Education. National Center for Education Statistics.

Integrated Postsecondary Education Data System (IPEDS). *Digest of Education Statistics, 2016.* Chapter 3.

The Integrated Postsecondary Education Data System (IPEDS) surveys approximately 10,000 postsecondary institutions, including universities, colleges, and institutions offering technical and vocational education beyond the high school level. This survey, which began in 1986, replaced the Higher Education General Information Survey (HEGIS). IPEDS is made up of eight integrated components that obtain information on who provides postsecondary education (institutions), who participates in it and completes it (students), what programs are offered and which ones are completed, and the specific human and financial resources involved in the provision of institutionally based postsecondary education. These components are organized into the following categories: Institutional Characteristics, including instructional activity; Fall Enrollment, including age and residence; Enrollment in Occupationally Specific Programs; Completions; Finance; Staff; Salaries of Full-Time Instructional Faculty; and Academic Libraries.

Institutions of higher education include those with courses leading to an associate's degree or higher, or those with courses accepted for credit toward such degrees. A public institution is controlled and operated by publicly elected or appointed officials and derives its primary support from public funds. A private institution is controlled by an individual or agency other than a state, a subdivision of a state, or the federal government; it is usually primarily supported by nonpublic funds, and the operation of its program does not rest with publicly elected or appointed officials. Private institutions comprise both not-for-profit and proprietary institutions.

Full-time students include undergraduate students enrolled for 12 or more semester credits, 12 or more quarter credits, or 24 or more contact hours a week each term; graduate students enrolled for 9 or more semester credits or 9 or more quarter credits, or students involved in thesis or dissertation preparation who are considered full time students by the institution; and first-professional students (as defined by the institution).

Types of institutions include the following:

- Degree-granting institutions, which offer associate's, bachelor's, master's, doctoral and/or first-professional degrees.

- Level categories include four-year and higher (four-year) institutions, at least two but less than four-year (two-year) institutions, and less than two-year institutions.

A four-year institution is a postsecondary institution that offers programs of at least four years' duration or programs at or above the baccalaureate level. This category includes schools that only offer post-baccalaureate certificates and those that only offer graduate programs. Also included are freestanding medical, law, and other first-professional schools.

A two-year institution is a postsecondary institution that offers programs of at least two years' duration but less than four years' duration. This category includes occupational and vocational schools with programs of at least 1,800 hours and academic institutions with programs of less than four years' duration. It does not include bachelor's degree–granting institutions where the baccalaureate program can be completed in three years.

Control categories are public, private not-for-profit, and private for-profit.

Undergraduate students are registered at an institution of higher education and are working in a program leading to a baccalaureate degree or other formal award below the baccalaureate, such as an associate degree.

Postbaccalaureate students are working towards master's or doctor's degree or are enrolled in graduate-level classes, but not enrolled in degree programs.

Race/ethnicity categories are categories used to describe groups to which individuals belong, identify with, or belong to in the eyes of the community. A person may be counted in only one group. Classification is based on self-identification. Race categories exclude persons of Hispanic ethnicity.

A nonresident alien is a person who is not a citizen or national of the United States, and who is in this country on a visa or temporary basis; a nonresident alien does not have the right to remain in the United States indefinitely.

Migration refers to the movement of students from their home state of residence to another state to attend a postsecondary institution. The percentages in columns 123 and 124 refer to all first-time postsecondary students enrolled in degree granting institutions in fall 2012.

An associate's degree is a degree granted for the successful completion of a sub-baccalaureate program of studies, and usually requires at least two years (or the equivalent) of full-time college-level study. This category also includes degrees granted in a cooperative or work-study program.

A bachelor's degree is a degree granted for the successful completion of a baccalaureate program of studies, and usually requires at least four years (or the equivalent) of full-time college-level study. This category includes degrees granted in a cooperative or work-study program.

A master's degree is awarded for successful completion of a program generally requiring

1 or 2 years of full-time, college-level study beyond the bachelor's degree. One type of master's degree, including the master of arts degree (M.A.), and the master of science degree (M.S.), is awarded in the liberal arts and sciences for advanced scholarship in a subject field or discipline and demonstrated ability to perform scholarly research. A second type of master's degree is awarded for the completion of a professionally oriented program. These include master's degrees in education (M.Ed.), business administration (M.B.A.), fine arts (M.F.A.), music (M.M.), social work (M.S.W.), and public administration (M.P.A.) A third type of master's degree is awarded in professional fields for study beyond the first-professional degree, such as the master of laws (L.L.M.) and the masters of science in various medical specializations. Some master's degrees—such as divinity degrees (M.Div. or M.H.L./Rav), which were formerly classified as "first-professional"—may require more than 2 years of full-time study beyond the bachelor's degree.

A doctor's degree is an earned degree that generally carries the title of Doctor. The Doctor of Philosophy degree (Ph.D.) is the highest academic degree and requires mastery within a field of knowledge and demonstrated ability to perform scholarly research.

Other doctor's degrees are awarded for fulfilling specialized requirements in professional fields, such as education (Ed.D.), musical arts (D.M.A.), business administration (D.B.A.), and engineering (D.Eng. or D.E.S.). Many doctor's degrees in academic and professional fields require an earned master's degree as a prerequisite. The doctor's degree classification includes most degrees that NCES formerly classified as first-professional degrees. Such degrees are awarded in the fields of dentistry (D.D.S. or D.M.D.), medicine (M.D.), optometry (O.D.), osteopathic medicine (D.O.), pharmacy (Pharm.D.), podiatry (D.P.M., Pod.D., or D.P.), veterinary medicine (D.V.M.), chiropractic (D.C. or D.C.M.), and law (L.L.B. or J.D.).

Tuition and required fees are payments or charges for instruction or compensation for services, privileges, or the use of equipment, books, or other goods. Data are for the entire academic year and are average charges. In-state tuition and fees were weighted by the number of full-time-equivalent undergraduates, but were not adjusted to reflect student residency. Out-of-state tuition and fees were weighted by the number of first-time freshmen attending the institution in fall 2015 from out of state.

PART C

COUNTY EDUCATION STATISTICS

PART C—COUNTY EDUCATION STATISTICS

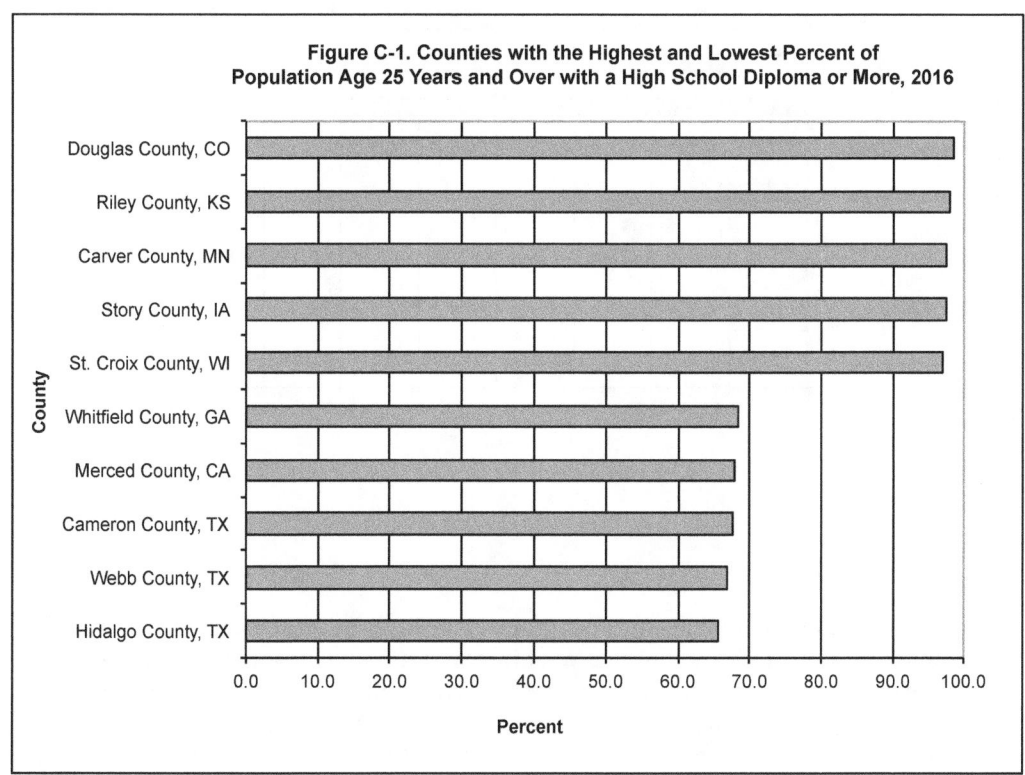

Figure C-1. Counties with the Highest and Lowest Percent of Population Age 25 Years and Over with a High School Diploma or More, 2016

There were 46 counties where more than 95 percent of the population age 25 years old and over had graduated from high school in 2016. The highest proportion was 98.5 percent in Douglas County, Colorado. Seven counties had high school attainment levels of less than 70 percent, including three counties in Texas and three in California.

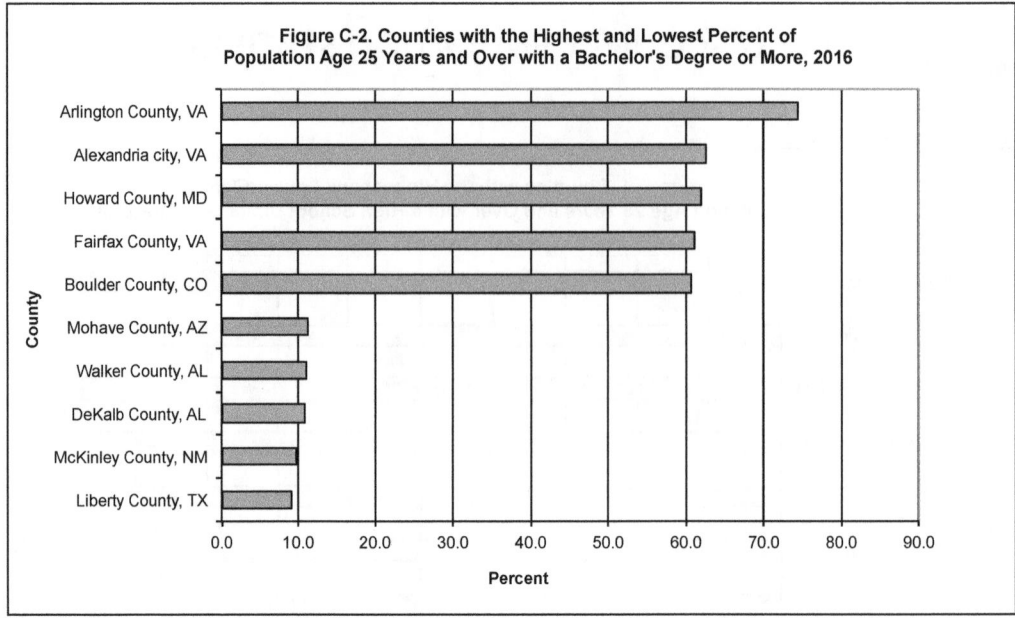

Figure C-2. Counties with the Highest and Lowest Percent of Population Age 25 Years and Over with a Bachelor's Degree or More, 2016

In 2016, 29 counties had college attainment levels that exceeded 60 percent, with Arlington County, Virginia, (which is in the Washington, DC, area) leading the way with 77.1 percent of population age 25 years and over having college degrees. Six of the top ten counties are in the Washington, DC metropolitan area. The others are Douglas County, Colorado (67.2 percent with college degrees); Boulder County, Colorado (66.7 percent college graduates); New York County, New York (64.5 percent); and Hamilton County, Indiana (64.2 percent). Liberty County, Texas, had the lowest college attainment rate at 16.1 percent. (Table C-2)

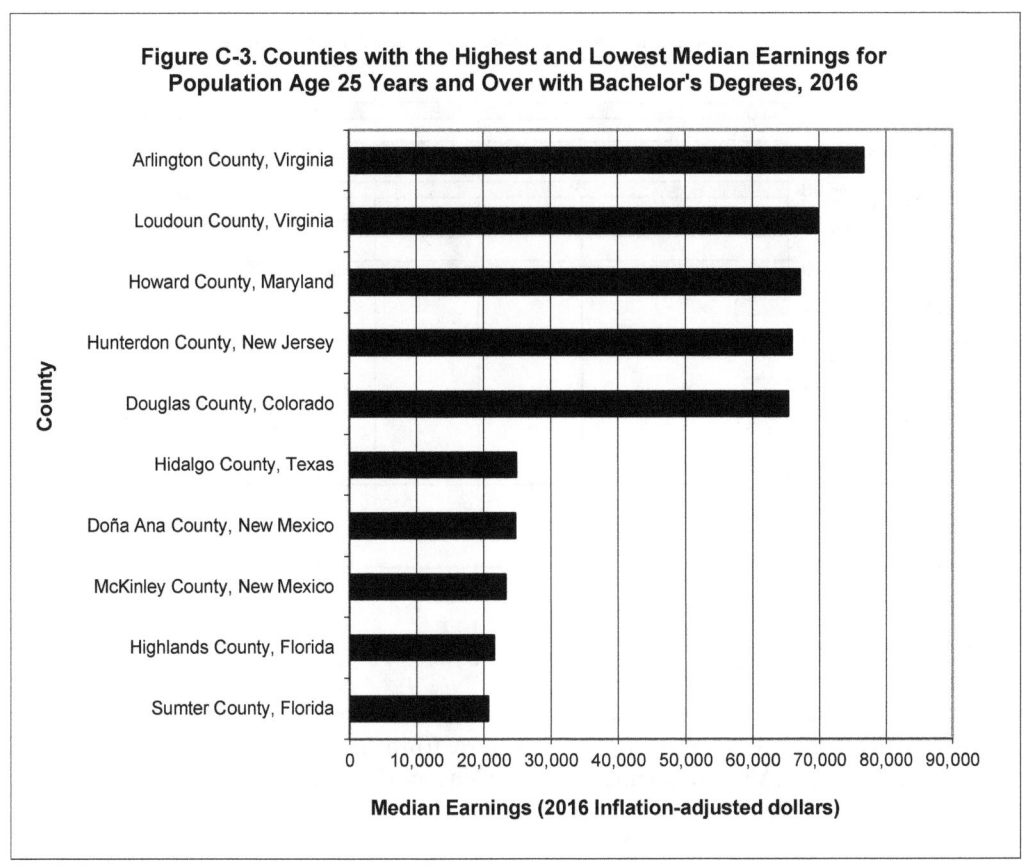

Figure C-3. Counties with the Highest and Lowest Median Earnings for Population Age 25 Years and Over with Bachelor's Degrees, 2016

Arlington County also had the highest median earnings for 2016 at $76,636. Five counties had median earnings of over $65,000. Sumter County, Florida, had the lowest median earnings, $20,619. Sixty-five counties had median earnings under $30,000. (Table C-2)

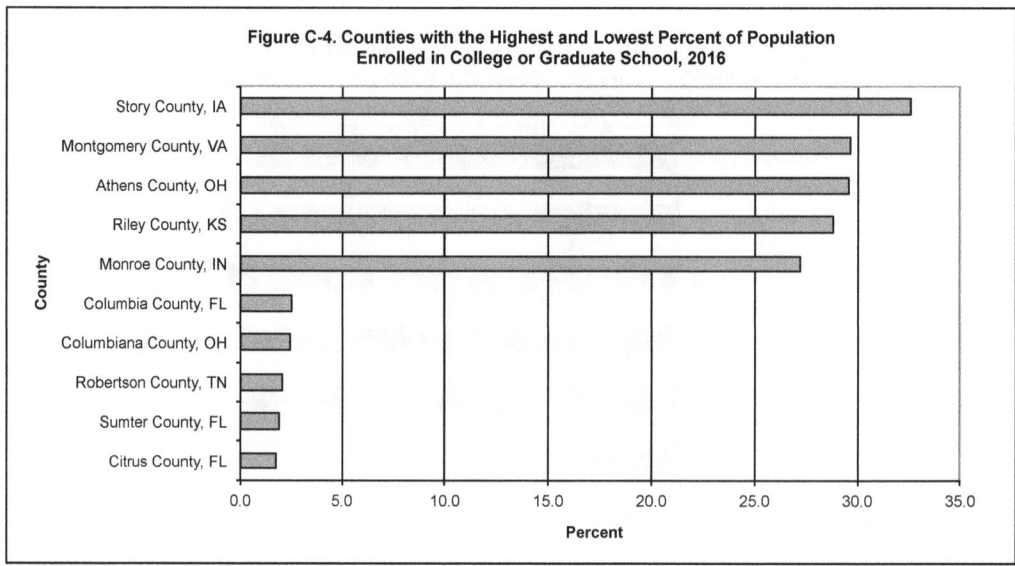

Figure C-4. Counties with the Highest and Lowest Percent of Population Enrolled in College or Graduate School, 2016

The counties with the highest percent of population enrolled in college or graduate school in 2016 were: Story County, Iowa, where Iowa State is located (32.6 percent), Montgomery County, Virginia, which contains Virginia Tech (29.7 percent), and Athens County, Ohio, home to Ohio University (29.6 percent).

Table C-1. Population and Poverty Characteristics, by State and Selected Counties, 2016

(Number; percent.)

State/County	Population		Children under 18 years old in poverty (percent)	Children under 18 years with no health insurance (percent)
	Total under 18 years old	Percent under 18 years old		
UNITED STATES	73,503,793	23.1	19.5	4.5
ALABAMA	1,098,052	23.0	24.5	2.4
Baldwin County, Alabama.................................	45,880	22.2	15.5	2.5
Calhoun County, Alabama................................	24,832	22.0	24.9	1.1
Cullman County, Alabama................................	17,941	22.0	19.2	1.0
DeKalb County, Alabama.................................	17,102	24.4	35.9	1.5
Elmore County, Alabama.................................	18,619	24.3	24.6	1.7
Etowah County, Alabama.................................	22,574	22.2	25.0	1.2
Houston County, Alabama...............................	24,379	23.6	29.7	2.9
Jefferson County, Alabama	151,541	23.2	21.3	2.9
Lauderdale County, Alabama............................	18,893	20.7	15.1	2.4
Lee County, Alabama......................................	34,070	21.6	17.3	0.3
Limestone County, Alabama............................	21,258	23.7	18.4	4.3
Madison County, Alabama...............................	78,764	22.4	19.6	1.6
Marshall County, Alabama...............................	23,493	24.9	38.0	3.3
Mobile County, Alabama	98,267	24.1	30.6	3.4
Montgomery County, Alabama..........................	52,334	23.6	27.9	1.8
Morgan County, Alabama.................................	27,295	23.3	24.8	4.2
St. Clair County, Alabama...............................	20,199	23.5	12.4	1.4
Shelby County, Alabama	50,551	24.2	10.3	1.6
Talladega County, Alabama.............................	17,517	22.7	17.1	0.7
Tuscaloosa County, Alabama...........................	43,367	21.2	21.6	0.7
Walker County, Alabama	14,386	22.4	34.8	1.7
ALASKA..	186,839	26.0	14.1	10.0
Anchorage Municipality, Alaska...........................	73,785	25.7	8.4	7.2
Fairbanks North Star Borough, Alaska	24,432	25.9	17.8	7.2
Matanuska-Susitna Borough, Alaska....................	28,328	27.7	9.0	10.4
ARIZONA	1,629,040	23.9	23.6	7.3
Apache County, Arizona	20,931	28.9	41.1	19.0
Cochise County, Arizona	27,697	23.7	38.3	4.6
Coconino County, Arizona................................	29,022	20.7	18.9	9.0
Maricopa County, Arizona	1,038,894	24.7	21.7	7.1
Mohave County, Arizona	36,807	18.3	24.5	4.3
Navajo County, Arizona	30,656	28.5	37.9	6.9
Pima County, Arizona	216,945	21.8	27.2	6.4
Pinal County, Arizona	98,129	25.0	22.8	5.9
Yavapai County, Arizona.................................	37,250	16.6	13.3	9.1
Yuma County, Arizona....................................	52,383	26.3	27.3	14.8
ARKANSAS...	705,155	24.0	23.8	3.6
Benton County, Arkansas................................	69,195	26.9	11.3	2.5
Craighead County, Arkansas	26,080	24.9	18.6	4.2
Faulkner County, Arkansas..............................	28,354	23.4	19.1	6.6
Garland County, Arkansas	20,272	21.1	36.4	1.2
Jefferson County, Arkansas.............................	15,777	24.0	27.4	4.0
Lonoke County, Arkansas................................	18,435	26.1	23.8	4.4
Pulaski County, Arkansas................................	92,566	23.9	27.0	2.5
Saline County, Arkansas.................................	27,671	23.6	10.0	1.2
Sebastian County, Arkansas............................	30,837	24.3	20.6	2.0
Washington County, Arkansas	56,130	24.8	17.4	8.7
White County, Arkansas	18,713	23.8	19.0	7.3
CALIFORNIA	9,079,778	23.4	19.9	2.9
Alameda County, California	345,092	21.1	12.4	1.8
Butte County, California..................................	45,588	20.4	22.0	2.4
Contra Costa County, California	261,155	23.1	10.2	1.9
El Dorado County, California	37,897	20.6	5.8	3.1
Fresno County, California	280,157	28.9	37.9	2.9
Humboldt County, California	26,510	19.5	17.1	4.5
Imperial County, California	51,728	30.1	33.7	2.7
Kern County, California	257,805	30.1	32.3	2.3
Kings County, California	40,910	30.8	20.1	2.0
Lake County, California	13,273	20.9	27.7	1.0
Los Angeles County, California.........................	2,249,080	22.3	23.4	3.7
Madera County, California...............................	42,532	28.9	32.4	1.6
Marin County, California..................................	53,019	20.7	9.6	0.8
Mendocino County, California	19,259	22.2	27.4	4.1

Table C-1. Population and Poverty Characteristics, by State and Selected Counties, 2016—*Continued*

(Number; percent.)

State/County	Population		Children under 18 years old in poverty (percent)	Children under 18 years with no health insurance (percent)
	Total under 18 years old	Percent under 18 years old		
CALIFORNIA—*(Continued)*				
Merced County, California	80,144	30.1	27.1	2.8
Monterey County, California	114,648	27.3	18.9	3.0
Napa County, California	30,062	21.4	5.2	1.7
Nevada County, California	17,720	18.0	8.3	5.0
Orange County, California	711,763	22.6	14.4	2.5
Placer County, California	85,313	22.6	7.3	3.3
Riverside County, California	613,052	25.9	21.1	4.0
Sacramento County, California	362,474	24.2	23.8	2.0
San Bernardino County, California	572,812	27.4	26.0	4.0
San Diego County, California	727,449	22.6	16.4	3.2
San Francisco County, California	117,817	13.6	9.0	1.4
San Joaquin County, California	201,144	27.7	18.6	2.0
San Luis Obispo County, California	50,644	18.3	6.6	2.7
San Mateo County, California	161,265	21.2	7.6	1.1
Santa Barbara County, California	99,964	22.8	15.3	3.9
Santa Clara County, California	432,805	22.7	11.1	1.5
Santa Cruz County, California	54,088	19.8	14.9	1.0
Shasta County, California	38,446	21.6	26.4	2.2
Solano County, California	98,774	23.1	18.9	2.4
Sonoma County, California	100,333	20.1	10.0	2.7
Stanislaus County, California	146,869	27.3	18.2	2.2
Sutter County, California	24,945	26.1	30.3	5.9
Tulare County, California	143,794	31.5	33.9	4.1
Ventura County, California	200,020	23.7	11.6	3.5
Yolo County, California	45,565	21.2	15.4	0.8
Yuba County, California	20,962	28.7	19.3	1.6
COLORADO	1,258,167	23.1	13.4	4.0
Adams County, Colorado	135,939	27.5	15.7	5.4
Arapahoe County, Colorado	152,429	24.2	11.8	5.1
Boulder County, Colorado	63,369	19.8	6.4	1.6
Broomfield County, Colorado	15,667	23.7	9.9	0.6
Denver County, Colorado	140,483	20.4	19.9	2.4
Douglas County, Colorado	89,406	27.3	3.1	1.7
El Paso County, Colorado	168,744	25.8	15.6	2.6
Jefferson County, Colorado	115,484	20.4	6.3	2.6
Larimer County, Colorado	67,948	20.1	9.7	6.7
Mesa County, Colorado	33,682	22.6	18.4	8.0
Pueblo County, Colorado	37,690	23.3	26.5	2.7
Weld County, Colorado	78,243	26.8	13.3	4.0
CONNECTICUT	751,459	21.3	12.9	2.8
Fairfield County, Connecticut	217,579	23.2	9.9	5.1
Hartford County, Connecticut	190,209	21.6	15.0	1.8
Litchfield County, Connecticut	34,218	18.9	7.8	3.2
Middlesex County, Connecticut	30,180	18.7	12.1	2.5
New Haven County, Connecticut	176,285	20.8	16.1	1.8
New London County, Connecticut	53,552	20.7	13.7	0.9
Tolland County, Connecticut	26,574	17.9	4.8	2.2
Windham County, Connecticut	22,862	20.0	14.2	1.3
DELAWARE	203,704	21.7	17.4	3.1
Kent County, Delaware	40,390	23.5	22.0	5.3
New Castle County, Delaware	121,478	22.1	14.1	2.5
Sussex County, Delaware	41,836	19.2	22.6	2.7
DISTRICT OF COLUMBIA	120,313	17.9	25.8	3.1
District of Columbia, District of Columbia	120,313	17.9	25.8	3.1
FLORIDA	4,136,345	20.4	21.0	6.2
Alachua County, Florida	47,703	18.3	23.1	4.2
Bay County, Florida	39,906	22.3	22.1	10.4
Brevard County, Florida	106,901	18.6	22.9	4.5
Broward County, Florida	406,743	21.4	18.3	7.0
Charlotte County, Florida	22,764	13.0	26.1	5.5
Citrus County, Florida	20,064	14.2	29.8	8.2
Clay County, Florida	49,345	24.1	12.9	5.4
Collier County, Florida	63,933	17.6	16.6	11.8
Columbia County, Florida	14,748	22.9	17.8	7.7
Duval County, Florida	209,470	23.2	20.0	5.0
Escambia County, Florida	65,678	22.0	24.3	4.6

Table C-1. Population and Poverty Characteristics, by State and Selected Counties, 2016—Continued

(Number; percent.)

State/County	Population		Children under 18 years old in poverty (percent)	Children under 18 years with no health insurance (percent)
	Total under 18 years old	Percent under 18 years old		
FLORIDA—(Continued)				
Flagler County, Florida	18,825	17.4	15.7	12.2
Hernando County, Florida	34,117	18.8	21.9	6.8
Highlands County, Florida	17,677	17.7	33.6	6.3
Hillsborough County, Florida	315,937	23.1	20.2	4.9
Indian River County, Florida	24,609	16.4	20.1	2.9
Lake County, Florida	65,222	19.6	18.3	2.8
Lee County, Florida	131,205	18.3	22.8	7.2
Leon County, Florida	53,425	18.8	16.0	2.6
Manatee County, Florida	70,899	19.0	21.2	5.7
Marion County, Florida	64,984	19.1	29.2	7.5
Martin County, Florida	26,951	17.4	16.2	10.0
Miami-Dade County, Florida	551,795	20.5	25.0	6.4
Monroe County, Florida	11,838	15.4	11.7	9.2
Nassau County, Florida	15,875	20.0	12.4	5.1
Okaloosa County, Florida	44,162	23.5	12.3	4.0
Orange County, Florida	295,446	22.7	22.7	5.7
Osceola County, Florida	82,888	24.8	22.7	7.3
Palm Beach County, Florida	279,302	19.5	19.1	7.3
Pasco County, Florida	103,765	20.5	18.0	4.6
Pinellas County, Florida	160,045	16.8	19.7	7.7
Polk County, Florida	149,219	22.7	25.9	5.8
Putnam County, Florida	15,591	21.9	33.4	5.7
St. Johns County, Florida	51,921	22.2	6.6	2.9
St. Lucie County, Florida	61,959	20.4	29.3	9.0
Santa Rosa County, Florida	37,854	23.7	14.9	3.4
Sarasota County, Florida	59,838	14.6	17.9	6.6
Seminole County, Florida	96,566	21.3	13.5	7.9
Sumter County, Florida	8,654	7.5	18.0	10.8
Volusia County, Florida	94,064	17.9	17.4	4.8
Walton County, Florida	12,928	20.3	14.1	10.3
GEORGIA	2,506,326	24.8	22.9	6.5
Barrow County, Georgia	20,522	26.7	20.4	9.1
Bartow County, Georgia	25,843	25.3	25.1	11.1
Bibb County, Georgia	37,910	25.4	37.2	4.3
Bulloch County, Georgia	14,638	19.8	28.4	7.2
Carroll County, Georgia	27,996	24.4	15.1	12.1
Catoosa County, Georgia	15,185	23.0	13.6	7.9
Chatham County, Georgia	63,261	22.5	24.5	3.6
Cherokee County, Georgia	61,109	25.4	10.0	9.2
Clarke County, Georgia	21,278	17.2	26.5	3.6
Clayton County, Georgia	78,935	28.6	31.5	10.6
Cobb County, Georgia	181,345	24.4	12.5	8.2
Columbia County, Georgia	38,238	26.8	8.1	1.8
Coweta County, Georgia	35,418	25.3	12.3	3.8
DeKalb County, Georgia	175,226	23.9	25.6	8.5
Dougherty County, Georgia	22,412	25.4	41.1	4.7
Douglas County, Georgia	37,105	26.3	17.5	3.6
Fayette County, Georgia	26,023	23.4	5.7	1.2
Floyd County, Georgia	22,334	23.7	14.1	1.6
Forsyth County, Georgia	62,003	28.2	8.0	2.9
Fulton County, Georgia	231,500	22.8	24.3	4.8
Glynn County, Georgia	19,397	23.2	30.9	8.2
Gwinnett County, Georgia	249,140	27.6	16.8	8.4
Hall County, Georgia	51,030	26.1	18.5	8.6
Henry County, Georgia	58,466	26.5	13.3	5.9
Houston County, Georgia	38,989	26.0	22.2	7.5
Liberty County, Georgia	17,582	31.2	18.8	4.9
Lowndes County, Georgia	27,378	25.4	29.0	4.4
Muscogee County, Georgia	48,002	25.7	29.1	3.6
Newton County, Georgia	28,495	26.8	36.5	4.5
Paulding County, Georgia	41,970	27.1	14.0	7.2
Richmond County, Georgia	46,728	24.4	40.2	3.4
Rockdale County, Georgia	22,459	25.4	22.6	4.9
Troup County, Georgia	17,455	25.5	32.4	5.9
Walker County, Georgia	15,296	23.0	27.7	4.2
Walton County, Georgia	22,773	25.5	20.0	5.0
Whitfield County, Georgia	28,257	27.2	23.9	11.4
HAWAII	307,561	22.3	10.1	2.2
Hawaii County, Hawaii	42,773	21.8	16.6	1.7

Table C-1. Population and Poverty Characteristics, by State and Selected Counties, 2016—*Continued*

(Number; percent.)

State/County	Population		Children under 18 years old in poverty (percent)	Children under 18 years with no health insurance (percent)
	Total under 18 years old	Percent under 18 years old		
HAWAII—(*Continued*)				
Honolulu County, Hawaii	211,751	22.4	9.6	2.3
Kauai County, Hawaii	16,190	22.7	3.9	2.6
Maui County, Hawaii	36,847	22.4	8.6	2.5
IDAHO	435,630	26.2	17.7	4.7
Ada County, Idaho	108,253	24.7	11.8	4.4
Bannock County, Idaho	22,492	27.0	20.3	1.5
Bonneville County, Idaho	34,721	31.3	14.5	2.9
Canyon County, Idaho	62,071	29.5	17.3	5.1
Kootenai County, Idaho	35,314	23.1	26.9	1.3
Twin Falls County, Idaho	23,174	28.0	18.6	6.1
ILLINOIS	2,919,863	23.1	17.7	2.4
Adams County, Illinois	15,029	23.0	14.4	3.4
Champaign County, Illinois	38,726	18.8	11.8	2.5
Cook County, Illinois	1,160,774	22.5	21.2	2.5
DeKalb County, Illinois	22,830	22.0	19.8	1.2
DuPage County, Illinois	213,714	23.1	9.6	2.5
Kane County, Illinois	139,489	26.4	16.2	4.2
Kankakee County, Illinois	25,852	24.0	21.9	2.0
Kendall County, Illinois	35,844	28.8	4.9	0.4
Lake County, Illinois	174,193	25.3	10.5	2.8
LaSalle County, Illinois	23,577	22.0	20.7	0.6
McHenry County, Illinois	74,287	24.3	11.3	2.3
McLean County, Illinois	37,553	21.9	11.4	1.4
Macon County, Illinois	23,624	22.7	29.4	3.0
Madison County, Illinois	58,209	22.1	18.3	3.7
Peoria County, Illinois	44,380	24.3	18.7	1.6
Rock Island County, Illinois	32,209	22.6	29.4	3.2
St. Clair County, Illinois	62,425	24.4	21.0	3.4
Sangamon County, Illinois	44,758	22.9	21.3	1.8
Tazewell County, Illinois	30,307	23.0	9.3	0.9
Vermilion County, Illinois	18,625	24.7	30.4	1.3
Will County, Illinois	177,102	26.0	10.3	1.3
Williamson County, Illinois	15,087	23.0	20.0	0.0
Winnebago County, Illinois	67,118	23.7	23.6	1.4
INDIANA	1,573,925	24.1	19.5	5.9
Allen County, Indiana	96,138	26.2	21.5	4.4
Bartholomew County, Indiana	19,394	24.0	18.4	9.3
Clark County, Indiana	26,671	23.3	14.9	3.2
Delaware County, Indiana	20,992	18.4	26.5	5.1
Elkhart County, Indiana	56,431	28.0	17.9	14.8
Floyd County, Indiana	17,075	22.5	10.2	1.8
Grant County, Indiana	13,914	21.0	33.2	1.0
Hamilton County, Indiana	87,890	27.9	6.9	3.0
Hancock County, Indiana	17,402	23.8	16.6	7.8
Hendricks County, Indiana	40,943	26.1	7.8	4.7
Howard County, Indiana	18,746	22.9	18.8	2.3
Johnson County, Indiana	38,507	25.6	7.7	5.4
Kosciusko County, Indiana	19,148	24.4	17.8	12.6
Lake County, Indiana	116,387	24.1	26.7	1.7
LaPorte County, Indiana	23,901	23.3	32.1	4.5
Madison County, Indiana	28,059	22.4	26.0	6.6
Marion County, Indiana	233,844	25.1	28.5	3.7
Monroe County, Indiana	22,876	15.8	21.2	4.7
Morgan County, Indiana	15,487	22.5	17.1	7.6
Porter County, Indiana	37,756	22.8	4.7	3.7
St. Joseph County, Indiana	64,229	24.1	23.3	6.1
Tippecanoe County, Indiana	39,106	21.0	16.2	5.2
Vanderburgh County, Indiana	39,636	22.1	24.1	1.6
Vigo County, Indiana	22,270	21.4	18.2	6.8
Wayne County, Indiana	14,544	22.2	24.5	8.7
IOWA	724,997	23.5	14.8	2.5
Black Hawk County, Iowa	28,415	21.6	21.6	5.9
Dallas County, Iowa	23,772	28.3	3.5	1.0
Dubuque County, Iowa	22,090	23.1	15.6	1.0
Johnson County, Iowa	29,513	20.4	14.5	3.9
Linn County, Iowa	52,195	23.8	14.1	1.6
Polk County, Iowa	119,061	25.4	15.6	2.3

Table C-1. Population and Poverty Characteristics, by State and Selected Counties, 2016—*Continued*

(Number; percent.)

	Population		Children under 18 years old in poverty (percent)	Children under 18 years with no health insurance (percent)
State/County	Total under 18 years old	Percent under 18 years old		
IOWA—*(Continued)*				
Pottawattamie County, Iowa	21,664	23.4	12.1	0.8
Scott County, Iowa	41,394	24.3	20.4	1.3
Story County, Iowa	15,476	16.1	7.5	0.0
Woodbury County, Iowa	27,102	26.6	16.9	1.0
KANSAS	713,102	25.0	14.1	4.3
Butler County, Kansas	16,958	26.3	9.2	10.9
Douglas County, Kansas	21,847	18.4	10.6	4.3
Johnson County, Kansas	144,935	25.0	5.7	2.9
Leavenworth County, Kansas	19,058	26.1	10.4	2.0
Riley County, Kansas	11,981	17.7	6.5	1.5
Sedgwick County, Kansas	133,393	26.3	19.9	4.1
Shawnee County, Kansas	42,468	24.3	10.5	3.6
Wyandotte County, Kansas	46,019	28.3	24.7	6.6
KENTUCKY	1,009,986	23.2	25.0	3.2
Boone County, Kentucky	34,566	27.2	12.5	0.0
Bullitt County, Kentucky	17,902	22.7	14.6	5.6
Campbell County, Kentucky	19,453	21.4	19.2	0.2
Christian County, Kentucky	19,749	31.5	24.6	9.0
Daviess County, Kentucky	23,888	24.5	20.7	1.6
Fayette County, Kentucky	66,652	21.3	24.8	4.6
Hardin County, Kentucky	26,426	25.5	17.0	0.9
Jefferson County, Kentucky	171,078	22.6	20.7	1.7
Kenton County, Kentucky	39,806	24.3	20.5	2.5
McCracken County, Kentucky	14,177	22.2	27.0	5.0
Madison County, Kentucky	19,018	21.4	28.4	1.9
Pike County, Kentucky	16,706	27.2	7.5	4.2
Warren County, Kentucky	28,421	22.9	25.4	0.4
LOUISIANA	1,115,457	24.4	28.6	3.0
Ascension Parish, Louisiana	33,356	27.6	11.3	3.3
Bossier Parish, Louisiana	31,803	26.9	26.6	4.5
Caddo Parish, Louisiana	60,350	24.7	40.6	2.8
Calcasieu Parish, Louisiana	49,813	25.1	30.9	2.4
East Baton Rouge Parish, Louisiana	100,911	22.7	29.1	1.6
Iberia Parish, Louisiana	19,711	27.2	30.2	1.8
Jefferson Parish, Louisiana	95,435	22.0	25.9	5.3
Lafayette Parish, Louisiana	57,345	24.0	25.5	3.7
Lafourche Parish, Louisiana	23,037	23.7	25.3	7.0
Livingston Parish, Louisiana	36,585	26.3	19.6	0.8
Orleans Parish, Louisiana	79,764	20.8	33.5	3.2
Ouachita Parish, Louisiana	39,503	25.8	38.9	2.9
Rapides Parish, Louisiana	33,101	25.6	27.9	3.4
St. Landry Parish, Louisiana	22,694	27.4	42.5	0.2
St. Tammany Parish, Louisiana	61,150	24.3	7.4	2.6
Tangipahoa Parish, Louisiana	31,844	24.5	28.7	2.4
Terrebonne Parish, Louisiana	29,108	26.0	36.1	2.4
MAINE	254,723	19.3	17.2	4.6
Androscoggin County, Maine	22,980	21.6	19.2	3.0
Aroostook County, Maine	12,518	18.7	23.2	4.7
Cumberland County, Maine	56,079	19.4	12.1	3.3
Kennebec County, Maine	23,766	20.0	23.0	3.8
Penobscot County, Maine	27,944	18.6	19.8	4.8
York County, Maine	39,429	19.7	8.1	5.1
MARYLAND	1,344,588	22.7	12.7	3.3
Allegany County, Maryland	12,716	19.1	20.7	2.1
Anne Arundel County, Maryland	127,234	23.2	9.7	2.3
Baltimore County, Maryland	179,048	21.8	11.5	3.8
Calvert County, Maryland	21,571	23.9	5.0	3.2
Carroll County, Maryland	36,607	22.1	5.3	0.6
Cecil County, Maryland	23,631	23.3	15.7	0.6
Charles County, Maryland	38,184	24.8	9.8	1.6
Frederick County, Maryland	58,093	23.7	6.9	4.0
Harford County, Maryland	56,270	22.7	7.2	1.7
Howard County, Maryland	77,981	24.9	5.6	1.9
Montgomery County, Maryland	244,110	23.6	8.2	2.4
Prince George's County, Maryland	203,527	22.6	12.3	5.3
St. Mary's County, Maryland	27,642	25.2	12.1	12.3

Table C-1. Population and Poverty Characteristics, by State and Selected Counties, 2016—*Continued*

(Number; percent.)

State/County	Population		Children under 18 years old in poverty (percent)	Children under 18 years with no health insurance (percent)
	Total under 18 years old	Percent under 18 years old		
MARYLAND—*(Continued)*				
Washington County, Maryland	33,278	23.5	18.4	6.2
Wicomico County, Maryland	22,612	22.3	29.2	1.7
Baltimore city, Maryland	128,946	21.3	32.2	4.0
MASSACHUSETTS	1,375,244	20.4	13.6	0.9
Barnstable County, Massachusetts	33,684	15.9	9.8	0.1
Berkshire County, Massachusetts	21,773	17.5	8.8	1.6
Bristol County, Massachusetts	115,867	21.0	14.3	0.5
Essex County, Massachusetts	168,121	21.8	14.5	1.1
Franklin County, Massachusetts	12,360	17.8	14.5	0.3
Hampden County, Massachusetts	102,856	22.2	27.7	1.6
Hampshire County, Massachusetts	24,499	15.3	13.6	1.1
Middlesex County, Massachusetts	320,981	20.4	8.8	1.0
Norfolk County, Massachusetts	148,358	21.6	5.7	0.6
Plymouth County, Massachusetts	112,343	22.1	11.3	0.9
Suffolk County, Massachusetts	133,778	17.2	28.7	1.0
Worcester County, Massachusetts	175,567	21.8	11.2	0.9
MICHIGAN	2,187,554	22.3	20.7	2.9
Allegan County, Michigan	28,409	24.8	8.2	1.3
Bay County, Michigan	21,398	20.6	26.5	3.7
Berrien County, Michigan	34,224	22.4	26.4	5.3
Calhoun County, Michigan	30,871	23.3	26.8	2.0
Clinton County, Michigan	17,820	23.0	12.0	1.3
Eaton County, Michigan	23,188	21.4	23.8	3.6
Genesee County, Michigan	93,940	23.1	28.9	3.9
Grand Traverse County, Michigan	19,057	21.1	15.4	7.1
Ingham County, Michigan	57,442	20.1	24.1	3.0
Isabella County, Michigan	12,350	17.5	20.7	3.7
Jackson County, Michigan	34,290	22.7	19.4	3.2
Kalamazoo County, Michigan	56,840	21.9	21.5	2.8
Kent County, Michigan	158,371	24.8	14.7	3.7
Lapeer County, Michigan	18,353	21.1	13.8	5.7
Lenawee County, Michigan	21,036	22.1	15.7	2.0
Livingston County, Michigan	41,556	22.1	5.4	0.9
Macomb County, Michigan	186,601	21.7	16.0	2.3
Marquette County, Michigan	12,358	19.1	12.3	0.7
Midland County, Michigan	17,852	21.6	5.5	4.2
Monroe County, Michigan	32,835	22.1	11.0	1.6
Muskegon County, Michigan	40,557	24.0	29.8	2.8
Oakland County, Michigan	267,556	21.6	10.6	1.9
Ottawa County, Michigan	68,918	24.5	10.7	1.2
Saginaw County, Michigan	41,154	21.8	22.3	1.6
St. Clair County, Michigan	34,117	21.5	20.9	1.2
Shiawassee County, Michigan	14,664	21.5	16.1	0.5
Van Buren County, Michigan	17,980	24.1	27.5	7.2
Washtenaw County, Michigan	69,178	19.3	12.1	1.0
Wayne County, Michigan	418,948	24.1	33.9	2.1
MINNESOTA	1,286,323	23.5	12.7	3.4
Anoka County, Minnesota	83,242	24.2	10.0	2.2
Blue Earth County, Minnesota	12,627	19.2	11.8	2.5
Carver County, Minnesota	26,717	26.7	1.6	4.4
Dakota County, Minnesota	102,930	24.8	6.6	3.3
Hennepin County, Minnesota	272,504	22.3	14.2	3.5
Olmsted County, Minnesota	37,666	24.9	10.7	3.2
Ramsey County, Minnesota	126,306	23.6	20.3	3.5
Rice County, Minnesota	14,077	22.3	16.6	2.3
St. Louis County, Minnesota	37,920	19.3	18.6	1.5
Scott County, Minnesota	40,359	28.5	9.6	3.4
Sherburne County, Minnesota	25,952	28.4	9.3	1.2
Stearns County, Minnesota	35,555	23.0	13.5	1.2
Washington County, Minnesota	62,931	25.2	4.6	2.6
Wright County, Minnesota	37,287	28.3	4.5	1.2
MISSISSIPPI	721,108	24.7	29.7	4.5
DeSoto County, Mississippi	45,837	26.3	14.3	3.4
Forrest County, Mississippi	17,380	23.1	45.8	6.8
Harrison County, Mississippi	48,974	25.1	36.8	5.6
Hinds County, Mississippi	58,776	24.6	29.6	2.6
Jackson County, Mississippi	34,099	24.4	27.0	6.4

Table C-1. Population and Poverty Characteristics, by State and Selected Counties, 2016—*Continued*

(Number; percent.)

State/County	Population		Children under 18 years old in poverty (percent)	Children under 18 years with no health insurance (percent)
	Total under 18 years old	Percent under 18 years old		
MISSISSIPPI—(*Continued*)				
Jones County, Mississippi	17,351	25.8	29.6	2.2
Lauderdale County, Mississippi	18,990	25.5	34.6	8.5
Lee County, Mississippi	21,765	25.8	20.8	2.3
Madison County, Mississippi	26,443	25.4	17.5	2.8
Rankin County, Mississippi	35,882	24.7	10.1	6.5
MISSOURI	1,386,471	23.2	19.2	4.5
Boone County, Missouri	35,845	20.5	16.9	2.3
Buchanan County, Missouri	20,024	23.3	26.3	0.9
Cape Girardeau County, Missouri	16,871	21.8	9.9	4.5
Cass County, Missouri	25,105	24.6	13.3	2.4
Christian County, Missouri	21,844	26.0	17.8	4.8
Clay County, Missouri	58,518	24.6	13.9	2.7
Cole County, Missouri	17,414	23.9	13.4	0.8
Franklin County, Missouri	23,877	23.4	17.9	2.5
Greene County, Missouri	60,154	21.1	17.4	4.6
Jackson County, Missouri	165,400	24.2	24.7	5.7
Jasper County, Missouri	29,948	25.3	21.9	3.5
Jefferson County, Missouri	53,205	23.9	13.4	2.9
Platte County, Missouri	23,439	24.1	5.6	2.0
St. Charles County, Missouri	93,160	24.0	5.7	1.4
St. Francois County, Missouri	13,891	23.1	8.6	1.6
St. Louis County, Missouri	221,134	22.4	12.3	3.2
St. Louis city, Missouri	61,564	20.1	38.2	3.7
MONTANA	227,631	22.2	15.1	4.7
Cascade County, Montana	18,267	23.4	18.5	2.5
Flathead County, Montana	21,759	22.3	16.4	3.1
Gallatin County, Montana	21,261	20.4	6.0	5.6
Lewis and Clark County, Montana	14,719	22.1	10.3	2.2
Missoula County, Montana	21,982	19.0	18.9	3.5
Yellowstone County, Montana	37,222	23.8	5.9	3.6
NEBRASKA	472,689	25.2	14.2	5.0
Douglas County, Nebraska	142,554	26.0	16.2	5.1
Lancaster County, Nebraska	71,090	23.3	14.2	3.3
Sarpy County, Nebraska	49,633	28.4	6.2	1.9
NEVADA	676,435	23.3	19.1	6.8
Clark County, Nevada	506,168	23.7	19.9	6.8
Washoe County, Nevada	99,508	22.1	16.0	5.8
NEW HAMPSHIRE	259,410	19.7	7.9	2.6
Cheshire County, New Hampshire	13,605	18.1	5.5	6.0
Grafton County, New Hampshire	14,591	16.6	11.7	3.3
Hillsborough County, New Hampshire	85,314	21.2	9.8	1.9
Merrimack County, New Hampshire	28,795	19.9	5.0	3.3
Rockingham County, New Hampshire	60,292	20.0	2.2	2.4
Strafford County, New Hampshire	23,977	19.0	3.1	1.6
NEW JERSEY	1,979,948	22.4	14.6	3.5
Atlantic County, New Jersey	58,932	21.9	24.2	3.5
Bergen County, New Jersey	201,136	21.6	7.7	4.2
Burlington County, New Jersey	93,872	21.6	7.8	1.5
Camden County, New Jersey	117,396	23.3	15.3	2.3
Cape May County, New Jersey	16,601	18.0	17.5	2.9
Cumberland County, New Jersey	36,561	25.9	25.5	6.2
Essex County, New Jersey	189,189	24.1	21.1	5.3
Gloucester County, New Jersey	65,441	22.5	7.7	1.6
Hudson County, New Jersey	138,448	20.6	22.3	6.4
Hunterdon County, New Jersey	24,197	20.0	6.2	1.5
Mercer County, New Jersey	79,552	21.7	15.1	2.4
Middlesex County, New Jersey	181,930	22.0	11.4	2.5
Monmouth County, New Jersey	135,294	21.7	8.9	2.8
Morris County, New Jersey	108,075	21.8	5.8	1.8
Ocean County, New Jersey	140,100	23.9	19.0	1.5
Passaic County, New Jersey	122,843	24.4	27.6	4.3
Salem County, New Jersey	13,693	22.0	25.2	3.3
Somerset County, New Jersey	74,491	22.5	5.0	4.6
Sussex County, New Jersey	29,208	20.6	6.6	1.4
Union County, New Jersey	131,136	23.8	15.0	5.3

Table C-1. Population and Poverty Characteristics, by State and Selected Counties, 2016—*Continued*

(Number; percent.)

State/County	Population		Children under 18 years old in poverty (percent)	Children under 18 years with no health insurance (percent)
	Total under 18 years old	Percent under 18 years old		
NEW JERSEY—(*Continued*)				
Warren County, New Jersey	21,853	20.6	15.4	6.4
NEW MEXICO	488,598	23.9	30.1	5.3
Bernalillo County, New Mexico	151,514	22.6	26.4	3.4
Chaves County, New Mexico	17,795	27.7	37.3	9.8
Doña Ana County, New Mexico	53,334	25.3	40.7	6.3
Lea County, New Mexico	21,228	31.3	34.6	6.5
McKinley County, New Mexico	22,418	30.0	50.6	9.7
Otero County, New Mexico	15,433	25.8	35.5	2.8
Sandoval County, New Mexico	33,947	24.1	21.4	10.3
San Juan County, New Mexico	29,598	26.0	25.5	8.1
Santa Fe County, New Mexico	27,761	18.9	24.8	4.9
Valencia County, New Mexico	18,209	24.6	27.8	4.4
NEW YORK	4,170,786	21.4	20.7	2.4
Albany County, New York	57,342	18.8	15.7	0.7
Bronx County, New York	367,900	25.6	40.1	1.5
Broome County, New York	38,503	20.0	26.1	1.6
Cattaraugus County, New York	17,559	22.8	16.3	7.0
Cayuga County, New York	15,336	20.6	15.5	2.4
Chautauqua County, New York	26,586	20.9	31.0	7.6
Chemung County, New York	18,286	22.2	20.3	12.4
Clinton County, New York	13,774	18.0	18.3	0.2
Dutchess County, New York	56,523	19.8	10.5	2.9
Erie County, New York	188,595	20.7	19.9	1.6
Jefferson County, New York	27,459	26.9	23.1	7.0
Kings County, New York	609,060	23.3	28.4	2.3
Livingston County, New York	11,124	18.1	19.1	2.2
Madison County, New York	13,592	19.2	6.0	2.8
Monroe County, New York	157,397	21.3	21.8	1.2
Nassau County, New York	295,875	21.9	7.6	1.8
New York County, New York	240,579	14.7	23.1	1.2
Niagara County, New York	42,766	20.4	17.9	1.8
Oneida County, New York	48,741	21.8	28.0	1.6
Onondaga County, New York	100,528	21.8	20.4	2.0
Ontario County, New York	22,469	20.6	16.9	1.6
Orange County, New York	97,120	26.1	19.6	2.7
Oswego County, New York	25,316	21.4	25.2	0.8
Putnam County, New York	20,181	20.5	3.9	1.8
Queens County, New York	476,209	20.6	17.4	2.6
Rensselaer County, New York	31,953	20.2	18.6	3.4
Richmond County, New York	104,843	22.2	19.1	1.5
Rockland County, New York	90,591	27.9	27.4	3.7
St. Lawrence County, New York	22,173	20.8	21.8	7.9
Saratoga County, New York	46,446	20.8	5.0	1.4
Schenectady County, New York	33,625	22.0	12.7	0.0
Steuben County, New York	21,095	22.0	20.9	6.3
Suffolk County, New York	322,562	21.8	10.1	2.7
Sullivan County, New York	16,043	22.2	17.3	2.1
Tompkins County, New York	15,274	14.7	17.9	4.0
Ulster County, New York	32,597	18.7	17.7	1.9
Warren County, New York	11,890	18.6	19.6	2.8
Wayne County, New York	19,610	21.8	17.1	4.9
Westchester County, New York	217,858	22.6	10.6	2.8
NORTH CARLOINA	2,292,483	23.0	21.7	4.5
Alamance County, North Carolina	35,675	22.5	27.5	4.4
Brunswick County, North Carolina	20,073	15.9	19.3	2.0
Buncombe County, North Carolina	48,440	19.2	17.9	3.6
Burke County, North Carolina	16,796	19.4	31.3	4.9
Cabarrus County, North Carolina	52,577	26.3	19.5	2.6
Caldwell County, North Carolina	16,345	20.3	19.6	1.6
Carteret County, North Carolina	12,514	18.5	8.5	5.7
Catawba County, North Carolina	35,252	22.8	15.3	2.1
Chatham County, North Carolina	14,876	20.8	19.6	3.4
Cleveland County, North Carolina	21,486	22.2	28.1	8.9
Craven County, North Carolina	22,603	23.4	22.6	2.7
Cumberland County, North Carolina	82,822	27.4	27.7	3.2
Davidson County, North Carolina	36,891	22.7	23.3	5.8
Durham County, North Carolina	66,050	22.0	25.0	8.8

Table C-1. Population and Poverty Characteristics, by State and Selected Counties, 2016—*Continued*

(Number; percent.)

State/County	Population		Children under 18 years old in poverty (percent)	Children under 18 years with no health insurance (percent)
	Total under 18 years old	Percent under 18 years old		
NORTH CARLOINA—*(Continued)*				
Forsyth County, North Carolina	87,260	23.7	25.7	4.9
Gaston County, North Carolina	49,422	23.0	23.4	6.1
Guilford County, North Carolina	117,989	22.8	26.8	2.9
Harnett County, North Carolina	35,046	28.0	19.8	3.8
Henderson County, North Carolina	21,790	19.3	14.6	2.3
Iredell County, North Carolina	40,540	23.6	12.6	5.1
Johnston County, North Carolina	49,956	26.3	20.9	6.0
Lincoln County, North Carolina	17,180	21.3	18.9	3.4
Mecklenburg County, North Carolina	254,831	24.3	18.0	6.4
Moore County, North Carolina	20,061	21.6	12.6	0.8
Nash County, North Carolina	20,178	21.7	23.0	2.7
New Hanover County, North Carolina	42,202	19.1	21.9	3.2
Onslow County, North Carolina	47,478	29.9	17.6	1.7
Orange County, North Carolina	28,734	20.4	7.6	7.1
Pitt County, North Carolina	38,678	22.0	21.9	6.4
Randolph County, North Carolina	32,904	23.2	18.6	4.9
Robeson County, North Carolina	34,139	26.0	38.6	1.6
Rockingham County, North Carolina	18,838	20.9	30.6	4.7
Rowan County, North Carolina	31,438	22.8	27.5	3.4
Rutherford County, North Carolina	13,510	20.6	19.9	2.5
Surry County, North Carolina	15,357	21.6	24.4	4.4
Union County, North Carolina	62,826	27.9	13.0	2.2
Wake County, North Carolina	256,665	24.7	11.7	3.4
Wayne County, North Carolina	29,858	24.9	32.9	6.9
Wilkes County, North Carolina	14,294	21.1	25.0	3.4
Wilson County, North Carolina	19,014	23.7	39.0	2.8
NORTH DAKOTA	174,130	23.5	12.4	7.8
Burleigh County, North Dakota	22,239	24.1	7.5	10.0
Cass County, North Dakota	39,163	22.6	15.2	3.1
Grand Forks County, North Dakota	14,088	20.5	13.4	6.4
Ward County, North Dakota	16,122	24.3	6.8	5.4
OHIO	2,605,997	22.8	20.5	3.6
Allen County, Ohio	23,917	23.7	21.3	4.0
Ashtabula County, Ohio	21,898	23.0	26.5	13.9
Athens County, Ohio	9,557	14.6	20.9	2.5
Belmont County, Ohio	12,989	20.0	22.3	6.3
Butler County, Ohio	89,395	23.9	17.0	2.5
Clark County, Ohio	30,422	22.9	20.6	4.9
Clermont County, Ohio	47,429	23.5	12.6	2.0
Columbiana County, Ohio	21,241	21.2	35.0	4.5
Cuyahoga County, Ohio	264,419	21.4	26.3	1.9
Delaware County, Ohio	53,032	27.1	4.9	1.4
Erie County, Ohio	15,309	20.7	16.9	4.8
Fairfield County, Ohio	37,178	24.8	14.1	1.7
Franklin County, Ohio	297,503	23.7	24.4	4.2
Geauga County, Ohio	21,568	23.1	5.7	15.1
Greene County, Ohio	34,051	21.1	17.2	0.6
Hamilton County, Ohio	187,727	23.4	23.5	2.2
Hancock County, Ohio	16,870	22.5	11.2	0.2
Jefferson County, Ohio	13,394	20.3	17.4	3.9
Lake County, Ohio	46,372	20.5	12.7	1.6
Licking County, Ohio	40,957	24.0	20.9	2.8
Lorain County, Ohio	68,641	22.9	17.3	1.6
Lucas County, Ohio	99,670	23.3	28.4	1.8
Mahoning County, Ohio	46,640	20.7	27.8	1.1
Marion County, Ohio	13,598	22.9	18.6	2.4
Medina County, Ohio	40,617	23.1	8.7	1.0
Miami County, Ohio	24,166	23.3	11.8	4.4
Montgomery County, Ohio	118,004	22.6	28.1	3.3
Muskingum County, Ohio	19,955	23.4	16.1	1.3
Portage County, Ohio	30,564	19.0	16.2	7.2
Richland County, Ohio	26,008	22.8	20.4	2.6
Ross County, Ohio	16,284	22.9	26.2	2.7
Scioto County, Ohio	16,686	22.8	30.4	1.5
Stark County, Ohio	80,785	21.9	19.7	1.3
Summit County, Ohio	114,657	21.4	20.0	4.9
Trumbull County, Ohio	41,818	21.1	34.2	3.8
Tuscarawas County, Ohio	20,973	22.9	17.1	13.6

Table C-1. Population and Poverty Characteristics, by State and Selected Counties, 2016—*Continued*

(Number; percent.)

State/County	Population		Children under 18 years old in poverty (percent)	Children under 18 years with no health insurance (percent)
	Total under 18 years old	Percent under 18 years old		
OHIO—(*Continued*)				
Warren County, Ohio	57,119	26.0	4.2	2.1
Wayne County, Ohio	28,253	24.5	17.2	15.2
Wood County, Ohio	26,546	20.6	11.7	1.4
OKLAHOMA	959,850	25.0	22.9	7.3
Canadian County, Oklahoma	35,879	26.6	12.0	3.5
Cleveland County, Oklahoma	61,269	22.5	10.3	4.8
Comanche County, Oklahoma	29,546	26.5	22.8	6.5
Creek County, Oklahoma	17,122	24.3	22.5	6.5
Muskogee County, Oklahoma	17,097	25.8	31.7	18.7
Oklahoma County, Oklahoma	201,621	26.2	25.2	4.3
Payne County, Oklahoma	15,676	19.6	21.1	6.0
Pottawatomie County, Oklahoma	17,402	24.7	25.5	8.4
Rogers County, Oklahoma	21,961	24.2	12.1	6.6
Tulsa County, Oklahoma	163,660	25.6	24.7	7.1
Wagoner County, Oklahoma	19,347	25.0	18.4	3.0
OREGON	866,585	21.4	17.0	3.3
Benton County, Oregon	14,918	16.7	14.5	2.1
Clackamas County, Oregon	88,893	21.9	11.5	1.8
Deschutes County, Oregon	37,378	20.7	15.0	3.3
Douglas County, Oregon	21,289	19.8	21.4	5.7
Jackson County, Oregon	44,855	20.8	16.2	4.3
Josephine County, Oregon	16,100	18.9	14.7	4.6
Klamath County, Oregon	14,571	22.1	29.7	9.1
Lane County, Oregon	69,347	18.8	21.2	5.0
Linn County, Oregon	27,951	22.9	13.8	5.8
Marion County, Oregon	83,519	25.3	19.5	3.5
Multnomah County, Oregon	154,030	19.4	19.8	2.4
Polk County, Oregon	18,432	22.6	8.3	4.3
Umatilla County, Oregon	19,771	27.5	20.2	7.3
Washington County, Oregon	137,559	23.7	12.9	1.2
Yamhill County, Oregon	23,961	23.3	18.5	1.3
PENNSYLVANIA	2,666,701	21.2	18.5	4.4
Adams County, Pennsylvania	20,723	20.5	16.9	3.9
Allegheny County, Pennsylvania	231,365	19.1	14.9	1.5
Armstrong County, Pennsylvania	12,683	19.2	20.9	5.8
Beaver County, Pennsylvania	32,514	19.6	13.1	1.5
Berks County, Pennsylvania	93,386	22.8	21.3	5.7
Blair County, Pennsylvania	25,677	20.8	19.9	2.4
Bucks County, Pennsylvania	130,357	21.0	8.3	2.3
Butler County, Pennsylvania	37,497	20.3	5.6	1.3
Cambria County, Pennsylvania	25,740	19.5	25.5	4.3
Carbon County, Pennsylvania	12,218	19.5	27.9	1.0
Centre County, Pennsylvania	24,435	15.6	11.0	4.8
Chester County, Pennsylvania	119,178	23.3	8.3	7.2
Clearfield County, Pennsylvania	14,773	19.6	23.2	7.2
Columbia County, Pennsylvania	11,750	17.9	14.6	9.5
Crawford County, Pennsylvania	18,058	21.3	18.6	9.5
Cumberland County, Pennsylvania	50,522	20.9	10.9	4.7
Dauphin County, Pennsylvania	61,165	22.6	16.8	3.1
Delaware County, Pennsylvania	124,560	22.4	15.8	1.6
Erie County, Pennsylvania	59,615	22.1	24.4	2.2
Fayette County, Pennsylvania	25,867	20.0	29.6	2.5
Franklin County, Pennsylvania	34,600	22.7	12.1	12.2
Indiana County, Pennsylvania	15,632	18.4	28.3	12.6
Lackawanna County, Pennsylvania	42,677	20.6	17.7	2.4
Lancaster County, Pennsylvania	128,270	24.1	17.8	17.1
Lawrence County, Pennsylvania	17,350	20.1	16.9	3.9
Lebanon County, Pennsylvania	32,099	23.4	12.9	6.6
Lehigh County, Pennsylvania	82,453	23.0	21.9	2.7
Luzerne County, Pennsylvania	61,730	20.0	24.0	1.7
Lycoming County, Pennsylvania	23,692	21.2	25.0	3.4
Mercer County, Pennsylvania	21,504	19.7	29.3	9.8
Monroe County, Pennsylvania	33,553	20.3	17.6	2.3
Montgomery County, Pennsylvania	177,687	22.0	7.9	2.2
Northampton County, Pennsylvania	61,125	20.4	15.1	4.6
Northumberland County, Pennsylvania	18,137	20.5	22.1	3.1
Philadelphia County, Pennsylvania	345,404	22.2	37.3	3.5
Schuylkill County, Pennsylvania	27,884	20.4	17.3	2.8
Somerset County, Pennsylvania	13,593	19.4	24.7	8.3
Washington County, Pennsylvania	40,932	19.9	9.4	1.6

Table C-1. Population and Poverty Characteristics, by State and Selected Counties, 2016—*Continued*

(Number; percent.)

State/County	Population		Children under 18 years old in poverty (percent)	Children under 18 years with no health insurance (percent)
	Total under 18 years old	Percent under 18 years old		
PENNSYLVANIA—*(Continued)*				
Westmoreland County, Pennsylvania	65,712	18.6	14.3	1.9
York County, Pennsylvania	98,087	22.4	13.5	3.6
RHODE ISLAND	208,268	20.0	17.0	1.9
Kent County, Rhode Island	31,113	19.0	13.5	2.3
Newport County, Rhode Island	14,994	19.0	7.3	3.8
Providence County, Rhode Island	131,420	21.1	21.0	1.8
Washington County, Rhode Island	21,434	17.1	8.7	1.6
SOUTH CAROLINA	1,097,385	22.6	23.0	4.0
Aiken County, South Carolina	36,035	21.7	28.9	5.2
Anderson County, South Carolina	45,008	23.1	23.5	2.9
Beaufort County, South Carolina	35,428	20.2	16.4	4.8
Berkeley County, South Carolina	50,973	24.8	18.3	2.8
Charleston County, South Carolina	79,208	20.4	20.5	2.9
Darlington County, South Carolina	15,275	23.0	28.8	6.6
Dorchester County, South Carolina	38,702	25.7	10.3	2.9
Florence County, South Carolina	33,162	24.2	26.7	1.0
Greenville County, South Carolina	115,710	23.4	14.4	4.3
Greenwood County, South Carolina	17,097	24.8	48.0	16.3
Horry County, South Carolina	59,945	18.7	28.5	5.1
Lancaster County, South Carolina	19,288	22.1	23.2	1.2
Laurens County, South Carolina	14,569	22.3	25.2	0.7
Lexington County, South Carolina	66,996	23.7	16.4	2.4
Oconee County, South Carolina	15,288	20.2	28.1	5.2
Orangeburg County, South Carolina	20,454	23.5	32.8	3.2
Pickens County, South Carolina	24,220	19.8	14.8	4.2
Richland County, South Carolina	88,344	22.9	22.4	2.7
Spartanburg County, South Carolina	70,079	23.6	27.9	5.6
Sumter County, South Carolina	26,045	25.3	28.8	5.2
York County, South Carolina	63,037	24.5	13.7	3.5
SOUTH DAKOTA	212,981	25.1	16.9	4.5
Minnehaha County, South Dakota	47,056	25.5	12.5	3.0
Pennington County, South Dakota	25,420	23.8	24.3	3.1
TENNESSEE	1,500,902	22.9	22.6	3.5
Anderson County, Tennessee	15,657	20.9	13.7	2.4
Blount County, Tennessee	26,663	20.9	13.0	3.9
Bradley County, Tennessee	22,451	21.7	17.7	3.1
Davidson County, Tennessee	145,789	21.5	22.3	5.8
Greene County, Tennessee	12,757	19.0	25.5	3.0
Hamilton County, Tennessee	75,034	21.2	18.3	1.0
Knox County, Tennessee	96,703	21.4	17.3	2.2
Madison County, Tennessee	22,143	23.0	27.9	5.5
Maury County, Tennessee	21,008	23.6	14.1	6.7
Montgomery County, Tennessee	52,726	29.3	16.4	4.5
Putnam County, Tennessee	16,205	21.6	27.5	2.7
Robertson County, Tennessee	16,972	24.8	13.1	0.9
Rutherford County, Tennessee	76,716	25.1	14.1	3.1
Sevier County, Tennessee	21,119	22.0	26.3	2.8
Shelby County, Tennessee	235,160	25.5	34.5	4.6
Sullivan County, Tennessee	30,659	19.8	25.6	1.6
Sumner County, Tennessee	43,216	24.2	13.3	3.3
Washington County, Tennessee	24,828	19.8	20.7	1.8
Williamson County, Tennessee	60,547	27.7	6.8	3.9
Wilson County, Tennessee	31,565	24.0	11.1	0.8
TEXAS	7,282,033	26.6	22.4	9.2
Angelina County, Texas	22,672	26.5	27.6	11.3
Bastrop County, Texas	19,703	24.5	13.1	11.2
Bell County, Texas	94,979	29.7	18.5	5.1
Bexar County, Texas	500,037	26.3	22.1	7.7
Bowie County, Texas	22,507	25.5	35.3	5.7
Brazoria County, Texas	94,207	27.4	12.5	7.4
Brazos County, Texas	45,119	20.9	25.2	6.0
Cameron County, Texas	130,909	31.2	41.5	16.1
Collin County, Texas	250,439	26.7	7.2	6.0
Comal County, Texas	30,167	22.6	14.9	7.8
Coryell County, Texas	17,646	31.0	17.3	2.2
Dallas County, Texas	686,427	26.8	25.3	10.6
Denton County, Texas	205,479	25.6	10.1	4.7
Ector County, Texas	47,383	30.4	17.1	16.4

Table C-1. Population and Poverty Characteristics, by State and Selected Counties, 2016—*Continued*

(Number; percent.)

State/County	Population		Children under 18 years old in poverty (percent)	Children under 18 years with no health insurance (percent)
	Total under 18 years old	Percent under 18 years old		
TEXAS—*(Continued)*				
Ellis County, Texas	44,990	26.9	13.2	9.6
El Paso County, Texas	232,168	28.6	32.0	7.8
Fort Bend County, Texas	204,850	27.8	12.0	5.4
Galveston County, Texas	80,753	24.9	18.8	8.1
Grayson County, Texas	30,633	24.1	16.4	13.3
Gregg County, Texas	31,832	26.3	26.5	7.9
Guadalupe County, Texas	39,949	26.1	14.2	8.5
Harris County, Texas	1,238,348	27.1	24.9	10.2
Harrison County, Texas	16,843	25.6	26.0	11.1
Hays County, Texas	47,209	23.3	16.8	6.3
Henderson County, Texas	17,381	22.0	18.5	8.9
Hidalgo County, Texas	282,769	33.5	44.2	12.6
Hunt County, Texas	22,266	24.4	25.7	10.4
Jefferson County, Texas	60,570	25.3	32.3	10.4
Johnson County, Texas	42,502	26.4	13.1	11.0
Kaufman County, Texas	32,373	27.6	17.7	6.9
Liberty County, Texas	20,835	28.4	21.9	12.3
Lubbock County, Texas	72,700	24.4	21.0	8.7
McLennan County, Texas	60,895	25.0	25.1	14.4
Midland County, Texas	46,457	28.9	9.5	14.4
Montgomery County, Texas	148,226	26.8	14.9	10.0
Nacogdoches County, Texas	15,492	23.8	38.6	11.4
Nueces County, Texas	90,355	25.4	21.5	6.9
Orange County, Texas	21,272	25.3	16.5	2.7
Parker County, Texas	32,191	25.1	9.6	10.6
Potter County, Texas	33,175	29.1	27.2	11.2
Randall County, Texas	31,882	24.2	9.1	5.6
Rockwall County, Texas	25,708	27.6	3.6	8.8
San Patricio County, Texas	18,116	27.1	26.8	7.4
Smith County, Texas	55,545	25.0	21.5	6.0
Tarrant County, Texas	539,187	26.9	20.1	8.4
Taylor County, Texas	33,334	25.2	19.2	6.3
Tom Green County, Texas	27,658	24.3	14.9	10.3
Travis County, Texas	269,559	22.6	16.5	8.2
Victoria County, Texas	23,322	25.5	18.6	6.2
Walker County, Texas	10,828	18.8	13.8	5.9
Webb County, Texas	92,198	34.3	45.0	11.2
Wichita County, Texas	29,108	25.0	20.1	9.1
Williamson County, Texas	139,144	26.5	6.0	6.1
UTAH	918,971	30.4	11.1	5.8
Cache County, Utah	37,628	30.8	11.2	5.5
Davis County, Utah	111,944	33.0	7.0	4.4
Salt Lake County, Utah	312,335	28.0	10.6	7.9
Utah County, Utah	201,710	34.3	9.5	4.7
Washington County, Utah	43,052	27.1	18.4	4.0
Weber County, Utah	71,123	29.1	11.8	4.9
VERMONT	118,351	19.1	14.8	1.6
Chittenden County, Vermont	29,465	18.4	9.3	1.8
VIRGINIA	1,864,852	22.7	14.3	4.8
Albemarle County, Virginia	21,609	20.5	11.4	10.6
Arlington County, Virginia	40,828	18.1	7.6	1.5
Augusta County, Virginia	14,664	20.5	11.2	7.6
Bedford County, Virginia	16,113	20.8	13.9	1.2
Chesterfield County, Virginia	81,154	24.1	8.8	2.2
Fairfax County, Virginia	270,764	24.1	7.1	4.6
Fauquier County, Virginia	16,148	23.5	2.0	1.7
Frederick County, Virginia	19,429	23.4	4.0	1.2
Hanover County, Virginia	23,011	22.1	7.2	0.8
Henrico County, Virginia	75,369	23.2	10.9	4.5
James City County, Virginia	15,275	21.0	4.1	1.1
Loudoun County, Virginia	110,761	28.9	3.3	5.7
Montgomery County, Virginia	15,823	16.2	8.2	0.3
Prince William County, Virginia	125,705	28.1	11.3	7.9
Roanoke County, Virginia	19,121	20.7	11.0	3.7
Rockingham County, Virginia	17,660	22.2	13.2	8.4
Spotsylvania County, Virginia	33,053	25.2	9.9	6.1
Stafford County, Virginia	37,858	27.3	7.9	2.6
York County, Virginia	16,586	26.2	6.7	1.4

Table C-1. Population and Poverty Characteristics, by State and Selected Counties, 2016—*Continued*

(Number; percent.)

State/County	Population		Children under 18 years old in poverty (percent)	Children under 18 years with no health insurance (percent)
	Total under 18 years old	Percent under 18 years old		
VIRGINIA—*(Continued)*				
Alexandria city, Virginia	28,454	18.7	21.8	14.0
Chesapeake city, Virginia	57,520	25.3	14.7	5.8
Hampton city, Virginia	28,461	21.9	25.8	2.1
Lynchburg city, Virginia	15,381	19.6	17.6	5.2
Newport News city, Virginia	41,902	24.3	17.1	7.4
Norfolk city, Virginia	49,562	22.7	32.8	6.1
Portsmouth city, Virginia	22,379	24.9	32.5	3.8
Richmond city, Virginia	39,960	18.1	42.7	3.1
Roanoke city, Virginia	22,265	22.6	31.5	4.7
Suffolk city, Virginia	22,099	25.3	17.2	5.8
Virginia Beach city, Virginia	101,727	23.9	10.8	2.9
WASHINGTON	1,627,304	22.7	13.7	2.5
Benton County, Washington	51,853	27.0	10.9	3.1
Chelan County, Washington	18,293	24.2	9.1	3.3
Clallam County, Washington	13,468	18.3	23.9	6.2
Clark County, Washington	115,060	24.8	9.6	2.6
Cowlitz County, Washington	23,803	22.8	19.6	0.8
Franklin County, Washington	30,659	34.8	25.9	3.6
Grant County, Washington	27,257	29.3	25.1	3.6
Grays Harbor County, Washington	14,589	21.3	16.4	5.7
Island County, Washington	14,954	19.5	20.2	4.3
King County, Washington	443,121	20.7	11.1	1.9
Kitsap County, Washington	54,625	21.7	11.9	3.2
Lewis County, Washington	16,148	21.2	14.4	1.5
Pierce County, Washington	204,295	24.3	16.2	2.7
Skagit County, Washington	27,109	22.1	6.7	2.1
Snohomish County, Washington	179,458	23.1	9.0	2.7
Spokane County, Washington	110,648	22.6	15.4	2.0
Thurston County, Washington	59,631	22.1	11.7	2.5
Whatcom County, Washington	42,550	19.8	10.4	4.3
Yakima County, Washington	74,606	30.2	26.6	2.3
WEST VIRGINIA	375,790	20.8	24.0	2.1
Berkeley County, West Virginia	27,182	24.0	19.3	2.5
Cabell County, West Virginia	19,323	20.4	25.3	1.5
Harrison County, West Virginia	14,747	21.8	15.7	0.6
Kanawha County, West Virginia	37,779	20.5	22.6	2.1
Monongalia County, West Virginia	17,359	16.9	15.4	4.9
Raleigh County, West Virginia	16,143	21.7	19.6	1.4
Wood County, West Virginia	18,105	21.3	33.8	1.0
WISCONSIN	1,283,539	22.5	15.7	3.5
Brown County, Wisconsin	62,586	24.3	11.6	4.3
Dane County, Wisconsin	110,899	21.0	10.4	0.9
Dodge County, Wisconsin	17,818	21.2	15.7	2.4
Eau Claire County, Wisconsin	21,432	21.0	11.8	6.3
Fond du Lac County, Wisconsin	22,280	22.2	9.3	2.4
Jefferson County, Wisconsin	18,492	22.0	11.0	2.6
Kenosha County, Wisconsin	39,431	23.7	23.1	3.2
La Crosse County, Wisconsin	23,517	20.1	11.3	0.7
Manitowoc County, Wisconsin	16,533	20.9	7.1	2.4
Marathon County, Wisconsin	31,088	23.1	17.3	5.7
Milwaukee County, Wisconsin	230,743	24.5	28.0	2.0
Outagamie County, Wisconsin	43,991	24.0	13.5	1.9
Ozaukee County, Wisconsin	19,140	21.8	7.5	0.6
Portage County, Wisconsin	13,485	19.2	11.4	3.1
Racine County, Wisconsin	45,524	23.9	21.9	2.2
Rock County, Wisconsin	38,225	23.9	21.2	2.4
St. Croix County, Wisconsin	22,404	25.7	7.7	3.6
Sheboygan County, Wisconsin	25,928	22.9	6.3	1.5
Walworth County, Wisconsin	22,153	21.7	7.1	2.4
Washington County, Wisconsin	30,391	22.7	5.7	3.6
Waukesha County, Wisconsin	86,662	21.9	5.8	1.7
Winnebago County, Wisconsin	34,909	21.2	16.0	1.9
Wood County, Wisconsin	15,514	21.4	9.8	4.2
WYOMING	140,464	24.4	11.1	8.8
Laramie County, Wyoming	22,869	24.1	10.5	3.8
Natrona County, Wyoming	19,835	24.8	7.7	6.6

Table C-2. Educational Attainment of the Population, by Selected Counties, 2016

(Number; percent; dollars.)

State/County	Total	Population 18 to 24 years			
		Less than high school graduate (percent)	High school graduate (includes equivalency) (percent)	Some college or associate's degree	Bachelor's degree or higher
ALABAMA					
Baldwin County, Alabama	15,621	20.8	25.6	45.9	7.7
Calhoun County, Alabama	11,440	12.2	35.4	43.0	9.4
Cullman County, Alabama	7,002	26.4	33.4	36.8	3.3
DeKalb County, Alabama	5,564	12.9	40.0	46.6	0.4
Elmore County, Alabama	6,948	13.9	46.1	35.4	4.6
Etowah County, Alabama	8,798	14.4	22.3	62.6	0.8
Houston County, Alabama	8,150	17.5	33.4	43.7	5.4
Jefferson County, Alabama	58,627	12.3	28.5	47.9	11.3
Lauderdale County, Alabama	10,073	7.3	24.1	65.1	3.5
Lee County, Alabama	29,916	5.4	22.1	55.8	16.8
Limestone County, Alabama	7,522	30.7	28.3	37.6	3.4
Madison County, Alabama	34,226	12.1	24.9	53.8	9.2
Marshall County, Alabama	7,267	26.4	39.1	32.1	2.4
Mobile County, Alabama	37,976	15.6	37.7	42.0	4.7
Montgomery County, Alabama	22,724	11.0	38.4	43.3	7.3
Morgan County, Alabama	9,459	17.5	44.8	33.5	4.2
St. Clair County, Alabama	6,398	16.7	41.6	30.9	10.8
Shelby County, Alabama	16,231	13.2	32.2	47.9	6.7
Talladega County, Alabama	6,391	12.7	44.7	42.6	0.1
Tuscaloosa County, Alabama	34,738	2.6	25.2	60.0	12.1
Walker County, Alabama	5,125	24.7	21.5	53.9	0.0
ALASKA					
Anchorage Municipality, Alaska	30,695	10.7	36.2	45.0	8.2
Fairbanks North Star Borough, Alaska	14,987	9.6	33.6	48.6	8.1
Matanuska-Susitna Borough, Alaska	9,795	17.2	44.9	34.2	3.8
ARIZONA					
Apache County, Arizona	6,982	28.1	31.7	40.2	0.0
Cochise County, Arizona	10,138	18.3	43.3	33.4	5.0
Coconino County, Arizona	29,998	5.9	31.6	56.0	6.5
Maricopa County, Arizona	396,041	14.8	33.3	42.7	9.2
Mohave County, Arizona	13,112	29.8	42.2	25.6	2.4
Navajo County, Arizona	8,553	33.1	35.4	31.5	0.0
Pima County, Arizona	121,619	14.0	29.4	48.8	7.7
Pinal County, Arizona	32,581	21.4	36.6	37.9	4.1
Yavapai County, Arizona	16,013	6.4	37.1	53.6	2.9
Yuma County, Arizona	23,513	18.2	35.6	42.9	3.3
ARKANSAS					
Benton County, Arkansas	20,576	14.3	42.1	36.0	7.5
Craighead County, Arkansas	12,218	13.9	26.6	55.5	4.1
Faulkner County, Arkansas	19,181	5.5	26.1	58.5	9.9
Garland County, Arkansas	7,656	23.1	35.2	34.3	7.5
Jefferson County, Arkansas	7,388	15.5	45.5	38.2	0.9
Lonoke County, Arkansas	5,768	13.4	45.8	25.2	15.5
Pulaski County, Arkansas	35,507	19.1	31.8	35.4	13.7
Saline County, Arkansas	9,101	21.5	35.6	41.5	1.4
Sebastian County, Arkansas	10,715	13.6	42.2	37.5	6.7
Washington County, Arkansas	35,117	6.9	23.2	55.9	14.0
White County, Arkansas	9,203	3.9	20.4	68.3	7.4
CALIFORNIA					
Alameda County, California	143,035	8.7	26.1	48.4	16.8
Butte County, California	33,430	7.1	25.8	57.1	9.9
Contra Costa County, California	94,402	12.3	27.6	47.4	12.7
El Dorado County, California	13,415	9.6	39.5	43.2	7.6
Fresno County, California	100,475	15.3	30.9	49.5	4.3
Humboldt County, California	18,358	2.8	28.5	64.4	4.3
Imperial County, California	19,708	19.3	18.8	58.6	3.2
Kern County, California	93,724	13.9	40.8	41.1	4.3
Kings County, California	16,766	19.6	36.0	36.3	8.1
Lake County, California	3,219	7.4	53.2	37.0	2.4
Los Angeles County, California	1,006,771	12.9	27.4	49.3	10.5
Madera County, California	16,151	17.1	32.9	45.9	4.2
Marin County, California	17,266	11.9	22.2	49.3	16.6
Mendocino County, California	6,386	14.4	36.7	40.4	8.6
Merced County, California	30,354	8.6	32.0	55.3	4.1
Monterey County, California	45,003	19.7	28.0	46.7	5.5
Napa County, California	12,919	10.7	26.2	58.2	4.9
Nevada County, California	5,656	6.8	29.8	59.1	4.3

Table C-2. Educational Attainment of the Population, by Selected Counties, 2016—*Continued*

(Number; percent; dollars.)

State/County	Total	Population 25 years and over							
		Less than 9th grade	9th to 12th grade, no diploma	High school graduate (includes equivalency)	Some college, no degree	Associate's degree	Bachelor's degree	Graduate or professional degree
ALABAMA									
Baldwin County, Alabama	146,987	2.9	7.1	28.5	21.2	10.6	17.4	12.3
Calhoun County, Alabama	78,218	6.5	11.3	31.7	27.1	7.0	9.3	7.2
Cullman County, Alabama	57,469	8.0	14.6	32.2	18.3	10.0	11.4	5.5
DeKalb County, Alabama	48,227	10.3	15.3	31.8	22.1	9.7	6.8	4.1
Elmore County, Alabama	56,224	4.0	9.3	30.3	21.4	9.1	15.8	10.2
Etowah County, Alabama	71,104	6.3	12.2	34.8	23.5	7.7	9.7	5.9
Houston County, Alabama	71,469	4.5	11.4	30.1	24.2	9.5	13.1	7.2
Jefferson County, Alabama	449,112	2.8	7.8	26.3	21.7	8.5	20.0	12.9
Lauderdale County, Alabama	63,320	6.3	7.6	36.2	20.9	7.1	14.3	7.5
Lee County, Alabama	94,996	4.3	7.9	22.1	22.1	7.9	19.7	16.0
Limestone County, Alabama	63,911	6.0	13.1	30.2	21.4	7.0	14.5	7.7
Madison County, Alabama	243,888	3.9	5.8	22.6	20.0	7.1	23.8	16.8
Marshall County, Alabama	64,390	6.5	11.0	33.4	24.8	8.0	11.0	5.4
Mobile County, Alabama	278,541	2.8	10.6	32.1	21.7	9.1	15.8	7.8
Montgomery County, Alabama	151,057	4.2	10.4	24.3	23.3	6.1	18.9	12.9
Morgan County, Alabama	82,212	8.5	11.0	29.8	22.0	9.0	13.2	6.5
St. Clair County, Alabama	61,405	5.0	12.8	36.1	21.0	7.7	12.2	5.2
Shelby County, Alabama	143,840	2.6	5.5	19.4	23.1	7.4	27.7	14.3
Talladega County, Alabama	56,133	5.1	13.5	32.5	25.7	8.3	9.8	5.2
Tuscaloosa County, Alabama	127,997	2.8	8.2	28.0	23.3	7.7	17.1	12.9
Walker County, Alabama	45,447	8.5	12.6	38.4	20.1	9.5	6.7	4.4
ALASKA									
Anchorage Municipality, Alaska	193,529	1.9	4.2	23.2	25.4	8.8	23.3	13.3
Fairbanks North Star Borough, Alaska	61,109	1.7	2.5	24.1	30.5	9.7	21.8	9.7
Matanuska-Susitna Borough, Alaska	66,199	1.6	4.2	31.8	32.4	10.7	12.7	6.7
ARIZONA									
Apache County, Arizona	45,180	9.0	9.4	31.1	31.3	7.6	6.9	4.8
Cochise County, Arizona	87,838	6.1	7.3	26.1	26.1	10.2	15.5	8.8
Coconino County, Arizona	81,866	3.7	6.8	22.1	24.6	7.5	20.5	14.9
Maricopa County, Arizona	2,806,841	5.9	6.9	22.4	24.6	8.3	20.4	11.5
Mohave County, Arizona	155,272	3.3	12.0	34.4	30.2	8.8	7.3	4.0
Navajo County, Arizona	70,759	7.6	11.5	29.8	28.6	8.2	8.6	5.8
Pima County, Arizona	676,920	4.8	7.2	22.1	25.4	8.6	18.0	13.8
Pinal County, Arizona	287,719	5.4	9.1	28.1	27.2	9.9	13.1	7.1
Yavapai County, Arizona	172,269	2.0	5.8	27.3	30.8	10.0	13.7	10.4
Yuma County, Arizona	129,735	14.8	11.0	26.6	26.3	5.8	10.2	5.2
ARKANSAS									
Benton County, Arkansas	168,509	6.1	5.7	29.2	21.0	5.8	22.2	10.0
Craighead County, Arkansas	67,521	4.9	7.1	37.5	21.1	5.9	15.3	8.2
Faulkner County, Arkansas	74,676	2.4	6.1	32.0	24.1	6.5	17.1	11.8
Garland County, Arkansas	69,426	2.7	9.3	29.6	30.8	9.3	12.5	5.8
Jefferson County, Arkansas	46,788	6.9	12.2	34.4	19.9	8.0	12.4	6.2
Lonoke County, Arkansas	48,025	3.6	6.8	35.1	23.8	9.6	13.6	7.6
Pulaski County, Arkansas	265,108	2.8	6.0	26.0	24.4	6.7	21.0	13.1
Saline County, Arkansas	81,777	1.5	6.4	32.6	22.9	8.1	18.5	9.9
Sebastian County, Arkansas	86,125	6.9	8.9	33.9	25.0	8.0	11.7	5.6
Washington County, Arkansas	136,698	7.2	7.3	26.1	21.7	5.0	18.2	14.5
White County, Arkansas	51,306	3.2	8.8	39.4	20.4	6.7	10.7	10.8
CALIFORNIA									
Alameda County, California	1,159,183	6.7	5.5	17.6	18.3	6.5	26.3	19.1
Butte County, California	147,756	4.5	6.8	23.6	30.4	8.9	15.5	10.3
Contra Costa County, California	779,169	6.1	4.6	17.1	22.3	8.3	25.8	15.7
El Dorado County, California	134,269	2.7	3.9	22.2	26.5	10.7	21.1	12.9
Fresno County, California	598,981	14.6	10.7	23.3	23.0	8.2	13.2	7.0
Humboldt County, California	91,712	1.8	7.5	25.8	25.7	9.6	20.3	9.2
Imperial County, California	109,421	15.5	15.3	23.8	25.0	6.5	9.5	4.3
Kern County, California	532,865	13.2	12.9	27.1	23.0	7.5	11.2	5.1
Kings County, California	92,081	11.7	13.8	30.7	25.2	7.1	7.9	3.7
Lake County, California	47,610	5.7	9.8	24.8	32.9	10.8	10.0	6.0
Los Angeles County, California	6,878,029	12.9	8.8	20.8	19.0	7.0	20.5	11.0
Madera County, California	96,004	16.8	12.2	25.2	28.0	6.0	7.8	4.0
Marin County, California	190,225	5.0	2.0	10.4	18.6	5.0	34.5	24.6
Mendocino County, California	61,924	8.0	8.5	24.5	28.6	8.2	14.8	7.3
Merced County, California	158,046	19.5	12.7	24.3	23.4	6.6	8.2	5.3
Monterey County, California	275,443	20.9	8.9	19.0	17.9	8.4	14.9	9.9
Napa County, California	99,152	9.2	5.7	17.5	23.4	9.0	22.6	12.5
Nevada County, California	75,724	1.4	6.2	17.1	27.9	10.8	23.8	12.8

Table C-2. Educational Attainment of the Population, by Selected Counties, 2016—*Continued*

(Number; percent; dollars.)

State/County		Population 18 to 24 years			
	Total	Less than high school graduate (percent)	High school graduate (includes equivalency) (percent)	Some college or associate's degree	Bachelor's degree or higher
CALIFORNIA—*(Continued)*					
Orange County, California	300,195	9.8	26.1	52.7	11.4
Placer County, California	28,508	8.6	31.9	49.9	9.6
Riverside County, California	239,190	11.5	37.1	45.7	5.7
Sacramento County, California	133,677	12.9	31.0	46.8	9.2
San Bernardino County, California	229,818	14.7	36.1	43.5	5.7
San Diego County, California	353,693	9.6	32.3	47.9	10.2
San Francisco County, California	63,216	5.9	19.0	38.2	36.9
San Joaquin County, California	71,788	14.2	37.4	44.3	4.1
San Luis Obispo County, California	43,444	4.1	24.2	64.4	7.3
San Mateo County, California	55,956	10.6	24.0	44.2	21.1
Santa Barbara County, California	70,077	10.6	19.5	60.2	9.6
Santa Clara County, California	165,205	9.1	26.8	43.2	20.9
Santa Cruz County, California	41,476	7.1	25.3	57.7	9.9
Shasta County, California	14,809	11.3	33.5	49.6	5.6
Solano County, California	40,408	10.7	38.5	45.4	5.4
Sonoma County, California	41,935	10.2	33.5	50.1	6.2
Stanislaus County, California	51,928	10.1	42.1	43.8	4.1
Sutter County, California	9,823	18.9	38.4	41.7	1.0
Tulare County, California	46,929	16.0	34.0	47.3	2.7
Ventura County, California	81,736	12.9	29.9	49.5	7.7
Yolo County, California	42,451	4.7	21.8	63.0	10.5
Yuba County, California	7,321	9.7	30.2	56.2	3.9
COLORADO					
Adams County, Colorado	44,114	20.8	40.4	32.4	6.4
Arapahoe County, Colorado	54,493	13.2	32.9	41.8	12.1
Boulder County, Colorado	48,199	6.5	17.8	59.9	15.7
Broomfield County, Colorado	5,503	10.9	25.6	39.9	23.5
Denver County, Colorado	57,773	13.3	29.2	39.8	17.7
Douglas County, Colorado	23,465	17.5	34.1	34.6	13.9
El Paso County, Colorado	77,482	9.4	35.1	44.4	11.1
Jefferson County, Colorado	46,820	15.9	27.5	44.0	12.6
Larimer County, Colorado	49,922	6.4	24.8	53.6	15.2
Mesa County, Colorado	15,625	10.1	32.6	49.4	7.8
Pueblo County, Colorado	15,102	17.5	38.4	40.0	4.1
Weld County, Colorado	28,455	11.5	36.8	46.5	5.3
CONNECTICUT					
Fairfield County, Connecticut	87,040	10.9	30.3	39.9	18.8
Hartford County, Connecticut	82,172	13.1	26.0	45.5	15.5
Litchfield County, Connecticut	13,527	9.8	33.7	39.4	17.2
Middlesex County, Connecticut	15,218	5.6	22.3	55.4	16.7
New Haven County, Connecticut	87,211	8.6	33.2	41.7	16.5
New London County, Connecticut	28,574	6.3	35.9	44.6	13.2
Tolland County, Connecticut	30,088	2.7	22.0	67.3	8.1
Windham County, Connecticut	12,723	8.8	29.7	56.3	5.2
DELAWARE					
Kent County, Delaware	17,575	18.2	38.3	38.2	5.3
New Castle County, Delaware	53,228	15.3	32.9	40.7	11.1
Sussex County, Delaware	14,478	20.8	36.9	33.9	8.4
DISTRICT OF COLUMBIA					
District of Columbia, District of Columbia	80,230	7.8	28.9	39.3	24.0
FLORIDA					
Alachua County, Florida	56,157	8.7	14.4	62.1	14.9
Bay County, Florida	15,320	14.8	32.2	51.4	1.6
Brevard County, Florida	42,571	15.6	32.5	41.0	10.9
Broward County, Florida	153,952	16.5	29.9	43.6	9.9
Charlotte County, Florida	10,253	19.9	39.7	34.8	5.5
Citrus County, Florida	7,729	24.7	51.5	16.3	7.5
Clay County, Florida	17,167	15.3	34.3	38.4	12.0
Collier County, Florida	25,446	21.1	40.2	27.5	11.2
Columbia County, Florida	7,173	25.4	39.9	34.0	0.7
Duval County, Florida	84,791	17.0	30.6	41.6	10.8
Escambia County, Florida	38,828	13.9	28.8	49.6	7.7
Flagler County, Florida	7,339	14.6	48.6	32.8	4.0
Hernando County, Florida	11,794	11.3	42.9	41.4	4.5

Table C-2. Educational Attainment of the Population, by Selected Counties, 2016—*Continued*

(Number; percent; dollars.)

State/County	Total	Less than 9th grade	9th to 12th grade, no diploma	High school graduate (includes equivalency)	Some college, no degree	Associate's degree	Bachelor's degree	Graduate or professional degree
CALIFORNIA—*(Continued)*								
Orange County, California	2,159,696	8.4	6.8	17.1	20.0	7.8	25.9	14.0
Placer County, California	266,649	2.0	2.9	17.3	26.6	12.2	25.8	13.2
Riverside County, California	1,534,614	9.5	9.5	26.2	24.9	8.1	13.8	8.0
Sacramento County, California	1,017,725	7.1	6.6	22.7	24.5	9.4	19.3	10.4
San Bernardino County, California	1,336,971	9.5	11.8	26.3	24.1	8.4	13.2	6.8
San Diego County, California	2,235,728	7.0	6.7	18.4	22.7	7.9	23.3	14.0
San Francisco County, California	689,696	7.4	4.7	12.3	13.7	4.7	34.1	23.2
San Joaquin County, California	460,561	11.7	11.2	27.5	23.5	9.4	11.4	5.4
San Luis Obispo County, California	188,750	3.6	4.6	18.6	25.6	11.5	23.3	12.9
San Mateo County, California	547,316	6.4	4.5	15.3	16.8	6.6	29.3	21.1
Santa Barbara County, California	275,969	13.4	6.4	17.3	22.6	7.9	18.6	13.8
Santa Clara County, California	1,321,019	7.6	5.2	15.0	14.9	6.3	28.1	22.9
Santa Cruz County, California	179,041	8.9	3.8	15.7	23.0	8.1	23.1	17.5
Shasta County, California	126,208	2.6	5.7	25.3	33.9	10.6	14.9	6.9
Solano County, California	300,893	5.4	6.9	23.4	28.6	10.3	17.8	7.6
Sonoma County, California	360,452	6.2	5.9	18.6	25.7	9.7	21.4	12.4
Stanislaus County, California	342,516	13.0	10.6	27.5	24.7	7.9	11.2	5.0
Sutter County, California	61,873	14.1	10.1	21.9	26.5	11.3	11.7	4.4
Tulare County, California	269,538	17.3	13.3	25.9	22.3	7.5	8.8	4.9
Ventura County, California	567,552	9.6	6.3	18.5	22.8	9.2	20.4	13.2
Yolo County, California	127,671	7.7	7.4	17.9	19.7	6.4	21.1	19.7
Yuba County, California	46,987	5.7	10.0	23.0	31.8	11.0	13.8	4.8
COLORADO								
Adams County, Colorado	318,077	7.9	9.4	29.1	21.7	9.0	15.8	7.1
Arapahoe County, Colorado	429,459	2.7	4.6	21.9	20.4	8.9	26.3	15.2
Boulder County, Colorado	210,587	1.8	3.0	13.3	15.2	6.0	32.4	28.3
Broomfield County, Colorado	45,359	1.4	1.8	15.4	21.3	8.2	31.5	20.4
Denver County, Colorado	494,647	5.9	6.9	18.2	16.3	5.3	28.9	18.5
Douglas County, Colorado	215,761	0.6	0.9	11.4	19.9	7.7	37.0	22.5
El Paso County, Colorado	441,771	2.0	3.6	19.8	24.0	11.9	23.5	15.2
Jefferson County, Colorado	409,083	1.8	4.0	19.9	22.9	7.8	28.2	15.3
Larimer County, Colorado	222,045	1.2	2.5	20.7	19.8	9.0	27.4	19.4
Mesa County, Colorado	100,672	2.6	8.8	30.4	24.1	9.1	15.9	9.1
Pueblo County, Colorado	112,202	3.3	9.0	28.1	26.1	12.4	13.7	7.5
Weld County, Colorado	188,160	5.0	7.6	28.9	22.5	8.8	19.1	8.1
CONNECTICUT								
Fairfield County, Connecticut	639,468	5.2	4.7	22.1	15.0	6.4	26.9	19.7
Hartford County, Connecticut	619,835	4.6	6.0	28.0	16.4	7.8	21.4	15.8
Litchfield County, Connecticut	134,791	2.4	4.4	29.0	18.1	9.4	22.0	14.7
Middlesex County, Connecticut	117,918	2.4	3.0	27.3	16.4	9.1	25.3	16.5
New Haven County, Connecticut	593,082	4.0	6.2	30.6	17.1	7.0	18.6	16.5
New London County, Connecticut	187,622	2.2	5.1	30.7	21.1	8.4	18.2	14.3
Tolland County, Connecticut	94,427	1.2	3.6	27.7	17.8	9.7	22.7	17.4
Windham County, Connecticut	80,594	4.3	8.5	34.0	19.9	9.3	14.1	9.9
DELAWARE								
Kent County, Delaware	116,721	4.6	8.3	35.9	19.8	8.9	14.1	8.5
New Castle County, Delaware	381,908	2.6	6.0	31.4	17.4	7.1	20.6	14.8
Sussex County, Delaware	163,918	4.2	9.6	30.9	20.0	8.9	16.1	10.3
DISTRICT OF COLUMBIA								
District of Columbia, District of Columbia	480,158	3.6	6.0	17.8	13.0	2.9	24.0	32.9
FLORIDA								
Alachua County, Florida	159,567	3.4	5.6	23.2	17.7	10.5	19.5	20.2
Bay County, Florida	128,694	2.3	6.6	32.7	25.7	9.4	15.5	7.7
Brevard County, Florida	429,390	2.6	5.5	28.3	22.1	12.2	18.6	10.7
Broward County, Florida	1,348,321	5.4	6.8	26.7	20.5	9.8	19.3	11.5
Charlotte County, Florida	145,407	2.7	7.2	32.7	24.6	9.1	14.8	8.9
Citrus County, Florida	115,626	3.1	9.7	36.6	20.9	9.3	12.8	7.6
Clay County, Florida	141,743	2.1	4.8	34.4	23.4	11.8	16.1	7.4
Collier County, Florida	275,724	8.2	6.7	25.9	17.3	7.9	19.6	14.3
Columbia County, Florida	47,365	6.0	11.0	36.2	24.1	9.2	9.1	4.5
Duval County, Florida	631,705	3.2	8.0	27.2	22.2	10.0	20.2	9.2
Escambia County, Florida	210,492	2.3	6.9	26.7	24.3	13.0	17.3	9.6
Flagler County, Florida	82,146	2.2	6.8	32.0	25.2	10.7	12.9	10.1
Hernando County, Florida	136,874	3.8	8.8	35.8	23.1	9.8	12.6	6.1

Table C-2. Educational Attainment of the Population, by Selected Counties, 2016—*Continued*

(Number; percent; dollars.)

State/County		Population 18 to 24 years			
	Total	Less than high school graduate (percent)	High school graduate (includes equivalency) (percent)	Some college or associate's degree	Bachelor's degree or higher
FLORIDA—*(Continued)*					
Highlands County, Florida	6,284	18.6	40.8	34.1	6.5
Hillsborough County, Florida	124,798	14.7	30.2	44.1	11.0
Indian River County, Florida	13,786	21.6	30.4	41.2	6.9
Lake County, Florida	23,889	20.3	35.5	37.1	7.1
Lee County, Florida	50,372	15.2	32.5	44.1	8.3
Leon County, Florida	63,941	7.1	15.9	65.6	11.4
Manatee County, Florida	26,853	17.4	45.7	30.0	6.9
Marion County, Florida	23,637	18.7	52.0	24.6	4.7
Martin County, Florida	10,944	22.3	33.4	37.0	7.4
Miami-Dade County, Florida	234,322	14.7	28.6	48.1	8.6
Monroe County, Florida	7,260	29.3	25.7	42.1	3.0
Nassau County, Florida	5,028	19.7	34.1	41.3	4.9
Okaloosa County, Florida	19,560	12.3	36.1	45.8	5.8
Orange County, Florida	143,474	11.4	21.9	55.5	11.2
Osceola County, Florida	32,135	10.5	39.3	43.1	7.2
Palm Beach County, Florida	109,955	16.9	29.2	44.5	9.4
Pasco County, Florida	36,046	17.8	35.2	40.5	6.5
Pinellas County, Florida	64,992	14.8	35.0	39.6	10.6
Polk County, Florida	55,570	17.5	33.7	41.5	7.2
Putnam County, Florida	5,603	20.6	43.2	32.4	3.7
St. Johns County, Florida	16,668	12.8	35.0	44.2	8.0
St. Lucie County, Florida	25,623	16.9	42.1	35.7	5.2
Santa Rosa County, Florida	12,589	18.5	32.5	36.9	12.1
Sarasota County, Florida	24,182	18.8	35.2	39.8	6.3
Seminole County, Florida	38,260	8.7	27.5	57.8	5.9
Sumter County, Florida	6,503	24.6	35.7	39.8	0.0
Volusia County, Florida	42,990	12.8	23.1	52.2	11.8
Walton County, Florida	5,149	33.5	39.6	17.7	9.2
GEORGIA					
Barrow County, Georgia	6,002	21.1	37.9	38.8	2.2
Bartow County, Georgia	8,173	23.7	38.3	32.8	5.2
Bibb County, Georgia	15,540	16.7	27.7	49.7	5.9
Bulloch County, Georgia	18,972	12.2	25.2	59.1	3.6
Carroll County, Georgia	15,654	12.5	35.7	43.5	8.2
Catoosa County, Georgia	4,844	8.2	36.6	52.2	3.0
Chatham County, Georgia	32,541	12.8	25.5	48.0	13.7
Cherokee County, Georgia	18,778	12.3	33.7	45.4	8.6
Clarke County, Georgia	34,875	5.2	23.3	56.5	15.0
Clayton County, Georgia	27,736	20.7	47.2	26.6	5.5
Cobb County, Georgia	68,336	11.3	25.3	50.1	13.3
Columbia County, Georgia	12,381	21.1	36.9	33.2	8.8
Coweta County, Georgia	11,618	19.3	44.0	31.8	4.9
DeKalb County, Georgia	64,917	16.8	32.2	35.1	15.9
Dougherty County, Georgia	10,310	11.4	30.5	56.1	2.0
Douglas County, Georgia	13,320	9.6	28.8	48.4	13.1
Fayette County, Georgia	9,263	15.9	29.5	40.0	14.6
Floyd County, Georgia	10,343	21.0	16.0	52.0	11.0
Forsyth County, Georgia	16,192	14.9	34.4	42.3	8.4
Fulton County, Georgia	103,973	10.1	25.2	46.7	17.9
Glynn County, Georgia	6,876	21.8	47.4	24.0	6.8
Gwinnett County, Georgia	82,748	17.2	30.4	40.1	12.3
Hall County, Georgia	18,155	23.4	32.5	35.6	8.4
Henry County, Georgia	19,696	15.3	40.2	40.1	4.4
Houston County, Georgia	12,191	13.2	31.1	49.3	6.4
Liberty County, Georgia	9,626	14.1	42.0	40.0	3.9
Lowndes County, Georgia	19,735	8.6	22.2	61.0	8.1
Muscogee County, Georgia	20,997	15.1	35.9	42.8	6.2
Newton County, Georgia	11,309	20.9	41.0	28.7	9.3
Paulding County, Georgia	15,241	17.6	46.9	32.2	3.3
Richmond County, Georgia	23,183	12.3	31.0	48.7	7.9
Rockdale County, Georgia	8,004	16.0	26.7	46.6	10.8
Troup County, Georgia	7,065	38.2	37.1	19.5	5.3
Walker County, Georgia	4,922	21.7	43.7	31.1	3.5
Walton County, Georgia	9,404	21.2	50.1	26.3	2.4
Whitfield County, Georgia	10,609	17.2	41.3	32.6	8.9
HAWAII					
Hawaii County, Hawaii	15,836	14.3	34.9	40.6	10.1
Honolulu County, Hawaii	96,590	6.3	39.9	43.8	9.9

Table C-2. Educational Attainment of the Population, by Selected Counties, 2016—*Continued*

(Number; percent; dollars.)

State/County	Total	Less than 9th grade	9th to 12th grade, no diploma	High school graduate (includes equivalency)	Some college, no degree	Associate's degree	Bachelor's degree	Graduate or professional degree
FLORIDA—*(Continued)*								
Highlands County, Florida	76,952	7.0	7.3	44.1	19.5	9.1	8.5	4.5
Hillsborough County, Florida	934,670	4.8	7.2	27.9	18.9	8.9	20.7	11.6
Indian River County, Florida	112,931	5.3	7.4	28.8	20.2	9.6	16.9	11.8
Lake County, Florida	246,107	3.3	7.2	33.7	23.0	9.7	13.5	9.5
Lee County, Florida	540,614	5.1	7.6	30.4	19.8	8.9	18.2	10.1
Leon County, Florida	170,317	1.9	4.4	18.5	18.1	9.5	26.7	20.8
Manatee County, Florida	277,852	3.5	7.7	31.4	21.6	8.1	17.4	10.3
Marion County, Florida	260,102	4.3	9.3	38.3	22.3	7.9	11.8	6.2
Martin County, Florida	120,799	3.9	5.6	25.6	23.4	11.2	18.3	12.0
Miami-Dade County, Florida	1,926,417	10.2	8.6	28.2	15.7	9.4	17.7	10.2
Monroe County, Florida	59,979	3.7	6.3	27.4	19.6	9.6	21.8	11.6
Nassau County, Florida	59,714	2.6	5.5	29.7	22.1	9.9	18.8	11.4
Okaloosa County, Florida	137,299	2.6	5.8	25.7	24.7	10.7	18.1	12.4
Orange County, Florida	875,092	5.4	7.8	24.3	18.4	10.4	22.5	11.2
Osceola County, Florida	220,880	5.2	7.8	32.5	22.0	12.5	14.4	5.6
Palm Beach County, Florida	1,054,130	6.1	6.5	24.6	18.5	9.2	21.8	13.2
Pasco County, Florida	372,432	3.7	7.6	34.3	20.5	10.9	15.6	7.4
Pinellas County, Florida	735,561	3.1	6.4	28.1	23.2	9.9	19.2	10.1
Polk County, Florida	461,083	6.8	8.9	35.9	20.5	7.7	13.3	6.8
Putnam County, Florida	51,052	6.3	14.3	37.9	19.1	6.9	8.7	6.8
St. Johns County, Florida	166,186	1.4	2.9	21.5	20.5	10.8	27.3	15.5
St. Lucie County, Florida	218,832	5.3	8.3	33.4	22.7	9.7	13.9	6.7
Santa Rosa County, Florida	119,962	2.6	7.6	26.3	23.2	12.8	17.6	9.9
Sarasota County, Florida	328,503	2.5	4.5	30.3	20.1	9.0	20.2	13.4
Seminole County, Florida	320,502	1.9	3.9	21.4	22.5	13.3	24.1	12.9
Sumter County, Florida	108,728	3.2	5.2	32.4	23.7	6.5	15.4	13.7
Volusia County, Florida	392,036	2.7	7.6	31.3	22.8	11.5	15.7	8.4
Walton County, Florida	47,812	3.6	9.8	25.4	24.0	9.1	19.5	8.6
GEORGIA								
Barrow County, Georgia	50,599	5.7	10.8	34.0	23.0	8.2	11.1	7.2
Bartow County, Georgia	69,782	5.5	11.6	33.7	22.7	7.0	13.7	5.7
Bibb County, Georgia	99,061	5.4	10.4	29.8	19.8	8.7	14.9	10.9
Bulloch County, Georgia	41,106	3.6	11.1	25.1	23.9	9.1	14.3	12.9
Carroll County, Georgia	72,598	5.8	11.6	31.7	24.1	5.6	13.3	8.0
Catoosa County, Georgia	46,369	2.0	9.9	33.1	22.7	9.0	16.8	6.5
Chatham County, Georgia	193,126	2.9	8.0	23.3	25.7	8.1	20.9	11.1
Cherokee County, Georgia	161,757	3.6	5.9	21.8	23.7	7.3	26.7	11.1
Clarke County, Georgia	68,541	4.1	7.8	21.4	18.3	7.4	18.1	22.9
Clayton County, Georgia	172,693	6.9	8.1	32.4	23.4	8.8	13.7	6.8
Cobb County, Georgia	498,306	4.7	4.2	18.2	19.9	6.4	29.7	16.9
Columbia County, Georgia	96,831	2.7	3.3	26.9	21.3	10.1	21.0	14.8
Coweta County, Georgia	93,478	2.9	8.5	30.0	22.0	7.7	20.2	8.7
DeKalb County, Georgia	499,806	4.8	6.2	20.8	18.0	6.9	24.7	18.7
Dougherty County, Georgia	57,249	5.3	10.0	29.3	24.7	9.5	12.5	8.8
Douglas County, Georgia	91,716	3.2	7.9	31.5	22.5	7.9	17.2	9.8
Fayette County, Georgia	76,341	2.2	2.4	20.2	18.9	7.5	29.5	19.2
Floyd County, Georgia	63,782	6.2	11.0	31.1	20.1	7.4	13.8	10.4
Forsyth County, Georgia	142,799	4.0	4.3	16.6	18.0	6.8	33.9	16.4
Fulton County, Georgia	687,737	2.4	5.6	18.3	16.9	5.6	30.2	21.1
Glynn County, Georgia	58,184	5.8	9.2	26.1	23.5	7.7	18.5	9.1
Gwinnett County, Georgia	575,081	6.6	5.7	23.0	20.8	9.2	22.7	11.9
Hall County, Georgia	127,397	10.8	12.0	29.5	18.2	7.9	13.2	8.3
Henry County, Georgia	143,597	2.8	8.2	27.6	23.1	9.3	16.9	12.1
Houston County, Georgia	100,776	3.0	7.1	22.5	28.0	9.5	16.9	13.0
Liberty County, Georgia	35,357	3.1	6.6	30.7	30.0	11.8	12.5	5.3
Lowndes County, Georgia	67,466	3.3	9.5	35.3	20.9	6.9	13.9	10.3
Muscogee County, Georgia	127,871	3.5	8.6	26.6	24.4	9.5	16.2	11.3
Newton County, Georgia	67,161	6.2	12.5	31.1	25.6	7.6	10.8	6.3
Paulding County, Georgia	98,550	3.2	6.3	33.5	24.9	8.4	16.5	7.2
Richmond County, Georgia	131,589	4.7	11.2	31.1	22.4	8.5	13.6	8.5
Rockdale County, Georgia	58,783	5.0	6.6	36.1	16.7	11.2	17.7	6.8
Troup County, Georgia	45,415	6.1	15.4	31.4	19.1	7.0	13.5	7.4
Walker County, Georgia	47,666	4.8	16.7	33.0	21.1	7.8	11.4	5.3
Walton County, Georgia	58,004	3.7	10.2	34.3	20.9	8.0	15.5	7.4
Whitfield County, Georgia	65,693	14.6	17.0	27.6	22.3	6.0	8.4	4.1
HAWAII								
Hawaii County, Hawaii	139,834	2.8	4.5	32.9	21.5	10.8	19.2	8.4
Honolulu County, Hawaii	684,066	3.9	4.6	25.9	20.9	10.4	22.6	11.8

Table C-2. Educational Attainment of the Population, by Selected Counties, 2016—*Continued*

(Number; percent; dollars.)

State/County	Total	Population 18 to 24 years			
		Less than high school graduate (percent)	High school graduate (includes equivalency) (percent)	Some college or associate's degree	Bachelor's degree or higher
HAWAII—*(Continued)*					
Kauai County, Hawaii	5,411	5.4	41.0	37.8	15.8
Maui County, Hawaii	12,012	6.3	60.7	27.9	5.1
IDAHO					
Ada County, Idaho	37,923	9.4	35.0	47.5	8.1
Bannock County, Idaho	8,575	7.6	20.6	62.7	9.2
Bonneville County, Idaho	9,290	15.4	41.8	36.8	5.9
Canyon County, Idaho	20,175	12.1	45.8	40.3	1.8
Kootenai County, Idaho	13,121	15.2	42.2	36.0	6.5
Twin Falls County, Idaho	7,364	12.8	35.7	49.3	2.2
ILLINOIS					
Adams County, Illinois	5,051	7.3	34.1	52.0	6.7
Champaign County, Illinois	48,880	2.2	16.4	64.5	16.9
Cook County, Illinois	476,909	12.6	27.5	42.7	17.3
DeKalb County, Illinois	20,899	8.1	26.0	55.3	10.5
DuPage County, Illinois	82,635	8.8	26.4	44.7	20.1
Kane County, Illinois	47,718	16.3	33.7	40.6	9.5
Kankakee County, Illinois	11,715	12.9	29.7	52.3	5.1
Kendall County, Illinois	10,299	19.1	42.4	30.0	8.5
Lake County, Illinois	73,389	11.7	32.8	41.6	13.9
LaSalle County, Illinois	9,630	19.1	37.4	39.1	4.5
McHenry County, Illinois	26,663	15.7	21.4	50.0	13.0
McLean County, Illinois	29,035	7.3	16.5	62.8	13.4
Macon County, Illinois	10,085	19.3	30.8	44.2	5.7
Madison County, Illinois	21,576	10.9	24.3	53.5	11.4
Peoria County, Illinois	16,984	12.1	23.1	56.2	8.6
Rock Island County, Illinois	12,551	15.1	31.9	46.6	6.4
St. Clair County, Illinois	22,302	13.1	40.3	35.4	11.3
Sangamon County, Illinois	16,863	10.9	26.8	50.0	12.4
Tazewell County, Illinois	9,524	15.9	30.7	46.6	6.8
Vermilion County, Illinois	6,655	29.5	24.5	42.7	3.3
Will County, Illinois	64,619	9.1	36.7	39.8	14.4
Williamson County, Illinois	4,958	4.2	48.3	43.8	3.7
Winnebago County, Illinois	23,973	18.2	35.9	37.6	8.3
INDIANA					
Allen County, Indiana	34,179	17.3	31.1	46.2	5.4
Bartholomew County, Indiana	7,466	23.4	25.6	28.4	22.6
Clark County, Indiana	9,584	19.0	31.8	36.3	12.9
Delaware County, Indiana	23,747	6.6	18.4	63.5	11.5
Elkhart County, Indiana	17,385	26.9	30.4	35.0	7.6
Floyd County, Indiana	7,082	16.5	31.3	45.4	6.8
Grant County, Indiana	8,825	5.0	40.4	46.0	8.6
Hamilton County, Indiana	22,162	16.1	20.4	38.8	24.8
Hancock County, Indiana	6,214	14.8	44.6	38.8	1.7
Hendricks County, Indiana	12,907	18.5	28.8	40.4	12.4
Howard County, Indiana	6,484	28.1	34.1	34.1	3.7
Johnson County, Indiana	13,279	18.9	32.7	38.5	9.9
Kosciusko County, Indiana	7,050	22.5	39.4	35.7	2.3
Lake County, Indiana	42,826	22.0	35.5	35.4	7.0
LaPorte County, Indiana	9,428	25.1	45.1	25.8	4.0
Madison County, Indiana	11,130	22.0	38.4	35.5	4.1
Marion County, Indiana	88,941	19.1	29.0	39.5	12.4
Monroe County, Indiana	40,591	4.2	15.8	66.5	13.6
Morgan County, Indiana	5,884	18.5	44.5	30.8	6.2
Porter County, Indiana	15,939	8.5	40.7	40.7	10.2
St. Joseph County, Indiana	30,753	13.4	27.4	47.2	12.0
Tippecanoe County, Indiana	45,619	3.3	20.5	63.0	13.3
Vanderburgh County, Indiana	18,314	14.7	26.6	46.3	12.4
Vigo County, Indiana	16,308	9.9	23.9	58.3	7.9
Wayne County, Indiana	6,024	7.1	43.3	46.5	3.1
IOWA					
Black Hawk County, Iowa	20,730	4.3	18.6	65.0	12.1
Dallas County, Iowa	5,853	8.5	29.3	33.9	28.3
Dubuque County, Iowa	9,819	11.1	19.7	59.8	9.4
Johnson County, Iowa	30,196	6.8	18.9	58.3	16.0
Linn County, Iowa	19,771	8.2	31.1	48.9	11.7
Polk County, Iowa	41,759	13.6	28.3	43.7	14.5

Table C-2. Educational Attainment of the Population, by Selected Counties, 2016—*Continued*

(Number; percent; dollars.)

State/County	Population 25 years and over							
	Total	Less than 9th grade	9th to 12th grade, no diploma	High school graduate (includes equivalency)	Some college, no degree	Associate's degree	Bachelor's degree	Graduate or professional degree
HAWAII—*(Continued)*								
Kauai County, Hawaii	50,428	3.6	3.3	33.3	20.3	11.6	21.0	6.9
Maui County, Hawaii	116,520	3.4	3.7	32.7	25.0	10.5	17.0	7.7
IDAHO								
Ada County, Idaho	297,773	1.3	3.5	22.5	23.5	11.1	26.0	12.1
Bannock County, Idaho	53,292	4.2	5.8	28.2	26.3	7.9	19.7	7.9
Bonneville County, Idaho	68,163	1.3	6.0	23.7	27.2	9.5	20.9	11.4
Canyon County, Idaho	129,307	6.4	9.8	32.3	25.5	6.8	14.1	5.0
Kootenai County, Idaho	105,789	1.2	6.1	27.3	29.9	9.5	16.6	9.4
Twin Falls County, Idaho	52,959	3.5	6.9	26.9	26.2	14.5	14.5	7.4
ILLINOIS								
Adams County, Illinois	46,467	1.7	6.6	34.7	24.3	7.3	16.3	9.0
Champaign County, Illinois	120,365	1.1	3.4	20.8	21.3	7.6	23.3	22.6
Cook County, Illinois	3,564,871	6.8	6.6	23.4	19.1	6.4	22.9	14.9
DeKalb County, Illinois	60,799	2.3	6.2	25.6	23.6	10.5	19.9	11.9
DuPage County, Illinois	632,930	3.6	3.8	18.5	18.6	6.8	30.2	18.4
Kane County, Illinois	344,178	8.6	6.5	22.0	20.9	8.2	21.2	12.4
Kankakee County, Illinois	72,379	4.9	8.4	34.4	24.7	8.5	11.4	7.7
Kendall County, Illinois	78,552	4.7	5.5	21.6	22.2	11.1	22.4	12.6
Lake County, Illinois	455,465	4.9	4.6	20.5	18.8	6.6	26.0	18.5
LaSalle County, Illinois	77,423	3.3	8.2	35.1	23.7	10.6	12.2	6.8
McHenry County, Illinois	206,054	3.2	4.3	26.5	23.8	8.5	23.4	10.3
McLean County, Illinois	105,815	1.1	2.0	25.1	19.5	8.3	27.4	16.5
Macon County, Illinois	72,841	3.4	7.1	34.0	24.4	9.4	13.0	8.6
Madison County, Illinois	185,936	1.5	6.0	28.8	26.8	10.6	16.5	9.9
Peoria County, Illinois	123,600	2.2	7.4	26.5	24.1	9.2	19.2	11.5
Rock Island County, Illinois	100,024	3.1	7.7	28.4	27.3	10.6	16.0	6.9
St. Clair County, Illinois	177,988	2.6	5.6	29.6	23.3	10.9	16.4	11.7
Sangamon County, Illinois	135,861	2.4	5.4	26.4	22.0	8.2	22.0	13.7
Tazewell County, Illinois	94,554	3.0	5.5	31.2	24.9	11.7	17.0	6.8
Vermilion County, Illinois	52,831	3.9	7.9	39.2	23.8	11.1	9.8	4.3
Will County, Illinois	447,552	3.9	4.9	26.6	21.7	8.3	22.2	12.5
Williamson County, Illinois	47,515	2.0	6.4	27.5	29.3	10.2	15.0	9.5
Winnebago County, Illinois	194,735	3.4	10.1	31.1	25.1	7.8	14.2	8.2
INDIANA								
Allen County, Indiana	239,861	4.1	6.5	28.4	22.7	9.4	19.3	9.6
Bartholomew County, Indiana	54,455	3.6	9.4	29.2	16.9	7.6	18.9	14.4
Clark County, Indiana	79,711	3.2	8.1	33.8	25.6	8.9	13.2	7.2
Delaware County, Indiana	70,681	2.5	7.5	36.7	22.0	8.6	12.5	10.1
Elkhart County, Indiana	129,898	8.6	12.7	36.1	18.4	5.6	12.3	6.3
Floyd County, Indiana	52,823	3.2	7.3	31.1	22.2	8.2	17.9	10.1
Grant County, Indiana	44,188	4.1	10.2	39.2	22.4	7.5	9.3	7.3
Hamilton County, Indiana	206,314	1.0	3.2	15.5	16.2	6.6	37.0	20.6
Hancock County, Indiana	50,101	1.0	5.1	32.4	20.9	10.0	21.7	8.7
Hendricks County, Indiana	106,721	1.1	6.4	28.5	16.5	9.9	23.7	13.8
Howard County, Indiana	57,271	1.6	7.4	39.1	22.7	7.9	12.9	8.4
Johnson County, Indiana	100,100	2.6	7.2	30.7	18.9	8.3	20.2	12.2
Kosciusko County, Indiana	52,883	7.0	11.7	35.1	17.8	7.5	12.5	8.4
Lake County, Indiana	326,446	3.5	7.6	35.0	22.7	9.1	14.3	7.8
LaPorte County, Indiana	76,614	2.5	7.6	39.6	22.2	9.9	12.1	6.1
Madison County, Indiana	89,848	3.1	9.5	40.4	21.2	8.8	11.6	5.4
Marion County, Indiana	617,575	4.7	8.2	28.2	21.0	7.9	19.9	10.2
Monroe County, Indiana	82,029	1.8	7.0	24.2	16.4	7.2	24.0	19.5
Morgan County, Indiana	48,327	2.3	7.8	42.9	21.7	9.3	10.5	5.5
Porter County, Indiana	114,080	2.6	5.8	33.1	22.9	9.7	16.8	9.0
St. Joseph County, Indiana	174,051	3.9	8.5	32.1	20.2	7.1	17.1	11.1
Tippecanoe County, Indiana	103,323	2.8	5.6	26.3	20.9	7.5	21.4	15.6
Vanderburgh County, Indiana	123,731	2.4	10.0	30.4	21.7	9.9	15.8	9.8
Vigo County, Indiana	69,206	3.4	8.2	31.2	23.2	8.4	15.8	9.8
Wayne County, Indiana	45,950	5.4	7.0	41.6	20.2	8.5	10.1	7.3
IOWA								
Black Hawk County, Iowa	83,720	3.6	5.1	31.7	21.5	9.9	18.4	9.7
Dallas County, Iowa	54,891	3.3	1.7	16.6	18.1	10.7	32.6	17.0
Dubuque County, Iowa	65,015	2.2	5.0	33.0	22.0	8.7	18.7	10.4
Johnson County, Iowa	86,838	3.1	3.1	15.7	16.3	7.8	28.1	26.0
Linn County, Iowa	149,512	1.8	4.0	26.4	20.4	12.0	25.2	10.2
Polk County, Iowa	313,040	4.2	5.0	23.7	22.2	9.1	24.3	11.5

Table C-2. Educational Attainment of the Population, by Selected Counties, 2016—*Continued*

(Number; percent; dollars.)

| State/County | Population 18 to 24 years | | | | |
	Total	Less than high school graduate (percent)	High school graduate (includes equivalency) (percent)	Some college or associate's degree	Bachelor's degree or higher
IOWA—(*Continued*)					
Pottawattamie County, Iowa...........................	9,155	11.0	40.7	41.4	6.9
Scott County, Iowa.......................................	14,550	14.5	37.1	38.8	9.6
Story County, Iowa.......................................	29,894	2.9	17.9	72.0	7.2
Woodbury County, Iowa................................	10,206	12.3	25.4	54.0	8.3
KANSAS					
Butler County, Kansas..................................	5,978	14.5	30.9	49.2	5.4
Douglas County, Kansas	28,355	1.9	24.7	61.3	12.1
Johnson County, Kansas...............................	46,386	10.7	28.4	38.3	22.6
Leavenworth County, Kansas	7,238	13.4	19.4	58.0	9.2
Riley County, Kansas...................................	24,392	1.4	23.4	65.6	9.5
Sedgwick County, Kansas	48,212	16.7	28.2	45.4	9.7
Shawnee County, Kansas	14,918	16.2	33.0	41.0	9.9
Wyandotte County, Kansas	14,313	23.6	30.4	40.1	5.9
KENTUCKY					
Boone County, Kentucky	11,462	10.9	34.3	46.4	8.4
Bullitt County, Kentucky	7,124	17.4	45.7	28.1	8.9
Campbell County, Kentucky..........................	9,820	11.6	22.3	48.3	17.8
Christian County, Kentucky	11,018	9.9	48.1	32.0	9.9
Daviess County, Kentucky............................	9,070	23.1	25.7	47.8	3.4
Fayette County, Kentucky.............................	45,471	5.6	25.7	55.6	13.1
Hardin County, Kentucky..............................	10,096	20.3	35.6	36.4	7.7
Jefferson County, Kentucky..........................	66,066	10.4	29.8	44.6	15.2
Kenton County, Kentucky.............................	13,619	10.4	25.7	52.1	11.8
McCracken County, Kentucky.......................	5,723	22.9	29.9	37.1	10.1
Madison County, Kentucky...........................	15,721	3.6	29.3	61.8	5.4
Pike County, Kentucky.................................	5,796	18.7	30.7	42.6	8.0
Warren County, Kentucky.............................	21,322	5.8	30.4	57.3	6.5
LOUISIANA					
Ascension Parish, Louisiana	10,442	19.1	46.6	34.3	0.0
Bossier Parish, Louisiana.............................	11,988	11.8	40.5	37.6	10.0
Caddo Parish, Louisiana	21,742	17.8	33.9	38.9	9.4
Calcasieu Parish, Louisiana..........................	18,284	14.5	43.0	38.5	4.0
East Baton Rouge Parish, Louisiana	62,284	9.4	28.2	52.6	9.9
Iberia Parish, Louisiana................................	7,196	12.8	57.5	29.3	0.4
Jefferson Parish, Louisiana...........................	34,414	18.0	34.5	35.9	11.6
Lafayette Parish, Louisiana	22,978	12.8	24.7	56.0	6.4
Lafourche Parish, Louisiana..........................	8,920	23.0	37.5	35.0	4.6
Livingston Parish, Louisiana	12,174	20.9	44.0	31.8	3.3
Orleans Parish, Louisiana	36,224	14.7	25.0	44.9	15.4
Ouachita Parish, Louisiana...........................	15,366	17.3	37.5	37.0	8.2
Rapides Parish, Louisiana............................	11,834	20.7	43.5	34.5	1.3
St. Landry Parish, Louisiana	7,841	28.0	43.6	25.7	2.7
St. Tammany Parish, Louisiana	19,093	12.5	36.1	42.4	9.0
Tangipahoa Parish, Louisiana........................	15,235	20.2	36.3	40.1	3.4
Terrebonne Parish, Louisiana........................	10,491	27.7	37.4	32.3	2.7
MAINE					
Androscoggin County, Maine	9,485	16.4	34.0	39.3	10.4
Aroostook County, Maine..............................	5,555	14.7	33.2	48.7	3.4
Cumberland County, Maine...........................	26,023	8.5	20.4	54.6	16.4
Kennebec County, Maine..............................	10,475	15.1	33.4	42.0	9.6
Penobscot County, Maine	16,422	10.1	28.5	55.9	5.5
York County, Maine.....................................	14,582	10.9	28.3	43.4	17.5
MARYLAND					
Allegany County, Maryland............................	8,964	7.9	29.6	50.4	12.0
Anne Arundel County, Maryland....................	50,197	10.6	31.6	44.2	13.6
Baltimore County, Maryland..........................	74,705	9.7	30.3	46.9	13.1
Calvert County, Maryland.............................	7,210	12.2	28.8	45.2	13.8
Carroll County, Maryland..............................	14,246	8.2	35.9	37.8	18.1
Cecil County, Maryland................................	8,421	9.8	41.3	39.3	9.6
Charles County, Maryland	14,205	6.0	39.0	49.9	5.1
Frederick County, Maryland..........................	21,427	12.0	29.3	45.5	13.2
Harford County, Maryland.............................	21,088	11.5	37.3	42.4	8.8
Howard County, Maryland............................	26,721	8.3	25.1	48.4	18.2
Montgomery County, Maryland......................	83,894	12.1	26.9	37.9	23.1
Prince George's County, Maryland	92,616	13.6	24.9	48.0	13.5

Table C-2. Educational Attainment of the Population, by Selected Counties, 2016—*Continued*

(Number; percent; dollars.)

State/County	Population 25 years and over							
	Total	Less than 9th grade	9th to 12th grade, no diploma	High school graduate (includes equivalency)	Some college, no degree	Associate's degree	Bachelor's degree	Graduate or professional degree
IOWA—*(Continued)*								
Pottawattamie County, Iowa	62,692	1.6	6.9	33.5	24.6	11.7	14.1	7.4
Scott County, Iowa	116,457	2.1	4.6	31.7	19.6	10.7	19.0	12.3
Story County, Iowa	51,648	0.4	2.0	18.5	15.8	8.4	31.5	23.3
Woodbury County, Iowa	65,375	6.2	9.0	30.2	21.7	10.2	14.0	8.6
KANSAS								
Butler County, Kansas	44,088	1.3	7.3	27.2	23.6	11.7	19.7	9.2
Douglas County, Kansas	69,181	1.3	3.7	18.4	18.3	6.2	28.4	23.6
Johnson County, Kansas	392,961	1.7	2.6	14.2	18.9	7.2	34.6	20.7
Leavenworth County, Kansas	53,908	1.5	4.1	28.4	23.7	8.7	16.5	17.1
Riley County, Kansas	36,970	0.5	1.5	17.0	24.2	7.8	25.1	23.9
Sedgwick County, Kansas	330,105	3.8	7.2	25.9	24.1	7.7	20.1	11.4
Shawnee County, Kansas	120,401	2.5	5.3	33.2	23.3	5.7	17.2	12.7
Wyandotte County, Kansas	103,325	9.6	12.6	32.5	20.8	6.5	12.6	5.3
KENTUCKY								
Boone County, Kentucky	82,493	2.0	4.5	25.2	27.7	9.9	20.5	10.1
Bullitt County, Kentucky	54,125	3.1	10.8	39.7	21.2	9.8	9.1	6.3
Campbell County, Kentucky	62,855	3.6	4.4	29.9	18.3	7.9	24.4	11.4
Christian County, Kentucky	41,511	4.7	8.9	32.3	28.6	10.2	8.7	6.5
Daviess County, Kentucky	66,665	3.7	6.3	31.3	23.8	11.6	14.2	9.2
Fayette County, Kentucky	206,147	4.0	5.7	20.0	19.6	6.9	24.5	19.2
Hardin County, Kentucky	70,693	3.0	6.3	29.2	23.2	14.7	13.0	10.5
Jefferson County, Kentucky	527,688	2.9	7.1	26.0	23.8	8.2	19.1	12.8
Kenton County, Kentucky	111,449	3.6	7.4	27.1	24.0	7.3	20.2	10.5
McCracken County, Kentucky	45,174	3.0	8.1	28.2	23.7	16.5	13.1	7.3
Madison County, Kentucky	54,808	5.4	8.2	29.2	19.1	9.7	17.2	11.3
Pike County, Kentucky	43,058	1.3	3.9	20.7	25.1	8.0	25.6	15.4
Warren County, Kentucky	75,726	4.6	7.3	26.7	20.9	8.7	18.4	13.3
LOUISIANA								
Ascension Parish, Louisiana	77,789	3.6	9.0	32.3	21.1	9.5	15.6	9.0
Bossier Parish, Louisiana	82,255	2.9	8.4	29.0	25.5	7.9	17.2	9.0
Caddo Parish, Louisiana	166,694	4.1	9.9	34.2	22.5	7.1	13.4	8.8
Calcasieu Parish, Louisiana	132,409	4.3	10.3	33.4	23.9	7.7	12.5	7.9
East Baton Rouge Parish, Louisiana	283,615	2.9	6.3	27.6	22.9	6.0	22.1	12.2
Iberia Parish, Louisiana	46,366	8.8	12.9	41.5	17.5	4.3	10.2	4.7
Jefferson Parish, Louisiana	306,368	6.2	9.3	31.7	22.5	4.8	17.2	8.3
Lafayette Parish, Louisiana	160,955	3.5	7.7	30.1	21.0	5.8	22.6	9.3
Lafourche Parish, Louisiana	66,342	8.5	13.6	39.4	17.4	3.5	11.9	5.7
Livingston Parish, Louisiana	91,371	5.0	10.7	40.5	19.5	7.2	11.4	5.7
Orleans Parish, Louisiana	275,465	4.1	10.2	21.8	21.0	4.6	22.2	16.2
Ouachita Parish, Louisiana	101,778	3.1	12.4	37.3	21.3	5.0	13.0	7.9
Rapides Parish, Louisiana	87,408	5.0	9.1	37.0	23.0	4.7	14.0	7.2
St. Landry Parish, Louisiana	53,326	9.9	13.7	43.3	13.6	5.0	10.0	4.5
St. Tammany Parish, Louisiana	173,330	2.7	7.5	26.9	25.4	6.5	20.3	10.8
Tangipahoa Parish, Louisiana	83,564	4.4	15.9	33.1	20.5	6.0	14.0	6.1
Terrebonne Parish, Louisiana	73,540	9.7	10.7	40.3	19.3	5.3	11.2	3.5
MAINE								
Androscoggin County, Maine	74,841	3.5	6.0	38.1	21.6	9.1	13.3	8.3
Aroostook County, Maine	49,878	5.8	6.7	35.3	21.9	10.3	14.3	5.7
Cumberland County, Maine	209,899	1.6	3.3	23.8	16.7	9.0	27.4	18.2
Kennebec County, Maine	86,306	3.6	5.6	34.0	19.7	10.5	15.0	11.5
Penobscot County, Maine	107,403	2.2	4.5	36.1	21.6	10.6	16.8	8.2
York County, Maine	148,283	2.4	4.7	31.2	20.8	10.5	20.0	10.5
MARYLAND								
Allegany County, Maryland	50,410	2.7	6.6	40.7	20.2	11.9	9.5	8.5
Anne Arundel County, Maryland	390,828	1.4	5.3	23.8	19.7	7.5	24.8	17.6
Baltimore County, Maryland	576,783	2.9	5.4	26.8	19.7	7.2	22.2	15.9
Calvert County, Maryland	62,470	1.3	4.6	31.7	25.6	6.7	14.0	16.1
Carroll County, Maryland	116,780	2.1	6.2	30.4	19.8	7.5	22.3	11.8
Cecil County, Maryland	70,522	2.4	8.9	35.6	22.7	6.3	14.4	9.6
Charles County, Maryland	105,303	2.5	3.9	35.0	23.6	7.7	14.6	12.8
Frederick County, Maryland	167,966	3.2	5.0	24.9	17.9	8.2	22.2	18.6
Harford County, Maryland	173,658	3.1	5.1	26.6	21.5	7.6	22.1	14.1
Howard County, Maryland	212,505	2.0	2.2	14.2	13.8	6.0	29.0	32.9
Montgomery County, Maryland	715,672	4.8	3.2	14.3	13.2	5.2	26.9	32.3
Prince George's County, Maryland	611,828	7.5	6.5	26.0	22.4	5.6	17.7	14.2

Table C-2. Educational Attainment of the Population, by Selected Counties, 2016—*Continued*

(Number; percent; dollars.)

State/County	Total	Population 18 to 24 years			
		Less than high school graduate (percent)	High school graduate (includes equivalency) (percent)	Some college or associate's degree	Bachelor's degree or higher
MARYLAND—*(Continued)*					
St. Mary's County, Maryland	10,688	8.3	38.5	40.2	13.0
Washington County, Maryland	11,721	16.4	47.8	27.2	8.5
Wicomico County, Maryland	15,017	9.9	24.9	60.9	4.3
MASSACHUSETTS					
Baltimore city, Maryland	62,526	15.8	27.7	42.6	
Barnstable County, Massachusetts	14,762	8.2	38.4	37.3	16.1
Berkshire County, Massachusetts	12,555	10.0	28.2	53.9	8.0
Bristol County, Massachusetts	52,622	13.2	30.6	44.6	11.6
Essex County, Massachusetts	73,944	13.8	31.7	39.6	14.9
Franklin County, Massachusetts	4,972	8.1	41.1	36.8	14.0
Hampden County, Massachusetts	50,402	14.1	28.9	47.5	9.5
Hampshire County, Massachusetts	37,107	2.1	10.5	76.2	11.2
Middlesex County, Massachusetts	158,249	9.1	27.1	39.2	24.6
Norfolk County, Massachusetts	62,099	12.4	26.4	38.1	23.1
Plymouth County, Massachusetts	45,235	17.5	27.6	41.9	13.0
Suffolk County, Massachusetts	108,798	10.1	18.9	49.8	21.2
Worcester County, Massachusetts	81,888	9.8	35.2	41.2	13.8
MICHIGAN					
Allegan County, Michigan	8,658	11.9	41.3	39.9	6.9
Bay County, Michigan	8,114	15.0	39.3	40.7	4.9
Berrien County, Michigan	12,725	16.1	28.8	44.0	11.1
Calhoun County, Michigan	12,702	12.9	38.3	42.4	6.4
Clinton County, Michigan	6,946	10.8	25.4	54.5	9.3
Eaton County, Michigan	9,960	9.9	27.2	52.0	10.9
Genesee County, Michigan	35,811	17.8	31.2	42.8	8.1
Grand Traverse County, Michigan	6,616	23.6	20.7	46.6	9.1
Ingham County, Michigan	57,705	6.9	20.6	60.9	11.7
Isabella County, Michigan	20,552	5.0	22.8	64.0	8.2
Jackson County, Michigan	14,189	14.6	34.5	45.6	5.3
Kalamazoo County, Michigan	41,858	7.9	24.5	57.0	10.6
Kent County, Michigan	61,384	12.8	27.2	48.5	11.5
Lapeer County, Michigan	6,947	28.2	31.7	36.5	3.6
Lenawee County, Michigan	9,077	11.6	42.8	42.2	3.4
Livingston County, Michigan	15,586	11.7	29.0	48.5	10.8
Macomb County, Michigan	71,828	14.1	33.2	43.1	9.5
Marquette County, Michigan	9,892	3.8	18.4	69.3	8.5
Midland County, Michigan	6,999	7.5	29.4	50.6	12.4
Monroe County, Michigan	12,091	13.3	28.0	54.9	3.7
Muskegon County, Michigan	15,078	22.3	40.5	32.3	5.0
Oakland County, Michigan	101,633	10.9	25.7	46.0	17.4
Ottawa County, Michigan	38,140	14.3	23.7	51.0	11.0
Saginaw County, Michigan	19,657	12.2	31.7	50.2	5.9
St. Clair County, Michigan	13,042	17.4	44.6	34.0	4.0
Shiawassee County, Michigan	5,604	8.6	45.3	41.3	4.7
Van Buren County, Michigan	5,576	23.1	34.1	34.4	8.5
Washtenaw County, Michigan	68,582	5.9	17.9	55.7	20.6
Wayne County, Michigan	158,938	17.3	32.1	43.5	7.1
MINNESOTA					
Anoka County, Minnesota	28,609	13.3	35.3	43.2	8.2
Blue Earth County, Minnesota	15,624	3.0	25.9	65.8	5.2
Carver County, Minnesota	7,742	16.9	26.8	39.9	16.4
Dakota County, Minnesota	33,145	13.5	30.6	40.6	15.3
Hennepin County, Minnesota	107,498	11.1	22.3	44.7	21.8
Olmsted County, Minnesota	12,312	12.6	29.2	38.6	19.6
Ramsey County, Minnesota	55,529	10.4	25.6	46.5	17.5
Rice County, Minnesota	9,485	7.0	14.2	73.0	5.8
St. Louis County, Minnesota	26,142	7.2	20.7	63.0	9.1
Scott County, Minnesota	10,726	12.9	36.1	40.0	11.0
Sherburne County, Minnesota	7,490	13.7	38.2	38.9	9.2
Stearns County, Minnesota	23,456	8.6	17.3	63.5	10.5
Washington County, Minnesota	21,248	9.6	30.2	42.6	17.5
Wright County, Minnesota	9,971	13.7	27.4	50.4	8.4
MISSISSIPPI					
DeSoto County, Mississippi	15,373	20.8	33.1	43.0	3.1
Forrest County, Mississippi	11,506	9.2	26.3	57.3	7.2
Harrison County, Mississippi	20,840	13.7	35.9	47.3	3.2

Table C-2. Educational Attainment of the Population, by Selected Counties, 2016—*Continued*

(Number; percent; dollars.)

State/County	Total	Less than 9th grade	9th to 12th grade, no diploma	High school graduate (includes equivalency)	Some college, no degree	Associate's degree	Bachelor's degree	Graduate or professional degree
MARYLAND—(*Continued*)								
St. Mary's County, Maryland	74,257	4.2	9.3	30.0	20.1	10.3	14.0	12.1
Washington County, Maryland	105,207	4.1	10.2	37.0	21.3	7.1	11.8	8.5
Wicomico County, Maryland	64,937	4.1	7.1	36.3	20.7	7.0	14.4	10.5
MASSACHUSETTS								
Baltimore city, Maryland	422,984	5.1	9.9	29.6	19.6	5.0	16.5	14.4
Barnstable County, Massachusetts	165,674	1.4	2.8	25.9	17.4	9.1	25.6	17.8
Berkshire County, Massachusetts	92,219	2.5	6.2	30.8	17.6	9.1	18.8	14.9
Bristol County, Massachusetts	389,535	7.8	6.5	28.9	18.3	9.3	18.1	11.2
Essex County, Massachusetts	536,624	5.8	5.3	24.9	17.0	8.6	22.8	15.6
Franklin County, Massachusetts	52,999	1.0	4.6	29.3	18.3	10.1	18.6	18.1
Hampden County, Massachusetts	314,950	6.1	8.2	29.7	19.4	10.3	16.1	10.3
Hampshire County, Massachusetts	100,134	2.3	3.5	24.6	14.9	8.8	22.4	23.4
Middlesex County, Massachusetts	1,109,915	3.7	3.2	19.4	12.6	6.0	27.4	27.7
Norfolk County, Massachusetts	486,480	2.3	3.8	20.4	13.3	7.5	28.2	24.5
Plymouth County, Massachusetts	355,763	2.8	4.8	29.5	17.8	8.9	23.3	12.8
Suffolk County, Massachusetts	541,459	8.0	6.5	22.9	12.9	4.9	25.6	19.3
Worcester County, Massachusetts	561,264	3.2	6.7	28.0	17.6	8.6	21.6	14.3
MICHIGAN								
Allegan County, Michigan	78,462	4.4	4.8	37.5	21.8	9.7	14.2	7.6
Bay County, Michigan	75,219	2.6	7.0	35.1	26.6	11.0	12.4	5.4
Berrien County, Michigan	107,048	3.1	7.4	27.1	23.6	10.5	16.3	12.0
Calhoun County, Michigan	90,638	3.0	6.4	37.9	23.3	9.1	13.3	6.9
Clinton County, Michigan	53,069	1.4	3.5	28.0	24.4	9.9	19.8	13.0
Eaton County, Michigan	75,984	2.2	5.0	27.7	28.0	11.5	17.5	8.0
Genesee County, Michigan	278,737	2.1	7.3	32.5	26.6	11.5	12.5	7.6
Grand Traverse County, Michigan	66,411	1.4	3.9	24.9	26.3	10.7	18.8	14.0
Ingham County, Michigan	172,712	2.4	5.4	22.3	23.4	8.3	20.1	18.1
Isabella County, Michigan	38,341	3.7	4.7	29.1	22.6	9.7	16.7	13.6
Jackson County, Michigan	109,953	2.1	7.2	28.6	29.1	11.2	15.2	6.7
Kalamazoo County, Michigan	162,834	1.9	4.4	22.9	23.8	9.1	21.7	16.3
Kent County, Michigan	421,948	4.5	5.5	24.6	21.3	9.4	23.2	11.5
Lapeer County, Michigan	62,968	3.4	7.4	38.4	22.3	10.9	11.6	6.0
Lenawee County, Michigan	68,240	2.6	6.2	36.9	23.6	8.5	13.7	8.4
Livingston County, Michigan	131,443	1.7	3.6	27.6	23.4	9.7	23.1	11.0
Macomb County, Michigan	609,181	3.6	6.1	31.2	23.4	10.8	16.7	8.1
Marquette County, Michigan	44,140	2.4	2.9	29.7	23.2	8.6	22.9	10.2
Midland County, Michigan	58,599	1.6	4.2	27.9	23.3	9.3	21.0	12.7
Monroe County, Michigan	104,248	2.2	6.8	35.7	24.2	11.8	13.4	5.9
Muskegon County, Michigan	117,747	2.7	7.9	34.9	26.1	11.9	11.3	5.3
Oakland County, Michigan	874,502	2.0	4.1	18.5	21.4	7.8	26.4	19.8
Ottawa County, Michigan	175,169	3.2	4.4	30.4	21.7	8.4	21.7	10.1
Saginaw County, Michigan	131,280	2.3	7.7	33.3	24.5	9.5	14.3	8.5
St. Clair County, Michigan	112,409	2.7	8.6	35.6	26.3	10.4	10.6	5.8
Shiawassee County, Michigan	48,286	1.4	5.0	37.1	26.8	13.7	10.6	5.4
Van Buren County, Michigan	51,667	4.3	8.3	33.0	24.3	10.2	13.4	6.5
Washtenaw County, Michigan	226,851	1.3	3.2	14.9	18.5	7.2	25.5	29.3
Wayne County, Michigan	1,170,984	4.4	9.8	29.9	24.7	8.1	13.7	9.3
MINNESOTA								
Anoka County, Minnesota	233,951	1.8	4.1	29.5	23.6	13.8	19.0	8.2
Blue Earth County, Minnesota	38,188	1.9	3.9	29.0	20.7	11.8	21.5	11.2
Carver County, Minnesota	65,797	0.6	1.8	18.2	18.8	12.7	35.5	12.4
Dakota County, Minnesota	281,359	2.5	3.2	19.8	21.5	12.0	28.3	12.7
Hennepin County, Minnesota	852,117	3.2	3.9	16.6	18.7	9.0	31.2	17.5
Olmsted County, Minnesota	103,088	2.7	3.2	19.5	18.7	13.1	26.1	16.5
Ramsey County, Minnesota	358,650	5.3	4.4	22.3	18.6	8.5	24.7	16.1
Rice County, Minnesota	42,052	3.7	7.5	29.5	19.2	13.1	15.2	11.9
St. Louis County, Minnesota	135,585	1.3	4.8	28.5	24.5	13.6	18.0	9.4
Scott County, Minnesota	92,581	2.8	1.3	23.7	20.0	12.1	29.3	10.8
Sherburne County, Minnesota	60,083	1.6	3.3	28.0	25.9	15.3	18.3	7.6
Stearns County, Minnesota	96,576	3.4	3.7	28.7	25.2	13.1	18.6	7.3
Washington County, Minnesota	168,928	1.7	2.5	22.6	21.3	10.1	27.1	14.6
Wright County, Minnesota	85,184	2.2	3.7	26.8	22.1	14.5	21.7	9.1
MISSISSIPPI								
DeSoto County, Mississippi	114,337	2.8	6.5	28.9	26.1	10.7	16.6	8.4
Forrest County, Mississippi	47,052	3.6	7.3	28.4	23.9	11.9	13.9	11.0
Harrison County, Mississippi	133,354	3.7	9.0	29.7	26.6	10.8	13.2	7.0

Table C-2. Educational Attainment of the Population, by Selected Counties, 2016—*Continued*

(Number; percent; dollars.)

State/County	Population 18 to 24 years				
	Total	Less than high school graduate (percent)	High school graduate (includes equivalency) (percent)	Some college or associate's degree	Bachelor's degree or higher
MISSISSIPPI—*(Continued)*					
Hinds County, Mississippi	27,255	18.5	19.9	53.4	8.1
Jackson County, Mississippi	12,946	11.3	44.3	40.8	3.6
Jones County, Mississippi	5,693	10.1	51.5	37.8	0.7
Lauderdale County, Mississippi	7,152	22.5	27.4	41.4	8.7
Lee County, Mississippi	6,666	11.4	39.2	44.7	4.7
Madison County, Mississippi	10,021	16.2	29.0	48.4	6.4
Rankin County, Mississippi	12,114	9.9	26.1	46.5	17.5
MISSOURI					
Boone County, Missouri	34,797	6.4	17.9	58.2	17.5
Buchanan County, Missouri	7,948	14.3	26.1	47.8	11.8
Cape Girardeau County, Missouri	10,911	5.0	15.6	65.5	13.9
Cass County, Missouri	7,998	15.6	37.8	42.2	4.4
Christian County, Missouri	6,174	17.5	38.7	39.8	4.1
Clay County, Missouri	19,556	11.0	37.1	37.0	14.9
Cole County, Missouri	7,315	25.1	18.3	50.6	6.1
Franklin County, Missouri	7,977	17.0	42.9	37.6	2.5
Greene County, Missouri	41,302	7.1	19.9	65.0	8.0
Jackson County, Missouri	58,259	13.9	30.7	44.1	11.3
Jasper County, Missouri	11,523	8.0	54.5	32.6	4.9
Jefferson County, Missouri	16,592	17.1	37.8	40.7	4.4
Platte County, Missouri	8,454	10.4	20.9	53.7	14.9
St. Charles County, Missouri	33,565	9.3	28.4	52.7	9.7
St. Francois County, Missouri	5,776	18.4	50.5	26.5	4.6
St. Louis County, Missouri	86,310	13.8	27.1	44.9	14.2
St. Louis city, Missouri	30,815	14.7	23.1	45.0	17.1
MONTANA					
Cascade County, Montana	7,986	10.4	37.1	37.4	15.2
Flathead County, Montana	6,999	17.3	41.4	35.0	6.4
Gallatin County, Montana	16,714	2.2	17.3	62.5	18.0
Lewis and Clark County, Montana	5,372	14.7	22.2	54.4	8.8
Missoula County, Montana	16,155	4.9	41.3	48.9	4.9
Yellowstone County, Montana	13,348	11.9	42.4	41.9	3.9
NEBRASKA					
Douglas County, Nebraska	51,329	10.6	31.5	47.3	10.6
Lancaster County, Nebraska	46,558	7.3	18.0	60.1	14.6
Sarpy County, Nebraska	15,486	9.3	35.4	49.0	6.3
NEVADA					
Clark County, Nevada	184,374	17.4	36.6	40.6	5.4
Washoe County, Nevada	41,600	14.2	29.7	48.2	7.9
NEW HAMPSHIRE					
Cheshire County, New Hampshire	9,401	8.2	20.3	60.4	11.0
Grafton County, New Hampshire	11,029	7.7	26.3	51.9	14.2
Hillsborough County, New Hampshire	35,860	13.3	37.1	32.4	17.2
Merrimack County, New Hampshire	14,151	6.7	30.4	51.2	11.7
Rockingham County, New Hampshire	23,107	14.9	27.6	36.6	20.9
Strafford County, New Hampshire	20,334	2.8	29.3	55.5	12.4
NEW JERSEY					
Atlantic County, New Jersey	25,386	16.7	25.7	48.3	9.3
Bergen County, New Jersey	77,062	9.0	25.0	41.2	24.8
Burlington County, New Jersey	39,205	11.3	30.3	44.2	14.2
Camden County, New Jersey	43,509	13.7	32.0	38.9	15.4
Cape May County, New Jersey	7,301	13.3	35.6	39.3	11.9
Cumberland County, New Jersey	12,749	21.0	35.9	35.0	8.2
Essex County, New Jersey	73,366	14.0	28.9	45.0	12.2
Gloucester County, New Jersey	26,205	4.7	37.3	44.2	13.8
Hudson County, New Jersey	57,219	8.8	28.7	41.7	20.8
Hunterdon County, New Jersey	11,239	23.1	21.5	31.2	24.1
Mercer County, New Jersey	41,628	13.6	27.4	44.3	14.8
Middlesex County, New Jersey	79,888	7.6	21.3	57.8	13.3
Monmouth County, New Jersey	53,525	10.5	28.0	41.0	20.5
Morris County, New Jersey	43,088	8.7	25.5	41.0	24.8
Ocean County, New Jersey	44,133	13.7	31.8	44.0	10.4
Passaic County, New Jersey	50,503	12.5	31.3	43.1	13.1

Table C-2. Educational Attainment of the Population, by Selected Counties, 2016—*Continued*

(Number; percent; dollars.)

State/County	Population 25 years and over							
	Total	Less than 9th grade	9th to 12th grade, no diploma	High school graduate (includes equivalency)	Some college, no degree	Associate's degree	Bachelor's degree	Graduate or professional degree
MISSISSIPPI—*(Continued)*								
Hinds County, Mississippi	154,693	3.8	8.1	24.9	25.1	8.4	17.5	12.2
Jackson County, Mississippi	94,196	4.1	6.9	32.3	23.8	10.3	14.5	8.1
Jones County, Mississippi	44,884	7.6	9.2	27.8	25.3	11.4	11.4	7.4
Lauderdale County, Mississippi	51,577	5.2	8.6	30.5	24.0	10.2	12.5	9.1
Lee County, Mississippi	56,893	3.5	13.1	25.8	24.7	9.2	14.3	9.5
Madison County, Mississippi	68,611	2.1	6.7	16.3	19.9	8.5	27.6	18.8
Rankin County, Mississippi	102,143	3.3	7.6	29.7	21.0	9.2	19.2	10.0
MISSOURI								
Boone County, Missouri	105,860	1.9	3.3	21.3	21.1	8.5	25.2	18.7
Buchanan County, Missouri	60,912	5.7	7.8	33.6	24.7	5.8	14.6	7.8
Cape Girardeau County, Missouri	51,042	2.3	6.5	30.7	24.9	5.1	17.3	13.1
Cass County, Missouri	69,730	2.1	4.4	33.6	27.2	8.6	15.3	8.8
Christian County, Missouri	56,354	1.6	7.9	27.6	27.8	9.3	18.2	7.6
Clay County, Missouri	160,909	1.7	4.0	29.4	22.1	8.8	24.2	9.8
Cole County, Missouri	51,887	2.7	5.7	29.7	19.9	8.4	20.1	13.4
Franklin County, Missouri	70,984	3.6	6.9	31.9	23.7	10.5	15.5	7.8
Greene County, Missouri	187,052	2.4	5.4	29.0	25.4	8.1	19.2	10.5
Jackson County, Missouri	467,734	3.0	6.0	29.6	23.3	7.0	19.8	11.3
Jasper County, Missouri	77,593	4.3	8.8	36.2	21.9	7.7	14.8	6.3
Jefferson County, Missouri	154,362	2.4	10.2	31.5	25.2	12.1	13.1	5.5
Platte County, Missouri	66,410	1.7	3.3	20.7	23.5	8.1	28.2	14.5
St. Charles County, Missouri	264,104	1.2	3.6	24.1	22.6	9.1	25.6	13.8
St. Francois County, Missouri	46,902	4.0	10.8	39.9	24.5	7.4	9.2	4.3
St. Louis County, Missouri	690,608	2.2	4.6	21.2	20.6	7.9	24.9	18.6
St. Louis city, Missouri	218,935	3.0	10.0	23.8	21.9	7.2	18.4	15.7
MONTANA								
Cascade County, Montana	55,456	2.8	6.0	29.9	27.0	11.1	17.0	6.3
Flathead County, Montana	69,263	0.6	5.1	28.1	24.5	11.4	19.2	11.1
Gallatin County, Montana	66,512	1.4	2.7	16.9	19.6	10.0	32.8	16.5
Lewis and Clark County, Montana	47,137	0.7	2.6	24.9	23.9	10.3	23.7	13.9
Missoula County, Montana	77,932	0.9	5.7	20.4	23.4	8.5	25.3	15.7
Yellowstone County, Montana	107,635	1.9	4.3	32.8	21.5	7.6	22.1	9.8
NEBRASKA								
Douglas County, Nebraska	360,304	5.2	5.2	22.2	21.5	7.7	25.8	12.5
Lancaster County, Nebraska	191,838	2.9	4.0	21.2	20.6	11.0	25.6	14.6
Sarpy County, Nebraska	113,848	1.8	3.2	22.4	23.7	9.4	26.1	13.4
NEVADA								
Clark County, Nevada	1,464,406	6.5	8.0	29.7	25.0	7.5	15.6	7.6
Washoe County, Nevada	312,348	5.5	7.0	24.5	26.3	7.5	17.6	11.6
NEW HAMPSHIRE								
Cheshire County, New Hampshire	52,767	2.3	5.6	32.6	17.4	9.1	19.2	13.8
Grafton County, New Hampshire	63,203	2.2	5.0	26.3	15.9	7.0	21.5	22.2
Hillsborough County, New Hampshire	286,364	2.8	5.7	25.5	18.6	10.2	24.1	13.1
Merrimack County, New Hampshire	105,578	2.0	5.0	26.4	19.0	11.8	20.5	15.3
Rockingham County, New Hampshire	219,845	1.7	3.4	25.3	18.1	11.2	25.1	15.2
Strafford County, New Hampshire	83,065	1.8	4.2	27.0	21.6	10.5	21.5	13.5
NEW JERSEY								
Atlantic County, New Jersey	186,643	4.3	7.1	33.1	21.2	6.7	18.5	9.2
Bergen County, New Jersey	660,788	4.2	3.7	22.3	14.8	5.8	30.4	18.8
Burlington County, New Jersey	315,389	2.0	4.3	29.7	18.4	8.4	23.6	13.6
Camden County, New Jersey	349,245	3.9	7.3	30.5	20.2	6.7	20.1	11.3
Cape May County, New Jersey	70,487	3.5	5.6	31.9	19.2	8.4	20.8	10.7
Cumberland County, New Jersey	104,422	10.1	12.7	38.7	17.2	7.4	10.0	3.8
Essex County, New Jersey	534,056	7.2	6.9	27.9	17.8	6.0	20.1	14.0
Gloucester County, New Jersey	200,633	2.7	4.9	34.1	18.0	9.3	20.6	10.5
Hudson County, New Jersey	482,166	9.4	6.0	26.5	12.8	4.6	25.0	15.7
Hunterdon County, New Jersey	88,182	2.0	3.1	22.4	14.8	5.2	29.9	22.7
Mercer County, New Jersey	249,778	5.8	5.2	25.3	15.6	5.4	22.1	20.6
Middlesex County, New Jersey	574,999	4.8	5.3	26.5	15.3	6.1	25.6	16.6
Monmouth County, New Jersey	436,927	3.5	4.4	24.1	17.2	6.8	26.4	17.6
Morris County, New Jersey	347,166	3.0	3.2	20.3	13.1	7.1	31.8	21.4
Ocean County, New Jersey	408,164	3.0	6.1	33.5	20.8	7.8	18.7	10.0
Passaic County, New Jersey	334,398	9.8	8.4	33.1	15.6	5.2	19.2	8.7

Table C-2. Educational Attainment of the Population, by Selected Counties, 2016—*Continued*

(Number; percent; dollars.)

State/County	Total	Population 18 to 24 years			
		Less than high school graduate (percent)	High school graduate (includes equivalency) (percent)	Some college or associate's degree	Bachelor's degree or higher
NEW JERSEY—*(Continued)*					
Salem County, New Jersey	5,675	29.2	29.4	33.1	8.3
Somerset County, New Jersey	28,462	8.4	25.5	40.4	25.7
Sussex County, New Jersey	11,586	14.1	33.8	38.7	13.3
Union County, New Jersey	48,376	11.5	32.8	42.9	12.9
Warren County, New Jersey	8,753	6.5	45.2	39.4	8.9
NEW MEXICO					
Bernalillo County, New Mexico	61,999	15.7	26.6	48.5	9.1
Chaves County, New Mexico	6,583	18.5	38.4	30.0	13.2
Doña Ana County, New Mexico	30,583	12.7	23.4	56.1	7.8
Lea County, New Mexico	6,739	19.2	24.0	53.9	3.0
McKinley County, New Mexico	7,839	25.8	40.8	31.6	1.9
Otero County, New Mexico	6,723	30.7	29.8	38.7	0.8
Sandoval County, New Mexico	10,707	23.1	26.2	46.0	4.7
San Juan County, New Mexico	9,656	14.7	33.5	48.1	3.6
Santa Fe County, New Mexico	11,235	21.6	26.4	49.5	2.5
Valencia County, New Mexico	6,013	24.6	44.9	27.7	2.8
NEW YORK					
Albany County, New York	46,237	7.1	22.6	47.8	22.6
Bronx County, New York	156,130	22.0	26.1	44.3	7.6
Broome County, New York	26,611	7.9	20.8	57.9	13.4
Cattaraugus County, New York	7,468	13.1	40.5	43.9	2.5
Cayuga County, New York	7,799	13.6	37.9	42.4	6.1
Chautauqua County, New York	13,301	13.7	28.3	50.4	7.7
Chemung County, New York	7,710	14.3	37.0	39.2	9.4
Clinton County, New York	11,371	9.2	38.2	45.8	6.9
Dutchess County, New York	33,485	14.4	29.4	44.5	11.7
Erie County, New York	88,219	10.1	28.7	45.8	15.4
Jefferson County, New York	14,389	8.3	42.5	42.7	6.4
Kings County, New York	228,226	13.0	26.8	40.3	19.9
Livingston County, New York	10,525	7.8	27.9	61.0	3.2
Madison County, New York	9,773	8.6	39.5	45.6	6.3
Monroe County, New York	77,486	10.7	23.8	49.1	16.4
Nassau County, New York	123,028	8.4	20.5	48.5	22.6
New York County, New York	152,197	8.4	16.9	40.8	33.9
Niagara County, New York	18,039	8.4	32.7	45.5	13.4
Oneida County, New York	22,759	15.2	31.6	44.8	8.4
Onondaga County, New York	49,343	9.1	24.6	51.0	15.2
Ontario County, New York	9,745	8.1	35.9	42.1	13.9
Orange County, New York	40,223	14.4	29.9	45.1	10.6
Oswego County, New York	13,432	9.3	29.0	54.7	7.0
Putnam County, New York	8,082	12.1	42.9	26.4	18.6
Queens County, New York	195,366	10.0	25.7	48.1	16.2
Rensselaer County, New York	17,348	8.1	34.1	44.7	13.1
Richmond County, New York	41,202	13.6	27.1	46.8	12.4
Rockland County, New York	30,885	14.9	24.2	47.3	13.6
St. Lawrence County, New York	15,576	6.1	21.2	70.1	2.6
Saratoga County, New York	20,240	6.4	26.2	54.1	13.3
Schenectady County, New York	15,090	10.4	35.5	40.1	14.0
Steuben County, New York	7,788	16.3	44.8	30.5	8.3
Suffolk County, New York	138,374	10.5	27.4	45.6	16.6
Sullivan County, New York	7,246	25.1	26.0	40.0	8.9
Tompkins County, New York	28,662	3.0	14.2	61.0	21.8
Ulster County, New York	17,155	12.2	27.8	50.7	9.2
Warren County, New York	4,642	9.9	22.8	56.4	10.8
Wayne County, New York	7,018	12.4	47.5	30.5	9.7
Westchester County, New York	88,332	11.4	26.2	44.6	17.9
NORTH CAROLINA					
Alamance County, North Carolina	15,551	9.8	21.4	62.8	6.1
Brunswick County, North Carolina	7,123	19.6	45.6	30.4	4.4
Buncombe County, North Carolina	20,267	13.1	38.5	38.1	10.3
Burke County, North Carolina	7,370	21.4	47.6	25.4	5.6
Cabarrus County, North Carolina	16,219	21.9	36.4	33.9	7.8
Caldwell County, North Carolina	6,520	21.4	28.2	46.1	4.3
Carteret County, North Carolina	4,586	33.4	22.4	35.6	8.6
Catawba County, North Carolina	12,742	12.5	33.4	45.8	8.4
Chatham County, North Carolina	4,367	3.3	42.2	50.9	3.7
Cleveland County, North Carolina	9,926	20.4	21.5	47.2	10.9

Table C-2. Educational Attainment of the Population, by Selected Counties, 2016—*Continued*

(Number; percent; dollars.)

State/County	Population 25 years and over							
	Total	Less than 9th grade	9th to 12th grade, no diploma	High school graduate (includes equivalency)	Some college, no degree	Associate's degree	Bachelor's degree	Graduate or professional degree
NEW JERSEY—*(Continued)*								
Salem County, New Jersey	43,935	3.3	10.0	39.5	18.5	10.0	12.8	5.9
Somerset County, New Jersey	230,267	3.5	3.7	21.2	13.7	6.4	27.9	23.7
Sussex County, New Jersey	101,611	1.7	3.7	32.3	20.3	8.0	23.9	10.1
Union County, New Jersey	375,954	7.7	6.3	28.6	16.3	6.1	21.6	13.4
Warren County, New Jersey	75,962	5.2	5.7	30.9	19.5	7.6	21.3	9.9
NEW MEXICO								
Bernalillo County, New Mexico	463,147	4.3	6.8	23.6	23.4	8.4	18.7	14.9
Chaves County, New Mexico	40,870	13.1	11.3	25.6	18.2	9.5	15.9	6.4
Doña Ana County, New Mexico	130,157	11.6	8.4	23.8	22.4	7.7	15.8	10.3
Lea County, New Mexico	41,761	16.9	13.1	29.5	19.4	6.9	10.2	4.0
McKinley County, New Mexico	44,598	10.2	16.5	34.1	22.7	6.7	5.2	4.6
Otero County, New Mexico	43,247	5.1	8.9	28.8	28.1	11.1	10.5	7.5
Sandoval County, New Mexico	97,355	3.0	8.2	22.0	24.3	10.8	18.5	13.2
San Juan County, New Mexico	75,728	6.0	8.6	28.6	30.0	10.2	9.1	7.5
Santa Fe County, New Mexico	109,637	5.3	5.0	24.2	18.0	5.7	21.8	19.9
Valencia County, New Mexico	51,370	4.4	12.1	33.6	24.5	7.6	11.4	6.4
NEW YORK								
Albany County, New York	204,813	2.5	5.9	22.9	14.8	11.3	22.1	20.5
Bronx County, New York	931,269	14.0	14.0	28.6	17.8	7.3	12.0	6.3
Broome County, New York	130,194	2.6	7.1	31.0	18.3	11.4	16.1	13.6
Cattaraugus County, New York	52,613	3.7	8.2	39.6	16.8	13.0	9.6	9.2
Cayuga County, New York	54,630	2.9	10.1	31.3	19.0	13.3	14.9	8.4
Chautauqua County, New York	89,506	4.1	7.9	36.0	17.8	12.6	11.7	9.8
Chemung County, New York	60,288	3.5	5.3	33.3	18.7	11.7	14.6	12.9
Clinton County, New York	55,928	3.3	7.9	38.1	17.4	12.0	10.7	10.6
Dutchess County, New York	203,914	2.6	7.7	26.3	17.3	11.3	19.8	15.0
Erie County, New York	643,909	2.6	6.0	28.3	17.6	12.3	18.8	14.4
Jefferson County, New York	72,123	3.0	5.4	37.7	21.7	11.6	12.1	8.6
Kings County, New York	1,791,538	8.9	9.8	25.1	13.5	6.2	22.0	14.4
Livingston County, New York	42,505	1.4	8.9	33.6	18.7	11.9	15.1	10.4
Madison County, New York	47,964	2.1	6.5	34.3	14.7	13.2	17.0	12.1
Monroe County, New York	512,340	3.2	6.8	22.7	18.1	11.8	21.0	16.4
Nassau County, New York	942,318	4.9	3.6	23.1	15.4	8.0	24.7	20.2
New York County, New York	1,250,801	7.2	5.6	12.7	10.1	4.0	31.3	29.2
Niagara County, New York	150,900	2.4	6.2	33.9	20.1	13.1	14.4	9.9
Oneida County, New York	159,553	4.2	8.1	32.3	16.7	12.1	16.4	10.2
Onondaga County, New York	316,286	3.3	6.2	25.2	18.6	11.8	19.7	15.3
Ontario County, New York	77,601	2.1	4.8	28.3	17.8	13.3	18.5	15.3
Orange County, New York	241,750	4.1	6.6	29.6	20.1	10.6	16.3	12.7
Oswego County, New York	80,239	3.8	9.3	38.6	18.9	11.6	9.7	8.0
Putnam County, New York	70,568	4.0	3.2	25.2	13.6	10.5	24.2	19.2
Queens County, New York	1,661,279	10.1	8.3	27.9	14.3	7.9	19.5	11.9
Rensselaer County, New York	110,749	3.6	5.1	26.9	17.3	13.9	19.1	14.0
Richmond County, New York	329,911	4.8	6.7	30.5	18.2	7.4	19.4	13.1
Rockland County, New York	205,190	7.4	7.0	21.7	16.5	7.9	21.5	18.0
St. Lawrence County, New York	72,162	3.6	8.9	35.3	16.9	11.9	11.0	12.4
Saratoga County, New York	160,185	1.9	4.3	24.4	17.3	11.4	24.1	16.7
Schenectady County, New York	105,829	3.6	7.0	32.9	14.9	11.2	18.6	11.7
Steuben County, New York	67,999	3.2	7.4	36.2	17.2	13.4	11.9	10.9
Suffolk County, New York	1,031,076	4.1	5.1	29.0	17.6	9.4	19.1	15.7
Sullivan County, New York	51,496	4.4	9.7	30.8	21.7	11.2	11.8	10.5
Tompkins County, New York	60,604	1.1	4.3	21.6	12.5	8.8	22.4	29.3
Ulster County, New York	129,290	3.9	5.5	29.9	17.5	10.4	18.3	14.6
Warren County, New York	48,009	2.7	5.1	33.6	20.4	8.4	17.9	12.0
Wayne County, New York	64,170	4.2	6.3	32.7	20.8	14.3	11.9	9.8
Westchester County, New York	666,907	6.9	5.9	19.4	13.9	6.3	24.1	23.5
NORTH CAROLINA								
Alamance County, North Carolina	108,448	4.8	9.0	25.5	26.4	11.8	15.1	7.4
Brunswick County, North Carolina	99,746	2.1	6.4	29.2	23.6	11.6	17.4	9.7
Buncombe County, North Carolina	187,268	2.6	6.7	23.7	21.3	8.0	23.0	14.7
Burke County, North Carolina	64,276	8.0	10.9	31.7	22.2	11.1	11.2	5.0
Cabarrus County, North Carolina	132,652	4.4	6.6	22.7	24.4	10.0	20.3	11.5
Caldwell County, North Carolina	58,577	6.0	15.5	33.4	21.4	10.2	9.4	4.2
Carteret County, North Carolina	51,780	4.2	4.1	29.0	26.7	10.4	14.5	11.1
Catawba County, North Carolina	108,433	4.4	10.0	30.4	22.4	11.8	14.4	6.5
Chatham County, North Carolina	52,984	6.0	6.5	20.1	16.2	8.7	21.7	20.8
Cleveland County, North Carolina	65,716	4.7	11.6	30.1	22.8	10.9	10.9	9.0

Table C-2. Educational Attainment of the Population, by Selected Counties, 2016—*Continued*

(Number; percent; dollars.)

State/County	Population 18 to 24 years				
	Total	Less than high school graduate (percent)	High school graduate (includes equivalency) (percent)	Some college or associate's degree	Bachelor's degree or higher
NORTH CAROLINA—*(Continued)*					
Craven County, North Carolina	13,146	13.4	46.5	34.9	5.3
Cumberland County, North Carolina	40,273	12.1	37.6	45.9	4.4
Davidson County, North Carolina	12,835	23.6	38.2	33.9	4.3
Durham County, North Carolina	30,116	11.2	24.6	37.7	26.5
Forsyth County, North Carolina	36,326	15.6	30.1	44.5	9.9
Gaston County, North Carolina	18,196	18.5	35.0	38.3	8.2
Guilford County, North Carolina	55,361	10.5	27.9	52.9	8.7
Harnett County, North Carolina	11,688	20.7	31.2	40.1	8.0
Henderson County, North Carolina	7,086	13.4	38.3	29.6	18.7
Iredell County, North Carolina	14,766	18.6	36.7	40.6	4.1
Johnston County, North Carolina	16,052	21.8	26.9	47.9	3.3
Lincoln County, North Carolina	5,757	17.2	42.9	25.5	14.3
Mecklenburg County, North Carolina	95,599	12.6	23.9	46.7	16.9
Moore County, North Carolina	6,523	23.4	35.9	37.5	3.2
Nash County, North Carolina	7,437	8.2	35.9	50.4	5.6
New Hanover County, North Carolina	28,618	8.2	27.5	46.7	17.7
Onslow County, North Carolina	38,871	8.7	55.2	33.7	2.5
Orange County, North Carolina	25,281	2.9	18.3	54.8	24.0
Pitt County, North Carolina	32,094	5.1	24.3	59.1	11.6
Randolph County, North Carolina	10,989	18.0	36.0	42.5	3.5
Robeson County, North Carolina	13,463	16.0	42.5	38.4	3.1
Rockingham County, North Carolina	7,610	25.5	25.9	47.4	1.3
Rowan County, North Carolina	12,519	13.5	37.2	43.8	5.5
Rutherford County, North Carolina	5,661	11.8	42.2	35.5	10.6
Surry County, North Carolina	5,668	14.3	38.6	42.4	4.7
Union County, North Carolina	19,757	11.8	41.2	39.3	7.7
Wake County, North Carolina	96,599	8.8	26.3	45.6	19.2
Wayne County, North Carolina	11,790	19.6	32.5	45.0	3.0
Wilkes County, North Carolina	5,432	18.5	33.3	41.9	6.3
Wilson County, North Carolina	7,168	30.1	35.2	31.3	3.4
NORTH DAKOTA					
Burleigh County, North Dakota	8,982	6.5	38.8	46.0	8.8
Cass County, North Dakota	26,285	3.3	20.2	56.2	20.2
Grand Forks County, North Dakota	14,722	1.5	25.9	63.5	9.2
Ward County, North Dakota	10,051	11.5	39.3	37.3	11.9
OHIO					
Allen County, Ohio	11,410	12.7	39.0	43.2	5.2
Ashtabula County, Ohio	7,336	24.8	36.9	30.4	7.9
Athens County, Ohio	20,707	3.4	20.6	71.3	4.7
Belmont County, Ohio	4,861	14.3	36.6	41.4	7.8
Butler County, Ohio	46,287	7.1	34.4	48.9	9.6
Clark County, Ohio	12,061	15.1	37.3	42.8	4.8
Clermont County, Ohio	16,578	14.9	43.2	34.7	7.2
Columbiana County, Ohio	7,768	17.4	40.6	23.0	19.1
Cuyahoga County, Ohio	113,362	14.5	31.2	39.8	14.5
Delaware County, Ohio	15,297	8.1	32.5	43.8	15.6
Erie County, Ohio	6,090	11.2	51.6	29.9	7.3
Fairfield County, Ohio	11,860	12.7	34.2	44.9	8.2
Franklin County, Ohio	124,946	9.7	26.1	49.5	14.7
Geauga County, Ohio	8,153	32.8	24.1	30.7	12.4
Greene County, Ohio	20,795	10.0	15.1	66.1	8.8
Hamilton County, Ohio	75,466	12.4	35.9	37.1	14.7
Hancock County, Ohio	7,426	12.1	32.0	38.7	17.3
Jefferson County, Ohio	6,144	5.7	42.9	45.6	5.9
Lake County, Ohio	17,197	12.4	29.2	43.2	15.1
Licking County, Ohio	15,552	14.2	41.0	39.7	5.1
Lorain County, Ohio	27,688	14.8	39.3	39.3	6.7
Lucas County, Ohio	40,697	16.4	32.8	42.0	8.7
Mahoning County, Ohio	19,361	17.6	40.1	35.5	6.8
Marion County, Ohio	5,581	16.7	40.1	40.6	2.5
Medina County, Ohio	13,252	13.3	36.0	42.0	8.7
Miami County, Ohio	7,660	15.2	43.0	30.7	11.1
Montgomery County, Ohio	48,829	11.5	27.9	52.4	8.2
Muskingum County, Ohio	7,494	8.4	29.7	55.4	6.6
Portage County, Ohio	27,503	8.6	25.9	50.8	14.7
Richland County, Ohio	9,793	19.0	51.0	27.0	3.0
Ross County, Ohio	6,023	23.1	43.8	27.5	5.5
Scioto County, Ohio	6,574	23.7	40.8	32.8	2.6

Table C-2. Educational Attainment of the Population, by Selected Counties, 2016—*Continued*

(Number; percent; dollars.)

State/County	Population 25 years and over							
	Total	Less than 9th grade	9th to 12th grade, no diploma	High school graduate (includes equivalency)	Some college, no degree	Associate's degree	Bachelor's degree	Graduate or professional degree
NORTH CAROLINA—*(Continued)*								
Craven County, North Carolina	67,687	4.9	8.1	23.8	22.9	13.9	17.2	9.2
Cumberland County, North Carolina	203,807	3.1	6.2	25.9	28.1	11.4	16.7	8.7
Davidson County, North Carolina	115,176	5.8	11.0	33.4	23.0	9.5	12.4	4.9
Durham County, North Carolina	209,945	5.1	7.3	17.7	15.1	7.0	26.1	21.7
Forsyth County, North Carolina	247,842	4.6	6.2	24.6	21.5	8.8	21.5	12.8
Gaston County, North Carolina	149,258	4.6	11.4	30.1	22.1	10.2	15.2	6.5
Guilford County, North Carolina	347,807	5.3	6.9	24.7	21.4	7.2	22.0	12.4
Harnett County, North Carolina	84,127	4.5	8.2	29.7	25.7	12.0	13.2	6.7
Henderson County, North Carolina	85,288	4.8	7.0	26.1	22.5	9.2	19.1	11.3
Iredell County, North Carolina	117,528	4.7	7.4	29.6	21.7	10.3	19.0	7.4
Johnston County, North Carolina	125,406	4.8	9.1	27.0	21.8	13.2	17.4	6.6
Lincoln County, North Carolina	58,231	3.4	8.3	32.1	26.3	9.0	14.6	6.3
Mecklenburg County, North Carolina	704,185	4.1	5.3	17.2	20.2	8.6	29.8	14.8
Moore County, North Carolina	69,160	2.8	4.4	21.8	22.4	10.9	23.3	14.5
Nash County, North Carolina	66,362	5.3	11.7	33.9	17.2	11.5	11.6	8.7
New Hanover County, North Carolina	152,648	1.8	6.1	23.2	21.1	8.7	26.5	12.5
Onslow County, North Carolina	100,734	2.2	7.1	29.2	31.1	11.7	13.3	5.3
Orange County, North Carolina	87,775	4.2	4.3	12.8	14.7	6.0	26.0	32.1
Pitt County, North Carolina	106,388	3.1	6.9	22.7	24.4	11.4	18.6	13.1
Randolph County, North Carolina	99,506	7.0	12.0	32.2	23.7	8.8	11.8	4.5
Robeson County, North Carolina	85,584	7.4	14.7	35.1	21.3	8.3	9.6	3.7
Rockingham County, North Carolina	64,907	4.8	14.6	33.9	24.2	8.1	9.6	4.8
Rowan County, North Carolina	95,890	5.0	8.9	31.9	25.5	8.9	14.9	4.9
Rutherford County, North Carolina	47,248	6.2	11.2	33.1	19.9	11.4	12.5	5.7
Surry County, North Carolina	51,044	11.3	12.5	29.7	20.9	10.6	9.9	5.1
Union County, North Carolina	143,989	3.7	8.5	24.6	21.0	8.3	23.5	10.4
Wake County, North Carolina	693,438	3.2	3.8	14.2	17.3	8.3	33.7	19.5
Wayne County, North Carolina	82,498	6.9	9.6	30.1	21.9	13.8	11.7	5.9
Wilkes County, North Carolina	48,946	6.2	11.4	33.3	24.1	9.9	10.3	4.8
Wilson County, North Carolina	55,331	8.7	12.0	34.0	18.2	8.5	12.9	5.5
NORTH DAKOTA								
Burleigh County, North Dakota	63,201	2.3	5.4	22.9	19.9	16.1	25.0	8.4
Cass County, North Dakota	109,732	1.9	3.5	18.8	20.6	14.0	29.5	11.6
Grand Forks County, North Dakota	42,251	1.2	4.1	26.9	20.9	13.8	23.4	9.8
Ward County, North Dakota	43,991	2.2	4.7	32.6	23.0	9.6	20.5	7.3
OHIO								
Allen County, Ohio	68,415	1.5	10.2	37.8	20.3	13.6	10.0	6.7
Ashtabula County, Ohio	68,989	5.9	9.3	42.6	20.6	8.0	8.2	5.4
Athens County, Ohio	35,883	2.7	10.0	36.5	16.9	7.9	14.1	12.0
Belmont County, Ohio	50,739	3.1	7.2	39.4	19.5	11.8	12.3	6.7
Butler County, Ohio	241,769	2.9	7.4	32.1	20.8	7.1	19.3	10.4
Clark County, Ohio	92,244	1.6	10.1	38.8	23.1	8.5	11.6	6.3
Clermont County, Ohio	139,006	3.7	8.5	31.3	19.5	8.9	17.9	10.2
Columbiana County, Ohio	74,657	2.7	8.9	43.5	20.6	11.3	8.4	4.7
Cuyahoga County, Ohio	871,344	2.5	7.5	29.0	22.3	7.5	18.2	13.0
Delaware County, Ohio	128,032	1.0	2.7	20.1	15.3	6.0	34.3	20.6
Erie County, Ohio	53,666	1.5	6.7	37.5	22.7	9.9	13.5	8.2
Fairfield County, Ohio	103,502	2.2	5.4	32.4	22.4	10.4	17.1	10.1
Franklin County, Ohio	841,899	2.8	6.4	25.5	19.1	7.0	25.1	14.0
Geauga County, Ohio	64,333	9.2	2.4	26.1	18.6	7.6	23.3	12.8
Greene County, Ohio	109,844	2.1	4.2	24.6	23.5	8.6	19.8	17.2
Hamilton County, Ohio	545,596	2.5	6.4	26.7	19.4	8.1	21.7	15.2
Hancock County, Ohio	51,576	1.5	4.1	36.0	21.9	10.8	16.3	9.4
Jefferson County, Ohio	47,136	3.2	8.5	44.1	17.2	10.5	11.4	5.1
Lake County, Ohio	165,027	1.9	5.7	31.9	22.6	9.1	17.5	11.1
Licking County, Ohio	115,689	1.6	6.9	34.2	21.8	10.4	16.7	8.3
Lorain County, Ohio	209,967	2.4	8.7	30.3	21.8	12.2	14.9	9.7
Lucas County, Ohio	292,076	2.3	8.2	28.2	24.8	10.4	16.2	9.9
Mahoning County, Ohio	163,942	2.0	7.1	37.4	21.7	6.7	17.1	8.0
Marion County, Ohio	45,879	1.5	11.4	45.8	22.3	7.3	7.9	3.8
Medina County, Ohio	123,346	1.1	3.9	31.0	21.9	8.9	22.6	10.5
Miami County, Ohio	72,843	3.0	7.4	36.6	21.1	10.2	12.3	9.4
Montgomery County, Ohio	364,377	2.8	7.6	27.8	26.3	10.0	16.0	9.7
Muskingum County, Ohio	58,596	3.5	10.7	41.8	21.3	10.0	8.0	4.7
Portage County, Ohio	103,843	1.7	5.2	36.2	19.2	8.1	17.5	12.1
Richland County, Ohio	85,196	2.8	10.3	39.9	21.6	7.8	11.7	5.9
Ross County, Ohio	54,542	2.7	9.5	43.9	20.3	7.5	10.8	5.3
Scioto County, Ohio	52,762	3.7	9.2	42.3	22.5	8.6	8.1	5.7

Table C-2. Educational Attainment of the Population, by Selected Counties, 2016—*Continued*

(Number; percent; dollars.)

State/County	Population 18 to 24 years				
	Total	Less than high school graduate (percent)	High school graduate (includes equivalency) (percent)	Some college or associate's degree	Bachelor's degree or higher
OHIO—*(Continued)*					
Stark County, Ohio	32,945	10.6	39.6	41.7	8.2
Summit County, Ohio	46,820	16.1	30.0	40.9	13.0
Trumbull County, Ohio	16,614	19.3	43.9	26.4	10.5
Tuscarawas County, Ohio	7,773	29.3	43.5	22.0	5.2
Warren County, Ohio	17,677	19.3	40.3	30.0	10.4
Wayne County, Ohio	11,431	18.6	31.6	45.7	4.1
Wood County, Ohio	22,838	4.9	17.7	69.4	8.0
OKLAHOMA					
Canadian County, Oklahoma	10,924	12.8	37.1	40.4	9.8
Cleveland County, Oklahoma	41,306	8.3	21.2	61.9	8.6
Comanche County, Oklahoma	16,765	11.6	48.4	34.8	5.2
Creek County, Oklahoma	6,099	17.8	59.3	21.6	1.4
Muskogee County, Oklahoma	6,554	24.7	49.6	23.8	1.9
Oklahoma County, Oklahoma	71,264	15.7	33.1	43.0	8.2
Payne County, Oklahoma	21,372	4.3	22.0	64.5	9.3
Pottawatomie County, Oklahoma	7,095	15.0	26.0	51.2	7.9
Rogers County, Oklahoma	7,796	13.6	35.2	44.2	7.1
Tulsa County, Oklahoma	57,659	18.0	34.3	38.9	8.8
Wagoner County, Oklahoma	5,892	26.5	32.0	35.5	6.0
OREGON					
Benton County, Oregon	20,570	3.6	13.1	67.7	15.6
Clackamas County, Oregon	31,083	13.6	37.1	37.9	11.4
Deschutes County, Oregon	12,331	19.8	17.5	45.2	17.5
Douglas County, Oregon	7,550	19.9	42.5	37.6	0.0
Jackson County, Oregon	17,282	13.5	38.5	42.8	5.2
Josephine County, Oregon	5,955	20.9	37.0	42.1	0.0
Klamath County, Oregon	5,974	21.5	21.9	49.0	7.6
Lane County, Oregon	46,915	8.5	28.0	55.7	7.7
Linn County, Oregon	9,495	13.4	30.9	48.9	6.8
Marion County, Oregon	32,033	16.6	34.5	44.5	4.4
Multnomah County, Oregon	66,267	9.2	28.4	46.5	15.9
Polk County, Oregon	11,184	8.0	22.5	59.5	10.1
Umatilla County, Oregon	7,346	18.2	37.5	41.8	2.5
Washington County, Oregon	47,762	11.6	33.2	40.7	14.5
Yamhill County, Oregon	11,233	6.6	35.3	53.5	4.6
PENNSYLVANIA					
Adams County, Pennsylvania	9,737	12.4	40.5	37.2	9.8
Allegheny County, Pennsylvania	109,705	9.1	28.3	42.2	20.4
Armstrong County, Pennsylvania	4,488	18.2	38.0	29.3	14.5
Beaver County, Pennsylvania	12,043	13.2	29.3	44.1	13.4
Berks County, Pennsylvania	40,519	14.0	40.6	36.1	9.3
Blair County, Pennsylvania	9,802	11.4	38.2	40.2	10.3
Bucks County, Pennsylvania	49,897	11.1	33.1	37.2	18.5
Butler County, Pennsylvania	16,076	7.7	30.8	47.7	13.7
Cambria County, Pennsylvania	12,779	13.8	25.8	51.5	8.9
Carbon County, Pennsylvania	4,131	11.1	60.7	18.5	9.6
Centre County, Pennsylvania	37,644	3.5	26.2	61.0	9.3
Chester County, Pennsylvania	47,324	9.8	32.9	41.7	15.6
Clearfield County, Pennsylvania	6,406	7.9	62.1	20.5	9.5
Columbia County, Pennsylvania	10,929	5.0	26.7	58.3	10.1
Crawford County, Pennsylvania	8,119	19.2	32.4	42.5	6.0
Cumberland County, Pennsylvania	23,795	9.5	29.5	51.0	10.0
Dauphin County, Pennsylvania	22,799	13.7	39.4	33.2	13.7
Delaware County, Pennsylvania	57,303	7.2	28.3	51.7	12.7
Erie County, Pennsylvania	27,843	11.6	31.4	44.9	12.1
Fayette County, Pennsylvania	9,561	13.1	48.0	30.7	8.2
Franklin County, Pennsylvania	12,462	19.1	46.1	25.7	9.1
Indiana County, Pennsylvania	14,238	10.7	24.9	52.3	12.1
Lackawanna County, Pennsylvania	19,106	6.8	32.6	48.9	11.7
Lancaster County, Pennsylvania	49,282	19.8	35.8	32.5	11.9
Lawrence County, Pennsylvania	7,323	9.7	36.8	48.4	5.2
Lebanon County, Pennsylvania	12,451	16.8	46.1	34.4	2.7
Lehigh County, Pennsylvania	32,671	22.2	30.8	37.6	9.5
Luzerne County, Pennsylvania	28,507	13.1	33.4	44.5	9.0
Lycoming County, Pennsylvania	10,922	15.0	39.5	39.1	6.4
Mercer County, Pennsylvania	11,125	12.7	38.1	43.3	5.9
Monroe County, Pennsylvania	19,380	10.3	36.7	44.6	8.4

Table C-2. Educational Attainment of the Population, by Selected Counties, 2016—*Continued*

(Number; percent; dollars.)

State/County	Population 25 years and over							
	Total	Less than 9th grade	9th to 12th grade, no diploma	High school graduate (includes equivalency)	Some college, no degree	Associate's degree	Bachelor's degree	Graduate or professional degree
OHIO—*(Continued)*								
Stark County, Ohio	259,702	2.4	6.3	38.5	20.8	7.8	14.8	9.4
Summit County, Ohio	378,788	2.7	5.8	31.5	19.2	9.4	20.1	11.2
Trumbull County, Ohio	143,360	3.5	6.7	44.6	18.5	7.0	13.8	5.8
Tuscarawas County, Ohio	63,630	6.9	7.2	43.5	17.5	6.3	11.9	6.7
Warren County, Ohio	152,254	2.0	5.3	25.8	15.9	8.2	27.8	15.1
Wayne County, Ohio	76,693	6.0	6.7	40.0	18.3	8.5	12.7	7.8
Wood County, Ohio	80,806	0.9	5.3	28.3	20.7	10.3	19.2	15.2
OKLAHOMA								
Canadian County, Oklahoma	89,682	3.0	5.7	29.3	26.1	9.6	20.1	6.2
Cleveland County, Oklahoma	175,831	1.8	6.1	23.3	25.9	9.7	21.5	11.7
Comanche County, Oklahoma	75,748	2.1	9.3	32.9	27.2	8.0	12.3	8.3
Creek County, Oklahoma	48,085	3.0	10.4	42.0	21.2	7.2	12.1	4.2
Muskogee County, Oklahoma	45,808	3.1	10.1	35.5	22.5	8.1	14.8	5.8
Oklahoma County, Oklahoma	509,852	5.5	7.7	25.4	23.3	6.9	19.9	11.3
Payne County, Oklahoma	44,075	2.9	5.5	25.4	22.7	7.1	18.5	18.0
Pottawatomie County, Oklahoma	47,709	2.5	10.4	36.7	25.1	8.4	11.7	5.2
Rogers County, Oklahoma	61,972	2.4	5.8	33.5	25.6	9.9	15.9	7.0
Tulsa County, Oklahoma	421,335	4.4	6.4	25.9	23.6	8.5	21.1	10.1
Wagoner County, Oklahoma	52,440	2.0	7.5	33.5	24.0	7.9	18.2	7.0
OREGON								
Benton County, Oregon	53,831	1.2	3.0	10.5	23.4	7.6	29.6	24.6
Clackamas County, Oregon	287,965	2.4	3.9	20.5	27.2	10.0	22.9	13.1
Deschutes County, Oregon	131,527	1.2	6.5	28.1	22.5	8.9	20.2	12.5
Douglas County, Oregon	79,588	2.8	8.2	31.3	29.9	10.3	9.4	8.1
Jackson County, Oregon	154,339	4.0	7.2	25.1	30.2	6.9	16.7	9.9
Josephine County, Oregon	63,758	1.1	10.8	27.5	32.9	8.2	12.8	6.8
Klamath County, Oregon	45,866	5.9	8.4	31.8	27.0	8.6	10.9	7.4
Lane County, Oregon	253,107	2.2	6.4	24.5	28.4	9.7	17.3	11.5
Linn County, Oregon	85,318	2.4	5.9	27.8	34.7	7.5	14.5	7.2
Marion County, Oregon	220,446	8.0	6.7	26.7	27.4	8.5	14.8	7.9
Multnomah County, Oregon	579,147	4.1	4.8	16.4	22.5	7.1	27.3	17.9
Polk County, Oregon	52,192	3.6	6.0	24.2	26.9	9.6	17.4	12.3
Umatilla County, Oregon	49,339	9.2	9.0	28.5	28.0	9.5	8.2	7.5
Washington County, Oregon	397,353	4.0	4.5	17.8	21.7	9.0	26.0	17.0
Yamhill County, Oregon	69,819	2.9	7.9	27.3	26.6	8.8	18.4	8.0
PENNSYLVANIA								
Adams County, Pennsylvania	71,649	4.9	8.4	40.6	15.7	8.7	12.2	9.4
Allegheny County, Pennsylvania	883,649	1.7	3.9	27.3	16.1	9.4	24.8	16.7
Armstrong County, Pennsylvania	49,294	2.4	9.0	47.1	15.5	9.7	10.4	5.8
Beaver County, Pennsylvania	122,808	1.6	6.0	36.5	18.1	12.2	17.7	7.9
Berks County, Pennsylvania	280,522	5.9	7.7	37.3	15.7	8.4	16.1	8.9
Blair County, Pennsylvania	89,160	1.7	6.6	48.1	17.3	8.0	13.1	5.3
Bucks County, Pennsylvania	445,411	2.0	4.4	29.6	15.9	7.9	24.0	16.1
Butler County, Pennsylvania	132,863	1.5	3.5	31.9	16.6	10.1	22.8	13.5
Cambria County, Pennsylvania	96,044	2.4	5.7	43.5	15.7	10.5	13.5	8.7
Carbon County, Pennsylvania	47,157	2.9	8.1	46.4	15.8	9.7	11.3	6.0
Centre County, Pennsylvania	99,337	1.8	3.0	29.3	11.0	6.7	26.5	21.8
Chester County, Pennsylvania	349,419	2.6	4.1	21.8	13.6	6.8	31.2	19.9
Clearfield County, Pennsylvania	59,403	4.3	9.7	49.3	13.3	9.3	8.8	5.3
Columbia County, Pennsylvania	43,741	2.4	8.3	40.6	17.6	8.2	13.7	9.2
Crawford County, Pennsylvania	59,971	3.4	7.1	46.2	13.6	7.6	12.6	9.5
Cumberland County, Pennsylvania	174,144	2.1	6.3	31.2	16.6	7.6	22.8	13.2
Dauphin County, Pennsylvania	189,682	3.2	6.7	32.3	16.7	8.7	20.2	12.2
Delaware County, Pennsylvania	380,990	2.2	4.8	31.0	16.1	7.5	22.1	16.3
Erie County, Pennsylvania	188,454	2.2	5.6	41.2	15.0	7.9	18.4	9.7
Fayette County, Pennsylvania	97,293	2.2	10.0	50.0	13.2	8.3	11.5	4.8
Franklin County, Pennsylvania	106,597	3.2	8.7	42.3	15.0	9.2	13.1	8.6
Indiana County, Pennsylvania	56,494	3.3	7.4	43.7	14.7	9.0	12.7	9.2
Lackawanna County, Pennsylvania	149,504	3.6	6.2	37.3	16.7	9.2	16.8	10.2
Lancaster County, Pennsylvania	360,762	6.4	8.7	36.9	14.9	8.1	16.2	8.8
Lawrence County, Pennsylvania	62,570	2.9	6.9	43.1	16.6	7.7	14.4	8.5
Lebanon County, Pennsylvania	94,270	2.9	8.4	45.3	16.0	6.8	13.4	7.2
Lehigh County, Pennsylvania	247,963	4.5	6.3	34.0	17.4	8.4	18.2	11.2
Luzerne County, Pennsylvania	226,048	3.1	7.5	39.0	16.5	10.9	14.7	8.4
Lycoming County, Pennsylvania	80,588	2.6	6.6	37.5	20.6	11.5	13.8	7.4
Mercer County, Pennsylvania	79,823	2.8	6.9	42.7	16.3	9.3	12.7	9.3
Monroe County, Pennsylvania	113,148	3.0	6.7	35.8	21.1	7.6	16.2	9.4

Table C-2. Educational Attainment of the Population, by Selected Counties, 2016—*Continued*

(Number; percent; dollars.)

| State/County | Population 18 to 24 years | | | | |
	Total	Less than high school graduate (percent)	High school graduate (includes equivalency) (percent)	Some college or associate's degree	Bachelor's degree or higher
PENNSYLVANIA—*(Continued)*					
Montgomery County, Pennsylvania	66,538	10.2	29.4	41.5	18.9
Northampton County, Pennsylvania	30,037	9.2	32.9	48.3	9.6
Northumberland County, Pennsylvania	6,416	17.8	37.0	36.6	8.6
Philadelphia County, Pennsylvania	164,132	13.0	30.9	44.5	11.6
Schuylkill County, Pennsylvania	10,024	18.7	46.8	27.9	6.6
Somerset County, Pennsylvania	5,501	17.8	46.6	25.8	9.9
Washington County, Pennsylvania	17,624	14.2	33.4	38.7	13.7
Westmoreland County, Pennsylvania	27,982	9.1	29.6	47.0	14.3
York County, Pennsylvania	37,221	15.2	43.9	34.7	6.3
RHODE ISLAND					
Kent County, Rhode Island	11,663	13.8	25.8	48.8	11.6
Newport County, Rhode Island	7,712	6.5	18.6	35.8	39.1
Providence County, Rhode Island	70,423	11.5	32.0	45.1	11.4
Washington County, Rhode Island	18,408	12.5	29.1	45.9	12.6
SOUTH CAROLINA					
Aiken County, South Carolina	13,865	14.6	33.5	47.0	4.9
Anderson County, South Carolina	16,983	18.0	37.4	35.0	9.7
Beaufort County, South Carolina	16,909	18.5	40.7	34.7	6.1
Berkeley County, South Carolina	20,934	13.2	37.8	37.1	11.9
Charleston County, South Carolina	35,844	10.2	25.7	47.5	16.6
Darlington County, South Carolina	5,920	7.6	46.8	39.0	6.7
Dorchester County, South Carolina	12,747	18.2	35.8	32.7	13.4
Florence County, South Carolina	11,884	13.6	36.5	44.3	5.6
Greenville County, South Carolina	43,892	13.5	28.6	44.0	13.9
Greenwood County, South Carolina	7,419	38.0	12.9	44.0	5.2
Horry County, South Carolina	25,034	14.1	32.5	47.7	5.6
Lancaster County, South Carolina	6,583	12.4	44.7	41.0	1.9
Laurens County, South Carolina	6,522	10.5	37.9	44.1	7.5
Lexington County, South Carolina	21,956	11.5	31.8	46.1	10.6
Oconee County, South Carolina	6,226	8.7	46.9	38.1	6.3
Orangeburg County, South Carolina	8,925	10.4	30.4	56.4	2.8
Pickens County, South Carolina	20,824	9.2	20.1	64.3	6.4
Richland County, South Carolina	65,261	6.5	34.1	48.7	10.7
Spartanburg County, South Carolina	28,876	14.1	33.3	44.8	7.8
Sumter County, South Carolina	11,536	10.2	33.5	50.0	6.2
York County, South Carolina	22,129	14.3	28.5	46.8	10.5
SOUTH DAKOTA					
Minnehaha County, South Dakota	17,416	14.3	28.7	46.1	10.9
Pennington County, South Dakota	9,485	13.1	29.8	44.7	12.4
TENNESSEE					
Anderson County, Tennessee	5,952	4.0	46.4	38.7	10.9
Blount County, Tennessee	9,817	10.0	30.8	52.9	6.3
Bradley County, Tennessee	10,371	7.6	33.2	53.8	5.4
Davidson County, Tennessee	69,236	10.1	25.4	45.1	19.3
Greene County, Tennessee	6,370	14.2	35.9	43.2	6.6
Hamilton County, Tennessee	32,611	11.0	22.6	55.2	11.1
Knox County, Tennessee	54,439	8.6	27.8	50.5	13.1
Madison County, Tennessee	10,830	7.8	49.3	34.9	8.0
Maury County, Tennessee	6,953	12.1	36.7	44.7	6.6
Montgomery County, Tennessee	21,993	7.4	41.6	41.5	9.4
Putnam County, Tennessee	10,409	4.5	30.7	59.7	5.1
Robertson County, Tennessee	4,925	14.2	47.3	31.7	6.8
Rutherford County, Tennessee	39,887	6.6	31.4	49.2	12.8
Sevier County, Tennessee	7,358	18.5	40.7	36.1	4.8
Shelby County, Tennessee	90,608	13.7	33.2	43.5	9.6
Sullivan County, Tennessee	12,121	16.8	37.7	37.7	7.9
Sumner County, Tennessee	14,100	14.0	35.3	40.9	9.8
Washington County, Tennessee	15,304	7.3	28.6	51.1	13.0
Williamson County, Tennessee	16,274	22.5	30.6	25.2	21.7
Wilson County, Tennessee	10,126	12.9	38.0	36.8	12.3
TEXAS					
Angelina County, Texas	8,404	10.4	39.8	45.0	4.7
Bastrop County, Texas	8,524	28.1	43.9	27.3	0.8
Bell County, Texas	39,312	12.7	40.2	39.6	7.4
Bexar County, Texas	202,503	13.4	34.4	44.2	8.1
Bowie County, Texas	7,654	18.8	47.1	33.1	1.0
Brazoria County, Texas	29,546	12.7	38.5	40.1	8.7

Table C-2. Educational Attainment of the Population, by Selected Counties, 2016—*Continued*

(Number; percent; dollars.)

State/County	Population 25 years and over							
	Total	Less than 9th grade	9th to 12th grade, no diploma	High school graduate (includes equivalency)	Some college, no degree	Associate's degree	Bachelor's degree	Graduate or professional degree
PENNSYLVANIA—*(Continued)*								
Montgomery County, Pennsylvania	576,833	1.9	3.9	24.2	15.2	6.9	27.5	20.6
Northampton County, Pennsylvania	211,011	3.2	6.0	35.4	17.1	9.4	18.8	10.1
Northumberland County, Pennsylvania	67,758	3.2	9.7	50.2	12.0	7.4	11.7	6.0
Philadelphia County, Pennsylvania	1,057,805	5.8	11.0	31.8	17.4	5.5	16.9	11.7
Schuylkill County, Pennsylvania	105,640	2.6	8.9	47.3	15.8	9.7	9.7	6.0
Somerset County, Pennsylvania	55,951	5.4	7.0	47.9	14.5	9.1	10.8	5.2
Washington County, Pennsylvania	149,408	2.5	5.1	38.8	16.1	8.1	20.0	9.4
Westmoreland County, Pennsylvania	261,528	1.9	3.9	37.4	17.2	11.5	17.8	10.3
York County, Pennsylvania	308,230	2.9	7.4	41.0	16.2	8.4	15.7	8.5
RHODE ISLAND								
Kent County, Rhode Island	121,800	2.7	5.4	29.0	20.5	10.2	20.0	12.1
Newport County, Rhode Island	60,041	2.2	3.1	21.8	19.9	7.7	28.3	17.1
Providence County, Rhode Island	431,584	7.2	7.3	30.1	18.0	8.0	18.1	11.3
Washington County, Rhode Island	86,400	1.1	3.7	23.6	18.1	6.9	25.7	20.9
SOUTH CAROLINA								
Aiken County, South Carolina	117,504	4.9	9.8	32.6	21.3	7.9	14.5	9.0
Anderson County, South Carolina	134,544	5.0	11.0	33.7	19.0	10.2	12.8	8.4
Beaufort County, South Carolina	130,743	1.9	3.6	22.9	22.3	7.5	23.6	18.1
Berkeley County, South Carolina	138,969	3.6	9.1	27.4	24.3	10.4	16.3	9.0
Charleston County, South Carolina	281,282	2.7	7.5	22.1	17.7	8.5	27.2	14.4
Darlington County, South Carolina	46,018	6.8	14.6	33.2	19.4	8.7	10.9	6.4
Dorchester County, South Carolina	102,255	4.1	8.0	25.9	21.9	10.9	19.6	9.5
Florence County, South Carolina	93,661	5.9	10.8	30.8	20.7	9.5	14.6	7.7
Greenville County, South Carolina	338,862	4.2	8.4	22.9	21.6	8.9	21.9	12.1
Greenwood County, South Carolina	45,548	3.7	10.4	30.1	20.6	11.2	16.5	7.5
Horry County, South Carolina	237,363	3.5	6.9	31.7	25.8	9.7	15.0	7.4
Lancaster County, South Carolina	63,699	3.5	9.5	33.0	17.1	10.3	18.1	8.4
Laurens County, South Carolina	45,545	7.7	13.1	31.2	23.9	10.1	9.4	4.5
Lexington County, South Carolina	197,188	4.0	6.5	29.6	20.8	8.6	19.6	10.9
Oconee County, South Carolina	54,652	5.2	9.5	29.9	22.8	8.1	14.8	9.6
Orangeburg County, South Carolina	58,483	4.2	10.0	31.9	20.5	15.3	12.1	6.0
Pickens County, South Carolina	77,764	5.4	10.8	26.6	19.3	10.4	17.1	10.3
Richland County, South Carolina	255,352	3.2	6.2	22.1	21.5	8.1	23.1	15.8
Spartanburg County, South Carolina	202,391	5.1	10.0	31.3	20.2	11.2	14.3	8.0
Sumter County, South Carolina	69,787	4.4	9.8	31.6	25.6	9.2	13.2	6.3
York County, South Carolina	173,199	4.1	6.5	25.8	22.8	10.9	19.9	9.9
SOUTH DAKOTA								
Minnehaha County, South Dakota	122,560	3.5	4.8	25.4	21.9	11.0	23.0	10.4
Pennington County, South Dakota	74,338	2.2	6.3	26.2	23.4	11.7	19.6	10.6
TENNESSEE								
Anderson County, Tennessee	54,291	5.0	7.0	32.0	25.6	7.2	13.2	9.9
Blount County, Tennessee	92,123	3.7	7.6	33.7	22.4	9.7	14.8	8.1
Bradley County, Tennessee	71,667	5.3	8.7	34.8	20.4	7.8	15.1	7.9
Davidson County, Tennessee	468,932	4.2	8.2	22.3	19.6	5.8	24.9	14.9
Greene County, Tennessee	49,412	6.1	8.3	44.0	19.4	6.0	10.1	6.2
Hamilton County, Tennessee	249,883	4.0	7.2	29.3	19.2	9.5	21.1	9.5
Knox County, Tennessee	304,869	2.9	6.3	24.1	20.2	8.1	23.8	14.6
Madison County, Tennessee	64,646	3.3	8.6	40.5	21.3	5.3	13.4	7.6
Maury County, Tennessee	61,953	3.0	5.8	34.1	24.8	10.1	13.6	8.6
Montgomery County, Tennessee	120,879	2.3	5.9	29.8	27.7	8.4	18.4	7.4
Putnam County, Tennessee	49,287	6.0	7.8	38.2	16.2	3.8	16.9	11.2
Robertson County, Tennessee	47,268	5.6	8.7	37.8	20.4	7.8	13.0	6.7
Rutherford County, Tennessee	191,596	2.3	4.7	29.6	23.4	8.1	22.0	9.9
Sevier County, Tennessee	68,175	5.3	8.4	38.4	22.8	6.7	11.6	6.7
Shelby County, Tennessee	608,402	4.2	7.5	25.7	24.4	7.4	19.2	11.5
Sullivan County, Tennessee	113,824	4.8	9.2	37.3	20.8	8.0	12.1	7.8
Sumner County, Tennessee	122,747	4.0	5.5	32.3	21.9	9.3	18.2	8.8
Washington County, Tennessee	87,299	3.9	8.6	30.4	19.2	6.2	19.6	12.1
Williamson County, Tennessee	142,284	2.6	3.5	13.6	17.5	6.8	36.9	19.0
Wilson County, Tennessee	91,054	3.3	6.9	26.4	25.3	9.0	19.7	9.4
TEXAS								
Angelina County, Texas	56,702	9.3	12.4	29.1	25.1	8.1	10.9	5.0
Bastrop County, Texas	54,506	8.9	8.9	27.2	26.7	8.2	13.3	6.8
Bell County, Texas	206,073	3.8	6.1	25.7	31.4	10.7	14.7	7.6
Bexar County, Texas	1,225,485	7.8	9.6	25.3	21.7	7.8	17.8	10.1
Bowie County, Texas	63,684	2.9	8.4	36.8	23.7	7.2	14.6	6.4
Brazoria County, Texas	230,238	5.3	6.9	28.0	23.3	8.9	17.1	10.4

Table C-2. Educational Attainment of the Population, by Selected Counties, 2016—*Continued*

(Number; percent; dollars.)

State/County		Population 18 to 24 years			
	Total	Less than high school graduate (percent)	High school graduate (includes equivalency) (percent)	Some college or associate's degree	Bachelor's degree or higher
TEXAS—*(Continued)*					
Brazos County, Texas	59,167	4.1	14.6	68.7	12.6
Cameron County, Texas	45,231	23.8	37.0	36.1	3.1
Collin County, Texas	75,782	12.4	29.5	40.3	17.8
Comal County, Texas	12,048	20.6	35.4	31.3	12.8
Coryell County, Texas	9,468	8.3	57.8	32.3	1.6
Dallas County, Texas	249,071	16.1	32.5	39.4	12.0
Denton County, Texas	76,329	10.9	29.8	50.0	9.3
Ector County, Texas	16,648	9.4	37.4	48.9	4.3
Ellis County, Texas	15,774	16.3	37.1	40.1	6.5
El Paso County, Texas	95,052	11.8	29.7	53.4	5.2
Fort Bend County, Texas	61,383	12.9	23.1	49.6	14.4
Galveston County, Texas	28,844	14.8	30.2	45.8	9.2
Grayson County, Texas	10,976	14.4	38.1	41.9	5.5
Gregg County, Texas	12,058	9.3	32.0	54.3	4.4
Guadalupe County, Texas	14,309	13.5	42.4	35.2	8.9
Harris County, Texas	437,962	17.3	31.6	41.4	9.7
Harrison County, Texas	6,175	21.1	40.8	32.1	6.0
Hays County, Texas	35,898	7.9	31.7	53.6	6.8
Henderson County, Texas	6,571	19.2	25.9	47.7	7.2
Hidalgo County, Texas	93,585	19.0	28.0	46.3	6.7
Hunt County, Texas	9,621	14.1	28.4	49.0	8.5
Jefferson County, Texas	25,026	15.0	37.6	39.0	8.4
Johnson County, Texas	14,086	22.3	43.2	29.7	4.8
Kaufman County, Texas	9,728	14.2	34.1	42.2	9.4
Liberty County, Texas	6,908	17.7	47.2	29.3	5.8
Lubbock County, Texas	51,656	7.7	20.9	62.5	8.9
McLennan County, Texas	36,883	8.4	28.3	53.6	9.7
Midland County, Texas	14,787	16.5	36.7	41.3	5.5
Montgomery County, Texas	46,424	23.9	37.4	30.0	8.7
Nacogdoches County, Texas	13,332	5.8	27.3	63.1	3.8
Nueces County, Texas	37,143	9.5	37.6	45.1	7.8
Orange County, Texas	7,028	20.2	21.8	53.2	4.9
Parker County, Texas	10,011	9.4	52.3	30.9	7.4
Potter County, Texas	11,258	17.5	37.4	41.7	3.5
Randall County, Texas	13,706	7.8	34.8	49.3	8.1
Rockwall County, Texas	8,257	7.7	31.2	45.0	16.1
San Patricio County, Texas	6,621	19.3	46.7	29.7	4.3
Smith County, Texas	22,159	18.0	33.0	44.5	4.5
Tarrant County, Texas	188,971	14.5	32.3	42.9	10.3
Taylor County, Texas	18,949	12.7	33.7	45.2	8.4
Tom Green County, Texas	14,813	5.9	25.6	64.7	3.7
Travis County, Texas	113,223	9.5	21.9	50.7	17.8
Victoria County, Texas	8,697	20.7	32.5	44.0	2.8
Walker County, Texas	14,803	6.2	16.3	70.1	7.5
Webb County, Texas	30,675	18.6	40.9	37.4	3.2
Wichita County, Texas	18,346	8.2	45.3	43.8	2.7
Williamson County, Texas	41,753	14.9	26.0	47.1	12.1
UTAH					
Cache County, Utah	22,965	10.9	21.6	59.7	7.9
Davis County, Utah	31,925	11.5	35.1	45.7	7.8
Salt Lake County, Utah	107,161	14.0	33.8	43.9	8.3
Utah County, Utah	99,206	6.8	27.0	59.5	6.7
Washington County, Utah	15,440	12.8	26.5	59.6	1.1
Weber County, Utah	24,103	13.6	32.0	50.9	3.6
VERMONT					
Chittenden County, Vermont	25,800	4.8	18.6	58.2	18.4
VIRGINIA					
Albemarle County, Virginia	13,051	8.1	23.3	53.6	15.0
Arlington County, Virginia	18,392	13.1	15.5	22.4	49.0
Augusta County, Virginia	6,036	13.7	43.4	24.8	18.0
Bedford County, Virginia	5,650	17.5	30.8	39.9	11.8
Chesterfield County, Virginia	29,977	11.8	32.9	41.0	14.4
Fairfax County, Virginia	94,919	13.9	23.7	40.7	21.6
Fauquier County, Virginia	5,326	14.5	48.5	25.8	11.1
Frederick County, Virginia	7,062	11.1	48.5	31.4	9.0
Hanover County, Virginia	9,526	3.7	40.2	47.5	8.6
Henrico County, Virginia	25,204	15.1	29.2	40.9	14.7
James City County, Virginia	5,506	27.9	40.2	25.3	6.6
Loudoun County, Virginia	28,628	11.4	24.8	44.5	19.3
Montgomery County, Virginia	27,806	1.6	12.9	66.0	19.5
Prince William County, Virginia	40,132	12.9	32.7	41.6	12.8
Roanoke County, Virginia	7,123	11.6	34.6	38.4	15.4

Table C-2. Educational Attainment of the Population, by Selected Counties, 2016—*Continued*

(Number; percent; dollars.)

	Population 25 years and over							
State/County	Total	Less than 9th grade	9th to 12th grade, no diploma	High school graduate (includes equivalency)	Some college, no degree	Associate's degree	Bachelor's degree	Graduate or professional degree
TEXAS—(*Continued*)								
Brazos County, Texas	116,055	6.9	6.7	19.9	21.1	6.5	20.0	18.9
Cameron County, Texas	245,943	19.2	13.2	27.1	16.3	7.2	12.0	5.0
Collin County, Texas	613,358	3.4	3.1	15.1	19.3	7.4	33.4	18.3
Comal County, Texas	92,508	2.6	3.8	26.1	22.3	8.8	24.6	11.9
Coryell County, Texas	47,572	6.9	6.2	28.0	31.4	11.5	11.3	4.6
Dallas County, Texas	1,638,570	11.9	9.8	22.0	20.1	5.8	19.5	10.9
Denton County, Texas	524,239	3.7	4.1	17.6	22.6	7.4	30.7	13.9
Ector County, Texas	93,324	8.9	15.4	31.3	22.4	6.7	11.4	3.9
Ellis County, Texas	107,633	6.0	9.5	27.3	27.2	8.2	15.1	6.7
El Paso County, Texas	510,580	13.6	9.4	23.3	23.4	8.3	14.7	7.3
Fort Bend County, Texas	474,935	4.2	5.0	19.0	19.6	7.2	28.1	16.9
Galveston County, Texas	219,771	4.6	7.5	23.9	24.0	10.8	18.3	10.9
Grayson County, Texas	86,626	3.3	7.9	28.0	30.1	11.3	14.9	4.5
Gregg County, Texas	79,826	7.6	12.0	28.0	25.5	5.6	13.9	7.4
Guadalupe County, Texas	100,974	5.6	6.1	32.2	19.7	9.1	17.9	9.5
Harris County, Texas	2,912,844	10.8	8.1	23.6	20.0	6.5	20.0	11.0
Harrison County, Texas	43,374	5.8	10.9	32.8	27.8	5.8	11.9	5.0
Hays County, Texas	121,051	6.0	6.3	21.5	24.0	6.0	21.4	14.7
Henderson County, Texas	55,949	7.3	9.4	33.5	26.1	5.2	11.3	7.1
Hidalgo County, Texas	473,366	21.4	13.1	23.3	19.6	4.4	12.8	5.5
Hunt County, Texas	60,159	5.9	12.3	29.9	25.3	6.4	12.1	8.1
Jefferson County, Texas	168,925	7.7	9.0	33.7	22.5	8.6	12.4	6.1
Johnson County, Texas	106,686	5.3	9.1	37.6	23.1	5.3	15.0	4.5
Kaufman County, Texas	76,218	7.0	7.0	36.6	21.9	8.1	12.8	6.6
Liberty County, Texas	53,961	9.6	14.4	40.5	19.6	7.0	6.9	2.2
Lubbock County, Texas	178,621	6.1	8.4	24.6	24.5	5.5	19.5	11.4
McLennan County, Texas	149,696	6.7	10.3	29.1	22.8	9.2	13.5	8.3
Midland County, Texas	101,188	7.2	9.1	27.4	21.3	8.5	19.4	7.1
Montgomery County, Texas	361,549	4.7	8.3	23.6	22.1	7.9	21.2	12.2
Nacogdoches County, Texas	36,960	6.2	14.6	24.8	23.2	5.4	17.3	8.4
Nueces County, Texas	233,620	6.9	10.1	28.0	25.1	7.9	14.4	7.7
Orange County, Texas	56,658	3.8	7.8	39.5	24.6	8.8	12.1	3.4
Parker County, Texas	87,198	4.5	7.3	31.3	26.9	8.1	14.7	7.2
Potter County, Texas	76,399	11.1	13.2	32.1	22.0	6.8	9.9	4.8
Randall County, Texas	86,683	2.4	7.2	19.5	27.4	11.9	21.0	10.6
Rockwall County, Texas	60,013	4.1	4.1	20.0	22.6	9.0	25.2	15.0
San Patricio County, Texas	42,902	9.2	11.7	29.6	27.9	7.0	11.0	3.6
Smith County, Texas	147,441	6.4	7.9	23.7	27.3	9.8	17.4	7.5
Tarrant County, Texas	1,288,602	6.9	7.7	24.7	22.5	7.4	20.4	10.3
Taylor County, Texas	84,075	5.1	6.2	36.0	23.2	7.0	15.2	7.4
Tom Green County, Texas	75,857	4.7	11.0	28.2	24.8	6.3	17.0	8.0
Travis County, Texas	816,263	6.2	5.0	16.7	19.6	5.4	30.3	16.9
Victoria County, Texas	60,364	6.6	9.0	31.2	26.7	7.3	13.1	6.1
Walker County, Texas	45,665	5.9	6.5	40.2	21.1	5.0	13.7	7.6
Webb County, Texas	148,275	18.2	14.8	28.7	14.6	6.5	12.3	4.9
Wichita County, Texas	84,259	5.6	8.7	29.4	24.9	7.6	16.1	7.7
Williamson County, Texas	347,601	2.7	3.4	20.4	24.0	8.8	27.9	12.7
UTAH								
Cache County, Utah	62,058	4.0	4.7	18.7	26.7	7.4	27.7	10.9
Davis County, Utah	198,180	1.0	3.1	21.3	25.9	11.1	25.2	12.5
Salt Lake County, Utah	701,154	4.0	5.9	22.8	24.2	9.2	21.1	12.6
Utah County, Utah	290,596	1.8	3.7	16.2	28.7	10.9	26.4	12.3
Washington County, Utah	101,498	2.4	3.4	22.1	30.4	13.6	17.6	10.7
Weber County, Utah	152,217	3.1	6.8	29.6	28.5	9.8	15.1	7.2
VERMONT								
Chittenden County, Vermont	106,218	2.2	2.8	20.3	16.1	8.3	28.9	21.5
VIRGINIA								
Albemarle County, Virginia	72,178	4.8	5.6	15.4	17.9	3.9	26.3	26.2
Arlington County, Virginia	170,778	3.9	2.2	9.2	7.7	2.8	33.9	40.4
Augusta County, Virginia	54,196	4.1	11.1	34.8	19.5	7.1	14.4	9.0
Bedford County, Virginia	56,184	2.6	6.5	30.7	21.8	8.9	17.3	12.4
Chesterfield County, Virginia	227,539	2.8	4.0	23.7	20.1	8.7	25.5	15.1
Fairfax County, Virginia	772,823	4.7	3.5	12.1	13.5	5.2	31.1	30.0
Fauquier County, Virginia	47,595	3.3	6.3	24.7	22.4	8.8	22.2	12.5
Frederick County, Virginia	57,872	3.0	6.2	33.2	19.0	10.0	16.3	12.2
Hanover County, Virginia	71,796	2.1	6.1	24.1	19.4	7.7	26.3	14.3
Henrico County, Virginia	225,821	2.5	5.6	22.1	20.3	7.6	26.5	15.5
James City County, Virginia	53,623	1.1	3.5	17.0	20.0	8.1	28.5	21.8
Loudoun County, Virginia	246,461	3.9	3.1	12.6	14.8	6.0	34.5	25.2
Montgomery County, Virginia	54,973	2.2	3.8	21.9	15.9	5.9	24.3	26.0
Prince William County, Virginia	289,294	6.4	5.7	21.1	18.6	7.6	24.5	16.0
Roanoke County, Virginia	67,778	3.4	5.4	23.6	19.9	14.5	21.5	11.6

Table C-2. Educational Attainment of the Population, by Selected Counties, 2016—*Continued*

(Number; percent; dollars.)

State/County	Population 18 to 24 years				
	Total	Less than high school graduate (percent)	High school graduate (includes equivalency) (percent)	Some college or associate's degree	Bachelor's degree or higher
VIRGINIA —*(Continued)*					
Rockingham County, Virginia	7,261	12.3	39.2	40.9	7.7
Spotsylvania County, Virginia	11,553	17.8	35.0	39.2	8.0
Stafford County, Virginia	14,610	10.9	33.3	43.7	12.2
York County, Virginia	6,403	17.5	17.4	55.8	9.2
Alexandria city, Virginia	10,348	15.1	22.4	41.9	20.5
Chesapeake city, Virginia	19,685	9.7	35.0	47.6	7.6
Hampton city, Virginia	15,956	7.3	40.5	48.1	4.1
Lynchburg city, Virginia	20,711	2.9	29.4	44.2	23.4
Newport News city, Virginia	23,566	8.7	36.5	47.5	7.3
Norfolk city, Virginia	43,765	6.4	29.2	58.7	5.7
Portsmouth city, Virginia	10,378	11.3	38.9	45.1	4.7
Richmond city, Virginia	29,333	7.3	19.3	59.4	14.0
Roanoke city, Virginia	7,523	24.8	26.9	42.8	5.5
Suffolk city, Virginia	7,671	16.5	30.5	44.9	8.0
Virginia Beach city, Virginia	44,237	6.6	33.6	51.1	8.7
WASHINGTON					
Benton County, Washington	16,978	23.9	30.2	41.2	4.7
Chelan County, Washington	6,505	29.0	17.3	40.9	12.8
Clallam County, Washington	5,130	21.6	27.3	48.2	2.9
Clark County, Washington	37,857	16.4	38.1	38.9	6.5
Cowlitz County, Washington	8,176	21.5	43.3	33.3	1.9
Franklin County, Washington	8,500	39.0	27.6	32.8	0.6
Grant County, Washington	10,065	31.8	26.0	40.3	1.9
Grays Harbor County, Washington	4,850	14.7	55.0	29.2	1.2
Island County, Washington	7,225	12.9	40.2	39.4	7.5
King County, Washington	180,302	12.4	23.5	41.0	23.1
Kitsap County, Washington	26,625	12.5	38.6	42.4	6.4
Lewis County, Washington	6,444	21.1	35.0	35.8	8.1
Pierce County, Washington	80,665	14.5	39.0	38.1	8.4
Skagit County, Washington	10,613	22.7	34.7	38.7	3.9
Snohomish County, Washington	64,554	15.0	33.1	39.2	12.7
Spokane County, Washington	49,657	13.0	29.8	49.4	7.8
Thurston County, Washington	21,021	12.6	32.9	43.7	10.7
Whatcom County, Washington	31,711	10.2	22.8	56.0	11.0
Yakima County, Washington	24,113	29.3	29.5	38.1	3.1
WEST VIRGINIA					
Berkeley County, West Virginia	7,867	16.1	41.2	31.9	10.7
Cabell County, West Virginia	13,583	5.8	22.5	52.5	19.2
Harrison County, West Virginia	4,785	7.3	40.0	42.8	10.0
Kanawha County, West Virginia	13,458	20.8	30.3	42.2	6.7
Monongalia County, West Virginia	22,846	4.9	22.3	61.5	11.3
Raleigh County, West Virginia	5,271	22.5	48.9	28.6	0.0
Wood County, West Virginia	6,585	15.1	36.6	39.4	8.9
WISCONSIN					
Brown County, Wisconsin	24,074	8.4	33.9	42.8	14.9
Dane County, Wisconsin	73,399	3.9	23.7	48.3	24.1
Dodge County, Wisconsin	6,986	19.1	34.0	41.4	5.5
Eau Claire County, Wisconsin	17,489	6.7	30.9	52.1	10.3
Fond du Lac County, Wisconsin	8,795	9.0	35.1	48.4	7.5
Jefferson County, Wisconsin	8,488	3.8	34.6	48.1	13.6
Kenosha County, Wisconsin	17,055	13.1	34.6	44.0	8.3
La Crosse County, Wisconsin	19,193	4.6	32.2	54.4	8.7
Manitowoc County, Wisconsin	6,135	14.2	37.6	41.9	6.3
Marathon County, Wisconsin	11,259	11.6	37.6	40.6	10.2
Milwaukee County, Wisconsin	93,881	12.2	29.4	48.1	10.2
Outagamie County, Wisconsin	16,035	13.3	32.1	42.6	12.0
Ozaukee County, Wisconsin	7,924	10.0	28.6	51.3	10.0
Portage County, Wisconsin	11,726	3.8	25.6	61.0	9.6
Racine County, Wisconsin	16,742	19.5	42.0	30.6	7.9
Rock County, Wisconsin	13,963	8.9	45.1	40.7	5.3
St. Croix County, Wisconsin	6,239	8.4	27.9	55.5	8.2
Sheboygan County, Wisconsin	8,823	15.6	33.6	40.0	10.8
Walworth County, Wisconsin	13,352	8.6	33.8	48.8	8.8
Washington County, Wisconsin	9,583	12.2	27.0	49.0	11.8
Waukesha County, Wisconsin	31,161	12.5	27.4	41.8	18.3
Winnebago County, Wisconsin	20,674	7.0	32.4	51.2	9.4
Wood County, Wisconsin	5,366	14.5	41.6	37.9	5.9
WYOMING					
Laramie County, Wyoming	8,007	17.6	38.5	32.5	11.4
Natrona County, Wyoming	7,196	10.7	37.8	47.2	4.3

Table C-2. Educational Attainment of the Population, by Selected Counties, 2016—*Continued*

(Number; percent; dollars.)

State/County	Total	Less than 9th grade	9th to 12th grade, no diploma	High school graduate (includes equivalency)	Some college, no degree	Associate's degree	Bachelor's degree	Graduate or professional degree
VIRGINIA —*(Continued)*								
Rockingham County, Virginia	54,823	7.3	9.4	34.4	15.9	6.4	15.5	11.1
Spotsylvania County, Virginia	87,404	4.2	5.8	30.2	22.2	7.4	18.8	11.5
Stafford County, Virginia	91,847	1.4	5.2	22.1	23.9	7.9	21.4	18.1
York County, Virginia	44,987	2.3	2.7	21.1	17.2	10.3	25.5	20.9
Alexandria city, Virginia	116,979	4.6	3.6	10.9	12.8	5.5	28.9	33.7
Chesapeake city, Virginia	160,682	2.7	6.2	25.7	24.2	9.6	20.5	11.0
Hampton city, Virginia	90,993	2.3	6.5	29.7	25.2	9.0	15.6	11.7
Lynchburg city, Virginia	44,029	4.2	8.3	26.3	20.4	7.4	19.5	14.0
Newport News city, Virginia	116,209	2.1	7.2	26.7	26.7	10.0	17.0	10.3
Norfolk city, Virginia	151,771	3.3	8.3	25.7	26.6	7.9	17.9	10.2
Portsmouth city, Virginia	62,369	3.9	9.0	30.2	29.0	6.8	14.1	7.1
Richmond city, Virginia	153,809	4.4	9.4	21.9	18.2	7.3	22.0	16.8
Roanoke city, Virginia	69,862	3.1	9.7	35.3	20.2	10.6	13.4	7.6
Suffolk city, Virginia	59,503	2.3	7.2	28.9	25.6	9.6	15.9	10.6
Virginia Beach city, Virginia	306,588	1.9	4.7	21.2	26.3	10.9	22.7	12.3
WASHINGTON								
Benton County, Washington	124,831	5.4	3.8	23.5	27.0	10.6	18.2	11.6
Chelan County, Washington	51,524	9.1	10.2	26.5	17.6	10.3	14.5	11.7
Clallam County, Washington	55,957	1.3	8.3	29.2	27.3	9.8	15.0	9.1
Clark County, Washington	314,097	2.2	5.4	24.2	27.2	11.5	19.1	10.5
Cowlitz County, Washington	73,161	3.2	8.8	31.4	29.3	10.2	10.8	6.3
Franklin County, Washington	50,994	15.5	9.3	23.8	26.2	8.9	9.0	7.2
Grant County, Washington	56,205	14.6	8.8	26.2	25.6	6.7	11.7	6.5
Grays Harbor County, Washington	52,168	5.1	8.1	35.0	24.9	10.3	12.1	4.6
Island County, Washington	60,457	1.6	3.2	23.4	28.8	11.7	17.8	13.3
King County, Washington	1,526,042	3.6	4.1	15.1	17.9	7.9	30.8	20.6
Kitsap County, Washington	183,529	2.1	4.3	22.8	28.9	10.0	20.9	11.1
Lewis County, Washington	54,318	4.3	6.9	30.0	29.4	12.6	11.3	5.4
Pierce County, Washington	576,216	3.2	5.9	27.0	25.9	11.1	17.9	9.0
Skagit County, Washington	85,910	4.6	5.8	26.1	28.0	11.2	15.7	8.7
Snohomish County, Washington	543,473	2.7	5.2	24.3	26.0	10.5	21.4	10.1
Spokane County, Washington	338,520	1.5	4.2	23.5	27.1	12.8	19.4	11.5
Thurston County, Washington	194,426	2.0	4.1	20.6	25.9	12.2	22.3	12.9
Whatcom County, Washington	142,486	3.6	5.0	25.1	23.6	9.8	21.0	11.8
Yakima County, Washington	150,873	14.2	11.0	28.7	22.2	8.1	9.6	6.3
WEST VIRGINIA								
Berkeley County, West Virginia	78,451	2.0	10.9	37.7	21.7	7.0	12.3	8.5
Cabell County, West Virginia	62,994	4.4	8.9	31.6	20.3	9.2	14.0	11.6
Harrison County, West Virginia	48,823	3.7	7.9	38.2	18.5	6.6	16.4	8.8
Kanawha County, West Virginia	134,965	3.3	9.4	35.9	19.4	6.8	14.1	11.1
Monongalia County, West Virginia	64,393	1.3	6.2	31.0	15.6	5.4	21.0	19.6
Raleigh County, West Virginia	55,155	3.4	7.8	40.8	20.8	7.6	12.9	6.7
Wood County, West Virginia	60,885	2.6	5.8	32.4	25.1	8.8	14.7	10.5
WISCONSIN								
Brown County, Wisconsin	173,698	2.8	4.0	31.7	20.0	13.2	20.6	7.7
Dane County, Wisconsin	346,949	1.5	2.2	17.8	15.9	10.7	31.1	20.9
Dodge County, Wisconsin	63,264	2.6	6.8	39.7	22.9	11.4	11.0	5.4
Eau Claire County, Wisconsin	63,980	2.5	4.2	25.2	22.0	15.4	20.0	10.8
Fond du Lac County, Wisconsin	71,069	2.7	5.8	37.2	20.0	10.6	16.7	7.1
Jefferson County, Wisconsin	57,644	3.6	6.3	32.5	21.4	11.8	16.7	7.8
Kenosha County, Wisconsin	111,676	3.9	8.5	30.2	22.9	9.5	15.4	9.6
La Crosse County, Wisconsin	75,372	1.6	3.7	21.8	22.6	13.6	22.8	14.0
Manitowoc County, Wisconsin	56,868	2.5	5.6	43.0	19.4	10.3	13.5	5.7
Marathon County, Wisconsin	93,256	3.2	5.6	35.3	18.4	12.8	16.8	7.9
Milwaukee County, Wisconsin	626,433	4.2	7.7	28.5	21.0	7.9	19.4	11.2
Outagamie County, Wisconsin	124,500	2.5	3.9	31.5	21.8	13.1	19.1	8.1
Ozaukee County, Wisconsin	61,250	1.1	2.8	21.4	19.3	7.4	28.2	19.7
Portage County, Wisconsin	45,236	1.6	4.0	30.9	20.8	11.3	22.6	8.9
Racine County, Wisconsin	132,870	2.9	7.1	35.3	21.1	10.5	15.1	7.9
Rock County, Wisconsin	109,432	2.7	6.9	34.3	23.4	11.0	14.3	7.3
St. Croix County, Wisconsin	59,386	1.4	1.6	23.1	22.4	15.7	25.4	10.4
Sheboygan County, Wisconsin	80,642	2.2	4.3	36.1	21.8	10.0	18.8	6.9
Walworth County, Wisconsin	67,454	2.4	5.1	32.0	22.1	9.1	18.0	11.3
Washington County, Wisconsin	94,307	1.2	3.9	29.6	22.5	12.2	21.3	9.4
Waukesha County, Wisconsin	280,191	1.1	2.8	23.7	19.8	9.7	27.8	15.1
Winnebago County, Wisconsin	114,281	2.1	5.7	34.0	19.7	10.1	20.3	8.1
Wood County, Wisconsin	52,220	2.6	5.6	37.2	20.2	13.1	12.6	8.7
WYOMING								
Laramie County, Wyoming	67,239	1.7	4.3	25.3	26.5	14.9	17.4	9.9
Natrona County, Wyoming	53,993	0.6	5.2	33.9	24.9	11.9	14.3	9.2

Table C-2. Educational Attainment of the Population, by Selected Counties, 2016—*Continued*

(Number; percent; dollars.)

State/County	Population 25 to 34 years			Population 35 to 44 years		
	Total	High school graduate or more	Bachelor's degree or more	Total	High school graduate or more	Bachelor's degree or more
ALABAMA						
Baldwin County, Alabama	24,663	91.4	31.1	23,384	89.6	30.0
Calhoun County, Alabama	14,623	91.3	19.4	14,083	83.8	25.3
Cullman County, Alabama	10,351	75.6	19.4	10,056	76.2	13.0
DeKalb County, Alabama	8,571	90.5	10.4	9,329	70.8	10.5
Elmore County, Alabama	11,622	82.5	22.6	10,823	89.1	25.8
Etowah County, Alabama	11,409	83.2	13.8	12,262	83.7	15.9
Houston County, Alabama	13,593	89.1	20.8	12,681	87.2	20.3
Jefferson County, Alabama	95,118	89.8	37.9	83,165	90.2	37.5
Lauderdale County, Alabama	10,704	91.9	22.9	10,779	88.7	30.9
Lee County, Alabama	23,465	88.2	37.9	17,921	90.5	42.5
Limestone County, Alabama	12,571	77.5	25.1	12,241	80.8	21.7
Madison County, Alabama	48,747	91.8	40.0	44,813	89.9	48.3
Marshall County, Alabama	12,517	80.1	15.7	11,469	79.5	16.0
Mobile County, Alabama	57,734	86.9	26.1	49,476	89.0	30.5
Montgomery County, Alabama	33,610	89.7	25.7	28,374	82.7	35.9
Morgan County, Alabama	13,931	80.7	13.2	15,726	80.6	26.8
St. Clair County, Alabama	11,539	89.2	18.7	11,032	90.5	19.3
Shelby County, Alabama	25,994	92.2	37.7	31,160	89.6	42.0
Talladega County, Alabama	9,874	82.8	14.8	10,184	87.1	23.7
Tuscaloosa County, Alabama	31,080	90.7	37.4	24,939	89.0	26.6
Walker County, Alabama	7,778	78.9	3.2	7,530	84.4	13.5
ALASKA						
Anchorage Municipality, Alaska	52,809	94.4	30.5	39,268	95.6	40.2
Fairbanks North Star Borough, Alaska	17,886	97.3	36.2	11,544	94.0	29.1
Matanuska-Susitna Borough, Alaska	14,812	97.4	11.3	13,397	90.8	19.6
ARIZONA						
Apache County, Arizona	8,994	89.5	7.9	8,398	87.4	10.1
Cochise County, Arizona	16,154	88.3	14.5	13,584	89.6	27.7
Coconino County, Arizona	17,194	91.6	31.3	15,174	94.0	38.0
Maricopa County, Arizona	608,882	87.5	30.8	552,398	84.6	33.2
Mohave County, Arizona	21,037	78.8	14.8	18,042	81.2	10.3
Navajo County, Arizona	14,279	84.7	9.1	11,511	83.4	21.1
Pima County, Arizona	125,100	89.1	27.6	113,791	87.4	31.0
Pinal County, Arizona	53,102	76.9	13.6	55,455	84.8	17.1
Yavapai County, Arizona	19,565	94.7	16.5	19,362	92.7	19.0
Yuma County, Arizona	27,534	82.6	13.5	22,430	81.3	23.6
ARKANSAS						
Benton County, Arkansas	37,940	91.6	39.4	36,806	87.0	38.9
Craighead County, Arkansas	15,318	94.2	28.5	13,812	91.5	20.2
Faulkner County, Arkansas	17,224	96.0	31.5	15,527	94.8	28.8
Garland County, Arkansas	10,783	79.4	15.9	10,940	89.3	25.1
Jefferson County, Arkansas	8,113	76.1	9.4	8,505	85.7	16.1
Lonoke County, Arkansas	10,190	89.5	17.6	9,399	94.4	29.4
Pulaski County, Arkansas	57,408	93.3	37.9	48,680	90.5	36.9
Saline County, Arkansas	15,477	95.9	33.8	14,927	92.2	32.0
Sebastian County, Arkansas	17,553	87.8	13.9	16,070	76.1	15.9
Washington County, Arkansas	33,502	87.6	33.0	28,949	83.6	30.2
White County, Arkansas	10,489	92.5	35.6	9,352	89.7	21.0
CALIFORNIA						
Alameda County, California	272,967	92.3	52.3	243,462	88.7	52.1
Butte County, California	27,079	90.3	22.0	23,961	86.5	29.9
Contra Costa County, California	144,333	90.2	37.3	151,293	87.0	46.5
El Dorado County, California	17,660	95.0	23.1	21,081	92.1	40.4
Fresno County, California	148,909	81.4	20.4	119,815	74.0	19.5
Humboldt County, California	17,593	89.9	27.0	17,010	93.9	29.9
Imperial County, California	26,063	84.3	15.0	21,409	80.7	18.7
Kern County, California	136,121	79.8	13.8	110,617	71.3	17.0
Kings County, California	24,398	79.3	11.1	19,366	78.9	10.6
Lake County, California	6,166	77.7	6.1	8,149	84.1	17.2
Los Angeles County, California	1,613,327	87.6	36.8	1,383,874	79.0	33.5
Madera County, California	21,397	75.2	7.5	18,625	70.9	9.4
Marin County, California	21,624	89.4	47.0	33,876	85.0	64.1
Mendocino County, California	10,321	83.7	13.2	9,764	80.2	21.6
Merced County, California	38,805	81.0	14.2	32,870	66.7	13.0
Monterey County, California	63,220	72.3	23.2	56,134	61.8	21.7
Napa County, California	17,179	90.1	34.5	17,715	75.9	36.0

Table C-2. Educational Attainment of the Population, by Selected Counties, 2016—*Continued*

(Number; percent; dollars.)

State/County	Population 45 to 64 years			Population 65 years and over		
	Total	High school graduate or more	Bachelor's degree or more	Total	High school graduate or more	Bachelor's degree or more
ALABAMA						
Baldwin County, Alabama	58,319	88.7	28.6	40,621	90.8	30.0
Calhoun County, Alabama	30,550	78.0	12.0	18,962	80.7	14.9
Cullman County, Alabama	21,978	78.5	16.4	15,084	77.8	18.7
DeKalb County, Alabama	18,463	73.8	10.4	11,864	66.6	12.2
Elmore County, Alabama	21,789	88.5	29.5	11,990	85.6	23.4
Etowah County, Alabama	28,748	81.6	17.5	18,685	78.9	13.6
Houston County, Alabama	27,692	83.2	21.3	17,503	79.2	18.4
Jefferson County, Alabama	170,948	90.8	31.3	99,881	85.8	27.0
Lauderdale County, Alabama	24,682	86.8	20.2	17,155	79.8	17.8
Lee County, Alabama	36,034	90.7	32.9	17,576	78.6	31.5
Limestone County, Alabama	25,656	82.2	23.9	13,443	81.5	17.1
Madison County, Alabama	98,832	92.0	40.9	51,496	85.9	33.7
Marshall County, Alabama	24,414	84.9	16.0	15,990	83.1	17.6
Mobile County, Alabama	107,708	87.0	21.2	63,623	83.7	20.3
Montgomery County, Alabama	57,224	86.6	34.1	31,849	81.4	30.5
Morgan County, Alabama	32,386	82.3	21.3	20,169	77.6	16.2
St. Clair County, Alabama	24,413	78.1	15.1	14,421	77.1	18.7
Shelby County, Alabama	57,014	93.1	44.3	29,672	92.0	41.4
Talladega County, Alabama	22,278	85.9	13.9	13,797	69.0	10.4
Tuscaloosa County, Alabama	46,587	90.4	29.2	25,391	84.8	26.1
Walker County, Alabama	17,651	81.1	12.9	12,488	72.5	11.9
ALASKA						
Anchorage Municipality, Alaska	72,367	94.1	38.7	29,085	90.1	37.0
Fairbanks North Star Borough, Alaska	23,073	94.8	29.2	8,606	97.8	31.1
Matanuska-Susitna Borough, Alaska	27,327	95.1	22.3	10,663	92.1	22.9
ARIZONA						
Apache County, Arizona	17,155	82.2	13.3	10,633	69.4	13.4
Cochise County, Arizona	31,548	86.2	25.7	26,552	84.6	26.8
Coconino County, Arizona	32,851	89.1	33.8	16,647	84.3	40.4
Maricopa County, Arizona	1,025,632	87.7	32.3	619,929	88.6	31.3
Mohave County, Arizona	57,252	88.1	10.0	58,941	84.6	11.6
Navajo County, Arizona	26,639	83.1	13.6	18,330	73.5	15.4
Pima County, Arizona	244,295	86.6	31.6	193,734	89.3	35.3
Pinal County, Arizona	95,752	88.3	22.6	83,410	88.1	23.8
Yavapai County, Arizona	65,962	90.9	21.0	67,380	92.7	30.7
Yuma County, Arizona	41,775	67.2	14.9	37,996	71.7	12.6
ARKANSAS						
Benton County, Arkansas	60,173	88.3	29.5	33,590	85.7	21.4
Craighead County, Arkansas	23,933	90.3	21.3	14,458	74.3	25.1
Faulkner County, Arkansas	27,260	90.8	28.9	14,665	83.7	25.7
Garland County, Arkansas	26,216	89.7	15.3	21,487	89.5	19.7
Jefferson County, Arkansas	18,783	85.5	21.5	11,387	72.8	22.1
Lonoke County, Arkansas	18,459	94.8	18.7	9,977	75.7	21.7
Pulaski County, Arkansas	102,469	92.0	33.4	56,551	88.4	29.0
Saline County, Arkansas	30,507	91.9	26.5	20,866	89.4	24.7
Sebastian County, Arkansas	33,008	85.2	17.6	19,494	86.1	21.0
Washington County, Arkansas	47,758	86.2	36.4	26,489	83.2	28.2
White County, Arkansas	19,084	87.0	19.2	12,381	84.5	13.4
CALIFORNIA						
Alameda County, California	427,336	86.6	41.8	215,418	83.2	36.1
Butte County, California	55,660	90.2	23.5	41,056	86.9	28.9
Contra Costa County, California	313,703	90.1	41.6	169,840	89.3	40.5
El Dorado County, California	59,899	94.9	36.2	35,629	90.8	31.7
Fresno County, California	214,163	72.3	19.6	116,094	71.1	21.6
Humboldt County, California	34,158	89.1	31.2	22,951	91.1	28.5
Imperial County, California	38,816	64.5	13.2	23,133	49.6	9.2
Kern County, California	194,554	71.2	16.8	91,573	73.6	18.2
Kings County, California	33,942	73.5	11.6	14,375	63.2	13.6
Lake County, California	18,162	85.9	17.1	15,133	85.6	18.1
Los Angeles County, California	2,572,255	75.5	29.0	1,308,573	71.9	27.8
Madera County, California	35,523	69.0	14.6	20,459	70.4	13.8
Marin County, California	80,879	95.2	60.8	53,846	96.3	58.1
Mendocino County, California	24,358	79.8	17.5	17,481	90.4	34.3
Merced County, California	57,388	63.3	13.7	28,983	60.1	12.7
Monterey County, California	100,848	71.0	23.4	55,241	74.8	32.3
Napa County, California	38,471	84.5	33.1	25,787	88.7	37.9

Table C-2. Educational Attainment of the Population, by Selected Counties, 2016—*Continued*

(Number; percent; dollars.)

State/County	Population 25 to 34 years			Population 35 to 44 years		
	Total	High school graduate or more	Bachelor's degree or more	Total	High school graduate or more	Bachelor's degree or more
CALIFORNIA—*(Continued)*						
Nevada County, California	10,611	88.8	23.7	10,027	94.5	35.4
Orange County, California	453,741	89.2	41.7	413,720	82.9	41.0
Placer County, California	41,749	97.2	40.3	48,228	95.7	49.1
Riverside County, California	329,408	86.6	20.7	301,969	80.7	22.0
Sacramento County, California	235,323	90.5	30.3	196,255	85.0	32.3
San Bernardino County, California	318,466	85.8	19.5	272,885	77.1	21.2
San Diego County, California	544,022	90.9	39.1	434,359	86.9	42.0
San Francisco County, California	203,463	95.9	75.9	137,227	92.9	66.8
San Joaquin County, California	101,966	81.4	16.2	93,623	76.6	16.9
San Luis Obispo County, California	32,508	93.2	38.5	30,078	86.1	34.1
San Mateo County, California	111,731	93.7	56.2	109,407	88.3	58.9
Santa Barbara County, California	59,548	80.5	31.3	50,648	71.8	26.0
Santa Clara County, California	303,241	91.2	58.5	278,434	88.2	56.6
Santa Cruz County, California	31,610	90.9	37.8	32,347	83.9	36.8
Shasta County, California	21,921	91.3	21.5	19,101	94.0	25.1
Solano County, California	64,381	90.4	24.6	53,652	80.5	23.1
Sonoma County, California	65,058	86.4	26.9	62,392	83.4	32.7
Stanislaus County, California	78,543	85.9	19.1	67,064	78.0	17.2
Sutter County, California	11,893	91.1	16.3	12,302	71.4	12.7
Tulare County, California	64,708	77.9	13.7	57,068	67.2	14.2
Ventura County, California	112,032	85.3	26.2	105,191	82.9	33.4
Yolo County, California	29,809	89.5	41.1	26,118	84.2	41.3
Yuba County, California	12,259	88.4	14.9	8,833	87.1	25.6
COLORADO						
Adams County, Colorado	79,882	83.6	21.7	71,775	81.0	25.7
Arapahoe County, Colorado	97,034	91.6	38.1	89,412	92.4	39.8
Boulder County, Colorado	43,246	94.3	58.9	40,939	94.5	68.2
Broomfield County, Colorado	9,524	95.7	58.7	9,564	96.3	64.3
Denver County, Colorado	156,779	90.4	56.0	108,276	86.2	48.2
Douglas County, Colorado	34,825	99.1	61.3	50,509	98.4	62.7
El Paso County, Colorado	107,430	94.8	32.9	85,319	92.4	39.4
Jefferson County, Colorado	81,348	94.6	45.8	74,391	94.6	51.9
Larimer County, Colorado	48,148	96.4	49.2	40,973	95.5	50.7
Mesa County, Colorado	17,723	90.1	20.9	17,887	79.5	21.3
Pueblo County, Colorado	20,976	84.0	19.8	19,603	89.8	19.6
Weld County, Colorado	43,063	89.4	24.7	39,319	83.8	31.7
CONNECTICUT						
Fairfield County, Connecticut	108,109	91.6	45.8	118,652	88.2	52.8
Hartford County, Connecticut	117,223	93.9	44.7	108,062	91.3	40.6
Litchfield County, Connecticut	17,750	95.9	46.3	20,340	94.3	42.6
Middlesex County, Connecticut	16,802	94.6	50.0	17,848	96.5	53.0
New Haven County, Connecticut	114,097	92.6	43.2	100,218	92.3	40.8
New London County, Connecticut	33,029	94.9	34.6	31,456	94.5	34.3
Tolland County, Connecticut	14,951	97.7	37.0	14,416	98.2	51.1
Windham County, Connecticut	14,635	91.8	33.3	13,500	93.3	23.0
DELAWARE						
Kent County, Delaware	24,759	86.0	21.3	19,849	83.9	28.5
New Castle County, Delaware	80,958	92.1	38.2	68,205	90.5	39.7
Sussex County, Delaware	22,852	81.6	24.3	21,964	79.6	17.9
DISTRICT OF COLUMBIA						
District of Columbia, District of Columbia	154,662	94.7	70.2	98,911	91.7	61.7
FLORIDA						
Alachua County, Florida	40,611	92.7	45.2	27,453	92.8	47.8
Bay County, Florida	25,253	90.7	18.9	22,037	92.1	26.8
Brevard County, Florida	64,314	92.3	28.7	58,300	92.2	30.0
Broward County, Florida	259,466	90.7	31.4	252,541	89.9	34.5
Charlotte County, Florida	13,182	90.2	20.9	12,780	89.5	17.9
Citrus County, Florida	11,833	81.9	11.6	11,921	83.3	19.3
Clay County, Florida	24,742	94.1	25.8	27,530	94.0	28.7
Collier County, Florida	35,066	82.0	19.0	36,645	78.0	30.4
Columbia County, Florida	8,425	80.9	7.7	7,686	84.1	21.3
Duval County, Florida	152,526	90.9	30.7	116,254	88.6	33.9
Escambia County, Florida	44,275	93.6	28.6	35,255	90.6	28.3
Flagler County, Florida	9,899	94.7	13.1	9,773	98.7	16.6
Hernando County, Florida	19,087	84.0	20.7	17,445	88.6	19.6
Highlands County, Florida	9,250	80.7	8.1	8,259	91.8	14.5

Table C-2. Educational Attainment of the Population, by Selected Counties, 2016—*Continued*

(Number; percent; dollars.)

State/County	Population 45 to 64 years			Population 65 years and over		
	Total	High school graduate or more	Bachelor's degree or more	Total	High school graduate or more	Bachelor's degree or more
CALIFORNIA—*(Continued)*						
Nevada County, California	29,418	91.4	38.6	25,668	94.3	40.0
Orange County, California	849,037	83.8	39.5	443,198	84.3	38.0
Placer County, California	104,521	95.5	37.8	72,151	92.7	33.5
Riverside County, California	571,679	78.4	21.4	331,558	80.4	23.5
Sacramento County, California	379,905	86.8	29.2	206,242	82.1	27.7
San Bernardino County, California	508,534	76.5	19.5	237,086	75.9	20.3
San Diego County, California	811,524	84.8	34.9	445,823	83.3	35.2
San Francisco County, California	219,669	85.4	46.3	129,337	74.2	36.4
San Joaquin County, California	174,119	77.1	16.8	90,853	72.9	17.1
San Luis Obispo County, California	72,010	91.4	33.8	54,154	94.9	39.0
San Mateo County, California	209,942	90.2	48.8	116,236	83.5	39.4
Santa Barbara County, California	100,543	80.2	31.6	65,230	86.4	39.5
Santa Clara County, California	493,801	86.5	48.8	245,543	82.9	39.8
Santa Cruz County, California	74,238	86.1	42.3	40,846	89.3	42.3
Shasta County, California	48,693	91.8	21.0	36,493	90.6	21.4
Solano County, California	118,264	90.1	26.0	64,596	86.5	26.9
Sonoma County, California	140,907	88.4	33.6	92,095	91.1	40.0
Stanislaus County, California	127,746	72.6	15.1	69,163	70.8	14.3
Sutter County, California	23,179	73.5	16.9	14,499	70.4	17.7
Tulare County, California	97,568	65.8	13.9	50,194	68.0	12.8
Ventura County, California	226,599	83.8	36.9	123,730	84.5	34.2
Yolo County, California	45,818	84.9	40.3	25,926	80.4	41.1
Yuba County, California	17,752	82.2	16.1	8,143	80.2	21.9
COLORADO						
Adams County, Colorado	116,639	83.9	22.3	49,781	81.5	22.4
Arapahoe County, Colorado	163,301	93.3	44.4	79,712	93.1	41.6
Boulder County, Colorado	83,519	95.5	60.4	42,883	95.7	55.7
Broomfield County, Colorado	17,705	98.1	51.3	8,566	95.8	32.0
Denver County, Colorado	152,177	85.6	41.7	77,415	84.9	40.1
Douglas County, Colorado	94,343	99.1	59.3	36,084	96.2	53.4
El Paso County, Colorado	165,591	96.1	42.3	83,431	92.6	38.2
Jefferson County, Colorado	163,984	94.0	40.9	89,360	93.9	39.3
Larimer County, Colorado	82,771	96.8	44.8	50,153	96.0	44.7
Mesa County, Colorado	38,112	90.2	23.5	26,950	91.5	32.4
Pueblo County, Colorado	42,134	91.5	23.5	29,489	83.6	19.9
Weld County, Colorado	71,330	88.7	26.8	34,448	86.5	26.1
CONNECTICUT						
Fairfield County, Connecticut	272,932	92.9	48.1	139,775	85.1	38.9
Hartford County, Connecticut	249,718	90.3	37.0	144,832	82.6	28.8
Litchfield County, Connecticut	60,254	95.2	35.4	36,447	88.2	31.2
Middlesex County, Connecticut	52,661	96.4	40.6	30,607	90.3	32.9
New Haven County, Connecticut	239,433	91.2	33.3	139,334	82.9	27.5
New London County, Connecticut	77,808	93.0	32.4	45,329	89.3	30.0
Tolland County, Connecticut	42,729	95.2	39.6	22,331	91.8	36.2
Windham County, Connecticut	34,474	87.8	22.2	17,985	77.9	20.5
DELAWARE						
Kent County, Delaware	43,175	89.5	25.4	28,938	86.6	15.6
New Castle County, Delaware	151,595	93.3	34.1	81,150	87.8	31.6
Sussex County, Delaware	62,516	88.8	27.7	56,586	87.8	29.1
DISTRICT OF COLUMBIA						
District of Columbia, District of Columbia	147,488	88.2	47.6	79,097	84.9	41.9
FLORIDA						
Alachua County, Florida	57,116	89.6	32.0	34,387	90.1	39.5
Bay County, Florida	50,581	90.9	24.4	30,823	91.1	22.5
Brevard County, Florida	172,596	93.3	30.0	134,180	89.7	28.4
Broward County, Florida	529,073	88.4	31.3	307,241	82.8	26.5
Charlotte County, Florida	50,008	90.9	20.2	69,437	89.5	27.8
Citrus County, Florida	41,042	89.8	20.2	50,830	87.3	23.0
Clay County, Florida	58,249	93.1	22.9	31,222	91.9	18.3
Collier County, Florida	91,041	82.2	29.4	112,972	90.6	43.3
Columbia County, Florida	18,674	85.6	15.6	12,580	80.1	9.8
Duval County, Florida	237,871	88.6	28.3	125,054	86.9	25.7
Escambia County, Florida	79,361	92.1	27.2	51,601	86.5	23.8
Flagler County, Florida	29,218	90.5	19.1	33,256	88.0	31.3
Hernando County, Florida	49,790	88.4	20.1	50,552	87.2	16.5
Highlands County, Florida	25,080	86.3	10.9	34,363	85.2	15.5

Table C-2. Educational Attainment of the Population, by Selected Counties, 2016—*Continued*

(Number; percent; dollars.)

State/County	Population 25 to 34 years			Population 35 to 44 years		
	Total	High school graduate or more	Bachelor's degree or more	Total	High school graduate or more	Bachelor's degree or more
FLORIDA—*(Continued)*						
Hillsborough County, Florida	208,933	89.6	34.7	185,452	89.3	37.1
Indian River County, Florida	12,160	91.2	19.3	11,665	83.5	21.8
Lake County, Florida	34,726	90.2	24.4	36,117	88.6	28.9
Lee County, Florida	78,301	85.3	24.2	74,705	83.1	24.2
Leon County, Florida	41,685	95.3	50.3	31,294	91.7	45.3
Manatee County, Florida	37,399	86.2	21.9	39,250	84.9	26.4
Marion County, Florida	38,061	87.2	13.9	32,505	86.1	18.9
Martin County, Florida	14,224	85.3	20.6	14,464	83.2	27.2
Miami-Dade County, Florida	390,085	89.3	31.2	375,803	87.3	31.5
Monroe County, Florida	8,733	95.9	31.4	9,623	84.1	29.3
Nassau County, Florida	9,223	95.7	20.4	9,867	91.3	33.3
Okaloosa County, Florida	31,025	89.3	30.4	23,155	91.2	31.1
Orange County, Florida	220,809	91.1	39.0	184,048	87.3	34.7
Osceola County, Florida	50,249	89.5	19.1	45,672	91.5	23.4
Palm Beach County, Florida	172,561	88.4	32.0	164,543	84.9	34.5
Pasco County, Florida	55,456	90.8	24.2	61,890	91.7	32.0
Pinellas County, Florida	114,255	91.3	29.5	104,393	91.9	33.8
Polk County, Florida	85,549	88.3	21.0	77,580	84.1	20.2
Putnam County, Florida	7,238	82.1	7.0	7,442	75.2	7.8
St. Johns County, Florida	24,369	96.5	35.1	29,795	98.7	55.6
St. Lucie County, Florida	30,381	86.4	17.0	34,419	89.8	21.3
Santa Rosa County, Florida	23,313	85.7	28.2	21,774	91.6	29.3
Sarasota County, Florida	33,613	94.7	22.2	35,699	87.7	30.3
Seminole County, Florida	65,714	97.0	34.2	61,062	95.2	42.0
Sumter County, Florida	6,136	72.3	9.3	7,233	79.8	8.3
Volusia County, Florida	60,095	89.1	20.4	55,345	91.2	30.4
Walton County, Florida	7,119	87.7	19.7	7,827	85.2	24.9
GEORGIA						
Barrow County, Georgia	11,421	89.2	23.4	11,339	86.9	22.3
Bartow County, Georgia	14,162	81.5	24.0	14,433	87.3	25.4
Bibb County, Georgia	21,062	90.1	30.2	17,294	88.7	34.1
Bulloch County, Georgia	9,771	91.6	31.6	8,360	83.8	31.9
Carroll County, Georgia	15,114	90.7	29.1	14,676	84.9	20.3
Catoosa County, Georgia	8,373	93.8	28.8	9,023	87.2	35.4
Chatham County, Georgia	47,222	92.5	35.9	35,780	88.2	26.4
Cherokee County, Georgia	28,045	88.9	32.8	35,241	89.7	45.8
Clarke County, Georgia	21,363	91.2	44.8	12,079	89.9	49.7
Clayton County, Georgia	42,679	87.8	22.6	37,739	85.2	17.8
Cobb County, Georgia	107,531	91.1	48.1	107,228	88.9	47.3
Columbia County, Georgia	20,134	96.8	40.7	21,239	94.3	43.2
Coweta County, Georgia	17,528	83.7	33.9	18,875	89.5	35.3
DeKalb County, Georgia	124,232	87.8	45.2	106,730	89.0	45.1
Dougherty County, Georgia	12,009	82.6	15.4	11,267	88.4	23.0
Douglas County, Georgia	18,274	89.9	20.8	18,946	88.8	37.6
Fayette County, Georgia	10,437	95.7	58.1	12,845	97.4	48.0
Floyd County, Georgia	11,725	91.0	26.0	12,303	79.5	27.7
Forsyth County, Georgia	20,465	92.6	48.2	35,920	92.1	63.8
Fulton County, Georgia	168,838	92.7	56.0	148,098	92.8	56.5
Glynn County, Georgia	10,792	80.7	25.7	8,506	78.6	29.4
Gwinnett County, Georgia	119,222	88.9	29.7	134,241	83.9	35.3
Hall County, Georgia	24,652	78.3	20.0	25,742	69.8	20.6
Henry County, Georgia	28,378	87.8	29.7	30,511	91.1	38.5
Houston County, Georgia	23,106	91.1	24.3	20,657	85.6	38.6
Liberty County, Georgia	11,165	93.5	24.6	7,265	94.1	7.8
Lowndes County, Georgia	17,617	92.9	26.4	12,975	90.7	21.4
Muscogee County, Georgia	32,339	90.8	27.1	24,685	89.5	33.5
Newton County, Georgia	11,546	85.8	10.4	14,411	86.3	18.4
Paulding County, Georgia	17,815	92.9	15.6	23,577	92.8	35.9
Richmond County, Georgia	33,335	84.9	24.9	22,988	87.1	19.5
Rockdale County, Georgia	9,419	89.1	11.3	11,906	89.6	36.1
Troup County, Georgia	9,166	79.4	13.5	8,510	78.3	16.1
Walker County, Georgia	8,225	84.5	12.4	8,722	85.9	26.0
Walton County, Georgia	9,568	85.7	19.1	11,597	85.8	35.7
Whitfield County, Georgia	13,316	71.0	9.9	13,415	72.3	15.4
HAWAII						
Hawaii County, Hawaii	23,298	91.5	24.0	23,497	97.2	26.9
Honolulu County, Hawaii	153,870	95.5	33.6	124,187	95.7	40.2

Table C-2. Educational Attainment of the Population, by Selected Counties, 2016—*Continued*

(Number; percent; dollars.)

State/County	Population 45 to 64 years			Population 65 years and over		
	Total	High school graduate or more	Bachelor's degree or more	Total	High school graduate or more	Bachelor's degree or more
FLORIDA—*(Continued)*						
Hillsborough County, Florida	351,747	88.9	31.8	188,538	83.3	25.7
Indian River County, Florida	40,630	86.8	24.4	48,476	87.6	36.3
Lake County, Florida	86,237	88.4	19.6	89,027	90.6	23.3
Lee County, Florida	189,652	88.6	26.7	197,956	88.6	33.0
Leon County, Florida	61,406	94.0	46.9	35,932	93.0	47.6
Manatee County, Florida	101,946	88.9	28.2	99,257	91.2	29.9
Marion County, Florida	89,911	85.9	15.9	99,625	86.8	21.2
Martin County, Florida	44,221	91.2	30.0	47,890	93.5	34.3
Miami-Dade County, Florida	727,448	83.5	28.0	433,081	64.5	21.5
Monroe County, Florida	24,414	91.4	35.4	17,209	88.5	33.9
Nassau County, Florida	23,296	93.4	29.3	17,328	88.2	34.8
Okaloosa County, Florida	51,552	94.6	28.5	31,567	89.3	33.4
Orange County, Florida	322,796	87.4	32.3	147,439	78.6	27.6
Osceola County, Florida	81,073	89.0	21.3	43,886	75.5	15.1
Palm Beach County, Florida	380,675	88.2	34.5	336,351	87.2	37.3
Pasco County, Florida	138,144	90.2	22.8	116,942	84.2	17.8
Pinellas County, Florida	287,850	91.7	29.0	229,063	88.0	27.6
Polk County, Florida	164,468	83.6	20.2	133,486	82.6	19.4
Putnam County, Florida	20,558	80.6	19.6	15,814	78.6	17.8
St. Johns County, Florida	67,787	93.9	41.6	44,235	95.9	40.3
St. Lucie County, Florida	81,832	87.4	21.3	72,200	83.6	21.1
Santa Rosa County, Florida	49,068	91.4	26.1	25,807	89.0	28.0
Sarasota County, Florida	113,468	93.1	31.1	145,723	93.7	38.8
Seminole County, Florida	124,581	94.9	38.5	69,145	89.5	32.5
Sumter County, Florida	25,536	91.4	23.2	69,823	94.7	35.1
Volusia County, Florida	149,645	90.2	22.9	126,951	88.8	24.5
Walton County, Florida	19,895	85.0	26.8	12,971	89.3	36.9
GEORGIA						
Barrow County, Georgia	18,940	79.7	14.5	8,899	79.8	15.0
Bartow County, Georgia	27,464	83.2	16.7	13,723	79.2	13.9
Bibb County, Georgia	38,235	85.1	23.2	22,470	73.7	19.9
Bulloch County, Georgia	14,734	87.5	28.3	8,241	75.5	15.0
Carroll County, Georgia	27,699	83.6	21.5	15,109	70.6	14.0
Catoosa County, Georgia	17,598	88.3	17.5	11,375	84.0	18.3
Chatham County, Georgia	68,320	89.2	30.1	41,804	85.6	35.0
Cherokee County, Georgia	67,127	92.4	37.5	31,344	89.0	33.7
Clarke County, Georgia	22,657	84.7	32.9	12,442	87.2	40.9
Clayton County, Georgia	67,164	86.9	21.6	25,111	75.2	18.1
Cobb County, Georgia	197,897	92.8	49.7	85,650	90.0	36.8
Columbia County, Georgia	36,859	96.9	35.1	18,599	85.0	23.3
Coweta County, Georgia	39,386	92.5	25.6	17,689	83.9	24.5
DeKalb County, Georgia	186,555	91.1	43.2	82,289	86.6	38.9
Dougherty County, Georgia	21,039	88.6	23.8	12,934	77.3	21.1
Douglas County, Georgia	38,572	92.6	29.7	15,924	79.4	14.9
Fayette County, Georgia	33,701	96.5	55.6	19,358	92.1	32.4
Floyd County, Georgia	24,197	85.9	20.9	15,557	74.5	25.1
Forsyth County, Georgia	59,756	92.4	49.8	26,658	88.9	34.5
Fulton County, Georgia	257,488	92.6	49.4	113,313	88.9	41.4
Glynn County, Georgia	23,662	86.7	27.3	15,224	88.7	28.4
Gwinnett County, Georgia	236,915	89.7	37.7	84,703	86.6	32.4
Hall County, Georgia	48,864	75.9	19.7	28,139	84.9	26.8
Henry County, Georgia	60,762	90.1	28.0	23,946	84.8	18.4
Houston County, Georgia	37,791	95.4	33.5	19,222	82.2	20.2
Liberty County, Georgia	11,657	90.0	19.9	5,270	79.1	12.9
Lowndes County, Georgia	23,354	84.1	26.3	13,520	82.1	20.4
Muscogee County, Georgia	45,730	89.4	28.8	25,117	79.9	19.4
Newton County, Georgia	27,916	82.4	21.2	13,288	69.6	12.7
Paulding County, Georgia	40,303	90.4	22.9	16,855	85.0	17.3
Richmond County, Georgia	48,384	87.9	23.6	26,882	73.7	18.2
Rockdale County, Georgia	25,241	92.0	27.2	12,217	79.3	17.6
Troup County, Georgia	17,899	80.8	30.0	9,840	73.4	15.6
Walker County, Georgia	18,842	77.9	16.7	11,877	69.8	12.6
Walton County, Georgia	23,396	90.7	21.6	13,443	78.8	16.7
Whitfield County, Georgia	24,910	67.6	12.6	14,052	63.8	12.2
HAWAII						
Hawaii County, Hawaii	55,080	93.0	29.1	37,959	90.3	27.9
Honolulu County, Hawaii	241,358	92.0	35.0	164,651	84.1	29.7

Table C-2. Educational Attainment of the Population, by Selected Counties, 2016—*Continued*

(Number; percent; dollars.)

State/County	Population 25 to 34 years			Population 35 to 44 years		
	Total	High school graduate or more	Bachelor's degree or more	Total	High school graduate or more	Bachelor's degree or more
HAWAII—(*Continued*)						
Kauai County, Hawaii	7,708	94.3	29.7	9,621	96.5	26.4
Maui County, Hawaii	20,957	98.4	16.9	22,034	91.9	22.5
IDAHO						
Ada County, Idaho	63,825	95.9	38.0	60,001	96.2	43.5
Bannock County, Idaho	11,944	96.9	23.8	10,917	86.4	33.2
Bonneville County, Idaho	15,911	88.7	30.4	13,702	93.6	38.1
Canyon County, Idaho	28,186	88.7	18.1	26,304	76.5	20.6
Kootenai County, Idaho	19,496	92.2	16.8	18,644	95.2	33.6
Twin Falls County, Idaho	11,536	94.4	21.7	10,201	86.6	24.3
ILLINOIS						
Adams County, Illinois	7,915	96.3	37.8	7,818	96.1	31.5
Champaign County, Illinois	31,316	96.0	53.8	22,269	98.5	53.6
Cook County, Illinois	847,524	92.8	49.7	703,176	88.0	40.7
DeKalb County, Illinois	13,871	94.8	29.2	12,157	91.9	33.0
DuPage County, Illinois	117,476	93.3	52.5	118,953	93.1	55.9
Kane County, Illinois	63,224	85.6	28.4	72,696	79.9	35.3
Kankakee County, Illinois	12,822	89.1	25.3	12,722	90.0	26.9
Kendall County, Illinois	15,668	93.8	46.6	20,368	92.9	39.1
Lake County, Illinois	76,763	90.9	38.6	88,932	88.6	50.5
LaSalle County, Illinois	13,334	88.2	23.6	12,321	88.9	20.4
McHenry County, Illinois	33,230	92.8	38.0	39,115	93.3	39.3
McLean County, Illinois	23,555	98.3	46.9	20,660	98.0	52.4
Macon County, Illinois	12,046	87.7	18.0	11,501	92.5	32.4
Madison County, Illinois	36,189	94.9	33.8	32,369	92.9	32.9
Peoria County, Illinois	24,513	91.4	36.7	24,041	94.8	40.1
Rock Island County, Illinois	19,563	87.5	24.8	17,353	91.4	23.9
St. Clair County, Illinois	34,867	95.0	30.7	32,710	93.2	34.7
Sangamon County, Illinois	24,302	93.3	40.8	24,821	93.8	42.0
Tazewell County, Illinois	16,661	93.6	28.6	17,430	94.7	33.8
Vermilion County, Illinois	9,181	87.8	16.5	9,012	87.9	13.6
Will County, Illinois	78,927	92.2	36.2	95,608	92.2	41.6
Williamson County, Illinois	8,823	97.8	27.7	8,772	97.4	29.1
Winnebago County, Illinois	35,354	88.6	25.1	34,556	86.3	25.7
INDIANA						
Allen County, Indiana	50,488	91.5	35.9	45,503	89.1	27.2
Bartholomew County, Indiana	11,285	84.4	41.7	10,091	94.1	43.5
Clark County, Indiana	16,291	87.6	23.5	15,221	91.3	21.6
Delaware County, Indiana	12,736	91.3	25.4	11,217	90.6	22.8
Elkhart County, Indiana	25,530	80.6	20.3	26,678	74.3	18.0
Floyd County, Indiana	9,641	91.1	36.5	9,353	93.9	29.4
Grant County, Indiana	6,788	84.5	11.4	7,001	85.4	16.8
Hamilton County, Indiana	38,927	94.7	62.6	46,968	97.4	68.7
Hancock County, Indiana	8,491	99.8	35.5	9,329	97.6	40.1
Hendricks County, Indiana	21,314	89.2	45.7	21,896	97.2	53.1
Howard County, Indiana	9,748	90.8	22.5	8,961	87.0	22.2
Johnson County, Indiana	19,446	91.1	33.4	20,915	91.2	44.8
Kosciusko County, Indiana	10,222	80.3	28.4	8,873	81.0	21.7
Lake County, Indiana	59,855	90.0	26.7	61,557	89.5	25.5
LaPorte County, Indiana	13,822	87.4	17.5	14,283	92.8	15.1
Madison County, Indiana	16,720	87.6	12.4	15,154	87.2	22.6
Marion County, Indiana	157,064	88.6	35.1	119,872	85.3	33.6
Monroe County, Indiana	21,250	93.4	51.0	14,039	93.6	52.4
Morgan County, Indiana	7,529	91.6	16.9	8,188	92.3	17.8
Porter County, Indiana	19,943	96.3	31.4	22,057	92.2	36.5
St. Joseph County, Indiana	33,740	88.8	37.6	32,948	85.4	26.6
Tippecanoe County, Indiana	25,975	94.9	42.6	19,663	86.8	38.2
Vanderburgh County, Indiana	26,306	87.3	26.1	20,607	83.8	25.7
Vigo County, Indiana	14,092	85.1	32.8	12,676	89.6	30.9
Wayne County, Indiana	7,941	85.3	19.2	7,539	95.6	19.7
IOWA						
Black Hawk County, Iowa	16,834	95.4	34.3	14,500	93.3	36.2
Dallas County, Iowa	12,421	96.4	55.2	13,100	95.3	62.2
Dubuque County, Iowa	12,406	94.1	31.5	10,582	93.6	36.8
Johnson County, Iowa	24,800	94.8	61.5	17,273	94.0	62.1
Linn County, Iowa	30,656	93.4	43.6	28,342	96.1	42.8
Polk County, Iowa	73,770	91.1	39.9	64,040	89.8	40.3
Pottawattamie County, Iowa	10,930	93.5	22.1	10,841	94.7	34.6

Table C-2. Educational Attainment of the Population, by Selected Counties, 2016—*Continued*

(Number; percent; dollars.)

State/County	Population 45 to 64 years			Population 65 years and over		
	Total	High school graduate or more	Bachelor's degree or more	Total	High school graduate or more	Bachelor's degree or more
HAWAII—*(Continued)*						
Kauai County, Hawaii	19,585	98.5	26.9	13,514	82.2	29.5
Maui County, Hawaii	46,133	94.1	25.6	27,396	87.6	31.0
IDAHO						
Ada County, Idaho	112,617	95.8	36.7	61,330	92.3	35.5
Bannock County, Idaho	19,106	89.4	25.2	11,325	87.3	30.4
Bonneville County, Idaho	23,538	93.5	32.1	15,012	94.9	29.3
Canyon County, Idaho	46,678	83.9	19.1	28,139	85.4	18.9
Kootenai County, Idaho	39,949	93.1	27.7	27,700	90.7	24.5
Twin Falls County, Idaho	18,678	89.5	24.4	12,544	87.7	16.7
ILLINOIS						
Adams County, Illinois	17,846	90.8	21.9	12,888	87.5	18.8
Champaign County, Illinois	42,242	96.0	41.7	24,538	91.2	35.8
Cook County, Illinois	1,308,186	85.7	34.1	705,985	79.5	27.1
DeKalb County, Illinois	22,749	92.3	30.7	12,022	85.8	35.7
DuPage County, Illinois	263,004	93.6	48.8	133,497	89.5	38.3
Kane County, Illinois	141,165	87.4	36.8	67,093	84.1	30.2
Kankakee County, Illinois	29,677	84.8	16.3	17,158	85.8	13.6
Kendall County, Illinois	29,713	89.8	32.0	12,803	80.3	21.2
Lake County, Illinois	197,777	92.0	46.8	91,993	88.3	38.7
LaSalle County, Illinois	31,589	90.2	19.9	20,179	86.0	13.8
McHenry County, Illinois	93,983	94.0	34.0	39,726	88.2	24.1
McLean County, Illinois	40,822	97.4	43.4	20,778	93.4	33.2
Macon County, Illinois	29,218	91.6	18.9	20,076	85.8	21.5
Madison County, Illinois	73,998	93.8	24.9	43,380	87.8	17.9
Peoria County, Illinois	46,004	88.5	28.1	29,042	89.2	21.9
Rock Island County, Illinois	36,553	90.2	22.9	26,555	87.7	21.1
St. Clair County, Illinois	71,889	93.1	27.7	38,522	85.6	20.5
Sangamon County, Illinois	53,823	91.9	33.8	32,915	90.9	30.2
Tazewell County, Illinois	36,311	93.4	22.1	24,152	84.8	15.7
Vermilion County, Illinois	20,258	89.4	13.0	14,380	86.8	14.1
Will County, Illinois	189,649	93.2	35.7	83,368	84.6	23.2
Williamson County, Illinois	17,628	92.6	25.0	12,292	81.6	18.5
Winnebago County, Illinois	77,349	87.1	19.8	47,476	83.9	22.2
INDIANA						
Allen County, Indiana	93,047	90.3	28.5	50,823	85.7	24.0
Bartholomew County, Indiana	20,553	87.0	29.1	12,526	83.6	24.2
Clark County, Indiana	30,882	88.9	18.9	17,317	87.0	19.1
Delaware County, Indiana	27,640	92.5	23.3	19,088	84.9	19.8
Elkhart County, Indiana	49,280	80.0	18.0	28,410	79.0	18.8
Floyd County, Indiana	21,764	89.7	25.0	12,065	84.6	25.7
Grant County, Indiana	17,882	87.6	17.7	12,517	83.6	17.7
Hamilton County, Indiana	83,705	96.3	55.5	36,714	93.8	43.0
Hancock County, Indiana	20,827	92.1	33.0	11,454	89.4	14.0
Hendricks County, Indiana	42,871	92.9	31.5	20,640	89.7	25.2
Howard County, Indiana	22,783	93.7	20.3	15,779	89.4	21.4
Johnson County, Indiana	38,061	93.5	31.7	21,678	82.9	20.6
Kosciusko County, Indiana	21,170	82.8	16.4	12,618	80.0	21.9
Lake County, Indiana	130,136	91.4	20.7	74,898	83.0	18.2
LaPorte County, Indiana	30,304	92.1	20.9	18,205	85.9	16.7
Madison County, Indiana	35,088	89.9	16.6	22,886	84.0	17.1
Marion County, Indiana	229,903	88.5	29.0	110,736	84.0	21.6
Monroe County, Indiana	29,491	92.0	42.4	17,249	84.8	28.5
Morgan County, Indiana	21,510	90.6	16.9	11,100	85.8	12.5
Porter County, Indiana	45,640	93.1	22.2	26,440	85.0	19.0
St. Joseph County, Indiana	67,579	90.0	28.8	39,784	84.4	20.5
Tippecanoe County, Indiana	37,645	92.2	34.9	20,040	91.1	32.5
Vanderburgh County, Indiana	47,928	89.5	27.7	28,890	87.6	21.8
Vigo County, Indiana	25,489	90.9	22.6	16,949	86.6	20.3
Wayne County, Indiana	17,879	90.4	17.9	12,591	80.4	14.2
IOWA						
Black Hawk County, Iowa	31,676	90.2	25.3	20,710	88.1	21.7
Dallas County, Iowa	19,508	92.1	47.5	9,862	98.5	29.9
Dubuque County, Iowa	25,523	95.1	28.3	16,504	87.8	23.7
Johnson County, Iowa	29,497	92.3	45.4	15,268	94.9	49.4
Linn County, Iowa	57,478	96.5	33.0	33,036	89.5	25.7
Polk County, Iowa	117,065	92.0	34.6	58,165	89.3	28.0
Pottawattamie County, Iowa	25,486	93.2	19.1	15,435	84.8	16.1

Table C-2. Educational Attainment of the Population, by Selected Counties, 2016—*Continued*

(Number; percent; dollars.)

State/County	Population 25 to 34 years			Population 35 to 44 years		
	Total	High school graduate or more	Bachelor's degree or more	Total	High school graduate or more	Bachelor's degree or more
IOWA—*(Continued)*						
Scott County, Iowa	22,793	94.6	32.5	22,697	96.3	35.8
Story County, Iowa	13,347	98.3	65.8	8,819	97.2	66.5
Woodbury County, Iowa	13,844	86.3	18.5	12,292	81.0	24.8
KANSAS						
Butler County, Kansas	7,864	93.6	36.4	8,517	91.8	36.1
Douglas County, Kansas	17,889	95.9	57.8	13,248	93.9	58.8
Johnson County, Kansas	79,101	95.0	58.1	81,016	95.3	55.9
Leavenworth County, Kansas	11,064	93.8	34.4	12,248	97.0	40.2
Riley County, Kansas	13,153	99.5	47.9	6,353	99.0	49.8
Sedgwick County, Kansas	73,045	91.2	32.5	61,894	88.5	35.4
Shawnee County, Kansas	22,617	91.2	28.1	20,892	92.5	35.8
Wyandotte County, Kansas	24,151	80.9	20.8	21,673	67.7	14.8
KENTUCKY						
Boone County, Kentucky	15,840	91.5	32.0	17,321	96.1	38.5
Bullitt County, Kentucky	9,727	95.5	12.1	10,303	90.5	19.3
Campbell County, Kentucky	13,196	92.1	44.4	11,243	92.3	50.9
Christian County, Kentucky	12,142	95.9	16.6	7,509	86.5	14.3
Daviess County, Kentucky	12,722	92.7	30.0	11,914	96.5	35.9
Fayette County, Kentucky	49,522	90.8	47.2	41,856	91.9	48.0
Hardin County, Kentucky	14,589	95.0	18.9	14,259	92.9	34.5
Jefferson County, Kentucky	112,463	91.7	35.6	95,313	93.9	38.0
Kenton County, Kentucky	23,893	93.9	47.0	21,079	88.6	32.7
McCracken County, Kentucky	7,614	93.4	19.7	7,568	95.7	27.6
Madison County, Kentucky	11,287	90.1	32.9	10,544	90.1	40.2
Pike County, Kentucky	6,446	98.6	38.8	10,307	89.7	46.1
Warren County, Kentucky	16,354	90.0	34.1	15,402	87.7	37.0
LOUISIANA						
Ascension Parish, Louisiana	16,660	92.8	29.0	17,307	90.2	33.8
Bossier Parish, Louisiana	19,929	87.8	31.3	15,294	90.9	33.2
Caddo Parish, Louisiana	35,012	86.5	24.2	29,953	87.0	21.4
Calcasieu Parish, Louisiana	29,262	87.7	16.6	24,839	87.7	19.9
East Baton Rouge Parish, Louisiana	69,563	90.9	38.6	50,721	91.6	36.5
Iberia Parish, Louisiana	7,416	87.6	12.8	8,901	74.6	20.8
Jefferson Parish, Louisiana	65,073	86.7	30.0	53,540	83.0	26.0
Lafayette Parish, Louisiana	42,724	87.4	30.6	31,422	90.7	30.0
Lafourche Parish, Louisiana	14,167	85.9	23.6	11,720	83.0	19.5
Livingston Parish, Louisiana	19,363	88.3	16.4	19,953	83.8	17.7
Orleans Parish, Louisiana	73,170	90.5	46.8	51,089	87.9	42.9
Ouachita Parish, Louisiana	22,277	84.7	17.7	19,386	85.4	22.8
Rapides Parish, Louisiana	17,033	86.2	21.3	16,278	93.7	22.3
St. Landry Parish, Louisiana	9,878	80.3	16.2	9,189	84.7	13.2
St. Tammany Parish, Louisiana	29,444	91.4	33.9	33,506	92.5	33.7
Tangipahoa Parish, Louisiana	16,734	75.4	20.5	17,492	81.1	19.2
Terrebonne Parish, Louisiana	16,403	81.5	14.3	13,528	88.5	22.0
MAINE						
Androscoggin County, Maine	13,300	95.4	30.4	12,934	92.7	29.1
Aroostook County, Maine	6,857	90.8	23.6	6,812	95.9	25.8
Cumberland County, Maine	38,530	97.6	48.1	35,690	96.1	50.0
Kennebec County, Maine	14,063	91.9	31.9	13,997	95.5	28.4
Penobscot County, Maine	20,535	94.7	32.6	16,651	94.1	29.1
York County, Maine	23,756	96.7	37.0	23,638	94.5	34.4
MARYLAND						
Allegany County, Maryland	9,100	88.3	11.6	8,001	96.1	22.6
Anne Arundel County, Maryland	80,834	95.6	43.5	74,478	94.8	49.6
Baltimore County, Maryland	116,426	93.7	38.4	100,476	93.3	45.7
Calvert County, Maryland	10,497	95.2	36.2	11,315	96.1	40.0
Carroll County, Maryland	18,146	94.3	40.0	18,813	96.5	45.4
Cecil County, Maryland	13,064	91.0	21.7	12,660	89.0	30.7
Charles County, Maryland	20,392	92.2	28.1	20,182	95.1	33.5
Frederick County, Maryland	30,761	92.2	43.0	32,104	94.9	50.7
Harford County, Maryland	30,431	93.7	40.7	30,055	93.8	46.0
Howard County, Maryland	37,341	97.3	61.6	44,924	97.3	69.0
Montgomery County, Maryland	134,705	92.8	60.6	143,552	90.9	59.1
Prince George's County, Maryland	134,627	87.2	33.5	121,578	80.8	34.3
St. Mary's County, Maryland	16,523	89.4	26.4	13,259	86.0	27.3
Washington County, Maryland	20,096	85.2	18.1	18,672	87.4	24.5

Table C-2. Educational Attainment of the Population, by Selected Counties, 2016—*Continued*

(Number; percent; dollars.)

State/County	Population 45 to 64 years			Population 65 years and over		
	Total	High school graduate or more	Bachelor's degree or more	Total	High school graduate or more	Bachelor's degree or more
IOWA—(*Continued*)						
Scott County, Iowa	44,622	92.6	31.2	26,345	90.9	26.8
Story County, Iowa	18,356	97.3	46.7	11,126	97.2	45.9
Woodbury County, Iowa	24,039	85.4	25.6	15,200	85.6	20.0
KANSAS						
Butler County, Kansas	18,044	91.2	27.4	9,663	89.8	19.6
Douglas County, Kansas	24,670	94.6	48.2	13,374	95.3	44.6
Johnson County, Kansas	152,856	96.5	58.4	79,988	95.3	46.0
Leavenworth County, Kansas	19,905	94.2	33.4	10,691	92.3	25.6
Riley County, Kansas	11,293	97.0	49.6	6,171	95.7	49.4
Sedgwick County, Kansas	125,987	88.5	30.4	69,179	88.4	28.8
Shawnee County, Kansas	46,379	93.3	33.2	30,513	90.9	22.2
Wyandotte County, Kansas	38,698	80.9	18.0	18,803	78.9	17.6
KENTUCKY						
Boone County, Kentucky	33,772	95.1	32.1	15,560	89.4	17.4
Bullitt County, Kentucky	22,607	86.3	15.8	11,488	73.9	13.6
Campbell County, Kentucky	25,096	94.0	30.5	13,320	87.8	24.9
Christian County, Kentucky	14,001	86.5	12.6	7,859	71.3	18.4
Daviess County, Kentucky	25,617	90.5	19.2	16,412	82.5	15.8
Fayette County, Kentucky	76,146	90.1	42.9	38,623	88.5	36.4
Hardin County, Kentucky	27,638	92.3	23.6	14,207	80.7	17.4
Jefferson County, Kentucky	203,095	89.9	30.4	116,817	85.3	26.3
Kenton County, Kentucky	44,505	90.1	25.6	21,972	81.8	20.9
McCracken County, Kentucky	17,640	89.3	20.0	12,352	81.4	17.1
Madison County, Kentucky	21,416	89.2	27.0	11,561	74.5	16.2
Pike County, Kentucky	18,281	96.9	44.5	8,024	93.8	28.3
Warren County, Kentucky	28,345	89.4	28.3	15,625	84.1	30.6
LOUISIANA						
Ascension Parish, Louisiana	30,373	88.2	21.9	13,449	75.7	13.5
Bossier Parish, Louisiana	30,209	90.7	23.7	16,823	84.0	18.5
Caddo Parish, Louisiana	62,339	87.4	20.3	39,390	82.6	24.1
Calcasieu Parish, Louisiana	50,385	85.4	21.3	27,923	80.6	23.0
East Baton Rouge Parish, Louisiana	104,602	92.4	32.3	58,729	86.9	30.6
Iberia Parish, Louisiana	19,626	81.1	11.2	10,423	69.2	18.5
Jefferson Parish, Louisiana	117,845	84.8	24.6	69,910	83.2	22.6
Lafayette Parish, Louisiana	58,391	90.4	34.0	28,418	85.8	31.5
Lafourche Parish, Louisiana	26,358	76.3	15.8	14,097	68.3	13.3
Livingston Parish, Louisiana	34,305	83.5	19.7	17,750	82.3	12.1
Orleans Parish, Louisiana	100,274	84.6	32.6	50,932	78.8	33.3
Ouachita Parish, Louisiana	37,961	84.2	21.0	22,154	84.4	22.3
Rapides Parish, Louisiana	33,731	88.3	23.2	20,366	75.4	16.8
St. Landry Parish, Louisiana	21,321	76.5	12.0	12,938	67.1	18.1
St. Tammany Parish, Louisiana	69,962	88.3	29.1	40,418	88.9	30.1
Tangipahoa Parish, Louisiana	31,607	81.9	22.3	17,731	78.3	16.7
Terrebonne Parish, Louisiana	28,479	79.9	13.5	15,130	69.1	11.3
MAINE						
Androscoggin County, Maine	30,637	91.9	18.6	17,970	82.7	15.0
Aroostook County, Maine	20,940	88.6	18.0	15,269	80.8	18.4
Cumberland County, Maine	85,573	95.1	46.2	50,106	92.6	39.6
Kennebec County, Maine	36,581	92.5	24.4	21,665	84.1	25.5
Penobscot County, Maine	43,690	94.8	23.0	26,527	89.3	19.8
York County, Maine	62,362	94.2	26.2	38,527	87.7	30.7
MARYLAND						
Allegany County, Maryland	19,212	92.1	19.0	14,097	87.2	17.9
Anne Arundel County, Maryland	156,094	93.2	41.5	79,422	90.0	35.9
Baltimore County, Maryland	222,336	93.1	38.3	137,545	86.8	31.9
Calvert County, Maryland	27,629	96.5	27.2	13,029	86.5	22.8
Carroll County, Maryland	52,495	92.8	33.7	27,326	84.5	23.0
Cecil County, Maryland	29,817	89.0	23.0	14,981	85.6	22.1
Charles County, Maryland	45,859	96.4	26.7	18,870	86.8	21.7
Frederick County, Maryland	71,255	94.0	40.2	33,846	83.9	30.9
Harford County, Maryland	74,612	93.5	33.9	38,560	85.9	29.7
Howard County, Maryland	88,830	96.2	63.5	41,410	92.0	51.1
Montgomery County, Maryland	285,806	92.3	59.3	151,609	91.4	57.8
Prince George's County, Maryland	243,798	88.3	31.8	111,825	85.1	27.7
St. Mary's County, Maryland	30,510	88.7	25.8	13,965	78.8	25.2
Washington County, Maryland	41,955	88.8	20.9	24,484	79.4	17.9

Table C-2. Educational Attainment of the Population, by Selected Counties, 2016—*Continued*

(Number; percent; dollars.)

State/County	Population 25 to 34 years			Population 35 to 44 years		
	Total	High school graduate or more	Bachelor's degree or more	Total	High school graduate or more	Bachelor's degree or more
MARYLAND—(*Continued*)						
Wicomico County, Maryland	12,743	91.5	17.3	11,244	91.9	27.0
Baltimore city, Maryland	116,182	90.4	45.2	74,745	89.8	36.8
MASSACHUSETTS						
Barnstable County, Massachusetts	18,401	95.1	34.1	18,388	94.8	38.4
Berkshire County, Massachusetts	13,409	89.9	39.4	12,607	91.3	39.7
Bristol County, Massachusetts	69,840	91.8	31.7	69,479	90.1	36.4
Essex County, Massachusetts	93,218	89.6	38.7	92,521	89.0	41.2
Franklin County, Massachusetts	8,266	94.1	37.0	8,523	95.1	44.4
Hampden County, Massachusetts	60,618	87.6	28.0	52,895	87.7	29.4
Hampshire County, Massachusetts	16,891	96.4	46.7	16,216	98.1	53.0
Middlesex County, Massachusetts	242,002	95.8	65.6	206,889	94.7	63.2
Norfolk County, Massachusetts	86,150	96.0	63.5	86,619	95.8	64.5
Plymouth County, Massachusetts	54,463	90.9	35.2	59,179	94.6	45.4
Suffolk County, Massachusetts	180,999	92.8	64.9	100,568	87.9	44.2
Worcester County, Massachusetts	103,151	90.9	38.0	99,002	92.9	44.6
MICHIGAN						
Allegan County, Michigan	14,085	90.1	21.1	13,625	92.8	23.8
Bay County, Michigan	12,611	91.8	22.6	12,227	93.9	21.5
Berrien County, Michigan	18,051	89.1	26.5	17,434	92.1	36.8
Calhoun County, Michigan	16,269	90.6	14.5	15,271	91.1	27.7
Clinton County, Michigan	8,901	94.6	28.4	9,134	94.4	46.6
Eaton County, Michigan	13,926	94.5	33.6	12,023	95.3	21.4
Genesee County, Michigan	48,504	91.1	20.2	48,826	93.8	22.7
Grand Traverse County, Michigan	12,027	99.0	31.5	10,574	91.8	35.0
Ingham County, Michigan	39,774	93.0	46.9	31,326	92.0	41.5
Isabella County, Michigan	9,300	89.5	28.1	6,152	96.6	43.0
Jackson County, Michigan	19,044	87.4	22.2	18,704	91.6	23.3
Kalamazoo County, Michigan	33,247	95.5	43.5	29,922	94.5	43.6
Kent County, Michigan	99,586	91.6	40.1	79,640	88.8	37.4
Lapeer County, Michigan	9,743	87.1	21.0	9,395	86.9	24.7
Lenawee County, Michigan	11,409	89.3	27.1	11,676	94.6	28.0
Livingston County, Michigan	19,465	94.3	31.2	21,499	97.2	43.1
Macomb County, Michigan	112,350	91.4	31.6	106,367	91.7	31.3
Marquette County, Michigan	8,062	93.3	33.4	6,912	98.4	41.3
Midland County, Michigan	10,071	94.3	33.7	10,131	96.9	42.2
Monroe County, Michigan	16,725	93.3	24.4	17,643	94.3	23.1
Muskegon County, Michigan	21,946	89.1	12.9	20,306	89.6	18.1
Oakland County, Michigan	159,354	95.3	52.5	155,408	95.7	54.4
Ottawa County, Michigan	34,124	94.3	30.9	32,155	94.3	40.4
Saginaw County, Michigan	22,865	93.1	24.9	20,989	92.1	32.1
St. Clair County, Michigan	17,331	92.8	17.8	18,089	90.7	19.8
Shiawassee County, Michigan	8,061	95.7	18.0	7,800	94.9	16.1
Van Buren County, Michigan	8,344	88.8	21.9	9,053	83.7	19.8
Washtenaw County, Michigan	52,330	94.7	60.5	40,803	96.8	61.0
Wayne County, Michigan	237,381	88.2	24.6	210,238	86.2	25.3
MINNESOTA						
Anoka County, Minnesota	43,929	94.9	28.8	45,858	96.1	33.0
Blue Earth County, Minnesota	8,595	95.4	34.8	6,582	94.1	42.7
Carver County, Minnesota	12,005	97.9	52.3	13,991	99.7	57.0
Dakota County, Minnesota	53,909	94.6	42.2	55,677	92.1	46.5
Hennepin County, Minnesota	210,356	94.8	55.0	161,814	91.0	54.7
Olmsted County, Minnesota	21,933	93.7	54.1	19,839	93.5	49.9
Ramsey County, Minnesota	89,381	90.2	43.0	64,337	88.5	44.8
Rice County, Minnesota	7,210	85.1	30.5	7,979	82.0	30.9
St. Louis County, Minnesota	22,336	93.7	31.6	21,659	97.0	29.1
Scott County, Minnesota	16,855	95.4	37.1	21,840	94.0	50.6
Sherburne County, Minnesota	12,117	96.4	25.7	13,306	96.3	33.5
Stearns County, Minnesota	19,583	96.6	29.6	17,570	94.6	28.9
Washington County, Minnesota	28,266	97.2	48.3	32,715	95.9	47.9
Wright County, Minnesota	15,221	96.3	37.3	18,421	97.6	32.2
MISSISSIPPI						
DeSoto County, Mississippi	21,453	90.1	23.3	26,930	94.6	35.5
Forrest County, Mississippi	11,359	91.1	31.6	8,985	95.2	21.6
Harrison County, Mississippi	29,790	88.0	18.8	24,847	91.3	22.5
Hinds County, Mississippi	35,590	89.9	30.2	29,159	89.8	24.8
Jackson County, Mississippi	17,799	92.0	30.0	17,167	94.6	27.1
Jones County, Mississippi	9,129	79.3	8.2	8,411	90.1	20.6
Lauderdale County, Mississippi	9,299	91.9	30.2	11,177	91.8	20.9
Lee County, Mississippi	11,322	89.0	25.6	11,252	89.7	32.2

Table C-2. Educational Attainment of the Population, by Selected Counties, 2016—*Continued*

(Number; percent; dollars.)

State/County	Population 45 to 64 years			Population 65 years and over		
	Total	High school graduate or more	Bachelor's degree or more	Total	High school graduate or more	Bachelor's degree or more
MARYLAND—(*Continued*)						
Wicomico County, Maryland	25,557	87.4	30.3	15,393	86.6	20.4
Baltimore city, Maryland	152,809	84.2	21.7	79,248	74.1	21.6
MASSACHUSETTS						
Barnstable County, Massachusetts	65,575	96.6	40.6	63,310	95.5	50.6
Berkshire County, Massachusetts	38,447	91.7	29.0	27,756	91.4	35.0
Bristol County, Massachusetts	158,890	87.4	28.9	91,326	74.9	22.5
Essex County, Massachusetts	223,437	91.2	40.0	127,448	84.1	33.2
Franklin County, Massachusetts	22,444	94.7	35.2	13,766	93.7	34.0
Hampden County, Massachusetts	127,194	86.6	25.9	74,243	81.1	23.6
Hampshire County, Massachusetts	40,709	95.8	47.3	26,318	87.8	38.6
Middlesex County, Massachusetts	429,248	93.5	52.4	231,776	88.0	41.9
Norfolk County, Massachusetts	200,119	94.9	51.3	113,592	89.2	37.8
Plymouth County, Massachusetts	153,476	93.5	35.7	88,645	89.9	31.2
Suffolk County, Massachusetts	170,948	82.6	33.1	88,944	73.6	27.3
Worcester County, Massachusetts	237,295	91.7	35.2	121,816	84.0	28.2
MICHIGAN						
Allegan County, Michigan	32,403	92.7	20.1	18,349	86.8	23.8
Bay County, Michigan	30,220	92.8	18.9	20,161	83.9	10.8
Berrien County, Michigan	43,141	89.9	26.2	28,422	87.4	27.2
Calhoun County, Michigan	35,859	91.2	19.8	23,239	89.3	20.2
Clinton County, Michigan	22,335	97.4	32.5	12,699	91.7	26.3
Eaton County, Michigan	31,377	94.1	25.1	18,658	87.6	23.2
Genesee County, Michigan	114,099	91.5	19.7	67,308	86.8	18.8
Grand Traverse County, Michigan	26,602	94.2	31.2	17,208	94.4	34.8
Ingham County, Michigan	65,633	93.1	33.5	35,979	89.8	34.4
Isabella County, Michigan	14,689	93.6	29.5	8,200	86.8	24.7
Jackson County, Michigan	45,594	92.5	22.4	26,611	89.4	19.8
Kalamazoo County, Michigan	62,378	92.9	31.6	37,287	92.6	39.0
Kent County, Michigan	160,584	90.9	32.8	82,138	87.4	29.4
Lapeer County, Michigan	28,781	91.9	16.5	15,049	86.9	13.2
Lenawee County, Michigan	27,901	92.9	20.8	17,254	87.2	17.0
Livingston County, Michigan	60,493	95.7	34.9	29,986	91.2	28.0
Macomb County, Michigan	249,490	92.0	23.4	140,974	84.9	17.2
Marquette County, Michigan	17,318	96.4	32.5	11,848	90.8	29.3
Midland County, Michigan	23,840	94.6	31.5	14,557	91.6	31.4
Monroe County, Michigan	44,678	93.8	18.0	25,202	82.3	15.6
Muskegon County, Michigan	47,755	91.3	16.5	27,740	86.7	18.7
Oakland County, Michigan	361,538	94.8	45.9	198,202	89.8	35.3
Ottawa County, Michigan	69,638	92.6	30.4	39,252	88.5	28.2
Saginaw County, Michigan	52,302	91.2	22.4	35,124	84.9	16.3
St. Clair County, Michigan	48,954	89.7	15.3	28,035	83.0	15.3
Shiawassee County, Michigan	20,635	95.2	18.2	11,790	88.6	10.8
Van Buren County, Michigan	21,614	90.5	19.7	12,656	83.9	19.1
Washtenaw County, Michigan	86,725	96.8	51.7	46,993	92.6	48.8
Wayne County, Michigan	471,559	86.4	22.9	251,806	81.7	19.8
MINNESOTA						
Anoka County, Minnesota	99,595	95.1	26.2	44,569	88.9	21.9
Blue Earth County, Minnesota	14,165	94.4	28.6	8,846	93.0	29.9
Carver County, Minnesota	28,849	98.3	48.3	10,952	92.5	30.7
Dakota County, Minnesota	116,820	96.2	41.8	54,953	92.3	32.3
Hennepin County, Minnesota	317,248	93.2	46.4	162,699	92.1	39.3
Olmsted County, Minnesota	38,484	96.5	39.1	22,832	90.8	31.3
Ramsey County, Minnesota	131,332	90.5	40.1	73,600	91.5	36.3
Rice County, Minnesota	17,075	94.1	24.9	9,788	88.1	25.5
St. Louis County, Minnesota	55,539	95.8	28.3	36,051	89.3	22.6
Scott County, Minnesota	40,094	98.4	40.5	13,792	91.7	25.5
Sherburne County, Minnesota	24,836	96.8	24.7	9,824	87.5	18.9
Stearns County, Minnesota	37,602	94.7	24.7	21,821	85.1	22.1
Washington County, Minnesota	72,528	96.2	41.0	35,419	93.6	32.3
Wright County, Minnesota	35,526	93.5	30.1	16,016	89.7	24.3
MISSISSIPPI						
DeSoto County, Mississippi	44,391	91.7	22.8	21,563	84.6	18.7
Forrest County, Mississippi	16,834	90.7	24.5	9,874	78.4	20.8
Harrison County, Mississippi	51,085	86.8	20.0	27,632	84.0	20.1
Hinds County, Mississippi	58,665	89.3	29.1	31,279	82.0	34.9
Jackson County, Mississippi	38,565	89.3	18.9	20,665	81.1	19.2
Jones County, Mississippi	16,469	83.4	22.8	10,875	80.7	20.1
Lauderdale County, Mississippi	18,458	82.1	20.4	12,643	83.1	17.6
Lee County, Mississippi	21,872	85.5	23.7	12,447	68.9	14.7

Table C-2. Educational Attainment of the Population, by Selected Counties, 2016—*Continued*

(Number; percent; dollars.)

State/County	Population 25 to 34 years			Population 35 to 44 years		
	Total	High school graduate or more	Bachelor's degree or more	Total	High school graduate or more	Bachelor's degree or more
MISSISSIPPI—*(Continued)*						
Madison County, Mississippi	13,266	91.8	40.0	14,573	94.5	46.7
Rankin County, Mississippi	22,025	93.4	33.1	20,122	91.6	34.1
MISSOURI						
Boone County, Missouri	27,430	99.4	49.9	19,897	98.3	51.9
Buchanan County, Missouri	12,723	90.9	27.6	10,969	83.6	20.2
Cape Girardeau County, Missouri	10,523	93.5	26.3	8,733	95.7	39.0
Cass County, Missouri	11,934	94.0	19.2	12,752	93.2	32.7
Christian County, Missouri	10,631	96.5	35.1	11,868	94.2	23.3
Clay County, Missouri	31,584	94.8	36.5	33,901	96.2	45.1
Cole County, Missouri	9,441	91.2	26.4	10,071	90.5	29.6
Franklin County, Missouri	12,522	93.7	32.0	11,504	85.3	26.5
Greene County, Missouri	39,318	94.4	35.9	32,449	92.4	27.5
Jackson County, Missouri	106,356	94.6	40.6	85,653	89.0	32.0
Jasper County, Missouri	15,829	92.5	22.7	15,560	82.3	24.9
Jefferson County, Missouri	28,119	89.4	22.6	29,678	90.4	22.7
Platte County, Missouri	11,996	94.5	36.0	13,777	98.6	56.1
St. Charles County, Missouri	50,893	95.4	43.8	52,993	95.6	50.4
St. Francois County, Missouri	9,576	79.0	10.1	8,992	89.9	17.9
St. Louis County, Missouri	127,221	94.2	45.8	117,454	94.2	49.6
St. Louis city, Missouri	61,779	94.6	47.3	40,790	87.6	36.7
MONTANA						
Cascade County, Montana	11,496	94.2	21.7	8,879	94.5	22.8
Flathead County, Montana	11,580	95.2	29.0	11,939	92.3	30.4
Gallatin County, Montana	16,469	96.1	40.0	13,957	96.8	55.4
Lewis and Clark County, Montana	7,810	96.5	44.5	8,061	97.3	40.5
Missoula County, Montana	17,524	92.3	42.1	14,583	94.5	46.8
Yellowstone County, Montana	20,271	91.7	31.6	18,945	94.6	37.2
NEBRASKA						
Douglas County, Nebraska	87,096	89.1	43.5	72,324	87.0	44.1
Lancaster County, Nebraska	45,326	92.0	42.6	36,840	93.1	45.5
Sarpy County, Nebraska	25,118	98.0	46.1	25,107	95.3	49.2
NEVADA						
Clark County, Nevada	320,855	87.3	22.5	298,072	84.1	23.4
Washoe County, Nevada	66,885	87.2	26.5	54,217	85.6	29.8
NEW HAMPSHIRE						
Cheshire County, New Hampshire	8,793	91.6	23.5	7,781	94.1	40.9
Grafton County, New Hampshire	11,036	96.8	56.0	9,019	90.2	40.6
Hillsborough County, New Hampshire	53,963	93.1	42.8	49,508	92.4	41.7
Merrimack County, New Hampshire	17,643	93.3	39.0	17,441	93.7	43.5
Rockingham County, New Hampshire	34,032	95.7	48.5	35,482	96.7	44.1
Strafford County, New Hampshire	16,056	96.6	44.0	14,133	97.1	42.3
NEW JERSEY						
Atlantic County, New Jersey	31,954	93.7	28.4	31,296	87.6	26.5
Bergen County, New Jersey	109,676	95.4	56.2	123,746	94.8	58.2
Burlington County, New Jersey	55,483	96.1	43.2	55,008	95.4	44.2
Camden County, New Jersey	70,864	90.0	36.4	63,822	92.0	35.3
Cape May County, New Jersey	9,096	92.5	37.2	9,161	91.0	33.0
Cumberland County, New Jersey	22,685	78.9	13.9	20,391	73.9	10.6
Essex County, New Jersey	109,390	91.2	34.0	111,751	90.0	37.7
Gloucester County, New Jersey	36,434	93.1	37.7	36,587	96.3	37.9
Hudson County, New Jersey	144,220	95.2	59.7	106,604	88.2	45.9
Hunterdon County, New Jersey	11,092	95.3	54.5	12,923	97.0	57.6
Mercer County, New Jersey	47,379	86.5	42.3	47,642	90.2	47.2
Middlesex County, New Jersey	117,109	93.8	51.7	114,720	92.4	52.3
Monmouth County, New Jersey	66,870	93.8	50.1	72,065	92.4	51.1
Morris County, New Jersey	53,096	95.2	57.4	62,351	94.4	60.7
Ocean County, New Jersey	64,502	92.4	35.7	60,206	91.5	33.1
Passaic County, New Jersey	67,844	88.7	31.2	65,070	81.9	26.9
Salem County, New Jersey	6,888	94.7	20.7	7,468	88.2	22.5
Somerset County, New Jersey	34,171	95.1	49.3	44,685	91.9	57.7
Sussex County, New Jersey	14,511	98.2	39.9	16,278	97.6	41.9
Union County, New Jersey	71,809	90.3	37.5	76,937	87.1	41.2
Warren County, New Jersey	11,989	92.0	38.3	12,677	87.2	32.8
NEW MEXICO						
Bernalillo County, New Mexico	101,234	90.6	30.9	84,789	87.8	35.0
Chaves County, New Mexico	8,156	85.0	24.2	7,895	80.0	26.1

Table C-2. Educational Attainment of the Population, by Selected Counties, 2016—*Continued*

(Number; percent; dollars.)

State/County	Population 45 to 64 years			Population 65 years and over		
	Total	High school graduate or more	Bachelor's degree or more	Total	High school graduate or more	Bachelor's degree or more
MISSISSIPPI—(*Continued*)						
Madison County, Mississippi	27,154	94.0	50.6	13,618	81.3	44.1
Rankin County, Mississippi	39,049	84.9	24.7	20,947	89.7	28.6
MISSOURI						
Boone County, Missouri	37,965	90.4	39.0	20,568	93.1	37.1
Buchanan County, Missouri	23,496	87.3	19.5	13,724	83.1	24.4
Cape Girardeau County, Missouri	19,151	92.2	31.1	12,635	84.6	27.0
Cass County, Missouri	28,334	95.6	21.6	16,710	89.7	25.4
Christian County, Missouri	21,041	86.6	24.3	12,814	88.5	23.1
Clay County, Missouri	62,997	95.2	32.5	32,427	89.8	22.8
Cole County, Missouri	20,685	94.5	40.0	11,690	87.8	31.0
Franklin County, Missouri	29,876	92.7	23.1	17,082	83.4	15.1
Greene County, Missouri	69,437	93.1	29.6	45,848	88.8	26.5
Jackson County, Missouri	178,402	91.7	29.1	97,323	87.4	23.8
Jasper County, Missouri	29,087	86.6	20.3	17,117	86.3	17.4
Jefferson County, Missouri	64,728	87.7	16.9	31,837	82.3	14.8
Platte County, Missouri	27,078	94.5	43.2	13,559	93.2	34.4
St. Charles County, Missouri	104,759	97.1	38.1	55,459	90.9	27.2
St. Francois County, Missouri	17,623	87.5	12.8	10,711	82.8	13.8
St. Louis County, Missouri	273,573	94.6	43.9	172,360	89.3	37.0
St. Louis city, Missouri	79,728	83.9	26.6	36,638	80.1	25.1
MONTANA						
Cascade County, Montana	20,202	91.9	27.7	14,879	86.1	19.0
Flathead County, Montana	28,149	95.5	30.2	17,595	93.2	31.3
Gallatin County, Montana	23,557	95.9	52.8	12,529	94.8	48.3
Lewis and Clark County, Montana	19,219	96.8	35.4	12,047	96.3	34.7
Missoula County, Montana	29,102	92.0	36.5	16,723	95.9	43.1
Yellowstone County, Montana	42,795	96.8	33.0	25,624	89.8	26.5
NEBRASKA						
Douglas County, Nebraska	133,356	90.4	34.8	67,528	91.8	32.2
Lancaster County, Nebraska	69,598	94.2	38.2	40,074	92.3	36.5
Sarpy County, Nebraska	43,725	94.4	36.6	19,898	92.0	25.3
NEVADA						
Clark County, Nevada	541,832	85.1	22.7	303,647	85.7	24.8
Washoe County, Nevada	120,092	86.9	26.9	71,154	90.4	35.0
NEW HAMPSHIRE						
Cheshire County, New Hampshire	22,239	93.8	35.0	13,954	88.5	31.6
Grafton County, New Hampshire	25,558	94.4	38.7	17,590	89.2	44.8
Hillsborough County, New Hampshire	122,039	93.1	36.0	60,854	86.1	31.4
Merrimack County, New Hampshire	44,438	93.5	31.5	26,056	91.7	35.8
Rockingham County, New Hampshire	100,270	96.2	39.6	50,061	90.6	33.5
Strafford County, New Hampshire	34,775	93.8	31.1	18,101	89.9	28.7
NEW JERSEY						
Atlantic County, New Jersey	77,603	89.8	30.1	45,790	83.5	23.7
Bergen County, New Jersey	272,624	93.7	50.2	154,742	84.9	35.2
Burlington County, New Jersey	131,688	94.8	37.1	73,210	88.5	27.4
Camden County, New Jersey	138,441	89.6	30.0	76,118	83.9	26.0
Cape May County, New Jersey	27,972	93.6	30.8	24,258	87.3	29.7
Cumberland County, New Jersey	38,912	81.9	15.3	22,434	70.0	14.1
Essex County, New Jersey	210,345	85.2	34.9	102,570	76.8	29.0
Gloucester County, New Jersey	83,764	92.3	30.6	43,848	88.7	20.5
Hudson County, New Jersey	157,022	81.5	28.2	74,320	65.3	22.5
Hunterdon County, New Jersey	43,334	97.1	55.3	20,833	89.0	42.5
Mercer County, New Jersey	101,542	91.9	44.9	53,215	84.8	34.9
Middlesex County, New Jersey	224,632	90.1	37.8	118,538	83.5	31.2
Monmouth County, New Jersey	194,231	93.4	44.1	103,761	88.5	35.3
Morris County, New Jersey	151,149	95.1	54.0	80,570	89.8	43.2
Ocean County, New Jersey	151,609	93.0	28.0	131,847	87.3	23.9
Passaic County, New Jersey	132,055	83.4	29.6	69,429	71.8	22.2
Salem County, New Jersey	18,163	87.2	18.6	11,416	80.2	15.1
Somerset County, New Jersey	101,793	94.8	54.4	49,618	87.8	41.5
Sussex County, New Jersey	48,298	94.5	31.5	22,524	90.2	29.8
Union County, New Jersey	151,862	87.6	34.9	75,346	77.6	26.2
Warren County, New Jersey	33,528	91.4	32.6	17,768	84.2	22.6
NEW MEXICO						
Bernalillo County, New Mexico	174,113	89.4	33.9	103,011	87.5	34.6
Chaves County, New Mexico	15,025	73.9	20.9	9,794	66.9	19.9

Table C-2. Educational Attainment of the Population, by Selected Counties, 2016—*Continued*

(Number; percent; dollars.)

State/County	Population 25 to 34 years			Population 35 to 44 years		
	Total	High school graduate or more	Bachelor's degree or more	Total	High school graduate or more	Bachelor's degree or more
NEW MEXICO—*(Continued)*						
Doña Ana County, New Mexico	27,641	88.1	24.1	22,642	78.8	21.9
Lea County, New Mexico	10,243	71.5	11.0	9,260	75.7	14.2
McKinley County, New Mexico	10,136	84.6	5.4	9,110	79.9	9.3
Otero County, New Mexico	9,552	93.9	16.8	7,346	83.2	20.4
Sandoval County, New Mexico	18,257	89.0	23.8	17,852	86.8	35.5
San Juan County, New Mexico	15,629	86.1	10.3	14,344	88.1	16.9
Santa Fe County, New Mexico	17,070	92.0	34.5	16,522	85.9	32.0
Valencia County, New Mexico	9,452	80.9	14.5	9,288	73.9	16.3
NEW YORK						
Albany County, New York	39,492	92.1	49.1	35,494	93.6	49.5
Bronx County, New York	231,644	82.2	21.6	184,048	75.3	21.6
Broome County, New York	22,595	89.4	30.5	19,602	89.4	28.4
Cattaraugus County, New York	8,418	93.5	22.8	8,330	91.7	21.2
Cayuga County, New York	9,325	87.1	26.3	8,675	87.2	21.8
Chautauqua County, New York	15,924	83.0	21.0	13,022	89.8	22.8
Chemung County, New York	10,127	91.8	29.0	10,537	93.8	36.3
Clinton County, New York	10,674	86.7	17.2	9,015	87.8	29.2
Dutchess County, New York	33,868	88.9	34.1	32,790	89.7	38.2
Erie County, New York	129,214	92.8	41.2	101,335	92.8	40.4
Jefferson County, New York	18,802	95.8	22.5	12,676	92.6	21.4
Kings County, New York	483,666	88.8	49.9	365,561	85.2	40.7
Livingston County, New York	6,744	87.1	27.3	6,646	89.7	28.1
Madison County, New York	7,597	89.1	28.6	7,465	96.8	39.2
Monroe County, New York	103,865	90.9	43.0	83,295	91.5	41.0
Nassau County, New York	155,840	91.3	51.5	162,437	91.8	52.7
New York County, New York	372,335	94.9	74.4	239,181	90.6	66.1
Niagara County, New York	25,309	92.9	29.4	24,019	93.6	29.9
Oneida County, New York	28,214	89.1	29.2	25,030	88.5	36.1
Onondaga County, New York	61,136	92.4	40.1	53,055	90.7	41.2
Ontario County, New York	11,868	93.5	33.6	11,989	95.0	46.2
Orange County, New York	43,854	90.2	27.2	45,161	89.2	33.8
Oswego County, New York	14,545	90.2	18.6	12,524	89.7	23.0
Putnam County, New York	10,169	95.8	39.4	12,914	86.0	49.6
Queens County, New York	381,573	90.1	44.1	325,901	85.3	35.2
Rensselaer County, New York	22,217	93.8	43.7	18,065	94.0	39.0
Richmond County, New York	63,666	89.2	40.2	60,389	91.3	42.5
Rockland County, New York	36,242	84.5	40.0	36,934	79.1	36.7
St. Lawrence County, New York	13,042	82.8	27.0	11,583	90.4	27.2
Saratoga County, New York	27,101	96.1	44.3	27,958	94.7	45.7
Schenectady County, New York	19,528	96.7	38.0	18,322	84.5	25.5
Steuben County, New York	11,026	90.4	31.0	11,144	90.3	27.0
Suffolk County, New York	171,566	92.3	39.1	178,774	88.5	39.8
Sullivan County, New York	7,436	89.7	28.8	7,563	78.5	24.6
Tompkins County, New York	13,780	95.5	61.2	10,383	93.1	55.2
Ulster County, New York	21,402	90.4	31.0	19,763	91.8	38.3
Warren County, New York	7,940	91.8	35.0	6,582	91.3	28.4
Wayne County, New York	9,631	91.2	22.0	10,359	91.9	25.5
Westchester County, New York	109,889	88.4	48.2	124,664	87.6	51.9
NORTH CAROLINA						
Alamance County, North Carolina	19,163	87.5	23.5	19,468	81.9	20.7
Brunswick County, North Carolina	12,195	91.4	13.0	12,303	90.1	22.5
Buncombe County, North Carolina	35,093	92.4	35.7	33,392	91.4	44.8
Burke County, North Carolina	9,993	83.5	10.6	9,827	82.6	21.3
Cabarrus County, North Carolina	24,777	90.5	34.6	28,676	92.5	39.9
Caldwell County, North Carolina	9,637	86.7	6.7	10,148	73.2	15.9
Carteret County, North Carolina	7,191	95.4	23.0	7,861	87.6	28.7
Catawba County, North Carolina	17,317	90.9	21.1	20,163	90.4	25.0
Chatham County, North Carolina	6,196	87.3	36.7	8,537	75.8	43.3
Cleveland County, North Carolina	10,283	86.4	19.7	11,426	83.7	31.4
Craven County, North Carolina	12,978	84.2	21.5	11,366	90.3	28.1
Cumberland County, North Carolina	55,003	94.2	24.6	38,761	94.0	30.1
Davidson County, North Carolina	18,632	88.4	20.9	19,451	85.6	20.0
Durham County, North Carolina	56,190	89.5	58.9	42,602	85.5	45.9
Forsyth County, North Carolina	47,580	89.6	33.2	45,237	89.2	38.1
Gaston County, North Carolina	27,358	84.1	24.1	27,722	85.1	27.0
Guilford County, North Carolina	71,413	90.8	33.0	65,043	87.1	39.6
Harnett County, North Carolina	20,687	92.7	24.4	17,485	83.6	21.4
Henderson County, North Carolina	11,058	86.2	16.0	13,130	78.7	24.2
Iredell County, North Carolina	19,343	90.4	27.5	22,454	88.9	29.8
Johnston County, North Carolina	21,358	95.1	27.5	26,890	83.4	23.4
Lincoln County, North Carolina	8,624	87.8	16.4	10,222	94.5	35.1

Table C-2. Educational Attainment of the Population, by Selected Counties, 2016—*Continued*

(Number; percent; dollars.)

State/County	Population 45 to 64 years			Population 65 years and over		
	Total	High school graduate or more	Bachelor's degree or more	Total	High school graduate or more	Bachelor's degree or more
NEW MEXICO—(*Continued*)						
Doña Ana County, New Mexico	47,411	79.4	28.6	32,463	74.8	27.2
Lea County, New Mexico	14,988	66.8	17.8	7,270	67.4	11.9
McKinley County, New Mexico	17,011	73.3	12.3	8,341	52.0	10.7
Otero County, New Mexico	15,387	85.6	18.0	10,962	81.5	17.5
Sandoval County, New Mexico	37,996	89.9	30.5	23,250	88.4	36.9
San Juan County, New Mexico	28,394	89.1	18.7	17,361	76.2	18.4
Santa Fe County, New Mexico	43,104	89.6	41.5	32,941	90.4	50.5
Valencia County, New Mexico	20,078	86.9	16.1	12,552	87.3	24.3
NEW YORK						
Albany County, New York	80,981	92.0	40.2	48,846	89.0	36.5
Bronx County, New York	344,596	72.4	17.5	170,981	53.7	12.2
Broome County, New York	52,512	92.3	31.4	35,485	88.4	27.3
Cattaraugus County, New York	21,989	88.8	18.2	13,876	81.5	15.9
Cayuga County, New York	23,040	86.9	23.0	13,590	86.8	22.7
Chautauqua County, New York	36,115	88.5	21.2	24,445	89.3	21.5
Chemung County, New York	23,909	91.7	22.1	15,715	88.4	28.8
Clinton County, New York	23,063	90.7	20.2	13,176	87.9	21.1
Dutchess County, New York	89,077	92.2	35.9	48,179	85.5	30.7
Erie County, New York	255,974	93.1	30.8	157,386	86.6	25.9
Jefferson County, New York	25,649	90.8	17.4	14,996	87.1	23.3
Kings County, New York	608,626	79.4	29.6	333,685	69.5	24.4
Livingston County, New York	18,300	92.4	23.6	10,815	86.5	26.0
Madison County, New York	20,934	91.9	28.5	11,968	88.4	24.4
Monroe County, New York	202,554	91.3	36.4	122,626	86.3	31.8
Nassau County, New York	392,275	94.0	45.1	231,766	87.1	34.8
New York County, New York	393,662	85.5	53.5	245,623	74.8	44.8
Niagara County, New York	63,225	93.9	22.3	38,347	85.0	20.9
Oneida County, New York	64,662	87.0	22.5	41,647	87.2	25.6
Onondaga County, New York	127,416	91.7	33.6	74,679	86.8	28.4
Ontario County, New York	32,716	90.9	33.0	21,028	95.4	28.1
Orange County, New York	102,731	91.6	28.7	50,004	84.0	26.8
Oswego County, New York	35,109	87.1	15.5	18,061	81.8	17.8
Putnam County, New York	31,693	94.7	47.4	15,792	92.3	32.7
Queens County, New York	621,255	80.3	26.5	332,550	70.6	22.4
Rensselaer County, New York	45,181	90.7	30.8	25,286	88.0	23.7
Richmond County, New York	132,725	91.1	28.9	73,131	81.1	24.2
Rockland County, New York	81,605	88.8	44.3	50,409	86.3	33.7
St. Lawrence County, New York	29,409	89.7	21.4	18,128	85.5	21.6
Saratoga County, New York	67,426	93.5	42.6	37,700	92.0	31.3
Schenectady County, New York	42,688	91.0	31.3	25,291	84.4	26.4
Steuben County, New York	28,206	88.9	21.5	17,623	89.2	17.0
Suffolk County, New York	441,136	92.5	34.0	239,600	88.2	29.5
Sullivan County, New York	22,848	87.9	20.4	13,649	84.8	20.7
Tompkins County, New York	23,024	95.7	47.9	13,417	92.8	45.8
Ulster County, New York	54,910	90.8	30.8	33,215	89.5	34.1
Warren County, New York	19,873	95.3	28.0	13,614	88.4	30.2
Wayne County, New York	28,062	91.7	20.6	16,118	83.0	20.6
Westchester County, New York	274,747	89.1	50.3	157,607	82.8	39.1
NORTH CAROLINA						
Alamance County, North Carolina	43,246	87.6	24.0	26,571	86.1	20.4
Brunswick County, North Carolina	37,143	92.2	26.5	38,105	91.2	33.6
Buncombe County, North Carolina	70,119	90.9	39.2	48,664	88.5	32.0
Burke County, North Carolina	26,761	81.3	16.9	17,695	78.5	15.5
Cabarrus County, North Carolina	53,247	89.1	33.5	25,952	83.5	17.0
Caldwell County, North Carolina	23,540	82.2	15.1	15,252	71.1	13.9
Carteret County, North Carolina	20,394	92.2	24.4	16,334	91.6	26.7
Catawba County, North Carolina	43,699	85.8	24.2	27,254	78.3	12.8
Chatham County, North Carolina	20,329	91.9	43.2	17,922	88.0	43.3
Cleveland County, North Carolina	26,668	87.5	16.9	17,339	76.3	17.1
Craven County, North Carolina	24,283	85.9	26.1	19,060	88.5	29.1
Cumberland County, North Carolina	72,331	91.5	27.6	37,712	81.2	17.7
Davidson County, North Carolina	47,659	83.6	17.2	29,434	77.8	13.4
Durham County, North Carolina	74,361	89.4	44.2	36,792	83.3	40.1
Forsyth County, North Carolina	99,308	90.6	35.1	55,717	86.9	30.8
Gaston County, North Carolina	60,286	86.3	20.6	33,892	79.2	17.5
Guilford County, North Carolina	135,821	88.4	36.0	75,530	84.6	28.8
Harnett County, North Carolina	30,577	89.9	18.8	15,378	78.9	14.3
Henderson County, North Carolina	31,912	91.4	32.1	29,188	89.8	36.9
Iredell County, North Carolina	49,543	90.2	27.5	26,188	81.0	20.5
Johnston County, North Carolina	53,037	86.5	26.7	24,121	79.8	15.4
Lincoln County, North Carolina	26,093	87.8	19.8	13,292	84.8	15.4

Table C-2. Educational Attainment of the Population, by Selected Counties, 2016—*Continued*

(Number; percent; dollars.)

State/County	Population 25 to 34 years			Population 35 to 44 years		
	Total	High school graduate or more	Bachelor's degree or more	Total	High school graduate or more	Bachelor's degree or more
NORTH CAROLINA—*(Continued)*						
Mecklenburg County, North Carolina	176,519	91.5	49.2	156,976	89.0	48.1
Moore County, North Carolina	10,520	94.0	33.2	10,407	96.1	44.1
Nash County, North Carolina	12,102	82.6	15.5	10,854	94.0	27.3
New Hanover County, North Carolina	29,352	93.0	42.8	28,274	93.8	44.0
Onslow County, North Carolina	33,173	96.2	24.4	20,270	93.2	22.6
Orange County, North Carolina	17,928	93.4	59.6	16,087	92.3	64.4
Pitt County, North Carolina	24,692	94.3	33.2	20,731	93.2	34.4
Randolph County, North Carolina	16,222	86.5	18.1	16,923	80.4	19.5
Robeson County, North Carolina	17,000	77.4	11.5	16,332	79.4	17.2
Rockingham County, North Carolina	9,310	85.3	15.4	11,242	83.8	12.7
Rowan County, North Carolina	16,648	88.6	18.6	17,349	84.7	18.8
Rutherford County, North Carolina	6,285	89.5	22.0	7,210	86.1	21.8
Surry County, North Carolina	7,098	77.1	15.5	8,590	78.7	21.2
Union County, North Carolina	21,288	86.3	26.3	32,574	85.4	44.4
Wake County, North Carolina	153,563	93.0	54.6	158,514	92.6	59.8
Wayne County, North Carolina	16,923	82.8	17.4	14,585	76.4	22.1
Wilkes County, North Carolina	7,106	81.7	9.3	7,948	81.1	19.6
Wilson County, North Carolina	9,691	75.7	20.0	9,912	82.0	28.5
NORTH DAKOTA						
Burleigh County, North Dakota	13,887	91.6	36.0	11,737	92.4	36.8
Cass County, North Dakota	30,530	96.3	51.7	21,065	96.3	46.1
Grand Forks County, North Dakota	12,020	99.8	38.7	7,081	91.3	42.5
Ward County, North Dakota	13,299	93.8	30.1	8,203	92.9	32.6
OHIO						
Allen County, Ohio	12,737	89.1	17.0	11,831	86.1	18.2
Ashtabula County, Ohio	10,904	78.3	15.4	10,998	83.6	15.6
Athens County, Ohio	7,575	87.5	27.6	6,277	91.3	31.8
Belmont County, Ohio	8,677	93.7	24.2	8,263	90.0	21.0
Butler County, Ohio	44,829	88.8	30.9	46,036	92.6	33.2
Clark County, Ohio	15,725	86.6	14.5	14,257	88.2	23.5
Clermont County, Ohio	24,869	91.0	32.7	25,629	87.6	31.5
Columbiana County, Ohio	11,415	86.1	16.5	12,725	93.8	9.5
Cuyahoga County, Ohio	169,697	91.9	36.5	142,613	91.1	36.4
Delaware County, Ohio	20,368	98.1	58.6	29,040	98.1	67.8
Erie County, Ohio	7,914	98.6	20.1	7,418	93.0	26.9
Fairfield County, Ohio	18,065	94.5	24.2	19,524	94.5	34.0
Franklin County, Ohio	229,437	92.8	44.2	167,912	91.0	45.2
Geauga County, Ohio	7,853	80.7	36.3	9,515	88.6	49.1
Greene County, Ohio	22,016	95.7	42.1	18,360	92.6	40.1
Hamilton County, Ohio	121,584	94.7	42.6	94,038	90.9	42.6
Hancock County, Ohio	10,480	96.7	36.2	8,927	94.2	24.6
Jefferson County, Ohio	6,911	92.5	19.2	7,268	91.2	29.8
Lake County, Ohio	27,340	95.9	37.4	25,979	93.5	34.6
Licking County, Ohio	18,993	95.0	28.8	20,560	90.0	29.4
Lorain County, Ohio	32,884	91.4	26.1	37,703	91.3	30.8
Lucas County, Ohio	60,371	90.2	32.6	50,046	90.4	27.8
Mahoning County, Ohio	25,908	94.3	30.5	26,535	92.1	26.4
Marion County, Ohio	8,473	89.2	13.2	8,064	87.2	8.4
Medina County, Ohio	18,739	96.8	41.7	22,099	96.3	46.0
Miami County, Ohio	12,265	89.0	23.5	12,402	91.7	21.8
Montgomery County, Ohio	71,119	92.5	27.9	60,567	91.9	26.7
Muskingum County, Ohio	10,394	88.1	13.6	9,944	90.2	14.3
Portage County, Ohio	17,911	95.4	39.7	17,253	96.1	33.4
Richland County, Ohio	15,604	83.4	16.0	13,878	84.2	21.6
Ross County, Ohio	9,827	87.0	12.6	10,270	88.5	21.5
Scioto County, Ohio	9,966	85.1	17.1	9,251	91.1	14.8
Stark County, Ohio	43,602	94.8	27.9	42,003	92.1	33.0
Summit County, Ohio	70,651	93.4	37.5	62,326	95.1	35.6
Trumbull County, Ohio	23,115	88.8	23.2	21,291	89.6	20.4
Tuscarawas County, Ohio	10,412	90.0	20.9	11,081	82.5	24.8
Warren County, Ohio	25,834	89.9	47.3	31,098	95.8	59.5
Wayne County, Ohio	13,464	85.0	24.1	13,351	86.8	20.9
Wood County, Ohio	15,914	95.6	41.2	13,664	95.6	38.3
OKLAHOMA						
Canadian County, Oklahoma	20,011	95.2	30.2	18,475	87.6	30.5
Cleveland County, Oklahoma	40,536	94.5	38.7	34,832	92.8	38.2
Comanche County, Oklahoma	17,626	88.8	17.0	14,954	90.1	19.7
Creek County, Oklahoma	7,803	85.1	14.6	8,715	89.5	20.7
Muskogee County, Oklahoma	8,774	86.2	18.1	8,129	94.0	19.6
Oklahoma County, Oklahoma	124,707	86.2	34.4	99,258	85.5	32.2
Payne County, Oklahoma	11,945	94.5	42.1	7,916	94.8	40.2

Table C-2. Educational Attainment of the Population, by Selected Counties, 2016—*Continued*

(Number; percent; dollars.)

State/County	Population 45 to 64 years			Population 65 years and over		
	Total	High school graduate or more	Bachelor's degree or more	Total	High school graduate or more	Bachelor's degree or more
NORTH CAROLINA—*(Continued)*						
Mecklenburg County, North Carolina	259,248	92.6	43.8	111,442	86.8	34.0
Moore County, North Carolina	24,968	92.5	33.3	23,265	91.2	41.9
Nash County, North Carolina	26,817	86.9	23.6	16,589	69.6	13.7
New Hanover County, North Carolina	57,673	92.6	35.8	37,349	89.5	37.5
Onslow County, North Carolina	29,978	87.0	13.0	17,313	83.5	12.5
Orange County, North Carolina	36,431	93.5	58.3	17,329	84.9	50.0
Pitt County, North Carolina	40,178	91.0	33.1	20,787	80.2	24.0
Randolph County, North Carolina	41,907	83.0	15.5	24,454	74.1	14.1
Robeson County, North Carolina	33,614	81.7	11.5	18,638	70.2	14.5
Rockingham County, North Carolina	26,788	81.4	16.5	17,567	74.5	11.6
Rowan County, North Carolina	38,464	87.6	21.9	23,429	83.1	17.8
Rutherford County, North Carolina	19,576	83.8	17.4	14,177	76.3	16.0
Surry County, North Carolina	20,790	84.6	14.6	14,566	62.3	11.5
Union County, North Carolina	62,967	90.6	36.0	27,160	85.0	22.3
Wake County, North Carolina	269,712	94.8	54.2	111,649	89.2	39.5
Wayne County, North Carolina	32,333	88.7	17.3	18,657	80.5	14.8
Wilkes County, North Carolina	20,106	88.2	13.1	13,786	75.0	18.6
Wilson County, North Carolina	21,877	85.2	16.3	13,851	70.5	13.7
NORTH DAKOTA						
Burleigh County, North Dakota	23,523	95.2	34.8	14,054	87.9	25.6
Cass County, North Dakota	38,697	95.5	38.4	19,440	88.2	24.4
Grand Forks County, North Dakota	14,660	95.0	27.3	8,490	89.9	27.4
Ward County, North Dakota	14,168	94.1	25.3	8,321	90.3	23.7
OHIO						
Allen County, Ohio	26,676	92.0	17.0	17,171	83.3	14.7
Ashtabula County, Ohio	28,834	85.5	10.5	18,253	88.3	16.1
Athens County, Ohio	14,409	87.6	24.6	7,622	83.2	22.3
Belmont County, Ohio	20,200	90.9	18.5	13,599	85.4	15.5
Butler County, Ohio	98,101	91.3	30.1	52,803	84.8	24.6
Clark County, Ohio	37,015	90.3	18.2	25,247	86.6	16.3
Clermont County, Ohio	57,806	89.5	26.8	30,702	82.3	24.2
Columbiana County, Ohio	30,678	90.1	13.3	19,839	83.8	13.1
Cuyahoga County, Ohio	344,443	91.5	30.1	214,591	85.4	25.3
Delaware County, Ohio	54,283	96.2	54.8	24,341	92.7	36.4
Erie County, Ohio	22,137	94.7	22.4	16,197	84.1	19.0
Fairfield County, Ohio	43,006	93.4	29.6	22,907	87.0	19.4
Franklin County, Ohio	301,171	91.7	35.6	143,379	85.4	31.0
Geauga County, Ohio	29,066	92.1	37.3	17,899	85.5	27.0
Greene County, Ohio	42,661	94.1	36.5	26,807	92.1	31.3
Hamilton County, Ohio	211,395	92.1	34.5	118,579	85.8	30.8
Hancock County, Ohio	19,604	95.7	23.8	12,565	90.6	20.7
Jefferson County, Ohio	19,661	89.3	12.8	13,296	83.1	13.2
Lake County, Ohio	69,064	93.7	28.2	42,644	87.2	20.1
Licking County, Ohio	48,563	93.4	25.2	27,573	86.6	18.6
Lorain County, Ohio	86,665	89.5	24.5	52,715	84.1	19.3
Lucas County, Ohio	115,166	91.1	23.7	66,493	85.5	23.3
Mahoning County, Ohio	65,575	92.2	26.8	45,924	86.3	19.0
Marion County, Ohio	18,341	90.3	11.7	11,001	80.1	13.1
Medina County, Ohio	53,106	95.1	31.2	29,402	92.6	21.4
Miami County, Ohio	29,321	91.3	21.0	18,855	86.0	21.6
Montgomery County, Ohio	140,806	91.1	26.8	91,885	83.9	21.7
Muskingum County, Ohio	23,313	87.8	11.9	14,945	78.2	12.2
Portage County, Ohio	43,994	94.5	26.0	24,685	87.0	26.2
Richland County, Ohio	33,244	91.4	16.5	22,470	84.1	17.7
Ross County, Ohio	22,245	92.7	16.1	12,200	79.0	14.4
Scioto County, Ohio	20,561	91.7	15.2	12,984	78.7	8.5
Stark County, Ohio	104,761	93.1	22.6	69,336	85.8	19.0
Summit County, Ohio	153,389	92.3	31.1	92,422	86.1	24.4
Trumbull County, Ohio	57,786	93.1	21.3	41,168	85.7	14.9
Tuscarawas County, Ohio	25,065	88.1	17.2	17,072	82.6	15.4
Warren County, Ohio	64,274	95.6	41.1	31,048	86.1	26.4
Wayne County, Ohio	30,292	89.0	20.3	19,586	86.8	18.1
Wood County, Ohio	31,959	96.1	33.6	19,269	87.2	27.7
OKLAHOMA						
Canadian County, Oklahoma	33,853	92.8	27.4	17,343	88.0	15.0
Cleveland County, Oklahoma	65,279	92.5	29.9	35,184	87.6	28.2
Comanche County, Oklahoma	28,992	88.8	23.1	14,176	86.6	21.1
Creek County, Oklahoma	19,274	87.4	15.7	12,293	84.4	14.9
Muskogee County, Oklahoma	17,509	87.4	22.1	11,396	81.3	21.2
Oklahoma County, Oklahoma	184,818	87.7	30.7	101,069	87.1	27.3
Payne County, Oklahoma	14,296	91.4	33.9	9,918	86.2	30.6

Table C-2. Educational Attainment of the Population, by Selected Counties, 2016—*Continued*

(Number; percent; dollars.)

State/County	Population 25 to 34 years			Population 35 to 44 years		
	Total	High school graduate or more	Bachelor's degree or more	Total	High school graduate or more	Bachelor's degree or more
OKLAHOMA —*(Continued)*						
Pottawatomie County, Oklahoma	9,048	88.5	14.2	8,826	88.9	15.3
Rogers County, Oklahoma	10,933	96.0	21.8	10,945	93.1	25.0
Tulsa County, Oklahoma	95,331	90.1	30.8	81,958	86.3	31.7
Wagoner County, Oklahoma	9,615	93.0	17.7	10,339	89.2	34.2
OREGON						
Benton County, Oregon	12,230	98.0	55.1	8,462	99.1	52.2
Clackamas County, Oregon	50,163	95.1	36.5	52,716	93.7	36.3
Deschutes County, Oregon	23,012	94.9	30.0	23,198	91.9	35.9
Douglas County, Oregon	11,587	88.5	20.6	10,660	88.2	14.0
Jackson County, Oregon	26,474	88.2	22.8	25,765	81.6	25.3
Josephine County, Oregon	8,281	93.6	9.4	9,918	85.6	13.7
Klamath County, Oregon	8,000	89.0	16.7	6,614	84.5	21.9
Lane County, Oregon	48,416	90.4	24.2	43,208	93.7	31.9
Linn County, Oregon	16,283	92.8	21.1	14,937	88.5	23.8
Marion County, Oregon	45,859	87.0	21.7	42,900	82.8	23.2
Multnomah County, Oregon	149,211	93.6	50.7	128,310	91.9	50.8
Polk County, Oregon	9,220	93.6	25.5	8,556	90.1	36.7
Umatilla County, Oregon	10,521	80.2	14.0	8,750	78.4	17.8
Washington County, Oregon	89,684	93.8	46.5	87,768	88.7	44.7
Yamhill County, Oregon	12,453	90.0	28.6	13,047	84.7	29.3
PENNSYLVANIA						
Adams County, Pennsylvania	10,712	89.5	22.8	10,525	90.4	31.7
Allegheny County, Pennsylvania	187,568	96.9	56.0	139,558	96.8	53.9
Armstrong County, Pennsylvania	7,238	88.7	18.9	7,361	94.9	24.2
Beaver County, Pennsylvania	20,568	92.6	38.3	18,632	92.1	36.0
Berks County, Pennsylvania	51,096	88.5	27.2	47,307	86.2	30.1
Blair County, Pennsylvania	14,774	90.9	23.3	14,304	94.4	25.9
Bucks County, Pennsylvania	69,141	95.6	46.2	72,659	95.4	45.3
Butler County, Pennsylvania	20,915	97.0	45.9	21,977	97.6	52.4
Cambria County, Pennsylvania	13,864	95.9	29.3	14,638	96.6	30.2
Carbon County, Pennsylvania	6,929	86.9	20.7	7,351	96.3	21.4
Centre County, Pennsylvania	24,229	95.8	59.6	16,842	94.9	54.8
Chester County, Pennsylvania	58,354	93.5	50.6	62,930	92.2	60.7
Clearfield County, Pennsylvania	9,387	89.2	22.7	9,909	87.8	15.9
Columbia County, Pennsylvania	6,692	96.8	33.2	6,979	91.9	26.6
Crawford County, Pennsylvania	9,736	91.1	28.9	9,170	91.9	25.5
Cumberland County, Pennsylvania	32,573	93.4	43.5	29,971	93.3	40.9
Dauphin County, Pennsylvania	37,473	89.7	39.2	33,290	91.8	34.1
Delaware County, Pennsylvania	72,341	95.3	41.4	66,123	93.0	48.1
Erie County, Pennsylvania	35,974	93.2	35.7	30,203	90.9	33.5
Fayette County, Pennsylvania	15,319	88.8	19.7	16,056	88.8	17.8
Franklin County, Pennsylvania	16,572	89.7	19.4	18,616	88.4	26.2
Indiana County, Pennsylvania	9,296	87.6	18.3	8,153	88.6	31.3
Lackawanna County, Pennsylvania	26,897	94.1	33.8	23,248	91.8	33.7
Lancaster County, Pennsylvania	69,728	85.3	30.3	60,922	86.8	27.8
Lawrence County, Pennsylvania	9,302	93.6	29.1	9,664	89.6	32.7
Lebanon County, Pennsylvania	15,866	90.3	22.0	15,255	92.0	28.4
Lehigh County, Pennsylvania	47,317	91.1	31.2	45,322	93.2	38.2
Luzerne County, Pennsylvania	38,737	91.5	26.0	35,898	91.2	29.2
Lycoming County, Pennsylvania	15,356	93.7	29.7	12,332	91.2	26.4
Mercer County, Pennsylvania	11,508	89.6	21.5	11,702	90.7	25.2
Monroe County, Pennsylvania	17,522	96.1	33.5	17,913	90.5	25.0
Montgomery County, Pennsylvania	101,652	95.7	54.6	101,394	96.2	58.9
Northampton County, Pennsylvania	35,822	94.8	33.5	34,815	94.4	36.3
Northumberland County, Pennsylvania	10,721	80.8	19.1	11,166	92.6	28.6
Philadelphia County, Pennsylvania	295,799	91.0	44.2	191,490	86.4	29.1
Schuylkill County, Pennsylvania	17,355	87.8	21.1	17,905	87.9	21.1
Somerset County, Pennsylvania	8,781	88.4	19.1	8,837	91.6	19.4
Washington County, Pennsylvania	23,432	94.1	37.3	23,238	95.6	42.6
Westmoreland County, Pennsylvania	36,524	95.7	38.4	39,274	97.0	37.0
York County, Pennsylvania	54,087	92.2	30.1	52,902	93.0	31.7
RHODE ISLAND						
Kent County, Rhode Island	22,048	95.0	37.9	20,032	93.4	36.4
Newport County, Rhode Island	9,612	99.6	45.1	8,569	99.4	49.1
Providence County, Rhode Island	94,719	93.3	38.7	77,500	87.4	32.9
Washington County, Rhode Island	11,045	99.2	50.4	11,931	96.9	56.9
SOUTH CAROLINA						
Aiken County, South Carolina	21,235	83.6	18.9	19,877	80.7	16.7
Anderson County, South Carolina	23,518	78.7	21.6	23,563	89.7	21.5

Table C-2. Educational Attainment of the Population, by Selected Counties, 2016—*Continued*

(Number; percent; dollars.)

State/County	Population 45 to 64 years			Population 65 years and over		
	Total	High school graduate or more	Bachelor's degree or more	Total	High school graduate or more	Bachelor's degree or more
OKLAHOMA —*(Continued)*						
Pottawatomie County, Oklahoma	18,263	86.3	18.5	11,572	86.0	17.8
Rogers County, Oklahoma	24,931	94.4	25.6	15,163	83.6	17.5
Tulsa County, Oklahoma	157,141	90.5	32.3	86,905	88.7	29.1
Wagoner County, Oklahoma	20,620	92.8	26.4	11,866	85.8	21.1
OREGON						
Benton County, Oregon	19,521	94.0	53.5	13,618	94.3	55.6
Clackamas County, Oregon	115,467	94.2	36.9	69,619	91.9	34.1
Deschutes County, Oregon	49,934	91.9	32.0	35,383	91.4	33.6
Douglas County, Oregon	30,919	92.6	18.5	26,422	85.2	16.2
Jackson County, Oregon	56,697	92.5	27.5	45,403	88.6	28.3
Josephine County, Oregon	23,394	82.2	21.2	22,165	93.2	24.1
Klamath County, Oregon	17,858	83.1	18.5	13,394	87.6	17.2
Lane County, Oregon	93,442	90.6	27.6	68,041	91.7	31.6
Linn County, Oregon	31,580	94.2	22.9	22,518	89.5	18.9
Marion County, Oregon	80,431	82.9	21.2	51,256	89.5	25.5
Multnomah County, Oregon	200,637	90.1	41.7	100,989	88.8	37.1
Polk County, Oregon	19,953	87.0	22.6	14,463	93.4	38.2
Umatilla County, Oregon	18,741	82.6	12.0	11,327	84.1	21.9
Washington County, Oregon	146,238	91.7	42.9	73,663	91.8	37.2
Yamhill County, Oregon	27,162	90.0	24.0	17,157	90.7	26.7
PENNSYLVANIA						
Adams County, Pennsylvania	30,241	88.9	18.7	20,171	79.8	20.1
Allegheny County, Pennsylvania	335,685	95.2	37.7	220,838	89.5	27.3
Armstrong County, Pennsylvania	20,527	90.6	15.9	14,168	82.2	10.9
Beaver County, Pennsylvania	49,302	95.8	21.8	34,306	87.7	18.0
Berks County, Pennsylvania	113,849	88.9	26.5	68,270	80.7	17.4
Blair County, Pennsylvania	34,852	93.5	19.3	25,230	88.0	9.8
Bucks County, Pennsylvania	193,307	94.8	41.3	110,304	89.0	30.9
Butler County, Pennsylvania	56,353	95.4	35.5	33,618	91.3	21.4
Cambria County, Pennsylvania	38,538	93.1	20.2	29,004	86.1	17.3
Carbon County, Pennsylvania	20,065	90.8	16.9	12,812	83.4	13.6
Centre County, Pennsylvania	37,091	96.5	44.8	21,175	92.8	36.6
Chester County, Pennsylvania	148,758	94.7	52.3	79,377	91.4	41.7
Clearfield County, Pennsylvania	24,232	88.5	11.2	15,875	79.0	12.2
Columbia County, Pennsylvania	17,976	91.4	21.5	12,094	80.4	17.1
Crawford County, Pennsylvania	24,497	91.8	21.2	16,568	83.9	17.5
Cumberland County, Pennsylvania	67,907	93.0	36.2	43,693	86.6	26.9
Dauphin County, Pennsylvania	75,765	92.2	33.1	43,154	85.3	24.4
Delaware County, Pennsylvania	154,344	94.0	37.5	88,182	89.1	30.2
Erie County, Pennsylvania	76,770	93.4	26.6	45,507	90.2	20.7
Fayette County, Pennsylvania	39,627	91.1	17.6	26,291	81.5	11.2
Franklin County, Pennsylvania	42,193	91.0	19.2	29,216	83.0	23.5
Indiana County, Pennsylvania	23,188	94.9	23.1	15,857	82.5	17.5
Lackawanna County, Pennsylvania	57,861	90.5	27.7	41,498	86.6	17.8
Lancaster County, Pennsylvania	138,425	87.4	24.6	91,687	79.3	19.8
Lawrence County, Pennsylvania	25,567	92.8	20.5	18,037	85.2	17.9
Lebanon County, Pennsylvania	37,383	89.9	20.3	25,766	83.8	15.4
Lehigh County, Pennsylvania	95,734	91.3	27.5	59,590	81.5	24.4
Luzerne County, Pennsylvania	90,229	91.4	24.0	61,184	84.2	16.1
Lycoming County, Pennsylvania	31,584	91.8	17.5	21,316	86.8	17.5
Mercer County, Pennsylvania	33,284	92.5	24.0	23,329	87.3	17.9
Monroe County, Pennsylvania	50,964	89.8	23.5	26,749	86.9	24.8
Montgomery County, Pennsylvania	232,491	95.6	47.0	141,296	89.7	37.2
Northampton County, Pennsylvania	85,946	92.6	29.0	54,428	83.0	20.8
Northumberland County, Pennsylvania	27,245	92.1	15.4	18,626	80.5	13.5
Philadelphia County, Pennsylvania	368,911	81.2	20.9	201,605	72.6	19.4
Schuylkill County, Pennsylvania	41,846	89.9	15.9	28,534	87.2	8.6
Somerset County, Pennsylvania	22,438	91.5	14.9	15,895	79.4	14.0
Washington County, Pennsylvania	62,425	93.1	26.5	40,313	88.6	21.7
Westmoreland County, Pennsylvania	108,389	96.0	26.7	77,341	89.4	20.7
York County, Pennsylvania	127,021	91.8	22.6	74,220	82.0	17.3
RHODE ISLAND						
Kent County, Rhode Island	50,138	94.4	34.5	29,582	84.3	21.0
Newport County, Rhode Island	24,634	94.7	45.7	17,226	89.8	43.1
Providence County, Rhode Island	166,192	85.4	25.4	93,173	75.9	24.3
Washington County, Rhode Island	38,758	95.0	44.4	24,666	93.0	43.4
SOUTH CAROLINA						
Aiken County, South Carolina	45,863	88.9	24.5	30,529	83.7	29.6
Anderson County, South Carolina	52,959	88.2	21.5	34,504	77.5	20.1

Table C-2. Educational Attainment of the Population, by Selected Counties, 2016—*Continued*

(Number; percent; dollars.)

State/County	Population 25 to 34 years			Population 35 to 44 years		
	Total	High school graduate or more	Bachelor's degree or more	Total	High school graduate or more	Bachelor's degree or more
SOUTH CAROLINA—(*Continued*)						
Beaufort County, South Carolina	20,433	94.7	30.8	18,984	92.5	33.0
Berkeley County, South Carolina	30,167	89.2	26.1	27,735	84.8	26.1
Charleston County, South Carolina	68,697	90.5	45.9	51,674	90.4	47.6
Darlington County, South Carolina	7,664	82.5	18.0	8,053	81.3	22.9
Dorchester County, South Carolina	20,573	94.6	33.5	21,977	86.4	34.7
Florence County, South Carolina	17,773	82.5	19.1	17,786	90.7	28.0
Greenville County, South Carolina	69,012	88.9	37.9	64,587	88.2	40.7
Greenwood County, South Carolina	7,870	89.3	21.3	8,047	85.3	27.9
Horry County, South Carolina	38,192	87.8	22.9	36,779	83.7	20.1
Lancaster County, South Carolina	9,910	93.2	30.5	12,496	80.3	27.8
Laurens County, South Carolina	8,210	85.1	11.9	7,294	84.3	16.2
Lexington County, South Carolina	38,263	89.8	31.3	37,882	86.6	36.3
Oconee County, South Carolina	9,345	84.3	13.0	7,397	78.5	16.7
Orangeburg County, South Carolina	10,307	94.0	18.0	9,121	89.0	17.6
Pickens County, South Carolina	14,620	88.3	33.4	13,566	83.6	25.4
Richland County, South Carolina	60,653	91.1	40.6	50,514	92.2	41.7
Spartanburg County, South Carolina	38,799	87.0	26.8	37,149	86.8	23.6
Sumter County, South Carolina	14,528	89.9	16.1	11,673	91.1	26.3
York County, South Carolina	31,931	93.1	31.1	35,431	89.1	32.9
SOUTH DAKOTA						
Minnehaha County, South Dakota	29,232	93.7	42.7	24,220	91.9	36.9
Pennington County, South Dakota	15,099	87.7	26.8	11,950	95.8	25.6
TENNESSEE						
Anderson County, Tennessee	8,725	97.0	27.6	8,997	89.5	19.4
Blount County, Tennessee	15,453	87.8	22.3	14,254	94.8	33.9
Bradley County, Tennessee	13,323	91.4	26.6	12,973	85.7	30.6
Davidson County, Tennessee	134,458	91.7	51.3	93,672	86.2	40.7
Greene County, Tennessee	6,985	93.3	32.0	8,290	90.8	12.2
Hamilton County, Tennessee	49,364	90.5	37.8	45,244	91.7	35.6
Knox County, Tennessee	61,463	94.9	44.8	56,792	91.8	39.9
Madison County, Tennessee	10,755	92.7	18.7	12,244	93.4	22.5
Maury County, Tennessee	11,696	92.2	25.5	11,358	93.0	25.4
Montgomery County, Tennessee	37,596	95.1	28.4	24,491	93.4	27.6
Putnam County, Tennessee	10,134	92.2	38.8	8,354	89.5	30.0
Robertson County, Tennessee	9,480	82.5	21.3	8,786	92.7	24.6
Rutherford County, Tennessee	43,743	96.0	33.9	43,924	94.0	35.8
Sevier County, Tennessee	12,318	83.1	13.6	11,045	87.6	18.6
Shelby County, Tennessee	135,342	89.9	32.7	117,341	89.1	30.8
Sullivan County, Tennessee	17,234	89.0	16.2	18,192	88.2	24.9
Sumner County, Tennessee	21,327	95.5	37.2	24,293	94.1	26.9
Washington County, Tennessee	14,869	92.7	36.1	15,557	92.0	37.0
Williamson County, Tennessee	20,090	94.0	57.2	32,869	94.4	64.0
Wilson County, Tennessee	15,200	97.9	37.1	17,901	90.5	36.0
TEXAS						
Angelina County, Texas	9,754	92.0	21.9	11,017	76.8	10.7
Bastrop County, Texas	8,189	84.5	17.4	11,820	78.0	21.9
Bell County, Texas	57,857	90.1	17.9	43,627	93.9	26.7
Bexar County, Texas	304,334	87.5	28.6	256,376	84.8	31.1
Bowie County, Texas	14,077	89.7	13.8	11,657	91.0	24.4
Brazoria County, Texas	48,479	89.8	27.1	52,048	88.3	28.6
Brazos County, Texas	35,446	89.8	39.5	23,763	83.8	40.4
Cameron County, Texas	50,179	83.2	18.4	52,529	70.0	20.2
Collin County, Texas	118,559	94.1	51.6	149,597	93.3	57.2
Comal County, Texas	13,034	94.6	30.6	16,589	91.8	33.3
Coryell County, Texas	14,508	84.9	15.3	10,775	87.9	18.4
Dallas County, Texas	415,787	83.6	34.2	356,378	73.5	29.0
Denton County, Texas	119,677	93.5	46.8	124,349	92.8	50.3
Ector County, Texas	25,669	80.4	18.5	18,997	79.3	14.0
Ellis County, Texas	21,414	84.8	20.8	22,025	85.5	24.2
El Paso County, Texas	125,016	90.4	25.4	104,160	82.7	25.7
Fort Bend County, Texas	91,859	93.5	47.3	112,298	92.7	48.0
Galveston County, Texas	43,928	92.5	31.7	42,971	83.7	29.9
Grayson County, Texas	14,998	86.2	17.9	15,709	91.4	20.7
Gregg County, Texas	16,751	84.8	15.7	15,256	77.3	17.7
Guadalupe County, Texas	19,560	92.0	27.1	20,956	93.5	28.7
Harris County, Texas	742,905	86.4	33.0	652,816	79.4	31.5
Harrison County, Texas	7,933	83.3	12.5	7,946	85.8	20.2
Hays County, Texas	29,332	88.6	35.5	25,474	85.9	37.9
Henderson County, Texas	8,836	88.9	18.1	8,110	88.7	12.5
Hidalgo County, Texas	110,931	79.7	18.1	109,591	67.9	19.8
Hunt County, Texas	10,743	86.1	26.4	10,677	76.0	21.5

Table C-2. Educational Attainment of the Population, by Selected Counties, 2016—*Continued*

(Number; percent; dollars.)

State/County	Population 45 to 64 years			Population 65 years and over		
	Total	High school graduate or more	Bachelor's degree or more	Total	High school graduate or more	Bachelor's degree or more
SOUTH CAROLINA—*(Continued)*						
Beaufort County, South Carolina	43,884	94.8	34.5	47,442	94.9	56.6
Berkeley County, South Carolina	53,599	89.9	25.8	27,468	82.7	22.2
Charleston County, South Carolina	100,352	90.4	39.2	60,559	87.8	35.7
Darlington County, South Carolina	18,353	81.0	18.1	11,948	70.4	11.8
Dorchester County, South Carolina	39,802	86.6	25.4	19,903	85.2	25.8
Florence County, South Carolina	35,752	87.9	24.9	22,350	70.9	16.2
Greenville County, South Carolina	130,115	89.3	32.2	75,148	82.4	27.9
Greenwood County, South Carolina	17,375	90.7	24.3	12,256	77.3	22.6
Horry County, South Carolina	90,740	90.7	21.0	71,652	92.3	25.3
Lancaster County, South Carolina	23,491	89.0	23.4	17,802	85.3	27.6
Laurens County, South Carolina	18,377	80.4	15.1	11,664	69.8	11.9
Lexington County, South Carolina	77,951	92.4	29.7	43,092	86.7	26.1
Oconee County, South Carolina	20,701	88.8	33.0	17,209	84.5	23.6
Orangeburg County, South Carolina	23,255	89.0	20.5	15,800	73.8	14.9
Pickens County, South Carolina	29,942	85.8	28.8	19,636	77.2	22.1
Richland County, South Carolina	94,630	91.3	37.8	49,555	86.9	35.8
Spartanburg County, South Carolina	78,982	86.5	21.6	47,461	78.9	18.4
Sumter County, South Carolina	26,882	87.2	21.6	16,704	76.3	14.1
York County, South Carolina	70,260	90.7	31.7	35,577	83.7	22.2
SOUTH DAKOTA						
Minnehaha County, South Dakota	45,125	92.4	30.7	23,983	87.8	23.3
Pennington County, South Dakota	28,881	91.3	31.2	18,408	92.3	34.4
TENNESSEE						
Anderson County, Tennessee	21,973	88.1	24.7	14,596	81.3	20.4
Blount County, Tennessee	37,385	90.5	18.9	25,031	83.0	22.7
Bradley County, Tennessee	28,402	87.2	20.3	16,969	80.2	19.1
Davidson County, Tennessee	162,139	86.4	34.2	78,663	84.6	30.5
Greene County, Tennessee	19,586	87.3	15.0	14,551	76.9	12.9
Hamilton County, Tennessee	96,270	89.7	30.2	59,005	83.5	21.7
Knox County, Tennessee	116,852	91.9	38.0	69,762	84.6	32.4
Madison County, Tennessee	26,040	88.7	21.2	15,607	79.6	21.0
Maury County, Tennessee	24,683	91.2	21.2	14,216	88.6	18.5
Montgomery County, Tennessee	41,202	93.6	22.6	17,590	78.3	25.5
Putnam County, Tennessee	18,008	88.5	27.1	12,791	76.4	19.6
Robertson County, Tennessee	19,285	88.5	19.6	9,717	76.9	13.8
Rutherford County, Tennessee	72,578	92.6	30.3	31,351	88.5	27.1
Sevier County, Tennessee	26,973	92.1	17.7	17,839	78.9	22.1
Shelby County, Tennessee	238,426	89.8	31.8	117,293	82.7	26.6
Sullivan County, Tennessee	45,502	86.6	21.6	32,896	82.2	16.8
Sumner County, Tennessee	49,579	89.5	25.6	27,548	85.1	21.7
Washington County, Tennessee	34,160	88.1	31.8	22,713	80.0	25.0
Williamson County, Tennessee	62,894	94.1	57.2	26,431	92.4	41.9
Wilson County, Tennessee	37,587	90.4	28.4	20,366	82.0	18.6
TEXAS						
Angelina County, Texas	22,121	75.2	15.4	13,810	74.4	16.2
Bastrop County, Texas	22,273	86.6	18.7	12,224	76.8	23.0
Bell County, Texas	69,045	90.9	22.6	35,544	83.7	23.4
Bexar County, Texas	438,139	82.0	27.9	226,636	74.8	23.1
Bowie County, Texas	22,636	87.5	19.0	15,314	88.0	28.3
Brazoria County, Texas	90,099	88.3	27.8	39,612	83.1	25.7
Brazos County, Texas	37,040	86.7	40.2	19,806	82.9	33.5
Cameron County, Texas	87,772	66.5	16.1	55,463	52.8	14.2
Collin County, Texas	246,648	94.3	53.0	98,554	90.7	40.2
Comal County, Texas	38,665	92.9	35.8	24,220	95.5	42.9
Coryell County, Texas	14,999	89.1	12.9	7,290	84.7	19.6
Dallas County, Texas	606,014	77.5	29.0	260,391	78.3	29.7
Denton County, Texas	204,257	92.1	42.9	75,956	89.7	36.2
Ector County, Texas	33,551	70.5	12.9	15,107	75.1	17.1
Ellis County, Texas	43,005	85.3	23.9	21,189	81.5	16.0
El Paso County, Texas	181,552	75.5	21.8	99,852	57.1	14.3
Fort Bend County, Texas	193,320	91.4	45.7	77,458	83.2	35.9
Galveston County, Texas	88,870	88.6	30.3	44,002	86.1	23.5
Grayson County, Texas	33,355	89.5	18.7	22,564	87.9	20.6
Gregg County, Texas	29,700	78.2	22.6	18,119	82.6	27.5
Guadalupe County, Texas	39,331	90.0	31.8	21,127	76.9	18.2
Harris County, Texas	1,069,381	79.5	29.7	447,742	78.5	30.3
Harrison County, Texas	17,092	82.1	14.2	10,403	83.3	22.1
Hays County, Texas	44,752	89.4	34.0	21,493	84.6	39.4
Henderson County, Texas	21,931	82.0	20.4	17,072	79.4	19.0
Hidalgo County, Texas	159,084	63.5	19.3	93,760	49.1	14.7
Hunt County, Texas	24,780	83.0	17.3	13,959	81.0	19.7

Table C-2. Educational Attainment of the Population, by Selected Counties, 2016—*Continued*

(Number; percent; dollars.)

State/County	Population 25 to 34 years			Population 35 to 44 years		
	Total	High school graduate or more	Bachelor's degree or more	Total	High school graduate or more	Bachelor's degree or more
TEXAS—*(Continued)*						
Jefferson County, Texas	37,871	87.7	19.4	32,996	83.2	16.0
Johnson County, Texas	20,805	90.6	16.5	20,721	82.2	27.1
Kaufman County, Texas	15,925	91.6	15.6	16,847	87.6	25.3
Liberty County, Texas	11,279	82.9	11.2	10,402	70.4	7.0
Lubbock County, Texas	45,002	89.7	35.0	33,978	86.5	33.6
McLennan County, Texas	31,375	88.3	25.6	27,804	79.9	20.7
Midland County, Texas	28,604	89.9	27.9	20,784	83.5	23.2
Montgomery County, Texas	69,629	87.0	27.3	75,780	87.4	36.1
Nacogdoches County, Texas	7,388	78.6	28.2	6,792	72.0	19.7
Nueces County, Texas	52,869	89.1	22.6	43,909	84.3	23.5
Orange County, Texas	11,130	96.2	12.0	9,953	91.6	26.3
Parker County, Texas	15,685	84.8	18.8	14,350	90.5	30.9
Potter County, Texas	17,984	79.9	11.1	15,996	70.8	11.8
Randall County, Texas	19,021	91.9	26.5	17,393	86.7	31.2
Rockwall County, Texas	9,289	92.8	43.6	14,959	93.3	45.8
San Patricio County, Texas	8,376	82.6	13.3	8,702	88.9	17.6
Smith County, Texas	30,196	86.5	24.5	27,073	86.3	21.4
Tarrant County, Texas	300,187	87.7	31.3	274,487	83.1	32.0
Taylor County, Texas	20,474	94.2	19.1	14,423	86.5	19.7
Tom Green County, Texas	18,668	92.8	25.1	12,836	85.9	23.7
Travis County, Texas	241,015	91.6	50.0	188,479	86.6	49.4
Victoria County, Texas	12,431	87.8	22.8	11,491	93.5	22.0
Walker County, Texas	10,827	91.4	14.7	9,017	90.5	15.9
Webb County, Texas	36,551	80.9	14.8	35,076	69.0	19.4
Wichita County, Texas	20,854	89.2	21.9	14,772	87.5	23.3
Williamson County, Texas	73,224	95.2	41.2	85,696	95.2	45.8
UTAH						
Cache County, Utah	17,065	94.7	35.9	14,681	87.2	41.7
Davis County, Utah	48,122	97.0	41.9	48,341	95.6	40.9
Salt Lake County, Utah	184,154	91.8	35.6	162,085	87.2	35.7
Utah County, Utah	84,672	95.0	39.3	73,741	94.8	41.2
Washington County, Utah	19,184	94.2	21.7	17,678	94.4	36.8
Weber County, Utah	37,331	92.9	23.8	33,483	90.2	24.8
VERMONT						
Chittenden County, Vermont	21,811	95.5	58.5	18,845	98.3	59.9
VIRGINIA						
Albemarle County, Virginia	14,047	89.2	46.7	12,115	95.7	55.8
Arlington County, Virginia	56,669	98.0	82.9	38,998	94.8	77.4
Augusta County, Virginia	8,202	84.9	20.6	8,292	92.8	26.3
Bedford County, Virginia	7,838	96.3	32.5	8,286	92.7	37.7
Chesterfield County, Virginia	40,331	92.9	35.0	45,324	94.8	42.9
Fairfax County, Virginia	152,599	92.7	59.8	165,011	91.1	64.0
Fauquier County, Virginia	7,426	96.1	29.4	8,154	87.7	40.2
Frederick County, Virginia	10,345	89.7	26.7	9,800	92.3	29.4
Hanover County, Virginia	10,359	93.5	45.5	11,618	98.8	51.9
Henrico County, Virginia	47,225	93.2	47.1	43,645	94.7	50.1
James City County, Virginia	6,985	93.2	44.2	7,841	98.0	47.8
Loudoun County, Virginia	46,386	95.1	57.9	66,370	94.3	69.3
Montgomery County, Virginia	14,447	96.0	56.5	10,084	94.5	63.6
Prince William County, Virginia	62,728	89.7	41.2	69,085	86.4	42.6
Roanoke County, Virginia	10,493	92.7	41.6	11,692	97.0	35.5
Rockingham County, Virginia	9,597	87.3	29.8	8,934	92.4	40.5
Spotsylvania County, Virginia	15,404	90.6	28.9	17,700	91.0	32.4
Stafford County, Virginia	17,670	94.9	35.6	20,209	96.3	42.2
York County, Virginia	6,883	99.0	33.8	9,442	100.0	51.9
Alexandria city, Virginia	33,476	94.6	70.8	29,727	87.9	60.7
Chesapeake city, Virginia	35,676	92.3	34.4	30,620	92.0	34.7
Hampton city, Virginia	21,867	95.8	32.6	14,623	93.7	31.7
Lynchburg city, Virginia	10,284	95.6	47.6	6,251	90.1	36.6
Newport News city, Virginia	29,759	93.4	29.7	20,136	92.2	29.4
Norfolk city, Virginia	47,028	93.7	31.9	27,187	92.6	29.1
Portsmouth city, Virginia	14,774	91.4	24.4	11,010	92.1	20.9
Richmond city, Virginia	48,358	91.6	50.8	26,049	86.3	35.5
Roanoke city, Virginia	14,750	92.6	24.1	13,422	88.0	29.2
Suffolk city, Virginia	10,924	94.3	28.1	11,780	93.7	30.7
Virginia Beach city, Virginia	75,365	94.8	31.7	58,150	94.0	35.6
WASHINGTON						
Benton County, Washington	25,765	94.9	24.4	24,281	89.1	34.9
Chelan County, Washington	8,489	78.8	24.8	8,621	72.6	32.4

Table C-2. Educational Attainment of the Population, by Selected Counties, 2016—*Continued*

(Number; percent; dollars.)

State/County	Population 45 to 64 years			Population 65 years and over		
	Total	High school graduate or more	Bachelor's degree or more	Total	High school graduate or more	Bachelor's degree or more
TEXAS—(*Continued*)						
Jefferson County, Texas	63,156	84.3	17.2	34,902	76.9	22.2
Johnson County, Texas	42,244	86.7	16.8	22,916	82.0	20.5
Kaufman County, Texas	29,357	84.2	17.8	14,089	81.3	19.8
Liberty County, Texas	21,640	76.3	8.7	10,640	73.8	9.6
Lubbock County, Texas	63,122	87.1	29.1	36,519	76.9	26.4
McLennan County, Texas	56,025	82.7	21.2	34,492	80.9	20.1
Midland County, Texas	35,124	80.8	27.6	16,676	79.3	26.1
Montgomery County, Texas	145,597	87.2	35.5	70,543	86.3	32.4
Nacogdoches County, Texas	13,968	80.4	25.1	8,812	83.5	29.5
Nueces County, Texas	86,940	83.9	22.0	49,902	74.3	20.5
Orange County, Texas	22,501	85.7	13.7	13,074	84.0	13.5
Parker County, Texas	37,093	91.4	24.7	20,070	83.3	12.5
Potter County, Texas	27,642	76.2	16.1	14,777	75.0	19.9
Randall County, Texas	31,862	92.3	34.1	18,407	89.0	33.1
Rockwall County, Texas	24,095	90.4	36.0	11,670	92.4	39.3
San Patricio County, Texas	15,894	79.6	11.0	9,930	66.8	18.8
Smith County, Texas	54,326	83.8	23.8	35,846	87.4	29.5
Tarrant County, Texas	496,272	85.8	30.3	217,656	83.8	29.3
Taylor County, Texas	29,673	88.5	25.2	19,505	84.6	24.3
Tom Green County, Texas	26,540	78.9	23.2	17,813	82.4	28.6
Travis County, Texas	278,342	88.4	44.6	108,427	87.4	44.0
Victoria County, Texas	21,954	80.1	16.0	14,488	80.6	18.4
Walker County, Texas	17,734	83.3	22.7	8,087	88.6	33.1
Webb County, Texas	52,087	65.5	18.6	24,561	46.6	14.7
Wichita County, Texas	29,831	85.2	24.1	18,802	80.9	25.7
Williamson County, Texas	125,658	93.6	39.2	63,023	90.9	35.5
UTAH						
Cache County, Utah	19,205	89.9	36.9	11,107	93.8	41.2
Davis County, Utah	69,589	96.2	32.9	32,128	94.5	36.9
Salt Lake County, Utah	241,120	90.4	31.9	113,795	90.3	32.1
Utah County, Utah	88,230	93.9	36.4	43,953	94.9	37.9
Washington County, Utah	31,949	92.3	23.7	32,687	96.1	32.0
Weber County, Utah	53,326	89.4	20.7	28,077	88.0	20.2
VERMONT						
Chittenden County, Vermont	43,080	94.2	46.0	22,482	93.6	43.0
VIRGINIA						
Albemarle County, Virginia	27,572	87.1	56.6	18,444	89.8	48.6
Arlington County, Virginia	52,999	90.3	68.9	22,112	90.9	59.9
Augusta County, Virginia	22,884	84.6	22.9	14,818	80.8	24.5
Bedford County, Virginia	23,886	92.0	31.1	16,174	85.8	21.7
Chesterfield County, Virginia	94,112	94.4	44.0	47,772	89.4	36.0
Fairfax County, Virginia	313,706	92.6	62.9	141,507	90.2	55.1
Fauquier County, Virginia	21,071	88.8	31.3	10,944	91.8	40.5
Frederick County, Virginia	24,150	92.5	27.7	13,577	87.8	30.8
Hanover County, Virginia	32,440	93.3	41.2	17,379	83.6	29.3
Henrico County, Virginia	86,631	91.7	40.1	48,320	88.7	33.0
James City County, Virginia	19,939	95.8	54.8	18,858	94.8	49.1
Loudoun County, Virginia	100,034	92.2	57.8	33,671	90.4	48.5
Montgomery County, Virginia	19,255	95.5	48.1	11,187	88.4	33.6
Prince William County, Virginia	116,070	87.8	41.2	41,411	87.6	34.1
Roanoke County, Virginia	26,088	93.4	33.0	19,505	83.7	27.4
Rockingham County, Virginia	21,389	78.4	20.6	14,903	82.1	24.9
Spotsylvania County, Virginia	36,825	91.7	30.0	17,475	85.0	29.9
Stafford County, Virginia	39,702	93.4	43.6	14,266	87.6	29.0
York County, Virginia	18,378	95.2	52.3	10,284	87.5	39.5
Alexandria city, Virginia	38,068	92.5	59.4	15,708	91.1	56.4
Chesapeake city, Virginia	64,669	93.3	32.4	29,717	83.7	22.8
Hampton city, Virginia	35,208	91.7	26.5	19,295	83.3	19.3
Lynchburg city, Virginia	16,001	88.0	27.5	11,493	78.0	27.2
Newport News city, Virginia	44,097	91.5	25.6	22,217	84.1	25.7
Norfolk city, Virginia	52,273	87.1	25.9	25,283	76.5	24.7
Portsmouth city, Virginia	23,203	86.5	17.7	13,382	79.5	24.0
Richmond city, Virginia	52,819	85.9	34.9	26,583	76.3	28.1
Roanoke city, Virginia	26,500	90.6	17.2	15,190	75.2	17.7
Suffolk city, Virginia	24,579	90.2	27.0	12,220	84.7	20.0
Virginia Beach city, Virginia	113,483	93.0	37.7	59,590	91.9	33.5
WASHINGTON						
Benton County, Washington	47,370	91.9	30.7	27,415	86.6	28.8
Chelan County, Washington	20,331	81.4	27.9	14,083	85.7	21.1

Table C-2. Educational Attainment of the Population, by Selected Counties, 2016—*Continued*

(Number; percent; dollars.)

	Population 25 to 34 years			Population 35 to 44 years		
State/County	Total	High school graduate or more	Bachelor's degree or more	Total	High school graduate or more	Bachelor's degree or more
WASHINGTON—*(Continued)*						
Clallam County, Washington	7,453	84.5	16.7	7,080	79.7	20.1
Clark County, Washington	60,930	93.2	27.1	61,261	89.7	34.1
Cowlitz County, Washington	11,787	89.4	17.5	12,453	87.3	10.8
Franklin County, Washington	13,547	85.3	13.8	12,088	72.0	18.6
Grant County, Washington	12,288	71.8	13.0	10,936	78.3	16.3
Grays Harbor County, Washington	8,240	88.1	21.1	8,714	79.5	10.6
Island County, Washington	11,313	95.0	19.1	7,659	96.0	21.0
King County, Washington	376,944	94.4	57.7	316,291	91.7	56.4
Kitsap County, Washington	38,325	95.3	26.8	29,872	95.7	35.3
Lewis County, Washington	8,189	90.7	17.7	8,752	83.3	13.4
Pierce County, Washington	130,456	90.2	25.7	110,665	90.6	28.5
Skagit County, Washington	14,076	85.8	12.7	14,611	88.2	26.0
Snohomish County, Washington	114,272	92.6	33.9	108,857	90.3	34.1
Spokane County, Washington	72,685	93.3	27.2	60,118	95.3	30.8
Thurston County, Washington	41,208	93.9	31.6	34,150	92.8	36.2
Whatcom County, Washington	28,300	89.6	30.0	24,771	89.6	36.4
Yakima County, Washington	32,288	79.0	12.5	29,325	73.1	16.8
WEST VIRGINIA						
Berkeley County, West Virginia	16,565	88.5	21.3	15,128	90.2	22.9
Cabell County, West Virginia	11,846	92.8	33.4	10,869	92.8	32.7
Harrison County, West Virginia	8,502	95.8	33.8	8,269	88.8	27.0
Kanawha County, West Virginia	23,417	87.6	29.8	22,377	90.5	30.1
Monongalia County, West Virginia	18,051	94.7	49.2	11,687	94.0	43.2
Raleigh County, West Virginia	9,228	90.7	23.0	11,014	90.2	24.4
Wood County, West Virginia	9,939	94.4	27.5	10,118	91.9	30.9
WISCONSIN						
Brown County, Wisconsin	35,457	93.1	31.7	32,264	94.6	37.9
Dane County, Wisconsin	81,622	97.5	65.3	70,093	96.8	55.2
Dodge County, Wisconsin	11,022	91.6	17.3	10,940	90.0	21.2
Eau Claire County, Wisconsin	13,975	95.1	28.2	10,740	90.0	26.6
Fond du Lac County, Wisconsin	12,155	90.0	31.7	11,594	94.9	31.2
Jefferson County, Wisconsin	9,878	91.4	25.1	9,866	93.8	35.5
Kenosha County, Wisconsin	20,713	90.7	26.7	20,116	89.2	31.8
La Crosse County, Wisconsin	15,601	97.2	40.8	12,997	95.4	42.3
Manitowoc County, Wisconsin	8,529	93.6	21.8	8,988	88.2	23.3
Marathon County, Wisconsin	15,803	91.2	32.8	16,016	94.7	29.6
Milwaukee County, Wisconsin	155,894	92.1	38.0	120,143	86.9	33.3
Outagamie County, Wisconsin	24,488	95.6	31.3	23,363	94.1	37.3
Ozaukee County, Wisconsin	8,716	96.9	39.8	9,937	100.0	69.7
Portage County, Wisconsin	8,491	96.1	40.0	7,480	95.9	39.7
Racine County, Wisconsin	23,514	93.9	20.3	23,114	90.2	26.2
Rock County, Wisconsin	19,491	90.7	27.5	18,833	90.0	21.1
St. Croix County, Wisconsin	10,217	97.9	40.1	12,251	98.7	35.0
Sheboygan County, Wisconsin	13,273	92.5	26.2	14,453	96.8	26.8
Walworth County, Wisconsin	10,716	93.8	37.2	11,499	89.5	24.0
Washington County, Wisconsin	13,960	98.9	40.0	16,464	93.5	39.5
Waukesha County, Wisconsin	41,653	95.5	51.6	47,853	95.8	52.6
Winnebago County, Wisconsin	21,888	94.9	35.2	19,925	93.7	35.8
Wood County, Wisconsin	8,451	93.0	26.6	7,960	89.6	18.8
WYOMING						
Laramie County, Wyoming	16,097	93.3	26.7	10,820	98.8	34.8
Natrona County, Wyoming	11,947	95.1	13.7	10,590	96.6	25.8

Table C-2. Educational Attainment of the Population, by Selected Counties, 2016—*Continued*

(Number; percent; dollars.)

State/County	Population 45 to 64 years			Population 65 years and over		
	Total	High school graduate or more	Bachelor's degree or more	Total	High school graduate or more	Bachelor's degree or more
WASHINGTON—*(Continued)*						
Clallam County, Washington	20,522	94.9	24.5	20,902	91.6	27.6
Clark County, Washington	123,360	93.7	29.9	68,546	91.5	26.9
Cowlitz County, Washington	28,889	91.5	17.2	20,032	82.5	20.8
Franklin County, Washington	18,153	66.4	14.5	7,206	83.4	21.1
Grant County, Washington	20,345	78.4	20.0	12,636	77.1	21.7
Grays Harbor County, Washington	20,783	88.0	19.5	14,431	88.8	13.6
Island County, Washington	21,897	95.7	30.7	19,588	94.3	42.5
King County, Washington	559,675	92.2	48.7	273,132	90.0	42.5
Kitsap County, Washington	70,784	92.3	32.3	44,548	93.1	33.6
Lewis County, Washington	20,850	92.2	17.8	16,527	86.3	16.6
Pierce County, Washington	220,171	91.9	26.0	114,924	90.1	28.7
Skagit County, Washington	33,138	88.9	22.3	24,085	93.5	32.9
Snohomish County, Washington	219,070	93.5	30.2	101,274	90.8	28.4
Spokane County, Washington	128,854	95.4	31.3	76,863	92.7	33.9
Thurston County, Washington	73,845	95.1	35.7	45,223	92.7	36.9
Whatcom County, Washington	53,775	92.7	30.3	35,640	91.9	36.5
Yakima County, Washington	55,628	72.0	17.4	33,632	77.0	16.1
WEST VIRGINIA						
Berkeley County, West Virginia	30,746	89.1	19.6	16,012	78.8	20.1
Cabell County, West Virginia	23,532	86.8	19.9	16,747	78.6	23.6
Harrison County, West Virginia	19,259	86.6	24.2	12,793	85.9	19.4
Kanawha County, West Virginia	53,737	88.3	23.6	35,434	83.6	21.7
Monongalia County, West Virginia	22,170	91.0	37.9	12,485	90.6	30.3
Raleigh County, West Virginia	19,977	89.2	20.0	14,936	86.1	13.4
Wood County, West Virginia	24,190	96.3	26.5	16,638	82.8	18.5
WISCONSIN						
Brown County, Wisconsin	70,332	93.2	25.6	35,645	92.1	21.9
Dane County, Wisconsin	127,418	96.4	46.0	67,816	94.2	44.0
Dodge County, Wisconsin	26,259	90.7	12.5	15,043	89.8	19.3
Eau Claire County, Wisconsin	24,197	95.0	33.8	15,068	91.3	31.3
Fond du Lac County, Wisconsin	29,574	93.3	20.9	17,746	87.3	18.2
Jefferson County, Wisconsin	24,410	90.3	24.0	13,490	86.3	16.5
Kenosha County, Wisconsin	48,944	86.6	23.6	21,903	85.4	20.4
La Crosse County, Wisconsin	28,553	95.1	34.4	18,221	91.6	33.1
Manitowoc County, Wisconsin	23,956	94.1	19.9	15,395	89.7	14.4
Marathon County, Wisconsin	38,494	91.9	24.0	22,943	87.5	16.8
Milwaukee County, Wisconsin	229,980	87.9	27.9	120,416	84.5	23.6
Outagamie County, Wisconsin	51,282	94.1	23.9	25,367	90.3	20.7
Ozaukee County, Wisconsin	26,028	96.9	46.0	16,569	92.0	42.3
Portage County, Wisconsin	18,272	94.6	27.5	10,993	91.8	25.9
Racine County, Wisconsin	55,250	91.6	23.8	30,992	83.8	21.3
Rock County, Wisconsin	45,436	92.2	22.5	25,672	87.1	16.2
St. Croix County, Wisconsin	25,275	97.5	35.0	11,643	93.4	34.8
Sheboygan County, Wisconsin	32,796	95.2	26.7	20,120	89.1	22.5
Walworth County, Wisconsin	28,562	94.9	27.6	16,677	89.6	30.5
Washington County, Wisconsin	41,161	95.7	27.9	22,722	92.0	23.3
Waukesha County, Wisconsin	120,612	97.5	42.5	70,073	94.3	31.7
Winnebago County, Wisconsin	45,988	93.5	25.1	26,480	86.4	22.7
Wood County, Wisconsin	21,591	94.1	25.1	14,218	88.9	13.8
WYOMING						
Laramie County, Wyoming	25,495	94.4	24.6	14,827	90.3	27.1
Natrona County, Wyoming	20,498	92.5	24.0	10,958	93.6	31.1

Table C-2. Educational Attainment of the Population, by Selected Counties, 2016—*Continued*

(Number; percent; dollars.)

| | Educational attainment by race/ethnicity, 25 years and over | | | | | | | | |
| | White alone | | | White alone, not Hispanic | | | Black alone | | |
State/County	Total	High school graduate or more	Bachelor's degree or more	Total	High school graduate or more	Bachelor's degree or more	Total	High school graduate or more	Bachelor's degree or more
ALABAMA									
Baldwin County, Alabama	130,158	90.8	31.4	126,860	91.5	32.0	11,637	81.4	11.1
Calhoun County, Alabama	60,939	83.3	16.6	60,430	83.4	16.7	14,392	80.4	14.4
Cullman County, Alabama	55,223	77.0	16.9	54,217	77.8	17.1	N	N	N
DeKalb County, Alabama	43,083	76.3	11.3	40,995	77.1	11.9	N	N	N
Elmore County, Alabama	43,150	87.5	27.8	42,940	87.8	27.9	12,370	84.8	20.2
Etowah County, Alabama	60,214	81.4	15.6	58,269	82.8	15.8	9,661	83.1	15.4
Houston County, Alabama	51,909	87.7	23.8	50,723	87.9	24.1	17,195	73.8	10.3
Jefferson County, Alabama	246,764	92.6	42.9	241,548	93.1	43.3	182,251	86.8	19.5
Lauderdale County, Alabama	56,142	85.9	22.1	55,244	86.5	22.4	6,150	87.3	18.2
Lee County, Alabama	66,281	89.9	37.3	64,571	89.7	37.9	23,500	81.2	26.6
Limestone County, Alabama	52,874	84.1	24.4	51,080	85.6	24.8	9,791	63.0	8.9
Madison County, Alabama	175,033	90.9	42.0	168,374	91.9	42.5	53,994	90.2	34.9
Marshall County, Alabama	61,027	82.5	16.8	55,458	85.4	18.3	N	N	N
Mobile County, Alabama	173,523	88.1	27.2	169,712	88.0	27.1	91,779	85.5	16.6
Montgomery County, Alabama	61,497	93.0	41.9	59,645	94.1	42.6	82,264	80.7	24.0
Morgan County, Alabama	67,671	83.5	21.8	66,039	84.5	22.3	9,505	78.3	8.8
St. Clair County, Alabama	54,463	83.1	18.3	53,698	83.3	18.5	5,889	73.1	6.7
Shelby County, Alabama	118,069	93.9	43.5	115,597	94.0	43.3	16,964	92.4	37.4
Talladega County, Alabama	37,406	82.2	16.1	37,060	82.3	16.0	17,675	78.8	11.4
Tuscaloosa County, Alabama	85,392	90.9	35.8	83,247	91.2	36.5	38,131	86.2	17.5
Walker County, Alabama	42,308	78.9	11.5	41,526	79.9	11.7	1,667	87.3	3.8
ALASKA									
Anchorage Municipality, Alaska	131,316	96.6	44.2	125,361	97.1	45.2	10,114	91.0	10.0
Fairbanks North Star Borough, Alaska	48,337	96.7	35.2	46,351	97.0	36.3	N	N	N
Matanuska-Susitna Borough, Alaska	57,765	94.6	20.7	55,796	94.4	20.8	N	N	N
ARIZONA									
Apache County, Arizona	11,593	96.3	18.8	10,159	96.6	20.3	N	N	N
Cochise County, Arizona	77,380	86.3	23.5	54,066	91.8	28.4	3,915	96.2	29.1
Coconino County, Arizona	54,952	94.4	46.4	48,927	97.1	49.8	N	N	N
Maricopa County, Arizona	2,236,660	89.8	33.7	1,778,478	94.9	38.7	139,222	89.9	24.5
Mohave County, Arizona	144,583	84.7	10.9	127,184	85.7	11.2	N	N	N
Navajo County, Arizona	36,554	89.7	22.9	33,432	89.0	24.2	N	N	N
Pima County, Arizona	542,084	90.6	34.5	407,542	94.2	39.9	21,444	88.6	21.2
Pinal County, Arizona	240,988	87.0	21.2	185,520	92.3	24.9	11,887	85.3	22.7
Yavapai County, Arizona	162,307	92.4	24.3	147,783	93.6	25.9	N	N	N
Yuma County, Arizona	79,892	80.8	17.8	52,060	91.4	21.3	N	N	N
ARKANSAS									
Benton County, Arkansas	151,109	89.0	30.8	131,988	93.7	33.6	2,398	80.3	40.6
Craighead County, Arkansas	57,466	88.9	23.5	56,315	89.5	24.0	7,614	82.1	22.4
Faulkner County, Arkansas	63,613	91.3	29.3	62,828	91.9	29.5	7,147	95.3	24.3
Garland County, Arkansas	62,373	90.7	19.0	60,654	90.8	19.3	4,492	68.3	13.2
Jefferson County, Arkansas	21,297	86.4	19.6	20,647	87.1	19.7	24,644	75.5	17.6
Lonoke County, Arkansas	43,033	90.9	21.7	42,085	91.3	21.8	2,374	84.3	15.9
Pulaski County, Arkansas	161,912	94.2	41.7	155,320	94.8	42.5	86,842	87.6	20.1
Saline County, Arkansas	74,228	91.9	26.8	72,778	92.1	27.2	5,371	95.3	44.8
Sebastian County, Arkansas	66,694	88.9	19.2	64,550	89.5	19.5	5,518	87.6	11.5
Washington County, Arkansas	112,421	90.3	35.5	107,043	91.9	36.4	3,820	93.6	14.9
White County, Arkansas	48,003	87.9	20.5	46,583	88.7	20.9	N	N	N
CALIFORNIA									
Alameda County, California	514,045	91.5	50.9	415,011	96.3	57.4	124,126	90.5	27.6
Butte County, California	128,274	91.1	27.8	115,973	93.3	28.9	N	N	N
Contra Costa County, California	476,358	91.9	44.2	383,654	97.1	50.5	65,328	91.6	24.8
El Dorado County, California	119,354	94.6	33.2	109,354	95.8	34.1	N	N	N
Fresno County, California	404,221	78.0	21.5	219,804	91.0	30.9	28,167	82.5	18.2
Humboldt County, California	78,413	91.8	31.0	73,741	92.6	31.1	N	N	N
Imperial County, California	68,245	73.8	16.6	15,422	93.2	20.6	N	N	N
Kern County, California	398,454	74.5	16.2	222,893	90.3	23.2	28,252	80.1	14.2
Kings County, California	62,208	78.1	14.0	35,005	89.5	20.2	6,665	71.6	6.2
Lake County, California	37,919	86.3	16.4	35,481	88.7	16.9	N	N	N
Los Angeles County, California	3,587,356	80.6	34.5	2,100,790	94.6	49.6	576,020	89.4	25.9
Madera County, California	69,561	78.0	13.6	41,717	90.0	19.7	3,056	67.6	8.1
Marin County, California	152,428	97.5	65.6	143,260	98.0	67.0	4,499	83.3	12.7

N = Data for this geographic area cannot be displayed because the number of sample cases is too small.

Table C-2. Educational Attainment of the Population, by Selected Counties, 2016—*Continued*

(Number; percent; dollars.)

State/County	American Indian or Alaska Native alone			Asian alone			Native Hawaiian or Other Pacific Islander alone		
	Total	High school graduate or more	Bachelor's degree or more	Total	High school graduate or more	Bachelor's degree or more	Total	High school graduate or more	Bachelor's degree or more
ALABAMA									
Baldwin County, Alabama	N	N	N	N	N	N	N	N	N
Calhoun County, Alabama	N	N	N	N	N	N	N	N	N
Cullman County, Alabama	N	N	N	N	N	N	N	N	N
DeKalb County, Alabama	N	N	N	N	N	N	N	N	N
Elmore County, Alabama	N	N	N	N	N	N	N	N	N
Etowah County, Alabama	N	N	N	N	N	N	N	N	N
Houston County, Alabama	N	N	N	780	87.7	39.0	N	N	N
Jefferson County, Alabama	N	N	N	6,166	89.7	65.9	N	N	N
Lauderdale County, Alabama	N	N	N	N	N	N	N	N	N
Lee County, Alabama	N	N	N	3,967	96.0	59.5	N	N	N
Limestone County, Alabama	N	N	N	N	N	N	N	N	N
Madison County, Alabama	1,991	91.5	40.9	5,735	89.8	59.1	N	N	N
Marshall County, Alabama	N	N	N	N	N	N	N	N	N
Mobile County, Alabama	2,406	59.9	4.3	5,321	80.8	37.9	N	N	N
Montgomery County, Alabama	N	N	N	4,293	84.6	43.2	N	N	N
Morgan County, Alabama	N	N	N	N	N	N	N	N	N
St. Clair County, Alabama	N	N	N	N	N	N	N	N	N
Shelby County, Alabama	N	N	N	2,891	69.0	51.0	N	N	N
Talladega County, Alabama	N	N	N	N	N	N	N	N	N
Tuscaloosa County, Alabama	N	N	N	N	N	N	N	N	N
Walker County, Alabama	N	N	N	N	N	N	N	N	N
ALASKA									
Anchorage Municipality, Alaska	14,651	84.0	15.7	17,701	86.2	29.5	4,119	92.2	10.4
Fairbanks North Star Borough, Alaska	N	N	N	N	N	N	N	N	N
Matanuska-Susitna Borough, Alaska	3,087	89.6	11.4	N	N	N	N	N	N
ARIZONA									
Apache County, Arizona	31,533	76.8	8.4	N	N	N	N	N	N
Cochise County, Arizona	N	N	N	2,448	90.0	45.3	N	N	N
Coconino County, Arizona	21,110	76.8	8.1	N	N	N	N	N	N
Maricopa County, Arizona	47,094	86.8	16.5	117,801	86.6	56.6	5,976	90.4	22.0
Mohave County, Arizona	2,858	88.9	11.8	N	N	N	N	N	N
Navajo County, Arizona	27,698	72.9	5.3	N	N	N	N	N	N
Pima County, Arizona	18,964	76.8	12.9	18,827	87.7	53.0	N	N	N
Pinal County, Arizona	11,958	69.8	5.0	6,275	83.1	39.6	N	N	N
Yavapai County, Arizona	1,842	94.3	13.5	N	N	N	N	N	N
Yuma County, Arizona	1,637	51.1	15.1	1,919	90.6	55.3	N	N	N
ARKANSAS									
Benton County, Arkansas	1,706	93.5	24.5	6,346	92.9	73.6	N	N	N
Craighead County, Arkansas	N	N	N	N	N	N	N	N	N
Faulkner County, Arkansas	N	N	N	N	N	N	N	N	N
Garland County, Arkansas	N	N	N	N	N	N	N	N	N
Jefferson County, Arkansas	N	N	N	N	N	N	N	N	N
Lonoke County, Arkansas	N	N	N	N	N	N	N	N	N
Pulaski County, Arkansas	N	N	N	5,787	93.1	57.5	N	N	N
Saline County, Arkansas	N	N	N	N	N	N	N	N	N
Sebastian County, Arkansas	N	N	N	3,712	76.9	6.9	N	N	N
Washington County, Arkansas	N	N	N	3,314	84.0	61.6	N	N	N
White County, Arkansas	N	N	N	N	N	N	N	N	N
CALIFORNIA									
Alameda County, California	5,936	86.7	21.9	352,635	87.9	55.2	9,258	84.6	19.8
Butte County, California	1,640	88.3	10.4	5,305	62.1	24.3	N	N	N
Contra Costa County, California	2,622	91.1	8.1	133,722	89.2	56.7	3,246	61.4	20.2
El Dorado County, California	N	N	N	6,476	83.7	54.1	N	N	N
Fresno County, California	7,075	82.5	18.3	63,143	73.1	30.0	N	N	N
Humboldt County, California	3,435	79.9	14.5	N	N	N	N	N	N
Imperial County, California	1,273	64.6	11.5	1,882	84.9	30.3	N	N	N
Kern County, California	5,391	82.6	3.5	27,415	81.9	39.0	N	N	N
Kings County, California	1,255	69.1	0.7	3,856	89.7	24.0	N	N	N
Lake County, California	N	N	N	N	N	N	N	N	N
Los Angeles County, California	44,017	66.4	15.2	1,120,166	87.4	50.9	16,975	87.8	16.7
Madera County, California	N	N	N	N	N	N	N	N	N
Marin County, California	N	N	N	11,408	93.4	55.9	N	N	N

N = Data for this geographic area cannot be displayed because the number of sample cases is too small.

Table C-2. Educational Attainment of the Population, by Selected Counties, 2016—*Continued*

(Number; percent; dollars.)

	Educational attainment by race/ethnicity, 25 years and over								
	White alone			White alone, not Hispanic			Black alone		
State/County	Total	High school graduate or more	Bachelor's degree or more	Total	High school graduate or more	Bachelor's degree or more	Total	High school graduate or more	Bachelor's degree or more
CALIFORNIA—(*Continued*)									
Mendocino County, California	52,779	87.1	24.1	45,337	91.8	26.8	N	N	N
Merced County, California	92,572	78.4	15.6	55,705	87.5	21.0	5,218	88.4	9.2
Monterey County, California	166,025	79.9	30.5	103,315	93.0	41.9	7,642	86.8	17.0
Napa County, California	79,464	86.7	36.5	59,870	95.5	43.8	1,929	85.0	34.8
Nevada County, California	71,105	93.5	36.9	66,672	94.1	38.5	N	N	N
Orange County, California	1,386,802	87.9	39.2	994,106	96.2	48.9	37,728	90.4	34.8
Placer County, California	224,803	95.8	38.1	205,244	96.4	39.0	4,388	97.2	31.8
Riverside County, California	963,669	85.0	23.4	659,004	92.7	29.0	98,643	91.0	25.8
Sacramento County, California	629,325	89.9	31.7	517,558	93.8	34.6	95,167	89.0	21.8
San Bernardino County, California	846,099	80.3	19.0	464,444	91.0	26.0	111,548	86.5	18.5
San Diego County, California	1,644,465	86.8	38.1	1,146,637	96.1	48.0	107,425	91.8	25.1
San Francisco County, California	338,426	96.3	73.3	299,734	98.2	77.1	33,229	91.6	24.7
San Joaquin County, California	276,225	78.4	16.4	180,027	89.1	21.7	33,306	87.0	12.3
San Luis Obispo County, California	164,337	93.8	37.8	140,738	97.0	40.7	3,577	76.8	14.6
San Mateo County, California	290,000	92.1	52.5	233,818	96.6	59.5	13,819	92.7	27.7
Santa Barbara County, California	219,425	81.1	35.2	144,690	97.4	48.4	5,986	83.0	19.8
Santa Clara County, California	614,553	90.4	49.9	475,871	96.1	58.4	32,020	92.1	39.4
Santa Cruz County, California	140,772	92.6	45.1	117,001	97.9	50.3	N	N	N
Shasta County, California	114,840	92.6	22.0	106,969	93.4	22.7	N	N	N
Solano County, California	161,064	90.3	26.1	130,241	94.6	27.9	42,362	91.4	17.4
Sonoma County, California	283,031	93.3	38.1	254,388	95.7	40.2	5,265	87.5	26.3
Stanislaus County, California	258,713	79.7	16.5	170,528	87.9	21.4	9,959	89.3	13.0
Sutter County, California	44,973	80.2	16.3	32,924	89.7	18.5	N	N	N
Tulare County, California	204,604	71.4	14.7	97,867	88.7	23.4	4,633	89.9	19.4
Ventura County, California	462,574	83.7	32.1	295,144	96.4	43.3	10,050	92.1	44.3
Yolo County, California	95,407	86.3	40.5	68,389	95.3	50.9	3,498	93.9	31.4
Yuba County, California	36,986	84.0	17.8	29,579	87.7	19.4	N	N	N
COLORADO									
Adams County, Colorado	264,118	84.2	24.1	184,116	93.9	30.1	9,877	91.4	22.6
Arapahoe County, Colorado	321,611	94.8	46.2	287,688	97.5	49.4	42,722	91.5	25.6
Boulder County, Colorado	191,387	95.8	61.0	172,929	98.0	65.1	N	N	N
Broomfield County, Colorado	40,048	98.2	53.4	36,951	98.7	54.6	N	N	N
Denver County, Colorado	386,897	90.0	52.4	302,565	96.8	62.7	44,326	83.5	25.9
Douglas County, Colorado	194,463	98.8	58.7	182,723	99.0	59.2	2,933	97.9	56.3
El Paso County, Colorado	368,760	95.4	41.1	329,327	96.6	43.0	25,495	93.8	23.9
Jefferson County, Colorado	378,070	94.7	44.0	335,965	96.7	47.0	4,336	89.8	29.0
Larimer County, Colorado	205,661	97.0	47.8	192,046	97.5	49.3	N	N	N
Mesa County, Colorado	95,524	89.0	25.6	87,445	91.9	26.7	N	N	N
Pueblo County, Colorado	92,404	89.0	23.2	64,679	92.0	26.3	N	N	N
Weld County, Colorado	175,137	88.1	27.4	136,106	95.0	33.1	N	N	N
CONNECTICUT									
Fairfield County, Connecticut	487,375	92.8	51.7	420,244	95.6	56.3	71,052	86.0	19.5
Hartford County, Connecticut	464,184	91.5	40.2	415,820	93.8	43.0	77,610	86.4	19.3
Litchfield County, Connecticut	127,541	93.6	37.0	122,974	94.3	37.2	N	N	N
Middlesex County, Connecticut	107,889	95.3	42.6	103,332	96.1	42.5	5,700	85.6	25.8
New Haven County, Connecticut	459,723	91.5	37.1	410,257	93.2	39.4	69,992	86.7	20.3
New London County, Connecticut	158,733	93.9	33.4	150,999	94.2	33.9	10,161	82.6	12.8
Tolland County, Connecticut	87,316	96.0	40.7	84,140	96.1	40.5	N	N	N
Windham County, Connecticut	73,921	88.2	24.3	70,545	89.0	24.9	N	N	N
DELAWARE									
Kent County, Delaware	82,574	86.7	21.9	78,670	87.4	22.7	26,464	89.1	24.4
New Castle County, Delaware	259,551	92.3	38.3	239,324	94.4	40.1	88,181	89.5	21.5
Sussex County, Delaware	139,996	88.1	27.8	131,472	90.1	28.9	17,375	74.7	12.3
DISTRICT OF COLUMBIA									
District of Columbia, District of Columbia	209,538	97.4	88.9	189,306	99.4	92.0	217,411	86.4	25.6
FLORIDA									
Alachua County, Florida	115,402	94.3	42.7	105,558	95.5	42.8	29,884	81.4	22.2
Bay County, Florida	109,829	91.6	24.7	104,045	91.8	25.0	12,904	91.0	8.9
Brevard County, Florida	367,992	93.3	30.0	339,289	94.0	30.2	37,260	82.7	19.6
Broward County, Florida	873,308	91.0	34.3	564,395	94.1	37.0	344,977	81.4	20.0
Charlotte County, Florida	134,693	91.6	24.8	128,113	91.9	24.4	6,957	77.3	9.2
Citrus County, Florida	107,011	87.3	19.3	103,616	87.2	19.4	4,797	88.1	34.5

N = Data for this geographic area cannot be displayed because the number of sample cases is too small.

Table C-2. Educational Attainment of the Population, by Selected Counties, 2016—*Continued*

(Number; percent; dollars.)

| | Educational attainment by race/ethnicity, 25 years and over | | | | | | | | |
| State/County | American Indian or Alaska Native alone | | | Asian alone | | | Native Hawaiian or Other Pacific Islander alone | | |
	Total	High school graduate or more	Bachelor's degree or more	Total	High school graduate or more	Bachelor's degree or more	Total	High school graduate or more	Bachelor's degree or more
CALIFORNIA—(*Continued*)									
Mendocino County, California	2,108	76.0	4.4	N	N	N	N	N	N
Merced County, California	N	N	N	12,481	63.3	26.0	N	N	N
Monterey County, California	1,405	81.6	15.1	18,827	90.2	42.1	N	N	N
Napa County, California	N	N	N	7,919	89.5	45.8	N	N	N
Nevada County, California	N	N	N	N	N	N	N	N	N
Orange County, California	8,852	77.5	20.4	460,740	88.2	56.0	7,300	95.4	22.4
Placer County, California	1,480	81.4	22.4	19,182	95.8	59.9	N	N	N
Riverside County, California	11,356	77.4	17.0	104,904	89.6	46.0	4,628	87.4	32.3
Sacramento County, California	7,111	74.6	18.3	160,153	80.5	37.9	11,225	80.2	8.4
San Bernardino County, California	9,966	82.0	10.5	107,906	89.5	50.9	3,530	98.1	20.8
San Diego County, California	15,753	76.2	14.9	281,082	88.1	48.5	9,851	96.0	34.6
San Francisco County, California	2,534	74.4	32.4	241,085	78.4	45.7	N	N	N
San Joaquin County, California	3,358	70.9	7.1	72,345	80.5	29.6	N	N	N
San Luis Obispo County, California	N	N	N	6,529	91.8	46.2	N	N	N
San Mateo County, California	1,991	59.9	20.7	163,896	91.6	61.1	7,297	90.7	21.8
Santa Barbara County, California	3,170	80.9	11.2	14,577	90.0	45.7	N	N	N
Santa Clara County, California	5,060	77.2	14.8	494,323	90.4	64.9	5,280	87.0	17.7
Santa Cruz County, California	N	N	N	7,390	95.6	56.8	N	N	N
Shasta County, California	N	N	N	3,822	80.7	41.4	N	N	N
Solano County, California	N	N	N	50,103	88.5	40.1	2,427	87.4	24.4
Sonoma County, California	3,343	71.7	7.0	16,186	89.0	43.5	N	N	N
Stanislaus County, California	2,839	80.8	20.8	21,093	73.8	29.5	2,271	73.1	10.7
Sutter County, California	N	N	N	10,421	58.0	16.6	N	N	N
Tulare County, California	3,614	81.7	3.8	11,173	77.4	28.1	N	N	N
Ventura County, California	3,710	71.3	9.7	44,587	94.6	61.7	N	N	N
Yolo County, California	N	N	N	14,610	89.6	59.2	N	N	N
Yuba County, California	N	N	N	2,084	96.0	44.4	N	N	N
COLORADO									
Adams County, Colorado	4,791	70.6	22.0	13,354	81.1	27.1	N	N	N
Arapahoe County, Colorado	2,317	85.9	22.1	26,152	85.5	47.1	N	N	N
Boulder County, Colorado	N	N	N	9,335	92.8	74.6	N	N	N
Broomfield County, Colorado	N	N	N	2,756	91.9	48.8	N	N	N
Denver County, Colorado	4,071	70.8	16.1	18,552	81.8	50.4	N	N	N
Douglas County, Colorado	N	N	N	11,199	94.3	80.7	N	N	N
El Paso County, Colorado	2,176	72.9	24.3	12,613	89.1	45.7	N	N	N
Jefferson County, Colorado	2,115	87.0	11.8	12,060	87.2	52.1	N	N	N
Larimer County, Colorado	N	N	N	4,513	93.2	49.1	N	N	N
Mesa County, Colorado	N	N	N	N	N	N	N	N	N
Pueblo County, Colorado	4,377	90.9	11.7	N	N	N	N	N	N
Weld County, Colorado	N	N	N	2,810	75.1	43.8	N	N	N
CONNECTICUT									
Fairfield County, Connecticut	2,238	64.7	17.2	35,104	88.7	63.8	N	N	N
Hartford County, Connecticut	N	N	N	31,326	91.4	71.6	N	N	N
Litchfield County, Connecticut	N	N	N	2,733	92.6	38.0	N	N	N
Middlesex County, Connecticut	N	N	N	2,510	94.9	57.6	N	N	N
New Haven County, Connecticut	N	N	N	22,913	91.9	70.9	N	N	N
New London County, Connecticut	N	N	N	8,622	89.2	50.9	N	N	N
Tolland County, Connecticut	N	N	N	N	N	N	N	N	N
Windham County, Connecticut	N	N	N	N	N	N	N	N	N
DELAWARE									
Kent County, Delaware	N	N	N	2,324	91.7	30.2	N	N	N
New Castle County, Delaware	N	N	N	21,313	94.5	67.8	N	N	N
Sussex County, Delaware	N	N	N	1,872	78.9	61.8	N	N	N
DISTRICT OF COLUMBIA									
District of Columbia, District of Columbia	N	N	N	19,965	96.5	85.6	N	N	N
FLORIDA									
Alachua County, Florida	769	88.8	23.7	8,898	89.8	65.9	N	N	N
Bay County, Florida	N	N	N	3,318	78.6	39.5	N	N	N
Brevard County, Florida	N	N	N	10,631	81.8	40.9	N	N	N
Broward County, Florida	4,603	71.0	14.8	49,987	87.2	54.9	N	N	N
Charlotte County, Florida	N	N	N	N	N	N	N	N	N
Citrus County, Florida	N	N	N	N	N	N	N	N	N

N = Data for this geographic area cannot be displayed because the number of sample cases is too small.

Table C-2. Educational Attainment of the Population, by Selected Counties, 2016—*Continued*

(Number; percent; dollars.)

State/County	Educational attainment by race/ethnicity, 25 years and over								
	White alone			White alone, not Hispanic			Black alone		
	Total	High school graduate or more	Bachelor's degree or more	Total	High school graduate or more	Bachelor's degree or more	Total	High school graduate or more	Bachelor's degree or more
FLORIDA—(*Continued*)									
Clay County, Florida	117,213	93.4	22.7	109,086	93.1	22.9	14,211	92.5	22.5
Collier County, Florida	249,585	86.9	35.5	196,348	94.2	43.1	15,602	67.6	13.4
Columbia County, Florida	37,427	85.6	14.4	35,848	86.9	14.8	7,983	79.7	11.7
Duval County, Florida	408,114	90.6	32.2	370,627	91.6	32.9	167,848	86.1	19.4
Escambia County, Florida	153,143	93.1	30.7	146,075	93.7	30.7	42,992	85.0	11.8
Flagler County, Florida	70,193	91.4	22.5	64,605	91.6	23.0	7,911	87.9	26.2
Hernando County, Florida	124,952	87.3	18.4	112,749	88.4	18.2	6,782	88.6	15.7
Highlands County, Florida	64,778	88.3	13.5	57,463	90.5	14.5	6,417	78.5	6.8
Hillsborough County, Florida	689,881	89.7	34.2	513,293	93.4	38.7	142,581	87.6	22.3
Indian River County, Florida	101,072	89.0	30.3	94,739	91.2	31.9	7,009	76.6	13.8
Lake County, Florida	213,919	90.0	23.2	188,142	91.9	23.4	21,678	83.0	11.3
Lee County, Florida	479,273	88.7	29.5	405,047	91.9	32.1	35,614	75.2	16.8
Leon County, Florida	112,225	96.8	53.3	105,490	97.5	53.3	46,992	86.1	29.5
Manatee County, Florida	245,530	89.4	28.4	218,462	92.3	29.1	18,568	88.6	15.9
Marion County, Florida	222,372	87.9	18.2	198,296	89.1	18.5	28,200	78.9	14.4
Martin County, Florida	109,715	92.5	32.2	102,749	93.3	32.6	6,049	80.9	7.0
Miami-Dade County, Florida	1,465,069	81.9	30.3	260,373	94.7	49.2	311,900	78.2	16.2
Monroe County, Florida	54,332	89.4	34.5	43,131	93.8	38.8	4,100	97.0	13.9
Nassau County, Florida	53,444	92.2	31.1	52,472	92.2	30.7	4,900	90.1	21.2
Okaloosa County, Florida	111,438	93.5	32.1	107,942	93.7	32.6	12,214	85.5	19.9
Orange County, Florida	590,813	88.2	36.6	397,064	93.6	42.7	170,865	83.6	21.2
Osceola County, Florida	167,422	86.9	20.1	83,483	90.6	24.5	25,206	87.5	16.7
Palm Beach County, Florida	828,055	90.0	37.8	653,221	94.5	42.1	166,265	76.6	21.3
Pasco County, Florida	336,584	89.1	21.7	297,996	90.1	22.1	17,400	87.1	30.5
Pinellas County, Florida	625,627	92.1	30.0	581,227	92.7	30.4	64,329	82.0	19.4
Polk County, Florida	375,532	85.7	21.0	307,533	88.1	22.7	61,488	76.9	10.7
Putnam County, Florida	42,768	82.2	17.0	39,618	84.6	18.1	7,686	66.9	6.7
St. Johns County, Florida	151,108	96.3	43.1	142,830	96.6	43.5	7,582	88.5	32.3
St. Lucie County, Florida	172,007	88.2	21.9	144,003	91.7	22.9	35,811	78.1	11.3
Santa Rosa County, Florida	104,288	90.7	29.2	100,554	90.8	29.6	8,100	78.6	9.0
Sarasota County, Florida	305,361	94.1	34.5	285,482	94.6	35.3	10,759	79.9	12.7
Seminole County, Florida	256,461	95.9	38.6	210,304	96.8	41.5	34,392	86.3	23.5
Sumter County, Florida	100,224	93.1	31.1	96,961	93.4	31.9	6,632	76.2	2.2
Volusia County, Florida	340,457	90.0	24.1	304,913	91.2	25.3	33,764	86.4	18.2
Walton County, Florida	42,956	88.5	30.0	41,693	88.9	29.5	2,400	79.9	11.7
GEORGIA									
Barrow County, Georgia	41,401	86.0	20.3	38,361	87.2	19.3	5,294	83.0	11.3
Bartow County, Georgia	60,489	83.0	19.9	56,734	83.5	19.1	6,929	86.5	17.2
Bibb County, Georgia	45,131	89.9	33.6	43,758	90.0	33.9	49,868	80.0	17.9
Bulloch County, Georgia	28,717	87.8	31.4	28,354	87.6	30.5	10,460	78.5	14.2
Carroll County, Georgia	57,258	83.0	23.0	54,996	83.7	23.1	11,339	82.7	12.9
Catoosa County, Georgia	43,105	89.2	23.3	42,523	89.1	22.6	N	N	N
Chatham County, Georgia	110,428	91.8	40.3	104,910	92.4	40.1	69,538	86.2	17.1
Cherokee County, Georgia	142,699	91.6	38.3	133,882	93.5	39.3	9,771	96.4	34.5
Clarke County, Georgia	43,680	90.9	50.5	38,752	96.9	54.2	20,519	83.0	18.9
Clayton County, Georgia	30,441	76.7	15.0	24,212	81.7	15.4	118,183	92.6	22.1
Cobb County, Georgia	311,450	92.5	50.0	285,395	94.2	52.3	129,000	93.1	40.3
Columbia County, Georgia	73,016	94.0	34.1	70,198	94.5	34.4	16,536	96.1	35.5
Coweta County, Georgia	72,733	90.0	31.0	69,353	91.0	30.5	15,409	84.8	23.2
DeKalb County, Georgia	188,382	91.1	63.9	164,875	96.8	69.6	263,215	89.5	27.7
Dougherty County, Georgia	18,506	90.3	29.3	17,548	90.5	29.2	37,396	82.0	17.2
Douglas County, Georgia	47,283	85.0	18.2	43,416	86.6	18.8	39,531	94.6	36.7
Fayette County, Georgia	54,188	95.1	46.8	50,346	96.4	48.9	16,348	96.0	51.7
Floyd County, Georgia	50,499	85.8	26.9	48,470	86.5	27.6	9,630	74.2	10.2
Forsyth County, Georgia	117,794	92.4	46.7	108,907	94.5	47.7	4,475	94.9	61.5
Fulton County, Georgia	328,616	95.6	66.8	302,259	97.5	69.6	287,694	88.7	30.4
Glynn County, Georgia	42,389	85.9	30.3	39,805	88.8	31.2	13,002	79.4	17.4
Gwinnett County, Georgia	296,602	90.9	36.5	247,532	96.1	40.2	147,422	92.8	33.2
Hall County, Georgia	112,579	77.9	22.8	88,139	87.6	27.5	8,922	81.1	8.0
Henry County, Georgia	76,183	88.2	24.8	70,260	90.5	25.9	58,516	90.8	34.3
Houston County, Georgia	64,684	91.1	30.0	61,011	93.5	31.5	29,275	87.1	24.5
Liberty County, Georgia	16,951	91.3	15.6	14,967	91.6	17.3	14,875	89.7	17.6
Lowndes County, Georgia	41,790	92.4	30.9	39,164	93.2	31.9	24,072	78.7	12.7
Muscogee County, Georgia	60,096	91.4	35.3	56,891	91.9	35.7	56,526	84.4	17.8
Newton County, Georgia	37,561	78.7	17.9	35,175	83.0	18.7	28,316	84.1	15.4

N = Data for this geographic area cannot be displayed because the number of sample cases is too small.

Table C-2. Educational Attainment of the Population, by Selected Counties, 2016—*Continued*

(Number; percent; dollars.)

State/County	Educational attainment by race/ethnicity, 25 years and over								
	American Indian or Alaska Native alone			Asian alone			Native Hawaiian or Other Pacific Islander alone		
	Total	High school graduate or more	Bachelor's degree or more	Total	High school graduate or more	Bachelor's degree or more	Total	High school graduate or more	Bachelor's degree or more
FLORIDA—*(Continued)*									
Clay County, Florida	N	N	N	4,348	86.3	38.0	N	N	N
Collier County, Florida	N	N	N	3,338	91.3	49.5	N	N	N
Columbia County, Florida	N	N	N	N	N	N	N	N	N
Duval County, Florida	N	N	N	31,233	88.5	49.2	N	N	N
Escambia County, Florida	N	N	N	6,036	87.3	43.8	N	N	N
Flagler County, Florida	N	N	N	N	N	N	N	N	N
Hernando County, Florida	N	N	N	N	N	N	N	N	N
Highlands County, Florida	N	N	N	N	N	N	N	N	N
Hillsborough County, Florida	2,679	81.4	21.4	38,677	88.8	58.3	N	N	N
Indian River County, Florida	N	N	N	N	N	N	N	N	N
Lake County, Florida	N	N	N	5,268	98.2	57.1	N	N	N
Lee County, Florida	N	N	N	8,132	92.8	43.3	N	N	N
Leon County, Florida	N	N	N	N	N	N	N	N	N
Manatee County, Florida	N	N	N	5,480	89.4	51.2	N	N	N
Marion County, Florida	N	N	N	3,072	79.0	29.5	N	N	N
Martin County, Florida	N	N	N	N	N	N	N	N	N
Miami-Dade County, Florida	N	N	N	33,080	82.3	46.3	N	N	N
Monroe County, Florida	N	N	N	N	N	N	N	N	N
Nassau County, Florida	N	N	N	N	N	N	N	N	N
Okaloosa County, Florida	N	N	N	4,739	79.9	42.4	N	N	N
Orange County, Florida	N	N	N	48,831	87.7	58.2	N	N	N
Osceola County, Florida	N	N	N	7,014	75.7	31.8	N	N	N
Palm Beach County, Florida	N	N	N	28,326	85.2	44.9	N	N	N
Pasco County, Florida	N	N	N	8,832	89.2	54.4	N	N	N
Pinellas County, Florida	2,538	96.4	19.4	24,371	78.7	39.0	N	N	N
Polk County, Florida	N	N	N	9,717	80.2	49.6	N	N	N
Putnam County, Florida	N	N	N	N	N	N	N	N	N
St. Johns County, Florida	N	N	N	N	N	N	N	N	N
St. Lucie County, Florida	N	N	N	N	N	N	N	N	N
Santa Rosa County, Florida	N	N	N	2,801	86.8	15.0	N	N	N
Sarasota County, Florida	N	N	N	4,996	76.6	35.7	N	N	N
Seminole County, Florida	N	N	N	13,787	91.2	45.6	N	N	N
Sumter County, Florida	N	N	N	N	N	N	N	N	N
Volusia County, Florida	N	N	N	6,606	93.2	58.2	N	N	N
Walton County, Florida	N	N	N	N	N	N	N	N	N
GEORGIA									
Barrow County, Georgia	N	N	N	1,562	66.0	9.5	N	N	N
Bartow County, Georgia	N	N	N	N	N	N	N	N	N
Bibb County, Georgia	N	N	N	1,691	67.4	51.2	N	N	N
Bulloch County, Georgia	N	N	N	N	N	N	N	N	N
Carroll County, Georgia	N	N	N	N	N	N	N	N	N
Catoosa County, Georgia	N	N	N	N	N	N	N	N	N
Chatham County, Georgia	N	N	N	4,955	85.5	57.6	N	N	N
Cherokee County, Georgia	N	N	N	3,387	89.6	59.6	N	N	N
Clarke County, Georgia	N	N	N	N	N	N	N	N	N
Clayton County, Georgia	N	N	N	10,317	68.8	33.6	N	N	N
Cobb County, Georgia	N	N	N	27,574	92.4	66.4	N	N	N
Columbia County, Georgia	N	N	N	5,023	87.5	65.6	N	N	N
Coweta County, Georgia	N	N	N	N	N	N	N	N	N
DeKalb County, Georgia	2,966	61.9	5.3	30,987	81.5	60.3	N	N	N
Dougherty County, Georgia	N	N	N	N	N	N	N	N	N
Douglas County, Georgia	N	N	N	N	N	N	N	N	N
Fayette County, Georgia	N	N	N	3,381	95.9	64.1	N	N	N
Floyd County, Georgia	N	N	N	N	N	N	N	N	N
Forsyth County, Georgia	N	N	N	16,268	92.3	76.1	N	N	N
Fulton County, Georgia	5,034	52.5	6.6	47,049	95.9	77.4	N	N	N
Glynn County, Georgia	N	N	N	N	N	N	N	N	N
Gwinnett County, Georgia	N	N	N	71,560	83.0	46.5	N	N	N
Hall County, Georgia	N	N	N	2,147	73.4	37.4	N	N	N
Henry County, Georgia	N	N	N	5,510	89.7	43.5	N	N	N
Houston County, Georgia	N	N	N	N	N	N	N	N	N
Liberty County, Georgia	N	N	N	N	N	N	N	N	N
Lowndes County, Georgia	N	N	N	N	N	N	N	N	N
Muscogee County, Georgia	N	N	N	3,177	90.1	42.5	N	N	N
Newton County, Georgia	N	N	N	N	N	N	N	N	N

N = Data for this geographic area cannot be displayed because the number of sample cases is too small.

Table C-2. Educational Attainment of the Population, by Selected Counties, 2016—*Continued*

(Number; percent; dollars.)

	Educational attainment by race/ethnicity, 25 years and over								
	White alone			White alone, not Hispanic			Black alone		
State/County	Total	High school graduate or more	Bachelor's degree or more	Total	High school graduate or more	Bachelor's degree or more	Total	High school graduate or more	Bachelor's degree or more
GEORGIA—(*Continued*)									
Paulding County, Georgia	77,438	90.2	22.5	75,484	90.5	22.3	18,163	95.4	27.9
Richmond County, Georgia	54,351	83.5	24.7	51,162	84.0	25.7	70,889	84.6	19.0
Rockdale County, Georgia	26,183	87.2	22.5	23,239	90.7	24.9	29,608	92.0	25.9
Troup County, Georgia	28,381	82.4	26.4	27,547	82.9	26.9	15,297	71.6	9.4
Walker County, Georgia	44,349	77.4	16.0	43,996	77.3	16.1	N	N	N
Walton County, Georgia	48,181	89.0	23.9	47,252	89.6	24.1	8,190	72.9	16.2
Whitfield County, Georgia	58,633	68.9	13.0	44,567	79.4	15.9	2,754	80.9	3.8
HAWAII									
Hawaii County, Hawaii	54,778	94.8	36.6	51,210	95.1	38.4	N	N	N
Honolulu County, Hawaii	146,889	97.0	45.7	133,192	97.1	47.9	14,856	94.9	24.9
Kauai County, Hawaii	18,502	97.9	47.1	17,458	97.7	48.6	N	N	N
Maui County, Hawaii	48,147	96.1	37.5	42,281	98.0	41.1	N	N	N
IDAHO									
Ada County, Idaho	274,867	95.7	38.2	261,725	96.2	39.1	N	N	N
Bannock County, Idaho	48,422	92.2	28.5	46,524	93.6	29.7	N	N	N
Bonneville County, Idaho	61,471	94.9	33.4	59,032	95.5	34.3	N	N	N
Canyon County, Idaho	111,809	87.8	21.0	99,838	90.3	22.9	N	N	N
Kootenai County, Idaho	100,673	92.4	25.6	98,867	92.3	25.6	N	N	N
Twin Falls County, Idaho	49,568	90.7	22.9	44,811	93.2	24.3	N	N	N
ILLINOIS									
Adams County, Illinois	43,648	92.1	25.9	43,342	92.3	25.6	N	N	N
Champaign County, Illinois	94,128	96.7	46.1	89,469	97.0	45.9	13,468	88.6	22.3
Cook County, Illinois	2,114,221	89.8	43.8	1,689,031	94.4	50.5	806,725	86.7	22.7
DeKalb County, Illinois	54,105	93.1	32.9	51,268	92.8	34.0	N	N	N
DuPage County, Illinois	499,838	94.3	48.1	451,718	96.7	51.0	28,064	94.0	31.0
Kane County, Illinois	256,621	91.2	39.5	220,657	95.7	44.3	17,010	88.2	16.6
Kankakee County, Illinois	59,751	89.8	19.5	55,836	92.2	20.6	9,645	74.6	14.7
Kendall County, Illinois	64,584	92.5	37.0	57,952	94.8	38.4	4,184	92.4	34.5
Lake County, Illinois	356,530	93.3	46.2	308,652	97.0	51.0	28,618	87.6	24.6
LaSalle County, Illinois	74,217	89.2	19.1	69,240	91.1	20.0	1,679	59.8	0.0
McHenry County, Illinois	192,175	93.1	33.1	175,843	94.9	34.6	2,400	98.3	44.8
McLean County, Illinois	88,978	97.4	42.4	86,268	97.4	43.0	8,203	93.9	30.8
Macon County, Illinois	60,546	92.2	23.1	59,553	92.4	23.3	8,156	78.4	11.8
Madison County, Illinois	167,478	92.9	27.2	164,131	92.8	27.4	13,044	90.0	13.8
Peoria County, Illinois	97,572	92.4	32.8	94,469	92.9	32.9	18,535	78.2	7.2
Rock Island County, Illinois	84,999	90.9	23.7	78,253	92.2	24.7	8,391	85.2	16.4
St. Clair County, Illinois	121,600	93.8	31.4	118,476	94.1	31.2	48,608	87.9	18.8
Sangamon County, Illinois	117,607	93.0	36.6	116,215	93.0	36.5	13,341	84.8	23.7
Tazewell County, Illinois	90,920	92.1	24.1	89,458	92.1	24.4	N	N	N
Vermilion County, Illinois	45,498	89.7	14.9	44,368	90.1	15.3	5,864	77.3	5.0
Will County, Illinois	341,037	93.3	35.8	307,627	95.3	37.3	47,821	91.3	27.2
Williamson County, Illinois	44,312	91.3	25.2	43,947	91.3	25.4	N	N	N
Winnebago County, Illinois	161,671	88.0	22.4	147,967	90.1	24.0	21,472	77.5	16.3
INDIANA									
Allen County, Indiana	200,414	91.9	30.8	190,469	92.8	31.7	24,295	82.4	15.9
Bartholomew County, Indiana	47,376	89.4	29.7	46,462	89.4	29.3	N	N	N
Clark County, Indiana	72,146	88.8	21.4	69,949	90.1	22.1	5,528	92.1	7.6
Delaware County, Indiana	64,403	90.4	22.4	63,937	90.5	22.3	3,935	90.0	19.1
Elkhart County, Indiana	117,935	79.5	19.3	104,634	83.7	21.1	6,730	78.4	11.2
Floyd County, Indiana	49,130	90.2	28.5	48,203	90.0	29.0	2,116	83.2	19.4
Grant County, Indiana	39,849	86.7	16.9	38,996	86.4	17.1	3,405	72.9	10.6
Hamilton County, Indiana	182,032	96.6	57.0	176,094	96.8	57.1	8,202	93.9	53.1
Hancock County, Indiana	48,799	94.0	30.6	48,383	94.0	30.6	N	N	N
Hendricks County, Indiana	95,066	93.9	39.7	93,429	94.2	39.5	7,878	78.3	12.9
Howard County, Indiana	51,402	91.2	22.3	50,597	91.0	21.7	4,235	94.5	8.5
Johnson County, Indiana	93,335	91.2	32.1	92,692	91.6	32.2	N	N	N
Kosciusko County, Indiana	50,889	81.2	20.5	47,973	83.1	21.0	N	N	N
Lake County, Indiana	214,772	91.2	25.5	193,525	92.4	26.3	73,134	88.2	13.6
LaPorte County, Indiana	66,408	91.5	19.8	64,005	91.8	20.3	7,359	82.2	4.4
Madison County, Indiana	80,544	88.2	17.5	78,698	88.6	17.6	6,361	81.9	12.4
Marion County, Indiana	411,018	89.4	36.1	385,108	91.1	37.6	157,736	86.3	16.0
Monroe County, Indiana	73,667	91.3	42.5	72,826	91.4	42.4	N	N	N
Morgan County, Indiana	47,294	89.7	16.0	46,747	89.6	16.2	N	N	N

N = Data for this geographic area cannot be displayed because the number of sample cases is too small.

Table C-2. Educational Attainment of the Population, by Selected Counties, 2016—*Continued*

(Number; percent; dollars.)

	Educational attainment by race/ethnicity, 25 years and over								
	American Indian or Alaska Native alone			Asian alone			Native Hawaiian or Other Pacific Islander alone		
State/County	Total	High school graduate or more	Bachelor's degree or more	Total	High school graduate or more	Bachelor's degree or more	Total	High school graduate or more	Bachelor's degree or more
GEORGIA—*(Continued)*									
Paulding County, Georgia....................	N	N	N	N	N	N	N	N	N
Richmond County, Georgia	N	N	N	2,783	85.9	59.0	N	N	N
Rockdale County, Georgia	N	N	N	N	N	N	N	N	N
Troup County, Georgia	N	N	N	N	N	N	N	N	N
Walker County, Georgia......................	N	N	N	N	N	N	N	N	N
Walton County, Georgia	N	N	N	N	N	N	N	N	N
Whitfield County, Georgia	N	N	N	N	N	N	N	N	N
HAWAII									
Hawaii County, Hawaii........................	N	N	N	37,161	91.7	29.9	16,395	91.2	13.1
Honolulu County, Hawaii.....................	N	N	N	332,054	89.1	37.1	56,996	84.9	13.3
Kauai County, Hawaii..........................	N	N	N	18,658	89.4	21.3	3,493	81.7	11.7
Maui County, Hawaii...........................	N	N	N	38,822	87.9	20.2	12,272	95.7	8.8
IDAHO									
Ada County, Idaho..............................	N	N	N	8,001	87.8	43.3	N	N	N
Bannock County, Idaho	N	N	N	N	N	N	N	N	N
Bonneville County, Idaho....................	N	N	N	N	N	N	N	N	N
Canyon County, Idaho.........................	N	N	N	N	N	N	N	N	N
Kootenai County, Idaho.......................	N	N	N	N	N	N	N	N	N
Twin Falls County, Idaho	N	N	N	N	N	N	N	N	N
ILLINOIS									
Adams County, Illinois........................	N	N	N	N	N	N	N	N	N
Champaign County, Illinois..................	N	N	N	10,041	94.0	75.9	N	N	N
Cook County, Illinois	9,287	70.6	18.5	269,867	89.5	63.2	N	N	N
DeKalb County, Illinois.......................	N	N	N	N	N	N	N	N	N
DuPage County, Illinois.......................	N	N	N	73,825	91.6	70.3	N	N	N
Kane County, Illinois	N	N	N	14,157	88.7	55.1	N	N	N
Kankakee County, Illinois....................	N	N	N	N	N	N	N	N	N
Kendall County, Illinois.......................	N	N	N	N	N	N	N	N	N
Lake County, Illinois...........................	N	N	N	36,131	94.0	73.4	N	N	N
LaSalle County, Illinois.......................	N	N	N	N	N	N	N	N	N
McHenry County, Illinois.....................	N	N	N	6,176	93.1	61.4	N	N	N
McLean County, Illinois.......................	N	N	N	N	N	N	N	N	N
Macon County, Illinois........................	N	N	N	N	N	N	N	N	N
Madison County, Illinois......................	N	N	N	N	N	N	N	N	N
Peoria County, Illinois	N	N	N	N	N	N	N	N	N
Rock Island County, Illinois.................	N	N	N	2,251	67.1	28.1	N	N	N
St. Clair County, Illinois......................	N	N	N	2,815	95.5	69.1	N	N	N
Sangamon County, Illinois...................	N	N	N	2,603	91.3	51.1	N	N	N
Tazewell County, Illinois.....................	N	N	N	N	N	N	N	N	N
Vermilion County, Illinois....................	N	N	N	N	N	N	N	N	N
Will County, Illinois............................	N	N	N	24,547	94.4	67.3	N	N	N
Williamson County, Illinois..................	N	N	N	N	N	N	N	N	N
Winnebago County, Illinois..................	N	N	N	4,572	83.9	48.7	N	N	N
INDIANA									
Allen County, Indiana	N	N	N	8,042	54.7	31.7	N	N	N
Bartholomew County, Indiana	N	N	N	N	N	N	N	N	N
Clark County, Indiana	N	N	N	N	N	N	N	N	N
Delaware County, Indiana...................	N	N	N	N	N	N	N	N	N
Elkhart County, Indiana	N	N	N	1,607	83.6	30.4	N	N	N
Floyd County, Indiana.........................	N	N	N	N	N	N	N	N	N
Grant County, Indiana	N	N	N	N	N	N	N	N	N
Hamilton County, Indiana....................	N	N	N	12,312	87.4	73.7	N	N	N
Hancock County, Indiana.....................	N	N	N	N	N	N	N	N	N
Hendricks County, Indiana	N	N	N	N	N	N	N	N	N
Howard County, Indiana......................	N	N	N	N	N	N	N	N	N
Johnson County, Indiana.....................	N	N	N	3,452	71.2	30.7	N	N	N
Kosciusko County, Indiana..................	N	N	N	N	N	N	N	N	N
Lake County, Indiana..........................	N	N	N	4,924	94.2	50.7	N	N	N
LaPorte County, Indiana......................	N	N	N	N	N	N	N	N	N
Madison County, Indiana.....................	N	N	N	N	N	N	N	N	N
Marion County, Indiana.......................	N	N	N	17,502	75.6	43.3	N	N	N
Monroe County, Indiana......................	N	N	N	N	N	N	N	N	N
Morgan County, Indiana......................	N	N	N	N	N	N	N	N	N

N = Data for this geographic area cannot be displayed because the number of sample cases is too small.

Table C-2. Educational Attainment of the Population, by Selected Counties, 2016—*Continued*

(Number; percent; dollars.)

	Educational attainment by race/ethnicity, 25 years and over								
	White alone			White alone, not Hispanic			Black alone		
State/County	Total	High school graduate or more	Bachelor's degree or more	Total	High school graduate or more	Bachelor's degree or more	Total	High school graduate or more	Bachelor's degree or more
INDIANA—*(Continued)*									
Porter County, Indiana	106,307	91.8	25.3	99,364	92.9	26.2	3,514	95.6	17.4
St. Joseph County, Indiana	144,456	90.1	30.1	138,108	91.0	30.7	18,900	74.9	13.5
Tippecanoe County, Indiana	88,488	92.4	36.9	84,818	93.2	37.9	4,366	97.3	13.9
Vanderburgh County, Indiana	109,854	88.1	26.4	108,381	88.5	26.6	9,382	85.6	19.8
Vigo County, Indiana	61,937	89.8	26.3	61,053	89.8	26.4	3,850	76.9	17.5
Wayne County, Indiana	42,176	87.8	17.3	41,936	88.1	17.4	N	N	N
IOWA									
Black Hawk County, Iowa	73,462	92.5	27.5	71,890	92.7	27.5	6,659	85.1	29.4
Dallas County, Iowa	50,419	95.3	49.2	48,644	98.2	50.7	N	N	N
Dubuque County, Iowa	61,970	93.3	29.4	61,079	93.4	29.6	N	N	N
Johnson County, Iowa	72,741	95.9	55.6	71,180	96.2	55.9	5,050	89.6	24.2
Linn County, Iowa	137,382	95.1	35.4	134,391	95.3	35.5	6,319	76.6	16.8
Polk County, Iowa	272,388	92.9	37.4	260,446	94.5	38.4	18,122	80.1	18.7
Pottawattamie County, Iowa	60,455	91.7	21.5	57,818	92.0	22.1	N	N	N
Scott County, Iowa	103,304	94.3	31.7	98,373	95.0	32.5	7,176	85.1	14.4
Story County, Iowa	44,826	97.6	50.3	43,676	97.7	50.7	N	N	N
Woodbury County, Iowa	58,314	87.1	22.8	52,726	91.4	24.8	N	N	N
KANSAS									
Butler County, Kansas	41,369	91.9	29.1	40,232	92.2	28.9	N	N	N
Douglas County, Kansas	58,346	95.2	52.3	56,835	95.7	52.9	N	N	N
Johnson County, Kansas	348,060	96.1	55.7	328,919	97.7	57.1	16,868	95.0	38.4
Leavenworth County, Kansas	45,042	95.4	35.2	44,221	95.5	35.5	4,636	81.8	19.8
Riley County, Kansas	30,770	98.1	50.6	29,569	98.6	51.7	N	N	N
Sedgwick County, Kansas	268,887	91.1	33.5	245,711	93.9	35.3	27,002	85.6	17.3
Shawnee County, Kansas	102,255	93.1	32.5	96,071	93.2	33.4	8,045	93.1	12.7
Wyandotte County, Kansas	64,918	79.7	19.5	50,080	87.9	22.8	23,993	85.8	16.8
KENTUCKY									
Boone County, Kentucky	76,734	94.0	30.1	75,593	94.8	30.3	N	N	N
Bullitt County, Kentucky	52,984	86.4	15.7	52,618	86.4	15.6	N	N	N
Campbell County, Kentucky	60,475	92.3	35.9	59,799	92.4	36.1	N	N	N
Christian County, Kentucky	30,576	85.3	18.4	28,978	85.3	18.2	9,326	90.7	6.8
Daviess County, Kentucky	62,906	90.3	22.9	61,782	90.4	22.8	N	N	N
Fayette County, Kentucky	160,414	92.5	48.9	153,883	93.8	50.1	27,878	85.2	14.8
Hardin County, Kentucky	57,839	89.9	23.2	56,208	89.6	22.7	8,585	94.0	20.2
Jefferson County, Kentucky	400,268	91.4	35.5	384,763	91.8	35.6	101,950	86.5	16.6
Kenton County, Kentucky	103,463	89.7	31.6	102,196	89.6	31.3	4,362	83.5	5.4
McCracken County, Kentucky	40,729	89.7	21.8	39,994	90.1	22.2	3,984	82.2	9.3
Madison County, Kentucky	51,110	85.8	28.8	50,362	86.8	29.0	N	N	N
Pike County, Kentucky	39,914	95.0	42.7	38,881	95.9	43.1	N	N	N
Warren County, Kentucky	65,114	90.1	35.1	63,578	90.9	35.3	6,352	83.3	9.0
LOUISIANA									
Ascension Parish, Louisiana	58,559	91.8	26.1	56,075	92.6	26.5	14,154	74.2	23.2
Bossier Parish, Louisiana	62,319	89.9	26.0	58,693	91.1	27.5	16,965	84.4	25.2
Caddo Parish, Louisiana	84,639	92.5	30.0	83,020	92.6	29.7	76,378	78.9	12.8
Calcasieu Parish, Louisiana	97,166	88.6	20.6	95,074	88.3	20.7	30,531	76.8	18.9
East Baton Rouge Parish, Louisiana	144,162	95.1	46.5	139,409	95.7	47.3	120,658	86.6	18.1
Iberia Parish, Louisiana	30,748	81.7	17.3	30,276	82.2	17.4	12,308	77.0	8.5
Jefferson Parish, Louisiana	202,631	88.2	29.8	177,033	90.1	31.5	73,925	78.9	14.8
Lafayette Parish, Louisiana	118,798	92.0	37.8	112,738	93.0	39.2	37,146	78.4	12.9
Lafourche Parish, Louisiana	54,566	81.4	19.7	53,582	81.1	20.0	8,053	57.9	7.8
Livingston Parish, Louisiana	84,284	84.1	17.5	82,809	84.6	17.8	5,265	90.8	11.4
Orleans Parish, Louisiana	106,024	96.1	65.7	96,494	97.2	67.5	153,157	79.0	19.4
Ouachita Parish, Louisiana	65,802	89.2	25.7	64,297	89.3	26.0	33,549	74.9	11.3
Rapides Parish, Louisiana	58,429	90.0	22.9	56,952	90.7	23.1	25,266	77.4	16.3
St. Landry Parish, Louisiana	30,967	76.5	17.4	30,738	76.6	17.1	21,734	75.9	10.2
St. Tammany Parish, Louisiana	146,844	91.4	33.3	140,997	91.7	33.7	18,238	85.8	18.0
Tangipahoa Parish, Louisiana	61,406	82.7	22.7	58,341	82.6	21.8	20,472	70.4	10.3
Terrebonne Parish, Louisiana	55,594	82.6	16.6	53,464	83.3	17.1	12,055	76.4	12.9
MAINE									
Androscoggin County, Maine	71,052	91.4	22.3	70,417	91.4	22.4	1,569	51.3	8.7
Aroostook County, Maine	48,283	87.6	20.1	48,078	87.6	19.9	N	N	N
Cumberland County, Maine	197,220	95.6	46.4	195,304	95.7	46.3	3,764	91.0	29.6
Kennebec County, Maine	83,410	91.0	26.5	83,092	91.1	26.4	N	N	N

N = Data for this geographic area cannot be displayed because the number of sample cases is too small.

Table C-2. Educational Attainment of the Population, by Selected Counties, 2016—*Continued*

(Number; percent; dollars.)

State/County	Educational attainment by race/ethnicity, 25 years and over								
	American Indian or Alaska Native alone			Asian alone			Native Hawaiian or Other Pacific Islander alone		
	Total	High school graduate or more	Bachelor's degree or more	Total	High school graduate or more	Bachelor's degree or more	Total	High school graduate or more	Bachelor's degree or more
INDIANA—*(Continued)*									
Porter County, Indiana	N	N	N	N	N	N	N	N	N
St. Joseph County, Indiana	N	N	N	N	N	N	N	N	N
Tippecanoe County, Indiana	N	N	N	N	N	N	N	N	N
Vanderburgh County, Indiana	N	N	N	N	N	N	N	N	N
Vigo County, Indiana	N	N	N	1,044	92.1	50.4	N	N	N
Wayne County, Indiana	N	N	N	N	N	N	N	N	N
IOWA									
Black Hawk County, Iowa	N	N	N	N	N	N	N	N	N
Dallas County, Iowa	N	N	N	N	N	N	N	N	N
Dubuque County, Iowa	N	N	N	N	N	N	N	N	N
Johnson County, Iowa	N	N	N	N	N	N	N	N	N
Linn County, Iowa	N	N	N	N	N	N	N	N	N
Polk County, Iowa	N	N	N	13,244	74.8	35.3	N	N	N
Pottawattamie County, Iowa	N	N	N	N	N	N	N	N	N
Scott County, Iowa	N	N	N	3,164	80.9	48.8	N	N	N
Story County, Iowa	N	N	N	N	N	N	N	N	N
Woodbury County, Iowa	N	N	N	N	N	N	N	N	N
KANSAS									
Butler County, Kansas	N	N	N	N	N	N	N	N	N
Douglas County, Kansas	N	N	N	N	N	N	N	N	N
Johnson County, Kansas	N	N	N	18,334	94.1	67.3	N	N	N
Leavenworth County, Kansas	N	N	N	N	N	N	N	N	N
Riley County, Kansas	N	N	N	N	N	N	N	N	N
Sedgwick County, Kansas	3,292	79.6	14.9	14,213	79.8	36.4	N	N	N
Shawnee County, Kansas	N	N	N	N	N	N	N	N	N
Wyandotte County, Kansas	N	N	N	3,531	70.4	33.1	N	N	N
KENTUCKY									
Boone County, Kentucky	N	N	N	N	N	N	N	N	N
Bullitt County, Kentucky	N	N	N	N	N	N	N	N	N
Campbell County, Kentucky	N	N	N	N	N	N	N	N	N
Christian County, Kentucky	N	N	N	N	N	N	N	N	N
Daviess County, Kentucky	N	N	N	N	N	N	N	N	N
Fayette County, Kentucky	N	N	N	8,027	88.9	70.4	N	N	N
Hardin County, Kentucky	N	N	N	N	N	N	N	N	N
Jefferson County, Kentucky	N	N	N	13,804	83.6	53.5	N	N	N
Kenton County, Kentucky	N	N	N	N	N	N	N	N	N
McCracken County, Kentucky	N	N	N	N	N	N	N	N	N
Madison County, Kentucky	N	N	N	N	N	N	N	N	N
Pike County, Kentucky	N	N	N	N	N	N	N	N	N
Warren County, Kentucky	N	N	N	2,226	70.5	26.7	N	N	N
LOUISIANA									
Ascension Parish, Louisiana	N	N	N	N	N	N	N	N	N
Bossier Parish, Louisiana	N	N	N	N	N	N	N	N	N
Caddo Parish, Louisiana	N	N	N	N	N	N	N	N	N
Calcasieu Parish, Louisiana	N	N	N	N	N	N	N	N	N
East Baton Rouge Parish, Louisiana	N	N	N	10,137	88.1	64.8	N	N	N
Iberia Parish, Louisiana	N	N	N	N	N	N	N	N	N
Jefferson Parish, Louisiana	N	N	N	12,864	85.2	36.8	N	N	N
Lafayette Parish, Louisiana	N	N	N	N	N	N	N	N	N
Lafourche Parish, Louisiana	1,689	60.1	6.3	N	N	N	N	N	N
Livingston Parish, Louisiana	N	N	N	N	N	N	N	N	N
Orleans Parish, Louisiana	N	N	N	8,490	75.4	40.5	N	N	N
Ouachita Parish, Louisiana	N	N	N	N	N	N	N	N	N
Rapides Parish, Louisiana	N	N	N	N	N	N	N	N	N
St. Landry Parish, Louisiana	N	N	N	N	N	N	N	N	N
St. Tammany Parish, Louisiana	N	N	N	N	N	N	N	N	N
Tangipahoa Parish, Louisiana	N	N	N	N	N	N	N	N	N
Terrebonne Parish, Louisiana	3,850	65.7	0.0	N	N	N	N	N	N
MAINE									
Androscoggin County, Maine	N	N	N	N	N	N	N	N	N
Aroostook County, Maine	N	N	N	N	N	N	N	N	N
Cumberland County, Maine	N	N	N	4,373	86.1	38.9	N	N	N
Kennebec County, Maine	N	N	N	N	N	N	N	N	N

N = Data for this geographic area cannot be displayed because the number of sample cases is too small.

Table C-2. Educational Attainment of the Population, by Selected Counties, 2016—*Continued*

(Number; percent; dollars.)

State/County	White alone			White alone, not Hispanic			Black alone		
	Total	High school graduate or more	Bachelor's degree or more	Total	High school graduate or more	Bachelor's degree or more	Total	High school graduate or more	Bachelor's degree or more
MAINE—(*Continued*)									
Penobscot County, Maine	103,181	93.4	25.0	102,733	93.4	25.0	N	N	N
York County, Maine	143,236	93.2	30.3	141,458	93.3	30.4	N	N	N
MARYLAND									
Allegany County, Maryland	45,390	91.7	19.3	44,722	91.8	19.5	3,976	77.6	1.9
Anne Arundel County, Maryland	296,984	94.5	44.6	282,944	94.6	44.8	60,950	89.1	32.4
Baltimore County, Maryland	375,696	91.2	38.9	359,231	92.2	39.7	152,342	94.4	32.0
Calvert County, Maryland	51,492	95.2	30.5	49,907	95.1	30.3	8,576	85.9	17.5
Carroll County, Maryland	108,576	91.6	33.1	106,229	91.8	33.1	4,165	88.6	36.3
Cecil County, Maryland	63,290	89.1	24.1	62,095	89.6	24.0	4,526	85.1	17.5
Charles County, Maryland	51,494	92.4	26.5	48,128	93.8	27.5	45,051	95.1	27.4
Frederick County, Maryland	140,768	92.4	42.4	131,243	94.8	43.6	15,401	87.7	27.8
Harford County, Maryland	142,234	92.7	36.8	138,827	92.7	36.9	20,414	92.6	31.1
Howard County, Maryland	131,396	96.2	61.9	121,846	97.3	64.3	35,860	96.8	50.9
Montgomery County, Maryland	411,423	94.8	65.3	345,502	98.1	71.6	125,324	94.3	49.1
Prince George's County, Maryland	112,154	86.4	39.0	88,988	92.9	45.2	394,654	93.1	32.3
St. Mary's County, Maryland	60,003	89.4	27.9	57,628	89.9	28.2	11,072	79.4	16.4
Washington County, Maryland	90,420	86.7	20.4	87,658	87.7	20.7	10,975	75.6	14.0
Wicomico County, Maryland	44,424	89.0	26.8	43,064	90.9	27.5	17,025	91.8	17.7
Baltimore city, Maryland	143,796	88.3	53.8	132,237	90.3	55.8	255,214	83.2	15.9
MASSACHUSETTS									
Barnstable County, Massachusetts	155,072	96.4	44.3	152,103	96.9	44.7	3,303	88.9	11.6
Berkshire County, Massachusetts	88,033	91.7	34.2	85,618	91.9	34.8	N	N	N
Bristol County, Massachusetts	341,841	86.4	30.1	335,251	86.5	30.2	12,385	90.4	27.3
Essex County, Massachusetts	452,998	91.3	41.2	411,739	93.8	44.0	18,782	84.5	23.0
Franklin County, Massachusetts	50,000	94.5	36.1	49,158	94.7	36.0	N	N	N
Hampden County, Massachusetts	269,521	86.5	27.6	221,022	91.2	31.1	25,558	85.1	19.4
Hampshire County, Massachusetts	91,881	94.4	46.6	88,323	94.8	46.3	2,739	93.6	14.4
Middlesex County, Massachusetts	878,973	94.8	56.4	840,363	95.5	57.2	53,797	87.4	29.6
Norfolk County, Massachusetts	390,194	96.1	53.7	379,098	96.3	53.9	28,417	89.3	35.0
Plymouth County, Massachusetts	306,942	94.8	38.4	300,938	95.2	38.7	27,549	79.5	21.0
Suffolk County, Massachusetts	315,415	92.0	59.1	271,275	95.5	64.3	116,939	83.2	20.9
Worcester County, Massachusetts	483,817	91.5	35.8	457,061	93.0	37.2	23,596	85.6	37.6
MICHIGAN									
Allegan County, Michigan	74,982	91.2	22.1	71,780	93.1	22.9	N	N	N
Bay County, Michigan	71,867	90.8	18.0	69,671	90.7	18.1	1,740	85.5	8.9
Berrien County, Michigan	88,221	91.4	29.3	85,673	92.2	29.5	12,990	80.7	13.9
Calhoun County, Michigan	77,149	90.7	19.9	74,828	91.4	20.3	9,193	91.6	22.4
Clinton County, Michigan	51,395	95.4	32.7	49,723	95.4	33.2	N	N	N
Eaton County, Michigan	67,920	92.8	24.6	65,313	92.8	24.5	4,266	90.5	36.9
Genesee County, Michigan	217,531	90.9	21.6	212,508	91.3	21.9	50,890	89.6	10.7
Grand Traverse County, Michigan	63,528	95.0	33.2	62,066	94.9	33.8	N	N	N
Ingham County, Michigan	136,516	94.5	39.1	130,199	95.1	39.7	17,721	84.7	25.5
Isabella County, Michigan	34,581	92.3	29.9	34,265	92.3	29.6	N	N	N
Jackson County, Michigan	98,451	92.1	22.4	96,280	92.3	22.6	8,114	74.0	18.3
Kalamazoo County, Michigan	138,781	95.1	39.5	134,939	96.0	40.0	14,826	83.0	24.7
Kent County, Michigan	354,189	92.4	37.5	336,070	94.1	38.6	35,916	84.9	20.9
Lapeer County, Michigan	60,366	89.7	17.3	58,288	90.2	17.3	N	N	N
Lenawee County, Michigan	64,398	91.6	22.3	60,967	92.4	23.1	1,830	73.8	6.6
Livingston County, Michigan	128,086	95.0	34.0	125,848	95.2	34.0	N	N	N
Macomb County, Michigan	514,878	90.9	24.7	506,277	91.1	24.7	60,359	89.5	18.5
Marquette County, Michigan	41,822	94.8	33.6	41,661	94.8	33.6	N	N	N
Midland County, Michigan	55,239	93.9	33.0	54,440	93.9	33.2	N	N	N
Monroe County, Michigan	99,665	91.0	19.1	97,796	91.1	19.1	2,190	88.1	10.9
Muskegon County, Michigan	98,198	91.5	18.1	95,106	91.9	18.4	14,784	77.9	9.4
Oakland County, Michigan	674,294	94.3	46.0	655,919	94.6	46.1	114,748	92.4	30.7
Ottawa County, Michigan	161,547	93.4	32.8	153,482	94.7	33.9	N	N	N
Saginaw County, Michigan	103,352	91.2	25.0	98,020	91.4	25.5	21,391	85.0	9.9
St. Clair County, Michigan	107,073	89.1	16.2	105,199	89.1	16.4	2,343	84.6	18.8
Shiawassee County, Michigan	46,826	93.7	16.1	45,832	93.6	16.0	N	N	N
Van Buren County, Michigan	45,822	90.3	21.1	44,247	91.0	21.6	1,824	82.2	12.3
Washtenaw County, Michigan	174,453	96.7	57.5	168,303	97.0	57.7	25,237	88.4	21.9
Wayne County, Michigan	654,195	88.8	28.2	624,424	89.8	28.9	436,345	82.9	13.5
MINNESOTA									
Anoka County, Minnesota	206,547	95.3	27.6	202,721	95.6	27.9	9,952	89.5	21.4
Blue Earth County, Minnesota	36,524	94.7	33.1	35,724	96.0	33.7	N	N	N

N = Data for this geographic area cannot be displayed because the number of sample cases is too small.

Table C-2. Educational Attainment of the Population, by Selected Counties, 2016—*Continued*

(Number; percent; dollars.)

State/County	American Indian or Alaska Native alone			Asian alone			Native Hawaiian or Other Pacific Islander alone		
	Total	High school graduate or more	Bachelor's degree or more	Total	High school graduate or more	Bachelor's degree or more	Total	High school graduate or more	Bachelor's degree or more
MAINE—*(Continued)*									
Penobscot County, Maine	1,443	89.5	9.8	N	N	N	N	N	N
York County, Maine	N	N	N	3,130	90.4	42.7	N	N	N
MARYLAND									
Allegany County, Maryland	N	N	N	N	N	N	N	N	N
Anne Arundel County, Maryland	N	N	N	14,666	90.3	54.8	N	N	N
Baltimore County, Maryland	N	N	N	34,331	89.1	57.5	N	N	N
Calvert County, Maryland	N	N	N	N	N	N	N	N	N
Carroll County, Maryland	N	N	N	N	N	N	N	N	N
Cecil County, Maryland	N	N	N	N	N	N	N	N	N
Charles County, Maryland	N	N	N	3,336	87.1	39.9	N	N	N
Frederick County, Maryland	N	N	N	7,388	90.3	42.9	N	N	N
Harford County, Maryland	N	N	N	4,467	86.6	54.3	N	N	N
Howard County, Maryland	N	N	N	38,802	94.4	73.4	N	N	N
Montgomery County, Maryland	N	N	N	114,271	92.3	67.3	N	N	N
Prince George's County, Maryland	2,302	79.0	20.5	27,549	86.0	51.8	N	N	N
St. Mary's County, Maryland	N	N	N	2,216	56.2	32.2	N	N	N
Washington County, Maryland	N	N	N	1,472	88.0	39.9	N	N	N
Wicomico County, Maryland	N	N	N	2,124	77.1	53.9	N	N	N
Baltimore city, Maryland	N	N	N	11,012	89.6	66.0	N	N	N
MASSACHUSETTS									
Barnstable County, Massachusetts	N	N	N	N	N	N	N	N	N
Berkshire County, Massachusetts	N	N	N	N	N	N	N	N	N
Bristol County, Massachusetts	N	N	N	8,043	82.2	52.1	N	N	N
Essex County, Massachusetts	N	N	N	18,260	86.5	49.0	N	N	N
Franklin County, Massachusetts	N	N	N	N	N	N	N	N	N
Hampden County, Massachusetts	N	N	N	7,127	77.2	29.1	N	N	N
Hampshire County, Massachusetts	N	N	N	3,095	89.7	40.5	N	N	N
Middlesex County, Massachusetts	1,564	98.0	13.8	125,502	88.9	68.2	N	N	N
Norfolk County, Massachusetts	N	N	N	52,088	83.0	56.8	N	N	N
Plymouth County, Massachusetts	N	N	N	4,166	90.9	63.5	N	N	N
Suffolk County, Massachusetts	N	N	N	46,367	76.9	47.7	N	N	N
Worcester County, Massachusetts	N	N	N	25,882	86.6	57.7	N	N	N
MICHIGAN									
Allegan County, Michigan	N	N	N	N	N	N	N	N	N
Bay County, Michigan	N	N	N	N	N	N	N	N	N
Berrien County, Michigan	N	N	N	N	N	N	N	N	N
Calhoun County, Michigan	N	N	N	N	N	N	N	N	N
Clinton County, Michigan	N	N	N	N	N	N	N	N	N
Eaton County, Michigan	N	N	N	N	N	N	N	N	N
Genesee County, Michigan	N	N	N	2,936	93.9	72.3	N	N	N
Grand Traverse County, Michigan	N	N	N	N	N	N	N	N	N
Ingham County, Michigan	N	N	N	9,686	88.4	68.5	N	N	N
Isabella County, Michigan	732	77.7	10.4	N	N	N	N	N	N
Jackson County, Michigan	N	N	N	N	N	N	N	N	N
Kalamazoo County, Michigan	N	N	N	4,104	92.2	59.3	N	N	N
Kent County, Michigan	N	N	N	11,783	74.9	35.1	N	N	N
Lapeer County, Michigan	N	N	N	N	N	N	N	N	N
Lenawee County, Michigan	N	N	N	N	N	N	N	N	N
Livingston County, Michigan	N	N	N	N	N	N	N	N	N
Macomb County, Michigan	N	N	N	21,391	77.8	46.5	N	N	N
Marquette County, Michigan	N	N	N	N	N	N	N	N	N
Midland County, Michigan	N	N	N	N	N	N	N	N	N
Monroe County, Michigan	N	N	N	N	N	N	N	N	N
Muskegon County, Michigan	N	N	N	N	N	N	N	N	N
Oakland County, Michigan	2,504	89.8	31.8	60,058	95.3	80.0	N	N	N
Ottawa County, Michigan	N	N	N	4,694	85.9	24.6	N	N	N
Saginaw County, Michigan	N	N	N	N	N	N	N	N	N
St. Clair County, Michigan	N	N	N	N	N	N	N	N	N
Shiawassee County, Michigan	N	N	N	N	N	N	N	N	N
Van Buren County, Michigan	N	N	N	N	N	N	N	N	N
Washtenaw County, Michigan	N	N	N	18,078	95.8	81.1	N	N	N
Wayne County, Michigan	3,797	82.3	5.1	36,343	82.9	55.7	N	N	N
MINNESOTA									
Anoka County, Minnesota	1,817	94.1	7.8	8,942	84.3	34.7	N	N	N
Blue Earth County, Minnesota	N	N	N	N	N	N	N	N	N

N = Data for this geographic area cannot be displayed because the number of sample cases is too small.

Table C-2. Educational Attainment of the Population, by Selected Counties, 2016—*Continued*

(Number; percent; dollars.)

| | Educational attainment by race/ethnicity, 25 years and over | | | | | | | | |
| | White alone | | | White alone, not Hispanic | | | Black alone | | |
State/County	Total	High school graduate or more	Bachelor's degree or more	Total	High school graduate or more	Bachelor's degree or more	Total	High school graduate or more	Bachelor's degree or more
MINNESOTA—(*Continued*)									
Carver County, Minnesota	60,508	97.9	49.1	59,292	98.0	49.7	N	N	N
Dakota County, Minnesota	242,513	96.5	42.6	234,641	97.2	43.2	13,870	87.3	25.3
Hennepin County, Minnesota	665,329	96.7	53.7	645,120	97.5	54.5	87,115	81.1	20.5
Olmsted County, Minnesota	90,312	96.0	42.9	87,965	96.8	43.5	4,381	74.2	23.1
Ramsey County, Minnesota	265,300	95.9	47.1	255,040	96.9	48.2	33,863	82.4	18.4
Rice County, Minnesota	37,105	94.0	28.5	36,627	94.3	28.8	N	N	N
St. Louis County, Minnesota	128,300	94.6	28.1	127,516	94.6	28.2	1,562	83.9	14.3
Scott County, Minnesota	79,974	97.1	41.5	78,490	97.3	41.6	N	N	N
Sherburne County, Minnesota	57,062	95.8	26.1	56,562	95.7	26.1	N	N	N
Stearns County, Minnesota	88,771	94.0	26.2	87,771	94.4	26.0	3,725	76.1	7.3
Washington County, Minnesota	150,612	97.0	42.1	147,246	97.4	42.2	5,775	83.0	28.3
Wright County, Minnesota	81,026	95.8	30.7	80,478	95.8	30.7	N	N	N
MISSISSIPPI									
DeSoto County, Mississippi	81,865	91.6	26.0	79,355	92.4	26.3	27,594	90.8	21.1
Forrest County, Mississippi	29,909	91.2	30.8	28,940	91.1	31.0	16,109	85.9	11.7
Harrison County, Mississippi	96,547	88.1	21.5	92,428	88.4	21.8	28,700	86.8	16.9
Hinds County, Mississippi	45,379	95.0	45.4	44,390	95.1	46.0	106,127	85.7	22.8
Jackson County, Mississippi	70,106	90.0	24.8	68,635	90.5	24.9	19,188	89.1	15.6
Jones County, Mississippi	32,051	85.6	23.3	30,852	86.3	24.0	11,757	79.4	6.7
Lauderdale County, Mississippi	30,167	92.7	26.5	29,693	92.6	26.7	20,932	77.3	14.0
Lee County, Mississippi	40,301	87.1	27.9	39,690	87.8	28.2	15,184	74.2	11.9
Madison County, Mississippi	41,558	96.4	58.8	40,876	96.9	59.0	23,207	82.8	23.4
Rankin County, Mississippi	80,113	92.4	32.4	78,965	92.3	32.4	19,690	78.3	17.3
MISSOURI									
Boone County, Missouri	88,484	95.5	45.2	87,281	95.6	45.2	9,540	88.2	19.0
Buchanan County, Missouri	53,833	89.2	24.4	52,406	89.6	24.2	3,493	76.3	4.0
Cape Girardeau County, Missouri	46,372	90.9	31.2	45,733	90.9	31.5	3,054	93.1	12.5
Cass County, Missouri	64,616	93.5	24.1	63,036	94.1	24.5	N	N	N
Christian County, Missouri	54,604	90.2	25.8	53,652	90.0	26.2	N	N	N
Clay County, Missouri	142,103	95.8	34.0	136,745	95.8	35.0	9,084	90.5	38.4
Cole County, Missouri	45,537	92.1	34.5	44,927	92.5	34.7	4,933	89.7	21.8
Franklin County, Missouri	68,683	89.7	23.5	67,951	89.7	23.2	N	N	N
Greene County, Missouri	173,365	92.9	30.8	170,905	93.0	30.8	5,454	87.3	10.8
Jackson County, Missouri	334,433	93.3	36.0	316,090	94.6	37.0	101,949	87.5	17.0
Jasper County, Missouri	71,597	88.2	21.0	68,468	90.1	21.9	N	N	N
Jefferson County, Missouri	149,691	87.4	18.4	147,965	87.5	18.4	N	N	N
Platte County, Missouri	58,752	96.4	43.1	56,453	96.5	43.0	4,005	85.3	27.9
St. Charles County, Missouri	241,738	95.3	38.5	236,570	95.7	38.9	11,665	94.4	41.0
St. Francois County, Missouri	43,416	85.9	14.2	43,389	85.9	14.3	N	N	N
St. Louis County, Missouri	498,982	94.7	48.8	486,892	95.1	49.1	147,977	89.5	21.5
St. Louis city, Missouri	113,290	91.7	48.5	108,173	92.5	49.4	92,964	81.7	15.0
MONTANA									
Cascade County, Montana	50,620	91.4	24.1	49,379	92.2	24.4	N	N	N
Flathead County, Montana	66,129	94.6	30.8	65,576	94.8	31.1	N	N	N
Gallatin County, Montana	64,047	96.0	49.3	62,389	95.9	49.8	N	N	N
Lewis and Clark County, Montana	44,919	96.6	38.6	44,096	96.6	38.2	N	N	N
Missoula County, Montana	71,904	93.8	40.9	70,827	94.3	41.1	N	N	N
Yellowstone County, Montana	100,753	94.0	31.7	97,896	94.4	32.0	N	N	N
NEBRASKA									
Douglas County, Nebraska	299,886	91.6	40.6	273,901	96.1	43.4	35,157	88.1	25.3
Lancaster County, Nebraska	170,999	94.7	41.4	163,560	95.9	41.9	7,081	85.0	17.0
Sarpy County, Nebraska	103,485	95.4	39.8	96,473	96.7	41.3	4,159	89.4	25.0
NEVADA									
Clark County, Nevada	951,120	87.1	23.8	729,108	93.4	28.0	157,322	90.8	18.7
Washoe County, Nevada	254,443	89.5	30.8	218,420	94.4	33.4	6,975	89.6	17.6
NEW HAMPSHIRE									
Cheshire County, New Hampshire	51,206	92.3	33.5	50,717	92.2	33.3	N	N	N
Grafton County, New Hampshire	59,309	92.6	41.5	58,413	93.1	41.7	N	N	N
Hillsborough County, New Hampshire	262,964	92.0	37.0	252,020	93.0	37.7	5,756	84.0	29.8
Merrimack County, New Hampshire	100,956	93.3	35.5	99,926	93.4	35.5	N	N	N

N = Data for this geographic area cannot be displayed because the number of sample cases is too small.

Table C-2. Educational Attainment of the Population, by Selected Counties, 2016—*Continued*

(Number; percent; dollars.)

State/County	Educational attainment by race/ethnicity, 25 years and over								
	American Indian or Alaska Native alone			Asian alone			Native Hawaiian or Other Pacific Islander alone		
	Total	High school graduate or more	Bachelor's degree or more	Total	High school graduate or more	Bachelor's degree or more	Total	High school graduate or more	Bachelor's degree or more
MINNESOTA—(*Continued*)									
Carver County, Minnesota	N	N	N	N	N	N	N	N	N
Dakota County, Minnesota	N	N	N	13,768	79.8	46.4	N	N	N
Hennepin County, Minnesota	5,769	84.6	16.8	55,309	84.5	51.9	N	N	N
Olmsted County, Minnesota	N	N	N	6,172	84.2	59.0	N	N	N
Ramsey County, Minnesota	2,030	78.8	14.8	40,904	67.6	28.4	N	N	N
Rice County, Minnesota	N	N	N	N	N	N	N	N	N
St. Louis County, Minnesota	2,924	83.5	12.8	N	N	N	N	N	N
Scott County, Minnesota	N	N	N	5,283	93.0	46.0	N	N	N
Sherburne County, Minnesota	N	N	N	N	N	N	N	N	N
Stearns County, Minnesota	N	N	N	N	N	N	N	N	N
Washington County, Minnesota	N	N	N	6,913	81.1	52.8	N	N	N
Wright County, Minnesota	N	N	N	N	N	N	N	N	N
MISSISSIPPI									
DeSoto County, Mississippi	N	N	N	N	N	N	N	N	N
Forrest County, Mississippi	N	N	N	N	N	N	N	N	N
Harrison County, Mississippi	N	N	N	3,678	76.4	7.0	N	N	N
Hinds County, Mississippi	N	N	N	N	N	N	N	N	N
Jackson County, Mississippi	N	N	N	N	N	N	N	N	N
Jones County, Mississippi	N	N	N	N	N	N	N	N	N
Lauderdale County, Mississippi	N	N	N	N	N	N	N	N	N
Lee County, Mississippi	N	N	N	N	N	N	N	N	N
Madison County, Mississippi	N	N	N	N	N	N	N	N	N
Rankin County, Mississippi	N	N	N	N	N	N	N	N	N
MISSOURI									
Boone County, Missouri	N	N	N	5,193	96.2	74.5	N	N	N
Buchanan County, Missouri	N	N	N	N	N	N	N	N	N
Cape Girardeau County, Missouri	N	N	N	N	N	N	N	N	N
Cass County, Missouri	N	N	N	N	N	N	N	N	N
Christian County, Missouri	N	N	N	N	N	N	N	N	N
Clay County, Missouri	N	N	N	3,634	69.9	29.7	N	N	N
Cole County, Missouri	N	N	N	N	N	N	N	N	N
Franklin County, Missouri	N	N	N	N	N	N	N	N	N
Greene County, Missouri	N	N	N	2,367	90.0	34.6	N	N	N
Jackson County, Missouri	N	N	N	8,853	81.7	44.7	N	N	N
Jasper County, Missouri	N	N	N	N	N	N	N	N	N
Jefferson County, Missouri	N	N	N	N	N	N	N	N	N
Platte County, Missouri	N	N	N	N	N	N	N	N	N
St. Charles County, Missouri	N	N	N	7,261	94.0	61.7	N	N	N
St. Francois County, Missouri	N	N	N	N	N	N	N	N	N
St. Louis County, Missouri	N	N	N	28,024	90.7	70.7	N	N	N
St. Louis city, Missouri	N	N	N	7,539	89.0	58.3	N	N	N
MONTANA									
Cascade County, Montana	1,565	80.9	6.6	N	N	N	N	N	N
Flathead County, Montana	N	N	N	N	N	N	N	N	N
Gallatin County, Montana	N	N	N	N	N	N	N	N	N
Lewis and Clark County, Montana	N	N	N	N	N	N	N	N	N
Missoula County, Montana	N	N	N	N	N	N	N	N	N
Yellowstone County, Montana	3,230	91.6	34.9	N	N	N	N	N	N
NEBRASKA									
Douglas County, Nebraska	N	N	N	11,633	64.2	41.9	N	N	N
Lancaster County, Nebraska	N	N	N	6,666	78.1	47.0	N	N	N
Sarpy County, Nebraska	N	N	N	2,693	89.2	42.0	N	N	N
NEVADA									
Clark County, Nevada	8,568	84.8	15.8	161,040	90.8	37.7	9,767	93.4	12.4
Washoe County, Nevada	4,166	92.8	8.0	18,645	85.8	42.1	N	N	N
NEW HAMPSHIRE									
Cheshire County, New Hampshire	N	N	N	N	N	N	N	N	N
Grafton County, New Hampshire	N	N	N	N	N	N	N	N	N
Hillsborough County, New Hampshire	N	N	N	9,991	87.7	54.3	N	N	N
Merrimack County, New Hampshire	N	N	N	N	N	N	N	N	N

N = Data for this geographic area cannot be displayed because the number of sample cases is too small.

Table C-2. Educational Attainment of the Population, by Selected Counties, 2016—*Continued*

(Number; percent; dollars.)

State/County	White alone			White alone, not Hispanic			Black alone		
	Total	High school graduate or more	Bachelor's degree or more	Total	High school graduate or more	Bachelor's degree or more	Total	High school graduate or more	Bachelor's degree or more
NEW HAMPSHIRE—*(Continued)*									
Rockingham County, New Hampshire	209,784	94.9	40.2	206,302	95.1	40.2	N	N	N
Strafford County, New Hampshire	78,390	94.3	35.0	76,870	94.3	34.8	N	N	N
NEW JERSEY									
Atlantic County, New Jersey	129,740	91.5	30.5	115,003	94.2	33.3	26,431	85.1	14.8
Bergen County, New Jersey	483,166	91.7	46.4	390,843	94.1	51.1	38,939	92.4	34.5
Burlington County, New Jersey	235,359	94.6	37.6	223,456	94.7	38.1	50,330	93.5	30.8
Camden County, New Jersey	235,266	91.8	35.3	217,702	92.8	36.3	62,557	88.8	20.8
Cape May County, New Jersey	65,583	92.0	32.8	62,299	92.4	33.9	2,406	89.4	11.6
Cumberland County, New Jersey	72,864	77.3	16.0	55,510	86.6	18.9	19,528	79.8	6.0
Essex County, New Jersey	248,154	87.5	45.9	181,776	92.7	54.2	208,921	86.2	19.2
Gloucester County, New Jersey	167,576	93.3	31.2	164,171	93.5	31.4	19,020	92.1	27.6
Hudson County, New Jersey	273,495	84.6	40.4	152,875	92.1	57.7	53,567	87.5	29.1
Hunterdon County, New Jersey	82,087	95.2	51.8	78,030	96.0	53.0	N	N	N
Mercer County, New Jersey	166,195	89.0	43.0	135,552	95.4	49.9	48,818	85.9	20.2
Middlesex County, New Jersey	350,880	88.7	33.6	275,658	93.3	38.2	55,000	93.7	35.7
Monmouth County, New Jersey	366,698	93.6	45.2	341,292	95.4	47.0	30,089	83.7	24.3
Morris County, New Jersey	285,710	94.6	52.7	255,489	96.3	55.9	10,963	92.3	34.2
Ocean County, New Jersey	376,418	92.0	28.9	356,101	93.3	29.7	11,177	84.3	20.9
Passaic County, New Jersey	227,266	84.4	32.8	153,026	91.5	41.4	37,211	85.8	11.3
Salem County, New Jersey	36,258	88.2	20.1	35,097	89.5	20.5	5,356	78.0	6.2
Somerset County, New Jersey	160,229	94.1	48.6	139,007	96.1	52.9	20,514	90.5	37.8
Sussex County, New Jersey	95,652	94.9	33.6	89,805	94.6	33.9	2,002	82.1	24.6
Union County, New Jersey	217,413	87.7	41.5	161,997	92.3	49.5	79,895	90.7	23.7
Warren County, New Jersey	68,904	89.8	30.4	64,600	91.3	31.4	2,924	93.0	36.6
NEW MEXICO									
Bernalillo County, New Mexico	340,983	90.6	37.4	209,733	96.1	47.1	11,674	91.0	30.5
Chaves County, New Mexico	37,682	76.8	23.3	19,434	90.5	30.4	N	N	N
Doña Ana County, New Mexico	117,144	80.1	25.3	43,483	94.7	43.4	N	N	N
Lea County, New Mexico	37,208	69.9	14.2	18,498	88.9	23.7	N	N	N
McKinley County, New Mexico	7,816	85.4	32.0	5,199	87.0	38.1	N	N	N
Otero County, New Mexico	35,260	84.8	19.1	24,624	91.3	24.0	N	N	N
Sandoval County, New Mexico	69,771	93.5	38.9	48,531	96.5	45.4	N	N	N
San Juan County, New Mexico	43,597	90.5	21.0	35,839	93.3	23.8	N	N	N
Santa Fe County, New Mexico	93,859	90.8	43.1	55,038	98.0	60.8	N	N	N
Valencia County, New Mexico	42,066	86.2	18.5	20,150	92.9	23.4	N	N	N
NEW YORK									
Albany County, New York	163,069	94.5	45.4	158,052	94.8	45.9	22,768	78.0	15.4
Bronx County, New York	220,217	73.9	22.8	99,417	86.3	35.6	322,680	77.9	19.7
Broome County, New York	116,192	92.0	30.2	114,686	92.3	30.2	6,688	83.6	18.5
Cattaraugus County, New York	49,765	88.5	19.1	49,371	88.8	19.2	N	N	N
Cayuga County, New York	51,681	89.2	24.5	50,960	89.7	24.8	N	N	N
Chautauqua County, New York	85,044	89.1	21.8	81,793	90.2	22.2	1,734	78.5	16.7
Chemung County, New York	53,971	92.4	27.5	53,300	92.9	27.7	N	N	N
Clinton County, New York	50,430	91.0	22.2	49,946	91.0	21.9	N	N	N
Dutchess County, New York	165,923	91.7	36.7	152,871	92.5	37.1	20,967	78.3	17.3
Erie County, New York	528,498	93.8	35.4	516,671	94.1	35.7	76,137	83.4	15.9
Jefferson County, New York	64,196	91.9	20.9	62,348	92.5	21.1	3,179	85.8	18.9
Kings County, New York	788,349	87.7	50.5	663,751	91.6	56.1	586,918	84.7	24.0
Livingston County, New York	40,017	90.0	26.2	39,502	90.2	26.4	N	N	N
Madison County, New York	46,529	91.4	29.2	45,908	91.2	29.5	N	N	N
Monroe County, New York	411,059	93.1	41.3	389,535	94.0	42.8	67,603	77.1	14.5
Nassau County, New York	664,756	94.0	46.8	599,096	95.7	49.0	106,997	90.9	34.9
New York County, New York	743,429	93.8	75.4	625,117	98.1	83.2	176,242	81.8	29.2
Niagara County, New York	135,819	92.3	25.2	134,239	92.3	25.2	9,233	81.6	11.4
Oneida County, New York	142,270	90.6	27.7	138,392	91.4	28.0	8,113	66.8	12.8
Onondaga County, New York	266,892	93.1	37.3	260,476	93.1	37.0	29,444	78.8	12.2
Ontario County, New York	72,664	93.8	33.8	71,458	93.9	34.1	N	N	N
Orange County, New York	183,307	90.4	30.1	164,160	91.5	31.0	25,442	94.1	25.3
Oswego County, New York	78,287	87.1	17.7	77,239	87.0	17.7	N	N	N
Putnam County, New York	62,155	94.8	44.7	57,340	95.6	46.6	N	N	N
Queens County, New York	677,669	85.2	36.5	456,381	90.6	44.5	292,365	86.5	25.2
Rensselaer County, New York	99,689	92.6	33.7	97,606	92.8	34.1	5,949	86.9	14.4
Richmond County, New York	251,768	90.1	32.2	216,123	92.3	34.7	30,638	86.9	29.1

N = Data for this geographic area cannot be displayed because the number of sample cases is too small.

Table C-2. Educational Attainment of the Population, by Selected Counties, 2016—*Continued*

(Number; percent; dollars.)

State/County	American Indian or Alaska Native alone			Asian alone			Native Hawaiian or Other Pacific Islander alone		
	Total	High school graduate or more	Bachelor's degree or more	Total	High school graduate or more	Bachelor's degree or more	Total	High school graduate or more	Bachelor's degree or more
NEW HAMPSHIRE—(*Continued*)									
Rockingham County, New Hampshire	N	N	N	4,160	96.5	49.3	N	N	N
Strafford County, New Hampshire	N	N	N	N	N	N	N	N	N
NEW JERSEY									
Atlantic County, New Jersey	N	N	N	15,193	83.7	41.0	N	N	N
Bergen County, New Jersey	1,319	85.2	26.8	110,510	95.3	69.8	N	N	N
Burlington County, New Jersey	N	N	N	16,461	90.8	62.3	N	N	N
Camden County, New Jersey	N	N	N	20,185	86.8	50.1	N	N	N
Cape May County, New Jersey	N	N	N	N	N	N	N	N	N
Cumberland County, New Jersey	N	N	N	N	N	N	N	N	N
Essex County, New Jersey	N	N	N	30,184	95.0	67.1	N	N	N
Gloucester County, New Jersey	N	N	N	5,534	81.1	48.0	N	N	N
Hudson County, New Jersey	N	N	N	78,553	93.5	72.6	N	N	N
Hunterdon County, New Jersey	N	N	N	3,385	97.9	68.1	N	N	N
Mercer County, New Jersey	N	N	N	27,544	97.5	87.5	N	N	N
Middlesex County, New Jersey	N	N	N	136,713	93.3	71.0	N	N	N
Monmouth County, New Jersey	N	N	N	24,449	91.0	63.6	N	N	N
Morris County, New Jersey	N	N	N	36,416	92.3	73.2	N	N	N
Ocean County, New Jersey	N	N	N	8,505	92.1	54.2	N	N	N
Passaic County, New Jersey	N	N	N	18,336	86.9	55.0	N	N	N
Salem County, New Jersey	N	N	N	N	N	N	N	N	N
Somerset County, New Jersey	N	N	N	39,808	94.0	77.6	N	N	N
Sussex County, New Jersey	N	N	N	N	N	N	N	N	N
Union County, New Jersey	N	N	N	20,204	93.5	70.4	N	N	N
Warren County, New Jersey	N	N	N	2,166	90.2	53.8	N	N	N
NEW MEXICO									
Bernalillo County, New Mexico	21,473	90.4	21.4	13,274	89.9	44.2	N	N	N
Chaves County, New Mexico	N	N	N	N	N	N	N	N	N
Doña Ana County, New Mexico	N	N	N	N	N	N	N	N	N
Lea County, New Mexico	N	N	N	N	N	N	N	N	N
McKinley County, New Mexico	33,415	71.6	3.7	N	N	N	N	N	N
Otero County, New Mexico	2,363	84.4	10.1	N	N	N	N	N	N
Sandoval County, New Mexico	10,495	82.3	9.5	N	N	N	N	N	N
San Juan County, New Mexico	25,581	79.7	8.1	N	N	N	N	N	N
Santa Fe County, New Mexico	3,208	97.6	41.6	N	N	N	N	N	N
Valencia County, New Mexico	N	N	N	N	N	N	N	N	N
NEW YORK									
Albany County, New York	N	N	N	12,309	82.7	62.3	N	N	N
Bronx County, New York	5,242	68.4	11.0	37,452	82.1	39.4	N	N	N
Broome County, New York	N	N	N	3,915	83.3	43.6	N	N	N
Cattaraugus County, New York	1,451	87.5	8.8	N	N	N	N	N	N
Cayuga County, New York	N	N	N	N	N	N	N	N	N
Chautauqua County, New York	N	N	N	N	N	N	N	N	N
Chemung County, New York	N	N	N	N	N	N	N	N	N
Clinton County, New York	N	N	N	N	N	N	N	N	N
Dutchess County, New York	N	N	N	7,236	92.3	64.9	N	N	N
Erie County, New York	2,933	76.9	15.3	19,530	79.9	55.7	N	N	N
Jefferson County, New York	N	N	N	N	N	N	N	N	N
Kings County, New York	5,458	60.8	19.1	223,329	65.0	32.6	N	N	N
Livingston County, New York	N	N	N	N	N	N	N	N	N
Madison County, New York	N	N	N	N	N	N	N	N	N
Monroe County, New York	N	N	N	15,923	81.9	45.8	N	N	N
Nassau County, New York	N	N	N	87,665	92.8	64.0	N	N	N
New York County, New York	3,644	63.3	17.5	160,413	81.1	64.1	N	N	N
Niagara County, New York	N	N	N	N	N	N	N	N	N
Oneida County, New York	N	N	N	5,282	54.3	28.1	N	N	N
Onondaga County, New York	N	N	N	9,685	70.5	49.0	N	N	N
Ontario County, New York	N	N	N	N	N	N	N	N	N
Orange County, New York	N	N	N	7,665	95.7	50.8	N	N	N
Oswego County, New York	N	N	N	N	N	N	N	N	N
Putnam County, New York	N	N	N	N	N	N	N	N	N
Queens County, New York	6,160	68.9	12.5	436,122	77.8	36.9	N	N	N
Rensselaer County, New York	N	N	N	N	N	N	N	N	N
Richmond County, New York	N	N	N	29,408	82.2	45.8	N	N	N

N = Data for this geographic area cannot be displayed because the number of sample cases is too small.

Table C-2. Educational Attainment of the Population, by Selected Counties, 2016—*Continued*

(Number; percent; dollars.)

| | Educational attainment by race/ethnicity, 25 years and over | | | | | | | | |
| | White alone | | | White alone, not Hispanic | | | Black alone | | |
State/County	Total	High school graduate or more	Bachelor's degree or more	Total	High school graduate or more	Bachelor's degree or more	Total	High school graduate or more	Bachelor's degree or more
NEW YORK—(*Continued*)									
Rockland County, New York	141,815	90.7	42.8	128,742	92.4	44.0	26,227	80.6	26.5
St. Lawrence County, New York	68,350	88.3	23.3	67,414	88.7	23.5	N	N	N
Saratoga County, New York	151,605	93.9	40.0	148,770	94.0	40.1	N	N	N
Schenectady County, New York	86,424	91.4	31.7	82,903	92.3	32.7	8,565	78.8	12.2
Steuben County, New York	64,826	89.4	21.9	64,464	89.5	21.8	N	N	N
Suffolk County, New York	853,953	92.6	36.0	746,204	95.1	38.6	70,399	90.7	24.8
Sullivan County, New York	43,421	89.1	24.1	39,936	91.2	24.8	4,009	80.0	12.1
Tompkins County, New York	52,671	96.3	50.9	50,845	96.2	50.0	1,764	74.7	30.0
Ulster County, New York	113,391	91.9	34.1	107,925	92.2	34.8	7,314	84.9	12.6
Warren County, New York	46,324	92.3	30.2	45,487	92.6	30.1	N	N	N
Wayne County, New York	60,428	90.2	22.0	58,906	90.4	21.9	1,906	87.5	5.7
Westchester County, New York	447,917	90.0	53.8	381,379	94.0	58.7	97,380	87.3	31.3
NORTH CAROLINA									
Alamance County, North Carolina	78,619	89.8	27.0	74,991	91.5	28.0	20,152	86.1	11.0
Brunswick County, North Carolina	86,371	92.0	29.8	84,491	92.0	29.6	10,017	85.2	9.5
Buncombe County, North Carolina	170,250	90.5	39.1	163,406	92.0	39.7	10,253	93.7	17.6
Burke County, North Carolina	56,056	82.8	17.9	55,136	82.7	17.6	N	N	N
Cabarrus County, North Carolina	98,502	91.3	33.5	95,926	91.5	33.6	21,372	85.0	22.8
Caldwell County, North Carolina	53,055	80.4	14.0	52,632	80.5	14.0	N	N	N
Carteret County, North Carolina	47,228	92.1	26.0	46,055	93.1	26.3	2,638	82.7	18.7
Catawba County, North Carolina	88,963	88.5	22.8	87,518	88.8	23.1	9,067	72.7	7.5
Chatham County, North Carolina	43,954	88.6	47.9	40,759	92.2	50.1	6,919	85.7	14.6
Cleveland County, North Carolina	51,326	86.9	22.4	50,924	87.1	22.4	12,279	71.1	9.1
Craven County, North Carolina	49,270	91.3	30.7	47,638	91.7	31.7	12,831	79.3	12.4
Cumberland County, North Carolina	106,560	92.8	28.2	96,223	93.3	28.4	76,873	88.8	22.3
Davidson County, North Carolina	99,589	84.1	18.4	96,932	84.5	18.7	9,370	82.0	12.1
Durham County, North Carolina	114,931	89.6	55.7	100,529	95.7	62.3	74,917	87.0	35.1
Forsyth County, North Carolina	172,152	90.1	37.6	156,590	93.2	39.7	60,510	89.4	24.6
Gaston County, North Carolina	120,067	84.8	21.9	115,817	85.6	21.7	22,355	83.9	19.5
Guilford County, North Carolina	209,739	90.7	40.3	197,176	92.7	41.7	108,725	86.8	24.1
Harnett County, North Carolina	58,707	89.6	23.2	55,735	90.5	23.3	17,421	85.9	12.4
Henderson County, North Carolina	80,254	88.9	31.4	74,493	92.6	32.8	3,375	79.4	10.6
Iredell County, North Carolina	100,110	88.3	27.0	94,080	90.3	27.7	13,101	85.9	19.5
Johnston County, North Carolina	101,668	87.6	25.0	92,624	90.6	26.2	20,015	79.9	20.0
Lincoln County, North Carolina	51,922	89.4	22.4	50,533	90.3	23.0	N	N	N
Mecklenburg County, North Carolina	409,819	93.4	52.7	367,360	96.4	56.1	211,377	90.6	29.3
Moore County, North Carolina	58,596	94.0	42.4	56,362	94.3	43.2	8,391	88.8	10.2
Nash County, North Carolina	37,116	88.0	23.8	35,551	89.0	24.1	25,570	78.7	14.2
New Hanover County, North Carolina	127,185	93.6	42.2	122,567	94.0	42.9	18,977	82.4	16.9
Onslow County, North Carolina	78,106	91.6	20.1	72,164	91.2	19.8	14,961	89.1	10.6
Orange County, North Carolina	67,585	92.5	63.3	63,326	95.5	65.6	10,032	85.4	24.5
Pitt County, North Carolina	64,013	94.0	39.8	61,194	93.9	39.7	36,949	84.3	19.1
Randolph County, North Carolina	86,222	83.7	16.5	83,063	85.5	17.2	6,276	81.1	16.6
Robeson County, North Carolina	27,045	81.0	16.7	25,478	84.5	17.5	19,968	82.3	9.4
Rockingham County, North Carolina	51,740	82.1	16.6	49,634	83.1	17.0	11,807	72.5	3.0
Rowan County, North Carolina	76,635	88.3	21.0	74,396	88.2	21.3	14,265	85.7	15.1
Rutherford County, North Carolina	42,293	83.4	19.4	40,537	84.8	19.7	3,806	73.0	5.5
Surry County, North Carolina	46,791	76.6	15.2	44,873	78.6	15.7	2,339	83.9	10.3
Union County, North Carolina	120,899	88.9	35.4	109,706	92.7	37.9	16,447	78.9	17.5
Wake County, North Carolina	477,555	95.7	58.6	446,101	97.4	60.3	133,832	89.6	33.9
Wayne County, North Carolina	54,209	86.0	21.9	47,991	91.7	23.8	24,656	80.2	9.6
Wilkes County, North Carolina	45,381	83.0	15.4	44,598	83.4	15.5	N	N	N
Wilson County, North Carolina	30,485	88.5	27.9	29,159	89.3	28.5	21,256	73.1	8.1
NORTH DAKOTA									
Burleigh County, North Dakota	59,478	93.2	34.9	58,772	93.5	35.0	N	N	N
Cass County, North Dakota	98,483	95.5	43.3	97,502	95.6	43.2	5,172	89.4	11.7
Grand Forks County, North Dakota	37,512	96.2	34.1	36,190	96.9	35.0	N	N	N
Ward County, North Dakota	38,955	94.9	29.1	38,204	95.6	29.5	N	N	N
OHIO									
Allen County, Ohio	58,989	89.2	17.3	58,394	89.0	17.3	7,115	81.0	8.1
Ashtabula County, Ohio	64,520	85.3	13.9	63,240	86.0	14.1	2,752	75.7	0.0
Athens County, Ohio	34,092	86.7	24.5	33,854	86.6	24.5	N	N	N
Belmont County, Ohio	47,622	90.5	19.0	47,410	90.6	19.0	2,691	75.7	18.2
Butler County, Ohio	211,262	89.7	30.1	204,878	90.4	30.6	18,166	93.0	20.6

N = Data for this geographic area cannot be displayed because the number of sample cases is too small.

Table C-2. Educational Attainment of the Population, by Selected Counties, 2016—*Continued*

(Number; percent; dollars.)

| | Educational attainment by race/ethnicity, 25 years and over | | | | | | | | |
| | American Indian or Alaska Native alone | | | Asian alone | | | Native Hawaiian or Other Pacific Islander alone | | |
State/County	Total	High school graduate or more	Bachelor's degree or more	Total	High school graduate or more	Bachelor's degree or more	Total	High school graduate or more	Bachelor's degree or more
NEW YORK—(*Continued*)									
Rockland County, New York	N	N	N	14,460	92.2	67.5	N	N	N
St. Lawrence County, New York	N	N	N	N	N	N	N	N	N
Saratoga County, New York	N	N	N	4,253	94.2	78.5	N	N	N
Schenectady County, New York	N	N	N	4,688	92.3	59.5	N	N	N
Steuben County, New York	N	N	N	N	N	N	N	N	N
Suffolk County, New York	2,509	66.4	8.1	38,568	90.5	59.3	N	N	N
Sullivan County, New York	N	N	N	N	N	N	N	N	N
Tompkins County, New York	N	N	N	N	N	N	N	N	N
Ulster County, New York	N	N	N	N	N	N	N	N	N
Warren County, New York	N	N	N	N	N	N	N	N	N
Wayne County, New York	N	N	N	N	N	N	N	N	N
Westchester County, New York	N	N	N	42,680	91.9	71.5	N	N	N
NORTH CAROLINA									
Alamance County, North Carolina	N	N	N	N	N	N	N	N	N
Brunswick County, North Carolina	N	N	N	N	N	N	N	N	N
Buncombe County, North Carolina	N	N	N	N	N	N	N	N	N
Burke County, North Carolina	N	N	N	2,341	66.3	10.0	N	N	N
Cabarrus County, North Carolina	N	N	N	N	N	N	N	N	N
Caldwell County, North Carolina	N	N	N	N	N	N	N	N	N
Carteret County, North Carolina	N	N	N	N	N	N	N	N	N
Catawba County, North Carolina	N	N	N	N	N	N	N	N	N
Chatham County, North Carolina	N	N	N	N	N	N	N	N	N
Cleveland County, North Carolina	N	N	N	N	N	N	N	N	N
Craven County, North Carolina	N	N	N	N	N	N	N	N	N
Cumberland County, North Carolina	3,503	74.0	8.3	5,454	84.8	31.1	N	N	N
Davidson County, North Carolina	N	N	N	N	N	N	N	N	N
Durham County, North Carolina	N	N	N	11,626	93.0	72.6	N	N	N
Forsyth County, North Carolina	N	N	N	5,545	90.3	71.9	N	N	N
Gaston County, North Carolina	N	N	N	2,268	90.6	45.9	N	N	N
Guilford County, North Carolina	N	N	N	16,244	71.5	41.4	N	N	N
Harnett County, North Carolina	N	N	N	N	N	N	N	N	N
Henderson County, North Carolina	N	N	N	N	N	N	N	N	N
Iredell County, North Carolina	N	N	N	2,380	88.0	42.1	N	N	N
Johnston County, North Carolina	N	N	N	N	N	N	N	N	N
Lincoln County, North Carolina	N	N	N	N	N	N	N	N	N
Mecklenburg County, North Carolina	2,048	58.3	16.5	40,662	89.4	64.0	N	N	N
Moore County, North Carolina	N	N	N	N	N	N	N	N	N
Nash County, North Carolina	N	N	N	N	N	N	N	N	N
New Hanover County, North Carolina	N	N	N	N	N	N	N	N	N
Onslow County, North Carolina	N	N	N	N	N	N	N	N	N
Orange County, North Carolina	N	N	N	6,489	91.4	67.5	N	N	N
Pitt County, North Carolina	N	N	N	N	N	N	N	N	N
Randolph County, North Carolina	N	N	N	982	81.7	35.0	N	N	N
Robeson County, North Carolina	33,733	76.6	12.8	N	N	N	N	N	N
Rockingham County, North Carolina	N	N	N	N	N	N	N	N	N
Rowan County, North Carolina	N	N	N	N	N	N	N	N	N
Rutherford County, North Carolina	N	N	N	N	N	N	N	N	N
Surry County, North Carolina	N	N	N	N	N	N	N	N	N
Union County, North Carolina	N	N	N	3,804	91.5	65.0	N	N	N
Wake County, North Carolina	2,498	90.3	35.1	45,607	91.7	73.9	N	N	N
Wayne County, North Carolina	N	N	N	N	N	N	N	N	N
Wilkes County, North Carolina	N	N	N	N	N	N	N	N	N
Wilson County, North Carolina	N	N	N	N	N	N	N	N	N
NORTH DAKOTA									
Burleigh County, North Dakota	N	N	N	N	N	N	N	N	N
Cass County, North Dakota	N	N	N	2,289	67.7	39.1	N	N	N
Grand Forks County, North Dakota	N	N	N	N	N	N	N	N	N
Ward County, North Dakota	N	N	N	N	N	N	N	N	N
OHIO									
Allen County, Ohio	N	N	N	N	N	N	N	N	N
Ashtabula County, Ohio	N	N	N	N	N	N	N	N	N
Athens County, Ohio	N	N	N	N	N	N	N	N	N
Belmont County, Ohio	N	N	N	N	N	N	N	N	N
Butler County, Ohio	N	N	N	6,246	89.8	49.8	N	N	N

N = Data for this geographic area cannot be displayed because the number of sample cases is too small.

Table C-2. Educational Attainment of the Population, by Selected Counties, 2016—*Continued*

(Number; percent; dollars.)

| | Educational attainment by race/ethnicity, 25 years and over | | | | | | | | |
| | White alone | | | White alone, not Hispanic | | | Black alone | | |
State/County	Total	High school graduate or more	Bachelor's degree or more	Total	High school graduate or more	Bachelor's degree or more	Total	High school graduate or more	Bachelor's degree or more
OHIO—(*Continued*)									
Clark County, Ohio	82,407	87.9	18.3	81,013	88.1	18.4	6,647	90.2	14.1
Clermont County, Ohio	134,018	87.9	27.7	132,323	88.2	27.8	N	N	N
Columbiana County, Ohio	71,150	89.0	13.6	70,831	89.0	13.5	N	N	N
Cuyahoga County, Ohio	580,784	92.4	36.9	556,138	93.2	37.6	237,252	85.4	15.3
Delaware County, Ohio	114,494	96.6	53.5	112,460	96.9	54.1	3,848	86.9	41.0
Erie County, Ohio	47,663	93.7	22.6	46,740	93.6	22.8	4,396	79.3	9.5
Fairfield County, Ohio	92,845	92.0	26.1	92,149	92.0	25.8	7,136	98.7	36.7
Franklin County, Ohio	605,060	92.5	43.7	582,337	93.1	44.3	168,683	86.1	19.6
Geauga County, Ohio	62,372	88.6	36.0	61,782	88.5	35.8	N	N	N
Greene County, Ohio	98,000	93.6	35.5	96,848	93.6	35.4	6,129	93.8	36.7
Hamilton County, Ohio	387,252	93.4	43.5	380,010	93.7	43.5	129,914	86.2	15.4
Hancock County, Ohio	48,377	94.6	25.4	47,421	94.7	25.5	N	N	N
Jefferson County, Ohio	43,981	88.0	17.1	43,894	87.9	17.2	2,737	92.1	7.1
Lake County, Ohio	152,335	92.8	28.9	150,150	93.1	29.1	6,183	92.3	18.5
Licking County, Ohio	108,945	91.4	24.7	108,034	91.3	24.7	4,321	90.1	29.1
Lorain County, Ohio	185,973	89.6	25.6	174,956	90.5	26.4	15,682	83.8	9.8
Lucas County, Ohio	224,121	91.9	29.3	217,198	92.1	29.1	51,250	80.7	13.2
Mahoning County, Ohio	136,868	92.6	28.0	131,410	93.7	28.5	21,729	81.1	9.0
Marion County, Ohio	41,837	88.5	11.7	41,303	88.7	11.6	2,338	77.0	14.1
Medina County, Ohio	117,841	95.1	32.7	116,919	95.0	32.6	N	N	N
Miami County, Ohio	69,408	90.0	21.6	68,623	90.6	21.8	1,386	74.3	21.1
Montgomery County, Ohio	277,193	91.0	27.7	271,817	91.2	27.8	71,261	85.5	16.1
Muskingum County, Ohio	54,813	85.9	12.8	54,802	85.9	12.8	2,551	79.1	16.6
Portage County, Ohio	97,764	93.0	28.9	96,660	93.4	29.0	3,508	94.0	31.8
Richland County, Ohio	75,068	87.9	18.7	74,410	88.2	18.6	7,934	80.1	7.0
Ross County, Ohio	49,594	88.8	16.8	49,269	88.8	16.6	2,683	72.1	3.9
Scioto County, Ohio	50,745	87.6	13.9	49,980	87.4	14.1	N	N	N
Stark County, Ohio	235,064	92.0	25.0	232,896	92.2	25.0	16,480	86.2	13.5
Summit County, Ohio	311,682	92.7	33.3	307,080	92.9	33.3	49,057	89.2	16.8
Trumbull County, Ohio	130,303	90.0	20.3	129,123	89.9	20.0	10,399	89.0	7.3
Tuscarawas County, Ohio	62,472	85.7	18.4	61,903	86.0	18.5	N	N	N
Warren County, Ohio	136,709	93.1	41.9	134,290	93.1	41.6	4,822	76.5	19.5
Wayne County, Ohio	73,137	87.4	20.4	72,752	87.4	20.4	N	N	N
Wood County, Ohio	75,700	94.5	34.3	73,676	94.9	34.6	N	N	N
OKLAHOMA									
Canadian County, Oklahoma	76,139	93.1	28.2	72,963	93.8	28.4	N	N	N
Cleveland County, Oklahoma	145,162	92.3	32.6	135,934	92.7	33.5	7,252	90.3	36.7
Comanche County, Oklahoma	50,806	90.0	23.0	47,604	90.1	23.9	12,457	88.6	16.7
Creek County, Oklahoma	40,496	87.8	16.4	39,390	88.2	16.4	N	N	N
Muskogee County, Oklahoma	30,520	86.1	20.8	29,555	86.5	20.6	4,634	85.6	21.9
Oklahoma County, Oklahoma	370,007	87.2	33.4	323,188	92.8	36.5	72,435	90.4	20.7
Payne County, Oklahoma	36,132	91.3	33.2	35,410	92.2	33.6	N	N	N
Pottawatomie County, Oklahoma	38,425	88.7	18.2	37,434	88.9	18.3	1,194	79.6	6.4
Rogers County, Oklahoma	48,931	92.4	23.7	47,796	92.8	23.2	N	N	N
Tulsa County, Oklahoma	313,037	92.2	34.6	291,855	94.2	36.1	38,578	88.2	18.0
Wagoner County, Oklahoma	41,944	90.4	25.6	40,546	91.1	26.3	1,722	94.3	23.5
OREGON									
Benton County, Oregon	48,831	96.1	53.7	46,473	96.8	54.9	N	N	N
Clackamas County, Oregon	258,508	94.0	36.2	246,772	94.6	36.7	3,465	81.2	26.7
Deschutes County, Oregon	123,446	93.4	33.4	118,970	94.3	34.0	N	N	N
Douglas County, Oregon	74,475	89.0	17.6	72,545	89.3	17.6	N	N	N
Jackson County, Oregon	142,293	90.6	26.6	132,774	92.0	28.0	N	N	N
Josephine County, Oregon	59,530	87.6	19.6	56,981	88.0	20.5	N	N	N
Klamath County, Oregon	41,757	87.2	19.0	38,828	89.8	20.4	N	N	N
Lane County, Oregon	230,398	92.5	28.6	219,667	93.0	28.9	2,229	80.5	17.1
Linn County, Oregon	78,188	93.1	22.1	75,779	93.4	22.3	N	N	N
Marion County, Oregon	183,743	89.4	24.6	162,931	93.6	26.5	2,342	79.3	3.9
Multnomah County, Oregon	472,648	93.4	48.3	437,976	95.6	50.3	28,068	84.4	17.6
Polk County, Oregon	47,769	90.5	29.6	43,931	93.8	31.7	N	N	N
Umatilla County, Oregon	43,701	81.6	15.9	36,663	88.1	18.2	N	N	N
Washington County, Oregon	312,967	93.6	43.5	285,656	96.5	46.2	7,431	95.2	43.9
Yamhill County, Oregon	62,405	89.3	27.8	57,159	93.0	29.9	N	N	N
PENNSYLVANIA									
Adams County, Pennsylvania	67,993	87.7	22.2	66,329	88.0	22.5	N	N	N
Allegheny County, Pennsylvania	738,547	95.2	43.0	728,520	95.4	43.1	99,357	90.5	22.0

N = Data for this geographic area cannot be displayed because the number of sample cases is too small.

Table C-2. Educational Attainment of the Population, by Selected Counties, 2016—*Continued*

(Number; percent; dollars.)

State/County	Educational attainment by race/ethnicity, 25 years and over								
	American Indian or Alaska Native alone			Asian alone			Native Hawaiian or Other Pacific Islander alone		
	Total	High school graduate or more	Bachelor's degree or more	Total	High school graduate or more	Bachelor's degree or more	Total	High school graduate or more	Bachelor's degree or more
OHIO—*(Continued)*									
Clark County, Ohio	N	N	N	N	N	N	N	N	N
Clermont County, Ohio	N	N	N	N	N	N	N	N	N
Columbiana County, Ohio	N	N	N	N	N	N	N	N	N
Cuyahoga County, Ohio	1,542	70.3	28.9	25,427	86.5	60.4	N	N	N
Delaware County, Ohio	N	N	N	N	N	N	N	N	N
Erie County, Ohio	N	N	N	N	N	N	N	N	N
Fairfield County, Ohio	N	N	N	N	N	N	N	N	N
Franklin County, Ohio	N	N	N	42,033	89.0	60.6	N	N	N
Geauga County, Ohio	N	N	N	N	N	N	N	N	N
Greene County, Ohio	N	N	N	N	N	N	N	N	N
Hamilton County, Ohio	N	N	N	14,350	83.1	60.9	N	N	N
Hancock County, Ohio	N	N	N	N	N	N	N	N	N
Jefferson County, Ohio	N	N	N	N	N	N	N	N	N
Lake County, Ohio	N	N	N	N	N	N	N	N	N
Licking County, Ohio	N	N	N	N	N	N	N	N	N
Lorain County, Ohio	N	N	N	N	N	N	N	N	N
Lucas County, Ohio	N	N	N	5,066	92.9	53.8	N	N	N
Mahoning County, Ohio	N	N	N	N	N	N	N	N	N
Marion County, Ohio	N	N	N	N	N	N	N	N	N
Medina County, Ohio	N	N	N	N	N	N	N	N	N
Miami County, Ohio	N	N	N	985	98.8	24.4	N	N	N
Montgomery County, Ohio	N	N	N	8,202	81.8	48.5	N	N	N
Muskingum County, Ohio	N	N	N	N	N	N	N	N	N
Portage County, Ohio	N	N	N	N	N	N	N	N	N
Richland County, Ohio	N	N	N	N	N	N	N	N	N
Ross County, Ohio	N	N	N	N	N	N	N	N	N
Scioto County, Ohio	N	N	N	N	N	N	N	N	N
Stark County, Ohio	N	N	N	N	N	N	N	N	N
Summit County, Ohio	N	N	N	11,242	71.8	43.3	N	N	N
Trumbull County, Ohio	N	N	N	N	N	N	N	N	N
Tuscarawas County, Ohio	N	N	N	N	N	N	N	N	N
Warren County, Ohio	N	N	N	8,197	99.1	69.9	N	N	N
Wayne County, Ohio	N	N	N	N	N	N	N	N	N
Wood County, Ohio	N	N	N	N	N	N	N	N	N
OKLAHOMA									
Canadian County, Oklahoma	3,187	88.5	10.1	3,256	89.9	21.4	N	N	N
Cleveland County, Oklahoma	6,624	88.9	26.3	6,979	89.7	49.4	N	N	N
Comanche County, Oklahoma	4,137	85.5	10.0	1,915	72.2	28.5	N	N	N
Creek County, Oklahoma	4,343	79.5	8.4	N	N	N	N	N	N
Muskogee County, Oklahoma	6,658	91.5	19.7	N	N	N	N	N	N
Oklahoma County, Oklahoma	15,739	87.7	24.0	17,189	85.1	49.3	N	N	N
Payne County, Oklahoma	1,760	81.5	36.4	N	N	N	N	N	N
Pottawatomie County, Oklahoma	5,623	79.8	14.4	N	N	N	N	N	N
Rogers County, Oklahoma	6,612	92.7	18.7	N	N	N	N	N	N
Tulsa County, Oklahoma	19,159	82.3	23.2	12,879	82.5	37.3	N	N	N
Wagoner County, Oklahoma	3,903	88.9	24.2	N	N	N	N	N	N
OREGON									
Benton County, Oregon	N	N	N	N	N	N	N	N	N
Clackamas County, Oregon	N	N	N	10,642	94.9	58.3	N	N	N
Deschutes County, Oregon	N	N	N	N	N	N	N	N	N
Douglas County, Oregon	N	N	N	N	N	N	N	N	N
Jackson County, Oregon	N	N	N	N	N	N	N	N	N
Josephine County, Oregon	N	N	N	N	N	N	N	N	N
Klamath County, Oregon	N	N	N	N	N	N	N	N	N
Lane County, Oregon	2,466	76.0	8.7	5,570	84.2	53.8	N	N	N
Linn County, Oregon	N	N	N	N	N	N	N	N	N
Marion County, Oregon	N	N	N	4,875	80.0	38.2	N	N	N
Multnomah County, Oregon	3,349	71.5	16.0	41,241	75.2	41.7	3,118	82.9	17.8
Polk County, Oregon	N	N	N	N	N	N	N	N	N
Umatilla County, Oregon	1,142	95.0	6.9	N	N	N	N	N	N
Washington County, Oregon	N	N	N	42,829	92.0	60.0	N	N	N
Yamhill County, Oregon	N	N	N	N	N	N	N	N	N
PENNSYLVANIA									
Adams County, Pennsylvania	N	N	N	N	N	N	N	N	N
Allegheny County, Pennsylvania	N	N	N	28,758	87.9	72.4	N	N	N

N = Data for this geographic area cannot be displayed because the number of sample cases is too small.

Table C-2. Educational Attainment of the Population, by Selected Counties, 2016—*Continued*

(Number; percent; dollars.)

	Educational attainment by race/ethnicity, 25 years and over								
	White alone			White alone, not Hispanic			Black alone		
State/County	Total	High school graduate or more	Bachelor's degree or more	Total	High school graduate or more	Bachelor's degree or more	Total	High school graduate or more	Bachelor's degree or more
PENNSYLVANIA—*(Continued)*									
Armstrong County, Pennsylvania	48,142	88.9	16.2	47,964	88.9	16.2	N	N	N
Beaver County, Pennsylvania	113,818	93.3	26.2	112,336	93.2	25.9	6,457	87.4	18.3
Berks County, Pennsylvania	244,350	88.2	26.1	222,595	91.0	27.6	11,123	88.5	16.8
Blair County, Pennsylvania	86,198	91.7	18.1	85,878	91.6	18.1	1,528	91.2	12.0
Bucks County, Pennsylvania	398,924	94.3	40.0	386,291	94.8	40.3	15,315	93.5	30.0
Butler County, Pennsylvania	128,699	95.1	35.7	127,607	95.0	35.4	N	N	N
Cambria County, Pennsylvania	92,002	92.0	22.5	91,405	92.0	22.6	1,789	86.4	4.8
Carbon County, Pennsylvania	45,696	88.8	17.2	44,124	89.5	17.8	N	N	N
Centre County, Pennsylvania	88,934	95.5	47.2	86,981	95.7	46.9	3,893	93.0	39.8
Chester County, Pennsylvania	305,187	93.9	51.5	290,819	95.7	53.1	18,491	89.8	28.2
Clearfield County, Pennsylvania	56,291	86.7	14.7	55,346	87.3	15.0	N	N	N
Columbia County, Pennsylvania	41,918	90.1	22.7	41,817	90.1	22.7	N	N	N
Crawford County, Pennsylvania	57,983	89.7	22.2	57,702	89.9	22.3	N	N	N
Cumberland County, Pennsylvania	156,202	92.6	36.0	154,616	92.7	36.1	5,788	82.1	13.2
Dauphin County, Pennsylvania	143,658	92.4	35.0	137,202	93.6	35.9	31,251	83.8	20.7
Delaware County, Pennsylvania	279,012	95.0	41.4	272,960	95.2	41.4	72,233	87.7	22.6
Erie County, Pennsylvania	171,101	93.4	29.1	167,243	94.2	29.6	11,543	85.0	14.9
Fayette County, Pennsylvania	91,103	88.2	16.3	90,967	88.2	16.2	4,013	76.0	10.8
Franklin County, Pennsylvania	101,412	88.6	21.7	98,406	88.7	21.7	3,746	80.8	19.8
Indiana County, Pennsylvania	54,346	88.9	21.6	53,974	89.0	21.5	N	N	N
Lackawanna County, Pennsylvania	140,040	90.7	27.2	134,474	91.4	27.8	3,349	84.0	10.8
Lancaster County, Pennsylvania	330,456	85.6	25.2	310,838	86.3	26.3	12,700	77.4	16.5
Lawrence County, Pennsylvania	59,632	90.3	23.2	59,103	90.4	23.1	2,417	94.8	14.3
Lebanon County, Pennsylvania	85,968	88.8	21.6	83,120	88.9	21.6	N	N	N
Lehigh County, Pennsylvania	204,796	90.3	30.4	179,390	92.4	33.2	15,562	84.1	16.9
Luzerne County, Pennsylvania	210,905	90.4	23.3	199,434	91.8	24.0	7,024	81.0	7.5
Lycoming County, Pennsylvania	76,629	91.1	22.0	75,806	91.1	22.0	2,608	84.5	4.3
Mercer County, Pennsylvania	74,266	90.8	22.9	73,448	90.8	23.1	4,028	95.4	11.0
Monroe County, Pennsylvania	90,141	91.1	25.5	81,876	91.9	26.4	14,229	90.5	26.4
Montgomery County, Pennsylvania	471,946	95.2	48.5	456,932	95.8	49.1	48,977	91.2	33.1
Northampton County, Pennsylvania	188,854	90.7	28.6	173,179	92.4	29.6	10,078	96.7	29.4
Northumberland County, Pennsylvania	64,972	87.4	17.5	63,704	87.9	17.2	N	N	N
Philadelphia County, Pennsylvania	472,211	88.2	40.1	421,043	91.2	42.7	423,802	83.0	16.8
Schuylkill County, Pennsylvania	99,213	89.5	16.1	97,772	89.8	16.3	3,418	76.6	1.4
Somerset County, Pennsylvania	53,454	87.8	16.2	53,044	88.0	16.3	N	N	N
Washington County, Pennsylvania	141,763	92.8	29.6	140,520	92.8	29.6	3,787	92.9	19.3
Westmoreland County, Pennsylvania	251,989	94.5	27.9	250,496	94.5	27.9	5,620	84.5	23.2
York County, Pennsylvania	280,280	90.2	24.2	271,056	90.4	24.4	14,870	90.5	24.6
RHODE ISLAND									
Kent County, Rhode Island	113,391	92.1	31.3	110,721	91.9	31.3	2,312	94.3	32.1
Newport County, Rhode Island	55,330	95.0	45.5	53,616	94.9	45.6	2,064	92.1	19.3
Providence County, Rhode Island	334,374	87.6	31.8	295,522	89.5	34.7	35,820	83.7	20.4
Washington County, Rhode Island	81,690	95.4	47.5	80,377	95.7	47.6	N	N	N
SOUTH CAROLINA									
Aiken County, South Carolina	86,882	86.2	25.4	82,795	87.9	26.3	26,949	82.0	14.8
Anderson County, South Carolina	110,576	86.7	23.9	108,616	86.9	24.2	19,879	72.5	6.3
Beaufort County, South Carolina	103,622	95.6	48.6	96,421	96.7	51.0	20,955	90.3	14.1
Berkeley County, South Carolina	97,180	87.6	27.3	93,767	88.5	27.7	33,125	86.4	18.0
Charleston County, South Carolina	199,085	94.9	51.5	190,776	96.4	52.8	72,250	77.6	13.9
Darlington County, South Carolina	27,667	84.4	19.0	27,123	85.0	19.4	17,606	69.1	14.9
Dorchester County, South Carolina	72,339	90.9	33.0	69,332	90.7	33.3	24,578	82.5	20.4
Florence County, South Carolina	54,160	86.7	25.8	52,304	87.9	25.8	37,001	78.6	15.5
Greenville County, South Carolina	262,162	89.1	37.2	245,059	91.8	38.8	57,542	83.1	18.8
Greenwood County, South Carolina	31,701	87.7	28.1	30,557	90.9	29.1	12,716	81.1	12.4
Horry County, South Carolina	201,188	91.1	24.0	193,807	92.3	24.6	26,864	85.1	13.4
Lancaster County, South Carolina	47,961	91.8	32.8	47,233	92.2	32.3	13,120	69.2	4.1
Laurens County, South Carolina	33,059	79.2	15.6	32,639	79.2	15.7	10,601	77.5	9.0
Lexington County, South Carolina	161,762	90.3	32.2	155,556	91.6	33.0	26,576	89.1	22.0
Oconee County, South Carolina	49,897	86.0	26.6	48,589	86.4	26.8	3,867	80.5	1.0
Orangeburg County, South Carolina	22,350	89.8	21.9	22,156	90.2	22.1	35,382	83.3	15.6
Pickens County, South Carolina	69,573	84.7	27.8	68,100	85.1	28.1	5,250	72.4	13.5
Richland County, South Carolina	122,400	94.1	49.3	116,578	94.7	50.1	116,995	87.9	28.0
Spartanburg County, South Carolina	153,850	86.1	24.8	146,893	87.6	25.6	39,550	81.8	13.5

N = Data for this geographic area cannot be displayed because the number of sample cases is too small.

Table C-2. Educational Attainment of the Population, by Selected Counties, 2016—*Continued*

(Number; percent; dollars.)

State/County	Educational attainment by race/ethnicity, 25 years and over								
	American Indian or Alaska Native alone			Asian alone			Native Hawaiian or Other Pacific Islander alone		
	Total	High school graduate or more	Bachelor's degree or more	Total	High school graduate or more	Bachelor's degree or more	Total	High school graduate or more	Bachelor's degree or more
PENNSYLVANIA—(*Continued*)									
Armstrong County, Pennsylvania	N	N	N	N	N	N	N	N	N
Beaver County, Pennsylvania	N	N	N	N	N	N	N	N	N
Berks County, Pennsylvania	N	N	N	3,501	87.6	57.8	N	N	N
Blair County, Pennsylvania	N	N	N	N	N	N	N	N	N
Bucks County, Pennsylvania	N	N	N	20,631	87.4	58.4	N	N	N
Butler County, Pennsylvania	N	N	N	N	N	N	N	N	N
Cambria County, Pennsylvania	N	N	N	N	N	N	N	N	N
Carbon County, Pennsylvania	N	N	N	N	N	N	N	N	N
Centre County, Pennsylvania	N	N	N	N	N	N	N	N	N
Chester County, Pennsylvania	N	N	N	16,995	94.0	80.3	N	N	N
Clearfield County, Pennsylvania	N	N	N	N	N	N	N	N	N
Columbia County, Pennsylvania	N	N	N	N	N	N	N	N	N
Crawford County, Pennsylvania	N	N	N	N	N	N	N	N	N
Cumberland County, Pennsylvania	N	N	N	7,308	87.5	66.3	N	N	N
Dauphin County, Pennsylvania	N	N	N	8,203	78.5	35.1	N	N	N
Delaware County, Pennsylvania	N	N	N	21,666	88.6	54.8	N	N	N
Erie County, Pennsylvania	N	N	N	3,056	51.0	23.3	N	N	N
Fayette County, Pennsylvania	N	N	N	N	N	N	N	N	N
Franklin County, Pennsylvania	N	N	N	N	N	N	N	N	N
Indiana County, Pennsylvania	N	N	N	N	N	N	N	N	N
Lackawanna County, Pennsylvania	N	N	N	3,510	78.0	37.4	N	N	N
Lancaster County, Pennsylvania	N	N	N	7,117	76.9	45.1	N	N	N
Lawrence County, Pennsylvania	N	N	N	N	N	N	N	N	N
Lebanon County, Pennsylvania	N	N	N	N	N	N	N	N	N
Lehigh County, Pennsylvania	N	N	N	8,464	93.0	63.8	N	N	N
Luzerne County, Pennsylvania	N	N	N	2,224	89.3	65.9	N	N	N
Lycoming County, Pennsylvania	N	N	N	N	N	N	N	N	N
Mercer County, Pennsylvania	N	N	N	N	N	N	N	N	N
Monroe County, Pennsylvania	N	N	N	2,591	77.5	52.8	N	N	N
Montgomery County, Pennsylvania	N	N	N	41,869	94.1	67.1	N	N	N
Northampton County, Pennsylvania	N	N	N	4,923	87.1	51.6	N	N	N
Northumberland County, Pennsylvania	N	N	N	N	N	N	N	N	N
Philadelphia County, Pennsylvania	3,806	63.0	11.2	75,381	70.5	39.9	N	N	N
Schuylkill County, Pennsylvania	N	N	N	N	N	N	N	N	N
Somerset County, Pennsylvania	N	N	N	N	N	N	N	N	N
Washington County, Pennsylvania	N	N	N	N	N	N	N	N	N
Westmoreland County, Pennsylvania	N	N	N	2,213	85.4	51.0	N	N	N
York County, Pennsylvania	N	N	N	4,352	67.2	38.2	N	N	N
RHODE ISLAND									
Kent County, Rhode Island	N	N	N	N	N	N	N	N	N
Newport County, Rhode Island	N	N	N	N	N	N	N	N	N
Providence County, Rhode Island	N	N	N	16,567	90.3	41.7	N	N	N
Washington County, Rhode Island	N	N	N	N	N	N	N	N	N
SOUTH CAROLINA									
Aiken County, South Carolina	N	N	N	N	N	N	N	N	N
Anderson County, South Carolina	N	N	N	N	N	N	N	N	N
Beaufort County, South Carolina	N	N	N	N	N	N	N	N	N
Berkeley County, South Carolina	N	N	N	3,522	98.5	47.2	N	N	N
Charleston County, South Carolina	N	N	N	4,694	89.9	66.1	N	N	N
Darlington County, South Carolina	N	N	N	N	N	N	N	N	N
Dorchester County, South Carolina	N	N	N	N	N	N	N	N	N
Florence County, South Carolina	N	N	N	N	N	N	N	N	N
Greenville County, South Carolina	N	N	N	8,350	89.6	63.3	N	N	N
Greenwood County, South Carolina	N	N	N	N	N	N	N	N	N
Horry County, South Carolina	N	N	N	N	N	N	N	N	N
Lancaster County, South Carolina	N	N	N	N	N	N	N	N	N
Laurens County, South Carolina	N	N	N	N	N	N	N	N	N
Lexington County, South Carolina	N	N	N	3,328	85.0	38.5	N	N	N
Oconee County, South Carolina	N	N	N	N	N	N	N	N	N
Orangeburg County, South Carolina	N	N	N	N	N	N	N	N	N
Pickens County, South Carolina	N	N	N	N	N	N	N	N	N
Richland County, South Carolina	N	N	N	6,732	89.8	54.1	N	N	N
Spartanburg County, South Carolina	N	N	N	4,017	83.5	14.9	N	N	N

N = Data for this geographic area cannot be displayed because the number of sample cases is too small.

Table C-2. Educational Attainment of the Population, by Selected Counties, 2016—*Continued*

(Number; percent; dollars.)

	Educational attainment by race/ethnicity, 25 years and over								
	White alone			White alone, not Hispanic			Black alone		
State/County	Total	High school graduate or more	Bachelor's degree or more	Total	High school graduate or more	Bachelor's degree or more	Total	High school graduate or more	Bachelor's degree or more
SOUTH CAROLINA—(*Continued*)									
Sumter County, South Carolina	34,983	89.5	21.7	34,152	89.3	21.8	32,602	81.7	16.1
York County, South Carolina	134,036	91.4	33.8	129,042	92.5	34.6	30,687	83.7	14.2
SOUTH DAKOTA									
Minnehaha County, South Dakota	110,204	94.8	35.4	107,828	95.2	35.9	4,738	61.3	13.6
Pennington County, South Dakota	65,284	94.2	32.2	64,079	94.5	32.4	N	N	N
TENNESSEE									
Anderson County, Tennessee	50,278	87.7	22.9	49,560	87.8	22.6	N	N	N
Blount County, Tennessee	87,180	89.2	23.0	85,479	90.2	23.1	N	N	N
Bradley County, Tennessee	66,225	86.2	23.9	63,515	87.2	24.5	4,091	89.4	9.6
Davidson County, Tennessee	321,239	89.5	44.8	291,489	93.0	48.1	117,060	85.1	26.0
Greene County, Tennessee	47,520	85.6	16.9	47,082	85.5	17.1	N	N	N
Hamilton County, Tennessee	196,064	90.8	34.3	188,516	91.7	34.7	45,106	80.2	13.9
Knox County, Tennessee	267,222	91.1	38.8	260,001	91.6	38.9	23,856	88.6	25.1
Madison County, Tennessee	41,240	89.1	24.2	40,022	89.8	24.1	21,910	87.1	15.3
Maury County, Tennessee	53,195	91.2	24.3	51,271	91.3	25.2	7,319	90.4	8.0
Montgomery County, Tennessee	90,394	92.6	26.1	82,070	93.5	27.2	21,949	89.6	24.1
Putnam County, Tennessee	46,947	86.0	27.0	44,561	86.7	27.8	N	N	N
Robertson County, Tennessee	42,807	85.9	20.4	40,698	87.0	21.0	3,304	80.0	6.8
Rutherford County, Tennessee	154,251	92.8	32.0	145,971	94.5	33.2	25,704	96.0	31.8
Sevier County, Tennessee	66,060	86.0	18.5	63,937	86.2	19.1	N	N	N
Shelby County, Tennessee	261,121	94.0	43.3	247,777	95.4	44.4	308,557	85.5	19.6
Sullivan County, Tennessee	108,842	86.0	20.1	108,374	86.0	20.1	2,370	93.5	5.7
Sumner County, Tennessee	111,280	90.6	27.2	107,772	91.2	27.1	7,982	87.7	21.1
Washington County, Tennessee	81,179	87.8	32.1	79,669	87.9	32.1	N	N	N
Williamson County, Tennessee	127,842	94.1	55.5	123,033	95.9	56.7	5,917	85.8	37.5
Wilson County, Tennessee	82,103	90.9	28.7	80,214	90.9	28.4	5,615	84.2	36.2
TEXAS									
Angelina County, Texas	45,103	79.8	17.0	38,327	84.1	17.1	8,019	78.8	9.7
Bastrop County, Texas	40,236	86.8	23.0	32,139	94.3	27.2	N	N	N
Bell County, Texas	138,062	90.8	24.0	106,976	93.9	27.8	46,941	89.4	17.9
Bexar County, Texas	973,067	83.1	28.6	395,670	94.6	43.4	93,137	90.0	26.9
Bowie County, Texas	46,052	89.9	23.2	43,034	91.3	24.3	14,702	86.0	14.3
Brazoria County, Texas	173,333	86.8	22.7	122,129	94.3	26.8	31,185	93.4	38.7
Brazos County, Texas	87,701	86.7	41.2	67,322	95.4	49.0	12,649	90.9	15.4
Cameron County, Texas	231,990	68.2	17.1	31,154	92.7	34.8	N	N	N
Collin County, Texas	443,318	93.6	49.0	381,551	97.4	53.1	55,408	93.6	44.2
Comal County, Texas	84,831	94.0	36.2	68,419	96.1	41.2	N	N	N
Coryell County, Texas	35,327	88.7	18.6	29,640	91.7	19.1	5,462	71.3	9.4
Dallas County, Texas	1,034,726	75.6	32.3	592,630	93.8	48.9	370,158	89.4	21.6
Denton County, Texas	399,058	93.6	44.4	338,197	96.6	47.4	46,957	94.1	35.1
Ector County, Texas	80,751	77.2	15.9	37,289	90.6	25.0	4,582	86.0	5.6
Ellis County, Texas	91,974	84.3	21.4	72,748	90.9	25.7	10,317	90.0	25.7
El Paso County, Texas	413,519	77.0	22.2	72,474	94.4	36.7	18,340	94.4	19.9
Fort Bend County, Texas	249,345	91.4	44.4	174,032	96.1	52.1	95,590	95.8	34.7
Galveston County, Texas	175,937	89.2	30.5	136,775	94.0	33.9	26,606	85.9	17.2
Grayson County, Texas	76,393	89.4	20.6	70,474	91.0	21.2	4,438	88.8	10.4
Gregg County, Texas	61,964	80.6	23.1	51,278	90.6	27.4	15,129	78.4	11.7
Guadalupe County, Texas	72,039	90.5	30.6	56,263	93.4	33.7	7,140	95.8	31.6
Harris County, Texas	1,853,570	80.4	32.6	1,027,228	95.4	47.7	548,592	89.9	26.5
Harrison County, Texas	33,204	85.5	18.2	30,028	87.4	20.0	9,241	76.2	12.7
Hays County, Texas	111,255	87.8	36.0	72,314	96.4	45.3	3,808	96.7	42.6
Henderson County, Texas	51,740	83.7	18.5	46,931	86.8	20.3	3,282	74.6	12.3
Hidalgo County, Texas	396,270	67.0	18.3	44,202	92.0	29.1	N	N	N
Hunt County, Texas	50,509	85.7	21.2	47,676	86.0	21.3	4,061	77.6	10.4
Jefferson County, Texas	102,615	84.1	21.5	78,678	93.6	25.9	54,544	85.0	11.1
Johnson County, Texas	98,875	85.6	19.7	83,301	89.4	21.5	3,515	89.5	11.9
Kaufman County, Texas	64,967	85.4	19.4	53,899	91.2	21.2	7,661	88.7	17.1
Liberty County, Texas	45,847	76.1	9.8	37,030	82.8	12.1	5,793	84.8	3.8
Lubbock County, Texas	146,722	87.5	33.0	104,728	94.7	41.3	11,020	86.6	15.7
McLennan County, Texas	119,010	84.5	24.9	93,422	93.6	30.4	20,816	81.8	6.9
Midland County, Texas	87,037	83.5	26.2	53,068	94.8	38.0	7,235	87.9	16.2
Montgomery County, Texas	317,372	87.4	32.5	261,899	92.6	34.7	17,174	97.0	40.2
Nacogdoches County, Texas	28,924	80.9	29.4	24,579	88.4	32.9	6,830	73.8	8.8

N = Data for this geographic area cannot be displayed because the number of sample cases is too small.

Table C-2. Educational Attainment of the Population, by Selected Counties, 2016—*Continued*

(Number; percent; dollars.)

	Educational attainment by race/ethnicity, 25 years and over								
	American Indian or Alaska Native alone			Asian alone			Native Hawaiian or Other Pacific Islander alone		
State/County	Total	High school graduate or more	Bachelor's degree or more	Total	High school graduate or more	Bachelor's degree or more	Total	High school graduate or more	Bachelor's degree or more
SOUTH CAROLINA—*(Continued)*									
Sumter County, South Carolina	N	N	N	N	N	N	N	N	N
York County, South Carolina	1,364	87.8	19.5	3,498	77.8	30.4	N	N	N
SOUTH DAKOTA									
Minnehaha County, South Dakota	1,992	75.2	0.0	2,554	80.2	44.8	N	N	N
Pennington County, South Dakota	5,322	64.4	14.1	N	N	N	N	N	N
TENNESSEE									
Anderson County, Tennessee	N	N	N	N	N	N	N	N	N
Blount County, Tennessee	N	N	N	N	N	N	N	N	N
Bradley County, Tennessee	N	N	N	N	N	N	N	N	N
Davidson County, Tennessee	N	N	N	16,915	82.3	51.7	N	N	N
Greene County, Tennessee	N	N	N	N	N	N	N	N	N
Hamilton County, Tennessee	N	N	N	4,595	85.6	43.0	N	N	N
Knox County, Tennessee	N	N	N	7,272	91.9	77.7	N	N	N
Madison County, Tennessee	N	N	N	N	N	N	N	N	N
Maury County, Tennessee	N	N	N	N	N	N	N	N	N
Montgomery County, Tennessee	N	N	N	3,274	74.2	24.2	N	N	N
Putnam County, Tennessee	N	N	N	N	N	N	N	N	N
Robertson County, Tennessee	N	N	N	N	N	N	N	N	N
Rutherford County, Tennessee	N	N	N	5,702	89.0	26.7	N	N	N
Sevier County, Tennessee	N	N	N	N	N	N	N	N	N
Shelby County, Tennessee	N	N	N	16,506	87.7	61.5	N	N	N
Sullivan County, Tennessee	N	N	N	N	N	N	N	N	N
Sumner County, Tennessee	N	N	N	N	N	N	N	N	N
Washington County, Tennessee	N	N	N	N	N	N	N	N	N
Williamson County, Tennessee	N	N	N	N	N	N	N	N	N
Wilson County, Tennessee	N	N	N	1,706	54.9	26.3	N	N	N
TEXAS									
Angelina County, Texas	N	N	N	N	N	N	N	N	N
Bastrop County, Texas	N	N	N	N	N	N	N	N	N
Bell County, Texas	N	N	N	6,449	84.5	34.8	N	N	N
Bexar County, Texas	9,100	60.2	11.0	38,135	88.3	50.7	N	N	N
Bowie County, Texas	N	N	N	N	N	N	N	N	N
Brazoria County, Texas	N	N	N	15,405	95.0	70.8	N	N	N
Brazos County, Texas	N	N	N	N	N	N	N	N	N
Cameron County, Texas	N	N	N	N	N	N	N	N	N
Collin County, Texas	2,549	90.2	27.7	87,228	94.7	76.8	N	N	N
Comal County, Texas	N	N	N	N	N	N	N	N	N
Coryell County, Texas	N	N	N	N	N	N	N	N	N
Dallas County, Texas	4,662	77.9	20.3	108,723	82.2	56.1	N	N	N
Denton County, Texas	2,771	88.9	30.4	43,360	92.7	65.4	N	N	N
Ector County, Texas	N	N	N	N	N	N	N	N	N
Ellis County, Texas	N	N	N	N	N	N	N	N	N
El Paso County, Texas	3,678	87.5	15.0	7,431	88.0	41.2	N	N	N
Fort Bend County, Texas	N	N	N	96,942	91.5	65.0	N	N	N
Galveston County, Texas	N	N	N	8,460	82.6	51.7	N	N	N
Grayson County, Texas	N	N	N	N	N	N	N	N	N
Gregg County, Texas	N	N	N	N	N	N	N	N	N
Guadalupe County, Texas	N	N	N	N	N	N	N	N	N
Harris County, Texas	9,269	80.2	22.5	225,669	85.6	49.7	N	N	N
Harrison County, Texas	N	N	N	N	N	N	N	N	N
Hays County, Texas	N	N	N	N	N	N	N	N	N
Henderson County, Texas	N	N	N	N	N	N	N	N	N
Hidalgo County, Texas	N	N	N	5,747	96.3	62.9	N	N	N
Hunt County, Texas	N	N	N	N	N	N	N	N	N
Jefferson County, Texas	N	N	N	6,393	68.3	39.4	N	N	N
Johnson County, Texas	N	N	N	N	N	N	N	N	N
Kaufman County, Texas	N	N	N	N	N	N	N	N	N
Liberty County, Texas	N	N	N	N	N	N	N	N	N
Lubbock County, Texas	2,233	59.5	1.8	N	N	N	N	N	N
McLennan County, Texas	N	N	N	2,189	71.7	38.6	N	N	N
Midland County, Texas	N	N	N	N	N	N	N	N	N
Montgomery County, Texas	N	N	N	10,996	86.1	63.1	N	N	N
Nacogdoches County, Texas	N	N	N	N	N	N	N	N	N

N = Data for this geographic area cannot be displayed because the number of sample cases is too small.

Table C-2. Educational Attainment of the Population, by Selected Counties, 2016—*Continued*

(Number; percent; dollars.)

	Educational attainment by race/ethnicity, 25 years and over								
	White alone			White alone, not Hispanic			Black alone		
State/County	Total	High school graduate or more	Bachelor's degree or more	Total	High school graduate or more	Bachelor's degree or more	Total	High school graduate or more	Bachelor's degree or more
TEXAS—*(Continued)*									
Nueces County, Texas	210,764	82.8	22.1	80,592	93.1	34.9	8,960	91.0	18.9
Orange County, Texas	50,785	89.0	15.6	47,925	90.6	15.8	4,545	83.8	10.3
Parker County, Texas	82,907	89.1	21.9	76,310	90.0	23.2	N	N	N
Potter County, Texas	60,973	78.5	16.1	39,988	90.5	22.9	7,864	72.0	6.3
Randall County, Texas	79,178	90.8	31.9	67,394	94.6	35.5	N	N	N
Rockwall County, Texas	52,623	93.2	42.3	46,281	95.7	43.9	3,270	94.3	23.7
San Patricio County, Texas	40,355	79.0	14.7	18,698	91.8	23.7	N	N	N
Smith County, Texas	114,982	86.8	27.1	97,982	93.9	29.7	23,627	84.1	13.2
Tarrant County, Texas	907,534	87.1	33.6	696,518	94.6	39.5	196,619	90.7	22.7
Taylor County, Texas	68,563	90.8	24.1	57,501	92.6	26.6	5,561	85.6	12.7
Tom Green County, Texas	68,765	84.8	25.9	45,060	92.9	31.5	3,144	86.9	11.9
Travis County, Texas	627,032	90.4	50.9	449,921	97.2	60.9	64,080	90.0	26.0
Victoria County, Texas	52,868	84.8	19.6	30,761	94.6	29.0	4,008	91.7	9.2
Walker County, Texas	33,563	87.1	24.0	27,454	91.8	28.1	11,247	91.2	14.0
Webb County, Texas	140,905	66.5	16.9	6,666	95.9	50.6	N	N	N
Wichita County, Texas	70,014	87.9	24.3	59,731	90.8	26.2	7,809	74.3	17.9
Williamson County, Texas	284,953	94.7	39.4	226,177	97.2	42.7	20,262	91.5	34.1
UTAH									
Cache County, Utah	55,820	95.0	40.5	52,628	96.6	41.7	N	N	N
Davis County, Utah	179,616	96.5	38.9	170,844	96.9	39.8	N	N	N
Salt Lake County, Utah	573,767	94.2	36.3	535,040	95.2	37.5	9,987	81.4	17.6
Utah County, Utah	271,869	94.9	38.8	245,690	97.2	41.1	N	N	N
Washington County, Utah	94,001	95.5	28.8	91,098	96.0	29.4	N	N	N
Weber County, Utah	140,257	90.7	22.6	123,295	94.0	25.1	1,658	91.6	29.3
VERMONT									
Chittenden County, Vermont	97,450	95.7	50.6	96,277	95.7	50.7	N	N	N
VIRGINIA									
Albemarle County, Virginia	60,121	90.8	56.5	58,401	91.4	57.0	6,879	84.5	15.8
Arlington County, Virginia	123,880	97.7	82.4	110,747	99.3	86.1	14,313	86.6	46.6
Augusta County, Virginia	50,872	85.5	24.3	50,449	85.6	24.4	2,358	77.6	14.8
Bedford County, Virginia	50,776	92.0	29.9	50,322	91.9	29.8	4,178	81.6	21.8
Chesterfield County, Virginia	160,182	93.8	43.8	150,951	95.5	45.2	47,347	94.5	29.7
Fairfax County, Virginia	492,569	94.8	65.8	418,348	98.2	71.7	72,665	92.3	47.9
Fauquier County, Virginia	41,765	91.4	34.0	39,463	92.8	34.2	3,432	81.8	25.1
Frederick County, Virginia	53,736	91.3	29.4	50,957	92.4	30.3	N	N	N
Hanover County, Virginia	63,091	93.3	42.2	61,550	93.7	42.3	6,605	79.8	25.4
Henrico County, Virginia	136,532	94.1	47.1	129,562	94.8	48.6	63,235	87.8	24.6
James City County, Virginia	44,387	97.3	56.4	42,773	97.2	57.1	6,156	83.9	16.9
Loudoun County, Virginia	168,405	94.1	57.8	144,980	97.3	62.6	17,010	93.5	48.9
Montgomery County, Virginia	49,681	93.6	47.3	48,603	93.7	46.8	N	N	N
Prince William County, Virginia	168,952	90.5	43.0	137,671	95.5	48.0	58,574	93.8	41.3
Roanoke County, Virginia	60,464	91.6	34.1	59,698	91.7	34.4	4,068	90.9	27.7
Rockingham County, Virginia	51,980	83.2	27.0	50,313	84.8	27.4	N	N	N
Spotsylvania County, Virginia	65,366	91.9	34.7	63,307	92.9	35.2	14,008	92.8	18.1
Stafford County, Virginia	63,739	95.0	43.7	60,756	95.1	44.1	16,501	93.9	28.0
York County, Virginia	34,509	98.0	48.5	33,382	97.9	48.0	5,736	81.5	26.9
Alexandria city, Virginia	73,528	95.5	73.4	65,055	98.9	78.1	24,677	91.7	41.4
Chesapeake city, Virginia	102,838	93.7	33.3	97,000	93.6	33.1	47,769	86.1	25.5
Hampton city, Virginia	41,021	92.0	27.4	38,603	91.7	27.8	44,232	91.4	27.1
Lynchburg city, Virginia	29,553	89.9	43.1	28,990	90.0	43.4	13,280	81.8	11.1
Newport News city, Virginia	59,835	94.2	33.5	55,833	94.3	34.3	45,572	86.6	20.3
Norfolk city, Virginia	77,636	92.4	37.7	72,968	92.5	38.5	59,166	83.2	14.0
Portsmouth city, Virginia	28,358	92.2	26.4	27,118	92.5	26.9	30,809	82.8	16.1
Richmond city, Virginia	75,946	92.6	59.1	69,561	95.3	63.6	69,332	79.6	15.8
Roanoke city, Virginia	48,301	85.8	24.9	45,154	88.7	25.4	18,206	88.9	7.0
Suffolk city, Virginia	33,181	93.0	30.7	31,934	93.4	31.3	23,389	87.5	20.6
Virginia Beach city, Virginia	213,429	95.0	37.5	201,265	95.2	38.4	54,980	93.0	22.5
WASHINGTON									
Benton County, Washington	107,795	93.6	30.7	97,415	95.1	32.4	N	N	N
Chelan County, Washington	47,915	82.6	26.6	39,756	90.6	31.6	N	N	N
Clallam County, Washington	51,397	90.9	24.9	49,611	91.3	25.5	N	N	N
Clark County, Washington	272,845	94.0	29.5	261,969	94.8	29.9	5,798	90.9	28.2

N = Data for this geographic area cannot be displayed because the number of sample cases is too small.

Table C-2. Educational Attainment of the Population, by Selected Counties, 2016—*Continued*

(Number; percent; dollars.)

| | Educational attainment by race/ethnicity, 25 years and over | | | | | | | | |
| | American Indian or Alaska Native alone | | | Asian alone | | | Native Hawaiian or Other Pacific Islander alone | | |
State/County	Total	High school graduate or more	Bachelor's degree or more	Total	High school graduate or more	Bachelor's degree or more	Total	High school graduate or more	Bachelor's degree or more
TEXAS—*(Continued)*									
Nueces County, Texas	N	N	N	4,964	90.8	46.2	N	N	N
Orange County, Texas	N	N	N	N	N	N	N	N	N
Parker County, Texas	N	N	N	N	N	N	N	N	N
Potter County, Texas	N	N	N	3,251	52.7	22.3	N	N	N
Randall County, Texas	N	N	N	N	N	N	N	N	N
Rockwall County, Texas	N	N	N	1,639	74.8	38.1	N	N	N
San Patricio County, Texas	N	N	N	N	N	N	N	N	N
Smith County, Texas	N	N	N	N	N	N	N	N	N
Tarrant County, Texas	6,338	88.9	21.7	73,007	83.8	41.7	N	N	N
Taylor County, Texas	N	N	N	2,262	85.4	17.5	N	N	N
Tom Green County, Texas	N	N	N	N	N	N	N	N	N
Travis County, Texas	3,861	82.3	22.1	53,495	92.3	62.4	N	N	N
Victoria County, Texas	N	N	N	N	N	N	N	N	N
Walker County, Texas	N	N	N	N	N	N	N	N	N
Webb County, Texas	N	N	N	N	N	N	N	N	N
Wichita County, Texas	N	N	N	2,134	81.5	57.8	N	N	N
Williamson County, Texas	N	N	N	23,341	88.6	70.0	N	N	N
UTAH									
Cache County, Utah	N	N	N	N	N	N	N	N	N
Davis County, Utah	N	N	N	4,115	94.1	38.0	N	N	N
Salt Lake County, Utah	3,778	95.6	18.9	30,471	85.0	50.5	8,769	90.1	10.9
Utah County, Utah	N	N	N	4,349	99.2	67.3	3,018	90.3	5.1
Washington County, Utah	N	N	N	N	N	N	N	N	N
Weber County, Utah	N	N	N	2,103	87.9	38.9	N	N	N
VERMONT									
Chittenden County, Vermont	N	N	N	3,898	77.8	49.7	N	N	N
VIRGINIA									
Albemarle County, Virginia	N	N	N	N	N	N	N	N	N
Arlington County, Virginia	N	N	N	18,148	92.7	74.2	N	N	N
Augusta County, Virginia	N	N	N	N	N	N	N	N	N
Bedford County, Virginia	N	N	N	N	N	N	N	N	N
Chesterfield County, Virginia	N	N	N	9,605	88.4	58.2	N	N	N
Fairfax County, Virginia	N	N	N	153,343	88.7	61.2	N	N	N
Fauquier County, Virginia	N	N	N	N	N	N	N	N	N
Frederick County, Virginia	N	N	N	N	N	N	N	N	N
Hanover County, Virginia	N	N	N	N	N	N	N	N	N
Henrico County, Virginia	N	N	N	18,977	91.7	67.7	N	N	N
James City County, Virginia	N	N	N	N	N	N	N	N	N
Loudoun County, Virginia	N	N	N	44,235	91.2	73.8	N	N	N
Montgomery County, Virginia	N	N	N	N	N	N	N	N	N
Prince William County, Virginia	N	N	N	27,838	85.7	49.0	N	N	N
Roanoke County, Virginia	N	N	N	1,901	76.3	9.9	N	N	N
Rockingham County, Virginia	N	N	N	N	N	N	N	N	N
Spotsylvania County, Virginia	N	N	N	N	N	N	N	N	N
Stafford County, Virginia	N	N	N	3,904	88.3	42.9	N	N	N
York County, Virginia	N	N	N	N	N	N	N	N	N
Alexandria city, Virginia	N	N	N	7,646	91.1	62.7	N	N	N
Chesapeake city, Virginia	N	N	N	5,047	90.8	44.5	N	N	N
Hampton city, Virginia	N	N	N	2,467	78.8	30.2	N	N	N
Lynchburg city, Virginia	N	N	N	N	N	N	N	N	N
Newport News city, Virginia	N	N	N	3,342	78.8	20.4	N	N	N
Norfolk city, Virginia	N	N	N	6,118	92.0	46.6	N	N	N
Portsmouth city, Virginia	N	N	N	N	N	N	N	N	N
Richmond city, Virginia	N	N	N	N	N	N	N	N	N
Roanoke city, Virginia	N	N	N	N	N	N	N	N	N
Suffolk city, Virginia	N	N	N	1,284	69.0	36.2	N	N	N
Virginia Beach city, Virginia	N	N	N	22,214	87.0	44.2	N	N	N
WASHINGTON									
Benton County, Washington	N	N	N	3,681	80.5	42.2	N	N	N
Chelan County, Washington	N	N	N	N	N	N	N	N	N
Clallam County, Washington	1,916	81.2	8.1	N	N	N	N	N	N
Clark County, Washington	1,486	81.8	28.3	15,724	88.2	46.6	N	N	N

N = Data for this geographic area cannot be displayed because the number of sample cases is too small.

Table C-2. Educational Attainment of the Population, by Selected Counties, 2016—*Continued*

(Number; percent; dollars.)

	Educational attainment by race/ethnicity, 25 years and over								
	White alone			White alone, not Hispanic			Black alone		
State/County	Total	High school graduate or more	Bachelor's degree or more	Total	High school graduate or more	Bachelor's degree or more	Total	High school graduate or more	Bachelor's degree or more
WASHINGTON—*(Continued)*									
Cowlitz County, Washington	67,331	88.7	17.3	64,556	88.6	17.8	N	N	N
Franklin County, Washington	34,370	85.9	20.8	25,710	92.7	26.0	N	N	N
Grant County, Washington	40,041	86.5	22.9	36,368	90.1	24.9	N	N	N
Grays Harbor County, Washington	46,327	88.3	17.8	43,596	91.5	18.0	N	N	N
Island County, Washington	53,149	96.3	32.3	50,329	96.3	33.2	N	N	N
King County, Washington	1,049,772	95.9	54.3	999,068	96.7	55.3	82,294	82.9	27.8
Kitsap County, Washington	153,124	94.9	33.4	148,505	94.8	33.5	4,768	90.1	12.5
Lewis County, Washington	50,372	90.0	17.3	48,128	91.1	17.4	N	N	N
Pierce County, Washington	445,138	93.0	28.6	420,421	93.9	29.2	36,819	91.7	20.9
Skagit County, Washington	75,189	93.7	26.5	70,716	94.8	27.2	N	N	N
Snohomish County, Washington	429,493	94.0	30.5	407,908	94.9	31.2	15,486	84.4	22.0
Spokane County, Washington	306,298	95.3	31.6	299,383	95.6	31.7	5,071	94.4	37.9
Thurston County, Washington	163,799	94.5	36.3	153,765	95.7	37.0	6,336	92.9	33.3
Whatcom County, Washington	122,343	94.5	33.7	119,214	95.0	34.3	N	N	N
Yakima County, Washington	120,951	77.0	17.1	82,076	90.7	23.2	N	N	N
WEST VIRGINIA									
Berkeley County, West Virginia	69,730	87.5	21.1	68,093	87.6	21.5	6,469	87.6	15.8
Cabell County, West Virginia	59,068	86.7	25.8	58,676	86.6	25.9	2,480	92.6	10.0
Harrison County, West Virginia	46,828	88.2	24.6	46,362	88.1	24.5	N	N	N
Kanawha County, West Virginia	121,741	87.2	24.6	120,818	87.2	24.5	8,568	91.6	22.7
Monongalia County, West Virginia	59,062	92.6	39.3	58,067	93.7	39.6	N	N	N
Raleigh County, West Virginia	48,287	87.6	19.1	47,754	87.7	19.3	4,609	99.7	15.7
Wood County, West Virginia	59,419	91.7	24.9	58,897	91.8	25.0	N	N	N
WISCONSIN									
Brown County, Wisconsin	154,321	95.3	29.8	150,035	95.6	30.2	3,125	79.9	6.5
Dane County, Wisconsin	302,425	97.4	53.0	293,403	98.0	53.3	14,484	88.0	26.9
Dodge County, Wisconsin	60,901	91.4	16.7	59,160	92.5	17.0	N	N	N
Eau Claire County, Wisconsin	60,981	94.3	31.4	60,029	94.6	31.4	N	N	N
Fond du Lac County, Wisconsin	67,417	92.8	23.5	66,333	93.3	23.6	N	N	N
Jefferson County, Wisconsin	55,384	91.3	25.0	53,841	92.1	25.2	N	N	N
Kenosha County, Wisconsin	99,238	88.9	25.3	91,531	90.6	27.0	6,772	79.1	14.1
La Crosse County, Wisconsin	70,215	95.0	37.5	69,866	95.0	37.5	N	N	N
Manitowoc County, Wisconsin	54,669	92.8	19.5	53,595	93.5	19.5	N	N	N
Marathon County, Wisconsin	88,114	92.2	25.3	86,673	93.2	25.7	N	N	N
Milwaukee County, Wisconsin	412,531	93.1	37.7	374,571	95.2	39.9	144,690	82.3	14.4
Outagamie County, Wisconsin	114,830	95.0	27.8	113,268	95.5	27.7	N	N	N
Ozaukee County, Wisconsin	58,283	96.6	47.0	57,052	97.0	47.6	N	N	N
Portage County, Wisconsin	43,181	94.8	31.5	42,432	95.4	31.6	N	N	N
Racine County, Wisconsin	111,494	91.7	25.1	104,251	93.6	26.4	13,009	81.7	6.8
Rock County, Wisconsin	99,036	91.6	22.0	96,225	92.3	22.5	4,387	85.3	21.8
St. Croix County, Wisconsin	57,735	97.1	35.7	56,597	97.3	36.2	N	N	N
Sheboygan County, Wisconsin	74,790	94.8	26.2	71,452	95.3	26.8	N	N	N
Walworth County, Wisconsin	65,006	93.1	29.7	60,421	94.4	30.4	N	N	N
Washington County, Wisconsin	90,764	95.0	30.1	89,649	95.1	29.9	N	N	N
Waukesha County, Wisconsin	262,719	96.9	42.1	255,379	97.1	42.5	3,446	59.0	17.3
Winnebago County, Wisconsin	107,679	92.8	28.7	104,971	93.2	28.7	1,940	78.6	11.9
Wood County, Wisconsin	50,184	91.9	20.3	49,267	92.0	20.2	N	N	N
WYOMING									
Laramie County, Wyoming	61,071	94.4	28.1	54,263	96.1	29.1	N	N	N
Natrona County, Wyoming	52,029	94.3	23.6	48,914	95.1	25.2	N	N	N

N = Data for this geographic area cannot be displayed because the number of sample cases is too small.

Table C-2. Educational Attainment of the Population, by Selected Counties, 2016—*Continued*

(Number; percent; dollars.)

State/County	Educational attainment by race/ethnicity, 25 years and over								
	American Indian or Alaska Native alone			Asian alone			Native Hawaiian or Other Pacific Islander alone		
	Total	High school graduate or more	Bachelor's degree or more	Total	High school graduate or more	Bachelor's degree or more	Total	High school graduate or more	Bachelor's degree or more
WASHINGTON—*(Continued)*									
Cowlitz County, Washington	N	N	N	N	N	N	N	N	N
Franklin County, Washington	N	N	N	N	N	N	N	N	N
Grant County, Washington	N	N	N	N	N	N	N	N	N
Grays Harbor County, Washington	1,387	88.8	14.3	N	N	N	N	N	N
Island County, Washington	N	N	N	2,859	87.2	27.7	N	N	N
King County, Washington	7,829	77.0	12.9	258,554	88.3	59.7	10,367	80.3	12.9
Kitsap County, Washington	1,798	90.9	29.6	9,394	81.6	35.4	N	N	N
Lewis County, Washington	N	N	N	N	N	N	N	N	N
Pierce County, Washington	6,189	84.6	13.6	38,304	78.8	30.8	7,320	95.3	11.2
Skagit County, Washington	1,287	89.0	6.2	1,621	82.5	35.3	N	N	N
Snohomish County, Washington	4,932	89.3	14.5	57,960	90.8	49.7	2,991	70.3	6.3
Spokane County, Washington	4,559	97.0	13.2	7,049	75.3	34.5	N	N	N
Thurston County, Washington	N	N	N	11,075	88.0	36.9	N	N	N
Whatcom County, Washington	3,533	79.9	17.8	6,149	91.9	59.7	N	N	N
Yakima County, Washington	6,081	80.7	11.3	1,820	93.4	43.1	N	N	N
WEST VIRGINIA									
Berkeley County, West Virginia	N	N	N	N	N	N	N	N	N
Cabell County, West Virginia	N	N	N	N	N	N	N	N	N
Harrison County, West Virginia	N	N	N	N	N	N	N	N	N
Kanawha County, West Virginia	N	N	N	N	N	N	N	N	N
Monongalia County, West Virginia	N	N	N	N	N	N	N	N	N
Raleigh County, West Virginia	N	N	N	N	N	N	N	N	N
Wood County, West Virginia	N	N	N	N	N	N	N	N	N
WISCONSIN									
Brown County, Wisconsin	3,889	78.6	19.0	4,287	83.6	39.9	N	N	N
Dane County, Wisconsin	N	N	N	17,438	88.8	68.2	N	N	N
Dodge County, Wisconsin	N	N	N	N	N	N	N	N	N
Eau Claire County, Wisconsin	N	N	N	N	N	N	N	N	N
Fond du Lac County, Wisconsin	N	N	N	N	N	N	N	N	N
Jefferson County, Wisconsin	N	N	N	N	N	N	N	N	N
Kenosha County, Wisconsin	N	N	N	N	N	N	N	N	N
La Crosse County, Wisconsin	N	N	N	3,040	92.4	30.2	N	N	N
Manitowoc County, Wisconsin	N	N	N	N	N	N	N	N	N
Marathon County, Wisconsin	N	N	N	3,475	73.1	14.6	N	N	N
Milwaukee County, Wisconsin	3,741	83.9	15.2	23,870	78.5	40.6	N	N	N
Outagamie County, Wisconsin	1,749	84.3	14.1	3,782	65.2	35.3	N	N	N
Ozaukee County, Wisconsin	N	N	N	N	N	N	N	N	N
Portage County, Wisconsin	N	N	N	N	N	N	N	N	N
Racine County, Wisconsin	N	N	N	N	N	N	N	N	N
Rock County, Wisconsin	N	N	N	N	N	N	N	N	N
St. Croix County, Wisconsin	N	N	N	N	N	N	N	N	N
Sheboygan County, Wisconsin	N	N	N	N	N	N	N	N	N
Walworth County, Wisconsin	N	N	N	N	N	N	N	N	N
Washington County, Wisconsin	N	N	N	N	N	N	N	N	N
Waukesha County, Wisconsin	N	N	N	8,982	96.9	84.0	N	N	N
Winnebago County, Wisconsin	N	N	N	2,652	83.2	33.0	N	N	N
Wood County, Wisconsin	N	N	N	N	N	N	N	N	N
WYOMING									
Laramie County, Wyoming	N	N	N	N	N	N	N	N	N
Natrona County, Wyoming	N	N	N	N	N	N	N	N	N

N = Data for this geographic area cannot be displayed because the number of sample cases is too small.

Table C-2. Educational Attainment of the Population, by Selected Counties, 2016—*Continued*

(Number; percent; dollars.)

State/County	Educational attainment by race/ethnicity, 25 years and over								
	Some other race alone			Two or more races alone			Hispanic or Latino (of any race)		
	Total	High school graduate or more	Bachelor's degree or more	Total	High school graduate or more	Bachelor's degree or more	Total	High school graduate or more	Bachelor's degree or more
ALABAMA									
Baldwin County, Alabama	N	N	N	N	N	N	4,382	67.6	10.0
Calhoun County, Alabama	N	N	N	N	N	N	N	N	N
Cullman County, Alabama	N	N	N	N	N	N	N	N	N
DeKalb County, Alabama	N	N	N	N	N	N	N	N	N
Elmore County, Alabama	N	N	N	N	N	N	N	N	N
Etowah County, Alabama	N	N	N	N	N	N	N	N	N
Houston County, Alabama	N	N	N	761	81.1	5.4	1,663	74.9	7.8
Jefferson County, Alabama	6,462	47.9	2.2	5,729	91.2	38.5	12,441	55.9	10.9
Lauderdale County, Alabama	N	N	N	N	N	N	N	N	N
Lee County, Alabama	N	N	N	N	N	N	N	N	N
Limestone County, Alabama	N	N	N	N	N	N	N	N	N
Madison County, Alabama	N	N	N	4,794	87.6	40.7	9,233	60.4	24.3
Marshall County, Alabama	N	N	N	N	N	N	6,047	55.5	1.8
Mobile County, Alabama	2,588	59.5	19.1	2,904	84.1	28.9	6,940	80.4	26.2
Montgomery County, Alabama	N	N	N	N	N	N	3,403	51.1	18.3
Morgan County, Alabama	N	N	N	N	N	N	4,732	22.6	2.0
St. Clair County, Alabama	N	N	N	N	N	N	N	N	N
Shelby County, Alabama	4,523	52.7	19.5	N	N	N	6,716	64.8	30.5
Talladega County, Alabama	N	N	N	N	N	N	N	N	N
Tuscaloosa County, Alabama	N	N	N	N	N	N	3,865	78.5	4.7
Walker County, Alabama	N	N	N	1,236	64.1	4.2	N	N	N
ALASKA									
Anchorage Municipality, Alaska	4,543	84.7	11.0	11,085	94.0	29.6	13,330	81.1	14.5
Fairbanks North Star Borough, Alaska	N	N	N	N	N	N	N	N	N
Matanuska-Susitna Borough, Alaska	N	N	N	3,658	92.4	7.8	2,467	97.5	13.7
ARIZONA									
Apache County, Arizona	N	N	N	N	N	N	2,426	77.7	9.6
Cochise County, Arizona	N	N	N	N	N	N	25,441	73.4	12.3
Coconino County, Arizona	N	N	N	N	N	N	8,269	75.4	21.3
Maricopa County, Arizona	202,099	56.3	7.5	57,989	89.6	29.7	686,675	66.5	12.6
Mohave County, Arizona	N	N	N	2,780	96.0	27.0	19,837	77.8	7.5
Navajo County, Arizona	3,528	54.0	2.2	2,120	77.7	2.9	7,296	75.9	5.4
Pima County, Arizona	54,460	67.5	11.5	20,198	83.6	25.4	205,327	75.7	16.2
Pinal County, Arizona	11,091	74.2	8.8	4,372	87.1	11.0	69,362	70.2	9.4
Yavapai County, Arizona	2,968	80.8	2.0	N	N	N	17,692	80.0	7.4
Yuma County, Arizona	41,399	59.8	9.1	2,406	97.0	20.9	70,654	60.2	10.0
ARKANSAS									
Benton County, Arkansas	2,203	55.8	9.9	4,283	82.4	29.3	21,626	57.3	11.2
Craighead County, Arkansas	N	N	N	N	N	N	N	N	N
Faulkner County, Arkansas	N	N	N	N	N	N	N	N	N
Garland County, Arkansas	N	N	N	N	N	N	N	N	N
Jefferson County, Arkansas	N	N	N	N	N	N	N	N	N
Lonoke County, Arkansas	N	N	N	N	N	N	N	N	N
Pulaski County, Arkansas	4,276	58.9	22.0	5,691	83.9	17.9	11,473	66.2	14.9
Saline County, Arkansas	N	N	N	N	N	N	N	N	N
Sebastian County, Arkansas	6,866	36.3	5.4	2,245	96.0	30.0	9,409	46.3	8.4
Washington County, Arkansas	10,785	35.8	8.1	3,369	87.4	25.0	16,979	44.2	11.4
White County, Arkansas	N	N	N	N	N	N	N	N	N
CALIFORNIA									
Alameda County, California	103,801	65.0	11.4	49,382	88.9	42.3	218,972	69.7	18.0
Butte County, California	5,202	62.1	3.7	5,118	81.9	9.6	18,570	68.7	12.2
Contra Costa County, California	62,149	66.9	11.7	35,744	93.1	35.8	165,427	69.9	15.8
El Dorado County, California	2,308	66.7	18.5	2,727	97.1	51.7	12,855	80.0	22.1
Fresno County, California	79,685	54.1	6.8	15,884	82.8	18.7	276,084	60.6	9.5
Humboldt County, California	N	N	N	5,186	89.0	31.1	7,176	81.4	23.8
Imperial County, California	31,927	57.9	7.5	2,769	60.3	2.7	87,729	64.0	12.3
Kern County, California	57,554	59.4	7.9	14,567	80.3	17.4	242,795	56.2	7.5
Kings County, California	14,872	56.8	2.1	2,945	76.6	6.7	43,884	60.7	4.4
Lake County, California	5,380	78.1	14.5	N	N	N	8,151	69.4	13.4
Los Angeles County, California	1,344,136	58.7	9.3	189,359	88.9	39.1	2,944,413	60.5	11.8
Madera County, California	16,147	38.4	6.2	2,999	79.2	4.6	46,929	52.8	4.9
Marin County, California	14,534	46.5	13.3	6,817	97.7	51.9	24,076	63.7	23.8

N = Data for this geographic area cannot be displayed because the number of sample cases is too small.

Table C-2. Educational Attainment of the Population, by Selected Counties, 2016—*Continued*

(Number; percent; dollars.)

State/County	Median earnings in the past 12 months (2016 inflation-adjusted dollars)					
	Population 25 years and over with earnings					
	Total	Less than high school graduate	High school graduate (includes equivalency)	Some college or associate's degree	Bachelor's degree	Graduate or professional degree
ALABAMA						
Baldwin County, Alabama	38,174	25,198	29,985	32,211	55,804	53,423
Calhoun County, Alabama	31,177	15,302	25,377	31,883	46,061	51,174
Cullman County, Alabama	30,670	21,557	24,857	37,815	37,912	52,770
DeKalb County, Alabama	26,402	18,638	26,685	26,339	41,412	50,150
Elmore County, Alabama	37,194	15,786	28,832	35,747	42,225	62,402
Etowah County, Alabama	30,381	19,736	26,586	30,714	50,399	55,231
Houston County, Alabama	30,082	20,828	23,471	29,621	42,181	54,302
Jefferson County, Alabama	36,744	20,024	26,548	31,628	50,712	61,320
Lauderdale County, Alabama	31,171	22,930	25,418	28,763	41,781	51,165
Lee County, Alabama	36,041	16,700	30,901	31,168	41,484	58,401
Limestone County, Alabama	35,155	19,106	28,834	32,122	51,362	60,743
Madison County, Alabama	41,601	18,864	25,836	34,795	60,446	90,875
Marshall County, Alabama	30,317	19,239	28,030	30,407	44,107	49,857
Mobile County, Alabama	32,900	20,999	29,372	29,640	49,445	55,657
Montgomery County, Alabama	33,133	19,344	24,315	29,987	46,717	52,070
Morgan County, Alabama	31,917	16,519	25,574	40,300	41,563	52,228
St. Clair County, Alabama	36,068	23,384	35,521	33,196	60,725	50,054
Shelby County, Alabama	46,909	20,800	36,646	39,131	54,732	61,795
Talladega County, Alabama	29,629	20,664	25,880	28,789	36,604	48,791
Tuscaloosa County, Alabama	35,007	19,848	30,015	31,498	45,745	50,971
Walker County, Alabama	30,546	20,678	27,042	32,022	42,226	50,574
ALASKA						
Anchorage Municipality, Alaska	48,149	30,503	37,493	42,168	60,531	82,154
Fairbanks North Star Borough, Alaska	41,159	40,709	31,759	45,408	41,630	68,556
Matanuska-Susitna Borough, Alaska	37,447	35,200	31,151	36,818	46,754	76,440
ARIZONA						
Apache County, Arizona	35,333	17,479	26,674	35,465	46,408	55,607
Cochise County, Arizona	26,492	14,764	19,749	25,664	47,027	51,335
Coconino County, Arizona	35,029	21,368	27,000	31,387	41,131	51,975
Maricopa County, Arizona	38,457	22,110	30,378	36,279	52,077	66,763
Mohave County, Arizona	30,255	22,106	26,854	30,937	35,899	46,276
Navajo County, Arizona	28,901	25,226	18,328	29,820	40,179	46,505
Pima County, Arizona	31,975	19,220	24,685	31,314	43,319	58,427
Pinal County, Arizona	31,196	17,531	26,964	31,307	43,997	53,011
Yavapai County, Arizona	27,174	23,384	23,504	25,864	40,439	42,251
Yuma County, Arizona	28,633	18,596	28,787	28,405	47,367	45,939
ARKANSAS						
Benton County, Arkansas	39,352	25,402	27,217	37,680	61,958	68,311
Craighead County, Arkansas	30,688	20,104	22,460	26,938	42,710	55,296
Faulkner County, Arkansas	35,309	31,335	25,465	31,855	46,858	60,402
Garland County, Arkansas	27,449	13,188	26,323	27,095	36,926	56,804
Jefferson County, Arkansas	31,137	14,027	28,188	30,449	46,190	60,446
Lonoke County, Arkansas	36,217	21,677	29,055	36,970	45,222	51,762
Pulaski County, Arkansas	35,850	22,504	26,198	31,126	47,322	61,525
Saline County, Arkansas	40,340	26,022	30,713	36,750	57,917	60,482
Sebastian County, Arkansas	28,563	20,596	25,253	31,103	41,035	57,012
Washington County, Arkansas	32,402	25,595	29,756	30,485	45,746	52,630
White County, Arkansas	31,450	27,344	29,478	26,230	41,921	48,491
CALIFORNIA						
Alameda County, California	51,139	25,086	34,354	44,039	67,951	92,310
Butte County, California	32,357	21,745	23,962	31,606	46,777	64,138
Contra Costa County, California	51,059	23,964	33,951	45,557	71,331	93,650
El Dorado County, California	44,637	20,135	32,194	41,846	64,035	80,289
Fresno County, California	30,793	18,532	26,113	31,963	50,587	75,666
Humboldt County, California	29,711	21,294	25,425	27,582	38,650	50,627
Imperial County, California	26,434	15,105	23,644	26,580	40,101	60,098
Kern County, California	31,464	20,366	30,472	35,638	55,828	80,054
Kings County, California	31,489	21,708	31,092	31,114	54,048	75,288
Lake County, California	30,382	21,313	27,226	31,913	36,916	34,570
Los Angeles County, California	35,502	20,650	27,330	35,493	52,003	75,820
Madera County, California	26,683	17,234	26,108	35,103	54,312	70,377
Marin County, California	60,534	20,830	26,802	42,889	75,717	100,269

N = Data for this geographic area cannot be displayed because the number of sample cases is too small.

Table C-2. Educational Attainment of the Population, by Selected Counties, 2016—*Continued*

(Number; percent; dollars.)

	Educational attainment by race/ethnicity, 25 years and over								
	Some other race alone			Two or more races alone			Hispanic or Latino (of any race)		
State/County	Total	High school graduate or more	Bachelor's degree or more	Total	High school graduate or more	Bachelor's degree or more	Total	High school graduate or more	Bachelor's degree or more
CALIFORNIA—*(Continued)*									
Mendocino County, California	3,591	26.6	0.0	N	N	N	11,354	48.2	6.1
Merced County, California	42,718	42.4	5.6	3,441	86.7	22.6	82,029	53.2	6.5
Monterey County, California	72,457	38.3	6.3	8,067	91.2	41.1	137,619	48.0	9.1
Napa County, California	6,763	58.1	10.7	2,016	88.0	34.5	27,022	59.6	12.8
Nevada County, California	N	N	N	N	N	N	5,884	78.0	13.4
Orange County, California	204,512	54.0	10.2	53,762	90.6	43.7	618,761	63.1	13.6
Placer County, California	8,502	70.7	21.5	7,931	97.3	41.3	29,901	84.0	26.8
Riverside County, California	306,098	61.3	6.7	45,316	90.0	26.5	636,578	65.5	9.2
Sacramento County, California	67,097	63.2	9.8	47,647	89.5	27.3	191,141	69.6	15.5
San Bernardino County, California	212,859	61.0	9.3	45,063	85.7	20.5	623,437	65.6	10.2
San Diego County, California	102,417	65.5	12.7	74,735	92.0	35.3	635,448	66.2	15.2
San Francisco County, California	47,499	70.2	21.8	25,324	95.6	65.5	92,286	75.4	32.4
San Joaquin County, California	41,180	55.5	4.9	31,131	79.0	12.2	160,110	59.7	5.9
San Luis Obispo County, California	8,799	64.0	7.3	3,605	92.6	46.2	33,859	72.6	16.9
San Mateo County, California	51,841	63.1	15.1	18,472	93.0	50.8	115,233	69.1	20.7
Santa Barbara County, California	25,259	63.1	7.9	7,500	89.3	25.5	105,820	54.4	9.3
Santa Clara County, California	130,948	59.0	11.7	38,835	90.2	43.4	286,929	65.7	16.7
Santa Cruz County, California	22,017	48.6	5.1	5,264	93.0	43.2	48,560	59.0	13.4
Shasta County, California	N	N	N	3,702	85.6	10.6	9,232	82.5	11.4
Solano County, California	25,814	60.7	9.2	17,778	92.1	20.0	63,652	69.7	14.5
Sonoma County, California	40,373	50.5	6.0	10,724	86.2	25.8	74,308	59.6	12.5
Stanislaus County, California	38,624	51.1	8.0	9,017	81.1	16.1	131,235	60.1	7.1
Sutter County, California	1,766	50.1	10.3	2,673	70.5	18.4	14,747	54.5	10.8
Tulare County, California	40,028	52.9	4.0	5,240	74.2	18.2	151,045	54.6	5.7
Ventura County, California	28,913	65.7	11.1	16,529	95.6	38.0	205,075	62.8	12.8
Yolo County, California	6,382	53.6	15.9	5,763	85.1	42.0	35,916	62.4	15.5
Yuba County, California	N	N	N	N	N	N	10,703	70.7	11.0
COLORADO									
Adams County, Colorado	18,061	59.2	7.3	7,672	87.6	16.4	105,062	62.3	9.4
Arapahoe County, Colorado	26,504	76.8	8.6	9,167	95.3	35.5	63,878	74.5	15.3
Boulder County, Colorado	3,008	68.4	24.4	3,908	89.1	60.1	22,493	73.3	22.8
Broomfield County, Colorado	N	N	N	N	N	N	4,221	82.5	35.3
Denver County, Colorado	28,570	58.8	13.1	11,870	88.8	54.1	119,594	64.3	16.0
Douglas County, Colorado	N	N	N	3,065	100.0	54.1	15,831	96.6	47.8
El Paso County, Colorado	14,463	76.0	12.4	16,602	95.8	29.5	58,762	83.0	20.5
Jefferson County, Colorado	6,172	83.4	25.0	6,089	90.3	41.3	50,857	79.5	20.4
Larimer County, Colorado	3,408	82.2	23.8	4,363	88.5	33.7	19,338	86.5	28.8
Mesa County, Colorado	1,648	74.8	3.5	N	N	N	10,226	61.4	12.3
Pueblo County, Colorado	8,945	75.5	7.4	2,952	74.9	23.1	41,941	81.0	13.6
Weld County, Colorado	4,859	71.1	9.5	3,107	81.3	31.0	44,717	65.2	7.4
CONNECTICUT									
Fairfield County, Connecticut	32,770	62.3	13.6	10,562	88.9	42.2	108,427	71.2	19.5
Hartford County, Connecticut	34,035	66.0	9.6	11,029	86.7	26.8	88,125	69.8	13.6
Litchfield County, Connecticut	N	N	N	N	N	N	6,196	71.9	31.6
Middlesex County, Connecticut	N	N	N	N	N	N	5,816	74.6	34.4
New Haven County, Connecticut	27,214	66.4	12.0	12,145	89.4	31.6	82,500	73.8	16.3
New London County, Connecticut	5,091	81.5	27.9	3,907	93.0	13.6	14,221	86.0	25.1
Tolland County, Connecticut	N	N	N	N	N	N	4,452	80.7	36.0
Windham County, Connecticut	N	N	N	N	N	N	6,785	69.7	14.3
DELAWARE									
Kent County, Delaware	N	N	N	3,180	79.5	29.4	6,542	74.4	9.5
New Castle County, Delaware	6,467	74.2	13.2	4,569	88.5	30.8	29,160	69.5	18.1
Sussex County, Delaware	N	N	N	N	N	N	10,026	58.6	14.6
DISTRICT OF COLUMBIA									
District of Columbia, District of Columbia	21,627	56.9	24.1	9,884	96.1	74.4	47,175	67.8	41.5
FLORIDA									
Alachua County, Florida	N	N	N	3,359	75.1	32.5	12,544	81.4	37.8
Bay County, Florida	N	N	N	N	N	N	6,527	86.1	18.6
Brevard County, Florida	6,355	77.1	23.4	6,288	93.1	34.2	35,310	83.6	27.0
Broward County, Florida	42,445	85.0	22.4	31,957	78.7	28.8	371,516	84.4	28.0
Charlotte County, Florida	N	N	N	N	N	N	7,866	80.3	28.8
Citrus County, Florida	N	N	N	N	N	N	N	N	N

N = Data for this geographic area cannot be displayed because the number of sample cases is too small.

Table C-2. Educational Attainment of the Population, by Selected Counties, 2016—*Continued*

(Number; percent; dollars.)

State/County	Median earnings in the past 12 months (2016 inflation-adjusted dollars)					
	Population 25 years and over with earnings					
	Total	Less than high school graduate	High school graduate (includes equivalency)	Some college or associate's degree	Bachelor's degree	Graduate or professional degree
CALIFORNIA—*(Continued)*						
Mendocino County, California	26,364	18,111	23,925	30,162	31,690	50,917
Merced County, California	30,782	21,880	24,887	36,848	56,663	62,493
Monterey County, California	31,168	20,670	28,410	35,854	50,909	81,386
Napa County, California	42,066	22,558	31,829	40,949	61,830	93,371
Nevada County, California	37,052	23,590	28,845	31,883	41,726	64,722
Orange County, California	42,356	22,049	30,347	40,925	61,897	86,855
Placer County, California	51,710	25,777	32,837	47,713	68,057	87,994
Riverside County, California	35,473	21,867	30,738	36,244	52,002	75,687
Sacramento County, California	38,844	21,207	28,806	36,185	56,576	72,883
San Bernardino County, California	33,827	22,995	30,053	35,406	50,976	67,755
San Diego County, California	40,688	21,712	30,660	35,835	57,464	80,040
San Francisco County, California	61,426	23,129	30,349	41,057	76,065	100,774
San Joaquin County, California	36,332	22,365	31,792	41,405	53,467	72,593
San Luis Obispo County, California	42,336	26,153	34,726	40,829	52,777	66,297
San Mateo County, California	56,000	26,812	33,492	44,728	69,856	107,863
Santa Barbara County, California	35,326	22,139	30,478	35,929	52,487	70,151
Santa Clara County, California	60,543	25,238	33,794	43,316	81,539	115,610
Santa Cruz County, California	41,183	20,581	30,479	40,478	53,204	72,454
Shasta County, California	32,184	22,858	31,852	30,946	40,730	60,945
Solano County, California	41,447	24,965	35,696	40,751	57,181	76,726
Sonoma County, California	40,213	25,618	30,587	40,270	50,933	66,705
Stanislaus County, California	33,507	25,288	28,411	36,011	55,762	74,097
Sutter County, California	30,049	20,647	26,275	32,116	46,094	67,158
Tulare County, California	29,187	19,082	26,425	33,569	51,549	71,628
Ventura County, California	41,178	21,712	31,386	40,963	61,877	80,333
Yolo County, California	41,802	26,547	34,101	41,029	45,686	80,835
Yuba County, California	33,668	20,994	24,140	37,514	37,229	65,833
COLORADO						
Adams County, Colorado	39,657	26,386	34,733	40,430	55,765	59,384
Arapahoe County, Colorado	41,480	26,235	31,888	37,139	52,677	70,002
Boulder County, Colorado	45,900	23,466	32,512	36,515	51,083	66,210
Broomfield County, Colorado	54,385	22,415	40,135	39,592	66,877	90,939
Denver County, Colorado	41,986	23,803	30,017	35,818	51,822	65,852
Douglas County, Colorado	65,247	45,444	37,223	50,148	75,013	87,117
El Paso County, Colorado	37,724	23,128	29,907	32,029	46,114	68,449
Jefferson County, Colorado	45,563	27,294	35,047	40,941	56,513	66,025
Larimer County, Colorado	40,110	28,386	30,806	35,762	41,610	58,223
Mesa County, Colorado	32,535	31,322	28,302	29,655	39,767	51,745
Pueblo County, Colorado	33,777	23,528	29,685	34,110	41,547	53,155
Weld County, Colorado	40,079	26,847	32,728	37,470	55,494	59,602
CONNECTICUT						
Fairfield County, Connecticut	50,402	20,880	32,078	40,654	70,419	93,279
Hartford County, Connecticut	47,438	25,196	36,229	41,768	59,815	81,459
Litchfield County, Connecticut	45,456	23,636	40,247	39,580	54,782	71,364
Middlesex County, Connecticut	53,235	17,820	36,929	47,424	65,267	80,019
New Haven County, Connecticut	46,337	24,967	35,380	41,003	57,739	71,004
New London County, Connecticut	43,239	30,335	31,630	44,400	51,681	78,267
Tolland County, Connecticut	51,500	19,627	40,087	45,943	67,728	78,913
Windham County, Connecticut	41,753	26,319	37,435	41,282	62,309	59,576
DELAWARE						
Kent County, Delaware	35,755	25,975	32,550	32,912	45,149	60,697
New Castle County, Delaware	42,467	25,969	31,492	40,833	58,862	75,393
Sussex County, Delaware	36,152	27,598	31,786	34,421	49,168	66,065
DISTRICT OF COLUMBIA						
District of Columbia, District of Columbia	60,200	22,167	30,311	35,313	65,886	89,436
FLORIDA						
Alachua County, Florida	35,361	16,950	25,952	31,232	43,703	50,200
Bay County, Florida	30,612	18,120	25,747	30,358	45,136	56,338
Brevard County, Florida	33,374	19,955	25,740	30,382	50,125	70,318
Broward County, Florida	33,955	20,931	27,262	32,194	45,717	61,736
Charlotte County, Florida	28,452	16,602	26,278	26,344	41,415	37,114
Citrus County, Florida	28,452	18,763	23,927	30,073	41,022	80,127

N = Data for this geographic area cannot be displayed because the number of sample cases is too small.

Table C-2. Educational Attainment of the Population, by Selected Counties, 2016—*Continued*

(Number; percent; dollars.)

State/County	Some other race alone Total	Some other race alone High school graduate or more	Some other race alone Bachelor's degree or more	Two or more races alone Total	Two or more races alone High school graduate or more	Two or more races alone Bachelor's degree or more	Hispanic or Latino (of any race) Total	Hispanic or Latino (of any race) High school graduate or more	Hispanic or Latino (of any race) Bachelor's degree or more
FLORIDA—*(Continued)*									
Clay County, Florida	N	N	N	2,787	98.6	41.4	12,230	96.3	15.3
Collier County, Florida	5,009	40.0	12.4	N	N	N	58,722	58.8	7.6
Columbia County, Florida	N	N	N	N	N	N	2,566	39.6	4.9
Duval County, Florida	10,151	67.3	23.6	12,487	84.9	30.4	50,534	77.0	25.1
Escambia County, Florida	N	N	N	5,289	93.9	19.2	9,389	77.0	29.2
Flagler County, Florida	N	N	N	N	N	N	6,629	90.4	15.7
Hernando County, Florida	N	N	N	2,352	83.5	32.7	14,125	78.1	20.8
Highlands County, Florida	N	N	N	N	N	N	12,001	65.6	5.2
Hillsborough County, Florida	40,411	63.8	11.7	19,577	81.8	31.1	231,895	76.4	19.6
Indian River County, Florida	N	N	N	N	N	N	8,750	59.7	6.5
Lake County, Florida	N	N	N	2,991	95.6	39.9	28,347	76.0	22.1
Lee County, Florida	10,842	67.2	8.0	5,739	81.7	14.0	87,390	71.6	14.9
Leon County, Florida	N	N	N	N	N	N	8,248	87.3	49.2
Manatee County, Florida	4,693	61.0	10.4	2,550	90.3	29.0	32,393	65.8	20.9
Marion County, Florida	N	N	N	4,920	75.6	23.3	26,072	77.6	15.3
Martin County, Florida	N	N	N	N	N	N	10,574	63.0	16.8
Miami-Dade County, Florida	88,561	77.7	22.5	23,330	84.8	29.3	1,332,338	78.8	25.6
Monroe County, Florida	N	N	N	N	N	N	12,034	72.9	18.7
Nassau County, Florida	N	N	N	N	N	N	1,894	81.9	30.3
Okaloosa County, Florida	4,821	68.2	16.2	3,535	98.2	22.2	9,473	78.5	19.5
Orange County, Florida	42,850	80.2	19.0	20,517	85.2	29.9	250,017	78.2	23.1
Osceola County, Florida	14,872	89.6	17.6	5,902	93.4	24.2	107,972	84.5	15.2
Palm Beach County, Florida	16,233	70.9	21.1	13,247	86.3	27.6	195,689	73.0	21.8
Pasco County, Florida	3,765	68.4	16.5	4,618	78.6	27.5	44,290	80.7	18.8
Pinellas County, Florida	9,699	77.5	18.8	8,372	84.8	36.8	55,466	83.5	24.7
Polk County, Florida	6,498	79.9	17.7	6,201	89.0	21.3	78,618	75.9	13.8
Putnam County, Florida	N	N	N	N	N	N	3,277	52.0	3.9
St. Johns County, Florida	N	N	N	N	N	N	10,141	88.5	36.3
St. Lucie County, Florida	3,210	70.7	4.9	N	N	N	32,983	71.2	18.0
Santa Rosa County, Florida	N	N	N	3,054	94.3	26.1	5,793	86.6	30.7
Sarasota County, Florida	N	N	N	N	N	N	22,733	83.3	22.4
Seminole County, Florida	8,568	82.2	25.5	6,719	92.5	41.8	58,989	89.7	25.2
Sumter County, Florida	N	N	N	N	N	N	4,035	83.2	7.6
Volusia County, Florida	4,754	87.7	16.9	4,627	89.8	22.6	41,969	80.4	15.1
Walton County, Florida	N	N	N	N	N	N	N	N	N
GEORGIA									
Barrow County, Georgia	N	N	N	N	N	N	4,479	62.0	24.1
Bartow County, Georgia	N	N	N	N	N	N	N	N	N
Bibb County, Georgia	N	N	N	N	N	N	N	N	N
Bulloch County, Georgia	N	N	N	N	N	N	N	N	N
Carroll County, Georgia	N	N	N	N	N	N	N	N	N
Catoosa County, Georgia	N	N	N	N	N	N	N	N	N
Chatham County, Georgia	N	N	N	4,541	96.3	26.8	9,882	76.4	39.6
Cherokee County, Georgia	N	N	N	N	N	N	13,062	55.0	18.0
Clarke County, Georgia	N	N	N	N	N	N	6,241	46.0	17.6
Clayton County, Georgia	10,117	38.5	8.5	N	N	N	17,586	48.3	13.1
Cobb County, Georgia	19,410	56.1	7.3	7,823	91.1	45.9	50,352	64.7	17.6
Columbia County, Georgia	N	N	N	N	N	N	4,099	84.3	22.8
Coweta County, Georgia	N	N	N	N	N	N	5,678	70.6	28.5
DeKalb County, Georgia	4,908	58.6	22.8	9,247	85.7	38.9	32,575	51.9	21.5
Dougherty County, Georgia	N	N	N	N	N	N	N	N	N
Douglas County, Georgia	N	N	N	N	N	N	6,660	72.6	10.8
Fayette County, Georgia	N	N	N	N	N	N	4,832	78.7	24.7
Floyd County, Georgia	N	N	N	N	N	N	3,807	49.0	6.3
Forsyth County, Georgia	N	N	N	2,073	90.0	58.5	11,240	62.9	31.9
Fulton County, Georgia	6,719	59.6	27.1	11,854	94.3	56.9	41,230	69.9	31.2
Glynn County, Georgia	N	N	N	N	N	N	3,455	52.4	21.4
Gwinnett County, Georgia	47,663	57.2	10.7	10,980	97.5	32.5	100,515	61.9	14.9
Hall County, Georgia	N	N	N	N	N	N	27,128	42.4	5.9
Henry County, Georgia	N	N	N	N	N	N	8,519	64.9	12.6
Houston County, Georgia	N	N	N	N	N	N	5,800	61.0	16.5
Liberty County, Georgia	N	N	N	N	N	N	3,381	85.8	8.5
Lowndes County, Georgia	N	N	N	N	N	N	3,387	71.1	14.3
Muscogee County, Georgia	3,345	81.6	22.8	4,201	90.1	33.1	8,103	85.3	24.7
Newton County, Georgia	N	N	N	N	N	N	N	N	N
Paulding County, Georgia	N	N	N	N	N	N	N	N	N

N = Data for this geographic area cannot be displayed because the number of sample cases is too small.

Table C-2. Educational Attainment of the Population, by Selected Counties, 2016—*Continued*

(Number; percent; dollars.)

| State/County | Median earnings in the past 12 months (2016 inflation-adjusted dollars) | | | | | |
| | Population 25 years and over with earnings | | | | | |
	Total	Less than high school graduate	High school graduate (includes equivalency)	Some college or associate's degree	Bachelor's degree	Graduate or professional degree
FLORIDA—*(Continued)*						
Clay County, Florida	38,142	22,721	32,141	36,993	51,009	70,616
Collier County, Florida	29,832	20,892	26,305	32,443	42,490	62,055
Columbia County, Florida	31,411	16,297	26,678	31,097	46,535	52,297
Duval County, Florida	35,848	22,569	27,951	33,036	47,913	61,658
Escambia County, Florida	30,681	20,274	24,759	28,737	40,521	50,022
Flagler County, Florida	28,472	17,354	24,773	31,065	31,814	56,491
Hernando County, Florida	32,167	21,062	31,277	31,289	43,168	43,324
Highlands County, Florida	21,506	18,852	19,436	29,356	30,789	51,061
Hillsborough County, Florida	36,112	20,498	26,551	34,312	49,316	66,038
Indian River County, Florida	28,148	20,705	25,935	29,426	50,659	50,594
Lake County, Florida	30,607	21,508	26,609	31,029	38,561	46,849
Lee County, Florida	30,796	22,541	26,774	30,629	41,455	51,803
Leon County, Florida	37,562	19,361	26,461	30,474	44,071	52,125
Manatee County, Florida	32,118	23,062	26,366	32,076	47,191	53,602
Marion County, Florida	26,119	19,748	26,242	25,321	37,003	50,118
Martin County, Florida	33,872	19,109	24,032	37,097	42,886	61,848
Miami-Dade County, Florida	30,508	20,012	23,489	31,276	41,179	61,583
Monroe County, Florida	35,351	20,532	26,536	36,304	42,007	48,594
Nassau County, Florida	37,702	24,600	30,856	35,979	47,145	52,003
Okaloosa County, Florida	35,430	18,667	29,063	32,292	40,323	71,922
Orange County, Florida	32,246	22,508	25,907	30,754	45,740	56,086
Osceola County, Florida	28,115	21,031	25,584	28,948	42,247	45,510
Palm Beach County, Florida	35,144	20,938	26,279	34,246	45,953	61,988
Pasco County, Florida	34,829	19,477	25,229	33,978	47,081	61,540
Pinellas County, Florida	34,065	21,935	26,946	31,934	46,548	57,774
Polk County, Florida	31,459	23,900	26,896	32,194	42,332	50,648
Putnam County, Florida	26,411	21,297	23,593	29,649	45,376	42,867
St. Johns County, Florida	42,049	20,170	30,121	38,667	51,383	77,258
St. Lucie County, Florida	27,806	19,426	22,225	33,012	40,396	44,285
Santa Rosa County, Florida	36,761	20,335	26,107	36,929	60,762	80,505
Sarasota County, Florida	31,916	21,274	28,061	31,108	41,412	57,154
Seminole County, Florida	40,008	21,314	31,212	32,103	50,699	60,119
Sumter County, Florida	20,619	16,305	20,382	17,231	22,492	46,474
Volusia County, Florida	30,790	21,842	26,621	30,294	41,289	52,956
Walton County, Florida	32,372	27,653	32,073	29,344	43,914	80,566
GEORGIA						
Barrow County, Georgia	35,150	26,512	35,158	31,812	44,716	47,056
Bartow County, Georgia	32,397	15,802	31,514	35,135	47,625	83,028
Bibb County, Georgia	30,055	11,825	23,360	26,979	40,109	64,226
Bulloch County, Georgia	31,332	19,334	27,749	29,180	37,929	49,941
Carroll County, Georgia	37,180	24,313	31,395	35,319	51,700	52,118
Catoosa County, Georgia	35,214	22,108	31,802	29,338	49,429	53,398
Chatham County, Georgia	35,596	19,911	28,449	32,387	42,404	51,432
Cherokee County, Georgia	46,252	20,656	36,514	41,491	59,830	72,724
Clarke County, Georgia	26,940	19,014	20,292	24,489	38,229	45,008
Clayton County, Georgia	31,062	22,424	24,875	31,074	41,184	50,571
Cobb County, Georgia	42,332	22,594	30,057	34,389	55,076	71,074
Columbia County, Georgia	41,749	28,606	28,234	41,814	46,595	69,372
Coweta County, Georgia	45,288	31,221	33,525	41,869	61,178	67,054
DeKalb County, Georgia	38,568	20,360	26,253	31,739	51,323	65,292
Dougherty County, Georgia	28,318	12,216	21,655	27,403	48,935	60,291
Douglas County, Georgia	36,123	22,399	27,433	35,320	49,778	54,826
Fayette County, Georgia	50,831	14,117	30,551	47,383	55,739	75,221
Floyd County, Georgia	32,151	21,149	26,694	30,666	47,652	57,055
Forsyth County, Georgia	56,138	21,374	31,801	44,739	75,142	90,706
Fulton County, Georgia	45,310	17,051	25,462	30,758	57,906	76,432
Glynn County, Georgia	30,622	16,265	25,036	30,523	40,702	57,520
Gwinnett County, Georgia	37,351	24,117	30,537	37,317	50,091	61,002
Hall County, Georgia	31,714	24,268	30,841	34,467	40,819	51,286
Henry County, Georgia	41,103	19,724	34,370	37,185	45,075	61,790
Houston County, Georgia	42,113	20,454	30,993	38,587	58,496	75,780
Liberty County, Georgia	32,149	22,664	31,926	31,607	31,496	50,337
Lowndes County, Georgia	32,143	18,110	28,678	29,880	35,402	56,168
Muscogee County, Georgia	30,867	16,548	22,869	27,910	45,261	62,025
Newton County, Georgia	32,874	13,028	32,039	34,882	45,114	58,876
Paulding County, Georgia	40,443	20,252	30,671	40,868	55,577	63,753

N = Data for this geographic area cannot be displayed because the number of sample cases is too small.

Table C-2. Educational Attainment of the Population, by Selected Counties, 2016—*Continued*

(Number; percent; dollars.)

State/County	Educational attainment by race/ethnicity, 25 years and over								
	Some other race alone			Two or more races alone			Hispanic or Latino (of any race)		
	Total	High school graduate or more	Bachelor's degree or more	Total	High school graduate or more	Bachelor's degree or more	Total	High school graduate or more	Bachelor's degree or more
GEORGIA—*(Continued)*									
Richmond County, Georgia	N	N	N	N	N	N	5,254	79.9	8.5
Rockdale County, Georgia	N	N	N	N	N	N	N	N	N
Troup County, Georgia	N	N	N	N	N	N	N	N	N
Walker County, Georgia	N	N	N	N	N	N	N	N	N
Walton County, Georgia	N	N	N	N	N	N	N	N	N
Whitfield County, Georgia	N	N	N	N	N	N	17,707	38.2	3.9
HAWAII									
Hawaii County, Hawaii	N	N	N	28,646	92.2	16.1	11,917	89.8	9.0
Honolulu County, Hawaii	5,484	90.7	15.4	126,715	94.4	25.6	47,821	92.7	20.4
Kauai County, Hawaii	N	N	N	8,590	94.7	9.7	4,077	88.6	9.6
Maui County, Hawaii	N	N	N	16,141	94.6	10.4	9,682	85.0	10.2
IDAHO									
Ada County, Idaho	N	N	N	6,122	87.3	52.7	18,793	84.2	16.9
Bannock County, Idaho	N	N	N	N	N	N	3,317	53.1	9.6
Bonneville County, Idaho	3,684	61.0	5.4	N	N	N	6,503	66.4	10.4
Canyon County, Idaho	11,898	45.4	1.2	N	N	N	25,018	56.7	3.8
Kootenai County, Idaho	N	N	N	N	N	N	2,845	99.6	18.3
Twin Falls County, Idaho	N	N	N	N	N	N	6,128	64.4	7.2
ILLINOIS									
Adams County, Illinois	N	N	N	N	N	N	N	N	N
Champaign County, Illinois	N	N	N	1,932	92.5	42.8	5,200	92.1	50.5
Cook County, Illinois	302,738	61.4	11.1	60,598	89.9	47.1	756,670	67.6	15.3
DeKalb County, Illinois	N	N	N	N	N	N	4,976	86.4	7.3
DuPage County, Illinois	19,419	54.6	9.7	10,823	86.5	39.7	71,970	67.2	17.7
Kane County, Illinois	50,304	49.8	3.2	4,919	90.4	39.7	88,817	56.1	6.7
Kankakee County, Illinois	N	N	N	N	N	N	5,733	53.9	4.0
Kendall County, Illinois	N	N	N	N	N	N	11,743	60.6	16.1
Lake County, Illinois	28,269	53.2	7.4	4,737	85.3	42.9	77,766	63.7	12.1
LaSalle County, Illinois	N	N	N	N	N	N	5,513	63.5	8.6
McHenry County, Illinois	2,670	48.4	8.8	2,380	100.0	34.1	19,502	70.4	15.5
McLean County, Illinois	N	N	N	N	N	N	3,715	92.9	21.6
Macon County, Illinois	N	N	N	2,817	70.6	6.7	N	N	N
Madison County, Illinois	N	N	N	2,294	87.2	36.1	4,343	95.3	14.2
Peoria County, Illinois	N	N	N	N	N	N	4,350	79.8	30.4
Rock Island County, Illinois	N	N	N	N	N	N	9,974	74.2	13.9
St. Clair County, Illinois	2,350	59.9	2.9	1,947	100.0	21.6	5,846	74.8	19.4
Sangamon County, Illinois	N	N	N	1,582	100.0	36.0	2,067	91.8	42.0
Tazewell County, Illinois	N	N	N	N	N	N	N	N	N
Vermilion County, Illinois	N	N	N	N	N	N	1,714	73.8	4.6
Will County, Illinois	26,220	61.1	7.5	6,645	92.4	24.5	61,903	69.4	15.4
Williamson County, Illinois	N	N	N	N	N	N	N	N	N
Winnebago County, Illinois	2,799	56.0	16.4	4,004	96.9	30.3	17,628	64.6	8.8
INDIANA									
Allen County, Indiana	2,519	66.2	13.7	4,066	90.0	13.3	13,157	72.6	14.7
Bartholomew County, Indiana	N	N	N	N	N	N	N	N	N
Clark County, Indiana	N	N	N	N	N	N	3,001	47.5	0.7
Delaware County, Indiana	N	N	N	N	N	N	N	N	N
Elkhart County, Indiana	N	N	N	N	N	N	14,820	45.0	4.9
Floyd County, Indiana	N	N	N	N	N	N	N	N	N
Grant County, Indiana	N	N	N	N	N	N	1,116	88.1	14.4
Hamilton County, Indiana	N	N	N	N	N	N	7,216	89.3	44.0
Hancock County, Indiana	N	N	N	N	N	N	N	N	N
Hendricks County, Indiana	N	N	N	N	N	N	N	N	N
Howard County, Indiana	N	N	N	N	N	N	N	N	N
Johnson County, Indiana	N	N	N	N	N	N	N	N	N
Kosciusko County, Indiana	N	N	N	N	N	N	N	N	N
Lake County, Indiana	27,552	70.9	14.1	4,840	89.7	14.5	51,325	75.5	14.9
LaPorte County, Indiana	N	N	N	N	N	N	3,917	71.0	6.7
Madison County, Indiana	N	N	N	N	N	N	2,607	69.0	9.7
Marion County, Indiana	18,584	54.1	7.4	10,927	86.1	23.6	45,619	60.2	11.6
Monroe County, Indiana	N	N	N	N	N	N	N	N	N
Morgan County, Indiana	N	N	N	N	N	N	N	N	N
Porter County, Indiana	N	N	N	N	N	N	8,806	77.6	14.5

N = Data for this geographic area cannot be displayed because the number of sample cases is too small.

Table C-2. Educational Attainment of the Population, by Selected Counties, 2016—*Continued*

(Number; percent; dollars.)

| State/County | Median earnings in the past 12 months (2016 inflation-adjusted dollars) | | | | | |
| | Population 25 years and over with earnings | | | | | |
	Total	Less than high school graduate	High school graduate (includes equivalency)	Some college or associate's degree	Bachelor's degree	Graduate or professional degree
GEORGIA—*(Continued)*						
Richmond County, Georgia	27,594	13,612	22,824	27,450	39,749	51,604
Rockdale County, Georgia	35,350	24,777	28,072	35,370	51,835	50,739
Troup County, Georgia	28,067	13,515	24,834	29,802	40,866	57,408
Walker County, Georgia	30,616	26,510	25,754	30,638	45,253	54,907
Walton County, Georgia	35,817	21,992	30,556	32,241	47,304	55,772
Whitfield County, Georgia	31,117	23,185	30,092	36,595	39,100	51,687
HAWAII						
Hawaii County, Hawaii	34,489	24,660	30,706	34,761	45,125	52,236
Honolulu County, Hawaii	41,570	23,145	31,670	40,315	50,991	66,466
Kauai County, Hawaii	36,649	19,569	28,094	39,969	45,012	65,249
Maui County, Hawaii	35,786	25,936	32,172	33,592	45,341	62,509
IDAHO						
Ada County, Idaho	39,142	25,079	30,385	36,309	45,775	66,014
Bannock County, Idaho	31,277	30,276	26,429	30,184	35,995	54,409
Bonneville County, Idaho	35,371	24,642	23,245	30,349	54,526	72,279
Canyon County, Idaho	29,630	26,349	27,492	28,566	40,259	44,184
Kootenai County, Idaho	29,611	17,469	23,733	28,448	47,011	51,041
Twin Falls County, Idaho	31,984	20,553	28,076	32,381	38,801	62,083
ILLINOIS						
Adams County, Illinois	38,137	27,692	32,116	32,395	42,390	56,205
Champaign County, Illinois	40,363	18,242	32,146	32,205	47,848	52,519
Cook County, Illinois	41,216	22,280	30,149	35,698	55,680	72,076
DeKalb County, Illinois	37,264	27,594	26,714	35,215	48,333	60,490
DuPage County, Illinois	50,204	24,754	31,555	41,204	61,211	77,373
Kane County, Illinois	40,404	23,394	29,402	38,498	65,049	71,352
Kankakee County, Illinois	36,555	21,782	32,876	37,742	45,481	50,875
Kendall County, Illinois	50,951	25,810	42,459	36,843	68,815	67,699
Lake County, Illinois	47,043	22,195	31,092	40,754	67,330	91,156
LaSalle County, Illinois	37,761	21,452	29,299	40,205	41,929	62,183
McHenry County, Illinois	43,675	21,250	35,866	42,330	63,054	72,252
McLean County, Illinois	43,918	16,201	30,778	36,696	60,803	65,108
Macon County, Illinois	35,823	19,281	30,292	31,360	50,763	61,850
Madison County, Illinois	39,173	18,858	27,221	36,755	49,461	65,170
Peoria County, Illinois	36,189	19,242	21,871	33,002	50,256	80,185
Rock Island County, Illinois	35,552	20,231	30,300	35,287	45,022	58,771
St. Clair County, Illinois	36,284	16,475	26,693	33,410	49,601	64,569
Sangamon County, Illinois	37,614	20,845	26,776	35,574	48,586	61,534
Tazewell County, Illinois	40,277	22,166	34,026	34,196	55,404	68,955
Vermilion County, Illinois	32,468	29,653	31,288	32,176	49,565	51,457
Will County, Illinois	47,108	25,312	35,089	41,303	60,418	76,975
Williamson County, Illinois	36,085	26,450	26,364	32,079	47,016	61,159
Winnebago County, Illinois	32,324	20,387	27,674	30,906	46,992	65,938
INDIANA						
Allen County, Indiana	36,221	22,439	31,041	33,332	45,821	60,663
Bartholomew County, Indiana	35,428	18,618	30,453	30,160	52,712	85,431
Clark County, Indiana	35,381	25,396	31,198	33,401	51,652	50,809
Delaware County, Indiana	33,361	30,103	30,706	30,714	41,665	55,361
Elkhart County, Indiana	31,996	30,126	30,339	32,033	40,048	50,024
Floyd County, Indiana	38,555	22,541	32,598	35,907	51,659	63,896
Grant County, Indiana	27,671	13,578	24,837	28,232	34,092	61,634
Hamilton County, Indiana	53,539	22,215	30,757	40,372	66,463	81,084
Hancock County, Indiana	43,388	2,500-	30,689	41,118	62,032	65,308
Hendricks County, Indiana	46,083	26,573	32,280	41,740	60,269	55,196
Howard County, Indiana	34,564	21,395	25,710	37,814	44,040	52,855
Johnson County, Indiana	40,319	22,110	32,345	37,303	50,189	60,721
Kosciusko County, Indiana	34,421	23,069	31,933	35,992	42,180	56,667
Lake County, Indiana	36,641	22,031	32,840	32,027	47,355	59,445
LaPorte County, Indiana	36,912	22,010	31,139	35,603	50,096	62,037
Madison County, Indiana	33,254	20,533	31,301	33,841	40,224	54,767
Marion County, Indiana	35,080	20,419	28,679	32,105	46,724	61,012
Monroe County, Indiana	32,485	16,139	27,549	28,265	37,469	49,140
Morgan County, Indiana	36,187	28,025	32,916	36,427	48,549	67,468
Porter County, Indiana	41,944	31,307	35,525	42,177	47,689	62,291

N = Data for this geographic area cannot be displayed because the number of sample cases is too small.

Table C-2. Educational Attainment of the Population, by Selected Counties, 2016—*Continued*

(Number; percent; dollars.)

State/County	Some other race alone			Two or more races alone			Hispanic or Latino (of any race)		
	Total	High school graduate or more	Bachelor's degree or more	Total	High school graduate or more	Bachelor's degree or more	Total	High school graduate or more	Bachelor's degree or more
INDIANA—*(Continued)*									
St. Joseph County, Indiana	4,062	54.4	6.5	N	N	N	10,546	64.2	11.6
Tippecanoe County, Indiana	3,523	58.8	2.8	N	N	N	6,943	66.0	7.7
Vanderburgh County, Indiana	N	N	N	N	N	N	2,404	49.4	10.1
Vigo County, Indiana	N	N	N	N	N	N	N	N	N
Wayne County, Indiana	N	N	N	N	N	N	N	N	N
IOWA									
Black Hawk County, Iowa	N	N	N	N	N	N	2,156	73.7	22.8
Dallas County, Iowa	N	N	N	N	N	N	N	N	N
Dubuque County, Iowa	N	N	N	N	N	N	N	N	N
Johnson County, Iowa	N	N	N	N	N	N	3,894	58.9	22.6
Linn County, Iowa	N	N	N	N	N	N	3,461	85.3	34.2
Polk County, Iowa	5,254	58.7	15.0	3,059	91.8	34.6	18,492	59.9	15.4
Pottawattamie County, Iowa	N	N	N	N	N	N	3,174	81.1	15.0
Scott County, Iowa	N	N	N	N	N	N	5,772	80.8	14.4
Story County, Iowa	N	N	N	N	N	N	N	N	N
Woodbury County, Iowa	N	N	N	N	N	N	7,208	45.1	3.5
KANSAS									
Butler County, Kansas	N	N	N	N	N	N	N	N	N
Douglas County, Kansas	N	N	N	N	N	N	3,712	88.8	35.0
Johnson County, Kansas	3,090	60.1	18.1	5,694	98.0	62.3	22,727	68.0	30.7
Leavenworth County, Kansas	N	N	N	N	N	N	2,661	95.9	12.5
Riley County, Kansas	N	N	N	N	N	N	N	N	N
Sedgwick County, Kansas	10,026	61.3	15.5	6,685	88.5	27.8	34,579	61.8	15.2
Shawnee County, Kansas	4,833	79.8	8.7	2,761	87.9	8.6	10,996	88.2	11.6
Wyandotte County, Kansas	7,817	40.4	6.0	N	N	N	23,096	48.7	7.9
KENTUCKY									
Boone County, Kentucky	N	N	N	N	N	N	N	N	N
Bullitt County, Kentucky	N	N	N	N	N	N	N	N	N
Campbell County, Kentucky	N	N	N	N	N	N	N	N	N
Christian County, Kentucky	N	N	N	N	N	N	N	N	N
Daviess County, Kentucky	N	N	N	N	N	N	N	N	N
Fayette County, Kentucky	5,504	50.4	6.8	3,043	93.4	47.9	10,982	60.2	13.6
Hardin County, Kentucky	N	N	N	N	N	N	3,200	100.0	40.0
Jefferson County, Kentucky	4,023	68.2	15.5	6,418	92.1	24.3	20,990	77.9	28.6
Kenton County, Kentucky	N	N	N	N	N	N	N	N	N
McCracken County, Kentucky	N	N	N	N	N	N	N	N	N
Madison County, Kentucky	N	N	N	N	N	N	N	N	N
Pike County, Kentucky	N	N	N	N	N	N	N	N	N
Warren County, Kentucky	N	N	N	N	N	N	N	N	N
LOUISIANA									
Ascension Parish, Louisiana	N	N	N	N	N	N	N	N	N
Bossier Parish, Louisiana	N	N	N	N	N	N	4,431	69.8	2.0
Caddo Parish, Louisiana	N	N	N	N	N	N	3,901	69.0	20.5
Calcasieu Parish, Louisiana	N	N	N	N	N	N	3,715	82.8	11.0
East Baton Rouge Parish, Louisiana	N	N	N	N	N	N	10,396	73.7	18.3
Iberia Parish, Louisiana	N	N	N	N	N	N	N	N	N
Jefferson Parish, Louisiana	11,798	54.2	7.4	4,277	90.2	29.1	39,530	68.8	14.8
Lafayette Parish, Louisiana	N	N	N	N	N	N	6,712	72.6	12.0
Lafourche Parish, Louisiana	N	N	N	N	N	N	N	N	N
Livingston Parish, Louisiana	N	N	N	N	N	N	N	N	N
Orleans Parish, Louisiana	3,202	77.4	21.9	4,093	93.4	49.0	14,660	82.1	37.3
Ouachita Parish, Louisiana	N	N	N	N	N	N	N	N	N
Rapides Parish, Louisiana	N	N	N	N	N	N	2,287	68.1	22.4
St. Landry Parish, Louisiana	N	N	N	N	N	N	N	N	N
St. Tammany Parish, Louisiana	N	N	N	N	N	N	8,273	76.8	18.3
Tangipahoa Parish, Louisiana	N	N	N	N	N	N	3,306	85.3	36.9
Terrebonne Parish, Louisiana	N	N	N	N	N	N	3,196	56.3	3.1
MAINE									
Androscoggin County, Maine	N	N	N	N	N	N	N	N	N
Aroostook County, Maine	N	N	N	N	N	N	N	N	N
Cumberland County, Maine	N	N	N	3,238	85.1	34.0	N	N	N
Kennebec County, Maine	N	N	N	N	N	N	N	N	N

N = Data for this geographic area cannot be displayed because the number of sample cases is too small.

Table C-2. Educational Attainment of the Population, by Selected Counties, 2016—*Continued*

(Number; percent; dollars.)

State/County	Median earnings in the past 12 months (2016 inflation-adjusted dollars)					
	Population 25 years and over with earnings					
	Total	Less than high school graduate	High school graduate (includes equivalency)	Some college or associate's degree	Bachelor's degree	Graduate or professional degree
INDIANA—*(Continued)*						
St. Joseph County, Indiana	35,283	24,759	29,825	31,762	48,991	52,239
Tippecanoe County, Indiana	36,472	23,714	31,666	31,161	47,299	55,838
Vanderburgh County, Indiana	32,837	17,927	25,817	32,077	44,634	51,433
Vigo County, Indiana	29,640	16,809	23,821	27,434	41,214	61,018
Wayne County, Indiana	30,933	15,575	28,983	30,035	42,349	61,325
IOWA						
Black Hawk County, Iowa	36,241	25,943	29,675	35,785	41,377	65,378
Dallas County, Iowa	51,328	29,907	31,587	41,041	65,569	84,038
Dubuque County, Iowa	37,103	20,563	31,589	32,960	49,703	69,295
Johnson County, Iowa	42,112	25,304	27,687	37,025	46,162	60,006
Linn County, Iowa	41,644	22,649	35,755	36,904	50,234	80,365
Polk County, Iowa	40,980	23,232	31,221	37,003	52,363	70,232
Pottawattamie County, Iowa	39,671	31,917	31,656	37,602	53,429	65,456
Scott County, Iowa	37,441	28,419	30,767	33,422	52,199	73,926
Story County, Iowa	41,944	29,008	34,450	41,897	41,498	51,579
Woodbury County, Iowa	36,113	31,906	31,045	33,175	45,425	57,224
KANSAS						
Butler County, Kansas	40,656	21,278	27,609	40,602	45,586	45,431
Douglas County, Kansas	36,432	19,779	27,073	28,983	39,007	51,915
Johnson County, Kansas	48,822	22,830	30,397	39,589	55,611	70,436
Leavenworth County, Kansas	40,447	31,180	31,080	32,005	60,185	77,318
Riley County, Kansas	35,515	12,826	25,470	33,468	35,713	48,009
Sedgwick County, Kansas	36,904	23,584	29,112	34,889	47,504	56,928
Shawnee County, Kansas	36,916	16,994	30,488	33,007	45,862	57,024
Wyandotte County, Kansas	30,440	21,561	26,952	30,545	43,421	57,211
KENTUCKY						
Boone County, Kentucky	43,773	27,081	34,375	39,506	71,089	53,611
Bullitt County, Kentucky	39,431	21,048	36,103	37,821	65,792	63,910
Campbell County, Kentucky	44,510	19,692	36,679	37,139	58,222	61,060
Christian County, Kentucky	31,805	25,503	25,973	31,413	41,577	59,671
Daviess County, Kentucky	39,440	21,506	34,138	36,373	45,375	59,637
Fayette County, Kentucky	36,368	21,289	25,672	29,436	46,145	59,166
Hardin County, Kentucky	37,154	15,417	24,680	38,261	47,885	59,543
Jefferson County, Kentucky	37,151	18,995	29,318	34,255	50,366	61,415
Kenton County, Kentucky	41,239	24,418	33,465	39,788	49,763	56,592
McCracken County, Kentucky	31,020	17,123	25,857	30,105	40,876	50,833
Madison County, Kentucky	35,242	20,658	29,234	29,210	43,255	54,862
Pike County, Kentucky	46,477	20,927	29,117	34,767	60,378	90,948
Warren County, Kentucky	31,829	21,746	30,665	28,754	41,786	51,159
LOUISIANA						
Ascension Parish, Louisiana	47,457	21,050	39,358	48,268	50,385	77,414
Bossier Parish, Louisiana	34,373	17,279	25,351	33,259	46,234	60,958
Caddo Parish, Louisiana	29,975	15,419	20,434	29,810	43,874	52,369
Calcasieu Parish, Louisiana	35,650	23,510	26,793	36,528	42,122	53,508
East Baton Rouge Parish, Louisiana	36,666	18,706	26,801	32,792	47,739	63,042
Iberia Parish, Louisiana	31,992	31,771	29,266	31,618	40,830	40,357
Jefferson Parish, Louisiana	35,587	21,725	30,794	32,062	47,960	54,881
Lafayette Parish, Louisiana	36,443	14,238	26,602	33,712	51,382	51,466
Lafourche Parish, Louisiana	37,887	21,276	37,868	35,010	50,503	51,448
Livingston Parish, Louisiana	39,936	22,109	35,000	36,722	47,560	60,787
Orleans Parish, Louisiana	32,312	19,845	23,484	27,537	40,452	55,964
Ouachita Parish, Louisiana	30,137	15,617	22,044	27,325	50,239	45,225
Rapides Parish, Louisiana	34,777	14,787	24,577	33,192	48,628	77,966
St. Landry Parish, Louisiana	30,014	16,936	25,934	35,110	40,549	46,373
St. Tammany Parish, Louisiana	41,148	27,424	30,875	39,221	49,744	76,041
Tangipahoa Parish, Louisiana	36,458	19,932	30,679	35,738	52,080	48,438
Terrebonne Parish, Louisiana	30,975	24,431	25,010	30,255	52,150	65,190
MAINE						
Androscoggin County, Maine	35,678	19,922	31,595	35,299	45,094	46,221
Aroostook County, Maine	31,510	16,868	25,009	35,404	40,764	39,571
Cumberland County, Maine	41,146	20,250	30,359	36,835	51,234	63,547
Kennebec County, Maine	35,845	18,358	24,580	35,066	41,001	62,413

N = Data for this geographic area cannot be displayed because the number of sample cases is too small.

Table C-2. Educational Attainment of the Population, by Selected Counties, 2016—*Continued*

(Number; percent; dollars.)

State/County	Educational attainment by race/ethnicity, 25 years and over								
	Some other race alone			Two or more races alone			Hispanic or Latino (of any race)		
	Total	High school graduate or more	Bachelor's degree or more	Total	High school graduate or more	Bachelor's degree or more	Total	High school graduate or more	Bachelor's degree or more
MAINE—(*Continued*)									
Penobscot County, Maine	N	N	N	N	N	N	N	N	N
York County, Maine	N	N	N	N	N	N	N	N	N
MARYLAND									
Allegany County, Maryland	N	N	N	N	N	N	N	N	N
Anne Arundel County, Maryland	8,003	85.6	19.9	9,264	95.1	35.9	22,901	88.3	33.3
Baltimore County, Maryland	3,580	79.9	27.2	8,862	89.6	37.5	23,522	68.9	22.5
Calvert County, Maryland	N	N	N	N	N	N	N	N	N
Carroll County, Maryland	N	N	N	N	N	N	2,836	85.9	27.5
Cecil County, Maryland	N	N	N	N	N	N	N	N	N
Charles County, Maryland	N	N	N	4,469	97.4	23.8	4,724	78.7	18.7
Frederick County, Maryland	N	N	N	2,309	88.1	39.7	12,407	65.1	23.6
Harford County, Maryland	N	N	N	3,652	91.5	34.4	6,463	77.4	26.0
Howard County, Maryland	N	N	N	N	N	N	11,876	82.6	33.4
Montgomery County, Maryland	46,940	60.4	13.7	16,265	92.0	58.4	117,404	70.7	24.6
Prince George's County, Maryland	60,547	39.1	7.1	14,442	86.8	35.7	90,214	46.9	10.1
St. Mary's County, Maryland	N	N	N	N	N	N	N	N	N
Washington County, Maryland	N	N	N	1,712	96.2	36.0	3,422	60.3	16.0
Wicomico County, Maryland	N	N	N	N	N	N	N	N	N
Baltimore city, Maryland	5,313	72.4	27.6	5,821	91.0	55.4	17,083	65.7	27.3
MASSACHUSETTS									
Barnstable County, Massachusetts	N	N	N	N	N	N	3,650	77.4	20.2
Berkshire County, Massachusetts	N	N	N	N	N	N	N	N	N
Bristol County, Massachusetts	20,255	73.5	10.5	6,788	82.6	20.9	20,946	72.6	11.1
Essex County, Massachusetts	36,934	66.5	10.1	8,340	75.0	25.8	84,910	65.9	11.4
Franklin County, Massachusetts	N	N	N	N	N	N	N	N	N
Hampden County, Massachusetts	7,993	66.8	3.7	3,958	92.2	31.1	60,202	66.0	11.1
Hampshire County, Massachusetts	N	N	N	N	N	N	4,022	84.5	49.2
Middlesex County, Massachusetts	34,013	72.9	17.1	15,781	90.9	51.4	70,707	77.4	29.4
Norfolk County, Massachusetts	8,383	76.1	27.0	6,757	93.4	68.8	17,287	86.9	39.8
Plymouth County, Massachusetts	12,802	64.5	7.2	3,699	83.1	27.9	10,506	67.7	18.2
Suffolk County, Massachusetts	26,322	65.6	13.7	34,336	61.2	16.3	104,983	64.7	18.9
Worcester County, Massachusetts	19,318	65.5	9.4	7,202	93.4	26.8	48,534	66.3	11.5
MICHIGAN									
Allegan County, Michigan	N	N	N	1,390	83.9	19.9	4,177	55.8	6.5
Bay County, Michigan	N	N	N	N	N	N	2,759	91.5	10.7
Berrien County, Michigan	N	N	N	2,321	76.4	17.5	4,085	60.4	26.2
Calhoun County, Michigan	N	N	N	1,809	91.7	34.5	3,291	70.3	4.8
Clinton County, Michigan	N	N	N	N	N	N	1,909	94.8	18.1
Eaton County, Michigan	N	N	N	N	N	N	3,150	95.2	27.5
Genesee County, Michigan	N	N	N	4,476	92.2	24.4	7,223	77.8	8.5
Grand Traverse County, Michigan	N	N	N	N	N	N	N	N	N
Ingham County, Michigan	3,582	60.3	9.0	4,253	88.1	25.3	11,333	74.8	19.6
Isabella County, Michigan	N	N	N	1,442	88.1	25.7	756	85.3	27.4
Jackson County, Michigan	N	N	N	N	N	N	3,119	82.5	15.7
Kalamazoo County, Michigan	N	N	N	3,768	93.1	14.4	5,368	61.7	21.5
Kent County, Michigan	10,733	49.0	5.6	7,749	81.8	19.5	31,685	58.2	11.9
Lapeer County, Michigan	N	N	N	N	N	N	2,642	74.4	19.0
Lenawee County, Michigan	N	N	N	1,011	96.6	39.2	4,181	79.7	8.9
Livingston County, Michigan	N	N	N	1,331	80.2	32.7	2,373	85.8	29.3
Macomb County, Michigan	N	N	N	8,811	90.3	31.0	11,493	77.8	25.8
Marquette County, Michigan	N	N	N	N	N	N	N	N	N
Midland County, Michigan	N	N	N	N	N	N	N	N	N
Monroe County, Michigan	N	N	N	N	N	N	2,530	89.0	32.3
Muskegon County, Michigan	N	N	N	2,092	95.7	6.5	4,718	77.7	6.7
Oakland County, Michigan	6,446	78.7	48.8	16,220	91.1	42.5	26,420	83.2	39.4
Ottawa County, Michigan	4,463	56.8	16.9	2,545	96.3	17.3	12,947	65.5	13.0
Saginaw County, Michigan	2,533	81.0	9.8	1,906	90.0	35.4	8,186	86.3	13.5
St. Clair County, Michigan	N	N	N	1,401	84.0	27.1	2,870	88.5	14.0
Shiawassee County, Michigan	N	N	N	N	N	N	N	N	N
Van Buren County, Michigan	N	N	N	1,544	83.6	13.6	4,138	52.9	4.4
Washtenaw County, Michigan	N	N	N	6,778	90.8	42.1	8,979	88.6	49.4
Wayne County, Michigan	18,948	60.6	6.7	21,093	77.8	19.9	52,660	65.5	11.2
MINNESOTA									
Anoka County, Minnesota	3,205	59.4	13.7	3,348	93.9	23.5	7,575	71.3	13.4
Blue Earth County, Minnesota	N	N	N	N	N	N	N	N	N

N = Data for this geographic area cannot be displayed because the number of sample cases is too small.

Table C-2. Educational Attainment of the Population, by Selected Counties, 2016—*Continued*

(Number; percent; dollars.)

State/County	Median earnings in the past 12 months (2016 inflation-adjusted dollars)					
	Population 25 years and over with earnings					
	Total	Less than high school graduate	High school graduate (includes equivalency)	Some college or associate's degree	Bachelor's degree	Graduate or professional degree
MAINE—*(Continued)*						
Penobscot County, Maine	32,074	15,625	23,800	31,956	39,288	57,117
York County, Maine	38,546	21,835	30,250	36,770	50,574	54,187
MARYLAND						
Allegany County, Maryland	30,542	35,156	25,223	26,626	47,143	59,189
Anne Arundel County, Maryland	53,490	29,256	37,432	45,765	70,216	82,637
Baltimore County, Maryland	46,482	26,693	35,994	41,215	60,153	72,525
Calvert County, Maryland	61,841	24,264	49,131	63,067	71,675	88,564
Carroll County, Maryland	51,141	21,966	39,050	52,309	65,517	80,827
Cecil County, Maryland	43,041	22,255	40,490	43,728	55,554	72,828
Charles County, Maryland	56,244	28,589	41,532	55,453	67,021	92,389
Frederick County, Maryland	51,784	33,122	35,513	45,700	70,187	83,903
Harford County, Maryland	52,097	28,406	35,368	47,151	71,283	80,180
Howard County, Maryland	67,055	29,156	30,654	44,039	70,109	100,216
Montgomery County, Maryland	55,095	26,086	30,139	41,090	62,158	92,887
Prince George's County, Maryland	45,389	26,156	34,773	45,490	59,056	79,327
St. Mary's County, Maryland	51,681	32,189	40,572	53,673	71,970	98,604
Washington County, Maryland	37,160	27,388	30,921	35,982	50,609	70,595
Wicomico County, Maryland	32,491	29,010	27,308	27,296	51,831	60,717
Baltimore city, Maryland	38,472	21,782	26,992	36,234	49,845	65,402
MASSACHUSETTS						
Barnstable County, Massachusetts	40,168	26,230	31,272	36,170	48,058	59,589
Berkshire County, Massachusetts	39,369	30,277	31,894	35,919	45,652	55,985
Bristol County, Massachusetts	43,828	31,722	35,001	41,686	53,657	71,980
Essex County, Massachusetts	46,641	27,133	35,485	41,194	59,155	77,568
Franklin County, Massachusetts	38,206	19,614	31,205	36,085	40,623	56,277
Hampden County, Massachusetts	38,755	22,476	32,631	36,192	52,426	60,753
Hampshire County, Massachusetts	41,204	30,952	32,640	38,796	47,483	61,230
Middlesex County, Massachusetts	54,998	24,966	35,170	41,816	62,464	83,626
Norfolk County, Massachusetts	56,381	25,607	38,776	41,606	66,332	83,070
Plymouth County, Massachusetts	49,428	25,287	37,945	43,577	66,424	82,391
Suffolk County, Massachusetts	44,993	21,800	30,618	36,333	60,848	71,955
Worcester County, Massachusetts	46,779	26,363	36,007	41,546	59,383	76,199
MICHIGAN						
Allegan County, Michigan	35,942	31,741	31,699	35,687	42,886	59,448
Bay County, Michigan	32,281	16,194	28,383	30,263	50,918	75,427
Berrien County, Michigan	32,497	16,464	22,488	32,068	47,419	63,582
Calhoun County, Michigan	32,328	15,571	30,629	32,045	49,112	67,637
Clinton County, Michigan	41,942	11,655	35,152	32,346	58,712	68,636
Eaton County, Michigan	37,289	23,305	30,166	39,221	47,867	52,855
Genesee County, Michigan	31,420	16,346	25,914	30,866	47,308	64,691
Grand Traverse County, Michigan	33,304	24,236	24,005	33,791	44,549	60,697
Ingham County, Michigan	33,911	21,682	26,981	30,718	42,022	55,693
Isabella County, Michigan	30,942	12,629	24,066	26,696	31,076	64,883
Jackson County, Michigan	33,029	10,000	26,833	32,619	42,937	65,449
Kalamazoo County, Michigan	36,803	17,140	26,914	31,032	51,086	67,289
Kent County, Michigan	36,099	20,107	27,554	33,158	46,704	63,308
Lapeer County, Michigan	32,938	16,128	24,039	35,724	55,052	63,996
Lenawee County, Michigan	32,493	22,319	25,822	33,241	45,794	60,933
Livingston County, Michigan	48,211	20,765	33,035	43,143	62,860	77,153
Macomb County, Michigan	40,162	21,687	30,541	38,069	53,203	71,777
Marquette County, Michigan	35,674	10,253	26,055	31,871	48,060	58,718
Midland County, Michigan	35,866	18,432	24,386	31,368	56,714	67,652
Monroe County, Michigan	41,728	21,906	36,658	41,267	51,981	55,335
Muskegon County, Michigan	30,480	20,813	24,033	30,606	45,343	61,671
Oakland County, Michigan	47,576	19,820	27,939	35,588	60,486	81,422
Ottawa County, Michigan	37,857	26,662	29,188	36,773	52,233	61,766
Saginaw County, Michigan	32,233	21,942	25,677	31,068	46,784	53,952
St. Clair County, Michigan	33,956	20,963	30,146	34,801	48,541	59,984
Shiawassee County, Michigan	34,769	20,638	29,883	36,232	37,653	60,983
Van Buren County, Michigan	33,552	16,050	27,619	32,469	52,228	56,505
Washtenaw County, Michigan	45,655	21,392	30,185	30,693	50,706	70,134
Wayne County, Michigan	33,815	20,532	26,650	31,588	51,535	71,593
MINNESOTA						
Anoka County, Minnesota	45,101	30,692	35,710	41,700	59,162	71,720
Blue Earth County, Minnesota	37,891	38,706	27,396	36,995	42,044	59,832

N = Data for this geographic area cannot be displayed because the number of sample cases is too small.

Table C-2. Educational Attainment of the Population, by Selected Counties, 2016—*Continued*

(Number; percent; dollars.)

State/County	Educational attainment by race/ethnicity, 25 years and over								
	Some other race alone			Two or more races alone			Hispanic or Latino (of any race)		
	Total	High school graduate or more	Bachelor's degree or more	Total	High school graduate or more	Bachelor's degree or more	Total	High school graduate or more	Bachelor's degree or more
MINNESOTA—*(Continued)*									
Carver County, Minnesota	N	N	N	N	N	N	N	N	N
Dakota County, Minnesota	6,238	59.9	12.9	4,093	92.8	26.0	14,155	66.3	19.0
Hennepin County, Minnesota	21,129	48.0	12.2	17,098	92.6	43.8	43,236	58.5	18.2
Olmsted County, Minnesota	N	N	N	N	N	N	3,525	66.0	15.6
Ramsey County, Minnesota	8,264	58.7	9.2	8,121	89.4	33.1	20,151	66.4	15.1
Rice County, Minnesota	N	N	N	N	N	N	2,370	50.5	11.0
St. Louis County, Minnesota	N	N	N	1,328	84.8	16.4	N	N	N
Scott County, Minnesota	N	N	N	N	N	N	3,618	70.9	14.6
Sherburne County, Minnesota	N	N	N	N	N	N	N	N	N
Stearns County, Minnesota	N	N	N	N	N	N	2,119	61.4	37.5
Washington County, Minnesota	1,933	85.6	22.9	2,888	99.0	41.0	5,462	81.9	33.2
Wright County, Minnesota	N	N	N	N	N	N	N	N	N
MISSISSIPPI									
DeSoto County, Mississippi	N	N	N	N	N	N	4,128	63.3	17.2
Forrest County, Mississippi	N	N	N	N	N	N	N	N	N
Harrison County, Mississippi	N	N	N	2,892	95.1	27.8	5,521	75.6	15.7
Hinds County, Mississippi	N	N	N	N	N	N	2,061	82.7	10.1
Jackson County, Mississippi	N	N	N	N	N	N	N	N	N
Jones County, Mississippi	N	N	N	N	N	N	N	N	N
Lauderdale County, Mississippi	N	N	N	N	N	N	N	N	N
Lee County, Mississippi	N	N	N	N	N	N	N	N	N
Madison County, Mississippi	N	N	N	N	N	N	N	N	N
Rankin County, Mississippi	N	N	N	N	N	N	N	N	N
MISSOURI									
Boone County, Missouri	N	N	N	N	N	N	N	N	N
Buchanan County, Missouri	N	N	N	N	N	N	3,127	60.2	17.7
Cape Girardeau County, Missouri	N	N	N	N	N	N	N	N	N
Cass County, Missouri	N	N	N	N	N	N	2,315	71.4	16.6
Christian County, Missouri	N	N	N	N	N	N	N	N	N
Clay County, Missouri	N	N	N	N	N	N	8,712	87.7	12.3
Cole County, Missouri	N	N	N	N	N	N	N	N	N
Franklin County, Missouri	N	N	N	N	N	N	N	N	N
Greene County, Missouri	N	N	N	N	N	N	4,951	75.2	23.8
Jackson County, Missouri	11,168	63.9	8.3	8,180	88.8	25.8	31,696	69.0	14.8
Jasper County, Missouri	N	N	N	N	N	N	4,021	38.6	1.9
Jefferson County, Missouri	N	N	N	N	N	N	N	N	N
Platte County, Missouri	N	N	N	N	N	N	3,374	89.3	42.3
St. Charles County, Missouri	N	N	N	2,536	97.8	54.0	6,020	76.2	20.6
St. Francois County, Missouri	N	N	N	N	N	N	N	N	N
St. Louis County, Missouri	3,951	73.0	36.9	10,722	84.9	31.2	15,623	75.8	34.9
St. Louis city, Missouri	N	N	N	2,710	87.0	33.8	6,955	76.0	30.3
MONTANA									
Cascade County, Montana	N	N	N	N	N	N	1,753	66.1	13.9
Flathead County, Montana	N	N	N	N	N	N	N	N	N
Gallatin County, Montana	N	N	N	N	N	N	N	N	N
Lewis and Clark County, Montana	N	N	N	N	N	N	N	N	N
Missoula County, Montana	N	N	N	N	N	N	N	N	N
Yellowstone County, Montana	N	N	N	N	N	N	4,210	81.7	28.3
NEBRASKA									
Douglas County, Nebraska	6,138	56.5	9.0	6,163	86.8	28.3	32,567	46.6	11.0
Lancaster County, Nebraska	2,634	62.9	14.0	3,492	84.6	38.9	10,230	67.5	24.4
Sarpy County, Nebraska	N	N	N	2,080	100.0	55.2	8,131	78.4	20.2
NEVADA									
Clark County, Nevada	129,674	58.7	8.1	46,915	90.4	23.2	370,657	64.3	9.6
Washoe County, Nevada	17,812	60.6	4.1	8,972	84.2	26.5	58,081	60.7	11.4
NEW HAMPSHIRE									
Cheshire County, New Hampshire	N	N	N	N	N	N	N	N	N
Grafton County, New Hampshire	N	N	N	N	N	N	N	N	N
Hillsborough County, New Hampshire	3,031	78.1	35.8	4,200	89.9	27.9	14,029	70.9	21.8
Merrimack County, New Hampshire	N	N	N	N	N	N	N	N	N

N = Data for this geographic area cannot be displayed because the number of sample cases is too small.

Table C-2. Educational Attainment of the Population, by Selected Counties, 2016—*Continued*

(Number; percent; dollars.)

| State/County | Median earnings in the past 12 months (2016 inflation-adjusted dollars) | | | | | |
| | Population 25 years and over with earnings | | | | | |
	Total	Less than high school graduate	High school graduate (includes equivalency)	Some college or associate's degree	Bachelor's degree	Graduate or professional degree
MINNESOTA—*(Continued)*						
Carver County, Minnesota	54,694	29,567	39,159	41,878	70,061	83,139
Dakota County, Minnesota	47,644	25,993	36,322	42,220	59,916	76,411
Hennepin County, Minnesota	46,663	22,542	31,004	38,969	57,844	74,915
Olmsted County, Minnesota	46,661	15,953	30,616	39,456	60,351	72,341
Ramsey County, Minnesota	40,172	21,637	30,898	35,432	50,168	65,721
Rice County, Minnesota	40,446	22,125	31,669	41,756	42,451	60,839
St. Louis County, Minnesota	37,003	19,800	29,558	35,114	47,196	70,268
Scott County, Minnesota	51,096	31,455	30,435	43,861	68,264	81,846
Sherburne County, Minnesota	45,158	23,826	40,476	42,108	46,728	77,898
Stearns County, Minnesota	38,779	24,414	31,081	36,785	47,798	54,264
Washington County, Minnesota	51,993	24,554	40,355	50,320	63,244	82,100
Wright County, Minnesota	44,444	21,849	38,866	40,167	60,970	72,347
MISSISSIPPI						
DeSoto County, Mississippi	38,543	25,691	30,976	37,455	50,813	55,117
Forrest County, Mississippi	30,587	9,158	22,196	26,268	37,403	45,189
Harrison County, Mississippi	29,945	16,774	24,605	30,175	45,544	50,543
Hinds County, Mississippi	31,261	17,162	25,980	30,425	40,052	50,230
Jackson County, Mississippi	39,314	30,515	26,893	38,688	48,929	67,573
Jones County, Mississippi	31,135	15,505	27,439	30,046	51,632	55,024
Lauderdale County, Mississippi	31,744	21,604	24,112	29,734	43,373	47,720
Lee County, Mississippi	33,046	19,392	28,214	31,289	38,018	54,358
Madison County, Mississippi	40,184	22,464	25,489	31,177	51,465	61,770
Rankin County, Mississippi	40,837	22,057	32,349	36,603	50,860	61,242
MISSOURI						
Boone County, Missouri	37,168	25,767	29,951	32,759	41,116	55,214
Buchanan County, Missouri	32,393	16,252	31,599	31,081	46,025	53,603
Cape Girardeau County, Missouri	36,172	25,893	31,475	31,096	41,702	46,976
Cass County, Missouri	38,197	25,867	33,553	36,752	46,554	53,230
Christian County, Missouri	31,703	29,404	31,361	26,966	36,910	57,169
Clay County, Missouri	40,492	17,970	33,213	36,444	47,389	61,787
Cole County, Missouri	36,696	22,369	29,250	35,339	42,148	50,897
Franklin County, Missouri	38,627	21,664	32,082	39,784	42,077	60,134
Greene County, Missouri	31,391	17,213	25,457	28,361	40,387	50,467
Jackson County, Missouri	36,801	21,025	29,770	35,401	46,302	58,904
Jasper County, Missouri	31,526	22,011	31,176	29,494	35,628	52,957
Jefferson County, Missouri	37,052	29,618	33,498	35,949	56,465	51,733
Platte County, Missouri	45,112	31,894	37,331	37,124	55,606	63,214
St. Charles County, Missouri	46,644	27,293	35,208	41,907	57,136	63,120
St. Francois County, Missouri	30,243	20,992	25,722	32,739	33,553	54,572
St. Louis County, Missouri	42,074	23,376	30,125	35,491	51,533	68,021
St. Louis city, Missouri	33,699	17,608	25,755	30,066	43,868	56,752
MONTANA						
Cascade County, Montana	31,499	11,966	25,064	31,131	37,459	55,909
Flathead County, Montana	30,616	26,694	22,658	25,543	37,715	66,028
Gallatin County, Montana	37,591	24,148	27,903	31,535	41,994	61,425
Lewis and Clark County, Montana	38,656	12,050	27,145	35,805	48,655	63,180
Missoula County, Montana	29,997	17,816	24,401	25,575	32,175	49,568
Yellowstone County, Montana	38,658	20,505	31,457	37,401	43,037	53,312
NEBRASKA						
Douglas County, Nebraska	40,967	24,677	31,279	36,475	51,086	67,133
Lancaster County, Nebraska	36,924	21,793	29,231	34,556	43,639	52,478
Sarpy County, Nebraska	42,831	31,344	31,991	39,939	47,410	68,169
NEVADA						
Clark County, Nevada	34,974	25,446	30,975	35,306	46,577	62,161
Washoe County, Nevada	35,125	24,293	30,322	33,159	50,344	62,136
NEW HAMPSHIRE						
Cheshire County, New Hampshire	34,786	27,308	30,249	30,795	37,237	56,646
Grafton County, New Hampshire	37,435	22,018	26,984	34,444	42,358	65,671
Hillsborough County, New Hampshire	45,313	28,565	32,457	41,987	55,611	69,616
Merrimack County, New Hampshire	42,144	22,781	35,068	38,067	48,830	66,834

N = Data for this geographic area cannot be displayed because the number of sample cases is too small.

Table C-2. Educational Attainment of the Population, by Selected Counties, 2016—*Continued*

(Number; percent; dollars.)

State/County	Educational attainment by race/ethnicity, 25 years and over								
	Some other race alone			Two or more races alone			Hispanic or Latino (of any race)		
	Total	High school graduate or more	Bachelor's degree or more	Total	High school graduate or more	Bachelor's degree or more	Total	High school graduate or more	Bachelor's degree or more
NEW HAMPSHIRE—(*Continued*)									
Rockingham County, New Hampshire	N	N	N	N	N	N	4,837	87.2	45.5
Strafford County, New Hampshire	N	N	N	N	N	N	1,695	93.9	43.0
NEW JERSEY									
Atlantic County, New Jersey	11,717	71.3	8.7	2,930	81.3	27.3	28,559	70.7	9.9
Bergen County, New Jersey	13,860	80.7	22.1	12,248	94.5	49.9	115,963	82.4	26.8
Burlington County, New Jersey	5,960	68.3	11.1	6,868	93.3	31.0	20,351	86.2	24.1
Camden County, New Jersey	25,193	62.6	6.9	5,581	91.8	31.5	45,818	71.3	14.8
Cape May County, New Jersey	N	N	N	N	N	N	3,922	78.9	9.9
Cumberland County, New Jersey	6,628	60.6	4.1	2,461	94.5	4.8	25,596	51.5	6.3
Essex County, New Jersey	36,387	67.7	15.1	9,211	77.5	27.7	109,806	71.1	19.8
Gloucester County, New Jersey	3,855	68.0	11.2	4,554	94.4	36.8	9,325	78.9	19.6
Hudson County, New Jersey	61,094	70.5	12.0	12,901	88.1	42.1	193,047	73.8	16.6
Hunterdon County, New Jersey	N	N	N	N	N	N	4,678	81.9	28.4
Mercer County, New Jersey	2,955	81.6	13.1	3,403	84.8	23.2	36,066	63.1	12.7
Middlesex County, New Jersey	20,934	80.8	15.3	10,114	87.5	39.7	101,797	74.5	18.0
Monmouth County, New Jersey	10,366	67.0	10.8	4,366	89.6	43.9	37,998	70.0	20.1
Morris County, New Jersey	10,340	78.1	16.4	3,634	89.0	55.5	41,180	80.3	23.9
Ocean County, New Jersey	8,600	46.2	7.6	N	N	N	29,921	63.6	12.7
Passaic County, New Jersey	44,972	65.3	6.3	5,970	65.8	24.9	124,122	68.1	12.0
Salem County, New Jersey	N	N	N	N	N	N	2,273	69.9	14.9
Somerset County, New Jersey	6,312	65.9	6.1	2,633	86.9	55.5	29,140	76.1	18.1
Sussex County, New Jersey	N	N	N	N	N	N	7,131	97.1	26.6
Union County, New Jersey	50,482	69.6	12.7	6,550	77.1	21.4	107,086	71.5	13.8
Warren County, New Jersey	N	N	N	N	N	N	5,586	61.8	16.2
NEW MEXICO									
Bernalillo County, New Mexico	63,928	77.7	15.5	11,474	96.0	37.7	203,824	81.0	20.0
Chaves County, New Mexico	N	N	N	N	N	N	20,244	61.3	15.8
Doña Ana County, New Mexico	4,889	54.8	11.3	N	N	N	79,826	70.5	14.3
Lea County, New Mexico	1,912	42.4	2.6	N	N	N	20,743	50.8	4.5
McKinley County, New Mexico	N	N	N	N	N	N	5,217	65.3	12.2
Otero County, New Mexico	N	N	N	N	N	N	13,677	74.9	8.0
Sandoval County, New Mexico	9,373	58.2	6.9	4,767	92.7	31.2	33,629	79.2	17.7
San Juan County, New Mexico	4,342	60.7	11.0	N	N	N	12,863	71.8	8.9
Santa Fe County, New Mexico	7,371	69.8	11.0	2,775	90.0	49.5	48,464	79.7	18.5
Valencia County, New Mexico	5,638	64.0	12.9	N	N	N	28,188	76.8	13.8
NEW YORK									
Albany County, New York	2,692	76.6	17.2	3,530	93.8	49.7	8,818	80.6	26.7
Bronx County, New York	315,865	63.2	10.7	29,473	74.4	26.3	494,733	64.2	12.1
Broome County, New York	N	N	N	N	N	N	3,575	61.0	21.7
Cattaraugus County, New York	N	N	N	N	N	N	N	N	N
Cayuga County, New York	N	N	N	N	N	N	N	N	N
Chautauqua County, New York	N	N	N	N	N	N	4,605	57.0	9.9
Chemung County, New York	N	N	N	N	N	N	N	N	N
Clinton County, New York	N	N	N	N	N	N	1,533	68.6	25.0
Dutchess County, New York	5,756	69.0	10.3	3,047	92.7	29.1	20,290	78.0	22.7
Erie County, New York	9,486	59.6	15.1	7,160	82.1	25.4	25,099	71.3	21.2
Jefferson County, New York	N	N	N	N	N	N	3,342	79.7	11.3
Kings County, New York	144,815	58.0	13.7	41,903	81.6	45.0	318,198	64.0	17.7
Livingston County, New York	N	N	N	N	N	N	N	N	N
Madison County, New York	N	N	N	N	N	N	N	N	N
Monroe County, New York	7,680	69.9	21.4	8,708	82.7	33.5	33,325	73.4	15.3
Nassau County, New York	61,184	67.8	17.9	19,268	77.4	35.4	138,375	72.6	22.5
New York County, New York	121,176	66.7	18.3	44,990	78.1	39.9	294,995	68.3	25.1
Niagara County, New York	N	N	N	1,784	79.7	18.4	3,065	97.1	24.9
Oneida County, New York	N	N	N	2,222	73.4	18.6	5,945	60.2	12.2
Onondaga County, New York	3,073	63.3	22.5	5,788	83.2	25.3	10,550	82.9	35.3
Ontario County, New York	N	N	N	N	N	N	2,711	72.2	24.9
Orange County, New York	19,234	71.2	15.8	4,674	88.2	32.7	42,077	77.1	19.6
Oswego County, New York	N	N	N	N	N	N	N	N	N
Putnam County, New York	3,803	56.5	11.5	N	N	N	8,977	73.2	17.8
Queens County, New York	203,303	71.7	12.4	44,752	78.1	31.3	425,758	73.5	17.6
Rensselaer County, New York	N	N	N	1,426	85.0	19.5	3,385	66.9	13.1
Richmond County, New York	13,402	78.2	15.6	3,982	83.7	38.9	51,052	77.5	18.0

N = Data for this geographic area cannot be displayed because the number of sample cases is too small.

Table C-2. Educational Attainment of the Population, by Selected Counties, 2016—*Continued*

(Number; percent; dollars.)

State/County	Median earnings in the past 12 months (2016 inflation-adjusted dollars)					
	Population 25 years and over with earnings					
	Total	Less than high school graduate	High school graduate (includes equivalency)	Some college or associate's degree	Bachelor's degree	Graduate or professional degree
NEW HAMPSHIRE—*(Continued)*						
Rockingham County, New Hampshire	50,054	31,948	35,775	42,397	60,212	75,097
Strafford County, New Hampshire	41,181	30,513	32,468	37,047	49,944	62,577
NEW JERSEY						
Atlantic County, New Jersey	35,082	21,065	30,573	32,070	56,334	77,192
Bergen County, New Jersey	54,810	22,178	36,563	45,227	65,868	89,846
Burlington County, New Jersey	50,889	27,276	35,935	43,223	65,046	85,640
Camden County, New Jersey	42,190	20,286	31,462	40,635	59,205	79,172
Cape May County, New Jersey	40,539	18,275	32,527	35,081	52,365	80,466
Cumberland County, New Jersey	27,312	20,402	25,742	27,563	54,873	54,968
Essex County, New Jersey	40,861	22,056	28,783	35,129	57,714	85,850
Gloucester County, New Jersey	50,788	22,089	37,130	44,495	61,537	81,376
Hudson County, New Jersey	43,640	20,200	29,136	35,109	63,220	84,757
Hunterdon County, New Jersey	65,809	17,171	43,523	51,417	74,348	92,589
Mercer County, New Jersey	50,409	21,516	30,608	41,982	62,596	93,444
Middlesex County, New Jersey	50,283	23,618	35,391	41,499	61,322	87,411
Monmouth County, New Jersey	52,282	25,065	31,987	47,586	65,427	89,500
Morris County, New Jersey	61,162	30,292	36,158	47,173	76,869	98,543
Ocean County, New Jersey	41,543	25,873	32,009	40,444	54,727	66,930
Passaic County, New Jersey	37,864	21,769	30,798	37,397	56,947	77,132
Salem County, New Jersey	37,681	27,022	34,510	37,786	52,927	60,845
Somerset County, New Jersey	58,926	25,015	32,084	43,671	73,993	101,931
Sussex County, New Jersey	51,720	36,399	42,300	45,184	66,937	90,494
Union County, New Jersey	45,339	24,076	30,323	41,912	62,345	90,260
Warren County, New Jersey	47,338	28,582	37,294	47,452	56,834	76,449
NEW MEXICO						
Bernalillo County, New Mexico	32,727	19,738	26,591	30,773	42,218	60,925
Chaves County, New Mexico	27,155	15,666	22,530	28,928	39,431	50,672
Doña Ana County, New Mexico	24,660	16,116	20,969	25,081	39,912	51,231
Lea County, New Mexico	37,794	19,977	37,576	40,274	45,654	65,960
McKinley County, New Mexico	23,238	15,892	20,700	25,366	44,634	42,994
Otero County, New Mexico	27,718	22,872	26,887	24,193	30,159	61,438
Sandoval County, New Mexico	38,102	19,909	30,735	36,362	47,751	61,436
San Juan County, New Mexico	35,672	25,635	26,546	36,409	43,589	53,062
Santa Fe County, New Mexico	37,171	21,647	27,463	36,171	45,303	56,906
Valencia County, New Mexico	32,051	25,424	26,476	31,774	41,119	58,390
NEW YORK						
Albany County, New York	42,640	24,230	30,225	39,118	51,485	71,546
Bronx County, New York	30,336	19,466	25,932	31,275	45,302	62,145
Broome County, New York	34,948	20,779	27,530	31,835	50,870	56,818
Cattaraugus County, New York	35,266	19,615	27,295	35,957	45,922	53,761
Cayuga County, New York	37,658	36,641	32,841	35,438	48,944	60,963
Chautauqua County, New York	31,925	21,052	29,252	31,600	40,988	55,475
Chemung County, New York	36,414	14,785	33,068	31,871	46,559	65,455
Clinton County, New York	35,558	25,092	28,102	36,876	55,666	60,033
Dutchess County, New York	43,615	19,667	34,814	41,124	60,740	81,705
Erie County, New York	40,426	20,713	30,931	35,116	49,949	65,234
Jefferson County, New York	31,517	26,239	27,059	30,333	41,834	60,098
Kings County, New York	40,105	20,339	27,425	36,011	54,100	71,253
Livingston County, New York	37,080	16,217	30,416	38,279	51,515	50,580
Madison County, New York	41,528	25,724	36,180	37,171	49,613	64,291
Monroe County, New York	39,073	19,112	25,962	33,210	51,403	62,813
Nassau County, New York	54,737	25,132	37,154	46,392	69,373	85,093
New York County, New York	61,878	19,432	26,207	33,660	76,549	95,252
Niagara County, New York	37,962	19,183	32,482	36,107	53,265	58,200
Oneida County, New York	36,003	20,271	30,739	33,667	47,966	61,827
Onondaga County, New York	40,751	20,228	31,240	36,132	50,346	62,745
Ontario County, New York	38,336	21,897	28,542	35,652	50,080	55,500
Orange County, New York	42,637	21,499	32,424	40,762	62,758	79,879
Oswego County, New York	34,575	22,384	30,194	33,725	37,341	62,911
Putnam County, New York	52,219	21,003	35,888	50,304	61,206	90,365
Queens County, New York	38,323	21,376	30,084	38,088	51,955	67,102
Rensselaer County, New York	43,714	18,672	38,353	40,294	52,092	64,189
Richmond County, New York	51,213	25,676	40,549	47,425	61,439	75,494

N = Data for this geographic area cannot be displayed because the number of sample cases is too small.

Table C-2. Educational Attainment of the Population, by Selected Counties, 2016—*Continued*

(Number; percent; dollars.)

State/County	Some other race alone			Two or more races alone			Hispanic or Latino (of any race)		
	Total	High school graduate or more	Bachelor's degree or more	Total	High school graduate or more	Bachelor's degree or more	Total	High school graduate or more	Bachelor's degree or more
NEW YORK—(*Continued*)									
Rockland County, New York	19,573	51.1	11.9	2,474	92.8	60.3	32,865	60.6	20.2
St. Lawrence County, New York	N	N	N	N	N	N	N	N	N
Saratoga County, New York	N	N	N	N	N	N	3,772	85.4	36.3
Schenectady County, New York	4,044	68.6	10.1	N	N	N	4,958	75.2	8.2
Steuben County, New York	N	N	N	N	N	N	750	73.6	23.5
Suffolk County, New York	52,674	65.2	13.8	12,468	85.4	31.4	164,385	71.7	16.6
Sullivan County, New York	N	N	N	N	N	N	5,635	55.1	12.3
Tompkins County, New York	N	N	N	N	N	N	N	N	N
Ulster County, New York	3,088	69.7	13.9	2,678	79.4	29.9	9,864	78.1	17.8
Warren County, New York	N	N	N	N	N	N	N	N	N
Wayne County, New York	N	N	N	N	N	N	2,209	62.4	20.7
Westchester County, New York	64,495	65.6	15.7	13,020	84.3	40.4	143,666	67.4	21.8
NORTH CAROLINA									
Alamance County, North Carolina	5,975	43.0	0.2	1,512	87.2	18.1	10,105	47.7	3.4
Brunswick County, North Carolina	N	N	N	N	N	N	N	N	N
Buncombe County, North Carolina	N	N	N	N	N	N	8,460	55.2	21.8
Burke County, North Carolina	N	N	N	N	N	N	2,779	68.6	16.3
Cabarrus County, North Carolina	5,640	57.1	13.0	N	N	N	8,861	66.7	18.8
Caldwell County, North Carolina	N	N	N	N	N	N	N	N	N
Carteret County, North Carolina	N	N	N	N	N	N	1,474	61.2	21.1
Catawba County, North Carolina	5,082	54.7	4.6	N	N	N	6,796	57.7	5.1
Chatham County, North Carolina	N	N	N	N	N	N	3,976	38.8	15.6
Cleveland County, North Carolina	N	N	N	N	N	N	N	N	N
Craven County, North Carolina	N	N	N	N	N	N	3,081	59.8	3.3
Cumberland County, North Carolina	4,385	88.5	22.8	6,652	96.6	25.0	18,850	87.3	23.5
Davidson County, North Carolina	N	N	N	N	N	N	5,490	74.8	4.2
Durham County, North Carolina	5,313	37.3	4.4	2,426	90.7	42.0	20,835	46.1	8.7
Forsyth County, North Carolina	4,860	61.6	4.2	3,673	86.7	27.0	21,736	61.1	14.9
Gaston County, North Carolina	2,522	44.7	5.8	N	N	N	7,279	57.8	18.4
Guilford County, North Carolina	7,808	58.4	13.7	3,490	100.0	33.8	20,061	58.4	14.9
Harnett County, North Carolina	4,733	59.5	1.6	1,790	90.1	23.2	7,969	65.7	10.5
Henderson County, North Carolina	N	N	N	N	N	N	6,220	44.5	12.3
Iredell County, North Carolina	N	N	N	N	N	N	7,091	59.8	16.3
Johnston County, North Carolina	N	N	N	N	N	N	11,579	59.1	10.7
Lincoln County, North Carolina	N	N	N	N	N	N	3,474	49.7	4.7
Mecklenburg County, North Carolina	29,348	54.1	14.7	10,626	94.0	48.8	72,607	61.6	17.7
Moore County, North Carolina	N	N	N	N	N	N	N	N	N
Nash County, North Carolina	N	N	N	N	N	N	N	N	N
New Hanover County, North Carolina	N	N	N	N	N	N	6,332	82.3	22.4
Onslow County, North Carolina	N	N	N	4,162	94.3	18.1	8,985	95.7	21.6
Orange County, North Carolina	N	N	N	N	N	N	5,764	57.2	27.5
Pitt County, North Carolina	N	N	N	N	N	N	5,730	91.4	19.6
Randolph County, North Carolina	N	N	N	N	N	N	7,571	41.3	6.4
Robeson County, North Carolina	3,184	39.0	3.8	N	N	N	5,059	36.1	3.2
Rockingham County, North Carolina	N	N	N	N	N	N	2,724	63.2	12.0
Rowan County, North Carolina	N	N	N	N	N	N	5,397	59.7	7.2
Rutherford County, North Carolina	N	N	N	N	N	N	N	N	N
Surry County, North Carolina	N	N	N	N	N	N	3,248	34.0	1.9
Union County, North Carolina	N	N	N	1,482	77.8	35.7	12,310	54.2	10.7
Wake County, North Carolina	18,980	53.9	16.3	14,809	90.1	41.4	54,342	66.0	27.1
Wayne County, North Carolina	N	N	N	N	N	N	N	N	N
Wilkes County, North Carolina	N	N	N	N	N	N	N	N	N
Wilson County, North Carolina	N	N	N	N	N	N	4,021	37.4	4.2
NORTH DAKOTA									
Burleigh County, North Dakota	N	N	N	N	N	N	N	N	N
Cass County, North Dakota	N	N	N	N	N	N	N	N	N
Grand Forks County, North Dakota	N	N	N	N	N	N	N	N	N
Ward County, North Dakota	N	N	N	N	N	N	N	N	N
OHIO									
Allen County, Ohio	N	N	N	N	N	N	N	N	N
Ashtabula County, Ohio	N	N	N	N	N	N	2,133	46.7	0.7

N = Data for this geographic area cannot be displayed because the number of sample cases is too small.

Table C-2. Educational Attainment of the Population, by Selected Counties, 2016—*Continued*

(Number; percent; dollars.)

	Median earnings in the past 12 months (2016 inflation-adjusted dollars)					
	Population 25 years and over with earnings					
State/County	Total	Less than high school graduate	High school graduate (includes equivalency)	Some college or associate's degree	Bachelor's degree	Graduate or professional degree
NEW YORK—*(Continued)*						
Rockland County, New York.................	46,422	20,474	26,702	41,780	70,600	82,046
St. Lawrence County, New York............	35,197	20,476	25,769	33,335	43,782	57,050
Saratoga County, New York.................	48,522	26,986	33,949	41,199	63,970	75,285
Schenectady County, New York............	35,235	20,883	24,189	32,241	45,602	70,141
Steuben County, New York.................	31,269	15,346	26,314	31,426	37,459	61,287
Suffolk County, New York.................	50,250	26,762	39,829	46,432	61,241	87,222
Sullivan County, New York.................	32,195	23,131	26,729	32,428	46,570	51,561
Tompkins County, New York	36,777	16,982	22,002	33,372	40,399	51,319
Ulster County, New York	40,424	22,613	27,499	40,522	51,172	61,576
Warren County, New York..................	37,651	28,435	31,045	36,538	45,845	60,066
Wayne County, New York..................	35,995	27,013	27,814	36,638	42,421	54,547
Westchester County, New York	51,662	21,695	31,694	41,254	67,611	96,040
NORTH CAROLINA						
Alamance County, North Carolina..........	32,328	17,477	26,440	32,253	45,415	56,786
Brunswick County, North Carolina	29,121	15,178	23,252	32,301	43,783	44,845
Buncombe County, North Carolina	31,501	18,783	25,002	30,469	37,540	42,951
Burke County, North Carolina..............	28,325	18,291	26,158	28,307	37,575	51,912
Cabarrus County, North Carolina..........	40,192	21,436	31,081	36,202	52,335	61,134
Caldwell County, North Carolina...........	27,216	14,229	28,693	26,197	41,377	41,920
Carteret County, North Carolina...........	31,010	21,161	22,038	29,190	44,764	48,750
Catawba County, North Carolina..........	32,216	22,785	27,448	31,167	42,107	52,360
Chatham County, North Carolina..........	43,242	25,918	29,962	36,264	53,626	81,975
Cleveland County, North Carolina.........	30,586	13,442	24,103	26,827	41,781	46,421
Craven County, North Carolina............	33,493	21,721	27,437	37,082	39,769	76,457
Cumberland County, North Carolina.......	30,719	16,243	22,230	29,710	42,178	54,819
Davidson County, North Carolina	34,048	26,944	26,528	34,874	42,226	56,349
Durham County, North Carolina...........	36,552	19,673	23,474	34,176	42,237	57,087
Forsyth County, North Carolina	32,266	19,916	25,586	30,426	42,479	56,619
Gaston County, North Carolina............	32,441	17,866	30,479	31,694	47,266	55,618
Guilford County, North Carolina...........	33,632	19,521	26,309	30,674	47,409	53,232
Harnett County, North Carolina	35,316	21,927	29,226	36,430	43,165	50,360
Henderson County, North Carolina........	33,831	17,681	29,562	32,379	42,217	55,648
Iredell County, North Carolina	36,632	25,417	30,271	36,105	56,332	62,542
Johnston County, North Carolina..........	32,442	17,076	28,327	33,117	45,313	61,732
Lincoln County, North Carolina............	36,502	25,576	29,065	36,363	49,575	60,994
Mecklenburg County, North Carolina	40,925	21,409	28,460	33,073	53,632	70,403
Moore County, North Carolina.............	37,318	19,405	29,233	35,038	41,955	55,452
Nash County, North Carolina..............	31,189	19,147	23,752	30,061	49,621	53,883
New Hanover County, North Carolina......	36,988	22,857	30,955	31,347	47,051	60,371
Onslow County, North Carolina............	31,697	25,285	26,637	30,592	37,170	60,925
Orange County, North Carolina............	42,409	21,023	30,068	27,229	43,657	70,199
Pitt County, North Carolina...............	36,571	16,425	23,363	31,817	47,554	65,967
Randolph County, North Carolina.........	31,024	23,785	27,150	31,557	42,013	43,812
Robeson County, North Carolina..........	27,370	18,923	25,172	28,677	40,016	50,514
Rockingham County, North Carolina	30,136	19,425	24,566	30,994	47,111	66,044
Rowan County, North Carolina............	31,901	22,281	29,044	32,107	40,985	46,293
Rutherford County, North Carolina........	26,372	21,545	21,770	26,579	35,979	38,802
Surry County, North Carolina	30,954	19,159	29,966	31,250	46,745	45,907
Union County, North Carolina.............	40,833	21,773	31,182	39,138	56,146	77,103
Wake County, North Carolina	46,569	21,735	30,531	36,610	54,058	72,095
Wayne County, North Carolina............	31,340	22,258	24,609	32,037	47,859	55,069
Wilkes County, North Carolina	29,525	21,836	27,036	31,553	39,423	45,392
Wilson County, North Carolina............	29,982	19,782	26,839	31,049	42,254	61,150
NORTH DAKOTA						
Burleigh County, North Dakota............	44,446	38,832	33,533	41,530	52,670	62,637
Cass County, North Dakota...............	40,626	30,706	29,313	36,345	44,082	67,271
Grand Forks County, North Dakota........	39,368	20,347	36,152	36,628	48,210	56,942
Ward County, North Dakota...............	39,003	25,725	34,739	37,331	48,192	70,849
OHIO						
Allen County, Ohio.......................	32,200	22,119	27,174	32,723	40,132	57,215
Ashtabula County, Ohio...................	34,342	21,109	28,323	33,618	44,599	80,912

N = Data for this geographic area cannot be displayed because the number of sample cases is too small.

Table C-2. Educational Attainment of the Population, by Selected Counties, 2016—*Continued*

(Number; percent; dollars.)

State/County	Educational attainment by race/ethnicity, 25 years and over								
	Some other race alone			Two or more races alone			Hispanic or Latino (of any race)		
	Total	High school graduate or more	Bachelor's degree or more	Total	High school graduate or more	Bachelor's degree or more	Total	High school graduate or more	Bachelor's degree or more
OHIO—*(Continued)*									
Athens County, Ohio	N	N	N	N	N	N	N	N	N
Belmont County, Ohio	N	N	N	N	N	N	N	N	N
Butler County, Ohio	N	N	N	3,884	86.2	27.9	8,450	63.3	12.5
Clark County, Ohio	N	N	N	N	N	N	1,939	80.4	11.1
Clermont County, Ohio	N	N	N	N	N	N	N	N	N
Columbiana County, Ohio	N	N	N	N	N	N	N	N	N
Cuyahoga County, Ohio	12,188	72.1	11.3	13,828	90.7	28.9	39,592	73.9	17.2
Delaware County, Ohio	N	N	N	N	N	N	2,424	73.0	16.5
Erie County, Ohio	N	N	N	N	N	N	N	N	N
Fairfield County, Ohio	N	N	N	N	N	N	1,914	84.4	39.9
Franklin County, Ohio	7,573	61.8	11.7	17,054	92.4	31.3	33,189	74.9	25.7
Geauga County, Ohio	N	N	N	N	N	N	N	N	N
Greene County, Ohio	N	N	N	2,043	96.9	31.1	1,644	95.7	37.5
Hamilton County, Ohio	5,601	65.1	24.1	7,920	92.9	32.5	12,451	73.3	32.8
Hancock County, Ohio	N	N	N	N	N	N	N	N	N
Jefferson County, Ohio	N	N	N	N	N	N	N	N	N
Lake County, Ohio	N	N	N	2,468	77.9	17.4	4,708	64.9	5.9
Licking County, Ohio	N	N	N	N	N	N	N	N	N
Lorain County, Ohio	2,435	66.8	26.2	4,015	82.0	26.7	15,079	76.7	17.3
Lucas County, Ohio	6,522	80.7	8.2	4,349	82.1	11.8	14,243	83.8	20.9
Mahoning County, Ohio	N	N	N	2,754	88.4	7.2	7,706	71.6	14.9
Marion County, Ohio	N	N	N	N	N	N	N	N	N
Medina County, Ohio	N	N	N	N	N	N	N	N	N
Miami County, Ohio	N	N	N	N	N	N	N	N	N
Montgomery County, Ohio	N	N	N	5,380	91.2	15.8	7,614	81.4	19.5
Muskingum County, Ohio	N	N	N	N	N	N	N	N	N
Portage County, Ohio	N	N	N	N	N	N	N	N	N
Richland County, Ohio	N	N	N	N	N	N	N	N	N
Ross County, Ohio	N	N	N	N	N	N	N	N	N
Scioto County, Ohio	N	N	N	N	N	N	N	N	N
Stark County, Ohio	N	N	N	4,325	85.3	12.2	3,904	55.1	17.1
Summit County, Ohio	N	N	N	5,516	88.2	33.3	5,661	79.5	36.2
Trumbull County, Ohio	N	N	N	N	N	N	1,880	91.2	41.4
Tuscarawas County, Ohio	N	N	N	N	N	N	N	N	N
Warren County, Ohio	N	N	N	N	N	N	N	N	N
Wayne County, Ohio	N	N	N	N	N	N	N	N	N
Wood County, Ohio	N	N	N	N	N	N	3,632	75.5	18.2
OKLAHOMA									
Canadian County, Oklahoma	N	N	N	2,636	94.1	22.2	5,230	62.0	17.6
Cleveland County, Oklahoma	N	N	N	8,165	94.7	36.7	11,864	86.8	20.7
Comanche County, Oklahoma	N	N	N	4,524	89.6	14.4	7,356	85.9	7.7
Creek County, Oklahoma	N	N	N	1,883	79.2	25.7	1,299	68.6	13.3
Muskogee County, Oklahoma	N	N	N	2,854	86.6	25.1	N	N	N
Oklahoma County, Oklahoma	12,589	51.6	7.9	21,334	89.0	34.2	62,555	50.3	11.4
Payne County, Oklahoma	N	N	N	1,957	95.2	52.5	N	N	N
Pottawatomie County, Oklahoma	N	N	N	1,876	84.4	9.2	1,576	84.4	9.9
Rogers County, Oklahoma	N	N	N	4,130	92.2	21.3	2,293	78.0	23.9
Tulsa County, Oklahoma	14,127	47.6	5.8	23,276	86.4	26.1	37,847	57.9	10.0
Wagoner County, Oklahoma	N	N	N	3,680	93.9	24.4	2,232	77.6	7.2
OREGON									
Benton County, Oregon	N	N	N	N	N	N	2,886	79.2	25.4
Clackamas County, Oregon	3,686	66.6	8.1	8,964	96.9	28.6	17,699	78.0	19.2
Deschutes County, Oregon	N	N	N	3,005	85.8	23.4	7,159	63.7	15.8
Douglas County, Oregon	N	N	N	2,697	92.4	8.9	3,216	74.7	16.8
Jackson County, Oregon	N	N	N	4,254	86.8	31.4	13,651	58.8	7.9
Josephine County, Oregon	N	N	N	N	N	N	N	N	N
Klamath County, Oregon	N	N	N	N	N	N	3,849	48.5	0.9
Lane County, Oregon	3,171	62.5	6.4	8,903	86.6	34.4	15,773	76.6	20.3
Linn County, Oregon	2,873	50.5	9.3	N	N	N	5,371	64.2	12.9
Marion County, Oregon	13,585	52.6	7.0	13,127	61.4	12.9	42,510	52.0	7.6
Multnomah County, Oregon	11,132	75.8	26.4	19,591	94.9	36.9	49,503	69.0	23.9
Polk County, Oregon	N	N	N	N	N	N	4,671	57.0	8.7
Umatilla County, Oregon	N	N	N	N	N	N	9,209	51.9	9.1
Washington County, Oregon	18,282	54.5	10.8	13,220	89.3	26.8	49,420	61.7	13.6
Yamhill County, Oregon	N	N	N	2,795	95.6	24.8	8,472	63.0	6.2
PENNSYLVANIA									
Adams County, Pennsylvania	N	N	N	N	N	N	3,377	54.5	7.8
Allegheny County, Pennsylvania	3,208	91.1	14.0	12,748	93.8	43.7	14,634	84.9	36.8

N = Data for this geographic area cannot be displayed because the number of sample cases is too small.

Table C-2. Educational Attainment of the Population, by Selected Counties, 2016—*Continued*

(Number; percent; dollars.)

State/County	Median earnings in the past 12 months (2016 inflation-adjusted dollars)					
	Population 25 years and over with earnings					
	Total	Less than high school graduate	High school graduate (includes equivalency)	Some college or associate's degree	Bachelor's degree	Graduate or professional degree
OHIO—*(Continued)*						
Athens County, Ohio	28,493	18,827	22,146	28,853	29,910	57,092
Belmont County, Ohio	28,684	15,232	22,461	28,282	40,650	54,388
Butler County, Ohio	41,153	21,516	31,689	40,236	60,407	71,818
Clark County, Ohio	31,588	16,937	29,275	30,904	45,300	70,094
Clermont County, Ohio	39,328	21,434	31,710	37,186	52,044	71,286
Columbiana County, Ohio	30,981	16,088	30,977	29,522	37,795	58,296
Cuyahoga County, Ohio	37,048	20,722	27,016	33,653	51,057	66,246
Delaware County, Ohio	57,716	31,711	32,168	44,722	68,425	85,506
Erie County, Ohio	33,100	16,957	26,953	33,721	39,763	68,769
Fairfield County, Ohio	41,798	29,571	32,647	35,348	62,126	69,835
Franklin County, Ohio	38,500	20,638	28,342	33,482	51,511	66,626
Geauga County, Ohio	45,555	35,616	40,135	41,321	60,875	70,789
Greene County, Ohio	41,842	21,761	30,541	36,622	47,014	74,059
Hamilton County, Ohio	39,531	18,734	30,659	33,347	51,654	66,598
Hancock County, Ohio	34,352	11,685	21,932	35,285	51,687	61,984
Jefferson County, Ohio	31,830	16,788	27,006	31,363	47,251	47,098
Lake County, Ohio	40,867	21,648	32,155	36,850	56,452	64,632
Licking County, Ohio	35,760	13,322	27,289	35,132	56,064	61,199
Lorain County, Ohio	36,865	24,351	30,716	31,859	53,348	71,659
Lucas County, Ohio	35,198	19,241	31,960	30,407	45,980	60,799
Mahoning County, Ohio	31,882	17,018	27,244	26,298	44,218	51,357
Marion County, Ohio	31,481	19,076	28,834	34,495	44,653	36,995
Medina County, Ohio	43,713	26,861	32,182	40,824	56,130	67,490
Miami County, Ohio	37,082	19,948	32,092	34,782	51,547	69,299
Montgomery County, Ohio	35,420	20,996	26,813	32,213	48,133	64,503
Muskingum County, Ohio	29,918	31,387	26,791	29,167	31,859	52,343
Portage County, Ohio	33,726	24,161	28,836	29,536	50,679	61,557
Richland County, Ohio	30,977	19,036	26,379	31,295	43,635	54,604
Ross County, Ohio	32,300	12,542	29,362	36,087	41,091	71,575
Scioto County, Ohio	31,270	15,021	25,890	35,471	40,888	52,006
Stark County, Ohio	33,266	18,161	29,281	30,984	49,427	61,609
Summit County, Ohio	37,891	21,418	30,502	32,450	50,734	70,749
Trumbull County, Ohio	32,252	20,435	28,909	31,209	45,487	55,947
Tuscarawas County, Ohio	32,017	26,836	30,079	31,130	36,258	52,204
Warren County, Ohio	50,458	23,868	37,093	41,351	68,158	82,580
Wayne County, Ohio	33,618	32,468	30,918	30,121	42,566	55,744
Wood County, Ohio	40,619	21,587	30,333	36,695	52,217	61,273
OKLAHOMA						
Canadian County, Oklahoma	38,680	26,476	28,439	39,076	50,212	56,799
Cleveland County, Oklahoma	38,910	26,795	29,651	37,394	42,889	61,485
Comanche County, Oklahoma	32,536	17,138	28,500	38,333	37,050	50,793
Creek County, Oklahoma	36,572	26,814	32,498	35,935	43,400	58,166
Muskogee County, Oklahoma	30,439	21,517	27,379	27,086	47,435	48,841
Oklahoma County, Oklahoma	35,022	21,590	26,551	32,539	50,377	61,732
Payne County, Oklahoma	32,674	19,384	26,573	28,016	40,305	63,034
Pottawatomie County, Oklahoma	31,344	21,129	25,421	30,311	40,967	51,255
Rogers County, Oklahoma	40,244	21,393	31,882	39,681	46,690	62,476
Tulsa County, Oklahoma	36,127	22,434	27,191	34,684	49,373	64,515
Wagoner County, Oklahoma	36,789	17,875	31,285	35,228	52,221	55,465
OREGON						
Benton County, Oregon	40,109	31,484	26,963	32,034	40,307	61,024
Clackamas County, Oregon	42,402	28,988	33,249	37,742	58,590	71,424
Deschutes County, Oregon	34,441	21,044	29,713	34,326	40,332	57,228
Douglas County, Oregon	30,036	19,497	29,900	25,045	38,208	60,173
Jackson County, Oregon	30,237	19,258	28,257	28,277	41,592	56,943
Josephine County, Oregon	25,262	18,961	20,986	25,469	47,996	55,182
Klamath County, Oregon	31,277	11,488	31,498	30,070	50,078	54,080
Lane County, Oregon	31,397	23,014	28,625	28,420	41,330	55,020
Linn County, Oregon	34,468	19,303	28,765	35,305	47,653	51,266
Marion County, Oregon	31,353	23,575	26,624	30,594	48,391	60,402
Multnomah County, Oregon	40,135	24,783	31,432	32,682	43,078	65,167
Polk County, Oregon	35,864	18,250	30,261	36,572	45,145	52,235
Umatilla County, Oregon	28,892	22,115	25,155	31,679	45,281	33,952
Washington County, Oregon	42,091	22,297	30,226	37,094	55,823	81,716
Yamhill County, Oregon	36,449	25,409	26,881	38,119	50,747	60,040
PENNSYLVANIA						
Adams County, Pennsylvania	35,212	25,039	31,910	35,559	41,727	65,952
Allegheny County, Pennsylvania	41,296	18,584	27,489	34,935	50,727	69,364

N = Data for this geographic area cannot be displayed because the number of sample cases is too small.

Table C-2. Educational Attainment of the Population, by Selected Counties, 2016—*Continued*

(Number; percent; dollars.)

State/County	Educational attainment by race/ethnicity, 25 years and over								
	Some other race alone			Two or more races alone			Hispanic or Latino (of any race)		
	Total	High school graduate or more	Bachelor's degree or more	Total	High school graduate or more	Bachelor's degree or more	Total	High school graduate or more	Bachelor's degree or more
PENNSYLVANIA—*(Continued)*									
Armstrong County, Pennsylvania	N	N	N	N	N	N	N	N	N
Beaver County, Pennsylvania	N	N	N	N	N	N	N	N	N
Berks County, Pennsylvania	7,649	66.4	8.3	11,417	71.9	14.8	41,254	60.6	9.6
Blair County, Pennsylvania	N	N	N	N	N	N	N	N	N
Bucks County, Pennsylvania	4,346	63.2	20.4	5,421	85.8	30.0	18,247	76.1	24.5
Butler County, Pennsylvania	N	N	N	N	N	N	N	N	N
Cambria County, Pennsylvania	N	N	N	N	N	N	968	83.7	24.0
Carbon County, Pennsylvania	N	N	N	N	N	N	N	N	N
Centre County, Pennsylvania	N	N	N	N	N	N	N	N	N
Chester County, Pennsylvania	3,816	64.0	8.5	4,440	89.3	47.0	19,633	59.5	15.7
Clearfield County, Pennsylvania	N	N	N	N	N	N	N	N	N
Columbia County, Pennsylvania	N	N	N	N	N	N	N	N	N
Crawford County, Pennsylvania	N	N	N	N	N	N	N	N	N
Cumberland County, Pennsylvania	2,958	58.4	8.9	1,771	99.2	34.3	5,358	67.8	14.7
Dauphin County, Pennsylvania	3,697	71.9	24.0	2,307	96.7	33.7	11,971	72.9	19.3
Delaware County, Pennsylvania	3,432	68.8	18.2	4,109	91.1	47.7	10,654	81.4	31.5
Erie County, Pennsylvania	N	N	N	1,295	95.5	37.7	5,171	66.5	10.9
Fayette County, Pennsylvania	N	N	N	N	N	N	N	N	N
Franklin County, Pennsylvania	N	N	N	N	N	N	N	N	N
Indiana County, Pennsylvania	N	N	N	N	N	N	N	N	N
Lackawanna County, Pennsylvania	N	N	N	N	N	N	6,999	74.8	13.1
Lancaster County, Pennsylvania	5,419	69.6	4.4	4,757	77.5	23.7	28,438	70.1	8.0
Lawrence County, Pennsylvania	N	N	N	N	N	N	N	N	N
Lebanon County, Pennsylvania	4,395	82.4	2.0	N	N	N	8,131	86.0	10.1
Lehigh County, Pennsylvania	14,479	77.6	10.5	4,374	90.7	26.1	44,586	75.4	10.8
Luzerne County, Pennsylvania	3,329	47.6	10.2	2,193	91.4	24.5	16,484	62.1	10.8
Lycoming County, Pennsylvania	N	N	N	N	N	N	N	N	N
Mercer County, Pennsylvania	N	N	N	N	N	N	N	N	N
Monroe County, Pennsylvania	N	N	N	N	N	N	13,467	84.5	16.3
Montgomery County, Pennsylvania	5,308	46.0	10.2	7,845	96.6	42.0	21,958	70.9	24.6
Northampton County, Pennsylvania	2,899	72.7	19.8	3,937	96.7	19.8	21,170	75.1	18.2
Northumberland County, Pennsylvania	N	N	N	N	N	N	N	N	N
Philadelphia County, Pennsylvania	59,111	61.9	6.9	23,074	85.9	33.0	123,124	63.3	12.9
Schuylkill County, Pennsylvania	N	N	N	N	N	N	3,073	59.5	7.2
Somerset County, Pennsylvania	N	N	N	N	N	N	N	N	N
Washington County, Pennsylvania	N	N	N	1,726	92.5	27.3	1,983	75.0	18.9
Westmoreland County, Pennsylvania	N	N	N	N	N	N	2,278	87.1	24.3
York County, Pennsylvania	3,807	74.4	4.2	3,863	92.3	27.0	15,219	85.1	14.6
RHODE ISLAND									
Kent County, Rhode Island	N	N	N	N	N	N	4,116	100.0	30.0
Newport County, Rhode Island	N	N	N	N	N	N	N	N	N
Providence County, Rhode Island	31,404	63.6	11.8	10,256	82.9	24.8	76,056	69.6	10.5
Washington County, Rhode Island	N	N	N	N	N	N	N	N	N
SOUTH CAROLINA									
Aiken County, South Carolina	N	N	N	N	N	N	4,745	54.5	9.2
Anderson County, South Carolina	N	N	N	N	N	N	N	N	N
Beaufort County, South Carolina	N	N	N	N	N	N	10,252	81.8	14.8
Berkeley County, South Carolina	2,984	71.5	14.7	1,656	91.0	22.9	6,679	68.4	15.0
Charleston County, South Carolina	N	N	N	3,487	65.3	26.3	10,672	63.5	18.4
Darlington County, South Carolina	N	N	N	N	N	N	N	N	N
Dorchester County, South Carolina	N	N	N	N	N	N	N	N	N
Florence County, South Carolina	N	N	N	N	N	N	2,144	54.6	26.4
Greenville County, South Carolina	5,977	58.2	16.4	3,635	84.6	14.9	24,573	54.1	15.0
Greenwood County, South Carolina	N	N	N	N	N	N	N	N	N
Horry County, South Carolina	N	N	N	N	N	N	10,008	57.7	11.6
Lancaster County, South Carolina	N	N	N	N	N	N	N	N	N
Laurens County, South Carolina	N	N	N	N	N	N	N	N	N
Lexington County, South Carolina	N	N	N	2,610	91.3	13.2	9,055	56.2	16.2
Oconee County, South Carolina	N	N	N	N	N	N	1,922	65.0	12.9
Orangeburg County, South Carolina	N	N	N	N	N	N	N	N	N
Pickens County, South Carolina	N	N	N	N	N	N	N	N	N
Richland County, South Carolina	3,940	57.0	18.5	4,761	95.0	37.5	10,529	68.9	21.8
Spartanburg County, South Carolina	2,275	56.9	10.2	2,508	84.5	26.4	9,735	55.2	9.8

N = Data for this geographic area cannot be displayed because the number of sample cases is too small.

Table C-2. Educational Attainment of the Population, by Selected Counties, 2016—*Continued*

(Number; percent; dollars.)

State/County	Median earnings in the past 12 months (2016 inflation-adjusted dollars)					
	Population 25 years and over with earnings					
	Total	Less than high school graduate	High school graduate (includes equivalency)	Some college or associate's degree	Bachelor's degree	Graduate or professional degree
PENNSYLVANIA—(*Continued*)						
Armstrong County, Pennsylvania	31,734	20,279	30,141	30,962	50,421	65,709
Beaver County, Pennsylvania	37,360	21,229	29,414	38,243	51,081	61,188
Berks County, Pennsylvania	38,669	24,866	31,877	36,387	50,026	72,573
Blair County, Pennsylvania	31,517	22,532	27,970	34,725	42,128	56,275
Bucks County, Pennsylvania	46,790	26,143	34,294	41,046	59,975	85,025
Butler County, Pennsylvania	45,704	25,296	35,563	40,262	61,238	70,597
Cambria County, Pennsylvania	31,744	16,750	27,340	31,074	42,095	51,737
Carbon County, Pennsylvania	35,790	21,689	31,257	38,032	48,834	51,963
Centre County, Pennsylvania	39,934	25,169	25,614	35,005	46,976	70,973
Chester County, Pennsylvania	52,655	22,499	36,511	40,246	67,177	91,125
Clearfield County, Pennsylvania	30,070	24,153	26,179	30,865	36,764	60,518
Columbia County, Pennsylvania	36,522	22,340	30,284	36,111	46,932	56,905
Crawford County, Pennsylvania	31,644	23,807	25,598	32,853	33,592	59,599
Cumberland County, Pennsylvania	41,938	17,032	29,809	41,748	53,804	67,553
Dauphin County, Pennsylvania	40,628	21,984	32,389	38,566	48,869	65,936
Delaware County, Pennsylvania	43,975	21,848	31,520	40,694	55,488	75,133
Erie County, Pennsylvania	32,523	17,515	27,976	31,704	39,410	57,093
Fayette County, Pennsylvania	31,908	15,874	27,461	32,429	39,914	65,791
Franklin County, Pennsylvania	38,919	41,006	31,705	39,888	52,105	62,148
Indiana County, Pennsylvania	31,030	20,272	25,597	30,259	45,421	60,630
Lackawanna County, Pennsylvania	36,430	20,214	26,820	36,718	46,034	60,880
Lancaster County, Pennsylvania	37,605	27,042	31,724	36,275	48,151	67,710
Lawrence County, Pennsylvania	34,917	25,927	26,014	33,864	42,234	63,659
Lebanon County, Pennsylvania	36,205	34,712	31,611	34,798	46,868	54,302
Lehigh County, Pennsylvania	40,895	21,382	30,720	38,475	56,098	76,582
Luzerne County, Pennsylvania	35,673	24,222	29,018	33,739	50,376	63,163
Lycoming County, Pennsylvania	33,375	23,021	28,486	31,705	45,403	52,862
Mercer County, Pennsylvania	32,435	20,153	26,854	30,673	50,929	52,330
Monroe County, Pennsylvania	38,188	25,393	31,722	37,085	42,884	69,758
Montgomery County, Pennsylvania	51,338	25,904	36,506	40,188	59,659	85,143
Northampton County, Pennsylvania	39,612	30,017	31,659	35,842	51,987	62,885
Northumberland County, Pennsylvania	32,081	21,603	27,500	36,935	43,825	60,522
Philadelphia County, Pennsylvania	35,143	21,864	26,323	31,639	47,496	60,593
Schuylkill County, Pennsylvania	37,151	23,438	35,014	35,685	50,561	56,202
Somerset County, Pennsylvania	30,500	22,460	27,107	32,091	41,668	51,362
Washington County, Pennsylvania	39,888	17,133	31,010	36,390	50,508	66,302
Westmoreland County, Pennsylvania	40,059	23,814	31,446	35,183	50,865	66,145
York County, Pennsylvania	40,791	26,424	33,491	37,695	54,755	70,508
RHODE ISLAND						
Kent County, Rhode Island	41,357	24,826	29,599	40,487	51,794	69,825
Newport County, Rhode Island	44,455	45,591	32,218	39,381	54,270	81,104
Providence County, Rhode Island	40,597	25,581	33,955	36,123	52,687	68,743
Washington County, Rhode Island	49,964	20,804	36,046	37,377	51,538	73,244
SOUTH CAROLINA						
Aiken County, South Carolina	31,781	20,991	29,065	30,867	46,497	51,326
Anderson County, South Carolina	32,430	22,953	24,990	34,993	51,391	61,383
Beaufort County, South Carolina	34,333	19,805	27,851	32,806	41,940	50,682
Berkeley County, South Carolina	38,025	25,137	36,556	33,148	50,014	62,500
Charleston County, South Carolina	40,963	19,819	29,443	32,042	51,519	65,410
Darlington County, South Carolina	30,036	21,681	30,262	27,321	31,244	49,735
Dorchester County, South Carolina	37,274	26,438	35,146	36,047	48,373	51,531
Florence County, South Carolina	32,172	21,322	26,120	35,682	36,939	51,371
Greenville County, South Carolina	35,995	18,409	28,179	34,321	47,100	57,802
Greenwood County, South Carolina	30,020	17,478	25,734	30,370	31,224	60,160
Horry County, South Carolina	27,324	20,758	25,661	25,383	37,124	50,836
Lancaster County, South Carolina	34,315	29,251	30,771	31,491	61,140	49,234
Laurens County, South Carolina	30,603	19,877	25,825	31,956	45,013	50,086
Lexington County, South Carolina	38,474	21,699	31,107	36,568	49,793	60,044
Oconee County, South Carolina	29,569	18,612	22,766	30,549	48,494	68,803
Orangeburg County, South Carolina	24,933	17,076	17,463	23,255	35,883	49,080
Pickens County, South Carolina	32,230	23,719	26,731	32,697	41,444	52,404
Richland County, South Carolina	35,867	14,153	25,047	31,800	45,699	52,444
Spartanburg County, South Carolina	32,231	24,148	25,991	31,319	45,645	55,917

N = Data for this geographic area cannot be displayed because the number of sample cases is too small.

Table C-2. Educational Attainment of the Population, by Selected Counties, 2016—*Continued*

(Number; percent; dollars.)

	Educational attainment by race/ethnicity, 25 years and over								
	Some other race alone			Two or more races alone			Hispanic or Latino (of any race)		
State/County	Total	High school graduate or more	Bachelor's degree or more	Total	High school graduate or more	Bachelor's degree or more	Total	High school graduate or more	Bachelor's degree or more
SOUTH CAROLINA—*(Continued)*									
Sumter County, South Carolina	N	N	N	N	N	N	N	N	N
York County, South Carolina	N	N	N	N	N	N	7,022	61.4	15.4
SOUTH DAKOTA									
Minnehaha County, South Dakota	N	N	N	N	N	N	4,442	58.3	9.0
Pennington County, South Dakota	N	N	N	N	N	N	N	N	N
TENNESSEE									
Anderson County, Tennessee	N	N	N	N	N	N	N	N	N
Blount County, Tennessee	N	N	N	N	N	N	2,098	46.9	13.3
Bradley County, Tennessee	N	N	N	N	N	N	3,055	60.9	12.6
Davidson County, Tennessee	5,298	54.3	16.3	7,200	84.2	31.5	35,354	55.3	13.1
Greene County, Tennessee	N	N	N	N	N	N	N	N	N
Hamilton County, Tennessee	N	N	N	3,248	88.7	30.3	9,037	68.0	20.3
Knox County, Tennessee	N	N	N	2,944	86.4	43.4	9,527	76.2	30.1
Madison County, Tennessee	N	N	N	N	N	N	N	N	N
Maury County, Tennessee	N	N	N	N	N	N	2,438	86.9	4.1
Montgomery County, Tennessee	N	N	N	3,155	98.5	36.9	9,818	85.4	17.5
Putnam County, Tennessee	N	N	N	N	N	N	N	N	N
Robertson County, Tennessee	N	N	N	N	N	N	2,241	68.5	7.6
Rutherford County, Tennessee	2,339	74.0	13.5	2,978	98.5	52.2	10,945	66.5	11.0
Sevier County, Tennessee	N	N	N	N	N	N	2,849	81.7	2.7
Shelby County, Tennessee	13,136	44.3	6.4	7,009	94.8	37.8	27,511	54.4	12.7
Sullivan County, Tennessee	N	N	N	N	N	N	N	N	N
Sumner County, Tennessee	N	N	N	N	N	N	3,934	71.4	27.3
Washington County, Tennessee	N	N	N	N	N	N	N	N	N
Williamson County, Tennessee	N	N	N	N	N	N	5,447	51.1	24.7
Wilson County, Tennessee	N	N	N	N	N	N	2,627	83.1	41.3
TEXAS									
Angelina County, Texas	N	N	N	N	N	N	9,301	51.7	13.9
Bastrop County, Texas	7,243	63.4	1.9	N	N	N	15,888	60.1	4.4
Bell County, Texas	4,410	76.9	13.3	7,656	89.7	17.4	42,824	80.2	12.5
Bexar County, Texas	85,093	67.7	12.5	25,900	88.1	28.6	685,084	74.2	17.6
Bowie County, Texas	N	N	N	N	N	N	N	N	N
Brazoria County, Texas	6,107	76.5	4.4	N	N	N	59,099	69.7	12.0
Brazos County, Texas	3,900	69.7	20.3	N	N	N	26,201	59.7	15.1
Cameron County, Texas	9,058	47.2	5.5	1,266	72.0	33.6	211,286	63.6	14.0
Collin County, Texas	12,491	79.5	16.3	11,901	94.6	48.4	77,619	72.1	22.9
Comal County, Texas	3,487	82.3	17.7	N	N	N	20,305	84.5	16.2
Coryell County, Texas	N	N	N	4,419	89.4	6.5	7,762	75.1	13.7
Dallas County, Texas	85,429	54.0	10.8	33,620	88.2	38.7	542,692	52.3	10.2
Denton County, Texas	20,330	60.9	21.9	11,529	92.6	52.9	83,424	72.9	26.0
Ector County, Texas	4,741	47.7	7.7	N	N	N	49,909	63.7	7.8
Ellis County, Texas	1,560	83.2	13.4	2,218	69.4	9.1	22,601	60.3	6.0
El Paso County, Texas	57,761	67.1	16.1	9,552	91.3	40.3	408,360	72.8	18.9
Fort Bend County, Texas	22,938	63.1	8.6	8,053	83.5	45.1	102,257	76.6	22.6
Galveston County, Texas	4,392	59.6	8.1	N	N	N	45,081	71.5	17.6
Grayson County, Texas	N	N	N	N	N	N	7,525	72.0	11.1
Gregg County, Texas	N	N	N	N	N	N	11,113	33.5	2.5
Guadalupe County, Texas	17,350	76.4	10.0	N	N	N	33,793	78.3	13.9
Harris County, Texas	224,733	60.0	10.3	49,513	85.3	35.1	1,079,323	61.6	13.1
Harrison County, Texas	N	N	N	N	N	N	4,018	68.4	3.2
Hays County, Texas	N	N	N	N	N	N	41,411	71.7	19.1
Henderson County, Texas	N	N	N	N	N	N	5,023	53.5	0.6
Hidalgo County, Texas	63,325	51.0	13.9	4,096	72.9	18.8	420,642	62.1	16.6
Hunt County, Texas	4,124	32.5	8.0	N	N	N	6,970	52.8	12.9
Jefferson County, Texas	2,792	57.3	6.1	N	N	N	27,779	53.7	7.2
Johnson County, Texas	N	N	N	N	N	N	17,474	66.3	9.5
Kaufman County, Texas	N	N	N	N	N	N	12,886	60.9	10.2
Liberty County, Texas	N	N	N	N	N	N	10,423	45.6	0.5
Lubbock County, Texas	10,702	62.2	4.0	3,127	79.1	36.7	55,489	67.7	10.5
McLennan County, Texas	5,067	56.6	3.1	1,893	87.2	26.8	31,853	52.7	4.8
Midland County, Texas	3,454	75.0	20.3	N	N	N	38,882	67.0	10.4
Montgomery County, Texas	8,716	70.4	18.8	4,535	83.7	41.7	68,081	64.0	21.6
Nacogdoches County, Texas	N	N	N	N	N	N	4,871	35.1	8.5
Nueces County, Texas	4,574	69.8	10.6	3,289	83.0	13.7	137,782	76.3	14.0

N = Data for this geographic area cannot be displayed because the number of sample cases is too small.

Table C-2. Educational Attainment of the Population, by Selected Counties, 2016—*Continued*

(Number; percent; dollars.)

State/County	Median earnings in the past 12 months (2016 inflation-adjusted dollars)					
	Population 25 years and over with earnings					
	Total	Less than high school graduate	High school graduate (includes equivalency)	Some college or associate's degree	Bachelor's degree	Graduate or professional degree
SOUTH CAROLINA—*(Continued)*						
Sumter County, South Carolina	28,182	18,041	21,088	28,814	40,182	55,112
York County, South Carolina	40,833	22,738	30,722	37,021	58,805	63,456
SOUTH DAKOTA						
Minnehaha County, South Dakota	38,571	26,710	31,437	37,687	45,879	55,548
Pennington County, South Dakota	31,564	14,566	27,999	31,928	37,145	37,494
TENNESSEE						
Anderson County, Tennessee	34,266	23,883	30,158	32,014	36,389	63,632
Blount County, Tennessee	34,335	16,637	26,137	36,396	40,442	59,384
Bradley County, Tennessee	32,251	17,343	31,945	31,917	36,475	47,068
Davidson County, Tennessee	36,499	22,384	28,227	32,104	46,678	56,166
Greene County, Tennessee	29,616	22,973	27,278	28,000	28,349	52,151
Hamilton County, Tennessee	36,998	19,575	26,882	35,439	46,544	60,416
Knox County, Tennessee	35,959	17,137	28,433	31,360	44,483	56,238
Madison County, Tennessee	35,063	27,107	31,366	30,250	44,689	55,421
Maury County, Tennessee	35,998	31,480	26,239	35,803	41,398	50,541
Montgomery County, Tennessee	36,963	20,236	30,940	37,874	44,966	50,569
Putnam County, Tennessee	31,690	13,327	24,488	33,394	38,056	44,863
Robertson County, Tennessee	36,075	26,543	30,573	34,840	49,766	60,149
Rutherford County, Tennessee	39,450	25,318	34,074	36,722	49,975	53,990
Sevier County, Tennessee	26,153	15,096	26,544	25,192	32,819	41,886
Shelby County, Tennessee	34,755	20,653	25,373	31,772	50,200	61,356
Sullivan County, Tennessee	29,741	15,908	25,674	30,574	38,271	55,610
Sumner County, Tennessee	39,489	21,647	31,192	36,108	51,020	58,728
Washington County, Tennessee	32,241	30,411	21,690	28,774	47,136	50,553
Williamson County, Tennessee	53,639	23,354	36,663	41,572	66,934	91,866
Wilson County, Tennessee	41,360	31,352	32,475	41,167	50,335	66,132
TEXAS						
Angelina County, Texas	30,093	15,422	26,139	31,415	47,823	70,885
Bastrop County, Texas	39,730	22,403	40,315	36,022	56,357	65,342
Bell County, Texas	32,104	18,193	27,165	31,594	49,466	75,412
Bexar County, Texas	33,018	20,765	26,427	33,916	47,774	62,772
Bowie County, Texas	35,131	17,809	29,802	31,799	52,530	62,416
Brazoria County, Texas	49,451	31,451	30,683	48,667	66,513	79,718
Brazos County, Texas	35,262	24,163	25,310	32,978	48,928	56,316
Cameron County, Texas	25,025	17,431	20,841	27,385	41,672	60,055
Collin County, Texas	55,250	22,993	33,997	46,422	64,006	90,123
Comal County, Texas	41,444	17,885	30,802	46,029	56,914	61,957
Coryell County, Texas	31,663	14,054	23,225	33,083	40,381	44,639
Dallas County, Texas	35,603	23,688	26,417	35,920	55,242	71,938
Denton County, Texas	50,079	25,636	32,157	41,385	61,591	76,421
Ector County, Texas	36,983	30,104	33,005	40,670	50,114	55,703
Ellis County, Texas	41,130	27,199	34,303	41,026	52,085	59,911
El Paso County, Texas	28,011	16,738	23,192	27,417	44,331	56,962
Fort Bend County, Texas	50,777	22,288	33,827	41,563	66,662	81,981
Galveston County, Texas	44,983	21,930	34,206	40,151	66,696	69,946
Grayson County, Texas	33,886	22,462	32,272	33,853	41,548	65,278
Gregg County, Texas	31,028	19,997	26,674	35,333	35,166	76,388
Guadalupe County, Texas	40,472	24,815	30,722	40,976	54,308	70,094
Harris County, Texas	37,118	21,325	26,867	36,314	57,434	76,481
Harrison County, Texas	31,326	24,701	27,385	36,856	36,930	53,665
Hays County, Texas	41,429	26,439	31,334	40,627	46,749	62,361
Henderson County, Texas	28,006	23,098	22,909	23,898	44,362	56,828
Hidalgo County, Texas	24,812	15,655	21,403	27,004	46,327	55,755
Hunt County, Texas	31,109	24,351	26,973	34,859	46,728	52,512
Jefferson County, Texas	36,228	22,624	30,510	36,955	51,267	54,548
Johnson County, Texas	38,567	30,955	36,458	35,838	50,124	63,896
Kaufman County, Texas	40,380	22,438	31,541	43,470	52,325	61,262
Liberty County, Texas	39,010	26,402	45,031	37,305	49,907	73,443
Lubbock County, Texas	32,712	20,749	27,120	30,617	45,670	56,922
McLennan County, Texas	31,537	20,185	26,572	32,137	46,273	52,015
Midland County, Texas	44,075	26,769	34,773	42,036	57,515	76,377
Montgomery County, Texas	45,626	25,266	31,343	45,078	63,648	71,813
Nacogdoches County, Texas	30,203	21,301	29,727	29,667	45,979	51,028
Nueces County, Texas	35,647	18,682	29,650	34,623	52,300	60,885

N = Data for this geographic area cannot be displayed because the number of sample cases is too small.

Table C-2. Educational Attainment of the Population, by Selected Counties, 2016—*Continued*

(Number; percent; dollars.)

State/County	Educational attainment by race/ethnicity, 25 years and over								
	Some other race alone			Two or more races alone			Hispanic or Latino (of any race)		
	Total	High school graduate or more	Bachelor's degree or more	Total	High school graduate or more	Bachelor's degree or more	Total	High school graduate or more	Bachelor's degree or more
TEXAS—(*Continued*)									
Orange County, Texas	N	N	N	N	N	N	3,087	62.1	10.9
Parker County, Texas	N	N	N	N	N	N	8,333	73.0	7.8
Potter County, Texas	2,073	64.7	2.9	1,783	53.5	3.4	24,129	56.7	3.4
Randall County, Texas	N	N	N	N	N	N	14,781	71.5	11.9
Rockwall County, Texas	N	N	N	N	N	N	8,440	73.1	27.3
San Patricio County, Texas	N	N	N	N	N	N	22,508	68.1	7.1
Smith County, Texas	3,599	53.3	10.0	N	N	N	20,941	47.1	10.9
Tarrant County, Texas	77,962	52.5	7.5	25,057	87.3	30.6	301,005	60.3	13.0
Taylor County, Texas	5,381	67.3	14.5	N	N	N	17,080	76.5	11.9
Tom Green County, Texas	2,101	61.0	2.7	N	N	N	26,394	68.3	14.4
Travis County, Texas	47,280	62.0	14.4	19,783	89.2	43.3	233,737	70.8	22.8
Victoria County, Texas	N	N	N	N	N	N	24,437	70.3	7.2
Walker County, Texas	N	N	N	N	N	N	6,528	64.6	5.6
Webb County, Texas	5,314	71.8	17.9	N	N	N	140,317	65.3	15.3
Wichita County, Texas	N	N	N	N	N	N	12,883	67.2	11.1
Williamson County, Texas	9,727	87.2	23.5	8,212	97.2	36.6	71,167	85.8	26.4
UTAH									
Cache County, Utah	N	N	N	N	N	N	5,503	61.3	19.0
Davis County, Utah	6,098	84.0	9.5	3,248	100.0	44.4	16,092	87.4	16.8
Salt Lake County, Utah	61,413	55.9	10.7	12,969	82.8	26.1	103,292	65.5	13.7
Utah County, Utah	2,985	57.5	8.6	4,789	97.3	58.6	30,606	72.5	15.9
Washington County, Utah	N	N	N	N	N	N	7,167	71.8	21.9
Weber County, Utah	4,564	74.4	3.8	N	N	N	22,037	68.6	5.0
VERMONT									
Chittenden County, Vermont	N	N	N	N	N	N	N	N	N
VIRGINIA									
Albemarle County, Virginia	N	N	N	N	N	N	2,659	64.3	29.8
Arlington County, Virginia	8,614	57.9	13.8	N	N	N	23,468	74.8	38.6
Augusta County, Virginia	N	N	N	N	N	N	N	N	N
Bedford County, Virginia	N	N	N	N	N	N	N	N	N
Chesterfield County, Virginia	5,311	70.8	20.4	4,488	93.0	25.5	15,236	67.4	19.5
Fairfax County, Virginia	30,853	59.0	16.3	20,733	93.1	64.4	108,842	71.1	27.8
Fauquier County, Virginia	N	N	N	N	N	N	2,841	64.4	30.8
Frederick County, Virginia	N	N	N	N	N	N	3,385	68.3	14.8
Hanover County, Virginia	N	N	N	N	N	N	N	N	N
Henrico County, Virginia	N	N	N	4,001	91.9	32.3	9,920	80.4	20.8
James City County, Virginia	N	N	N	N	N	N	N	N	N
Loudoun County, Virginia	7,611	80.2	44.6	7,926	96.7	62.9	30,103	74.7	28.3
Montgomery County, Virginia	N	N	N	N	N	N	N	N	N
Prince William County, Virginia	24,459	58.1	11.3	8,202	88.2	45.5	57,987	64.7	18.1
Roanoke County, Virginia	N	N	N	N	N	N	N	N	N
Rockingham County, Virginia	N	N	N	N	N	N	N	N	N
Spotsylvania County, Virginia	3,897	65.7	1.2	1,661	85.7	26.1	6,429	64.3	8.8
Stafford County, Virginia	5,370	77.5	25.1	N	N	N	9,255	82.1	28.4
York County, Virginia	N	N	N	N	N	N	N	N	N
Alexandria city, Virginia	6,540	47.1	17.6	N	N	N	16,553	64.3	30.2
Chesapeake city, Virginia	N	N	N	3,358	95.9	47.1	7,882	88.2	34.5
Hampton city, Virginia	N	N	N	N	N	N	4,495	93.1	30.7
Lynchburg city, Virginia	N	N	N	N	N	N	N	N	N
Newport News city, Virginia	N	N	N	4,512	100.0	26.8	7,834	86.8	17.3
Norfolk city, Virginia	4,519	76.5	14.8	3,582	92.0	36.0	9,427	86.6	21.8
Portsmouth city, Virginia	N	N	N	N	N	N	N	N	N
Richmond city, Virginia	N	N	N	4,101	75.2	33.0	7,832	65.3	12.5
Roanoke city, Virginia	N	N	N	N	N	N	N	N	N
Suffolk city, Virginia	N	N	N	N	N	N	2,258	89.2	12.8
Virginia Beach city, Virginia	6,016	63.1	18.3	9,072	94.4	36.7	20,342	83.9	21.0
WASHINGTON									
Benton County, Washington	8,432	59.1	14.4	2,389	90.3	33.3	19,198	72.7	16.6
Chelan County, Washington	N	N	N	N	N	N	9,912	42.5	3.8
Clallam County, Washington	N	N	N	N	N	N	1,950	80.4	6.6
Clark County, Washington	7,715	53.3	7.3	7,997	90.8	27.2	20,368	66.0	14.9
Cowlitz County, Washington	N	N	N	2,807	98.6	21.1	3,950	70.8	6.9
Franklin County, Washington	13,103	46.6	5.0	N	N	N	22,403	54.4	5.8

N = Data for this geographic area cannot be displayed because the number of sample cases is too small.

Table C-2. Educational Attainment of the Population, by Selected Counties, 2016—*Continued*

(Number; percent; dollars.)

State/County	Median earnings in the past 12 months (2016 inflation-adjusted dollars)					
	Population 25 years and over with earnings					
	Total	Less than high school graduate	High school graduate (includes equivalency)	Some college or associate's degree	Bachelor's degree	Graduate or professional degree
TEXAS—(*Continued*)						
Orange County, Texas	37,282	41,667	35,438	32,093	46,065	54,413
Parker County, Texas	41,453	26,258	28,410	41,915	53,067	90,412
Potter County, Texas	31,044	24,349	29,480	32,858	48,859	60,979
Randall County, Texas	40,650	24,492	33,642	36,138	50,007	65,865
Rockwall County, Texas	56,215	31,076	51,244	46,299	65,765	81,673
San Patricio County, Texas	32,428	24,171	30,591	31,992	41,737	50,381
Smith County, Texas	31,555	20,537	22,577	31,319	46,382	61,385
Tarrant County, Texas	38,331	23,637	30,560	37,101	53,724	69,581
Taylor County, Texas	31,040	15,527	25,931	35,208	42,058	60,740
Tom Green County, Texas	31,334	18,905	27,161	32,444	37,264	61,004
Travis County, Texas	42,394	23,735	29,895	38,678	52,806	72,676
Victoria County, Texas	33,488	21,436	24,526	39,466	47,207	74,930
Walker County, Texas	36,521	26,283	24,211	40,603	45,913	61,678
Webb County, Texas	26,050	16,753	22,820	31,873	45,888	55,669
Wichita County, Texas	31,765	17,282	26,992	31,110	44,237	57,056
Williamson County, Texas	45,443	26,597	30,743	39,485	57,422	66,960
UTAH						
Cache County, Utah	32,365	26,042	31,831	24,405	39,328	67,936
Davis County, Utah	41,600	23,388	31,232	36,541	52,707	74,089
Salt Lake County, Utah	38,411	25,395	31,024	36,391	49,044	68,351
Utah County, Utah	38,169	25,556	26,905	32,009	46,238	70,312
Washington County, Utah	30,096	21,646	25,051	26,611	31,687	73,496
Weber County, Utah	36,574	27,138	31,829	34,545	47,484	65,273
VERMONT						
Chittenden County, Vermont	43,530	21,696	34,539	40,121	48,428	60,989
VIRGINIA						
Albemarle County, Virginia	46,903	25,296	29,885	38,096	53,876	67,609
Arlington County, Virginia	76,636	19,851	30,018	36,549	75,941	102,322
Augusta County, Virginia	35,910	23,809	31,105	36,128	47,623	56,412
Bedford County, Virginia	36,686	23,663	27,030	36,322	51,752	62,125
Chesterfield County, Virginia	42,258	21,983	32,104	40,225	51,715	60,448
Fairfax County, Virginia	61,564	25,641	31,414	41,968	72,431	100,831
Fauquier County, Virginia	51,324	33,573	49,425	42,204	62,219	76,250
Frederick County, Virginia	40,899	29,035	30,087	42,227	52,218	71,544
Hanover County, Virginia	50,283	25,947	35,738	45,361	61,771	56,063
Henrico County, Virginia	41,623	19,459	30,424	36,989	53,856	64,625
James City County, Virginia	41,972	22,198	24,484	31,596	51,358	62,696
Loudoun County, Virginia	69,749	30,125	35,481	50,757	86,612	101,431
Montgomery County, Virginia	43,206	25,774	25,664	34,379	36,952	80,126
Prince William County, Virginia	50,523	27,575	35,514	43,260	65,330	93,149
Roanoke County, Virginia	42,206	19,556	33,152	40,677	50,651	66,234
Rockingham County, Virginia	36,448	31,622	30,841	35,372	52,730	51,786
Spotsylvania County, Virginia	43,225	31,500	36,735	40,172	58,098	71,168
Stafford County, Virginia	52,808	19,046	31,317	41,930	71,708	109,082
York County, Virginia	49,980	20,824	31,419	40,281	52,785	91,156
Alexandria city, Virginia	61,434	20,742	26,564	38,094	70,342	92,243
Chesapeake city, Virginia	42,250	21,994	31,818	40,046	52,301	73,347
Hampton city, Virginia	36,400	27,018	30,683	35,060	42,138	52,631
Lynchburg city, Virginia	30,435	17,147	23,667	31,850	33,844	45,681
Newport News city, Virginia	34,105	25,833	28,348	32,710	40,642	54,241
Norfolk city, Virginia	31,688	21,199	27,192	29,380	42,540	59,085
Portsmouth city, Virginia	34,840	24,137	31,009	33,549	37,299	62,683
Richmond city, Virginia	34,584	18,928	23,470	28,691	46,427	52,048
Roanoke city, Virginia	30,762	22,856	22,706	31,329	36,889	56,282
Suffolk city, Virginia	42,042	22,500	31,512	42,106	52,520	75,745
Virginia Beach city, Virginia	40,667	24,332	31,755	37,371	49,152	69,828
WASHINGTON						
Benton County, Washington	42,252	21,683	32,385	36,973	60,548	71,984
Chelan County, Washington	34,373	19,530	23,781	36,403	40,439	63,756
Clallam County, Washington	32,437	17,140	30,645	31,775	45,659	57,449
Clark County, Washington	41,275	29,946	33,973	37,129	57,350	67,320
Cowlitz County, Washington	35,221	27,253	35,183	30,663	50,374	66,180
Franklin County, Washington	30,864	23,720	26,441	35,515	62,584	60,271

N = Data for this geographic area cannot be displayed because the number of sample cases is too small.

Table C-2. Educational Attainment of the Population, by Selected Counties, 2016—*Continued*

(Number; percent; dollars.)

State/County	Some other race alone			Two or more races alone			Hispanic or Latino (of any race)		
	Total	High school graduate or more	Bachelor's degree or more	Total	High school graduate or more	Bachelor's degree or more	Total	High school graduate or more	Bachelor's degree or more
WASHINGTON—*(Continued)*									
Grant County, Washington	13,346	47.3	5.5	N	N	N	17,547	48.9	4.7
Grays Harbor County, Washington	N	N	N	N	N	N	3,322	47.4	13.2
Island County, Washington	N	N	N	N	N	N	3,367	91.1	14.5
King County, Washington	53,962	59.1	16.4	63,264	93.1	40.5	113,252	70.6	25.3
Kitsap County, Washington	4,476	83.5	19.9	8,500	93.0	21.7	10,257	91.0	24.1
Lewis County, Washington	N	N	N	N	N	N	3,164	61.6	12.3
Pierce County, Washington	14,395	59.4	8.1	28,051	90.1	20.3	44,498	72.2	14.9
Skagit County, Washington	5,081	29.5	3.6	2,081	92.9	7.4	10,160	53.0	8.4
Snohomish County, Washington	14,473	59.7	9.4	18,138	90.7	29.0	39,682	71.6	15.0
Spokane County, Washington	5,105	72.8	17.0	9,153	89.3	21.7	13,835	78.4	20.1
Thurston County, Washington	1,896	79.4	24.6	7,305	96.8	23.3	13,221	78.6	26.0
Whatcom County, Washington	5,369	41.4	1.1	3,640	75.2	24.1	9,302	52.9	8.9
Yakima County, Washington	16,167	51.2	7.3	4,002	89.4	12.5	57,846	50.4	4.9
WEST VIRGINIA									
Berkeley County, West Virginia	N	N	N	N	N	N	2,509	74.9	2.2
Cabell County, West Virginia	N	N	N	N	N	N	N	N	N
Harrison County, West Virginia	N	N	N	N	N	N	N	N	N
Kanawha County, West Virginia	N	N	N	2,438	78.2	35.4	N	N	N
Monongalia County, West Virginia	N	N	N	N	N	N	N	N	N
Raleigh County, West Virginia	N	N	N	N	N	N	N	N	N
Wood County, West Virginia	N	N	N	N	N	N	N	N	N
WISCONSIN									
Brown County, Wisconsin	5,812	59.1	2.5	N	N	N	10,529	70.9	7.0
Dane County, Wisconsin	6,076	90.7	16.4	5,176	91.2	59.1	16,422	80.8	32.5
Dodge County, Wisconsin	N	N	N	N	N	N	1,944	51.4	5.0
Eau Claire County, Wisconsin	N	N	N	N	N	N	N	N	N
Fond du Lac County, Wisconsin	N	N	N	N	N	N	2,379	63.7	23.8
Jefferson County, Wisconsin	N	N	N	N	N	N	N	N	N
Kenosha County, Wisconsin	N	N	N	N	N	N	9,905	66.5	8.2
La Crosse County, Wisconsin	N	N	N	N	N	N	N	N	N
Manitowoc County, Wisconsin	N	N	N	N	N	N	1,344	62.3	18.0
Marathon County, Wisconsin	N	N	N	N	N	N	N	N	N
Milwaukee County, Wisconsin	30,181	57.3	6.3	11,252	84.0	27.1	72,514	65.0	12.1
Outagamie County, Wisconsin	1,924	74.6	0.0	N	N	N	3,977	72.3	15.8
Ozaukee County, Wisconsin	N	N	N	N	N	N	N	N	N
Portage County, Wisconsin	N	N	N	N	N	N	N	N	N
Racine County, Wisconsin	3,926	70.0	14.2	N	N	N	12,173	67.6	9.7
Rock County, Wisconsin	3,238	56.3	5.2	N	N	N	6,166	61.4	5.6
St. Croix County, Wisconsin	N	N	N	N	N	N	N	N	N
Sheboygan County, Wisconsin	N	N	N	N	N	N	3,796	84.2	11.9
Walworth County, Wisconsin	N	N	N	N	N	N	5,738	76.5	18.2
Washington County, Wisconsin	N	N	N	N	N	N	1,943	83.0	38.3
Waukesha County, Wisconsin	N	N	N	N	N	N	9,805	85.3	26.1
Winnebago County, Wisconsin	N	N	N	N	N	N	3,154	76.3	25.1
Wood County, Wisconsin	N	N	N	N	N	N	N	N	N
WYOMING									
Laramie County, Wyoming	N	N	N	N	N	N	8,578	81.0	17.4
Natrona County, Wyoming	N	N	N	N	N	N	3,291	81.4	0.9

N = Data for this geographic area cannot be displayed because the number of sample cases is too small.

Table C-2. Educational Attainment of the Population, by Selected Counties, 2016—*Continued*

(Number; percent; dollars.)

| State/County | Median earnings in the past 12 months (2016 inflation-adjusted dollars) | | | | | |
| | Population 25 years and over with earnings | | | | | |
	Total	Less than high school graduate	High school graduate (includes equivalency)	Some college or associate's degree	Bachelor's degree	Graduate or professional degree
WASHINGTON—*(Continued)*						
Grant County, Washington	26,932	23,975	26,243	29,627	31,501	67,414
Grays Harbor County, Washington	30,087	18,468	29,167	25,589	60,351	40,833
Island County, Washington	36,508	28,193	28,108	38,854	39,697	53,148
King County, Washington	51,702	25,777	33,599	40,536	66,785	82,291
Kitsap County, Washington	41,603	24,889	33,776	38,613	54,395	71,320
Lewis County, Washington	31,746	24,151	30,890	30,971	39,085	55,643
Pierce County, Washington	41,609	26,897	34,417	40,474	52,248	71,587
Skagit County, Washington	37,140	22,061	34,886	35,959	52,353	71,211
Snohomish County, Washington	46,842	30,625	36,873	42,314	61,998	80,051
Spokane County, Washington	35,011	26,981	29,798	31,238	46,849	60,141
Thurston County, Washington	41,212	25,537	30,102	37,462	51,724	62,163
Whatcom County, Washington	37,144	30,993	35,391	32,483	40,925	65,254
Yakima County, Washington	30,637	22,107	30,386	32,239	50,014	62,169
WEST VIRGINIA						
Berkeley County, West Virginia	37,027	30,314	26,511	37,815	52,171	68,082
Cabell County, West Virginia	31,116	27,051	21,565	27,254	39,109	49,145
Harrison County, West Virginia	34,582	20,238	26,263	32,722	49,854	56,503
Kanawha County, West Virginia	32,490	18,505	26,709	30,359	42,132	60,630
Monongalia County, West Virginia	40,950	28,438	27,355	30,078	47,560	62,464
Raleigh County, West Virginia	32,370	21,985	24,775	32,585	42,370	48,925
Wood County, West Virginia	31,575	11,612	22,185	27,965	42,084	52,049
WISCONSIN						
Brown County, Wisconsin	38,463	25,787	30,970	36,205	49,711	61,580
Dane County, Wisconsin	45,123	24,302	33,957	36,883	51,199	64,083
Dodge County, Wisconsin	35,418	26,383	33,641	35,456	42,279	61,949
Eau Claire County, Wisconsin	36,439	18,633	30,736	35,044	45,698	55,708
Fond du Lac County, Wisconsin	38,504	28,879	32,646	38,414	50,745	54,512
Jefferson County, Wisconsin	37,172	22,426	32,560	36,551	45,741	52,361
Kenosha County, Wisconsin	36,896	21,748	31,139	34,914	60,244	62,929
La Crosse County, Wisconsin	37,954	21,350	30,432	31,982	42,348	56,828
Manitowoc County, Wisconsin	34,407	26,831	31,363	35,572	47,722	58,173
Marathon County, Wisconsin	35,741	17,934	30,838	32,997	50,368	67,405
Milwaukee County, Wisconsin	36,657	22,368	28,758	32,254	49,379	63,253
Outagamie County, Wisconsin	40,158	25,557	34,506	37,117	51,283	57,360
Ozaukee County, Wisconsin	52,096	50,862	34,226	41,788	62,068	90,095
Portage County, Wisconsin	36,175	30,038	31,878	31,230	41,623	60,465
Racine County, Wisconsin	36,870	26,444	30,957	35,204	54,080	67,348
Rock County, Wisconsin	35,218	20,944	30,596	36,534	41,426	57,306
St. Croix County, Wisconsin	46,442	28,482	33,858	46,982	52,348	69,213
Sheboygan County, Wisconsin	40,226	32,931	31,901	38,828	49,891	70,369
Walworth County, Wisconsin	37,151	22,753	31,297	34,454	50,219	61,119
Washington County, Wisconsin	45,087	30,023	35,902	42,229	59,329	70,030
Waukesha County, Wisconsin	50,196	23,323	35,884	41,593	60,795	81,726
Winnebago County, Wisconsin	40,526	22,303	32,170	40,901	50,287	57,386
Wood County, Wisconsin	38,954	24,174	29,317	40,321	46,651	75,333
WYOMING						
Laramie County, Wyoming	40,444	26,861	31,376	36,386	50,099	62,274
Natrona County, Wyoming	36,082	16,429	25,581	38,598	47,286	61,642

N = Data for this geographic area cannot be displayed because the number of sample cases is too small.

Table C-3. College Enrollment of the Population, by Selected Counties, 2016

(Number.)

State/County	Total population	Population enrolled in college or graduate school	Male Total population	Male Enrolled in public college or graduate school	Male Enrolled in private college or graduate school	Female Total population	Female Enrolled in public college or graduate school	Female Enrolled in private college or graduate school
ALABAMA								
Baldwin County, Alabama	208,563	9,301	100,902	3,228	1,006	107,661	4,038	1,029
Calhoun County, Alabama	114,611	7,490	55,491	2,861	586	59,120	3,834	209
Cullman County, Alabama	82,471	2,823	40,699	1,264	188	41,772	1,129	242
DeKalb County, Alabama	70,900	3,165	34,509	1,171	14	36,391	1,767	213
Elmore County, Alabama	81,799	3,907	39,956	1,092	687	41,843	1,592	536
Etowah County, Alabama	102,564	4,937	49,861	1,929	44	52,703	2,834	130
Houston County, Alabama	104,056	4,904	50,015	2,072	301	54,041	1,959	572
Jefferson County, Alabama	659,521	44,540	310,913	15,423	4,838	348,608	17,939	6,340
Lauderdale County, Alabama	92,318	7,848	45,121	3,521	314	47,197	3,410	603
Lee County, Alabama	158,991	27,926	79,257	12,246	936	79,734	12,957	1,787
Limestone County, Alabama	92,753	4,954	47,635	1,801	224	45,118	2,929	0
Madison County, Alabama	356,967	31,819	174,569	11,766	886	182,398	15,325	3,842
Marshall County, Alabama	95,157	3,455	46,338	1,799	132	48,819	1,369	155
Mobile County, Alabama	414,836	22,595	197,818	6,827	2,568	217,018	10,945	2,255
Montgomery County, Alabama	226,349	16,226	107,250	4,103	2,344	119,099	8,048	1,731
Morgan County, Alabama	119,012	4,519	59,211	1,713	37	59,801	1,988	781
St. Clair County, Alabama	88,019	3,694	44,199	1,067	423	43,820	2,023	181
Shelby County, Alabama	210,622	13,839	101,886	5,674	831	108,736	5,624	1,710
Talladega County, Alabama	80,103	3,062	39,813	991	302	40,290	1,305	464
Tuscaloosa County, Alabama	206,102	28,410	99,017	12,913	606	107,085	14,163	728
Walker County, Alabama	64,967	3,065	32,091	1,572	0	32,876	1,493	0
ALASKA								
Anchorage Municipality, Alaska	298,192	22,887	152,882	8,960	1,833	145,310	10,952	1,142
Fairbanks North Star Borough, Alaska	100,605	8,628	55,651	3,944	484	44,954	3,869	331
Matanuska-Susitna Borough, Alaska	104,365	4,533	54,259	1,664	427	50,106	1,976	466
ARIZONA								
Apache County, Arizona	73,112	3,563	35,514	1,223	166	37,598	1,988	186
Cochise County, Arizona	125,770	5,904	63,326	2,114	601	62,444	2,382	807
Coconino County, Arizona	140,908	26,635	70,483	12,129	325	70,425	13,265	916
Maricopa County, Arizona	4,242,997	279,133	2,097,936	103,706	22,836	2,145,061	122,759	29,832
Mohave County, Arizona	205,249	6,107	103,278	1,926	157	101,971	3,471	553
Navajo County, Arizona	110,026	3,151	55,099	1,452	267	54,927	1,377	55
Pima County, Arizona	1,016,206	93,406	499,791	41,227	3,833	516,415	42,744	5,602
Pinal County, Arizona	418,540	19,637	217,387	5,975	1,681	201,153	8,822	3,159
Yavapai County, Arizona	225,562	15,702	110,885	4,357	3,402	114,677	6,056	1,887
Yuma County, Arizona	205,631	10,984	106,203	4,558	296	99,428	5,722	408
ARKANSAS								
Benton County, Arkansas	258,291	11,348	128,175	3,913	1,355	130,116	4,852	1,228
Craighead County, Arkansas	105,835	8,384	52,521	3,854	197	53,314	4,180	153
Faulkner County, Arkansas	122,227	13,915	59,273	5,817	1,310	62,954	5,562	1,226
Garland County, Arkansas	97,477	3,957	47,024	1,110	346	50,453	2,247	254
Jefferson County, Arkansas	70,016	4,307	34,819	805	705	35,197	1,812	985
Lonoke County, Arkansas	72,228	3,179	35,917	1,554	43	36,311	964	618
Pulaski County, Arkansas	393,250	24,056	188,529	7,092	1,388	204,721	12,622	2,954
Saline County, Arkansas	118,703	5,083	59,231	1,742	301	59,472	2,234	806
Sebastian County, Arkansas	127,793	7,964	61,949	3,376	74	65,844	3,741	773
Washington County, Arkansas	228,049	26,604	113,146	12,437	870	114,903	12,073	1,224
White County, Arkansas	79,263	8,079	38,113	1,115	2,080	41,150	1,807	3,077
CALIFORNIA								
Alameda County, California	1,647,704	145,293	809,120	58,973	9,681	838,584	61,824	14,815
Butte County, California	226,864	29,331	111,727	13,540	475	115,137	14,872	444
Contra Costa County, California	1,135,127	80,447	554,517	29,612	6,001	580,610	35,316	9,518
El Dorado County, California	185,625	10,541	93,447	4,105	835	92,178	4,921	680
Fresno County, California	979,915	75,386	489,186	31,475	4,361	490,729	35,154	4,396
Humboldt County, California	136,646	14,868	67,540	6,279	407	69,106	7,843	339
Imperial County, California	180,883	15,212	92,611	6,285	157	88,272	7,579	1,191
Kern County, California	884,788	56,546	454,117	17,009	6,597	430,671	27,460	5,480
Kings County, California	149,785	8,972	82,378	4,466	1,084	67,407	2,767	655
Lake County, California	64,116	3,556	31,258	874	274	32,858	2,165	243
Los Angeles County, California	10,137,915	874,383	4,994,405	311,342	87,242	5,143,510	360,043	115,756
Madera County, California	154,697	9,235	74,406	3,011	196	80,291	5,400	628
Marin County, California	260,651	17,082	126,528	6,483	1,012	134,123	6,887	2,700
Mendocino County, California	87,628	4,246	42,946	1,239	690	44,682	2,062	255
Merced County, California	268,672	23,860	135,524	10,169	575	133,148	12,250	866
Monterey County, California	435,232	33,358	222,251	11,341	4,027	212,981	14,971	3,019

Table C-3. College Enrollment of the Population, by Selected Counties, 2016—*Continued*

(Number.)

State/County	Total population	Population enrolled in college or graduate school	Male Total population	Male Enrolled in public college or graduate school	Male Enrolled in private college or graduate school	Female Total population	Female Enrolled in public college or graduate school	Female Enrolled in private college or graduate school
CALIFORNIA—*(Continued)*								
Napa County, California	142,166	11,214	70,550	4,192	1,155	71,616	4,203	1,664
Nevada County, California	99,107	5,645	50,350	2,561	274	48,757	2,208	602
Orange County, California	3,172,532	278,530	1,565,562	109,471	22,385	1,606,970	116,803	29,871
Placer County, California	380,531	24,147	185,096	10,165	1,844	195,435	9,508	2,630
Riverside County, California	2,387,741	186,156	1,187,627	66,366	19,702	1,200,114	79,739	20,349
Sacramento County, California	1,514,460	109,780	739,516	40,787	7,011	774,944	52,654	9,328
San Bernardino County, California	2,140,096	153,384	1,063,881	54,967	16,106	1,076,215	59,407	22,904
San Diego County, California	3,317,749	305,786	1,667,581	120,243	29,142	1,650,168	122,292	34,109
San Francisco County, California	870,887	71,057	443,777	24,955	7,423	427,110	27,259	11,420
San Joaquin County, California	733,709	44,128	365,605	15,375	4,132	368,104	17,172	7,449
San Luis Obispo County, California	282,887	36,079	142,925	17,051	1,526	139,962	17,030	472
San Mateo County, California	764,797	52,218	377,751	18,859	4,973	387,046	21,372	7,014
Santa Barbara County, California	446,170	56,243	223,041	25,263	2,516	223,129	25,854	2,610
Santa Clara County, California	1,919,402	164,322	968,824	59,275	22,540	950,578	59,839	22,668
Santa Cruz County, California	274,673	36,247	136,118	15,736	1,404	138,555	17,399	1,708
Shasta County, California	179,631	11,669	88,646	3,969	1,148	90,985	4,654	1,898
Solano County, California	440,207	32,332	219,221	13,429	2,793	220,986	12,789	3,321
Sonoma County, California	503,070	40,807	245,647	16,685	1,799	257,423	18,270	4,053
Stanislaus County, California	541,560	35,170	266,537	13,474	2,556	275,023	16,412	2,728
Sutter County, California	96,651	5,712	48,681	1,874	330	47,970	3,075	433
Tulare County, California	460,437	26,662	228,947	8,082	1,536	231,490	14,678	2,366
Ventura County, California	849,738	63,267	420,103	22,998	5,109	429,635	27,592	7,568
Yolo County, California	215,802	43,991	105,035	18,334	1,613	110,767	22,989	1,055
Yuba County, California	75,275	5,596	37,967	1,769	724	37,308	2,481	622
COLORADO								
Adams County, Colorado	498,187	23,770	250,881	8,478	2,358	247,306	9,902	3,032
Arapahoe County, Colorado	637,068	38,145	316,007	13,255	3,264	321,061	16,551	5,075
Boulder County, Colorado	322,226	42,963	161,728	20,660	1,589	160,498	18,488	2,226
Broomfield County, Colorado	66,529	4,076	32,659	1,821	140	33,870	1,781	334
Denver County, Colorado	693,060	49,771	347,500	16,045	6,514	345,560	18,590	8,622
Douglas County, Colorado	328,632	17,167	164,070	4,610	1,772	164,562	8,269	2,516
El Paso County, Colorado	688,284	52,931	348,155	21,966	4,585	340,129	21,526	4,854
Jefferson County, Colorado	571,837	34,016	284,185	12,827	3,397	287,652	13,481	4,311
Larimer County, Colorado	339,993	39,342	170,498	17,041	1,062	169,495	19,379	1,860
Mesa County, Colorado	150,083	9,994	74,153	3,681	305	75,930	5,122	886
Pueblo County, Colorado	165,123	8,556	81,828	3,096	330	83,295	4,679	451
Weld County, Colorado	294,932	22,000	148,543	7,678	936	146,389	11,486	1,900
CONNECTICUT								
Fairfield County, Connecticut	944,177	66,398	459,940	15,472	12,713	484,237	20,685	17,528
Hartford County, Connecticut	892,389	63,448	433,714	18,714	9,170	458,675	23,798	11,766
Litchfield County, Connecticut	182,571	10,468	90,394	3,458	906	92,177	4,903	1,201
Middlesex County, Connecticut	163,329	14,258	80,205	2,493	3,116	83,124	5,146	3,503
New Haven County, Connecticut	856,875	69,365	413,588	17,476	13,901	443,287	19,400	18,588
New London County, Connecticut	269,801	16,437	134,326	4,043	3,293	135,475	5,868	3,233
Tolland County, Connecticut	151,118	25,754	75,753	10,780	1,714	75,365	10,654	2,606
Windham County, Connecticut	116,192	9,901	57,233	3,959	1,115	58,959	4,450	377
DELAWARE								
Kent County, Delaware	174,827	12,833	83,893	3,281	806	90,934	6,975	1,771
New Castle County, Delaware	556,987	41,694	269,580	14,219	4,004	287,407	19,031	4,440
Sussex County, Delaware	220,251	8,185	106,759	3,081	603	113,492	3,742	759
DISTRICT OF COLUMBIA								
District of Columbia, District of Columbia	681,170	74,095	323,591	7,857	23,890	357,579	9,695	32,653
FLORIDA								
Alachua County, Florida	263,496	55,061	126,827	25,308	790	136,669	28,292	671
Bay County, Florida	183,974	10,995	91,650	4,422	662	92,324	5,038	873
Brevard County, Florida	579,130	35,013	281,982	12,014	5,668	297,148	13,569	3,762
Broward County, Florida	1,909,632	137,750	929,377	43,098	18,358	980,255	52,822	23,472
Charlotte County, Florida	178,465	7,803	87,345	1,923	453	91,120	4,456	971
Citrus County, Florida	143,621	2,560	69,132	830	0	74,489	1,116	614
Clay County, Florida	208,311	14,513	101,957	5,554	1,133	106,354	6,027	1,799
Collier County, Florida	365,136	14,733	178,667	4,224	2,431	186,469	5,004	3,074
Columbia County, Florida	69,299	1,763	36,080	290	86	33,219	1,275	112
Duval County, Florida	926,255	67,938	448,891	22,936	5,586	477,364	31,343	8,073
Escambia County, Florida	315,187	27,519	156,201	9,199	4,214	158,986	10,101	4,005

Table C-3. College Enrollment of the Population, by Selected Counties, 2016—*Continued*

(Number.)

State/County	Total population	Population enrolled in college or graduate school	Male Total population	Male Enrolled in public college or graduate school	Male Enrolled in private college or graduate school	Female Total population	Female Enrolled in public college or graduate school	Female Enrolled in private college or graduate school
FLORIDA—(*Continued*)								
Flagler County, Florida	108,310	4,907	52,422	1,907	769	55,888	2,126	105
Hernando County, Florida	182,835	8,292	87,602	2,038	877	95,233	4,138	1,239
Highlands County, Florida	100,917	2,951	47,825	679	282	53,092	1,847	143
Hillsborough County, Florida	1,376,238	101,537	670,193	31,592	13,428	706,045	41,027	15,490
Indian River County, Florida	151,563	6,073	72,644	2,655	187	78,919	3,095	136
Lake County, Florida	335,396	12,496	163,604	3,552	770	171,792	6,509	1,665
Lee County, Florida	722,336	37,149	354,048	12,852	4,008	368,288	13,468	6,821
Leon County, Florida	287,822	59,495	136,318	26,730	557	151,504	30,317	1,891
Manatee County, Florida	375,888	17,376	181,270	6,037	1,577	194,618	6,660	3,102
Marion County, Florida	349,020	13,683	168,449	4,262	1,287	180,571	6,464	1,670
Martin County, Florida	158,701	6,239	78,291	2,478	676	80,410	2,726	359
Miami-Dade County, Florida	2,712,945	200,786	1,315,759	61,755	23,173	1,397,186	80,817	35,041
Monroe County, Florida	79,077	3,526	41,660	1,117	661	37,417	1,186	562
Nassau County, Florida	80,622	2,854	38,905	349	570	41,717	1,098	837
Okaloosa County, Florida	201,170	12,075	102,605	4,189	1,047	98,565	5,920	919
Orange County, Florida	1,314,367	130,436	646,317	49,225	10,794	668,050	56,536	13,881
Osceola County, Florida	336,015	17,009	163,661	5,333	1,337	172,354	7,795	2,544
Palm Beach County, Florida	1,443,810	85,736	698,414	26,172	7,772	745,396	41,455	10,337
Pasco County, Florida	512,368	22,718	249,613	8,098	2,413	262,755	8,749	3,458
Pinellas County, Florida	960,730	54,308	460,325	17,915	6,264	500,405	23,317	6,812
Polk County, Florida	666,149	35,295	325,981	10,783	4,746	340,168	12,393	7,373
Putnam County, Florida	72,277	2,920	36,698	1,388	71	35,579	1,007	454
St. Johns County, Florida	235,087	13,365	115,221	3,606	1,652	119,866	5,169	2,938
St. Lucie County, Florida	306,507	15,797	148,782	5,371	2,354	157,725	6,897	1,175
Santa Rosa County, Florida	170,497	8,624	86,775	3,035	621	83,722	4,257	711
Sarasota County, Florida	412,569	15,178	197,570	4,455	1,719	214,999	7,100	1,904
Seminole County, Florida	455,479	36,637	219,626	14,437	2,431	235,853	14,979	4,790
Sumter County, Florida	123,996	2,379	61,477	637	314	62,519	1,064	364
Volusia County, Florida	529,364	37,584	258,972	9,352	8,627	270,392	12,585	7,020
Walton County, Florida	65,889	3,064	34,195	918	217	31,694	1,751	178
GEORGIA								
Barrow County, Georgia	77,126	3,971	37,956	1,400	165	39,170	2,062	344
Bartow County, Georgia	103,807	3,435	51,468	370	210	52,339	2,030	825
Bibb County, Georgia	152,760	11,376	71,693	2,236	1,973	81,067	4,413	2,754
Bulloch County, Georgia	74,722	16,769	37,678	8,089	243	37,044	8,094	343
Carroll County, Georgia	116,261	12,165	57,902	4,703	512	58,359	5,621	1,329
Catoosa County, Georgia	66,398	3,510	32,948	1,143	184	33,450	1,828	355
Chatham County, Georgia	289,082	30,963	139,200	6,779	5,355	149,882	11,992	6,837
Cherokee County, Georgia	241,689	12,004	119,033	4,068	1,556	122,656	5,504	876
Clarke County, Georgia	124,707	30,882	60,024	13,615	430	64,683	16,329	508
Clayton County, Georgia	279,462	19,020	128,772	5,905	1,754	150,690	8,828	2,533
Cobb County, Georgia	748,150	56,611	361,331	21,523	4,177	386,819	25,747	5,164
Columbia County, Georgia	147,450	7,948	71,884	2,788	848	75,566	3,980	332
Coweta County, Georgia	140,526	6,091	68,236	2,305	197	72,290	2,614	975
DeKalb County, Georgia	740,321	56,202	350,328	12,460	9,100	389,993	19,662	14,980
Dougherty County, Georgia	90,017	9,041	40,903	2,882	293	49,114	5,367	499
Douglas County, Georgia	142,224	7,554	68,772	1,947	694	73,452	2,848	2,065
Fayette County, Georgia	111,627	5,232	53,888	1,937	788	57,739	2,169	338
Floyd County, Georgia	96,560	6,497	47,010	1,257	1,059	49,550	2,202	1,979
Forsyth County, Georgia	221,009	11,727	109,708	4,560	1,039	111,301	4,557	1,571
Fulton County, Georgia	1,023,336	88,474	495,020	30,866	10,512	528,316	33,119	13,977
Glynn County, Georgia	84,502	3,136	39,690	1,295	613	44,812	962	266
Gwinnett County, Georgia	907,135	57,646	443,379	18,985	6,263	463,756	25,214	7,184
Hall County, Georgia	196,637	10,163	97,493	3,515	797	99,144	4,613	1,238
Henry County, Georgia	221,768	11,600	106,026	4,832	130	115,742	5,627	1,011
Houston County, Georgia	152,122	13,879	74,525	5,696	448	77,597	6,659	1,076
Liberty County, Georgia	62,570	6,918	32,287	2,475	646	30,283	2,922	875
Lowndes County, Georgia	114,628	13,112	56,100	4,523	1,155	58,528	6,434	1,000
Muscogee County, Georgia	197,485	16,081	96,919	5,746	552	100,566	8,602	1,181
Newton County, Georgia	106,999	6,470	49,949	2,522	650	57,050	2,648	650
Paulding County, Georgia	155,825	8,748	75,737	4,171	427	80,088	3,144	1,006
Richmond County, Georgia	201,647	16,244	97,382	5,545	743	104,265	8,387	1,569
Rockdale County, Georgia	89,355	6,837	42,098	2,217	0	47,257	3,969	651
Troup County, Georgia	70,005	2,152	34,260	399	78	35,745	1,040	635
Walker County, Georgia	67,896	2,583	34,263	397	835	33,633	961	390
Walton County, Georgia	90,184	5,129	44,482	814	411	45,702	3,208	696
Whitfield County, Georgia	104,589	5,420	52,233	2,082	46	52,356	2,880	412
HAWAII								
Hawaii County, Hawaii	198,449	9,915	98,955	4,110	671	99,494	4,796	338

Table C-3. College Enrollment of the Population, by Selected Counties, 2016—*Continued*

(Number.)

State/County	Total population	Population enrolled in college or graduate school	Male			Female		
			Total population	Enrolled in public college or graduate school	Enrolled in private college or graduate school	Total population	Enrolled in public college or graduate school	Enrolled in private college or graduate school
HAWAII—*(Continued)*								
Honolulu County, Hawaii	992,605	80,459	501,898	30,276	9,509	490,707	31,219	9,455
Kauai County, Hawaii	72,029	2,593	35,051	705	110	36,978	1,184	594
Maui County, Hawaii	165,379	6,929	82,112	2,450	307	83,267	3,280	892
IDAHO								
Ada County, Idaho	444,028	33,488	222,150	12,739	2,189	221,878	15,492	3,068
Bannock County, Idaho	84,377	9,319	41,577	4,146	399	42,800	4,172	602
Bonneville County, Idaho	112,232	5,255	56,459	2,182	405	55,773	1,938	730
Canyon County, Idaho	211,698	12,282	104,116	2,762	1,744	107,582	4,614	3,162
Kootenai County, Idaho	154,311	8,094	76,312	2,329	502	77,999	4,501	762
Twin Falls County, Idaho	83,514	4,409	40,607	1,064	225	42,907	2,695	425
ILLINOIS								
Adams County, Illinois	66,578	2,174	32,707	306	364	33,871	840	664
Champaign County, Illinois	208,419	48,386	103,293	23,892	878	105,126	21,605	2,011
Cook County, Illinois	5,203,499	376,954	2,526,484	98,397	68,457	2,677,015	118,630	91,470
DeKalb County, Illinois	104,528	16,613	52,811	6,912	874	51,717	8,489	338
DuPage County, Illinois	929,368	65,069	455,769	19,284	11,735	473,599	20,237	13,813
Kane County, Illinois	531,715	32,049	265,152	12,691	3,117	266,563	12,026	4,215
Kankakee County, Illinois	110,008	7,917	53,865	2,422	709	56,143	2,508	2,278
Kendall County, Illinois	124,695	6,403	61,405	1,581	842	63,290	2,228	1,752
Lake County, Illinois	703,047	43,985	351,612	15,676	5,507	351,435	14,500	8,302
LaSalle County, Illinois	110,642	4,107	55,778	1,790	255	54,864	1,765	297
McHenry County, Illinois	307,004	16,511	152,689	5,662	1,507	154,315	6,326	3,016
McLean County, Illinois	172,418	25,107	84,537	9,398	1,912	87,881	12,171	1,626
Macon County, Illinois	106,550	5,224	51,064	1,530	949	55,486	1,856	889
Madison County, Illinois	265,759	20,637	128,886	8,099	1,462	136,873	9,082	1,994
Peoria County, Illinois	185,006	13,982	89,857	2,671	2,945	95,149	5,395	2,971
Rock Island County, Illinois	144,784	7,937	70,339	2,104	1,349	74,445	2,480	2,004
St. Clair County, Illinois	262,759	15,597	126,820	4,698	1,504	135,939	7,698	1,697
Sangamon County, Illinois	197,499	13,087	95,069	4,181	1,241	102,430	6,209	1,456
Tazewell County, Illinois	134,385	6,622	66,304	2,464	695	68,081	2,834	629
Vermilion County, Illinois	78,111	3,987	39,079	1,285	144	39,032	2,269	289
Will County, Illinois	689,529	43,621	342,171	13,324	6,559	347,358	16,254	7,484
Williamson County, Illinois	67,560	2,590	34,537	1,123	186	33,023	1,200	81
Winnebago County, Illinois	285,873	16,093	139,747	4,186	2,196	146,126	6,121	3,590
INDIANA								
Allen County, Indiana	370,404	21,675	180,930	8,471	1,976	189,474	8,374	2,854
Bartholomew County, Indiana	81,402	4,434	41,383	1,037	209	40,019	2,875	313
Clark County, Indiana	116,031	6,557	56,178	2,572	98	59,853	3,037	850
Delaware County, Indiana	115,603	19,088	56,422	9,022	243	59,181	9,415	408
Elkhart County, Indiana	203,781	6,171	100,665	1,971	1,131	103,116	1,726	1,343
Floyd County, Indiana	76,990	4,249	37,782	1,840	558	39,208	1,756	95
Grant County, Indiana	66,937	6,187	32,352	575	1,859	34,585	616	3,137
Hamilton County, Indiana	316,373	14,558	153,095	4,516	1,712	163,278	7,163	1,167
Hancock County, Indiana	73,717	3,103	36,577	1,526	321	37,140	777	479
Hendricks County, Indiana	160,610	7,181	79,683	2,753	630	80,927	2,894	904
Howard County, Indiana	82,568	3,867	40,320	1,085	173	42,248	2,301	308
Johnson County, Indiana	151,982	8,354	73,792	3,318	1,063	78,190	3,038	935
Kosciusko County, Indiana	79,092	2,656	39,019	546	647	40,073	741	722
Lake County, Indiana	485,846	24,210	234,662	8,674	2,120	251,184	10,381	3,035
LaPorte County, Indiana	110,015	3,143	57,378	383	621	52,637	1,781	358
Madison County, Indiana	129,296	6,686	63,677	2,195	390	65,619	2,600	1,501
Marion County, Indiana	941,229	60,144	453,482	19,398	5,890	487,747	25,638	9,218
Monroe County, Indiana	145,496	39,607	72,895	19,280	423	72,601	19,054	850
Morgan County, Indiana	69,698	2,116	34,325	685	35	35,373	1,327	69
Porter County, Indiana	167,791	10,627	82,455	2,882	2,365	85,336	3,371	2,009
St. Joseph County, Indiana	269,141	21,567	130,979	4,066	5,891	138,162	4,015	7,595
Tippecanoe County, Indiana	188,059	43,099	96,352	23,650	786	91,707	17,318	1,345
Vanderburgh County, Indiana	181,721	13,252	88,429	3,926	1,070	93,292	6,823	1,433
Vigo County, Indiana	107,931	13,127	54,647	4,996	1,233	53,284	6,301	597
Wayne County, Indiana	66,568	3,565	31,948	772	575	34,620	1,727	491
IOWA								
Black Hawk County, Iowa	132,904	15,769	66,262	6,216	996	66,642	7,872	685
Dallas County, Iowa	84,516	4,488	41,755	1,657	633	42,761	1,464	734
Dubuque County, Iowa	97,003	7,027	47,974	1,155	1,966	49,029	2,042	1,864
Johnson County, Iowa	146,547	32,541	72,310	13,779	1,187	74,237	15,933	1,642
Linn County, Iowa	221,661	13,052	109,457	3,370	1,853	112,204	4,587	3,242
Polk County, Iowa	474,045	27,988	233,139	8,911	3,917	240,906	8,960	6,200

Table C-3. College Enrollment of the Population, by Selected Counties, 2016—*Continued*

(Number.)

State/County	Total population	Population enrolled in college or graduate school	Male			Female		
			Total population	Enrolled in public college or graduate school	Enrolled in private college or graduate school	Total population	Enrolled in public college or graduate school	Enrolled in private college or graduate school
IOWA—*(Continued)*								
Pottawattamie County, Iowa	93,582	5,474	46,344	1,999	413	47,238	2,126	936
Scott County, Iowa	172,474	10,699	84,922	2,919	1,607	87,552	4,090	2,083
Story County, Iowa	97,090	31,646	49,721	16,303	402	47,369	14,611	330
Woodbury County, Iowa	102,779	7,594	51,248	2,019	1,355	51,531	2,944	1,276
KANSAS								
Butler County, Kansas	67,025	5,087	33,810	1,806	487	33,215	2,282	512
Douglas County, Kansas	119,440	25,929	59,518	13,010	656	59,922	12,018	245
Johnson County, Kansas	584,451	35,444	286,329	12,258	4,452	298,122	14,811	3,923
Leavenworth County, Kansas	80,204	5,819	43,829	2,883	629	36,375	2,013	294
Riley County, Kansas	73,343	21,157	39,642	11,010	450	33,701	9,517	180
Sedgwick County, Kansas	511,995	33,609	253,144	12,161	2,875	258,851	15,322	3,251
Shawnee County, Kansas	178,146	8,637	86,464	3,466	409	91,682	3,874	888
Wyandotte County, Kansas	163,831	7,659	81,019	2,094	1,338	82,812	2,696	1,531
KENTUCKY								
Boone County, Kentucky	128,536	6,178	63,585	2,000	294	64,951	3,553	331
Bullitt County, Kentucky	79,151	3,031	39,161	1,026	268	39,990	1,412	325
Campbell County, Kentucky	92,211	6,888	44,630	2,611	157	47,581	3,683	437
Christian County, Kentucky	72,351	4,845	38,489	2,300	203	33,862	2,161	181
Daviess County, Kentucky	99,674	5,168	48,401	1,968	552	51,273	1,736	912
Fayette County, Kentucky	318,449	42,038	156,230	15,591	1,775	162,219	21,258	3,414
Hardin County, Kentucky	107,316	9,556	53,126	3,875	1,209	54,190	3,363	1,109
Jefferson County, Kentucky	765,352	47,238	370,139	16,172	4,164	395,213	19,212	7,690
Kenton County, Kentucky	164,945	9,774	81,187	3,009	773	83,758	5,221	771
McCracken County, Kentucky	65,162	4,756	31,405	1,983	0	33,757	2,270	503
Madison County, Kentucky	89,547	13,513	42,697	5,127	892	46,850	6,079	1,415
Oldham County, Kentucky	65,560	2,891	33,660	1,020	485	31,900	947	439
Warren County, Kentucky	125,532	17,787	61,841	7,040	830	63,691	9,596	321
LOUISIANA								
Ascension Parish, Louisiana	121,587	5,273	60,951	2,133	236	60,636	2,904	0
Bossier Parish, Louisiana	126,057	7,091	63,404	2,530	270	62,653	3,925	366
Caddo Parish, Louisiana	248,851	10,935	118,005	3,537	218	130,846	5,785	1,395
Calcasieu Parish, Louisiana	200,601	11,269	98,097	3,764	129	102,504	6,860	516
East Baton Rouge Parish, Louisiana	447,037	50,444	213,382	19,822	2,691	233,655	24,513	3,418
Iberia Parish, Louisiana	73,273	2,167	34,529	706	65	38,744	993	403
Jefferson Parish, Louisiana	436,523	23,317	211,470	5,896	3,068	225,053	8,962	5,391
Lafayette Parish, Louisiana	241,398	16,304	117,655	6,039	485	123,743	8,559	1,221
Lafourche Parish, Louisiana	98,305	4,466	48,019	1,933	284	50,286	1,732	517
Livingston Parish, Louisiana	140,138	5,538	70,223	1,597	628	69,915	2,348	965
Orleans Parish, Louisiana	391,495	35,880	186,998	6,630	6,716	204,497	12,688	9,846
Ouachita Parish, Louisiana	156,983	8,757	75,476	3,189	259	81,507	5,098	211
Rapides Parish, Louisiana	132,424	7,091	64,622	2,042	565	67,802	3,412	1,072
St. Landry Parish, Louisiana	83,883	2,188	40,045	483	377	43,838	589	739
St. Tammany Parish, Louisiana	253,602	11,639	123,200	2,926	974	130,402	6,661	1,078
Tangipahoa Parish, Louisiana	130,710	9,772	63,659	3,331	218	67,051	5,661	562
Terrebonne Parish, Louisiana	113,220	4,637	55,974	1,541	127	57,246	2,496	473
MAINE								
Androscoggin County, Maine	107,319	5,725	52,369	1,365	1,039	54,950	2,335	986
Aroostook County, Maine	67,959	3,627	33,609	892	735	34,350	1,183	817
Cumberland County, Maine	292,041	21,360	141,354	5,637	3,386	150,687	6,689	5,648
Kennebec County, Maine	120,569	8,414	59,398	2,526	1,560	61,171	2,581	1,747
Penobscot County, Maine	151,806	14,439	74,920	5,186	1,695	76,886	5,994	1,564
York County, Maine	202,343	11,375	98,366	2,481	1,667	103,977	4,510	2,717
MARYLAND								
Allegany County, Maryland	72,130	7,279	37,688	3,541	92	34,442	3,569	77
Anne Arundel County, Maryland	568,346	42,683	281,988	18,339	2,781	286,358	17,282	4,281
Baltimore County, Maryland	831,026	63,370	393,924	23,010	5,003	437,102	26,980	8,377
Calvert County, Maryland	91,251	5,625	45,190	1,871	312	46,061	2,437	1,005
Carroll County, Maryland	167,656	12,250	83,174	3,895	1,655	84,482	4,625	2,075
Cecil County, Maryland	102,603	5,302	51,190	2,013	698	51,413	2,233	358
Charles County, Maryland	157,705	9,479	76,601	3,540	231	81,104	4,246	1,462
Frederick County, Maryland	247,591	19,216	121,850	6,216	2,323	125,741	7,577	3,100
Harford County, Maryland	251,032	15,223	122,387	5,367	1,491	128,645	7,205	1,160
Howard County, Maryland	317,233	24,784	154,895	9,955	2,294	162,338	9,920	2,615
Montgomery County, Maryland	1,043,863	77,753	503,189	28,886	7,394	540,674	29,177	12,296

Table C-3. College Enrollment of the Population, by Selected Counties, 2016—*Continued*

(Number.)

State/County	Total population	Population enrolled in college or graduate school	Male Total population	Male Enrolled in public college or graduate school	Male Enrolled in private college or graduate school	Female Total population	Female Enrolled in public college or graduate school	Female Enrolled in private college or graduate school
MARYLAND—(*Continued*)								
Prince George's County, Maryland	908,049	86,108	437,076	31,962	7,481	470,973	37,952	8,713
St. Mary's County, Maryland	112,587	9,645	55,251	3,708	1,268	57,336	4,201	468
Washington County, Maryland	150,292	5,961	76,188	1,936	283	74,104	2,986	756
Wicomico County, Maryland	102,577	12,577	48,998	5,179	290	53,579	6,575	533
Baltimore city, Maryland	614,664	52,759	289,086	13,508	7,973	325,578	19,722	11,556
MASSACHUSETTS								
Barnstable County, Massachusetts	214,276	9,488	102,271	3,372	1,515	112,005	3,777	824
Berkshire County, Massachusetts	126,903	8,762	60,848	1,737	1,885	66,055	2,874	2,266
Bristol County, Massachusetts	558,324	39,111	271,369	11,511	5,968	286,955	14,809	6,823
Essex County, Massachusetts	779,018	53,792	376,004	13,649	10,198	403,014	17,646	12,299
Franklin County, Massachusetts	70,382	3,491	34,446	1,236	100	35,936	1,484	671
Hampden County, Massachusetts	468,467	34,610	226,014	9,570	3,977	242,453	13,011	8,052
Hampshire County, Massachusetts	161,816	33,612	75,944	11,979	1,676	85,872	12,784	7,173
Middlesex County, Massachusetts	1,589,774	148,484	776,787	26,892	42,395	812,987	29,608	49,589
Norfolk County, Massachusetts	697,181	51,710	334,100	9,006	12,336	363,081	12,110	18,258
Plymouth County, Massachusetts	513,565	30,359	249,720	9,022	3,438	263,845	12,089	5,810
Suffolk County, Massachusetts	784,230	111,082	380,262	12,725	36,803	403,968	15,780	45,774
Worcester County, Massachusetts	819,589	59,763	404,691	14,655	11,807	414,898	18,564	14,737
MICHIGAN								
Allegan County, Michigan	115,548	4,000	57,740	1,024	266	57,808	2,374	336
Bay County, Michigan	104,747	5,211	51,999	2,004	431	52,748	2,215	561
Berrien County, Michigan	154,010	9,358	75,592	2,612	2,035	78,418	2,868	1,843
Calhoun County, Michigan	134,386	8,213	64,953	2,640	824	69,433	3,275	1,474
Clinton County, Michigan	77,888	6,405	38,323	2,430	334	39,565	3,497	144
Eaton County, Michigan	109,160	7,790	53,471	3,293	520	55,689	2,609	1,368
Genesee County, Michigan	408,615	24,650	196,719	8,832	1,555	211,896	12,050	2,213
Grand Traverse County, Michigan	92,084	5,495	44,676	2,481	327	47,408	2,274	413
Ingham County, Michigan	288,051	53,295	139,189	26,156	861	148,862	25,249	1,029
Isabella County, Michigan	71,282	18,717	34,754	7,889	572	36,528	9,695	561
Jackson County, Michigan	158,460	7,955	80,892	2,806	278	77,568	3,379	1,492
Kalamazoo County, Michigan	261,654	32,774	127,763	15,278	766	133,891	15,330	1,400
Kent County, Michigan	642,173	41,124	316,715	13,907	5,108	325,458	14,316	7,793
Lapeer County, Michigan	88,340	3,374	45,360	942	299	42,980	2,025	108
Lenawee County, Michigan	98,504	5,592	50,221	1,124	1,449	48,283	1,857	1,162
Livingston County, Michigan	188,624	11,234	94,740	4,489	1,143	93,884	4,702	900
Macomb County, Michigan	867,730	54,683	422,671	19,688	2,336	445,059	28,013	4,646
Marquette County, Michigan	66,435	8,903	33,826	4,184	546	32,609	3,989	184
Midland County, Michigan	83,462	5,154	41,095	1,841	735	42,367	1,601	977
Monroe County, Michigan	149,208	8,209	73,674	3,159	377	75,534	3,808	865
Muskegon County, Michigan	173,408	6,459	86,153	1,986	877	87,255	2,311	1,285
Oakland County, Michigan	1,243,970	88,835	606,839	33,778	8,181	637,131	37,235	9,641
Ottawa County, Michigan	282,250	25,660	138,278	9,613	2,031	143,972	11,449	2,567
Saginaw County, Michigan	192,326	14,214	94,082	5,479	545	98,244	7,823	367
St. Clair County, Michigan	159,587	5,854	79,340	2,522	267	80,247	2,470	595
Shiawassee County, Michigan	68,554	3,353	33,880	1,070	439	34,674	1,341	503
Van Buren County, Michigan	75,223	3,188	37,503	1,372	268	37,720	1,395	153
Washtenaw County, Michigan	364,709	69,334	180,083	34,072	1,385	184,626	32,542	1,335
Wayne County, Michigan	1,749,366	112,942	841,906	42,975	8,408	907,460	50,816	10,743
MINNESOTA								
Anoka County, Minnesota	345,957	20,616	172,322	6,839	2,374	173,635	8,879	2,524
Blue Earth County, Minnesota	66,441	10,703	33,206	4,758	218	33,235	5,411	316
Carver County, Minnesota	100,262	4,659	49,993	1,320	595	50,269	2,035	709
Dakota County, Minnesota	417,486	22,098	205,671	6,257	2,522	211,815	9,584	3,735
Hennepin County, Minnesota	1,232,483	92,548	609,092	35,292	8,584	623,391	35,413	13,259
Olmsted County, Minnesota	153,102	8,535	74,975	2,382	651	78,127	3,920	1,582
Ramsey County, Minnesota	540,649	46,275	263,213	12,662	8,548	277,436	15,886	9,179
Rice County, Minnesota	65,622	8,815	33,703	986	2,753	31,919	1,447	3,629
St. Louis County, Minnesota	199,980	19,102	100,287	8,641	1,293	99,693	7,024	2,144
Scott County, Minnesota	143,680	5,698	71,431	1,559	443	72,249	2,667	1,029
Sherburne County, Minnesota	93,528	5,814	47,597	1,324	149	45,931	3,639	702
Stearns County, Minnesota	155,652	19,103	78,735	7,983	2,291	76,917	6,492	2,337
Washington County, Minnesota	253,117	14,705	125,629	5,529	1,337	127,488	5,343	2,496
Wright County, Minnesota	132,550	5,965	66,963	1,902	851	65,587	2,854	358
MISSISSIPPI								
DeSoto County, Mississippi	175,611	9,285	85,225	2,724	1,376	90,386	4,298	887

Table C-3. College Enrollment of the Population, by Selected Counties, 2016—*Continued*

(Number.)

State/County	Total population	Population enrolled in college or graduate school	Male Total population	Male Enrolled in public college or graduate school	Male Enrolled in private college or graduate school	Female Total population	Female Enrolled in public college or graduate school	Female Enrolled in private college or graduate school
MISSISSIPPI—*(Continued)*								
Forrest County, Mississippi	75,979	9,691	35,478	2,716	81	40,501	5,989	905
Harrison County, Mississippi	203,234	14,075	99,744	6,720	295	103,490	5,933	1,127
Hinds County, Mississippi	241,229	21,091	112,687	7,063	1,585	128,542	9,317	3,126
Jackson County, Mississippi	141,241	7,354	67,681	2,304	372	73,560	3,365	1,313
Jones County, Mississippi	67,953	2,287	32,765	863	113	35,188	1,076	235
Lauderdale County, Mississippi	77,755	4,630	38,539	1,635	127	39,216	2,773	95
Lee County, Mississippi	85,381	4,230	41,057	1,176	287	44,324	2,533	234
Madison County, Mississippi	105,114	5,690	50,550	1,678	814	54,564	2,313	885
Rankin County, Mississippi	150,228	8,272	72,542	2,848	554	77,686	3,524	1,346
MISSOURI								
Boone County, Missouri	176,594	31,379	86,362	13,127	665	90,232	16,122	1,465
Buchanan County, Missouri	88,938	5,827	45,511	2,953	352	43,427	2,407	115
Cape Girardeau County, Missouri	78,913	10,282	38,137	4,979	19	40,776	4,523	761
Cass County, Missouri	102,845	4,195	49,757	1,585	275	53,088	1,738	597
Christian County, Missouri	84,401	3,534	41,057	550	415	43,344	2,102	467
Clay County, Missouri	239,085	13,687	117,726	4,090	1,314	121,359	6,347	1,936
Cole County, Missouri	76,631	4,951	38,876	1,442	953	37,755	2,033	523
Franklin County, Missouri	102,838	3,554	51,683	1,072	393	51,155	1,791	298
Greene County, Missouri	288,690	33,195	141,178	11,581	2,300	147,512	16,119	3,195
Jackson County, Missouri	691,801	38,286	334,478	12,676	4,143	357,323	15,442	6,025
Jasper County, Missouri	119,111	7,771	57,629	2,696	607	61,482	3,174	1,294
Jefferson County, Missouri	224,226	9,972	111,045	1,849	1,636	113,181	5,142	1,345
Platte County, Missouri	98,309	5,723	48,678	1,905	482	49,631	2,452	884
St. Charles County, Missouri	390,918	26,466	191,755	6,630	3,969	199,163	6,663	9,204
St. Francois County, Missouri	66,627	2,715	36,256	506	190	30,371	1,514	505
St. Louis County, Missouri	998,581	66,100	474,218	15,603	14,849	524,363	19,611	16,037
St. Louis city, Missouri	311,404	24,809	150,976	3,779	7,046	160,428	6,659	7,325
MONTANA								
Cascade County, Montana	81,755	3,897	41,495	1,164	257	40,260	2,131	345
Flathead County, Montana	98,082	3,540	48,402	859	143	49,680	1,505	1,033
Gallatin County, Montana	104,502	14,240	54,254	7,870	136	50,248	5,984	250
Lewis and Clark County, Montana	67,282	4,044	32,723	1,160	497	34,559	958	1,429
Missoula County, Montana	116,130	12,832	59,269	5,759	0	56,861	6,760	313
Yellowstone County, Montana	158,437	6,722	78,855	2,034	526	79,582	3,217	945
NEBRASKA								
Douglas County, Nebraska	554,995	42,718	274,299	13,296	5,502	280,696	15,042	8,878
Lancaster County, Nebraska	309,637	37,051	155,106	15,690	3,377	154,531	13,911	4,073
Sarpy County, Nebraska	179,023	12,419	89,675	4,110	1,465	89,348	5,752	1,092
NEVADA								
Clark County, Nevada	2,155,664	117,983	1,076,144	42,091	10,307	1,079,520	53,485	12,100
Washoe County, Nevada	453,616	37,292	228,410	14,694	1,567	225,206	18,119	2,912
NEW HAMPSHIRE								
Cheshire County, New Hampshire	75,774	6,838	37,376	769	1,218	38,398	3,506	1,345
Grafton County, New Hampshire	88,888	9,889	43,711	2,073	3,425	45,177	1,930	2,461
Hillsborough County, New Hampshire	407,761	25,413	203,705	5,390	6,855	204,056	6,033	7,135
Merrimack County, New Hampshire	148,582	11,773	73,820	3,173	2,321	74,762	3,103	3,176
Rockingham County, New Hampshire	303,251	17,431	150,446	5,501	3,111	152,805	5,555	3,264
Strafford County, New Hampshire	127,428	14,671	62,491	5,655	780	64,937	6,950	1,286
NEW JERSEY								
Atlantic County, New Jersey	270,991	20,667	131,134	7,870	2,101	139,857	8,158	2,538
Bergen County, New Jersey	939,151	60,009	455,140	18,104	8,806	484,011	20,182	12,917
Burlington County, New Jersey	449,284	28,894	221,357	9,431	3,584	227,927	10,327	5,552
Camden County, New Jersey	510,150	30,912	247,142	9,919	2,198	263,008	13,038	5,757
Cape May County, New Jersey	94,430	3,749	46,576	1,012	355	47,854	2,048	334
Cumberland County, New Jersey	153,797	5,987	78,770	2,399	355	75,027	2,758	475
Essex County, New Jersey	796,914	56,063	383,430	17,171	7,540	413,484	20,474	10,878
Gloucester County, New Jersey	292,330	21,092	141,848	7,919	1,115	150,482	9,259	2,799
Hudson County, New Jersey	677,983	49,909	337,305	13,998	8,817	340,678	17,034	10,060
Hunterdon County, New Jersey	124,676	5,254	62,582	1,304	798	62,094	2,052	1,100
Mercer County, New Jersey	371,023	29,850	181,379	5,710	6,109	189,644	11,719	6,312
Middlesex County, New Jersey	837,073	71,881	412,318	29,864	5,345	424,755	30,287	6,385
Monmouth County, New Jersey	625,846	37,245	304,738	10,664	5,236	321,108	12,819	8,526
Morris County, New Jersey	498,423	31,427	244,273	7,407	6,625	254,150	10,363	7,032

Table C-3. College Enrollment of the Population, by Selected Counties, 2016—*Continued*

(Number.)

			Male			Female		
State/County	Total population	Population enrolled in college or graduate school	Total population	Enrolled in public college or graduate school	Enrolled in private college or graduate school	Total population	Enrolled in public college or graduate school	Enrolled in private college or graduate school
NEW JERSEY—*(Continued)*								
Ocean County, New Jersey	592,497	32,257	285,718	8,261	9,294	306,779	9,592	5,110
Passaic County, New Jersey	507,945	35,689	247,924	12,381	4,598	260,021	14,181	4,529
Salem County, New Jersey	63,436	2,892	31,035	1,122	98	32,401	1,377	295
Somerset County, New Jersey	333,751	22,594	162,691	8,666	2,314	171,060	9,227	2,387
Sussex County, New Jersey	142,522	8,584	71,095	2,537	1,375	71,427	3,661	1,011
Union County, New Jersey	555,630	35,258	271,004	11,749	4,383	284,626	13,268	5,858
Warren County, New Jersey	106,617	6,772	52,752	1,521	995	53,865	2,746	1,510
NEW MEXICO								
Bernalillo County, New Mexico	676,953	56,023	331,988	24,397	2,887	344,965	25,186	3,553
Chaves County, New Mexico	65,282	3,252	33,230	788	887	32,052	1,092	485
Doña Ana County, New Mexico	214,207	25,237	105,526	12,886	546	108,681	11,276	529
Lea County, New Mexico	69,749	2,814	35,234	828	94	34,515	1,800	92
McKinley County, New Mexico	74,923	4,152	35,991	1,659	57	38,932	2,286	150
Otero County, New Mexico	65,410	2,698	33,001	632	580	32,409	1,373	113
Sandoval County, New Mexico	142,025	11,424	69,889	4,992	856	72,136	3,946	1,630
San Juan County, New Mexico	115,079	5,965	56,584	2,355	388	58,495	2,891	331
Santa Fe County, New Mexico	148,651	10,230	72,532	3,697	407	76,119	4,641	1,485
Valencia County, New Mexico	75,626	3,517	38,367	1,731	229	37,259	1,381	176
NEW YORK								
Albany County, New York	308,846	36,583	150,008	14,943	4,864	158,838	11,569	5,207
Bronx County, New York	1,455,720	115,870	686,382	30,563	16,260	769,338	46,086	22,961
Broome County, New York	195,334	23,262	95,998	9,961	957	99,336	11,174	1,170
Cattaraugus County, New York	77,677	4,356	38,420	1,029	789	39,257	1,803	735
Cayuga County, New York	77,861	4,287	40,044	1,457	608	37,817	1,044	1,178
Chautauqua County, New York	129,504	8,931	63,937	4,241	270	65,567	4,021	399
Chemung County, New York	86,322	4,602	43,024	520	1,002	43,298	1,908	1,172
Clinton County, New York	81,073	6,347	41,503	2,481	228	39,570	3,537	101
Dutchess County, New York	294,473	25,310	145,770	4,718	6,757	148,703	6,779	7,056
Erie County, New York	921,046	70,085	446,090	24,523	6,810	474,956	27,793	10,959
Jefferson County, New York	114,006	5,979	59,129	1,982	520	54,877	3,023	454
Kings County, New York	2,629,150	178,401	1,247,152	47,130	31,240	1,381,998	62,800	37,231
Livingston County, New York	64,257	7,876	32,140	2,826	350	32,117	4,334	366
Madison County, New York	71,329	6,674	35,319	1,794	1,434	36,010	1,545	1,901
Monroe County, New York	747,727	65,514	361,383	13,985	15,729	386,344	20,112	15,688
Nassau County, New York	1,361,500	101,098	661,023	24,474	22,292	700,477	28,986	25,346
New York County, New York	1,643,734	144,553	779,699	22,439	39,699	864,035	26,998	55,417
Niagara County, New York	211,758	12,191	103,889	3,954	1,948	107,869	3,782	2,507
Oneida County, New York	231,190	13,542	114,737	4,213	2,283	116,453	4,298	2,748
Onondaga County, New York	466,194	40,931	224,766	7,873	10,529	241,428	9,401	13,128
Ontario County, New York	109,828	7,819	53,977	1,124	1,993	55,851	2,232	2,470
Orange County, New York	379,210	22,294	189,312	6,778	3,620	189,898	8,183	3,713
Oswego County, New York	118,987	9,191	59,716	3,978	259	59,271	4,552	402
Putnam County, New York	98,900	3,794	48,854	1,259	367	50,046	1,530	638
Queens County, New York	2,333,054	184,791	1,131,856	56,610	25,770	1,201,198	69,567	32,844
Rensselaer County, New York	160,070	12,182	78,869	1,951	4,429	81,201	1,976	3,826
Richmond County, New York	476,015	33,204	230,553	11,816	3,631	245,462	12,762	4,995
Rockland County, New York	326,780	22,371	159,480	5,919	5,643	167,300	5,386	5,423
St. Lawrence County, New York	110,038	13,500	55,511	5,130	1,295	54,527	5,892	1,183
Saratoga County, New York	227,053	13,008	113,487	3,594	2,110	113,566	5,077	2,227
Schenectady County, New York	154,553	11,190	74,263	2,142	2,328	80,290	3,883	2,837
Steuben County, New York	96,940	3,378	48,179	902	214	48,761	1,611	651
Suffolk County, New York	1,492,583	102,522	734,100	34,076	14,178	758,483	34,958	19,310
Sullivan County, New York	74,801	2,731	38,420	1,221	160	36,381	1,121	229
Tompkins County, New York	104,871	28,098	51,667	3,977	10,577	53,204	3,989	9,555
Ulster County, New York	179,225	10,642	89,419	2,710	836	89,806	5,774	1,322
Warren County, New York	64,567	2,801	31,800	1,162	314	32,767	1,000	325
Wayne County, New York	90,798	3,134	44,497	515	86	46,301	1,916	617
Westchester County, New York	974,542	66,129	471,884	16,827	10,586	502,658	19,099	19,617
NORTH CAROLINA								
Alamance County, North Carolina	159,688	11,881	76,240	3,415	2,015	83,448	3,066	3,385
Brunswick County, North Carolina	126,953	5,112	61,148	1,227	172	65,805	3,084	629
Buncombe County, North Carolina	256,088	16,434	123,522	4,584	1,386	132,566	8,315	2,149
Burke County, North Carolina	88,851	3,890	44,093	1,048	303	44,758	1,836	703
Cabarrus County, North Carolina	201,590	10,840	97,770	3,094	939	103,820	3,722	3,085
Caldwell County, North Carolina	81,449	3,184	40,169	1,271	0	41,280	1,759	154
Carteret County, North Carolina	68,890	3,387	33,599	1,471	147	35,291	1,571	198

Table C-3. College Enrollment of the Population, by Selected Counties, 2016—*Continued*

(Number.)

State/County	Total population	Population enrolled in college or graduate school	Male Total population	Male Enrolled in public college or graduate school	Male Enrolled in private college or graduate school	Female Total population	Female Enrolled in public college or graduate school	Female Enrolled in private college or graduate school
NORTH CAROLINA—(*Continued*)								
Catawba County, North Carolina	156,459	8,706	77,838	2,496	1,376	78,621	3,018	1,816
Chatham County, North Carolina	72,243	2,646	34,139	902	0	38,104	1,604	140
Cleveland County, North Carolina	97,144	6,627	47,494	2,086	754	49,650	2,964	823
Craven County, North Carolina	103,445	5,377	52,824	2,590	389	50,621	1,835	563
Cumberland County, North Carolina	327,127	29,648	160,604	9,053	3,650	166,523	13,144	3,801
Davidson County, North Carolina	164,926	6,612	79,467	2,113	415	85,459	3,503	581
Durham County, North Carolina	306,212	30,469	146,455	5,625	7,184	159,757	10,634	7,026
Forsyth County, North Carolina	371,511	26,974	176,789	7,676	3,090	194,722	9,648	6,560
Gaston County, North Carolina	216,965	10,800	104,655	3,109	1,244	112,310	5,144	1,303
Guilford County, North Carolina	521,330	48,059	246,962	15,789	4,133	274,368	22,452	5,685
Harnett County, North Carolina	130,881	10,957	65,600	2,846	1,679	65,281	4,373	2,059
Henderson County, North Carolina	114,209	4,789	54,745	1,455	388	59,464	2,044	902
Iredell County, North Carolina	172,916	7,567	85,047	2,124	1,061	87,869	3,635	747
Johnston County, North Carolina	191,450	10,965	94,352	4,296	575	97,098	4,913	1,181
Lincoln County, North Carolina	81,168	2,376	39,677	558	251	41,491	1,448	119
Mecklenburg County, North Carolina	1,054,835	74,781	506,610	26,718	5,349	548,225	33,071	9,643
Moore County, North Carolina	95,776	4,817	45,342	1,739	421	50,434	2,130	527
Nash County, North Carolina	94,005	6,059	46,638	1,302	343	47,367	3,506	908
New Hanover County, North Carolina	223,483	20,050	106,521	10,051	638	116,962	8,688	673
Onslow County, North Carolina	187,136	12,598	101,034	4,814	1,443	86,102	5,292	1,049
Orange County, North Carolina	141,796	27,792	67,401	11,707	343	74,395	14,305	1,437
Pitt County, North Carolina	177,220	29,708	83,449	11,432	357	93,771	17,512	407
Randolph County, North Carolina	143,416	6,733	70,702	2,122	102	72,714	3,622	887
Robeson County, North Carolina	133,235	6,572	63,685	2,261	74	69,550	3,695	542
Rockingham County, North Carolina	91,393	3,473	44,333	1,165	123	47,060	2,112	73
Rowan County, North Carolina	139,933	6,695	68,758	2,101	875	71,175	2,649	1,070
Rutherford County, North Carolina	66,421	1,939	32,104	N	N	34,317	N	N
Surry County, North Carolina	72,113	2,405	35,755	698	172	36,358	1,057	478
Union County, North Carolina	226,606	11,206	110,942	2,916	1,250	115,664	5,412	1,628
Wake County, North Carolina	1,046,791	81,611	508,628	34,893	5,173	538,163	33,018	8,527
Wayne County, North Carolina	124,150	7,982	60,609	3,235	455	63,541	3,709	583
Wilkes County, North Carolina	68,740	1,988	33,877	746	114	34,863	1,128	0
Wilson County, North Carolina	81,661	3,758	38,874	1,029	253	42,787	1,547	929
NORTH DAKOTA								
Burleigh County, North Dakota	94,487	5,398	46,686	1,351	857	47,801	1,472	1,718
Cass County, North Dakota	175,249	19,961	90,877	8,313	768	84,372	9,758	1,122
Grand Forks County, North Dakota	71,083	12,865	36,679	7,729	117	34,404	4,883	136
Ward County, North Dakota	70,210	6,099	37,182	2,533	186	33,028	2,822	558
OHIO								
Allen County, Ohio	103,742	6,406	51,453	2,316	1,333	52,289	1,736	1,021
Ashtabula County, Ohio	98,231	3,787	49,800	918	402	48,431	2,081	386
Athens County, Ohio	66,186	19,560	32,687	9,269	135	33,499	9,838	318
Belmont County, Ohio	68,673	2,576	35,233	943	119	33,440	1,134	380
Butler County, Ohio	377,537	33,633	185,576	13,539	1,232	191,961	17,471	1,391
Clark County, Ohio	134,786	6,877	64,502	1,504	1,072	70,284	2,512	1,789
Clermont County, Ohio	203,022	8,504	100,441	2,608	616	102,581	3,949	1,331
Columbiana County, Ohio	103,685	2,509	52,716	851	171	50,969	1,269	218
Cuyahoga County, Ohio	1,249,352	86,374	595,362	18,677	15,012	653,990	34,111	18,574
Delaware County, Ohio	196,463	11,170	97,536	3,245	2,038	98,927	3,519	2,368
Erie County, Ohio	75,107	3,041	36,681	1,119	367	38,426	1,273	282
Fairfield County, Ohio	152,597	8,858	76,224	2,908	698	76,373	3,749	1,503
Franklin County, Ohio	1,264,518	109,906	617,615	40,476	9,453	646,903	47,189	12,788
Geauga County, Ohio	94,060	4,177	46,402	1,836	363	47,658	1,454	524
Greene County, Ohio	164,765	21,724	80,408	7,897	2,049	84,357	8,571	3,207
Hamilton County, Ohio	809,099	54,403	390,081	20,200	5,930	419,018	21,062	7,211
Hancock County, Ohio	75,872	4,705	37,258	970	1,071	38,614	1,128	1,536
Jefferson County, Ohio	66,704	4,084	32,371	1,105	711	34,333	1,040	1,228
Lake County, Ohio	228,614	13,156	110,785	3,824	1,173	117,829	5,134	3,025
Licking County, Ohio	172,198	11,046	84,022	2,532	1,145	88,176	3,892	3,477
Lorain County, Ohio	306,365	19,002	150,841	6,442	2,550	155,524	6,874	3,136
Lucas County, Ohio	432,488	28,917	209,933	11,578	1,885	222,555	12,706	2,748
Mahoning County, Ohio	230,008	14,380	112,268	5,027	764	117,740	7,169	1,420
Marion County, Ohio	65,096	3,346	34,365	980	157	30,731	1,823	386
Medina County, Ohio	177,221	9,603	87,625	3,245	718	89,596	4,701	939
Miami County, Ohio	104,679	3,812	51,654	1,365	485	53,025	1,703	259
Montgomery County, Ohio	531,239	40,494	256,395	10,962	7,776	274,844	14,639	7,117
Muskingum County, Ohio	86,068	4,486	41,853	1,165	685	44,215	1,638	998
Portage County, Ohio	161,921	22,500	78,973	9,266	591	82,948	11,747	896

Table C-3. College Enrollment of the Population, by Selected Counties, 2016—*Continued*

(Number.)

			Male			Female		
State/County	Total population	Population enrolled in college or graduate school	Total population	Enrolled in public college or graduate school	Enrolled in private college or graduate school	Total population	Enrolled in public college or graduate school	Enrolled in private college or graduate school
OHIO—(*Continued*)								
Richland County, Ohio	121,107	4,373	61,776	1,014	981	59,331	1,707	671
Ross County, Ohio	77,000	2,763	40,376	1,011	54	36,624	1,017	681
Scioto County, Ohio	76,088	3,402	36,953	1,026	444	39,135	1,405	527
Stark County, Ohio	373,612	20,570	181,115	5,814	2,174	192,497	7,911	4,671
Summit County, Ohio	540,300	35,930	262,227	14,598	1,931	278,073	16,240	3,161
Trumbull County, Ohio	201,825	7,625	97,484	2,479	400	104,341	4,117	629
Tuscarawas County, Ohio	92,420	2,828	45,251	1,386	201	47,169	1,137	104
Warren County, Ohio	227,063	10,282	114,367	3,476	405	112,696	5,017	1,384
Wayne County, Ohio	116,470	7,637	58,249	3,443	652	58,221	2,231	1,311
Wood County, Ohio	130,219	19,461	65,280	7,349	1,353	64,939	10,412	347
OKLAHOMA								
Canadian County, Oklahoma	136,532	7,179	67,095	2,486	889	69,437	2,830	974
Cleveland County, Oklahoma	278,655	36,129	139,897	16,142	1,001	138,758	17,824	1,162
Comanche County, Oklahoma	122,136	8,660	63,777	3,487	504	58,359	4,379	290
Creek County, Oklahoma	71,312	2,254	35,301	758	113	36,011	1,159	224
Muskogee County, Oklahoma	69,477	3,348	33,850	1,528	284	35,627	1,434	102
Oklahoma County, Oklahoma	782,970	45,232	382,993	14,373	4,352	399,977	20,875	5,632
Payne County, Oklahoma	81,131	21,059	41,436	12,203	247	39,695	8,458	151
Pottawatomie County, Oklahoma	72,290	4,794	35,089	1,173	435	37,201	2,014	1,172
Rogers County, Oklahoma	91,766	5,174	45,366	2,038	273	46,400	2,681	182
Tulsa County, Oklahoma	642,940	38,786	313,474	12,277	5,541	329,466	14,354	6,614
Wagoner County, Oklahoma	77,679	2,934	38,042	882	451	39,637	1,244	357
OREGON								
Benton County, Oregon	89,385	20,979	44,722	10,983	457	44,663	9,303	236
Clackamas County, Oregon	408,062	23,209	200,839	8,611	1,182	207,223	9,693	3,723
Deschutes County, Oregon	181,307	7,502	89,988	2,622	1,140	91,319	3,529	211
Douglas County, Oregon	108,457	3,900	54,065	1,265	485	54,392	2,022	128
Jackson County, Oregon	216,527	10,845	105,721	4,562	714	110,806	5,187	382
Josephine County, Oregon	85,904	4,203	41,022	1,122	0	44,882	2,393	688
Klamath County, Oregon	66,443	3,541	33,623	1,321	118	32,820	2,009	93
Lane County, Oregon	369,519	35,255	181,794	15,042	1,241	187,725	17,593	1,379
Linn County, Oregon	122,849	6,523	61,175	2,712	288	61,674	3,109	414
Marion County, Oregon	336,316	18,976	165,756	5,386	1,874	170,560	7,906	3,810
Multnomah County, Oregon	799,766	65,261	396,875	22,287	5,693	402,891	26,944	10,337
Polk County, Oregon	81,823	9,841	38,468	2,850	353	43,355	6,280	358
Umatilla County, Oregon	76,456	2,936	39,719	801	319	36,737	1,649	167
Washington County, Oregon	582,779	35,906	286,494	14,403	2,808	296,285	12,912	5,783
Yamhill County, Oregon	105,035	8,206	53,168	1,139	2,233	51,867	2,443	2,391
PENNSYLVANIA								
Adams County, Pennsylvania	102,180	6,709	50,359	732	2,389	51,821	1,603	1,985
Allegheny County, Pennsylvania	1,225,365	95,071	592,374	25,176	17,548	632,991	33,455	18,892
Armstrong County, Pennsylvania	66,486	2,695	33,041	555	146	33,445	1,216	778
Beaver County, Pennsylvania	167,429	8,455	81,612	3,385	1,008	85,817	2,278	1,784
Berks County, Pennsylvania	414,812	26,124	204,372	7,810	2,108	210,440	11,996	4,210
Blair County, Pennsylvania	124,650	5,207	61,100	2,016	782	63,550	1,921	488
Bucks County, Pennsylvania	626,399	35,985	307,346	9,096	6,455	319,053	11,141	9,293
Butler County, Pennsylvania	186,847	12,435	92,823	4,977	579	94,024	5,608	1,271
Cambria County, Pennsylvania	134,732	8,720	66,143	2,570	984	68,589	2,886	2,280
Carbon County, Pennsylvania	63,594	1,693	32,121	373	220	31,473	653	447
Centre County, Pennsylvania	161,464	38,935	85,208	20,842	727	76,256	16,312	1,054
Chester County, Pennsylvania	516,312	36,799	254,127	12,662	3,941	262,185	14,776	5,420
Clearfield County, Pennsylvania	80,596	2,149	42,229	866	92	38,367	909	282
Columbia County, Pennsylvania	66,420	8,301	31,694	2,846	238	34,726	5,104	113
Crawford County, Pennsylvania	86,257	4,386	42,103	966	1,106	44,154	1,174	1,140
Cumberland County, Pennsylvania	248,506	16,960	123,073	5,028	2,930	125,433	4,855	4,147
Dauphin County, Pennsylvania	273,707	12,455	131,911	4,189	1,241	141,796	5,358	1,667
Delaware County, Pennsylvania	563,402	49,369	270,782	8,775	12,628	292,620	12,263	15,703
Erie County, Pennsylvania	276,207	18,904	136,372	5,670	2,702	139,835	6,383	4,149
Fayette County, Pennsylvania	132,733	4,757	65,462	1,721	141	67,271	2,466	429
Franklin County, Pennsylvania	153,851	5,026	76,604	1,531	583	77,247	2,258	654
Indiana County, Pennsylvania	86,364	9,648	43,621	4,223	104	42,743	4,580	741
Lackawanna County, Pennsylvania	211,321	13,408	101,894	1,699	3,862	109,427	1,721	6,126
Lancaster County, Pennsylvania	538,500	26,426	264,057	5,592	4,308	274,443	10,293	6,233
Lawrence County, Pennsylvania	87,294	4,730	42,742	1,430	770	44,552	1,465	1,065
Lebanon County, Pennsylvania	138,863	5,837	67,675	632	2,308	71,188	1,965	932
Lehigh County, Pennsylvania	363,147	21,848	177,485	4,543	3,839	185,662	6,264	7,202
Luzerne County, Pennsylvania	316,383	17,725	155,463	4,100	4,638	160,920	4,481	4,506

Table C-3. College Enrollment of the Population, by Selected Counties, 2016—*Continued*

(Number.)

State/County	Total population	Population enrolled in college or graduate school	Male Total population	Male Enrolled in public college or graduate school	Male Enrolled in private college or graduate school	Female Total population	Female Enrolled in public college or graduate school	Female Enrolled in private college or graduate school
PENNSYLVANIA—*(Continued)*								
Lycoming County, Pennsylvania...............	115,248	7,488	56,210	2,001	1,301	59,038	2,690	1,496
Mercer County, Pennsylvania...............	112,913	5,750	55,637	568	1,507	57,276	1,676	1,999
Monroe County, Pennsylvania...............	166,098	11,636	82,312	5,232	1,170	83,786	4,501	733
Montgomery County, Pennsylvania...............	821,725	52,033	399,488	12,055	10,742	422,237	14,701	14,535
Northampton County, Pennsylvania...............	302,294	23,285	149,254	3,915	6,380	153,040	5,229	7,761
Northumberland County, Pennsylvania	92,541	2,454	47,301	446	272	45,240	1,319	417
Philadelphia County, Pennsylvania...............	1,567,872	137,807	743,380	23,843	34,167	824,492	35,754	44,043
Schuylkill County, Pennsylvania...............	143,573	4,171	73,503	1,523	432	70,070	1,249	967
Somerset County, Pennsylvania...............	75,061	1,953	38,762	621	128	36,299	980	224
Washington County, Pennsylvania...............	207,981	9,954	101,664	2,976	1,670	106,317	4,028	1,280
Westmoreland County, Pennsylvania	355,458	18,378	173,607	5,657	2,689	181,851	6,143	3,889
York County, Pennsylvania...............	443,744	20,270	218,703	5,728	2,698	225,041	7,040	4,804
RHODE ISLAND								
Kent County, Rhode Island...............	164,614	9,076	79,351	3,122	1,213	85,263	3,053	1,688
Newport County, Rhode Island...............	82,784	6,447	40,195	2,130	831	42,589	1,491	1,995
Providence County, Rhode Island	633,673	60,670	307,712	11,803	14,033	325,961	15,995	18,839
Washington County, Rhode Island...............	126,288	14,202	60,512	4,114	1,547	65,776	7,422	1,119
SOUTH CAROLINA								
Aiken County, South Carolina...............	167,458	7,755	81,683	2,767	451	85,775	4,109	428
Anderson County, South Carolina	196,569	10,276	94,805	2,581	1,358	101,764	4,662	1,675
Beaufort County, South Carolina...............	183,149	9,708	89,378	3,054	488	93,771	5,163	1,003
Berkeley County, South Carolina...............	210,898	10,729	104,553	2,837	1,644	106,345	5,275	973
Charleston County, South Carolina...............	396,484	28,544	190,528	11,731	1,735	205,956	10,971	4,107
Darlington County, South Carolina...............	67,234	3,486	31,105	682	758	36,129	1,903	143
Dorchester County, South Carolina	153,773	8,186	75,358	3,170	316	78,415	3,947	753
Florence County, South Carolina	138,742	9,801	64,489	2,345	175	74,253	6,564	717
Greenville County, South Carolina...............	498,766	30,308	242,098	8,658	4,975	256,668	9,371	7,304
Greenwood County, South Carolina	70,133	4,269	32,128	1,106	126	38,005	2,716	321
Horry County, South Carolina	322,342	17,415	155,255	7,108	697	167,087	8,300	1,310
Lancaster County, South Carolina...............	89,594	4,396	44,583	869	515	45,011	2,541	471
Laurens County, South Carolina...............	66,777	4,444	32,541	753	685	34,236	1,682	1,324
Lexington County, South Carolina...............	286,196	15,094	139,230	4,907	1,202	146,966	7,403	1,582
Oconee County, South Carolina...............	76,355	4,124	36,795	1,781	110	39,560	1,977	256
Orangeburg County, South Carolina...............	87,903	7,589	41,321	1,854	340	46,582	3,456	1,939
Pickens County, South Carolina...............	122,863	19,527	60,735	8,393	1,202	62,128	9,429	503
Richland County, South Carolina...............	409,549	46,211	198,431	17,542	3,155	211,118	20,749	4,765
Spartanburg County, South Carolina...............	301,463	19,011	146,664	5,472	1,936	154,799	8,534	3,069
Sumter County, South Carolina...............	107,396	8,073	52,411	2,846	487	54,985	3,999	741
York County, South Carolina	258,526	17,447	124,462	6,883	580	134,064	9,475	509
SOUTH DAKOTA								
Minnehaha County, South Dakota	187,318	9,953	94,159	2,811	1,584	93,159	3,822	1,736
Pennington County, South Dakota	109,372	7,475	54,783	3,706	330	54,589	2,929	510
TENNESSEE								
Anderson County, Tennessee	75,936	3,146	37,839	480	253	38,097	2,051	362
Blount County, Tennessee	128,670	4,282	62,288	954	918	66,382	1,591	819
Bradley County, Tennessee...............	104,490	8,084	50,653	1,714	1,505	53,837	2,607	2,258
Davidson County, Tennessee...............	684,410	56,475	329,473	11,852	12,443	354,937	16,418	15,762
Greene County, Tennessee...............	68,615	3,476	33,969	1,342	435	34,646	1,245	454
Hamilton County, Tennessee...............	357,738	27,935	173,590	10,879	2,443	184,148	11,469	3,144
Knox County, Tennessee	456,132	41,072	222,119	17,712	2,769	234,013	18,098	2,493
Madison County, Tennessee...............	97,663	6,820	46,549	582	1,622	51,114	2,270	2,346
Maury County, Tennessee...............	89,981	3,306	44,105	1,252	81	45,876	1,886	87
Montgomery County, Tennessee	195,734	19,885	96,375	7,740	1,428	99,359	9,365	1,352
Putnam County, Tennessee...............	75,931	8,016	37,714	4,313	60	38,217	3,548	95
Robertson County, Tennessee...............	69,165	1,426	33,717	393	124	35,448	493	416
Rutherford County, Tennessee...............	308,251	26,854	151,436	11,115	1,922	156,815	13,116	701
Sevier County, Tennessee...............	96,673	3,020	48,504	1,553	171	48,169	977	319
Shelby County, Tennessee...............	934,603	63,230	445,343	19,853	6,824	489,260	27,243	9,310
Sullivan County, Tennessee...............	156,667	6,763	75,796	2,520	612	80,871	2,880	751
Sumner County, Tennessee...............	180,063	7,373	87,834	2,885	600	92,229	2,973	915
Washington County, Tennessee...............	127,440	10,243	62,924	4,359	313	64,516	5,067	504
Williamson County, Tennessee...............	219,107	10,443	107,205	2,831	1,567	111,902	3,796	2,249
Wilson County, Tennessee...............	132,781	6,162	65,113	2,031	573	67,668	2,848	710
TEXAS								
Angelina County, Texas	87,791	3,965	42,273	1,234	38	45,518	2,375	318
Bastrop County, Texas...............	82,733	2,403	42,343	364	90	40,390	1,770	179

Table C-3. College Enrollment of the Population, by Selected Counties, 2016—*Continued*

(Number.)

			Male			Female		
State/County	Total population	Population enrolled in college or graduate school	Total population	Enrolled in public college or graduate school	Enrolled in private college or graduate school	Total population	Enrolled in public college or graduate school	Enrolled in private college or graduate school
TEXAS—(*Continued*)								
Bell County, Texas	340,411	28,705	169,564	9,348	1,709	170,847	13,777	3,871
Bexar County, Texas	1,928,680	140,398	951,190	49,733	16,931	977,490	54,806	18,928
Bowie County, Texas	93,860	5,004	47,367	1,503	1,106	46,493	2,047	348
Brazoria County, Texas	354,195	18,070	178,453	7,982	1,025	175,742	7,519	1,544
Brazos County, Texas	220,417	59,195	112,020	31,324	668	108,397	26,806	397
Cameron County, Texas	422,135	19,479	204,626	9,269	790	217,509	8,591	829
Collin County, Texas	939,585	59,273	461,416	25,613	3,601	478,169	25,182	4,877
Comal County, Texas	134,788	4,797	66,708	1,427	397	68,080	2,179	794
Coryell County, Texas	74,686	4,059	37,817	1,868	0	36,869	1,883	308
Dallas County, Texas	2,574,984	144,291	1,267,526	49,854	15,933	1,307,458	62,342	16,162
Denton County, Texas	806,180	66,188	396,322	22,910	3,737	409,858	34,056	5,485
Ector County, Texas	157,462	9,072	80,102	4,296	96	77,360	4,580	100
Ellis County, Texas	168,499	8,988	83,163	2,692	700	85,336	4,398	1,198
El Paso County, Texas	837,918	71,377	411,497	29,311	3,555	426,421	33,502	5,009
Fort Bend County, Texas	741,237	52,644	364,149	21,867	3,360	377,088	22,249	5,168
Galveston County, Texas	329,431	22,583	162,548	9,735	1,091	166,883	10,737	1,020
Grayson County, Texas	128,235	7,154	62,706	2,239	1,275	65,529	3,353	287
Gregg County, Texas	123,745	7,833	61,139	2,780	1,377	62,606	2,215	1,461
Guadalupe County, Texas	155,265	10,166	76,684	3,748	986	78,581	4,580	852
Harris County, Texas	4,589,928	306,456	2,281,026	113,294	29,225	2,308,902	127,357	36,580
Harrison County, Texas	66,534	3,169	31,892	572	789	34,642	1,279	529
Hays County, Texas	204,470	26,564	100,110	11,005	493	104,360	14,545	521
Henderson County, Texas	79,901	3,165	38,440	760	131	41,461	2,056	218
Hidalgo County, Texas	849,843	55,025	415,546	22,845	3,795	434,297	22,550	5,835
Hunt County, Texas	92,073	6,759	45,503	2,725	313	46,570	3,355	366
Jefferson County, Texas	254,679	11,354	130,673	5,246	404	124,006	5,409	295
Johnson County, Texas	163,274	4,506	81,331	1,884	232	81,943	1,978	412
Kaufman County, Texas	118,350	6,425	58,708	2,028	372	59,642	3,566	459
Liberty County, Texas	81,704	2,452	41,468	909	0	40,236	917	626
Lubbock County, Texas	303,137	48,235	149,132	23,782	1,762	154,005	21,430	1,261
McLennan County, Texas	247,934	27,188	120,728	5,641	6,391	127,206	6,521	8,635
Midland County, Texas	162,565	8,629	81,341	2,016	822	81,224	4,905	886
Montgomery County, Texas	556,203	25,509	276,246	8,507	1,497	279,957	13,524	1,981
Nacogdoches County, Texas	65,806	11,282	31,281	3,942	0	34,525	7,291	49
Nueces County, Texas	361,350	23,874	178,469	10,054	212	182,881	12,639	969
Orange County, Texas	84,964	3,947	41,889	1,623	185	43,075	2,077	62
Parker County, Texas	129,441	5,240	64,651	1,307	369	64,790	3,275	289
Potter County, Texas	120,832	6,012	62,406	2,037	157	58,426	3,630	188
Randall County, Texas	132,501	11,593	65,222	4,333	530	67,279	5,955	775
Rockwall County, Texas	93,978	6,464	45,729	2,827	797	48,249	2,307	533
San Patricio County, Texas	67,655	2,563	34,245	1,018	99	33,410	1,294	152
Smith County, Texas	225,290	14,283	108,293	5,525	1,120	116,997	6,252	1,386
Tarrant County, Texas	2,016,872	138,218	985,977	47,923	13,166	1,030,895	60,401	16,728
Taylor County, Texas	136,535	11,375	67,109	1,645	3,217	69,426	1,900	4,613
Tom Green County, Texas	118,386	10,435	58,379	4,798	501	60,007	5,000	136
Travis County, Texas	1,199,323	99,408	604,685	43,218	5,283	594,638	43,260	7,647
Victoria County, Texas	92,467	4,485	45,014	1,656	0	47,453	2,704	125
Walker County, Texas	71,484	13,183	42,074	5,819	55	29,410	6,675	634
Webb County, Texas	271,193	15,287	131,568	6,458	461	139,625	7,179	1,189
Wichita County, Texas	131,838	8,501	68,077	3,318	251	63,761	4,681	251
Williamson County, Texas	528,718	32,734	259,891	13,352	3,209	268,827	13,516	2,657
UTAH								
Cache County, Utah	122,753	16,671	60,795	7,456	679	61,958	8,020	516
Davis County, Utah	342,281	22,012	173,129	10,358	1,759	169,152	8,584	1,311
Salt Lake County, Utah	1,121,354	77,326	562,661	33,642	6,348	558,693	29,154	8,182
Utah County, Utah	592,299	79,576	299,911	21,969	19,744	292,388	16,899	20,964
Washington County, Utah	160,245	13,106	79,883	5,038	902	80,362	6,127	1,039
Weber County, Utah	247,560	15,647	124,784	6,561	881	122,776	6,913	1,292
VERMONT								
Chittenden County, Vermont	161,531	21,202	79,754	5,730	3,684	81,777	7,400	4,388
VIRGINIA								
Albemarle County, Virginia	106,878	11,264	50,994	5,092	704	55,884	5,077	391
Arlington County, Virginia	230,050	15,606	114,984	4,375	2,950	115,066	3,909	4,372
Augusta County, Virginia	74,997	2,523	37,498	497	352	37,499	1,213	461
Bedford County, Virginia	77,960	2,924	38,851	374	449	39,109	862	1,239
Chesterfield County, Virginia	339,009	24,016	163,650	9,332	2,301	175,359	9,413	2,970
Fairfax County, Virginia	1,138,652	82,726	564,379	32,994	8,318	574,273	32,333	9,081
Fauquier County, Virginia	69,069	2,656	34,383	805	160	34,686	1,158	533

Table C-3. College Enrollment of the Population, by Selected Counties, 2016—*Continued*

(Number.)

State/County	Total population	Population enrolled in college or graduate school	Male			Female		
			Total population	Enrolled in public college or graduate school	Enrolled in private college or graduate school	Total population	Enrolled in public college or graduate school	Enrolled in private college or graduate school
VIRGINIA—*(Continued)*								
Frederick County, Virginia	84,421	3,455	41,801	944	547	42,620	1,425	539
Hanover County, Virginia	104,392	5,806	51,683	1,887	1,027	52,709	1,612	1,280
Henrico County, Virginia	326,501	19,109	153,668	5,912	1,823	172,833	8,747	2,627
James City County, Virginia	74,404	4,544	34,824	1,330	141	39,580	2,513	560
Loudoun County, Virginia	385,945	22,721	191,567	9,142	1,647	194,378	9,299	2,633
Montgomery County, Virginia	98,602	29,273	50,997	15,806	1,052	47,605	11,605	810
Prince William County, Virginia	455,210	33,029	226,532	12,317	2,803	228,678	13,922	3,987
Roanoke County, Virginia	94,031	5,475	45,071	2,114	351	48,960	1,862	1,148
Rockingham County, Virginia	79,744	4,287	38,921	651	650	40,823	1,788	1,198
Spotsylvania County, Virginia	132,010	7,810	65,365	2,720	138	66,645	4,399	553
Stafford County, Virginia	144,361	10,235	72,808	3,958	1,432	71,553	4,095	750
York County, Virginia	67,976	5,910	32,325	2,421	1,073	35,651	1,908	508
Alexandria city, Virginia	155,810	12,235	74,560	3,688	1,747	81,250	5,202	1,598
Chesapeake city, Virginia	237,940	16,077	116,137	5,082	1,237	121,803	8,063	1,695
Hampton city, Virginia	135,410	15,396	64,156	3,445	2,458	71,254	6,215	3,278
Lynchburg city, Virginia	80,212	14,550	35,920	910	6,617	44,292	527	6,496
Newport News city, Virginia	181,825	17,886	88,786	5,267	1,951	93,039	8,037	2,631
Norfolk city, Virginia	245,115	29,975	127,741	13,986	1,813	117,374	11,564	2,612
Portsmouth city, Virginia	95,252	7,248	45,634	2,502	749	49,618	3,359	638
Richmond city, Virginia	223,170	28,178	106,262	9,388	2,496	116,908	14,128	2,166
Roanoke city, Virginia	99,660	5,437	47,335	2,249	498	52,325	2,386	304
Suffolk city, Virginia	89,273	5,804	43,617	2,024	490	45,656	2,531	759
Virginia Beach city, Virginia	452,602	37,693	222,398	12,516	4,707	230,204	14,724	5,746
WASHINGTON								
Benton County, Washington	193,686	9,877	96,102	3,507	975	97,584	4,406	989
Chelan County, Washington	76,338	2,381	38,152	537	241	38,186	1,250	353
Clallam County, Washington	74,570	3,269	36,554	1,350	45	38,016	1,657	217
Clark County, Washington	467,018	23,269	230,670	8,303	1,234	236,348	11,683	2,049
Cowlitz County, Washington	105,160	4,567	51,052	1,713	270	54,108	2,124	460
Franklin County, Washington	90,160	4,174	46,542	2,096	111	43,618	1,853	114
Grant County, Washington	93,546	4,535	47,037	2,023	130	46,509	1,867	515
Grays Harbor County, Washington	71,628	2,261	37,737	747	162	33,891	1,195	157
Island County, Washington	82,636	4,574	42,597	1,899	295	40,039	1,828	552
King County, Washington	2,149,970	147,574	1,075,509	56,622	12,792	1,074,461	58,026	20,134
Kitsap County, Washington	264,811	16,252	134,237	7,379	1,381	130,574	6,192	1,300
Lewis County, Washington	77,066	3,598	38,991	1,200	293	38,075	1,776	329
Pierce County, Washington	861,312	49,964	427,539	17,451	5,742	433,773	21,662	5,109
Skagit County, Washington	123,681	6,187	61,569	1,994	150	62,112	3,476	567
Snohomish County, Washington	787,620	45,767	394,394	17,191	3,170	393,226	19,007	6,399
Spokane County, Washington	499,072	36,556	248,100	13,046	4,127	250,972	14,831	4,552
Thurston County, Washington	275,222	17,702	135,063	5,912	1,998	140,159	7,880	1,912
Whatcom County, Washington	216,800	26,073	107,399	10,956	962	109,401	13,553	602
Yakima County, Washington	249,636	10,451	124,709	3,279	849	124,927	5,199	1,124
WEST VIRGINIA								
Berkeley County, West Virginia	113,525	6,402	55,447	1,719	487	58,078	3,438	758
Cabell County, West Virginia	95,987	9,346	46,975	3,790	326	49,012	5,019	211
Harrison County, West Virginia	68,400	2,504	33,222	667	144	35,178	1,232	461
Kanawha County, West Virginia	186,241	8,858	88,537	4,029	500	97,704	3,561	768
Monongalia County, West Virginia	104,622	21,986	53,431	10,904	389	51,191	9,861	832
Raleigh County, West Virginia	76,601	3,581	38,557	765	299	38,044	2,240	277
Wood County, West Virginia	85,643	4,148	40,920	1,719	232	44,723	1,752	445
WISCONSIN								
Brown County, Wisconsin	260,401	18,329	130,129	5,860	2,398	130,272	7,197	2,874
Dane County, Wisconsin	531,273	62,102	263,187	27,565	1,800	268,086	28,147	4,590
Dodge County, Wisconsin	88,068	3,801	46,565	1,139	234	41,503	1,973	455
Eau Claire County, Wisconsin	102,965	12,321	50,998	5,311	250	51,967	6,162	598
Fond du Lac County, Wisconsin	102,144	5,769	49,848	1,346	1,432	52,296	1,939	1,052
Jefferson County, Wisconsin	84,625	6,261	42,562	2,277	887	42,063	2,512	585
Kenosha County, Wisconsin	168,183	13,306	82,871	4,119	1,503	85,312	5,164	2,520
La Crosse County, Wisconsin	118,122	15,001	56,961	6,177	531	61,161	6,382	1,911
Manitowoc County, Wisconsin	79,536	3,122	39,441	1,063	186	40,095	1,313	560
Marathon County, Wisconsin	135,603	5,812	67,858	2,686	274	67,745	2,545	307
Milwaukee County, Wisconsin	951,448	73,374	460,687	18,813	12,258	490,761	25,933	16,370
Outagamie County, Wisconsin	184,526	10,638	91,828	3,265	620	92,698	4,919	1,834
Ozaukee County, Wisconsin	88,314	6,482	42,960	1,805	816	45,354	2,338	1,523
Portage County, Wisconsin	70,447	9,342	34,966	3,720	311	35,481	5,183	128

Table C-3. College Enrollment of the Population, by Selected Counties, 2016—*Continued*

(Number.)

State/County	Total population	Population enrolled in college or graduate school	Male			Female		
			Total population	Enrolled in public college or graduate school	Enrolled in private college or graduate school	Total population	Enrolled in public college or graduate school	Enrolled in private college or graduate school
WISCONSIN—(*Continued*)								
Racine County, Wisconsin	195,140	10,106	96,418	2,998	1,352	98,722	4,561	1,195
Rock County, Wisconsin	161,620	8,894	79,531	2,554	1,373	82,089	2,400	2,567
St. Croix County, Wisconsin	88,029	4,843	43,967	1,388	603	44,062	2,329	523
Sheboygan County, Wisconsin	115,427	5,691	58,200	1,857	475	57,227	2,398	961
Walworth County, Wisconsin	102,959	10,612	51,364	4,366	382	51,595	5,368	496
Washington County, Wisconsin	134,296	6,644	66,215	2,445	780	68,081	2,219	1,200
Waukesha County, Wisconsin	398,424	22,344	195,314	6,868	2,996	203,110	7,185	5,295
Winnebago County, Wisconsin	169,886	15,782	86,078	7,356	447	83,808	7,080	899
Wood County, Wisconsin	73,107	2,433	35,526	939	161	37,581	1,079	254
WYOMING								
Laramie County, Wyoming	98,136	6,427	50,128	2,786	280	48,008	3,015	346
Natrona County, Wyoming	81,039	5,735	39,821	2,482	122	41,218	2,955	176

Table C-4. Primary and Secondary School Enrollment, by Sex and Selected Counties, 2016

(Number.)

State/County	Population 3 years and over	Male Nursery school, Pre-school	Male Kindergarten	Male Grades 1 to 4	Male Grades 5 to 8	Male Grades 9 to 12	Female Nursery school, Pre-school	Female Kindergarten	Female Grades 1 to 4	Female Grades 5 to 8	Female Grades 9 to 12
ALABAMA											
Baldwin County, Alabama................	202,654	1,956	1,163	5,464	6,002	4,852	580	1,095	5,075	5,312	5,701
Calhoun County, Alabama	110,492	423	496	3,429	3,118	3,156	667	874	2,432	2,783	2,863
Cullman County, Alabama	79,650	466	313	1,536	2,051	2,145	369	546	1,331	2,310	2,437
DeKalb County, Alabama................	68,766	479	102	1,922	2,951	1,807	189	228	2,117	1,756	2,030
Elmore County, Alabama................	79,235	294	598	2,369	1,922	2,750	620	147	2,404	2,448	1,565
Houston County, Alabama................	100,144	357	761	3,020	3,146	2,945	768	736	2,802	2,369	2,766
Jefferson County, Alabama	633,429	5,316	5,826	17,724	14,894	16,862	5,666	3,765	17,122	17,009	16,306
Lauderdale County, Alabama............	89,431	452	659	2,451	1,803	2,629	427	313	1,693	2,232	1,691
Lee County, Alabama................	153,304	742	1,297	4,342	4,664	3,190	1,535	907	3,322	3,211	3,353
Limestone County, Alabama................	89,802	556	233	2,657	3,284	4,103	177	138	1,766	2,250	2,453
Madison County, Alabama................	344,834	2,535	2,249	8,529	10,049	9,344	2,560	2,750	8,404	8,147	7,719
Marshall County, Alabama................	91,414	967	412	2,734	3,236	2,496	684	1,009	2,590	2,100	2,830
Mobile County, Alabama	398,315	2,957	1,850	11,719	10,920	12,390	3,501	2,956	11,918	9,458	10,603
Montgomery County, Alabama.........	217,720	1,574	2,398	6,947	4,350	5,339	2,596	1,989	5,456	5,196	5,736
Morgan County, Alabama	115,411	1,035	1,280	3,839	2,839	3,759	638	541	2,298	2,892	2,928
St. Clair County, Alabama................	84,854	1,365	620	1,908	2,007	2,541	652	380	2,345	2,033	1,836
Shelby County, Alabama	203,284	1,436	994	5,266	7,679	5,910	1,468	1,728	4,669	5,729	7,567
Tuscaloosa County, Alabama............	198,481	751	1,579	4,753	5,241	3,947	1,132	1,386	4,474	4,808	4,677
ALASKA											
Anchorage Municipality, Alaska........	284,706	1,839	1,560	8,437	8,065	9,129	1,699	1,681	7,104	7,149	7,628
Fairbanks North Star Borough, Alaska	96,121	286	500	2,752	3,507	3,142	986	687	3,527	1,661	1,516
Matanuska-Susitna Borough, Alaska.	100,281	695	412	3,224	3,946	3,744	907	731	3,167	3,123	2,862
ARIZONA											
Apache County, Arizona	70,304	454	568	2,581	2,733	2,417	625	743	2,202	2,512	3,226
Cochise County, Arizona	120,615	623	837	3,732	2,218	3,502	606	705	2,758	4,018	2,992
Coconino County, Arizona................	136,047	712	576	3,280	4,033	3,580	1,069	492	2,984	3,215	3,533
Maricopa County, Arizona	4,083,018	30,197	28,236	120,434	117,506	120,162	25,647	29,161	111,322	111,969	118,836
Mohave County, Arizona	200,438	1,320	1,675	4,099	4,359	4,597	1,406	517	4,105	4,828	4,992
Navajo County, Arizona................	105,459	451	770	4,288	3,430	4,176	915	1,029	3,278	3,647	3,484
Pima County, Arizona................	982,197	6,212	5,240	24,783	27,077	26,661	5,947	7,310	21,775	23,174	26,795
Pinal County, Arizona................	403,577	1,939	1,357	13,160	12,281	11,201	2,233	2,693	13,177	9,625	9,893
Yavapai County, Arizona................	220,564	188	1,389	5,417	4,738	3,927	202	897	4,111	4,012	4,044
Yuma County, Arizona................	196,316	1,737	1,534	6,302	5,315	6,811	753	1,686	5,996	5,241	5,271
ARKANSAS											
Benton County, Arkansas................	247,162	1,798	1,815	8,572	7,782	7,495	1,741	1,671	7,504	7,672	6,884
Craighead County, Arkansas	101,917	615	601	3,608	2,980	2,600	916	1,183	2,839	2,391	2,880
Faulkner County, Arkansas................	118,108	1,408	353	2,815	3,655	3,007	1,422	728	3,489	2,705	3,471
Jefferson County, Arkansas................	67,596	545	165	1,906	1,923	2,280	594	796	1,243	1,778	2,173
Lonoke County, Arkansas................	69,276	681	257	2,105	2,438	2,238	747	179	1,480	2,075	2,171
Pulaski County, Arkansas................	378,049	3,264	3,951	11,061	9,273	10,412	2,904	4,252	9,939	8,336	10,427
Saline County, Arkansas................	114,561	1,213	632	4,042	2,768	3,216	917	442	2,528	3,679	2,985
Sebastian County, Arkansas................	122,982	1,404	864	4,014	2,739	3,233	376	925	3,244	3,744	4,239
Washington County, Arkansas	218,685	1,225	1,843	6,299	6,417	5,173	2,210	1,554	5,776	6,997	5,465
White County, Arkansas................	75,890	264	842	1,815	2,233	2,050	792	122	1,669	3,002	1,761
CALIFORNIA											
Alameda County, California................	1,590,501	13,764	10,006	41,287	36,918	38,210	14,008	10,416	34,271	38,187	36,896
Butte County, California................	220,040	1,278	1,646	5,939	4,902	5,899	2,168	1,394	5,049	3,985	6,005
Contra Costa County, California	1,099,760	10,491	8,201	27,837	31,361	33,390	10,519	7,354	29,530	29,091	30,512
El Dorado County, California	180,829	1,554	1,269	4,957	4,210	4,438	1,064	965	4,780	3,897	4,492
Fresno County, California................	933,879	7,346	9,300	29,023	34,331	30,990	8,882	7,814	30,115	31,124	30,702
Humboldt County, California................	132,729	477	575	2,909	3,606	2,782	1,339	759	2,923	2,798	3,565
Imperial County, California................	171,575	1,509	2,214	5,765	5,642	5,870	2,271	2,025	3,578	5,667	7,112
Kern County, California................	841,501	5,421	6,455	27,397	32,290	29,837	4,904	7,415	27,762	27,708	27,807
Kings County, California................	142,818	827	878	4,643	4,827	6,859	1,063	1,093	3,777	4,907	6,180
Los Angeles County, California.........	9,769,241	85,490	71,163	236,264	249,357	283,527	76,538	61,383	236,514	236,519	265,658
Madera County, California................	146,845	467	1,897	3,445	4,257	6,255	673	1,015	5,085	5,308	3,872
Marin County, California................	252,768	1,808	1,097	6,112	6,693	6,854	2,523	1,744	5,851	6,864	5,446
Mendocino County, California	84,587	394	613	1,664	2,690	2,322	640	298	2,703	2,226	2,423
Merced County, California................	256,493	3,635	2,901	9,373	7,883	9,936	2,681	2,918	8,666	7,950	9,778
Monterey County, California............	416,770	3,296	3,334	12,389	14,065	15,075	2,437	3,171	12,356	11,798	11,925
Napa County, California................	137,717	759	1,170	2,836	3,774	3,406	559	1,512	2,437	3,166	3,348
Nevada County, California................	97,008	1,067	240	1,991	1,850	3,990	425	336	1,565	2,208	1,826

Table C-4. Primary and Secondary School Enrollment, by Sex and Selected Counties, 2016—*Continued*

(Number.)

State/County	Population 3 years and over	Male					Female				
		Nursery school, Pre-school	Kindergarten	Grades 1 to 4	Grades 5 to 8	Grades 9 to 12	Nursery school, Pre-school	Kindergarten	Grades 1 to 4	Grades 5 to 8	Grades 9 to 12
CALIFORNIA—*(Continued)*											
Orange County, California	3,063,415	25,499	21,403	76,242	82,615	89,170	25,980	18,303	70,202	80,259	86,234
Placer County, California	368,317	3,491	1,847	9,455	10,803	10,208	3,040	3,435	8,144	10,286	10,384
Riverside County, California	2,295,368	15,732	17,477	69,980	69,629	79,777	12,656	16,525	62,613	71,783	71,988
Sacramento County, California	1,454,167	10,068	12,020	36,543	43,845	43,042	11,827	9,856	38,497	40,622	39,255
San Bernardino County, California	2,054,506	13,835	14,609	60,809	67,960	72,958	17,053	16,426	61,247	62,007	67,087
San Diego County, California	3,188,012	26,894	21,370	77,769	84,132	87,896	25,253	23,731	72,174	78,734	79,511
San Francisco County, California	844,623	5,340	4,216	11,787	11,526	11,697	6,157	4,389	10,772	11,977	11,217
San Joaquin County, California	705,043	4,946	7,249	21,978	24,027	22,592	5,470	6,885	22,630	20,457	23,415
San Luis Obispo County, California	274,685	1,632	981	5,848	5,773	5,573	1,356	1,158	5,158	6,753	5,570
San Mateo County, California	737,655	6,074	4,744	18,925	19,132	18,741	7,201	4,535	16,020	19,732	16,768
Santa Barbara County, California	429,024	3,943	2,599	11,976	10,702	11,076	3,460	2,655	10,397	10,499	10,803
Santa Clara County, California	1,850,653	17,654	14,059	48,616	49,892	49,650	17,081	10,605	46,644	48,880	48,359
Santa Cruz County, California	266,174	1,421	981	6,519	5,823	6,880	1,666	1,447	5,535	5,415	6,773
Shasta County, California	172,417	1,263	1,086	3,711	5,153	4,964	894	1,607	4,150	4,236	3,319
Solano County, California	424,338	2,974	2,725	9,550	10,852	12,837	2,877	2,112	10,442	10,337	11,446
Sonoma County, California	488,063	3,294	4,341	9,795	10,608	12,582	2,653	2,468	10,532	12,484	10,870
Stanislaus County, California	518,319	3,821	3,856	14,252	18,747	17,150	4,620	4,480	16,031	16,175	17,743
Sutter County, California	92,881	571	1,174	2,607	3,394	3,276	281	561	3,000	2,746	3,167
Tulare County, California	437,827	3,022	4,224	17,331	15,286	16,180	4,745	5,049	13,189	16,659	16,660
Ventura County, California	820,378	6,931	6,445	22,192	24,332	24,813	6,855	6,496	21,912	20,136	25,727
Yolo County, California	209,494	1,365	2,026	4,865	4,861	5,279	2,115	1,010	5,238	5,423	4,415
Yuba County, California	72,603	1,123	638	2,835	2,472	1,497	1,428	539	2,174	2,054	1,703
COLORADO											
Adams County, Colorado	476,841	2,620	5,376	14,284	16,059	15,147	3,930	3,588	14,848	15,845	14,562
Arapahoe County, Colorado	613,003	5,095	4,983	18,363	17,019	18,230	4,672	4,127	17,021	16,677	15,841
Boulder County, Colorado	313,388	2,327	1,770	7,934	6,873	7,452	3,098	1,400	6,868	7,753	8,154
Broomfield County, Colorado	64,441	691	164	1,577	2,059	1,950	495	510	1,981	1,889	1,841
Denver County, Colorado	663,517	5,281	4,685	17,051	14,352	13,107	4,037	3,748	15,587	15,050	11,685
Douglas County, Colorado	318,591	3,302	2,588	11,151	11,908	11,001	3,521	2,275	10,226	11,265	10,589
El Paso County, Colorado	660,895	5,035	4,942	20,556	18,560	19,345	5,123	4,581	19,533	17,084	18,134
Jefferson County, Colorado	552,608	5,111	3,062	13,906	12,647	14,494	4,003	2,683	13,124	12,723	14,189
Larimer County, Colorado	328,801	2,219	1,217	8,092	8,376	8,737	1,637	2,025	7,620	7,268	6,291
Mesa County, Colorado	145,122	845	927	4,493	3,338	4,239	654	756	3,917	3,078	3,634
Pueblo County, Colorado	159,883	936	1,256	4,342	4,336	4,260	1,323	930	4,484	3,585	4,305
Weld County, Colorado	281,915	3,272	1,436	10,993	7,460	9,122	2,446	2,015	9,331	8,112	7,765
CONNECTICUT											
Fairfield County, Connecticut	912,840	8,981	7,463	23,184	26,342	31,511	7,487	5,914	25,279	24,872	27,770
Hartford County, Connecticut	864,715	7,631	4,242	20,366	22,998	25,929	7,652	4,340	21,152	22,631	23,055
Litchfield County, Connecticut	177,631	1,147	781	3,981	4,788	4,702	1,006	618	2,681	4,774	4,334
Middlesex County, Connecticut	158,799	1,042	994	3,287	3,627	4,254	772	537	2,280	4,797	3,780
New Haven County, Connecticut	832,287	6,831	5,496	19,818	21,844	22,784	5,847	4,987	17,055	21,634	21,878
New London County, Connecticut	262,054	2,146	1,218	6,779	6,120	6,708	2,510	1,631	5,333	6,492	6,662
Tolland County, Connecticut	147,771	1,989	572	3,285	2,974	3,411	953	823	2,501	3,057	3,138
Windham County, Connecticut	112,954	944	752	1,652	2,479	3,630	682	850	3,031	2,861	2,388
DELAWARE											
Kent County, Delaware	166,967	1,690	861	4,517	4,775	4,841	837	1,992	4,215	3,994	4,329
New Castle County, Delaware	539,984	5,425	3,231	12,270	14,756	14,892	4,645	3,946	12,436	15,642	12,829
Sussex County, Delaware	212,268	859	1,248	4,832	4,758	4,968	841	833	4,589	3,563	5,898
DISTRICT OF COLUMBIA											
District of Columbia, District of Columbia	654,704	8,060	4,640	13,758	9,818	11,984	6,695	3,132	13,431	10,717	12,100
FLORIDA											
Alachua County, Florida	253,962	2,094	893	6,427	4,093	5,053	2,040	581	5,596	4,513	4,419
Bay County, Florida	175,874	1,283	1,145	5,162	2,828	5,381	910	814	5,889	3,421	3,577
Brevard County, Florida	563,002	4,238	3,614	11,308	12,115	13,784	4,565	3,182	10,531	12,384	13,961
Broward County, Florida	1,843,920	16,040	12,287	45,284	45,753	50,362	13,308	9,859	41,513	49,364	50,436
Charlotte County, Florida	175,897	798	461	2,413	3,545	3,813	599	427	2,678	1,942	2,939
Citrus County, Florida	140,556	906	593	2,337	3,030	2,723	431	554	1,766	2,186	2,763
Clay County, Florida	201,908	1,002	2,156	5,347	5,282	6,469	1,191	781	6,806	6,545	4,703
Collier County, Florida	355,095	1,730	1,994	6,315	7,452	7,305	1,570	1,533	7,665	7,012	8,092
Duval County, Florida	886,693	9,070	4,619	26,042	22,216	22,040	6,164	6,560	23,187	20,950	22,819
Escambia County, Florida	303,882	1,847	1,854	8,448	7,769	7,409	2,227	1,183	6,206	8,454	8,047

Table C-4. Primary and Secondary School Enrollment, by Sex and Selected Counties, 2016—*Continued*

(Number.)

State/County	Population 3 years and over	Male Nursery school, Pre-school	Male Kindergarten	Male Grades 1 to 4	Male Grades 5 to 8	Male Grades 9 to 12	Female Nursery school, Pre-school	Female Kindergarten	Female Grades 1 to 4	Female Grades 5 to 8	Female Grades 9 to 12
FLORIDA—*(Continued)*											
Hernando County, Florida	178,219	638	893	4,693	3,868	4,563	1,019	431	3,706	4,163	4,028
Hillsborough County, Florida	1,321,324	12,364	9,280	36,527	35,381	37,996	9,623	9,222	33,467	34,111	33,499
Indian River County, Florida	148,860	1,321	901	2,511	2,745	3,839	413	181	2,760	4,012	4,446
Lake County, Florida	325,357	1,767	2,035	6,589	8,794	8,106	1,158	2,034	6,141	8,745	7,940
Lee County, Florida	700,892	3,761	3,059	14,527	17,209	14,334	3,793	3,510	11,769	17,927	14,039
Leon County, Florida	278,674	2,698	2,062	4,805	6,805	5,520	2,631	1,200	6,063	6,666	5,508
Manatee County, Florida	364,188	2,012	2,911	7,620	7,659	7,661	1,865	2,720	7,053	8,136	8,437
Marion County, Florida	338,680	1,161	1,556	7,130	9,222	8,146	1,312	1,337	7,391	6,308	7,367
Martin County, Florida	154,536	648	721	3,349	3,166	3,220	993	392	2,917	2,531	4,276
Miami-Dade County, Florida	2,617,135	21,369	16,937	61,554	61,871	65,484	22,927	17,310	57,961	57,648	62,608
Nassau County, Florida	78,583	866	330	2,561	1,414	1,852	423	284	1,952	1,838	1,896
Okaloosa County, Florida	191,636	1,585	1,467	4,527	4,853	4,852	1,588	1,382	4,112	4,521	4,820
Orange County, Florida	1,265,040	13,162	8,590	35,092	33,027	30,647	8,870	7,623	31,967	31,645	33,999
Osceola County, Florida	323,634	2,995	2,361	7,683	8,389	8,835	1,220	2,050	8,464	9,768	10,736
Palm Beach County, Florida	1,399,821	11,152	6,346	32,369	31,664	37,426	9,708	8,237	31,381	28,978	33,549
Pasco County, Florida	495,995	3,374	2,439	12,725	11,670	12,972	2,710	2,735	10,730	12,140	11,623
Pinellas County, Florida	935,587	5,548	4,214	16,597	17,957	19,710	5,571	5,387	15,636	17,564	19,519
Polk County, Florida	642,052	3,958	5,105	16,675	16,903	17,374	4,335	3,948	15,901	16,540	18,027
Putnam County, Florida	70,124	398	558	2,417	1,849	2,408	378	118	1,508	2,113	1,240
St. Johns County, Florida	228,929	2,482	2,060	4,853	8,126	6,370	2,101	1,108	5,659	6,500	7,001
St. Lucie County, Florida	298,534	1,341	1,841	7,551	7,048	7,603	2,035	1,809	7,025	5,698	8,665
Santa Rosa County, Florida	165,460	867	605	4,519	5,238	5,306	2,198	798	4,448	3,791	4,236
Sarasota County, Florida	404,737	1,582	1,933	6,905	9,412	7,806	1,025	1,007	7,179	5,672	8,432
Seminole County, Florida	441,213	3,151	2,697	10,970	10,956	12,590	4,248	2,838	12,495	8,469	11,371
Volusia County, Florida	515,379	2,891	2,069	12,166	10,076	13,230	2,934	3,535	9,120	10,054	10,554
GEORGIA											
Barrow County, Georgia	74,083	483	556	2,659	2,800	2,691	1,036	530	2,934	1,766	2,100
Bibb County, Georgia	146,181	1,298	979	4,209	3,887	4,583	1,187	1,256	4,195	3,989	3,611
Bulloch County, Georgia	72,100	506	584	1,375	1,775	1,597	181	94	1,819	1,760	2,668
Carroll County, Georgia	112,916	965	331	2,646	4,299	4,271	657	1,245	2,186	3,403	3,088
Chatham County, Georgia	276,829	2,976	1,475	8,400	6,639	7,319	2,495	1,875	6,304	6,538	5,909
Cherokee County, Georgia	233,160	2,765	1,218	7,046	8,338	8,313	2,538	752	7,220	6,878	6,150
Clarke County, Georgia	118,745	874	1,344	1,984	2,093	1,927	662	819	2,108	2,036	1,190
Clayton County, Georgia	266,120	2,769	2,191	8,477	8,617	8,004	3,253	1,977	9,620	7,856	8,968
Cobb County, Georgia	717,291	7,721	5,225	19,925	19,995	20,479	6,512	5,803	19,531	20,648	19,656
Columbia County, Georgia	141,149	783	1,560	3,753	4,333	4,123	1,164	1,268	3,835	3,619	4,793
Coweta County, Georgia	135,505	1,166	1,000	4,715	4,393	4,032	852	712	3,552	4,524	4,712
DeKalb County, Georgia	709,575	7,308	4,414	20,967	18,798	18,768	7,034	5,279	19,631	18,959	17,791
Dougherty County, Georgia	86,479	1,119	167	2,579	3,031	2,938	654	517	1,910	3,018	2,815
Douglas County, Georgia	136,633	1,253	825	4,373	4,087	5,191	718	1,869	3,678	4,709	4,067
Fayette County, Georgia	108,908	985	598	3,969	2,687	3,736	488	547	2,121	4,464	3,794
Floyd County, Georgia	94,165	646	1,013	1,505	3,303	2,954	688	684	2,302	3,019	3,025
Forsyth County, Georgia	213,677	2,985	1,440	6,981	8,381	7,479	2,543	1,520	7,272	7,601	7,260
Fulton County, Georgia	985,405	9,479	6,744	24,381	28,599	26,163	8,279	7,680	24,483	24,495	26,665
Glynn County, Georgia	81,795	682	895	2,841	1,588	2,253	902	600	2,196	2,442	1,659
Gwinnett County, Georgia	872,484	7,564	6,309	27,411	30,367	31,301	7,013	4,849	27,950	30,874	30,965
Hall County, Georgia	189,083	1,164	1,652	5,951	6,466	4,899	1,265	791	6,434	5,516	5,857
Henry County, Georgia	214,787	1,694	1,164	8,042	7,039	8,491	1,951	2,364	4,439	7,496	8,419
Houston County, Georgia	146,026	1,815	1,930	4,118	4,523	3,986	1,211	1,610	4,889	4,263	3,639
Liberty County, Georgia	58,833	822	603	1,763	2,305	2,261	309	471	1,466	2,496	1,390
Lowndes County, Georgia	109,320	762	271	3,965	2,701	3,158	779	828	3,156	3,004	2,382
Muscogee County, Georgia	189,423	2,770	1,430	5,244	5,331	6,255	1,474	850	6,153	5,383	4,305
Newton County, Georgia	102,597	352	805	4,236	2,739	3,127	1,477	358	3,913	3,161	3,194
Paulding County, Georgia	149,299	724	1,009	4,509	5,834	4,729	485	1,175	4,755	5,027	5,293
Richmond County, Georgia	193,988	1,644	998	6,657	4,852	4,882	1,436	1,064	5,140	5,280	5,224
Rockdale County, Georgia	85,741	272	267	3,405	2,588	2,978	193	484	3,145	1,878	3,343
Troup County, Georgia	67,344	1,094	360	1,869	2,451	3,146	1,131	527	1,649	2,125	1,259
Walker County, Georgia	65,585	1,689	768	1,111	1,412	2,577	118	171	2,142	1,432	1,918
Walton County, Georgia	87,212	897	782	3,064	2,724	2,820	699	99	2,751	2,350	3,262
HAWAII											
Hawaii County, Hawaii	192,048	1,205	1,239	4,947	4,473	4,206	1,339	1,147	4,895	4,548	4,777
Honolulu County, Hawaii	954,072	7,994	5,864	21,561	24,651	22,433	9,752	5,356	18,574	22,606	22,676
Kauai County, Hawaii	69,165	156	353	1,944	1,370	1,701	1,026	297	1,385	2,139	909
Maui County, Hawaii	159,502	1,346	1,130	4,070	3,818	3,442	810	859	3,676	4,099	2,857
IDAHO											
Ada County, Idaho	429,407	3,923	2,185	13,134	12,987	12,596	3,977	2,496	12,210	12,490	11,719
Bannock County, Idaho	81,059	689	618	1,859	3,036	2,470	791	615	2,691	1,989	2,886
Bonneville County, Idaho	107,257	1,165	2,219	3,447	4,085	3,779	1,046	830	4,004	4,130	3,429

Table C-4. Primary and Secondary School Enrollment, by Sex and Selected Counties, 2016—Continued

(Number.)

State/County	Population 3 years and over	Male Nursery school, Preschool	Male Kindergarten	Male Grades 1 to 4	Male Grades 5 to 8	Male Grades 9 to 12	Female Nursery school, Preschool	Female Kindergarten	Female Grades 1 to 4	Female Grades 5 to 8	Female Grades 9 to 12
IDAHO—(*Continued*)											
Canyon County, Idaho	202,514	912	2,379	7,710	6,014	6,533	887	1,660	6,280	7,691	6,195
Kootenai County, Idaho	148,125	941	504	5,172	3,698	4,325	735	862	3,944	3,432	4,052
Twin Falls County, Idaho	79,614	602	416	2,505	2,507	2,328	822	628	2,584	2,579	2,243
ILLINOIS											
Adams County, Illinois	64,070	381	663	1,647	2,193	1,384	845	243	1,680	1,272	1,869
Champaign County, Illinois	201,819	1,782	1,487	4,187	3,970	4,161	1,528	965	4,701	4,615	3,382
Cook County, Illinois	5,006,199	49,427	36,964	127,260	131,840	132,937	45,191	30,522	125,300	124,456	131,705
DeKalb County, Illinois	100,934	1,013	464	3,595	2,228	3,053	464	405	2,417	2,408	3,377
DuPage County, Illinois	896,733	8,673	4,948	25,842	23,894	26,855	9,095	6,720	24,270	22,726	24,361
Kane County, Illinois	512,336	5,628	3,781	14,225	17,349	18,652	4,232	4,360	12,950	17,385	18,037
Kankakee County, Illinois	106,125	1,233	1,259	2,777	2,992	3,277	864	552	2,931	3,090	2,665
Kendall County, Illinois	120,167	1,473	184	4,883	4,760	3,245	1,225	766	3,595	4,859	4,173
Lake County, Illinois	679,919	5,919	3,517	21,374	21,396	23,423	6,105	4,387	18,363	21,873	22,234
LaSalle County, Illinois	106,978	871	1,102	2,192	2,675	3,404	950	1,051	2,419	2,259	3,304
McHenry County, Illinois	297,569	2,403	1,376	9,246	9,286	10,699	2,353	1,388	8,692	9,633	9,238
McLean County, Illinois	166,500	1,245	821	5,375	4,037	4,952	930	1,326	4,073	3,624	4,174
Macon County, Illinois	102,422	1,123	967	2,384	2,834	2,423	998	488	2,504	2,685	2,841
Madison County, Illinois	258,225	2,496	748	7,063	7,848	5,787	2,889	1,415	6,667	5,772	6,664
Peoria County, Illinois	177,050	2,383	1,082	5,415	4,692	4,686	1,677	1,244	5,317	3,976	4,911
Rock Island County, Illinois	138,787	924	1,264	2,842	3,875	3,159	944	700	4,362	3,251	3,714
St. Clair County, Illinois	252,571	1,759	1,859	8,640	5,276	7,231	2,081	1,851	6,439	7,296	6,525
Sangamon County, Illinois	191,287	2,559	1,235	5,122	5,107	4,882	1,222	1,574	5,045	4,953	5,748
Tazewell County, Illinois	129,977	1,318	916	3,896	2,697	3,700	1,045	643	3,119	3,420	3,846
Vermilion County, Illinois	75,009	315	467	2,454	1,689	2,271	736	441	1,720	2,376	2,310
Will County, Illinois	664,864	6,119	4,923	19,051	22,534	24,797	4,847	3,370	20,996	20,971	22,444
Williamson County, Illinois	64,923	560	386	1,553	1,575	1,529	341	307	929	2,503	1,530
Winnebago County, Illinois	275,326	2,644	2,831	8,486	6,453	8,662	2,098	970	6,991	7,988	7,287
INDIANA											
Allen County, Indiana	354,345	2,948	2,710	10,650	10,569	10,286	3,329	1,917	9,817	9,753	11,253
Bartholomew County, Indiana	78,659	883	720	2,351	1,861	3,018	637	254	2,157	1,319	2,921
Clark County, Indiana	111,586	990	377	3,610	2,915	2,821	741	977	3,914	1,980	3,402
Delaware County, Indiana	111,717	234	678	2,425	2,378	3,085	327	1,041	1,877	2,154	2,382
Elkhart County, Indiana	195,204	1,676	1,759	7,206	5,066	6,411	1,583	2,099	5,580	7,502	5,856
Floyd County, Indiana	74,306	637	324	1,748	2,518	2,228	812	317	2,524	1,733	2,101
Grant County, Indiana	65,575	1,197	443	1,401	1,593	1,586	725	330	1,291	1,479	1,300
Hamilton County, Indiana	303,720	3,299	1,489	10,436	10,729	10,405	2,891	2,767	9,109	10,228	10,610
Hancock County, Indiana	70,980	230	965	1,984	1,622	2,712	515	646	1,751	1,874	2,016
Hendricks County, Indiana	154,387	997	781	3,640	5,502	5,348	2,267	730	5,115	4,605	5,431
Howard County, Indiana	79,949	727	510	2,368	2,444	2,058	632	327	1,960	2,426	2,445
Johnson County, Indiana	147,231	1,529	1,599	3,974	3,365	4,343	1,109	2,396	5,204	3,088	3,916
Kosciusko County, Indiana	76,008	593	1,120	1,468	1,904	2,402	494	265	2,440	2,475	1,651
Lake County, Indiana	468,180	2,897	1,565	15,792	13,075	14,060	3,624	3,475	13,108	12,521	14,199
LaPorte County, Indiana	106,828	875	538	2,909	2,958	3,794	283	653	1,897	3,216	2,577
Madison County, Indiana	124,745	776	745	3,657	3,577	3,447	870	1,130	2,539	3,394	2,682
Marion County, Indiana	898,979	10,168	7,897	26,804	24,356	24,315	7,143	7,592	27,121	24,925	24,476
Monroe County, Indiana	142,700	1,620	491	2,506	2,552	2,557	2,116	468	2,337	2,294	2,217
Morgan County, Indiana	67,539	311	432	2,275	1,731	1,994	825	301	1,331	1,825	2,315
Porter County, Indiana	162,772	807	1,583	4,564	4,777	4,007	1,159	1,034	4,459	4,010	4,781
St. Joseph County, Indiana	258,490	1,716	1,836	7,302	8,087	7,104	2,128	1,845	6,573	8,155	7,064
Tippecanoe County, Indiana	180,850	1,280	1,600	4,295	4,889	2,922	1,848	615	4,993	3,053	3,304
Vanderburgh County, Indiana	175,467	1,328	1,073	4,940	4,447	4,478	819	763	4,548	4,254	4,223
Vigo County, Indiana	104,404	716	776	3,002	1,954	2,775	602	405	3,075	2,266	1,665
Wayne County, Indiana	64,856	600	560	1,370	1,527	1,573	681	357	1,869	1,339	1,301
IOWA											
Black Hawk County, Iowa	128,168	715	1,300	3,609	3,140	2,584	625	707	3,269	2,441	2,502
Dallas County, Iowa	80,693	1,196	1,207	2,393	2,378	2,261	1,287	402	3,248	2,875	2,110
Dubuque County, Iowa	93,136	1,221	620	2,129	3,095	2,653	1,264	529	2,395	2,177	2,144
Johnson County, Iowa	140,739	900	352	4,161	3,003	2,640	1,205	853	3,232	3,037	3,105
Linn County, Iowa	212,275	1,616	1,491	5,661	6,161	5,431	1,678	1,989	5,465	6,018	5,109
Polk County, Iowa	454,313	5,128	4,145	14,748	11,114	12,488	4,837	2,731	11,592	14,370	13,199
Pottawattamie County, Iowa	90,277	670	639	2,144	3,015	2,855	647	802	2,070	2,338	2,537
Scott County, Iowa	165,617	1,314	1,690	4,420	4,627	4,939	1,783	1,115	4,714	4,636	3,747
Story County, Iowa	94,562	244	489	2,062	1,533	2,203	465	320	1,488	2,186	1,572
Woodbury County, Iowa	97,956	1,261	306	3,250	2,901	2,706	643	319	2,925	2,807	3,222
KANSAS											
Butler County, Kansas	64,804	434	786	1,438	2,196	2,004	249	508	1,659	2,461	1,833
Douglas County, Kansas	115,600	1,714	326	1,333	2,883	2,856	1,139	611	2,743	1,637	2,281

Table C-4. Primary and Secondary School Enrollment, by Sex and Selected Counties, 2016—*Continued*

(Number.)

State/County	Population 3 years and over	Male — Nursery school, Pre-school	Male — Kindergarten	Male — Grades 1 to 4	Male — Grades 5 to 8	Male — Grades 9 to 12	Female — Nursery school, Pre-school	Female — Kindergarten	Female — Grades 1 to 4	Female — Grades 5 to 8	Female — Grades 9 to 12
KANSAS—*(Continued)*											
Johnson County, Kansas	562,453	6,790	4,133	16,128	17,482	17,028	5,230	4,130	15,091	16,170	16,402
Leavenworth County, Kansas	76,615	318	1,044	2,271	2,295	3,577	670	548	1,881	1,996	1,027
Riley County, Kansas	70,040	749	296	989	1,062	1,129	364	226	1,525	641	623
Sedgwick County, Kansas	490,881	5,129	3,671	15,844	13,899	14,817	4,111	3,011	15,433	14,588	15,394
Shawnee County, Kansas	171,743	1,590	1,035	4,723	5,176	4,671	1,719	1,263	4,956	3,855	4,107
Wyandotte County, Kansas	155,531	1,426	751	5,399	6,209	3,898	752	1,076	4,601	5,390	5,248
KENTUCKY											
Boone County, Kentucky	124,068	2,055	868	3,724	3,818	4,830	781	1,087	3,501	4,536	3,848
Bullitt County, Kentucky	76,894	569	327	2,948	1,811	2,305	279	604	2,069	1,898	1,784
Campbell County, Kentucky	89,349	761	774	2,439	1,959	2,163	727	828	2,270	1,605	2,254
Christian County, Kentucky	68,012	969	637	2,262	1,917	1,802	700	366	1,805	2,247	1,202
Daviess County, Kentucky	96,166	867	890	2,641	2,575	2,548	1,216	82	3,072	2,528	3,668
Fayette County, Kentucky	307,270	2,729	2,352	8,136	6,898	6,536	2,151	2,112	7,371	7,214	6,270
Hardin County, Kentucky	102,864	668	417	2,352	4,177	3,548	804	904	2,887	3,042	2,387
Jefferson County, Kentucky	734,419	4,447	5,123	21,019	18,537	18,421	5,637	3,006	19,077	19,082	18,489
Kenton County, Kentucky	158,681	2,445	990	4,630	4,476	4,370	798	1,152	5,508	3,405	4,254
Madison County, Kentucky	87,353	640	1,042	2,090	1,877	2,183	375	854	1,974	1,715	1,858
Oldham County, Kentucky	63,665	773	235	1,196	2,672	3,023	403	345	2,440	1,978	2,174
Warren County, Kentucky	120,770	544	329	3,283	3,187	3,100	1,005	567	2,710	3,397	2,878
LOUISIANA											
Ascension Parish, Louisiana	117,758	1,574	485	5,337	3,829	4,114	1,101	472	4,459	2,370	2,430
Bossier Parish, Louisiana	120,092	1,108	1,107	3,622	3,275	3,740	1,307	734	3,664	3,214	2,127
Caddo Parish, Louisiana	236,724	2,269	1,823	5,851	7,239	5,863	1,728	981	6,305	7,003	6,407
Calcasieu Parish, Louisiana	191,578	1,294	1,493	7,286	4,467	6,006	1,832	1,729	5,104	4,988	4,949
East Baton Rouge Parish, Louisiana .	429,272	3,563	2,280	12,938	10,996	10,898	4,435	2,208	11,283	11,474	10,659
Jefferson Parish, Louisiana	419,086	2,515	2,403	10,198	11,646	11,366	3,329	2,865	11,735	9,204	9,816
Lafayette Parish, Louisiana	231,764	1,822	663	6,364	6,051	6,764	3,329	1,023	6,871	4,625	6,759
Lafourche Parish, Louisiana	94,511	140	573	1,972	4,251	2,519	461	369	2,524	3,162	3,224
Livingston Parish, Louisiana	134,182	1,050	1,264	4,499	4,730	5,255	901	802	5,060	3,096	3,924
Orleans Parish, Louisiana	376,727	3,011	1,830	9,953	8,702	8,406	3,426	2,947	9,309	7,895	8,000
Ouachita Parish, Louisiana	149,573	1,526	1,882	3,849	5,221	3,496	942	567	4,923	3,283	5,277
Rapides Parish, Louisiana	126,987	716	960	3,924	3,939	4,370	1,053	880	2,857	4,335	3,720
St. Landry Parish, Louisiana	79,495	1,152	1,096	1,956	2,749	2,666	364	567	2,779	2,087	2,707
St. Tammany Parish, Louisiana	245,655	2,209	1,808	6,349	7,824	8,737	3,443	831	6,379	7,857	8,038
Tangipahoa Parish, Louisiana	125,098	1,670	1,007	2,719	3,795	3,019	1,662	874	4,642	1,915	3,451
Terrebonne Parish, Louisiana	107,691	781	1,048	2,457	3,843	3,545	727	894	4,322	2,635	2,791
MAINE											
Androscoggin County, Maine	104,271	673	430	3,025	2,453	2,418	1,224	753	2,840	1,677	3,246
Aroostook County, Maine	65,975	205	539	1,146	1,550	1,486	466	423	1,556	1,083	1,740
Cumberland County, Maine	284,467	3,462	1,742	7,843	4,949	7,240	2,281	1,010	6,559	5,842	6,072
Kennebec County, Maine	117,515	851	814	2,804	2,731	3,553	944	867	2,176	2,305	2,404
Penobscot County, Maine	147,413	1,337	1,362	3,176	2,666	3,723	677	600	3,166	3,064	2,685
York County, Maine	195,868	684	912	3,266	5,895	6,191	607	820	3,805	5,397	4,710
MARYLAND											
Allegany County, Maryland	70,073	646	556	1,351	1,200	1,868	262	260	1,444	1,240	1,358
Anne Arundel County, Maryland	548,534	4,845	4,078	13,454	14,426	14,383	5,902	3,110	13,231	14,732	14,152
Baltimore County, Maryland	801,062	5,568	4,560	21,089	18,058	20,847	6,121	4,067	18,944	19,804	20,049
Calvert County, Maryland	88,416	677	408	3,201	2,317	3,662	607	420	2,476	2,522	2,909
Carroll County, Maryland	162,779	1,497	976	3,861	4,847	4,920	1,436	859	3,473	4,971	4,585
Cecil County, Maryland	99,537	1,022	1,174	2,969	2,431	2,402	447	271	2,260	3,221	3,278
Charles County, Maryland	152,221	1,223	1,157	3,969	5,654	3,963	998	818	4,385	4,735	3,632
Frederick County, Maryland	239,431	2,464	1,121	6,732	7,065	8,030	2,249	2,104	6,603	6,186	6,542
Harford County, Maryland	242,243	2,591	1,712	5,897	6,234	7,361	1,288	1,515	5,209	7,448	6,060
Howard County, Maryland	306,604	3,191	1,693	9,089	10,193	9,539	3,565	1,211	8,536	10,117	8,832
Montgomery County, Maryland	1,002,211	8,818	6,099	29,161	26,862	28,883	7,895	6,572	27,289	24,169	28,284
Prince George's County, Maryland	873,327	5,773	5,883	23,739	21,676	22,721	5,878	5,732	25,389	18,880	18,921
St. Mary's County, Maryland	108,651	683	453	2,910	3,590	2,858	933	433	3,003	3,196	3,481
Washington County, Maryland	145,999	1,134	1,120	3,670	3,995	4,305	1,135	485	4,099	3,463	3,513
Wicomico County, Maryland	98,877	331	642	3,619	2,323	3,132	520	808	1,769	2,797	2,497
Baltimore city, Maryland	591,817	4,243	3,097	15,485	13,263	14,121	5,920	4,248	12,232	14,532	12,631
MASSACHUSETTS											
Barnstable County, Massachusetts ...	209,334	1,543	439	3,583	4,363	4,152	1,835	2,053	3,187	3,745	3,835

Table C-4. Primary and Secondary School Enrollment, by Sex and Selected Counties, 2016—*Continued*

(Number.)

State/County	Population 3 years and over	Male Nursery school, Pre-school	Male Kindergarten	Male Grades 1 to 4	Male Grades 5 to 8	Male Grades 9 to 12	Female Nursery school, Pre-school	Female Kindergarten	Female Grades 1 to 4	Female Grades 5 to 8	Female Grades 9 to 12
MASSACHUSETTS—*(Continued)*											
Berkshire County, Massachusetts	124,230	622	259	3,124	3,073	2,831	983	612	2,707	2,438	2,885
Bristol County, Massachusetts..........	543,421	6,109	3,469	13,139	13,716	16,318	4,410	3,404	12,275	12,349	13,334
Essex County, Massachusetts..........	754,026	4,740	4,568	19,831	20,742	20,468	5,219	4,792	16,137	20,248	20,273
Franklin County, Massachusetts........	68,489	672	271	1,370	1,437	1,877	349	73	1,256	1,644	1,455
Hampden County, Massachusetts.....	453,071	2,889	3,237	12,526	10,807	14,143	3,838	3,375	9,570	11,678	13,408
Hampshire County, Massachusetts ...	158,899	874	1,352	2,453	3,388	2,431	792	682	3,125	2,336	2,675
Middlesex County, Massachusetts ...	1,538,767	16,187	7,652	35,338	38,663	41,326	14,358	8,374	33,976	35,321	38,632
Norfolk County, Massachusetts	677,505	8,073	3,578	16,212	18,553	19,867	5,718	3,482	16,225	17,601	18,932
Plymouth County, Massachusetts.....	496,259	4,587	2,817	12,139	13,562	17,161	4,005	2,528	10,574	14,091	15,734
Suffolk County, Massachusetts.........	758,459	5,114	5,411	12,385	15,676	15,788	3,269	4,158	15,530	13,210	15,089
Worcester County, Massachusetts....	794,430	6,817	6,142	17,500	20,915	23,314	6,309	4,865	20,428	19,203	21,863
MICHIGAN											
Allegan County, Michigan..................	111,023	690	535	3,200	3,336	3,478	688	708	2,790	3,309	3,066
Bay County, Michigan	101,785	731	503	2,763	2,161	2,988	664	955	2,090	1,964	2,292
Berrien County, Michigan..................	148,369	1,057	1,006	4,159	3,628	4,340	971	1,351	3,728	3,672	3,861
Calhoun County, Michigan	129,170	691	631	2,836	3,873	3,029	659	982	3,007	3,367	4,540
Clinton County, Michigan..................	75,683	824	801	2,352	1,679	2,043	381	453	1,923	2,052	2,348
Eaton County, Michigan	105,821	400	600	2,286	3,041	3,118	594	604	2,773	2,504	2,465
Genesee County, Michigan...............	394,823	3,836	3,652	11,191	10,314	10,963	3,658	2,326	10,100	10,687	11,649
Grand Traverse County, Michigan	88,915	522	823	2,145	2,056	1,936	387	774	1,617	2,698	2,328
Ingham County, Michigan..................	278,305	2,253	1,652	6,371	6,851	5,282	1,650	1,414	6,432	7,595	5,939
Isabella County, Michigan.................	69,530	348	246	1,643	1,613	1,456	354	159	1,764	1,364	1,507
Jackson County, Michigan.................	153,592	913	1,227	2,916	5,058	4,527	1,730	845	4,431	2,957	3,621
Kalamazoo County, Michigan	252,284	1,865	1,473	4,938	7,341	6,531	2,483	1,352	6,488	6,265	6,492
Kent County, Michigan......................	617,061	5,203	5,327	16,072	18,896	18,300	6,371	4,647	18,366	16,318	17,109
Lapeer County, Michigan...................	85,269	634	946	2,075	2,038	2,346	425	530	1,477	2,433	2,510
Lenawee County, Michigan	95,684	973	796	1,919	2,847	2,995	609	640	2,587	1,854	2,794
Livingston County, Michigan.............	182,148	1,092	1,468	3,840	5,518	5,579	1,123	1,189	4,441	3,778	6,389
Macomb County, Michigan	837,430	6,531	5,939	19,597	21,680	25,496	5,654	4,340	21,726	20,391	20,641
Marquette County, Michigan.............	64,710	490	294	1,398	1,390	1,206	701	74	1,321	1,380	1,311
Midland County, Michigan.................	80,784	619	672	2,275	1,965	2,212	227	464	1,585	2,094	2,443
Monroe County, Michigan.................	144,409	1,039	792	3,691	4,086	4,228	1,023	868	3,372	3,917	4,429
Muskegon County, Michigan.............	167,408	1,395	1,030	4,834	4,136	5,406	1,176	978	3,655	5,072	4,415
Oakland County, Michigan................	1,203,367	10,068	7,185	29,085	29,702	36,776	9,896	5,346	28,676	31,203	32,866
Ottawa County, Michigan	271,951	2,244	1,835	8,497	8,145	7,785	1,696	2,471	7,250	7,821	7,974
Saginaw County, Michigan...............	185,769	1,659	776	4,364	5,199	6,326	1,543	699	5,304	4,295	3,496
St. Clair County, Michigan................	154,912	845	575	3,725	4,410	4,904	1,127	944	3,363	4,404	3,945
Shiawassee County, Michigan..........	66,449	461	393	1,681	1,333	2,086	392	215	1,548	1,943	1,863
Van Buren County, Michigan............	72,365	410	410	1,891	2,582	2,717	639	508	1,419	2,020	2,189
Washtenaw County, Michigan	353,292	2,332	1,804	7,422	8,693	9,024	2,527	1,924	8,078	7,185	8,235
Wayne County, Michigan..................	1,682,554	13,129	13,352	47,142	44,520	50,179	14,108	10,234	43,872	45,233	48,790
MINNESOTA											
Anoka County, Minnesota	332,802	3,249	2,237	8,503	10,088	10,688	2,978	1,937	9,335	8,711	10,153
Blue Earth County, Minnesota	64,448	625	559	778	1,535	1,613	424	163	1,291	1,196	1,473
Carver County, Minnesota................	96,575	1,430	611	2,840	3,493	3,586	617	1,229	3,333	2,694	3,285
Dakota County, Minnesota	402,052	4,234	3,008	10,820	12,504	12,903	2,410	2,461	9,653	12,868	11,574
Hennepin County, Minnesota	1,182,974	10,984	7,139	31,234	30,081	30,014	10,110	6,795	31,741	27,654	29,642
Olmsted County, Minnesota	147,046	1,574	1,068	3,845	4,186	3,755	1,547	483	4,452	4,371	3,939
Ramsey County, Minnesota..............	519,006	3,729	4,295	13,447	14,367	13,854	4,957	3,356	14,043	12,500	12,549
Rice County, Minnesota	63,352	633	414	2,088	1,372	1,246	315	743	1,367	1,631	1,497
St. Louis County, Minnesota.............	193,962	1,204	881	3,512	4,853	4,758	843	1,515	3,537	4,483	4,112
Scott County, Minnesota..................	138,046	1,717	892	4,490	5,200	4,322	1,094	1,143	4,735	4,630	4,249
Sherburne County, Minnesota..........	89,970	1,075	1,096	2,560	3,295	2,945	668	575	3,968	2,065	2,698
Stearns County, Minnesota	149,592	1,630	1,473	3,768	3,791	3,562	720	1,365	3,471	3,692	4,438
Washington County, Minnesota	243,834	2,354	1,432	7,964	7,607	7,964	2,235	1,837	6,215	7,210	7,439
Wright County, Minnesota.................	127,254	1,222	1,100	4,771	3,856	4,520	951	1,079	3,263	5,168	4,505
MISSISSIPPI											
DeSoto County, Mississippi	169,963	948	1,751	4,701	6,641	5,919	1,707	1,001	5,722	4,922	5,782
Forrest County, Mississippi..............	72,640	237	128	2,876	1,591	1,441	143	223	1,998	3,078	1,477
Harrison County, Mississippi	194,484	1,743	1,251	5,336	6,526	5,464	1,187	652	5,945	5,219	5,272
Hinds County, Mississippi.................	232,037	1,983	1,978	6,395	8,140	5,927	3,293	1,574	7,842	5,357	7,519
Jackson County, Mississippi.............	136,493	767	1,214	3,306	4,000	4,883	1,298	1,518	3,784	4,360	4,565
Jones County, Mississippi.................	65,079	726	204	2,424	2,259	1,275	273	632	1,388	2,104	2,016
Lauderdale County, Mississippi........	75,094	288	1,450	1,954	1,856	2,408	257	571	2,034	2,059	1,479

Table C-4. Primary and Secondary School Enrollment, by Sex and Selected Counties, 2016—*Continued*

(Number.)

State/County	Population 3 years and over	Male					Female				
		Enrolled in school					Enrolled in school				
		Nursery school, Pre-school	Kindergarten	Grades 1 to 4	Grades 5 to 8	Grades 9 to 12	Nursery school, Pre-school	Kindergarten	Grades 1 to 4	Grades 5 to 8	Grades 9 to 12
MISSISSIPPI—*(Continued)*											
Lee County, Mississippi	81,831	486	654	2,757	2,437	2,621	767	621	2,532	2,328	1,948
Madison County, Mississippi	101,851	1,140	932	2,151	3,400	3,761	1,371	1,058	2,436	3,534	2,757
Rankin County, Mississippi	144,612	1,111	1,368	4,396	3,889	3,879	1,551	788	3,569	3,483	4,464
MISSOURI											
Boone County, Missouri	169,865	1,769	869	3,850	4,296	4,278	920	585	3,539	4,826	2,968
Buchanan County, Missouri	85,323	475	393	2,400	2,668	1,837	597	365	2,739	1,844	1,509
Cape Girardeau County, Missouri	76,087	1,169	884	2,020	1,311	1,736	462	517	2,106	1,932	1,617
Cass County, Missouri	99,158	1,068	973	2,709	2,618	2,556	675	914	2,691	3,013	2,916
Christian County, Missouri	81,275	779	966	2,477	2,414	2,721	1,114	447	2,973	2,177	2,347
Clay County, Missouri	231,361	2,621	2,186	6,555	5,862	6,474	2,273	1,644	7,625	5,709	5,776
Cole County, Missouri	74,676	768	179	2,803	1,977	2,906	597	541	1,965	1,876	2,043
Franklin County, Missouri	98,128	442	772	2,032	3,082	2,921	947	713	2,224	2,645	2,557
Greene County, Missouri	279,009	2,935	1,180	6,789	7,103	7,483	1,266	1,499	5,925	6,158	6,663
Jackson County, Missouri	664,224	5,725	5,434	17,376	19,773	16,843	3,977	3,676	18,298	18,189	17,596
Jasper County, Missouri	114,429	877	720	3,521	3,971	2,714	725	1,019	3,018	3,181	3,263
Jefferson County, Missouri	216,758	2,480	1,910	6,819	5,791	6,271	1,634	1,199	6,644	5,816	6,601
Platte County, Missouri	94,973	1,228	941	2,400	1,964	3,006	874	258	2,188	2,354	3,342
St. Charles County, Missouri	377,554	3,113	3,288	10,827	10,088	10,811	4,031	2,522	9,614	11,537	9,650
St. Louis County, Missouri	964,514	9,251	6,105	24,001	27,488	29,519	8,273	4,657	24,764	22,943	26,606
St. Louis city, Missouri	299,793	3,001	1,550	6,479	7,039	6,265	2,173	2,116	6,623	5,427	6,677
MONTANA											
Cascade County, Montana	78,828	466	645	2,009	2,013	1,921	631	509	1,721	2,420	1,779
Flathead County, Montana	94,536	500	738	2,247	2,467	2,573	339	473	3,590	1,727	2,433
Gallatin County, Montana	101,019	961	384	2,049	3,218	2,477	507	917	2,486	2,009	1,893
Lewis and Clark County, Montana	65,104	396	142	1,791	1,625	2,027	219	594	2,305	1,035	1,465
Missoula County, Montana	113,266	775	927	2,485	2,950	2,617	619	694	2,378	2,378	1,984
Yellowstone County, Montana	153,144	1,597	1,686	4,608	3,173	4,198	1,327	560	4,677	4,002	3,464
NEBRASKA											
Douglas County, Nebraska	528,852	4,923	5,151	15,887	15,323	14,522	4,416	3,277	15,230	15,058	15,443
Lancaster County, Nebraska	297,426	2,010	1,661	8,092	8,757	7,930	2,051	1,964	8,304	7,275	7,287
Sarpy County, Nebraska	171,399	1,516	1,687	5,090	6,410	5,538	1,844	1,253	6,489	4,356	5,263
NEVADA											
Clark County, Nevada	2,076,405	14,194	11,936	58,285	57,278	60,447	11,628	14,559	54,150	54,903	57,769
Washoe County, Nevada	437,429	3,631	1,414	11,269	11,588	12,002	2,791	2,548	10,819	11,342	10,370
NEW HAMPSHIRE											
Cheshire County, New Hampshire	73,196	608	791	1,249	1,586	2,012	536	409	1,449	1,261	1,308
Grafton County, New Hampshire	86,729	637	395	1,722	1,220	1,822	522	680	1,019	1,436	1,860
Hillsborough County, New Hampshire	394,594	3,295	1,793	10,100	10,719	11,750	2,530	2,469	9,748	9,448	9,632
Merrimack County, New Hampshire	144,250	1,025	1,054	3,541	2,874	3,535	1,138	745	3,095	2,889	3,270
Rockingham County, New Hampshire	295,606	2,140	1,300	6,404	8,258	8,793	1,934	1,412	7,470	6,640	6,946
Strafford County, New Hampshire	124,096	692	794	2,749	3,324	2,479	338	760	2,344	3,072	2,470
NEW JERSEY											
Atlantic County, New Jersey	262,576	2,281	2,000	6,609	6,855	7,821	2,877	1,171	4,920	8,203	7,577
Bergen County, New Jersey	910,166	9,887	7,555	20,610	23,257	25,928	7,602	6,272	21,268	21,173	25,377
Burlington County, New Jersey	436,647	3,857	1,971	9,896	12,587	12,334	3,769	2,099	10,420	11,419	12,053
Camden County, New Jersey	489,683	3,968	3,273	13,160	14,555	13,039	3,574	2,698	14,333	11,590	12,869
Cape May County, New Jersey	92,443	786	349	1,955	2,517	1,467	327	217	1,781	1,878	1,729
Cumberland County, New Jersey	148,424	1,945	490	3,976	4,431	5,554	948	833	4,212	4,321	3,268
Essex County, New Jersey	765,883	9,076	6,352	22,006	20,462	21,128	9,178	5,224	20,824	20,527	22,095
Gloucester County, New Jersey	282,774	2,342	2,079	7,221	8,452	7,371	2,320	2,641	6,375	6,778	7,909
Hudson County, New Jersey	649,839	8,210	4,980	14,029	13,952	13,619	6,362	3,621	15,223	13,660	12,582
Hunterdon County, New Jersey	121,991	1,124	555	2,908	3,407	5,077	928	365	2,488	3,264	3,397
Mercer County, New Jersey	358,726	2,869	2,555	9,023	9,221	9,382	3,863	2,581	8,223	9,255	9,881
Middlesex County, New Jersey	809,948	6,322	5,419	20,480	21,674	19,936	8,370	5,025	22,167	17,518	19,666
Monmouth County, New Jersey	608,104	6,211	3,051	15,896	16,016	19,434	6,361	3,739	14,305	15,176	17,889
Morris County, New Jersey	483,908	4,835	2,171	12,280	13,973	14,492	4,043	2,972	12,447	12,215	14,377
Ocean County, New Jersey	568,989	5,717	4,208	14,721	17,198	15,478	5,328	4,282	16,019	13,722	15,051
Passaic County, New Jersey	488,561	6,502	4,334	13,781	13,235	14,452	5,689	3,617	13,670	13,408	12,914
Salem County, New Jersey	60,982	679	561	1,870	1,171	1,982	301	255	1,324	1,658	1,590
Somerset County, New Jersey	323,461	2,704	1,594	8,068	9,784	11,010	2,680	1,455	9,036	8,225	9,637
Sussex County, New Jersey	138,551	351	968	3,426	3,468	5,247	1,147	454	2,634	3,627	4,963

Table C-4. Primary and Secondary School Enrollment, by Sex and Selected Counties, 2016—*Continued*

(Number.)

State/County	Population 3 years and over	Male — Nursery school, Pre-school	Male — Kindergarten	Male — Grades 1 to 4	Male — Grades 5 to 8	Male — Grades 9 to 12	Female — Nursery school, Pre-school	Female — Kindergarten	Female — Grades 1 to 4	Female — Grades 5 to 8	Female — Grades 9 to 12
NEW JERSEY—(*Continued*)											
Union County, New Jersey	535,086	6,573	4,055	15,525	13,420	15,671	5,099	3,763	12,394	17,270	14,073
Warren County, New Jersey	103,803	897	1,258	1,923	3,139	2,906	638	429	1,974	2,617	2,864
NEW MEXICO											
Bernalillo County, New Mexico	653,027	4,610	3,683	18,361	17,714	16,446	5,119	4,375	16,338	16,727	16,630
Chaves County, New Mexico	63,254	422	352	2,410	2,165	3,074	187	617	2,176	2,041	1,709
Doña Ana County, New Mexico	205,764	1,170	1,018	6,277	5,761	6,031	1,376	1,098	5,770	5,947	6,501
McKinley County, New Mexico	71,325	758	568	2,695	2,725	2,879	408	499	2,335	2,259	2,606
Otero County, New Mexico	62,667	439	967	882	1,801	2,734	152	930	1,551	1,053	1,610
Sandoval County, New Mexico	137,215	1,562	878	3,594	3,919	4,900	802	1,122	3,025	3,897	4,676
San Juan County, New Mexico	110,114	616	766	3,224	3,501	2,906	1,405	552	3,909	3,168	3,250
Santa Fe County, New Mexico	144,707	803	1,032	3,257	2,732	3,725	953	322	2,249	4,292	3,574
Valencia County, New Mexico	73,746	488	872	2,035	1,756	2,573	521	1,114	1,889	1,811	2,122
NEW YORK											
Albany County, New York	299,476	2,119	1,779	6,083	7,109	7,852	2,659	1,170	6,825	5,938	6,327
Bronx County, New York	1,390,790	13,217	12,012	43,714	39,864	43,179	10,194	9,729	41,329	40,184	41,426
Broome County, New York	189,854	1,296	1,486	4,632	5,022	4,860	1,683	646	4,227	3,963	4,547
Cattaraugus County, New York	75,303	400	251	2,382	1,876	2,262	811	476	2,036	1,959	1,977
Cayuga County, New York	75,774	162	450	1,704	1,700	1,905	520	235	1,407	1,772	2,593
Chautauqua County, New York	125,710	1,025	245	2,668	3,288	3,445	813	628	2,769	2,738	3,287
Chemung County, New York	83,649	754	271	2,279	1,869	2,684	437	229	2,111	2,239	2,606
Dutchess County, New York	287,393	1,646	1,250	6,411	6,147	9,886	1,878	1,429	6,752	6,065	7,640
Erie County, New York	889,960	6,092	5,134	21,651	21,211	23,646	4,866	4,459	20,428	20,465	22,238
Jefferson County, New York	108,539	507	648	3,135	2,670	2,197	970	442	3,223	2,534	2,942
Kings County, New York	2,512,989	25,664	20,910	69,739	62,883	65,122	24,997	20,255	67,784	57,210	62,465
Livingston County, New York	62,624	527	183	1,354	1,417	1,229	207	250	1,218	1,317	1,335
Madison County, New York	69,222	419	340	1,499	1,480	1,726	39	328	1,358	1,534	1,876
Monroe County, New York	722,562	5,032	4,794	17,962	17,302	20,911	4,540	4,592	15,223	18,603	18,144
Nassau County, New York	1,320,275	11,583	8,948	33,625	34,364	38,394	10,980	9,263	30,530	31,826	37,060
New York County, New York	1,594,918	12,418	8,040	27,199	23,233	25,316	12,251	7,117	25,546	25,125	22,791
Niagara County, New York	205,597	1,054	1,308	4,078	4,999	6,632	1,425	807	4,235	5,516	4,665
Oneida County, New York	223,955	2,083	1,552	6,093	4,571	5,464	1,000	1,393	5,986	5,324	5,410
Onondaga County, New York	451,317	3,084	2,784	12,075	11,198	11,432	2,603	2,690	11,140	10,389	13,202
Ontario County, New York	106,764	446	305	2,782	2,907	3,188	416	233	2,215	2,862	2,833
Orange County, New York	364,505	3,312	3,358	10,390	11,850	12,923	3,069	2,351	11,645	10,351	11,620
Oswego County, New York	114,318	327	722	2,470	2,829	3,175	776	813	3,133	2,037	3,153
Putnam County, New York	96,430	371	240	2,231	2,787	3,223	509	258	2,671	2,377	3,456
Queens County, New York	2,246,024	17,727	13,320	54,705	50,774	53,425	14,760	14,124	51,246	50,005	51,193
Rensselaer County, New York	154,133	712	1,085	4,282	2,938	3,487	799	668	2,598	4,782	3,381
Richmond County, New York	459,791	3,443	2,781	11,907	12,351	12,877	2,950	3,551	9,813	12,897	12,071
Rockland County, New York	312,786	3,246	3,381	10,952	9,231	11,101	3,579	2,242	9,866	10,016	10,587
St. Lawrence County, New York	106,893	885	674	2,056	2,816	2,548	707	386	2,411	2,905	2,194
Saratoga County, New York	220,252	2,281	1,702	5,857	4,279	5,784	1,624	2,177	5,101	4,110	5,563
Schenectady County, New York	148,813	1,219	1,404	3,888	3,940	3,774	1,424	588	4,305	3,447	3,269
Steuben County, New York	93,599	290	457	1,942	2,623	3,269	780	556	2,555	2,028	2,256
Suffolk County, New York	1,447,900	10,413	7,560	36,927	38,726	43,041	10,376	7,030	36,217	35,146	42,747
Tompkins County, New York	102,697	688	463	2,436	1,956	1,642	745	420	1,741	1,307	1,591
Ulster County, New York	174,779	1,042	1,019	3,836	3,670	4,338	744	1,015	4,002	4,131	3,438
Warren County, New York	62,772	348	186	1,055	2,023	1,403	355	35	914	1,085	2,172
Wayne County, New York	88,598	848	663	2,059	1,889	2,504	543	777	2,504	1,465	2,902
Westchester County, New York	943,449	9,121	7,092	24,670	25,141	27,619	8,179	5,329	22,441	25,058	26,660
NORTH CAROLINA											
Alamance County, North Carolina	154,854	1,146	1,671	4,244	3,062	4,930	1,166	525	2,986	4,836	4,388
Brunswick County, North Carolina	123,710	107	173	1,867	2,548	2,568	743	476	2,602	1,318	2,422
Buncombe County, North Carolina	249,484	1,328	1,632	7,005	4,573	5,958	1,183	1,243	5,369	4,975	6,302
Cabarrus County, North Carolina	193,738	1,508	1,139	6,343	7,114	5,914	1,253	1,263	5,346	6,533	7,749
Carteret County, North Carolina	67,284	323	670	1,443	1,487	1,812	549	378	1,537	962	1,632
Catawba County, North Carolina	151,174	917	475	4,262	4,852	4,668	674	977	3,655	3,750	3,844
Chatham County, North Carolina	70,822	351	220	1,808	2,253	2,137	655	552	1,268	1,860	2,171
Cleveland County, North Carolina	93,920	374	376	3,074	2,211	2,925	203	315	3,363	1,263	2,377
Craven County, North Carolina	100,007	1,095	438	3,124	2,574	3,238	314	430	2,969	2,365	2,192
Cumberland County, North Carolina	311,364	2,946	2,708	9,787	7,733	9,999	2,799	2,375	8,288	8,048	8,886
Davidson County, North Carolina	159,463	574	534	5,206	4,037	4,658	1,078	1,223	3,695	3,564	5,935
Durham County, North Carolina	294,004	2,248	1,560	8,668	6,221	5,938	1,936	1,198	7,201	6,719	6,067
Forsyth County, North Carolina	358,779	2,757	2,180	11,680	7,709	11,547	2,199	2,178	8,247	10,630	9,201
Gaston County, North Carolina	208,228	1,043	1,571	5,229	5,119	6,048	1,010	1,192	5,118	5,407	5,903

Table C-4. Primary and Secondary School Enrollment, by Sex and Selected Counties, 2016—*Continued*

(Number.)

State/County	Population 3 years and over	Male					Female				
		Enrolled in school					Enrolled in school				
		Nursery school, Pre-school	Kindergarten	Grades 1 to 4	Grades 5 to 8	Grades 9 to 12	Nursery school, Pre-school	Kindergarten	Grades 1 to 4	Grades 5 to 8	Grades 9 to 12
NORTH CAROLINA—*(Continued)*											
Guilford County, North Carolina	503,919	2,905	3,737	14,067	12,246	14,361	3,027	3,157	12,806	13,291	13,765
Harnett County, North Carolina	125,230	984	941	4,116	4,032	4,472	821	703	3,572	4,053	3,571
Henderson County, North Carolina	110,814	588	485	1,774	2,786	2,948	793	954	2,841	1,835	2,001
Iredell County, North Carolina	166,879	691	1,087	4,768	4,332	5,706	778	905	4,032	5,281	5,061
Johnston County, North Carolina	184,654	1,784	1,129	4,603	7,230	6,759	620	817	4,875	7,174	5,205
Lincoln County, North Carolina	78,801	516	345	1,620	2,131	2,729	733	297	2,287	1,852	1,674
Mecklenburg County, North Carolina	1,011,241	9,885	6,513	29,722	28,921	27,847	8,997	6,801	26,537	29,852	26,941
Moore County, North Carolina	92,602	827	511	2,416	2,294	3,391	951	241	2,379	2,214	2,921
Nash County, North Carolina	91,011	239	733	3,326	1,424	2,933	193	584	2,532	1,994	2,172
New Hanover County, North Carolina	217,248	683	1,555	5,615	3,986	4,598	1,168	517	4,320	4,348	5,170
Onslow County, North Carolina	175,141	1,314	1,366	5,182	4,282	4,398	1,608	1,316	4,429	5,070	4,027
Orange County, North Carolina	137,270	1,173	1,481	2,605	3,462	3,771	548	544	3,526	3,240	3,244
Pitt County, North Carolina	171,134	1,756	913	7,246	2,200	4,428	752	634	4,188	4,232	3,655
Randolph County, North Carolina	138,412	403	862	3,400	4,762	4,367	435	948	3,450	3,225	4,633
Robeson County, North Carolina	127,440	586	957	4,056	4,024	3,844	723	806	3,985	4,060	3,714
Rowan County, North Carolina	135,261	661	474	4,067	3,985	4,138	525	590	3,030	3,426	4,288
Surry County, North Carolina	69,845	518	295	1,861	1,500	2,269	406	395	1,953	1,568	1,697
Union County, North Carolina	217,986	1,681	1,266	7,577	8,294	8,581	2,043	1,280	6,976	7,419	8,378
Wake County, North Carolina	1,007,069	9,743	7,915	30,662	30,837	28,603	9,058	7,972	29,388	26,909	28,019
Wayne County, North Carolina	118,845	901	1,309	3,015	3,308	3,220	918	922	3,708	2,240	3,724
Wilson County, North Carolina	79,145	327	542	2,168	1,765	3,884	511	183	2,141	2,610	1,776
NORTH DAKOTA											
Burleigh County, North Dakota	90,844	737	373	2,676	2,310	2,046	597	919	2,307	1,751	1,850
Cass County, North Dakota	166,097	1,426	1,315	4,003	3,753	3,167	912	1,456	4,112	3,652	3,066
Grand Forks County, North Dakota	68,101	325	271	1,553	1,431	1,211	331	536	934	1,267	1,128
Ward County, North Dakota	66,776	791	296	1,959	1,517	1,696	184	558	2,175	1,038	1,489
OHIO											
Allen County, Ohio	99,863	1,159	673	2,691	2,269	2,553	700	502	2,744	2,633	2,851
Ashtabula County, Ohio	95,011	640	1,187	2,458	1,984	2,797	505	364	3,107	2,068	2,631
Belmont County, Ohio	66,865	673	428	1,533	1,034	2,619	390	336	1,508	1,364	1,474
Butler County, Ohio	364,082	4,059	2,000	9,972	10,061	10,818	2,609	2,691	9,528	10,145	8,769
Clark County, Ohio	129,885	897	562	3,767	3,249	3,276	972	857	3,464	3,167	4,022
Clermont County, Ohio	196,109	1,486	1,176	5,257	4,493	6,004	1,225	1,834	5,414	4,666	5,625
Columbiana County, Ohio	100,522	458	452	3,493	1,920	2,619	887	487	1,785	2,922	2,570
Cuyahoga County, Ohio	1,204,282	8,389	7,809	27,240	29,672	33,632	8,677	7,243	29,954	27,197	32,241
Delaware County, Ohio	188,607	1,567	1,999	6,829	6,079	6,188	1,827	1,935	5,982	5,765	6,453
Erie County, Ohio	72,954	233	1,289	1,181	1,851	2,565	297	357	1,066	1,946	2,404
Fairfield County, Ohio	148,428	1,454	1,170	4,102	4,149	4,834	1,313	1,265	2,998	5,216	4,238
Franklin County, Ohio	1,207,542	8,780	9,819	33,253	31,062	29,310	8,737	6,447	32,034	31,702	30,395
Geauga County, Ohio	91,402	613	361	2,951	2,243	2,576	171	275	2,050	2,984	1,965
Greene County, Ohio	159,118	1,503	754	2,980	4,831	3,809	1,313	1,421	3,419	3,723	4,195
Hamilton County, Ohio	776,467	6,772	5,775	20,703	20,966	21,494	5,672	5,572	22,407	18,725	18,609
Hancock County, Ohio	72,537	315	381	1,803	1,854	2,673	529	413	1,412	2,477	1,879
Jefferson County, Ohio	64,857	557	210	1,649	1,542	1,699	740	160	1,451	1,439	1,453
Lake County, Ohio	222,241	1,322	1,317	5,522	5,156	5,891	1,185	948	5,900	4,953	6,054
Licking County, Ohio	165,901	1,091	1,306	4,853	4,219	5,494	675	976	3,704	5,355	4,657
Lorain County, Ohio	295,264	2,338	1,590	7,866	8,232	8,058	2,365	1,971	7,024	7,297	7,578
Lucas County, Ohio	414,539	3,703	2,894	12,703	9,666	11,447	2,414	2,889	11,403	10,454	11,373
Mahoning County, Ohio	223,330	2,151	933	5,461	5,752	5,380	1,549	1,168	4,375	5,321	6,004
Medina County, Ohio	172,036	1,224	1,467	4,253	4,754	5,048	1,350	710	4,676	4,348	5,339
Miami County, Ohio	101,619	370	672	2,997	2,609	3,717	732	387	2,021	3,305	2,992
Montgomery County, Ohio	511,147	3,927	3,436	14,383	12,639	13,472	3,829	3,271	12,836	13,675	13,009
Muskingum County, Ohio	83,657	495	687	1,555	2,406	2,949	331	468	2,578	2,122	2,217
Portage County, Ohio	157,973	1,662	864	3,555	2,955	4,079	710	523	3,667	3,307	3,953
Richland County, Ohio	117,219	673	690	2,547	2,799	3,941	473	427	2,749	3,177	3,108
Ross County, Ohio	74,198	266	369	1,849	2,137	2,093	553	384	1,458	1,755	2,590
Scioto County, Ohio	73,751	388	511	1,632	2,322	2,360	714	40	1,313	2,088	2,587
Stark County, Ohio	362,571	3,253	2,071	9,214	8,380	10,128	2,309	2,334	9,117	9,489	9,063
Summit County, Ohio	521,581	4,162	2,489	11,617	14,927	13,805	4,281	1,940	12,549	12,785	14,332
Trumbull County, Ohio	195,435	622	1,356	4,724	3,542	4,642	1,154	1,367	5,141	4,224	4,590
Tuscarawas County, Ohio	89,142	647	461	1,936	2,374	2,612	498	338	2,512	2,206	2,756
Warren County, Ohio	219,782	1,451	1,590	6,470	6,733	8,452	1,406	1,513	6,407	6,537	6,728
Wayne County, Ohio	112,033	1,054	505	3,429	3,123	2,733	493	494	2,362	3,379	3,250
Wood County, Ohio	127,606	1,627	1,217	2,858	3,083	3,322	1,374	602	2,145	3,162	3,120
OKLAHOMA											
Canadian County, Oklahoma	131,110	991	1,477	3,984	3,346	3,663	1,235	802	5,019	2,975	4,830
Cleveland County, Oklahoma	268,918	1,997	1,696	7,855	6,322	7,123	1,559	1,785	7,138	6,378	7,153

Table C-4. Primary and Secondary School Enrollment, by Sex and Selected Counties, 2016—*Continued*

(Number.)

State/County	Population 3 years and over	Male — Nursery school, Pre-school	Male — Kindergarten	Male — Grades 1 to 4	Male — Grades 5 to 8	Male — Grades 9 to 12	Female — Nursery school, Pre-school	Female — Kindergarten	Female — Grades 1 to 4	Female — Grades 5 to 8	Female — Grades 9 to 12
OKLAHOMA—*(Continued)*											
Comanche County, Oklahoma	116,510	1,257	948	3,080	3,688	3,133	932	1,246	2,775	2,785	3,193
Creek County, Oklahoma	68,722	564	639	1,926	1,685	2,263	744	512	1,663	1,841	1,816
Muskogee County, Oklahoma	66,669	682	450	1,621	1,934	2,212	622	504	1,748	1,905	2,207
Oklahoma County, Oklahoma	747,380	5,987	5,251	22,059	23,843	20,202	6,384	4,795	25,453	20,026	19,490
Payne County, Oklahoma	78,382	721	411	2,023	1,848	1,685	741	676	1,608	1,492	1,172
Pottawatomie County, Oklahoma	69,978	662	304	2,433	2,075	2,121	461	443	2,087	1,668	2,214
Rogers County, Oklahoma	88,383	779	686	2,495	2,149	3,046	765	891	2,466	2,552	2,336
Tulsa County, Oklahoma	614,569	5,863	4,433	19,227	18,617	17,199	5,216	3,711	19,512	17,214	16,949
Wagoner County, Oklahoma	75,215	909	561	1,802	2,538	2,336	542	689	2,356	2,098	2,374
OREGON											
Benton County, Oregon	87,643	834	164	1,727	1,916	1,636	765	180	1,353	1,832	2,043
Clackamas County, Oregon	395,065	2,605	2,933	9,339	10,835	12,189	3,047	1,929	9,287	10,501	10,630
Deschutes County, Oregon	175,678	2,088	1,332	4,027	4,262	4,443	1,058	1,015	5,190	2,940	4,457
Douglas County, Oregon	104,524	465	675	2,552	2,812	2,589	373	483	1,808	2,374	2,323
Jackson County, Oregon	209,420	845	877	6,024	5,110	5,128	1,577	1,012	4,336	5,678	3,723
Josephine County, Oregon	83,703	766	192	1,767	1,879	1,965	539	319	1,752	2,334	1,800
Lane County, Oregon	358,351	2,075	1,880	6,763	7,864	8,834	1,570	1,402	7,144	7,957	8,722
Linn County, Oregon	118,511	828	1,299	3,575	2,593	3,186	248	797	3,365	2,046	2,992
Marion County, Oregon	322,204	2,262	2,307	9,516	8,106	10,176	2,375	1,305	10,078	10,670	8,630
Multnomah County, Oregon	773,932	8,463	4,704	17,362	15,842	15,733	5,929	4,596	15,577	16,494	15,189
Polk County, Oregon	78,333	815	474	1,819	1,722	1,915	265	421	2,409	2,188	2,880
Umatilla County, Oregon	74,009	467	385	2,434	2,644	1,947	675	694	1,510	2,572	2,199
Washington County, Oregon	560,363	4,334	3,993	14,932	15,028	14,942	5,265	4,573	14,407	14,669	15,238
Yamhill County, Oregon	102,055	761	874	3,106	3,025	2,695	911	799	3,322	1,688	2,642
PENNSYLVANIA											
Adams County, Pennsylvania	98,877	556	730	2,185	2,690	2,368	270	411	2,905	2,146	2,590
Allegheny County, Pennsylvania	1,184,719	10,960	5,590	25,377	25,673	28,070	8,706	5,509	23,404	25,189	27,193
Armstrong County, Pennsylvania	64,586	477	289	1,691	1,433	1,478	487	454	1,295	1,266	1,414
Beaver County, Pennsylvania	161,903	1,528	1,302	3,262	3,547	3,719	1,039	965	3,076	4,174	3,492
Berks County, Pennsylvania	400,903	2,558	2,523	10,278	10,572	12,004	3,242	2,020	9,871	10,499	10,352
Blair County, Pennsylvania	120,272	938	576	2,976	3,190	2,762	643	502	2,594	3,074	3,250
Bucks County, Pennsylvania	608,142	4,435	3,082	15,790	15,160	18,694	3,826	4,374	13,475	13,615	17,413
Butler County, Pennsylvania	181,096	1,467	1,102	4,111	4,625	4,888	1,378	1,307	4,352	3,562	4,064
Cambria County, Pennsylvania	130,882	1,399	607	3,232	2,476	2,942	1,012	854	3,351	2,388	3,235
Centre County, Pennsylvania	157,521	643	938	2,574	2,914	3,239	715	760	2,372	2,910	2,937
Chester County, Pennsylvania	500,228	4,925	3,438	12,908	15,045	14,553	5,095	2,833	13,317	13,493	14,621
Clearfield County, Pennsylvania	78,678	421	226	2,211	1,515	1,958	494	185	1,441	2,103	1,566
Columbia County, Pennsylvania	64,956	365	330	1,379	1,117	1,303	112	423	1,106	1,145	1,496
Crawford County, Pennsylvania	83,505	454	589	2,083	1,838	2,259	386	216	2,087	2,078	2,266
Cumberland County, Pennsylvania	240,666	918	1,275	5,796	6,227	6,282	2,113	1,211	4,714	6,120	6,165
Dauphin County, Pennsylvania	263,551	1,858	1,031	5,972	7,782	7,568	1,671	865	6,852	7,040	6,986
Delaware County, Pennsylvania	543,933	6,325	4,090	13,024	13,808	14,900	4,830	3,756	12,846	13,618	13,912
Erie County, Pennsylvania	267,349	1,883	1,490	7,580	6,903	7,006	2,001	2,205	6,715	6,320	5,808
Fayette County, Pennsylvania	128,337	442	373	2,142	3,617	3,876	841	563	2,665	3,009	2,559
Franklin County, Pennsylvania	149,174	258	1,073	3,531	5,356	4,470	657	318	4,282	3,214	3,046
Indiana County, Pennsylvania	84,179	598	325	1,550	2,189	1,835	700	414	1,530	1,958	1,720
Lackawanna County, Pennsylvania	204,985	1,420	1,045	5,224	5,141	4,185	1,647	1,060	4,687	5,141	4,828
Lancaster County, Pennsylvania	516,874	4,463	3,354	15,300	13,766	13,783	2,544	2,370	14,923	12,668	13,175
Lawrence County, Pennsylvania	85,030	830	406	1,786	2,346	1,854	978	324	1,822	1,606	2,181
Lebanon County, Pennsylvania	133,432	587	895	3,183	4,206	3,879	503	537	4,037	3,410	3,625
Lehigh County, Pennsylvania	350,726	1,969	3,032	8,941	9,574	11,094	1,467	2,471	8,872	8,850	9,662
Luzerne County, Pennsylvania	307,716	2,395	1,353	6,319	7,861	7,177	2,892	1,555	5,834	7,659	6,806
Lycoming County, Pennsylvania	111,078	549	398	2,403	3,321	2,994	372	822	2,474	2,562	2,238
Mercer County, Pennsylvania	109,586	553	424	2,591	2,620	3,328	849	807	1,881	2,364	2,876
Monroe County, Pennsylvania	161,863	775	1,382	3,728	4,012	4,477	942	1,266	3,430	3,376	4,693
Montgomery County, Pennsylvania	795,156	8,574	3,883	20,138	22,282	22,615	8,007	4,421	21,607	18,034	21,594
Northampton County, Pennsylvania	293,625	1,296	1,497	6,967	7,565	8,238	2,163	2,241	5,499	7,516	6,427
Northumberland County, Pennsylvania	89,844	483	565	2,160	2,267	1,986	359	582	1,974	1,827	1,924
Philadelphia County, Pennsylvania	1,499,561	12,122	10,289	38,675	36,584	37,984	12,170	10,418	33,971	34,470	36,302
Schuylkill County, Pennsylvania	139,542	629	744	3,148	3,387	3,448	995	745	3,249	3,306	3,378
Somerset County, Pennsylvania	72,740	445	260	1,709	1,320	1,602	623	263	1,326	1,335	1,479
Washington County, Pennsylvania	202,116	2,208	1,009	4,496	4,861	5,004	1,697	861	4,157	5,092	5,140
Westmoreland County, Pennsylvania	344,664	2,226	1,973	6,967	7,912	8,513	2,271	1,511	7,974	6,444	7,601
York County, Pennsylvania	428,454	3,803	3,049	10,780	11,692	11,875	2,553	1,612	11,568	11,776	11,595
RHODE ISLAND											
Kent County, Rhode Island	160,342	1,748	687	2,953	4,132	3,738	1,519	584	3,314	3,465	3,724
Newport County, Rhode Island	80,789	272	752	1,636	1,545	2,290	199	462	1,604	1,630	1,315

Table C-4. Primary and Secondary School Enrollment, by Sex and Selected Counties, 2016—*Continued*

(Number.)

State/County	Population 3 years and over	Male — Enrolled in school					Female — Enrolled in school				
		Nursery school, Pre-school	Kindergarten	Grades 1 to 4	Grades 5 to 8	Grades 9 to 12	Nursery school, Pre-school	Kindergarten	Grades 1 to 4	Grades 5 to 8	Grades 9 to 12
RHODE ISLAND—*(Continued)*											
Providence County, Rhode Island	612,571	3,856	2,969	13,891	16,076	16,468	5,139	2,484	13,589	14,408	15,511
Washington County, Rhode Island	123,432	656	728	1,442	3,226	3,454	1,076	186	1,914	3,141	3,258
SOUTH CAROLINA											
Aiken County, South Carolina...........	161,756	1,083	1,033	5,347	3,569	4,995	879	461	4,149	3,696	4,479
Anderson County, South Carolina	190,272	1,763	783	5,850	5,716	4,640	855	1,337	4,842	5,655	4,103
Beaufort County, South Carolina	177,721	1,997	1,057	4,396	3,546	4,068	1,769	614	5,360	3,586	3,773
Berkeley County, South Carolina	203,139	1,321	2,039	5,214	5,888	6,139	1,245	1,634	5,295	6,070	5,308
Charleston County, South Carolina	381,933	3,743	2,734	8,790	8,762	7,719	3,946	2,272	7,869	7,731	8,662
Darlington County, South Carolina	65,449	135	687	1,818	1,614	1,343	421	802	1,168	2,607	2,002
Dorchester County, South Carolina ...	148,696	1,924	646	4,040	5,801	5,895	1,361	927	4,275	4,147	4,582
Florence County, South Carolina	133,591	845	1,166	4,126	3,793	4,261	504	2,488	3,020	3,595	3,916
Greenville County, South Carolina	479,193	3,230	4,419	14,090	12,321	14,150	3,488	3,799	11,714	13,801	11,367
Horry County, South Carolina	313,437	1,952	1,260	7,242	7,682	6,550	2,249	2,553	6,167	6,439	8,107
Laurens County, South Carolina	64,509	318	389	2,169	1,633	1,414	92	712	1,684	1,749	1,111
Lexington County, South Carolina......	276,324	1,876	2,668	7,911	7,190	7,137	2,532	2,024	7,685	6,910	7,510
Orangeburg County, South Carolina..	84,487	666	866	2,444	1,903	2,615	350	869	1,605	3,112	1,779
Pickens County, South Carolina	118,467	888	1,043	2,197	3,107	3,187	336	433	2,881	2,712	2,025
Richland County, South Carolina	396,476	3,921	4,125	9,329	10,078	11,293	2,502	2,835	12,196	8,595	10,011
Spartanburg County, South Carolina.	291,253	1,216	1,739	9,372	7,164	9,943	1,521	2,322	7,407	6,789	8,362
Sumter County, South Carolina........	102,374	512	1,809	2,678	3,164	3,230	834	1,085	2,815	2,866	2,162
York County, South Carolina	247,596	1,749	1,741	6,291	8,809	6,829	1,328	1,525	7,066	8,125	6,542
SOUTH DAKOTA											
Minnehaha County, South Dakota	178,174	1,688	1,510	5,829	4,012	5,350	1,309	1,218	4,386	4,798	4,444
Pennington County, South Dakota	105,071	994	1,396	2,498	2,846	2,567	535	878	2,481	2,120	2,366
TENNESSEE											
Anderson County, Tennessee............	73,348	409	259	2,098	1,243	2,251	155	211	1,607	1,710	1,793
Blount County, Tennessee................	124,331	460	828	2,779	3,724	2,754	1,113	462	2,037	3,766	3,397
Bradley County, Tennessee..............	101,179	363	1,075	2,093	3,240	1,933	302	891	2,948	2,928	2,177
Davidson County, Tennessee............	654,774	5,143	4,460	14,438	16,304	14,372	4,126	5,060	15,941	14,558	13,967
Greene County, Tennessee...............	66,406	287	60	1,447	1,381	2,289	251	600	1,039	1,191	1,485
Hamilton County, Tennessee.............	346,260	2,757	1,818	6,360	11,437	7,912	2,372	1,928	7,270	8,077	8,762
Knox County, Tennessee	441,054	4,115	2,647	9,915	11,356	10,574	3,245	3,279	11,269	9,310	9,548
Madison County, Tennessee	93,938	832	397	1,900	3,161	2,915	573	780	1,788	2,278	2,473
Maury County, Tennessee	86,661	1,140	766	2,420	2,145	3,005	765	443	1,824	1,685	2,118
Montgomery County, Tennessee.......	185,971	2,242	2,472	4,674	5,062	4,732	1,541	1,635	5,289	5,442	6,329
Robertson County, Tennessee..........	66,563	768	137	2,788	1,623	2,018	347	470	1,717	1,796	2,230
Rutherford County, Tennessee..........	296,056	2,091	2,876	8,666	9,058	8,016	1,645	1,349	9,602	7,898	8,665
Shelby County, Tennessee................	894,734	7,255	6,827	21,981	29,917	26,706	6,011	4,495	25,019	26,457	26,215
Sullivan County, Tennessee..............	152,598	1,043	1,498	3,630	2,985	3,570	876	894	3,440	3,436	3,654
Sumner County, Tennessee..............	173,463	1,121	1,602	4,228	4,805	5,693	1,640	990	4,760	4,996	4,970
Washington County, Tennessee........	124,642	178	673	4,113	3,264	3,094	758	562	2,028	3,213	2,920
Williamson County, Tennessee..........	212,139	3,616	1,554	6,245	8,124	8,180	2,317	1,266	6,425	7,924	7,749
Wilson County, Tennessee	128,272	479	676	3,707	4,507	3,059	1,376	257	3,933	3,918	3,640
TEXAS											
Bell County, Texas...........................	323,027	2,905	2,435	10,955	10,262	9,058	2,467	2,033	10,736	8,275	8,777
Bexar County, Texas........................	1,839,075	15,976	14,222	56,740	57,257	54,091	15,288	13,748	56,448	54,477	53,952
Bowie County, Texas........................	91,486	1,784	509	3,108	2,696	2,629	966	560	2,671	3,148	2,210
Brazoria County, Texas....................	339,664	2,033	3,596	10,634	10,946	9,480	2,717	2,177	11,179	11,363	9,890
Brazos County, Texas.......................	212,375	1,264	810	5,647	5,120	5,218	2,070	1,260	5,190	3,766	3,879
Cameron County, Texas....................	401,287	4,944	3,074	14,032	15,518	16,770	3,562	4,575	12,460	14,698	16,370
Collin County, Texas.........................	905,977	9,425	6,889	28,478	31,229	30,236	9,018	7,203	29,304	28,885	29,811
Comal County, Texas........................	129,661	790	901	3,383	3,504	4,479	287	924	3,992	3,243	3,670
Coryell County, Texas.......................	71,142	565	322	2,484	1,694	1,785	675	426	2,123	2,339	2,170
Dallas County, Texas........................	2,455,363	21,825	21,260	84,327	75,107	69,842	24,259	19,141	78,503	72,160	70,645
Denton County, Texas.......................	776,283	8,509	5,654	20,868	27,674	23,450	6,997	5,735	25,219	19,890	21,490
Ector County, Texas..........................	147,942	1,087	1,483	6,162	5,177	4,963	1,371	1,909	4,905	4,388	3,543
Ellis County, Texas...........................	162,028	1,580	1,388	5,078	5,260	5,995	1,398	1,307	5,044	5,221	5,171
El Paso County, Texas	799,121	6,752	6,916	26,751	24,508	26,916	6,839	5,535	25,601	25,875	26,652
Fort Bend County, Texas..................	714,926	8,100	5,824	24,385	25,005	22,811	7,022	6,746	23,429	23,239	24,952
Galveston County, Texas	316,924	2,362	2,872	7,936	10,966	10,134	3,361	2,405	9,474	7,486	9,486
Grayson County, Texas.....................	122,706	190	975	4,293	2,700	3,834	419	595	3,820	2,861	3,502
Gregg County, Texas........................	117,938	663	867	4,821	2,954	2,947	1,200	861	3,248	3,155	2,468
Guadalupe County, Texas.................	149,061	1,065	1,234	5,066	3,774	5,346	1,355	449	4,182	5,013	4,872

Table C-4. Primary and Secondary School Enrollment, by Sex and Selected Counties, 2016—*Continued*

(Number.)

		Male					Female				
		Enrolled in school					Enrolled in school				
State/County	Population 3 years and over	Nursery school, Pre-school	Kindergarten	Grades 1 to 4	Grades 5 to 8	Grades 9 to 12	Nursery school, Pre-school	Kindergarten	Grades 1 to 4	Grades 5 to 8	Grades 9 to 12
TEXAS—(*Continued*)											
Harris County, Texas	4,373,342	38,905	30,087	150,449	137,533	135,779	37,092	39,224	137,430	129,577	128,751
Hays County, Texas	196,219	1,344	1,358	5,785	4,036	6,111	976	1,878	4,767	5,508	4,973
Henderson County, Texas	77,323	338	542	1,707	2,540	2,285	441	419	1,813	1,626	2,441
Hidalgo County, Texas	805,754	6,998	7,079	31,902	33,524	33,059	8,582	7,730	29,958	33,095	29,149
Hunt County, Texas	87,952	728	71	2,632	3,098	2,007	312	425	2,704	2,154	2,626
Jefferson County, Texas	244,557	1,772	1,517	7,287	6,442	6,794	2,483	1,285	6,771	6,981	5,924
Johnson County, Texas	157,141	1,526	902	4,457	4,547	4,829	998	827	4,292	5,032	4,685
Kaufman County, Texas	113,386	835	527	4,230	3,207	4,189	797	536	3,244	4,475	3,059
Lubbock County, Texas	289,589	2,754	3,119	7,629	7,528	6,665	1,833	2,370	8,757	7,738	7,592
McLennan County, Texas	238,297	2,277	2,460	6,642	7,396	6,742	1,803	1,081	7,996	5,899	6,582
Midland County, Texas	153,783	1,677	1,024	5,935	4,206	4,571	898	1,064	4,326	6,619	4,424
Montgomery County, Texas	532,241	4,128	2,152	19,593	16,628	19,006	5,587	3,612	15,724	15,866	16,034
Nueces County, Texas	345,792	1,916	2,565	11,370	8,548	9,255	1,693	1,660	10,101	11,175	9,175
Orange County, Texas	81,395	836	756	2,100	2,640	2,860	686	690	1,427	3,002	2,043
Parker County, Texas	124,390	1,529	1,035	3,501	3,898	3,583	392	684	2,431	4,648	3,351
Potter County, Texas	114,521	1,164	1,189	4,284	4,020	3,198	606	1,424	3,186	3,496	2,949
Randall County, Texas	127,950	804	913	3,696	3,868	3,900	940	940	3,221	3,909	3,430
Rockwall County, Texas	90,662	280	1,167	2,873	3,781	3,211	701	555	2,397	3,548	3,621
Smith County, Texas	214,937	2,131	1,865	6,708	5,900	6,772	1,198	1,565	6,494	5,458	5,838
Tarrant County, Texas	1,928,647	16,844	14,188	60,320	61,950	56,713	14,775	15,502	58,170	59,340	59,156
Taylor County, Texas	131,175	1,338	858	5,145	2,388	3,509	1,160	1,251	3,606	3,513	2,771
Tom Green County, Texas	113,296	542	654	3,255	3,172	3,009	1,250	497	3,109	3,117	2,970
Travis County, Texas	1,152,059	10,775	6,375	33,795	29,571	25,755	10,833	6,500	31,209	28,258	22,899
Victoria County, Texas	88,275	220	646	3,165	2,438	1,983	753	444	2,543	2,920	2,472
Webb County, Texas	255,278	2,787	2,952	9,151	11,540	10,315	3,205	1,936	11,643	9,945	10,533
Wichita County, Texas	125,691	783	1,090	2,897	3,658	2,597	225	663	3,908	3,294	2,887
Williamson County, Texas	509,543	5,986	4,421	15,347	16,792	16,991	5,421	3,148	15,787	17,363	15,494
UTAH											
Cache County, Utah	115,665	962	926	4,316	4,070	4,022	1,248	985	3,869	4,122	4,257
Davis County, Utah	325,007	4,091	3,625	13,216	13,075	12,791	3,483	3,886	12,099	11,701	10,033
Salt Lake County, Utah	1,068,571	11,629	10,821	36,189	33,859	34,088	10,030	8,618	35,720	32,561	34,919
Utah County, Utah	557,476	6,813	6,420	22,690	22,904	22,094	4,696	5,456	23,549	19,956	19,887
Washington County, Utah	153,435	935	1,411	6,687	3,613	6,040	1,150	1,401	4,429	4,691	4,159
Weber County, Utah	235,119	2,246	1,695	9,731	7,048	7,543	2,397	1,835	7,702	7,597	8,339
VERMONT											
Chittenden County, Vermont	156,937	1,437	932	3,457	3,364	3,714	1,079	908	2,827	3,200	3,286
VIRGINIA											
Albemarle County, Virginia	103,761	667	664	2,998	2,595	2,471	624	763	3,038	2,007	2,300
Arlington County, Virginia	221,951	2,658	1,608	4,688	3,973	3,394	2,581	1,462	4,561	3,247	3,267
Augusta County, Virginia	72,724	669	365	1,103	2,447	1,863	558	549	915	2,144	1,727
Bedford County, Virginia	76,141	637	1,013	1,398	2,351	2,013	112	286	1,370	2,593	1,718
Chesterfield County, Virginia	326,938	2,736	1,913	9,670	9,970	10,115	2,313	2,073	8,845	9,687	9,451
Fairfax County, Virginia	1,096,144	10,518	7,636	32,565	28,841	34,258	10,416	7,614	29,073	29,765	30,784
Fauquier County, Virginia	66,935	647	256	1,679	2,044	2,290	510	402	1,330	2,318	1,693
Frederick County, Virginia	81,433	591	182	2,294	2,609	2,450	780	874	1,714	1,740	1,914
Hanover County, Virginia	101,919	624	631	2,709	3,391	3,059	798	634	2,353	2,674	2,773
Henrico County, Virginia	315,071	2,763	1,935	8,630	8,768	9,133	1,931	1,763	9,565	7,314	9,291
James City County, Virginia	73,218	705	540	1,693	2,167	2,112	312	541	1,620	2,458	3,006
Loudoun County, Virginia	370,187	4,515	3,415	13,572	12,506	13,222	5,617	2,747	13,322	12,586	11,726
Montgomery County, Virginia	95,026	305	657	1,291	1,803	1,930	583	150	2,075	987	2,063
Prince William County, Virginia	433,935	2,766	3,608	14,494	14,782	13,681	3,282	3,251	13,740	14,517	13,988
Roanoke County, Virginia	91,716	309	635	1,414	2,795	2,912	480	373	2,613	1,934	2,611
Rockingham County, Virginia	76,699	662	440	1,726	2,856	1,858	174	565	1,905	1,770	1,966
Spotsylvania County, Virginia	127,515	696	1,274	3,840	4,224	4,390	1,016	744	3,143	4,201	4,656
Stafford County, Virginia	139,519	1,210	1,297	5,379	3,846	4,830	574	993	4,045	4,503	4,867
York County, Virginia	66,133	480	609	1,454	2,088	1,767	550	471	1,988	2,529	2,305
Alexandria city, Virginia	149,731	1,953	590	2,827	2,388	2,256	1,944	584	2,974	2,856	1,838
Chesapeake city, Virginia	228,863	1,685	1,554	7,496	6,348	7,061	2,851	1,515	6,450	5,435	6,772
Hampton city, Virginia	131,387	1,075	496	3,528	3,052	3,295	905	705	2,847	3,273	3,144
Lynchburg city, Virginia	77,809	411	971	1,005	1,252	1,623	940	979	1,680	938	2,029
Newport News city, Virginia	173,375	888	1,005	5,742	4,071	4,748	1,704	1,018	4,448	4,577	4,413
Norfolk city, Virginia	234,078	1,758	1,500	5,461	5,410	3,654	1,950	1,266	5,295	5,020	3,924
Portsmouth city, Virginia	91,041	752	220	2,998	2,151	2,218	321	908	3,262	2,173	2,077
Richmond city, Virginia	214,876	1,602	1,632	3,458	3,589	4,114	1,266	1,018	5,481	2,853	4,115

Table C-4. Primary and Secondary School Enrollment, by Sex and Selected Counties, 2016—*Continued*

(Number.)

		Male					Female				
		Enrolled in school					Enrolled in school				
State/County	Population 3 years and over	Nursery school, Pre-school	Kindergarten	Grades 1 to 4	Grades 5 to 8	Grades 9 to 12	Nursery school, Pre-school	Kindergarten	Grades 1 to 4	Grades 5 to 8	Grades 9 to 12
VIRGINIA—(*Continued*)											
Roanoke city, Virginia	95,662	1,137	777	3,137	1,760	2,202	962	388	2,545	2,185	2,359
Suffolk city, Virginia	85,446	639	256	2,175	3,332	2,796	650	433	2,137	2,895	2,573
Virginia Beach city, Virginia	435,464	3,191	2,202	10,284	12,974	12,281	3,825	2,890	10,798	11,151	10,493
WASHINGTON											
Benton County, Washington	186,922	1,706	1,103	8,097	5,335	4,949	1,016	1,798	6,646	5,444	6,477
Chelan County, Washington	74,248	493	960	2,143	2,093	1,783	908	131	2,503	1,407	2,498
Clallam County, Washington	72,969	622	512	1,201	1,241	1,624	534	643	1,841	1,019	1,686
Clark County, Washington	449,959	3,819	2,519	14,192	11,923	13,573	3,580	2,657	13,887	11,835	13,529
Franklin County, Washington	85,144	323	587	4,112	3,667	3,536	682	979	3,797	3,418	2,754
Grant County, Washington	88,063	340	990	2,751	3,046	3,142	201	299	3,947	2,866	3,837
Island County, Washington	80,560	696	587	2,286	1,449	1,934	542	309	1,232	1,253	1,767
King County, Washington	2,073,843	19,676	12,516	51,886	45,163	48,855	18,091	12,635	48,843	45,279	46,408
Kitsap County, Washington	255,661	2,527	1,789	5,984	6,131	5,382	1,788	1,149	5,741	6,229	5,696
Lewis County, Washington	74,774	431	197	2,330	1,904	2,564	476	204	1,744	1,578	1,968
Pierce County, Washington	825,499	6,334	5,580	21,959	21,831	21,472	5,503	4,155	21,644	21,722	22,476
Skagit County, Washington	119,710	1,182	481	2,999	2,960	3,702	1,019	742	2,650	3,368	2,439
Snohomish County, Washington	757,658	6,789	4,040	21,178	20,365	20,412	5,449	4,115	20,060	18,464	19,547
Spokane County, Washington	481,863	5,210	2,209	11,922	14,176	11,473	2,496	2,720	11,529	12,418	12,361
Thurston County, Washington	267,052	2,592	1,483	7,153	6,387	7,053	948	699	6,967	5,968	6,294
Whatcom County, Washington	210,053	1,717	848	5,406	4,475	4,814	1,396	1,148	5,150	3,775	5,213
Yakima County, Washington	237,520	2,553	1,617	8,275	8,546	8,836	892	2,631	9,381	7,184	8,107
WEST VIRGINIA											
Berkeley County, West Virginia	110,247	925	489	3,579	3,291	2,397	434	834	3,462	2,653	2,748
Cabell County, West Virginia	92,413	472	919	2,024	2,171	2,055	443	428	2,164	1,951	2,343
Kanawha County, West Virginia	179,666	1,155	1,252	4,873	2,892	4,573	693	1,147	4,639	4,824	3,857
Monongalia County, West Virginia	101,713	572	234	1,776	1,638	2,117	543	509	2,453	1,185	1,610
Wood County, West Virginia	82,947	901	517	1,229	2,594	1,943	810	434	1,710	2,555	2,141
WISCONSIN											
Brown County, Wisconsin	249,401	1,741	1,821	7,827	5,946	7,619	2,189	1,712	6,588	6,663	6,439
Dane County, Wisconsin	512,092	4,500	2,800	11,637	12,966	12,058	4,428	2,987	11,069	12,048	12,531
Dodge County, Wisconsin	85,666	612	409	1,820	2,214	2,328	676	201	2,251	1,977	2,315
Eau Claire County, Wisconsin	99,894	626	727	2,180	2,642	2,533	908	722	2,676	1,920	2,186
Fond du Lac County, Wisconsin	99,055	488	672	3,032	2,111	2,390	1,049	431	2,826	2,636	2,460
Jefferson County, Wisconsin	82,225	507	495	2,553	2,115	2,399	232	397	2,127	2,254	2,261
Kenosha County, Wisconsin	161,426	799	1,789	3,916	4,160	4,953	462	752	4,135	4,776	4,239
La Crosse County, Wisconsin	114,008	642	511	2,666	2,772	2,547	656	425	3,051	2,188	3,099
Manitowoc County, Wisconsin	77,105	745	478	2,232	1,995	1,716	885	482	1,851	1,849	2,016
Marathon County, Wisconsin	130,640	1,734	746	3,520	3,322	3,676	1,161	509	3,477	3,628	3,497
Milwaukee County, Wisconsin	910,558	4,846	9,143	26,992	26,119	25,718	5,207	11,245	26,040	23,697	22,207
Outagamie County, Wisconsin	177,898	1,774	1,264	4,638	5,517	6,004	635	1,257	4,711	5,123	4,575
Ozaukee County, Wisconsin	86,028	790	755	1,545	2,991	2,365	705	397	2,009	2,005	2,982
Portage County, Wisconsin	68,656	500	450	1,274	1,693	1,370	571	529	1,574	1,416	1,483
Racine County, Wisconsin	187,405	1,002	1,673	5,405	4,745	6,090	1,349	1,196	5,676	4,449	6,307
Rock County, Wisconsin	156,111	1,222	1,290	5,094	4,450	4,812	1,266	1,191	3,905	4,347	4,218
St. Croix County, Wisconsin	85,350	1,005	1,024	2,256	2,321	2,681	626	1,096	2,666	2,045	2,596
Sheboygan County, Wisconsin	111,667	1,209	668	3,357	2,760	2,932	744	779	3,317	2,105	3,527
Walworth County, Wisconsin	99,892	955	743	2,197	2,922	2,996	575	1,198	2,001	2,452	2,399
Washington County, Wisconsin	129,978	856	1,205	3,460	3,460	3,791	1,036	1,173	3,851	2,887	3,522
Waukesha County, Wisconsin	386,777	2,553	2,602	9,350	10,957	11,770	2,794	2,754	8,879	10,572	11,870
Winnebago County, Wisconsin	163,681	1,408	682	4,414	3,373	4,443	866	799	3,769	3,784	4,000
Wood County, Wisconsin	71,072	593	605	1,781	1,447	2,006	724	132	1,829	2,064	1,649
WYOMING											
Laramie County, Wyoming	94,324	586	836	3,216	1,676	2,190	583	390	3,287	2,346	2,351
Natrona County, Wyoming	78,159	440	482	2,215	2,213	2,068	619	656	2,161	2,404	2,634

NOTES AND DEFINITIONS: COUNTY EDUCATION STATISTICS

Part C presents data items for selected counties, county equivalents, and independent cities. The District of Columbia is included as both a county and a state.

GEOGRAPHIC IDENTIFICATION

A five-digit state and county code is assigned to each entity. The first two digits indicate the state; the remaining three identify the county. Within each state, the counties are numbered in alphabetical order, beginning with 001, with even numbers usually omitted. Independent cities follow the counties and begin with the number 510.

These codes have been established by the U.S. government as Federal Information Processing Standards and are often referred to as "FIPS codes." They are used by U.S. government agencies and many other organizations for data presentation. They are provided in this volume for use in matching the data given here with other data sources in which counties may be identified by FIPS codes.

Not all county equivalents are included in this publication.

County equivalents. In Louisiana, the primary divisions of the state are known as parishes rather than counties. In Alaska, the county equivalents are the organized boroughs, together with the census areas that were developed for general statistical purposes by the state of Alaska and the U.S. Census Bureau.

Several recent changes have occurred in Alaska's county equivalents:

The old Skagway-Hoonah-Angoon Census Area has been divided into the Skagway Municipality and the Hoonah-Angoon Census Area.

A new Prince of Wales-Hyder Census Area was created after part of the old Prince of Wales-Outer Ketchikan Census Area was annexed by the Ketchikan Gateway Borough.

The old Wrangell-Petersburg Census Area was divided into the Wrangell City and Borough and the Petersburg Census Area.

Independent cities. Independent cities are not included in any county; data are presented separately in this volume where available.

Maryland
Baltimore (separate from Baltimore County)

Missouri
St. Louis (separate from St. Louis County)

Nevada
Carson City

Virginia
Alexandria
Bedford
Bristol
Buena Vista
Charlottesville
Chesapeake
Colonial Heights
Covington
Danville
Emporia
Fairfax
Falls Church
Franklin
Fredericksburg
Galax
Hampton
Harrisonburg
Hopewell
Lexington
Lynchburg
Manassas
Manassas Park

Martinsville
Newport News
Norfolk
Norton
Petersburg
Poquoson
Portsmouth
Radford
Richmond
Roanoke
Salem
Staunton
Suffolk
Virginia Beach
Waynesboro
Williamsburg
Winchester

DATA SOURCES AND EXPLANATIONS

The population, characteristics, enrollment, and attainment data in Table C have been compiled from the detailed tables of the American Community Survey (2016 1-year) and can be found on the Census Bureau's website in the "American FactFinder" section.

ACS data are subject to sampling error, which can be especially large in small geographic areas or small population groups. Margins of error can be found on the Census Bureau website.

Table C-1. Population and Poverty Characteristics, by State and Selected Counties, 2016
Source: U.S. Census Bureau. American Community Survey, 1-Year Estimates.

The population data are Census Bureau estimates of the resident population as of July 1, 2016.

Table C-2. Educational Attainment of the Population, by Selected Counties, 2016
Source: U.S. Census Bureau. American Community Survey, 2016. factfinder2.census.gov.

ACS gathers demographic, social, economic, housing and financial information about the nation's people and communities on a continuous basis, providing the detailed characteristics that have previously come from the sample long form of the decennial census.

People are classified according to the highest degree or level of school completed. The order in which degrees were listed on the questionnaire suggested that doctorate degrees were "higher" than professional school degrees, which were "higher" than master's degrees. The question included instructions for people currently enrolled in school to report the level of the previous grade attended or the highest degree received. Respondents who did not report educational attainment or enrollment level were assigned the attainment of a person of the same age, race, Hispanic or Latino origin, occupation, and sex, where possible, who resided in the same area or nearby. Respondents who filled in more than one box were edited to the highest level or degree reported. The question included a response category that allowed respondents to report completing the 12th grade without receiving a high school diploma. It allowed people who received either a high school diploma or the equivalent, such as those who passed the Test of General Educational Development (G.E.D.) and did not attend college, to be reported as "high school graduate(s)."

High school diploma or less. This category includes all persons who have not received a high school diploma, as well as those high school graduates who never attended college.

High school diploma or more. This category includes people whose highest degree was a high school diploma or its equivalent, people who attended college but did not receive a degree, and people who received a college, university, or professional degree. People who reported completing the 12th grade but not receiving a diploma are not high school graduates.

Bachelor's degree or more. This category includes people whose highest degree was a bachelor's, master's, professional, or doctoral degree. Master's degrees include the traditional M.A. and M.S. degrees and field-specific degrees. Some examples of professional degrees include medicine, dentistry, chiropractic, optometry, osteopathic medicine, pharmacy, podiatry, veterinary medicine, law, and theology. Vocational and technical training, such as barber school training; business, trade, technical, and vocational schools; or other training for a specific trade are specifically excluded.

ACS data are subject to sampling error which can be especially large in small geographic areas or small population groups. Margins of error can be found on the Census Bureau website.

Table C-3. College Enrollment of the Population, by Selected Counties, 2016 and Table C-4. Primary and Secondary School Enrollment, by Sex and Selected Counties, 2016 Source: U.S. Census Bureau. American Community Survey, 2016. factfinder2.census.gov.

ACS gathers demographic, social, economic, housing and financial information about the nation's people and communities on a continuous basis, providing the detailed characteristics that have previously come from the sample long form of the decennial census.

People were classified as enrolled in school if they reported attending a "regular" public or private school or college during the three months prior to the interview. The question included instructions to "include only nursery school or preschool, kindergarten, elementary school, and schooling which leads to a high school diploma or a college degree" as regular school or college. Respondents who did not answer the enrollment question were assigned the enrollment status and type of school of a person with the same age, sex, and race/Hispanic or Latino origin whose residence was in the same or a nearby area. All persons 3 years old and over are included.

Public and private schools. Public and private schools include people who attended school during the reference period and who indicated they were enrolled by marking one of the questionnaire categories for either "public school, public college" or "private school, private college." Schools primarily supported and controlled by a federal, state, or local government are defined as public (including tribal schools). Those primarily supported and controlled by religious organizations or other private groups are considered private, as are home schools.

ACS data are subject to sampling error which can be especially large in small geographic areas or small population groups. Margins of error can be found on the Census Bureau website.

INDEX

INDEX